I0827747

Exposition of Ephesians

Volume 1 of Two Volumes

Exposition of Ephesians

Volume 1 of Two Volumes

Thomas Goodwin

Sovereign Grace Publishers, Inc.
P.O. Box 4998
Lafayette, IN 47903

Exposition of Ephesians By Thomas Goodwin
Volume 1 of 2 Volumes
Hardback Edition

ISBN 1-58960-139-4

Printed In the United States of America
By Lightning Source, Inc.

INTRODUCTION

This, the first complete reprinting of *The Works of Thomas Goodwin* in 130 years, stands as a fitting climax to the past half-century of the rediscovery and republication of the writings of the Puritans. Renowned for intelligent piety at its Puritan best, Thomas Goodwin, "the Atlas of independency," stands on a par with John Owen, "the prince of Puritans," as a theologian and an exegete, and often surpasses him in experimental depth. Slightly easier to read than Owen, Goodwin's writings demand concentration for maximum benefit. Any lover of the Biblical and experimental emphases of the Puritans will find Goodwin both readable and spiritually rewarding. He represents the cream of Puritanism, capturing the intellect, will, and heart of his readers. His treatises join the vigor of earlier Puritans such as William Perkins and Richard Sibbes to the matured thought of later Puritan divines, represented supremely by Owen.

Those influenced by Goodwin's writings include John Cotton, Jonathan Edwards, George Whitefield, and John Gill. Alexander Whyte confessed: "I have read no other author so much and so often. And I continue to read him to this day, as if I had never read him before." He calls Goodwin's sermon, "Christ Dwelling in Our Hearts by Faith," one of the "two very greatest sermons in the English language." Whyte aptly concludes:

> Goodwin is always an interpreter, and one of a thousand.... All his work, throughout his twelve volumes, is just so much pulpit exposition and pulpit application of the Word of God.... Full as Goodwin always is of the ripest scriptural and Reformation scholarship; full as he always is of the best theological and philosophical learning of his own day and of all foregoing days; full, also, as he always is of the deepest

> spiritual experience—all the same, he is always so simple, so clear, so direct, so untechnical, so personal, and so pastoral.[1]

In our generation, Puritan scholar J.I. Packer concurs: "Whyte called Goodwin 'the greatest pulpit exegete of Paul that has ever lived,' and perhaps justly; Goodwin's Biblical expositions are quite unique, even among the Puritans, in the degree to which they combine theological breadth with experimental depth. John Owen saw into the mind of Paul as clearly as Goodwin—sometimes, on points of detail, more clearly—but not even Owen ever saw so deep into Paul's heart."[2]

The Life of Thomas Goodwin

Thomas Goodwin was born in 1600, at Rollesby, Norfolk, in a county of England famed for Puritan resistance to religious persecution by the Crown. This Puritan climate impacted his God-fearing parents, who strove to rear him in preparation for the ministry by their own example and by providing him with the best classical education offered by neighboring schools. In early school days he had a tender conscience, experiencing from the age of six impressions of the Holy Spirit that produced tears for sin and "flashes of joy upon thoughts of the things of God."[3] At the age of twelve, one year before the usual time, he was able to enter Christ's College, Cambridge (1613), a "nest of Puritans" in those days. The young Goodwin found that the memory of the father of Puritanism, William Perkins (1558-1602), permeated Cambridge. Here too Richard Sibbes, the "sweet dropper of Israel," was preaching at Trinity Church, attracting those who yearned for spiritual edification rather than embellished rhetoric.

Goodwin's memoir, edited by his son, reveals a great deal about his induction into the Puritan movement at Cambridge

[1] *Thirteen Appreciations* (London: Oliphant, Anderson and Ferrier, 1913), 158ff.

[2] "The Witness of the Spirit: The Puritan Teaching," in *The Wisdom of Our Fathers* (London: Puritan Conference, 1956), 14; cf. J. C. Philpot, *Reviews by the late Mr. J. C. Philpot* (London: Frederick Kirby, 1901), 2:479ff., who comments, "Being a man of choice experience, Goodwin so blends with [his sound expositions of doctrine] the work of the Spirit, in all its various branches, as to enrich his exposition with a heavenly savour and unction which carries with it great force, and commends itself in a very sensible and profitable manner to the conscience."

[3] *The Works of Thomas Goodwin*, 2:xi.

under the direction of several godly and learned tutors.[4] At age fourteen, Goodwin eagerly anticipated Easter when he hoped to partake of the Lord's Supper for the second time because he thought he found those marks of saving grace within him which were expounded by Zacharius Ursinus in his *Commentary on the Heidelberg Catechism.* He also prepared himself by praying, attending Sibbes's lectures, and reading Calvin's *Institutes*. When the day arrived, however, his tutor, Mr. William Power, who had a profound influence upon him, lovingly restrained him from receiving Communion due to his age and spiritual immaturity.

Feeling rejected, the young Goodwin stopped attending Sibbes's sermons and lectures, ceased praying and reading the Scriptures and Puritan literature, and instead set his heart on becoming a successful preacher in the world. He determined to study the art and rhetoric of preachers who cared more for style than substance and were inclined to embrace the current brand of Arminianism being imported from the Netherlands.

In 1619 he continued his studies at St. Catherine's Hall in Cambridge, probably to obtain early promotion where scholars were not as abundant as at Christ's College. He became a fellow and lecturer in the Hall. Among the fellows there were John Arrowsmith, Andrew Perne, William Spurstowe, and William Strong, all future colleagues of Goodwin in the Westminster Assembly. Several of these and other Puritan friends sought to persuade him, somewhat successfully, that his pursuit of embel-

[4] *Ibid.*, 2:lii ff. For biographical material on Goodwin, see "Memoir of Thomas Goodwin, D.D.," by Robert Halley, and "Memoir of Thomas Goodwin, D.D., Composed out of his own papers and memoirs, by his son," *ibid.*, 2:ix-xlviii, lii-lxxv respectively. Also, consult Edmund Calamy, *The Nonconformist's Memorial*, ed. Samuel Palmer (London: Alex. Hogg, 1778), 1:183-87; James Reid, "Life of Thomas Goodwin," in *Memoirs of the Westminster Divines* (1811; reprint Edinburgh: Banner of Truth Trust, 1982), 319-43; Sir Leslie Stephen and Sir Sidney Lee, eds., *The Dictionary of National Biography [DNB]*, vol. 22 (1890; reprint Oxford: University Press, 1922), 148-50; A. G. Matthews, *Calamy Revised* (Oxford: Clarendon Press, 1934), 228-29; Whyte, *Thirteen Appreciations*, 157-76; Philip E. Hughes, gen. ed., *The Encyclopedia of Christianity* (Marshallton, DE: National Foundation for Christian Education, 1972), 4:392-94; Brian Freer, "Thomas Goodwin, the Peaceable Puritan," Graham Harrison, "Thomas Goodwin and Independency," in *Diversities of Gifts*, Westminster Conference Reports, 1980 (London: The Westminster Conference, 1981), 7-44.

lished rhetoric and flirtation with Arminianism could serve neither edification nor truth. Moreover, he never could fully free himself from the preaching of Sibbes at Trinity Church and the catechetical sermons of John Preston in the college chapel. Nevertheless, his interest in Puritan spirituality remained spasmodic for another year, usually intensifying prior to the Lord's Supper.

Hardness of heart increased until God finally brought Goodwin to a more profound conviction of sin and genuine conversion on October 2, 1620, just after his twentieth birthday. On that afternoon, as Thomas met with some friends to "make merry," one of the friends convinced the group to attend a funeral sermon preached by a Dr. Bainbridge, which focused on the need for personal repentance from Luke 19:41-42. God used this message to show Goodwin his dreadful sins both original and actual, the essential depravity of his heart, his averseness to all spiritual good, and his desperate Christless condition which left him exposed to the just wrath of God and an open hell.[5]

Happily, it was not many hours later "before God, who after we are regenerate is so faithful and mindful of his word,"[6] came and spoke to him a "speedy word" of deliverance from Ezekiel 16:

> '[Live,] yea, I said unto you, Live,'—so God was pleased on the sudden, and as it were in an instant, to alter the whole of his former dispensation towards me, and said of and to my soul, Yea, live; yea, live, I say, said God: and as he created the world and the matter of all things by a word, so he created and put a new life and spirit into my soul, and so great an alteration was strange to me....
>
> God [then] took me aside, and as it were privately said unto me, Do you now turn to me, and I will pardon all your sins though never so many, as I forgave and pardoned my servant Paul, and convert you unto me....[7]

Goodwin explains four reasons why he believed that "these instructions and suggestions [of deliverance and pardon] were immediately from God": (1) the condition of his heart prior to receiving the word of God's willingness to pardon—"the posture and condition of my spirit, and that this suggestion took me when my heart was fixed, and that unmoveably, in the contrary persuasions"; (2) the appropriateness of this divine word when it did

[5] *Works*, 2:lii-lx.

[6] *Ibid.*, lxi.

[7] *Ibid.*, lxi-lxii.

come—"it was a word in its proper season"; (3) that this word was "not an ungrounded fancy, but the pure word of God, which is the ground of faith and hope"; and (4) that this divine intimation had "consequents and effects after God's speaking to me," including an altered disposition of soul; a dissolution of the works of Satan; an enlightened understanding; a melted will disposed to turn to God; a new nature "inclining me to good"; the Spirit of God as "a new indweller"; and "an actual turning from all known sins, and my entertaining the truth of all godliness."[8]

Upon conversion, Goodwin aligned himself unequivocally for the remainder of his life with the theological tradition of Perkins, Bayne, Sibbes, and Preston. He resolved never to seek personal fame but "to part with all for Christ and make the glory of God the measure of all time to come." Consequently, he abandoned the polished style of preaching then common among Anglican divines, since it promoted the preacher, and adopted the Puritan plain style of preaching, which, in its self-conscious disuse of human embellishment, sought to give all glory to God. His preaching became earnest, didactic, experimental, and pastoral.

For the first seven years after his regeneration in 1620, Goodwin struggled for personal assurance of faith. During these years he was largely "intent on the conviction God had wrought in him, of the heinousness of sin, and of his own sinful and miserable state by nature; of the difference between the workings of natural conscience, though enlightened, and the motions of a holy soul, changed and acted by the Spirit, in an effectual work of peculiar saving grace. And accordingly he kept a constant diary."[9] Through letters and conversations with a godly minister, Mr. Price of Kings Lynn (of whom Goodwin "said that he was the greatest man for experimental acquaintance with Christ that ever he met"), he was led to see his need to "live by faith in Christ, and to derive from him life and strength for sanctification, and all comfort and joy through believing." Of this period of spiritual struggle and difficulty, he confessed: "I was diverted from Christ for several years, to search only into the signs of grace in me. It was almost seven years ere I was taken off to live by faith on Christ, and God's free love, which are alike the object of faith."[10]

[8] *Ibid.*, lxii-lxiv.

[9] *Ibid.*, lxviii.

[10] *Ibid.*

Goodwin's soul finally found rest in Christ alone. He learned that he could not live from marks of grace. Writing to Mr. Price, he states: "I am come to this pass now, that signs will do me no good alone; I have trusted too much to habitual grace for assurance of justification; I tell you Christ is worth all." His son concludes: "Thus coming unto Christ, his weary soul found rest, when in all its unquiet motions it could not find it anywhere else."[11]

Goodwin's preaching now became considerably more Christ-centered. He could now agree with Dr. Sibbes's advice: "Young man, if you ever would do good, you must preach the gospel and the free grace of God in Christ Jesus."[12]

Shortly before this time, Goodwin was licensed as a preacher in Cambridge University. The following year (1626) he was influential in bringing Sibbes to St. Catherine's Hall as Master. In 1628 he was appointed lecturer at Trinity Church, succeeding Sibbes and Preston at the age of twenty-seven! From 1632 to 1634 he served as vicar of this church. In 1634, not willing to submit to Archbishop William Laud's new articles of conformity and having become a target of Laudian repression, Goodwin resigned his offices and left Cambridge. Numerous people, including several who later became influential Puritan pastors, were converted under Goodwin's preaching and lecturing in Cambridge.

During the mid-1630s, largely under the influence of John Cotton, Goodwin adopted Independent principles of church government.[13] From 1634 to 1639 he was probably a Separatist preacher in London. In 1639, because of increasing preaching restrictions and the threat of fines and imprisonment, he took refuge in the Netherlands where he labored in Arnhem with other well-known Independent ministers in serving a group of more than one hundred refugees from Laud's persecution. For two years he also exchanged reflections with his Dutch colleagues and came to realize that the Dutch Second Reformation (*Nadere Reformatie*) divines were emphasizing the same kind of Reformed, experimental truths in preaching and pastoring as were

[11] *Ibid.*, lxx.

[12] *Ibid.*, lxxi.

[13] Cf. Freer, "Goodwin, the Peaceable Puritan," 12-13. "Cotton's Congregationalism was given a final expression in *The Keys of the Kingdom* (1644), about which Goodwin said it provided a middle way between Brownism and Presbyterianism" (*ibid.*, 13).

the English Puritans, and were provoking similar responses from many of their colleagues. Just as some of the orthodox Dutch Calvinists looked askance at pietists such as Gijsbertus Voetius, the Dutch Owen, so some Calvinistic clergy in the English establishment viewed the Puritans with a certain degree of suspicion. In Holland, however, there was more freedom to experiment in the area of church government, so Goodwin found opportunity to explore the "Congregational Way," knowing that Independency was at best a minority view among the Puritans in England.[14]

In 1641, after Laud had been impeached and the Long Parliament had convened, Goodwin responded to Parliament's invitation to all who had left England for nonconformity to return. Some have claimed he gathered a church on Anchor Lane in the parish of St. Dunstan's in the East, London, later to become one of the most influential of the Independent churches. There is no conclusive evidence to substantiate this claim although Goodwin was preaching to an Independent church in St. Michael's Crooked Lane in London in 1646.[15]

Goodwin's rise to fame began with an invitation to preach to Parliament on April 27, 1642. Subsequently, he was appointed a member of the Westminster Assembly, where he is said to have been "the most decisive figure and the great disturber of the Westminster Assembly," due to his continual promotion of the Independent view of church government. Records of the assembly covering 243 sessions held from August 1643 to December 1644, indicate that Goodwin gave more addresses than any other divine—357 in all![16] Goodwin, Philip Nye, Sydrach Simpson,

[14] At Arnhem he studied church order and church discipline extensively with his colleague, Philip Nye. For additional detail on Goodwin's stay in the Netherlands, see Joel R. Beeke, *Assurance of Faith: Calvin, English Puritanism, and the Dutch Second Reformation* (New York: Peter Lang, 1991), 330-32, 353-54.

[15] *The Registar-Booke of the Fourth Classis in the Province of London*, transcribed by Charles Surnam (London: Harleian Society, 1953), 143.

[16] Wayne R. Spear, "Covenanted Uniformity in Religion: The Influence of the Scottish Commissioners Upon the Ecclesiology of the Westminster Assembly" (Ph.D. dissertation, University of Pittsburgh, 1976), 362.

For Goodwin's role in the Presbyterian-Independent controversy, see Fienberg, "Thomas Goodwin: Puritan Pastor and Independent Divine," 80-265; Berndt Gustafsson, *The Five Dissenting Brethren: A Study of the Dutch Background of Their Independentism* (London: C. W. K. Gloerup, 1955); R. B. Carter, "The Presbyterian-Independent Controversy with

William Bridge, and Jeremiah Burroughs became nicknamed the five "Dissenting Brethren" on account of their Independent views which they also presented to the Westminster Assembly in their *Apologeticall Narration* (1644).[17] Despite Goodwin's prolonging of the debate on church government, he retained the respect of the Presbyterian majority as a capable and irenic Puritan.[18] He was chosen to pray in the solemn meeting of seven hours' duration in which the assembly prepared to enter on the debate concerning the discipline of the church. This respect is also evident by his being appointed in 1644 to present to Parliament *The Directory of Public Worship*, at which time (and on several other occasions) he preached before Parliament. Subsequently, the House of Lords gave Goodwin and Jeremiah Whitaker the oversight and examination of the papers to be printed for the assembly.[19]

After the assembly recessed, additional preferments followed in rapid succession for Goodwin. In 1649, Goodwin, Joseph Caryl, and Edward Reynolds were appointed lecturers at Oxford. On June 7, 1649, both Goodwin and Owen preached before the House of Commons on a special day of public thanksgiving and the next day the House put their names forward for promotion to the presidency of two Oxford colleges. In 1650, Goodwin became president of Magdalen College, Oxford, while Owen similarly became dean of Christchurch. The pair must have had considerable influence, since Cromwell yielded his power as Chancellor to a commission headed by Owen. At his post, Goodwin was made a close adviser to Cromwell and the protector's Oxford Commissioner.

Goodwin's influence shaped Magdalen College into an institution known for adherence to scriptural truth and Calvinistic, experimental doctrine. Demanding academic excellence and

Special Reference to Dr. Thomas Goodwin and the Years 1640 to 1660" (Ph.D. dissertation, Edinburgh, 1961); David R. Ehalt, "The Development of Early Congregational Theory of the Church with Special Reference to the Five 'Dissenting Brethren' at the Westminster Assembly" (Ph.D. dissertation, Claremont, 1969); J. R. De Witt, *Jus Divinum: The Westminster Assembly and the Divine Right of Church Government* (Kampen: Kok, 1969).

[17] *Ibid.*, 88-99.

[18] Freer, "Goodwin, the Peaceable Puritan," 15-18.

[19] Goodwin's own shorthand notes on the Assembly filled fourteen volumes!

dealing plainly with the spiritual lives of the students, he was soon accused of operating a "scruple shop" by those who did not appreciate his Puritan emphasis on intelligent piety. It was in these years, however, as even Lord Clarendon later pronounced, that "the University of Oxford yielded a harvest of extraordinary good and sound knowledge in all parts of learning."[20]

As he began his college presidency, Goodwin married for the second time. In 1638 he had married Elizabeth Prescott, the daughter of a London alderman, but she died in the 1640s, leaving him with one daughter. In 1650 he married Mary Hammond, "of ancient and honorable Shropshire lineage." Goodwin was forty-nine and she was in her seventeenth year. By this second marriage Goodwin had two sons, Thomas and Richard, and two daughters, both of whom died in infancy. Richard died as a young man on a voyage to the East Indies. Thomas followed in his father's footsteps as an Independent pastor and later established a private academy for the training of ministers.

Goodwin's ten years at Oxford were active and productive. During this time he and John Owen shared a Sunday afternoon lecture for the students at Oxford, and both were chaplains to Cromwell. Goodwin also formed an Independent church and preached to a unique mixture of hearers, uneducated and educated, including Stephen Charnock and Thankful Owen. In 1653 Goodwin was awarded a doctorate in divinity by Oxford University. The following year he was chosen by Cromwell to sit on the Board of Visitors of Oxford University, as well as to be one of the Triers on The Board for the Approbation of Public Preachers, whose task it was to examine men for both pulpit and public instructional work. He was also appointed to the Oxfordshire Commission for the Ejection of Scandalous Ministers. During this decade, Goodwin was probably closer to Cromwell than any other Independent divine and attended the Lord Protector on his deathbed.

Before Cromwell died (September 3, 1658), Goodwin secured his reluctant permission for the Independents to hold a synod and draft a confession of faith. On September 29, 1658 Goodwin, Owen, Philip Nye, William Bridge, Joseph Caryl, and William Greenhill were appointed to draw up a confession of faith to be used by some 120 Independent churches. Owen almost

[20] Cited by Peter Toon, *Puritans and Calvinism* (Swengel, PA: Reiner, 1973), 47.

certainly wrote the lengthy introduction, but it was Goodwin who probably had the most important hand in writing the first draft:

> Goodwin again was prominent and this declaration amounted to a statement of his convictions on Church faith and order spawned in his twenties, triggered into action by John Cotton, consolidated in his thirties, thrashed out in Holland, practised in London and Oxford, defended in the Westminster Assembly and thus at last given a definitive expression. Goodwin's star had reached its zenith.[21]

The resulting document was presented for approval to a group of representatives from over one hundred Independent churches. After eleven or twelve days of work, the *Savoy Declaration of* Faith and Order was adopted October 12, 1658, being unanimously approved. On October 14 Goodwin led a delegation to present the *Savoy Declaration* to Richard Cromwell. Closely resembling the Westminster Confession of Faith with the major exception of church polity, it became the confessional standard for British and American Congregationalism from that date.[22]

With the Rump Parliament restored in 1659 the Presbyterian state-church was restored as well, but one year later, with the support of many Presbyterians and Anglicans, Charles II landed at Dover on May 25. Due to the accession of Charles II and the accompanying loss of Puritan power, Goodwin felt compelled to leave his work at Oxford. He moved to London, together with a substantial part of his congregation, and formed a church there in 1660. Despite assurances to the contrary, the new king enacted strict acts of conformity. In 1662 two thousand godly ministers were ejected from the national church. Being in an Independent church, however, and holding no offices to which he had been appointed by the government, Goodwin was not among them. He was allowed by God's overruling providence to continue preaching throughout the many years of persecution under Charles II. He also was enabled to lead his London congregation through the dreaded Plague, when most Established Church pastors abandoned the city. He devoted his last years to preaching, pastoral work, and the writing of numerous treatises, of which we are

[21] Freer, "Goodwin, the Peaceable Puritan," 14.

[22] Cf. *The Savoy Declaration of Faith and Order*, edited by A. G. Matthews (London: Independent Press, Ltd., 1959); Beeke, *Assurance of Faith,* 237-38, 273.

beneficiaries more than three hundred years later with this timely reprint of his *Works*.

Reading Goodwin

Thomas Goodwin was a prolific author and editor. During the 1630s he coedited with John Ball the works of John Preston and Richard Sibbes. He began to publish some of his own sermons in 1636.[23] Prior to his death, he published at least twelve devotional works, most of which were collections of sermons.[24] The fact that they were reissued forty-seven times indicates the high demand and wide circulation of his publications.

Most of Goodwin's major theological writings were the fruit of his riper years and were published posthumously. His unusually large corpus of treatises displays a pastoral and scholarly zeal rivalled by few Puritans.

The first collection of Goodwin's works was published in five folio volumes in London from 1681 to 1704 under the editorship of Thankful Owen, Thomas Baron, and Thomas Goodwin, Jr. An abridged version of Goodwin's works, condensed by J. Rabb, was printed in four volumes (London, 1847-50). The presently reprinted twelve-volume authoritative edition was printed by James Nichol (Edinburgh, 1861-66) as his first choice in what would become known as the well-edited and highly regarded *Nichol's Series of Standard Divines*; not surprisingly, it is far superior to the original five folio volumes.

Goodwin's treatment of his subjects is massive, sometimes liable to exhaust the half-hearted. The pull of his writings is not always felt immediately. His first editors (1681) explained his occasional prolixity in these terms: "He had a genius to dive into the bottom of points, to 'study them down,' as he used to express it, not contenting himself with superficial knowledge, without wading into the depths of things."[25] Edmund Calamy put it this way: "It is evident from his writings, he studied not words, but things. His stile is plain and familiar; but very diffuse, homely and tedious."[26] Though Calamy has exaggerated the problem of

[23] *DNB*, 8:149.

[24] Reid, *op. cit.*, 1:341-43.

[25] For the reprinting of the original, succinct preface, see *Works*, 1:xxix-xxxii.

[26] *The Nonconformist's Memorial*, 1:186.

style, one does need patience to read Goodwin at times; along with depth and prolixity, however, he combines a wonderful sense of warmth, unction, and experience. The reader's patience will be amply rewarded.

How then ought a beginner in Goodwin's *Works* proceed? Here is a suggested plan:

First, begin by reading some of the shorter, more practical writings of Goodwin, such as these:

(1) *Patience and Its Perfect Work*, four sermons expounding James 1:1-5, was written after the loss of a large part of Goodwin's personal library by fire (volume 2, pages 429-467 [hereafter 2:429-467]) and is replete with practical instruction for enhancing a spirit of submission.

(2) *Certain Select Cases Resolved* includes three experimental treatises which unveil Goodwin's large pastoral heart for afflicted Christians, each of them aiming at specific struggles in the believer's soul: (a) *A Child of Light Walking in Darkness*, a classic treatise of Puritan encouragement for the spiritually depressed based on Isaiah 50:10-11 (3:241-350). Its subtitle summarizes its contents well: *A Treatise shewing The Causes by which, The Cases wherein, and the Ends for which, God leaves His Children to Distress of Conscience, Together with Directions How to Walk so as to Come Forth of Such a Condition.* (b) *The Return of Prayers*, based on Psalm 85:8, a uniquely practical work that affords discernment in ascertaining "God's answers to our prayers" (3:353-429). (c) *The Trial of a Christian's Growth* (3:433-506), based on John 15:1-2, a masterpiece on sanctification which focuses on the graces of mortification and vivification. For a mini-classic on spiritual growth, this gem remains unsurpassed until today.

(3) *The Vanity of Thoughts*, based on Jeremiah 4:14 (3:509-528), is a convicting little work, stressing the need for bringing every thought into captive obedience to Christ, and providing remedies on how to foster that obedience.

Second, read for instruction and edification some of Goodwin's great sermons which inevitably bear a strong, Biblical, Christological, and experimental stamp (2:359-425; 4:151-224; 5:439-548; 7:473-576; 9:499-514; 12:1-127).

Third, delve into Goodwin's great works which expound major doctrines, including the following:

(1) *An Unregenerate Man's Guiltiness Before God in Respect of Sin and Punishment* (10:1-567) is a weighty Puritan

treatment of human guilt, corruption, and the imputation and punishment of sin. For exposure of the total depravity of the natural man's heart, this treatise is unparalleled in all of Christian literature. It aims to produce a heartfelt sense of dire need for saving faith in Christ rather than the quick-fix approach of contemporary, superficial Christendom.

(2) *The Object and Acts of Justifying Faith* is a frequently reprinted classic (8:1-593). Part I, on the *objects of faith*, focuses on God's nature, Christ Himself, and the free grace of God revealed in His absolute promises. Part II deals with the *acts of faith*—what it means to believe in Christ, to obtain assurance, to find joy in the Holy Ghost, to make use of God's electing love. A concluding section beautifully expounds the "actings of faith in prayer." Part III addresses the *properties of faith*—its excellency, for it gives all honor to God and Christ; its difficulty, for it reaches beyond the natural abilities of man; its necessity, for we must endeavor to believe in the strength of God. A valuable, practical conclusion provides "directions to guide us in our endeavours to believe."

(3) *Christ the Mediator* (2 Corinthians 5:18-19), *Christ Set Forth* (Romans 8:34), and *The Heart of Christ in Heaven Towards Sinners on Earth* are great works of Christology (5:1-438; 4:1-92; 4:93-150). *Christ the Mediator* sets forth Jesus especially in His substitutionary work of humiliation, and rightly deserves to be called a classic as well; *Christ Set Forth* proclaims Him largely albeit briefly in His exaltation; *The Heart of Christ* expounds the neglected theme of the affectionate tenderness of Christ's glorified human nature shown to His people still on earth. In this latter work Goodwin waxes more mystical than anywhere else in his writings, but as Paul Cook has ably shown, his mysticism is confined within the boundaries of Scripture.[27] Here Goodwin is unapproached "in his combination of intellectual and theological power with evangelical and homiletical comfort."[28]

(4) *Gospel Holiness in Heart and Life* (7:129-336) is a convicting and stimulating masterpiece, based on Philippians 1:9-11, expounding the doctrine of sanctification in every sphere of life.

(5) *The Knowledge of God the Father, and His Son Jesus*

[27] Paul Cook, "Thomas Goodwin—Mystic?," in *Diversities of Gifts*, 45-56.

[28] Whyte, *Thirteen Appreciations*, 165.

Christ (4:347-569), combined with *The Work of the Holy Spirit* (6:1-522), speak much of a profound experimental acquaintance in the believer's soul of each of the three divine persons in their personhood and saving work. *The Work of the Spirit* is particularly helpful in the doctrines of regeneration and conversion, and in delicately yet lucidly discerning the work of "the natural conscience" from the Spirit's saving work.

(6) *The Glory of the Gospel* (4:227-346) consists of two sermons and a treatise based on Colossians 1:26-27, and ought to be read together with *The Blessed State of Glory Which the Saints Possess After Death* (7:339-472), based on Revelation 14:13.

(7) *A Discourse of Election* (9:1-498) is a profound work which delves deeply into questions such as the supralapsarian-infralapsarian debate which wrestles with the moral order of God's decree, but it also deals practically with the fruits of election (e.g., see Book IV on 1 Peter 5:10 and Book V on how God fulfils His covenant of grace in the generations of believers).

(8) In *The Creatures and the Condition of Their State by Creation* (7:1-128) Goodwin waxes more philosophical here than elsewhere.

Fourth, digest prayerfully and slowly Goodwin's profound 900+ page exposition of Ephesians 1:1 to 2:11 (1:1-564; 2:1-355)—a work of which has been justly concluded, "Not even Luther on the Galatians is such an expositor of Paul's mind and heart as is Goodwin on the Ephesians."[29]

Finally, save for last Goodwin's exposition of Revelation (3:1-226) and his sole polemical work, *The Constitution, Right Order, and Government of the Churches of Christ* (11:1-546). Independents, of course, would value this latter work highly, while Presbyterians would hold that Goodwin is a safe guide in nearly every area but church government. Happily, Goodwin's work does not degrade Presbyterians; in fact, one of his contemporaries who felt compelled to answer it confessed the author conveyed "a truly great and noble spirit" throughout the work.[30]

Goodwin's Distinctive Teachings: Sealing and Assurance

In discussing Goodwin's teaching, the pastoral context of his writing must be remembered. Most of his writing focuses on the

[29] *Ibid.*, 162.

[30] *Ibid.*, 169.

doctrine of salvation and its personal application; he is seldom interested in dogmatics or metaphysics for their own sake. All his teaching and theology are ultimately pulpit exposition and application. Consequently, he commences each book and usually each chapter of each book with a scriptural text that he first expounds and applies. He excels in drawing all his theology out of the fountainhead of Scripture. This renders his writings fresh, rich, and personal. In short, his sermons and treatises were written to help believers know their spiritual state and grow in their relationship with the Triune God.

Surprisingly little has been written on what Thomas Goodwin taught. Major studies on his theology are few.[31] Perhaps this is due to the fact that, for the most part, his doctrine of salvation was not original. Its basic feature was drawn from the classically Pauline-Augustinian-Puritan conviction that true happiness lay in the knowledge of and communion with God by faith, as well as in praise and obedience to Him in daily life. Throughout his life, the believer needs increasingly to grasp by faith the objective work of God in election and redemption as well as subjectively to experience God's work of justification and sanctification within him. There are two areas, however, in which Goodwin does chart his own course soteriologically: the sealing of the Spirit and personal assurance of faith.

On these matters, Goodwin has most to say in his *Exposition*

[31] For Goodwin on the covenant of grace, see Paul Edward Brown, "The Principle of the Covenant in the Theology of Thomas Goodwin" (Ph.D. dissertation, Drew University, 1950). Alexander McNally, "Some Aspects of Thomas Goodwin's Doctrine of Assurance" (Th.M., Westminster Theological Seminary, 1972) focuses on covenant, assurance of faith, and sealing of the Spirit. Stanley Fienberg, "Thomas Goodwin, Puritan Pastor and Independent Divine" (Ph.D. dissertation, University of Chicago, 1974) studies Goodwin's teaching on depravity, justification, and sanctification. Beeke, "Thomas Goodwin: The Merging of English-Dutch Thinking on Assurance," in *Assurance of Faith* (chapter 9), addresses Goodwin on assurance and compares his views on steps of grace experienced by the believer to the views of John Owen and Alexander Comrie. Michael Horton, "Christ Set Forth: Thomas Goodwin and the Puritan Doctrine of Assurance" (Ph.D. dissertation, Wycliffe Hall, Oxford and Coventry University, 1996) provides the most exhaustive look at Goodwin's theology to date, expounding his views on faith, assurance, predestination, justification, covenant, conversion, preparatory grace, temporary faith, perseverance, the church, and the sacraments.

of the Epistle to the Ephesians (sermons 13-17 on Ephesians 1:13-14), and *Of the Object and Acts of Justifying Faith* (Part II ["Of the Acts of Faith"], particularly Book II ["Of faith of assurance"]).[32] Additional thoughts on assurance are interwoven in several other works, most notably, *A Child of Light Walking in Darkness, The Return of Prayers*, and *The Trial of a Christian's Growth*.[33]

Goodwin's view on the sealing of the Spirit must be placed in light of its historical context. The seal of the Spirit was a common theme in the seventeenth century, and one which the majority of Puritans intimately conjoined with assurance. Not that this was always the case, however, for the early Reformers clearly maintained a one-to-one correlation between the "Spirit-regenerated" and the "Spirit-sealed." John Calvin (1509-1564), for example, denies what would become the general Puritan notion that it was possible to believe without being sealed with the Spirit; instead, he declares that the seal is the Holy Spirit Himself.[34] The sealing work of the Spirit also belongs to the essence of faith.

By the time of William Perkins (1558-1602), however, the focus was no longer on the Holy Spirit as seal, so much as on what the activity of the Spirit was in sealing the promise to the believer. Perkins taught that this personal sealing removes all

[32] *Works of Goodwin*, 1:206-252 and 8:338-419.

[33] E.g., *A Child of Light Walking in Darkness*, in which Goodwin affirms that the lack of assurance is compatible with faith (*Works of Goodwin* 3:238). In *The Return of Prayers*, Goodwin distinguishes assurance from "recumbency" (3:368), indicates that the doctrine of assurance will not make believers presumptuous unless it is abused (3:417), and stresses that assurance may be lost (3:422). In *The Trial of a Christian's Growth*, Goodwin asserts that God purges out corruption by assuring the believer of His love (3:480). In 4:207 Goodwin defines assurance as a persuasion that God and Christ "are prepared to save a man's own self in particular." In volume 5, he affirms that perseverance does not make the Christian less resolute in resisting temptation (p. 325), but acknowledges that many believers lack full assurance (p. 394). Moreover, assurance always presupposes a first act of faith's recumbency (5:403).

[34] Cf. Calvin's *Commentary* on Ephesians 1:13-14, 3:12 (reprint Grand Rapids: Baker, 1979), and his *Institutes of the Christian Religion*, ed. John T. McNeill, trans. F. L. Battles (Philadelphia: Westminster Press, 1960), 3.2.11, 34, 41.

doubt for the believer.[35] In sealing, which is mediated through the Word, the Spirit begets an assured "trust and confidence" in the promises so that the believer's will and understanding is moved to embrace the promises experimentally as his own.[36]

Perkins's successor, Paul Bayne (d. 1617), attempted to unite together both the Spirit as the seal Himself by being Indweller and the consequences of that sealing in the graces of the regenerate life, and thus bring some harmony to the diverse Reformed-Puritan heritage.[37] Bayne distinguished being sealed by the Spirit from being *made conscious* of such sealing. The former belonged to all true believers (Calvin's input); the latter, to some (Perkins's input).

Richard Sibbes (1577-1635), one of Bayne's converts and his successor, taught that the sealing of the Spirit was a "superadded work" and "superadded confirmation" of the believer's faith.[38] Sealing is comparable to the "sweet communion of marriage" with a perfect Bridegroom, Jesus Christ, whose own sealing by God the Father is the foundation of the believer's sealing.[39] For Christ's sake, seals serve for "confirmation, distinction, appropriation, estimation, secrecy," and remain "inviolable."[40] For Sibbes, the internal, sealing testimony of the Spirit is the supreme sign of grace.

Moving a step beyond Sibbes, John Preston (1587-1628) taught specifically that the sealing of the Spirit was a *second work*

[35] *William Perkins, 1558-1602; English Puritanist: His Pioneer Works on Casuistry*, ed. Thomas F. Merrill (Nieuwkoop: B. DeGraaf, 1966), 50-51.

[36] *The Workes of that Famous and VVorthy Minister of Christ, Mr. William Perkins* (London: John Legatt, 1612), 1:104-105.

[37] Paul Bayne, *An Entire Commentary vpon the whole Epistle of the Apostle Paul to the Ephesians* (London: Printed by M. F. for Milbourne and I. Bartlet, 1643), 80-81.

[38] *Complete Works* (1862; reprint Edinburgh: Banner of Truth Trust, 1973-82), 3:455. Sibbes preached often on the Spirit's sealing. First, a series of sermons transcribed by a noblewoman, Lady Elizabeth Brooke, was published in 1637 as *A Fountain Sealed* (*ibid.*, 5:409-456). Secondly, sermons on 2 Corinthians 1:22-23 in the *Exposition of Second Corinthians Chapter 1*, were published in 1655 (*ibid.*, 3:420-84). Thirdly, a sermon on Romans 8:15-16, *The Witness of the Spirit*, was first published in 1692 (*ibid.*, 7:367-85). Cf. *ibid.*, 2:453-64, 4:132ff., 6:374-79, 428-30.

[39] *Ibid.*, 5:433-34; 3:443.

[40] *Ibid.*, 434-37; 4:123.

given exclusively to those who overcome.[41] Influenced by this Sibbes-Preston tradition and by his own experience of full assurance, Thomas Goodwin carried the sealing of the Spirit as a second work to its fullest development. Consciously rejecting Calvin's position, Goodwin defines such sealing as a "light beyond the light of ordinary faith."[42] He expands as follows:

> The sealing of the Holy Spirit is an immediate assurance by a heavenly and divine light of a divine authority, which the Holy Ghost sheddeth in a man's heart, (not having relation to grace wrought or anything in a man's self,) whereby he sealeth him up to the day of redemption.[43]

And again:

> It is the next thing to heaven . . . you can have no more until you come thither.[44]

Sealing is the "whispering" of the Holy Spirit that I am elected of God, have my sins forgiven, and belong to Him forever—both intuitively and directly.[45] Thus, Goodwin made a direct tie between the sealing of the Spirit and full assurance of faith, contrary to Owen who rejected identifying the sealing of the Spirit with a post-regeneration experience of assurance.

Interestingly, the Westminster Assembly seems to have left this question open (*Westminster Confession of Faith*, chapter XVIII, paragraph 2). The divines agreed that assurance of faith is grounded primarily upon the promises of God and secondarily on "the inward evidences of those graces unto which these promises are made," but then they added these words without specifying whether they represent a continuation of the second ground or a distinct third ground: "the testimony of the Spirit of adoption witnessing with our spirits that we are the children of God, which Spirit is the earnest of our inheritance, whereby we are sealed to the day of redemption."

The Westminster divines knew that the witness of the Holy Spirit was the most difficult ground of assurance to comprehend. They freely confessed that "amazing variety" and vast mysteries

[41] *The New Covenant, or the Saint's Portion* (London: I.D. for Nicholas Bourne, 1639), 2:416-17.

[42] *The Works of Thomas Goodwin*, 1:236.

[43] *Ibid.*, 233.

[44] *Ibid.*, 236.

[45] *Ibid.*, 236-37.

surrounded them when they spoke of the leadings of the Spirit and how He dwells in believers. Consequently, the assembly desired to allow freedom for different opinions concerning some of the finer details of the Spirit's testimony. There were two, and possibly three schools of thought among the divines.

In the first group are those men, such as Jeremiah Burroughs, Anthony Burgess, and George Gillespie, who regarded the testimony of the Holy Spirit in assurance as exclusively His activity within syllogistic reasoning whereby He brings conscience to unite with His witness that the Christian is a child of God.[46] According to this view Romans 8:15 and 8:16 are regarded as synonymous: the witness of the Holy Spirit is always conjoined *with* the witness of the believer's spirit.[47] For these divines, the inward evidence of grace and the testimony of the Spirit are essentially one; they impart *full assurance*. These divines felt this view was important to maintain in opposition to mysticism and antinomianism which are prone to accent a direct testimony of the Spirit apart from the necessity of bringing forth practical fruits of faith and repentance.

In the second group are those divines such as Samuel Rutherford, William Twisse, Henry Scudder, and Thomas Goodwin, who believed that the witness of the Spirit described in Romans 8:15 contains something in addition to that of verse 16.[48] This group distinguishes the Spirit witnessing *with* the believer's spirit by syllogistic reasoning from His witnessing *to* the believer's spirit by direct applications of the Word. As Meyer points out, the former leaves in its wake the self-conscious conviction, "*I* am a child of God," and on the basis of such

[46] Burroughs, *The Saints' Happiness, together with the several steps leading thereunto. Delivered in Divers Lectures on the Beatitudes* (reprint ed., Beaver Falls, PA: Soli Deo Gloria, 1988), 196; Burgess, *Spiritual Refining: or, A Treatise of Grace and Assurance* (London: A. Miller, 1652), 44; Gillespie, *A Treatise of Miscellany Questions* (Edinburgh: Gedeon Lithgovv, 1649), 105-109.

[47] Cf. Burgess's exegesis of Romans 8:15-16, Ephesians 1:13, and 1 John 5:8 in *Spiritual Refining*, 49-50.

[48] Rutherford, *The Covenant of Life Opened* (Edinburgh: Andro Anderson, 1655), 65ff.; Twisse, *The Doctrine of the Synod of Dort and Arles, reduced to the practise* (Amsterdam: G. Thorp, 1631), 147ff.; Scudder, *The Christian's Daily Walk* (reprint Harrisburg, VA: Sprinkle, 1984), 338-42; *The Works of Thomas Goodwin*, 6:27; 7:66; 8:351, 363.

Spirit-worked syllogisms finds freedom to approach God as Father. The latter speaks the Spirit's pronouncement on behalf of the Father, "*You* are a child of God," and on this basis of hearing of its sonship from God's own Word by the Spirit, proceeds to approach Him with the familiarity of a child.[49] Henry Scudder's breakdown of the Spirit's witness is typical of this second group:

> This Spirit does witness to a man, that he is the child of God, two ways:
>
> First, By immediate witness and suggestion. Secondly, By necessary inferences, by signs from the infallible fruits of the said Spirit.[50]

This second group differed among themselves on whether the Spirit's direct testimony should be regarded as more spontaneous, durable, and powerful than His syllogistic testimony. The most common approach is Rutherford's, which allows for the direct testimony, but then stresses that the reflex act of faith is as a rule "more spiritual and helpful" than are direct acts.[51] Consequently, all believers should be regularly praying for the Spirit's illumination to guide them into syllogistic conclusions. Twisse and Scudder distinguish the Spirit's testifying with our spirit from His witnessing of personal adoption without determining which is most valuable.[52] Goodwin asserts, however, that the direct witness of the Spirit far supersedes the co-witnessing through the syllogisms.[53] For him, "full" assurance is more than *discursive*; it is also *intuitive*. Generally speaking, however, this second group (with the exception of Goodwin and a few others) does not conceive of the direct testimony of the Spirit as being

[49] Heinrich August Wilhelm Meyer, *Critical and Exegetical Hand-book to The Epistle of the Romans* (New York: Funk & Wagnalls, Publishers, 1889), 316.

[50] *The Christian's Daily Walk*, 338.

[51] *Catechisms of the Second Reformation*, ed. by Alexander F. Mitchell (London: James Nisbet, 1886), 207; Rutherford, *The Trial and Triumph of Faith* (Edinburgh: William Collins, 1845), 88ff. and *Christ Dying and Drawing Sinners to Himselfe* (London: J. D. for Andrew Cooke), 71, 94ff. Burgess agrees with Rutherford (*Spiritual Refining*, 672).

[52] Twisse, *The Doctrine of the Synod of Dort and Arles, reduced to the practise*, 156; Scudder, *The Christian's Daily Walk*, 338-42.

[53] *The Works of Thomas Goodwin*, 1:233; 8:366.

independent of the syllogisms, but as "superadded" to them. They are agreed that the syllogistic way of reaching assurance is more common and probably safer: "Some Divines do not indeed deny the possibility of such an immediate Testimony, but yet they conclude the ordinary and safe way, is, to look for that Testimony, which is by the effects, and fruits of God's Spirit."[54]

Goodwin and those he influenced may also be said to belong to a sub-group of the second group because though their views are intimately associated with the second group *theologically*, they place the event of "immediate" assurance by direct witness of the Holy Spirit on a higher level *practically*. Some Westminster divines, such as William Bridge and Samuel Rutherford, belonging to the second group, believe that such assurance becomes the portion of many Christians before they die.[55] Others, however, and most notably Goodwin, place this experience far beyond the pale of ordinary experience. In fact, Goodwin states that the experience of full assurance pronounced by the Spirit "immediately" is so profound that it is comparable to "a new conversion."[56]

For Goodwin this "full" assurance is the zenith of experimental life. Unlike the position adopted by most in the second group, such assurance is divorced from the syllogisms entirely:

> This witness is immediate, that is, it builds not his testimony on anything in us; it is not a testimony fetched out of a man's self, or the work of the Spirit in man, as the others were; for the Spirit speaks not by his effects, but speaks from himself.[57]

Goodwin repeatedly uses terms such as "immediate light," "joy unspeakable," "transcendent," "glorious," and "intuitive" in describing the experience of full assurance. Indeed, it is beyond human description:

> Those who have attained it cannot demonstrate it to others, especially not to those who have not experience of it, for it is a white stone which no one knows but he that receives it, Rev. 2:17.[58]

Goodwin nevertheless wholeheartedly concurred with his

[54] Burgess, *Spiritual Refining*, 52.

[55] Cf. *The Works of William Bridge* (reprint Beaver Falls, PA: Soli Deo Gloria, 1989), 2:140.

[56] *The Works of Thomas Goodwin*, 1:251.

[57] *Ibid.*, 8:366.

[58] *Ibid.*, 8:351.

fellow divines that the Spirit's testimony is always tied to, and may never contradict, the Word of God. "The Spirit is promised in the Word, and that promise is fulfilled in experience."[59] All the Westminster Assembly divines were most anxious to avoid antinomianism and unbiblical mysticism on the one hand, as well as to protect the freedom of the Spirit and the reality of Biblical-Pauline mystical experience on the other.

Goodwin's Homegoing and Epitaph

Goodwin died in London in his eightieth year embracing the Triune God by victorious faith and reminiscing of God's past faithfulness to him. More than fifty years before that time, he had experienced a sweet, "immediate" assurance sealed to his heart by the Holy Spirit which went far beyond anything he had previously experienced. Inseparable from this personal sense of full assurance, through which he felt almost as if he were "converted again," was an experimental realization of communing with each of the three divine Persons. This conviction strengthened with time and served him in good stead on his deathbed, as his son informs us:

> In all the violence of [his fever], he discoursed with that strength of faith and assurance of Christ's love, with that holy admiration of free grace, with that joy in believing, and such thanksgivings and praises, as he extremely moved and affected all that heard him.... He rejoiced in the thought that he was dying, and going to have a full and uninterrupted communion with God. 'I am going,' said he, 'to the three Persons, with whom I have had communion: they have taken me; I did not take them.... I could not have imagined I should ever have had such a measure of faith in this hour.... Christ cannot love me better than he doth; I think I cannot love Christ better than I do; I am swallowed up in God....' With this assurance of faith, and fulness of joy, his soul left this world.[60]

Throughout a long life, Thomas Goodwin not only attained celebrity or notoriety (depending on one's view) as a leader of Independency during the Civil War and Interregnum period, and as a principal architect of the Cromwellian domestic settlement; he also was known among the Puritan divines of the seventeenth

[59] John Von Rohr, *The Covenant of Grace in Puritan Thought* (Atlanta: Scholars Press, 1986), 165-66.

[60] *Works,* 2:lxxiv-lxxv.

century as an eminent believer, an able preacher, a caring pastor, and a profoundly spiritual writer. Buried in Bunhill Fields, his epitaph, written in long obliterated Latin, is most moving when read in full;[61] it summarizes well his most important gifts: He *was* by the grace of God knowledgeable in the Scriptures, sound in judgment, and enlightened by the Spirit to penetrate the mysteries of the gospel; he *was* a pacifier of troubled consciences, a dispeller of error, and a truly Christian pastor; he *did* edify numbers of souls whom he had first won to Christ. And is not the closing section of his epitaph being fulfilled even today by the reprinting of his works at the close of the second millenium of the Christian era?

> His writings..., the noblest monument of this great man's praise, will diffuse his name in a more fragrant odour than that of the richest perfume, to flourish in those distant ages, when this marble, inscribed with his just honour, shall have dropt into dust.

2115 Romence NE
Grand Rapids, Michigan 49503

Dr. Joel R. Beeke
Easter, 1996

[61] *Ibid.*, xlii-xliii.

CONTENTS.

GENERAL PREFACE.

BY

JOHN C. MILLER, D.D.,
LINCOLN COLLEGE, OXFORD; HONORARY CANON OF WORCESTER;
RECTOR OF ST MARTIN'S, BIRMINGHAM.

GENERAL PREFACE.

THE stores of theology, enriched by the accumulating treasures of successive generations, have of late years been thrown open widely to the Church of Christ. The Fathers, the Reformers, many of the great Puritan writers, no less than the later theologians of the Church of England and of the Nonconformist Churches, have been issued in a form and at a price which places them within general reach. In the departments of Hermeneutics and Exegetics, more especially, these stores are receiving constant and, with more or less of the alloy of human imperfection and error, most valuable additions. Among English scholars, the labours of Professor Ellicott, who, in philological acumen and attainments of the highest order, in combination with an absence of party bias, and with a profound reverence for the inspiration and authority of the Sacred Scriptures, is a very model of scholarship, sanctified to the honest and fearless interpretation of God's Word,—trusting Scripture, and anxious only to educe its meaning, to whatever conclusions it may lead; Dean Alford and Dr Wordsworth, in their great works; Dean Trench, Dr Peile, Professor Eadie, Dr Vaughan (whose unpretending Exposition of the Epistle to the Romans is sufficiently indicative of many of the qualifications of an expositor); Messrs Conybeare and Howson, in their well-known work; Dr Henderson on the Prophets; in America, Professor Stuart, with all his faults, and (though not as a philological scholar, yet as a sober, copious, and painstaking expositor) Albert Barnes,—have given to the Church *κτήματα ἐς ἀεί*.*

* In enumerating (not invidiously, and without the affectation of attempting to do it exhaustively) some of the most valuable modern additions to our expository theology, I cannot bring myself to omit Haldane's "Exposition of the Epistle to the Romans," though not agreeing with Mr Haldane on every point, any more than with the other writers specified above. No difference on particular points (where we recognise substantial orthodoxy on the capital truths of the gospel) should tempt us to withhold our meed of gratitude to such philologists and expositors. Their contributions should be recognised, not in a

Nor must our obligations to modern German theologians be forgotten. Their works, the best of them, need to be read with discrimination. And in those which have been brought within reach of the English student, some of which are deservedly in high esteem, there is even in the best, with scarcely an exception, not only much that is prolix and wearisome, but, specially to those of us who read them under the disadvantage of a translation, much that is misty, and not a little that is questionable. These are within our reach, and much used by many of our clergy and ministers. No theological library can be complete without them. To the student and to the preacher they are storehouses with which they can ill afford to dispense, if they are to be as scribes well "instructed unto the kingdom of heaven," bringing "forth out of" their "treasure things new and old."

For although there is something specious in the notion that the preacher can afford to be a man of one book, if that book be the Book of God,—and we doubt not that such men have been, and will be yet again, blessed to great usefulness in the Church of Christ,—it involves surely a blind and ungrateful misappreciation and disparagement of the gifts dispensed by that Divine Spirit whose "manifestation" is "given to every man to profit withal," when we underrate the treasures which have been left to us by men raised from time to time for the close study and investigation of the written Word, and for the enforcement and defence of the doctrines of our "most holy faith." Individual cases of "unlearned and ignorant men," lacking apostolic inspiration and endowments, may arise not seldom, in which, with humble gifts, and little or none of the assistance of human lore and training, they have been signally owned and honoured by God to do His work in the ingathering and edification of His people. But, as a rule, an ignorant clergy, a clergy undisciplined by habits of study and uninformed by reading, will fail to be effective in an enlightened and inquiring age. Their preaching will be vapid, superficial, and desultory, ultimately settling down into an iteration (fluent enough perhaps) of facile topics.

These remarks apply with peculiar force to a crisis in the Church's history in which heresy is rife, and the foundations of the faith are undermined and assailed by formidable errors. The Church then needs well-equipped champions. Such can be found only among

narrow-minded spirit of party, but with candour and large-hearted acknowledgments. Robert Haldane's grasp of the general scope of the Epistle to the Romans, and his lucid exposition of its *key-phrase*, "the righteousness of God," have long led me to value his work as one of the noblest pieces of exegetics in our language.

well-stored theologians, theologians "mighty in the Scriptures," but well versed also in the works of the great and gifted champions and exponents of the faith in every age—the Fathers and Reformers of old, and the later and the living contributors to the Church's stores.

Among these stores, it will not be denied that the writings of the Puritan Divines must ever be held in high estimation. Many of them are, *in extenso*, within our reach, widely circulated, and largely used; as Bishop Hopkins, Owen, Baxter, Howe, Bates, Flavel, &c. &c. Others, such as are to be published in this Series, are generally accessible in select works only; as Manton, Goodwin, Sibbes, Brooks, Charnock, Adams, &c. The works of the first four of these have never been published in a uniform edition; and of the works of Sibbes and Brooks, no complete collection exists in any public library of the kingdom, and probably in few, if in any, of the private libraries is a full set of either to be found.

The projector of the present scheme—a scheme to be followed up, should its success realise the expectations formed of it, by the issue of the works of Trapp, Swinnock, Gilpin, Trail, Bates, Burgess, and others which have been suggested—is conferring a great boon upon the Church of Christ, and one the influence of which may be felt throughout the Protestant pulpits of Christendom; by doing for the comparatively inaccessible works of these Puritan Divines what has been done for many of the Fathers, the Reformers, and the German Theologians, in collecting their works, and issuing them in a form and at a price which will place them on the shelves of thousands of our students and ministers, at home, in the colonies, and in the United States of America.

It would obviously be beyond the scope of this preface to enlarge upon the history of the Puritans, interwoven as it is with stirring events and times, more familiar to us probably than any others in the annals of England. From Bishop Hooper, down to the disastrous ejectment of 1662, their story has been often told. By none with greater candour, with more enlarged catholicity of spirit, or with more graceful diction, than by the historian of the Early and Later Puritans, the Rev. J. B. Marsden, in his standard volumes:—

"Wherever the religion, the language, or the free spirit of our country has forced its way, the Puritans of old have some memorial. They have moulded the character and shaped the laws of other lands, and tinged with their devouter shades unnumbered congregations of Christian worshippers, even where no allegiance is professed, or willing homage done to their peculiarities. It is a party that has numbered in its ranks many of the best, and not a few of the greatest men that England has enrolled upon her history. Amongst the Puritans were found, together with a crowd of our greatest divines, and a multitude of learned men, many of our most profound lawyers, some of our most able statesmen, of our most renowned soldiers, and (strangely out of place as they may seem) not a few of our greatest orators and poets. Smith and Owen, Baxter and Howe, were their ministers, and preached amongst them. Cecil revered and defended them while he lived; so did the illustrious Bacon; and the unfortunate Essex sought his consolations from them when he came to die." *

Mixed up as were the Puritans with keen and long-continued controversies, both political and religious, they have left behind them a vast mass of theology,—not controversial, but expository and hortatory,—which is the common property of the Church of Christ, and which Episcopalians and Presbyterians and Wesleyans, Independents and Baptists, may alike appreciate, use, and enjoy. Their works, developing and embodying the theology of the Reformation, form a department in our theological literature, and occupy a place so specific and important, that their absence from the student's shelves can be compensated neither by Fathers nor Reformers, nor by the richest stores of modern divinity, whether English or Continental.

They have ever been subjects of eulogy with those best acquainted with them. The *gustus spiritualis judicii* predicated of Goodwin by his editors, "Thankful Owen," and "James Barron,"†—the "genius to dive into the bottom of points," and "to study them down,"—"the happiness of high and intimate communion with God,"—the "deep insight into the grace of God and the covenant of grace,"—these are characteristic of the whole school; and, in an eminent degree, of those whose works have been selected for this Series. Of Manton writes the "silver-tongued Bates:"—

"God had furnished him with a rare union of those parts that are requisite to form an excellent minister of His Word. A clear judgment, rich fancy, strong memory, and happy elocution, met in him, and were excellently improved by his diligent study."

". . . . In the performing this work he was of that conspicuous eminence that none could detract from him, but from ignorance or envy.

"He was endowed with extraordinary knowledge in the Scriptures, those holy oracles from whence all spiritual light is derived; and in his preaching gave such a perspicuous account of the order

* Early Puritans, Second Edit., pp. 4, 5.

† Original Preface to folio, MDCLXXXI. See pp. xxix., xxx.

and dependence of divine truths, and with that felicity applied the Scriptures to confirm them, that every subject by his management was cultivated and improved. His discourses were so clear and convincing, that none, without offering voluntary violence to conscience, could resist their evidence. And from hence they were effectual, not only to inspire a sudden flame, and raise a short commotion in the affections, but to make a lasting change in the life."

"His doctrine was uncorrupt and pure; 'the truth according to goodness.' He was far from a guilty vile intention to prostitute that sacred ordinance for the acquiring any private secular advantage. Neither did he entertain his hearers with impertinent subtleties, empty notions, intricate disputes, dry and barren, without productive virtue; but as one that always had before his eyes the great end of the ministry, the glory of God and the salvation of men, his sermons were directed to open their eyes, that they might see their wretched condition as sinners, to hasten their 'flight from the wrath to come,' to make them humbly, thankfully, and entirely 'receive Christ as their Prince and all-sufficient Saviour.' And to build up the converted 'in their most holy faith,' and more excellent love, that is 'the fulfilling of the law.' In short, to make true Christians eminent in knowledge and universal obedience.

"As the matter of his sermons was designed for the good of souls, so his way of expression was proper to that end. Words are the vehicle of the heavenly light. As the Divine Wisdom was incarnate to reveal the eternal counsels of God to the world, so spiritual wisdom in the mind must be clothed with words to make it sensible to others. And in this he had a singular talent. His style was not exquisitely studied, not consisting of harmonious periods, but far distant from vulgar meanness. His expression was natural and free, clear and eloquent, quick and powerful, without any spice of folly, and always suitable to the simplicity and majesty of divine truths. His sermons afforded substantial food with delight, so that a fastidious mind could not disrelish them. He abhorred a vain ostentation of wit in handling sacred things, so venerable and grave, and of eternal consequence."

"His fervour and earnestness in preaching was such as might soften and make pliant the most stubborn, obdurate spirits. I am not speaking of one whose talent was only in voice, that labours in the pulpit as if the end of preaching were for the exercise of the body, and not for the profit of souls; but this man of God was inflamed with a holy zeal, and from thence such ardent expressions broke forth, as were capable to procure attention and consent in his hearers. He spake as one that had a living faith within him of divine truths. From this union of zeal with his knowledge, he was excellently qualified to convince and convert souls."

"His unparalleled assiduity in preaching declared him very sensible of those dear and strong obligations that lie upon ministers to be very diligent in that blessed work."

"This faithful minister 'abounded in the work of the Lord;' and, which is truly admirable, though so frequent in preaching, yet was always superior to others, and equal to himself."*

Of Clarkson, Bates spoke thus in his funeral sermon—

"In his preaching, how instructive and persuasive to convince and turn the carnal and worldly from the love of sin to the love of holiness, from the love of the earth to the love of heaven. The matter of his sermons was clear and deep, and always judiciously derived from the text. The language was neither gaudy and vain, with light trimmings, nor rude and neglected, but suitable to the oracles of God. Such were his chosen acceptable words, as to recommend heavenly truths, to make them more precious and amiable to the minds and affections of men, like the colour of the sky, that makes the stars to shine with a more sparkling brightness." †

Both are included by the admirable and lamented Angell James in an apostrophe to the "mighty shades" of those "illustrious and holy" Nonconformists, who have "bequeathed" to us "a rich legacy in their immortal works." Later, in the pages of his stirring "Earnest Ministry," he places Clarkson in the first rank of those who were "most distinguished as successful preachers of the Word of God." ‡ The work of Charnock on the Divine Attributes is thus spoken of by his early Editors: §—

"But thou hast in this book not only an excellent subject in the general, but great variety of matter for the employment of thy understanding, as well as enlivening thy affections, and that, too, such as thou wilt not readily find elsewhere: many excellent things which are out of the road of ordinary preachers and writers, and which may be grateful to the curious, no less than satisfactory to the wise and judicious. It is not, therefore, a book to be played with, nor slept over, but read with the most intent and serious mind; for though it afford much pleasure for the fancy, yet much more work for the

* Bates' Works, (Farmer's Edit.,) vol. iv., pp. 231-235.

† Bates' Works, vol. iv., p. 385.

‡ An Earnest Ministry the Want of the Times, pp. 56, 269 (Third Edition.)

§ Folio, 1699.

heart, and hath indeed enough in it to busy all the faculties. The dress is complete and decent, yet not garish or theatrical; the rhetoric masculine and vigorous, such as became a pulpit, and was never borrowed from the stage; the expressions full, clear, apt, and such as are best suited to the weightiness and spirituality of the truths here delivered. It is plain he was no empty preacher, but was more for sense than sound; filled up his words with matter, and chose rather to inform his hearers' minds than to claw any itching ears."

"In the doctrinal part of several of his discourses thou wilt find the depth of *polemical* divinity, and in his inferences from thence the sweetness of *practical;* some things which may exercise the profoundest scholar, and others which may instruct and edify the weakest Christian; nothing is more nervous than his reasonings, and nothing more affecting than his applications. Though he make great use of *school-men*, yet they are certainly more beholden to him than he to them."

"He is not like some *school writers*, who attenuate and rarefy the matter they discourse of to a degree bordering upon annihilation; at least beat it so thin that a puff of breath may blow it away; spin their threads so fine that the cloth, when made up, proves useless; solidity dwindles into niceties; and what we thought we had got by their assertions, we lose by their distinctions."*

Baxter enumerates the works of Reynolds among those which he considers as indispensably necessary to the library of a theological student. Dr Doddridge says that Reynolds' "are most elaborate both in thought and expression. Few men," he adds, "were more happy in the choice of their similitudes. He was . . . . of great learning, and a frequent preacher."†

"Distinguished by profound learning and elevated character, serious without gloom, and zealous without harshness, he stands out as one of the best ecclesiastical characters of his time; and, in a crisis which was most solemn and memorable for the Church of England, he bears a lofty contrast to most of the dignitaries which assembled around James."‡

"The divines of the Puritan school," writes the Rev. C. Bridges, with his wonted discrimination, "however, (with due allowance for the prevalent tone of scholastic subtleties,) supply to the ministerial

* Charnock's Works, folio, 1699.

† Reynolds' Works, (Chalmers' Edit.,) Preface, p. lxxi.

‡ Dr Tulloch's English Puritans, p. 33.

student a large fund of useful and edifying instruction. If they be less clear and simple in their doctrinal statements than the Reformers, they enter more deeply into the sympathies of Christian experience. Profoundly versed in spiritual tactics,—the habits and exercises of the human heart,—they are equally qualified to awaken conviction and to administer consolation, laying open the man to himself with peculiar closeness of application; stripping him of his false dependencies, and exhibiting before him the light and influence of the evangelical remedy for his distress." *

"I have learned far more from John Howe," said Robert Hall, "than from any other author I ever read. There is an astonishing magnificence in his conceptions." Having added—"He had not the same perception of the beautiful as of the sublime, and hence his endless subdivisions"—"There was, I think, an innate inaptitude in Howe's mind for discerning minute graces and proprieties, and hence his sentences are often long and cumbersome"—he declared him "unquestionably the greatest of the Puritan Divines." "Baxter," said Mr Hall, "enforces a particular idea with extraordinary clearness, force, and earnestness. His appeals to the conscience are irresistible. Howe, again, is distinguished by calmness, self-possession, majesty, and comprehensiveness; and, for my own part, I decidedly prefer him to Baxter." Owen, Mr Hall did not admire.†

It is curious to compare with this the criticism of another master-mind—

"Baxter," said Richard Cecil, "surpasses, perhaps, all others in the grand, impressive, and persuasive style. But he is not to be named with Owen, as to furnishing the student's mind. He is, however, multifarious, complex, practical." "Owen stands at the head of his class of divines. His scholars will be more profound and enlarged, and better furnished, than those of most other writers. His work on the Spirit has been my treasure-house, and one of my very first-rate books.'" ‡

It is not to be denied, however, that Puritan theology has, of late years, been comparatively little read, either by clergy or laity, in this country. Owen and Baxter—and perhaps Howe—are those best known to the present generation. Of the others a few select works only are accessible to the mass of readers. Nor has the present Series been projected under the anticipation that their works, as

* Christian Ministry, Third Edition, 12mo, pp. 53, 54.

† Robert Hall's Works, Bohn's Edition, vol. i., pp. 163, 164.

‡ Cecil's Remains, pp. 281, 282.

a whole, will be popular, in the wide sense of that term, in our own day. The current of theological literature has become wider, but shallower. Shorter books, books calling for little thought; the thoughts of the intellectual giants of former days diluted and watered down to our taste; these are best adapted to an age of much and rapid reading, but little study—an age marked by a pernicious taste for light reading, and content to derive too much of its learning and information at second-hand, from periodicals and newspapers. An age, too, in which even the multiplication of privileges, in the number of sermons preached and of public meetings held, in combination with the cheap publications with which the press teems, tends to diffuse, but not to deepen, thought. And ministers find in the multiplication of facilities for the composition of sermons a corresponding snare. Many a boy at school would grow up into a sounder, riper, and more independent scholar—certainly the process of acquirement would have proved a more healthful gymnasium to his mental powers and habits, as well as for the general disciplining of his character—if he had fewer crutches on which to lean, in lexicons and translations and copious English notes, which make everything easy, and enable him to dispense with personal and direct reference to the great fountain-heads of learning and scholarship. Thus the minister finds appliances so multiplied, the old theology of Fathers, Reformers, and Puritans so ready to his hand, in commentaries and in diluted forms, that he is tempted to a growing habit of indolence; takes all at second-hand; and finds it easier to manipulate into sermons and expositions the cheap commentary, than to study the ponderous folio for himself.

It must be confessed that while, in substance, the Puritan theology is of sterling value, it presents not a few characteristics which are drawbacks to general popularity among theologians of our habits of thought. They are over-copious and diffuse, and thus not seldom prolix to wearisomeness; solid, often to heaviness; and encumbered by references to works little known and altogether unread. "Due allowance," says Mr Bridges, in the passage just quoted, must be made "for the prevalent tone of scholastic subtleties;" and, in some, for "the occasional mixture of obscurity and bombast." And Mr James, in eulogising a sermon of Doolittle's as perhaps "the most solemn and awful sermon in the English or any other language," qualifies that high eulogium by a criticism on much of its "terminology," as expressive of a "familiarity with awful realities" which was a "vice" of the Puritan age and school.*

Neither their expository works nor their sermons are presented as

* Earnest Ministry, p. 103.

models. The former, looked upon *as expositions*, are marred occasionally by the endeavour to make them exhaustive treatises, and by a tiresome minuteness of division and subdivision. A sermon of Charnock's would be ill suited, *as such*, to a modern congregation: though not so much so as one of the English Chrysostom, Jeremy Taylor. But this very over-copiousness and attempts at exhaustiveness render them as storehouses invaluable. They are tomes of massive theology; theology with prolixity, and pedantry, and subtlety, but never as dry bones. It is experimental. There is unction. There is warmth. It is theology grasped and wrought out by great minds, but realised by loving hearts. The writers have *tasted* that the Lord is gracious. Their every page bears the impress of the *bene orasse est bene studuisse.* They are not theologians only but saints.

Nor are their characteristic excellencies hard to be accounted for. Not only were they pre-eminently men of God, and deep students of God's Word—"living and walking Bibles"*—and this in combination often with great secular erudition—but their lot was cast in troublous times, times in which great principles were at stake, to which they were called to witness, and for which they were called to suffer. As with the individual Christian, the time, not of his wealth and ease, but of his trial and suffering, is that which braces his power, and stimulates his health and growth, so is it with the aggregate Church. Stirring times produce stirring men. Christ's heroes are drawn out by conflicts. When we handle the doctrines of the gospel merely as the subject-matter of sermons, and treatises, and controversies, we are in danger of handling them drily and abstrusely. But when we are called to confess Christ by the actual bearing of His cross, and to suffer for His truth's sake, our theology must be experimental. We *then* want not Christianity but Christ. The gospel is *then* a reality, not a creed, nor a system only nor mainly, but an inner life, an indwelling, inworking power. "Christ—the Scripture—your own hearts—and Satan's devices," writes Thomas Brooks, "are the four things that should be first and most studied and searched; if any cast off the study of these, they can be neither safe here, nor happy hereafter." † His words are the key-note of Puritan theology.

These divines were diligent and profound students to a degree attained by few ministers of our own day, when, in all sections of the Christian Church, so much of their time is consumed in out-door work and quasi-secular duties. The organisation and maintenance

* Original Preface. See p. xxx.

† Preface to "Precious Remedies against Satan's Devices."

of parochial or congregational machinery,—the anxiety and labour merely of raising funds for their varied agencies and institutions,—the co-operation expected of them in the countless philanthropic schemes and multiplied religious societies of our age,—these drive or draw them from their studies. The mental tone and habits of the student are soon lost. A restless, desultory, excited spirit is engendered. And many an energetic minister falls into the fallacy that he is never working for his people, unless he is going up and down among them, and busy in schools, visitation, committees, and public meetings. No doubt it is a working age; working as distinguished from retirement, study, and meditation. But no minister should, under any stress of fancied duties, cease to be a student.

"Apart from practice, thought will become impoverished without study; the most active and fertile minds have perceived this. We cannot derive all the nourishment we need from ourselves; without borrowing we cannot create. It is true that there are other methods of study besides reading. When we have learned anything from books, and in the best of books as well as in others, we must make use of our native powers in order to assimilate it, as also we assimilate nourishment for the body. But when, without the aid of books, or in the absence of facts, we labour in solitude, on what materials shall we labour unless it be on those supplied by recollection? Whence do our thoughts arise except from facts, or from books, or from social intercourse? A great volume, which also demands our careful study. We must, therefore, study in order to excite and encircle our own thoughts by means of the thoughts of other men. Those who do not study will see their talent gradually fading away, and will become old and superannuated in mind before their time. Experience demonstrates this abundantly, so far as preaching is concerned. Whence comes it that preachers who were so admired when they entered upon their course, often deteriorate so rapidly, or disappoint many of the lofty expectations which they had excited? Very generally the reason is because they discontinue their studies. A faithful pastor will always keep up a certain amount of study; while he reads the Bible, he will not cease from reading the great book of humanity which is opened before him; but this empirical study will not suffice. Without incessant study, a preacher may make sermons, and even good sermons, but they will all resemble one another, and that increasingly as he continues the experiment. A preacher, on the other hand, who keeps up in his mind a constant flow of substantial ideas, who fortifies and nourishes his mind by various reading, will be always interesting. He who is governed by one pervading idea and purpose will find in all books, even in those which are not directly connected with the ministry, something that he may adapt to his special aim." *

"For a man who preaches much, without from time to time renewing the stock of matter with which he began his career, however sound or pious he may continue to be, will be almost sure ultimately to become a very barren preacher. And I only say *almost*, in consideration of a few rare instances, in which observation of life, and intercourse with varieties of character, seem to make an original and peculiar cast of mind, independent in a good measure of reading. But these are rare exceptions. Generally, and all but universally, a public teacher requires to have his own mind supplied and exercised by books. And to derive full advantage from them, I need hardly say, that he must not only read, but think. Undigested reading is better, I am sure, than none. I know that a different opinion is entertained by some, but this is mine. For there is no one who does not take away some matter from what he reads, and no mind can be so inert as not to be forced to some activity, while taking in new facts or thoughts. And, what is not to be put out of view, every mind becomes continually more unfurnished and more inert, when reading is wholly given up. But the benefit to be derived from reading without purpose and thought, of course falls far short of that which reflection will draw from the same, or from scantier stores. And this applies very particularly to the most fruitful, as well as the most important of the sources from which the preacher's materials are to be drawn. By reading the Holy Scriptures, without meditating upon them, a man may, no doubt, obtain considerable acquaintance with the facts and doctrines which they contain,—may become an adroit controversialist, and a well-furnished textuary,—but unless he studies the sacred volume with patient thought, (I need not add to you, my brethren, with earnest prayer,) until he becomes imbued with its spirit as well as acquainted with its contents, his use of Scripture will be comparatively jejune, and cold, and unprofitable. And so, you remember, the Apostle exhorts his beloved son in the faith: 'Meditate upon these things, give thyself wholly to them, that thy profiting may appear to all.' And, certainly, all do feel the difference which there is between one who is giving out crude materials, taken in hastily for the occasion, and one who is drawing from the stores which he has laid up in this meditative study of divine truth." †

* Vinet's Pastoral Theology, pp. 109, 110.

† Bishop O'Brien's Charge at Primary Visitation, 1842.

The Puritan writers were men engaged in stirring scenes, and had the conduct of questions and controversies involving great principles, and in which the liberties of this country and of the Church of Christ were at stake. They had to endure, in not a few cases, "a great fight of afflictions," persecution, imprisonment, ejectment. They were not students as living in stagnant times. But study, long, close, deep, sustained, was with them an integral part of their ministry. They toiled alike in rowing and in fishing; but they mended their nets. They gave themselves unto reading. They were not content with indolently picking up a few stray surface pieces of ore, which had been dropped by others at the mine's mouth. They sunk the shaft and went down and toiled and dug and smelted and refined and burnished for themselves, and for the Church Catholic.

We hear, in our own day, complaints loud and frequent of the feebleness of the pulpit. Not men of the world only, to whom, if they ever hear sermons, the sermon is a form with which they would gladly dispense, but an Angell James asks, "Has the modern evangelical pulpit lost, and is it still losing, any of its power?" *

Sir James Stephen writes †—

"Every seventh day a great company of preachers raise their voices in the land to detect our sins, to explain our duty, to admonish, to alarm, and to console. Compare the prodigious extent of this apparatus with its perceptible results, and inestimable as they are, who will deny that they disappoint the hopes which, antecedently to experience, the least sanguine would have indulged? The preacher has, indeed, no novelties to communicate. His path has been trodden hard and dry by constant use; yet he speaks as an ambassador from Heaven, and his hearers are frail, sorrowing, perplexed, and dying men. The highest interests of both are at stake. The preacher's eye rests on his manuscript; the hearer's turns to the clock; the half-hour glass runs out its sand; and the portals close on well-dressed groups of critics, looking for all the world as if just dismissed from a lecture on the tertiary strata."

No doubt, in many cases, our critics are not qualified. "The natural man receiveth not the things of the Spirit of God, for they are foolishness unto him; neither can he know them, because they are spiritually discerned." And the true power of the pulpit, be it remembered, is not in Paul, nor in Apollos, but with the Holy Ghost.

* Earnest Ministry, Preface, pp. vii., viii.

† Essays in Ecclesiastical Biography, (Fourth Edition,) p. 393.

And we cannot yield to the clamour for interesting sermons, if sermons are to be made attractive by smatterings of geology, and political economy, and geography, in an age in which intellect is a chief idol.

But that there is a want of *solid matter*, a flimsiness, in too many of our modern sermons is undeniable. They may be *faithful*, but they are too often, if not crude, meagre and vapid. There is a cry for simplicity. Too often in aiming at simplicity we fall into imbecility. Practical preaching is in demand. But Christian practice must be enforced on Christian motive; and Christian motive cannot be urged in all its fulness and power, unless Christian doctrine in its depth and variety be stated and enforced. The gospel must be offensive to the natural heart. But surely that scheme into which "angels desire to look," and which is to those lofty intelligences, surrounded by many evidences of the divine wisdom beyond man's present ken, the brightest manifestation of it,* must have matter capable of exercising (and that lawfully and profitably) man's highest intellectual powers. We call upon men to receive it with the simple faith of little children, but not necessarily as in itself unworthy of intellectual study and research. "To the Greek foolishness," is still true. But let it be "the foolishness of God," not the foolishness of our indolence and insipidity. "Preaching indeed, considered in regard to its sublime object, is at its best but foolishness after all; but this, we venture to think, is a reason why it should do its best, not its worst."† To this end ministers must be, as were the Puritan giants, students. Less public work. Fewer committees. Less serving of tables. A larger enlistment of the laity, specially in that which is secular. We must determine on this, or we shall have, in another generation, that of which we have but too threatening symptoms now—if indeed we have not passed beyond symptoms into a disastrous state of malady—an ill-stored, unlearned, untheological clergy.

Complaints of pulpit feebleness are not the only evil results. Our divinity students pass into the ministry and ascend our pulpits, having gone through their university curriculum, and "crammed up" the few authors required by their bishop or theological college, but unstored with experimental theology; too often with no discernment of distinctive truth, no well-proportioned and symmetrical view of Christian doctrine. Hence they are in danger of being "carried to and fro with

* Eph. iii. 10.

† Dean Alford's Lecture on "Pulpit Eloquence of the Seventeenth Century," (Lectures to Young Men's Christian Association, Exeter Hall, 1857–58,) p. 323.

every blast of vain doctrine." The mistiness and vagueness of negative theology, the husks of ritualism, would fail to satisfy men who had tasted "the living bread" and drunk deep into the wells of such theologians as this Series is designed to make accessible. Faults of prolixity, pedantry, scholastic subtlety, over-systematising, over-straining, and over-spiritualising, a familiarity and a homeliness running into a coarseness which would now shock where it did not provoke levity inconsistent with the reverence due to high and holy themes, are as trifles when weighed against the scriptural knowledge, the clear, distinct statement of doctrine, the close, masterly handling of all the subtle intricacies of the experiences of the inner life, in its varied conflicts, its hopes, its fears, its sorrows, its consolations, its joys. Contrast with a page of our modern negative theology,—an essay or sermon in which the writer, dealing with the fact of the death of Christ, at one time so employs the language of Holy Scripture as to leave no doubt of his orthodoxy, and, the next moment, so explains, and fences, and emasculates this language as to deprive the cross of its true efficacy, and to leave us in doubt as to any adequate *cui bono* for that unutterably solemn display of the divine perfections,—contrast with this a page of Charnock, or Reynolds, or Goodwin, or Clarkson, or—to go beyond the limits of this Series—of Thomas Jacomb,* or of Edward Polhill,† and we at once feel the difference of the atmosphere. If we seem to have been guided by the negative theologian to some height of intellectual power and philosophic research, we find it not to be a height from which, in flooding sunshine, we may survey the panorama of Christian truth, but a height on which we stand shivering amid the mists of un-

* Several Sermons preached on the whole Eighth Chapter of the Epistle to the Romans, by Thomas Jacomb, D.D. London, 1672.

"He was an excellent preacher of the gospel, and had a happy art of conveying saving truths into the minds and hearts of men.

"He did not entertain his hearers with curiosities, but with spiritual food. He dispensed the bread of life, whose vital sweetness and nourishing virtue is both productive and preservative of the life of souls. He preached 'Christ crucified, our only wisdom and righteousness, sanctification and redemption.' His great design was to convince sinners of their absolute want of Christ, that with flaming affections they might come to him, and 'from His fulness receive divine grace.'

"His sermons were clear, and solid, and affectionate. He dipped his words in his soul, in warm affections, and breathed a holy fire into the breasts of his hearers; of this many serious and judicious persons can give testimony, who so long attended upon his ministry with delight and profit."—*Bates' Works*, vol. iv., p. 286.

† The Works of Edward Polhill, Esq., of Burwash, in Sussex, are reprinted in a cheap form by Thomas Ward & Co., London. They form a grand volume of divinity. The author's preface is dated 1677.

satisfying negatives; and if, awhile, the mists seem ready to roll away and to disperse themselves, they return to cloud and chill us as before. When Manton expounds St James, or Goodwin St Paul,—when Sibbes is opening up the "Soul's Conflict," or dilating on the "Beloved" and His "Bride,"—when Brooks brings forth his "Precious Remedies" and "Heart's Ease,"—when Owen is analysing indwelling sin, or opening out the Epistle to the Hebrews,—or Polhill treating of election and redemption, we have massive theology baptized with all the rich unction of Christian experience. To travel still further beyond the limits of this particular Series, the Lectures of Bishop King on Jonas* present a combination of expository ability and pulpit power—specially in the element of uncompromising rebuke—which renders them a masterpiece and a model which modern preachers would do well to study. Contrasting these, and such as these, among our theological writers, with many whose unsound productions have for awhile unhappily superseded them, and are unsettling the minds of many in our universities and pulpits, we may employ the words of the editors of Goodwin, when they represent him as "wondering greatly at the daring attempts of some men of this age, unskilful in the word of righteousness, upon the great and momentous points of our religion, which are the glory of our Reformation; but these points will prove gold, silver, precious stones, when their wood, hay, and stubble will be burnt up. These will have a verdure and greenness on them, whilst the inventions of others will be blasted and wither. These will be firm, whilst others, wanting somewhat within, it will be with them as it was with the Jewish and heathenish worship, when a fate was upon them, all the efforts and endeavours of men could not make them stand."†

* Lectvres vpon Jonas, delivered at Yorke, in the yeare of ovr Lord 1594. London: Printed by Humfrey Lownes. 1618.

In the epistle addressed by the Christ Church students at Oxford to James I., in which they request that monarch to give Dr King the deanery, he is called "Clarissimum lumen Anglicanæ Ecclesiæ." Sir Edward Coke used to say of him that he was the best speaker in the Star Chamber in his time. "Deus bone, quam canora vox (saith one) vultus compositus, verba selecta, grandes sententiæ! Allicimur omnes lepore verborum, suspendimur gravitate sententiarum, orationis impetu et viribus flectimur."—*Wood's Athenæ Oxon.*, vol. i., p. 458, year 1621. Folio Edit., MDCCXXI.

Henry Smith, who died about 1600, (see Fuller's Life prefixed to Sermons, Edit. 1675,) was "esteemed the miracle and wonder of his age, for his . . . . fluent, eloquent, and practical way of preaching." "The Puritans flocked to hear him at St Clement Dane's, esteeming him the prime preacher of the nation. His sermons were taken into the hands of all the people."—*Wood's Athenæ Oxon.*, vol. i., p. 263, year 1593.

† Original Preface. See p. xxxii.

The controversial writings of the Puritans are beyond the province of this preface. If in one instance—that of a Treatise on Church Government by Goodwin—controversy has been included in this Series, it has been done to prevent his Works from being incomplete. As a whole, this class of subjects hardly enters into the writings of the authors whose Works are comprised in this Series. Of their abilities in polemical divinity Mr Marsden observes, with more immediate reference to the earlier among them, that "the student, after a wide search amongst the combatants of later times, finds to his surprise how insignificant are all their additions to a controversy opened, and, as far as learning and argument go, finally closed, by the earliest champions on either side."* Their style, if sometimes inflated and obscure, has a nervous pithiness and quaintness rarely found among the theologians and preachers of our own day. The commonplace book of the student will soon be filled up with terse and pointed sayings—those "words of the wise which are as goads." A strong, homely saying, quoted from an old Puritan, will be the sentence of all others, in many a modern sermon, which will fasten itself most readily on the memory, and retain the most lasting hold. "Several of them," says Mr Marsden, "write the English language in high, if not the highest, perfection, before it was degraded and Latinised by the feeble men of the last century."

Their homeliness, to call it by the mildest name, is nowhere more striking (nor, at times, more grotesque) than in the titles prefixed by them to treatises and sermons. Thomas Adams, for example, (following Luther,) designates a sermon on Judas, "The White Devil, or the Hypocrite Uncased;" another, "The Shot, or the Wofull Price which the Wicked pay for the Feast of Vanitie;" a third, on Jer. viii. 22, "The Sinner's Passing Bell, or a Complaint from Heaven for Man's Sinnes;" a fourth, on Matt. xii. 43, (the unclean spirit's return to the man from whom he had gone out,) "The Black Saint, or the Apostate;" a fifth, on Eccles. ix. 3, "Mysticall Bedlam, or the World of Madmen." We can hardly open a page of his sermons without finding quaintnesses of the most striking kind. The openings of the sermons, "The Fatall Banket" and "The Shot," are among the most singular. And not seldom, when we feel that the writer is running into fanciful conceit rather than exposition, the application is so full of power and beauty that, despite our judgment, it carries us with it. Take the following from Adams' sermon on "Christ his Starre, or the Wise Men's Oblation," folio, 1630, p. 165:—

* Christian Churches and Sects; article, *Puritans*, vol. ii., p. 139.

"Some will give *myrrh*, but not *frankincense;* some will give *frankincense*, but not *myrrh;* and some will give *myrrh* and *frankincense*, but not *gold.*

"1. Some will give *myrrh*, a strict moral life, not culpable of any gross eruption or scandalous impiety; but not frankincense. Their *prayers* are thin sown, therefore their *graces* cannot come up thick. Perhaps they feel no want, and then, you know, *raræ fumant felicibus aræ.* In their thought, they do not stand in any great need of God; when they do, they will offer Him some *incense.* These live a morally honest life, but are scant of religious *prayers;* and so may be said to offer *myrrh* without *frankincense.*

"2. Some will give *frankincense*, *pray* frequently, perhaps tediously; but they will give no myrrh, not mortify or restrain their concupiscence. The *Pharisees* had many prayers, but never the fewer sins. These mock God, that they so often beg of Him that His will may be done, when they never subdue their affections to it. There are too many such among us, that will often join with the Church in communion devotions, who yet join with the world in common vices. These make great smokes of *frankincense*, but let not fall one drop of *myrrh.*

"3. Some will give both *myrrh* and *frankincense*, but by no means their *gold.* I will give (saith the worldling) a sober life—there's my *myrrh;* I will say my prayers—there's my *frankincense;* but do you think I will part with my *gold?* This same *gold* lies closer in men's hearts than it doth in their purses. You may as well wring Hercules's club out of his fist as a penny from their heaps to charitable uses."

The skeleton of the sermon on "The Blacke Saint" is a most curious specimen of the over-elaborate division of a subject, specially as typographically displayed by the author (p. 352.)

It need hardly be remarked that "the Puritan was a Calvinist naturally and entirely." "Calvinism had been, if not the progenitor, the nursing-mother of Puritanism."* Our Calvinism may be more or less than theirs, but every lover of evangelical truth will be at one with them in their full exhibitions of the grace and glory of Emmanuel, as the Church's Head and the sinner's only Saviour. Their transcendent merit is their "sweet savour of Christ." Man, in his utter ruin in the first Adam, and his glorious salvation in the second Adam; the sovereign grace of the Triune Jehovah, in the eternal purpose and plan for man's recovery; the riches of the Father's love; the might and comfort, the peace and joy of the Spirit's

* English Puritanism and its Leaders, by John Tulloch, D.D., pp. 5, 41.

grace,—these are so taught as to fulfil the good pleasure of the Father, "that in all things" Christ "may have the pre-eminence." Their gospel is not "another gospel, which is not another," but the glorious gospel of the grace of the blessed God. "God in Christ reconciling the world unto himself;" the surrendered life of Christ; the penal and vicarious satisfaction by which the curse of the broken law was met; the blood of Christ the fountain opened for uncleanness and for the consecration of God's elect to their royal priesthood; the active obedience of Christ, as "made under the law," combining with his sufferings and blood-shedding to constitute Him "the Righteousness of God" to His people; present pardon and justification; the Spirit indwelling as the Sanctifier, the Teacher, the Comforter, the inward Witness to sonship, the Intercessor, the seal, the earnest; in a word, THE NEW COVENANT, with all its riches, and privileges, and strength, and peace, and hope, and joy,—these are their great and central theme. They discerned the difficulties presented, not by the implacableness of the Father, but by the laws of His moral government, based upon His own moral perfections, to the salvation of a fallen moral being; and how these were met by the counsels and provisions of that eternal scheme by which God is just, and the justifier of the ungodly—at once a Moral Governor of unsullied truth and purity, and a Saviour.

On the expulsion of the Puritans, on St Bartholomew's Day, in 1662, under the disastrous and suicidal Act of Uniformity, "they carried with them the spiritual light of the Church of England."* And "in the course of ninety years, the nation had descended to a state of irreligion which we now contemplate with feelings of dismay."†

"It was the opinion of those who lived in these evil days that had it not been for a small body of respectable clergymen who had been educated among the Puritans, and of whom Wilkins, Patrick, and Tillotson were the leaders, every trace of godliness would have been clean put out, and the land reduced to universal and avowed atheism. Indeed, the writings and sermons of the Church of England divines of this period confirm these statements. They are evidently addressed to hearers before whom it was necessary to prove not merely the providence, but the very being of a God—not only the soul's immortality, but the soul's existence. Their pains are chiefly spent not in defending any particular creed or system of doctrine, for they appear to have thought all points of doctrine beyond the attainment of the age. They take up the people of England where heathenism

* Marsden's Later Puritans, p. 473. † Ibid., p. 472.

might have left them a thousand years before; they teach the first elements of natural religion, and descant upon the nature of virtue, its present recompense, and the arguments in favour of a state of retribution, after the manner of Socrates and Plato. It is seldom that they rise beyond moral and didactic instructions. Theology languished, and spiritual religion became nearly unknown; and a few great and good men handed down to one another the practice and the traditions of a piety which was almost extinct. The restoration of civil liberty brought with it no return of spiritual life within the Church of England. The nation became less immoral without becoming more religious. Politics and party ate out the very vitals of what little piety remained. At length one of the most cautious of English writers, as well as the most profound of English divines, seventy years after the ejection of the Nonconformists, portrays the character of the age in those memorable words, in which he tells us that it had come, he knew not how, to be taken for granted by too many, that Christianity was not so much a subject of inquiry as that it was now at length discovered to be fictitious! How widely these opinions had infected the nation and its educated classes we may infer from the circumstance that he devoted his life to that wonderful book in which he proves by the argument from analogy that religion deserves at least a candid hearing. Bishop Newton, a few years afterwards, wrote his treatise on the fulfilment of prophecy, with the same intentions; while Doddridge, amongst Dissenters, deplored the prevalence of a fatal apathy, and the decay of real piety." *

The preaching with which these great and holy men aroused the nation was the preaching of Puritan doctrine, in place of the Christless ethics and semi- (or more than semi-) Socinian doctrine by which it had been supplanted. Substantially, it is the preaching by which the Sacramentalism and the Neology of our own day are to be met; for, substantially, not without its measure of "wood, hay, stubble," it is "gold, silver, precious stones," built upon the one foundation—Christ.

The present may seem, in some sense, an unfavourable moment for the issue of this Series. The theological taste of the day is not for systematic theology. Nevertheless, the cordial favour with which the design of this project has been greeted by divines of the greatest eminence, from nearly all sections of the Christian Church, both in this kingdom and in America, is in itself a token for good, and may well afford encouragement to those among us who are disposed

* Marsden's Later Puritans, pp. 470, 471.

to take a gloomy view of our prospects, by reason of the heresies and divisions which are rife. In the Puritan Theologians,—not, of course, in all their views and statements of doctrine, but substantially,—a large body of the most eminent and best qualified judges recognise a clear, rich, scriptural statement of evangelical truth. And, amid diversities of opinions and conflicting parties, no less than as affording hope that the power of the pulpit will be greatly strengthened among us, the accord of so large a body of Christian men and ministers is a hopeful and cheering sign. It will be an incalculably blessed result of this reprint, should our ministers catch something of the grandly SCRIPTURAL character of Puritan preaching and exposition. In this lay the secret of their strength.

No "Broad Church" divinity will be found in these pages. Our students and younger ministers are often attracted by more brilliant writers and bolder (not deeper) thinkers. They may pronounce the Puritans old-fashioned, behind the age, heavy. But the Series has been projected in the hope that a healthier tone may be fostered, and that facility may induce familiarity. Writings which must have been sought in rare and costly folios, or watched for at sales or at book-stalls, may now be upon our shelves without effort and at little cost. The supply will create a demand. A reaction in favour of Puritan theology—so far, at least, as to give it its due place—will indicate a healthier tone. The more spiritually-minded of our reading laity will find in these volumes truths and thoughts which may well tempt them to substitute them for those of writers who, if they make less demands upon the intellectual power of their readers, by presenting their matter in an easy and diluted form, repay the perusal in a proportionately moderate measure. But the main object and the paramount desire is that this Series may conduce to the soundness, solidity, and unction of the pulpit ministrations of our own day and of days to come; that, as these men were "mighty in the Scriptures," and proclaimed the gospel in all the riches of its grace, and exalted Christ, and honoured the Spirit of God, and entered, with a skilful and searching anatomy into the hidden secrets of the experience of God's saints, many a student and many a preacher may imbibe their spirit. No disparagement of the early Fathers nor of the Reformers, whose theology is here embodied and developed, is intended; nor any ungrateful undervaluing, by invidious comparison, of the treasures accumulated by later and living labourers. Still less are the Puritan theologians held up that we may call them fathers or masters, or make them an authoritative standard of appeal. Our first business, our solemn responsibility, is with THE WRITTEN WORD. "WHAT SAITH

THE SCRIPTURE?" Let that inquiry be first pursued, in lowly teachableness, in reliance upon no inner light, but upon the Spirit's promised teaching. Let it be pursued with diligent, honest study, not with a pedantic, but an exact and sound philology; and with a fearless trust in truth, no less than a sincere love of it. How few of us have full confidence in truth!

This Series, it is believed, supplies a lack. It comes forth in no ordinary crisis of the Church's history. If anywhere, within the Church the war of opinion rages. The ancient landmarks are being removed. The very foundations are threatened. The inspiration of the sacred oracles is controverted; their infallibility denied. The penmen of the Holy Ghost are deemed not to have been so inspired as to be preserved from error. Moses, Isaiah, and Paul—history, prophecy, doctrines—are alike assailed. Man brings his Maker's Book to the "verifying faculty" of his own inner light and moral consciousness. The death of the Son of God is an heroic self-sacrifice—not a penal satisfaction to the outraged law of the Moral Governor of the universe. Under our new interpreters, much of what we have received from our infancy, and have taught our children, as facts recorded in an inspired history, is relegated to the region of myth and ideology. At such a crisis, it is no slight boon to the Christian Church to make the voices of these witnesses to the truth be heard. Their testimony is, for the most part, silenced, because buried in costly folios; or comes to us only in the echoes of plagiarists. They will now speak in the library of many a pastor, upon whose shelves they have never yet found a place. And, while it is never to be forgotten that neither Father, nor Reformer, nor Puritan, is to share, much less to usurp, that homage which is due to the Scriptures of Truth alone, we believe that when the student and the preacher descend to the study of those uninspired, but gifted men who, in successive ages, have been raised up as exponents of those Scriptures and witnesses to that Truth, none are more calculated, under the divine blessing, to elevate and to deepen the tone of our theology, to preserve us from the deadly perils of old errors now revived, and to give distinctness, substance, unction, and experimental richness to our preaching, than the Puritan Divines.

PREFACE TO THE READER,

AS CONTAINED IN THE FOLIO EDITION, 1681.

THE design of this preface is not to acquaint the world with the worth of this great person; his works already extant sufficiently praise him; but to give the reader our just apprehensions of his eminent fitness for so great an undertaking, and of his happy performance of it.

Besides his eminent endowments, as to natural and acquired abilities, he had the happiness of an early and more than ordinary conversion, in which God favoured him with a marvellous light, especially in the mysteries of corrupt nature and of the gospel, which afterward shined through most of his works, and especially through this comment.

This light was attended, so far as we can judge, with an inward sense of spiritual things, with a *gustus spiritualis judicii*, which, after long experience, grew up into senses exercised to discern good and evil, and into an abounding in all knowledge and sense. And, indeed, that person is the best interpreter, who (besides other helps) hath a comment in his own heart; and he best interprets Paul's Epistles, who is himself the epistle of Christ written by the Spirit of God. He best understands Paul's Epistles, who hath Paul's sense, temptations, and experience.

He religiously observed the light he arrived to, and greatly abhorred to hold any truth in unrighteousness; but lived over the truths he knew, even to the hazard of what was most dear to him. And according to Christ's own aphorisms, the truest way of understanding his doctrine is to do it: as on the other side, there is no great distance between shipwreck of faith and a good conscience.

He had a genius to dive into the bottom of points which he intended to treat of; to "study them down," as he used to express it, not contenting himself with superficial knowledge, without wading into the depths of things. His way was to consult the weightiest, if not all the authors that had written upon the subject he was upon, greatly valuing the light which every man afforded, according to the manifold grace of God, and the various dispensations of his Spirit; yet confined himself to no man's sentiments, but made an advance from his own light and experience to the notions of others.

As he consulted with books, so he had the advantage of intimate converse with the greatest Christians of his age, those living and walking Bibles. And thus from reading the living word in himself and others, he rose up to a great improvement in the truths of God, and was able to speak more particularly and experimentally in cases of conscience and practical points, which did not a little qualify him for this work.

He was a person much addicted to retirements and deep contemplation, by which means he had the advantage of looking round the points and scriptures he was upon, and filling his head and heart with spiritual notions, as the sand of the sea.

He had the happiness of high and intimate communion with God, being a man mighty with him in prayer, to whom he had a frequent recourse in difficult points and cases; and such men wade further into the deep things of God who have such a leader.

He delighted much in searching into points and scriptures which were more abstruse and neglected by others, and removed from vulgar inquiry; and was very successful in opening such difficult texts, in discovering the depths of Satan, in anatomising the old man in himself and others.

He had been much exercised in the controversies that had been agitated in the age he lived in, having a piercing understanding, able to find out where the pinch and stress of controversies lay, when he stated them in his own heart from Scripture and experience, and had a peculiar faculty to bring them down to ordinary capacities in Scripture language, without hard and pedantic terms.

He had a deep insight into the grace of God, and the covenant of grace: a darkness in which was anciently, and still is, the cause of great errors in the Church. The ignorance of the Greek Fathers of the grace of God gave great occasion to the Pelagian errors, as Jansenius observes.

He had, before his undertaking this province, gone over, in the course of his ministry, the grand points of religion, and concocted them in his own head and heart. And this he had done in frequent and intelligent auditories, which greatly draws out the gifts of men, and fits them for such a work as this.

He had this further advantage, that God had exercised him not only with inward conflicts, but with sufferings for the truths he owned, leaving not only preferments, but, which was more precious to him, the exercise of his ministry in his native country: only he had this benefit by his recess, to review and study over again his notions and principles. And we never find God wanting in the discoveries of his secrets to such friends in their retirements.

After his return, he was made choice of to interpret this Epistle, to which work he was eminently suited upon all accounts, having a light into the deep and profound mysteries contained in it, beyond the elevation of those times.

As to his comment, it sufficiently commends itself, and therefore needs not our encomium. We shall only give you some remarks on it, which occurred in the perusal of his papers.

According to our observation, no man who hath been exercised in the same province doth more happily pitch upon the true, genuine, and full scope of the text. He is frequently guided to a scope unobserved by others, as to the latitude of it, and was much delighted to interpret Scripture into the most vast and comprehensive sense which the Spirit of God aimed at, adoring still the fulness of the Scripture, being curious and critical in observing the various references and aspects one place had upon others.

We find him dexterous at the opening of dark scriptures, having a peculiar faculty in comparing spiritual things with spiritual, one obscure place with another more clear and perspicuous; fetching light, as men do in optics, by various positions of glasses into a dark place; bringing light to gospel truths from dark types and prophecies, and reflecting back light again upon those dark shadows from gospel truths: that what places singly send out but some small rays, being happily gathered by him into a constellation, give now a glorious light.

He passeth by no difficulty of the text, till he assoils it and makes the place plain. He values the least iota, and makes it appear what great and momentous things depend upon little words in the Scripture, which others too carelessly pass by.

His observations are clear, genuine, and natural, and many times not of vulgar and common observation, which he usually confirms by one or more pertinent apposite scriptures, which he interprets as he goes along, to the great benefit and delight of the reader; still founding what he treats of upon Scripture, which is a way most satisfactory and blessed of God, and abides more on men's hearts.

He brings down the highest controverted point, and the most sublime mysteries of the gospel, in a plain and familiar way to discerning Christians, without affectation of hard and scholastic terms. Having stated those great controversies in his own heart, he makes them easy to the sense and experience of others.

He makes use of variety of learning, though in a concealed way; studying to bring his learning to Scripture, and not Scripture to his learning.

His language is natural, and expressive of his conceptions, being adapted to convey truths into the minds of men with clearness and delight.

He speaks the intimacies of things from an inward sense and feeling of them in his own heart, to the particular cases and experience of others.

He hath a vein of strong spiritual reason running through all these discourses, carrying its own light and evidence with it.

He discovers a deep insight into the mysteries of the gospel, and a great light in the discovery of them, such as is great in this age, but was much greater about forty years ago, when he preached these lectures. He breaketh open the mines of the glorious grace of God, and the unsearchable riches of Christ; and the further you search into them the greater treasures you will find: *Plenius responsura fodienti*, as one saith in a like case. No man's heart was more taken with the eternal designs of God's grace than his; and no man makes clearer schemes of it to others. None more clearly resolves the plot of man's salvation into pure grace than he.

His discourses all along are very evangelical, carrying the soul to a higher holiness, and from a higher spring and arguments than what are to be found in philosophers,—from the great pulleys and motives of the gospel, which are higher and nobler springs than what Adam himself had in innocency.

In the whole, he shews himself a "man of God throughly furnished to every good work," skilled in the whole compass of true divinity, speaking fully, clearly, and particularly to the points he undertakes to handle.

He hath frequently things out of the road and vulgar reach, and beyond the elevation of common writers, and unobserved by others; and yet well founded upon Scripture. There are diversities of gifts, dispensed by the same Spirit to divers persons, for the edification of the Church.

And if at any time he steps out of the road, he doth it with a due regard to the analogy of faith, and a just veneration for the Reformed religion; wondering greatly at the daring attempts of some men of this age, unskilful in the word of righteousness, upon the great and momentous points of our religion, which are the glory of our Reformation; but these points will prove gold, silver, precious stones, when their wood, hay, and stubble will be burnt up. These will have a verdure and greenness on them, whilst the inventions of others will be blasted and wither. These will be firm, whilst others, wanting somewhat within, it will be with them as it was with the Jewish and heathenish worship, when a fate was upon them, all the efforts and endeavours of men could not make them stand.

Upon the account of what of this excellent author hath been already and will hereafter be published, (by the good providence of God,) we think he may be looked upon as a person raised up by God for some eminent service in that age he lived in; as Augustine and others were in their times. And, therefore, we are not a little astonished at the unworthiness of some persons in this age, who have made use of all their arts and interest to suppress the light of this and other great luminaries of the Church; who have done what in them lay to eclipse stars, and of the first magnitude, and for little niceties and nothings, which the best and purest times of the Church were unacquainted with. But it is hard to dispute men out of corrupt interests; these controversies will have an easier decision at the great day.

We have added in the close some weighty discourses upon some other texts in the Ephesians and Colossians, (a parallel epistle to this of the Ephesians,) and upon some texts in the Hebrews, and other scriptures; either because of their congenialness to this comment, or the suitableness to the times we live in; and because his comment did not rise up to that bulk in the first projection, mentioned in the proposals.

That these discourses are his own, we need say no more, than that they bear his own signature; he having drawn to the life the picture of his own heart by his own hand.

THANKFUL OWEN.*

JAMES BARRON.†

For notices of these excellent men—

See * Owen— "The Nonconformists' Memorial" of Calamy, (by Palmer, 2d edit., 1802,) i. 235, iii. 128.
Hanbury's "Historical Memorials relating to the Independents," (1844,) iii. 422, 595.
Also, Wood's "Athenæ."

† Barron— "The Nonconformists' Memorial," *supra*, i. 288.

PUBLISHER'S ADVERTISEMENT.

In issuing the First Volume of this extensive Series of Standard Divines, the Publisher desires to acknowledge the obligations under which he has been placed by those whom he has consulted, for the hearty encouragement and ready aid which have been accorded to him so frankly and freely. The general approval which his Proposal met with from all sections of the Church, was a sufficient indication to him that the undertaking was likely to commend itself specially to those for whom it was designed. He has, accordingly, made arrangements for the publication of the Series with all the care he could exercise, so that, so far as was in his power, it should be worthy of the expectations formed of it. For details of the Scheme and Conditions of Publication, he begs respectfully to refer to his Prospectus, the issue of which he has deemed it better to defer till he could submit the First Volume to inspection. By adopting this course, intending Subscribers can judge fully of the scope of the Scheme, and of the manner in which the Works will be produced.

If to some the Publisher has appeared to be tardy in his movements, he can safely affirm he has not been unmindful of the responsibilities attaching to him in connexion with this enterprise. He has corresponded largely with distinguished Ministers, wherever the English language is spoken, and endeavoured to perfect his arrangements as far as possible before bringing out the First Volume, that no difficulty might arise to interfere with the regular production of the Series.

To those who are acquainted with the ponderous Folios of Goodwin, it does not require to be stated how numerous are the errors of the printer, how careless has been the punctuation, and how singularly inaccurate are the references to Scripture. To these points special attention has been given, and every text quoted has been verified. With the exception of changing the spelling to modern usage, adjusting the punctuation, and deleting redundant pronouns in such passages as the following,—"Adam *he* was created holy,"—the integrity of the text has been scrupulously preserved; and it is hoped the Edition will be recognised as possessing a great superiority over the original Folios.

The Editor's object has been to let the Author speak for himself, without attempting to explain his meaning by voluminous notes. The reader will thus be his own commentator. It is, however, designed to give, in the closing

Volume of Goodwin,—and similarly with the other Works in the Series,—whatever important information can be elicited during the progress of the Scheme. It is anxiously wished to explain all allusions, to give references to sources of information concerning names, places, and facts incidentally referred to by the Author, and, generally, to supply in an Appendix whatever information can be obtained regarding the Author or his Writings which will enhance the value of the Edition, and be of interest to the reader. Contributions to this Appendix will be gratefully received by the Publisher, as well as a note of any inaccuracy which may have escaped detection. It is known only to those who have undertaken the preparation of such copy for the press how toilsome a work it is, and how difficult to detect every flaw which exists.

The Volumes of this Series will probably present considerable difference in their thickness, as it will be an object to classify, as systematically as possible, the Writings of the Authors. Each Volume or consecutive Volumes will thus contain complete Treatises, or subjects of a cognate kind; but in each year it will be the Publisher's endeavour to supply the full average of pages stated in his Prospectus, in accordance with the number of Subscribers he may obtain. The Publisher places much reliance on the spontaneous pledges of co-operation he has received from numerous sources, and he trusts that various considerations will influence the friends of the Scheme to make it known to their acquaintance, and that Clergymen and Ministers will bring it under the notice of those laymen in their congregations who are likely to appreciate such a Series. The necessary extent of circulation would thus be attained, and all would derive the advantage of the full development of the Scheme.

EDINBURGH, *April* 1861.

AN EXPOSITION

OF THE

FIRST CHAPTER OF THE EPISTLE TO THE EPHESIANS.

A PREMISE CONCERNING THIS EPISTLE.

Something of custom uses to be premised by interpreters concerning the epistles or books they interpret, touching the argument, division of the whole, and occasion of the writing, and about the persons written to.

I shall only speak of two of these, as most necessary.

1. The excellency of this epistle.
2. The occasion of Paul's writing of it.

In the handling of which two, I shall yet wrap up all those other mentioned briefly.

1. For the excellency thereof,—It hath been esteemed among the choicest, and is accordingly placed in the midst of his epistles; as the most sparkling gem useth to be in a carkanet of many jewels: or, as Hierom's comparison of it is, *Quomodo cor animalis in medio est;* as the heart in the midst of the body, so he likened it, for the difficulties he observeth in it: but I rather, because, as the heart is the prime seat and fountain of spirits, and the fullest thereof; so this Epistle contains more of the spirits, the quintessence of the mysteries of Christ, than any other, and is made up of the most quickening cordials to the inward man. I shall say only, that I find our Apostle himself boasting, as it were, of none of his other writings but of this; and let his own judgment cast it, by what himself esteemed his masterpiece. Thus expressly in the third chapter of this epistle, at the third verse, he mentioning the grace of God vouchsafed him, in that rich treasury of knowledge dispensed to him as a steward for others, (as that word signifies,) and that transcendant way he came by it, more extraordinary than other Apostles, (who yet were in part taught it by Christ on earth,) Have you not heard (says he, by the common report went of it,) 'how that by revelation (namely immediate) he made known to me the mystery?' And thus far, indeed, I find him elsewhere speaking, as well as here, Gal. i. 12. But then in the following words he goes on yet further, and makes this very epistle the highest instance of this his knowledge and revelation: 'As I wrote afore,' προέγραψα ἐν ὀλίγῳ, a little afore, (namely in the two first chapters hereof, especially this first,) whereby in the reading you may understand 'my knowledge in the mystery of Christ;' that is, yourselves, not by hearsay only, as afore, but by and upon your own knowledge. There is not the like speech uttered by himself of any of his epistles; he makes this very epistle at once the most full evidence and demonstration of that transcendant

way of his receiving the gospel by immediate revelation. And so sublime was the matter contained in it, as it argued this original, and that it could come no other way but by immediate revelation, as afore he had affirmed of it, and likewise withal refers unto it, as the highest specimen of the depth and profoundness of his knowledge, and as his choicest exercise to shew his Christian learning by; so that, as elsewhere he professed to these same Ephesians that he had (when present with them) declared all the counsel of God to them, Acts xxvi. 27, so now absent, to have singled out to utter in this epistle the utmost depths of that counsel.

But what the reason should be, why Paul was thus more profoundly enlarged to them than others of the Gentiles to whom he also wrote, is worth our inquiry and observance. Some attribute the difference unto Paul's (the author's) own spirit, and the condition he was then in. It smells, say they, of the prison; Paul was a prisoner, as chap. iv. 1, and so more enlarged when most straitened, as in sufferings our spirits use to be. But I rather ascribe it to some difference in these Ephesians written to. Philostratus gives testimony of this city of Ephesus, that it excelled all other cities in wisdom and learning, and over-abounded in thousands of learned men.* And this their exquisiteness in human learning and search after knowledge was that which made them so addicted to curious arts, (as the Holy Ghost, speaking of these very Ephesians, calleth them, Acts xix. 19,) which were partly human, but vain, partly magical and devilish, as the Syriac renders the words; whence also *Ephesinæ literæ*, the letters of Ephesus, grew into a proverb. And Chrysostom says that, even unto his time, it abounded with philosophers above any other city, and that the chiefest philosophers and wise men of Asia had had their original and dwelling therein, and allegeth (in his preface of this epistle) that as the reason why Paul should write this epistle with more study and exactness, and why he uttered more profoundness of knowledge to them than unto others. But sure this his reason falls short of that which may theologically be supposed the true ground of his sublimeness therein, and it will be useful to improve it higher. To me it seems that that supereminent self-denial which appeared in many of these converted Ephesians, even in point of knowledge, in their renouncing all that excellency of learning which was then the glory of that city in the eyes of all the nations, the great Diana of their brains and hearts, (as the goddess was of their blind devotions,) as a testimony whereof they sacrificed the very books themselves unto the fire; as the Holy Ghost hath given testimony to their self-denial in this particular, Acts xix. 19;—this might be the reason why God honoured them with an epistle so sublime, by way of recompense. And it affords us this observation, grounded upon like instances—

Obs.—Whatever excellency any one hath been eminent in, or prized most, afore conversion, but now doth undervalue, and, as Christ's word is, hates and forsakes for Christ's sake, in that very thing Christ as apparently maketh recompense an hundred-fold.—These Ephesians forsook the most exquisite wisdom earthly, yea, the deepest that hell afforded; 'depths of Satan,' as John speaks in another case; and God therefore honours them with this divine epistle, made as public as their self-denial, to all the world, in which God from heaven enlarged this Apostle's heart, to make a professed discovery of the sublimest and deepest mysteries that heaven affordeth, that were to be communicated to any of the sons of men, and that were lawful to be

* 'Abundat bonarum artium studiis, philosophis, oratoribusque redundat, ut vere dici possit eam civitatem non equitum robore, sed clarorum hominum millibus cæteras superare, in eâque plurimum vigere sapientiam.'—Lib. 8, *de Vita Apol.* cap. 3.

uttered, as himself speaks, 2 Cor. xii., by him that was in heaven. They burn their very books, valued at many thousands, (for their price is on purpose valued, Acts xix. 19,) and therefore our Apostle's heart is enlarged towards them, to bring forth the bottom of that 'treasure of knowledge hid in Christ,' 'the unsearchable riches of Christ,' as ver. 8 of the third chapter. He calls them thus also himself, (the author of it,) having reckoned his learning when a Pharisee, wherein he profited above many of his equals, at so high a rate, as the account of the world then went; but now when converted, he accounting all but as dung and dogs' meat, for the excellency of the knowledge of Christ, Phil. iii. 8, was therefore accordingly enlarged and filled with an excellency in this knowledge above his fellow-apostles; though he complains of himself as born out of time, and as one put to this school long after them. Thus Moses also, undervaluing the Egyptian learning wherein he excelled, Acts vii. 22, as well as the pleasures of that court, having an eye to the recompense of reward to come, was accordingly in a proportion recompensed even in this life; as with being exalted to be a king over the people of God, a greater dignity than Egypt afforded, Deut. xxxiii. 5, for his leaving the Egyptian court, so with being made the prophet of the Old Testament for his renouncing of their learning; to whom God revealed himself and his law, as never to any other prophet, Num. xii. 6. He was the giver of that law, which by the confession of all the heathens excelled theirs; and therein made such an eminent type of Christ's prophetical office as no prophet was afore or after him, Deut. xviii. 15.

And so much for the excellency of this epistle. Yet let me add this, that of all epistles, that to the Colossians comes nearest to it in the matter and argument thereof; and in many things the one is a comment upon the other; only in the doctrine of God, free grace, and everlasting love, which is that mystery of the mystery of Christ, this far excels it.

2. In the second place, for the occasion of this epistle,—Interpreters are much put to it to find what it should have been; nor need we trouble our thoughts much, if we find not any; for perhaps the Apostle took one, as a good heart is apt when there is no set occasion given, for to do good; which seems all the occasion of that other Apostle's writing his, 2 Pet. i. 13, 'I think it meet, as long as I am in this tabernacle, to stir you up,' &c. But for any special one of this, the best and most probable which I by conjecture can find, is that which the Apostle by the spirit of prophesy foresaw, Acts xx., where calling all the elders of Ephesus together, (even the elders of this church which here he writeth unto, as you may see, ver. 17,) he tells them, ver. 29, 'I know this, that after my departure shall grievous wolves enter in among you; also of your own selves shall men arise, speaking perverse things, to draw away disciples after them.' He forewarns both that some of their own elders should rise up, (for oftentimes so it falleth out in churches,) and also that others from other churches and places should enter in among them, (wolves he calls them,) teaching perverse things. And I know this, says he; he knew it by the same spirit of prophesy and revelation that, ver. 25, he says he knew they should see his face no more. And although he perhaps knew not the particular errors which they should teach, yet in general you see he knew that gross errors, overthrowing the foundation of the gospel, should arise among them and be taught. Now therefore, to prevent their being carried away with any of these errors, whatever they might prove to be, he writeth this epistle in a positive way, to establish them aforehand in the greatest truths of the gospel. And what is the great and main argument of this epistle, especially in the first part of it? It is to

lay open the doctrine of free grace, and of God's eternal love in, and redemption by Christ, and the blessings issuing therefrom, and the dependence that our salvation hath on both. The Apostle not knowing what particular errors should arise, he yet chooseth to teach such doctrines as might be the most universal preventives to all whatever that were of any dangerous consequence; and for this purpose, of all other doctrines, he pitcheth upon this of free grace. The observation then is this—

Obs.—That if Christian judgments be well and thoroughly grounded in the doctrine of God's free grace and eternal love, and redemption through Jesus Christ alone, and in the most spiritual inward operations of God's Spirit, which he enumerates to have been experimentally communicated, that will fence them against all errors; you may then even venture them from taking in any falsehood of any great moment;—their souls being well shod with the preparation of the gospel of peace, (to use the Apostle's similitude, as it is in the 6th of this epistle, ver. 15.) Then, as they are tentation-proof in respect of sin or practical doubtings, (which is the Apostle's scope there,) so in like manner, when their judgments are thus shod with the doctrine of grace, they are error-proof also, (I speak in respect of taking in any dangerous heresy,) and this fully agrees with what the Apostle directs, Heb. xiii. 9: 'Be not,' saith he, 'carried away with divers and strange doctrines.' He calls them divers, or various doctrines, for though there is but one truth, yet errors about truth are divers; and he calls them strange, that are brought in differing from the faith the Apostles taught, and was 'once given.' And he instanceth in one, namely, the putting an holiness in an elective outward abstinence from some meats rather than others, (so in the next words.) But what any one thing was there that would, of all others, fix and balance their minds against this and all other such empty doctrines and waverings towards such superstitions? He adds, 'for it is a good thing that the heart be established with grace.' Both inherent grace in the soul itself, (for the new creature tastes and discerns truth as the palate doth meat;) as also with the doctrines of free grace without us, in God's heart toward us, as it is declared and taught in the Scriptures and in this chapter, and in the second of this epistle. And let their hearts be established and ballasted, and made steady with these, and they will not easily be 'tossed to and fro, and carried away with every wind of doctrine, by the sleight of men,' &c., as the Apostle speaks, chap. iv. 14 of this epistle. And the latter sense of grace, in that Heb. xiii., I understand to be principally meant; for the doctrine of God's grace revealed to us in the gospel is eminently styled 'the grace of God bringing salvation,' Titus ii. 11. But yet withal, take in those blessings and blessed operations wrought within us which our Apostle here enumerates in chap. i., and goes on to do it in chap. ii. to ver. 11 of that chapter; the working of which in these Ephesians he all along ascribes unto the grace, the exceeding riches of grace, mercy, and love in God, founded in election and redemption; and these, together with his doctrine of grace, will keep you steadfast and immovable.

I should now add, as the custom of expositors likewise is, some more general analysis or division of the whole epistle; but let that suffice which, in going over the particulars, will arise naturally to every man's observation: that the half of it, to the end of the third chapter, is doctrinal, laying down the mysteries of salvation and man's misery; the other half, to the end, is wholly practical, exhorting to several duties in all sorts of relations. I hasten to the exposition itself.

SERMON I.

Paul, an apostle of Jesus Christ, by the will of God, to the saints which are at Ephesus, and faithful in Christ Jesus. Grace be to you, and peace from God our Father, and from our Lord Jesus Christ.—VER. 1, 2.

ALTHOUGH the matter of the two first verses is found almost in every epistle, and is accordingly expounded by every interpreter, yet, that there may not be an uncomely vacuity at the very first entrance, I shall add some animadversions upon the words of them.

Paul, an Apostle.—The reason why in his epistles he usually prefixes both his name and office is, *first*, to ascertain them he wrote to that the epistles were his own, or genuine epistles—as you may perceive his intent to be by that closure of his second epistle to the Thessalonians, 2 Thess. iii. 17, 'The salutation of me, Paul, with my own hand, which is the sign or token in every epistle : so I write,' &c. So, then, this inscription is both a salutation and a blessing of these Ephesians ; of which afterwards.

Secondly, He adds his sacred office—'an apostle.' Apostleship was an office extraordinary in the Church of God, appointed for a time for the first rearing and governing of the Church of the New Testament, and to deliver that faith which was but once to be given to the saints, (as Jude speaks,) and the apostles are therefore entitled the foundation the Church is built on, Eph. ii. 20; which office, accordingly, had many extraordinary privileges annexed to it, suited (as all the callings by God and his institutions are) to attain that end which was so extraordinary—as, namely, unlimitedness of commission to teach all nations, Matt. xxviii. 19. They likewise had an infallibility and unerringness, whether in their preaching or in writing, (2 Cor. i. ver. 13 and 18 compared,) which was absolutely necessary for them to have, seeing they were to lay the foundation to all ages, 1 Cor. iii. 10, although in their personal walkings they might err, as Peter did, Gal. ii. 11. And, further, they had authority and jurisdiction committed to them, as elders in any church where Providence should cast them, 2 Cor. xi. 28, together with authority and power therein, 1 Cor. iv. 21, and 2 Cor. x. 8. And—

Thirdly, This our apostle had this special grace and honour from God vouchsafed him above most of the apostles, to be particularly moved and inspired by the Holy Ghost, the conscience of his own duty concurring, to edify not only the present churches then extant, but to write epistles to leave them to the ages to come, which every apostle did not; and there were none that did write any part of Scripture but as and when they were moved by the Holy Ghost, as Peter tells us, 2 Pet. i. 21. As 'no prophesy came in the old time'—*i. e.*, under the Old Testament—'by the will of man ; but holy men spake,' and so by like reason wrote, 'as they were moved by the Holy Ghost ;' and thus it is under the New as well as under the Old. But God was pleased to use this man to labour more than they all. We owe the third part of the New Testament to him, insomuch as he wrote epistles to some by special and personal inspiration, whom he never saw in the flesh, as the Colossians.

And this practice of affixing his name and office to his epistles, as well as the epistles themselves, is greatly to be heeded by us that do come in after ages. Excepting that to the Hebrews, for a special reason not setting down his office of apostle, which in two or three epistles, where it is less needed, is omitted also. It is to be heeded, I say, by us in after ages, for it has this instruction in it, (which was his scope of doing it,) that as the matter of them did bind and oblige those whom he wrote to, so all saints in after ages to come, for they do inherit these and other apostles' writings, to own them, and to embrace them, and to observe what is written in them, as of a divine authority; the word of God, as well as of man, and as intended to all saints and faithful in Christ Jesus, as well as those at Ephesus. As those instances declare, that the epistle that was writ to the Church of Colosse, Paul commands to be read to the Church of Laodicea. The inscription likewise to the Church at Corinth commands the same: 'To the church of Corinth, with all that call on the name of the Lord, both theirs and ours,' 1 Cor. i. 2.

Know, therefore, that when you read any epistle, the whole weight of their apostolical spirit and authority in them is to fall upon all our consciences and spirits, as it did on theirs, unto these purposes, both to assure our hearts of the unerring truth of every tittle of them, and their word in their writings to be as true as God is true, 2 Cor. i. 13, 18, as also to receive all their injunctions and commands therein, as coming with the same apostolical authority that it did to those to whom they were by name written, and as immediately warranting us in all those practices which their living commands did put them upon. In a word, to speak in the words of the Apostle to the Thessalonians, to receive them all as the word of God, 1 Thess. ii. 13, even as if we had heard them out of Paul's own mouth, as there he urged that they had heard; which work as effectually in you that believe as it did in them. So that as in these their writings we enjoy these apostles' ministry, and shall to the end of the world, Matt. xxviii. ult., and are therefore said to believe through their word, John xvii. 20; in like manner, their ordinary directions to believers to any duty belonging to them,—to become churches, or join themselves to churches, or else to churches how to demean themselves,—left us in their epistles, or the acts of the apostles recorded, have the same authority to bind us as they did them, and he gives the same warrants and commands to us which their persons, by living voice, did to those saints in their times; which their very commission, Matt. xxviii. 19, holds forth to us, 'Go and teach them to observe all that I have commanded,' says Christ, 'and, lo, I am with you to the end of the world.'

And in this respect these few words, *Paul, an apostle*, which we find prefixed, are of great use to us; and let this name, and title, and commands of his, which are from Christ, be for ever precious throughout all generations.

There are three things in these two first verses:—

1. The author of this epistle—*Paul.*

2. The persons to whom it was written—*Saints at Ephesus*, &c.

3. The salutation and blessing therein uttered, ordinary in all his epistles —*Grace and peace*, &c.

I. THE AUTHOR—*Paul.*—I will not speak much of his personal supereminent worth. In his own opinion he was the least of saints on earth; in mine, the highest saint in heaven, and next the man Christ Jesus. To whose labours (more abundant than of all the other apostles, 1 Cor. xv. 10) the one-half of the now Christian, then Roman world, doth owe, and the catholic

Church in all ages, the third part of that invaluable treasure of the New Testament; taking together all either written by him, as the Epistles, or written of him, as the greatest part of the Acts.

Only this name of his here, *Paul*, and the change thereof from that of *Saul*, is a difficulty among interpreters, which I shall not here meddle with, further than thus: that this change might be from his former Jewish name, Saul, into a Roman name, Paul; it being evident that several nations did use to alter men's names according to their own tongue, and very often the first letter of a man's name is changed in the same language; whom Jeremiah calls Merodach, him the writer of the Book of the Kings calls Berodach. So the eldest son of Simeon, whom Moses calls Jemuel, Gen. xlvi. 10 and Exod. vi. 15, the same man doth Moses call Nemuel in Num. xxvi. 12. The name Paul was a name usual among the Romans; given to a Roman deputy, Acts xiii. 7; and thus the name Saul might have been fitted unto the Roman mode, *S* being turned into *P;* and that which strengthens this conjecture is, that we read of this change of his name first when we read of his converse with that Roman deputy, Acts xiii.; but chiefly when he was anew separated to the work of preaching to the Gentiles by the command of the Holy Ghost, Acts xiii. 4.

It may be added that this new name hath been the rather given him by the Romans, and the more readily accepted by him, as fitly glancing at the littleness of his stature,* (which the more illustrated the glory of God's grace in the gifts of his mind,) of which antiquity gives testimony from tradition, and ancient images of him four hundred years after, in Chrysostom's time, Niceph. lib. ii., cap. 37. And Chrysostom, in his homily *De princip. Apostol.*, calls him ὁ τριπηχὺς ἄνθρωπος, a man of three cubits, whereas the ordinary proportion of men is four; which may most probably be thought to be that baseness and weakness of presence, which himself acknowledgeth in himself, 2 Cor. x. 1, 10. It is certain that the name Paulus was first given to the family of the Æmylians in Rome for the littleness of their stature. And this change himself might well permit and take on him: a new Gentile name instead of his Jewish, as an indication of his new office, the Apostle of the Gentiles, Rom. xi. 13: it being withal so fitly suited to express the character of his spirit and his most eminent grace, littleness in his own eyes; which, accordingly, you find him still inculcating, as if it were his motto, both interpreting his name and expressing his spirit, 'less than the least of saints,' Eph. iii. 8; 'least of apostles,' 1 Cor. xv. 9; perhaps in some allusion to his name, Paul; but this is only a conjecture, on which I insist not.

Paul, an Apostle.—It was made a wonder in the Old Testament, 'Is Saul among the prophets?' And it is as great a wonder of the New, that Saul the persecutor should be among the apostles; and so it was when Paul converted began first to preach that Christ was the Son of God, and was first heard at Damascus by the people. What the effect whereof was, the words of the hearers do shew, Acts ix. 21, 22, 'But all that heard him were amazed, and said, Is not this he that destroyed them which called on this name in Jerusalem, and came hither for that intent, that he might bring them bound unto the chief priests? But Saul increased the more in strength, and confounded the Jews which dwelt at Damascus, proving that this is very Christ.' Whose office in the Church was the first, 1 Cor. xii. 28, 'God hath set in the Church [first] apostles;' and therefore the highest under the gospel next Christ, even as the high-priesthood was the highest of the rank of priests under the law. Hence both these are coupled together, and in

* Paulum modicum quid. Aug. in Ps. lxxii.

way of honour given unto Christ himself, (God's first and great apostle sent out by him, John xx. 21,) 'The high priest and apostle of our profession, Jesus,' &c., Heb. iii. 1.

Obs.—No sins before, and I may add to it, nor yet after conversion, can hinder God's free grace from using men in the highest employments in the Church, but magnify it the more. David, after his adultery, was a penman of Scripture, Psalm li.; Solomon, after his fall, of Ecclesiastes; Peter, after his conversion, denied Christ with oaths and curses, is a chief apostle, and converts three thousand fifty days after, with the same mouth he had denied Christ; and Paul, after he had been a blasphemer, was made an apostle.

Of Jesus Christ.—This addition shews the author of this office, whose designment it was, Jesus Christ. 1. Christ, as the author and founder of his apostleship, so he was of all the other apostles, John xx. 21, 'As the Father sends me, I send you.' Apostle signifies *one sent;* Christ was God the Father's Apostle, Heb. iii. 1, and appointed by him, ver. 2; and, Eph. iv. 11, it is attributed to Christ that he, ascending, 'gave some to be apostles,' &c. It is the prerogative of a king, yea, every master of a family, to appoint what offices and officers shall be of his household. And, 2. It imports also the dignity of this office above human offices. The style of it runs, 'An apostle of Christ.' As the offices that belong to the king's person in court have a peculiar denomination, expressing a relation to his person, which other offices in the kingdom have not; as, the king's chamberlain, the king's steward, &c.; and as others in the kingdom are all subjects of the king as their prince, but courtiers in offices are peculiarly servants of the king as a master; so they write themselves servants to the king: and Paul, 'Christ Jesus my Lord,' Phil. iii. 8, as they in court, 'The king my master:' so though all Christians are subjects and members of Christ, yet apostles and ministers are in a more peculiar respect servants of Christ, as James and Jude style themselves in the first verse of their epistles.

But although he styles himself Christ's apostle, yet he leaves not out his commission also from, and the influence of God also into it, 'By the will of God,' that is both of the Godhead, and of all three Persons. For to apostleship and all offices in the Church they all concur, as well as to our salvation,—

To apostleship; so Gal. i. 1, 'Paul, an apostle of Jesus Christ, and God the Father;' there you see are two Persons. And then the Spirit, the third Person, said, 'Separate me Paul and Barnabas,' Acts xiii. 2. And so they concur *to all other officers* more inferior, 1 Cor. xii. 4–6, 'There are diversities of gifts, but the same Spirit.' (The gifts which officers are endued with, are ascribed to the Holy Ghost.) There are differences of administrations, and the same Lord—viz., Christ, who, as a Lord, appoints the several offices wherein gifts are exercised; and there are diversities of operations, but it is the same God—viz., the Father, who worketh all in all. The blessing upon gifts, and the success of all administrations or offices ministerial, are from the Father. Thus 'By the will of God;' all three Persons are at the ordination of every true minister, and lay their hands of blessing on each of them, and set their hands to every minister's commission.

More particularly, *By the will of God.*—This *first* imports that special decree of God in separating him to this office, which, Gal. i. 15 and Rom. i. 1, he with an emphasis expresseth, set apart to it; ἀφορίζειν is to select choice things: therefore choice sentences are called aphorisms. And in this respect our apostle is called a chosen vessel to bear his name; that is, a choice vessel for the purpose, Acts ix. 15. And thus the election of the Twelve at first is as expressly ascribed to Christ's will as here this is. So

Mark iii. 13, 'He called to him whom he would, and he ordained twelve;' and this out of mere grace, and the good pleasure of his will, so in the same Gal. i. 15, 'It pleased God,' &c. And that is one reason why he mentions it here, even to mind his own heart of the original of this his great dignity wholly to have been the will and grace of God, and nothing in himself, calling it therefore elsewhere, 'grace and apostleship,' Rom. i. 5, that is, the grace of apostleship; yea, he reckoning this as great a mercy well-nigh as his salvation, for so that great and solemn thanksgiving of his, 1 Tim. i., from the 11th to the 18th, where he relates his conversion, doth imply, it being chiefly for putting him into the ministry, ver. 12.

Of God.—This imports, *secondly*, the immediateness of his call, in distinction from other officers. And likewise for their direction whither to go and what to do, they were subordinate to none other. And this latter was peculiar to this office. Evangelists, though extraordinary ministers, yet were sent out by the apostles, as Titus, 2 Cor. xii. 18, and so Timothy; but apostles, they immediately by God; thus Gal. i. 1, (which place interprets this,) Paul, an apostle,' says he, 'not of men, neither by man, but by Jesus Christ and God the Father, who raised him from the dead.'

To interpret the words: *First*, 'Paul, an apostle, not of men,' that is, my office is not a human office, which men have instituted and invented; it is, saith he, of divine institution. And this is common to all ministerial offices in churches. And this he spake in distinction from offices in commonwealths. In a commonwealth, the offices thereof are (as the Apostle calls them by way of distinction from those in the Church) ἀνθρωπιναὶ κτίσεις, human creations, (we translate it, 'human ordinances,') whereas all Church-offices are divine, and not of men, in Paul's sense. But yet because this first requisite, 'not of men,' was common to all offices of the Church as well as apostleship, therefore, *secondly*, he adds, by way of further distinction from them also, 'neither by man.' The ordinary offices in the Church, although they are not of men,—*i. e.*, there ought to be an institution for every one of the offices themselves,—yet the man, the person, is usually put into the office by men, though guided in it by the Holy Ghost, Acts xx. 'By men,'—that is, the particular designation of the person, that is by men, though according to such rules in the Word as are to guide their choice, (and that is the difference of those two phrases, 'of men,' and 'by men.') But, saith he, this my office of apostleship is neither of men, nor by men, but as the text here saith, 'by the will of God;' that is, by God's immediate designation of my person to it; so it also there to the Galatians follows, but 'by Jesus Christ and God the Father.'

And, which was yet further a more peculiar prerogative above other apostles, this our Apostle was called into it by Jesus Christ, as risen from the dead, and ascended into heaven. Other apostles were called by Christ living here in the flesh, but I was born out of time, saith he, and so had like to have missed of being capable of this office, whereof one requisite was to have seen Christ; but to make up that requisite also, Christ deferred the calling of me unto it until himself came again. Christ rose again and converted me himself from heaven, when 'last of all he was seen of me,' 1 Cor. xv. 8. And this difference of himself from other apostles he seems to insinuate, ver. 12 of that Gal. i., that he 'neither received the gospel from men,' as evangelists did, 2 Tim. i. 13, 14, and as ordinary teachers do, 2 Tim. ii. 2, nor was taught it, namely by Christ in the flesh in the way of outward teaching, as the other apostles were by Christ himself; but merely and wholly by inward and immediate revelation; and this made him, as was observed, so much excel all the other apostles; his gifts were answerable to his call, which was so extraordinary.

If it be objected that he was ordained an apostle by laying on of hands of Ananias, Acts ix. 17, and again by the teachers of Antioch, Acts xiii. 3, the answer is, *First*, that he was ordained an apostle before, at his conversion, by Christ himself, Acts xxvi. 16–18, 'But rise, stand upon thy feet, for I have appeared unto thee for this purpose, to make thee a minister and a witness both of these things which thou hast seen, and of those things in the which I will appear unto thee, delivering thee from the people, and from the Gentiles, unto whom now I send thee, to open their eyes, and turn them from darkness to light, and from the power of Satan unto God,' &c. *Secondly*, That Ananias' laying on of hands was to minister the Holy Ghost, and fill him with it, Acts ix. *Thirdly*, That which was done at Antioch by man was for a blessing on the work and exercise of his apostleship, and of the office of apostleship itself, which was to spend his labour and endeavour upon the Gentiles, among whom they sent him. *Fourthly*, That even that was first appointed and declared by the Holy Ghost, 'Separate me Paul and Barnabas to the work I have called them.' The Holy Ghost (who is God) did immediately say this ere they laid their hands on him with fasting and prayer.

I hear there are apostles abroad, at least those that say there are to be apostles still in the Church, and to the end of the world; and those that affirm it are not of the Romish party only, who make the popedom a perpetual apostleship in the Church, but of those who would be in all other things most contrary unto the Pope. To refute whom, this here is sufficient, that the apostles' call is to be 'by the (immediate) will of God,' as hath been opened in Acts i. You read that when Judas was dead, all the eleven apostles could not have chosen another apostle; yea, they would never have thought of adding another, had not God by a prophecy said, 'Let another take his bishopric,' (and he quoteth a Psalm to warrant it, Ps. lxix.,) that is, his office of apostleship; and he there mentions a qualification that was to be in him that should be chosen to that office, which I am sure hath not been found in any man these fifteen hundred years; and he puts a necessity upon it that he that was to be chosen should be so qualified, a δεῖ, a *must*, upon it, ver. 21, 22, 'Of those men that have accompanied with us all the time that the Lord Jesus went in and out among us, beginning from the baptism of John, unto the same day that he was taken up, *must* one [if any] be ordained to be a witness with us of his resurrection.' And though they named two, for God to pick one, to shew that God's immediate call was requisite to authorise an apostle, that it might not be by man but God, they by prayer cast lots, and it fell upon Matthias; and it is God alone who, by an immediate hand, doth dispose the lot, as Solomon tells us: for apostles were to be by the will of God immediately.

But this is not a new imposture; this very church of Ephesus he writes to had those that came among them with this claim; for, Rev. ii. 2, it is made one of their chiefest commendations, 'that they had tried them that said they were apostles and were not, and had found them liars.' If therefore any be so impudent and presumptuous against Christ and his Church, as to arrogate the dignity and write themselves so, they may be tried, you see, and that by the marks of an apostle, as our true apostle speaks, 2 Cor. xii. 12. Let us examine these men: Have you the signs of an apostle? Have you seen Christ in the flesh? That is one sign of an apostle, 1 Cor. ix. 1. Yea, where are the miracles, wonders, and mighty deeds that confirm your preaching, which are made signs to prove your apostleship, as 2 Cor. xii. 12? I would fain see the man that dares say he is an apostle; he will be found a liar, as those at our Ephesus were.

II. The second head, THE PERSONS TO WHOM HE WRITES—*To the saints which are at Ephesus, and to the faithful in Christ Jesus.*

Here is a double appellation, saints and faithful, or believers, as I shall shew by and by. These two are seldom both thus joined together in the inscriptions of his epistles, (though singly elsewhere, sometimes he styling them whom he writes to, saints, sometimes believers,) only in that parallel epistle, Col. i. 2, you have it in like manner joined, 'To the saints and faithful brethren in Christ.' The scope in which words is to shew two distinct qualifications in those brethren at Colosse, that they were both saints, and also believers and faithful. Now in this here he placeth his words a little otherwise, 'To the saints which are at Ephesus, and the faithful in Christ,' insomuch as I a little considered whether his scope were not to inscribe this epistle, not to the saints at Ephesus only, but to others, even all the faithful in Christ elsewhere in the world; as if the particle καὶ, *and*, should import all other believing persons besides these Ephesians to have been written to, and so for him to intend this as an epistle general, as he inscribed that to the Corinthians to be, which he inscribes not only to the Corinthians, but adds, 'with all that in every place call on the name of Jesus Christ our Lord.' But he not prefixing the article, and also the comparing this with that to the Colossians, doth carry it rather that he should mean only another epithet or qualification he dignifies the same Ephesians with, superadded to that of saints, and so his intent to be (as in that to the Colossians) 'To the saints and faithful that are at Ephesus;' though, as I said, to be received and made use of by all saints to the end of the world.

Saints.—Thus he ordinarily styles those in the churches he writes to: as the Romans, chap. i. 7; those at Jerusalem, Rom. xv. 25; the Corinthians, both 1 Cor. i. 2 and also 2 Cor. i. 1. A title not to be appropriated to the Christians of those first times, but common to all that are saved in all after times also, as, Eph. iv. 12, the very naming which dasheth morality and formal profession out of countenance, as light doth a glow-worm, as importing a more divine workmanship created, and some singular thing, (as Christ's word is,) even holiness in truth, as Paul dignifies it in this epistle, and is the usual appellation of the New Testament. And we should keep up the name, that the reality of the true religion be not lowered (as it is) by avoiding this title, which in these times is out of use; but it is because true holiness is out of fashion. They are not only called saints which are in heaven, but that are on earth, Psalm xvi. 1; so these, whilst living in Ephesus.

At Ephesus.—Of all the cities of the Gentiles, the most generally dissolute and profuse, who banished Hermodorus,* a man of singular modesty and temperance, merely for his virtue; making this law when they did it, 'Let no man be frugal and temperate among us: let no one man excel another in virtue; or if he do, let him be gone from among us.' Yet out of these, doth God make saints: so free is grace, not calling according to works.

Again, *At Ephesus:* although he says not, To the church of Ephesus, saints, as elsewhere, 'To the church of Corinth, saints,' 1 Cor. i. 2, yet he

* 'Ephesii Hermodorum singularis modestiæ virum cum dejecissent, "Nemo, dixerunt, apud nos, frugi sit, nemo unus excellat, vel si excelluerit, abeat." Quo nomine dignos fuisse qui strangularentur cives suos Ephesianos pronunciavit Heraclitus in 5 Tusculum Cicero.'—*Ælius Rodig. Antiq.* l. 4, c. 25, *ex Strab.* l. 14.

intends it; for the saints at Ephesus were now a settled church when this was written. At first indeed at Ephesus there were but a few, about twelve, called disciples, that knew nothing of the way of the worship of the New Testament, nor so much as of the Holy Ghost, Acts xix. 1, whom our Apostle lays hands upon, and gathers into a body, a church, for so, chap. xx. 17, they are called. And after that it was that this epistle was written to them, who therefore, chap. ii. 22 of this epistle, are said to be 'built together for an habitation of God through the Spirit,' a little temple, (besides that general universal temple, whereof he says, ver. 20, 21, that they were a part in another consideration,) as the word 'also' in the 22d verse implies. In his writing to the churches he takes notice of no other but saints, for of such living stones only should this temple consist; so the Corinthians, 1 Cor. i. 2, 'To the church that is at Corinth, saints.' Yea, 1 Cor. xiv. 33, 'all the churches of the saints.' That was the primitive language, for that was the constitution of churches then. He says not, To all the saints in churches, but churches of the saints, as we say colleges of scholars, house of peers. The primitive constitution acknowledged no other members, and he speaks not of the universal catholic Church, but particular churches. They generally, when they had a sufficient number of converts in a place, put them into a church-state, for he says *churches*, and yet speaks catholicly or universally of them: 'all the churches,' for of such did all then by the apostles' direction consist; from which rule these times, how have they swerved, not only in practice, but in judgment! But let us take heed lest, whilst we make the Church more catholic, and take in all that will profess Christ, we leave out *holy*, which is a necessary attribute to church. Bellarmine hath even in this point a speech which made me wonder to hear from him.* 'The Church,' says he, 'in her intention gathers only true believers, and if she knew who were wicked and unbelievers, either she would never admit them, or being by chance admitted, would exclude them.'

Now surely there are many rules in the Word whereby it is meet for us to judge who are saints, (as Phil. i. 7,) and also, whereby the most of the Christian world may be discerned to 'lie in wickedness;' though professing to know God, their works are so abominable, and themselves 'to every good work reprobate;' by which rules those who are betrusted to receive men to ordinances in churches are to be guided, and so to separate between the precious and unclean, as the priests of old were enabled and commanded by ceremonial differences, which God then made to typify the like discrimination of persons, either by visible manifest sins are found that men are in, or visible possession of graces, so far as it is meet to judge of other men by. 'Some men's sins are open afore-hand and afar off,' as to Timothy; so that the common light of true Christianity is easily able to difference them from saints: 'We know we are of God, and that the whole world lieth in wickedness,' as John speaks. And we need not travel to Rome or Turkey to find the world. And though *de facto* other than such be received into churches, yet the churches are true churches considered as to their administration; for to be a church and fixed seat of worship is an ordinance of Divine institution.

And faithful.—The word πιστος, translated 'faithful,' is both of a passive and active signification; it signifies one that is really and truly faithful in what he professeth or undertaketh. So, according to the language of the Old Testament, godly men are called, as Prov. xx. 6, 'Many

* 'Ecclesia ex intentione fideles tantum colligit, et si nosset impios et incredulos, eos aut nunquam admitteret, aut casu admissos excluderet.'—*Bell.* l. 9, *de Ecc. Mil.* c. 12.

will boast of their own goodness, but who can find a faithful man?' Thus likewise in the New, 'The things that thou hast heard of me, commit to faithful men,' 2 Tim. ii. 2, with many other the like places.

Secondly, It signifies 'believing,' or one that is a believer, John xx. 27, 'Be not faithless, but believing;' in the original it is the same word that is here; yea, in the phrase of the New Testament it is an ordinary title given believers to express their very believing and having faith in them; see Acts x. 45, 1 Tim. iv. 12. There is nothing against it to take in both these here, so as the Apostle's meaning should be, 'To them at Ephesus that are believers,' and also constant and faithful, or true believers, which the Apostle elsewhere calls 'faith unfeigned,' and Heb. x. 22, 'a true heart.'

Obs.—What God has joined, as here Paul saith, let no man put asunder, —saints and believers,—neither really in our own hearts and lives, nor in our judgments either of ourselves or others. Do not think this enough, that they are true believers; that is, that they make a profession of the doctrine of faith; but see that further they hold forth a work of faith wrought by that doctrine; and not only so, but do approve themselves faithful (as here) in that profession, (as Lydia said, 'If ye have judged me faithful,') and that they add evidences of saintship, they must be saints too; saith he, were 'saints and faithful.' It is not a profession of faith joined with morality, and no grand scandal, but a profession of such a strictness as will rise to holiness, that you are to judge men saints by. Neither ought any other than such to be members of churches, which are the body of Christ; this word *saint*, and *faithful* added to that, dashes a formal, an outward, and a mere orthodox profession. These very words we love not; that men are believers or Christians, they can bear it; but to add and require being saints and true believers, or faithful in believing; these kind of denominations men think sound too high to be applied to the ordinary common sort of professors, whom yet they own. But much more, if you would judge of yourselves, do not look upon legal holiness in yourselves as a sign or mark of a good estate; be sure you have a work of faith too (from whence that holiness flows) distinctly working toward the Lord Jesus Christ, and your hearts drawn out to him, as much and more than ever, after holiness, 2 Thess. ii. 13: 'God,' saith he, 'hath chosen us to salvation through sanctification of the Spirit and belief of the truth;' there is faith and sanctification joined both together, and both made necessary to salvation; it is in effect one with what he says here, 'saints and faithful in Christ.'

In Jesus Christ.—Because these words follow next after *faithful*, or believers, therefore some would have Christ, as he is the object of faith, or of our believing, to be here intended, and so 'in Christ' to be all one with what elsewhere is expressed by believing 'in Christ Jesus.' But the scope of these words here rather is, to note out in whom the persons of these saints or believers are said to be, as members in the head; or, which is yet nearer, that they, considered as saints and believers, that even as such, they are what they are in him; and the reason why these words, 'in Christ Jesus,' import rather being in Christ as believers, than their believing in Christ as the object of their faith, is, from the like inscription from that parallel epistle to the Colossians, (which is so like, that in many things it will conduce to explain this epistle, as one evangelist doth another.) Now there, and there only, chap. i. 2, we find these two, 'saints and faithful,' joined together even as here, and 'in Christ' comes in too, but so as 'brethren' comes between; the words there being placed thus, 'To the saints and faithful brethren in Christ.' Now, 'in Christ' coming in after 'brethren,' cannot import the object of faith, but the subject rather, in whom those as brethren were, and as saints and faithful; so elsewhere, 1 Thess. i. 1, 'To the church in God, and in the Lord Jesus Christ'—that is, both their persons, and also as they were a church, they are in God and in Christ, so as these words here, 'in Christ Jesus,' refer both to their being saints, and to their being believers in him. And so, as I take it, it is not so much meant that the persons of these Ephesians were in Christ, (though that be true, and is after affirmed in every verse, yet that is not all,) but that, considered as saints and believers, and what they were as saints, they were it all *in Christ.*

Obs.—My brethren, all our grace must be grace in Christ; 'saints and faithful in Christ.' The apostle, speaking in a way of difference and distinction from the legal godliness of the formal Jews, (which many Christians take up and rest in,) useth this phrase, 'They that will live godly in Christ Jesus,' saith he, 2 Tim. iii. 12, implying that there is a holiness in Christ Jesus differing from all other, an holiness whereof the spring and rise is in him. All your holiness, it must be wrought in Christ; we are 'created in Christ Jesus to good works,' so the apostle saith, Eph. ii. 10. All your holiness must be acted in Christ, and by motives from Christ, and by strength fetched from Christ: so in that, 2 Tim. ii. 1, 'Be strong in the grace.' What? the grace that is dwelling in yourselves? No, 'which is in Christ Jesus;' so it follows; here lies your strength. And then, all your holiness and faith and every good thing in you must be accepted in Christ too, and you must go out of yourselves to God, to have your persons and graces accepted in Him, as the apostle, 1 Pet. ii. 5, calleth them 'spiritual sacrifices acceptable to God by Jesus Christ.'

Obs.—It is the nature of true faith to make men faithful unto God, as well as believing and depending upon God; the word 'faithful,' as you have heard, being ordinarily used for both in the New Testament, as here in this place. Look what faith eyes in God and expects to receive from him, that in a suitableness it frames the heart in a way of conformity unto, such is the ingenuity, the honesty (as the Scripture calls it) of genuine faith. As, if it looketh for the righteousness of Christ for justification, it bows the heart to imitate that righteousness for sanctification, and to hate all that sin it seeks the pardon of, as truly as it seeks for the pardon of it; it knows not upon what other terms to desire it; so in the instance in hand, faith eyeing God's faithfulness, and depending thereon for salvation, causeth the heart (in ingenuity) to be as faithful to God. Again, in all that he requires and commands, it could not look up steadily to God for his performance without framing the heart to this resolution.

Grace be to you, and peace from God our Father, and from the Lord Jesus Christ.—VER. 2.

III. Here is the third general head of these two first verses, the SALUTATION he gives them, or the blessing, as some would have it.

The main general scope.—I take these words to be both a salutation Christian, and also a blessing apostolical and ministerial, and both translated or continued (though with a heightening addition) from the like salutation of the Jews, and the blessings of the priests in the Old Testament.

1. *A salutation.*—So himself expressly terms it, ἀσπασμος, 'The salutation of me Paul, the grace of our Lord Jesus Christ,' 2 Thess. iii. 17, 18, and 1 Cor. xvi. 21, 23. Now, salutations both among Jews and Gentiles were well-wishes, by desiring some good thing, either when they met or parted, or in letters or epistles, at the beginning or end, or both; in which they still

wished the best things they knew of. The heathens wished health, joy, &c.; the Jews and Eastern nations, whose language the apostles more follow, all prosperity, and that under the name of peace, thereby understanding a perfection or integrity of good. This language the Gentiles used. Thus that Egyptian to Joseph's brethren, Gen. xliii. 23, 'Peace be to you;' so likewise the Assyrians, for Nebuchadnezzar, writing to all nations, Dan. iv. 1, begins thus, 'Peace be multiplied unto you;' also the Persians, for Artaxerxes, the king of Persia, in his letter, thus salutes them he writes to, Ezra iv. 17, 'Peace, and at such a time.' Both which are instances also, for their kind, of salutes in letters and epistles to have been then in use, as we see here. So the Jews used to inquire of one another's welfare when they met, under the name of peace, and also wished all outward prosperity under that name, at their meetings, and also partings, which they thus expressed, 'Go in peace,' 2 Sam. xv. 9. Not to name many places for either, I will instance in one that hath both together at once in it: 1 Sam. xxv. 5, when David intended to send to Nabal a kind message, he bids the man that went, 'Greet him in my name,' says he; the original hath it, 'Ask him in my name of peace;' like unto what we use to ask when we meet, How do you do? are you well? And then, ver. 6, further bids him wish peace to him, (as the manner then was,) 'Thus shalt thou say to him that liveth in prosperity, Peace be to thee and thy house, and peace be to all that thou hast;' where by peace is meant all good and prosperity, and in that notion is peace often elsewhere taken. And this same kind of salutation was in use in Christ's time, and prescribed by him to be used by his disciples, Luke x. 5, 'Salute them and say, Peace be unto this house.' (See also Judges vi. 23; 2 Sam. xviii. 28; 2 Kings ix. 17, 18; Jer. xxix. 7; Isa. liv. 12–14; Isa. lxvi. 12.)

Now, this duty of common friendship, which nature taught the Gentiles, and brotherhood, which religion taught the Jews, Christianity and the gospel teacheth us now. And this is one reason why these salutations are so frequently and solemnly used by the apostles in their epistles; and herein Christ himself instructed them when he sent them out, Luke x. 5, and by his own example also, as I shall shew by and by, using the same phrases and form of speech, yet so as, under the same expression of words, they intended to wish higher and greater good things than the Jews or Gentiles ordinarily either meant or understood, even as the gospel itself hath a clearer revelation of better good things, as our Apostle to the Hebrews speaks. Thus, whereas the Grecians usually saluted with χαῖρε, which the Latins express by *salutem*, 'health and salvation;' which is all one with our English of old, 'sending greeting,' or 'all hail,' or 'joy;' that very same word the angel himself useth to Mary in his saluting her, Luke i. 29, when he brought her the first news of the Messiah, 'Hail, Mary,' &c. And the very same do the apostles in the Church of Jerusalem in their letters, Acts xv. 23, which we translate, 'greeting;' the same also James i. 1; yea, Christ himself to the disciples after his resurrection, Matt. xxviii. 9, 'All hail,' says he. In all which phrases the Syriac, according to the phrase of the East, still renders those words, 'Peace be to you.' Now, by this heathenish salutation, thus turned Christian, they all did mean and intend a spiritual and heavenly joy, even joy in the Holy Ghost and eternal salvation; whereas the Gentiles meant only what was carnal and outward. So in like manner, whereas the Eastern nations, both Jew and Gentile, wished peace, the gospel retains the same; thus Christ himself, at another time after his resurrection, says to his disciples, John xx. 26, 'Peace be to you,' yet thereby meaning not a Jewish outward peace, but that heavenly peace which he doth, with an emphasis, and by way of distinction, call His peace, 'My peace I leave with you,' John xiv. 27, which place, because it opens and confirms this very notion I have been upon, I will a little open and explain.

Christ was then taking his farewell of them, having in that sermon first plainly told them he was to go away; and among other things whereby he expresseth his love and friendship to them, he, at his parting, condescends to frame his speech conformable to this very custom of men in the world, which we have been speaking of, in their farewells, thereby to take their hearts the more in a way of kindness, which was wont among men. His words are these, 'Peace I leave with you, my peace I give unto you; not as the world giveth, give I unto you.' The meaning of which words is, that whereas it is the custom of the world when they part with friends and take their leaves, to wish them peace, which they call giving peace, (as we in English call it giving joy, and sending greeting,) or sending away in peace, as Abimelech said to Isaac, Gen. xxvi. 29, I do the like, (says he,) 'Peace I leave' (that word imports farewell) 'with you.' And accordingly, as the manner of men in hearty farewells is to double their wish, and say it twice, as 'Farewell, farewell,' and the like, so there he doubles this, 'Peace I leave, and peace I give.' Yet withal, industriously instructing them both that it was another manner of peace than the men of the world in their farewells used to wish: 'My peace I give unto you;' *my peace*—that is, a peace with God, Rom. v. 1, purchased with my blood, a 'peace which passeth understanding,' Phil. iv. 7; and further withal intimating the difference between this last solemn farewell of his, and those which the world useth to make, 'Not as the world giveth, give I unto you'—that is, they use in their farewells to wish or give peace, but out of compliment; or if they be hearty, they cannot give what they wish; such wishes are but words in them, and have no force to convey a blessing; only they wish their goodwill, and at best it is but an outward peace they mean: but I am most hearty real in mine, and I am able to give what I wish, for it is *my peace*, a peace of my own purchasing, and in my power to make good, and I will give it indeed.

Now, all this tends but to open the salutation of the apostle here. Herein he followed Christ; for although he wisheth these Ephesians (as the Jews and Gentiles used to do) peace, yet I may say of it as Christ did of his, not as the world, or in their sense, doth he wish it; for it is both a further peace than they intended in their salutes, even the same that Christ wished, *his peace*. Therefore here, 'from Jesus Christ,' is added by our apostle; and he gives it them also not as the world by a bare well-wishing, but with an apostolical and ministerial blessing. And whereas the salutation of the Jews was but, 'Peace be to you,' the Apostle, as became the gospel and preachers of it, adds grace thereto, 'Grace be to you;' yea, grace as the first, and principal, and most comprehensive of all good else. And withal, as became the gospel also, he makes a distinct mention of those persons of the Trinity that were the fountain of that grace and peace, 'God the Father and the Son.'

Obs.—Thus religion doth not abolish, but spiritualise and improve civility and humanity, as it also turns all outward good things—which the Jews ordinarily intended, when they wished peace, and which were but 'the shadow of good things to come,' Heb. x. 1—into spiritual and heavenly; and the gospel further adds grace thereunto, and discovers it as the fountain of all, itself being called the 'grace of God,' Tit. ii. 11, (as the patent for a pardon is called a man's pardon,) as containing and revealing it: 'The law came by

Moses, but grace and truth by Jesus Christ,' John i. 17;—Grace and peace be to you, &c.—This for the *first*, as they are a salutation.

2. These words, say some, are not a bare salutation, but, in an apostle's mouth and pen, an apostolical blessing; and so, an institution, an ordinance to convey a blessing; such as that of the priests, Num. vi. 23. The apostles were the patriarchs of the Church of the New Testament, as the sons of Jacob of that of the Old, the 'foundation,' as they are called, Eph. ii. 20. And as there were thirteen tribes, reckoning the two sons of Joseph, so thirteen apostles, taking in this of ours; and these therefore, as patriarchs and spiritual fathers, 1 Cor. iv. 15, blessed their children, as here, with grace and peace. So our Apostle blessed Timothy under this very relation, 1 Tim. i. 2, 'To Timothy, my own son in the faith, Grace and peace,' &c.; the like he doth to Titus, and so to these Ephesians and others he wrote to.

And that which more confirms the taking it for a blessing, is the conformity which the matter of the blessing hath with that blessing the priests—the ministers of the Old Testament, as we are of the New—were to pronounce upon the people as an ordinance of God, Num. vi. 23–25. For if you more exactly view and compare the matter of their blessing there, and of this here, it comes all to one, and is the same for substance; which I the rather observe, that you may see how the words of blessing under the gospel were derived from the Jews, as the words of salutation were, as was afore observed. The blessing then ran thus, ver. 25, 'Jehovah make his face shine on thee, and be gracious to thee,' (his *face* imports his grace or favour, as Ps. lxxx. 19, 'Cause thy face to shine, and we shall be saved;' and so the words following interpret it, 'and be gracious to thee,') here you see is grace; then ver. 26, 'The Lord lift up his countenance, and give thee peace,' namely, as the fruit of that his favour, and as the conclusion of all blessings, as it is often made, (so Ps. xxix. 11, 'The Lord will bless his people with peace;' and likewise Ps. cxxv. 5, 'Peace be upon Israel,') which he pronounceth at last as the sum and substance of all blessings, there is peace also. But yet, whether it be a New Testament institution for ministers to pronounce such words as a blessing, or a farewell salutation only, is a question made by some; because in the New Testament there is no mention of any such ordinance under the term of blessing. There is of praying for them, James v. 14. There is of blessing the elements in the sacraments; so 1 Cor. x. 16; but nowhere of blessing (say they) the churches publicly; and further, say they, the priests in that were types of Christ, as in sacrificing also they were, who was 'sent to bless his people,' Acts iii. 26.

But the mistake I conceive lies in this, that that eminent way of blessing us, which is peculiar unto Jesus Christ, was typified out on purpose by a far greater priesthood than that of Aaron's sons, even by Melchisedec's priesthood, who therefore, as a more transcendent type of Christ, blessed Abraham, the father of the faithful, and so all faithful in him, Heb. vii. 6, 7, and in that blessing personated a greater person than Abraham, ver. 7, even Christ. But otherwise, to bless is a moral institution, and not merely typical, for one man blesseth another, and that as brethren; Ps. cxxix. 8, they that go by the reapers of corn, say, 'The blessing of the Lord be upon thee: we bless you in the name of the Lord.' And as thus one man may bless another, so those who have any special relations unto others may, according to the compass or extent of that relation, bless those they have relation to, and that with a special blessing suiting that their relation. Thus parents bless their children with a special blessing; thus kings, subjects; so David, 2 Sam. vi. 18, and Solomon, 1 Kings xviii. 55. And so in like manner the priests the people, in respect of their ministerial relation unto them; and therefore there is not the like reason for their blessing the people, and of their sacrificing for the people, which kings were not to do. Sacrifice was wholly a ceremonial action, but blessing a moral institution. And besides, the priests, as they are types of Christ, so of the ministers of the gospel also; as in the prophecy of the times of the gospel, Isa. lxvi. 21; and therefore in what was moral in their office, (as in teaching, &c., so in blessing,) what they did may safely be taken as types of those ministerial actions which we are to perform. And that which confirms me in it is, that the Apostle's blessing, as we have seen, for the matter of it, is the same that that of the priests' was, Num. vi., and so the action of blessing of the same morality with the matter itself.

And I see no reason but that if they bless the elements in our sacraments, as the priests did their ordinances then, but that they should bless the people also, and that as ministers, they being in Christ's stead in and unto both, as the Apostle speaks, 2 Cor. v. 20. And surely (as was said) every relation of receiving or doing good to others, is made by God a ground of conveying a blessing by the well-wishes of those in that relation. Thus, if a poor man receives relief from a rich man, so he is endowed with power, or rather privilege from God, to bless him that is the instrument of good to him, and by his hearty blessing him effectually to return that good which he received, and is an instrument of God so far to convey that blessing, of that promise made to those that consider the poor, Job xxix. 13. 'The blessing of him,' says Job, having relieved them, ver. 12, 'that was ready to perish, came upon me;' so in like manner those whom God hath made ordinances of some special good to others, God also accompanies their prayer and well-wishing with power to convey that good in a more special manner than others, that yet do in a common relation of brethren wish it. Thus, parents being instruments of conveying life in this world, and the good blessings of life to their children, and if godly, have the promises of the covenant of grace to them, thence they are especially honoured, that by blessing their children they should bring down those good things which they are in other respects really appointed the instruments of; and when through their children's obedience they are comforted, the promise of long life, &c., being made to such children, and they thereupon blessing them, as the patriarchs did, God regards that blessing of theirs so far as to fulfil those promises thereupon.

So it is in kings also blessing their people, being set up for their good, Rom. xiii. 4, &c. And answerably, ministers being set up as stewards of the good blessings of the gospel, 'to bring the glad tidings of peace,' &c., hence their well-wishings of grace and peace, and of all those blessings of the gospel, which in their preaching they bring, they are a special means sanctified by God to bring down those blessings upon those that obey their ministry: and therefore, as when they come to a people, they are said to come in the fulness of the blessing of the gospel, as Rom. xv. 29; so when they depart, their farewells and salutes and well-wishes, made up of those desires of the blessings of the gospel which they preach, have a special efficacy in their mouths above any other, as their ministry also hath, and their prayers are said to have, James v. 14, and therefore God bade them, as to preach peace, so to wish peace, Luke x. 5, even that peace which they preached. But however in that, as was shewn, 'grace and peace,' &c., are as well a salutation Christian, there is in that respect warrant enough for ministers to dismiss their congregations with them, or the like to them. And it is certain that so far as any such kind of well-wishes are warranted of God to be used, as it is acknowledged of all hands they are, either by way of farewell or institution, that there will an answerable blessing from God accompany them; for else holy things, and so God's name, should be used in vain.

Thus much as concerning the more general scope of this and the like apostolical salutations and blessings used sometimes at the beginning, sometimes at the end of their epistles, sometimes in both. What difference there is in this from those in other epistles (for they used a variety of words) I will not now take notice of, my work being to interpret this only. The parts thereof are these—

1. The good things wished, 'Grace and peace.'

2. The authors of both these, 'God the Father, and the Lord Jesus Christ.'

3. The persons to whom, 'to you,' whom he had afore styled 'saints and faithful.'

The particular exposition of the words:—

Grace and Peace.—For the understanding of these two, I shall shew the difference between them.

Grace is the free favour of God, and that importing here, not the attribute as it is in God, for that is incommunicable unto us, and so cannot be wished us, as those gracious acts of his favour and love towards us immanent in God, but set upon poor creatures, whom he hath chosen in Christ, even 'thoughts of grace and peace towards us,' as Jer. xxix. 11, which are the cause, the fountain of all the good things bestowed; which good things are therefore distinguished from this grace as it is in God towards us; thus, Rom. v. 15, 'The grace of God, and the gift by grace,' are made two distinct things; grace is there mentioned as the cause of bestowing the good things bestowed, or rather called gifts by grace. And thus grace and the free favour of God are held forth, in this very chapter, as the spring of all good to us, for he resolveth all the blessings bestowed upon us into the 'riches of his grace' as the efficient cause, ver. 7, and 'to the glory of his grace' as the final, ver. 6, and so likewise chap. ii. 7, 8; yea, and in the text here he says, 'Grace be to you,' singly, and apart, that only first; and not 'Grace and peace to you,' as usually elsewhere; and when he after adds 'and peace,' he seems to speak of it but as a thing cast in by grace, as all other things are said to be, to the kingdom of God sought first.

Peace, then, is the fruit and effect thence flowing, and one of the effects or gifts of grace, and that synecdochically mentioned for all the rest. Peace with God is the first benefit bestowed, that follows upon faith; so Rom. v. 1. The scope of that chapter being to enumerate the fruits of faith, he mentions that first, 'Being justified by faith we have peace with God;' and as it is put to express the first, so the last blessing bestowed also. 'The end of that man is peace,' saith the Psalmist, Ps. xxxvii. 37. So the joys of heaven are termed, Isa. lvii. 2. The righteous, when he dies, is said to enter into peace, and it is called 'peace in heaven,' Luke xix. 38, and accordingly peace is reckoned as the reward given the righteous at the latter day, Rom. ii. 10. Glory, saith he, and peace be to him, &c., and therefore it must needs comprehend all other blessings coming between, and so even all from the first to the last. It is a perfection of good, as in the acceptation of the Jews, and the perfection of all spiritual good in the sense of the apostles, Rom. xiv. 17. The whole kingdom of God consists in righteousness, and peace, and joy. Thus not justification only is called peace, but sanctification also, 1 Thess. v. 23, 'The very God of peace sanctify you.' Yea, and the growth and perfection of that is said there to be from God, as he is a God of peace; so it follows, 'Sanctify you wholly;' the word ὁλοτελεῖς is totally and finally, it signifies both. Thus likewise, joy in the Holy Ghost and communion with God is called peace, 'peace which passeth all understanding,' Phil. iv. 7.

To conclude then, as grace and peace are the sum of the gospel, so of this evangelical blessing here; and so express even the fulness of the blessing of the gospel, as the expression is, Rom. xv. 29. And more particularly and restrainedly, our reconciliation with God consists of two parts, *peace* and *good-will;* as with men also all reconciliation doth. Thus, if you would make an enemy to be friends with one, you must first make peace for him; and when you have done, because a man may still say, I will be at peace with him, but I can never love him again as I have done; therefore to have made him a friend, a favourite again, and so reconciled perfectly, you must obtain grace and favour and good-will for him too. Thus it is between God and us, Col. i. 20, 'Christ having made peace through the blood of his cross, he reconciled all things to himself;' when he had once made peace, then he reconciled them, made them friends, which is clear out of free grace. You have both in the song of the angels (for they began to preach the gospel.) Say they, Luke ii. 14, 'Peace on earth, good-will towards men.' Here is grace and peace, *i.e.*, good-will; that is, he will not only pardon you, and be at peace with you, but he will love you, and be a friend very gracious to you. These two are all one with what here are termed grace and peace.

Now for the *second* thing—the author of both these—

From God the Father, and from the Lord Jesus Christ.—You shall observe how in that blessing of the Old Testament, Num. vi., Jehovah is mentioned three times, 'Jehovah bless thee, &c., Jehovah be gracious, and Jehovah give thee peace,' &c., whereby the three Persons and their blessing of us are intended, though not explicitly mentioned. But here, as became the gospel, they are distinctly named, 'From God the Father, and from the Lord Jesus Christ.

Why God is called the Father, and Christ the Lord, I shall shew in opening the next verse. Only this here, that God bestows not this grace as he is a creator, or author of nature in common to men as his creatures, but as he is become a Father in Christ, and so bestows it in a peculiar love, out of which he will give all good things, 'How much more shall not your Father which is in heaven give good things?' Matt. vii. 11.

And although peace, as well as grace, are both of them from God the Father, and both also from the Son, (for God is the 'God of peace,' Heb. xiii. 20, as well as 'God of grace,' 1 Pet. v. 10.) And likewise Jesus Christ he is the Prince of peace, (and so peace is his gift,) so grace also, and therefore the grace of our Lord Jesus is wished in the end of all Epistles; of whom we are graciously accepted (says ver. 6 of this chapter.) Yet,

Grace from the Father.—It is more usually and especially attributed to him, for it is his free grace that chose us (ver. 4–6 of this chapter compared) that also justifies us, Rom. iii. 24, &c. And as he is the fountain of the Deity, so is his free grace the spring of peace, and also of all those works of the other two Persons for us.

Peace from Jesus Christ.—And this is from him in a more peculiar manner, for 'the chastisement of our peace was upon him,' Isa. liii. 5, and he is said to have 'made peace by the blood of his cross,' Col. i. 20; and thereupon God out of his free grace owns us, accepts, justifies us.

And although the particle 'from' Jesus Christ be not in the original, yet other Epistles warrant the putting it in. So 2 John 3 hath it expressly 'from the Father, and from Jesus Christ;' and the grammatical construction in those parallel salutations, Gal. i. 3 and 2 Tim. i. 2, do all evince it against the cavils of some heretics.

Now *lastly*, both grace and peace may be said to be from the Father and the Lord Christ in a double sense. *First*, efficiently; that is, in respect of real influence into these things themselves, as the authors and causes of both. Thus God the Father is the author of grace in his decreeing first to set his love upon us; and Christ our Lord in purchasing all that good which was out of this love decreed. And *secondly*, objectively; that is, this grace and love in God the Father, and this peace and satisfaction that is in Jesus Christ, as they come to be more and more apprehended by us, they thereby come to be more and more communicated unto us, and multiplied in us and upon us. This that benediction, 2 Pet. i. 2, evidently holds forth, 'Grace and peace (the same things there wished) be multiplied unto you, through the knowledge of God, and of Jesus Christ.' Mark how he says, 'through the knowledge,' &c. The meaning is, that as those two Persons are the cause of these things towards us, so through our apprehension of them, and of what they have done therein for us, and wrought in us, these are increased towards us, and multiplied upon us.

But then you will say, Where is the Holy Spirit? Here is only God the Father and Jesus Christ mentioned as those that he wished grace and peace unto from the Holy Ghost; what should be the reason of that?

For answer, *first*, it is not that the Holy Ghost is not the author of both these as well as the Father and the Son, nor that he is not intended here in this blessing. No, the works of the Trinity are undivided. If therefore from the Father and Son, then also from the Holy Ghost; and to this purpose it is observable, that by that forementioned form of blessing prescribed the priests in the Old Law, the word Jehovah, as we observed, is repeated thrice, to note it was pronounced in the name of all three Persons. And besides, once in the New Testament itself, you have grace and peace in one benediction wished from all three Persons, and therein the Spirit mentioned as well as God the Father and God the Son, and it is in the last of all apostolical benedictions in the last book of all, the Revelations, chap. i. *First*, from God the Father; and so in ver. 4, 'Grace and peace from him, that is, and was, and is to come.' Then *secondly*, from the Holy Ghost: so it follows, 'and from the seven Spirits,' the Holy Ghost being set forth by the fulness of those gifts (even a number of perfection) which he works in us, for though there be diversity of gifts, yet one and the same Spirit, 1 Cor. xii. 4. And then *thirdly*, from Christ, 'and from Jesus Christ,' &c., ver. 5.

Yet, *secondly*, so as ordinarily in all other Epistles, in their blessings prefixed, the mention of the Spirit is omitted; and the reason is, because it is both his office and work to reveal and communicate this grace from the Father, and peace from the Son. Hence in deed and in truth, blessing from the Holy Ghost comes to be wished in the very praying for a communication of grace and peace from God the Father and Christ; for, as Rom. v. 5, 'the love of God is shed abroad in our hearts by the Holy Ghost which is given us.' He is that Person that leadeth us out of ourselves unto the grace of God the Father, and the peace and satisfaction made by Jesus Christ. Those other two Persons are in their several works rather the objects of our faith and consolation, but the Holy Ghost is the author and efficient both of our faith on them, and comfort enjoyed in and from them. We look up to God the Father as the fountain of grace; and we look up to Jesus Christ as the fountain of our peace. But we are to look at the Holy Ghost as the revealer of both these from both. You will understand the justness of this reason, why he omitted the mention of him by this like instance: when you make your prayers, (and a blessing is a kind of prayer,) you use to pray to the Father, and likewise in the name of Christ, but you do not at all, or seldom, read in all the Scriptures of prayers made to the Holy Ghost. And why? Because it is his office to make the prayers themselves, which you thus put up to the other two Persons, and therein lieth his honour. Thus here, 'grace from God the Father, and peace from Jesus Christ;' but he that revealeth both these is the Spirit. I will shut up this with one scripture, wherein this our Apostle, making the same kind of prayer or blessing, confirmeth this notion, mentioning all these three several parts and influences of the three Persons in the same order and difference I have now given, and unto the same purpose: 2 Cor. xiii. 14, 'The grace of our Lord Jesus Christ, and the love of God, and the communion of the Holy Ghost, be with you,' &c. That which is attributed to the Holy Ghost is, as was said, to communicate and reveal all both that grace and love in God, and in Jesus Christ.

To you.—That is, every one of you in particular. I will not omit this mention of the persons to whom these are wished, which was the third thing mentioned. He had enstyled them saints and faithful in the first verse; and yet after that, wisheth grace and peace to them.

Obs.—The best Christians here need peace, and to that end Christ's blood and satisfaction, which is alone the procurer of all our peace, to wash their souls daily with the efficiency and spirits of that blood; and likewise for the acceptation even of their holiness and faithfulness they need grace too, the free favour of God. 'Grace and peace to you saints, and faithful Ephesians.' They both need the things themselves to be daily continued unto them; and their souls need to apprehend more of them, and about them, to have more enlarged revelation of them made to their faith. Hast thou peace already with God through faith? Yet still thou hast guilt and doubtings; thy faith is mixed with unbelief; therefore thou needest more of peace, 'Peace be to you.' Again, hast thou assurance of God's love? Yet, oh how little dost thou know of it! (as Job speaks.) This grace and love of God and Christ passeth knowledge, Eph. iii. 19. As in like manner this peace is said to pass understanding, 2 Pet. i. 2; Phil. iv. 7. And this is the Apostle's meaning in his benediction in both Epistles, 'Grace and peace be multiplied (says he) through the knowledge of God (the Father and his love) and of Jesus our Lord' (and his satisfaction for you.) Hence it is evident, that the communication of these to us is through our knowledge and apprehension thereof increased and multiplied; as also a further possession of them thereby.

Many are the observations that interpreters, upon several Epistles, do from hence raise, for which I refer the reader to their comments. I shall sum up that which I would commend to you in this one Meditation.

Seeing the grace and free favour of God cast upon us, and peace with God, as a fruit of that favour and of Christ's satisfaction, are the sum of the apostles' ordinary wishes and salutes, (who to be sure in such a breviary would wish the highest, who were willing to impart their own souls to those saints they wrote to,) let this be a directory to us what to make the more ordinary and continual scope of our desires and prosecutions, even the obtaining peace with God, and grace of God. Seek this peace and ensue it, peace with God through Christ. And yet learn, from this apostolical addition, to seek grace also, and not to rest in peace, but to seek God's favour. Good and evangelical spirits cannot content themselves with peace; they must have grace too; God's heart and love to be set upon them, his good-will. Seek to be pardoned, but above all seek to be beloved.

SERMON II.

Blessed be the God and Father of our Lord Jesus Christ, who hath blessed us with all spiritual blessings in heavenly places [or in heavenly things] in Christ.—Ver. 3.

The holy heart of this blessed Apostle was so full in his own person of being blessed by God, that he falls a blessing him as soon as he begins to speak. It is his first word he begins the body of this epistle with, and continues the same course and way of blessing God through the first half of the chapter unto ver. 15. And then he enters upon and opens another view of giving thanks, and pouring out prayers for these Ephesians, although this of blessing God far excels both thanksgiving and prayer, as I shall afterwards shew. But still under one or other of these ways of worshipping God, either prayer or thanksgiving or blessing, which are the highest strains of immediate worship we can perform to God, or at least with the materials for these, he goes on to fill up the rest of the first chapter. Yea, and after that being finished, he still continues matter of thanksgiving and blessing to the end of the second chapter throughout.

And here the occasion that inflamed him to pour forth such a flood of blessings, &c., comes duly to be noticed by us. And oh how abundantly did his heart use to overflow, if he fell but into this argument from that occasion, and entertained but the thoughts of it! You may for an instance thereof, though all his epistles testify it, but read over those passages of his in his first Epistle to the Thessalonians, which he begins even as he doth this chapter, Eph. i. 4, 'Knowing their election of God.' How? By the fruits of it throughout his ministry, as the instrument. 'For our gospel,' says he, 'came unto you, not in word only, but in power.' And how exemplarily they turned from idols to wait for Christ from heaven, through that his ministry, which brought forth all these fruits amongst them, as it hath done over the world! And having thus begun and fallen into this argument, as I said, he proves so concerned, as he knows not how to get out or to set bounds to his affections. Read on 1 Thess. ii. 8, 'So being affectionately desirous of you, we were willing to have imparted unto you, not the gospel of God only, but also our own souls;' and, chap. iii. 7, the joy hereof was so great, that it swallowed up the afflictions of all his sufferings, 'Therefore, brethren, we were comforted over you in all our afflictions and distress by your faith; for now we live, if you stand fast in the Lord: for what thanks can we render to God again for you, for all the joy wherewith we joy for your sakes before our God?' Thus he, when he took pen to write this Epistle, or otherwise to dictate it, the first thing the Holy Ghost filled him with was the consideration of all these blessings vouchsafed these Ephesians, which he enumerates together with this remembrance conjoined therewith. Thus all these blessings and matters of thanksgiving were all and every one of them the fruits of his own doings; that is, the very fruits of his own ministry and preaching; which, besides the glory and riches of God's grace towards those persons he writes to, did deeply affect him. Besides this, the memory of what had passed, and he had cause to remember them by a good token, he knew what he had preached, and remembered how they had been wrought upon thereby. For he had afore this Epistle, for three years' space, laboured amongst them night and day, publicly and privately, from house to house, in preaching and that with tears; as in his last farewell sermon to the elders of this very church himself relateth, when he told them they should see his face no more, and so that he should never any more preach to them again; and how much his heart and theirs was affected with that speech, the story of it and that his sermon doth sufficiently inform you.

Now, then, a little observe his speech in that farewell sermon, in which he makes a sum of his forepast ministry in that city, though but in general speeches; as how he had 'not shunned to declare all the counsel of God to them,' Acts xx. 27; and above all thereof to make a display of the grace of God in the gospel, wherewith he saith he had finished 'the ministry which I have received from our Lord Jesus, to testify the gospel of the grace of God,' ver. 24. And then let us but compare the first part of this Epistle, which contains the fruits I speak of; and they do answer to these his declarations of the matter of his preaching, related in that farewell sermon. In the fifth verse of this chapter, he mentions God's having chosen them in Christ, and having predestinated them to the adoption of children, to the praise of the glory of his grace. Whereby it sufficiently appears that the doctrines of election and predestination, in all the points of them, he certainly had in his ministry gone over, and were the points he had instructed them in, and had taught them fully; otherwise had he not declared all the counsel of God, (whereof specially the doctrines of election and predestination do eminently in the New Testament bear that very name of the counsel of the Almighty within himself,) and how could he have said, that He had elected and predestinated them, had he kept back anything that was profitable for them?

Well, he goes on first, 'In which glory and riches of his grace he hath abounded towards us, in all wisdom and prudence, having made known to us the mystery of his will,' in which words he tells us here again that this he had preached, 'according to his good pleasure, which he hath purposed in himself,' which in the eleventh verse he styles 'the counsel of his own will.' And again, ver. 11, out of which it was 'he had predestinated us to obtain an inheritance according to the purposes of him who worketh (both this, as) all things (else) according to the counsel of his own will.' So that the matter for which he here blesses God, wrought and accomplished in and upon their hearts, will be found answering, as the print does to the seal, that is, of his ministry. His doctrine namely, (as he recapitulates it in that sermon Acts xx., and that it has been the pith and principal sum of all his former sermons,) which had been to testify the grace of God in the gospel, and to open all the counsels of God in and about man's salvation; in which he had concealed nothing that was profitable unto them, (as he professeth,) that might work repentance towards God, and faith towards our Lord Jesus Christ, ver. 20, 21. Now behold, what you read, you find here in this Epistle, testified by the Holy Ghost, who had been the master workman of all grace in them, and towards them, to have been left from his preaching impressed upon their souls, verified on their persons; visibly to be read by all men, written in their hearts and lives, and openly avowed professions of themselves. There is no man that shall compare one with the other, but must say that as face answers to face in water, so those contents specified to have been the subject of his preaching in that sermon in the Acts, to be answerable to these impresses here in their hearts, the effects recorded in this Epistle, and the success of his ministry, answering to the other, as prints do unto their copy. As he had preached repentance toward God and faith toward our Lord Jesus Christ, as he had declared in that sermon of his there, so answerably here he says that 'the grace of God had abounded towards them in all wisdom and prudence;' the genuine meaning of which words is, that God had wrought all that belongs unto true faith, the truest wisdom and repentance, the only prudence accompanied with holiness; which are signified by these, as I shall shew, when I come to open those words. And by what means God had wrought it, he tells you in the 9th verse, that follows in his own words you meet with in that sermon in the Acts, ver. 20, whereby he had set out the matter of his preaching, 'having made known,' says he, 'to us the mystery and secret of his will,' 'the purpose and counsel of his will,' ver. 11, as to the matters namely of their salvation, and all to the 'praise and glory of that grace,' which in his preaching he had so much celebrated, and nowhere hath set forth more than in this paragraph of his blessing God for them.

In fine, as he elsewhere himself spake, so he had preached, and so they had believed, 1 Cor. xv. 11; so as in effect Paul's blessing of God by his enumerating these particular blessings of God bestowed upon them, proves to be indeed a preaching over to them the whole gospel of their salvation anew, the whole gospel in a new mode, in a new dress of thanksgiving, viz., for blessings of grace either shewed to them, and wrought in them, by the matter of his preaching. Instead of the seeds, the corn and grain he had sown, which were since grown up in their hearts, he returns the fruits of them—fruits of their own growth. And withal he doth in a covert manner mind them thereby, and brings fresh to their remembrance the principal materials, which God, by his preaching, and which while he was preaching them, God had wrought in them; and finally he provokes them upon the remembrance hereof afresh to bless God, by observing himself thus affectionately and passionately giving thanks, and praises, and blessing to God for them; that how much more should and ought they to do it anew for themselves? Than which course of proceeding herein held by him, there could not have been a greater artifice invented or used, whereby to affect their own hearts. This for the fitness and justness of the occasion of blessing God.

Nor let any man wonder that I make this kind of enumeration of gospel blessings to be as the preaching of the gospel itself. 'I am ready to preach the gospel to you at Rome also,' says Paul to the Romans, at the beginning of chap. i.; 'and I am sure,' says he, 'that when I come unto you I shall come in the fulness of the blessings of the gospel of Christ,' so speaks he at the end of that Epistle. The gospel is made up of blessings, is nothing but blessings, and the fulness of blessings.

Nor will it be out of our way or hinder us, to stand and observe, as touching the form of his blessing God, the vast difference that at this very entrance appears to be between the old dispensation among the Jews, and the dispensation under the New Testament. The form they used is, 'Blessed be the God of Israel.' And Zachary used this at a time when it was so near the expiring of the Old Testament and the approach of the New, at a time when the Messiah himself was conceived and come in the womb, though not yet born, and John the Baptist, that was to be his immediate forerunner, was already born. They all speak in this sort, till Christ were as the sun at his height, as if they generally knew no higher title to honour God by than the God of the Jews, the Lord God of Israel.

'Blessed be the Lord God of Israel,' that was the wonted note of old they used in the beginning, otherwhile in the middle, or else conclusion of their songs and worship. So David in the Psalms often, Zachary in his song, Luke i. 68. The difference is that they spake it according to the level of the Old Testament, 'Blessed be the God of Israel;' but the holy apostles Paul and Peter, according to the elevation of the New, the 'God and Father of our Lord Jesus Christ.' And this style the two great apostles begin with—our apostle here in the beginning of this Epistle, and Peter in the beginning of his first Epistle; and he used it then when he did write unto Jews, for unto them are his Epistles written, which makes the alteration of the style the more observable, 1 Peter i. 3, 'Blessed be the God and Father of our Lord Jesus Christ.' Yet the mercies which he there blesses God for are but one or two, 'who according to his abundant mercy hath begotten us again to a lively hope, to an inheritance,' &c. It is a blessing God for the first blessing in execution, regeneration, and the last performed, namely, the inheritance in heaven, as it followeth there.

He begins his doxology no higher than at that first spiritual mercy bestowed in this life, which estates us into that inheritance; but our apostle here prefixeth it before his 'Blessed be God,' and unto all blessings universally, whereof in his subsequent discourse he enumerates the particulars, and he takes the rise of his flight higher, 'according as he hath chosen us afore the world,' even at election; that first, original, and universally fundamental grace of all the other that follow; that vast womb of eternity, in which all blessings were conceived and shaped before the world was, and so from thence descends to redemption, regeneration, seal of the Spirit, glory.

And here in this place, since most interpreters generally have observed a correspondence held with that Jewish doxology in the Old Testament, I shall more specially add this one that appears to me to be the most direct and likeliest correspondent of the Old Testament, that ever the Apostle held intelligence with, in this of his of the New. And it was in a prophecy of the prophet David, Ps. lxxii., where, prophesying of Christ, ver. 17, 'Men shall be blessed in him,' (plainly meaning Christ,) and that 'all nations shall call him blessed,' he breaks forth thereupon, as here the apostle doth, 'Blessed be the Lord God, the God of Israel, (that latter is Old Testament language,) who only doth wondrous things; and blessed be his glorious name for ever, and let the whole earth be filled with his glory; Amen and Amen.' Wherein you see that the prophet blesseth God expressly for the times of the gospel, wherein he should bless us Gentiles, as well as Jews, in Christ; in whom, both to Abraham and again to David himself, God had promised to bless all the nations of the world. 'Let the whole earth be filled with his glory;' and this estate our holy apostles together having seen with their own eyes to have been in their days, (and especially Paul, the Apostle of the Gentiles, through his ministry so gloriously accomplished in these Ephesians and other Gentiles, as well as that other apostle had, on the Jews he wrote to,) the same Spirit of faith, 2 Cor. iv. 13, (in him and both, crowned and confirmed with so visible experience,) did burst out as you see into the same blessing for substance, but more full and explicit, which had been but by way of prophetical foresight uttered by David; thereby most passionately inciting these Ephesians, and with them all Christians in all nations, (so lately converted to Christ,) to join with him in this his manner of blessing God; the whole earth being now filled with his glory, and all nations being now blessed by

God, the God and Father of Christ, with all spiritual and heavenly blessings in him.

The words of this third verse divide themselves into three parts :—

1. A blessing God, as on our parts to be performed : 'Blessed be God.'

2. The style or titles under which Paul blesseth God : as 'the God and Father of Jesus Christ.'

3. The matter for which, or blessings bestowed on us : 'for all spiritual blessings in heavenly things in Christ.'

Blessed be God.

I. *What it is to bless God.*—Blessing of God is to wish well to, and speak well of God, out of good-will to God himself, and a sense of his goodness unto ourselves.

1. *To wish well to him, and speak well of him.*—There is *benedicere alicui*, which is, to invoke a blessing by prayer to another, as a father blesseth his child, one saint another : thus we are not capable of blessing God, nor God of being blessed by any. But there is *benedicere aliquem*, which is, to speak well of another, and to wish well to (as Ps. cxxix. 8), or to congratulate heartily the happiness of another ; and in this manner God gives us leave to bless him, εὐλογεῖν τὸν Θεόν, *in accusativo* Luc. i. 64, Jam. iii. 10. Yea, God loves your good word, that is, to be spoken of well by you, rejoiceth in your well-wishes, and to hear from you expressions of rejoicings in his own independent blessedness. Though God hath an infinite ocean of all blessedness, to which we can add nothing, who is therefore entitled by way of eminency, 'The Blessed One,' Mark xiv. 61, a title solely proper and peculiar to him, yet he delights to hear the *amen* of the saints, his creatures, resounding thereto ; that is, our 'so be it.' Thus our apostle having entitled him, Rom. i. 25, the 'God blessed for ever,' as in himself he is, and such in distinction from, and opposition to his whole creation, which is his scope there, yet he adds his own *amen*, or 'so be it,' thereto, 'God blessed for ever, Amen.' It is strange, that although so it is already, God is blessed in himself, and so it must be for evermore, that yet our 'so be it' is put to it ; we thereby uttering our good-will ; and it is well taken by him. It is not an *amen* set to a blessing of invocation, but it is an *amen* of joyful acclamation and congratulation, as expressing our rejoicing and complacency in his happiness, declaring that so we would have it.

Thus Christ, who is God with the Father, and so acknowledged in that 45th Psalm, (a psalm to his praise,) 'Thy throne, O God,' &c., ver. 6, (compare Heb. i. 8,) yet there we find that he is blessed by the Church, his spouse, in these words, ver. 4, 'Prosper thou, ride thou in thy majesty, or ride prosperously ;' which is a joyful shout and acclamation, as useth to be to kings, upon his passing by ; the people exulting in that glory and majestic state which they see him go forth in, wishing him prosperity in his expedition and undertakings, to make himself glorious, by doing wondrous things. The old translation expressed the intent of it, rather than the letter : 'Good luck have thou with thine honour.' The church there had withal in her eye all those gracious perfections his person was adorned with ; which thus won her heart to him, and drew this from her : for so it follows, 'Ride and prosper, because of truth, righteousness, and meekness.' And thus for us to take a view of all the absolute excellencies and perfections that are in God, to behold him crowned with glory and happiness that encircleth him round—a crown of glory made up of justice, truth, holiness, and other attributes ; to take a survey of all his proceedings and dispensations, and goings forth of every kind—his everlasting degrees of justice and mercy—all his ways and dealings in the variety of them, though never so cross to our particular; and to rejoice heartily in that glory of his, which is the result of them all: and inwardly to say, Oh, let him be thus glorious and blessed for ever, whatever shall become of me! to be glad of all, congratulate him and wish well to him in all, this is to bless him.

2. *When done out of good-will as the principle of it;* as indeed where such acts as those forementioned are, there must needs be good-will, the spring of them. And in this respect, blessing God superadds to confessing to his praise, yea or to give glory to him; it speaks more than either. The devils shall confess to his praise, Phil. ii. 10, 11, 'Every knee, and every tongue, even of things under the earth (in hell), shall confess Christ, to the glory of the Father;' but theirs is but extorted, although acknowledged by them to be justly his due. Hence if we would speak strictly, blessing God is appropriated properly to the saints, with a difference from praising God; Ps. cxlv. 10, 'All thy works shall praise thee, O Lord, and thy saints shall bless thee.' The saints alone, they bless him, and why? because they alone bear good-will to him. And they bless the Lord with their whole souls, and all that is within them, Ps. ciii. 1, and this God respects more than your 'giving him glory.' It was his very end in choosing forth a select company of saints; that he himself first blessing them, they then might bless him again. He could have been glorified however in them, but he loves to be blessed; he loves our good-will in it, more than the thing.

3. I added, *out of good-will to God himself;* that is, purely for what he is himself, and not only for what to ourselves; in this manner our apostle blesseth God here, even for this, that he is the God and Father of Christ. As loving God that ever he begot such a Son, he rejoiceth that so great a Father hath so great a Son; to the mutual honour of each. How often doth he in his Epistles come in with this, even in the midst or conclusion of a discourse, in which there was an occasion to magnify him, 'who is God blessed for ever,' which is a glorifying God as God, that is, in himself and by himself, thus blessed for ever. Thus Rom. i. 25, Rom. ix. 5, and elsewhere.

Yet, 4. together herewith, *out of a sense of his goodness also to us.* So here, though he blesseth him first for being the God of Christ, yet he withal after blesseth him for having blessed us with all blessings; and God gives us leave so to do. 'If you loved me [purely],' says Christ, John xiv. 28, 'you would rejoice, because I said, I go to my Father:' you would rejoice in my enjoyment of him, that is, in my blessedness in and through him, 'who is greater than I,' (as it follows,) and so is the fountain of that happiness I have. He takes it unkindly at our hands, if we rejoice not in his personal blessedness primarily, and in the first place. And thus as we love him because he loves us first, so we bless him because he blesseth us first: and yet it must rise higher in the end, (and in heaven it will do so,) even purely to bless him for himself, or else we love him not, nor bless him, as the great God is to be loved and blessed by us. A meditation or two:—

1st Meditation.

It is an infinite favour we are admitted to, and privilege vouchsafed to creatures, and indeed the highest, not only to pray to God to obtain all blessings, and to give thanks to him when we have them; and further to glorify him for the glory that is in him; but beyond all this, to bless him for all the blessedness that is in him, and for him to take in our *Amen*, our *Euge*, to his own blessedness, as in like manner he doth our faith as a seal to his truth and faithfulness. Oh, what is it! He was not content to be blessed alone, but he must bless us, and make us partakers thereof. But further, as if not perfect without us, he blesseth himself in our returns and echoes of blessing to his blessedness, that so we in him, and he in us, might be blessed together for evermore. Amen.

2D MEDITATION.

You have seen it a peculiar character of the saints, thus out of good-will to bless God, "Thy saints they bless thee.' It was his end why he had saints; said he with himself, They will do that which none of my other works will do—they will bless me, for none else have good-will to me: and whoever blesseth him, are first blessed of him. Hast thou, or dost thou find in thy heart, thus to bless God, and findest all within thee rising up in the doing of it? 'Bless God, O my soul, and all that is within me,' Ps. ciii. 1. Go home, thou art a saint I warrant thee. It was Job's grace, 'The Lord hath taken, yet blessed be the name of the Lord.' You will say, that was Old Testament grace: yea, and it is New Testament grace too; you see it in our Apostle, the greatest of saints; so we may write him, however he writes himself the least. His heart was full of this, and so it came out first; he could not hold at the first to utter it; when he was to speak to those he wrote to, he must needs begin to speak by way of blessing God: yea, it is the highest and best grace in heaven itself. The angels, though not themselves, but men only, have benefit by Christ's blood,—he died for men, not angels, and therefore it is only the chorus of men that sing, Rev. v. 9, 'Thou hast redeemed us by thy blood out of all nations'—yet, ver. 11, the angels are brought in blessing Christ also, and that for this, that he was slain, ver. 11, 12, 'And I beheld, and heard the voice of many angels round about the throne, and the beasts and the elders, and the number of them was ten thousand times ten thousand, and thousands of thousands; saying with a loud voice, Worthy is the Lamb that was slain to receive power, and riches, and wisdom, and strength, and honour, and glory, and blessing.' Worthy is the Lamb that was slain, (they mention nothing else of him,) and then blessing comes in at last as the *E, la*, the highest note that heavenly choir can reach to. The like at his birth, their song was to bless him for 'peace on earth, good-will to men,' (they mention not themselves,) but purely for good-will to men; because it brought 'glory to God on high,' (as there,) they heartily rejoiced in that glory God should have in his dispensations towards us.

This for our blessing of God on our parts, 'Blessed be God.'

II. *The person who, and the style under which our Apostle blesseth him*—'The God and Father of our Lord Jesus Christ.'

It is not only, Blessed be God the Father, but the God and Father of Christ: nor only the God who is the Father of Christ, but ὁ Θεὸς καὶ πατὴρ, the God and Father of Christ. Otherwise καὶ, *and*, were here redundant; but as conjoined thus between those two, shews that both these titles do speak each of them a several relation of God unto Christ; or what God is unto Christ—he is his God and his Father. The like manner of speech we have, (when elsewhere Christ is spoken of,) two titles of his in the same sort locked together with that καὶ· ὁ Θεὸς καὶ σωτὴρ, 2 Peter i. 1, 'Εν δικαιοσύνῃ τοὺ Θεοῦ ἡμῶν καὶ σωτῆρος ημων 'Ιησοῦ Χριστοῦ, speaking to them that believe in the righteousness of God, and our Saviour Jesus Christ, the Holy Ghost intending both those two attributes of Christ. And Titus ii. 13, Τοῦ μεγάλου Θεοῦ καὶ σωτῆρος ἡμῶν 'Ιησοῦ Χριστοῦ, 'Looking for the blessed hope, and the glorious appearing of the great God, and our Saviour Jesus Christ.' He speaks in both places of one and the same person, namely, Christ under two titles: and thus here he doth the like of God the Father, 'The God and Father of Christ.' And this parallel speech used to Christ in those places, compared with what the Apostle useth here, those places are strong proofs and assertions apostolical, that Christ is God as well as Saviour, the great God and Saviour; even as it is evident here in the like tenor of speech, that the person of God the Father is both the God and the Father of Christ: for in the very same strain and tenor of speech it is that both these are said of Christ, wherein here both are spoken of God the Father in his relation unto Christ. This for the phraseology; now as to the thing itself.

Two things are here to be apart spoken to for the explanation hereof:—

1. The matter itself: how God the Father is the God and the Father of Christ, and in what respects the one or the other, either of them.

2. The reason why here he singleth out these relations of God to Christ, and under the respects and considerations thereof he blesseth God here.

1. *The matter itself*, 'The God and Father of Christ.'—That the Father is both the God and Father of Christ, other Scriptures affirm, yea, accord also, in putting both relations thus together as well as here; yea, upon the cross he challengeth his interest in both, 'My God, my God,' Matt. xxvii. 46, and 'Father, into thy hands,' Luke xxiii. 46; and on the other side, when to enter into his glory, he mentions both, John xx. 17, 'I ascend unto my Father, and to my God.' There are both, you see, found in one sentence, only he puts Father first afore being his God; so there; but here the God afore the Father of Jesus Christ.

The difficulty about it is, how these two relations respectively are to be understood.

We all know and acknowledge Christ's person hath two natures. He is God, he is man; and we often find in one and the same sentence several things attributed to the person of Christ, whereof the one is spoken of him in respect of the human nature only, the other in relation to the Divine. I shall mention but one instance, because somewhat akin to this here; Heb. vii. 3, his person is described to be without father, without mother, and both are equally said of this one and the same person; yet the one in respect of one nature only, the other in relation to the other. It is evident the man Jesus had a mother, and yet he is said to be without mother, namely as God. It is evident that he called God his own Father, John v., as also he useth to do upon every occasion everywhere, and yet this person as man is said to be without father. And that both these should be thus attributed to, and said of one and the same person, all the wits in the world cannot otherwise reconcile than by affirming or acknowledging two natures to abide in this one person; and withal what is proper to each, yet to be in common and alike attributed to the person himself, respectively to these two natures. And therefore the Apostle elsewhere is fain to distinguish upon this matter with this or the like distinction: who, according to the flesh or human nature, came of the fathers by his mother Mary; and who, according to the spirit or Divine nature, is the declared Son of God, and God blessed for ever.* You have these distinctions *in terminis* thus applied, Rom. i. 3, 4, and Rom. ix. 5, and it is the sum of the scope of both places, as also of Acts ii. 30. In like manner here bring but these, the same distinctions tricked up, and insert them to each, and none will question this exposition, that question

* 'En Deus, et Pater unius et ejusdem Christi; Deus quidem ut incarnati, Pater, ut Dei Verbi.'—*Marlorat.*

not the verity of one of those his natures, that as Son of God, and so God equal with God, God is his Father: and that as Son of man, so the same God that is his Father is his God also. Thus Bishop Davenant expoundeth these words, 'God and Father of Christ.'

The God.—The Father is the God of Christ in relation to his being man, and that in these respects more peculiar to him—

1. Because he chose him to that grace and union, 1 Peter i. 20. Christ as man was predestinated as well as we, and so hath God to be his God by predestination and so by free grace, as well as he is our God in that respect.

2. Because God the Father made a covenant with him. Look, as because of that covenant with Abraham, &c., he is termed the God of Abraham, Isaac, and Jacob, so in respect of that covenant made with Christ, which we have specified, Isa. xlix., throughout, where Christ doth call him 'My God,' ver. 4, of which covenant, as also God's being his God, David was his type, Ps. lxxxix. 26.

3. Because God was his only refuge in all times of distress. Thus when hanging on the cross, he cries out to him, 'My God, my God,' Matt. xxvii. 46, compared with Ps. xxii. 1–5.

4. Because God is the author and immediately the matter of Christ's blessedness, (as he is man,) and therefore blessed be he as the God of Christ, who hath blessed our Lord Christ for ever and ever, as Ps. xlv. 2, whereupon, in the 7th verse, it follows, 'God, thy God, hath anointed thee with the oil of gladness above thy fellows.' The Psalmist satisfieth not himself to say, 'God hath anointed thee,' but with an emphasis, 'God, thy God:' and thy God he is in relation to this effect and fruit of it, 'anointing thee with gladness;' which, ver. 2, is synonymously expressed, 'God hath blessed thee for ever.' And then anointed by God as man he was when glorified, Acts iv. 27. And God thus blessed him by becoming himself his blessedness; which, in the 16th Psalm, Christ exults in, ver. 2, 'My soul, thou hast said unto the Lord, Thou art my Lord.' And, ver. 5, it follows, 'The Lord is the portion of mine inheritance;' and, ver. 6, 'I have,' says he, 'a goodly heritage,' that is, in having God to be my God and heritage to live upon for ever; for, as he further speaks in ver. 11, 'in thy presence is fulness of joy, and at thy right hand are pleasures for evermore.' The psalm is made in Christ's name, as the Apostle, Acts ii., and he speaks it of his human nature expressly in the 9th verse, 'My flesh,' says he, 'shall rest in hope,' namely this hope, by this my death to be advanced to the right hand of God, (which alone that man Christ Jesus is, for as God he was always at his right hand,) where those pleasures are: so then God is his happiness. Hence, therefore, when Christ was risen, and speaks of ascending, and was shortly to ascend, then it was he calls God his God, John xx. 17, 'I ascend to my God;' that is, to him in whom my happiness I now am going to enjoy consists. And therefore, John xiv. 28, he told his disciples, 'If ye loved me, you would rejoice that I go to my Father:' for I go to him that is able to make me happy, and is my immediate blessedness. For it follows, 'My Father is greater than I,' (namely, as I am a man,) and so I am to be blessed in him, the less being blessed of the greater. The human nature, though glorified, is not blessedness to itself, it is but finite in itself; but God immediately is. Nor is that human nature, though God dwells in it, the utmost blessedness of us; but God immediately also is: yet as to our right thereunto, it is because he is our God and his God first. Thus *his God*, as man.

But whether the Father is termed the God of Christ, as Christ is God, and so in relation to his divine nature, I will not debate it. There are that read that passage of the 45th Psalm thus: O God (as speaking to Christ as God) thy God, so terming his Father, *Deus de Deo*, God of God, is old: and the Father is *Deus gignens*, the Son *Deus genitus*, and *Deus Dei* is near to these; the Father is the God of the Son, who is God. But I pass it.

And the Father.—This is out of question spoken of Christ, and is true of him, both as God and also man.

1. As God: so he is his Son, his own Son, Rom. viii. 32, and reciprocally the Father, ἴδιος πατὴρ, his own Father, John v. 18, and therefore 'equal with God,' as it is emphatically there said; for the Jews objected against him, that πατέρα ἴδιον ἔλεγε τὸν Θεὸν, he said God was his own Father, (so in the Greek,) making himself equal with God. All which do imply, that he was such a Son as was begotten of the substance and essence of his Father, even as he that is said to be a man's own natural son useth to be, and is thereby distinguished from their adopted children; and in that respect also is Christ said to be God's only begotten Son, and ὁ υἱὸς, *Dei vivi*, that Son of the living God, Matt. xvi. 16; and so discriminated from all other. As from the angels, 'To which of all the angels did he say, Thou art my Son, this day have I begotten thee?' Heb. i., and so from all creatures. For whereas, John i. 18, he is termed the only-begotten Son, in distinction there from all creatures, which are said to be but made, ver. 1, 3, and believers to have received power from him to be sons, ver. 12. In fine, he is in such a respect the Son of God, and begotten of God, as being man he was the Son of David, because out of his loins. Thus Matt. xxii. 42. And that he was thus the Son of God, is the main and most fundamental point of the gospel, Rom. i. 3, 4, compared; and therefore is still brought in as the conclusion of all those several discourses of the last evangelist's Gospel, beginning at the first chapter, ver. 18, 49, chap. iii. 16, and so on to chap. xx. 31, where, in the conclusion of his book, he professeth this to have been the intended scope of the whole, 'These things are written that ye might believe that Jesus is the Christ, the Son of God, and that believing (thus of him) ye might have life through his name;' through that name of his that he is the Son of God, and thereby the fountain of life and sonship to us; for upon this very rock or foundation, Christ told his disciples he would build his Church.

2. As man and Son of man, God was his Father. That forementioned profession and answer in the name of all the rest of his disciples was setly pitched upon this in Christ's question as punctual thereunto: 'Whom do men say that I the Son of man am?' That was Christ's question. He answers thereupon, 'The Son of the living God.' Therefore as man he was the Son of the living God. The like ye have uttered by Christ himself, (for it was that point he died upon,) Mark xiv. 61, 62, compared.

But then as to this last point the question is, How it is to be understood that as man he was the Son of God; whether only but as other men, or in any transcendent privilege above us? Or thus, whether as man he was but the adopted son, as the saints are; or whether not the natural Son of God? Which is solved by these considerations:—

1. That the subject of this relation as Son to God, or the *terminus* of it, is not either his nature divine or human, but his person; for sonship is a personal property, not of the nature.

2. Hence, *secondly*, in the person of Christ there are not two Sons, or two sonships or relations of sonship unto God as a Father; but as God is but one, so the person of the Son but one, and so but one sonship in him.

3. Hence, *thirdly*, Christ as man is but one and the same Son of God;

that he is as he is God, that is, his style and honour is to be the natural Son of God, even as man. The sonship of the man Christ Jesus doth coalesce into one sonship with the Son of God, even as in like manner the man is taken up into one person with the Son of God, Luke i. 35, 'That holy thing which shall be born of thee (speaking of Christ's conception to the Virgin Mary) shall be called the Son of God.' For look as though he was man, yet that man was never a person of itself, but subsisted from the first in the personality of the second Person: so that the Son of man was never called or accounted a Son to God, of himself, as such; but his sonship was that of the person which he was taken up into. Only with this difference, that he is the Son of God as God, in that he was begotten of the Father's substance, but so the Son of man was not; but this Son of man becoming the Son of God, who was begotten of the substance of the Father by personal union, he the man, by being made one person with him, wears that dignity. The one is *per essentiæ communicationem*, the other *per unionem cum personâ*.

4. Hence, *fourthly*, he is not as man the Son of God naturally or essentially, but he is the Son of God personally. If we take *natural* for *essential*, so he is not, as man, God's natural Son; but take *natural* as in opposition to *adoption*, and so he is God's natural Son: and not by adoption, this being the title and honour he had from his conception and birth, and from his union with the person of the natural Son, as you heard from the angel, 'That holy thing which shall be born of thee shall be called the Son of God,' (and God calls things as they are.) And more distinctly, Gal. iv. 4, 'God sent forth his Son made of a woman, made under the law, that we might receive the adoption of sons,' where evidently his sonship and ours are set in these terms of distinction, that ours is the sonship of adoption received from his, and that his is primitive, original, and natural; yea, and this is true of him as he is man, for it is spoken of him that was 'made of a woman, made under the law.'

2. *The reason why under these relations of God and Father to Christ, he blesseth God.*

Although this will easily appear in many of the particulars that follow, yet one reason may be, to unvail the Old Testament and decipher it into the New, and bring forth the gospel in its substantial and real intendments, both of the promise of blessing, as also of God's relation to us men; God's being their God, this of old was typically set forth under this tenure, 'The God of Abraham, the God of Isaac, the God of Jacob,' Exod. iii. 6. And before them, 'The Lord God of Shem,' Gen. ix. 26; and in the names of these patriarchs the conveyance of the blessing ran, and answerably their return of praise and blessing unto God again then was, 'Blessed be the Lord God of Shem,' Gen. ix. 26. Thus before Abraham. After, when renewed in Jacob's name, 'Blessed be the Lord God of Israel,' as you heard out of David; and this form the Jews (upon whose hearts, as now in their synagogues, the veil remains, 2 Cor. iii. 14, in token thereof they wear it upon their heads,) in their worship keep to this day; but now that the substance is come, the shadows disappear. Abraham, and Isaac, and Israel are subdued. The days are come, as the prophet in another case speaks, that it shall no more be said, The God of Abraham, &c., but the God and Father of our Lord Jesus Christ; and as Isaiah foretold of the gospel times, Isa. lxv. 15, 16, look as my servants (or children of God) shall be called by another name, (namely Christians, as first at Antioch, and no longer Jews;) so also the terms of their covenant is altered, and so their form of blessing God, as was also foresignified there in the following words, 'He that blesseth himself in the earth, shall bless himself in the God of truth,' namely, when Christ, who is the truth and the life, shall come. Old Zachary, that lived in the expiration or extreme verge of the Old Testament, when Christ was not yet conceived, he then useth that Old Testament form which he found sanctified in the Scriptures of old. But had he stayed half a year longer, (for thereabouts was the distance between Christ's and his son John Baptist's conception,) his 'Blessed be the God of Israel' (which he useth in his song) had been out of date; and 'Blessed be the God and Father of Christ' had come in its room, and been in force.

MEDITATION.

Oh, let us, therefore, that live under the knowledge of Christ in the gospel, bless our God as the God and Father of Jesus Christ, which is the highest note of celebrating his praise which our hearts can reach to! For it is the most elevated strain of the gospel language, and of the glory of God, which any man, or all men, can rise up unto. It is said of Christ in the Psalms, Ps. lxxii. 17, 'All nations shall call him blessed.' In like manner it was spoken of and by herself, that was the mother of his human nature only, 'All generations shall call me blessed.' Oh, then, how should we all bless that God that is the Father of him, who in his person also is God blessed together with his Father for ever! Many good souls find this as an eternal evidence of their own future blessedness, that when wanting assurance of God's love to themselves, they can yet bless God for his being good to others in the same condition with themselves, out of their love to God and to the good of others' souls. If thou findest such elevations of spirit in thee, vent and spend them much more in blessing God, that he is the God and Father of Christ. This is high, and most divine.

Of our Lord Jesus Christ.—He having thus setly displayed these relations of God to Christ, he interweaves withal *our* special relation to Christ; to wit, his being our Lord; his scope therein being to shew the foundation and descent of those very same relations which God beareth to Christ; and of the same their coming down upon and unto us, namely of his being our God and our Father, which are the groundwork of the conveyance to us of all those particular blessings he doth after enumerate, by and through Jesus Christ's being our Lord or husband.

And it is observable how the Apostle carries on his discourse along. In the second verse he had called God our Father, and Jesus Christ barely the Lord; but then in this verse he styleth this God the Father of Christ, and then subjoins therewith, varying his style, this 'Jesus our Lord.' Thereby to shew the genealogy or descent of our being sons to God, and of God's being our Father, to lie in this, that Christ is our Lord, and so God becomes our Father by being his Father. And then, in the next verse, he answerably proceeds to shew how all other blessings do flow from this relation, first of God to Christ, then this of Christ to us; which in the fifth verse he doth more determinately discover to be his meaning in saying, 'He hath predestinated us by Jesus Christ to the adoption of children:' so that this mention of his being our Lord here, is not merely, as elsewhere, an appellative, or as the ordinary style that is given to the person of Christ, as that whereby he is described when he is spoken of or mentioned, when there is any occasion to name him. Thus frequently his disciples, 'We have seen the Lord,' say they all, John xx. 25. 'It is the Lord,' says he, when he spied him first, John xxi. 7. Yea, and this appellation of 'our Lord' is often used by the apostles, but barely to decipher his person, as in that speech, Heb. vii. 14, 'It is evident our Lord sprang out of Judah.' These in part are no more than as when men speak of the person of their prince, they say, The king, and, Our lord the king, so designing his person. But here in saying in this coherence, and in saying, 'The Father of our Lord Jesus Christ,' his intent is to draw the pedigree of our relation to God, as our Father also, even by descent from Christ; and this is the highest improvement, as to us, of this attribute here, 'Christ our Lord.' This for the general scope of these words.

To make good which general scope, two things are now particularly to be explicated :—

1. What special or peculiar relation there is of the saints unto Christ, as to their Lord.

2. That the relation of Christ to us as a Lord, is the foundation of God's being our God and Father, as well as he is Christ's God and Father.

For the first, that our Jesus is the Lord, and that one Lord, in distinction from God the Father; which title fully declareth his office of Mediator, and is attributed to him by way of eminency above and from all other lords; this I have elsewhere shewn upon 1 Cor. viii. 6. That which is more proper here is, that he is our Lord more peculiarly, and how we have these two apart attributed to Christ, both that he is the Lord, and our Lord, as in a special relation and appropriation, in the 4th verse of the Epistle of Jude; where speaking of the heresies of those times, he says, that they denied that only Lord God, and our Lord Jesus Christ. The question here hath been made by some, as also about the like parallel places, 2 Pet. i. 1, Tit. ii. 13, whether he here should speak of two persons distinct, viz., God and Christ, styling the first, the Lord God, but Christ, in distinction from him, our Lord; or whether that apostle should intend Christ only and alone as one and the same subject of two royal titles or relations; the one more general, namely his being the only Lord God, and then the other of his more special relation unto us, our Lord. Indeed as the English translation carries it, it leans more to that first interpretation, that he should speak of the Father in the one, whom he should signalise, the only Lord God; the other of Christ. But the Greek evidently inclines much rather to the latter, that Christ alone should be intended as the subject of both these styles.

Considering first, that though here be three attributes, 1, the only Lord, 2, God, 3, and our Lord; that yet there is but one article or note of designation affixed, or rather prefixed to all these at first, *τὸν μόνον*, as meaning evidently but one person pointed at in them all, as the subject of them: which the *Complutensis* copy of the Greek renders more plain, 'That only God and Lord, the Lord Jesus Christ'—*Τὸν μόνον Θεὸν καὶ δεσπότην, τὸν Κύριον*.

Which, secondly, the counterpart to this Apostle's epistle—namely, the second Epistle of Peter—helps to clear; where, speaking of the same heretics (whom both these apostles aimed to speak of, and do affirm these things of) there, in the latter he mentions Christ only as the person spoken of in these words, 'denying the Lord that bought them;' using there also the same word, *δεσπότην*, which the other epistle useth when he speaks of the lordship and dominion of Christ, which is in common over wicked men, and but such as over all things else, which Jude manifestly intended in calling him 'the Lord.' And the contradictions of all heretics, that professed Christianity in those times, were all and only bent against the person of Christ, and also against his being God, and not against the Father, or his being only Lord God.

So then that place of Jude holds forth two things distinctly and apart concerning Christ, which serves to clear the point in hand :—1. What he is absolutely and indeterminately in himself, and in his general relation to all things whatsoever, he is the only God and Lord of all. And, by the way, the word translated Lord in the first part of his style, is a differing word from that which follows in the second part. The first word is δεσπότην, supreme, sovereign disposer and governor, as by possession, and natural and more general right; such as a lord hath of his goods, his chattels, utensils, as 2 Tim. ii. 21. 2. But that other Κύριον, the latter word, which is joined with that special relation of his to us, with that addition of 'our' Lord; so noting out in this manifest distinction that sweet and special relation to his spouse and children of the sons of men. So then the meaning is, that besides that Jesus Christ is the sovereign Lord of all persons and things, (as Acts x. 36,) that he further hath a nearer and dearer relation of *our Lord*, so to us his saints.

So, then, he is the Lord of saints peculiarly, in the like sense and respect as he is called King of saints peculiarly, Rev. xv. 3, in distinction from his being King of nations, as, Jer. x. 7, the prophet had it.

Wicked men, as you have heard, are said to 'deny the Lord that bought them;' so then he is their Lord. And the devils are said to confess that Jesus is the Lord, Phil. ii. 11, but none of these do say, 'Our Lord.' The good angels, they come nearer to him, and surely they might say it upon better terms; he being their head, Col. ii. 10, and they our fellow-servants, Rev. xix. 10. Yet I find not that they speak thus of him, 'Our Lord,' but as it were, or would seem in a respect, both to him and us, the Holy Ghost should leave this to be alone said by us, and spoken by us of Christ. There was a full occasion once, if ever, for the good angels themselves to have assumed and uttered it, and said, 'Our Lord.' It is in Luke ii. 11, when they proclaimed him in the cradle; but their words there run thus, 'To you (speaking of men) is born a Saviour,' and so 'Christ the Lord;' for though a Saviour only to us men, yet those angels might have said, 'Our Lord,' for that their part in him forementioned. No; but when it did come in a comparison and competition with us men, they forbear to do it; they only say, Christ *the* Lord, not Christ *our* Lord; or anywhere else we read of. But believers and saints of the sons of men you find often, upon all occasions of mentioning him as the Lord, to assume the privilege to call him with this sweet additament, My Lord, or, Our Lord. David in the Old Testament, he began it, 'Jehovah said to my Lord,' Ps. cx. And he was in spirit when he did it, (as Christ tells us,) possessed with an evangelical spirit more than ordinary. Elizabeth followed him in the first break of day of the New Testament; she was in spirit, too, Luke i. 41, when she said it: 'Elizabeth was filled with the Holy Ghost,' and said, ver. 43, 'Whence is this to me, that the mother of my Lord is come?' Thomas, at last, for it was after the resurrection, with ravishment cries out, 'My Lord, and my God.' And our Apostle goes on, when his heart was as full as it could hold of glorying and rejoicing in this his interest in Christ, Phil. ii. 8, 'Yea, doubtless,' I that have known him so long, 'I do count all things but loss and dung, for the excellency of the knowledge of Christ Jesus my Lord.' The emphasis this comes in with argues his heart raised up to an infinite valuation of him, and also of this his spiritual relation unto him, 'My Lord.' These saints in their own persons, as particularly it fell out, first tasting the sweetness of it; but then after it grew, the common voice of all believers speaking in their own and other saints' names. So Paul was careful to observe to do, when he wrote to the Church of Corinth, ascribing and enlarging that title of 'Our Lord' unto all saints, as well as to the church of Corinth, as appears expressly in his inscription to that first epistle to that church, 1 Cor. i. 2, 'Unto the church of God that is at Corinth, called to be saints, with all that in every place call upon the name of our Lord;' and remarkably adds 'both theirs and ours,' thus appropriating it to the saints of mankind, as he does here, 'our Lord.'

I further only add, that when I thus term it a proper or more special relation with difference from other the sons of men, or the angels, I exemplify my meaning by the like language which the great officers and favourites of kings use, by way of distinction from other subjects, and glory so to do. They rejoice to style him, The king, my master, my lord. And I humbly submit the notion of it, if it appear singular to others. But I shall further add two special appropriate reasons why the saints do the like of Christ:—

1. His saving and redeeming them from sin and wrath. He is their Saviour, not of the angels: and 'to you,' say they, 'a Saviour is born, Christ the Lord;' and so your Lord more peculiarly, because your Saviour, which I insist not on.

2. Besides this obliging interest of redemption, proper to the saints of the sons of men, whereby he is our Lord, (though as a second-hand bargain he bought all the world, 2 Pet. ii. 1,) there is a further, more endearing consideration whereby he is our Lord; even because he is our husband, 'Thy Maker is thy husband,' and so thy Lord. And he is such a husband as did serve a servitude for his wife, yea, and bought her thereby of a slave and captive by the way of redemption, as in ver. 7 of this 1st of Ephesians; and again, Eph. v. 23, 'Even as Christ is head of the church, and Saviour of the body;' and ver. 25, 'He loved his church, and gave himself for her.' These things cannot be spoken of angels. A queen, the wife or spouse of a great king, when she mentions her relation to him, and says, My lord, or calls him her lord, she speaks it in that sense wherein none of her maids of honour or courtiers about her dare, or must take on them to speak it, though he be in other respects their lord also. For he is her lord as he is her husband, and not only as king; and so she imports, 'I am my beloved's, and my beloved is mine,' whilst she only calls him My lord. Sarah, you know, called Abraham, as her husband, lord, 1 Pet. iii. 6, which is applied to Christ and the church, Eph. v. 22, 23, 'Wives, submit yourselves unto your own husbands, as unto the Lord: for the husband is the head of the wife, even as Christ is the head of the church, and he is the Saviour of the body.' And in this conjugal respect it is that God the Father teacheth the Church to call Christ her Lord, Ps. xlv. 11, 'He is thy Lord, worship thou him: so shall the King greatly delight in thy beauty.' He speaks it of his conjugal relation, as that passage, 'delighting in her beauty,' argues. Now, as it is said of Christ's Sonship, 'To which of all the angels did he say, Thou art my Son, this day have I begotten thee?' though they are sons of God also, and he their Father, so say I of this lordship, To which of all the angels did he ever say, Christ is thy Lord,—that is, thy husband,—he shall greatly delight in thy beauty, as a husband in his spouse? Though they are the virgins that do attend her, yet that relation is reserved proper

between Christ and us. So, though he be a head to angels, Col. ii. 10, yet in a proper and a peculiar manner a head to his Church, the saints. So, in the 22d of this Eph. i., 'The Father hath given him to be a head over all to his church,' (even over 'all principalities and powers,' ver. 21,) and therefore in such a peculiar manner a head to them, as he is not to all or any else. He being said to be over all things else then, when withal his relation of headship to her is spoken of. And so it is in this.

For the second, I must now shew you, that this peculiar relation of his being our Lord in this near and endearing sense, is the foundation of God's being our God and our Father; even because he is the God and Father of Christ, who is this our Lord and husband.

1. The ὅτι, that so it is, that the foundation of these relations of God unto us is laid in these same like relations of ours unto Christ, (besides what by induction might be shewn to hold of all other titles or privileges communicated to us, how they all hold of Christ,) that one place afore cited, where Christ at once calls him both his God and his Father, John xx. 17, more fully and pertinently holds forth this to us, 'I ascend to my Father and your Father, to my God and your God.' He speaks at once, as that God is our God, &c., so that our relation of his being our God is founded upon God's being the God of Christ. And our Father, because his first. He says not, as Austin observes, I ascend to our Father, or to our God, as casting his own proper relation into the same common rank with ours. No, but apart, first mine and then yours. Mine primatively, naturally, and originally; yours derivatively by participation, or, as ver. 5 here expresseth it, 'sons of adoption by Jesus Christ;' or, as Gal. iv. 4, 'He sent his Son, (his own Son, as elsewhere,) that we might receive the adoption of sons.'

2. But secondly, if you will see how this doth spring from that special relation of Christ's being our Lord, that is, our Head, Husband, Redeemer, consult that Psalm xlv., which is an epithalamium, or marriage-song of Christ and his Church. God the Father, who gives all that good counsel there to the Church, (for all that come to Christ are taught of God, as Christ says,) in the 11th verse he teacheth her to call him her Lord, and in the 10th verse, to forsake her father's house, as spouses married use to do, and to cleave unto their husbands; and upon all this account, God himself there calls her his daughter, 'Hearken, O daughter,' &c. That is his compellation, (and parallel to this of a wife to her husband, My lord here,) God the Father, in the beginning of his speech to her, speaking as a father-in-law useth to do, who is giving counsel to his daughter new married unto his natural son. So then, from thence I infer that thus it is that we become sons and daughters to God, even by marriage with his natural Son, who in that conjugal respect doth become our Lord, and thereby also receive the adoption of sons, and so God takes on him the relation of Father. Thus Rom. viii. 17, 'heirs of God, joint-heirs with Christ.'

1st Meditation.

Let him then be Lord and King of saints, and level him not with saints, as some most cursedly in this age have done; even then when we are enjoying the highest advancement even of God himself in heaven, yet still Christ is our Lord, by means of whom God is our God. The Psalmist indeed says, that we are fellows in all with him: 'God, thy God, hath anointed thee above thy fellows,' xlv. 7. But if you would know of the Psalmist how far above his fellows, the Psalmist resolves you, 'He is thy

Lord, worship thou him,' ver 11. So as though we are his fellows, yet he hath the deserved honour, this title (and he alone) of being your Lord, yea and of the 'man, God's fellow,' given him by God himself in the prophet. Would you be all Christ's? Set your hearts at rest; there is but one Christ personally, as certainly as that God is but one. It is uttered as a fundamental maxim of Christian profession, universally received, 'To us (Christians namely) there is but one God and one Lord Jesus Christ,' 1 Cor. viii. 6, and because there is but one God, therefore God hath ordained but this one Lord; because he therein bears the image of God's sovereignty and oneness, being the brightness of his glory. Neither are we, the saints, considered as sharing with him herein, but himself is that one Lord alone. For it follows, 'And we in him,' we are all in him; and therefore not only reckoned distinct and apart from him, as he is that one Lord, but dependent on him, and not lords or Christs with him, but infinitely distant from him. It is true, we have all that Christ hath derivatively, but not in that kind he hath it. God is our Father as well as his Father, &c., but as Augustine well observes, commenting upon this passage, 'He says not, I ascend to our Father, but my Father and your Father, therefore he is in another respect my Father, and in another respect your Father; my Father by nature, yours by grace.'*

2D MEDITATION.

Let him be thy Lord, and worship thou him: thou hast now in this a greater tender made thee than ever was made to angels. Part with all for him, forsake thy former father's house, Ps. xlv. 10, this world, given to thy father Adam, and all things in it; for he is thy Lord, and thou shalt have by thy relation to him another Father, whose house hath many mansions, John xiv. 1. Account all things dross and dung that thou mayest win Christ, as Phil. iii. 8. Thou canst not win him else; he never becomes thy Lord, unless thou valuest him at the same rate he did thee, and partest in thy affections with all for him. Give thyself up to the Lord, as 2 Cor. viii. 5. Cast thy lot, thy interest together with his. Here thou shalt be sure never to lose thy love, as in cleaving to all else thou wilt. He is and must, however, be a Lord to thee, and thou must one day confess that Jesus is the Lord, whether thou wilt or no; for all must appear afore his judgment-seat. Oh, but if thy judge be become thy Lord and husband, thou art out of danger. And then give thyself up also to worship, and in all things to obey him, else he is not thy Lord, nor thou his lawful spouse, Eph. v. 24, 'As the Church is subject to Christ, so let wives be subject to their husbands;' why doth he speak with such an apparent difference? For what he speaks of wives is but as discoursing to them their duty: 'Let wives be subject,' he doth not say they cannot be saved else; but that other passage of the Church is spoken of as a taken for granted qualification, or essential property in the Church, if she be his lawful true spouse. 'As the Church is subject to Christ,' says he, so that it be the duty of both alike; the Church ought to be subject to Christ, as well as wives to their husbands. The reason and difference is perspicuous, because unless souls be subject to Christ, they are not the Church. A man's wife is his wife, though she be never so perverse and disobedient to him; but no soul is one of his Church and spouse, nor owned by Christ as such, unless she become subject to him,

* 'Non dicit Patrem nostrum, sed Patrem meum et patrem vestrum, aliter ergo meum, aliter vestrum, natura meum, gratia vestrum.'—*Tract.* 121, *in Joh.*

and subject too in everything, as the comparison there made sheweth. If thou sayest, thou wantest beauty, be not discouraged, he will take thee with all thy deformities, and put beauty on thee; for so the Apostle there goes on,—he washeth and cleanseth his Church, to present her to himself in the end, glorious, and without spot or wrinkle.

And being once married to him, take this for ever along with thee, thou art married to an husband risen from the dead, Rom. vii. 4. And oh, what holiness, heavenliness, should those have that would hold communion and intercourse with such a Lord and husband, the 'Lord from heaven,' and who is now in heaven!

SERMON III.

Who hath blessed us with all blessings.—VER. 3.

III. I COME to the third general head the text was divided into—the matter for which he blesseth God—namely, for his blessing us with all blessings: 'Who hath blessed us with all blessings.'

Who.—God, as he alone is blessed, styled therefore the Blessed One, ὁ εὐλογητός, Mark xiv. 61, so he alone blesseth, and is alone able to do it; and others, when they bless, their blessings are but invocations upon him, that he would bless some other person in what they desire for him. So all particular benedictions, made by parents or others, run in Scripture, as Gen. xlviii. 15, 16; which that saying, once for all other, shews, 'We bless you in the name of the Lord,' Ps. cxxix. 8. Yea, when man is made an instrument of conveying good things unto us, yet he cannot make them blessings; for this they have recourse to God. And in so doing, all have thereby acknowledged him the fountain of all blessings and blessedness; and so even Balaam himself confessed to Balak, Num. xxii. 38, and chap. xxiii. 8, 20. 'I wot that he whom thou blessest is blessed,' Num. xxii. 6.

Who.—I shewed afore, in general, that the apostle blesseth God under the consideration of being the God and Father of Christ, because thereby he becomes our God, and our Father also. I shall add now, how that under each of these considerations or relations it is that he blesseth us.

That which in general I shall premise, as common to the explication of these two particulars last mentioned, is that notion commonly received among the schoolmen, which I gladly took up from them:* That one requisite ingredient to move God to love, and to shew mercy unto us intelligent creatures of the sons of men, is an apprehending our misery, *ut suam*, as his own. And again, *Deus non miseretur nisi propter amorem, in quantum amat nos tanquam aliquid sui.* That God hath mercy on us, by apprehending our misery as his own, *quod fit per unionem affectûs*, which is done by an union of affection to us; and God is not executively merciful, but for his love, and is so far merciful to us, as he looks at us, *ut aliquid sui*, as we are something of his own, or something of himself.

This I greedily take hold of, to illustrate and carry on the ground and foundation of the special love he bears to his elect, and as agreeing with what the Scriptures say; both that love is in God, (which no man can deny to be in the nature of God to love, for he loves himself, his Son, &c.,) and that love is the ground of mercy, and, by the same reason, special electing love the ground of mercy in God to sinners. Thus, Eph. ii. 4, 'But God, who is rich in mercy,' (having in the foregoing verses set forth our sinfulness and misery,) 'for the great love wherewith he loved us,' &c. And Aquinas' *tantum in quantum*, is made the measure of the great and infinite difference of his love to creatures. There is a common love to men as creatures, so he loves every man and thing he hath made; but where he shews

* Aquinas secunda secundæ quæst. 30, art. 2, in respon. ad art. prim.

special mercies, as pardon of sin and the like, there is an *in quantum*, by an *how far* he loves, as the foundation of that, a special love. But still the question will be, What should be the ground of a special love in God to some, with such an infinite difference of that love from what it is to others in common? Aquinas resolves that, with this further foundation, to be *aliquid sui;* to make those he specially loves some way his own, and then the consequence of that to be, to look upon their misery as his own; and with that the Scriptures also agree, Isa. lxiii. 9, 'In all their affliction he was afflicted;' the like in Exod. iv. 31.

But then another question, (to drive the matter home to its head,) and that is, What is it in God, or in the creature, makes them to be in so special manner his own, who or what hath put so great a difference? Nothing but election, which follows in the next: 'according as he hath chosen us.' There is Aquinas' *in quantum*, so far as he loved us, so far he hath blessed us, with special blessings appropriate, suitable thereunto. Now the fundamental therefore of all, and of the difference is, he makes us first his own by love, by that special love specially his own. And, which is the head I approach next to, he became our God first, and our Father, and chose us so to be his as none else is. And then we were *aliquid sui*, something of himself and his own indeed, by special propriety. You have this in effect in that 63d of Isa. ver. 8, 9, 'So he was their Saviour,' and so redeemed them. But *in terminis*, in more express words, in the two particular relations specified, he first made himself, and became our God and our Father, and then to be sure we are his own.

1. *God blesseth us, as having first become our God.*—It is true, indeed, that God, as God, is full of blessedness in himself, and that is it which provokes him to communicate blessings to his creatures. God is good and doth good, says the Psalmist, and so God is blessed, (an all-sufficiency of all good,) and so bestoweth blessings; but yet know, that those he communicates himself in blessing unto, he first becomes their God. And then having taken that relation on him, he pours forth all his blessedness and blessings on them, so Ps. lxvii. 6, 'God, even our own God, shall bless us;' and when he is once so become, and hath taken upon him to be our God, he cannot but bless us. There is therefore, besides that emphasis put upon it, a duplicate made of it in the psalm; it is a second time repeated and said, God shall bless us; he cannot but do it, having made himself our God, and our own God to that, 'God, even our own God, shall bless us,' ver. 7. Yea, and they all would not be blessings to us at all, unless God had first become our God, and blessed us with giving himself to us. And whence came that, that he became our God, our own God? Why, by choosing us to be his, which was done by election entirely, both at once together; which is the very import of that speech, 'thine they were,' says Christ; those speeches or clauses, say interpreters, do mutually speak each other: as to say, Thine they were by election, and thou gavest them me; or to say, By election they became thine, thou electedst them. You have the like unto it in the same Isa. lxiii. 8, 'For he (God, namely) said (as within himself of old), Surely they are my people,' and therefore also 'children that will not lie; and so he was their Saviour.' And that which answereth and agrees to this, too, is that other speech of Christ's, Luke xviii. 7, 'His own elect;' and then you have election, by which they are made his own, and all to meet in their being something of his own indeed. This for the first, his becoming our God first, on purpose to bless us. If, therefore, we would have any or all blessings from God, we must first seek of him to be our God; and then, as the Psalmist,

God, even our God, will bless us; he will be sure to do it, upon the same account and for the same end and purpose he became our Father.

2. *God blesseth us under the relation of our Father.*—The first on earth that ever took upon them to bless others, and brought up that custom (or, as I may say, fashion) of blessing, were those that bore the relation of fathers. Their hearts were filled with the greatest love and good-will to their own children, a natural στόργη, did bless them, that is, wish well to them; and their hearts being enlarged to wish them more good than they found themselves able to bestow, they had recourse to God to bless them, and perform their desires, as that which was not in their own power to do. So the patriarchs, who blessed their children and posterity, and were the first of men that brought in this way of expressing their good-will which we call blessing,—as Moses termeth God's blessing, a manifestation of good-will borne to him whom he blesses, Deut. xxxiii. 16, in his blessing from God the several tribes: 'And for the good-will,' says he, 'of him that dwelt in the bush,' (which was Christ appearing to Moses, Exod. iii. 2–5; Acts vii. 32–34,) 'let the blessing come upon the head of Joseph, and upon the top of the head of him that was separated from his brethren,' (as Joseph was,) and thus singularly he blesseth Joseph, as separate from and above all the other tribes,—and thus God blesseth us out of infinite good-will, and thus it is a natural and a kindly act to come from fathers, and thus God blesseth us. It is the first fruit of good-will—that is, of that natural love and care which parents bear their children, it doth all. Love in fathers is that principle that doth of itself provoke them to wish the greatest good to their children, which if any good be in their own power to give, they give it from that principle; and when they have it not in their own power to bestow, if they are holy men, and have an interest in God the fountain of all good, they use that interest, and invocate God to bestow it; which invocating of God for them we use to call blessing a child, which is as much as in them lies to do.

Now, as Christ says of giving good things unto their children, (and parents' blessing is but a giving their children good things, by invocating of God to bestow them, as it is called in Isaac's blessing, Gen. xxvii. 27,) 'If you then being evil,' says Christ, Matt. vii. 11, that is, are full of self-love, that of itself would tempt you to keep and retain to yourselves, and not willingly to give away any good thing, yet ye know how, says Christ,—that is, you have the hearts and the affections by a natural instinct to spy out the best things for your children, which you judge to be such,—and 'if ye know how to give good things to your children, how much more,' says Christ, 'shall your Father which is in heaven,' who to this very end was pleased to become a Father to you, and has all in heaven to bestow, even that God who is styled the Blessed One in Scripture, who is an ocean of all blessedness, which seeks an outlet for itself to communicate to creatures, whom he hath loved and chosen, and hath been pleased to bear that relation towards us to this great end; he hath done all this to pour out his blessedness by and through that relation towards us, upon us his adopted sons; and who, by what he finds to be natural in himself towards his own natural Son, (whom he blesseth every day for ever, Ps. xlv. 2,) he for his sake and relation to us is further pleased to pour forth all blessings also upon us, having become in Christ a Father to us; and so to bear such a good-will to us in Christ, as members of him, and a spouse to him.

Hath blessed with all blessings.—You see here both the act of grace on God's part bestowing good on us is expressed by 'blessing,' and the things bestowed are called blessings. He gives one and the same denomination or name to either, which argues this expression of blessing to be full and as adequate as could be chosen forth. I shall endeavour to explicate both the *name* and *thing* itself—what it is to bless, as on God's part, and what is a blessing, and what it is that truly makes and constitutes good things to be blessings to us.

I. *For the word 'blessing,' or to bless.*—It is evident by that extensive comprehensiveness of speech which the Apostle here useth, that the whole, the total, and all particular good things, which he after enumerates, which God ever means to give, or the gospel promises, even all of them are to the utmost spoken of under and by this word of blessing. And it is worth our consideration that it is that original word under which the promise of the covenant of grace was at the first given to Abraham, the father of all the faithful; as which contained all particular good things, as his loins did that seed to whom that promise was made. And this I mention now at first as a fundamental consideration, that will have a great and necessary influence into the explication of the particulars that follow in this verse. The apostle here framing these words with an eye of allusion to, and comparison between those promises given them, and these promises which the gospel here declares; therefore unto that promise given them we shall have recourse again and again, to make our Apostle's meaning here the more manifest. That before me at the present is, that the sum and substance of gospel-promises began then to be set forth and expressed under this blessed word of *blessing*. 'I will bless thee,' said God to Abraham, 'and in thee all the families of the earth shall be blessed,' Gen. xii. 2, 3. And again, because it could not be better expressed by any other word, God doth but double the same, saying, 'In blessing I will bless thee,' Gen. xxii. 17; that is, I will bless thee and bless thee again, which is equivalent to the expression here, 'with all blessings hath he blessed us.' And what doth or can the great God say more? It is enough.

Now, that in God's intendment the whole total of the gospel was expressed to Abraham, and wrapt up in that term of blessing, the avowed explications and interpretations made thereof by the apostles do undeniably declare. Thus, presently after Christ's ascension, in one of the first made sermons, Acts iii., speaking to the Jews, ver. 25, 'Ye are the children of the covenant God made, saying to Abraham, In thy seed shall all the kindreds of the earth be blessed;' which he expounds unto them thus, that first God sent his Son Jesus to bless you, namely the Jews. And yet more expressly, Gal. iii. 8, 'God preached the gospel unto Abraham, saying, In thee shall all nations be blessed.' So that as Abraham's style was 'the blessed of the Lord,' Gen. xiv. 19, and also the children of God are all said to be blessed with faithful Abraham, in the following ver. 9; and again, Heb. vi. 13, 14, 'For when God made promise to Abraham, because he could swear by no greater, he sware by himself, saying, Surely blessing I will bless thee,' which, ver. 17, is said to contain the whole of his counsel to the heirs of promise, and that to shew the immutability of that his counsel, he confirmed it by an oath.

Hence therefore, although the gospel in most things speaks greater things than the Old Testament, and in higher terms, yet hath it not altered, nor can it better this. Christ himself, that began to preach this gospel in that his first large sermon that is recorded, it is the first word he therein utters, 'Blessed are the poor in spirit,' &c. Matt. v. 2, 3; and because he could not add to this, he does but repeat it over and over, as the general that contained in it the kingdom of heaven, ver. 3; comfort here, ver. 4; inheriting the earth, ver. 5; filling with all good, ver. 6; obtaining mercy, ver. 7;

seeing God, ver. 8; adoption and being God's children, ver. 9; and if there be any other particular, all are summed up in this word 'blessed.' Each and every particle of our salvation or happiness being blessings, as here, all the gospel can say is but blessing; which is therefore called in the lump of it, the fulness of the blessing of the gospel, Rom. xv. 29, for it cannot speak beyond what this word reacheth. All that Christ could do when he ascended was but to bless; and after Christ's ascension, the last book of the gospel, the Revelation, doth continually and throughout use the same style, and at the latter day, when heaven doors are to be set open for the righteous to enter in, their everlasting happiness is uttered by it, Come, ye blessed.

II. *For the thing, or what import this word carries with it.*—As you heard what it was for us to bless God, so now I am to shew what it is for God to bless us. God's blessing us, is his bestowing or communicating all good together with himself, with all hearty good-will, out of love to our persons.

1. *It is a bestowing or communicating of good.*—The Jews defined it in general *accessio boni*, grounded upon Psalm cxv., where what in ver. 12, 13 is expressed by blessing, in ver. 14 is *adjiciat super vos*, God add to you, namely, good or well-being, unto your being, or what is already given you. And the Scripture often useth the word blessing for a gift or present bestowed. Gen. xxxiii., that which Jacob calls his present or gift, ver. 10, he calls his blessing bestowed, ver. 11, 'Take, I pray thee, my blessing which is brought thee.' And, 2 Cor. ix. 5, 6, their bountiful gift to the churches he calls their blessing in the margin; you have the same, 2 Kings v. 15; the like, Lev. xxv. 21. And to be sure, whatever man's blessings are, all God's blessings are the giving and accumulation of good to us, or doing us good. And though the word εὐλογία signifies but his good word to and concerning us, yet God's word is his deed. And *Dei benedicere est benefacere*, for by a bare word of command he blesseth; Ps. cxxxiii. 3, 'there he commands the blessing,' that blessing of blessings, 'even life for evermore;' like as it is said, 'he commanded, and they were created,' Ps. cxlviii. 5. So he commands and we are blessed. Alas! when we creatures bless God, we express but our well-wishes or joyful acclamations to that blessedness is in himself already; but when God blesseth us, he altogether gives, he communicates.

2. *It is the communication of all good, yea of himself.*—God gives and blesseth like himself when he blesseth. He blesseth 'indeed,' as the phrase is, 1 Chron. iv. 10, and will not bless under giving all. He blesseth 'altogether,' as the phrase is, Num. xxiv. 10; therefore in the text here, 'with all blessings.' He cannot bless less, for he is God, and hath all to bestow. Thou art God, says David, and do thou bless me, 1 Chron. xvii. 26, 27. He urgeth that, for he knew what it was for God to bless, and that he blesseth as the great God and like himself, both with all that God himself is, and all that God can effect and do for us; or as he hath created and made all things, he hath all things to bestow; therefore to make up this total, I have put in both the communication of himself, and all good things with himself.

To this purpose I observe, that in the mention of the evangelical blessings,—Abraham's blessing, as I may call it,—both God's own all-sufficiency in himself, and God's power in his works and to effect all things, are still mentioned; sometimes the one, sometimes the other, because in blessing us he is considered as both; he both gives himself and all things else to us, and so we are blessed indeed. Thus to Abraham whom God in blessing blessed, 'I am El-shaddai,' says he, God that am and have all-sufficiency, Gen. xvii. 1. When Isaac would bless Jacob with this blessing of Abraham, he thus speaks, God all-sufficient bless thee, Gen. xxviii. 3, (the same word in both.) And though in the translation it is restrained to almightiness, yet it also imports God's all-sufficiency and abundance; and so this blessing intends a communication out of that riches and fulness of blessedness which God himself enjoys. This for the first.

Secondly, In other places his titles, that import power and sovereignty in making and possessing all in heaven and earth, are prefixed to his blessing. Thus, when Melchisedec pronounces Abraham blessed, Gen. xiv. 19, he calls him the blessed of God under this title, 'the most high God, possessor of heaven and earth,' who had therefore all things in heaven and earth to bless him withal. And the Jews used the same, Ps. cxv. 15, 'You are the blessed of the Lord, who made heaven and earth,' and so is able to do all things for you, by the same power whereby he made the world. The like Ps. cxxxiv.; these have been inferred out of Abraham's blessing.

Now, that not only God doth bless with all other good things, but above all by communicating himself and his own blessedness unto them, the Scriptures are elsewhere express, when this blessing is spoken of. They shall not only not want any good, as the Psalmist, Ps. xxxiv. 10, 'No good thing will he withhold;' as Ps. lxxxiv., but 'give both grace and glory;' but himself will be a sun unto them; as there, ver. 11, 'The Lord God is a sun and shield.' The sun doth not only enrich the earth with all good things which by its influence it produceth, (called the 'precious fruits brought forth by the sun,' Deut. xxxiii. 14,) but glads and refreshes all with shedding immediately its own wings of light and warmth, which is so pleasant to behold and enjoy. And thus doth God, and Christ the Sun of righteousness, and accordingly it follows there, 'Blessed is the man that trusts in him;' for in being our sun, himself becomes our blessedness. Thus his promise of blessing Abraham, God himself interprets, Gen. xv. 1, 'I am thy exceeding great and abundant reward;' I, that am El-shaddai,* that have infinite paps of sweetness for you to suck; breasts of consolation, as the prophet expresseth it; who am the God of all comforts, as 2 Cor. i. 3, lo, I hold them all forth naked to thee, for thee to draw and fetch comfort from. Thou shalt have all my blessedness to make thee blessed, which the Apostle fitly renders, Eph. iii., 'being filled with all the fulness of God;' and indeed all things else without God or besides God could never make us blessed. The Psalmist, after an enumeration of all sorts of blessings, having pronounced them happy that are in such a case or state, by way of correction adds, as not having uttered wherein the top of blessedness lies; he adds, 'yea, blessed is the people whose God is the Lord,' Ps. cxliv. 15.

And hence the people of God, as sensible wherein their interest of happiness lies, as they are termed the blessed of the Lord, so they are said to bless themselves in the Lord; which is to rejoice and make their boast in him alone, and how happy they are in him, (as Christ in the 16th Psalm doth,) 'The Lord is my portion, and my lines are fallen in a good ground; I have a goodly heritage.' And that promise of blessing to Abraham, to which I still have recourse, runs thus indifferently, either that in thy seed, that is, Christ, (Gal. iii. 16,) they shall be blessed, so Gen. xii. 3, xxviii. 14; or xxii. 18, they shall bless themselves, or *benedictos se reputent*, account themselves

* Some derive his name El-shaddai, 'God all-sufficient,' from שד, *mamma, quasi πολύμαστος*, having many paps or dugs to suck, (Rivet. Gen. exerc. 87, *ab initio;*) and as God takes the denomination of רחים, that is, 'most merciful,' from רחם, 'the womb,' and so bowels, so this name of 'all-sufficient' from breasts or paps, (A Lapide on Gen. xvii. 1;) so at once noting out God's fulness, and also his readiness to communicate to us.

blessed in him—so Junius upon that place—namely in Christ, who is God blessed for ever, Rom. ix., for else they could not bless themselves in him. And thus Isaiah makes it the top of evangelical perfection, which he prophesied of, chap. lxv. 16; yea, and of the state of the people of God in the new heaven and new earth, wherein righteousness dwells, of which ver. 17, 18, that he who should bless himself in the earth, should bless himself in the God of truth; that is, God and Christ, that is alone the truth and the firm substance of all blessedness and happiness; according to that also of the Psalmist, 'Whom have I in heaven but thee, and in earth in comparison of thee?' That as a wicked man is said to bless himself in his life, Ps. xlix. 18, that is, to applaud his own soul's happiness, (Soul, take thine ease,) in having goods laid up for many years, for to make him, as he judgeth, happy; so the saints bless themselves in their God, their glory, not in riches or wisdom or strength, but they glory in this, that they understand and know God, Jer. ix. 23, 24, and by knowing him are made happy in him. For that is eternal life, John xvii. 3. And so by having God and Christ for their blessedness, they have all things with them, and so are blessed with all blessings. 'I will be his God,' that first; then follows, 'and he shall inherit all things.'

Lastly, God blesseth out of hearty good-will and love to our persons. And this is as the soul or form of blessing, whether ye will take it for the act of blessing in God, or the matter of blessing bestowed upon us. It is the good-will of God that causeth each of these to have the denomination and nature of a blessing.

1. *It is the spring and fountain of that act of blessing*, as that which constitutes it such. To bless is to wish, or, wishing, to bestow all good out of good-will; as when we bless God, it is the good-will we express therein which makes it termed blessing him, and so to differ from praise, as was shewn. So in God's blessing us, (his blessing us to be sure at least answereth to our blessing of him, and infinitely exceeds it.) In him it is a fatherly act, and so proceeds from mere natural and pure good-will and affection. The Lord first loves, then blesseth; Jehovah thy God will love thee, and so will bless thee, Deut. vii. 12, 13. And so likewise in Ps. v. 12, God's blessing us is exegetically expressed and explained to be a compassing a man round about with favour and good-will, clasping and accepting him, as with everlasting arms, Deut. xxxiii. 27. Thou Jehovah wilt bless the righteous, thou wilt encompass him round with favour, or favourable acceptation, good-will or gracious good-liking and acceptance, joined with a delight in their persons, and rejoicing to do them good, as the same word (Isa. xl. 1, 'in whom my soul delights,' spoken of Christ,) imports. And it is an encompassing round, because that man hath nothing else from God but love and favour coming in upon him on every side and surrounding him, and hence it is that a man is blessed with all blessings. In these terms therefore doth Moses pour forth his prayers of blessing on Joseph's head, who was separated from his brethren, as the choicest of them all. 'The good-will of him that dwelt in the bush, let it come upon the head of Joseph, and upon the crown of the head of him that was separated from his brethren,' (Deut. xxxiii. 1, 16, compared.) He invocates the original, the fountain of all blessings; namely the good-will of that God who in the bush had appeared and said, 'I am the God of Abraham,' &c., Exod. iii. 2, 6. And surely if God communicates himself to whom he blesseth, his blessing of them must proceed from the deepest good-will; and indeed is the reason why he giveth himself, as in marriage they bestow themselves and all, to whom they bear their special good-will.

And, 2. This good-will of God, accompanying each thing bestowed, *is that which maketh a blessing of it*, and so to be more than merely gifts bestowed. The Hebrews termed their gifts or presents a blessing. Thus 1 Sam. xxv. 27, Abigail to David, 'This blessing which thine handmaid hath brought unto my Lord;' also 2 Kings v. 15; whereby they would have it understood by the receiver, that they proceeded from their free and most hearty good-will; and that to be more than the gift. Thou hast given long life to thy king, says David to God, and so blesseth him for that. But because long life in itself was as no blessing to him without God's favour, in another psalm he says, 'Thy loving-kindness is better than life,' and all the privileges of it better than the things bestowed. And therefore after that Jacob had wished his Joseph all the precious things, as he terms them, all the dainties heaven or earth afforded, both which he distinctly mentions, Deut. xxxiii., (read ver. 13, 14 afore,) then after all he prays, as without which these would not prove blessings, the good-will of our God, says he, come upon him, &c., so invocating this fountain of all. Thus take any particular outward mercy which hath the name of a blessing, and it is the blessing of God, that is, his favour accompanying it, that maketh it such. It is the blessing of God, as Solomon says, that maketh rich, Prov. x. 22; and so in all other, otherwise their blessings are turned into curses, as Mal. ii. 2.

Out of good-will, good-will to our persons themselves, it is that he blesseth us, as in our blessing of God we heard it imported pure good-will to himself; so in his blessing us. In that short and fervent prayer of Jabez, 'Oh that thou wouldest bless me indeed!' 1 Chron. iv. 10, this passage follows, 'that thou wouldest keep me from evil, that it may not grieve me!' I observe from thence, that our God who undertakes to bless us, loves us so well, that he is so moved (such is his love to our persons) with the pleas of self-love in us, when concurring with his own glory. For this holy man, in seeking God's blessing on him to be kept from evil, urgeth this to God, 'that it may not grieve me.' Such free and pure good-will doth God bear to us, that he loves we should love ourselves, and is affected with what proceeds from love to ourselves; for this request God granted; so then it is genuine to the nature of a blessing, and indeed to bless another doth naturally and evidently of all acts else imply a pure and candid aim in wishing and desiring another's good, out of a special love unto their persons. Thus much for what this word to bless, as an act of God's, as also what a blessing as the thing bestowed, holds forth to us.

'Us,'—who in and of ourselves are 'by nature children of wrath,' as in chap. ii. 3, and 'cursed children,' 2 Pet. ii. 14, to whom all the curses written and unwritten are due,—are yet rendered blessed in Christ, and blessed not with one sort or kind, but all blessings, termed therefore by way of distinction from other men that remain under the curse, the blessed of the Lord. So Abraham first, Gen. xiv. 19, Melchisedec gives it him as a most royal title for himself and his children to inherit, that it grew to be ordinarily their style and attribute by heathens themselves, who observed the blessing of Jehovah to environ them. Thus Abimelech treats Isaac, Gen. xxvi. 29, 'Thou blessed of the Lord;' yea, this appellation Laban gives Abraham's servant, Gen. xxiv. 31, and so it came to be given to all others of his seed, as Ps. cxv. 15. And as it is their name and denomination, so the end of their calling, even that which they are called unto, unto nothing else but blessing, 1 Pet. iii. 9, 'Ye are thereunto called, that you should inherit a blessing;' in relation to which it is Christ's own compellation, when they are to possess it, 'Come, ye blessed, inherit the kingdom,' Matt. xxv. 34. Yea, they are not blessed men only, but men of blessedness, as in the Hebrew it is;

made up of nothing else, ordained to nothing else; yea, to a surplusage flowing over; such as to be blessings to others with whom they live, and whom they have relation to; all they come near, says God to Abraham, Gen. xii. 2, and ushers it with a word of command, 'Be thou,' or thou shalt be, 'a blessing, and I will bless them that bless thee;' which is repeated to Jacob by his father Isaac, and so is true of all the seed, Gen. xxvii. 29, and fulfilled in Joseph, Gen. xxxix. 5, for whose sake God blessed Potiphar and all his house.

MEDITATION.

Oh, then, let your hearts be full of nothing but of blessing, both blessing God and blessing others; and let no cursing or reviling be found in our mouths, which is the Apostle's inference, 1 Pet. iii. 9.

'Us,'—whose persons he loved with a special love, and out of that love hath chosen from the rest of men, as it follows in the next verse; thus Ps. xxxiii. 12, 13, 'Blessed are the people whom he hath chosen for his own inheritance. The Lord looketh from heaven; he beholdeth all the sons of men;' that is, whereas he hath all the sons of men afore him, he loved and chose these out to bless, and it is said he loved and blessed them above all people, as Deut. vii. 14. Which discovered itself in the difference put between Jacob and Esau: Jacob have I loved, and out of love blessed him, peremptorily and unchangeably, for he added, 'Yea, and he shall be blessed,' Gen. xxvii. 33, which old Isaac, the father, spake as in the person of God; whereas Esau with much difficulty obtains a poor pittance of outward blessings for a season.

'Us.'—But these meditations on this word, though quickening, yet that which is more conjunct with the Apostle's intimate scope, and was the main provocation in his thoughts, with this vehemency of spirit to pour forth this offering of blessing to the Lord, was the fresh and recent experience of God's gracious performance of that great promise made to the patriarchs of blessing in Christ both Jew and Gentile of all nations with the fulness of the blessing of the gospel. And that which induceth me to this is, I consider that he writing to the Ephesians, Gentile converts, in whose hearts, as in other nations, the gospel had taken place, he so carrieth his following discourse, setly and intentionally, as still to involve both Jew and Gentile together in the same spiritual privileges, in making his applications sometimes to the one, sometimes to the other, all along his discourse, in this and the following chapters, which hath been the general observation of interpreters, sometimes speaking of the Jew, which himself was: 'we who first trusted in Christ,' ver. 11, 12; sometimes of the other, 'ye also,' ver. 13; and so chap. ii. throughout; and accordingly in this general introduction of blessing God, he wraps them both in one and the same 'us;' and we as in a community partake of all the same benefits, in ver. 4–9. The access of which Gentiles unto the Church, and to be made partakers of the blessing of Abraham according to the promise and prophecy, was but then effected in his days. Oh, blessed be God, says he, and the Father of Christ, that hath thus blessed us; and blessed are the ears and eyes of us that live in these days wherein we have and see these things fulfilled: the mystery opened and discovered, which in former ages was not made known, that the Gentiles should be fellow-heirs and partakers of his promise in Christ by the gospel, as himself, as referring to the things delivered here and the rest of this chapter, speaks, chap. iii. 3, compared with ver. 4–6. This was so vast a prospect, as he falls down at the first and general view and consideration thereof: Blessed be God the Father that hath blessed us, us Jews, and with us, you Gentiles, with the blessings promised Abraham. And so much for the persons blessed.

SERMON IV.

With all blessings.—VER. 3.

IN that old dispensation, when Jacob blessed his twelve sons, and in them their posterity, the twelve tribes, in the conclusion of his blessing it is said, 'These are the twelve tribes, and every man, according to his blessing, he blessed them.' That is, Joseph had some one eminent earthly blessing bestowed on his tribe, Reuben another, and Naphtali a third, and so the rest. None there are said to be blessed with *all blessings*. But when God comes to open his treasures of blessings in Christ, and to profess to bless indeed and altogether, he blesseth with all blessings. Every child of his he blesseth, even 'with the fulness of the blessing of the gospel,' as, Rom. xv. 29, it is called. For when God gives us Christ, and blesseth us in him, 'how shall he not with him freely give us all things?' Having given you my Son, nay then take all else, and take all freely; having given the greater so willingly, sure you shall have all the rest, which are the lesser, more willingly.

It is observable that when Esau approached his father, to ask the blessing like one that came to glean after another's harvest already reaped, Jacob having been before him, how hard, how difficult he found his father to be, and upon what low terms is Esau fain to beg something, anything of him. 'Hast thou not reserved a blessing for me?' that is, hast thou given all away? And ver. 38, 'Hast thou but one blessing, my father? bless me, me also, O my father.' And how doth Isaac his father speak? As having nothing now left he could think of to bestow; with these, and these things, says he, have I blessed him, 'and what shall I do now unto thee, my son?' He casts about with himself to think what should be left ungiven away. This had not been if Jacob had not gone away with all. Now, as our Apostle says in the Epistle to the Galatians, of Ishmael and Isaac, 'these things are an allegory;' so expressly the same Apostle affirmeth these also to have been, Heb. xii. 17. The father is God, whom in this dispensation Isaac the father represented; the elect, the 'us' here, are Jacob or Israel, as frequently they are called; whom God endues with all blessings *in solido*, at once makes over all to them alone, as their inheritance; so as for the rest there is not anything left, but things earthly and carnal, which is the superfluity and redundancy of that fulness bestowed on his own, and which they may well spare. Hast thou not reserved one blessing? No, not one. God hath blessed us with all. Oh, infinite goodness and special grace!

With all.—Even each saint with *all*. If with any one blessing, then with all; they hang together and go in a cluster. 'Whom he hath predestinated, them he hath called; whom he hath justified, them he hath glorified,' and not one is wanting. If thou hast one grace, thou hast all, and all gracious privileges together therewith; even all the things that belong to life and godliness; all the promises of this life and that to come.

MEDITATION.

O Christian! see and rejoice in thy lot and portion. God himself hath but all things, and so hast thou.

Sit miser, qui miser esse potest, 'Let him be miserable that can be, for I cannot,' may a believer say to all others in the world. For can that man be ever miserable that is blessed with all blessings? whereof, even to be thus blessed for ever must needs be one, or he hath not all; and to whom all things are turned into blessings, even the evils that befall thee. If men curse and revile thee, God will bless; as David spake, when Shimei cursed him; and if men envy thee for good, this shall turn to thy salvation, as Phil. i. 19. If the devils spite thee, God will bless thee; there is no witchcraft against Israel. He turned Balaam's society and dealing with the devil to curse into a blessing. It is an observation which Nehemiah, chap. xiii. 2, makes upon that passage of Moses' story: Balak 'hired Balaam against them, that he should curse them; howbeit our God turned the curse into a blessing.' God, who was able and did make that strange change in our persons, of cursed children to be men of blessedness, blessed with all blessings, can much more, as he doth, change and turn all things that befall us, though curses in themselves, into blessings unto us. That man cannot be miserable whom all passages whatever do call, yea make blessed, and who himself is called to nothing else but blessing; and oh, if God thus turneth all things into heavenly blessings unto us, how engaged are we to be heavenly in all things towards him!

Spiritual blessings.—This openeth the mystery of what was even now spoken of; for why should such a limitation and confinement or eminent designation rather be here specified? Hath not godliness all other temporal earthly blessings entailed upon it?

This is spoken in difference from the literal dispensation of the old covenant, (which notion doth still and will all along accompany us,) which ran in the letter, most in promises of blessings earthly and outward.

The Apostle Paul, in the third of the Galatians, treating of the blessings of Abraham, (or promised to Abraham, and in him to all nations, ver. 8, and now come upon them, ver. 14,) doth clearly in the 14th verse explain and declare it to be a spiritual blessing, or the promise of the Spirit: 'That the blessing of Abraham might come on the Gentiles through Jesus Christ, that we might receive the promise of the Spirit through faith.' The latter words, 'that we might receive the promise of the Spirit,' is a manifest exegesis or explanation of those former words, 'that the blessing of Abraham might come on the Gentiles,' thereby explaining what manner or kind of blessing that was which was intended to Abraham, and comes upon the Gentiles through Christ. It is the Spirit, which if taken of the Holy Ghost that is given us, the promise of the Spirit imports all spiritual blessings, as in the seed, the root, the fountain of them. To say we have the Spirit given us, or promised to us, is all one as to say that we have all spiritual things conveyed. He is the immediate author and effecter in us of all grace and glory. And then what Christ in one Evangelist calleth 'giving of the Spirit to them that ask him,' in another he termeth 'giving good things,' that is, the things which are truly good, which the Spirit brings with him, who is the author of things spiritual, the best of blessings. But Calvin, and Pareus after him, commenting on those words, Gal. iii. 14, are bold to interpret the promise of the Spirit, the promise of spiritual things. He says not, say they, 'the Spirit of promise,' but 'the promise of the Spirit,' which I take, says he, for spiritual *more Hebraico;* he speaking in opposition, says he, to things outward, and those words, 'through faith,' confirm it. That is, whereof faith is sensible and apprehensive, takes in, and receives, as it doeth all spiritual things, and is a principle suited to them. And so it is one and the same kind of blessing which comes on the Gentiles, who had not the promise of Canaan, and upon the Jews, which is his scope: 'that we Jews might receive,' &c., as well as the Gentiles, and both the same; and also which Abraham himself received, who had not a foot of land in Canaan, Acts vii. 5, and yet is said to have obtained, possessed, the promise, Heb. vi. 15, 'And so, after he had patiently endured, he obtained the promise;' which obtaining the promise, or thing promised, is evidently there spoken of as an actual enjoyment, or possession of it, after the making of it; as the word *obtained* implies, and after patient waiting, and it is the very promise of blessing, 'I will bless thee,' ver. 15. The things or blessings then promised to Abraham, consisted in things spiritual; and so the Gentiles, as well as the Jews, were capable of them, even all of one and the same blessing.

Thus, also, when Jacob was blessed by Isaac, and with so vast and great a difference put both in God's intention and Isaac's apprehension between him and that of Esau in his blessing of him, which Esau was also sensible of; and yet if we read that whole legacy of blessings bequeathed to Jacob, we find none but outward and earthly in the letter spoken of, Gen. xxvii. 28, 29, 'God give thee of the dew of heaven, and the fatness of the earth, and plenty of corn and wine. Let people serve thee, and nations bow down to thee; be lord over thy brethren, and let thy mother's sons bow down to thee. Cursed be every one that curseth thee, and blessed be he that blesseth thee.' Yea, if we compare herewith the blessing afterwards estated upon Esau, ver. 39, 40, 'Behold, thy dwelling shall be the fatness of the earth, and of the dew of heaven from above. And by thy sword shalt thou live, and shalt serve thy brother; and it shall come to pass, when thou shalt have the dominion, that thou shalt break his yoke from off thy neck;' this is, as to the point of earthly blessings, well-nigh as full a portion as that of Jacob was, so as, if that the spiritual blessings promised in Christ, the blessed seed, had not been typically and mystically intended and signified by and under those earthly unto Jacob, it could not have been collected by the Apostle from the story of it that Jacob inherited the blessing, and that Esau was rejected, for all such earthly blessings he inherited as well as Jacob; nor had Isaac reason so bitterly to lament that he had, as it were, nothing left of blessing to bestow upon Esau, 'What shall I do for thee, my son?' Nor could there be supposed any other ground why, notwithstanding the equality of these blessings for ought was visible, the difference between them should yet be held up at so high a disproportion.

This, therefore, evidently argues that there was another sort of blessings, which were latent and hid, even a substantial, spiritual, invisible kind of blessings for evermore, whereof these things were but the shadows, as that which put that difference. And so the Apostle expressly interprets it in the fore-cited Heb. xii. 17, 'Ye know that afterward, when he would have inherited the blessing, he was rejected,' or denied. Mark it, that which Jacob obtained is called the blessing, eminently such, or it was the 'blessing indeed,' 1 Chron. iv. 10, which was in Jabez' eye under all those veils; 'the blessing, even life for evermore,' as the Psalmist speaks by way of exposition, Ps. cxxxiii. 3. And, indeed, when Isaac afterwards with such vehemency doubles it, 'I have blessed him, yea, and he shall be blessed,' Gen. xxvii. 33, this imports a blessing indeed to have been contained and involved in that blessing; and therein Isaac also shewed that the same blessing that was promised to Abraham, which was spiritual, as I have shewn, was it that was made over by inheritance to Jacob. The words of Abraham's blessing have the same emphatical duplication that we find in Jacob's, 'In blessing, I will bless thee,' Gen. xxii. 17. Further, the last words in that blessing of Jacob's, ver. 29, which are left out in Esau's, manifestly refer to the blessing made to Abraham, 'Cursed be every one that curseth thee, and blessed be he that blesseth thee;' being part of the words that are used in Abraham's, Gen. xii. 2, 3, 'I will make thee a blessing, and I will bless thee, and thou shalt be a blessing, and I will bless them that bless thee, and curse them that curse thee.'

And in this like strain of outward blessings Moses afterwards goes on. Thus speaks the old covenant, 'Blessed art thou in thy store, blessed in thy basket, in the field,' &c. And so on the contrary, the curses, Deut. xxviii. throughout. Now, then, our Apostle comes, and, as became the gospel, which is the new spiritual covenant established upon better promises, shadowed forth by these, he overlooks all these things; his eye being, as the gospel intention is, not upon things that are seen, but at the things which are not seen; for the things which are seen are temporal, as all these are, but the things which are not seen are eternal; and therefore, instead of things temporal and earthly, he writes and sets down spiritual and heavenly. Instead of 'Blessed art thou in the fields,' write down, 'Blessed art thou in the assemblies of the saints, under the enjoyment of spiritual ordinances and communion of saints.' 'There the Lord commands,' and, commanding, communicates, 'the blessing, even life for evermore,' Ps. cxxxiii. 3. Instead of 'Blessed art thou in thy store,' set down, 'Blessed are the rich in good works;' and others accursed that are rich, and not towards God, as James and our Saviour speak. And thus the gospel throughout carries it, and as if those kind of outward blessings had utterly now ceased, passeth them over as not worth the naming or the intention of those that live under the bare and naked discovery of spiritual and heavenly, as the Apostle sets them forth in their native, real glory; and thus Christ and his apostles carry it all along in their publications of the gospel, even as in his celebration of praise here. When the Apostle preached the gospel to the Jews, Acts iii., he pitcheth upon opening this very blessing of Abraham. Read the words, ver. 25. And how doth he expound it? It follows, ver. 26, 'Unto you first God, having raised up his Son Jesus, sent him to bless you, in turning every one of you from your iniquities.'

How low doth this fall in the expectations of a carnal Jew, whose eyes are veiled with the outward letter of promises earthly, to hear that Jesus the Messiah was sent to bless them in turning them from their iniquities! They look for a kingdom in glory and pomp, to be brought with their Messiah; and for him to turn them from iniquities is so poor, and low, and mean a thing with them; whereas, indeed, to be converted to God and turned from iniquity is a greater blessing (spiritual) than if God should make every one of you kings and rulers of worlds, and create variety and multiplicity of them for each of you; for this is a spiritual and heavenly blessing. Peter, therefore, mentions but this one for all the rest, to shew what a sort they are all of; as also, because this is the first and foundation of all other, and all other the concomitants or consequents of this; even as, in correspondency to this very speech of his, the same Apostle makes mention of regeneration, or being born again, in his first Epistle to the converted Jews, cast out, for their cleaving to the gospel, of their land given them to inherit, entitling it, therefore, 'To the strangers,' namely, Jews, (for the Gentile Christians there were natives,) 'scattered throughout Asia;' notwithstanding, (to comfort their hearts,) 'Blessed be the God and Father of Christ, that hath begotten you again,' or turned them from their iniquities, 'to an inheritance immortal, reserved in the heavens for you,' better than Canaan; and this is the blessing of Abraham.

Now, as Christ in another case, all the rest of gospel blessings are like to this, spiritual all. If you will have David's description, says Paul, of the blessedness of his blessed man he so often speaks of, Rom. iv., 'even as David describeth the blessedness of the man,' &c., ver. 6, 'Blessed is the man whose sin is pardoned,' ver. 7, out of Ps. xxxii.; 'Blessed is the man that is poor in spirit, meek, pure in heart,' Matt. v. The blessedness, you see, lies in and is made unto spiritual graces and dispositions of holiness. As also blessed is he that walks holily, he is 'blessed in his deed,' James i. 25; yea, 'blessed is he that endures temptation,' ver. 12. And after this account and rule are we now blessed under and by the gospel; the gospel, not deigning so much as to mention any one earthly, carnal blessing as here, slips them over, and takes no notice of them, as not worthy to come into the catalogue of those more choice and divine blessings it makes promise of. Yea, it professeth to all its followers, that in this life we are of all men most miserable, the offscouring of the world; which carnal men observing, will be ready to say, as in another case our Apostle speaks, Where is the blessedness you speak of? It lies in a higher sort of things you wot not of, and therefore with the same breath pronounceth us most blessed when most miserable. 'Blessed are you when men revile you, and persecute you, both say and do all manner of evil against you,' says our Saviour; 'rejoice and be exceeding glad,' for as these are multiplied and enlarged, your treasures in those things, which are the real blessings, are increased, as it follows, 'for great is your reward in heaven:' greater, as the proportions of your persecutions are. Which hath brought me to the next word:—

I. *In heavenly places, or things.*—The phrase in the original is barely ἐν ἐπουρανίοις, 'in the heavenlies,' without this addition of either places or things. And it is a speech proper to this epistle, and nowhere else used, and four or five times used therein; and according as the context requires, we may add places or things, sometimes the one, sometimes the other; and perhaps in this place, which is so general and comprehensive, we may take in both, to fill up the Apostle's meaning:—

1. *In heavenly places.*—So twice in this and the ensuing chapter. Speaking of Christ, 'God hath set him at his right hand in heavenly,' ver. 20; here *places* must be added; the correspondency with the words 'set him' calls for it. So likewise, chap. ii. 6, he speaketh the same of us in a conformity to Christ our head, 'hath set us together in heavenly;' here *places* is to be added, as suited to 'setting.' The like he speaks of the good angels, the inhabitants of the heavenly world, to whom we being thus advanced, we are made like unto; as Christ says, chap. iii. 10, 'principalities and powers' that are constituted and set 'in heavenly places.'

2. *In heavenly things.*—Thus, chap. vi. 12, 'For we wrestle not against flesh and blood, but against principalities, against powers, against the rulers of the darkness of this world, against spiritual wickedness in high places.' It is translated 'high places' in your margin. According to the Greek, it is 'in heavenlies,' the same word that is here, and *places* is added, but not genuinely, but *things* rather should there be supplied. For this being spoken

concerning our contention with the devils, this passage, 'in heavenly,' is not an additional to note out the places wherein the devils are set, and have their station, as of the good angels, chap. iii. 10, you hear it spoken. Their place is designed and set out, chap. ii. 2, to be but the air or lower heavens. But the word reacheth there higher, far higher than is the air. It is not ἐν οὐρανίοις, simply 'in heavenly;' but in 'above-the-heavens,' ἐν ἐπουρανίοις, where Christ also sits at the right hand of God, and we with him, as you heard, ἐν ἐπουρανίοις, in supercelestial thrones, in the highest heavens. And as it must not be thought that the devils came up to the heaven of heavens at any time since they fell from thence, for no unclean thing enters thereinto; much less do they possess them for their place or station, which Jude, ver. 6, says they kept not; so it is hard to think that the Apostle using this phrase but in this epistle only, and everywhere else of Christ and us and the good angels, as advanced to heaven and the highest heavens, that in this one place at last it should be taken of that air, the habitation and seat of devils, and come in, too, but as a mere additional barely to express the place where these are with whom we contend. That phrase therefore there used, ἐν ἐπουρανίοις, refers to set out to us (the more to intend our spirits in this conflict against them) the infinite moment and weight of the things themselves, in or about which we are taken up or exercised in this our opposition against them; even things supercelestial, and that are all purely heavenly, is the matter of this strife, which they endeavour to spoil us of, and to cause us to lose in. Of no less value (more precious than diamonds and rubies) are the things that lie at the stake of this vying between them and us, which they strive with us about, to keep us or beat us off from them, and through their envy endeavouring to cause us to lose the things we may or have gained herein. To which sense the particle ἐν, translated *in*, fitly and properly serves, being often put for *about* or *concerning*, and denoting forth the direct matter about which we are conversant. 'Blessed,' says Christ, 'is he that is not offended *in me;*' that is, about or concerning me and my condition, as noting out the stone of stumbling, occasion, and matter of the offence. This for the phrase or speech itself; whether of these or both are to be taken in here, will appear in opening the thing itself.

II. *The thing itself.*—And here more specially why 'in heavenly' should be added to 'spiritual,' when these gospel blessings are spoken of; and so that all and every one of those blessings should be affirmed to be in heavenlies; not some spiritual, and some heavenly, but all both spiritual and also in heavenlies. That it is not a synonymous addition, as expressing the quality of these blessings by two words that signify one and the same, is evident, because he doth not say spiritual *and*, *or*, heavenly, but spiritual *in* heavenly. His scope must therefore be to carry our thoughts further than barely to consider the spirituality of those blessings, (so to set a value on them,) but further that they are heavenly also, and what heavenly import further than spiritual, that comes also to be the question.

1. In a further and more plain distinction from the tenure of the blessings promised in that old dispensation which in the letter, as they were in themselves outward and fleshly, so in giving forth the promises of them it is still added, 'in the land which the Lord thy God shall give thee,' so before their coming into Canaan; or 'in the land which the Lord thy God hath given thee,' after; as a land, partly from its own fertility, as also by reason of its situation and neighbourhood, flowing with all good blessings whatsoever, more than any other land, which God, that views from heaven all the plots and corners of earth below, is therefore said to have 'spied out for them,

flowing with milk and honey, which is the glory of all lands,' as God by the prophet speaks, Ezek. xx. 6. Now, the New Testament tells us that by this in the promise was foresignified, and in the expectation of the patriarchs to whom the promise was made, understood and apprehended, another country. They desired or expected, Heb. xi. 16, 'a better country, that is, a heavenly;' and such a city or country, says Paul there, was the import of God's styling himself in so vast a difference from other the sons of men, the God of Abraham, &c. For God being so great a God, so full of blessedness in himself, would never have appropriated or bestowed himself in so near a relation and style of being their God, their portion, and their inheritance, upon so low and mean conditions, so far below himself, as to give them only earthly things, and no other habitation than that one poor corner of the earth, Canaan, although never so abounding with all good things.

God, says the Apostle, would have been ashamed to have been called their God upon such terms only; as if that were all the great all-sufficient God, that is possessor of heaven and earth, as Melchisedec said to Abraham, was able to give, or had to bestow on them of whom he gloried to be called their God, and owned them as his eminently beloved ones. God therefore had prepared for them another manner of city or country than Jerusalem or Canaan; even an heavenly, where his own throne and glory is; and hath therefore appointed to take them up to himself, and to pay forth and give to them all good blessings in pure heavenlies; which the Psalmist clearly intimates, when he says, Ps. cxv. 15, 16, 'Blessed are ye of the Lord who hath made heaven and earth;' and accordingly hath given in common to all the children of men the earth, and the things therein, reserving heaven, which is his own peculiar habitation, to bestow upon these his blessedness, as it there follows, 'The heaven, even the heavens are the Lord's, but the earth hath he given to the children of men;' and therefore the Jews Peter wrote to are, as was observed, comforted with this by that holy apostle, that they were begotten to an inheritance reserved in the heaven for them, as in distinction from that given their fathers in Canaan, where the communication of God himself is so worthy, so suitable to and like himself, as the Apostle is bold to say of it: 'Wherefore God is not ashamed to be called their God, for he hath prepared for them a city,' namely this heavenly one, as he had termed it in the words just afore, and so there is an answerable communication of himself and all blessings given forth in heavenlies. And unto this notion will fitly suit that supplied addition, *places*—'in heavenly places.'

In heavenly places,—to make this intended opposition between these two full and complete, that look as Canaan of old was the designed seat, the place, the country, where all those fleshly outward blessings were enjoyed, and many of them grew, and so the promise thereof is made the additional unto all those promised blessings, (which is so frequently done throughout the Old Testament, as I need not quote any one testimony.) Now in like manner is heaven the ἑδραίωμα, the city, where both all these spiritual blessings have their full maturity and perfection, and is the place appointed to enjoy them in; where there is room and variety enough for all God's holy ones; 'heavenly places,' in the plural.

Places enough, 'many mansions,' John xiv. 1, &c. And in the meantime, till ye arrive there, those spiritual blessings we here partake in the first-fruits belong to, and come forth out of that country, all of them, where our conversation is said to be, even in this life, so far as we are made spiritual men. And in the type itself, when God did give forth the promise of blessing to Abraham, it is said, 'God called to Abraham from heaven,' Gen. xxii.

15–17, whereas he conferred with Adam but on earth, signifying that place from whence that blessing was to come, and in which to be enjoyed. Even as, in the like mystical intendment, heaven is said to have opened, when that voice came to Christ at his baptism, 'This is my well-beloved Son, in whom I am well pleased,' Matt. iii. 17, as from whence that blessed seed, in whom all are blessed, was to come,—Christ 'the Lord from heaven,' 1 Cor. xv. 47,—and so he to raise us to the same state and place.

2. *In heavenlies*, was added to spiritual, in a further distinction yet of the blessings wherewith in Christ we are blessed, from those wherewith in Adam in our first creation we and all his posterity were blessed of God; for blessed we are in him, as you read, Gen. i. 27, 28. Adam being made, as there, ver. 26, according to the image of God, which was the foundation of that charter of blessing him and his posterity, he was in that respect a spiritual man, for such is the image of God; his graces were all spiritual, and his life and communion with God was spiritual; and so of him it might be said, that he was blessed with spiritual blessings, as well as in those earthly, and so in respect thereof we in him, that were to come of him, being all to receive the same spiritual image from him; but yet still he, and so we in him, but blessed with all these as a man that was to live on earth only, and to enjoy God, though in a spiritual way, yet but as flesh and blood can in an earthly condition be capable of, which, whilst remaining such, cannot see or enjoy God, as in heaven he is to be seen or enjoyed, and live.

For Adam when in his best condition was but flesh and blood, and an earthly man, as he is termed in distinction from Christ, 1 Cor. xv. 47. And such as that earthly man was, such should we that are of him that was of earthly generation have been, and neither he nor we advanced higher, ver. 48. But our Lord Christ being the Lord from heaven, ver. 47, a heavenly man, ver. 48, therefore we being blessed in and together with him, we are blessed in heavenly things, or with heavenly blessings, and raised up to heavenly places with him; for as is the heavenly man Christ, such are (and is the condition) of those in him; even heavenly as himself is. Heaven is his native country, he is the Lord of it; and we being married to him, and he our Lord in that respect, as was said, the spouse must be where the husband is, and partake of the same good things which he is partaker of, and therefore he takes us, and carries us to his own home, to his Father's house, which being heaven, we thereby come to be blessed in Christ with all heavenly blessings, and not spiritual only, which Adam in his primitive condition was.

And this notion will fitly bring in that other supplement which interpreters have added, 'in heavenly things,' as that other took into itself 'in heavenly places.' All the graces we have are not only spiritual, to fit us for communion with God as on earth, but they are preparations, and making us more fit for the inheritance in light, to see God face to face. And they all tend to lead us in the way to heaven, and to bring us to heaven at last; and have all the promises of things heavenly annexed to and entailed upon them. 'Follow me, and thou shalt have treasure in heaven,' says Christ, and 'a more enduring substance in the heavens,' as Paul speaks, Heb. x. 34; even all things whatever that are in heaven, and are found growing there, are ours, and we have an interest in them, as they in Canaan had to all the earthly things that country afforded and abounded with; and for the enjoyment of those things there in that world, our very bodies at the resurrection will be made spiritual and heavenly, which Adam's was not. So in that 1 Cor. xv., 'it is raised a spiritual body.' 'There is a spiritual body,' namely, that received at the resurrection, 'and there is a natural body,' that which Adam was created in, ver. 44, alleging for proof of it, in ver. 45, 'and so it is written, The first Adam was made a living soul,' an earthly man, ver. 45, but Christ and his saints are made spiritual, heavenly, so ver. 48, and he evidently there applies this to the state of the body.

And accordingly, look as that natural body of Adam was framed with such inlets and capacities of outward senses as were suited to take in all the good things that God had made and provided in this world on purpose for him,—meats for the belly, and the belly for meats, 1 Cor. vi. 13, fitted each to other,—so he having provided and filled that other heavenly world, both with variety of heavenly places and of heavenly things in those habitations, (as, *more nostro*, the Scriptures express it,) which are called in the plural *τὰ ἄνω*, 'things above,' in answerable opposition unto *τὰ ἐπὶ τῆς γῆς*, 'things on earth,' Col. iii. 2, and *αὐτὰ δὲ τὰ ἐπουράνια*, the 'supercelestial things themselves,' Heb. ix. 23,—which opposition shews that, as on earth there is a plurality and a variety of things, so in heaven also there are,—and to the end we may be capable of like comfort from these things heavenly, though far more transcendent, as the things themselves are in goodness to afford it to us, our very bodies shall be fitted and suited thereunto, and made heavenly and spiritual, with inlets and capacities heavenly and spiritual. Even our bodies shall be made capable of pleasure in those created excellencies there, in the framing or contriving of which God hath shewed so much of his art and skill; (as those words, *τεχνίτης καὶ δημιουργὸς*, Heb. xi. 10, import;) and particularly our bodies to receive a glory and happiness in and from the presence of that heavenly body of Christ, these being in an heavenly manner and way suited each to other; which the following words of that 1 Cor. vi. 13, 14 clearly insinuate, of which I have elsewhere spoken.* And if our bodies, to how much more heavenly state and glorious capacity shall the soul be raised, to take in those pleasures which flow immediately from the face of God and the Godhead, whose fulness dwells in that human nature, the body and soul of Christ, 'in whose presence are rivers of pleasure for evermore!'

So then, to conclude, all in heaven, both places and things, God hath blessed us withal in the real donation of them hereafter to be enjoyed; and in the meantime furnished us with those graces and dispositions as in themselves are heavenly, and of an higher strain than Adam's,† though his were spiritual. Which graces God hath endued with a right unto all those things to be enjoyed in heaven, and entailed all upon them, and which will in the end bring us thither, and do render us meet for the enjoyment of them. There is a third reason of this addition of heavenly to spiritual, which will come in more fitly in the meditation that follows. And so much for the nature and condition of the blessings themselves.

Obs.—We may from hence at once learn to judge and discern, both what are the true and choicest and most desirable blessings, and by what rule to judge of God's dealings with us in this world; as also of our hearts and spirits, whether evangelised and made spiritual, yea or no.

1. *What are the choicest blessings.*—Take for this the true rate and estimate and price which the gospel sets upon things. It mentions not, you see, riches, honours, beauty, pleasures; it passeth these over in silence, which yet the Old Testament everywhere makes promise of. They were then children, as Gal. iv. 1–3, and God pleased them with the promise of these toys and rattles, as taking with them. But in the gospel hath shewn he hath 'provided some better things for us,' things spiritual and heavenly;

* Upon 1 Cor. xv. 45. † See my Sermons on Adam's State in Innocency.

both gracious and heavenly dispositions of spirit, that carry the soul to 'seek the things that are above, where Christ is;' and together therewith, those things themselves above that are the objects and inquest of them. You may judge of the superexcelling value of these blessings by what the devils, that are spiritual wickednesses, and so full both of envy and malice to us, do contend with us about. Now, what things are they which they oppose you in, and do make the ball of their contention with us, but these things spiritual and heavenly? As you heard, they malign you not, nor will they hinder you from being rich, honourable, to increase in and attain to a fulness of things worldly, or outward. Yea, all these sometimes he is used, as an instrument by God, to help men unto, as snares and baits to undo their souls. But as the devils themselves are spiritual wickednesses, so their envy, which sin is purely a spiritual wickedness, and which always hath for its object what is the chiefest excellency or good belonging to another, whom one envies or hates, is at and against you for none other things but spiritual good things, which therefore are, by this manifest acknowledgment of your greatest adversaries, the best things. *Fas est et ab hoste doceri.* If he knew any that were better, he would be sure to turn your opposite therein; and he knows the worth of them, by having fallen from them. These are, therefore, the best, yea, and the only true blessings indeed.

Yea further, there are a sort of things that are spiritual, which of themselves taken or found apart, severed from graces, are not spiritual blessings, though called spiritual gifts; as faith of miracles, gifts of tongues, and divine knowledge in the knowledge of the Scriptures, which yet are a fruit of Christ's ascending, Eph. iv. These the gospel condescends to commend to the Corinthians, as the objects of our desires, 'Desire spiritual gifts, yea, covet earnestly the best gifts,' 1 Cor. xii. 31; and these, chap. xiv. 1, as infinitely more desirable than all other earthly excellencies whatever, as being of immediate use in edifying the Church of God. Yet if you will have the Apostle speak his own heart, he undervalues all these but as toys which, when children, even under the gospel men are taken with, but in themselves are nothing in comparison of the least degree of true spiritual heavenly graces: as faith unfeigned and lively hope, which do entitle us to, and do accompany and carry us unto the very door of heaven; and sincere love, which goes in with us, and abides with us for ever. These other gifts, though spiritual, yet they are not of themselves spiritual blessings in heavenlies, if love and faith be wanting; for they interest not the person in whom they are in heavenlies, but men may go to hell with a rich portion had of them here. Here the Apostle himself speaks forth his own sense herein, 1 Cor. xiii. 1–3, 'Though I speak with the tongues of men and angels, and have not charity, I am become as sounding brass or a tinkling cymbal. And though I have the gift of prophecy, and understand all mysteries, and all knowledge, and though I have all faith, so that I could remove mountains, and have not charity, I am nothing.' These, when a man is a child in Christianity, he may for a while value, (ver. 1, 'When I was a child, I spake as a child,' &c.;) but after he is grown up, these other come in esteem with him.

To the like purpose we find him speaking, Heb. vi., of all those enlightenings and tastings of the heavenly gifts, which men that fall away do partake of, ver. 4, 5, preferring infinitely the least grain of true heavenly grace, such as sincere love to the saints, unto the greatest abundance of those other, as better things, infinitely better, upon the same account that here in the text, that they accompany salvation. So, ver. 9, 'We are persuaded better things of you, and things that accompany salvation,' instancing, ver. 10, in that of love to the saints: 'For God is not unrighteous, to forget your work and labour of love, which ye have shewed towards his name, in that ye have ministered to the saints, and do minister.' Even those elevations of the powers and principles in corrupt nature unto a tasting the heavenly gift, as also of the powers of the world to come, as the object of them, yet are they not in themselves spiritual blessings in heavenlies. Nor are they ordained as such, to bring the persons that have them thither, which true spiritual graces, that are the image of God and the new creature renewed in us, by our being begotten again, are ordained unto.

To distinguish, therefore, even these, though spiritual gifts, from those graces that are spiritual in heavenlies, and that appertain to and belong unto salvation, doth this addition, 'in heavenlies,' as pertinently and properly serve as either of the other two forementioned. And although they are from heaven as in respect of the giver, which is Christ as ascended into heaven, and the Holy Ghost who is from heaven; yet are they not ἐπουράνια, gifts supercelestial, in themselves or in the persons, so as to raise their hearts up unto things above the heavens,—that is, make their hearts heavenly,—nor will ever carry their persons thither. They are ἐκ, from heaven, not ἐν ἐπουρανίοις, not seated in, or constituted of heavenlies. But they are in the receivers of them, if their hearts be not renewed, but earthly, because they are but the stirrings of self-love in them (which is a corrupt member upon earth, as well as any other lust) by heavenly enlightenings; though elevating self to objects heavenly, so far as there is any consideration in them that suiteth self, as the greatest notion of joy, happiness, and blessedness doth; yet not unto τὰ αὐτὰ ἐπουράνια, 'to the heavenly things themselves,' Heb. ix. 23, in their spiritual nature considered, as the Apostle distinguisheth, 1 Cor. ii. 13, 14. And so the products of them in the spirits and affections of them in the receivers are heavenly no otherwise than the vapours and clouds or meteors that are exhaled by the sunbeams out of the earth and water may be said to be heavenly, because the light and influence of heaven extracts and elevates them above that sphere which otherwise they would not rise up unto. And so those are but *ex unâ parte*, but of one part heavenly, and so imperfectly; such merely *ex parte illuminantis et donantis*, on the part of the donor, because he is in heaven that gives them, and from heaven lets them down; as also, because they have a remoter tendency towards heaven and salvation. 'Thou art not far from the kingdom of heaven,' said Christ to one more than ordinarily enlightened among the Jews. But heavenly they are not, *ex parte recipientis*, the hearts of the receivers of them remaining still corrupt, as, whilst self remains the predominant agent and principle, a man must needs still remain, whatever his objects which self pursues be. They are earthly, as the affections themselves are that are stirred thereby in them; for if the root or soil be earthly, though the rain that falls on it and causeth it to sprout and bud be from heaven, yet the fruit must needs still be esteemed such; which comparison the Apostle hath an allusion to in Heb. vi. 7, 8, 'For the earth which drinketh in the rain that cometh oft upon it, and bringeth forth herbs meet for them by whom it is dressed, receiveth blessing from God: but that which beareth thorns and briars is rejected, and is nigh unto cursing; whose end is to be burned.'

And perhaps to put this or the like distinction between these spiritual gifts, thus imperfectly heavenly, from those graces of true regeneration, might be one great part of the Apostle's aim in that speech, James i. 16–18, 'Do not err, my beloved brethren,' (he speaks to the whole bulk and herd of professors and hearers of the word, in respect that many mistook imperfect workings on men, and actings by men from hearing the gospel, for true heavenly grace, and so by false reasonings deceived themselves, παραλογιζόμενοι ἑαυτούς, as ver. 22,)—'Do not err, my beloved brethren,' says he: 'every good gift and every perfect gift is from above, and cometh down from the Father of lights, with whom is no variableness, neither shadow of turning. Of his own will begat he us with the word of truth.' So making the distinction between true professors and false to consist in an innate difference in the gifts themselves; the one good and perfect, as regeneration is, which he instanceth in, and which alone brings forth fruit to perfection, as Christ says in the parable of the sower, which is every way good and perfect, both *ex parte dantis*, from above, and *ex parte recipientis*, changing the heart into an heavenly nature, as the 'engrafted word,' ver. 21, useth to do, so making the man holy and heavenly, as the Word and Spirit itself is. And that which confirms this is, that James's scope is evidently to distinguish seemingly true professors from true professors indeed. 'If any seem to be religious,' ver. 26; 'Pure religion and undefiled before God,' &c., ver. 27. Oh, therefore, let us all be moved to seek earnestly after these good and perfect gifts of true holiness and regeneration, and things that accompany salvation; to be blessed with these spiritual blessings in heavenlies, the possessors of which James twice in that chapter termeth blessed, and them alone!

2. Learn hence likewise, how to judge rightly of God's dealings with thee in this world, and to put a right and true interpretation thereupon, and of his heart towards thee therein. God often drives a clean contrary design to our expectations, desires, yea our very prayers, which perhaps have been drawn out and laid forth much upon things outward and earthly, which we have judged meet for us. But God perhaps hath broken thee in these, denied thy prayers, yea taken all away from thee, and done the clean contrary. But withal consider, what he hath been a doing all that while upon thy spirit in order to spiritual things in heavenlies. Hath God increased thee in faith, patience, submission to his will, humbling thyself under his mighty hand, keeping thee from sin? Hath he enlarged thy coast in joy in the Holy Ghost, communion with himself, and steady and close walking with him; and will not let thy heart go forth far after anything vain and carnal, but he comes upon thee with some cross, hedgeth up thy way, narrows thee in such comforts that would draw forth and increase thy lusts; but makes an open door, an enlarged abundant entrance into his own bosom, in accesses to him and converses with him? Or if not therein, yet increaseth thy secret store of gracious dispositions and holy compliances of spirit towards himself, such as his dealings with thee call for? Thy heart is kept in awe to sin, fearful to omit holy duties, dependent on him in all, loving of him, eyeing of him, walking with him, and aiming at him in all thy ways. So as whatever he doth to thee, as in relation to this world, and to thy worldly ends and desires, yet in relation to that other world and the things thereof thou observest that he still is sure to carry on that design strongly and hotly, and pursues it hard, to make thee more spiritual, and to bring thee nearer to himself. Oh, consider that even this is to bless thee, to bless thee indeed, to bless thee according to the tenure and dispensation of blessing men under the gospel! This is to bless thee in Christ, and with Christ, and the blessings of Christ, who was sent to bless us in things spiritual in heavenlies; and in these is the special good-will and love of God, as thy God and Father, and as the God and Father of Christ, laid forth and seen.

Thus he blessed Job, when he took all outward things from him. 'Blessed be the name of the Lord,' said he then, when all was gone. He could not have blessed God so heartily as he then did, if he had not found God blessing him most of all at that very time. Yea, with these he blessed his Son Christ himself, of whom it is said God 'blessed him for ever,' and yet had not a hole to hide his head in. With these [he blessed] the apostles, who had neither house nor home; suffered nakedness, hunger, and were at last appointed and set forth to death, as Paul expresseth it; when as other Christians in those times, less beloved and less blessed of him, as the Corinthians, babes in Christ, carnal, yet in a great measure were full, reigned, abounded in all earthly comforts. God allowed them these rattles then being as children: but take Paul's judgment, what though our outward man perish,—that is, our bodies, and the outward state and condition of the whole man, as we are men of this world,—what though we suffer loss in the things belonging thereto, so in lieu thereof our inward man be renewed daily? and the things belonging to this inward man are these spiritual blessings in things heavenly. Yea, we may well suffer the spoiling of our goods, as the Hebrews did, if instead thereof an enduring substance in the heaven be added unto us; as, if we obtain one degree of grace, (the least,) there is for certain withal such an addition, to an infinite disproportion, in heavenlies made.

The primitive Christians being possessed with such principles as these, cared not what they were to this world. If thou beest a servant, care not; yea, if thou wast of servants a slave, as some then that were called were, (for Paul says, 'whether bond or free in Christ,' &c., Col. iii., there were therefore such in Christ then;) and the condition of servants, especially slaves, in those times and places was hard and outwardly most miserable, their lords having power of life and death and to use them as they listed; yet how slightly doth the Apostle speak of that condition, and but in one short word: 'care not,' says he, 1 Cor. vii. 21; he spends no more words about it, nor no higher, as a thing so much taken for granted, not to be minded in comparison upon this consideration which follows, ver. 22, 'For he that is called in the Lord is the Lord's free man.' That is, Thy relation unto, and condition in, and privileges by Christ, are of such transcendant value in comparison of this other, as this should have no weight with thee to be regarded. Thou art blessed in Christ with all blessings in another world, so that it is no matter what thy condition be in this world. Only because outward things, joined with the favour of God, are in their kind blessings from God not to be contemned, yet so small as they come not into the gospel's inventory, therefore he there adds, that if such a one could be free, he should use it rather. And so if riches, or honours, or power be cast upon thee, use them rather. Yet still he speaks so slenderly of the difference between these, as if so little, and that which is, whether it be the good of the one, and evil that is in the other, so much swallowed up by that state and condition we have in Christ, as neither is much worth considering.

O my brethren, these men that talked and lived at this rate, as the apostles and Christians then did, how strangely and mightily must their minds be supposed to have been filled and possessed with the valuation and admiration of spiritual and heavenly blessings! Yea, insomuch as when they saw any man suffer much, they esteemed it a happiness, an addition of blessedness to that man. 'Behold, we account them happy that endure or suffer,' saith the Apostle James, chap. v. 11. He speaks it as the common thoughts and principle of '*us all*,' that are, or then were Christians, and speaks it in opposition to the thoughts of the world. They account them happy that have riches, have beautiful wives, fair houses, &c.; but, behold, we account them happy that endure. And if temptations of several kinds befell them, they aforehand were prepared and instructed to account it all joy. For their faith and experience prompted them that now God was about to bless them with an increase in such spiritual graces of faith and patience, &c., the least trial of which hereby, much more addition unto which, they accounted 'more precious than gold,' 1 Peter i. 6, 7; and 'blessed is the man that endures temptation;' and the more or greater these are, the more blessed he is.

Thus, God often makes but an advantage of a man's outward condition; sets up a man or woman that hath all affluences and accomplishments of riches, honours, abilities, pleasures, beauty, wit, &c., and bestows them on them but as it were only to afford but so many crosses and afflictions in the spoil of them, and to heighten these afflictions the more; when yet God's design in and by the loss or ruin of all these, is to make that man or woman great and rich and glorious in and unto this heavenly world, unto the higher and greater proportion, as he was in all these outward things in this world. Doth God greatly chastise and afflict thee, and withal teach thee out of his law, further instructing thee in thy duty, and framing thy heart thereupto? Hear David, Ps. xciv. 12, 'Blessed is the man whom thou chastenest, and teachest out of thy law.' Doth a great loss of a child, a wife, put thee upon making one more fervent prayer than otherwise thou shouldst have made? God hath really and more abundantly blessed thee thereby, than in the continuance of that outward enjoyment to thee. God often blesseth us when we are not aware of it. God lets thee fall into a sin perhaps, and that drives thee to the throne of grace, with outcries for help, Heb. iv. 16, βοήθειαν, as the Apostle's word is, as a man undone utterly and for ever, if God pity thee not. This prayer, though in itself a less good than thy sin was evil, yet unto thee is turned a far greater blessing than thy sin hath evil in it (as to thee:) such is his goodness. Thy sin shall be pardoned, and though it be a loss in itself, yet to thee, having this so great a consequent and effect of it, thou comest off a gainer. And, lo, God hath blessed thee by occasion of it with a further increase in heavenlies, which do abide for ever, and shall never be taken from thee.

3. Hereby also we may judge of our own spirits, whether yea or no at all made spiritual and heavenly, or to what degree; and so whether in this state of gospel blessedness, or the contrary. What blessings are they thy heart is drawn out to seek, when thy soul is in nearest approaches unto God, and thou findest thou hast hold of him in wrestling with him, as Jacob had usually at such times? What are the choicest desires of a man's soul he pours forth to him, and says, as Jacob there did, 'I will not let thee go, except thou bless me' thus or thus? And what are the blessings thy heart then with highest contention affecteth? Sometimes perhaps that God would communicate himself to thee, which, as you heard, was the sum and substance of all blessings and blessedness. Oh, bless me with thyself, thyself, Lord! And thy heart is so filled, and overpowered, and swallowed up with this, is so adequately filled and environed about with this, that thou canst not find in thy heart wherewith at that time to ask anything else; but the utmost sole intention of thy mind and soul are held up, fixed and united unto this, and this alone. Another time, or presently thereupon, as violently carried forth to be blessed in holiness and unblameableness in love towards this God. 'Oh that thou wouldest bless me indeed, and keep me from the evil!' So we find Jabez broke forth, 1 Chron. iv. 10, and his prayer is recorded for the eminent zeal and holiness of heart in it; and it stands there alone, like to a small fertile spot of earth in the midst of a long

tract of ground, that bears nothing but names and genealogies round about it. Oh, keep me from the evil, says he, that evil of evils, sin, (as Christ in the Lord's Prayer also expresseth it,) that it may not grieve me: for, Lord, to sin against thee would be to my spirit the greatest cross and affliction; though otherwise I abounded in all earthly blessings, and thou didst never so much enlarge my coast, as he had there also prayed; and to be kept from it is in my esteem and desire the greatest mercy I have to desire of thee,—to bless me; bless me, O Lord, 'by turning me from mine iniquities,' as Peter, Acts iii. 36, by enabling me to keep thy commandments, which is the greatest blessedness, as Rev. xxii. 14. Are these, and such as these, the top desires of thy soul? Thou art blessed in thy deeds, as James says. Go, and for thy comfort carry home with thee all the blessings which heaven itself affords thee therewith, and fall down on thy knees, and with the Apostle here bless thy God, who hath thus blessed thee with all (whilst thou hast thus a heart to prefer any one that is truly spiritual) blessings in heavenly things in Christ.

In Christ.—1. We before observed that God blesses us, as having taken upon him to bear the relation of our God, and of a Father unto us.

2. These two relations of God unto us are founded originally and firstly upon his said relations unto Christ—viz., of being his God and his Father first, and that in a transcendant manner higher than unto us; but descending down, and imparted to us in a lower, though true real degree.

3. Christ's bearing the title of being *Our Lord*, being joined to the last foregoing particular, do (both put together) become a joint foundation, both of God the Father's becoming our God and our Father also; and so upon those double relations of God the Father to us doth bring down a legally formal right, upon which the Father, according to that legal right, should bestow all sorts of blessings upon us, which his grace makes him willing to bestow. And this right is harmoniously and rationally grounded, though God the Father must be acknowledged original of all, on the superadded constitution last mentioned—viz., That God the Father did also therewith make and ordain his Son Christ to bear the relation of our Lord. Which relation Jesus Christ hath also taken upon him that he is indeed our husband, a Lord and husband of us the elect, by the Father given unto Christ to that end, so to be constituted his Church universal of men, to be his lawful spouse. And this is such a privilege as the good angels have not, although in respect of his dominion and their service to him Christ is said to be their Lord also; yet this more near conjugal relation and band of us to him is not communicated unto angels, but imported in these words, 'Our Lord.' Which words have this further emphasis, that God hath made his Christ to be our Lord and husband; that is, he hath made us sons and daughters in law by adoption to himself, which is expressed in the next verse, and Christ also doth thereupon bless us. So as, in fine, we are both the legal children of God the Father and rightful spouse of Christ, which is a sense and interpretation of the words 'Our Lord,' which, as far as I yet know of, has not been given to any mere creatures besides ourselves. And this is therefore a consideration of great weight and endearment both of God and Christ to us; besides that it is one of the architectonical pillars and buttresses of this fabric, and of all the particulars of this model.

SERMON V.

According as he hath chosen us in him before the foundation of the world: that we should be holy, &c.—VER. 4, 5, &c.

IN the third verse the Apostle premiseth a general proposition, which he afterwards breaks into particulars. His scope being to shew how all blessings depend both upon God's election before all worlds, and how likewise upon Jesus Christ, 'who hath blessed us with all spiritual blessings in heavenly things (or places) in Christ;' so saith the third verse. If you observe it, in those words there is the *act* of blessing, 'Who hath blessed us;' and there are the *blessings* themselves wherewith we are blessed.

I shewed before, both out of the coherence of these words with those that follow, ver. 4, and other scriptures, that the time when God bestowed all these blessings upon us in Christ was when he chose us, even before all worlds. To which accords that in 2 Tim. i. 9, 'He hath called us according to his own purpose and grace, which was given us in Jesus Christ before the world began.' That *grace* there is all one with these *blessings* here, they being all wrapped up in that one expression of grace. And that which is called a *gift* there, is called a *blessing* us here. And if you look into Gen. xxvii. 37, you shall find that to bless is all one with to give, (though it be not actually given till afterwards.) For so we read, that when Isaac speaks to Esau of his blessing of Jacob, he says, 'I have made him thy lord, and all his brethren have I *given* to him for servants,'—Jacob was but a poor man then, but Isaac had blessed him, and so had given him all these things,—'and with corn and wine have I sustained him,' or 'supported him,' as it is in the margin.

Now, what is here in the third verse expressed in the general, the Apostle cometh to explain particularly in the verses following.

There are two things, as I said before, in that third verse. There is the act of blessing, and there are the blessings wherewith God hath blessed us. Answerably in this 4th and 5th verses, the Apostle distinctly mentioneth, first, the act of blessing to be in electing and predestinating of us, 'according as he hath elected us,' so ver. 4; 'and predestinated us,' so ver. 5. And then he mentions two particular blessings with which in election and predestination he hath blessed us, holiness, ver. 4, and adoption of children, ver. 5, and all this in Jesus Christ. And so you have the coherence of these words.

I. *According as he hath chosen us in him.*—Those words, 'he hath chosen us in him,' have bred more controversy than any so few words almost in the whole Bible, and do therefore require some time to open them.

First, some say this choosing us in him implies that God chooseth us, as foreseeing us to believe in Christ, because by faith it is we are in Christ, and by faith only. And therefore this phrase, choosing us in him, namely in Christ, noteth out the state of the person of a believer, that he is in Christ, or one with Christ by faith. And so in God's choice we are considered as believers, according to this opinion; and this is one great place alleged for election to be out of faith foreseen. For, say they, no man is in Christ till such time as he believeth; and God chooseth us in Christ; therefore he chooseth only foreseeing them to be believers on Christ.

In a word or two, to confute this opinion, that this should not be the meaning of the place; and to take only such arguments as the text itself affords, (for that is proper to an exposition,)—

First, therefore, If the meaning were that God chooseth men as believers in Christ, or, which cometh all to one, chooseth upon faith foreseen, he should not choose persons, but graces; the principal object in God's election should be propositions, not persons; whereas in this verse, and all the three next verses, the primary object is the persons of men, 'He hath chosen us in him,' and so on, ver. 5, 6. God chooseth not propositions, as 'He that believeth shall be saved.' That proposition indeed is the consequent of election, and so declared to us, because it makes election visible to us. God declareth that, and such like propositions, to be true; but still the object of his choice is the person; for it is out of love, pure love. Nor did Christ die for propositions, but for persons.

Secondly, Again, the apostle had said in the verse before, ver. 3, that 'God hath blessed us with all spiritual blessings in Christ;' and then he subjoins here, 'according as he hath chosen us in him,' so making this of election one instance of a 'spiritual blessing' in ver. 3. Now, I ask this question, Whether is a man blessed with faith in Christ, yea or no, as one of those blessings wherewith we are said to be blessed in him? If they say, Yes; then a man must be supposed to be in Christ before he hath faith, (in some sense or other,) for faith itself is one of the blessings comprehended in that *all* of blessings. And so, if all be given us *in Christ*, then faith also, as we are considered already chosen in Christ; yea, otherwise, at the time when we have the blessing of faith given to us, we are considered out of Christ actually when it is first given us, if that is it which makes us to be first in Christ, according to the apostle's scope of it there. There must therefore be some sense or other intended whereby we are in Christ before we have faith. That is the second argument.

And then, *thirdly*, the apostle saith, he chose us in him 'that we should be holy and without blame before him in love,' &c.; and the same reason will carry it that he as well intends that he chose us to this end, *that we should believe on him.* And the reason lies in this: look as he doth not choose because we are holy in love, or that he foreseeth we will be holy in love, but he chooseth us that we should be holy and without blame in love; in like manner it may be said, he chooseth unto faith, for there is the same reason of the one that there is of the other. Besides that faith may be considered as a part of sanctification, 1 John v. 1, 'Whosoever believeth that Jesus is the Christ, is born of God,' &c. In 2 Thess. ii. 13, both faith and holiness are put in the like relation as to election, and we are said to be ordained to the one, as to the other; and therefore if we are chosen *to be holy*, (as here,) as being a fruit of election, then *to believe* also is a like fruit of election; for observe but the words there, and compare them with these here. It is there said, 'He hath appointed us unto salvation through justification and belief of the truth.' Holiness, you see, and faith are put both together, as being graces unto which we are alike ordained. And Acts xiii. 48, 'As many as were ordained to eternal life, believed.' So that this is not the meaning of the words; and that is the first interpretation.

The Popish divines and interpreters give another exposition: 'He hath chosen us in Christ'—that is, say they, for the merit's sake of Christ, foreseeing his death and passion. And yet the best of them that say it, put but a *forte*, an 'it may be,' upon it, as I remember Suarez doth.

Now this cannot be the meaning neither. We read, indeed, that we have redemption through the blood of Christ: so ver. 7, 'In whom we have redemption through his blood, and the forgiveness of sins.' But we nowhere read that we have election through the blood of Christ; no, not in the whole Book of God. Why? what is the reason of it? Because election is the first foundation of our salvation—it is the first act of God's going forth in intentions to save us, and hath no cause but the 'pleasure of his will,' so the text saith, ver. 5; and 'the praise of the glory of his grace,' so ver. 6. Hence, therefore, although the merits of Christ are the cause of our salvation, yet they are not the cause of our being ordained to salvation. They are the cause that purchaseth all things decreed unto us; but they are not the cause that first moved God to decree these things unto us; for if they were, there should be a derogation from God's free grace in the first act of it—he should not be free in it; for merit, you know, hath an obligation in it. Had God chosen us for Christ's merits, his election had not been of free grace. But having chosen us, and that out of his free grace, he ordained these merits as the cause of our salvation; which being thus a free gift of grace themselves, and the fruit of his grace, and nowise the cause or motive thereof, therefore now salvation, though merited, cometh to be altogether of free grace, because the foundation of it is such. And so you have this second interpretation taken away.

There is a third interpretation which some of our divines do give—

As, 1. That we are said to be elected in Christ—that is, to be in Christ in time to come. We are not elected, say they, as being in Christ when elected, or by election put into Christ, but elected to be in Christ in the fulness of time. And therefore—

2. They join this 'elected in Christ' with the words that follow, 'that we should be holy, and without blame before him in love.' So as the meaning of this interpretation tends only to this, that Jesus Christ is the great instrument to convey all the blessings to us which God hath decreed for us; that he is the great means indeed that God hath ordained, and the cause of all things that God hath appointed us unto. But he hath nothing to do with what concerneth the act of election itself. This 'in him' hath not relation so much to the act of God's choosing, as either to the blessings to be conveyed by him, which God hath chosen us unto; or else to shew that our future being in him is the *terminus* of that act of election. And so the whole that this place holds forth is no more in effect but what that in 1 Thess. v. 9 says, where you read that 'God hath appointed us to obtain salvation by our Lord Jesus Christ.' Mark it, the apostle there says, not that Jesus Christ, as God-man, hath any influence into the act of ordaining, but comes in only as a means subserving that act, to accomplish and bring about those ends which God in his decrees did pitch upon. The salvation God appointed us unto, he ordained us to obtain by Jesus Christ. So, then, 'he hath elected us in Christ to be holy'—that is, say they, in the fulness of time to be in him, and to be made holy in him, and he is to be the cause of our holiness. This is the other sense of his choosing us in Christ.

And, to explain their meaning, in the decrees of election there are two things to be considered—

1. *The act itself*, which is immanent, and remaineth in God himself, and floweth from himself from all eternity.

2. *The terminus, or the things that are decreed to be,* or to be brought to pass. Or, to express it in the same terms which I used and observed out of the third verse, there is the *act of blessing* itself, and there are the *blessings* wherewith we are blessed.

Now, when it is here said, that we are elected in Christ, that same 'in him' refers not, say they, to the act itself, as if it had any dependency on him, but only has relation to the things ordained by that act. And so they say that Christ is the foundation of election in this sense, that the *terminus electionis,* the things unto which we are elected, he is appointed in election to be the cause of. In a word, that God hath ordained that we should have them all in Christ, but *hath not in Christ ordained us, and them to us.*

So that now this is the great and universally-acknowledged glory given to Jesus Christ on all hands, that though God wholly and entirely reserveth to himself the glory of the act of choosing us, yet all the things that he chooseth us to, his Son (as God-man) is the cause of. He cometh in between election and the things, and we are ordained to have them all in him, even to obtain faith, grace, heaven, and all in Christ, as the deserver and purchaser of them. And it is a great glory that is given to our Lord and Saviour Jesus Christ, that God should set him up as the great engine to work all by. This, I say, is the third interpretation.

But though this be most true, and is one great part of the meaning of these words, yet this is not all, or the whole, as I shall prove by these three or four reasons; which, when I have done, I will shew you what I apprehend is to make up the full and clear scope and meaning of them. I shall only mention what reasons the text affordeth.

First, therefore, if you interpret the words, 'he hath chosen us in him,' that is, *to be* in him, you put in 'to be,' which is not in the text. Whereas this is the plain reading of the words, 'he hath chosen us in him;' and therefore if there be a sense wherein it may be absolutely said, as referring to the act of election itself, that we were chosen in him, without putting in any such words, it would be much fairer.

Secondly, it is said, 'he chose us in him before the foundation of the world.' Who, therefore, would not refer this 'in him' unto 'before the foundation of the world,' as well as that the act of choosing us to have been before the foundation of the world: and so God chose us then in him? Whereas if that had been the meaning, he only chose us to be in Christ in future times which were to come after the foundation of the world, the expression 'in him' should have come in after those words, 'the foundation of the world,' as well as the thing itself doth. But 'he chose us in him before the foundation of the world;' so as 'in him' seemeth to refer as well to 'before the foundation of the world,' as to God's choosing us before the foundation of the world.

Thirdly, whereas it is said, that 'in him' referreth to the words following, 'that we should be holy and without blame,' &c., we see here is a mighty *chasma,* a great gulf between these two, 'choosing us in him,' and 'that we should be holy:' for here is 'before the foundation of the world' comes between. If, indeed, the Apostle had said, 'he hath chosen us before the foundation of the world, in him that we should be holy,' &c., or 'that we should be holy in him,' there had then been some colour for it. But he saith plainly, 'he hath chosen us in him before the foundation of the world.' 'In him' cometh in before 'the foundation of the world.' So that it seemeth this 'in him' referreth to the act of choosing.

Fourthly, and then again there is this fourth great reason for it: he had said in the third verse, 'he hath blessed us with all spiritual blessings in Christ,' and then in the fourth and fifth verses he instanceth in election and predestination. *Sicut elegit*, as if he had said, for example's sake, or for explanation's sake, to give you an instance, 'according as he hath elected us in him.' Now, mark it by this coherence: either election is taken for the act of blessing us, as I said before, or for a blessing wherewith God hath blessed us. And if either of both, it is enough for the thing in hand; it must be in Christ, and this before the foundation of the world. And so we were elected in Christ then, as well as justified in Christ in the fulness of time.

And then, *Fifthly*, I find that other scriptures do back this interpretation, that 'in him' should have relation not only to the things decreed us, as the cause of them, but have reference to the act itself of choosing. And this not only that scripture I before mentioned, 2 Tim. i. 9, 'He hath given us grace in Christ before the world was,' but also that in the third of this Epistle, ver. 11, 'according to the eternal purpose which he purposed in Christ.' Mark it: 'in Christ' cometh in that place not only for the thing purposed, but in relation to the purpose itself; and this purpose is eternal, 'according to the eternal purpose which he purposed in Christ.' So that 'choosing us in him,' the meaning is not only, *to be in him* in the fulness of time, or that he should be the cause of all the things unto which we are chosen only; but the choice itself, in some sense or other, is in him,—that is, the act itself,—'according to the eternal purpose which he purposed in Christ.'

And then, for those places that are quoted to interpret it, which I before mentioned, as that in 1 Thess. v. 9, 'He hath appointed us to obtain salvation by our Lord Jesus Christ,' which, say they, is all one with this of the Apostle here, 'he hath elected us in him,' &c.; it is plainly not all one, and that for two reasons. For, 1. in that place of the Thessalonians there cometh in, 'to obtain salvation by our Lord Jesus Christ;' but not so here. Had he said so here, that 'he hath chosen us to obtain election,' or 'to be holy in Christ,' then I confess it had been plain; but he only saith 'he hath chosen us in him,' and then cometh in, 'that we should be holy before him in love;' and those words, 'before the foundation of the world,' come between both.

And then, 2. there is a great deal of difference between God's doing a thing *in* Christ and *through* Christ, ἐν Χριστῷ and διὰ τὸν Χριστὸν. It is Zanchie's observation, that when God is said to do a thing in Christ, it usually notes out some one of those immanent acts of God's towards us, that passed between him and Christ for us when they were alone, before we existed, and Jesus Christ was a Common Person representing us all, and God gave all to Christ for us; as it is said, 'the grace that was given us in Christ before the world was.' But the things that God doth 'through Christ,' which is the phrase in the Thessalonians, are usually some transient acts of God's towards us, or those things which he actually performeth and applieth to us through Christ. So that God redeemeth through Christ, justifieth through Christ, and saveth through Christ; but he chooseth in Christ. So that to choose in him, is not all one with that which the Apostle saith, 'he hath ordained us to obtain salvation through Christ.'

SECTION.

But now the question is, In what further sense we are said to be chosen in him; so that the act of choosing should be referred to 'in him,' and we to be in him at our election; and what subserviency Christ, considered as God-man, should be of to the act itself of electing us.

I shall endeavour to answer to, and to explain this, first, *negatively;* secondly, *affirmatively*. I will shew you, 1. What influence or subserviency he hath not; and, 2. I will shew you what he hath.

1. I will shew you what he hath not. He was not the cause of God's electing us, for the Apostle, in the 9th verse of this first chapter, saith that it was 'according to the good pleasure of his will, which he had purposed in himself.' What is the cause of all God's purposes towards us? Himself. There is no other cause. And in the same verse it is also added, 'according to his good pleasure,' &c. God, as he is the first being, so he and his own will are the first movers of himself. So that this, 'he chose us in Christ,' imports not that Jesus Christ was the cause of our predestination, (taking him as God-man, as here he is meant.) And I will give you this great reason for it; for he could not be the cause of our predestination who himself was predestinated. In 1 Pet. i. 20, it is plainly said of Christ, that he was pre-ordained before the world was founded. He himself was chosen as well as we; therefore he could not be the cause of our election. And both he and we being elected by one simple and entire act, the predestination, therefore, of one could not be the cause of the predestination of the other. And as Christ was not the cause of election for the substance of the act, so nor was he the cause of it for the persons elected. Jesus Christ, as God-man and Mediator, did not choose so much as one man. It was God that elected all those that are elected. 'Thine they were,' says Christ to his Father, 'and thou gavest them me.' And it were a much more fond conceit to think that God chose such to be saved as he foresaw the human nature of Christ would love and choose. This were to make the Divine will conformed to that of the human nature; whereas, 'Not my will, but thine be done,' said Christ unto God the Father.

This, therefore, is not the meaning, that Christ as God-man is the cause of the act of our election, as it was in God.

2. Affirmatively. The meaning is this, that Jesus Christ in election was the Head of the elect. He was from the first considered and ordained by God as a Common Person, to represent us. He undertook for us then, and so in him we were chosen, as in a Head. This is the sense that holy Baines giveth of it: To note out, saith he, the order of election, namely, that Christ was chosen first as a Head, and we in him; though both at the same time, yet, for priority of nature, he as a Common Person and a Head was first elected, and we in him.

For the clear understanding of this, I will, *first*, give you two cautions, to prevent a misunderstanding of it; and, *secondly*, explain how it might be that Christ should be considered as a Common Person in the act of election.

First, *For the cautions:*—

1. Learn to distinguish between being elected *with Christ*, and being elected *in Christ*. To be elected with Christ, is to be elected at the same time he was, for matter of time, for all was from eternity; but to be elected in Christ is with this difference, that Christ at God's first act of election was considered as a Common Person, a Head and Root, and we all as in him. This is common both to Christ and to us, that we were elected with him, and he with us, for matter of time. But this is proper to Christ, that we were elected in him, he not in us.

To explain this to you both out of Scripture, by his type Adam, and also by a similitude, that may convey it to your understanding.

First, by Scripture. So, Gen. i. 27, 'God created man, in his own image created he him (that is, Adam); male and female created he them.'

God in creating Adam created all mankind, as in blessing Adam he blessed all mankind. Yea, the creation of Adam was all the creation that the rest of mankind had. For though they exist by generation successively, yet in him were they created virtually, and then only. Thus in choosing Christ, God looked upon him as a Common Person, as a second Adam, and chose us in him. And therefore you shall find in 1 Cor. xv. 47, that God speaks of Christ and of Adam as if there had been but those two men in the world. 'The first man,' says he, 'and the second man.' Was there but a first man and a second man? Yes; but these two men stood for all the rest. Or, in a word, Jesus Christ was not only a Common Person in his dying for us, but in his being chosen also, (as I shall shew by and by,) and so we were elected in him. This is the meaning of it.

For the similitude which I spake of, I shall take it from amongst men. Suppose that a kingdom were now to be new set up, and a king to be chosen, and they meant so to choose him as they would choose his posterity, his eldest sons that should be after him, and that for ever. Now when they have made this covenant with this first man, the first king: We take you for our king, and your eldest son, and the eldest sons of all your posterity after you to the end of the world. In this case it may be said, that at the same time they chose his sons *with him;* and not so only, but that they chose his sons *in him* also. Why? Because he was the first, and they are considered as in his loins. What saith Christ? 'Here am I, and the children that thou hast given me.' And so God said to him, Here thou art, and in thee all my elect. I appoint thee as a root to as many men as I choose together with thee; but I choose them *in thee.* When God first said, Let there be a tree; for order of time both root and branches came up together, the branches were created with the root, and the root with the branches; yet the branches in the root, and not the root in the branches. Boast not thyself, as if thou wert chosen alone, and he alone, and that then thou wert given to him to be in him for time to come. No, that place I may allude unto in Rom. xi. 18, 'Boast not thyself, for thou bearest not the root, but the root thee;'—Thou bearest not Christ, he was not chosen in thee, but thou in him, and for him.

2. The second caution is, that you take heed how you understand it, as if that Christ alone were distinctly chosen, and that our persons were not as distinctly chosen too. Yes, both Christ and we too were distinctly and particularly thought of, and so individually elected. The meaning, I say, of this our being elected in him, is not as if he only had been distinctly and by name chosen, and we all but confusedly, and in gross, and as in his election only. God did not choose in the general, as a kingdom doth choose the children of a king that come after him, and are involved in him, in a general notion only, so as their distinct choice is of the king himself alone. No, the Scripture saith, 'God knoweth who are his;' he knoweth the very persons fully and particularly; yea, and distinctly viewed them when he elected them. And notwithstanding he thus chose us as distinct persons from Christ, yet still our election was in Christ. As suppose a kingdom, that chooseth a king and his children, should know by way of prophecy what manner of men all his sons to come would be, and how many he should have, and yet should choose him and them; though, I say, they did distinctly know all their persons and natures, yet still they chose them in him as the head of the family. Now, Christ is the head of all the family of them that are named, both in heaven and earth.

The second thing to be spoken to is, *How Jesus Christ may be rightly con-*

sidered to be a Common Person when he was chosen.—Some divines yield that he was chosen to be a Common Person when he should take up man's nature, and that we were chosen then to be by him represented. They acknowledge that he was a Common Person in his death, representing us, and is now a Common Person in heaven, and sits there as in our stead, representing us. But, say they, in the act of choosing, how should he be considered as a Common Person, in that he did not then exist as God-man? He might indeed be ordained to be a Common Person after he did exist as God-man, but how in election was he, or could he be such, he being as then only the Son of God, and not man?

To solve this difficulty, lay we out these few things together:—

1. That the person of the Son of God, who was ordained this Common Person, he was with God then, he was then existent. So, Prov. viii. 30, 'Then,' says Wisdom, namely Christ, 'I was by him,' &c. And the Evangelist John saith, 'He was in the beginning with God,' that is, from everlasting (as I shall shew afterwards.)

2. This Son of God that then existed (consider him as one that was to become man) was the object of election, as well as the manhood which was chosen to become one with God. That Divine person was, by an act and decree of God's will, pitched upon and singled out to assume our nature, and to sustain the person of a Head before God in the meanwhile.

3. At, or in the act of election, this Son of God, as he actually existed at the passing of that act of election upon himself, so he actually and solemnly undertook to be a Head and Common Person representing us, and to that end to assume our nature. And this is in order of nature to be supposed before our election, though coexistent together from eternity.

4. Upon this he was in repute such with God the Father. He was a Common Person in God's esteem, and that justly. So, Prov. viii. 23, 'I (namely, Christ) was set up from everlasting, ere ever the earth was,' &c.; I was set up, that is, in esteem with God for such. Now this cannot be understood of Christ, as he was the second Person only. But God did set him up from the beginning, as bearing and sustaining the person of God-man, (to which manhood he was chosen and undertook to assume,) and as a Head to his members, before God, who reputed him such. And of him considered as such are those words spoken; for so only he is called Wisdom, as there he is. For Christ is not called the Wisdom of God essentially taken, for that is one of his attributes, and not a person. But he is called God's Wisdom *manifestativè*, that is, as ordained to manifest God's wisdom unto us, he being to be 'God manifest in the flesh.' And such a person or relation as he then thus actually undertook, such did God then, and from that time, repute him to be, and actually entitled him by, as between himself and his Son. Therefore, in John xvii. 5, (observe the phrase there,) 'Glorify me,' says Christ to God, 'with the glory which I had with thee before the world was.' What glory was that? He doth not mean his glory as he was simply second Person, because he had that glory now, and therefore needed not to beg it. Nay, he could not beg it, it was too much for him so to beg, for so he is equal with God. Therefore it must be the glory of the mediatorship. 'Which I had before the world was;' that is, in thy repute; thou accountedst me thus and thus glorious in respect of the glory ordained me by my undertaking to be man and the Mediator of the Church. And this is plain, if you compare it with ver. 24, for there he speaks of that glory which was given him, which can be no other than the glory of the mediatorship.

So then, Jesus Christ, the second Person, being existent, and undertaking to be a Common Person and a Mediator for men, God did reckon him as such. He was in his account, at the choosing of him, as a Common Person and Head, and as a Mediator, too. And, indeed, there was this great advantage of our Mediator's being God, that thereby he was not only present at, and privy to the making of all God's decrees ; but was also by, to undertake for all that concerned his part in it which God should decree, and to enter upon the title and relation of our Head and Mediator then. And there is this reason why Christ must needs have been a Head to his members before his assuming our nature, or ascending up to heaven, (which I see not how it can be answered :) because otherwise Jesus Christ had not been a Head to the fathers under the Old Testament ; for he had not as then taken a human nature ; and yet was actually a Common Person for forgiving their sins, by virtue of that atonement he had engaged to perform for them ; which was such in God's repute existing before him in Job's time, 'Deliver him, I have found a ransom,' Job xxxiii. 24. And upon the account thereof God did as really and actually forgive the sins of the Old Testament as he did, Rom. iii. 25. Now, if he was a Head then, and they actually members of him, then he might be so, virtually and representatively, from everlasting, through his undertaking of it ; and this in as just a sense as he is said to be the 'Lamb slain from the beginning of the world.'

Why may not the promise of the second Person, then passed unto God, give as full, yea a fuller subsistence of those things which God decreed and which he undertook for, before God his Father, as God's promise, which was written in the Old Testament, gave to the fathers' faith then, in respect unto which Christ was as then already slain? God the Father, who was then present, had a certain assurance that Christ his Son, that gave his promise for performance, would and should perform it ; and Christ, as Son of God, who was God, having promised, I may say of both, that Christ's word then was as good as his bond, and the Father's assurance that he should perform it as good as if he had already seen it done, and his calling things that are not, as certain as if they were. And I may apply one and the same effect of the Apostle Paul equally to both. If of God the Father giving Christ his promise before the world began, it must be said, 'God that cannot lie,'—and so it is, and was as firm and sure as if done and fulfilled, and this because he is God, as Tit. i. 2, it is expressly there said, 'in hope of eternal life, which God, that cannot lie, promised before the world began,'—I may invert it, and say for the same reason, that that promise which Christ made the Father to undertake the mediatorship in man's nature before the world was, and to do all he did in the fulness of time ; that Christ's promise then must have been, and was reputed as sure and steadfast by God the Father as if it had been already done. And God the Father might as certainly build upon it to do anything that was to be done, depending upon what Christ undertook to do then, as if Christ had already performed all that promise and undertaking; and this upon as equal reasons, for Christ was God then, as well as the Father, and could no more lie than he ; for they both are equals, John x. 30, and all the terms of both sides are equal, 'before the world was,' &c. I might likewise urge that which followeth in the 10th verse of this 1st chapter to the Ephesians; there you have an ἀνακεφαλάιωσις, a gathering together again unto one head, both of Jew and Gentile. Why a gathering together unto one head? (for so the word signifieth.) One reason may be, because in election they were in Christ as a Head before. But I leave the discussing that till I come to the 10th verse.

So that, to conclude this point, that we are said to be 'elected in Christ,' the meaning of it is summed up in these particulars:—

1. That Jesus Christ was the Head of election, and of the elect of God; and so in order of nature elected first, though in order of time we were elected with him. In the womb of election he, the Head, came out first, and then we, the members. He is therefore said in predestination to be the first-born of all his brethren: Rom. viii. 29, 'Who hath predestinated us,' says the Apostle, 'to be conformed to the image of his Son, that he might be the first-born among many brethren.' Nay, in Col. i. 15, he is said to be the 'first-born of every creature.' How is that spoken of him? I have shewed it elsewhere to be plainly meant of Christ as God-man. Otherwise he is not said to be the first-born in respect of every creature. God would never have condescended so low, speaking of the eternal generation of his Son, as to compare him therein with creatures. But, saith he, he is the first-born of every creature, and 'the Head of the body, the Church,' as it followeth, ver. 18.

2. That God in that act of election looked not at us apart and singly as in ourselves, so as by one act to choose us, and by another act to give us to Christ. But, as we say of the soul, *infundendo creatur, et creando infunditur*, it is by one and the same act of God's both created and infused into the body, and so subsists not one moment apart; so God in the act of choosing us gave us to Christ, and in giving us to Christ he chose us. And thus, he never considering us apart, but as members of Christ and given to him in the very act of choosing; hence our very choice itself is said to be 'in him.' And so, on the other side, in the first view and purpose God took up concerning Christ, and in electing him, he looked not at him apart, as a single person in himself, but as a head to us his body, chosen in him, and with him. So that the meaning is not, that Jesus Christ, the second Person in the Trinity, was chosen by one act to be man, and then to be a Common Person by another. But at the very same instant that he was chosen the one, he was chosen the other; under that very consideration, to be a Common Person; which he then actually undertook. It was in this as in the creation of Adam, his shadow; who, when he was first made, was not made as a single man, he was made a living soul, 1 Cor. xv. 45. What is that? To be a public person, to convey life to others, as well as to have life personally in himself. That is the meaning, as appears by the following words, 'the last Adam,' that is, Christ, 'was made a quickening spirit;' that is, not to himself, but to others. So that the very first view that God in election took of Christ, was not of him only as a single person considered, but as a Common Person representing others. In a word, as in the womb head and members are not conceived apart, but together, as having relation each to other, so were we and Christ, as making up one mystical body unto God, formed together in that eternal womb of election. So that God's choice did completely terminate itself on him and us; us with him, and yet us in him; he having the priority to be constituted a Common Person and root to us: for that is the relation wherein we stand unto him, and in that relation we were first chosen.

3. And then the third thing which this phrase implieth, and which will make up the meaning of it, is this: that as God's decree gave us a subsisting beyond things merely possible to be,—that is, which God could make, but never decreed to make,—so we, by reason of this election of us with Christ, in this transaction, in this respect we came to have a further *representative being* and existence in Christ from everlasting, by virtue of his being then

considered as a common Head. So that in this did Jesus Christ subserve God's decree. I will, saith Christ, represent them; they are all virtually in me; and do thou, O Father, reckon them as having a subsistence in me. Jesus Christ, I say, did give thereby a subsistence to us, such as Adam, when he began to be, did give unto all mankind; they were all virtually in him. Now, make but the supposition that Adam had existed from everlasting, as Christ did, (the person, I mean, who took this title and relation on him,) and then how this might be is easily understood.

I will only add to this last thing mentioned the great ends and advantages that this subserviency of Christ unto the act of election was of, in his actual undertaking to be a root of a new ordained being to us, at that instant.

1. By means of this, our virtual or representative subsisting, or being looked at as in Christ, and as one with him, in and from God's first choosing us,—by means of this, God could then from everlasting make a covenant of grace, and also make that covenant sure unto us. A covenant, we know, is an agreement between two parties upon terms. Now, we then not existing in our single selves, though God might have taken up a purpose to do this or that for us, and in us, yet it could not be called a covenant unless we were some way extant before him; and the covenant of grace should otherwise not have been a covenant until men did believe. To help this, therefore, God chose us in Christ, and he represented us, standing before God in our stead, and offering to undertake to work in us all the terms that God should require on our part; as this here, 'to be holy before him in love,' &c. And so a covenant was as truly struck between God and us, through Christ's representing us, as the covenant of works was between God and us, as considered in Adam. And hence it is that Christ, by the prophet Isaiah, is called 'our covenant.'

2. Hence, likewise, secondly, it comes to pass that God might, upon this covenant, then give and bestow upon us all spiritual blessings, as we were thus considered in Christ. Had God chosen us in ourselves only and apart, then indeed he might have purposed them all unto us, but could not have been said, as then, to have *given* them unto us, or to have blessed us with them as then. But when as through Christ's actual undertaking this relation as then unto us, that we came to be considered in him as a Common Person, God might in him bless us with all these spiritual blessings, in the sense before given; even as Adam was created a Common Person, and so we considered virtually and representatively in him, God might and did bless us with all earthly blessings in him, as we before observed. God did purpose them unto Adam and us afore, by a bare decree, but could not have been said to bless us with them, unless he who should represent us was himself existent, and so we virtually and representatively in him, which was not until his creation; I speak of Adam. But now the Son of God, then actually existing, did voluntarily, and by God's appointment, personate us, that thereby all blessings, and the promises of them, might be virtually given us, by being then given to him for us, as that phrase, 2 Tim. i. 9, imports, 'the grace that was given us in Christ Jesus before the world began.' Even as a grandfather may give a portion to his son's child yet unborn, by giving it to his son, whom he makes his heir and executor—he personally subsisting before, and his child in him.

3. The third advantage is, that hereby our salvation had a sure foundation given it in election, not only in God's eternal love and purpose, (the foundation of the Lord remains sure, he knows who are his,) but further also, this

his first choice of us was a founding us on Christ, and in and together with choosing us, a setting us into him, so as then to be represented by him. So that now we are to run the same fortune, if I may so speak, with Christ himself for ever, our persons being made mystically one with his, and he a Common Person to us in election, as Adam was in his creation. Other men, as likewise the angels that fell, were ordained to be *in themselves*,—to stand or fall by themselves,—but we were, by a choice act of God's, culled out of the lump, and chosen in Christ, and not in ourselves apart. Hence they (the other mentioned) stood upon their own bottom, and in a single and naked relation unto God; and so, God dealing with them but as mere single creatures, according to that law that passeth between the Creator and the single creatures, they fell and perished. But we were considered in Christ from the first, and therefore, though we fall, we shall rise again in him and by him; for he is a Common Person for us, and to stand for us, and is for ever to look to us, to bring us to all that God ordained us unto; and so this foundation remains sure. We are chosen in Christ, and therefore are in as sure a condition, as for final perishing, as Christ himself.

4. There is a fourth end or subserviency of it, that God, looking on us thus represented in Christ, and bearing that relation to him, and he to us, God and Christ together might from that time delight in us, as you have it Prov. viii., and have a complacency between themselves beforehand in us. But of this when we come to the sixth verse.

There are two other things that go to make up this interpretation of these words, 'chosen in him,' yet fuller, which are added by some. I shall but name them now:—

1. That we were chosen in Christ as the pattern unto whom we should be conformed. God set him up as the pattern, and drew us, as so many little pictures, by him and his image. 'He hath predestinated us to be conformed to the image of his Son,' Rom. viii. 29. That is the first—'in him, as the pattern of us.

2. 'In him;' say some, this phrase noteth out *habitudinem causæ finalis;* said Anselm, long since, that he was the end of all those whom God chose. And therefore, whereas some copies have it ἐν αὐτῷ, others have it barely αὐτῷ, which accordingly may be read, 'to him. I shall meet with these two in the next verse, therefore I will no longer insist on them here.

I will now give you (for all this is but a doctrinal discourse to open the words) some useful observations.

Obs. 1.—Learn to give Jesus Christ his full honour, which God his Father hath given him. It is a mighty honour, that he is the cause of all the grace and glory that you have, and shall have. But that he should be the common Head, set up in election, too, before the world was, this honoureth him much more—this setteth another crown upon his head; and it is pity he should lose any honour that may be given him. Saith he, John xvii. 5, 'Glorify thou me with thy own self, with the glory which I had with thee before the world was'—that is, that glory which then, considered as God-man, I had in thy repute and estimation, and which thou thyself gavest me between me and thee, and which thou respectedst me for; accordingly, even as bearing that person of Head and Mediator, which, ere it be long, I shall visibly wear in heaven, give it me now in the sight of angels and men.

Now, since God thus glorified Christ then, do you likewise glorify him in your hearts with that glory which he had before the world was; part of which you have heard what it was, namely, that which is proper to the text, (for it would take up many sermons to lay it all open.) Men are afraid to derogate from God, whilst they give to Christ; but if we make God the sole cause of predestination, there is no danger of giving this honour unto Christ in the act of choosing us, that God (as the text hath it) should choose us in him. This is the Father's honour, that his will was the womb wherein lay both Christ and we too. But this is the Son's honour, that the Father set him up from everlasting as a Common Person for us to be chosen in him. He chose us in him, and never once considered us out of him.

2. *Observation*, or rather *Instruction.*—Let God the Father have the glory of the act, in that he is the fountain, the first mover in, and the sole cause of it. His will and good pleasure did cast it, for the substance of it, and singled out our persons, and ordained Christ a Head, and us in him. And remember, that as this election is unto this great privilege, to be in Christ, and one with him, (of all the highest, and fundamental to all other;) so that it is election, a choice, wherein others were left. God passed by, not only multitudes of persons whom he could have made, but did not, but also a vast number of those whom he did ordain to be. And were you so chosen in Christ, as that God never purposed you a being but as in Christ, and then gave you this subsistence in Christ, never casting a thought upon you out of him; then reckon of no other being but what you have in Christ. Reckon not of what you have in honours, or what you are in greatness or parts, but reckon of what you were in him before this world was, and of all the spiritual blessings wherewith he then blessed you; and likewise of what you are now in him, by an actual union, as then by a virtual and representative one. 'Of him,' namely God, 'you are in Christ,' saith the Apostle, in the forenamed place, 1 Cor. i. 30. Consider but the reference of the words to what was said before, and you will find that there is no being true and real to be valued by us but in Christ. 'Of him you *are*.' That phrase hath an emphasis in it; it is *verbum substantivum*, relating to other things that seem to have a being, but *are not*. So ver. 27, 'God hath chosen the weak things of the world to confound the mighty; things which are not to bring to nought the things which are.' There are other things spoken of, that 'are,' and 'are mighty,' and great things in the world's eye, as honours, wisdom, strength, &c., ver. 26; but glory not of these, says the apostle, as having any being. 'Of him you are in Christ,' 'that, according as it is written, He that glorieth let him glory in the Lord,' ver. 31. Here is your being, and all the being you have; and, says he, reckon of no being else; glory in nothing, but only in this, that you are in Christ. For God chose you in him; the being you had was in him before the world was.

And so much for that, which indeed is the greatest difficulty I am like to meet with in this chapter, or in this epistle.

II. Now, *in the second place*, as it is said, God hath chosen us in Christ, so the time when is specified next, *Before the foundation of the world.*

There are two senses which divines, with whom I have met, do give of these words. And I love still to give the largest sense that will hold.

First, say they, 'before the foundation of the world' signifies as much as from eternity. Why? Because before the world was, there was nothing but eternity. If you look past the world, you put your head up into eternity. And to make good this interpretation they cite John i. 1, where, when the Evangelist would express that Christ was eternal, he says, 'he was in the beginning.' And if he were in the beginning, at that very instant when the world was made, certainly he was from everlasting. Therefore, further to confirm this, Prov. viii. 23, Wisdom says, 'I was set up from everlasting;

from the beginning, ere ever the earth was.' These three phrases, you see, are equivalent, and all one.

The second interpretation that I have met withal, in the works of some who are yet alive, and which Mr Baines likewise hath, is this, that those words do note out the order of God's decree; namely, that God chose us in Christ in his own purpose, before the foundation of the world was laid in his decree or purpose; speaking herein of God after the manner of men. Not but that God thought of all at once; for all his works are known to him from the beginning. But because he did subordinate one thing to another; and so he did intend and make the world for his elect; and in that sense he chose Christ before them, and them before the world. They were 'set up,' as the phrase is, first and primarily, in his aim and intention, and the world subordinately unto them.

And there is a reason or two for this interpretation; for otherwise, where it is said, 1 Pet. i. 20, that God did 'pre-ordain Christ before the foundation of the world,' if the meaning were only this, before the world began to be, and not before the world was in God's purpose too, then there were no special thing said of God's ordaining Christ: for in that sense he likewise ordained the world before the world was; that is, he pre-ordained it to be ere it did actually exist. But, say they, this phrase importeth a special love from God unto Christ, in that he thought of him before he thought of the world, and ordained the world merely for him.

The other reason is, that otherwise it were incongruous to compare things in a like state with things in a different state. When therefore the Apostle speaks of God's decrees, and of our election in comparison of the world, he means the world as it also was in God's decrees. And perhaps it may be one reason why the word 'predestination' and 'foreknowledge' are used in Scripture only of God's decrees about man, and not about the world. I shall only add a scripture for the confirmation of this, 1 Cor. iii. 22, 'Whether Paul, or Apollos, or Cephas, or the world; all are yours, and you are Christ's, and Christ is God's.' Mark here the order of things; God ordained Christ for himself, 'Christ is God's.' He ordained you for Christ, 'you are Christ's.' And he ordained the world for you, 'Apollos, Cephas, and the world, all are yours.' So that the world was ordained both for you, and for Christ, and for God himself also.

I will give you an observation or two upon this place, and so pass on to the next.

Obs. 1.—First, therefore. If it be taken thus, that God chose you from eternity, you see then that God's love is everlasting. Do you therefore value it by the eternity of it, as Christ doth, John xvii. 24, 'Thou,' says he, 'lovedst me before the foundation of the world.' Christ, you see, makes a great matter of it, and why should not we? If a man were in love with a maid when she was a child, and his love towards her grew up together with her, it endears his love the more unto her. It is true of love, as it is of wine, that the older it is the better it is.

Obs. 2.—Secondly. Let God's love have the same valuation with you that the love of God himself had of you. You see, according to the interpretation given, that he chose you before he purposed to make the world; he preferred you to all the world. We speak not, as I said before, of the priority of time,—for all things came up at once before God,—but of what his aim and intention primarily pitched upon. The world was but cast in, as he saith, Matt. vi. 33. All other things shall be superadded. Have you the same valuation of God, and of his love? This David had. 'Whom,' says he, 'have I in heaven but thee? and there is none to me on earth in comparison of thee.' Value God and his love more than all the world, though there were millions of them. He valued you before the world, and therefore is beforehand with you in his love. He not only loved you from everlasting, (whereas your love is but of yesterday,) but in the valuation of it, he loved you before all worlds, and preferred you to all worlds: though you loved the world first, before you loved him. 'If any man love the world, the love of the Father is not in him,' 1 John ii. 15. Why is not the love of the Father in him? Because the Father loved us before the world was. And were a man's heart taken with the love of the Father, certainly he would prefer it before all the world; for the love of God the Father preferred him before all the world. Overlook we this world, no matter what becometh of it, or of us in it. We look not, says the Apostle, at things temporal. Look we to the other world, unto which God hath chosen and predestinated us.

Obs. 3.—A third observation or instruction. See the reason why all things in this world do further God's decree of election. 'All things work together for good to them that love God.' In God's purpose and intention you came first up before the world, as you may see in that Christian inventory, 1 Cor. iii. 22, (the place before cited;) all things are yours, Paul, Apollos, Cephas, the world, things present, things to come, life, death, and all are yours. And good reason why. God chose you before them all, and so plotted the business, that all things in this world should be so marshalled as to further and subserve the decree of election. He appointed that thou shouldst be poor, another rich; thou low, another honourable; one man to be deformed, another beautiful; one man to have these and these crosses and afflictions in the world, and another few or none at all. And all this variety is to further their salvation in a several way; all is subordinated unto election. God ordained our being and condition of living in this world, in subordination to that other world. James saith he chose the poor of this world. But how? Not as first foreseeing them poor, and so pitching on them for salvation; but having chosen their persons nakedly and simply considered, he ordained they should for the most part be poor, so to glorify his grace the more, (which is the end of election.) And so he ordained whose children we should be, which yet is the original of our being. This was not plotted first, and then we chosen to salvation; but we were chosen to salvation, and then God allotted or destinated the several times we should live in, who should be our parents, and what our conditions; and all as means subordinate to election, so to illustrate his grace the more. And therefore care not what thy parentage or what thy condition is here. Thou wert by God considered as that which he meant to make thee, even a brave and glorious creature, ere ever the consideration of what thy condition here should be came in; this estate of thine here being but the way unto that thy country and inheritance.

Obs. 4.—In the fourth place. See here the reason why nothing in this world can separate a man from the love of God. What says the Apostle, Rom. viii. 38? He makes a mighty challenge, he challengeth angels and men, dominions and principalities, &c., all things in this world, and in the world to come: and 'I am persuaded,' says he, 'that nothing shall be able to separate us from the love of God.' Why? He loved us before all worlds. That is a good reason. Should my covenant, says God, of night and day be lost? Let this world run into confusion; let heaven and earth cease to keep their laws; yet my covenant with you shall not cease. Why?

I chose you before all worlds. Here is the reason: 'Hills shall remove, and mountains depart; but my kindness shall not depart, neither shall the covenant of my peace be removed,' Isa. liv. 10. Why? Because my kindness was before the mountains, and before the hills were brought forth, (as Wisdom speaks, Prov. viii.)

Obs. 5.—Fear not the ruin of kingdoms, nor of the world, for your being depends not on either of them; God chose you before all worlds. Let kingdoms totter, and mountains be thrown into the midst of the sea, 'we have a kingdom that cannot be shaken,' Heb. xii. 28.

And thus much for the time of our election.

III. For the end unto which God chose us. The Apostle saith it is, *That we might be holy and unblameable before him in love.*

By 'holiness' here is meant, either that imperfect holiness of grace which we have in this life, or that perfect holiness which we are ordained to in the world to come. It is evidently meant of both.

First, Of that perfect holiness in the world to come, and this principally. For, saith the Apostle, he hath chosen us to be holy and blameless. The word signifieth such an innocence as no man can justly carp at; ἀμώμους, such as a captious Momus cannot take exceptions at; nay, such as God himself, who is more curious than man, shall find no fault with, or blame in; 'before him.' Therefore it must needs be meant of perfect holiness, which he hath ordained us unto in heaven; and, as I take it, is the same with that in the fifth chapter of this same epistle, ver. 27. Christ will 'sanctify and cleanse his church,' which is for the present but imperfectly holy, 'that he may present it to himself glorious, without spot or wrinkle, or any such thing; but that it may be holy, and without blemish.' It is the very same thing that here we are said to be ordained to in the end. And God will do this, to the end that he may look upon us with pleasure. Our imperfect holiness is indeed holiness before him in truth and sincerity; but it is not holiness before him *without blame.* It is not such as he can fully and perfectly delight in. So that this is the meaning of the place, that God hath ordained unto all those whom he hath chosen a perfect holiness, and that they should be blameless before him; which one day they shall certainly be. Paul, in Phil. iii. 12, wisheth that he might 'apprehend that for which also he was apprehended of Christ Jesus?' What is that? A perfection in grace. God, says he, gave me to Christ, that I might be perfectly holy. For, says he, ver. 14, 'I press towards the mark of the high calling of God in Christ Jesus,' 'if by any means I may attain to the resurrection of the dead.' He endeavoured to be as perfect as the just shall be at the resurrection, so ver. 11; for that is it for which God gave him unto Christ. Christ took us to bestow this upon us; and God ordained us unto this. God is so perfect in himself, and in his contrivements, that he looketh and pitcheth upon the perfection of his works at first. When we were chosen by him, we came not up sinful before him, or imperfectly holy as we are here; but God looked at the utmost end, what he would make us at the last; and so presented us unto Christ. Now Christ upon that presentation was so taken with our beauty, that never since can he absolutely delight in us, until he hath sanctified us and cleansed us, and made us perfect, having neither spot nor wrinkle, as at first we were presented to him.

Secondly, As he hath ordained us to perfect holiness in the world to come, to be blameless before him, so he hath ordained us to holiness in this life, or else we shall never come to heaven, 2 Thess. ii. 13, 'He hath chosen us unto salvation, through sanctification of the Spirit.' You must run through sanctification of the Spirit, or you shall never come to heaven. You must be pure in heart here, or else you shall never see God. This is the least intended of the two.

But you will say, How can our holiness here be called unblameableness?

I answer, Yes, in some sense it may be so called; namely, that evangelically it is such; for you are perfectly holy in desire. You pray that God's will may be done on earth as it is in heaven. It is the desire of every good soul to be unblameable. Again, you may be said to be unblameable, because if you sin you make it up again by repentance. So that you see, how by holiness and unblameableness are meant both holiness here and hereafter.

Accordingly 'before him' hath a double sense:—

1. If you understand the holiness mentioned of imperfect holiness here, the meaning is, that true holiness is not before men, it is before God, who approveth of sincerity only; such as your father Abraham was to you an example of, Gen. xvii. 1, 'Walk before me, and be upright.' That expression there is all one with this holiness before God here. If the heart be upright or sincere before God, that is all one as to be holy before him. In Col. iii. 22, servants are bidden to do their masters' service as before God, &c. But I cannot stand upon this now.

2. If that holiness be understood of the holiness of glory, as principally, if not only, it is, then 'before him' hath two meanings, and both good.

The one is this: God hath ordained us to be holy in his presence for ever, and there for ever to enjoy him, and delight ourselves in that enjoyment. 'In thy presence,' saith the Psalmist, 'there is fulness of joy,' &c.

Or, secondly, the meaning is this: that as we might delight in God, and enjoy his face and presence, so he might delight in us, we being perfectly holy before him, or in his account. The end of his choosing us was, that we might be in his presence, and he delight himself in us, and glory in his creatures as made thus holy and thus happy by him. *Dulce est amare, et amari*,—It is a sweet thing to love, and be beloved again. God, though he loved his children, yet could not rest in that love, nor heighten it to a delight in them, till he had made them blameless in love before him; till he had made them perfectly holy like himself.

And then lastly, 'in love' is added, as meant of perfect holiness in heaven, where there is no faith, nothing but love. And if you take it of imperfect holiness here, so all the principles of true holiness are nothing but love. 'Faith worketh by love.' So that the words may well bear both these senses.

I shall now give you some observations out of the words, as taken in either sense:—

Obs. 1.—If this holiness here be meant of perfect holiness, (as certainly it is,) see then what heaven is. It is perfect holiness and perfect love to God. To be holy before him in love, this is the foundation of the glory in heaven. If I should spend millions of years in describing heaven unto you, I could say no more, but only open these three things couched in the text, perfect holiness in God's presence, and enjoying and loving of him, even as we are beloved of him. This is heaven, and this is that which God hath pitched upon to bring us to. This is the chief thing in election, in which work of God's he looks to this unblameableness in holiness and love before him, as the end of it.

Obs. 2.—In the second place, whereas the Apostle in the next verse saith, 'He hath predestinated us to the adoption of children;' and in this verse foregoing it he saith, 'He hath chosen us to be holy before him in love,' so putting holiness before adoption; this is the reason of it: adoption is a privilege of ours, and does indeed contain all the privileges we have, as I may so speak, for ourselves; but holiness is that which is for God—it is to please and glorify him, and therefore it is justly here put before the other. From whence we may observe—

That it is God's first aim that we should be holy before him. Let it therefore be our great care too. That which was first in God's eye, let it be chiefly in ours. Though we be ordained to adoption and glory, yet we were first chosen to be 'holy before him in love.'

Art thou imperfectly holy? Comfort thyself with this, that though thou beest now full of blame, and men may lay many things to thy charge; yet God hath chosen thee to be one day holy and without blame before him. Yea, thou mayest comfort thyself against imperfect holiness in this, that when God chose thee, that first view he took of thee, that first idea wherein thou wert represented to him, was as he meant to make thee, even perfectly holy; such thou camest up before him in his first intention about thee, even clothed with all those jewels and embellishments which he meant one day to bestow upon thee. What is the reason that God is willing to pardon us, and that he pleaseth himself in us now? He knows that though we be sinful now, yet it will not be long ere we shall be perfectly holy before him. Christ cleanseth us, to 'present us to himself a glorious church, without spot or wrinkle.'

And on the other side, if it be meant of imperfect holiness, as the means to the end, there may these observations be raised from that:—

Obs. 1.—Without holiness here, there is no happiness to be expected hereafter. Without God's mercy we cannot be saved; and without holiness we are not under mercy, 1 Pet. i. 2, He hath chosen us to obedience of the truth. And without purity or holiness no man shall see God.

Obs. 2.—The ground of all true obedience is love: 'To be holy before him in love.' Faith works by love. As no duty is pleasing to God without faith, so neither without love. It was not the reason why God chose us, but the end unto which he chose us. He hath ordained us to be holy before him in love.

Obs. 3.—There remains one observation more, that is general to both interpretations, namely, that the foundation of God's love is not loveliness in us. Though in our love we cannot love a creature (as, not a child) until it is and hath a being,—and not then neither, unless we see something lovely in it which may draw out our affections towards it,—yet God can resolve to love such creatures as he can make thus and thus lovely, and so ordain them to be holy before him, that he may delight in them. He can therefore take things possible, in respect of being,—that is, which he can, or hath in his power to make and create,—and he can aforehand resolve thus and thus to love them; which we cannot do. And the reason of this is, for that his love is only from his own will, as our being his creatures also is; and so the first objects of election may be *res creabiles, non tantum quæ actu creatæ sunt et existunt*,—things that are looked upon by him but as yet to be created, not only those that are supposed actually to exist.

SERMON VI.

Having predestinated us unto adoption by Jesus Christ for himself, according to the good pleasure of his will, to the praise of the glory of his grace, wherein he hath made us accepted in the beloved.—VER. 5, 6.

THE coherence of these words with the former stands thus: they contain a second instance of that general of his premised, ver. 3, wherein the Apostle had said that God had blessed us with all spiritual blessings in heavenly things in Christ. Now, as in that verse he mentioneth both an act of blessing us, 'he hath blessed us,' and in the general or total speaks of certain blessings themselves wherewith God hath blessed us, 'with all spiritual blessing in heavenly things in Christ;' so in these following verses he accordingly instanceth in particulars, namely—

1. *Election*, ver. 4.
2. *Predestination*, ver. 5.

Both which are acts of blessing us.

His first instance is in election: 'according as he hath chosen us in him before the foundation of the world.' Here is the act of blessing, that God chose us in Christ, and so blessed us; for blessing was joined with choosing, as a concomitant of it; God then giving us all spiritual blessings when he chose us, as out of other scriptures I have shewed. So that the meaning is, that then, and in that act of choosing, God thus blessed us; and that particular blessing bestowed by that act is, that we were blessed with a perfect holiness, as it there follows, 'that we might be holy and without blame before him in love.'

The second instance he giveth is predestination: 'having predestinated us unto adoption,' &c. Herein again predestination is the act of blessing, and that from eternity; and adoption is the particular blessing wherewith we were blessed. And this is the fruit of predestination, as perfect holiness is of election.

Now, as an introduction to the opening of these words, you will expect I should first distinguish between *chosen* and *predestinated*, or between God's election and predestination. To choose, is to single and cull out from others, or out of a common lump; and to predestinate, is, in English, to fore-ordain, or fore-appoint to some end. Now, how do these differ, as they were then done by God?

1. It may be there was no difference intended; but the Apostle being to repeat the same thing, or one and the same act, his scope being apart to mention those particular blessings by that one word, as they are bestowed upon us by that one and eternal act of God's love, he takes occasion about them to use two several words or expressions thereof; especially considering that those eternal acts of choosing, predestinating, &c., were all but one entire act in God, even as his essence is one. And yet the Holy Ghost is pleased to express it by two acts; whereof the one notes out one thing more

eminently, and the other another thing, so to convey all of it the fuller unto our apprehensions, according to this latter conception.

2. Some distinguish them thus: that election or choice imports more eminently an act of God's will, for choice is an act of will; but that predestination is an act of his understanding, as working by counsel. So, ver. 11, this seems explained, 'Being predestinated according to the purpose of him who worketh all things after the counsel of his will.' But more expressly in Acts iv. 28, 'Whatever thy counsel did fore-determine to be done.' The word is the same that is here, προώρισε. So then the difference here should be, that election imports simply his decree to the end; but predestination should further note God's contrivement or preparation of means to the obtaining of that end.

3. But though other scriptures may hold forth this second difference, yet that it should be here in these two verses intended, I see not. For adoption here is set forth to be an end, as well as holiness; nor are there any means in this verse mentioned. And of the two, holiness is rather a means, or a foundation laid to adoption, than *è contra;* and therefore Rollock rather calls election, as here used, the decree of the means, and predestination the decree of the end. But yet that this notion of his should be the Apostle's scope here, I cannot wholly assent to neither; for the holiness unto which we are here said to be chosen is perfect holiness in heaven, which is the end we are ordained unto, as well as adoption. And, indeed, both of them are *decreta finis,* decrees about the end, as I shall afterwards shew.

Wherefore, the best difference that I can find out, and that is proper to the scope of the text, is, that election, although it be a decree about the end, or at least one main end concerning what God ultimately meaneth to do with us, as well as in predestination; yet together therewith it does eminently note forth a singling or culling out some persons with a special and peculiar love from others of the same rank and condition;* both out of things possible, which God had in his knowledge, which his power could have made, but he never decreed a being unto, which are as infinite as his knowledge and power are, (and even out of these there is an election,) as also out of all persons, whom he did make and actually give an existence unto, both men and angels, of whom some he laid aside, as in the case of the angels is undeniable. So that election being a preferring of some before others, doth connotate the *terminus à quo,* the term or mass of persons *from which;* but predestination more eminently notes out the *terminus ad quem,* the ultimate state *unto which* we are ordained.

And secondly, because by this election, or first calling out from others, we are not ordained to a sole and separate being in ourselves; such as other persons, whom he decreed not to save, are only to have,—they all stand upon their own bottom; but a being *in Christ,* as a Common Person and root to spring in and out of, and that in him we were considered and chosen to be in the very first act of God's choosing us, (as in God's heart we may be said to have stood, although, until converted, we have not an actual being in Christ, according to the rules of the Word, which God will judge us by, but are 'without God,' and 'without Christ,' as chap. ii. shews;) and therefore unto 'chosen' is added 'in him,' that being the first act that gives us a subsistence thus in God's mind, and that in Christ. Hence therefore election, the first act, having thus singled us out from all things, and decreed us a representative being in Christ as members in a head, together with our being,

* The proper object which election is carried unto are the persons. It is of persons as of persons. He hath chosen us to bring us to such an ultimate end, ordained for us.

predestination then further imports a second act of ordaining us to a glorious well-being in him, as the end God means to bring us to. It adds adoption, and by adoption is meant the right unto the glory of heaven, as I shall by and by shew you, and this is bestowed upon us as a privilege or dignity—ἐξουσία, as it is called, John i. 12—over and above our first being in him; for in him we must first be, ere we can partake of anything through him. Now, election was the first act that did put us into him, and then predestination was that which conveyed unto us all those privileges which we have through him, and union with him, whereof adoption and holiness are the highest and most eminent.

To illustrate this, we must know that things must be purposed to have a being ere they can be supposed to have a well-being from Christ; according to that maxim of him, that is, of the Father, whose work all this is, 'Of him you are,' and have a new being, 'in Christ,' which Christ is then 'made to us wisdom;' and many other privileges we have by him before we can come to have a well-being. In like manner, we must first be supposed to have a being in Christ—'Of him ye are in Christ Jesus,' 1 Cor. i. 30—ere we can be supposed to partake of anything from him, or of any extrinsical or intrinsical privilege that is his, or that cometh from him. You know, ere a man can have any privilege in the visible world, he must be a man, that is, a son of the first Adam. God indeed hath given the world to the sons of men, but yet the conveyance and the charter by which they hold it is their coming from Adam by multiplication, as it is Gen. i. 26, 28; so as, before any soul, if you could suppose it extant before it comes into the body, can come to enjoy the right or privilege of anything in this world, it must be by being united to a body that cometh from Adam by propagation, and so it becomes one of Adam's posterity. So is it here. Before ever you can come to have a right of inheritance in anything of the other world, you must first be supposed to be in Christ. Now, election is that which first gives you a being in Christ, and then God by the act of predestination did appoint you a well-being through him.

Again, look as God in his decrees about the creation did not consider the body of Adam singly or apart from his soul, nor yet the soul without his body, (I speak of his first creation and state thereby,) neither should either have so much as existed, but as the one in the other; so nor Christ and his Church in election, which gave the first existence both to Christ as a Head, and to the Church as his body, which each had in God's decrees.

And holiness, which is the fruit of election here, is the image of God, and a likeness unto him, which makes us capable of communion with him. As likeness in one man unto another makes him sociable and fit to converse with another man his superior, so holiness for communion with the great God; and therefore the Apostle says, 'without holiness no man shall see God,' nor indeed 'can see him,' as Christ, John iii. 3. Look as some colours are the groundwork to the laying on of other, and all colours to varnish, so is grace a groundwork unto glory and communion with himself. Look as reason is the foundation of learning, no man being able to attain it, unless he hath reason, so we cannot attain the glory of heaven, which is meant by adoption, till such time as we have holiness, and perfect holiness. 'Without holiness no man shall see God.' So that holiness is the image of God, which makes us like unto him, and fit for communion with him; and heaven is but communion with God.

But then, if you ask me what adoption is, it is plainly this: it is a right to the glory of heaven, and that is superadded to holiness. 'We groan within ourselves,' says the Apostle, Rom. viii. 23, 'waiting for the adoption, to wit, the redemption of our bodies;' that is, till we shall be brought to heaven, and to that full and consummate glory there, which not only the soul, now made perfect, hath, but which the soul and body together shall have when that last part of our redemption is finished, in the resurrection of the body. And therefore it is expressed by the redemption of the body, it being that glorious state that follows thereupon. And this we are by predestination ordained to, as the end that God would bring us unto. And so, some conjoin those two, adoption and glory, Rom. ix. 4, that is, glorious adoption, or adoption to glory. And if you look into 1 John iii. 2, you shall then see another place, where being the sons of God, or adopted, is put for heaven. 'Behold,' says the Apostle, 'what manner of love the Father hath shewed us, that we should be called the sons of God! Beloved, we are now the sons of God, but it doth not yet appear what we shall be; for we know that, when he shall appear, we shall be like unto him; for we shall see him as he is;' even the Lord Jesus Christ in glory. So then, adoption contains all the great dignity of a Christian in this life;* but ultimately, and more especially, as here, that fulness of glory whereby we shall be like to Christ in his glory; according to that in John xvii. 22, 'The glory thou hast given me, I have given them.' In a word, adoption and holiness here are all one with what the Psalmist speaks, 'He will give grace and glory; and no good thing will he withhold from them,' &c. Perfect grace and holiness, that is the fruit of election; and glory added to grace (that is the varnish of it) is meant by adoption. And so you have the first thing, the difference between perfect holiness and adoption.

But then the main question remaineth, Why is holiness made the fruit of putting us into Christ, or choosing us; and why is adoption or glory made the fruit of predestinating us? for so you see the words carry it.

You shall see a clear reason for this. Holiness must needs be the fruit or consequent of our being chosen in Christ; for it is essential to a being in Christ. It were an absurdity to say that God did ordain a man to be in Christ, and not ordain him to be holy. Because if God ordains him to be in Christ, he ordains him to be a member of Christ, and the spouse of Christ. Now the head and members must be homogeneal, and husband and spouse must be of the same kind and image. When Adam was to have a wife, she must be of the same species, she must have the same image upon her. None of the beasts was fit to be a wife for Adam. God brought them all unto him; but among them all 'there was not found a meet help for him,' Gen. ii. 20, because they had not the same image that he had. And whoever has his being from Adam, must likewise have reason from him, as a necessary concomitant of such a being. So if God chooseth a man in Christ, he must necessarily be holy. And this is the reason why holiness is annexed to our being chosen in him, the ordaining us to be holy being a natural and absolutely essential consequent of our being elected in him.

But then, why is glory the fruit of predestination?

Now I have given you the reason of the first, the second will easily follow. God might have made us perfectly holy in Christ, and not have added glory to it: Rom. vi. 22, 'You have your fruit unto holiness,' says the Apostle. If there had been holiness, there had been fruit enough; but here is more, 'and the end everlasting life.' So likewise, here is glory added to holiness as a further fruit and privilege. Therefore, as God by election

* There is *adoptio imperfecta* or *incompleta*, namely in the *jus* and title to it that is now bestowed.

putteth us into Christ, so he hath a further business about us; he predestinated us to glory and to the adoption of sons in him. It is a new grace, and therefore it is expressed to be the fruit of a new and second act, even predestination. *Plus est nos esse filios quam esse sanctos*, (it is Zanchy's speech,) It is a further thing to be sons than to be holy, to have heaven, and be received to the glory of God, than to be partaker of the holiness of God. Predestination therefore is here said to come over us after election a second time. God addeth thereby glory to grace, (as the Psalmist speaks,) as a fresh, new, and second gift; for gifts both and each are by the Psalmist said to be, 'He will give grace and glory.' Grace or holiness by election, glory by predestination.

And here, ere we go any further, let us pause a little, and view the harmony that is between these things here in the 4th and 5th verses, with what the Apostle had said before and ushered this in by. He began in the 3d verse, 'Blessed be the God and Father of our Lord Jesus Christ.' When I opened those words, I gave this meaning of them, that God is first and originally the God and Father of Christ, and so becomes our God and our Father, according to that in John xx. 17, 'I ascend to my God and your God, to my Father and your Father.' When I shewed you how he is the God and the Father of Jesus Christ himself, I gave this difference, that he was the God of Christ as man, because he chose the human nature unto that dignity. Nay, he chose the second Person to be the Mediator, 1 Peter i 20, and so was the God of Christ by election. But supposing that man to have been once chosen and united to the Son of God, and he becomes his Father by the relation of having begotten his Son; and that relation becomes natural between his Father and him. But he is not thus to us a Father by a natural relation as to Christ, but wholly by adoption,—which of Christ must not be said,—and so by predestination only, 'who hath predestinated us to the adoption of sons,' with difference from Christ. Adoption in us depends wholly and merely upon predestination and no natural relation. Again, as he is our God so considered, he chooseth us to be holy before him, according to that express saying, 'Be ye holy, for I the Lord your God am holy,' Lev. xix. 2. As he becometh our Father in Christ, he predestinateth us to adoption of sons. Here are two relations God beareth unto us in Christ; he is our God, and he is our Father, so ver. 3. And here are two acts of God towards us from everlasting that proceed from these: namely, election, ordaining us to be holy in conformity to him as our God; and predestination to the adoption of children, as he that thereby would and did become a Father to us.

I conclude this with what Zanchy observes, with what follows after. The two (saith he) acts of God for us, in this ver. 4 and 5, agree with those words which follow in ver. 6, 'to the praise of the glory of his grace.' That God should choose us in Christ to be perfectly holy, there was grace; but that he should add glory and heaven and sonship unto it too, this, says he, is to 'the glory of his grace.' And so he makes an *auxesis* of it, a further lightening of his love, that he not only chose us to be holy, but also predestinated us unto adoption and glory: to the shewing forth, not only of grace, as in holiness he did, that being the image of his grace; but the glory of his grace, as in adoption, that being the image of his glory. I will not much urge this, as here intended; I mention it only because he adds it; and certainly some such aim there might be, in that aspect which these words have to the former. And so I pass to some observations.

Obs. 1.—In the first place, from what hath been said, take notice how absolutely necessary holiness is unto salvation, which will appear to you, out of what I have said, by these four things :—

First, Not only that in these thoughts which God had towards us, he did first pitch upon holiness, and then upon adoption or glory; and so he preferred holiness to glory, and so should we prefer it to all other privileges which we have by Christ ;—

But, *secondly*, that holiness is a necessary and essential concomitant to being in Christ, and all other privileges superadded. There was no thought to be had of being in Christ, without being holy. Look how incongruous and absurd it were to make a beast a son and member of Adam; so incongruous and absurd were it to make one that is unholy to be a member of Christ. God never at first cast a thought on us to be in Christ, but with an intention that we should be holy. 'He hath chosen us in him to be holy,' saith ver. 4.

Yea, in the *third* place, God is not your God, unless you be holy: 'Be ye holy, as the Lord your God is holy.' God, as I told you, becomes your God by election, as he becomes your Father by predestination. If, therefore, God be your God, then be you holy as he is holy.

And, *fourthly*, grace is the foundation of glory. There is not a thought to be had of going to heaven without it; you must first be holy, ere you can be so much as capable of that glory; for the height and top of it is communion with God, and God is holy.

So you see, from what hath been said of predestination, he hath predestinated us unto adoption; that is, a sonship in law, in and through Christ, his natural Son. Do but think with yourselves, by way of inference, you that are believers indeed, what your privileges by your being in Christ will rise unto, by considering what is and needs must be included in this little word, *sonship* and *adoption*. No less than all privileges in this world and the world to come, every one of them in the present right to them; 'now,' says the Apostle, now at present, 'we are the sons of God, but what we,' by virtue of this our being sons, 'shall be,' none in the world, nor we ourselves, can know; none do or can come to know the consequents hereof. As we say of a mighty rich man, he knows not the end of his wealth; so we may say of a man's being an adopted son of God, none knows what this will bring a man to in the end. If a son then an heir, a co-heir with Christ, yea, an heir of God; to possess and enjoy God, as Christ doth. I say as Christ doth; for so it follows in that of John, 'When Christ shall appear, we shall be like unto him;' just like in our proportion; as he enjoys God, so shall we. Yea, and over and above, he shall have *all things* into boot. 'I will be his God, and he shall be my son;' and what further follows upon being a son? 'He shall inherit all things.' God himself hath but all things, and thou shalt have all things too; and this is to be predestinated unto adoption. Brethren, think of your privileges.

I have expounded what it is to be *chosen in him*, and what to be *predestinated to adoption.*

The division of the fifth verse :—

The rest that follows in the 5th and 6th verses is to set forth the causes of this our predestination. I call them causes in a large sense.

1. The *instrumental cause*, Christ: 'by (or through) Jesus Christ;' for in and through a relation unto him it is that we are sons and heirs of heaven, as in that Rom. viii. 17 it is declared, 'co-heirs with Christ.'

2. You have the *principal efficient cause*, and, in him, the mover of God thereunto, viz., the good pleasure of his will: 'according,' saith he, 'to the

good pleasure of his will.' All is resolved into that, as the supreme first mover of all, and you in your thoughts are to attribute all to that, when you think of your being made holy or happy.

3. The *final cause*, both for whom and for what.

(1.) *For whom;* and the word εἰς αὐτὸν is such as will serve either to signify 'for himself,' and so referring unto God the Father, or 'for him,' that is, for Jesus Christ the Son of God, who is also together with the Father one end of this our predestination unto adoption; therefore that which our translators translate 'to himself,' as referring to the person of God the Father, I would likewise render 'for him;' that is, for Jesus Christ; reading the words thus, 'who hath predestinated us to adoption by Jesus Christ, for him' as the second end; *for whom.*

(2.) *For what;* 'to the praise of the glory of his grace,' so ver. 6; that is, for the glory of his grace who did predestinate, which is God the Father.

And so you have the rest of these verses analysed to you.

There is nothing questionable herein, but only that I should translate it predestinated to adoption 'for him,' and so to carry it to Christ, that he was intended as one final cause of our predestination to adoption, as well as the instrumental; that is, that it was intended by God that contrived all in it, so as that it should be *for him* as well as *by him.*

I will give you the several interpretations or readings of the words '*for himself.*'

1. There are some would interpret it by ἐν ἑαυτῷ; to this sense, that he hath predestinated us 'in himself,' to shew that it was God's sole act immanent within himself, and in that respect to give him the glory of it as the contriver, &c., 'within himself.' But this will not hold; for, first, it is harsh in the phraseology of it, to render εἰς ἑαυτὸν by ἐν ἑαυτῷ.

2. That God was the cause of predestination, we see how that followeth after, for the Apostle attributeth it unto his will in the next words, 'according to the good pleasure of his will.' And certainly, in so brief an enumeration of causes, he could not use a repetition. And therefore—

3. Others read it, as here our translators have also turned it, 'unto himself,' to this sense: 'Having predestinated us unto adoption to himself,' that is, to be children adopted to himself.

Holy Baines, not being satisfied with this last reading of it, gives two reasons against this interpretation. *First*, saith he, that God did predestinate us to be children to himself, is sufficiently implied in the sole word 'adoption;' for to whom should we be children but to him? Not to Christ. Again, *secondly*, the Apostle, saith he, doth not say that He hath chosen us to be sons in the concrete, but he hath chosen us unto adoption in the abstract; so the words in the original do run. Now, says he, to add 'to himself' unto 'adoption' in the abstract, that is not proper. If indeed he had said, 'He hath chosen us to be sons to himself,' that had been proper; but the words run in that tenor: and therefore Mr Baines, to avoid this, rather chose that interpretation, which yet of all is the worst, 'He predestinated us in himself.'

That translation and interpretation therefore which remaineth is this, that God hath predestinated us either 'for himself' as the end thereof, or 'for him,' namely Christ, as the end of predestinating us to this adoption. And the words will fully bear the one as well as the other; for the preposition εἰς doth oft-times signify 'for,' as it doth denote the end or final cause; as in the very next verse, ver. 6, εἰς ἔπαινον δόξης τῆς χάριτος αὐτοῦ, 'to,' or for, 'the praise of the glory of his grace,' as noting out the final cause. It is the same preposition there that is here used, as likewise in that Rom. xi. 36, 'All things are of him, and through him, and for him,' εἰς αὐτὸν; they are the same words.

But then, if that particle εἰς be admitted to signify 'for,' as importing a final cause, the question will be, whether it be for himself,—that is, for God the Father, that he should make himself the end,—or whether it be for Christ, whom the Apostle had mentioned in the words immediately foregoing.

I confess, that when I expounded that verse in my lecture, and long after that, when I first perfected my notes upon that verse, I observed it not, as to such a purpose and issue as I shall now further drive at. But I understood it then as only to intend that we were predestinated to and for Christ, and to the glory of Christ, and so I handled it at large. But seeing the Greek word may as indifferently, with a variation of the aspirate, be rendered 'to himself,' and so refer unto God the Father; and finding that the Scriptures do frequently express God's electing of us by choosing us to himself and for himself, as I found when I lately handled the doctrine of election, (upon Rom. ii. 4–6,) and that there was so much and so great a matter comprehended and contained in that expression; I have been thereby moved to take that interpretation in also, it being a rule I have always measured the interpretation of Scripture by, as I have oft professed, to take Scripture phrases and words in the most comprehensive sense; yea, and in two senses, or more, that will stand together with the context and analogy of faith.

Junius, in his conference with Arminius, apprehended some great matter, beyond what was ordinarily pitched on, to lie intended in that small word. But he not explaining what, but groping at it, Dr Twiss, who wrote the defence of that conference, yet finds fault with him for obscurity, as not knowing what to make of Junius' meaning.

Others, to whose interpretation our translators seem to incline, do give this as the sole sense of these words, that God predestinated us unto adoption of children to himself: so as the whole intendment should be taken up in this particular, that he hath chosen us to be children to himself: the word 'to himself' referring only unto our being children to him; that is, his children.

But, says holy Baines, as I observed, it is not in the Greek said that he predestinated us to be 'sons' to himself in the concrete; but that he chose us to adoption in the abstract. Now, says he, to have added 'to adoption' in the abstract to 'himself,' is not so proper. Of which I have spoke before.

So that I understand the word 'to himself' not primarily or alone to refer to adoption of children to him, but to refer distinctly and as immediately unto his having predestinated us, and separated us to his own great and glorious self, and for and to his great and blessed Son. And that to have been another distinct and larger end of his predestinating us than adoption, over and above, and beyond that. And though that be as a special end mentioned first, yet that is but a more particular and lower end in comparison of this other, of God's predestinating us to himself.

Let us take up his meaning thus, as if he had said, 'He hath predestinated us to adoption,' that is one end, or benefit rather. But, which is more and further than that, he hath predestinated us even *to himself* also, in the full extent of what that will bear and hold forth. And truly, that which would further persuade unto this is, not only that it enlargeth the scope of the text to the utmost amplitude, but also, that 'by Jesus Christ' comes in between 'unto adoption' and 'to himself.' Whereas, if he had only intended that we were chosen unto adoption, that is, of children to himself, he would have placed them immediately together, and said, 'He hath predestinated us unto adoption to himself by Jesus Christ;' but he puts 'by Jesus Christ' between the one and the other.

FOR HIMSELF: THE END OF ELECTION.

I shall, for an enlargement and confirmation of this, run over some places in the Old and New Testament wherein the same expression is singly and in this general sense used, *that God chose us for himself*, and not limitedly unto this one particular, unto adoption to himself.

1. In the Old Testament, Ps. iv. 3, 'Know that the Lord hath set apart him that is godly for himself.' What is it to set apart, but to choose and sever from the rest, even as here in the text, to reserve, doth imply?

2. And, secondly, Who was it that he speaks of? David himself, whom elsewhere God had chosen, Ps. lxxxix. 19, 20.

3. And, thirdly, For what or whom did God choose him? Not to kingship only, but 'for himself,' says that text. And therein consists the height, the top-glory of our election, as it was of his. The word 'set apart' in the Hebrew signifies *magnifying* or *exalting;* and Ainsworth puts both together, and translates it thus, 'hath marvellously or wonderfully separated.' Now this great and wonderful exaltation lies in his separating, choosing us for himself. To have set us apart for kingdoms, for all the glories found in heaven and earth, had not been so much as to separate us for himself. And agreeing with this is that Isa. xliii. 20, 'My people, my chosen;' so he had styled them. And it immediately follows, ver. 21, 'This people have I formed for myself, they shall shew forth my praise;' which latter words are explicative of the former, 'My chosen.' There is a double formation, one in and by regeneration, &c., as that phrase, 'till Christ be formed in you,' shews. But this is but an imperfect formation, as those words also imply. Nor is it all the forming of Christ in us that is yet to be, for it is to be perfected in glory. But there was a foregoing one in God's everlasting decree of choosing us, 'My people, my chosen;' and that is the greatest formation of all. God's eternal choice was the womb wherein this birth was first conceived, and therein perfectly formed as to what we should be for ever. David, speaking of his body, maketh a double formation of it, Ps. cxxxix., first, one in the womb, which God saw and had an eye upon, that it should be done according to his mind and model; and of this he speaks, ver. 15, 'My substance was not hid from thee, when I was made in secret, and curiously wrought in the lowest parts of the earth.' The other in God's decree, ver. 16, 'In thy book all my members were written.' In like manner there is a double spiritual formation of the elect, and of their souls. One in election, which was the whole of what they should be to his praise; therein it was that we were blessed with all spiritual blessings at once. God cast the mould of all that we should be. All formations in this life are but imperfect draughts wrought by piecemeal, according to that pattern; they are all, to eternity, but several degrees of perfecting and filling up the idea of that first draught in God's heart of what he chose us to be, which he purposed within himself, Eph. i. 11. In that mould were all the prints engraven which we were, by being cast in, to bear the image of. And in this respect he is said in Isaiah to have formed them, 'They shall shew forth my praise;' which is the same tenor of language with Eph. i. 5, 6, 'Having predestinated us to himself, to the praise of the glory of his grace.'

If you desire yet a plainer scripture, wherein this phrase is, *in terminis*, applied unto God's choosing his people as the end thereof, take that in Ps. cxxxv. 4, 'For the Lord hath chosen Jacob for himself, and Israel for his peculiar treasure.' This for the Old Testament.

In the New you have the same. Besides this in the Epistle to the Ephesians, Rom. xi. 4, 'I have reserved to myself seven thousand men, who have not bowed the knee to the image of Baal.' Here is a precedent of election alleged of seven thousand men in Elijah's times, which is thus expressed there by God, 'I have left or reserved to myself,' &c. And this in the fifth verse he expressly terms 'an election of grace:' 'Even so then at this present time also there is a remnant according to the election of grace.' His 'even so then' interprets God's mind in that speech of his to Elijah, 1 Kings xix. 18, by way of parallel, and manifestly shews his saying, 'I have reserved to myself,' to be all one and equivalent unto, 'I have an election of grace of seven thousand, whom, by virtue of that election and separation to myself, I have kept from Baal's idolatry;' and thereby plainly infers his ultimate end in choosing was an election to himself. But this I have elsewhere more largely opened.

Again, when Christ himself from heaven was pleased to give Ananias an account of his so dearly beloved Paul, the truth of his conversion, to the end to assure him of it he brings forth his own and God's having elected him; from whence, as the original of all, he had now effectually called him, and meant and had designed to employ him in his greatest services. And how doth Christ express his election there? 'He is a chosen vessel to me,' saith Christ, Acts ix. 15.

So then, whether it be God the Father predestinating us to *himself*, or his predestinating by Jesus Christ to *him*,—that is, to Christ,—we have warrant to apply it unto either; and by applying it unto both, we make up the full comprehensive intent of the Apostle in that speech. I shall therefore, in the handling, speak to it—

1. As in relation to God himself.

2. As to Jesus Christ.

1. *For himself;* that is, *God the Father.*—What it carries with it as it relates to God the Father.

(1.) It notes out a special propriety: 'These I have chosen or reserved for myself,' is as to say, 'These I have laid my hands upon to be mine.' In that of Isa. xliii, 21, fore-cited, he had said just at the verse before, 'The beasts of the field shall honour me;' that is, they in their kind. And in another place, Ps. l., he sets his mark upon them, (as men do on their cattle;) they are his, ver. 10, 'For every beast of the forest is mine, and the cattle upon a thousand hills: I know all the fowls of the mountains, and the wild beasts of the field are mine,' and so shall honour him in their kind. Ay, but these are my people, my chosen; I have formed them for myself, &c., and are therefore dignified by being styled 'the first-fruits of his creatures,' James i. 18. Consecrated to him out of the whole, Jer. ii. 3, 'Israel is holiness to the Lord, the first-fruits of his increase.' Observe—

First, That he, the great God, though most blessed of himself without any of his creatures, and needed not have made them; yet he says of the whole lump, 'Ye are mine;' as if a rich man should say of his goods of his own getting, 'These are my increase.' But—

Secondly, Of his chosen people he says, 'These are the first-fruits of my increase, and holiness to the Lord.' Not only denoting their duty of devoting themselves, and all they are, unto his glory; but furthermore, it denotes his consecrating them to himself, as Num. xviii. in the type explains it. Our Saviour Christ, in John xvii. 9, makes a great matter of this, of God's taking them to be his: 'I pray for them: I pray not for the world, but for them which thou hast given me, for they are thine.' He had spoken before of a world of other men, whom he professeth not to pray for, but limits himself to that peculiar company who were his by election, the first-fruits of the whole; 'who,' says he, 'were thine,' and therefore also *mine*. By so vast a difference made between them and the world, as that he should profess to lay out the strength of his mediation for them, and not for the other; and that upon this ground and motive, 'For they were thine, O Father!' He gives it as the reason that moves him so to do; and that which Christ considers in our behalf, as that which had wrought so great and special an affection to us, how greatly ought it to affect us! Now, how is it that they are made his but by choice and election? For otherwise all the world is his. And you have this in Paul likewise, 'The Lord knows them that are his.' Which special propriety set upon them, and owning of them as his, is equivalent as to say, they are God's elect, Rom. viii. 33.

(2.) It is a choosing us to be *holy before him;* a consecrating us unto his service and worship. And this is especially instanced in and aimed at in Rom. xi. 4, which I fore-cited. 'These,' says he, 'I have reserved to myself,' whilst he left the rest unto the worshipping of Baal; but these I have reserved to cleave unto and worship me in purity and in truth. And besides what is here, heaven is an everlasting, perpetual worship of God. Thus also in Paul's instance, Acts ix. 15, there is his particular designment unto bearing Christ's name and sufferings for him; for which he is, in a special manner, set out as a chosen vessel: 'He is a chosen vessel unto me, to bear my name before the Gentiles, and kings, and the children of Israel.'

(3.) It is to choose them for *his glory.* For his glory, as manifested, is said to be himself; which therefore, he says, 'he will not give to another.' And here, in the following verse, it is added, 'unto the praise of the glory of his grace.' Of which I have spoken elsewhere, as it is conjoined with his choosing us for himself. But—

(4.) That which I most pitch upon as intended in this expression, is his designing us to the nearest *oneness* and entire communion with himself.* A man chooseth goods, and dwellings, and servants for his use, and kings used to make a collection of rarities and precious things for their special delight, Eccles. ii. 8. Yea, but to choose a spouse, a familar intimate friend, (as Zabud is called Solomon's friend, 1 Kings iv. 5,) imports something higher. And further, it is one thing for a king to choose to such or such an office or dignity, as to choose his lord chancellor, treasurer, chief justice, &c.; that is a choice unto things, to places, and but to outward privileges only: but it is another thing to choose his wife, to lie in his bosom, to be one flesh with him, and another self with himself; or an intimate companion, to be as one soul with him. This latter is to choose to and for himself, and for his own person, and unto the highest communion with himself, and a participation of himself; the other is but to outward honour, and for his business, his

* This head I have largely run out upon in that part of a discourse about election, 'That God hath made it his top and ultimate design in election to ordain us unto a super-creation, union with himself, and an immediate communication of himself;' unto which I refer the reader for the rest.

service, and the like. It is in such choices for himself, in which the grace and favour of a king in choosing is most seen and shewn; that is a choice indeed!

2. *For him;* that is, *for Jesus Christ.*—In the interpretation before, I said the words εἰς αὐτὸν would bear either 'for himself,' as referring to the Father, or 'for him,' referring to Jesus Christ, last mentioned. And the Holy Ghost intended both these senses; but yet, if we were to choose but one, this would make me think Christ rather to be here intended than God the Father, because the Father's being the end of predestination unto adoption, follows after 'to the praise of the glory of his grace,' namely, of the Father, whose free grace is thereby magnified; although it must be also acknowledged that his ordaining us for Christ is to the glory of his grace also.

So then let us consider whether it may not be intended of Christ, εἰς Χριστὸν, 'for Christ,' for which there are these reasons:—

1. The words αὑτὸν and αὐτὸν are promiscuously used, either for *him* or *himself.*

2. I find that many copies do so read it, εἰς αὐτὸν, 'for him,' even for Christ. So the Vulgar edition, and so some interpreters of all sorts do carry it, as Cornelius à Lapide, the Jesuit; Vorstius, Stapulensis, Castilio, Lubin, and others.

3. And, to conclude all, there is this reason for it: If Jesus Christ were in predestinating us aimed at by God, as an end thereof, as I shall presently make good unto you, then certainly he may be supposed to come in here. And so he doth. Where the Holy Ghost sets himself to enumerate all the causes of predestination, he mentioneth God the Father as the end of it, over and above, or besides, in those words, 'to the praise of the glory of his grace;' and if Christ should not come in here, he should come in nowhere, as a final cause. He cometh in as a Common Person, that is, as our Head, in those words, 'having elected us in him;' also, as a means, in those words, 'having predestinated us unto adoption by him;' but as an *end,* together with his Father, nowhere cometh in, unless here, by translating these words, εἰς αὐτὸν, *for him.*

I come now to some observations, the first of which shall be a general one; there being three following more particular, to make up this general one, which is this:—

Obs.—See here the fulness of Jesus Christ. We are elected in him, so says ver. 4, as a Common Head; so we are predestinated to adoption by or through him, so saith ver. 5; and we are predestinated likewise for him, as it follows in the same verse. He is made in God's aim the end for which he did predestinate us, as well as the glory of his own grace. Take notice of Christ's fulness, these three things being attributed unto him—in him, through him, and for him; that is his honour. But the Father hath this peculiar honour above him, that all things are said to be 'of him:' so, Rom. xi. 36, 'Of him, and through him, and to him are all things.' Now, in Christ, and through Christ, and for Christ are all things, but not of Christ. God the Father, as he is *Fons Personarum,* the fountain of the other two Persons, so he is the fountain and first mover of all the works of the other Persons—their motion comes from him. You have the same thing expressed, by way of difference, between God the Father and Christ, 1 Cor. viii. 6, 'There is but one God, the Father, of whom are all things, and we in him; and one Lord Jesus Christ, by whom are all things, and we by him.' So also, 2 Cor. v. 18, 'All things are of God, who hath reconciled us to himself by Jesus Christ.' I will only cast in this further observation, that as here, in the matter of election about our salvation, the honour of these three are given Christ,—in him, through him, and for him,—so the same three are likewise attributed to him to express his influence into the matter of creation and common providence towards all creatures. In that Col. i. 16, (an epistle of kin unto this,) ἐν αὐτῷ, δι' αὐτοῦ, εἰς αὐτὸν πάντα·—in him, for him, and through him all things are said to be created; of which I have spoken elsewhere.

This general being premised, I come to the particulars that here make up Christ's fulness.

I have before explained to you how we are chosen in him, and shall now further open what these two hold forth of glory unto Christ, that we are predestinated to adoption 'through him,' and 'for him.'

These words, εἰς αὐτὸν, will first of all bear this sense, *ad illius exemplum*, after his example or pattern; and if that phrase should not bear so much, yet this will, 'being predestinated to adoption through him.' The meaning is, that Christ being the natural Son, we are made sons *like him*, even as, in many other things, in that which he is in himself, we are made the like in him, and conformed therein to him. Is he chosen? so are we, thus ver. 4. Is he beloved? so are we, ver. 6. He first, and then we in a conformity to him; even as he is a Son, so are we in him, ver. 5.

1. The first particular then is, that Jesus Christ was set up by God as the *exemplary cause* of us in our predestination. The meaning whereof is this: I will (says God) make those whom I choose in Christ to be like unto him; he shall be their pattern. He is my natural Son, and I will make them my sons through him.

To prove that this is intended in this our being predestinated to adoption through him, I will only give that place in Rom. viii. 29, 'Whom he foreknew, he also predestinated to be conformed to the image of his Son;' that is, God did set up Christ as the prototype and principal masterpiece, and made us as little copies and models of him. That Christ came, and took frail flesh in this world, and suffered unto death as he did, therein we were his patterns; he was conformed unto us in that. He had never come into this world had we not first fallen into sin, and brought a frailty upon our nature: Heb. ii. 14, 'Forasmuch as the children are partakers of flesh and blood,' (that is, of the frailty of man's nature,—flesh and blood cannot inherit the kingdom of God,) 'he himself likewise took part of the same.' Here now our frailty is made the pattern of his. So likewise, Rom. viii. 3, 'He sent his Son in the likeness of sinful flesh.' Because we sinned, and so subjected ourselves to frailty, therefore God made his Son like us. Mark the phrase there used, God sent him 'in the likeness of sinful flesh.' But though we were patterns to Jesus Christ himself in all matters of frailty that befell him in his way to heaven,—wherein yet, in another sense, he is a pattern to us, in regard of the measure of afflictions wherein he exceeded, and therefore we are said to be conformed to him in sufferings,—yet I speak in respect of what was the consideration upon which God's ordaining of Christ unto afflictions and frailties was first founded, and that was, because we had sinned and become frail; and so, forasmuch as we partook of flesh and blood, he took part of the same. But take Christ as now in his glory, and invested with all his privileges as he is the Son of God, and as perfectly holy, &c., and thus he is our pattern. 'We are now the sons of God,' saith the apostle, 'but it appears not what we shall be; but this we know, we shall be like him when he shall appear.' I could amplify this unto you in the first and second Adam's conformity one to the other, from that place, 1 Cor. xv. 49: as we are conformed to the image of the first Adam—he was earthly and we are earthly; so we are to be conformed to the image of the second Adam—he is heavenly, and so are we to be.

And as Christ was thus set up by God, as our pattern and exemplar in our predestination, so—

2. He was set up as the *means* or *virtual cause through whom*, that is, by virtue of whom, God would adopt us by union with him. Jesus Christ, you know, is himself God's natural Son; but how shall we come to be sons? God putteth us into Christ, he chooseth us to be in Christ, to be married to him, and he betrothed us to him from everlasting; for Jesus Christ then betrothed himself unto us, when in election he undertook for us with his Father; and so we become sons-in-law unto God. So that Jesus Christ is the instrument, or rather virtual cause by or through whom God makes us sons. Even as a woman comes to be a man's daughter-in-law by marrying his son, or by his son's betrothing himself to her; so are we sons-in-law unto God,—as the word 'adoption' plainly signifieth,—even by a positive law; and this by marriage with his Son, which makes the relation nearer and stronger than those kind of adoptions among men do, when marriage with a child is not added to it.

Now, how is this being adopted through him to be understood? Of being made sons through his merits, or through the mere relation to his person?

I answer, through the relation to his person, and Christ's being a Son. I am in this of learned Mr Forbes's mind, that adoption, as primitively it was in predestination bestowed upon us, was not founded upon redemption, or Christ's obedience, but on Christ's personally being God's natural Son. Our justification indeed is built upon his obedience and sufferings, as ver. 7 hath it, 'in whom we have redemption, even the forgiveness of sins, through his blood.' But our adoption is through his being the natural Son of God, and we his brethren in relation to his person. To explain this: God ordained us to communion or fellowship with Jesus Christ in all things, so 1 Cor. i. 9, and so to partake of all his dignities, and whatever else in him we were capable of; as of all things in him, so likewise things even as they are in him, both in respect of order,—that in that order they are in him, are they also intended unto us,—and also in such manner as that which is bestowed on us doth answer to what is in him; and likewise in respect of causation, that anything which we have answering unto what is in him, is still founded upon that which is in Christ answering thereunto.

Now, as this privilege, to be the natural Son of God, was first in Christ himself, and was the foundation of merit in him; so this grace, to be God's adopted son, is first intended and founded upon his being God's natural Son; and then after that was intended what is the fruit of Christ's merit, namely justification founded upon his obedience.

Only let me add this caution, that we having indeed lost all our privileges, Christ was fain to purchase them anew. And so indeed it is true that adoption and all the rest are the fruits of his merits, as actually they come to be bestowed. Therefore the Apostle, Gal. iv. 5, saith, that he redeemed us, 'that we might receive the adoption of sons;' mark the phrase, that we might *receive* adoption. Our sins and bondage under the law and curse of it were an obstacle and impediment why God could not actually bestow adoption. And so indeed it is true, that our receiving adoption depends upon redemption; yet still intended it was, and founded upon our relation to Christ's person as he is God's natural Son, and we married unto him. And so, when sins are by his merits done out of the way, then this comes to take place. And so justification is by Junius rightly called *via adoptionis*.

Now then, election that gave us relation to Christ, did put us into him; God chose us in him. And then came predestination, and gave us this privilege. Is Christ my Son? says God. They shall be my sons, too; they shall be like him. Is he my heir? They shall be heirs, and co-heirs with him. And this may help to solve that question among divines, whether adoption or justification be the first benefit. For, I answer, that in God's intention of bestowing it from everlasting in predestination, adoption is the first, as being founded upon our mere relation to the person of Christ; and this without the consideration of merit. But for the actual bestowing it upon us, pardon of sins goes first. We are redeemed from under the law, that we might receive the adoption of sons, and that God might own us as such; so, John i. 12, to as many as believed he gave this privilege, that they should be the sons of God.

Now, take notice of this difference, to see your privilege yet further, as you are in Christ. Adam was created holy, perfectly holy; and, Luke iii. 38, we read that he was the son of God, but nowhere that he was the son of God by adoption through Christ. In the 38th of Job, the angels are called 'morning stars' and 'sons of God;' but nowhere are they called such by adoption through Christ. They were sons indeed, *per gratiam creationis*, because God made them, and in his own likeness, and so by creation was their Father. But they are not sons *per gratiam adoptionis*, especially not *in Christo, vel per Christum*, as divines speak. They are not sons by the grace of adoption, nor sons-in-law of God by being married unto Christ. No, this is proper only to believers. Now consider the greatness of this privilege. What, says David, is it a small thing to be son-in-law to a king? You may haply be a king's favourite or creature, as the term is; he may make you great; but to make you his son-in-law by marriage of his daughter, this is a further and more royal privilege. The angels are God's favourites and creatures; he made them what they are. But we exceed them; we are his sons, by being put into his Son Christ, and by a relation to his person. To which of all the angels hath it at any time been said, You are adopted sons through Christ? And which of them hath Christ called brethren? I will not say it is the meaning of that place, Heb. xii. 22, (I will but suggest it,) 'You are come,' says the Apostle, 'to the heavenly Jerusalem, to an innumerable company of angels, to the general assembly and church of the first-born that are written in heaven.' Why are we called God's first-born,—for the Apostle seems to intend the church of elect men as distinct from the angels, for he had mentioned them before,—but because that as Jesus Christ is called God's first-born comparatively unto us, he being God's natural Son, so it may be that we are called God's first-born in comparison of the angels, in regard that we have a higher privilege of sonship than they have? For we are sons through Christ. God hath predestinated us unto the adoption of sons through Christ.

And so I come to the third thing in the text, that as we are predestinated unto adoption *through* Christ, so also *for* Christ. So that Jesus Christ is likewise the end which God set up in predestinating us to this adoption and glory, and to perfect holiness. And this is the highest honour of the Lord Jesus Christ. It is a point of some difficulty, and therefore I shall somewhat the longer insist upon it.

The meaning of it is this. God having a natural Son, the second Person in the Trinity, whom he would make visibly glorious in a human nature, through an union of it with this divine nature, or second Person,—which human nature should by that union become his natural Son,—now upon the glorifying this second Person did God's decree primarily pitch; and for his greater glory, ordained us to be adopted sons through him, and as brethren unto him; for should he be alone? No; God will have his natural Son to have fellows; and therefore he predestinateth others *for* him, to be his companions; thus, Ps. xlv. 7, they are called. 'God,' saith the Psalmist unto Christ, 'hath anointed thee above thy fellows,' or peers. As, Zech. xiii. 7, the man Christ Jesus is called God's fellow, so in this psalm we are called Christ's fellows. And therefore God hath predestinated us to adoption of sons, as *through* him, so *for* him, that he might have company in heaven—to what end you shall see by and by. He is God's fellow; we are his fellows. He is God's natural son; we are sons by marriage with him. John xii. 24, Jesus Christ compares himself to a seed, which, saith he, if it dies not, it remains alone. His speech implies, that he was loth and had no mind to be in heaven alone; No, says he, I will have fellows there. Christ was to have company in heaven with him. And you shall see how this tended to the glory of Christ; for he is made the end of this decree of us and our adoption—

1. To greaten his glory and excellency the more, by comparison with younger brethren, that his glory might the more appear, as by comparison things do; in that he is, as Rom. viii. 29, 'the first-born among many brethren.'

2. God did ordain other sons besides him, for him as the end, that there might be those about him who might see his glory and magnify him, as you have it John xvii. 24. God had given Jesus Christ, by choosing him to the union with our nature, an infinite glory. Now, says Christ there, 'Father, I will that they whom thou hast given me be with me where I am, that they may behold my glory.' And, in 2 Thess. i. 10, it is said that Christ shall be 'glorified in his saints, and made wonderful in them that believe.' Those that believe are for this end, that Christ may be made wonderful in them, and also to them. And at the 10th verse of that 17th of John, 'I am,' says Christ, 'glorified in them.'

3. God thus ordained us to adoption that Christ might be glorified by being the cause of all our glory by adoption, and in that all we have, we have it *through him*, as it is here. And reason good that he should be the end of all, through whom we were to have all, and that we should be for him. So, Rom. xi. 36, they are conjoined, 'Through him, and for him, are all things'—namely, through and for God, of whom the apostle there speaks. And so it is said of Christ, διὰ αὐτοῦ, and εἰς αὐτὸν, as being therefore *for* him, because *through* him. In Col. i. 16, you read that God created all things 'in him' and 'for him.' I have shewed, in another place, that it is meant of Christ, as supposed to have a human nature. And it followeth at the 18th verse of that chapter, that 'he is the head of the body, the church, who is the beginning, the first-born from the dead; that in all things he might have the pre-eminence.' God set him up to be the head of the body; and if he be the head of his members, he is then their end. This I gather out of 1 Cor. xi. 3, compared with ver. 9: 'The head of every man is Christ; and the head of the woman is the man; and the head of Christ is God.' Part of the meaning whereof is, that God ordained Christ for himself, man for Christ, and woman for man; which is manifest by comparing this with

what is said at ver. 9, 'The man was not created for the woman, but the woman for the man;' he having said before, that the head of the woman is the man. He speaks this indeed of Christ's priority to man in common by the law of creation. Therefore he says, 'The head of every man is Christ,' not believers only. Yet I may well draw the like argument from that his common natural relation of headship to every man, into this his special relation of being a head to his Church: that if he be their head, that then they were created for him; they were ordained for him, and not he for them. Adam, you know, was Christ's type. Now he was not made for Eve, but Eve for him. And look what Adam was in creation, that was Christ in election, when we were put into him. God first made Adam; and then, seeing it was not fit for Adam to be alone, he brought Eve as a companion for him. So did God bring the Church unto Christ as a meet companion for him, for it was not meet that he should be alone; and so we were chosen *for* him. As therefore the woman is called 'the glory of the man,' in the same 1 Cor. xi. 7, so are the saints called 'the glory of Christ,' 2 Cor. viii. 23; and John xvii. 10, 'I am glorified in them,' says Christ, &c. So that in election Christ held the primacy, the firsthood,—as in dignity, so in order,—in that we were ordained for him. And so it follows in the conclusion of all, in that Col. i. 18, 'that in all things he might have the pre-eminence.'

Now to enlarge this a little. In the decrees of election, the consideration of Christ, as to assume man's nature, was not simply or only founded upon the supposition or the foresight of the Fall, as if occasioned only thereupon. For besides what the former explication of those words, that we were 'chosen in him,' does afford; this also, that we are 'predestinated for him' as the end of all, gives a sufficient ground against such an assertion. Now, mark my expression. I say, *not only* upon the consideration and foresight of the Fall; and that upon this ground, that all things were predestinated and created for him. Whereas to bring him into the world only upon occasion of man's sin, and for the work of redemption, were to subject Christ unto us, as he was to be incarnate and hypostatically united to a human nature, and to make us the end of that union, and of his personal dwelling in that nature. Whereas he, as so considered, is the end of us, and of all things else. This were also to have the person ordained for the benefits (as redemption, heaven, &c.) which we were to have by him, which are all far inferior to the gift of his person unto us, and much more to the glory of his person itself. His person is of infinite more worth than they all can be of.

Neither yet, on the other side, do I, or dare I, affirm that Christ should have been incarnate, and assumed our nature, though man had never fallen; because all things are ordained to fall out no otherwise than they do. God therefore never made such a single decree alone, that Christ should come into the world, but as always having the Fall in his eye, and his coming to redeem also. I account that opinion as great a chimera and fiction as many of those school questions and disputes, *What should have fallen out if Adam had stood?* &c., which are cut off with this, *That God never ordained his standing.* This is all that I affirm in this point, that God, in ordaining Christ, the second Person, to assume a human nature, had not Christ in his eye only or chiefly as a redeemer, but withal looked upon that infinite glory of the second Person to be manifested in that nature through this assumption. Both these ends moved him; and of the two, the glory of Christ's person, in and through that union, had the greatest sway, and that so as even redemption itself was subordinated to, and ordained for the glory of his person, as the end of all first and chiefly intended.

I shall open it unto you thus. When God went about to choose Christ and men, he had all his plot before him in his understanding, through the vast omnisciency of that his understanding, (by divines called his *Simple Intelligence*,) which represented unto him, as this plot which his will pitched upon, so infinite more frames of worlds which he could have made; and all these he must be supposed to have had in his view at once, afore ever his will concluded all that was ordained to come to pass. Now, he having Christ, and the work of redemption, and us, and all thus before him, the question is, which of all other projects he had most in his eye, and which his will chiefly and primarily pitched upon to ordain it? I say, it was Christ and the glory of his person. God's chief end was not to bring Christ into the world for us, but us for Christ. He is worth all creatures. And God contrived all things that do fall out, and even redemption itself, for the setting forth of Christ's glory, more than our salvation.

And the reasons for this are—

1. (Out of ver. 6.) That Christ is God's beloved, and beloved for himself. And *Deus unumquodque amat prout illud amabile est*,—God loves every thing according to that degree of loveliness that is in it. Now Christ, or the second Person dwelling in that human nature, is *per se amabilis*, amiable for and of himself, and so is by God *eligibilis per se, et propter se*, of and for himself, as being an absolute good, which no other creature is. Whereas the work of redemption performed by Christ was not *per se amabile*, not loved or pitched upon for itself. But that which gives the loveliness unto it is a remedy for sin, as Rom. vi. 10, and in that respect the goodness of it is not absolute and intrinsical, but accidental; but the goodness, the loveliness that is in Christ's person, is absolute, and in itself such. And therefore, to have ordained it for this work only, had been to have lowered and debased it.

2. (Out of ver. 5.) The grace of the hypostatical union infinitely transcends that of adoption. The being God's natural Son far surpasseth our being his adopted sons, and therefore was in order ordained first. And therefore it is that, as the text also hath it, we are said to be predestinated unto adoption through him; that is, through him as God's natural Son, and that as supposed man. For unto him as God-man is it that we have this or any other relation.

3. Yea, thirdly, the work of redemption itself was ordained principally for Christ's glory, more than for our salvation. In Phil. ii. 7, the Apostle tells us, that Jesus Christ took upon him the form of a servant, and became obedient to the death (there is the work of redemption;) 'wherefore,' saith he, 'God hath highly exalted him, and given him a name above every name,' &c. The plot of redemption therefore was subjected to the glory of Christ, and not Christ to it.

4. Now, fourthly, I might shew that then, when God took into his counsel and foreknowledge all his works projected by him, and this of Christ's assuming our nature as one among the rest, it was Christ's due that he should be the end of all, and that all God's decrees should be so framed as to make him the end of all, as well as God's own glory. So that in this there was that respect had unto Christ in those decrees of God, and he was so made the end of all therein, as no mere creature, no not the most eminent, could have been. There is a transcendency on Christ's part in this, that holdeth good in no creature. God might have made the angels and the elect, and not ordained the angels to serve the elect. That one creature

is any way made the end of another to serve it, was a matter of liberty unto God, and depended merely upon his arbitrary institution. But if God will ordain Christ and a world, angels and men elect, or whatever else together with him, it is due that God's decrees about all these be so shaped and cast that all should serve him; for they must all be his inheritance, and so he must be set up as the end of them all. And this is such reason as no man can deny. But I have spoken to this upon Col. i. 16, 17. That which I shall further add to this point, and which is more proper to this place, is, whether Christ's glory was considered by God as a motive unto God in predestinating, as God's own glory was. I know orthodox divines do grant that Christ was set up as the end of all things predestinated, who yet dispute and doubt whether Christ was so considered of God in the act of predestinating as to be the motive to move God's will to predestinate us, and ordain all things else with Christ. For, say they, nothing out of God is or can be any motive to him to predestinate; for he purposeth all things in himself.

For the resolution of this, I say—

1. That it is certain that the only determining or first moving cause that inclined God's will to predestinate both Christ and all things else with him, was his own will. He was so happy in himself, that he needed not that glory which is manifested in and by the union of the second Person with a human nature.

2. Yet, secondly, it is as certain that, so far as the manifestation of the glory of all or any of his attributes did or might move him to predestinate us, or ordain any of those works which he hath ordained, so far might the glory of the second Person move him to manifest it in and by this union, which was the highest way of glorifying him. In the sixth verse you read (and so in the thirteenth) that God predestinated us 'for the praise of the glory of his grace;' that is there made an end that moved him. Now, what is the glory of his grace? It is but the glory of one of God's attributes. Suppose then you put instead of it, 'to the praise of the glory of his Son.' Is not a person of the Trinity as near to him as one of his attributes? Is not his Son as much to him as his grace? Certainly he is. And then he might as well aim at the highest glory of the second Person, which ariseth from this personal union, as at the glory of his grace in predestinating us. Thus, John v. 22, 23, 'God hath given all judgment to the Son, that all might honour the Son as they honour the Father.' He therefore took his Son's glory into consideration, as well as his own.

And whereas it is objected, that nothing *out* of God can move God, it is true he predestinates all things by his own will and essence, even as he understands all things by his essence; so as that only was the cause that cast that determination in his will to the decreeing anything at all; yet so as, notwithstanding, the praise of the glory of his grace or power, &c., must be said to have moved him in the act: and this, although this praise of his glory be a thing out of himself,—as indeed it is, for it is that shine or result of his glory that arises out of all in the hearts of angels and men. But though this praise be not essentially God, yet it is God's; it is relatively his, and it is his peculiar. And so to say that it moves him in predestinating, is all one as to say that himself moves himself. For this praise relates to himself, and so he is said to make all things for himself, that is, for the praise of himself; which praise yet is not himself essentially, but his relatively. Now, even so the glory of the second Person, to be manifested in the human nature through that hypostatical union, is a thing out of God. It is not the person of his Son, but is relatively his Son's; and so moves him in the same order that the praise of the glory of his grace did. Only, to prevent mistakes, take in these four cautions:—

First, That take the human nature which was assumed, and that as in God's simple intelligence it came up before him, as all ours did, and it was not anything in that human nature that moved him to predestinate it, or any thing else for it. Nor was the glory of that human nature made the end in the act of predestinating; but it was the glory of the second Person only, which God saw might be more fully manifested in this personal union than any other way: that was it that moved him, and that was made the end of all. For otherwise the assuming of a human nature was as mere an act of grace as to predestinate any of us was. Yea, Christ might have assumed (take all things as they lay in a possibility before him) any human nature else unto that dignity, as well as that which he did assume.

The *second* caution is, That much less were Christ's merits considered as any motive unto God. They are but actions which are means of Christ's glory, and so far less than the glory of his person, and so are to him but as God's works are to himself. It was therefore the glory of his person alone that can, in the business we now speak of, be any way called a motive.

And that, *thirdly*, not *unto* the act, but *in* the act; for as for the act itself, God's will cast it beyond the force of the simple consideration of any such extrinsical glory that could arise unto him or any of the three Persons. Nothing without himself raised up that will in him; only, *inter prædestinandum*, in the act of predestinating, he set up this glory of the three Persons as the end for which he contrived and ordained all things: which must needs be; for if the *terminus*, or purpose of his will, was works without himself, then the encouraging motive to those works is suitably short of glory, which ariseth to him out of these.

And, *fourthly*, That Christ and his glory was set up as the end, is not to be understood as if God by one single act or decree did first predestinate Christ and his glory, and then by a new and distinct act chose us for him. But, that God having his whole platform, both about him and us, in one entire view before him, predestinated all by one entire act; yet so as in predestinating us, he was moved by the glory which Christ should have in us, whom he predestinated together with us, as both his end in predestinating us, and our end also; and accordingly did mould this whole contrivement so as we and all things else might most advance the glory of Jesus Christ, as was his due.

SERMON VII.

According to the good pleasure of his will; to the praise of the glory of his grace, wherein he hath made us accepted in the beloved.—VER. 5, 6.

I COME to those other two causes mentioned in the text; as—

1. The efficient and principal cause that cast it; and that is merely the 'good pleasure of his will.'

And, 2. here is another motive, besides the glory of Christ before-mentioned; and that is, 'the praise of the glory of God's grace.' 'According to the good pleasure of his will, to the praise of the glory of his grace.' The one is mentioned first, as that which did only cast the act, and move God to predestinate; the other, as that which yet moved him in the act itself.

Now, for the explication of both these in general, you may thus conceive the difference between them. God, blessed for ever, deliberating, as it were, with himself whether he should make any creature or no, whether he should decree any children unto himself, or his Son to take human nature; that which cast the matter was merely the good pleasure of his will. He might have been blessed for ever without this; he needed not have cared to make so much as one creature, nor to ordain the second Person's assumption of a human nature to glorify him. He needed not that external praise of the glory of his grace that ariseth from us. He was glorious enough without all this. What cast it then? Nothing but the good pleasure of his will. Here is God's prerogative and blessedness.

And the reason why nothing but God's own will could move him to it is, because all that the creature can be to him, or do for him, falleth short of him, and of the glory due unto him. Neh. ix. 5, 'Bless the Lord your God: blessed be his glorious name, which is exalted above all blessing and praise.' God is above all blessing and praise; for him, therefore, to aim at the praise of his grace, this was not motive sufficient to determine his will simply to do it. It was his own will that merely cast it, only it being determined to predestinate creatures, it propounded to itself the praise of the glory of God's grace, wisdom, and other his attributes; and so they move him in predestinating, though not to predestinate.

More particularly, for the first, *the efficient, determining cause of predestination.* If you observe it, it is not only put upon God's will, but upon the 'good pleasure of his will;' so saith the text. And this also is to be confined only to that part of his decrees of election, and predestinating men unto salvation; so as, between those decrees and all other there is this difference, that when other things, and making of other creatures are spoken of, the decrees about them are only put upon his will; as Eph. i. 11, 'He worketh all things according to the counsel of his own will'—barely 'his own will.' But when he comes to predestinate and to save poor creatures by Christ, there comes in the 'good pleasure of his will,' as the determining cause. 'He predestinated us according to the good pleasure of his will,' κατὰ τὴν εὐδοκίαν τοῦ θελήματος αὐτοῦ,—that is, this is the strength, the height of his whole will; this is the chief pleasure of it, even to predestinate us for Christ. Piscator, upon Matt. xi. 26, where the same word is used that here we meet with, 'Father, I thank thee that thou hast hid these things from the wise and prudent ones, and revealed them to babes; even so, Father, it pleased thee,' ὅτι οὕτως ἐγένετο εὐδοκία ἔμπροσθέν σου—therefore, says Piscator, reprobation is an act of God's good pleasure of his will, as well as election is.

My answer to this is, first, that when he there thanks his Father, and says it was his good pleasure, this hath not relation so much unto God's reprobating others as to his revealing of those things unto these babes; only this his good pleasure towards them is set off by his hiding it from others whom he reprobateth. The like manner of speech we have in many other scriptures, both in the Old Testament and the New; as, Rom. vi. 17, when Paul says, 'God be thanked ye were the servants of sin, but now have obeyed,' &c., his thanking God hath no reference at all to their having been the servants of sin, simply as such considered, but unto their having been now converted, and so obeyed, &c.; only, comparatively, the mercy of their conversion is set forth by their having been the servants of sin. So here, Christ gives thanks only for the converting of these babes, and not for the reprobating of any. Only he mentions their reprobation and rejection, as that which made this benefit the greater, and his good pleasure in shewing his free grace the more visible and apparent.

But, secondly, whatever God willeth may in a general sense be called his good pleasure; for if it did not please him, he would not will it. But still it is not said there, as here it is, that it was the good pleasure of his will. The phrase there hath not that *adjectum*, that addition to it, that here it hath. The meaning whereof is, that of all the things that God willeth, this alone (comparatively) is his good pleasure. He is pleased with nothing that he willeth so as he is with this. It is true he damneth men, but he doth it as a judge that condemneth a malefactor with a kind of regret and displeasure. And this may be truly said of it, that it is a mixed action. God hath something in him that moves him to the contrary, for he loveth his creature; only other ends prevail. But when he cometh to save men, here is the good pleasure of his will; his whole heart is poured forth in this: Jer. xxxii. 41, 'I will assuredly establish them with my whole heart, and with my whole soul.' God, when he shews mercy, when he predestinates unto glory, he doth it with his whole heart; there is nothing in him to contradict it; here is no mixture in this, all that is in him agreeth with it. It is therefore not only according to his good-will, but it is the top and height of his will; the most pleasing thing unto him of all the things that he willeth. It is 'according to the good pleasure of his will.'

Thus you have that which is the chief cause, which I call the determining cause—namely, the will of God, 'the good pleasure of his will;' that was it that caused him to predestinate.

Now, let us come to the other, *the end that moved God*, even 'the praise of the glory of his grace.' And here, for explication, take notice of the difference between the 'glory of his grace,' and the 'praise of that glory.'

This 'glory of his grace,' here spoken of, is that glorious attribute itself, which is God's essence, which was in itself glorious, and had continued so, though no creature had been predestinated. But the 'praise of that glory' is that holding forth of the glory of this grace, that men might praise it, and give glory to it. So, then, conceive thus of it. The Lord had grace in him, glorious grace; that was his essence. And that which moved him to predestinate us was, that this grace of his might be praised. This is the meaning of these words, 'to the praise of the glory of his grace.' It is all one with what you have Rom. ix. 22, 23, 'He was willing to make known the riches of his glory on the vessels of mercy.' God had riches of glory in him: yea, but, saith he, I will make it known. This was it that moved him; yet not so but that he could have done otherwise, he needed not to have cared for it. But his will determining to go forth of himself to glorify himself, he will do it to purpose; he will lay open all the riches that are in him 'to the praise of the glory of his grace,' as here you have it.

And the reason of this is, because as *bonum est sui diffusivum*, all goodness is communicative of itself, so glory is manifestive of itself, even as the light is; and this moves him to manifest this his glory.

You must know that God hath a double glory: an *essential glory*, namely, that of his attributes, as of wisdom, all-sufficiency, grace, &c.; and he hath a *manifestative glory*, whereby the glory of all these attributes is manifested unto the world. And this may move him; in that, although it be not his essence, yet it is his relatively, though not essentially.

Now observe further, that only the glory of God's grace is mentioned by the Apostle, when he speaks of that which moved him to predestinate. Why doth he not say, To the glory of his holiness? or, To the glory of his justice or power? All these were and are manifested in the things purposed in election too; but he sheweth his holiness elsewhere, and his power and justice elsewhere. He sheweth his holiness in making the law, his power in making the world, his justice in throwing men to hell. But his grace he shews nowhere so much as in the predestination of his children, and what he hath predestinated them to. He sheweth all his attributes therein, and grace over and above all the rest. Therefore that is here singled out and alone mentioned, especially because the act of predestinating itself, that is simply and only from free grace. And therefore you still find, that wherever election is spoken of, it is put upon his grace; both in that he chooseth freely, seeing nothing in the creature to move him, and in that he therein puts a difference between his elect and others. And therein lies the *formalis ratio* of grace, Rom. xi. 5, 6, 'There is a remnant according to the election of grace; and if by grace, then it is no more of works.' Other men God left, to deal with them according to their works; but in predestinating his children, he dealeth with them according to his free grace in Jesus Christ.

To come now to some observations.

Obs. 1.—You see that God is a glorious God: he hath glorious grace, so saith this text. He hath glorious power, so Rom. vi. 4. He hath glorious mercy, so Rom. ix. 23. All his attributes are glorious. 'Shew me thy glory,' said Moses, Exod. xxxiv. 6. Then 'the Lord passed by and proclaimed, The Lord, the Lord God, merciful and gracious,' &c. This is God's chief glory; his essential attributes are his glory.

Obs. 2.—You see that which moved God, in doing all that he doth, is his glory. He predestinated us for the glory of his grace; and certainly if in this, then in all things else he aimeth at his glory. If God should not, in all that he doth, aim more at his own glory than at our salvation, he were not a holy God. For what is holiness in God? It is that whereby he aimeth at himself; and he should descend from his being holy, if he should aim at our good more than at his own glory. This you have Isa. vi. 3, 'One angel cried unto another, Holy, holy, holy, is the Lord God of hosts; the whole earth is full of his glory.' God was to shew himself to be a holy God; that is, he was to glorify himself; that is the meaning of it. And therefore of all sinners he hates a proud man; 'He resists the proud,' because he is a competitor with God himself for glory, and contends with him for that which is most dear unto him, and his own prerogative alone, which the great and glorious God of all things cannot endure. And therefore of all sins God hateth pride and vain-glory; for all glory is his due, and justly belongeth to him alone.

Obs. 3.—You see that God was so perfect in himself that he needed not to have made any world, nor predestinated any unto the adoption of sons; for it was merely the act of his own will. Though his own glory moved him in the act, yet it was his will that cast and determined the act itself. If God will manifest himself, he will do it like God; he will make his own glory the end of all; and it becomes him so to do. He should not be a holy God else. But yet the thing that cast it was his will; because he could have done otherwise if it had pleased him, Rom. xi. 35, 'Who hath given to him, and it shall be recompensed to him again?' All that the creature doth is nothing to him. Paul challengeth all the creatures. Bring in your bills, saith he, and if you can say you have added anything unto him, you shall have it recompensed unto you again. All the righteousness that the angels have in heaven, and that the saints have on earth, what is it? It is nothing to him. Job xxxv. 7, 8, 'If thou beest righteous, what givest thou him? or what receiveth he of thine hand? Thy righteousness may profit a man as thou art,' but it can never profit God, he is blessed in himself. Nay, I go further; our Lord and Saviour Jesus Christ added nothing unto God by all that he did or suffered. It is true he sets forth the glory of God, but he addeth nothing to God. Ps. xvi. 2, 'My righteousness reacheth not to thee.' It is Christ that speaks those words, for that psalm is a psalm of his resurrection, and is quoted to that purpose by the Apostle, in Acts ii. 25–28. Now, says he, my goodness extends not to thee, O Father; it only reacheth to the saints that are on earth, to do them good; but as for thee, thou art above it. Therefore it must needs be God's own will, and his mere will, that moved him to predestinate any. Fall we therefore down before this great God, in that he minded us to choose us, notwithstanding he was completely happy in himself before the world was, and could have continued so still, and all his works add nothing unto him; for if they did, he would have made them sooner, he would certainly have created them from everlasting. But he let almost an eternity of time run out, ere he put forth his hand to make any of them, for indeed he had no need of them. The three Persons delighted one in another from all eternity, and needed no companions else save themselves. God cared not for what the creature could add unto him. Nothing moved him to elect us but merely the good pleasure of his will.

Obs. 4.—You see here that God predestinated us 'for the praise of the glory of his grace.' God's glory therefore is more interested in our salvation than our own good is, for not our benefit comes in here, in the mention of what moved God, but the praise of the glory of his grace only. You think it so difficult a thing to work God off to save you. Why, he hath that in him which moveth him now, and did move him from everlasting to do it! He hath the glory of his own grace to move him to it. This is to us the greatest ground of security in the world, that God's glory is interested with our good: Eph. i. 12, 'That we should be to the praise of his glory who first believed on Christ.' Wilt thou come and believe? Thou canst not do God a better turn; for this advanceth the praise of the glory of his grace; and God is for this reason more moved to save thee than thy heart can be to be saved thyself.

Obs. 5.—I told you it was the highest pleasure of his will; nothing pleased him so as this. Observe then, that of all things else which God purposeth, this, even to shew grace to poor sinners, pleaseth him the most. He willeth many things, and he works all things by the counsel of his own will; but this is according to the good pleasure of his will. There are many scriptures to this purpose. 'In these things,' speaking of acts of mercy, 'I delight,' Jer. ix. 24. 'Mercy is his delight,' Micah vii. 18. Yea, his delights are said to have been in this before the world was, Prov. viii. 31; where besides this there is nothing else mentioned.

Obs. 6.—Observe that God hath set up his Son, 'for him,' saith ver. 5; and his own free grace, 'to the praise of the glory of his grace,' saith ver. 6. These two are to share the glory between them; even Jesus Christ and himself. If Christ had not been his Son, and equal with himself, he would never have done it. No creature shall have a share in this glory, but all things are ordained for his Son, and for the praise of the glory of his own free grace. And accordingly, he hath wrought faith in our hearts to give all the glory unto free grace and to his Son. If you had been saved by love, that would have been diminishing from free grace and from Christ; and so would works and duties. But faith, that is a principle fully suited to God's own intent; which is, to set up his Son and free grace, and to magnify these two. You shall find in Scripture that God is said to be 'all in all,' and so is Christ said to be 'all in all' too. For these two share all the glory between them, that so men may honour the Son, even as they honour the Father, as I said even now. In 1 Cor. viii. 6, the Apostle says, 'To us there is but one God, the Father, of whom are all things, and we for him;' (as you have it in your margins;) 'and one Lord Jesus Christ, by whom are all things, and we by him.' Here, you see, they share it between them; only with this difference, that all things are said to be *of* God, and *by* him too; but all things are not said to be *of* Jesus Christ, but only *by* him.

We have seen and explicated two of those blessings intended to us, and bestowed on us from everlasting. *First, election* in Christ to be perfectly holy, as we shall be in heaven, for God looked at his works as he would like them to be at last; and, *secondly, predestination* to that glory that adoption, or being a son of God, bringeth with it. Now follows a *third* benefit: 'wherein,' saith the apostle, 'he hath made us accepted in the beloved.' This I am now to speak to; and so to proceed—

'Εχαρίτωσεν, 'He hath made us accepted.' I must open the force and signification of this word first. It is as much as if he had said, he hath made us *caros*, 'dear,' to him. Out of God's free grace he hath made us pleasant unto him in the beloved; so saith Calvin. The Papists, they would have the word to signify God's bestowing inherent grace of holiness upon us, and making us gracious or holy; and that which perverts them in this their interpretation is, their aiming to magnify the virgin Mary, for the word here in the original is used but once besides in all the New Testament, and that is Luke i. 28, 'Thou art highly favoured,' &c. It was spoken by the angel unto Mary. So we translate it; but they read it, 'Thou art full of grace.' They will needs carry this word to inherent grace in us, that so by this the fulness of grace in the virgin Mary may be extolled; that she being, and that God foreseeing her so full of grace, had therefore chosen her to be the mother of Christ. But the word is, in respect of us, a passive word, and indeed a made word, usurped by the apostle himself for his purpose; and there in Luke signifieth this, that God made her acceptable to him, and cast an infinite favour upon her; and this is proved by what is said in ver.

30 of the same chapter, 'Fear not, Mary, for thou hast found favour with God.' It was not that she had grace in her, but that God had cast grace and favour upon her; so that the meaning of the word is, he hath rendered us acceptable or gracious; or, most fitly in one word, he hath *ingratiated* us. The meaning is, not that God foresaw grace in us, but that he cast his favour upon us, and settled his delight in us—he made us dear, precious, and delightful to himself. And this to be the meaning of the word, and not that, as the Papists would have it, appears—

First, Because the apostle had mentioned the blessing of inherent holiness before, 'to be holy before him in love;' and also mentions conversion and regeneration, the imperfect work of faith and holiness in this life, afterwards, in ver. 18.

And, *secondly*, it appeareth likewise by what followeth, 'in his beloved;' that is, as he hath loved Jesus Christ, and delighted in him, so in this his beloved he loveth, pleaseth himself in, and delighteth in us. This is the meaning of his making us accepted in the beloved.

In the interpretation of these words, I have not a little been troubled unto what rank to refer this blessing: whether I should refer it to a part of justification, (which, we know, consisteth of these two particulars, forgiveness of sins and acceptation of our persons,) and so this to be a part of our justification in Christ, bestowed upon us in time here in this life; or whether I should interpret it of an action of God passed towards us from everlasting, (such as are election and predestination,) and that action as including also a blessing principally intended to our persons unto everlasting, and after this life, such as I have shewed you perfect holiness and adoption to be. I confess, in the end I inclined unto the latter, and found that Zanchy is with me in it; and I will give you these reasons for it, why it is not meant so much of that acceptation of our persons which is a part of justification,—though it may include that also, and that acceptation of our persons is the fruit of this,—but rather referreth to an eternal act towards us, and an eternal blessing, even to eternity, to be bestowed on us. For, *first*, it runneth in the same key with the other two, 'he hath blessed us,' and 'he hath chosen us;' so 'he hath accepted us"—they are all spoken in the time past; whereas, when he cometh to redemption or justification, he changeth the phrase and tense, 'in whom we *have* redemption.' Therefore, I cast this, 'having accepted us,' into the former rank, with having chosen and blessed us from eternity, as noting out three prime instances of God's eternal love.

Second, The order of the apostle's ranking of it, and his bringing of it in, would argue that he did not intend to speak of that acceptation of our persons which is a part of justification.

For, first, it comes in before forgiveness of sins, whereas that acceptation of our persons unto justification of life follows upon forgiveness, and doth necessarily first suppose it.

And, secondly, it is not only mentioned before forgiveness, but redemption comes in between it and forgiveness.

So that, I say, I rather account it to be one special act of God's love done towards us from everlasting, such as election and predestination was; and so it implieth both a third act and a third blessing, of the same sort with the two former.

It is not that acceptation of us which is the second part of our justification, for that is expressed by an accounting us righteous in Christ as our righteousness, and some such thing should have been put in as the ground of it; but this is an acceptation of our persons in Christ as he is God's beloved, and simply refers thereto, and so unto Christ's person as God's beloved one.

But then the question will be, both what distinct act of God's this is, differing from election and predestination, and what differing blessing it is from perfect holiness and adoption unto glory?

In the first place, some say, that it imports that love of God which was the foundation both of God's choice and of his predestination; that he hath therefore chosen and predestinated us, because he hath accepted us, that is, set his love upon us, in his beloved Son.

But that was supposed in God's *choosing* us; for *dilectio præsupponitur electioni*, as Aquinas well speaks. Yea, and this is also sufficiently expressed in the words foregoing, 'to the praise of the glory of his grace;' that is, of this his free love borne to us.

Again, this acceptance of our persons is not, as here it succeeds, that love or acceptation upon which he chose us, but is a branch or fruit following of it, and distinct from the act of his choosing us; it hath not an identity or sameness of act with choosing us itself. Though it is put forth in and together with choosing us,—yea, though it be said to have been in the beloved, Christ,—yet that first love that caused him to choose us, and not others, was immediately carried unto us in the act of choosing us as unto Christ himself, and moved him to choose our individual persons as immediately as he was moved to choose Christ himself; only, he was pleased to choose us in Christ, as a foundation or ground which he planted us into when he chose us, and by choosing, or when he chose us, he put us into Christ. But being thus chosen in Christ, then this fruit followed upon it, to accept us in Christ, as his beloved for ever after.

I take it, therefore, not so much to be an antecedent love to the election of our persons, as a consequent love or complacency, as I may so call it, or delighting in us, and accepting of us through his beloved, when he had chosen us in him, and set us into him; his delight even then was with the sons of men, Prov. viii., in his forethoughts about them.

And here I take not *antecedent* and *consequent love* in the Jesuitical or Arminian sense, whereby God should be said to love us with such a consequent love as ariseth from a foresight that we will believe, and so chooseth us, and in that sense should be said to choose us in Christ. There is a twofold love—*amor beneplaciti* and *amor complacentiæ*, an old distinction.

First, *a love of good-will*, whereby God doth bear a good-will to us, and so resolveth to choose us and give us to Christ; and this is spoken of in the former verse, 'He hath chosen us in him, according to the good pleasure of his will.'

And, secondly, there is *a love of acceptation* or *complacency*, or of delight and resting in what he hath done. God thereby delights himself in the creature which he hath thus set up and chosen in Christ, and this from everlasting, as I shall shew you by and by. It is called in Zeph. iii. 17, a 'resting in his love,' and supposeth election first. When God hath chosen us, he takes delight in and is infinitely well pleased, both with this design and contrivement he hath towards us, and with our persons also, as considered in and through his beloved Son; even as a father that means to bestow his son upon such a woman, first takes a liking to the woman, (here is the love of good-will,) which makes him choose her for his daughter, and pitch upon her, rather than upon any other, to make her his son's wife. But yet, when he hath betrothed her to his son, then he loves her with another and a further kind of love—he accepts her, he delights in her, and hath a complacency in her, as considering her to be his daughter, as wife unto this his son. This I take to be the orderly joining and meaning of these two words, 'having predestinated us unto adoption,' and 'accepted us in his beloved,' the latter act following upon the former.

The next question is, how this act of God towards us may be said to have been *from everlasting;* and how God may be said to have delighted in us before we were?

1. For this, that God did put forth such an act from everlasting, consider that scripture, Prov. viii. 30, 31. If you read the verses before, Christ tells you there what God and he did before the world was. 'I,' says Wisdom, or Christ, 'was by him, I was brought up with him, and I was daily his delight; rejoicing always before him in the habitable part of his earth; and my delights were with the sons of men.' All this was from everlasting, for read ver. 25–27, and he saith, 'it was before the mountains were settled, or the hills brought forth,' &c. So that Christ did then look upon us as delightful unto him, and God did the same in his Son.

2. For the clearing of it, we must remember what was said before; that when once God had first chosen us in Christ, look how far it may be said we had a being in him. So far God might take, and did take a view of us, as represented existing in him; and so please himself with us, as so viewed and considered, and look upon us with a gracious eye; and also rejoice and comfort himself in what he had done for us. And by this our representative being as in Christ, I mean not that kind of being before God which all other creatures he meant to produce had in their several ideas or appearances in his thoughts. But we further had a representative being in Christ, who actually stood before God, or 'by him,' as Solomon's word is. This representation becometh then real, when made in him and by him, by his undertaking to stand for us, and as in our stead undertaking as our head to represent us. And this gave us a real being in Christ, and as far differing and excelling those ideas of other creatures as the images or shadows of men, pictured for the ghosts of men when they are dead, do from those drawn with the brightest orient colours in oil, which painters make to set out men alive to the utmost life that may be. And by way of difference, we call the first but shadows; and such were the ideas of all other creatures in the mind of God, in comparison to what the elect had in God's mind, being set in Christ, who gives a being of him, yea, and in Christ Jesus. But still I must remember you of these two things I so often mentioned, that my meaning may be understood:—

The *first*, that this benefit of acceptation of our persons in the beloved I refer to those other antelapsarian benefits, severed from those of redemption, as hath been all along inculcated; that is, as flowing to us from Christ as our head of union with God; and to us as considered as purely creatures and abstractly before sin befell us, in that supernatural state which we were, at the first sight of us by him, ordained unto as creatures, and our persons also considered as one with Christ.

The *second*, that it is that acceptance of us in Christ which comes and flows merely from the person of Christ as God-man.

From which you may observe, that when the Apostle saith, God hath thus accepted us in the beloved, he doth not say that this acceptation of us is in the blood of the beloved, or the merits of the beloved. It is not so founded, but it is founded upon our relation to his person. God had chosen us in him to have relation to his person; and so, Jesus Christ being beloved, God accepteth us in him, for this our relation's sake unto him as the principal beloved. As a father when he hath betrothed his son unto a woman, he loves her for the relation she hath to the person of his son; so doth our God. This acceptation of us, even of our persons from everlasting, it is founded upon Christ's being beloved. And therefore you shall find, that the love wherewith God loved Christ, and the love wherewith he loved us, are said to be one and the same love, John xvii. 23, 'That the world may know that thou hast sent me, and hast loved them as thou hast loved me.' We were so represented by Christ, and considered in him, that we made up one Christ mystical; as the head and the body make up but one man.

Again, this seems to be some special favour and peculiar grace unto the sons of men elect, and not to the angels, as here it is spoken of. The angels, we read, are elect, 'the elect angels;' but we nowhere read of them that they are elect *in Christ*. Likewise that they are the sons of God, by creation namely; but not adopted sons through Christ, as we here are said to be. And so they are highly favoured of God; but nowhere that they are accepted in the beloved, as here we are said to be. It may be said, they are highly favoured as menial servants to God, but not as sons adopted. Many courtiers were in high favour with Saul; but David speaks of his being son to him as an higher matter by far. As in nobility there are higher ranks than other, so among the nobles in heaven. The angels, it may be said, God hath loved them with a special love, and he hath loved Christ and both from eternity; but it is nowhere said, that he hath loved the angels as Christ said there, 'Thou hast loved them, as thou hast loved me.' And how special a privilege this is I shall express to you by this similitude. The sun, you know, shines upon all the world; but if you take a burning-glass and hold it in the point of union or concentration, between the shining sun and something that you would have inflamed, hereby the sunbeams are contracted, and do fall upon that object with a more intense heat and fervour, even to an inflammation of it; and this by reason that the beams were first contracted in the centre of the glass, and then diffused and with more vehemency darted upon the object under it. Thus God loveth *all* his creatures; his love is 'over all his works,' so the Scripture expresseth it; but he loves them not in his beloved, he accepts them not in him. But now for the sons of men elect, that Son of God, who is his beloved, contracts all the beams of God's love into himself; they fall all upon him first, and then they through him shine and diffuse themselves upon us all, with a ray infinitely more strong and vigorous than they would have done if we had been considered in ourselves alone. And this is the advantage of being accepted in the beloved. God loves us with the same love wherewith he loved his Son.

To come now unto some observations from hence.

Obs. 1.—Observe here, that Jesus Christ is God's beloved in an eminent manner. Look, as God put all light into the sun, and that diffuseth and communicateth light unto all the stars; so Jesus Christ hath contracted all the love of God to himself, and through him it is diffused upon us. He is Υἱὸς τῆς ἀγάπης, the Son of his love, as he is called, Col. i. 13. You read it translated there 'his dear Son;' but the Greek hath it 'the Son of his love.' Christ hath, as it were, engrossed all God's love unto him: 'This is my well-beloved Son, in whom I am well pleased.' Yea, indeed and in truth God is not well pleased with any of the creatures, but as they have relation to him and are his servants. Otherwise, he findeth folly in his angels, Job iv. 18. They would not have pleased him, had they not come under his Son, and had relation unto him some way or other, and subserved for his glory. In loving his Son he loved them; but he loveth us as being planted into him. The Trinity could not please itself out of itself. He is the beloved.

Obs. 2.—Is Christ thus God's beloved, with and in whom he is so fully pleased; and is he not thy beloved, as it is in the Canticles? What is the matter? Is thy narrow soul more curious about an object for its love than God himself is? Oh, let him be to each of us our beloved! If he be God's beloved, he may as well be thine. Is he able to satisfy God's vast thoughts; and is he not able to satisfy thee, poor creature? God himself is satisfied and at rest in him: 'I was daily his delight,' says Christ, Prov. viii.; and wouldst thou be happier than God is? Is he God's beloved Son, in whom he is well pleased; and wilt thou be pleased in anything else save Christ?

Obs. 3.—Observe that Christ is said to be 'the beloved' simply in and for himself, and 'in whom we have redemption' comes afterward, as a superadded thing. So that, set aside the work and benefit of redemption that is to be had in and by Christ, and there is a loveliness in his very person beyond all, for which we should desire him. You that are sinners do love him because he hath redemption for you, and so you have need of him; and you do well so to love him, for he deserves it. But yet, let me tell you, *Est aliquid in Christo formosius salvatore*,—There is something in Christ more beautiful, more amiable and glorious, than his being a Saviour. God cannot love him for any benefit of redemption by him; and yet he is God's beloved. He is *primum amabile*, loved for himself; and so let him be to thee.

This is the first sort of observations from hence.

A second sort is this:—

Obs. 1.—If thou art in Christ, fear not sin; for God from everlasting saw all thy sins, and yet, for all that, he continued to accept thee in his beloved, It altered his mind not a whit. He was so much pleased with his beloved, that though in his own prescience he foresaw what we would be, yet, having chosen us in his Son, he accepteth us in him; and so, now that we actually exist and sin against him, he, notwithstanding, finds so much contentment at home in his Son, having him by him, that he can patiently bear with us, and please himself in Christ. And so, though he see thee sinful for the present, and foresaw thee sinful from everlasting, yet he still accepts thee in his beloved. And the reason is, because Jesus Christ is more beloved of him than sin is or can be hated by him. If ever sin should come to have more interest for hatred in the heart of God than Christ hath for love, thou mightest well fear: but he hath accepted thee in his beloved, therefore be not thou afraid.

Obs. 2.—Hath God accepted thee, and rendered thee thus dear unto himself in his beloved? No matter though the world hate thee. The world shall hate you, says Christ, John xvi. 33: 'In the world you shall have tribulation;' but it is no matter, 'in me you shall have peace,' &c. God accepts thee in Christ; he renders thee dear unto himself in his beloved.

Obs. 3.—Go therefore unto God, to be accepted only in and through his beloved. Here is the greatest and strongest argument for it that can be. It is said before, in ver. 4, that God chose us unto perfect holiness, and ordained us to perfect glory, and to be sons to him, ver. 5, and both these as we shall one day be in heaven. And yet, after both these, the acceptation of our persons in the beloved comes in as a third and distinct benefit; so that all this would not have pleased him so much as one look upon us in his beloved. It is not perfect holiness, nor that complete glory which we shall have in heaven, that makes us accepted with God comparatively to this, to be considered and accepted in the beloved. And wilt thou now go and bring thy imperfect graces and menstruous duties? Art thou in glory yet? Art thou perfectly holy? If thou wert, yet consider here is a third benefit besides all these, 'He hath accepted us in his beloved;' which let thy soul look out for, notwithstanding all thy grace and holiness.

And so I have gone over the three first blessings, which are eternal ones, and absolutely pitched upon our persons in the relation we have to the person of Christ. God *chose us* to be in him, and because he is holy, we must be holy: holiness, therefore, is essential to our being in Christ. God *predestinated* us in Christ, therefore we must be sons, as he is; and so we are predestinated to adoption in him, his natural Son. And then, God hath *accepted* us in his beloved; and therefore as he loveth him, so he loveth us. All these three blessings are not founded so much upon the merits of Christ as upon the relation we have unto his person. And they are the blessings which were first and absolutely intended to our persons, simply in the relation which by election we had given us to the person of Christ.

And so much for the sixth verse.

Come we now to the mercies which we have in relation to Christ's merits, couched in these three following verses:—

In whom we have redemption through his blood, the forgiveness of sins, according to the riches of his grace; wherein he hath abounded toward us in all wisdom and prudence; having made known unto us the mystery of his will, according to his good pleasure which he hath purposed in himself.—VER. 7–9.

The Apostle here changeth the key of his language: 'He hath chosen, he hath blessed, he hath accepted.' This was his language before; but here he beginneth to alter it. Here he varies the tense, and says, 'In whom we have redemption,' &c. Because he comes now to a new sort of blessings, therefore he speaks in a new key. And so interpreters almost generally observe.

Now for the general analysis, both of all these words from ver. 4, and likewise of these blessings.

There are two sorts of divisions, which these words and the former may be cast into.

The *first* is a *trichotomy*, or dividing of them into three parts.

You know there are three Persons in the Trinity, the Father, the Son, and the Holy Ghost. And these three Persons have three several works:—

1. *The Father's work* was to choose, to predestinate, and to accept in his beloved. His work therefore is in the 4th, 5th, and 6th verses.

2. *The work of the Son* is redemption, &c.: 'In whom we have redemption through his blood,' ver. 7, &c. It is not meant of redemption passive, or which we receive as the fruit of his having redeemed us; but of that redemption active, which was in him, and wrought by himself. And therefore it is not said '*by whom*,' but '*in whom* we have redemption through his blood.'

3. And then *the Holy Ghost's work* is the application of all these unto us, when the Spirit doth in and by conversion bring home all these to our hearts. And this you have in the 8th and 9th verses, 'Wherein he hath abounded toward us in all wisdom and prudence; having made known unto us the mystery of his will,' &c.—This is one division whereinto you may cast these verses and the blessings mentioned in them.

But there is a *second*, and that is a *dichotomy*, or division of them into two parts.

There is one sort of blessings from the 4th verse to the 7th, and another sort of blessings from the 7th verse to the 10th. And so, as there are three Persons, and their works described to be three, so there are also two triplicities of blessings, as I may so call them.

The first three are such blessings unto which God absolutely chose us in relation to Christ's person. And they are—

1. *Perfect holiness*, ver. 4.

2. *Perfect glory*, or *adoption*, ver. 5.

3. *Acceptation of our persons* in and upon that our relation to his beloved, ver. 6.

But then, secondly, there are three other blessings, founded upon our relation to Christ through his *merits*. As—

1. *Redemption*, taking it in the largest sense for whatever redemption may extend to; for redeeming us as well from misery as from sin, and for the purchasing of all those blessings which we had forfeited: 'In whom we have redemption through his blood,' ver. 7.

2. *Justification;* which is one fruit of redemption: 'The forgiveness of sins, according to the riches of his grace,' ver. 7.

3. *Vocation*, or *calling us;* which is the work of the Spirit: 'Wherein he hath abounded toward us in all wisdom and prudence; having made known to us,' &c., ver. 8, 9.

Calling, you know, is either external or internal. *External* is the preaching of the gospel; that you have in the 9th verse, 'Having made known to us the mystery of his will.' *Internal* is the working faith and holiness in us; which is mentioned in the 8th verse, 'He hath abounded to us in all wisdom,' the principle of faith; 'and prudence,' which is the principle of holiness, as interpreters carry it.

Now, observe what is common to these two several sorts of blessings.

First, They come from God's decree, both the three latter and the three former. How this is true of the three former you have already seen. We were elected to be holy, and predestinated to adoption, according to the good pleasure of his will, &c. And the three latter do depend upon the same good pleasure of his will from everlasting: 'In whom we have redemption, &c., according to the good pleasure of his will,' ver. 9. So that God's good pleasure is as well the fountain of these three latter sort of mercies, and therefore cometh in the rear of them too, as it was of the three former. And so Erasmus saith that this, 'according to the good pleasure of his will,' referreth as well unto redemption and forgiveness of sins, as it doth to calling us and giving us wisdom and prudence.

Secondly, They have this likewise common unto them, that there is *free grace* in them both. For the Apostle speaking of the first sort of blessings, he saith, 'He hath chosen us, and predestinated us, to the praise of the glory of his grace, wherein he hath made us accepted in the beloved;' and then coming to the other sort of blessings, at the 7th verse he saith, 'We have redemption and forgiveness of sins, according to the riches of his grace.' And then it follows, 'In which,' namely, grace, 'he hath abounded toward us,' in converting us also, ver. 8. So that still here is free grace in both.

And, *Thirdly*, They are both sorts *in Christ*. God chose us in Christ, predestinated us through Christ, and accepted us in the beloved: there is the first sort. 'In whom we have redemption, and the forgiveness of sins through his blood:' there is the second sort. We have all in and through

Christ, both the one sort of blessings and the other. These are common to them all.

But before I come to expound these words in the 7th, 8th, and 9th verses, and give you observations out of them, give me leave from the connexion, and the Apostle's thus ranking these blessings into these two sorts, to give you in my transition between them the greatest matter of note—that I know of—I can commend to you, and it shews their distinction.

In these verses (take them all together from the 4th verse to the 10th) the Apostle seems to hold forth unto us two several parts of God's decree—two designs contained in it; and these framed according to those two ranks of blessings before-mentioned. There are two parts, I say, of the mystery of God's will towards us from everlasting; two contrivements that God had towards us poor creatures; and both of them, as you will see in the handling of them, infinitely glorious.

The one is, the *decree of the end* that God hath ordained to bring us unto, *decretum finis.*

The other is *decretum viæ*, or *medii*, the *decree of the way* through which God leads us in bringing us to that end. Divines use to distinguish them thus, terming the one *decretum intentionis*, the decree of God's utmost intention to us: the other *decretum executionis*, the decree of his executing or bringing about the things intended, and is likewise by them called *decretum mediorum*, but I rather call it *decretum viæ.* The distinction is common among divines; but I find but few that apply it unto this scripture, though some do it. And we shall see these words naturally to part themselves into these two decrees:—

1. Here are God's decrees concerning the *end* unto which he meaneth to bring us, or about what he meaneth to do with us, and make us to be at the last. He intendeth to make us perfectly holy and perfectly glorious, like his Son; he meaneth to delight in us for ever, as considered in his beloved. And these decrees the 4th, 5th, and 6th verses do contain.

2. Here are the decrees of the *way* unto this end; that is, of what shall fall out to us in his leading us through this way unto this end—namely, perfect holiness, glory, &c.—and of what shall betide us ere we come to enjoy all this. The Apostle plainly intimates unto us, that we shall fall both into sin and into misery, and so have need of a Redeemer. This same Head we were chosen in must come to redeem us, and our sins must be forgiven, and we must be called, and must have faith; and all these things wrought in us before we can come to heaven. This is the decree of the means, *decretum viæ*, as the other is *decretum patriæ*, (*via* and *patria*, you know, is an old distinction;) and this latter is expressed in the 7th, 8th, and 9th verses.

For this distinction itself, you shall find it founded upon Scripture; as Heb. ii. 10, where the Apostle, speaking that God had ordained Christ to be the author, captain, and leader, ἀρχηγος, of our salvation, says, thus it became him 'in bringing many sons into glory.' So we translate it. The words in the original are πολλοὺς υἱοὺς εἰς δόξαν ἀγαγόντα, 'in leading many sons unto glory.' Here you see is the glory which God means to bring us unto as the end, and here is a way implied through which he leads us unto that glory. Here is the Canaan, and here is the wilderness through which we are to pass unto it. And as we are thus ordained to an end, and led through a way unto it; so is our Redeemer too. You shall find the Scripture speaking in the same language concerning him also. So, Ps. cx. 7, the Psalmist, speaking of Christ, tells us what he shall be in heaven, ver. 1, 'Sit thou at my right hand,' &c.; but before he comes thither, 'he shall drink of the brook in the way.' Our Saviour Christ is ordained to drink of fulness of pleasure in heaven at the end. 'At thy right hand,' says Christ, Ps. xvi. 11, which psalm was written of him, 'are pleasures for evermore:' rivers of pleasure, as they are called elsewhere. But he must drink of a bitter cup before he comes thither; he must 'drink of the brook by the way.' So that God had another decree about him too, even the decree of the way.

Now, to sum up all; if you speak of what God hath ordained us unto as the end and issue of all, it is contained in the 4th, 5th, and 6th verses: to be perfectly holy, and perfectly happy, and for God perfectly to delight in us; this is the end and upshot unto which God meaneth to bring us.

But by the way, to make the end and conclusion of all the more illustrious, God, in and by the same everlasting decree, ordained to permit the fall of these his elect. So that instead of these three, perfect holiness, perfect glory, and perfect acceptation with God, he throws you into a condition wherein you are perfectly unholy, perfectly unhappy, and perfectly hateful unto him, as in yourselves considered. This is an accident that falls out by the way; you shall see who will cure it presently. Instead of perfect holiness, here you have nothing but sin; instead of glory, and being the children of God by adoption, you have nothing but hell, and then being the children of wrath; and instead of being accepted by God, you are made a curse: 'Cursed is every one that continueth not in all that is written in this book to do it.' This curse seizeth upon all mankind, and upon yourselves although elected to the contrary. Here God's first design about the end unto which he means to bring us, seems utterly dashed and spoiled; and we are as far off from all that glory intended as possibly could be imagined. And what does God order then? Even that this Christ, God-man, he in whom he chose us, and he to be a Head unto us from everlasting, who is the 'Captain of our salvation,' as he is called in that place before-named; that he should come and take frail flesh, come 'in the likeness of sinful flesh,' and become our Redeemer: 'in whom we have redemption through his blood.' Through him, says God, I will forgive all their sins into which they are fallen, (as the word here used for sins fitly expresseth it, *παραπτώματα*,) and though they have nothing but unholiness, wickedness, and unbelief in them, yet I will abound towards them in all wisdom and prudence, and turn them unto me, and that in this life; and then bring them to that perfect holiness and glory, and to that perfect acceptation with me in the world to come, that I have ordained them unto.

SERMON VIII.

In whom we have redemption through his blood, the forgiveness of sins, according to the riches of his grace.—VER. 7.

I STAND here, at the 7th verse, between two of the greatest—what shall I call them?—heights or depths of God's wisdom and grace towards us; and as that angel in the Revelation had one foot upon the earth and another upon the sea, so I stand with one foot upon the blessings ordained us from eternity, and intended us when we come in heaven, and the other upon the blessings intended us here in this world. They are both of them two vast arguments, and therefore you shall give me leave to be somewhat larger than ordinary about them. For of all the mysteries of the gospel, since I knew it, this hath most swallowed up my thoughts.

Two things I shall observe about these two sorts of decrees and blessings.

First, I shall shew you how these blessings differ, as before I shewed you what was common unto them among themselves.

And, secondly, *I shall give you a glimpse of that infinitely glorious harmony between these two contrivements, and of the wisdom of God that shines in them both.* The greatness of the point deserves this.

For the first, *How these blessings differ.*

First, The first sort of blessings, perfect holiness, adoption, &c., were ordained us without the consideration of the Fall, though not before the consideration of the Fall; for all the things which God decrees are at once in his mind. They were all, both one and other, ordained to our persons. But God in the decrees about these first sort of blessings viewed us as *creabiles,* as creatures which he could and would make so and so glorious. For God can easily ordain the subject, and the utmost well-being of it both at once; and this might well be the first idea taken of us in God's purposes, because such is the perfection of God's understanding that he at first looks to the perfection and end of his work. But the second sort of blessings were ordained us merely upon consideration of the Fall, and to our persons considered as sinners and unbelievers. And the first sort were to the praise of God's grace, taking *grace* for the *freeness of love;* whereas the latter sort are to the praise of the glory of his grace, are with an ἄυξησις, an endearment of a greater degree of his grace, unto a further glory of his grace and an illustration of it, taking *grace* for *free mercy.*

Secondly, Those first sort of blessings are ordained to have their full and plenary accomplishment, and to take place in that other world, and are suited to that state into which we shall then be installed. And as in God's primary intention they are before the other, and therefore are said to have been 'before the foundation of the world,' ver. 4, so they are to take place after this world ended; they being the centre of all God's thoughts towards us. Then we shall be so holy as Satan himself shall find no ground to carp at us. Then we shall receive the adoption of children; and though we are now the sons of God, yet then it shall appear to us and all the world, by that infinite glory that God will then bestow upon us. But those second sort of blessings were ordained for our entertainment in this world, and are suited unto that condition which we shall run through unto the day of judgment.

Thirdly, The first sort are founded merely upon our relation to the person of Christ, as is manifested in all those three mentioned, ver. 4–6, 'chosen in him,' and therefore holy; because as he, being the Son of God, was to be holy, Luke i. 35, 'That holy thing which shall be born of thee shall be called the Son of God;' so are we, we being members of him. And as this is true of holiness, so of the other two it is more plain. But this second sort are founded merely upon the merits of Christ; as redemption through his blood, and so forgiveness, conversion, &c. In a word, these latter blessings are but the removings of those obstacles which by reason of sin stood in our way to that intended glory. In the fulness of time God sent his Son to redeem them that were under the law, that they might receive the adoption of sons, Gal. iv. 5.

I come now to the *second* thing propounded, *That glorious harmony of wisdom and grace, &c., that shines in these two designs,* and in the reducing them unto these two heads; the one subordinate and subserving the other.

It is true, if we speak rigidly, there is but one act and one entire object of God's decrees; for God doth all at once. Yet according to the language of the Scripture, wherein God condescendeth to our apprehensions, and hath plotted all things to our apprehension, to take us the better, you shall find that there are two plots or designs that God had towards us.

He had a primary plot, which was first in his intention; and he had an after plot, subordinate to the other. His first plot was to choose us to that state which we shall be in in heaven. His after plot, that he had towards us whilst we are in our way, was to redeem us and reconcile us unto himself by his Son Jesus Christ. To open the glory of this mystery unto you:—

First, God made two worlds for us. He made this world, and put us into it holy once, in Adam. But, alas! we stood not long in that state, but fell into sin. Then God hath made the world after the day of judgment. Now, answerably, he hath two designs about us. Whilst we are in this world, under sin and misery and imperfect holiness, he hath the design of redemption; to justify us, to forgive us our sins, and to abound towards us in all wisdom and prudence. And when we come into that other world, namely heaven, there he hath ordained perfect holiness for us, and acceptation with himself in Christ's person as the beloved. Again, answerably, as God hath two worlds into which he puts us, and two designs about us in those worlds, so he hath ordained us two sorts of blessings answerable to those two designs; the one for this world, the other for that to come. He hath perfect holiness, glory, and acceptation of our persons, for the world to come; and he hath other blessings, redemption, justification, forgiveness of sins, calling us, &c., for this life and this world.

Secondly, Answerably, Christ runs through a double state; one that was intended him first and simply, which, in John xvii. 5, he calls 'the glory he had with his Father before the world was;' that is, to speak the lowest sense of those words, the glory which God first and absolutely intended him before he had created the world, and before or without the consideration of Christ's coming into this wicked world or earth. For he cannot hereby mean the glory of the second Person, for that must not be begged or prayed for; and, ver. 24, it is said to be given him; and therefore it is a glory which he hath as God-man. He hath a glory now in heaven which was intended him before the world was. But then Christ had another state, even a frail state, clothed with our frail flesh and blood. He came down here, and takes upon him 'the likeness of sinful flesh,' in all the infirmities of it, and here he drinks of the brook by the way; he suffers, and so redeems us.

In the third place, Christ by both these states comes answerably to have a double relation to us: the one of a *Head* and Common Person, simply considered as an author of salvation (as he is called, Heb. ii. 10) more strictly considered; the other, as he is a *Redeemer.* You have them both in Col. i., ver. 18–20 compared together; where the Apostle describeth our Saviour Christ in both these his fulnesses. First, he tells what Christ is absolutely ordained unto, and his body with him, ver. 18, 'He is the head of the body, the church; he is the beginning, the first-born from the dead,' and so the founder of that state we shall have after the resurrection: 'that in all things he might have the pre-eminence: for it pleased the Father that in him should all fulness dwell,' even the fulness of all relations to us, ver. 19. And what followeth? 'And, having made peace through the blood of his cross, by him to reconcile all things to himself,' ver. 20. Here is the relation of a Head, and likewise the relation of a Redeemer and Reconciler too. God chose us in him, predestinated us in him, and accepted us in him; and besides this, 'in him we have redemption through his blood, the forgiveness of sins,' &c. That place in Colossians answereth this here in Ephesians.

In the fourth place, From both these doth arise unto Christ a double glory, which he is ordained to. The one intrinsical, due to him as he is the Son of God dwelling in a human nature, and being therein a Head of a glorious body, the Church; in whom, as such, and so beloved of God himself, and for his sake merely in respect of his person, they are beloved of God in him. And then, besides this, there is another glory more extrinsical, and acquired by the work of redemption; purchased and bought with the sweat of his soul, as, Phil. ii. 8, 9, 'He humbled himself, and became obedient unto the death of the cross; therefore God also hath highly exalted him,' &c.

And thus, *fifthly,* you see how these double sorts of blessings come to be bestowed upon a different ground. Those blessings which are the blessings of the end unto which God will bring us,—namely, perfect holiness, glory, and acceptation of our persons in heaven,—they are founded merely upon our relation to Christ's person. Therefore we see it is here said, that we are chosen in him to be holy before God in love; and we are predestinated through Jesus Christ unto the adoption of sons,—he being a natural Son, and we adopted in him; and we are accepted in him, he first being God's beloved; and it is merely our relation to his person that is the foundation of these blessings. But when the Apostle comes to the other sort of blessings, as redemption, forgiveness of sins, and the like; these he founds upon Christ's blood—'In whom we have redemption through his blood,' &c.

And thus, *in the sixth place,* we come doubly to be saved; saved over and over; and hereby we obtain a double right to heaven. We have one right founded upon our relation to Christ's person, being chosen in him, and accepted in him. And then we have all these bought over again, when we had forfeited them, by Christ's purchase in redeeming us. And for this you have a scripture in the 14th verse of this chapter, where you shall find that heaven is both an inheritance and purchased too: 'Which is the earnest of our inheritance, until the redemption of the purchased possession.' And therefore, Rom. viii. 23, heaven is called both 'the adoption,' in respect to its being an inheritance, by our being chosen heirs with Christ; and also a 'redemption,' as being purchased by his blood.

In the seventh place, Hereby God hath a double glory too. Here are two editions of his attributes besides that in the works of creation, and both in Christ. One in the person of Christ, simply and alone considered, in whom the glory of God doth shine: the other in the story of his mediation and the works thereof, in which all the same attributes are manifested over again and anew by works of his and the merit of them. It would be too long to go over them all; as to shew the double glory of his wisdom, the double glory of his grace, power, &c. A double glory riseth to God's wisdom, in that he could make one Jesus Christ serve for two designs, the greatest that ever were, and either of them worth the incarnation of his Son; I mean his taking our nature upon him. For I appeal to you, suppose that God should have created the man Christ Jesus in heaven, in that glory which now he hath, and he should never have come down hither to suffer and die, as he did; suppose withal, that God had taken up all his elect unto himself in heaven, or created them there at first with him, as he did the angels, so as they had never been in the other Adam, nor in this world, but had been made sons and heirs with Christ and members of him as their Head, and so God delighting himself in them, and they in him, from their first creation;—suppose God had done no more, I appeal to you if this had had not been worth the assumption of our nature? For here had all the attributes of God been manifested; here had been infinite love and free grace shewn; here had been the greatest power, the greatest goodness, the greatest holiness, and whatever else you will, in all these manifested. But you may haply say, here had the manifestation of one attribute been wanting, namely, *mercy to creatures in misery.* I answer, this mercy is but a further extension of the same love, causing God to continue to love them as sinners, whom he loved with a free love as creatures. Love is the foundation of mercy; and so that love in God was so great that it would have turned into mercy, if there had been need: Eph. ii. 4, 'God, who is rich in mercy, for the great love wherewith he hath loved us,' &c. Yet, the more evidently to shew forth this, he leaves us to sin and misery, and then sends his Son to take frail flesh upon him, and to suffer and die to redeem us. And in this work of redemption appear all these attributes anew, his power, justice, wisdom, holiness, &c., as I said before.

Eighthly, God ordered it thus so, to take us the more whom he would bring to heaven. Had we at first been brought to that communion with Christ which we shall have in heaven after the day of judgment, without having known either sin or misery, it had been a good and blessed condition indeed; we should infinitely have rejoiced in it, and had reason so to have done. But certainly heaven will be sweeter to us by reason of our having once fallen into sin and misery, and then having a Redeemer that came and freed us from all, and then brought us to heaven. Oh, how sweet will this make heaven to be unto you! Rom. ix. 23, before God brings the vessels of mercy unto heaven, it is said, he 'prepares them unto glory.' Now, what is it that prepares them to glory? It is couched in that expression therewith joined, that they were 'vessels of mercy,' that is, that once had been filled with misery, and then he takes them up to glory. This adds a shadow and a foil to glory, to make it the more glorious in their apprehensions. In an ante-masque you shall have hell first presented; and that being removed, you have heaven presently before you. Thus doth God with us. All that falls out to us here, together with the whole work of redemption, it is but an ante-masque and *prœludium* to take us up in our thoughts while we are here in this world: so to render that glory which we shall have in heaven the more resplendent and glorious.

This double plot serveth also to make the story of Christ's love the more illustrious to the Church, his spouse. Those that write romances and feigned stories, you shall have them set up some one man and some one woman, whom they mean to magnify and exalt to the dignity of a king and queen, and in the end marry them gloriously together. This they drive at; this is their first project when they set themselves to write such a book. But that they may take the reader the more, before this conclusion they will in their fiction throw this man and woman into the greatest and most desperate extremities that can be imagined, separate them in the greatest distance each from the other, that the reader shall judge it impossible these ever again should meet in a happy enjoyment and embraces. They will hurry them through all sorts of misfortunes and disasters, and make that lover to endure the greatest hardships, and run through the most hardy and heroical adventures and hazards for that his espoused love, that can be; so to effect and bring about in the end her and his liberty and mutual content in the enjoyment each of other. This makes the story to be read along with pleasure; to see all the way the constancy of them both in their begun loves, and in the end to see them both extricated out of the depths of miseries, and to meet together and enjoy each other, and become most great and glorious princes. This useth strongly to take those that are but readers, and that when they know it is but feigned; but if it were real, how would such a happy catastrophe take with and affect those lovers themselves! Now, just thus hath God set up Christ and the Church, his spouse, to be married together in heaven for ever; that is his plot. But he first throws her into sin and misery, and then sends his Son Jesus Christ to rescue and relieve her, so to shew his love unto her to the uttermost; and all this so to take our hearts the more when we shall come to see his person in heaven. 'God commendeth his love to us in this, that while we were yet sinners, he sent his Son for us,' &c. God loved us in ordaining us to life; but I will commend it yet more, says God, for they shall be in a state of death, and then I will give my Son for them to redeem them. So that this plot of redemption was but a further improvement or edition of the love of God and of Christ.

And then, *lastly*, God's love is set out unto us by a double gift of Christ to us and for us; whereof the gift of him as of a Redeemer to us is of the two the least. Thou art a good soul; tell me whether dost thou prize more the person of Jesus Christ given thee, or the benefits thou hast by his death? Thou wilt say, I prize the person of Christ most—and thou pitchest right; it is more worth than all his benefits. I use to say, and it is most certainly true, that Christ's love is more than his sufferings; his sufferings worth more than all his benefits; but his person is more than either benefits or sufferings. Now God, in choosing thee in him to be a son, and placing thee in him by election, and in him accepting thy person, gave thee in this, his person, and a relation to him, to live with him, and to have communion with him, and to be like to him for ever. And this is the first gift, and that which first he intended to thee. But then, over and besides this, God gave him as a Redeemer for thee; and this redemption is but a benefit which thou hast by him. And, indeed, it was but to remove objections that lay in the way unto that other great plot, as hindering the accomplishment of it; as I remember Cyril well expresseth it, *Præfunditur nobis Christus,* saith he, *ut possit natura humana, superatis malis quæ interim acciderant, ad pristinam gratiam Christi et dignitatem recurrere;*—It was to recover us out of those evils that fell out by the way, unto that dignity which God in Christ first chose us unto.

And, to conclude, the knowledge of Christ, and communion with his person and the glory thereof, is part of the happiness ordained for us in the world to come. But the knowledge of Christ in his benefits of redemption is that which takes up our thoughts here; and both do conduce to make him most glorious and most dear unto us, and us most completely happy in him.

Ver. 7, '*In whom we have redemption through his blood,*' &c.

Here is—

First, *Redemption itself.*

Secondly, *The Redeemer:* 'in whom.'

Thirdly, *The price of this redemption paid or laid down:* 'his blood.'

Fourthly, *One fruit of this redemption instanced in for all the rest:* 'the forgiveness of sin.'

Fifthly, *The spring or source of all this, the benefactor or founder of all this:* 'the riches of his grace.'

First, The redemption itself, which is larger than forgiveness of sins; for redemption reacheth to glory also. Glory was to be purchased anew. And why? Because, though we were predestinated to glory in our relation unto Christ's person as our head, yet we forfeited it all, and it must therefore be bought again; and therefore the glory of heaven, in Luke xxi. 28, is called redemption. 'Lift up your heads, for your redemption draws nigh,' saith Christ, speaking of the latter day. You have the like place, Rom. viii. 23, 'We groan within ourselves, waiting for the redemption of our bodies.' And, Tit. ii. 14, sanctification itself is called redemption, 'Who gave himself for us, that he might redeem us from all iniquity, and purify unto himself a peculiar people, zealous of good works.' Redemption is a large word; for Christ was fain to buy all that God intended us, because we lost it. That is for redemption.

Second, This redemption, as is said, we have it in Christ; 'in whom,' saith he, 'we have redemption.' He speaks not of the redemption we receive here, but of the work of redemption which Christ himself wrought—that is the cause of all the redemption we receive; for, he saith, it is redemption in Christ. There are some put this difference between being redeemed in Christ and redeemed through Christ: say they, the elect only are redeemed through Christ—that is, his redemption is applied to them. There is an universal redemption for all men, but it is only efficacious for them that are elected; they only are redeemed through Christ. But it is confuted here out of the text, by comparing the coherence. Who are redeemed? We, saith he. What *we?* Observe of whom he speaks before: according as he hath chosen us in him, and predestinated us in him, and accepted us in him; those *us* that were chosen, they are redeemed, and no other.

In the second place, he saith, 'we' have it 'in him.' What is the meaning of that? What doth that imply?

It is spoken, first, in a distinction from the fathers in the Old Testament. It is true they were redeemed virtually, but the thing was not done. They did not see Christ; 'they saw his day afar off' indeed, and he was 'the Lamb slain from the beginning of the world;' but he had not yet done it;

but we have it—Christ hath done it. We see Jesus, saith he, Heb. ii. 9, tasting of death for every man, and crowned with glory and honour. In Heb. ix. 15, you shall find there this expression, 'For this cause he is the Mediator of the new testament, that by means of death, for the redemption of the transgressions that were under the first testament—' Mark the expression: he was to die 'for the redemption of the transgressions that were under the first testament.' The meaning is this: that the world had gone upon the score with God, he received not one penny of money for all the fathers he had saved. They had been redeemed indeed; they had the fruit of that redemption that was afterward to be done; but as yet Jesus Christ had not paid his Father one penny of money. Now, then, he comes under the New Testament; and he is the Mediator, that by means of death he might be for the redemption of the transgressions that were under the Old Testament; that he might cancel all those bonds. You have the like expression in the 3d of the Romans.

So that, my brethren, it is a help to your faith in comparison of them; they had redemption only in the promise; they saw it afar off. We have redemption in Christ; it is done, it is past. We see Jesus tasting death, see him hang upon the cross, by faith, and see him now he is in heaven 'crowned with glory and honour;' so saith the Apostle in that place, Heb. ii. You have more help to believe than our forefathers had.

Secondly, we have redemption as in a Common Person in Christ. We have it not only when it is applied to us, but we have it in him as we had condemnation in Adam, before we were born in the world; so we had redemption in Christ when he died.

The next thing I would have you observe is this, and it may mightily and wonderfully instance the love of God towards us: The last words he had said of Christ, if you mark it, in ver. 6, was that he was God's beloved; 'He hath made us accepted in the beloved.' What is the next word after in this 7th verse? 'In whom we have redemption through his blood.' It is Chrysostom's observation: It is strange, infinite strange, that he that was God's beloved, whom he delighteth in as in himself, that God should ever send him to be a Redeemer, and to shed his blood for sinners. What! was he God's beloved, and have you redemption in him too? Should God sacrifice his beloved? God chose us to be holy in heaven with him, to be sons with him there, to delight in us there. Let that plot stand, let them never come to be sinful, let me have them up in heaven presently with my Son. One would have thought God might have said this. No, God would commend his love yet further. He would let them fall into sins; to redeem them, he would sacrifice this beloved. He had so much love in his heart that he could commend it to us no way but by sacrificing his beloved. He might have chosen whether he had done so or no; he might have made us as happy in heaven as now we shall be; it needed not have cost him the blood of his Son. But now he wonderfully sets out his love to us, in that we have redemption in his beloved.

So much for the Redeemer, which was the second head.

The third is, *The price;* and that is his 'blood:' 'redemption through his blood.'

The Hebrew word for *redemption* importeth somewhat more than redeeming by price; but the Greek word that is here used, and elsewhere, imports only a *redeeming by price*, not a *redeeming by force.* When God came to deal about our salvation, considering us sinners, saith he, I will have a full price, or I will not save you; I will be satisfied to the uttermost. He will have redemption by a price, so the word signifieth, ἀπολύτρωσις. He will have them bought. What I give I give, saith he; what I sell I sell. I will sell their salvation, and I will sell it to the uttermost. I will have a full price for it. 'You are bought with a price,' saith the Apostle, over-bought. And, 1 Tim. ii. 6, it is called ἀντίλυτρον, an adequate price, a price that if you weigh it in the balance it is heavy, it weighs down the other; it is sufficient for it, it was a full price. In Rom. iii. 26, and so on, you shall find there that when God came to justify a sinner, he saith he will be just too. I would fain save the sinner, but I would be just too. Therefore he will have a price, a full price, and therefore it is called *redemption by price.*

But what is meant by his blood? His blood is only mentioned; not that his active obedience doth not go into it. Take all Christ, good brethren. But because his blood was the last part of the payment that cancelled all the bond, therefore his blood is still mentioned in Scripture. And his blood is more mentioned than the other. Why? To answer the expression of the type in the old law. There was the blood poured out, you know, and there was blood laid upon the horns of the altar, and all things were sprinkled with blood. What did the blood signify in the Old Testament? Blood in the Old Testament signified the soul of the beast; saith he, the life of it, or the soul of it, lieth in the blood. So in the New Testament still, the blood of Christ is mentioned, to signify the sufferings of his soul; and it is mentioned, too, to answer the type. In the Lord's Supper you have bread, to signify the breaking of his body; but you shall find that he ascribeth more peculiarly his sufferings to his blood, signified by the wine, to represent the sufferings of his soul; and therefore his soul is said to be 'poured forth.' Fall down, my brethren, before the Lord Jesus Christ. 'Thou art worthy to receive all honour and glory, for thou hast redeemed us to God by thy blood,' say the angels and saints, Rev. v. 9.

Fourth, The Fruit. So much for the price. What is the fruit of it? Forgiveness of sins. What sins? Look in Col. ii. 13, 'Having forgiven you all trespasses'—all, past, present, and to come. He retaineth sin in your consciences to humble you, to break you; and when men are cast out of the Church, he then bindeth in heaven upon their consciences what is bound on earth; yet, considering you in Christ, he forgiveth all sins, strikes off all at once by his blood.

And what is this great business of the forgiveness of sins? We that are poor sinners, when we are first humbled and see our sins, oh, what a mercy is it that our sins were forgiven! True, but it is a small matter, my brethren, forgiveness of sins is; it is buried in the foundation; heaven, glory, eternity, communion with Christ and God, being all in all. I say, it is but a small thing, it is but the foundation of this great building; in heaven all sins will be remembered no more. Yet we poor souls, as we have reason, we come to Christ for forgiveness of sins first, and we do well, as we are sinners. He is the fittest object for us, as he is the Saviour of us from our sins, take him in his blood; but when we are come to Christ once, you find perfect holiness, you find adoption, glory, acceptation in his person; you find in his person more than in all his benefits, than in forgiveness, or whatsoever else.

Lastly, What is the cause he bestoweth all this? The riches of his grace; 'according,' saith he, 'to the riches of his grace.' Grace, you must know, signifieth properly God's freeness in doing it: 'He hath justified us freely by his grace,' Rom. iii. 24. Therefore the love of God is called grace, because it importeth a freeness of his love; and the mercy of God is called grace, because it importeth a freeness of his mercy. Grace is taken in the first sense in the 6th verse. It is taken in the second sense here in this 7th verse; for the freeness of shewing mercy, for mercy referreth to forgiveness. I shall have occasion to handle these things when I come to the second chapter, ver. 4–7. In a word, now observe what is the reason, when he said he did bless us first, it was 'to the praise of the glory of his grace;' when he speaks of the forgiveness of sins, then comes in 'the riches of his grace.' What is the reason of this difference?

This is the reason of it, saith God. My attributes they are mine, and they are yours; they are mine for my own glory, but they are yours for your benefit; all the riches of my grace, take them to your use, (riches, you know, are for use;) all the riches that are in me take them as they are riches, as they may be employed to the good of the creature take them—they are yours as much as mine, only the glory shall be mine. 'He hath predestinated us to the praise of the glory of his grace;' but he forgiveth sins 'according to the riches of his grace.'

And why *riches* of grace?

It is to help your unbelief. When you come and see your sins told out before you, set in order before you, and piled up as high as heaven, and as low as hell, thinks the poor soul, where is the wealth, where are the riches, where is that that shall forgive all these sins? Here it is; here is riches of grace told out before you; here is the blood of the Lord Jesus Christ manifested to you. *Riches of grace.* Thou needest not bring one penny. God is rich enough; what shouldest thou bring thy duties or anything to the forgiveness of sins? Here is riches of grace doth it, not a penny of ours; get but faith, it is the key to unlock this treasure, and to possess thee of these riches. There are multitudes of sins, here are multitudes of mercies; riches implieth multitudes, abundance: 'according to the riches of his grace.'

There is one difficulty I must open, and I have done with this verse. I shall be then over the greatest difficulty that I know in this chapter or epistle. I shall do it in a word.

There is this one objection or scruple: How doth God forgive sins according to the riches of his grace when he receiveth a price for it? Doth a man forgive freely when he is paid for it?

This stumbles the Socinians. Indeed, the gospel is made up, say they, with nothing but contradictions. God is paid for what he doth, and yet it is done freely. God chooseth men to life and salvation, and it is done immutably; ordaineth what their wills shall do, and yet they work freely. These are contradictions; we could name many more; amongst the rest this is one.

It is answered, *first*, It is true Justice had a satisfaction, but who called Christ to give this satisfaction? Not Justice, but it was Grace did it. Justice indeed stood upon it, kept her own distance. I will be satisfied, saith Justice. But who spake to Christ to pay this? Grace did. So that here is one reconciliation of it; it is according to the riches of his grace, because grace did move Christ to do all this for us.

Secondly, The merits of Christ, though they be a price of themselves, if Christ had offered, 'I will die for my people now they are sinners,' God might have refused it. *Quando aliud offertur*, &c. It is a law maxim, 'When another thing is offered than what is in the obligation, the satisfaction may be refused.' The meaning is this, as if God should say, I will be paid by them that sinned; I will not take your offer. It is true your merits are worth it, but I am at my liberty whether I will take them or no. Now here is grace; I will take my Son, I will sacrifice him, and accept of that satisfaction.

Again, *thirdly*, you must know this, That it is to God that Christ did all he did; he calls himself his servant,—'my elect,' saith he, my servant. 'I came down,' saith he, John vi., 'not to do mine own will, but the will of him that sent me.' He did it all upon his Father's cost, merely upon that motion. Hence then, because that the very death of Christ was the gift of God, as he is called, John iii. 16, 'He gave his only-begotten Son;' hence to us it is free grace.

And then, in the *fourth* place, That God should accept thee and me through his Son, and forgive us our sins through his merits, it is free grace. Thou art bought without any of thy money; it is free to thee. Though it cost Christ's soul dear, it cost thee nought, as the phrase is, Isa. lii. 3, 'You have sold yourselves for nought;' it is free to us. Thus you see grace and Christ's merits are reconciled. God takes a price, and yet he doth it freely.

And, *lastly*, let me add this, The more that God paid for to buy us, if it were his own he paid, the more grace it was to pay it. He gave his Son; he was his own, his only-begotten Son; he gave him, he gave him freely; he might have saved you without Christ's satisfaction, that is certain. Christ, when he was to go to suffer, useth this as the utmost argument with God: 'Father,' saith he, 'all things are possible with thee;' thou canst save the world another way; if thou wilt, thou mayest forgive them freely without my satisfaction; let this cup pass from me. No, saith God, I will do it this way to choose; I will have thee to die for them. Well, saith Christ, 'not my will, but thy will be done.' Here is free grace more than if he had no satisfaction made, because his grace giveth this satisfaction. He hath redeemed us 'by his blood,' yet according to 'the riches of his grace.' I have done with these words.

SERMON IX.

Wherein he hath abounded toward us in all wisdom and prudence; having made known unto us the mystery of his will, according to his good pleasure which he hath purposed in himself.—Ver. 8, 9.

The Apostle's scope in this chapter is an enumeration of the grand particular blessings which we have in Christ; which blessings are either such original blessings to which we are ordained from eternity, and shall enjoy in the end and issue of all, or they are such blessings as in the world were wrought for us in Christ, and are applied unto us in this life in and through Christ. There are *decreta finis*,—that is, of our journey's end, &c., that God means to bring us unto. Perfect holiness in the 4th verse; adoption or glory, through being sons, in the 5th verse; a perfect complacency of God for ever in us in his beloved Son, mentioned in the 6th verse, for the sake of his Son's person, and what he is in himself, the natural Son of God, and the beloved one of God, and communicated to us by our relation to him and union with him. There are likewise *decreta executionis*, the decrees of execution, or of the way to that end, heaven; which are these that follow in the 7th, 8th, and 9th verses—redemption through Christ's blood, &c. And these benefits depended upon what moreover Christ wrought and did for us; he redeemed us by his blood. And this he performed in this world; and in respect to this work he is to be considered as Redeemer, and our persons considered by God the Father as sinners, children of wrath, &c. And here begin the benefits of application.

Remission of sins is the first, and is the foundation, and is put for the whole of justification, as his blood speaks his whole obedience and redemption in parts,—viz., the price as paid by Christ, and the benefits purchased, which are redemption, &c. Then, secondly, there is the work of vocation, our first conversion to God, and of faith and sanctification;—the whole work, as it is imperfect from first, and wrought in us from first to last, which God hath begun to work, and will continue to perfect till the day of our death. And this is expressed by those words of the 8th verse, 'wherein he hath abounded in all wisdom and prudence.' He by these two words expresseth the chief and leading principles of sanctification wrought in us, and which comprehend in them the whole complex of the work of grace in this life wrought in us first and last. For the Apostle being to contract and crowd up these benefits into a compendium, he speaks *synecdoches*, and mentions parts for the whole of each kind, which he afterwards dilates upon in particulars.

I shall now repeat nothing more of what I delivered on the former verses. I come immediately to that which is the next benefit here before us; his having 'abounded toward us in all wisdom and prudence,' &c.

It is, as you will see by the opening of it, the blessing of conversion, and of our calling, and the working faith, and also our imperfect holiness, which God works in us here by the gospel. And he saith three things of it:—

I. HE SHEWETH YOU THE GREATNESS OF THE BLESSING; he saith that God hath abounded in grace in bestowing it: in which grace it is he hath abounded.

II. YOU HAVE THE BLESSING ITSELF, and both the parts of it: both the inward calling, working 'wisdom and prudence' in us; and the outward calling, 'having made known the mystery of his will,' &c., in the preaching of the gospel, and the revealing of it.

III. YOU HAVE THE CAUSE OF BOTH, and that is his good pleasure: 'according to his good pleasure.'

IV. And then, fourthly, (for I may add that,) you have THE CAUSE OF THAT GOOD PLEASURE TOO: 'which,' saith he, 'he had purposed in himself.' So you have the division of these 8th and 9th verses.

Divines, you know, make two parts of our calling. There is *vocatio externa,* that is common to all men that hear the gospel, and to whom the mystery of the will of God is made known. But then there is an internal calling, a work upon the heart, whereby he doth work wisdom and prudence in us to embrace this word, and to lay hold upon this mystery, and give up our souls unto it.

And then for the inward calling, you know divines reduce it to two heads. First, *the wor ing of faith;* secondly, *the working of holiness,* or *change oj heart and life.* All is reduced to these two, holiness and faith, as I shewed you out of the first verse of this chapter: there are the saints and faithful in Christ Jesus. Now accordingly the Apostle hath two words here. Here is *wisdom,* which is the principle of faith; and here is *prudence,* which, as I shall shew you, is the principle of sanctification, and is put for the whole work.

I. To begin first with that whereby he setteth out the *greatness of the blessing*—'wherein he hath abounded toward us,' ἐπερίσσευσεν. To open that word a little, 'abounded.' The word in the Greek is taken either to signify an abundance that one hath and hath received, taken *passively,* as I may so express it; as when in Scripture we are said to 'abound in grace,' as in some places we are; or else it is taken *actively,* as it implieth abounding in the giver, in the bestower, when one bestoweth out of abundance. As there is *plenitudo fontis,* and *plenitudo vasis,* a fulness in the fountain, and a fulness in the vessel; both are said to be full, but the fountain is said to be full as that which communicateth, as that which bestoweth, which fills the vessel, and the vessel is said to be full as having received all from the fountain; so we are said to abound in grace, when he has filled us with it. 'Of his fulness,' which is the fulness of the fountain, 'we have received grace for grace,' saith the Apostle, John i. 16. So now here is πλήρωμα *fontis,* and πλήρωμα *vasis.* Here is signified the abounding of the fountain, namely of God, as a fountain communicating; and the abundance of the vessel, of us receiving. Now it is the abounding of the fountain that is here meant. And of that there are two meanings too, which I find in Scripture; two significations or uses of the word.

First, It referreth to something abundantly or largely bestowed. When God doth largely or abundantly bestow, then he is said to abound; or as they do translate it, 2 Cor. ix. 8, where the same word is used, 'He is able to make all grace to abound towards you.' The meaning is not, he abounded in wisdom by making wisdom abound in us; for always when it is so taken it is joined with an accusative case, as it is there in that place of the Corinthians with πᾶσαν χάριν. But here it is not πᾶσαν σοφίαν, but ἐν πάσῃ σοφίᾳ, not making grace abound; but (which is the second meaning of the word or phrase, 'in which God abounded') it doth not only import that God did cause wisdom, &c., to abound, but that he out of abundance of grace in himself bestoweth wisdom. And so I find it to be used Luke xv. 17, abounding in bread, in my father's house, says the prodigal. It is in the genitive case, as it is here; 'bread enough,' so we translate it: so here God aboundeth in his grace, and it is all one as to say his grace aboundeth; or as the English phrase, when we say one 'aboundeth in love,' it is all one as to say 'his love is abundant.'

So that the meaning of it in a word is thus (to gather it up for the weaker understandings:) that God out of abundance of grace in himself bestoweth upon us, in converting us, wisdom and knowledge, wisdom and prudence, faith and holiness, as you shall hear afterwards; and his scope is to magnify the riches of grace that is in God, in bestowing such benefits on us. His grace aboundeth in the doing of it. And so it is all one with what Paul saith of himself in 1 Tim. i. 14 (a parallel place to this.) Paul speaks there of his conversion, as he speaks here of the Ephesians', and every Christian's calling and conversion and works inherent in him. He saith here, 'wherein God abounded,' namely in grace. So he saith there, 'The grace of God was exceeding abundant toward me' (exceeding abundant, ὑπερεπλεόνασε, it was over-full) 'with faith and love which is in Jesus Christ,' some way answerable to receive it. Here he reduceth the work of calling to two heads too, faith and love, faith and holiness, for love is the principle of holiness; and wisdom and prudence do, by a metonymy, or by a synecdoche rather, imply both these. So that that which Paul saith of his own calling there, the same he speaks of our calling here, and the one expresseth the other. There he saith the grace of God was over-full, it overflowed; so the word signifieth. And here his comparison is from a fountain. Grace gushed out from God's heart as a fountain, when he first bestowed saving wisdom and prudence, when he first converted them. This is the meaning of the words, 'wherein he hath abounded toward us.'

I should not have stayed so long upon the word but for the sake of some observations which this expression will afford.

Obs. 1.—When you would set a right value upon any blessing bestowed upon you, you are not to value it chiefly by the blessing itself bestowed, but by the grace in God out of which it comes. He doth not say here he gave abundance of wisdom and abundance of prudence, though all the quantity is noted here, but he saith he abounded in grace when he did it. The Apostle would have them set the value of this blessing upon the grace which was the fountain of it. 'Wherein,' saith he, or 'in which he hath abounded toward us.' My brethren, learn to value spiritual blessings and temporal blessings likewise, not by the things themselves, but by the love of God from which they come. A small blessing may be out of abundance of love. So in what we do for God, a cup of cold water, the widow's mite. God may abound in grace to thee in bestowing it, when the blessing is in the matter of it but little. What is the reason that many good souls, that have true grace wrought in their hearts, are so unthankful? They look to the grace wrought in them, and they see that there is but a little of that, and therefore they value all by what they find in themselves, by the blessing wrought: 'I find but little in me, if any at all.' And while thus they value the blessing by what they find in themselves, they prove unthankful to God. Whereas that little grace thou hast, that little faith, be it but as a grain of mustard-seed, it proceeds out of abundance of grace in God. 'Wherein he hath abounded toward us,' saith he here, in working the least beginning of true wisdom and prudence in the least saint. God abounds infinitely in his love to thee, when thou hast but the least beginnings of grace in thee, as small at first as Nicodemus had.

If you mark Paul's expression in 1 Tim. i. 14, the place even now quoted, he doth not say that his faith and love in Christ were exceeding abundant. No, but saith he, the grace of our Lord was exceeding abundant in bestowing faith and love upon me. He looks not to the quantity of his faith or his love, but he looks at the grace of both; and how doth he magnify that? He had said before two things of himself. First, saith he, 'I was a persecutor and injurious;' I hated the saints; there is the first. But, saith he, 'I did it ignorantly in unbelief;' I was an unbeliever, and I was a persecutor. Now, for God to work faith instead of unbelief, and love to the saints instead of persecution and hatred of them, in me, that was once an unbeliever and a persecutor, the grace of God was exceeding abundant herein. He looks not to the work wrought, but he looks to the grace that bestowed it, considering the circumstances of the condition he was in before.

Obs. 2.—Observe what thing it is that this big swelling word 'abounded,' overflowing, gushed out, as I may so say, is used about. What is it that he shewed abundance of grace in? It is the work of conversion, working in them wisdom and prudence, that is, faith and holiness; as you shall see by and by.

The observation, then, from thence is, That God sheweth abundance of mercy in converting of a man. It is an abundant grace he singleth out, that you see here eminently, and Paul, in that other place, said it was overfull; he was, saith he there, exceeding abundant, speaking of his conversion.

To give you another scripture for it, 1 Pet. i. 3, 'Blessed be the God and Father of our Lord Jesus Christ, who according to his abundant mercy hath'—done what for us?—'begotten us again.' There is an abundance of mercy eminently above all other works in a man shewed in his conversion.

I might enlarge upon this, but I will only give you one reason, and so pass from it. It is the fundamental mercy to all grace and glory. It is the first appearing of the love of God to a man: Tit. iii. 4, 5, 'After that the kindness and love of God our Saviour toward man appeared, not by works of righteousness which we have done, but according to his mercy he saved us, by the washing of regeneration, and renewing of the Holy Ghost.' God's love is like a river or a spring that runs under-ground, and hath done so from eternity. Where breaks it up first? Where bubbleth it first? (as the word in the text signifieth; it is a similitude I have used before, but the words in the text will bear it.) Where doth this fountain begin to bubble up or issue forth? When a man is first called, then that love that hath run from everlasting under-ground, and through the heart of Christ upon the cross, breaks out in a man's own heart too. And it is the fundamental mercy of all grace and glory whatsoever.

My brethren, the word here used doth compare God to a full fountain, which was restrained till the fulness of time came, when he would break forth in love to a man. Oh! when shall it once be? saith he. And when the time comes, his love and mercy gush out upon a man, when he calls and converts him. This is the meaning of the word in the Greek. It was the time of his espousals, a time of love. So much for the first thing in the text; that whereby he sets out the greatness of this blessing, 'wherein he hath abounded toward us.'

II. I come, secondly, to *the blessing itself;* wherein, as I told you, there are two parts. Here is first the internal part, the work of grace upon the heart, expressed here by *wisdom* and *prudence*. And here is the external calling, in the 9th verse, 'making known the mystery of his will,' &c.

He expresseth conversion, and the whole work inherently wrought in us, by the making of a man wise. It is usual in the Scriptures, and you may oft-times meet with it: Ps. xix. 7, 'converting the soul—making wise the simple;' Prov. ii. 10, the beginning of conversion, and so all along, the increase of all grace to the end, is expressed by wisdom entering into a man's heart, 'If wisdom enter into thy heart,' and so goes on to do more and more: not into thy head only,—a man may have all that, and be a fool in the end,—but when it entereth into the heart, and draws all the affections after it, and along with it, 'when knowledge is pleasant to thy soul,' then a man is converted; when God breaks open a man's heart, and makes wisdom fall in, enter in, and make a man wise.

Wisdom.—It is taken sometimes for the doctrine of the gospel, in which a stupendous divine wisdom is to be seen and adored: 1 Cor. ii. 7, 'We speak,' saith he, 'the wisdom of God in a mystery, even the hidden wisdom,' &c. Speaking of the doctrine of the gospel, he calls it the wisdom, and the hidden wisdom of God.

Or else, wisdom is taken for the gift of saving grace, working a principle in the soul, whereby our souls are made able to take in all the truths of the gospel effectually. And so it is taken in this very chapter, ver. 17, for the grace of wisdom in the knowledge of Christ, and to be wise to salvation. He prays there that they 'may have the Spirit of wisdom and revelation in the knowledge of Christ;' that is, to have the Holy Ghost working wisdom in them, and giving a principle to be capable of all the spiritual saving truths that discover the knowledge of Christ, and to enlighten that principle, to take them in and wisely to apply them to themselves; in one word, to be wise unto salvation.

Some have thought that in 1 Cor. i. 30, Christ is said to be made, in this sense, 'wisdom' to us, as particularly intending the grace of graces, namely the principle of faith,—now, it is certain it is a distinct thing from sanctification and justification, as there the apostle useth it,—and that it is made thus distinct from the other, and set first, because thereby we are enabled to take in all the spiritual truths of the gospel, so as to have a man's soul saved. Christ is made wisdom to us when the soul is humbled, emptied of itself; and when a man comes to himself, his eyes are enlightened to behold, and he is made wise to lay hold upon, that offer of mercy made to us in the Lord Jesus Christ. But we must not exclude that objective wisdom—that is, all that wisdom which God in the doctrine of the gospel contrived and prepared, which is called 'the wisdom of God in a mystery'—with which the apostle in that chapter had outfaced the Greeks that were so for wisdom; that, in comparison of which all the wisdom in this world, civil, moral, natural, he says, is foolishness and comes to nought, and which the doctrine of Christ utterly outshined. And so I judge that in that place, 1 Cor. i. 30, both this inherent spiritual wisdom in us, and objective wisdom which is in our Christ, as revealed in the gospel, are meant.

Now if you ask, which of the two are meant here, whether wisdom taken for the doctrine of the gospel, or for the gift of God working faith in the heart? I answer you, as I have said, it is taken for the *gift of wisdom* wrought in a man's soul, whereby he applies all the truths of the gospel and wisdom of the gospel to himself. For—

First, So it is taken plainly in the 17th verse, where he calls it the 'Spirit of wisdom and revelation,' by the Holy Ghost working wisdom in a man, and then revealing to that new eye of wisdom spiritual truths.

Then, secondly, it is taken rather for the *gift of wisdom* bestowed upon us, than for the *doctrine of wisdom* revealed in the gospel, because that follows in the 9th verse, 'having made known to us the mystery of his will;' therein the doctrine of wisdom is revealed. Therefore, when he speaks of wisdom and prudence in this 8th verse, he meaneth a heart made wise and prudent, the work of wisdom in a man's soul.

And then again, thirdly, there is this reason why it is meant of the gift of wisdom and of faith wrought in us, by that parallel place, and indeed almost parallel epistle, Col. i. 9, where the apostle prays that they may be 'filled with the knowledge of his will in all wisdom and spiritual understanding;' and that word, 'spiritual understanding,' puts it out of doubt that the knowledge of spirituals within us is meant.

Fourthly, And then that it is particularly meant faith, a fourth reason for that is this: that when the apostle comes to dilate this general head of the work of God, thus here expressed by 'wisdom,' &c., inherent in us, into diverse particular works wrought in them, which he doth in ver. 11–13, both to Jew and Gentile, he enumerates and instanceth in their believing on Christ. 'In whom,' saith he, 'we have obtained an inheritance'—viz., the Jews—'who first trusted in Christ.' The like saith the 12th verse. Then coming to the Gentiles, 'In whom,' saith he, 'ye also trusted, after that ye heard the word of truth, the gospel of your salvation.' So that his scope is to lay open the grace of faith and spiritual knowledge.

Now, brethren, to shew you how wisdom and prudence do differ, that is the second thing I must make good; for here are two things mentioned, 'He hath abounded toward us in wisdom and prudence.'

To open this, I shall difference them unto you by their objects. You know there are two sorts of things revealed; the first are *Credenda,* as we call them, things to be believed, all evangelical truths, the mysteries of salvation, the revelation of God's free grace, and of Christ, and of all he hath done and is made to us. Secondly, There are *Agenda,* things to be done and practised by us; that strictness and holiness of heart and life which they that do believe are to take up. Into these two is the whole will of God divided; it consists either in things to be believed by us, or in things to be done by us. It is that division the apostle makes, 1 Tim. i. 19, 'Holding faith and a good conscience.' By 'faith' he means the doctrine of faith; all things that are delivered to us to believe, we are to hold these fast. And by a 'good conscience' he means, by a *metonymy,* holiness and obedience, the things we know we ought to do, whereof a good conscience is the principle. Now then, as all things in the Word are reduced to these two heads, so all the works of grace upon a Christian's heart are reduced to two heads:—

First, A principle of wisdom, to take in and believe and see the worth and excellency, as by faith we do, of things that are to be believed by us, and which God revealeth for our salvation. And—

Secondly, To have a principle of prudence, savingly, spiritually, and effectually to see that holiness and obedience we owe to God, if we believe, and if we be saved, and so to see them as to have the heart taken with them. And that is prudence.

First, Wisdom is that gift of knowledge or faith whereby we believe all spiritual truths that are to be believed, and our hearts are affected with the goodness of them. For, brethren, therein lies wisdom, to see the excellency of a thing, and to be taken with it, and to choose it. A man is wise when he is wise for himself, as it is said, Prov. ix. 12; when a man knows what is good for him. That same merchant by whom and by whose carriage the conversion of a sinner is expressed to us, was a wise merchant; for he saw a pearl of great value, and he had the wisdom to like it, and to sell all he had for it; and this was by faith wrought, as I shall shew you by and by. When wisdom enters into the heart and becomes pleasant unto a man, as it is said, Prov. ii. 10,—takes the whole man,—when a man sees by faith those spiritual things so really as his whole heart is drawn after them, he chooseth them as excellent for him; this is wisdom. You have it expressed by the Apostle, in Phil. i. 9, 10, for he useth several expressions in several epistles, as his manner is, but intends one and the same thing. He prays, 'that their love may abound in knowledge and in all judgment, that they might approve the things that are excellent.' Where you have such a knowledge as works a love to the things known, and an approving of the excellency of them, this is spiritual knowledge, this is wisdom; for ἐπίγνωσις, the chiefest part of wisdom, as Aristotle saith well of it, is to discern what is good, and to pitch upon it and choose it. Now, when a man sees all the truths of the gospel and the excellencies of them spiritually, so as all his heart is taken with them, and they become pleasant to his soul, not the knowledge of them only, but the thing; when they are as the only pearl for which he sells all; then is a man made 'wise to salvation'—you have the expression, 2 Tim. iii. 15. When a man is made wise to save his own soul, sees the things of the gospel so as he is taken with them, and hath the wit never to leave them after, this is the first thing that is wrought.

Now, my brethren, it is faith that doth enable you thus to see the excellency of spiritual things, to choose them, to embrace them, and never to depart from them. Therefore faith is truly called wisdom here. I will give you a scripture in which you shall have two instances of it, to name no more. It is in Heb. xi. 13, 24. At the 13th verse, 'These all died in faith, not having received the promises, but seeing them [by faith] afar off, [for that is the meaning,] they were persuaded of them, [they believed the truth of them,] and they embraced them,' they laid hold upon them as good for them. This faith makes you to do, to see all the spiritual things in the Word really, and to embrace them as good for you. And the other instance is that of Moses, ver. 24, 'By faith Moses, when he was come to years, refused to be called the son of Pharaoh's daughter; choosing rather to suffer affliction with the people of God, than to enjoy the pleasures of sin for a season; esteeming the reproach of Christ greater riches than the treasures of Egypt.' Here faith made him wise. He saw what was the best bargain; it made him put a value upon the true riches; it made him to leave all the world, to refuse to be called the son of Pharaoh's daughter, or whatsoever preferment else he had at court, and to choose affliction rather with the people of God, because by faith he esteemed the reproach of Christ greater riches than the treasures of Egypt. So that now, to have that wisdom as to see spiritual things, the real nature of them, to set a value upon them, to approve the excellency of them, to be taken with them more than with all the things of the world, and he hath that light and knowledge of them begotten in his heart which he can never sell away again, but it works his heart off from all things else,—this man is a wise man; and this is wrought in your hearts by faith. This is the first thing.

Secondly, Prudence is that principle of wisdom that doth change the heart; which, as faith looks out to the truths of the gospel, and the promises of the gospel, to Christ and to God, and free grace, and the like; so this spiritual prudence looks out to all that is a man's duty, that God requires of him again,—to holiness, to obedience, to the whole law of God, to the whole will of God; and a man's heart is taken with them too, and that man whose heart is drawn by them, through seeing the excellency of them in his judgment, is a wise man, is a prudent man. What is it that turns a man's heart to righteousness and holiness? It is a spiritual knowledge of what holiness is, and what that obedience is that we ought to perform to the Lord. I will quote you one or two places for it: Luke i. 17, where the very same word is used that is used here. He tells us there that the end of John's ministry was to turn men; to what? 'The hearts of the fathers to the children,' that is the first that respecteth matters of faith. The Pharisees had in their doctrine led many from the gospel and from the faith of Abraham, and the children of Israel did not believe as their fathers did. He turns them to their fathers, to believe as Abraham did, and not as the Pharisees taught them. And then it follows, 'and the disobedient to the wisdom of the just,' of the righteous. It is the same word in the original that is translated here for prudence in my text. That wisdom that doth make a man righteous, that changeth his heart, makes him take in all that holy and righteous law of God, see an excellency in it, that it is right in all things, as the prophet David speaks, Ps. cxix.; this is *prudence*. And this is the second thing wherein conversion lies: to make a man a prudent man, prudent with the prudence of the just; to make a man righteous, to make a man just, to make a man holy. It is a practical skill, as I may so call it, which God imprints upon a man's understanding, that frames the heart and makes him wise to do good. You read in Jer. iv. 22, where the prophet, speaking of wicked men, saith, 'They are wise to do evil,' they are wise enough there; 'but to do good they have no knowledge.' Now to have an understanding to do good, to have such an understanding as changeth a man's heart and makes it conformable to the law; this is *prudence*. And it consists in two things, that I may open it unto you:—

First, It consists in enabling a man to take in all the rules of holiness, or the more fundamental rules of holiness, in a spiritual manner, to know the rule spiritually. A man's heart must be changed to do that. The Apostle prays, Rom. xii. 2, that they may be 'renewed in their minds,' (to be changed there, is to have their minds turned;) to what end? 'That you may approve,' saith he, 'of that good and acceptable will of God;' to take in the will of God, or any part of it, in the spiritualness of it, to approve it in the excellency of it, and to esteem it right in all things. My brethren, to know the rule spiritually, is from spiritual prudence; it is from grace to say the law is holy, spiritual, good. The carnal part of the law, carnal men say it is good. But to say of the spiritual, the holy part of the law that requires the whole heart to be obedient to God,—as such principles as these, to lie in no known sin, to aim at the glory of God more than at a man's self, and the like,—for a man to take in such principles as these, and to approve them from his very soul, this is wisdom, this is prudence, this is part of the prudence of the just that makes a man righteous.

Again, in the second place, it imports a skill that God imprints upon the mind of a man to manage his whole man, to do according to what he knows. 'We know not how to pray as we ought.' The Holy Ghost comes and imprints a skill upon a man's heart, and teacheth him how to pray acceptably to God, which no man in the world can do. To make an acceptable prayer to God, is as much as to make a world; to have the skill of it, to have the knack of it, as I may call it, to have the wisdom in the performance of any holy duty; for there is a skill, a wisdom that belongs to the performance of holy duties. When you take an apprentice you teach him two things; you teach him the rules of your trade, but when he hath learnt the rules he must by use get a skill in his fancy to enable him to work. Now, that which men get by time and use, which you call habits, that doth God imprint in every godly man's heart when he first turns him. As he teacheth him the rules, so he imprints the habit of skill, a spiritual wisdom to manage his heart. To be able to pray, to believe, to do all things acceptably, this is prudence, this is that holy skill, for God undertakes to teach us; he takes no apprentice but he teacheth him his trade. This is my covenant, saith he, 'they shall all know me, from the least to the greatest; they shall be all taught of God.' It is part of our indenture and his indenture with us, as Ps. xxv. 12. He imprints a holy skill in the heart, that guides a man's feet into the way of peace, as the expression is, Luke i. 79.

It is, my brethren, expounded in that parallel place I quoted but now, Col. i. 9, 10. He prays that they may be filled with all wisdom and spiritual understanding. For what end? 'That they might walk worthy of the Lord unto all well-pleasing, being fruitful in every good work.' Now, to have that skill as shall so guide and frame the heart to the law and will of God, that a man shall be able to walk worthy to well-pleasing, to do that which is acceptable to God in some measure, this is this spiritual prudence which is put for all sanctification, as wisdom is put for faith. So that here you have the two parts of conversion: here is wisdom, which is put for faith; here is prudence, which is put for that principle of sanctification which doth change and turn the whole man, make it obedient to the will and law of God.

And now I have opened it, I will cast in but this. Here you see four particular blessings, for now I shall so rank them in ver. 7, 8: here is redemption, 'in whom we have redemption through his blood;' here is justification, or forgiveness of sins, that is a second; here is wisdom, which is put for faith, believing spiritual truths revealed in the doctrine of the gospel; here is prudence, which is put for that principle of light which changeth a man's heart, and makes him holy, and sanctifies him, and so it is put for sanctification. Well, then, here you have the same four blessings which Christ is made to us, reckoned up, 1 Cor. i. 30, 'Of him are ye in Christ Jesus, who of God is made unto us wisdom,' there is one; 2. 'Righteousness,' there is justification, or forgiveness of sins; 3. Here is 'sanctification,' which prudence is put for; and, 4. 'Redemption.' And so I have done with the opening of the words.

You will ask me now, why doth the apostle express the work of grace, faith and sanctification, by wisdom and prudence?

One reason is this, because he useth several phrases in several epistles. Sometimes he calls it spiritual 'wisdom and knowledge,' sometimes 'wisdom and prudence,' sometimes he calls it 'sense,' αἴσθησις, as I remember he expresseth sanctification; so that light that sanctifieth a man is a spiritual sense, whereby a man tasteth the goodness of spiritual things; so he calls it in the Philippians, as the other is in the Colossians. This is one reason; he useth several expressions in several epistles.

Secondly, he wrote to the Grecians, and to the Asiatics, to those at Ephesus, who were all for wisdom, they liked nothing but what had wisdom in it. The Jews' humour was to seek for a sign, the Greeks were for wisdom, and therefore they refused the gospel, because to them it was foolishness, it had no wisdom in it. Saith the apostle, Here is wisdom ; seeing you prize wisdom so much, I will speak to you according to your own desires. Mark what a blessing God hath bestowed upon you ; he hath made you wise to salvation, he hath made you able to keep the law, and to obey the will of God; which prudence doth change your hearts, saith he ; therefore, he expresseth sanctification by wisdom and prudence. He speaks to them in their own language.

A third reason is this, because the truth is that the work of grace lies in working upon the understanding of a man ; it lies in working spiritual knowledge in a man ; however men little think of it, it is a light let into the heart that saveth a man, a different light from that wicked men have. Eph. iv. 22, he bids them 'put off the old man, and put on the new.' How must they do that ? 'Be renewed,' saith he, 'in the spirit of your mind.' If the spirit of a man's mind, if the understanding be renewed, it changeth the whole man presently. Therefore, because the main of the work of grace, or at least the first of it, lies in working upon or renewing the mind, therefore it is expressed here by wisdom and prudence. You have the like, Col. iii. 10. The image of God is renewed ; it is renewed in or by knowledge. God when he doth frame and paint his image upon the heart, what doth he ? He lets it in by the understanding, openeth a man's eye to see spiritually what true holiness is, and what the love of God is, and how a man must aim at the glory of God ; and with this light let into the mind and understanding, the heart being taken with it, the image of God is framed in men's spirits. Therefore it is expressed by *wisdom* and *prudence*.

But here is one particle yet more to be explained, 'all wisdom.' Do we receive all wisdom and prudence when we are turned unto God ?

The meaning therefore of that is this : it is taken, first, for all kinds, for all sorts, something of everything, as we use to say. They are made wise to believe truths, and they are made wise to do what they know ; their duties in their callings, their duties in their relations. There are several parts of the will and mind of God which God instructs a man in, so far forth as it is necessary for him to know to be saved. 1 John ii. 20, it is said, the Spirit teacheth us 'all things.' What is the meaning of that 'all things ?' Why, all things necessary to salvation, all things that go to save a man ; and so the poorest soul that is knoweth all things, hath all wisdom and prudence in him. He hath all necessary knowledge to save his soul if God should call him presently ; therefore it is called all wisdom and prudence.

And, in the second place, it is called all wisdom and prudence for the excellency of it ; it is instead of all wisdom, and better than all wisdom else, as, ver. 10, he calls the saints 'all things in heaven and in earth.' Why, there are more things in heaven and in earth besides them ? Yea, but they are worth them all ; God looks upon none else, cares for none else ; they are his all, as if there were no other thing. So here, 'all wisdom and prudence,' because this is instead of all, it is worth all ; this is the whole man, as the expression is, Eccles. xii. 13. For whatsoever else is in a man, whatsoever wisdom and knowledge he hath else, it is worth nothing ; he that hath this hath enough, he hath all.

Then, thirdly, take in all believers, whom he speaks of here collectively, and they have all wisdom and prudence amongst them. The Apostle speaks here of himself and of the rest of the apostles, and of all that are called by the gospel. He speaks generally and collectively of all saints ; they have amongst them received all wisdom and prudence ; it is in the pack of them.

And then in Christ there are all treasures of wisdom and knowledge laid up for us, and we are complete in him; so saith the apostle, Col. ii.

And all wisdom and knowledge is hid in this word, and if thou hast grace, thou hast a principle to understand it savingly more or less; if thou wilt dig for wisdom, thou hast a principle of wisdom which a wicked man wants; thou hast all wisdom and knowledge *in semine*. And though we know but in part, yet in Christ is hid all wisdom for us, and all the wisdom that is in Christ is made ours too, for our good; and we shall one day know it all, that is more. This wisdom and prudence will bring thee to know all the treasures that are in Christ, and therefore God hath abounded to thee, *in semine*, in all wisdom and prudence when first he turns thee.

All the gifts of the apostles and prophets, they are all ours, all thine when thou art once called; therefore God hath abounded toward us in all wisdom and prudence.

And then, lastly, and, it may be, chief of all. The apostle speaks of it in relation to them under the Old Testament; they received truths but by piecemeal, at 'sundry times,' as the expression is, Heb. i., now one and then another. But now, under the gospel, God hath hidden nothing, he hath unlocked all; therefore the least in the kingdom of heaven is said to be greater than John the Baptist, the least saint knows more than John Baptist did. So, comparatively to those under the Old Testament, God hath abounded toward us in all wisdom and knowledge. And so much for the opening of the words.

I will come now to gather some observations from them (for I see I cannot instance in all I meant.) The first observation is this :—

Obs. 1.—*A godly man only is a wise man.* He that is turned to God, he that is made wise to save his own soul, he only is a wise man, and all the rest of the world are fools; because let them seek for whatsoever excellency they will, yet they lose their souls in the end. 'Thou fool,' saith Christ,—he thought himself a wise man to get riches,—'thou fool,' saith he, 'where will thy soul be to-night?' He was a fool for his labour. A man that knows how to believe savingly, and that is wise for his soul, that man is only the wise man. Other men are wise in their generation, as Christ distinguisheth it; they are wise in their kind; take them in the world, and there they are wise indeed, and wiser than the children of light. But, saith the apostle, God hath chosen the fools of the world to confound the wise; he did it on purpose, it was his plot. The chiefest thing the wise ones of the world brag of is their wisdom. God hath taken out fools, that have less understanding, makes them able to save their souls; and at the latter day, who is the fool then? Thus he confounds all the wise ones in the world. They are only wise that are wise to salvation.

I will give you a scripture for it. It is in Job xxviii. 28, 'Behold the fear of the Lord, that is wisdom; and to depart from evil is understanding.' That is the understanding, the only understanding; and if men be wise never so much in anything else, they are fools.

Obs. 2.—*Whomsoever God saveth, he doth give them so much knowledge in spiritual things as shall make them wise.* Let them be never so ignorant before, they that are come to years of discretion, they shall be wise to save their souls. Do but observe it; men that had but little wit in them before, when they are turned they will speak of faith and of Christ and of the mysteries of salvation exceeding strongly and wisely. What is the reason of it? When God is master and teacheth a man, how soon is he learned whom he teacheth! No such schoolmaster as God is; he aboundeth toward a man in wisdom and prudence, so that a man hath abundance of knowledge the first day almost. You shall see it in many poor men that are turned to God. I will give you but a scripture for it, and so pass from it. Isa. xxxv. 8: the prophet speaks there of the times of the gospel, when Christ was to preach the word, as appears by the former verses. He tells us there that Christ is 'a way, and a highway,' that way that leads to life, 'and it shall be called, The way of holiness,' (which men miscall, and call by a thousand other nicknames, but that is the true name of it, The way of holiness,) 'and the unclean shall not pass over it.' Take an ungodly man, he shall never hit on the way, let him be never so wise; for so the opposition implies, as you shall see by and by. For whom, then, shall this way be? 'It shall be for the wayfaring men; though fools, they shall not err in it.' Art thou a wayfaring soul that art a-going to heaven, and hast a mind to go to heaven? And art thou simple, hath God given thee a heart to desire to be saved and to seek after Christ? Take the greatest doctor in the world; if wicked, he shall not find out the way that thou shalt find. Another man, a fool, shall find it; he shall not err in it, because God, whomsoever he doth save, himself is the master, and teacheth them this wisdom. And so much for that 8th verse; I will speak a little of the 9th, and so I will have done.

Ver. 9, *Having made known unto us the mystery of his will, according to his good pleasure*, &c.

Here, as I told you, he comes to external calling, the making known to us 'the mystery of his will,' whereby he doth work spiritual knowledge and understanding in a man. Now, to open this a little.

What is meant by making known? You all know that he did it by the preaching of the apostles; he doth it now by the preaching of the word, and by the Scriptures opened to you, whereby all that hear it and know it are called.

But what is meant by 'the mystery of his will?' for this is the only, the chief hard thing here.

Some men do take it thus, to shew the difference between the knowledge of believers and others. Others may know the will of God, they say, but there is a mystery in the will of God which only godly men know, and God reveals it to them. As in Col. i. 27, 'To whom God would make known'—speaking of the saints, as you shall see by comparing the 25th and 26th verses together—'the mystery which hath been hid from ages and from generations, but now is made manifest to his saints; to whom he hath made known the riches of the glory of this mystery.' My brethren, the mystery of God's will, and the riches and the glory of it, the saints only know.

But I rather think that the aim of it here, (though this be a truth, and I shall have occasion to mention it by and by,)—yet I think the main thing intended here is not to express the difference of wicked men's knowledge of the gospel, and godly men's. But it is taken for the substance of the gospel itself. The doctrine of the gospel is called the mystery of God's will, 1 Tim. iii. 16, 'Great is the mystery of godliness, God manifested in the flesh.' The doctrine of salvation by Christ was a great mystery.

Here I must open two things to you:—

1. *Why it is called a mystery.*

2. *Why the mystery of his will.*

First, Why it is called a *mystery*. A mystery is that which is a secret hidden, a thing unknown, which could no way have been known unless it had been revealed by him that knew it. A mystery is properly a thing hidden, 1 Cor. ii. 7, 'We preach the wisdom of God in a mystery, even the hidden wisdom, which God ordained before the world.' Therefore it is a mystery, because it is hidden. So a secret unknown is called a mystery in 1 Cor. xv. 51, 'Behold, I shew you a mystery.' What is that? 'We shall not all sleep, but we shall all be changed.' Some men shall not die at the latter day. Who knew this before? It was a thing unknown, it is not in all the prophets, nor in all the Old Testament; it is a thing we had not known, had not Paul told it us; it was a mystery.

Now to come to the gospel, it is a hidden mystery, the most hidden secret that ever was. It was hid where all the world could not have found it; no, all the wit of men and angels could not have found it where it was hid. It was hid in God's breast, in God's heart, 'hid in God.' You shall see the very expression in Eph. iii. 9, 'To make all men see what is the fellowship of the mystery, which from the beginning of the world hath been hid in God.' If you will know, saith he, in what field it lay, it was hidden in God.

Hid from whom?

First, From all the wise men in the world; they could never have found it out. Those that search into mysteries of state, and would know *arcana imperii*, think they are wise men, and that they know great matters. What saith the Apostle? 1 Cor. ii. 8, 'We speak the wisdom of God in a mystery, even the hidden wisdom, which none of the princes of this world knew.' They that have all secrets in their heads, and know how to govern states and kingdoms, none of them all knew this, nor could ever have known it.

Nay, secondly, the gospel was hid from all the saints in the Old Testament, as now it is revealed. In Col. i. 26, the Apostle saith it was hidden from 'ages and generations,' from all the generations past; hid from the beginning of the world, as you have it, Eph. iii. 10. You shall find in 1 Pet. i. 10, 11, that the very prophets that wrote the Scripture did not fully understand what themselves wrote in all things concerning the gospel. 'Of which salvation,' saith he, 'the prophets have inquired and searched diligently,'—they inquired by prayer, and searched diligently by study of their own writings,—'who prophesied of the grace that should come unto you: searching what, or what manner of time the Spirit of Christ which was in them did signify, when it testified beforehand the sufferings of Christ, and the glory that should follow. Unto whom it was revealed, that not unto themselves, but unto us, they did minister the things which are now reported unto you.' They had them in their writings indeed, but they ministered them to us, and that was the chief answer they could get upon all their prayers and study.

Lastly, It was hidden from the angels. The angels were near God, but they were not in his bosom; they were his favourites, indeed, they were courtiers, they stood round about him, but they knew none of it. No, God hid it from them. Not a creature knew it, not an angel in heaven knew it, as we now know it. Nay, the churches know it before the angels know it, and the angels do learn of the churches. That is part of the hiding mentioned, Eph. iii. 10: it was hidden in God, 'to the intent that now unto the principalities and powers in heavenly places'—that is, to angels—'might be known by the church the manifold wisdom of God.' They learned the gospel of the Church; therefore they come to hear sermons. Brethren, the churches are full of angels, they love to hear the gospel preached; and you know Peter tells us they pry, they bow down their necks; it is in 1 Pet. i. 12, 'which things the angels desire to look into.'

Thus the hidden gospel is a mystery so hidden as none could have known it. Adam knew the law; it was written in his heart. We have principles of the knowledge of the law in our consciences; when we hear the law preached, we have a principle in our own consciences within us that goes along with what we hear, and answers to it; we cannot deny it. But there is not the least footstep of the gospel in the wisdom of all the men in the world: there is nothing in the heart of man to answer to it. If the gospel be revealed, God must create light. When it was first discovered, he created light in their hearts to whom it was revealed. We were nothing but darkness. Saith the Apostle of himself as well as others, 2 Cor. iv. 6, 'God, that commanded the light to shine out of darkness, hath shined in our hearts, to give us the light of the knowledge of the glory of God in the face of Christ.' God must bring in a light, saith he, or else not we nor any of the apostles could ever have found it out.

What is the reason of this?

Because it is the 'mystery of God's will,' which reason we have in the text. Who could have known that God would ever have saved sinners? Who could ever have thought it? He had said, he had pronounced it as his will, it was gone out of his mouth, 'In the day thou eatest thereof, thou shalt die the death.' Here was a riddle now for all the angels in heaven. How could they have known the mystery of God's will, that he would save sinners? Adam stood trembling, poor man, and the devil thought all cocksure. I shall damn them, thought he, as sure as I have damned myself. And all the angels stood mute, till God himself came and makes the promise to us. Rom. xi. 32, saith the Apostle, 'God hath shut up all in unbelief, that he might have mercy upon all.' That God should let man sin, and permit sin to spoil his creature, and when he had done, should mean to save it, and have mercy upon those that are shut up under unbelief,—'O the depth,' saith he, 'of the riches both of the wisdom and knowledge of God!' so it follows in the next words, 'how unsearchable are his judgments, and his ways past finding out! Who hath known the mind of God? or who hath been his counsellor?' Who could ever have known this, had not God revealed it, that this was his will? No counsellor, my brethren, but one; that is 'the wonderful Counsellor, the mighty God,' as he is called, Isa. ix. 6. Therefore in John i. 18, where the Apostle speaking of the gospel of grace and truth that came by Jesus Christ, as the law came by Moses, (he speaks of the revelation of this gospel in opposition to the law;) saith he, 'No man hath seen God at any time,' that is, hath known the mind of God. That is meant by seeing God there, it is a Jewish proverb of knowing God's mind. 'The only-begotten Son, which is in the bosom of the Father, he hath declared it.' None in the world could have declared this will and mind of God, but only He that was in his bosom, that was familiar with him, his only Son; therefore he came down from heaven, and first broached the gospel: 'which was first preached by the Lord himself,' saith the Apostle, Heb. ii. 3.

Moses, my brethren,—St John speaks of him in the verses before, and he saith the law was given by Moses,—Moses was very intimate with God; he 'saw God face to face;' so the expression is, and God shewed him his glory. 'The law,' saith he, 'was given by Moses;' yea, 'but grace and truth,' the gospel, 'came by Jesus Christ.' Though Moses saw God face to face, he was not in his bosom, as Jesus Christ only was; and he only could reveal it, he only knew this mystery and mind of God.

I should likewise shew you that it is a mystery for the depth that is in it; but I shall let that pass. For an observation—

Obs. 1.—*Let all that live under the gospel, and saints especially, acknowledge what an infinite favour of God it is to know this mystery of his will, as you do; that God will save sinners, and that you see the reason of it too.* For it is brought down to you in a plain manner; you see such a satisfaction in Christ as will satisfy a man's reason. Bless God for that infinite mercy. You see how dainty God hath been of his gospel; he kept it hidden from all ages and generations till the apostles' times; above four thousand years. And saith our Saviour, Luke x. 24, Blessed are your eyes that you see, and your ears that you hear, such things as all the prophets and kings have desired to see and hear, and could not. 'I tell you,' saith he, 'many prophets and kings have desired to see those things which you see, and have not seen them; and to hear those things which you hear, and have not heard them.' Thou wouldst wish thyself to be a king, if thou desirest to be happy; or thou wouldst wish thyself to be a prophet, an old prophet, such a one as Elias was, or Isaiah, or Jeremiah, or some of them; nay, wish thyself as Solomon and David was, both prophet and king. Thine eyes and ears are more blessed than they. For these kings, saith he, and these prophets, neither could see nor hear those things which you both see and hear. Why? Because you hear and know the Mystery of His Will. My brethren, it is the greatest privilege in the world. Our Saviour Christ was a man of sorrows. We seldom find him rejoicing, but once; and upon what occasion was it? Look in the 21st verse of that 10th of Luke, just before these words: 'In that hour Jesus rejoiced in spirit, and said, I thank thee, O Father, Lord of heaven and earth, that thou hast hid these things from the wise and prudent, and hast revealed them unto babes.' And so he goeth on in his discourse, 'Blessed are your eyes,' &c.; that is the coherence of the words. Doth our Saviour Christ, our Head, bless God for revealing the gospel to us poor sinners, for to save our souls, and accounts it the greatest mercy of all others bestowed upon us, and shall not we? Doth Christ himself thus, as it were, fall down upon his knees and thank God for it, and shall not we?

You will object and say to me, But it is a common mercy; we see many wicked men partake of it.

I answer *first*, Why do wicked men partake of it? Because there are saints among them, and live in the places with them; therefore the gospel comes to them. 'I have much people in this city,' saith God, speaking of Corinth, and therefore he sent Paul to preach amongst them. And so, 2 Cor. iv. 15, 'For all things are for your sakes.' That Paul had all that knowledge, and all those gifts, it was for their sakes, it was for the elect; and therefore you have reason to be thankful for it; wicked men should not know a word of it else.

Secondly, Wicked men, though they hear the gospel, yet they hear, but understand not. There is a mystery in the gospel, which wicked men hear, and know not. There is, I say, a mystery in it; I passed it over before, I will speak but a word of it now: Matt. xiii. 11–14, 'To you it is given to know the mysteries of the kingdom of heaven, but to them it is not given.' Here Christ speaks of the mysteries of the gospel; a man must have it given him to know it, which is not done to wicked men. Here both heard the same parables: Christ, saith the evangelist, 'spake in parables;' and so he goeth on; saith he, 'Seeing, they see not; and hearing, they hear not, neither do they understand,'—that is, they do not understand savingly.

In 1 Cor. ii. 7, the place I quoted but now, 'We speak,' saith he, 'the wisdom of God in a mystery.' It is called wisdom in respect that wicked men may see and understand a rationality in it; but there is a mystery in this wisdom which godly men only see, and it must be given them to see it. 'The secret of the Lord is with them that fear him,' Ps. xxv. 14. So that now, though you think it a common mercy, yet it is a peculiar mercy to know the mystery of the gospel; to know the riches and the glory of it. It is a peculiar mercy to the saints.

Obs. 2.—*The mercy lies in this, to know the gospel, the mystery of his will.* He doth not say, to know the law. How slightly the apostle speaks of the law. 'The law,' saith he, 'came by Moses.' It is a slight speech, in comparison of 'grace and truth;' that, he saith, 'came by Jesus Christ.' It is the mystery of his will in the gospel that he purposed in himself, the knowledge of which a man should prize. This is the glory of Christ, and this is the glory of our preaching: 'He hath ordained it for our glory,' saith he, 1 Cor. ii. 7. The preaching of the gospel is that which brings in souls: Luke xvi. 16, 'The law and the prophets were until John,' but now the gospel is preached, men crowd into it, press into it, they come thick and threefold to it; men come in now when the gospel is preached infinitely more than when nothing but the law and the prophets were preached. 'The law and the prophets were until John; since that time,' saith he, 'the kingdom of God is preached, and every man presseth into it.' This is it that bringeth men in, my brethren. 'Woe is me,' saith the apostle. Why? He saith not simply, 'if I preach not,' but 'if I preach not the gospel;' that is the main thing.

Second, There is but one thing more to be opened, and that is, why it is called *the mystery of his will.*

One reason is this, because the will of God is the foundation of the gospel. What will you resolve it into? You must resolve it into his will, and into nothing else. 'I will have mercy;' this is the gospel, but his will is the foundation of it. 'I will have mercy upon whom I will have mercy;' and his will sets his understanding a work, as it were, to find out ways to bring about the salvation of mankind. 'He worketh all things after the counsel of his own will,' as it follows afterward in the 13th verse. Hence, therefore, it is called the mystery *of his will.*

I will give you another reason for it, which is the better reason for you, because the most comfortable thing we know in the gospel is the will of God to save sinners. Mark what I say, if thou knewest all that God knows, (it is a great word,) if thou didst not know this thing, that his mind and will were to save sinners, thou wert undone; the knowledge of this is worth all the rest. To know that God is merciful in his nature, this will not do it. You might have known that and despaired, for it might have been said, It is true, he is merciful in his nature, but the question is whether he will be merciful or no? 'Yea, but I will have mercy;' this word is worth all the world, this is the gospel.

It is called the mystery of his will, thirdly, because you might have known that Jesus Christ had died too, yet if you had not known it is the will of God to accept of that death for sinners, you had been undone still, if you could possibly have supposed this. What saith the apostle, Heb. x. 10, when he comes to speak of the sacrifice of Christ, what influence it had into our salvation? 'I came to do thy will,' saith he; 'by the which will we are sanctified through the offering of the body of Jesus Christ once for all.' What is it that saveth you, that sanctifieth you? It is not simply the offering of the blood of Christ; if you had heard Christ had died, that would not have comforted you, had it not been for this will: by this will you are sanctified through the offering of the body of Christ.

Take an observation or two from hence.

Obs. 1.—You see, my brethren, what is *the pith of the gospel.* It is the mystery of God's will; to know but this, that God will save sinners in the blood of Christ, this is the pith of the gospel. This is that which is essential to salvation; and you see too, that it is but a small thing to know that God will save sinners in Christ. How gracious hath God been! He hath not laid upon you to know all the hard things in the gospel, which scholars know, and many believers that have large understandings know, or else you cannot be saved. But this is the kernel of all, God will save sinners. It is the mystery of his will; dost thou know that? Hath that taken thy heart? Thou knowest that which will save thee, if thou knowest no more; thou knowest that which faith may feed upon, and which will make thee happy everlastingly.

But, saith a poor soul, Will God save sinners indeed? (when the soul begins to believe this in good earnest.) Hath God a mind to save such sinners as I am? saith he: I have reason to be content to be saved then. And so he giveth up his soul to God and to Christ, and so the bargain is made. Faith is to know the mystery of his will; it is resolved into that.

I will give you but a familiar instance, that the knowledge of this one thing is worth all the rest. Suppose that one had lived in Solomon's time, had been a subject to Solomon, a great favourite in his court, and had run into treason, so that it was in Solomon's power to take away his life, and Solomon should yet use him exceeding kindly, open to him all his heart,—you know that he had the most knowledge that ever man had, both in matters of nature and in the book of the law,—and he should tell him all his notions;—and he had as many notions in his head as there were sands on the sea-shore, for it is said he had a heart as large, he had a vast knowledge; —and suppose that Solomon should have told him all these, this poor man, being a traitor and in Solomon's power to put him to death when he would, if he had known but one thing of him, that Solomon would but say to him, 'I will pardon thy treason, I will save thee, thou shalt not die,'—this would have pleased him more than all the knowledge Solomon could have imparted to him. So I say here, we are traitors, and have deserved death, and it is in God's power to destroy us. If now God reveals unto thee that he hath an intent to save sinners, haply he doth conceal other things from thee; thou hast not a large understanding, thou canst not take in much; but this I know, that God hath a mind to save sinners in Christ, and I will give up myself unto him. But dost thou know further that he meaneth to save thee? It is worth all the knowledge else in the world. Why? Because it is the mystery of his will.

Obs. 2.—*See the grace of God in applying himself to all sorts of believers,* in revealing the gospel to weak as well as strong; he hath applied himself to weak capacities. If the gospel lay all in great hidden wisdom and rationalities, and that a man must know all the depths of wisdom in it, all the rationalities of it, the coherence of one truth with another, before he can be saved, many poor weak understandings should have been undone, and never should have come to be saved. God doth load your hearts but with one truth, *I will save sinners in and through Christ.* Hast thou learnt this in the gospel? This will save thee, the gospel is the mystery of his will. And, my brethren, he hath applied himself to weak understandings in faith too. Why did he choose faith of all graces to save a man by? Because the poorest in the world, the weakest understanding, can believe and trust. When he heareth that God will save sinners, he is able to trust God as strongly and as firmly as the wisest understanding man in the world. Nay, your weak men, they are aptest to believe, they are more suited for faith; let them but have this revealed to them, that God will save poor sinners, it lies but in a trust. When a man's heart is convinced of this, and a poor soul is able to do it, he doth it as strongly as the greatest understanding in the world can do. Thus God hath applied himself.

Obs. 3.—*Though the gospel be a mystery, yet you see God hath made it known.* Observe from hence, that God cares not who knows it; he kept it indeed hidden awhile, but now he would have all men see it. So it is, Eph. iii. 9, 10, 'That all men might see what is the fellowship of the mystery,' &c. It is the glory of God and of our religion, that we desire to have all known, all the mysteries of it. We do not as the Papists do, that keep things from the people. Know it to the uttermost in God's name, and let all God's people in their sphere and place prophesy; let them be all as prophets, to know the uttermost mystery of God's will. God hath abounded, not to ministers only, but to all his saints, in all wisdom and prudence, and hath made known the mystery of his will to them; let them all get what knowledge they can of it. It was not the nature of other religions to do so. The wise heathens, and the priests of the Egyptians and other heathen nations, had mysteries in their religion, but they kept them as mysteries, they never told the people of them. Popery, you know, is called a 'mystery of iniquity,' as this is called the mystery of God's will; for the devil hath made a gospel for his eldest son, as God hath for his Son. But what is the reason they will not let you know it, but keep you in ignorance? Because it is a mystery of iniquity, and people would come to see the iniquity of it, if they knew the mystery of it. But the gospel, it is the mystery of God's will. Saith God, All that ye know by me is, that I will save poor sinners, that I delight in mercy. I care not who knows this, saith God. It is a matter of grace, and therefore he makes known the mystery of his will. This is the glory of our God, and the glory of our religion, and the glory of the gospel. Would that all the saints in the world understood every tittle of this book! then our sermons would be understood, and we should preach with ease, my brethren. God desires this, and we desire it, to have all men know the mystery of his will.

According to his good pleasure, which he hath purposed in himself.

III. That which remaineth is this, that which was *the moving cause of making known the mystery of his will*, and of calling home those whom he had called, and shall call to the end of the world. It is 'according to his good pleasure, which he had purposed in himself.'

When I opened the 5th verse, I shewed that εὐδοκία, the 'good pleasure' of his will, was that which of all things else he is pleased most with, though he willeth other things. Here it is simply said, 'according to his good pleasure,' but the thing is all one. It was out of the good pleasure of his will that he did choose us and predestinate us to glory, to adoption, to perfect holiness, as the 4th and 5th verses have it. And it is out of the same good-will that he makes known the gospel savingly to any one's heart, and converts him, and turns him to him.

It is a known place, that in Matt. xi. 25, (to confirm this to you,) 'At that time Jesus answered and said, I thank thee, O Father, Lord of heaven and earth, that thou hast hid these things from the wise and prudent, and hast revealed them unto babes: even so, Father, for so it seemed good in thy sight,' ὅτι οὕτως ἐγένετο εὐδοκία. The word is the same that is here. It was thy good pleasure that thou shouldest put this difference, to reveal it unto some, and those babes, and pass by the wise and prudent. He speaks it of making known the mystery of his will, the thing in the text. Now, when he saith, 'I thank thee, because thou hast hid these things from the wise and prudent, and hast revealed them to babes, for so it seemed good in thy sight,' it is not that he doth make the ground, the *terminus* of it, to be in God's hiding of it simply from the wise or from the prudent; but the thing he giveth thanks for is his revealing it to babes. Only, here is the mercy set off the more, there is this foil cast upon it, that he hideth it from the wise and prudent, while he revealeth it unto babes; and herein is seen, by refusing some and taking others, the good pleasure of his will.

It is a like speech too, that in Rom. vi. 17, 'God be thanked, that you were the servants of sin, but you have obeyed from the heart that form of doctrine which you were delivered into.' He doth not thank God that they were the servants of sin simply; but that which he thanketh God for was, that they had obeyed that form of doctrine they were delivered unto; only seeing they were the servants of sin once, the mercy is set off by this so much the more. Just so here, 'Father, I thank thee, because thou hast hid these things from the wise and prudent, and hast revealed them unto babes; for even so it seemed good in thy sight.' I shall have recourse to this place by and by.

You have the like in 1 Cor. i. 21, where the same phrase is used, the same word of God's good pleasure that is here; and it is spoken of God's revealing the gospel to the babes of the world, as you may read there throughout the chapter. 'Not many wise, nor many noble,' &c.; and the reason was this, because God would confound wise men after the flesh, by enabling poor creatures to save their own souls.

I will make but an observation out of this, and so pass from it.

Obs.—God's making known the mystery of his will and the preaching of the gospel, and enlightening of men unto life by the gospel, doth not depend upon, nor is it dispensed according to, preparations in the creature, but it is according to his good pleasure. There are those that affirm otherwise, but this one place, compared with many others, sufficiently confutes it: 'Having made known unto us the mystery of his will, according to his good pleasure.' If you would know why the gospel is preached in that powerful manner in England or in London, and not in many other places of the world, and not in many other places of the kingdom, it is merely upon the good pleasure of God.

It is a thing that will never be answered. Why did God suffer the Gentiles so long, three thousand years, to walk in their own ways without revealing to them the mystery of his will,—for it was three thousand years and upward after Abraham,—and chose the Jews to whom he would make known his law? 'He dealt not so with any nation,' saith the Psalmist; 'neither had the heathen the knowledge of his law.' It was merely God's good pleasure. Moses tells them, Deut. ix. 6, that it was not for their righteousness; for they were a stiff-necked people. In obstinacy they surpassed all other nations; they were the most perverse and the most unbelieving people of any other in the world. And, Deut. x. 14, 'Behold,' saith he, 'the heaven of heavens is the Lord's thy God, the earth also, with all that therein is. Only the Lord had a delight in thy fathers to love them, and he chose their seed after them, even you above all people.' It was merely the good pleasure of his will that did it. And why doth Moses mention his title, of being Lord of heaven and earth, but to shew that this proceeded from his sovereignty, that he chose this people and revealed the word to them? All the earth, saith he, is mine, and I have angels in heaven; I need no man upon earth at all. He might have left them all to their own ways. 'The heaven of heavens is mine; the earth also, with all that is therein.'

You shall find in that place I quoted even now, Matt. xi. 25, that Christ resolveth it, why God revealed it to babes, into the same principle, by the title he giveth God there when he giveth him thanks: 'I thank thee, O Father, Lord of heaven and earth, because thou,' &c. God sheweth his liberty in this. And do but mark upon what occasion those words of Christ's come in. 'At that time,' saith the text, 'Jesus answered and said, Father, I thank thee,' &c. Our Saviour had in the 20th and 21st verses upbraided the cities wherein most of his mighty works were done, because they repented not. 'Woe to thee, Chorazin! woe to thee, Bethsaida! if the mighty works which were done in thee, had been done in Tyre and Sidon, they would have repented long ago, in sackcloth and ashes.' If God had gone and revealed the gospel according to preparations in men, certainly he would not have passed by Tyre and Sidon, and preached it to Chorazin and Bethsaida; for he saith that Tyre and Sidon would have made better use of it, they would have repented long ago. And Tyre was of all nations the most ingenuous to the Jews; they helped to build the temple, you know; yet God passed by them. 'At that time Jesus answered and said, I thank thee, O Father, Lord of heaven and earth, that thou hast hid these things from the wise and prudent, and revealed them to babes.' Thou goest in revealing the gospel by no such conditions in men, but dost it as the Lord of heaven and earth, out of thy good pleasure. And so much for that, 'according to his good pleasure.'

Which he purposed in himself.

IV. These words 'which he purposed in himself,' some copies, and as good as any other, leave προέθετο out, and so they do not refer them to the 9th verse, but to the 10th. 'He purposed in himself to gather together in one all things in Christ.' Yet because some have it, and thus you see it is read, and indeed more generally by interpreters, therefore by referring them to this 9th verse, let us see the reason why these words, 'which he purposed in himself,' come in after all as having relation to his good pleasure.

It might first be said, It is true God doth it out of his good pleasure, but yet notwithstanding, though his own will cast it, is there nothing at all he looks at in the creature why he doth it?

Nothing at all! It is, saith he, 'his good pleasure,' which he purposed in himself, merely in and out of himself. He looked to nothing but himself, when he did thus purpose eternal salvation to any, or to call them by the gospel.

And, secondly, whereas they might inquire, and say, Was it out of a fixed will, taken up from everlasting thus?

Yes, saith he, it was not a mere velleity, but it was a purpose, *secum statutum*, he purposed with himself, unalterably; so, indeed, Beza saith that God's purpose is mentioned to shew the firmness of election, as in Rom. viii. 28, where the purpose of God is mentioned, to shew the firmness and stability of his will and resolution in it: 'He purposed.'

If the words be referred to the 9th verse, then you may observe from thence these two things out of it:—

1. That effectual calling is the fruit of God's everlasting good-will to us, James i. 18, 'Of his own will he hath begotten us.' It was his will and his purpose he took up from everlasting. His begetting us is of his will, of his purpose, which he purposed, saith he, in himself. And therein now, our

begetting differeth from that of Christ's. Christ is his natural Son. As he is the second Person, he begat him not of his will; as he is man, indeed, so he came under God's decree as well as we; but as he is the natural Son of God, the second Person, he was not begotten of his will: but so are we by an everlasting purpose, by an everlasting decree, which he purposed in himself. So that, my brethren, look how you are called, and when you are called; it was all as God had plotted it from everlasting. He appointed that thou shouldest go to such a sermon, and there hear such a word spoken as should strike thy heart. It may be it was spoken by the by, or it may be thou camest into the church by the by, and thoughtest to go to another place, but God turned thee in. This was plotted from everlasting. God doth his great works by the by oftentimes, and so he converteth souls; yet they are plotted from everlasting. It is his purpose within himself.

There is one word yet in this 9th verse, 'which he purposed in himself.' Some read it ἐν αὐτῷ, which he purposed *in him*, namely, in Christ. But because that is so much before and after, certainly he meaneth ἐν αὑτῷ, *in himself*; the word signifieth either, as I have formerly shewed what is the meaning of that. He did not view anything in us, or out of himself, when he decreed anything concerning us. God hath no efficient cause to move him but his own will. He hath no final cause that ultimately moveth him, but his own glory and his Son's. He consults with nothing; he looks not out of himself. As he understandeth all things by himself and by his essence, so that, that casteth his will this way or that way, is himself. The meaning is not but that something out of God moved God, if we would speak strictly. I shall shew you why: for, take the glory of his grace, that you know moveth him; so the 6th verse telleth us, 'He did predestinate us, to the praise of the glory of his grace.' Now the praise of the glory of his grace is a thing out of God, for it is that manifestative glory that ariseth from the hearts of men and angels to him, upon his works that he declareth to the sons of men. It is that which ariseth out of all. He looked and saw that, in the creature which he made, there would be such a praise arising. This moveth him, and yet it is out of himself. How, then, is he said to purpose all in himself?

In one word, thus: although the praise of the glory of his grace is but a creature, yet relatively it is God, it is his own, it is himself, it hath relation to himself. 'My glory,' saith he, 'I will not give to another;' no, not this glory which thus ariseth out of the creature; not only his essential glory, but not that manifestative glory he hath out of all things. It is incommunicable to any creature. Though it be not essentially himself, yet relatively it is; therefore, Prov. xvi. 3, he is said to have 'made all things for himself, and the wicked for the day of evil.' And now to say that the praise of the glory of his grace moved him, is all one as to say himself moved himself; because it is his, and it is incommunicably his. So much now for that 9th verse.

SERMON X.

That in the dispensation of the fulness of times he might gather together in one all things in Christ, both which are in heaven, and which are on earth; even in him.—VER. 10.

THESE words contain the whole of God's everlasting purposes of grace (sever them from those of creation and providence) toward all or any, either in heaven or earth, whom he regards or loves.

This is his comprehensive scope; and that both the coherence of them with the former, and the matter itself, when opened, will discover and declare. *First*, the coherence these words have with the whole he had been discoursing of from ver. 3 until now. From ver. 3 unto ver. 7, he had been enumerating the particular purposes of God's grace to us men in Christ,—the things on earth,—how from everlasting he had chosen, predestinated, and graciously accepted us in his Son Christ. And then, from ver. 7 to this, how he had redeemed us, forgives us, and calls us according to the same rich grace in Christ. Which done and said of us men, whom this epistle was wholly wrote to and concerned, he then brings forth the whole of God's design in the utmost extent of it, so to glorify this grace and this Christ. 'To gather in him,'—not *us* only, you and us men, the things on earth, but all things that are in heaven also,—'in him I say;' and it is as if he had said, 'For a conclusion of these particulars, I will give you the total sum of all in comprehensive words.'

That particular account begun concerning us men, occasioned and drew out this general conclusion and glorious *coronis*.

The words immediately before, 'he purposed in himself,' there are two known variations of them, yet so as either stream falls into this scope.

1. Some copies, and those more ancient, have not that word 'which.' They render it not, '*which* he purposed in himself,' but simply thus, 'he purposed in himself.' And so those words before them, ver. 9, 'having made known the mystery of his will, according to his good pleasure,' they give a full period to his former sentence, ver. 8, and then these words, 'He purposed in himself,' begin anew, and do of right belong to this 10th verse, and are to be cut off from the 9th verse. And so the scope runs naturally to shew, as hath been said—

2. What was the whole, and all, and utmost, of what he purposed in himself—namely this, to gather all in Christ, the good angels, as well as us men, thereby to shew the fulness of Christ's glory. For, secondly, if that word 'which' prove to be that which fell from Paul's pen, (as most copies,) yet still the current empties itself into the same meaning: for whereas, in the 9th verse, he had set out the rich grace of God shewn to the Ephesians, as also himself in particular,—that he had called them unto Christ by the knowledge of his will, 'making known to them the mystery of his will;' which grace of gathering them personally first unto Christ he attributes unto the

good pleasure of his will, as it follows, 'according to his good pleasure,' κατὰ τὴν εὐδοκίαν, ἣν—that is, according to that, even that same good pleasure which, or out of which, he had purposed to gather universally all of them he loved in heaven or earth in his one Christ,—so as comfort yourselves, and adore that grace, which herein is the very same unto you which it is unto any or all of angels and men. And what love can be supposed greater? Yea, and this is your privilege, to be taken into that general account and number of that general assembly, consisting of a universal 'company of angels,' &c., the privilege of which the Apostle doth so celebrate, Heb. xii. What shall I say more? You have the bottom of God's heart, the centre and circumference of his decrees of grace, the greatest birth the heart of God was ever big with; so great, as God having been in travail with it from everlasting, as became so great a design, had also appointed a 'fulness of time,' a centre of time, for the delivery or discovery of it; which began when Christ was first revealed, 'seen of angels,' things in heaven—'believed on in the world,' both of Jews and Gentiles, which shall be gathered together in that last and general assembly in heaven. This is the coherence and general scope.

There are two eminent phrases to be opened:—

First, What is meant by 'all things in heaven, in earth.'

Secondly, What the import and signification of this word, of 'gathering together in one,' ἀνακεφαλαιώσασθαι, by which the Apostle undertakes to express the ultimate and most perfect design of God toward all his elect. What it signifies and extends itself unto I shall, for a clearer view of what I am to deliver—

First, Explain what is meant by 'all things.' And then—

Secondly, Set forth the particular heads I mean to treat on.

Thirdly, After that, I will give the import of that other phrase, 'gathering together in one;' the reason of doing which latter after the other will easily appear, because the variety of the signification of that phrase will be found to fall in with all these heads.

First, What is meant by 'all things.'

It expresseth those two sorts of intellectual creatures who are here set out and distinguished by their original countries they belong unto, the places of their habitation, heaven and earth. The Hebrews are wont thus to express them, as in the Second Commandment—

1. 'Thou shalt not make the likeness of things in heaven above;' whereby are meant angels, who sometimes took shapes;

2. 'Nor of things on the earth beneath,'

3. 'Nor under the earth;' devils, who appeared in the shapes of hairy ones, satyrs, &c. You have the very same, Phil. ii. 10.

Now of this third dominion of God's,—viz., that of devils, or of those in hell under the earth,—of this sin was the sole founder. But God only took out his original dominions, heaven and earth, for the subjects of this his choice. Those under the earth are left out, as they are said 'to be without;' there is no gathering thence. But two colonies he hath singled out of earth and heaven.

Secondly, These are two sorts of intelligent creatures, angels in heaven, and men on earth. Beza and others would have the souls of elect men, that were in heaven when Christ died and ascended, to be the 'things in heaven,' but without any instance of any scripture where they are so termed; and also that parallel place, Col. i. 18-20, that Christ is the head of the body, by whom God hath reconciled 'all things to himself, whether things in earth, or things in heaven;' the phrase is clearly interpreted by ver. 16, 'By him all things were created, that are in heaven, and that are on earth;' as being distinguished by the places which by their creation they belong unto.

If, secondly, you ask, Why the persons of angels and men are meant by *things?*

Resp.—It is ordinary in Scripture so to express it: Gal. iii. 32, God hath shut up 'all things under sin,' τὰ πάντα; which is elsewhere expressed, Rom. xi. 32, τοὺς πάντας, as meaning persons.

If, thirdly, why *all?* The answer is, the apostle intends all whom God cares for; and indeed those only *are*, whom God's favour gives being unto: 'Of him ye are in Christ Jesus,' 1 Cor. i. 30. Again, secondly, *all;* that is, all sorts in either. (1.) In heaven, there are several ranks of angels, which Col. i. 16 warrants, 'thrones and dominions;' as you see among peers, dukes, marquises, earls, although they are all of the same house; so here. Here are archangels, angels; the Scripture mentions both. (2.) On earth there are several ranks of men. Now God affects to have of all, 1 Tim. ii. 1, 2, of all nations, countries, families, conditions, that shall be made happy by him.

Secondly, The heads of the ensuing discourse.

The eminent particulars contained in this total of God's purposes of grace, the subjects of my discourse, are—

First, The utmost of that thing itself which God intended to bring all his unto. It is an union with himself, and a collection of all things to himself.

Secondly, His setting forth and singling out the person of Christ, the great *Him* here; 'in him,' I say, in whose very person he first purposed to gather up all sorts of things, and thereby to fit him to become a head or centre, in which he might gather all whom he loved.

Thirdly, That he hath taken his elect out of all sorts of persons that were in heaven or are in earth, and united them in Christ, as in, and through, and under one common head.

Fourthly, That to illustrate his grace, and the glory of his Christ the more, he ordained a first and second gathering or union of all these; and the first being slippery and failing, he ordained a firm and everlasting union at last, in and through his Son.

Fifthly, The manner of his effecting this, 'by Christ.' And so you have the heads to be treated on.

Thirdly, Let us consider the import and extent of this great word, ἀνακεφαλαιώσασθαι, and the several significations of it, which the Holy Ghost singled out on purpose to express this whole of God's design, and the several particulars forementioned therein.

I shall but give you what is collected from approved interpreters and critics, of which it is too large to give the account.

I. In general, it imports to join many things in one, and to bring them to an unity. This sense our translators favoured, rendering it simply thus, 'a gathering together in one.' And this general sense of the word falls fitly in with the first of those heads mentioned, viz., That God's utmost design was an union with himself.

II. Particularly. This more general contains many more particular significations under it:—

1. It is a similitude taken from arithmetic, and signifies a summing up many lesser broken numbers and accounts in one total sum, as merchants do. Thus the tale or total sum of bricks to be gathered by the Israelites,

Exod. v. 18, is rendered by the Septuagint, κεφάλαιον, which is a phrase akin to that of κεφαλή, the head. The Grecians placed the total sum of any account at the top, as we on the contrary at the bottom of it; and whereas we call it *pes computi*, discomputation, the foot of the account, they termed it κεφάλαιον, the head or top.

2. The word is a similitude from rhetoric,—that is, to sum or gather up many particulars, which have been largely and particularly dilated on, into one word or sentence, which is the brief or compendium of them all. Thus Rom. xiii. 9, having rehearsed many particular commandments, Thou shalt not steal, murder, &c., he concludes, 'And if there be any other commandment, it is briefly comprehended' (it is the same word that is here) 'in this one saying, Thou shalt love thy neighbour as thyself.' And these two significations do correspond with the second head, and fitly serve to express how that in the very person of Christ are summed so many particulars as in one sum, or one brief sentence.

3. It is a similitude taken from politics, as when we would express many nations or persons united under one prince, as their head. Thus Chrysostom understood it, and many since. And so in the natural body, ἀποκεφαλαιῶσαι is, 'to cut off the head,' *truncare caput;* opposite to which is this word here, 'to gather under one head.' And this signification suits and serves the third head, namely, that *all things*, all sorts of angels and men, are gathered up under Christ, as their head and natural prince.

Lastly, there is an ἀνὰ added, 'to gather again a second time,' to redeem or collect things or persons that were scattered asunder, as the dead bones in Ezekiel, which being disjointed came together miraculously again, and made up one body under one head.

And this serves fitly to the two last heads proposed, so as not one of them can be spared. You have the heads of my subject cut out, and the words opened as holding them forth. Now to give you the story of all these. For the first head:—

HEAD I.

That the great God purposed and designed an union with himself of those whom in a special manner he had set himself to love; and that this union is the deepest and furthest design of his heart, of any he hath toward them, or the whole creation. The full demonstration of his manifold wisdom and power moved him to make a variety of persons, things, yea, of worlds; but then his goodness and his love moved him to reduce out of that variety an *all* out of every sort, as a pledge of his respect to all, unto an unity again, and that with himself; and this union is the top perfection of all his works, as that, John xvii. 23, 'I in them, and they in me, that they may be made perfect in one.' It is the perfection of the creature, whereof the unity of the three Persons is the pattern, and the perfection of God's design.

HEAD II.

The next thing to be considered is, *what medium, means, or corner-stone and foundation it was which God laid and designed, in and by whom most efficaciously and harmoniously to accomplish this designed union between himself and all things in both worlds.* For the whole creation was at that distance from God, as God would have them know and retain the sense and remembrance of it, even when this union should be in its height and perfection; and to that end neither admits the generality, the *all* here, to an immediate union with himself; and those he doth admit but in and through another, and him the text names and holds up with the greatest eminence, 'in him, in him I say;' thereby shewing that it was this great He, and he alone, that was or could have been the foundation of this work.

Him, whom God hath made both Lord and Christ, and to that end singled forth and made up, and constituted him such a person as should be the centre, the compound of all things which he meant in and by him to unite.

And herein let us adore the infinite wisdom of God, to find out and contrive such a kind of person to be his instrument therein; remembering all along that we are not at present speaking of redemption, but only of union.

Now, to set forth this in general, let us consider, that if there were a general counsel of all sorts of intelligent natures, called by God, and commissionated to choose out a head to this *all* of themselves, they would certainly pitch upon such a one, if such a one could be found out by them, in whom all the interest and concernments of them all do meet. Now this hath God done for us, without us, in this choice of his Christ and our Lord. For what can, or could be supposed more harmonious than that, when God meant to unite the variety of all sorts in one head, he should ordain that one head in his person to be the sum of all their natures and conditions, and yet a person of himself, and distinct from them, and independent of them; and so Christ mystical, the Church, and Christ personal, who were to be espoused together, might suit and match, and alike consist of all things, to the end they might be like in all things as near as possible might be?

And this collection of *all* in the very person of Christ takes up two of those fore-mentioned significations of this word, ἀνακεφαλαιώσασθαι. First, the casting up of divers numbers in one total sum; secondly, the epitomising or summing up a variety of dilated discourses into one sentence.

Let us run through the divided numbers which 'all things, in heaven or earth,' are parted into.

The *first* great and more general division of all things is, *God and the creature,* and to cast up or bring in these two into one sum or total was the hardest piece of arithmetic that ever was. And yet none of us creatures had ever come into this after-account or second union with God under Christ, if God himself had not come into and made one of this first account and highest union, that is, *of God and a creature making one Person.*

Deny Christ to be God, and deny him to be head, and dissolve all our union with God, as also reconciliation unto God, the foundation of all is taken away. The mutable creature could never fix unto God, but by this sure and immutable foundation.

Secondly, Come we then to creatures. Among them there is another division; for as God hath made two worlds, so two possessors of them—the angels, the intellectual natures of the world above; and us men on earth, the lower world. It is true, that because the redemption of men was in his eye, as well as this of union of all things, therefore 'he took not the nature of angels;' and besides, therein there was a more special respect and inclination had unto men, rather than unto the angels, as Heb. ii. shews. Yet withal it must also be affirmed that, in order to the fetching in of this general union of all things both in earth and heaven, this was the only way to comprehend and grasp both and all,—to take into one person with him one individual nature of man, rather than any other. And hereby, and by this alone, he hath summed up all in heaven and earth in his person. Not only because in the nature of man, as in a little world, all things are summed up in both worlds; man having a spirit, which like the angels can subsist alone, out of the body, and live in their world, *i.e.*, in heaven; but he hath a body also, which consists of all sorts of creatures here below. The heathens observed, and their poets feigned, a piece of everything else went to make up man. Whereas, had he taken the nature of angels, then the 'all things on earth' had been quite left out of this account; for though man hath a spirit like that of the angelical nature, yet that spirit being ordained to dwell in a body, and that body being a part of man, and constitutive of him as such; (and therefore Christ proves the resurrection of the body of Abraham by this, that else it is not Abraham, the man Abraham, unless soul and body be joined.) But upon a further ground we shall see it was that in taking of man's nature he took in angels also, that is, *the condition of angels.*

It is true, had he been no more but an earthly man, as Adam his type, this design of taking in all had fallen short. But the person who assumes and takes into his person this individual nature of man being God, the Son of God, that man whom he so assumes is instantly a heavenly man, as to his condition, 1 Cor. xv. 47, 48. And although the substance of his nature is the same as ours, yet the state is heavenly, and to be ὡς ἄγγελοι, as angels; yea, 'far above all principalities and powers,' Eph. i.; yea, 'higher than the heavens,' Heb. vii. 25. It is not his right only to be in heaven, but he is Lord of it, 'the Lord from heaven,' as 1 Cor. xv. 47, and other scriptures speak, as John iii. 13, and is spoken as if, as he is man, he had first been actually in heaven, because it was a real condescension in him to take our nature with its frailty, by which he became for a little while 'lower than the angels,' Heb. ii. His natural due was that heavenly state, and to be as glorious as he is now. Here then is in an instant all in heaven and earth met, and all their interest. For though man could say, He hath our nature; yet the angels could withal instantly reply, But he is our countryman; by right we should have him here, and there he must in the end be, and live for ever. None of his creatures could say, We have a King and Head in whom ye have no share or alliance unto.

You know how sharp the contention grew between the men of Judah and the ten tribes, 2 Sam. xix., about David their king. 'He is nigh akin to us,' say the men of Judah, ver. 42, 'flesh of our flesh, and bone of our bone.' They of Judah plead, as he was David; so ver. 9, 'But he hath saved us out of the hands of our enemies, and delivered us out of the hands of the Philistines.' As he was king, say the ten tribes. And thereupon the men of Israel answered, 'We have ten parts in the king, and we have also more right in David than ye.' But, my brethren, here neither things on earth, neither things in heaven, need either of them to complain or quarrel about the like in Christ; for God hath summed up all in their King, Jesus, that so he might become their catholic King and universal Head. He is flesh of our flesh, and bone of our bone, and by birth akin to us, might man say, which the angels cannot. But this they can truly reply instead of it, But he is a heavenly man, and that by right of inheritance from a higher birth, which his person had from everlasting. Heaven is his country; his court is for ever to be there; his throne is there erected; and by birthright he is to sit at God's right hand. He is a spiritual man, 1 Cor. xv. 46; yea, and 'a quickening spirit' unto us, and to you the sons of men also: yea, and you men, if you will enjoy your King and his presence for ever, you must come up or be brought where we are, even as Christ prays they may, John xvii., 'be where I am, and see my glory;' and 'I have given it them.' So, then, neither can they say, 'they have no part in Jesse.'

Yea, here I may add that, in taking man's nature there was this further advantage: there was a gratification to all kinds of creatures else; they can all say, We have something of every one of us in him. Man's nature being the epitome of all, the centre of both worlds, higher and lower,—the elements, vegetatives, sensitive creatures,—man is the little idea of all species or kinds of things; and this great idea, the Son of God and the image of God, they married together; and a happy match it must needs prove, which brings God and all creatures thus into one person.

Thirdly, Come we to 'things on earth,' the sons of men. Amongst them we find one famous division of Jew and Gentile; and that Christ might be a meet head to both, God hath summed up both Jew and Gentile in him. And yet as touching the former, between men and angels, the election was that 'he took not the nature of angels,' Heb. ii. (which you have seen removed :) so here, that which follows, that he 'took on him the seed of Abraham,' serves wholly to exclude us Gentiles from having any portion in his person.

But the answer is as ready. It is true that, immediately and more eminently, he came of the Jewish race, Rom. ix. 5, 'Whose are the fathers, and of whom as concerning the flesh Christ came.' And as in that other division between angels and men, the portion that man hath in him preponderates; so it is here on the Jews' side also, yet withal not to the utter exclusion of the Gentiles. For, to allude to that speech of the ten tribes, concerning David, we Gentiles have ten parts in him. There were ten patriarchs that were his ancestors and ours, and came to us and the Jews, before this division of Abraham's seed was brought up in the world; and two thousand years or more before Abraham was styled the Father of the Faithful, and the Promised Seed, Eve was called the Mother of all Living: and so, that both Jew and Gentile had the first promise of the seed that should break the serpent's head, to be her seed. Yea, and after that division made from Abraham, you have two Gentiles mentioned in his very genealogy, Rahab and Ruth, as his great-grandmothers. So it was he would have some of the Gentiles' blood run in his veins, as well as that of the Jews.

Thus you have now seen, 1. God's most deep and comprehensive design to be the union of all things with himself. 2. The fulness of fulness in the person whom he singles forth to be the means or effecter of it; and therein two of the forementioned significations of the word ἀνακεφαλαιώσασθαι taken up therein.

HEAD III.

We come now to the persons gathered. The third head proposed was, *That God out of all sorts of persons, both in heaven and in earth, hath designed to collect a body and select company to union with himself, and through Christ as their Head.* Which the third particular import of this word gives warrant to; it signifies, 'gathering together as in one head.'

As he is an arithmetical head, so he is a political head. He is a Prince, and a Lord, and a Head to all things in heaven and in earth, and they are made all one, in being reduced to him as to a head. 'He hath given him to be the head over all things to the church,' Eph. i. 22. So that, my brethren, this is the second mystery I am to unfold to you, That as in the person of the Lord Jesus Christ there is God, and angels, and men, Jew and Gentile, summed up in him; he partakes in his person of all these: so his body, if you will so call it, or rather his family, whereof he is head,—(for I do not know that the angels are called members of his body, that is peculiarly the privilege of the saints),—but they are all gathered into one commonwealth, into one city, into one family, both angels and men, unto him as their head. And that same universal Church, that shall appear at the latter day when the fulness of time is out, when the glass is run; for then he will have them all about him, and they will all be under one head; and so that family of his, which shall all come unto him, will have a conformity to his person. Christ mystical will have a conformity to Christ personal; as Christ personal was summed up of all, so will that whole family of his, that whole commonwealth of his, whereof he is the head, be summed up of all too, both angels and men, Jew and Gentile, all sorts of men; all things in heaven, and all things in earth, shall all be gathered in one *in him.*

And this is that same great μυστήριον, as the Apostle calleth it, Eph. iii. 9: 'To make all men see,' saith he, 'what is the fellowship of the mystery,'—and the angels come in there too, at the 10th verse, for by the preaching of the gospel they have a fellowship with him as well as the Jew and Gentile,—'to the intent that now unto the principalities and powers in heavenly places might be known by the church the manifold wisdom of God.' This is that great association of all the creatures, whereby they are all, though they are two several kingdoms, as England and Scotland are, yet all united; there is an association under one monarch, so under one Christ, that they come all to have relation to one as their head, and all make up a family, and a commonwealth, and a kingdom too.

There are two things here to be treated of.

(1.) That the good angels, as well as men, are united and come into this society under Christ as a head, which alone I need insist upon; for of men there is no question.

(2.) That all of each—that is, all sorts of angels and all sorts of men—are taken in to make up this body or society.

(1.) Angels, as well as men; which I explain by these particulars:—

First, When I say they are 'gathered in one in Christ,' I mean not as a redeemer, but simply as a head. The difference of these two I shall in another section give the account of. I observe that, Rev. v. 9, 11, 12, when the two first rounds, or rings, gathered about the Lamb and the throne, the first and nearest is of men, of angels the second; and both celebrating the Lamb that was slain.

This in general, *That Christ is head both to angels and men.*

(2.) The second branch, That all sorts of each, both angels and men, were gathered unto him, as in that one head.

[1.] All sorts of angels. There are several ranks of angels, which Col. i. 16 doth give us the heraldry of: 'All things that are in heaven, and that are in earth, visible and invisible, whether they be thrones or dominions,' (there are things in heaven,) 'principalities or powers.' 1. Thrones speaks kingly power to be among them, Dan. x. 13, 'Lo, Michael, one of the chief princes,' as he is there called, which is spoken of a good angel; for it is Michael. 2. There are dominions, viceroys, as it were ranks, and orders under them; and this order in hell is kept, by which their kingdom is governed; there is one that is the Prince of Devils, even as under a king there are dukes, and marquises, and earls, &c. And these good angels are all of one house, consisting of the original peers of heaven. And this distinction of angels, for we presume not to give any more ranks of them, (as the counterfeit Dionysius and, from him, the Papists do;) we elsewhere find in Scripture that some are called archangels. One at least, Jude 9, who was a mere created angel, as is evident by this, that he 'durst not bring a railing accusation;' which must not be applied unto the second Person as God, as some have done. Likewise, 1 Thess. iv. 16, it is said, 'The Lord shall descend with the voice of an archangel;' which archangel is distinct from the Lord himself. The angels then are of several ranks, and there are of all sorts of them in heaven.

[2.] Men on earth. Christ hath a body of men, made up of all on earth, an elect of all sorts.

The first division of things on earth is into Jew and Gentile, in common; that the Church of men consists of both these, is known to all.

Secondly, Among the Gentiles there are many nations; and, Gen. xviii. 18, the promise is to Abraham, that in him (*i.e.*, in Christ) all the nations of the earth should be blessed, and it is repeated again in chap. xxii. It is not only that Christ should sprinkle 'many nations' with his blood, Isa. lii. 15; but the first promise saith, 'all nations.' Ps. lxxxvi. 9, 'All nations whom thou hast made shall come and worship before thee, O Lord, and shall glorify thy name.' Christ therefore gave commission that the gospel should be preached to all nations; and so it shall be before the end of the world.

Then, thirdly, in every several nation there are many kindreds, families, or fatherhoods, as Peter speaks of them, Acts iii. 25, out of Gen. xii. 3, 'In thy seed shall all the families of the earth be blessed;' and that is twice said, as well as the other of nations. And if you will hear the whole Church of the New Testament sum up all in their own names, Rev. v. 9, 'Thou wast slain, and hast redeemed us to God by thy blood, out of every kindred, and tongue, and people, and nation.' He multiplies words enough, even as lawyers use to do, that he might be sure to comprehend all.

Fourthly, There are other divisions. Sinners of all sorts; several ranks, kinds, and degrees of sinners. And God will save out of all these sorts, but of one; and they are such of the sons of men as join issue with the serpent, and sin the devil's sin, the sin against the Holy Ghost, and are in the state of the devils while they are upon earth; and therefore are not to be reckoned with things on earth. But of all sorts of sinners our Saviour Christ hath said, Matt. xii. 31, that they shall be forgiven. 'All manner of sin and blasphemy shall be forgiven unto men; but the blasphemy against the Holy Ghost shall not be forgiven unto men.' He doth not say that all manner of sins *may*, but he saith that all *shall* be forgiven in one or other. And he through whose hands all pardons run, it is he saith this. God hath ordered his elect, take the whole body and bulk of them, to fall into all sorts or sins, one or other of them; so as there is no sort, kind, or degree of sin, no way of sinning, manner of sinning, or aggravation of sin, but in some or other it shall be pardoned, and he doth it to glorify his grace in Christ, in whom he gathers them; and this was the mystery of that sheet which Peter saw coming down from heaven, tied at the four corners, as pointing to all the four quarters of the world; 'in which there were all manner of unclean creatures; four-footed beasts of the earth, and wild beasts, and creeping things, and fowls of the air,' Acts x. 11, 12. It imports all sorts of sinners, all the world over, the most venomous creatures, as many creeping things are; of those should the Church catholic consist.

Lastly, There is another division of the outward ranks of men; and out of all doth God take some. 1 Tim. ii. 1, he exhorts that prayers and thanks may be made for all men; for kings, and for all that are in authority. He takes up kings, and of all sorts and ranks that are in authority else; yea, and out of all men; and therefore he would have thanks given for all sorts, as well as prayers made. You know your calling, brethren, not many wise, not many noble; yet some. I am a debtor to the wise, and to the weak, saith Paul; and God takes fools as well as wise men. The fools shall not err therein, Isa. xxxv. 8; though they be natural fools, he can come at their hearts.

And so you have the third head in general mentioned, and the third signification of the word ἀνακεφαλαιώσασθαι filled up and made good.

HEAD IV.

That God, to illustrate the glory of his grace, and of his Christ, purposed a second gathering after a first, both of men and angels. This the word 'to gather again' implies; *recolligere.* This ἀνὰ, as Bishop Andrews on this text, must not be lost; it is an addition of infinite importance, to amplify the glory of God in this purpose of his. It imports—

1. A first and second gathering of these 'all things,' or a double union of these creatures to God; whereof the first being slippery and failing, he ordained the last firm and fixed in Christ, never to be broken or dissolved again. The first was not firm enough, but soon and easily dissoluble.

2. This ἀνὰ, or again, imports a miserable scattering of the first gathering to fall out between the first and second gathering; a dissolution of all first, on purpose decreed and permitted by God, to make this second gathering, and oneness with himself, and unity one with another, which was the ultimate aim of his design, more illustrious.

3. A third thing is the way, and manner, and means of doing it; it is *in Christ.*

The first serves to magnify his grace in Christ, the Head, to angels, who are *all things* in heaven. And the second to magnify his grace to the sons of men, the *all things* in earth, both as a Head and Redeemer. And all put together contains the whole counsel of God unto both. God united man and angels to himself in their first creation, and one to another. The elect angels stood in need of a second union, or gathering of them in Christ, as a head; to put them out of danger and possibility of being scattered, as their fellows had been; and therein lies their obligation. And elect men having all run into an actual riot and rebellion, and were separated from God, and scattered from one another, needed a gathering together again; and both in and through Christ, to fix either for ever from a perpetual hazard of departing. And the opening these things, and being added to the former, bring in an infinite revenue of glory unto God and Christ; and do give us indeed an account of the whole counsel of God: and still he renders it more and more complete.

For the first branch. There was an union of man and angels to God by the mere law of creation, and covenant of nature or works. And though the angels—for I speak of them now in common, and so of the *elect angels,* in the general condition with them that are fallen in their first creation—were created in heaven, and man upon earth, yet the same law of nature, and the same terms and tie of union, were alike enjoyed; and thereby they had an union and communion with God; but merely by their graces, and the exercise of them, according to the covenant of works. So, as long as that held, their union held, but not a moment longer.

For though the law of creation that was common both to men and angels had this meet dueness in it, as was said, that God should create them in that estate, and afford them help suitable thereunto; yet no law of nature or creation, either to angels or men, had a promise that God should keep them and preserve them in that estate from falling. They were as glasses without a bottom, which soon fell and broke; which by the event was made good, by the fall both of men and some angels: which shews the weakness and the slipperiness of this first union in either of them.

As concerning the ANGELS, if God would assure them to himself from the possibility of falling, they must be headed in Christ, or by Christ; they must be gathered by a gathering together in Christ as a head a second time, and then all is in sure hands. If therefore the query be, Wherein should the grace vouchsafed to them lie, so as they had need of Christ to interpose, and to make this second gathering of them, whereas they never had fallen actually?—for it may be thought needless—the necessity lay in this:—

First, If it were no more but the weakness and slipperiness of their first union: therefore, if there were no more, it was necessary they should be fixed in him by an immutable relation to him who is the Rock of Ages, and then they are in sure hands. For Christ is as sure and immutably fixed as the Son of God himself, by personal union with the Son of God; and they, if they be chosen in him, and accepted in him, and have a relation unto him as to their head, are made as immutable as Christ is. Job iv. 18, 'Behold, he put no trust in his servants, and his angels he charged with folly.' The Lord foresaw that if he kept to the laws that the condition of works required, and unto the dues of it, he could be sure of none; and he plainly saith he could put no confidence. And indeed he had little reason; for you know how all on earth served him, and how great a part of heaven (in the event) did serve him. Those morning stars fell. And this in Job is spoken of the good angels, his servants and courtiers he had about him. And all my creatures may serve me so, if they be left unto their first condition, to the law of their creation. And if they stand a thousand years, yet what Grotius dreams may be now, (upon those words, Gal. i. 8, 'If an angel from heaven, &c., let him be accursed;') as if angels might still fall; though that be false now since their confirmation in grace by Christ, yet it was true once; and he chargeth them with folly, because he saw their aptness to folly. He saw the possibility of it, and therefore could have no settled contentment in any of them in that estate, nor perfectly love them: but loved them *tanquam aliquando osurus*, as those whom he might one day hate, which prejudgeth perfect love; and therefore upon a foresight of their creature condition, he vouchsafed a second gathering of them in Christ, so to fix them. And hence arose *quædam simultas*, I will not say a grudge against them, for they had no sin; yet a kind of displicency with them, as mere creatures, if alone and apart considered. And then his charging them with folly might, and did arise, because he is so holy a God; and he is so infinitely holy, as that though in justice he hath nothing against them,—for he knows they are creatures, and whereof they are made,—yet still they are not of that holiness he would be pleased in, as Calvin doth interpret it. Upon all these grounds his grace first fixed them in Christ the Rock of Ages, as in their head, and a firm union with him as in that relation; for if he became and undertook to be a head to them, he would not lose his members.

And, secondly, thereby he pleased himself in them through him in whom only he is well pleased; which saying reaches the angels as well as men, even all intelligent creatures he is any way pleased withal; and he is pleased with the relation they bear to his person. Yea, thirdly, to take away all distaste aforesaid, they needed a kind of reconciliation, *reconciliatio analogica*, as learned Davenant. It was not a reconciliation by a price, so as to purchase their peace for sin actually committed; they needed not that. Reconciliation is a larger word; there is a reconciliation preventive of them that have any aptness or possibility to fall out, so as to make them fast friends for ever, and to make them sure unto himself, and to take away all occasion of jealousies; and so they were, as Bernard saith, *suo modo redempti*. Fourthly, I shall add this further, mercy does not lie only in pardoning, but in preventing. It cost Christ's blood to keep us from the sin we might have committed, as well as to obtain forgiveness for the sins we have committed; and therefore the Apostle saith he hath redeemed us from our vain conversation, even which we might have fallen into. God knows our thoughts afar off: and what they would be of ourselves. *Angelica natura egebat misericordiâ Dei, ne posset errare*, so saith Ambrose. So you have seen the need the angels had of their second gathering, and that by Christ.

I shall for the opening of this, do these three things

1. Prove it by other scriptures.

2. Explain it; and that by two things—

(1.) What fellowship and association angels and elect have, and shall have, one among another.

(2.) What communion, and fellowship, and relation angels have to Christ, as to a head.

3. Give some cautions, that you may not be mistaken in the point.

1. First, *For the proof of it*. There are many places brought, but the truth is, I know none come home to it so much, and therefore I will but name it, as that, Col. ii. 10, 'In him dwelleth all the fulness of the Godhead bodily; and you are complete in him, who is the head of all principality and power.' By principalities and powers, in the usual phrase of Scripture, is still meant the angels: Eph. i. 21, 'He hath raised him up,' speaking of Christ, 'and set him at his own right hand in the heavenly places, far above all principalities and powers, and might and dominion, and every name that is named, not only in this world, but also in that which is to come.' Now, saith he, what need you go out of Christ? you are complete in him. Why are we complete in him? Here is his reason: if the angels are complete in him, that are the highest creatures, that stand at God's right hand, and in his presence,—if he be their head, then you may very well be complete in him, you poor men that live on earth. 'You are complete in him, who is the head of all principalities and powers.'

I will give you some general expressions that will prove it and explain it. First, the angels and men do make up one family unto God, whereof Christ is the head, or the *pater-familias;* as you know it is the ordinary expression in all languages to call the master of the family the head of the family; so is Jesus Christ to angels and men, that make up one family to God. And, my brethren, so it falleth out, that the very text hinteth this to be the Apostle's meaning, for that which we translate, 'in the dispensation of the fulness of time,' is in the original εἰς οἰκονομίαν, the household dispensation, the family dispensation, as many read the words. That is, he hath gathered them all in one for a family dispensation, for a family government of them, into one family, so to order and govern them, and dispense to both, to angels and men, as to one family, now to be dispensed in these last times.

That which fitteth this interpretation, is that in the third of the Ephesians, ver. 15, 'Of whom,' saith he, 'the whole family in heaven and earth is named.' He had named Christ just before; saith he, ver. 14, 'Unto the Father of our Lord Jesus Christ, of whom (of Jesus Christ, namely) the whole family, (he takes all in, both angels and men,) in heaven and in earth is named.' They all hold of him. You know he that is the head of a family, they have all their name from him; as that of the Turks, they call the Ottoman family, because Ottoman was the first of them. It is spoken there by the Apostle in opposition to the Jews; for the Jews boasted that all God's family was in Abraham's house, in Abraham's children. No, saith he; not only is the family of God not restrained unto Abraham's children, but it is diffused and dispersed over all the earth, and not only so, but it reacheth to heaven, too; and all on earth, and all in heaven, make but one family to God—angels and all. For, otherwise, when the Apostle wrote this, there were few in heaven but Jews, and so he had not spoken so appositely to what the Jews intended, who would arrogate all to themselves. No, saith he, though God hath appointed Abraham, and erected a family in him, peculiar to the Jews, yet all in earth hold of Christ, and all in heaven, too, and all are named of him. He is the foundation of both families, and they make all but one family: 'The whole family in heaven and in earth.' I will not stand to open to you the meaning of the word 'named' any further; his meaning is general, universal. He had said two great things of Christ just before: he had said, in the 9th verse, that 'God created all things by Jesus Christ;' he had said, in the 11th verse, that 'God purposed all things in Jesus Christ;' now he telleth you that 'things both in heaven and earth,' that whole family, angels and men, (he bringeth it in here at the 15th verse, to honour Christ,) are all 'named of him.' They all hold of him, he owneth them all, and they all own him, and they have their being of him, as the word *named* oftentimes signifieth.

Again, another expression is, as they are called one family, whereof he is the head, so they are one city, both angels and men. They make one Jerusalem, saints on earth and angels in heaven, whereof Jesus Christ is the governor, and the king and head, a political head. For this, see Heb. xii. 22, 'You are come unto Mount Sion,' which was the place of worship before, 'and unto the city of the living God, the heavenly Jerusalem.' Here are the generals. Now who are the inhabitants of this city? Who are the citizens? Who are the worshippers in Mount Sion together? It followeth, 'to an innumerable company of angels, to the general assembly and company of the first-born.' All these make up one city to God, they make up one heavenly Jerusalem, they make up one company of worshippers, as you shall see afterward. Now, because when a man is converted, he cometh to all these; that is, he entereth into an association with all these, he is made free of the company of all these; therefore they are said to be gathered in one in Christ.

My brethren, the angels are part of the worshippers of Christ as well as we; as they are part of his family, as they are part of his city, whereof he is the King and Lord, so they are part of his worshippers; and, as you shall see anon, we, with all them, worship God and him together, both here, and shall do so hereafter. They are worshippers of him, and in that sense make a part of the Church; for *ecclesia colentium*, a church is properly for worship. If they be therefore part of the worshippers of Christ, they come under his Church, they are a part of it; particular churches are ordained for worship, and so is the general Church for a worship to be performed to Christ. And it is the proper expression of the members of a church, what they are designed unto—they are worshippers. Now, in Heb. i. 6, you shall find that the angels are all worshippers of Jesus Christ, 'And again, when he bringeth his first-begotten into the world, he saith, Let all the angels of God worship him,' speaking of Christ. I will not stand to open the phrase, whether it be at his first coming or his second, for some read the words thus—so Cameron doth, and to me it certainly seemeth the meaning—'When he bringeth his Son again into the world,' so the word εἰσαγάγῃ better beareth it; the second time, when he cometh to judge the world, then the angels of God shall worship him, together with all saints, and all the elect, before all the world. I will not further open the place; I only allege it for this, that they are worshippers of Christ.

See but the reason of this head; you have seen Scripture for it. *First*, it is due to Christ. If that man Christ shall be the Son of God and the heir of all things, it is his due that he should be the head of the best of God's creatures, of angels that are saved as well as men, that he should be the head of God's family. The eldest, you know, were the head of the family. Are the angels a part of God's family? Will you shut them out? No; they are a part of God's family as well as you, (how, you shall see afterward.) If they be, then the eldest son, the heir of all, is the head of that family, and so of the angels, by the law of nature. It is Christ's due, and therefore they all hold and depend upon him.

Secondly, That all, thus gathered together to one head, to make up one family, and one city and church to God, it was for the infinite glory and splendour of this church. What could be greater than that all in heaven and all in earth should be united one day in one to worship God, and all to bow at the name of Christ, as the apostle telleth us, Phil. ii.? God appointed his Church to be all in one place; he would have them all up to heaven; and therefore he appointed them all one happiness. He hath appointed them to be all one city, therefore they shall have one head, they shall be united all together in one. He loves not scattering and distraction, to have two companies of worshippers at last, for God is one. It is therefore for their perfection, it is therefore for their greater splendour, as you shall see in the observations that I shall raise.

Thirdly, Men and angels were capable of this union, to be knit together thus under one head. Why? For we agree both in an intellectual nature; we have the same understanding, and will, and affections as they have, (take us as we are souls;) we are capable of the same common happiness that they have, to see God and to see Christ; we shall one day, after the resurrection, be made like unto them—so the expression is, Matt. xxii. 30. If we be brought up to the same condition with them, shall have the same happiness, shall live in the same place, why should we not have the same Head, and be joined all together, that as God is the head of Christ, Christ may be the head of all, both angels and men?

Last of all, By this is made up a most complete parallel opposition with Satan, who is the head of wicked men and of the devils. So God ordaineth it; he made two heads, and all the world falls to one of them. The devil, you know, that great devil, is the head of the evil angels; therefore, Matt. xii. 24, he is called the prince of the devils. He is the head of all wicked men; therefore, John xii. 31, he is called the prince of this world. And when the world is at an end, let that devil take all his angels and wicked men, and he as a head is tormented with them for ever; they are cast into the fire with the devil and his angels, you know it is said of wicked men. Answerably, as this great devil, whom God setteth up against Christ, is the great—I cannot call him Antichrist, because he is no way for Christ—but he is the great one that opposeth Christ, whom God setteth up against him to share the world with him. As he is the head of all that are wicked on earth, and of all in hell, so is Christ opposite, the head of all that are godly on earth, and of all in heaven; and though the devil is not of the same nature with men, yet he is the head of wicked men, he is the prince of the world, and he rules effectually in the children of disobedience, Eph. ii. 2. So likewise, though Jesus Christ is not of the same nature or substance with the angels, yet he is the head of angels, of all principalities and powers, and rules as effectually, nay, ten thousand times more effectually, for Satan is not such a head as Christ is. And when Jesus Christ hath taken up his all, the devil will take all the rest. Christ is made the head of all things in heaven and in earth; he takes out his saints, and the devil takes all the rest; they share the world between them. So you have the thing proved both by Scripture and by reason.

2. The second thing, then, that I am to do is this, to *explain this association between men and angels, under one Christ.*

(1.) And, first, as I said, I shall explain the association between men and angels one amongst another, what the fellowship is between angels and men, as making up one family to God. And then, secondly, what communion, what relation, what union and communion, the angels have with Christ, as with a head. This I must explain.

First, *Men and angels, amongst themselves, have this fellowship under Christ their head, that they are all worshippers of God and Christ together.* They are so in this world, and they shall be so more completely and fully in the world to come, when that fulness of the dispensation of all time shall take place at the latter day. First, I say, there is an association in worship in this world between angels and saints. Little do we think it, but the angels fill our churches as well as men, and are present at all our congregations and assemblies. Because we are to be with them hereafter, and to worship God together with them, therefore they come down and are present at the worship of God here with us. I could give you many proofs for it; I will but name one or two.

What was the reason that the tabernacle and temple at Jerusalem was all full of cherubim? Read Exod. xxv. 19; there were to be two cherubim over the mercy-seat, in the Holy of Holies. Read Exod. xxvi. 1; all the curtains that were to be for the tabernacle, they were all to have cherubim wrought in them. Cherubim are angels. Go from thence to the temple of Solomon, 1 Kings vi. 23, there you have cherubim again, at the mercy-seat too; and then, ver. 29, all the walls of the house round about were carved with carved figures of cherubim, with angels still; nay, the very doors for the entering into the Holy of Holies, and the doors of the temple, had cherubim carved upon them. All this betokened that angels still filled the temple as well as men; and therefore, 1 Cor. xi. 10, (surely it is the meaning of it,) he biddeth women to be modest, to be veiled, to shew subjection, not only because of men, but because of the angels—so the text is there—that are present at their Christian assemblies. He instanceth in the least misdemeanour, and argueth from the lesser to the greater, to make this a motive, that men should behave themselves religiously and holily in the churches of Christ, because the angels are present. If, saith he, you are not to suffer the angels to espy in you the least immodesty, then much more, any other misbehaviour.

In Rev. v. 11, you have the Church of Christ described, and there you have twenty-four elders and four beasts, which are the people and officers of congregations, and they sing a new song unto Christ, ver. 9, 'Thou art worthy to take the book, and to open the seals thereof: for thou wast slain, and hast redeemed us unto God by thy blood out of every kindred, and tongue, and people, and nation; and hast made us unto our God kings and priests, and we shall reign on the earth. And I beheld,' saith he, 'and I heard the voice of many angels round about the throne.' Angels are round about the throne; they are present at the courts of God's house; still they are worshippers, you see, together with us on earth.

Secondly, *They do delight to hear Christ preached, because Christ is their Head, and therefore are present.* The text is express, Eph. iii. 10; he sheweth there the end why to him was committed, and so to others, the preaching of the gospel: 'To the intent that now unto the principalities and powers in heavenly places might be known by the church the manifold wisdom of God.' They do not know it out of the Scripture simply, but as it is opened in the church, by the ministers of the church, for the good of the church, so they come to know it; and they delight to do so, for so you have it, 1 Pet. i. 12. Saith he, speaking of the fathers before in the Old Testament, 'It was revealed unto them, that not unto themselves, but unto us they did minister the things which are now reported unto you' (he speaks in general) 'by them that preached the gospel with the Holy Ghost sent down from heaven; which things the angels desire to look into.' The angels are present, and they are glad to hear Christ laid open and preached unto men, to hear their Head spoken of. They are worshippers together with us of Christ.

Then, thirdly, *Here on earth they have joy when any poor soul is converted.* As they come to church, so they observe who is wrought upon. When they see a poor soul go home and humble himself, fall down upon his knees and become a new creature, news is presently carried up to heaven; for the text saith, Luke xv. 10, that 'there is joy in the presence of the angels of God'—that is, in the court of heaven, amongst them all, so the word signifieth, ἐνώπιον, in the face of all the angels; it is the same word used, Luke xii. 8, 'him shall the Son of man confess before the angels of God,' he will own him in his court, and confess him in the presence, in the face of all the angels; so there is joy amongst the angels, they rejoice before God—'over one sinner that is converted,' over a poor soul that is gathered unto Christ their Head.

This association, my brethren, we have with them, besides all the services they do us, which I cannot stand to repeat and reckon up unto you; for all the angels are our fellow-servants; so that angel calleth himself, Rev. xxii. 9. And Jacob's ladder that touched heaven, the angels ascended and descended upon it; and Christ himself, John i. 51, interprets it that he is the ladder; they all come down upon him and ascend upon him, for the service of men. He is their head, their ruler, their governor.

But as we have in this world this association with them, so in the world to come we shall all worship God with one worship, both angels and men together. Such he there in Heb. xii., the place I quoted before; 'you are come to the Mount Sion,'—so he calleth the Church, which consisteth both of angels and men, as I observed before. Mount Sion, you know, was the place of God's worship. What is his meaning, then, when he saith, 'you are come to the Mount Sion, to the heavenly Jerusalem?' You are all come, saith he, to the place of worship whither angels are come up; for all the tribes came up there, to that Mount Sion, to worship God—the mount where all the angels are, and where all the souls of just men made perfect shall come up in their succession, and all to worship God. It is called Mount Sion, because it is the place of God's worship. And that which we translate the company of angels, μυριάσιν, it is the solemn assembly of angels; so the word signifieth, such an assembly as was at a solemn feast of the Jews, whither all the people came up. The men that dwelt at Jerusalem, he compareth them to the angels, for that is their standing seat and dwelling; and we that are upon earth, he compareth to the tribes that came up to the solemn assembly, to the solemn feast. And he calleth them the general assembly, for there God will have all his children about him. So that both angels and we one day shall be common worshippers, live in one kingdom together; we shall be as angels; so Matt. xxii. 30.

We are beholden to the man Christ for doing this, for he hath blessed us with heavenly blessings, as the third verse hath it. We shall live in one city, in one place. I will give you but one scripture for it, and so I will end. It is Zech. iii. 7. There our Saviour Christ, the Angel of the Covenant, makes this promise to Joshua the high priest, and to Zerubbabel, 'If thou wilt walk in my ways, and keep my charge,'—in my house, my material house, while thou art here below, I will give thee a better house than this,—'I will give thee places to walk amongst these that stand by,'—I will give thee a place amongst the angels; for they were they that stood by, and appeared upon the speckled horses, as chap. i.,—I will give thee a better house, a better temple; thou shalt live with angels, and dwell with them, and worship with them; thou shalt be raised up to a heavenly court, even to holy angels, if thou wilt keep my courts here below. Thus you see what an association men and angels have amongst themselves, both in this world, and in the world to come.

(2.) Well, let us see what communion they have with Christ as a Head. *First*, some say that Jesus Christ is a head to them only *by way of eminency and external government*, because he is the principal and the head of all power, he hath all power in him; therefore, because he governeth them and ruleth them externally as a king doth his subjects, in that respect only they say he is a head.

But, my brethren, he is a head in a nearer relation to them than so. Why? For, first, so he is to all creatures in respect of government; all creatures are subject to him.

Again, secondly, the angels are a part of his family, as I shewed before. Now, though he that is master of the family be a lord to all the things in the house, and the master of them all, yet he is a head only to the persons, for he hath a more near relation to the persons in the family than he hath to all the goods. God ruleth all the world, he ruleth all the goods belonging to this family in heaven and in earth, and they are all subject unto him; but he is a head of the persons in this family, of which angels are a part as well as men.

Thirdly, this were to make Christ the head of the angels, as the Papists do make the Pope head of the Church, but by external government; certainly he is more than so. Nay, it were to make Jesus Christ head of the angels in heaven, as the devil is head of evil angels and wicked men, by ruling of them only externally. Certainly he is more than so, when they are made part of the family, when the Scripture saith that he is the head of all principalities and powers. Therefore—

In the *second* place, he is a head to them *by way of secret influence of grace and glory*. If Jesus Christ be a head, it is fit that he should do something for them, that they should be beholden to him, that he should not only have that headship by virtue of his dignity and excellency, but that they should have some benefit, some influence arising to them from Christ, if that thus he shall be advanced to be a head over them; for God will never advance Christ to be a head over any but they shall have benefit by him.

First, they had their creation by him, Col. i. 15, 16. The apostle telleth us there that all things, whether visible or invisible, are created by him. 'By him,' saith he, 'were all things created, that are in heaven, and that are in earth,' here is the same enumeration, 'visible and invisible,' here is angels and men, 'whether they be thrones or dominions, or principalities or powers, all things were created by him and for him.'

Yea, and, my brethren, they were virtually created by him as supposed to take man's nature; for of him, as supposed to take man's nature, doth the Apostle there speak: 'who is the image,' saith he, 'of the invisible God, the first-born of every creature,' which can be ascribed to Christ no way but as he is God-man, and so all the rest likewise; but I will not stand upon that.

In the second place, he is the common principle of their grace, as well as their being. Eph. i. 23, it is said, that Christ 'filleth all in all,' speaking of him as he is a head, and as he hath a body; it is the same phrase that is used of God after the day of judgment: 1 Cor. xv. 28, he saith, that God will be 'all in all.' God is all in angels, and all in men then; so is Jesus Christ—he is that universal principle of all grace.

And there is this reason for it; for whatsoever hath anything by way of participation, it is reducible to something that hath it *per se*, of itself. The angels have grace, but they have it by participation; therefore they are reduced, as well as men, to something, to some head, to *aliquid primum*, which hath grace in him *per se*. That only Christ hath; he only is of himself beloved; he only is the sun, the Church is the moon, and the angels are the stars. They are the 'morning stars,' as they are called, Job xxxviii. He enlighteneth both the moon and stars. But, however, this may be certainly said, that they were kept from falling by virtue of Jesus Christ to come. In the same first of the Colossians, having reckoned up all things in heaven and in earth, as created by him, he addeth, 'and by him all things consist.' Angels and men are all kept by him; the station they have is in and through the Lord Jesus Christ.

And there is this great reason for it: because to stand in grace and not to fall, is a supernatural gift, more than was due to the angels, as creatures, though they were never so excellent. The devils fell, the other angels stood; what put the difference? It must be some supernatural grace. Now Christ is the fountain of all grace, the great beloved, the universal principle. Job iv. 18, it is said there that God 'charged his angels with folly;' he put no confidence in his servants. The good angels had a possible folly in them, though they had not an actual folly; they might have sinned, yea, it was impossible, being but creatures, but that they should have a possibility to sin of themselves, take them as creatures. They were indeed a house of stone, whereas man is but a house of clay: 'how much less,' saith he, ver. 19, 'we that dwell in houses of clay?' But though they were as a house of stone, yet that stood upon a quagmire, the shocky weak will of a creature. And so they were apt to fall without propping. Now, what hath underpropped these creatures that they stand? What putteth the difference? It is because they are united, they are headed in Christ, they belong to him. Only Christ of all creatures could not sin; for if that man could have sinned, there had been a person in the Trinity wanting. The second Person must have come down from heaven himself, if that man could have sinned, for he was united to it; and as the blood is called the 'blood of God,' so the sin would have been the *sin of God*, which would have been blasphemy to imagine. He only could not sin. And the angels, as they stand now, it may be said of them that they are impeccable; they cannot sin, and they shall never sin to all eternity, because they are underpropped by this corner-stone, that is the basis of all parts of the family both in heaven and in earth. It is Jesus Christ that underprops them; both things visible and invisible, things in heaven and things in earth.

Now, my brethren, if they had had no grace from him at first, or had none now, but that which they had only by a covenant of creation; yet, notwithstanding, to have this privilege annexed to their grace, that they should never fall as the devils did, and be out of all danger of sinning as they did; this is an infinite privilege, it is worth their acknowledging Christ their Head, if they had no more by him. It is said of glass, that if it could be made a metal that would not break, it were worth all the gold and silver in the world; and therefore it is reported of an emperor that put a man to death for making of glass that could not be broken, as being an invention that would spoil all the gold and silver in the world. My brethren, the angels are glorious vessels, but they are as glass. What doth Christ now? He makes them that they cannot fall, they cannot be broken, and this is more than all their grace; and this they have from Christ, as he is their head, and as they belong unto him.

Lastly, They have a happiness in Christ, in *seeing of him* as well as we. I take that to be part of the meaning of that 1 Tim. iii. 16. I have often wondered at the expression there; I shall give you what I think to be the meaning of it. Speaking of Christ, and of the great mystery of godliness in him, saith he, 'God, who was manifested in the flesh,'—and there was more of God manifested in the flesh in the person of Christ, than there is in all creatures that were made, or possibly could be made,—'justified in the Spirit,' which was spoken of his resurrection, 'seen of angels, preached unto the Gentiles, believed on in the world, received up into glory.' Here are two principles, faith and vision. Here is faith attributed to men; they cleave to Christ their head by faith, 'believed on in the world.' The angels cleave unto him by vision, 'seen of angels;' admiring him with infinite joy, looking upon him as their Head. They saw more of God manifested in that man Christ Jesus, than they had seen in heaven before. We cleave to him by faith; they cleave to him by sense: that which we shall have, for we shall see him one day as he is, that the angels do, and are made happy in him; the same eternal life that we have, they have, 'and this is eternal life, to know God, and to know Jesus Christ,' John xvii. 3. Their happiness lieth, as our happiness, in seeing God incarnate, in seeing God in the flesh, in seeing God face to face, and his Christ for ever.—And so much for the association which the angels and the elect have, and shall have, one among another, and what communion and relation they have with and to Christ, as a Head.

3. I will give you but a caution or two, which is the *third* thing I am to do, and so I will conclude.

The first caution is this, That Jesus Christ is only a Head to them, he is not a Redeemer. The expression here, ver. 7, is not, that he redeemed angels and men. No, saith he, 'in whom *we* have redemption,' we only; but both they and we are gathered to him, as a Head, as the word here signifieth. You know I told you, that there are two sorts of benefits we have by Christ, the one founded upon our relation to his person, the other founded upon his merit and redemption. Now, the benefits that angels have by him are not founded so much upon his redemption, (how far it is, I shall discourse upon the third thing when I handle this, 'hath gathered together all things to himself;') but the benefits they have by him are founded upon their relation to his person. That is the first caution.

The second caution is this, That it is certain that Jesus Christ is so a head unto men, as he is not unto angels. Though he is a head both to them and to us, and all, both angels and men, are gathered together in one head in him, yet he is so a head to us as not to them. You shall see a wonderful privilege that we have in this same first of the Ephesians, ver. 21. This chapter holds forth this unto us; for there the Apostle telleth us that God hath advanced Christ 'far above all principality and power, and might and dominion,' meaning angels, 'and hath put all things under his feet, and hath given him to be the head over all things to the church.' Here the Church, and his headship of the Church, is a distinct thing from that relation he beareth to angels, as here it is mentioned: he hath a superiority over angels for the good of the Church; he is so a Head to his Church as not to angels. I know they are mentioned as well as men in that verse. But how are they mentioned? Not that he is the head of them as he is of men, that is not the scope of it; but the scope of this place is only this, that he that is above principalities and powers is the Head of the Church; he beareth a more special relation to them than he doth to principalities and powers, and is above them in order to his headship of the Church. Hence it is that the angels are not called the *members of Christ;* you have not such an expression in the whole Book of God. As God is said to be the 'head of Christ,' 1 Cor. xi. 3, having an influence into Christ, yet Christ is not a member of God. So, though the angels are said to come unto Christ as a head, and he is their head, yet members of him nowhere you read it; for that is peculiar only to the saints, to the elect here on earth, to the sons of men.

I will give you more things wherein we differ from them. Jesus Christ is not a Common Person representing them as he represented us, as he did while he was here below. We obeyed in him, we died with him, we rose with him. Not so the angels; he did not act their part, he was not a Common Person to them; therefore they are nowhere said to be elected in him: but we are said to be elected in him, and he did sustain a Common Person while he was here below.

Thirdly, We are brethren to Christ, and so not the angels; you have nowhere that said. I will give you a scripture or two for it; one is that in Heb. ii., and the scripture is exceeding express. The Apostle there goeth to prove that Jesus Christ took the same nature with us. How doth he prove it? 'Because,' saith he, ver. 11, 'he calleth us brethren, saying,'—he takes a place out of Ps. xxii. 22,—'I will declare thy name unto my brethren, in the midst of the church I will sing praise unto thee.' And at ver. 14, 'Forasmuch then as the children are partakers of flesh and blood, he also himself likewise took part of the same.' And ver. 16, 'For verily he took not on him the nature of angels, but he took on him the seed of Abraham.' So that the place is clear and express, that therefore we are brethren to Christ, and Christ to us, he having the same nature with us; therefore the angels are nowhere said to be adopted sons to God, as men are said to be, as not having relation to Christ, as to a husband, and in that relation being sons of God. To give you another scripture for this, Rev. xix. 10; you shall find there that the angel indeed calleth himself *fellow-servant* with John, but he doth not call himself *brother;* nay, he doth not call himself brother, though he mentioneth the saints as John's brethren, 'I am thy fellow-servant, and of thy brethren.' The like you have, Rev. xxii. 9, 'I am thy fellow-servant, and of thy brethren the prophets, and of them which keep the sayings of this book.' The saints of God are brethren one to another, and unto Jesus Christ. The angels are but their fellow-servants.

Much less are they the spouse of Christ, much less have they the relation of a wife to him as a husband; this is proper to the headship of Christ over believers: Eph. v. 23, 'The husband is the head of the wife, as Christ is the head of the church, and the Saviour of the body.' He is not a Saviour of the angels in a way of redemption, for he speaks of the Church which hath 'spots and wrinkles' in it, as ver. 27. The Church is the queen, the angels are but his guard round about his throne, Rev. v. 11.

I will give you one caution more. Though they have not these relations to Christ, yet they have the relation of servants, and servants are a part of the family. The family, you know, is usually made up of servants, and sons, and the wife. Now the relation of sons and the relation of wife, this the sons of men bear unto God and unto Christ, and of being brethren too unto him; but the angels are but servants sent out. They are his angels, and indeed in that respect he is called their father and their head, as the master is called the father of the servants, 2 Kings v. 13. So I have expressed to you what association the angels have with Jesus Christ, and one with another.

I will make some uses of what hath been delivered, and give you some observations, and so end this great point.

Obs. 1.—You heard how that all things are the elect of angels and men, which God summeth up in Christ. The first observation then is this, See what reckoning God putteth upon things he calleth his elect children, angels and men, *all things;* he looks upon all things else as nothing, they are of no esteem, they have no value with him. They are God's *all* that belong to Christ, both angels and men, and the rest are the devil's, as I said; therefore you know the Scripture calleth souls that are damned, *lost;* they *are not:* 'The men whom thou rememberest no more,' Ps. lxxxviii. 5. God makes no reckoning of them, he accounts them not. The things in heaven and in earth that belong to Christ are the 'all things;' they are the choice of all, they are the first-fruits, as they are called, James i. 18.

Let us therefore, if we would have a being, get into Christ; let us gather ourselves to that Head. You are lost else, you are of no reckoning with God, nor shall not be to all eternity.

Obs. 2.—A second observation is this. Have we this association with angels? Shall we be as angels hereafter? Let us live as angels now. We must live with angels for ever, we must be made like to them, we are come with them unto one Head, Christ. Be as angels now.

And, my brethren, let it be one motive to you to keep you from sinning. If men were by, you would not sin. Think with yourselves. Angels may be by while I am sinning, whom I am gathered unto, and with whom I must live for ever. 1 Tim. v. 21; what is the meaning there, 'I charge thee before God, and his elect angels?' He chargeth him that he should not in the execution and exercise of government in the Church be partial, 'I charge thee before God,' he seeth thee; 'and before the Lord Jesus Christ,' he sees thee; and 'the elect angels,' some or other of them see thee too. What is the reason of this? If that angels did not see and were not witnesses, many of them, or some of them, of men's carriages, why should this charge be laid upon Timothy? 'I charge thee before God, and the Lord Jesus Christ, and the elect angels, that thou observe these things, without preferring one before another, doing nothing by partiality.'

Obs. 3.—Observe again, in the third place, from what hath been delivered, That the saints are nearer unto Christ than angels are, as I told you before; he is so a head to men as he is not to them. Both their union and ours with God is by Christ; now, if we be more united to Christ than they are, then we are more nearly united to God too; more nearly united to Christ we are, for he is our brother, he hath our nature, he hath more of ours, he hath done more for us; we are sons by adoption in him, he is our husband. To which of all the angels was it said that Christ is their husband? Of which of all the angels is it said that Christ is their Saviour? The Church of God is the queen; the angels are our guardians. We belong to one family, we are worshippers together; yet you shall find in Rev. v. 11, where the Church is described, that the angels are farther off from the throne than the four-and-twenty elders; and the like you have Rev. vii. 9–11.

SERMON XI.

That in the dispensation of the fulness of times he might gather together in one all things in Christ, both which are in heaven, and which are on earth; even in him.—VER. 10.

THE coherence of these words I have formerly shewed you to be a relation unto what is said just before, 'He had purposed in himself.' What was it he purposed in himself but this, as the words may be truly read, 'to gather together in one all things in Christ?' I told you my thoughts were, that the Apostle did here, having spoken of God's decrees, of election in Christ, and redemption in Christ, &c., in the conclusion of the doctrinal part of his discourse, give you the sum of all God's purposes in himself, both towards Christ and us; and he expresseth it in this, that it was to 'gather all things in one in Christ, both which are in heaven, and which are on earth.'

The great thing to be opened (which I have made entrance into) is, what is meant here by *gathering together in one*, which seemeth to be the adequate design and project of God's heart towards Christ and us for ever, and comprehensively to contain all under it.

That by 'all things in heaven,' and 'all things on earth,' angels and men are meant, I shewed the last time. I told you the word ἀνακεφαλαιώσασθαι implieth, first, a summing up of many numbers into one. I gave you an account of this.

God, intending to sum up all things in heaven and in earth in Christ, summeth up first all things in heaven and in earth in Christ's person, as the foundation of the other summing up of a mystical body too.

All sorts of divisions God summed up in Christ. God and the creature first, he cast them up into one sum; for he made God and the creature one Person.

He takes, in the second place,—whereas he had two reasonable creatures, angels and men,—the nature of a man and uniteth it unto God, and the condition of an angel; for that is his due too. That man (if he be united unto God) is called The heavenly man; he is not an earthly man, nor to be an earthly man, though for our sins he took frail flesh; but that which is his due is to be a man, and like an angel for condition. He summeth up the condition of things in heaven, and the nature of men on earth, in his own person.

Then come down to earth, and there you have Jew and Gentile; he summed up both in Christ, for Christ came of both. Jew and Gentile, all the world, Christ and all, had the very same great-grandfathers, those ten men that were from Adam to Noah. Thus he summed up all in his person.

When he had done, he summeth up of all a body to him answerable to his person; or rather a church, a city of the living God, a family to him, as the Scripture expresseth it. He takes of all things in heaven, and of all things in earth, and he makes them up unto Christ, as a Head, one body.

That Christ was the Head of angels, I shewed in the last discourse. That there is an association between angels and the saints, I shewed likewise; and this under Christ as a Head. All these particulars I have largely opened; I shall not stand to repeat them. Only there is one thing which I added not in the last discourse, concerning that of angels, and that is this, Why it is said *all things in heaven?* You know, when we say all things on earth, it is all sorts of men, all ranks of men upon earth. Are there any several sorts of angels in heaven?

My brethren, for certain there are several ranks of them; what they are we cannot define, but that there are several ranks of them, that known place, and many others might be brought, Col. i. 16, 'By him were all things created, that are in heaven, and that are in earth, visible and invisible, whether they be thrones, or dominions, or principalities, or powers.' The angels are called principalities and powers; that we have an express place for in this first chapter of the Ephesians, ver. 21, 'He set him at his own right hand in the heavenly places, far above all principality, and power, and might, and dominion, and every name that is named, not only in this world, but also in that which is to come.' He expresseth these several ranks of angels, for there is *acies ordinata* of them, by the ranks that are here on earth, by way of similitude, so to convey it to our apprehensions. Some, he saith, are *thrones.* Thrones importeth kingly power, as we read in Dan. x. 13, 'He was the first of the princes,' speaking of one of the angels; and likewise we read of an archangel. Some, he saith, are *dominions,* which are as viceroys; and *principalities,* which among men were governors of provinces; and *powers,* which were ordinary lower magistrates. He expresseth it by these ranks, not that there are but four, or how many we know not, but he conveyeth what is in heaven to us by what is on earth. Now, of all these sorts of angels, he hath taken some, (as perhaps of all these angels some fell, as of all sorts of things in earth some are gathered to Satan,) but of all sorts of things on earth, he gathereth some to Christ, and so in heaven too.—So much for that.

Now I must come to shew, that he hath gathered all things on earth *to Him.* That which I handled in the last discourse was but the gathering to *a Head,* as the word signifieth, of all things in heaven, with things on earth. Now, God hath taken all sorts of men on earth, and meaneth to make out of them a body unto Christ. And therefore he expresseth it by the word τὰ πάντα, all things; because he takes all sorts of things and conditions whatsoever; therefore he expresseth it, I say, rather by things than by persons, as implying all conditions of men.

The first great division upon earth, what is it? It is both of Jew and Gentile. He will take of both these. I shall not need to prove it, for I shall meet with it again and again in opening of this place. In the very next words to my text, which therefore argueth that to be his meaning, he speaks of the calling of the Jews first, at the 12th verse, 'That we should be to the praise of his glory, who first trusted in Christ;' there is the Jews. 'In whom ye also trusted,' ver. 13, 'after that ye heard the word of truth;' there is the Gentile. It is a thing I must often speak to, therefore I will speak little to it now.

Come to the Gentiles. They are divided, we know, into many nations, which God hath made here upon earth. God takes, first and last, of all the nations upon the earth, to make up a body to his Son Christ. In Gen xviii. 18, there is a promise made to Abraham, that in his seed all the nations of the earth shall be blessed. The like you have, chap. xxii., repeated again;

for you have two places for it. And in Prov. viii. it is said, the delights of Christ were in the habitable parts of his earth, so the expression is, ver. 31. Wherever God hath earth inhabited, there Jesus Christ hath some from everlasting whom he did delight in, and shall do to everlasting.

Then come to nations; and there you have several kindreds. Now go, take all the kindreds of men that continue from the beginning of the world unto the end; God will take of all families and kindreds too. You shall find that the promise made to Abraham, as it runneth that *all nations* shall be blessed in him, so it runneth that *all families* of the earth shall be blessed in him too, and, as Peter interpreteth it, 'all fatherhoods;' so the expression is, Acts iii. 25. In Gen. xii. 3, 'In thee shall all the families of the earth be blessed.' The like you have in Gen. xxviii. 14. Twice it is said that all *nations* shall be blessed in Abraham, and in his seed; and twice it is said, all *families* shall be blessed—that is, all kindreds shall be blessed in him and his seed.

Then there are other divisions besides. There are several sorts and ranks of sinners. God hath excepted but one; and what is that one? Those that on earth become the serpent's seed, and so join issues with hell; those that sin against the Holy Ghost, and have the venom of this sin in their spirits, of revenge against God, such as the devil hath: except those, God takes of all sorts. It is a known place, Matt. xii. 31: He, through whose hands all the pardons of the world go, Jesus Christ, that stands at the sealing of them, saith, that 'all manner of sin and blasphemy shall be forgiven unto men.' He doth not only say, it *may be* forgiven, but he expressly saith, it *shall be* forgiven. God hath so ordered it, that as all mankind shall fall into all sorts of sin, so shall some of his elect do, some into some, and some into another; that you can instance in no sin, or way of sinning, or aggravation of sinning, which shall not be pardoned to some of the sons of men.

Then go, take all ranks, (there are other divisions yet,) take all ranks of poor and rich, kings and nobles, wise and fools; God takes of all these. He takes of fools, as he saith, Isa. xxxv. 8, 'Though fools, they shall not err' in that way. Natural fools, God takes some of them, and teacheth them to know Christ. 'Pray,' saith he, 'for kings, and all in authority,' 1 Tim. ii. 2; for God would have all men to be saved, all sorts of ranks.

Obs. 1.—See now, my brethren, of whom the Church universal consisteth, and see the glory and splendour of it: all things in heaven, and all things on earth; all nations, all families, all kindreds; whatsoever divisions you can make. You have it, Rev. v. 9, and likewise Rev. vii., where the Church universal is represented, perhaps under a particular way; yet, I say, you shall find it represented there. First, in the fifth chapter, the four beasts and the four-and-twenty elders, they cry unto Christ, they give glory unto him; 'for,' say they, 'thou wast slain, and hast redeemed us unto God by thy blood out of every kindred,'—there is families,—'and tongue, and people, and nation.' And all things in heaven come in too, ver. 11, 'And I heard the voice of many angels round about the throne.' You have the like words, chap. vii. 9, 'I beheld, and, lo, a great multitude, which no man could number, of all nations, and kindreds, and people, and tongues, stood before the throne, and before the Lamb.' And ver. 11, 'All the angels stood round about the throne, and about the elders.' The angels come in too. Men are nearer the throne; for if you observe it, the angels do stand about the elders. Men are nearer, because, as I said before, they have a nearer relation to Christ; he is in such a way a head to them as he is not to angels.

This, my brethren, is the glory and the splendour of this universal Church, of the body of our Lord Jesus Christ. And what should this teach us, by way of use and observation, but to long for that day when we shall all meet thus together; when God will bring men out of all parts of the earth, where thou shalt meet with some of thy kindred, some of thy nation, some that have been just such sinners as thou art? What a glorious day will that be! We account it a glorious day when the fulness of the Gentiles shall come in, and Jew and Gentile shall make up one sheepfold, and Christ be one shepherd; and it will be a glorious day indeed. But the day that is to come, when Christ shall have all his children about him; when God-man, in whom all things are summed up in his person for excellency; and when men and angels and all shall be gathered up to him, that have been from the beginning of the world to the end of it, when that general assembly shall be full and complete, and he shall not want, no not the least joint, the least member; what a glorious day will this be, when God hath all his sons about him! He forbeareth now opening the fulness of his glory, because he hath not all his sons about him: but when he hath them all about him, then he will bring forth all his riches, all the treasures of his glory. As you know Ahasuerus did, when he had the princes of the provinces before him in his great palace, Esth. i. 2. He was king of a hundred and twenty-seven provinces; and the text saith, 'He sat on the throne of his kingdom, which was in Shushan the palace; and he made a feast to all his princes and his servants; the power of Persia and Media, the nobles and princes of the provinces, being before him.' It seems it was a great occasion; whether to shew the greatness of his glory, or for what other end he calleth them up, they were all before him; and then he makes a feast, such a feast as never was read of. So, when God shall have all the princes of the earth, the first-born, before him; when men shall 'come from the east, and from the west, and sit down with Abraham, Isaac, and Jacob in his kingdom;' then will God feast, then will he bring forth all his glory, and empty himself for ever.

Obs. 2.—Therefore, my brethren, long for this day, and let your hearts seek to be one of this number, not to be left out of this *all*. For your encouragement herein consider this, which is a second observation, That no condition can be said to be any hindrance to you from being in Christ. Thou canst object nothing against thyself, neither poverty, nor folly, nor want of memory and understanding, nor weakness, nor sinfulness,—I say there is nothing at all thou canst object against thyself, which may hinder thy salvation. Why? Because God takes all sorts of things on earth. Thou canst say nothing of thyself, but that there are some whom God hath saved just like thee. 'There is no difference,' saith he, Rom. iii. 22; he 'justifieth freely by his grace.' There is no difference; take a beggar and a king, they have the same shadow in the sun. Sins, my brethren, make no difference, the greatness or the smallness of them, to hinder salvation. Mountains bear no proportion, more than mole-hills, to the heavens, they are so high. If one were in the heavens, the earth would seem as a round globe; mountains would not be seen more than mole-hills are.

Obs. 3.—Again, in the third place, you may see here the infinite goodness of God to all, that he takes of all sorts of things, of all sorts of ranks; of angels in heaven, he takes of all things there; of all sorts of things on earth, in all their several varieties. This is a great respect God hath to his creation, in that he will do so. He created and made all things, and he made them all by Jesus Christ, and therefore he shall have the first-fruits of every one, and of every sort of thing. I take it to be part of the meaning, though not all, of that Eph. iii., where, speaking of this mystery, 'that all men,' saith he, ver. 9, 'should see the fellowship of the mystery,' (having spoken of the calling of the Jew and Gentile before, ver. 8,) that mystery 'which from the beginning of the world hath been hid in God.' What cometh in afterward?—'who created all things by Jesus Christ.' He made all things by him, saith he, and therefore he will save of all sorts by him. He hath respect to the whole creation; he will have some of all sorts in it. Therefore, Acts x. 34, when they saw that God did save the Gentiles as well as Jews, what conclusion do they make out of it? 'Then Peter opened his mouth and said, Of a truth I perceive that God is no respecter of persons; but in every nation he that feareth him, and worketh righteousness, is accepted of him.' And there is another reason intimated in the next verse following, ver. 36, 'The word,' saith he, 'which God sent unto the children of Israel, preaching peace by Jesus Christ; he is Lord of all.' Is he Lord of all? He will save of all sorts by him.

God, as he hateth nothing that he hath made, as it is his creature; so he will shew the freeness of his grace by saving all varieties of his creatures. For therein lieth the freeness of his grace, that no condition shall hinder. I conclude with that which the Apostle concludeth (Rom. xi.) all the doctrinal part of his epistle. He had shewed that Jews and Gentiles were both corrupt, in chap. ii. and iii. He had shewed that God would save both of Jew and Gentile, in chap. ix., x., and xi. How concludeth he? Ver. 30 of that 11th chapter, 'As you in time past' (speaking to the Gentiles, they take their turns) 'have not believed God, yet have now obtained mercy through their unbelief: even so have these also' (speaking of the Jews) 'now not believed, that through your mercy they also might obtain mercy,' that both they and you might have mercy together; 'for God hath concluded' (it is translated *them*, but the word πάντα is) '*all*,' Jew and Gentile, 'in unbelief, that he might have mercy upon all.' And upon this he doth, as we all should do: 'O the depth of the riches both of the wisdom and knowledge of God!' (and mercy too;) 'how unsearchable are his judgments, and his ways past finding out!'

So much now for that part of gathering a body out of all sorts of things on earth and things in heaven. I have shewed you, in opening these words, first, that God hath summed up all in Christ, he cast up all as into one number in his person; which was the first signification of the words. He gathereth all things, both in heaven and on earth, as a church, as a family to him, as unto one head; that the word likewise signifieth.

There is a *third thing* that is to be added to the signification of this word; there is ἀνὰ, that he doth this again; there is a gathering together under one head again the second time; so the word signifieth. This same ἀνακεφαλαιώσασθαι, (as I remember Bishop Andrews in a sermon upon this text hath it,) saith he, the force of it is not only to signify a collection, a gathering of all; but it is a re-collection. It is true, our translators took not notice of it, they translate it simply, 'gather together in one;' but all know that the word signifieth *again;* 'to gather together again under one head.'

Now this gathering together again may import two things. *First,* a gathering a second time of all things in heaven and in earth. *Secondly,* it doth imply a scattering first; that he doth after his first gathering of them scatter all a-pieces as it were, severeth them one from another, and from himself. They are like members *disjecta,* like members rent and separated from their head; and then he gathereth them all together again, ἀνακεφαλαιώσασθαι importeth *recollectionem;* they were scattered from Christ, and so gathered again to him, as to a head.

Against this interpretation there is this great rub in the way—that the angels, the things in heaven, never were scattered; why should they be said to be gathered together again, with all things on earth, unto Christ as a head? Therefore interpreters have been exceeding shy of interpreting 'all things in heaven' to be meant of angels. I must first remove this rub; it is the main difficulty.

There are two interpretations that may help to remove it. The first is this, that although both things in heaven and things on earth were not both scattered, yet if things on earth were, it may be said to be a gathering together of all; take them altogether *in sensu composito*, though not *in sensu diviso*. Some explain it by this similitude. Suppose two nations were united under one monarch, and one of them falls off, and turn all rebels unto him, and rend themselves away from that other nation with which they were at peace and union under that one head. As when those seven provinces revolted from the Spaniard, there were ten remained still firm unto him. If ever these seventeen, the seven and the ten, unite themselves together again, and subject themselves, as before, to him as their head and monarch, and lay down hostility against him, it might be said that here is a gathering of them all, a reducing of them all to their former obedience, though but one part fell off. This is a similitude that one giveth of it to explain it. The like you find in Calvin. Suppose you find, saith he, a house, a great part whereof were fallen down, and some stood still; if that part that is fallen be built up again, the whole house is said to be rebuilt. So it is here. And this is the first interpretation to reconcile this difficulty: that because men were scattered, that part of the house on earth, the family on earth, were scattered from him, which were once joined unto him, unto one head, unto Christ, (God united all, angels and men unto him,) yet now being gathered together again, all is said to be gathered together in one unto him.

There is a second, which I do find that both Calvin and others have, and is more hard to explain. I will do it as clearly and as briefly as I can. I shall express my meaning perhaps in somewhat a differing way from theirs, yet it comes all to one. And it is this. That even of the angels themselves there is a double knitting of them unto God. First, a common, that they and the devils (created once holy) had, and that Adam in innocency, and all mankind in him, had in common together. And the other is a special union unto God, and that by Christ. So that though there was not an actual scattering of them from that first union of theirs, but even that also held and continued firm; yet it was prevented by a further union, by a gathering of them in one in Christ as their head, unto God, that did fix them for ever to stand firm unto him.

I may express it unto you well thus: that God, to magnify his grace the more,—both his glorifying grace to angels and men, and supernatural grace to stand for ever, which is a supernatural grace,—did ordain, to exalt this grace, two several knittings, two unions and communions of his creatures, (made holy at first,) to himself: whereof the first was not sure nor steadfast, nor would not perhaps have held to eternity. They would have dropped off one after another, if God had let things go on so; there would have been a perpetual hazard of the angels departing and scattering from him. The things on earth actually fell from him, the other were in danger; and therefore God, to make all fast and sure, ordaineth a second union, and a gathering together again in Christ.

To explain both these knittings to God;—it will, as I said it would, contain the whole design of God, both of creation and the instauration of the creature in Christ, and redemption and whatever else;—to explain, I say, this double knitting to God, this knitting the first time, and knitting again, I shall do these two things:—I shall, *first,* shew you what union at first in common the good angels, and those that are now bad, and man, and all had with God. And then, *secondly,* the necessity of a further union for their perpetual and everlasting standing in grace, and their enjoying their full glory in heaven.

For the first, To shew what this same first union and gathering of all creatures both in heaven and on earth in common was.—It was by their creation and the covenant thereof; that covenant that passeth between God merely as a Creator, unto them as his creatures, which was common both to good angels that stand, and them that fell, and man in his innocency, who also fell. Now, my brethren, this you must know, that although man was created on earth, and the angels created in heaven, in a higher condition of knowing and enjoying God; yet so as, take them merely as creatures, and as a covenant shall pass between God the Creator and them, they are both under the same law of nature, so as they may fall from their condition as well as man; and there was no law, either of nature or justice, between God and the creature, could any way oblige God to uphold and to maintain them. Thus slippery was the first union, simply considered as creatures. I need not stand to shew you how both angels and men were first united to God. Adam is called the son of God, Luke iii. 38, by creation. And the angels are called the sons of God, as they were first made, when they were holy and standing holy, Job xxxviii. 7. United then they were both to God.

And, in the second place, although we cannot say that there was a perfect association between angels and men then in the state of innocency, as now under the state of grace there is, (which I shewed you before,) and shall be for ever; but that angels should remain in their heaven, and man should have remained on his earth: 'The first man,' saith he, 'is of the earth earthly;' he speaks of man at best. I am not of the mind of some of those modern divines that have said, that the sin of the angels was this, that God did send them down upon earth to attend man; this they stomached, and tempted man to sin, and that was their sin. There is no ground of that at all, to think that, under the law of nature, the elder should serve the younger. It is a privilege we have by Christ; they are his 'ministering spirits, sent forth to minister for them that shall be the heirs of salvation,' Heb. i. 14. Yet concerning the association of both then, we may say this, that it is most certain that the same things whereby Adam knew God, by the same things did they know God; though also in a further degree, and in a higher measure. And therefore, as before I said there was an association both of angels and men in this respect, that angels themselves do pry into the things of the gospel, and so are present to our assemblies; so likewise in this respect both angels and man then had a kind of association in this, that the angels themselves took in the glory of God from things here below., They rejoiced when they saw the world made, when they saw God to limn out the world, and fill up that first draught of the chaos as he did, and when he brought man in the lord of all. That you have an express place for, Job xxxviii. 7. He saith, that when the foundations of the earth were laid, the angels, that were created the first day with the heavens, shouted for joy: 'The morning stars sang together, and all the sons of God shouted for joy.' They are called the morning stars, because they began early to glorify God, they were *matutinæ;* and they are called sons of God: it is said they all shouted for joy; and if they shouted for joy when the foundations of the earth were laid, certainly then when man was made they stood by as spectators to see God, I say, limn out the world, and perfect it in man's creation. So that though man should not have known, nor knew things from heaven, yet they knew things on earth; and therefore in that respect there was some kind of fellowship, they partaking of the same things that we did, though not we that they did.

And then, again, if there were not a fellowship, nor ever should have been,—and we have no ground at all to think so that I know of,—yet this is certain, there was a peace amongst them in these two kingdoms of God, of which he was monarch and lord. Though they remained distinct and divided, yet notwithstanding they were at peace, they were not at hostility, they were gathered in peace under one Lord then, both men and angels, and so united unto God. And they did glory in the good of man certainly; as they sung at the birth of Christ, 'Peace on earth, and good-will towards men;' they shouted when man was made, if they shouted when the foundations of the earth were laid. So that you see there was a common union, both to God, and some way among themselves; there was a peace at least.

But you will say unto me, This first union, was this in Christ? The word *again*, you will urge, will imply so much,—they are gathered again to a Head in one in Christ. Was he the Head, then, both of angels and men in creation?

For that I answer, *first*, it was not absolutely necessary, (though the force of the word will hold.) They were gathered unto one Head, God; for in 1 Cor. xi. 3, you shall find that God is called the 'Head of Christ,' and so of all things else, of all men and angels; he is the supreme Head of all, above the rest. They were gathered unto one Head, God; that is certain then. But that they should be gathered first unto Jesus Christ as a Head, as God-man, that is not necessary. It is true that the second gathering is in him as a Head.

Yet, in the *second* place, there is much in the current of the Scripture, which I shall have, sometime or other, opportunity to allege, that even Jesus Christ was the 'corner-stone' of the creation, both to men and angels. If he would not have been a creature, God would not have made a creature else. The meaning of it is not as if that he should not have been incarnate, if man had never fallen; but that neither men nor angels should have been made if Christ had not been to have been incarnate, which was at once ordained together with him. I could name many places for it. Rev. iii. 14, speaking of Christ, 'These things saith the Amen, the faithful and true Witness, the beginning of the creation of God.' You have the like, Col. i. He reckoneth up all the uses of God-man, and he saith, ver. 16, that 'by him all things were created, visible and invisible,' (there is the first gathering unto him;) and then, ver. 20, he speaks of reconciling all things in heaven and on earth, which is the second gathering, and the same with that in the text.

But then another question will be this: Was Jesus Christ the Head of the creation? What scripture is there for that?

For that I will give you but this place, 1 Cor. xi. 3, &c. Saith he, I would have you know, for perhaps it was a thing they did not so much consider, that the head of every man is Christ, the head of the woman is the man, and the head of Christ is God. He speaks of Christ as God-man; for so only God is said to be his head. He doth not only say he is the head of the elect angels and men, but of every man, and that by the law of creation;

for as the man by creation is the head of the woman, so is Jesus Christ the head of the man; therefore ver. 8, 9, saith he, 'The man was not created for the woman, but the woman for the man.' He speaks of creation expressly. So we elsewhere read, 'All things were created by Christ, and for Christ,'—that is, by virtue of him. For as he was the 'Lamb slain from the beginning of the world,' that he might redeem it, as he did those that were before he was incarnate, so virtually he might have an influence into the creation also, he being to be incarnate.

So now, my brethren, you see the *first gathering* how it was. But then you will say, If he was their head in creation, there is this difficulty yet, why did they not then stand? Why did not he preserve them, being their head, by virtue of being the head of the creation also?

The answer to that is easy, and it is this. He was their head by creation, but in a common relation, but by way of eminency, as being the chief of the creation of God, and as the Lord and heir of all, in a natural way, by a natural due; and therefore, notwithstanding it was his due thus to be their head, it went no further; he left them to the course of nature. But now his being a head a second time, in this second gathering, it is by a special protection, undertaking to preserve them in a more peculiar manner, and that in a supernatural way, to bestow supernatural glory, and if they fall to redeem them, as he did the sons of men. So that now, by a natural due of his, he was the head in creation; by a special undertaking, by a special protection, (as I may so express it,) he becometh a head in the second gathering; and therefore he will be sure now to hold them fast enough. Thus you see what this first gathering in Christ was; you have that explained as briefly and as plainly as possibly I could.

Secondly, We come now to the necessity of a second gathering, both of angels and men.—Still the difficulty will be on the angels' part; of men, (you know they falling,) there is no difficulty at all about them.

To represent this necessity unto you, my brethren, it is thus in a word. All things, angels and men, though they were by the common tie of creation, being made holy, knit unto God; yet only by no other term of justice or union, no stronger than what was simply due to the creature as the creature, and as it was meet for God as a creator to carry himself towards the creature. It was not *ultra debitum*, beyond the due of the creature, as the school-men express it. Now, therefore, it was not a due to the creature, nor no obligation by the law of creation that was between God and the creature, that he must uphold it; but that he might leave it to shew itself what it was to be a creature. What assistance, therefore, he giveth to uphold and to confirm in grace, and perpetually to stand, is above the bargain, above the covenant of creation, above the obligation of nature; it is wholly supernatural, and it is of grace; it is more than nature's due. So that, as I said before, though the angels themselves were created in heaven, as man upon earth, yet they stood by the same common law, and no otherwise, that man did upon earth. It is true, indeed, this of the angels, they had stronger natures and were built of stronger matter, and so were less subject to fall; they were more able to stand; yet still, if left but to the mere assistance that by the covenant of nature God was to give them, though in heaven, they would fall as well as man. See a scripture for this, wherein angels and men are compared together, Job iv. 18. It is a scripture which in this argument divines have recourse unto, and I shall have recourse unto it afterward. 'Behold,' saith he, 'he put no trust in his servants; his angels he charged with folly: how much less in them that dwell in houses of clay?'

Comparing men and angels together, saith he, the angels had two advantages: they were, first, by nature made of stronger stuff; alas! man dwells in a house of clay, a house of cards, that is easily tumbled or blown down; but they are built of a house of marble, that is stronger and abler to stand. Secondly, they had this advantage, that they were God's servants in a more peculiar manner; so they are called his, because they were his servants about his throne, at court. Man was his subject, but they were his household servants then in a more peculiar manner, and therefore nearer God. Yet, notwithstanding these advantages, saith he, God could put no confidence in them, he could put no trust in them; and he had a great deal of reason not to trust them, for you know how a great part of things in heaven served him when they fell. He chargeth them that fell with folly, with damnable folly; he spared them not, for he laid the guilt of sin upon them, and threw them down to hell, as Peter saith; and he chargeth the other with possible folly, as I shall shew anon.

So that you see by the law of creation—(for it is that law which he disputeth there; 'Shall a man be more pure than his maker?' It is the words immediately before, in the 17th verse; he bringeth it in, indeed, to another purpose; yea, but take God as he is a Maker, the one as the clay, the other as the potter)—he is no way obliged to make them stand as they are of themselves, but they are creatures that are not *stable*, as the word signifieth, and as some translations have it. You see then the angels,—and there was sufficient proof for it,—that by that law wherein they were first gathered to God, by that knot, by that covenant—it was too slippery—God could put no trust in them; all the angels might have served him as the devils did.

Again, there is this infallible reason, for it is an inseparable property of the creature, by an essential defect that cleaveth to it, that it is mutable, it is changeable, and may be tempted to sin. I call it a property of the creature, for in James i. 13, 17, compared together, you shall find that it is made the property of God alone to be immutable and without shadow of turning.

Now then, my brethren, you see that for these angels, if God would be sure of them, if he would put confidence in them, there must be some further knitting of them to him, by some further covenant, some further medium, by some higher law than this merely of creation, that passed between them as creatures and him as their Creator. There needed therefore a second gathering. Out of this that hath been said, you see then, that although they were not actually scattered, yet they were in danger; they had need therefore be fixed in a head; they are glasses, and they had need of a bottom, which might keep them from falling; and these morning stars, the Lord Jesus Christ had need hold them in his hand, or they may fall down from heaven, as Lucifer, that great devil, did. They needed supernatural grace to confirm them; it is not their due by nature; it is not their due by creation. And by whom should they have this grace? By whom should they have this protection? Why, from him whose ministering spirits they are; his ministering spirits, he calleth them so because he hath a special interest in them; they are not our ministering spirits, it is nowhere said so. They are sent indeed for our good, but they are his ministering spirits; he hath a proper interest and title in them; he is the fountain of grace, and everything that hath anything by participation is reduced to that which hath it of itself. Now the Lord Jesus Christ is that man of grace; he is the fountain of all grace; therefore if they have supernatural grace, they must have it from him, and therefore in him. When the Apostle had reckoned that he had created all things in heaven and in earth, he addeth that still in him all things consist, angels and all; the standing they have, this consistency, it is from the Lord Jesus Christ, Col. i. 17. He is the corner-stone of both the buildings, both that in heaven and that in earth.

For, my brethren, let me give you the reason of it. It is only Jesus Christ's natural due,—it is his natural due, only being the natural Son of God,—that after he is united to the Son of God, God should be engaged by a law, a law of nature, to uphold him, to be impeccable, to be put out of the danger of falling. It is only proper unto Jesus Christ; it is his law of nature, for he is the natural Son of God. It is his privilege to have life in himself; so you have it, John v. 26, 'For as the Father hath life in himself, so hath he given to the Son to have life in himself.' No creature hath so that it can stand of itself; therefore he having life in himself, if they stand and continue to have life, they have it from him.

Likewise, let me say this unto you, that the fulness of the glory in heaven, which is by a union with God, the angels could not attain to it, nor had it by the law of their creation; it is supernatural to them. The Papists ascribe it to the use of free-will, and to their merit; but it is above the due of the creature, as the best divines hold it. This utmost glory in heaven, that beatifical vision which we shall have after the day of judgment, and which the angels are brought unto *tanquam ad terminum,* as unto their utmost happiness, this is only Jesus Christ's natural due. So to see God as Jesus Christ himself doth, (and with the same kind of sight shall his members see him, though for degree he exceedeth, as we are anointed with the same Spirit that he is, though in degree, he above measure;) that sight which is thus proper to Christ, is the transcendent privilege of the Son of God. It is peculiar unto him, and it is by virtue of him we have it, both angels and men.

I will give you both Scripture for it and reason. John i. 18, 'No man hath seen God at any time.' It is translated *no man,* but it is *none,* οὐδεὶς, hath seen God; you may take it of all creatures at any time. 'The only-begotten Son, which is in the bosom of the Father, he hath declared him.' If angels had seen God as Christ seeth him, they might have declared him: it had not been Christ's peculiar prerogative to help us to that sight, if the angels had had the fulness of that beatifical vision which the Lord Jesus Christ hath, and bringeth all unto at last.

And, my brethren, I will give you this reason for it. (Another scripture there is, it is Ps. xvi., it is a psalm of Christ, and he it is that saith, 'At thy right hand there is fulness of joy, and pleasures for evermore;' he was able first to speak that speech.) There is, I say, the greatest reason for it that can be. The angels did not, by the law of their creation, receive that full sight which now they have in heaven, not by the law of their creation; though they that stood might have it at first, but it is probable otherwise. There is this evident reason, for otherwise those angels that fell had never fallen. Had they been filled with the sight of God which the saints of heaven shall be for ever filled with, it had kept them from sinning. Why? Because there had not been a possibility of thinking there was any other good, not a possibility of it. If the creature knew God to the uttermost,—knew God as we shall know him one day, as we are known of him,—and saw his face with that clearness as Christ, the saints, and angels in heaven now do, they could not have turned their thoughts upon anything else. Therefore you must suppose there was but such a sight and knowledge of God as they might entertain a thought of some better good thing; for the will of any creature, whether sinning or otherwise, must still be pitched upon some good. Therefore the school-men do rightly say that the utmost beatifical vision of God doth captivate, doth swallow up the mind. When we see God to the full, we shall be so in love with him that the heart shall never turn off from him. That 'fulness of pleasure,' those 'rivers of joy,' carry the soul away with a torrent for ever; it can never go back against the stream. The love of God constraineth. Now you see the angels did fall, and therefore certainly that fulness of the sight of God they had not; and if it had been by virtue of their creation they would have had it. To think that it should be by their own works, we know no such covenant; it is that, as you see, that is proper to the Lord Jesus Christ so to see God, he only lying in his bosom: by virtue of him men see God, and shall see God; by virtue of him angels see God.

And so much now for that, why there was a necessity of their being gathered unto Christ, as unto a head, a second time: both that they might have confirmation in grace, that God might put trust in them; and, secondly, that they might have fulness of glory, and that beatifical vision, that might make them impeccable, and without danger of sinning for ever.

There is yet somewhat more in that first of Colossians, (I confess I need not meddle with it, for it is out of my text, but yet it cometh fitly in.) It is said, 'He reconciled all things, both in heaven and in earth.' Interpreters are very shy here of interpreting it of angels, because they needed, they say, no reconciliation, for reconciliation doth suppose enmity. Therefore to speak to this a little.

This reconciliation, you see, is more than a second gathering; what need had they of this? Bishop Davenant saith of it that there was *reconciliatio analogica*, something that had the shadow of it, something like it. I shall give you my sense of it thus: when God had experience that the angels fell from him, and fell from him so at a clap, Why, might he think, they will all serve me thus, if they be left to the law of their creation; they may drop away thus, and turn rebels one after another, and as I have lost man, so I may lose all the angels too; it is in their nature to do it, the creature is apt to do it; I see experience in some of their natures already, made of the same metal with them. Now, my brethren, this must needs be supposed, that God is not contented with his creature, taken merely in itself, it breedeth a kind of *simultas*, a kind—I cannot call it of grudge, because there is no sin—but a kind of unsatisfiedness and displicence. Therefore the Scripture doth not only speak of the evil angels that fell, that God put no confidence in them; but it speaks plainly of the good angels, that God put no confidence in them, seeing the evil angels' fall, Job xv. 15, compared with that place I quoted before, Job iv. 18, 'Behold,' saith he, 'he putteth no trust in his saints; yea, the heavens are not clean in his sight: how much more abominable and filthy is man?' Whom doth he call saints here? He meaneth the angels. It is the same paralleled speech with the other, 'He put no trust in his servants, and his angels he chargeth with folly.' And it is plain he meaneth the angels by saints here, for he opposeth them to man; 'how much more abominable and filthy is man?' They are called in Scripture the *saints of God* oftentimes, as in Dan. viii. 13, 'I heard one saint speaking, and another saint said to that certain saint that spake,' &c. Then saith he, 'the heavens are not clean in his sight.' By heavens he meaneth angels too, or at leastwise they may be meant by heavens, for in Scripture often they are; as the devils are called the *gates of hell*, so the angels are called *heaven*, from the place where they are.

Now, saith he, these heavens, these heavenly creatures, these holy ones, the angels, they are not clean in his sight; he seeth a possibility in them of sinning. And as he repented that he made man when he saw man fall from him, so when he saw some of the angels fall from him, there was just ground of repenting for making angels; for, saith he, all these may fall too, if let alone. He could take no contentment in them. Here is some ground for a reconciliation, to take away all this discontent. God could not love them perfectly, unless they could stand for ever. Why? Because he must so love as some time he must hate; and that, you know, is not every way perfect love; *amare tanquam aliquando osurus.* Therefore now, as it is not only called mercy to deliver the creature out of misery, but it is truly mercy to prevent from misery; it is more than goodness to do so—it is mercy. Mercy respecteth misery, either misery that it may fall into, as well as mercy to deliver out of it; it is analogically mercy, though the other is more properly mercy. So there is *quædam analogica reconciliatio;* whether this was by the blood of Christ or no, I will not now stand to dispute. This is certain, Christ needed not to have died to preserve angels in their standing; the necessity was only on man's part for satisfaction; there is a plain place for it, 2 Cor. v. 14, 'In that he died for all, we conclude that all were dead.' That he died thus out of necessity, it must be for them only that are dead. Yet, dying for men, there might be this overplus in it, that for the merit of his obedience' sake, he having relation to angels, they might have, not a satisfaction, but a benefit by it. And if it be true, which some divines—not Papists only—say, that he did *mereri sibi,* merit for himself, he hath the benefit of his death; being exalted on high, he hath a double right to glory; so likewise he might for them too.—And so I have done with this thing, *things in heaven,* the angels; and thus much for them.

I will but anticipate a use, or observation or two.

Obs. 1.—The first is this, Has God now purposed in himself, as the text telleth you here, such a great and vast price as this is, and is this the story of the purpose of his heart? (and I have not told it out.) My brethren, I appeal to you all, whether the heart of man could ever have invented such a story as this is: One God, making the creature one with himself; and, the creature falling from him, making him one again; in making of all things, in summing up of all in Christ, that is the founder of this gathering again, making up a body of all things in heaven and in earth unto the Lord Jesus Christ. I cannot stand to lay open the particulars of it; you have heard it. The text saith, 'He purposed it in himself;' it could have come into no one's heart but his; it was hid in God, it was purposed in himself; the 'wisdom of God,' therefore, it is called, Eph. iii. 10.

Dost thou not believe that there is a God? Come hither, let this convince thee. Could all intelligible natures, all reasonable creatures, invent such a story as this? You think the Gunpowder-Plot to have been a plot so desperate that it must have been hatched in hell, it could not be formed in any man's brain. My brethren, this plot here could be hatched nowhere but in heaven, and in the heart of God. Go, and take angels and men, lay all your heads together and make such another. Such a God, such a Christ, thus great, having such a kingdom made out of all, both in heaven and earth, scattered from him, and reduced again; how infinitely doth this set out God and Christ! It is beyond the thoughts of men and angels to invent such a thing as this. No story ever had such a winding up as this. Read all histories, all romances, that men are pleased withal, they have not the shadow of such a plot as this. Take all the plots of all the great ones of the earth, and all their petty plots come to nothing. The wisdom of the world is foolishness in comparison of this. We preach wisdom, saith the Apostle, in a mystery, which none of the princes of the world knew; their wisdom comes to nothing before this, it all vanisheth. To set up so great a monarch that hath alliance to all his subjects, and to make him king of all the world, of both worlds, and to have some out of all in heaven and in earth to be made subjects unto him, and he in his own person to have all things in him; and they falling from God, he being able to knit them all again a second time. 'Without controversy,' saith he, 1 Tim. iii. 16, 'great is the mystery of godliness.' What is it? This very thing I have spoken of. It is first, 'God manifested in the flesh,' God and man summed up in one. It could never have entered into the heart of man or angel to have a thought that the Son of God should have taken a creature up into his own person thus, and such a creature as all should be summed up in him. 'Justified in the Spirit,' that is, at his resurrection. 'Seen of angels,' to be their head. 'Preached unto the Gentiles, believed on in the world,' to be the head of them on earth by faith too. This is a mystery without controversy; no man that readeth it or heareth it, but he must fall down before it. This is not man; this is not the wit of angels; this is, without controversy, from an omniscient understanding that knoweth all things, and hath infinite depth in him. Nay, my brethren, of all the arguments that ever fell upon my understanding to convince me that there is a God, there is none like unto this.

Obs. 2.—A second observation is this, See the several steps of the goodness of God to his creatures in these three particulars, which that which I have handled doth shew. First, there is his simple goodness as he is a Creator, communicating himself unto them as to creatures by the law of creation, but not beyond their due as creatures. This was the state of Adam in innocency, and this was the state of the angels that fell. Then, secondly, there is a further degree of goodness shewed,—which becometh grace, which hath a peculiarness in it, it is supernatural, it is beyond the common tie of creation,—to keep them from falling; this he shewed to the angels that stood, when he let the other fall, which prevented them from falling. Well, but there is a third degree beyond all; that is, when actually they did fall, as the elect of the sons of men did, then here is riches of mercy, to gather them all to himself, in him again, and that by his blood. This is the mercy, this is the top of the mercies of God; and the truth is, to shew forth this, he shut up all under sin, that he might have mercy upon all. It was but to shew mercy so much the further. There was his mercy in preventing this, but there is infinite depth of mercy in recovering out of this; when they were all scattered from him, to gather them together again.

SERMON XII.

According to his good pleasure which he hath purposed in himself, in the dispensation of the fulness of times to gather together in one all things in Christ, both which are in heaven, and which are on earth; even in him. —VER. 10.

THESE words, as I have formerly, in opening the coherence of them, shewed, do hold forth the full purpose, the whole birth, that lay hid in God's eternal purposes and decrees. All that God purposed, both concerning Christ and concerning us,—him as a Head, and us as members,—are all gathered into this one expression, 'He purposed to gather all in one in Christ, both things in heaven and things on earth.' That by things in heaven are meant angels, I have shewed. That by things on earth are meant men, I have shewed also. There are 'all things in heaven,' for there are several offices of angels at least; and there are 'all things on earth,' there are several sorts of men. Now, God hath gathered together all things in one. The great thing to be opened, as I promised at first, which containeth in it all that God intended both toward Christ and us, is this word, which is translated *to gather together in one*, *ἀνακεφαλαιώσασθαι*. It is a teeming word, a pregnant word, that containeth all that God intended toward Christ and us in the womb of it.

At the first, I did give you four approved significations of it, that none that knoweth and studieth the meaning of the word can deny.

The first; it signifieth a *summing up*, a casting up of several figures into one total sum.

The second is, it is a *gathering together* of several members or parts unto one head.

The third, which is rather an addition unto the second; it is a *gathering of them again*. There is ἀνά, a doing of it the second time.

The fourth is, a reducing things unto their *first principles*, to their first estate, *instaurare*, as I shall shew you anon.

I gave you these, when I made entrance into the words, to be the four several meanings of it. There is a fifth, which I will not stand upon. And these four contain all that God intended both towards Christ and us.

First, as a foundation to the great restoration of all things, the great recapitulation and gathering of all under one head, God layeth this foundation—he summeth up all things in Christ's person. He was to make him a head, and he would make him a head that should partake of all the body; one that should be a fit and a meet head, fit to be King of both worlds. He casteth up, summeth up in him, into one total, all divisions whatsoever, all things in earth and all things in heaven.

He summeth up in him God and the creature. That was the first great division.

He summeth up in him the nature of man and the condition of angels; for he is a heavenly man and far above angels. It is his due, and he possesseth it now.

He summeth up, in man's nature assumed, both Jew and Gentile; for he came of both.

Thus he cast up all sorts of divisions into one total sum in Christ's person first, and made that a foundation unto a second; and that is this, to gather together all things in earth and in heaven under one head, that is both head of angels and men; that angels and men do make up one great association under this one Head and Monarch, Christ; and that of all sorts of angels, and of all sorts of men, make what division you will,—nations, tongues, kindreds, sinners, ranks, whatsoever,—he gathereth together of all such, and makes up a body to Christ. That is the second.

The third was this, which I entered upon in the last discourse, that he hath made a second gathering of all things in one. In Christ there is a second gathering. There is a twofold union of creatures reasonable, with God, and amongst themselves, a first and a second; ἀνὰ is not to be lost. Yea, and he hath gathered together again the second time after a scattering, when they were dispersed, broken all in pieces; he makes up all again in Christ, to make his glory so much the more illustrious.

In the first place there was a first gathering of all things unto God, as under a head, which was that gathering of all in heaven and in earth by the law of creation; which I explained in four things.

First, that both angels and men were, by that law of creation, united to God. It was their due so to be; a natural due, if he would make them creatures reasonable.

Yet, secondly, so, as they were both united to God, but by the same like common tie, they might both fall in pieces.

Then, thirdly, there was a peace between both these among themselves, if not an association; which indeed the Scripture holds not forth; but a peace there was.

And then, fourthly, in some respect this might be said to be in Christ; not as a head undertaking for both, but by his natural due. It was his right, if he were to be a creature, to be the head of that creation, the 'beginning of the creation of God,' as he is called, Rev. iii. 24.

Now, I shewed there is a second gathering in Christ, as a head undertaking both for men and angels.

First, for the angels' parts, it was the thing I shewed you, the necessity of second union, and that in Christ. I cannot stand to repeat the particulars. They needed both confirming grace, as I shewed out of Job iv. 18, compared with Job xv. 15. They needed elevating grace, to that fulness of the vision of God which is only Christ's natural due, as John i. 18, 'None hath seen the Father,'—it is not only *no man*, but it is οὐδεὶς, *none*,—but only by way of participation from him who lay in the bosom of the Father. There is a vision of God which the angels were not created unto, which in Christ they are raised up unto.

Then, again, I shewed there was a kind of reconciliation of them, a gathering together in that respect, as the phrase, Col. i. 20, importeth, where all things are said to be reconciled, both in heaven and in earth. It is not a proper reconciliation indeed; but when God saw that his angels served him so, the most part of them, he chargeth the rest with folly. It was in their nature to do it, he could not trust them; it might have made him repent that ever he made angels. Christ takes this off, it is not an actual falling, but a possible falling, and fixeth them to God for ever. Thus he gathered all things in heaven to himself by a second gathering; for that is the point.

Now, that which I am to handle is this, *That there is a second gathering of men, of all things on earth;* and that is clearer than the other.

God doth not preserve men only from a danger of scattering by a second union with himself in and through Christ, but he actually preserveth them. He sheweth not his grace of preservation only; he withdraweth, or he leaveth them unto themselves, suffereth them all to turn head against him, to turn rebels, to the end he might get glory by a further degree of grace toward them, to shew forth the riches of his mercy in their recovery.

And, my brethren, this gathering of all things on earth in Christ, of men to himself, is the great gathering of all the rest. It was the greatest work of Christ. That of angels was but an overflow of it, cast into the bargain, to confirm them; but that which did draw forth all that was in Christ, to satisfy his Father, was to reconcile men unto him. This was the great scattering, for it divided heaven from earth, angels from men, men amongst themselves, as I shall shew you by and by. Therefore, when this cometh to be added unto the other, it makes it an universal gathering: it makes Christ a catholic King, the only catholic King, the only universal Head, to all things in heaven and in earth, when all come in again to him.

I shall explain or present unto you this gathering again in one of all things, all sorts of men on earth, by these four particulars:—

I. I told you, first, it implied a dispersion, a scattering; therefore I will briefly lay forth the desperate, miserable, forlorn, scattered condition of the sons of men, by the sin of Adam; how all in earth and in heaven were fallen in pieces, divided, and at enmity.

II. I shall, secondly, shew you the making up of all this again; what a complete, full, and entire gathering together in one there is of all that were scattered.

III. And then, thirdly, because God's second works always exceed the first, therefore this gathering again is with an addition of a more near, and entire, and more glorious union than at first; a more indissoluble union, never to part again.

IV. And, fourthly, that all this was done in Christ, or by Christ, as you shall hear anon; and by what it was in Christ that all was thus gathered together, when they were all scattered and broken in pieces.

These are the four heads which I shall now insist upon; and all are necessary to open this text.

I. *First, I shall shew you the division, the scattering, that was of things on earth, both from what is in heaven, and from amongst themselves.*

First, What is in heaven? There is God there, he is the chief in heaven. Why, they were all cut off from God. It is called a 'departing' from God, in Jer. xvii. 5, and Heb. iii. 12. It is called a 'going astray, like sheep,' after a thousand vanities, in Isa. liii. 6. 'This people,' saith he, Jer. v. 23, 'hath a revolting and a rebellious heart; they are revolted and gone;' clean gone from God, and gone for ever, if God take not the care of them: so the phrase is there. And, Col. i. 21, there are three degrees, which indeed comprehend all: 'You were,' saith he, 'alienated and enemies;' once they were friends, God and they were one; now they are strangers; not only so, but 'enemies in their minds;' yea, thirdly, 'in evil works,' all sort of hostility, not only in outward actions, but in inward dispositions; and by means of this, an eternal wall of separation is set up between God and man, Isa. lix. 2.

Here now is one division, all on earth cut off from him, 'without God in the world;' it is the expression the Apostle useth, Eph. ii. 12.

Secondly, What else is there in heaven? There are angels. Men are scattered utterly from them, because, as I told you, though there were not an association, yet there was a peace; though there were two worlds divided, distinct, though there was no trade, yet there was no enmity. But through man's fall there was; for the angels cannot but hate where God hateth, and they cannot but be angry where God is angry. And therefore you read, Gen. iii. 24, when man by sin was cast out of paradise, then cherubim came, with their swords turned every way to keep man out, with their swords drawn upon him. You never read of angels till then. When Balaam went on in a perverse way, Num. xxii. 22, it is said, 'The angel of the Lord stood in the way for an adversary against him.' They are adversaries, they are enemies to men in their evil courses and ways; and howsoever some divines have thought that all executions of judgments here below have been by evil angels, yet the Scripture evidently sheweth that they ordinarily and mostly be good; we have more instances of the one than the other. Those that destroyed Sodom were good angels, and Lot entertained them as such: 'The Lord,' say they, 'hath sent us to destroy Sodom,' Gen. xix. 13. They were angels created; therefore, Heb. xiii. 2, Lot is said to have 'entertained angels.' The like may be said of that, 1 Chron. xxi. 15; of that that struck Herod, Acts xii. 23; and of that smote the camp of the Assyrians, 2 Kings xix. 35. It is evident, for in all those places they are still called the angel of the Lord, which is never spoken of Satan.

There is once, indeed, mention of an 'evil spirit' from the Lord, but it is with an addition of evil; but the angels of the Lord are still good angels. And that angel that destroyed Jerusalem, which David saw with a drawn sword in his hand stretched out over the city, 1 Chron. xxi. 15, was evidently a good angel; for, ver. 18, he directs Gad to tell David where the temple should stand, and biddeth him worship; which an evil angel, God would never have used him to do it.

And, my brethren, if men be enemies to the Church of God, as wicked men by nature are, angels will revenge it. 'Take heed,' saith Christ, Matt. xviii. 10, 'that you offend not one of these little ones;' and he giveth the reason of it; 'for,' saith he, 'their angels do always behold the face of my Father which is in heaven:' they have angels that take their part. Thus they are enemies in this life unto wicked men; and at the day of judgment, you shall read in Matt. xiii. 41, 42, 49: 'The angels are the reapers,' saith he, ver. 39; and he sheweth there how they take the bodies and souls of wicked men. The good angels are their gatherers, but it is for hell. They gather all together, and 'cast them into the furnace of fire; there shall be wailing and gnashing of teeth.' It is attributed unto the angels.

Thus you see, I say, that angels and men are at odds, and all by sin; all is broken now. God is gone, angels are divided from us, and at enmity with us. All in heaven and earth is broken to pieces.

Well, come to *things on earth;* nothing but divisions there. There is not a man in the world but by nature is divided from all men. 'We, like sheep, have gone astray, every one after his own way;' so it is Isa. liii. 6. All went one way once, we all cleaved to God; we have left God, and are fallen all in pieces. 'God made man righteous;' there was but one way then, for so the opposition implieth; 'but they have sought out many inventions,' even as many as there are men, Eccles. vii. 29; and, Tit. iii. 3, 'serving divers lusts and pleasures.'

Then again, secondly, men are at enmity one with another, it is certain, more or less, *homo homini lupus.* Tit. iii. 3, 'We,' saith he, describing man's natural condition,—'We ourselves lived in malice and in envy, hateful, and hating one another.' Hateful every man is to another more or less, he is hated of another, and he hateth another more or less; and if his nature were let out to the full, there is that in him, 'every man is against every man,' as it is said of Ishmael. Self-love, my brethren, that ruleth all the world, is the greatest monopolist that ever was in the world. 'Men shall be lovers of themselves,' as you have it 2 Tim. iii. 2, 3; and what followeth? 'Covetous, boasters, proud, blasphemers, disobedient to parents, without natural affection, truce-breakers,' &c. Self-love breaks all bonds; all things in earth are scattered.

Go amongst all nations; there is nothing else but a fatal confusion amongst them; the Jew at enmity with the Gentile, and the Gentile with the Jew. All have heard how the Scripture sets it out, they were an abomination and curse each to other; of which I have treated elsewhere.*

And, thirdly, in religions, nothing but divisions, before our Lord and Saviour Christ came in the fulness of time. Look upon all nations, so many nations, so many gods; nay, so many cities, so many gods, as it is Jer. ii. 28; nay, so many families, so many gods; there was not a family but chose a several god to itself; and therefore, 1 Cor. viii. 5, 'there are lords many, and gods many.' Many indeed; for there was as many almost as there were men to worship them; each chose what god he pleased. And the Apostle in that place I last quoted, if you read it, you shall find, instanceth in both things in heaven and things in earth. All things in heaven and in earth, from stars to serpents that creep on the earth, the very onions were made gods amongst them! Thus was all the world divided; this was the shattered condition of all mankind, of all things in earth, when Jesus Christ came.

Nay, my brethren, fourthly, there is another division yet. There was a fatal sentence to scatter men's souls from their bodies, their bodies to go to the grave, and to return to dust, which also is scattered up and down with winds, God knows where, and their souls to hell; called their own place.

And, lastly, to conclude; by all these gatherings, they are gathered to the devil, as their head and prince, though they know not of it; who is the prince of the world, that rules it; and the 'god of this world,' that is worshipped by the 'children of disobedience.' What a miserable shattering is here; all in earth broken in pieces, and all in heaven! And thus have I represented to you the state and condition of man dispersed.

II. *Now I must shew you, secondly, that Jesus Christ hath made all one again;* I must go over all these particulars, and make it good; that is the second thing.

First, as I told you, all things on earth were cut off from God. What doth Christ do first? He makes peace with God, that was the great business of all the rest; make peace with him, and all else will fall in. This Christ did, Col. i. 20, 'Having made peace through the blood of his cross, by him to reconcile all things unto himself, whether they be things in earth, or things in heaven.' Here you see it: I need name no more scriptures, for I might give you many for it.

In the second place, angels come to be reconciled; you heard before they were enemies. I will shew you it in the general first, and secondly in the particulars.

First, *in the general.* They were enemies before, you heard; you shall see that the angels in Christ are made friends to souls and bodies. Read Luke xv. 8–10: Christ makes there a comparison of a woman that had lost

* *Vide* Sermon of Christ's being the Universal Peacemaker, on Eph. ii. 14.

her groat, and she lights a candle and sweeps her house; and when she had found it, she calls in her friends and neighbours, and, said she, 'Rejoice with me, for I have found my groat which was lost.' Who are those friends? the next words shew that they are angels; for it is added in the very next verse, 'There is joy in the presence of the angels of God over a sinner that repenteth.' They are made friends you see, the text is express for it. And in token of it what do they? Look in the second of Luke; they are so far friends, that as soon as they knew the Saviour of the world was born, they came flying down, a whole troop of them,—their hearts were full of it,—to bring men the news of it; and to shew their rejoicing, they sing; they were glad at heart, and sing, 'Peace on earth, good-will towards men.' They are the first messengers of that glad tidings: ver. 10, 'Suddenly there was with the angel a multitude of the heavenly host praising God, and saying, Glory to God in the highest, peace on earth, and good-will towards men.'

Everywhere you shall find angels described throughout the whole Scripture to be the *heavenly host*, because they are the men of war, they are the militia of heaven, to speak in the language of the age; so they are called in that second of Luke, and they are everywhere else so called: 1 Kings xxii. 19, 2 Kings vi. 17, Matt. xxvi. 53. Christ calls them legions, as the devils are called. Now, my brethren, what do these angels that were soldiers, enemies, warriors against devils and men? They come in all their warlike habit and attire down to earth, and proclaim peace. It became them so to do. 'A multitude of heavenly soldiers,' saith he, 'praising God, and saying, Glory,' &c. What do they say? God is at peace with men, and we are at peace with men; we are in our armour still, but it is to fight for this gospel we preach. As in the Revelation, 'I am thy fellow-servant,' saith he, 'and of thy brethren, that have the testimony of Jesus.' If any man have the testimony of Jesus and hold it forth; if you be for Jesus, we are for Jesus and for you too, saith he. Angels and men are friends: Ps. xxxiv. 7, 'They encamp about the saints.' All that heavenly host turn all their weapons now for Christ, and for the saints. Therefore, when Ahab went to fight, in that 1 Kings xxii. 19, the whole host of heaven appeared; for the whole host of heaven standeth ready to defend the gospel; they are all friends to Christ and the saints; so that you see that all in heaven is for them. See another place, Gen. xxxii. 1, 2. When poor Jacob went out to meet Esau, he went out trembling before; but the angels of God met him, and saith he, 'This is God's host;' there were two hosts of them, *Mahanaim*, two troops, so he calleth them.

Now, what is the cause of this, that angels come thus to be reconciled with us; that they come down upon the earth to serve men, and to be friends with them thus? It is Christ. Gen. xxviii. 12, Jacob saw a ladder that touched heaven and touched earth. Who is that ladder? Christ himself is that ladder, and himself interpreteth it so, John i. 51, 'You shall see the angels ascending and descending upon the Son of man,' as they did there ascend and descend upon that ladder that appeared to Jacob. The ladder, it touched heaven, it touched earth, for Jesus Christ hath both in him; he is a heavenly man, and he hath the nature of a man, he hath made up heaven and earth. You heard before how Christ was partaker of both natures, and by the one he hath a foot on earth, whereof the top is in heaven; and it is he that hath made the highway between heaven and earth an open passage. Therefore now angels are reconciled to men, heaven is reconciled to earth, and there is an intercourse, a trade, a highway, they ascend and descend familiarly; it was there to defend Jacob, and for many other ends they do it. Before, you heard, they kept man out of Paradise with a sword; but now you read, that they carry into Paradise the souls of men: as of Lazarus, Luke xvi. 22, and at the latter day, as in Matt. xxiv. 31, 'And he shall send his angels with a great sound of a trumpet, and they shall gather together his elect from the four winds, from one end of heaven to the other.'

This is the general. Now see it in the *particulars,* that angels are, in all the particulars wherein they are at enmity that I instanced in, reconciled to men. In the first place, I told you before that they execute judgments and plagues. It was a good angel that destroyed in Jerusalem with the plague. Now read Ps. xci. 10, 11, it is a pat instance of the contrary: 'There shall no evil befall thee, neither shall the plague come nigh thy dwelling: for he shall give his angels charge over thee, to keep thee in all thy ways.' You heard before that when man fell and was cast out of Paradise, angels stood there with a flaming sword to keep him out. Now you shall see the angels stand to let him in. Rev. xxi. 12, describing there the new Jerusalem, he saith there were 'twelve gates, and at the gates twelve angels.' It was Paradise, as appears, chap. xxii. 14, because there was the tree of life, for so it is described: 'Blessed are they that do his commandments, that they may have right to the tree of life, and may enter in through the gates into the city.' It is an allusion to Paradise; there angels kept out, here angels carry in. The angels, you know, fetched the soul of Lazarus, and carried it into Abraham's bosom, Luke xvi. And so at the latter day, Matt. xxiv. 31, the angels shall take the saints that rise, and bring them all to Christ; so the text saith there. Here you see it, I say, in all the particulars wherein they are enemies, how they are made friends. Here is then angels and men reconciled after being broken to pieces.

Well, I shewed you in the third place, that all on earth were shattered to pieces, the Jew from the Gentile, one man from another. Now Christ hath made up this division too. Take any man, my brethren, that is the greatest enemy to any; let them have had the most desperate enmity that ever was between two mortal men; let these two men be turned to God, let them meet in Christ, they will love one another, it is certain. Take a godly man, set before him the greatest enemy he hath in the earth; do but put that question to him, What will you say if this man should be turned to God? Oh, saith he, I could fall down before him! He would do anything in the world to procure it and bring it about.

My brethren, the Jew and the Gentile were two, so they are called; it is the very word used, Eph. ii. 15. They were two indeed, saith he, 'He hath made of twain one,' he hath reconciled both. Christ did it; it was by the blood of his cross he broke down the partition wall. The μεσότοιχον, the partition wall, of the ceremonial law is broken down: which is elegantly signified, alluding to the wall in the temple that kept the Gentiles from the Court of the Jews. The Jews were such enemies to the Gentiles, that they could not endure the gospel to be preached to them. They were all 'filled with envy;' so you read in the Acts the carnal Jews were. Well, but when Peter goeth and preacheth the gospel to the Gentiles, what say the godly Jews? See what they say, Acts xi. 18, good souls, 'When they heard these things,'—namely, that the Gentiles believed, that is the context,—'they held their peace, and glorified God, saying, Then hath God given also unto the Gentiles repentance unto life.' They fell down and glorified God. Here Jew and Gentile, that would not eat one with another before, are made friends; now they eat together at the same table, at the same Lord's Supper.

Now there is one body, one supper, one sacrament, one God, one Lord Jesus Christ, both Jew and Gentile one.

Go over particulars. Amongst the Jews themselves there were great divisions. There was the ten tribes opposite to the two tribes. Ephraim and Judah extremely opposite; you have it, Isa. xi. 13. He speaks there of the envy of Ephraim, and how they were adversaries to Judah; but I will order it so, saith he, that 'the envy of Ephraim shall depart, and the adversaries of Judah shall be cut off; Ephraim shall not envy Judah, and Judah shall not vex Ephraim.' This is in Christ; for if you mark it, he speaks of the 'root of Jesse' in the 10th verse. Here now both these are reconciled. You have the like, Ezek. xxxvii. 19. There are two sticks, the one is Ephraim, and the other is Judah. Take these sticks, saith he, and make them one; for I will make them one nation, and they shall have one king, and they shall be no more divided into two kingdoms. You may read it there at large, ver. 21–24. And you read how these are scattered as dry bones used to be; so as none knows who these Jews of the ten tribes are, as in a charnel-house none knows what bones are of such and such men. 'These bones are the whole house of Israel,' saith God to the prophet, ver. 11. Bones that were dried, their hope lost and cut off, and they scattered one from another.

Well, you heard that the Gentiles were dispersed one amongst another, and had a thousand religions; by the death of Jesus Christ they are all gathered into one. Take one place for it; it is John xi. 50, 51. The high priest there prophesying of Christ's death, and shewing the end of it, saith he, 'It is necessary that Jesus should die for this nation,' (for the Jews.) And what followeth, added by the Evangelist? It may be it was the prophecy of the high priest at that time, but this followeth: 'and not for this nation only, but that also he should gather together in one the children of God that were scattered abroad.' All the Gentiles that were scattered, scattered in place, scattered in religion, thus divided, Christ dieth to gather them together in one, all them that belong to God's election, both in that age, and in all ages to the end of the world. Therefore now, when Christ came into the world you have it fulfilled; in the apostles' time there were as many gods as men, as many gods as cities, as many gods as families,—1 Cor. viii. 5, 'There are lords many, and gods many,'—as many as there were 'things in heaven and things in earth,' as I said before he intimateth it there. Their religion lay in having *lords* that were mediators unto their *gods*. But, saith he now to us, 'There is but one God, and there is but one Lord.' This alteration did God make in the very apostles' times. And, my brethren, let me add this to it. Since the greatest part of the world hath one God, though it have not one Lord; the Turks and we have one God, we have not one Lord indeed; but yet over all Turkey, over all the Roman empire, there is still one God to this day, and those heathen gods are all gone.

Thus he hath gathered together things in earth in one, in Jesus Christ; he hath reconciled the nations; and he will never leave till such time as he hath been the God of the whole earth, of the whole world. He saith, Isa. xi. 9, when both Jew and Gentile shall come in, that 'the earth shall be full of the knowledge of the Lord, as the waters cover the sea.' Isa. liv. 5, he saith that 'the Redeemer, the Holy One of Israel, shall be called the God of the whole earth.' Dan. vii. 14, 27, he saith, there shall come a kingdom, after all the kingdoms, after the fourth monarchy, which is now a-destroying, (for the Pope is the last head of it,)—there shall come a kingdom of all nations, and tongues, and languages, and they shall serve him, and he shall possess all the kingdoms under the whole heavens, (it is not a kingdom in heaven.) He shall gather all in one, and there shall be but one kingdom, and one Lord, through the whole earth. This God will do in the end. Thus you see, I say, that Jesus Christ hath reconciled all on earth, he hath made them up all again; he meaneth to do it by the virtue of his death.

Well, there was one division more that I named; as great a scattering as any of the former is not yet made up: and it is of things that are yet both in heaven and earth, and remain divided one from another; and it is of the saints from the very beginning of the world, and will continue so to the very end. For death and the grave hold and keep the bodies of them, remaining still in the earth, whilst their souls, being 'spirits made perfect,' are lodged together in heaven. Here is a great scattering. All the patriarchs that did die before Christ came, all that have died since, their bodies are in one place, and their souls in another; one is in heaven, and the other is laid in the grave, and there resteth. Death hath scattered all the saints into two worlds, it hath reigned over all; and though he will be the God of all the earth, and join all nations together, yet souls and bodies are still divided of all that are dead, and of all the saints from the beginning of the world, and that shall be to the end. Now, what will Jesus Christ do? He will raise up all, and bring them all together, make up that division too. 1 Thess. iv. 16, compared with Matt. xxiv. 31. He saith there, the angels shall go into all the four corners of the world, when the great sound of the trumpet cometh,—he speaks of the latter day,—'and they shall gather together his elect from the four winds, from one end of heaven to the other.'

My brethren, the bodies of the elect, where are they? Some burnt and turned to ashes, all dispersed into the elements; who knoweth where every man's body is, and all the parts of it? All those atoms, all those bones, will God bring together again, and gather them all in one, and join their souls to them, and, saith he, we shall ever be with the Lord. There will be then a gathering together that shall never be dissolved. Thus, I say, he hath gathered together all in one that were all shattered and fallen to pieces.

III. *The third head, as I told you, was this, That this second gathering shall exceed the first infinitely.* I mentioned four particulars, you know, to explain. First, that all were fallen in pieces; secondly, that all shall be gathered together again; and that this second gathering shall exceed the first. It exceedeth it in two things; I will name no more. It exceedeth, first, in sureness and stability. That same first union with God by creation was upon slippery grounds. 'He putteth,' saith he, 'no trust in his saints,' Job xv. 15. He could trust none of them. He could not send an angel down,—for he speaks of angels there, as I shewed before,—he could not send them on an errand to earth, but they might have fallen and been in hell before they came up again. It was a slippery knot, that of creation. But now they are headed in Christ. God would never trust creature more, he will make sure work; and what doth he? He headeth them all in Christ; and what saith Christ? 'My sheep shall no man take out of my hand.' If angels and men be once bottomed on Christ, they can never be parted again. Who shall separate us, now we are again the second time gathered, from the love of God in Christ? It exceedeth in sureness, you see.

It exceedeth in nearness of the union too. We have a more near union with God, and one with another, than we had. First, a nearer union one with another; for in the first gathering by creation, as I told you at first, men and angels were at peace indeed, but they should have lived in two worlds. Man should have lived upon the earth, and they in heaven. They should not have come one at another, that is certain; man was an earthly creature, and he must have continued upon earth, as I have often hinted out of 1 Cor. But when we are gathered together the second time, angels and men live together in one world: men shall be like angels, Matt. xxii. 30; they shall 'bear the image of the heavenly man,' 1 Cor. xv. 49; and 'we are come to angels,' Heb. xii. 22; and we shall have places where they are, as I shewed out of Zech. iii. 7. There is a nearer union now one amongst another than was before. And a nearer union with God too. For, my brethren, let me tell you this, that men that were thus shattered from God and fallen into this great misery, shall be raised up to the nearest union with God that can be; for aught I know, nearer than the angels. Rev. vii. 11, there is the throne; the four beasts next that; the four-and-twenty elders next them; and the angels round about the throne and the elders. They are more remote from the throne than the beasts are, than the men are. Therefore, as I shewed before, Christ is our brother, which is nowhere said of angels; they are nowhere called brother; it is proper unto men, Heb. ii. Christ is our husband. It is not said of any of the angels that Christ is their husband, and that God is a Father to them by adoption through the marriage with Christ; there is a nearer union that these scattered ones have with God through Christ, upon this second gathering. So there is the third head explained.

IV. There is a fourth head, which shall be, and deserves to be, the *coronis* of this glorious story: *They are said to be gathered together in Christ.*

Well, *in Christ.* What will this hold forth? It holdeth forth that they are not only all gathered in Christ as unto a Head, but they are gathered by virtue of him. Not only gathered to him, but in him, efficiently, meritoriously, by something he hath done to gather all together again, when they were all shattered in pieces. You heard how all things both in heaven and earth were gathered together and summed up in the person of Christ, who is the founder of this their gathering. We shall now see that ere he himself could effect a gathering together of all in heaven and earth, himself must be made the subject of a fatal scattering; and as the gathering of all things in his person is the fundamental *medium unionis*, means of union, of all things else that are united to God by him, that so this scattering is the means of all that reconciliation of things scattered, as hath been said. Christ had his ἀνὰ too; he had his gathering again in his own person; and therefore a scattering first that befell his own person; and what is true of us is first true of him. And by virtue of this it was that we were all gathered; for it is a sure rule, that what is done in us by him, the like was first done for us in Christ himself; as, if we that are poor be made rich, it is because he that was rich was made poor. So in like manner, if he would gather all things that are out of himself into one in himself, himself must be scattered in himself. As his incarnation was the summing up of all, so his death the scattering of all, and his resurrection is his gathering of all again; and we had not God's design complete without all these. Now, to shew that he was scattered and shattered in all but the personal union—

First, That his death was a scattering of him; it was a taking down all, as I may so express it. Indeed, the union could never be taken down; the union with the Godhead could never be dissolved, but it went as near as possibly could be. You shall see the expression the Scripture hath, John xi. 51, 52. When he speaks of gathering all in one that were dispersed, he saith he must do it by his death. It is necessary, saith he, that Jesus should die for that nation. 'And not for that nation only; but that also he should gather together in one the children of God that were scattered abroad.' You know that death is a separation of all things, and so it was to Christ. Were we cut off from God? Look to that phrase, Dan. ix. 26, 'Messiah shall be cut off.' There was a division, a separation made. There were these *three* things summed up in him—God, the condition of angels, the nature of man. They are all dissolved, there was a kind of dissolution; it came as nigh as could be, so as he might still hold a personal union, for that was necessary.

First, *God*. God, you know, is called the Head of Christ, 1 Cor. xi. 3. Now, when Jesus Christ came to die, as we were cut off by sin from God our Head, so there was as near a cutting off of Christ from God as possibly could be. 'My God, my God, why hast thou forsaken me?' saith he. 'My God, my God,' still; yet he was turned enemy to him. Zech. xiii. 7, 'Awake, thou sword, against the man that is my fellow.' He strikes him, runneth his sword through his soul. Here God was gone, yet God is his God still. You see here was one scattering of that was once summed up in him.

Secondly, all the creatures left him; first his disciples, as it followeth there in Zechariah, 'Smite the shepherd, and the sheep shall be scattered.' When he hung upon the cross, not an angel durst come to comfort him; though whilst in his agony in the garden, when the curse came not on him unto its height, not so until he hung upon the tree; and then when the curse came in its fulness upon him, no angel did or durst appear to comfort him. If the light of the sun would comfort him, God withdrew it; and, in Dan. ix. 26, it is expressly said the Messiah had nothing. So in your margins.

In the third place, he was born, as I said, unto the condition of angels. He was a heavenly man, 'the Lord from heaven,' 1 Cor. xv.; and it was his due to be advanced, as now he is, 'far above all principality and power;' and therein he hath but his due. This I shewed at first, when I told you there was a summing up of all in him. Now what saith Heb. ii. 9? Saith he there, 'We see Jesus, who was made a little lower than the angels for the suffering of death, crowned with glory and honour,' &c. To give you the exposition that learned Camero hath given it, and certainly it is the right; the Apostle had shewed in the first chapter that Christ was above the angels, and that both as God and man it was his inheritance, his due, as he saith, ver. 4, 6. And, chap. ii. 5, he sheweth that the 'world to come' is not put into subjection to the angels, but to Christ; 'so that,' saith he, 'he hath that glory and that honour above the angels, as due to him.' What did God make him now? 'He made him,' saith he, 'lower than the angels,' when he came to die. You will say, 'a little lower.' But that same βραχύ τι is but for 'a little time;' *per illud tempus passionis*, for the time of his suffering, that is the meaning of it; for otherwise he was made a great deal lower than the angels. 'I am,' saith he, 'a worm and no man,' Ps. xxii. 6; that is lower than the angels, infinitely lower; but βραχύ τι, for 'a little while,' so interpreters many of them carry it. 'A little while,' saith he; that is, while he suffered death, as Camero interpreteth it. That man that had an inheritance above angels, to whom all things should be put in subjection under his feet, angels and all; this man, saith he, was for a little while made lower than the angels, and this while he suffered death. So that now, my brethren, you see that, as God hath forsaken him, so likewise, in the next place, here is the condition of the angels that he was born unto, that is gone too, while he tasteth of death for every man.

Well, but he is man yet? Why, but that is scattered too. What is man? He is the result of soul and body. Take the soul from the body, the humanity ceaseth; there is a body indeed and a soul still, but where is the man? Though he was personally united to the body in the grave, and the soul in Paradise, yet in a proper and strict sense there was a ceasing to be man. You know death is the dissolution of man into his soul and body. Take Christ's own expression, John ii. 19; he calls it an *unbuilding*, or destroying of himself. 'Destroy this temple,' saith he; take it in pieces, fling one stone from another,—for when he died, his soul went one way and his body another,—and, saith he, 'I will build it again.' The stones were pulled down, it was but unbuilt. It is true, it may be said that he is God-man when dead, but it cannot be said he was man when dead. Man he was indeed, in respect that his soul and body must be united again; but yet in a proper and strict sense, man he was not then. Here, I say, all is gone; here is a shattering even in Christ himself, so far as possibly may be. The union could not be dissolved, for then it could not have been said that God died, and that God was buried, and that God was raised, if the Godhead had not been united to the body. The union of the Godhead ceased not; the union of the soul and body, the man, ceased. Though it is true that the Godhead was united personally to his body in the grave, and to his soul in Paradise, and that union was never interrupted; yet our divines, speaking in a strict sense, say *in triduo desiit homo,* he ceased to be man; as man consisted of body and soul united in one together, so he ceased to be man, during the time he lay in the grave. Here, I say, you see all is gone in his death. Here is his manhood scattered too.

Second, But what followeth? In his resurrection all was made up again; he gathereth all together again in one, and by virtue of this we are gathered together in him; for what is done in us is done first in Jesus Christ. To give you an express scripture for it: Acts xiii., when Peter speaks of his rising again, saith he, at the 33d verse, 'God hath raised up Jesus again.' How doth he prove it? 'As it is written,' saith he, 'in the second psalm, Thou art my Son, this day have I begotten thee.' As if all had been shattered, dissolved, and taken in pieces, and he was, as it were, new born; God never saw his Son look like his Son till now; he begets him anew when he raiseth him, bringeth soul and body, and all is knit and made up again.

1. His body and soul came together again. 'He was declared to be the Son of God,' in that he was raised up by the eternal Spirit,—that is, the Godhead. Rom. i. 4, 'Destroy this temple;' he spake it of his body; and then at his resurrection it was verified that he built it up again; so then he was an entire man again, with soul and body united. 2. He is made now a heavenly man in qualities, not only such as the angels have, but far above the angels, and is become a quickening Spirit. 3. God is come again, and never so near him as now, for he hath admitted him to sit at his right hand. 4. He is advanced above all principalities and powers, 1 Pet. iii. 22; yea, 'far above all principalities and powers,' Eph. i. 21. And let us see the same place that spake of his abasement, that 'he was made a little lower than the angels,' to give testimony of his glory; we see him 'crowned with glory and honour,' Heb. ii. And in heaven he sits as a Head and Redeemer, to draw all men to him in all times and ages to come, until he is complete in respect of his body, which is his fulness.

Thus you see, my brethren, how all is made up, when all was shattered, and all broken to pieces, by the shattering of Christ himself; God, and the condition of angels, and the nature of man, in a sense, all being as it were dissolved, although the union with the Godhead was kept.—So you see now this third interpretation made good, that there is a gathering together again, when all in earth and all in heaven were shattered, in and through Christ.

There is a fourth interpretation, a fourth signification rather, to make up all complete. I shall give it you in a word; for it is a thing cast in by Christ, and therefore I will not insist upon it. I told you this, that he would restore all things to the first original,—I laid open that, when I expounded the words, I remember, at first. And, therefore, many translators read it *instaurare*, to restore all things, which is reserved, as the complement of all, in the fulness of time; and others, though they do not reject it, yet they say it is not the full meaning of the words, but it falleth short.

Well, my brethren, what doth this hold forth to us? You see all is in Christ's person; here are angels and men made a body to him. Well, take all things in heaven and in earth, all creatures else, and they shall all be restored to him; and when that is done, there is all God's full plot, all that was in his heart toward Christ, and us, and the whole creation. There is a time a-coming wherein the creatures shall be restored, all things in heaven and in earth, to their first original, and a more glorious condition, in and through Christ. It is a thing indeed that cometh in by accident; it was but cast into his bargain: he came to gather together men and angels; but yet this is cast together into the bargain.

To open this unto you a little. Man falleth. With his fall what should have fallen? The world should have fallen about his ears; as traitors' houses, you know, should be pulled down and made a jakes. What doth Jesus Christ? He buyeth the world of his Father. I will pay for it, saith he, and will have it into the bargain. He payeth for wicked men that live in the world; therefore it is said they deny the Lord that bought them: that is the meaning of that, 2 Pet. ii. 1. He buyeth wicked men and all the world, at one lump, of God. In the meantime he upholdeth it. It was said of David, Christ's type, Ps. lxxv. 3, 'The earth is dissolved, and the inhabitants thereof; I bear up the pillars of it:' and Christ 'upholdeth all things,' so saith the text, Heb. i. 3, 'by the word of his power;' it is spoken of Christ. And, my brethren, when he hath governed the world, and made it serve, though indirectly, that all works together for good; though wicked men have it directly, and the devils they carry the world away with them, and have done since the creation, but they shall not do so always; there is a time a-coming wherein all things in heaven and in earth shall be restored to their first condition, to a glorious condition, in and through Christ.

Read but Rom. viii. 19–21. There the Apostle is express for it: 'For the earnest expectation of the creature,' saith he, 'waiteth for the manifestation of the sons of God. For the creature was made subject to vanity, not willingly, but by reason of him who hath subjected the same in hope, because the creature itself also shall be delivered from the bondage of corruption into the glorious liberty of the children of God. For we know that the whole creation groaneth and travaileth in pain together until now.' And delivered, saith he, they shall be, if not before the day of judgment, yet certainly while the day of judgment lasteth, which will be a long day, while Christ will be upon earth and judge angels and men. As the first Adam did bring them all into bondage by reason of sin,—for as all was created for him, so most justly the whole frame and fabric of what was made for him was subjected to bondage by reason of his sin, and would have fallen to nothing had not Christ upheld it,—so the second Adam shall restore all unto a liberty; and this, in Acts iii. 21, is called 'the restitution of all things,'—not of angels and men only, but of all things.* It was meet that Christ, having taken the nature of man,—that is, the sum of all things,—that therefore all things should have some benefit thereby in their several kinds and capacities, and be in their kind gathered and restored according to their capacity; and when this shall be done, then God's design of *gathering* is fully accomplished. And though the time was full in respect of the centre of it when Christ came; and therefore it is said that in the fulness of time he might gather all, in the text; yet the fulness of time in the circumference is yet to come, and is then when we shall be gathered to Christ, as, in 2 Thess. ii. 1, the time of the resurrection and judgment is called.

And, my brethren, it became Christ thus, into the bargain, to restore all things in heaven and in earth. He created all things, therefore it is fit he should restore all things; they were all created by him and for him. The first Adam lost them, so saith Rom. viii.; but they were subjected under hope of a second Adam, that should come and restore them.

So now I shewed you the splendour of the universal Church out of Rev. v., and we will add the creatures to them, at that general assembly at the last day. I shewed you that all things on earth will meet then, and the angels will meet then; a representation of it you have there, though I will not say it is the full intendment of the place, yet it will hold forth much unto us. Read over Rev. v. 9–13, you shall see all things brought into Christ's presence. First, you have men, 'all things on earth,' ver. 9. 'They sung a new song, saying, Worthy art thou to take the book, and to open the seals thereof; for thou wast slain, and hast redeemed us to God by thy blood out of every kindred, and tongue, and people, and nation.' Here is all on earth gathered together, as I shewed you before. 'And I beheld,' saith he, ver. 11, 'and I heard the voice of many angels round about the throne,' (here angels come in too,) 'saying, Worthy is the Lamb that was slain, to receive power,' &c. Here you see God hath gathered both angels and men together; they both come in. Well, now there is but the creatures wanting. Read the next verse, 'And every creature which is in heaven, and on the earth, and under the earth, and such as are in the sea, and all that are in them, heard I saying, Blessing, honour, glory, and power, be unto him that sitteth upon the throne, and unto the Lamb for ever and ever.' Because not only angels and men are thus gathered in one unto him, but all the creatures shall be restored; every creature that is in heaven, and in earth, and under the earth, they all afford and administer matter of glory to man to praise God.—My brethren, now you see the sum of *gathering all in Christ.*

A MEDITATION OR TWO.

First, View and contemplate, with admiration and astonishment, the glory and splendour of Christ and his universal Church, to move your hearts to seek to be one thereof, and not left out of this number and gathering up of all things. You have the representation of this Church universal, during this world, in Rev. v. And, chap. vii., you have, first, the Church of men—four beasts, and four-and-twenty elders, next the throne—falling down and worshipping him that is on the throne, and the Lamb. 'Thou hast redeemed us,' say they—there are all things on earth—'out of every kindred, tongue, nation, and people,' chap. v. 9. Secondly, you have a round of all in heaven; they come in too, ver. 11, 12, 'And I beheld, and I heard the

* And unto this doth Bishop Davenant, as divers others, extend this word, because of the word πάντα, speaking of things; and not πάντας, speaking of persons only.

voice of many angels round about the throne and the beasts and the elders: and the number of them was ten thousand times ten thousand, and thousands of thousands; saying with a loud voice, Worthy is the Lamb that was slain to receive power, and riches, and wisdom, and strength, and honour, and glory, and blessing.' You have the like, chap. vii. 9–11. Then, thirdly, you have a ring of all the creatures that are round about both angels and men, that afford matter of praise unto God for his creating them, chap. v. 13, 14. This is the scheme and representations, as in this world. Oh, but what will it be at the great day, when Christ will come in his own and his Father's glory, with all his holy angels,—when Christ, that hath all things in his person, shall appear in his fulness! And all the holy angels, and saints of the sons of men that have been existent from the beginning of the world to that day, and not one wanting, but that Christ will raise it up at the last day; and then when all these shall go to heaven, and be ever together, when God shall have all his sons about him, and his eldest Son in the midst of them, then he will bring forth all his treasures of glory, that shall last, and not be spent to all eternity.

Secondly, Make sure to be one of this great assembly; let men flock unto and get into Christ by clusters; Gen. xlix. 10, 'To him shall the gathering of the people be.' Jesus Christ setteth up his standard; come into Jesus Christ, not to be as Judas, who fell short by iniquity from this lot. It is a fatal saying of Peter's to Simon Magus, 'Thou hast no part nor portion in this matter;' that so innumerable a company should be gathered under this one Head, and that thou shouldest be shut out. I have but further, to move you to it, two things out of the text: you must be gathered one way, either to Christ or Satan; you must fall either to Christ's or the devil's allotment and share. As Christ is the head of all that shall be saved, Eph. i. 22, so the devil is the head of all the children of disobedience, Eph. ii. 2. And as Christ is the head of the angels, though he be not of the same nature with them, so is the devil of men; and at the end of the world, when Christ shall have taken out all these his own, all the rest shall be cast into the fire prepared for the devil and his angels. The old expression in the Old Testament was, that men were gathered to their fathers; the wicked unto *cœtus gigantum*—unto the company of the giants, those wicked ones before the flood, from whom hell hath its denomination, as the first inhabitants of it, in Prov. xxi. 16. So the language of the New is, to be gathered to the devil and his angels, to the fire prepared for them.

Obs.—I will give you but one observation, and so I will end. The observation is this,—it is from this same gathering together again,—That God, to shew forth his glory, and his skill, and his grace the more, goeth over his works again the second time, spoils them, shatters them in pieces, and then makes them better than ever. This is his manner. Shattered, you see, are all things in heaven and in earth; here is his glory now to make them up again. This makes his glory illustrious, and his work illustrious. To give you an instance or two, and then to make a little use of it, and so conclude—

God created man according to his image, you know, at first, (and certainly had you lived with Adam, you would not have known how you could have been happier.) A glorious creature he was; he had the image of God drawn upon him, he was God's herald, he had his arms upon his breast. On a sudden, after God had drawn this picture, he dasheth it, breaketh it in pieces, strikes out all he had done. What was the reason of this? He meaneth to make it up better; he meaneth to frame upon man the image of Christ, and make him like unto him. 'You bore the image of the earthly, but I will make a better image for you; you shall bear the image of the heavenly, you shall be changed from glory to glory.' Thus he goes over his work again, after he had spoiled the first.

So, likewise, he createth man at first immortal; there was a possibility he should die, but by the providence of God he should not have died. What doth God? He takes and divides soul and body, and flings the body into the grave, there to rot. What is his end in this? He will raise it up a spiritual body, more glorious ten thousand times than it was at first. What saith the Apostle, 1 Cor. xv. 46? First, saith he, that which is natural, and then that which is spiritual.

Go, take his chosen people, the Jews; they were the only nation, his darling; theirs were the oracles of God, the promises, the covenant, and they were all in all with him for many thousand years. Why? He scatters them, breaks them all in pieces; the ten tribes he carrieth captive away long before the two tribes, and then the two tribes. And when he had thus scattered them all, what is his promise? Isa. xi. 11, 12, 'It shall come to pass,' saith the text, 'that the Lord shall set his hand again the second time to recover the remnant of his people. And he shall gather together the dispersed of Judah from the four corners of the earth.' He will gather them together in one again. What saith the Apostle, Rom. xi. 11? 'Have they stumbled,' saith he, 'that they should fall?' Or, as the prophet Jeremiah expresseth it,—we may allude to it, if it be not the meaning of the place,—chap. viii. 4, 'Shall they fall, and not rise?' He compareth the casting off of the Jews but to a stumbling, it was no more; yet it was the greatest stumble that ever was, for they stumbled upon the Rock, Christ: they crucified him, and yet God calls it but a stumbling; but it was a stumbling of a long stride, for it was sixteen hundred years. But, shall they stumble, saith he, that they shall fall? No, he will recover them again. Shall they fall, and not rise? Yes, and their rising shall be 'life from the dead,' as it followeth, ver. 15. In Ezek. xxxvii. 3, God compareth them to dry bones: 'Can these dry bones live?' saith he. Their hope was gone, all was gone. 'Behold,' saith he, ver. 5, 'I will cause breath to enter into these bones, and they shall live.' He comes over them the second time, and makes all these bones come together, and flesh comes upon them, and they shall live, and he will never cast them off again. Compare but Rom. xi. 26, the apostle quoteth but one Scripture to prove the calling of the Jews there; it is out of Isa. lix. 20. Read but that chapter, and you shall find that when they are once called, he will never cast them off again; but their seed's seed shall remain for ever. And, Isa. lxv. 17, he saith that the former heaven and earth shall no more be remembered, nor come into mind.

This, my brethren, is the manner of God. I should give you the reason of it, but I must pass on. I will conclude with a short use. You see here how all mankind ran into a confusion; here is a shattering in pieces of heaven and earth, and God gathered up all again. Fear not God's shattering nor breaking things in pieces. You think our kingdom now is running into confusion—confusion in opinions; the saints are divided, one runs one way, and another runneth another; one holdeth one opinion, and another holdeth another. My brethren, although the revealed will of God is that they should all agree, yet, notwithstanding all this scattering and division, God will in the end bring forth a glorious gathering together in one. If he pull down the tabernacle set up, and the frame and form of it, he will set up a better. If he pull down the temple, it is in three days to build it up again, and make it better, as Christ's body was when he rose again. Never fear, I say, God's shattering things, God's unbuilding.

To give you an instance. God set up a glorious church in the primitive times, and it was according to the pattern. What doth he do? He sendeth Antichrist into the world, and he pulls it down and defiles all the worship of God; there is a falling away to be, saith he,—so he calls it, 2 Thess. ii. 3,—both in worship and doctrine. And what hath God done? He hath reasonably well built it up again, recovered this temple out of the hands of Antichrist; he had once all nations following him, as you have it, Rev. xiii. 4, 7. Why, ere Christ hath done, all nations shall worship him; he had lost them all, he gathers all again. Fear not his scattering then.

There was a reformation made when first we came out of Popery. My brethren, what is imperfect God will pull down certainly; he will scatter you, he will melt you: and what is his end? To fetch out the dross, and when he hath done, you shall have a purer reformation come out of all. This is his manner. Fear not, I say, therefore, his scattering. And he will never cease till he hath brought the Church, not only to that purity that was in the primitive times, but to a purer. When the whore is burnt and cast off, and the bride cometh to dress herself for the Lamb, as you have it, Rev. xiv. and xviii., the Apostle saith he fell down and worshipped the angel that brought this news. This, saith he, is better than ever I saw, than ever was in his time; he would never have worshipped for it else; nay, he could scarce be brought to believe it, the angel was fain to say, 'These are the true sayings of God.' Thus, when God goeth to break all, he meaneth to mend all, and he will never cease till he hath brought the Church to the full stature of a perfect man in Christ. Fear not confusions, therefore, for the issue of them will be a closing in the end; it will be a gathering together of all again in one.

Again, after the reformation, the Church is to get power against Antichrist, and against all his adherents. The witnesses, saith he, shall have power to do thus and thus, Rev. xi. Yea, but after that power, when they have gotten it and carried it as you think they shall do, there will be an unbuilding, a scattering of the power of the holy people; so it is expressed, Dan. xii. 7. He speaks there of these latter times. Fear it not, for if God pull down one temple, he will set up the Holy of Holiest afterward. And as it followeth in that same 12th of Daniel, 'Blessed are those that come to those days;' and thrice blessed indeed are they, for they shall see better times. Fear not therefore God's scattering. What a miserable confusion was there when man fell! All was scattered; man divided from God, from angels, from himself. Christ came into the world when all nations were divided, men from men, and things on earth from things in heaven. So he will do in the Church; scatter all, that he may make all up again; melt all, that he may mend all. Fear not then his scattering.

I have done, you see, with the design itself which God had. I am now to come to *the time when this great dispensation began*, when God did break up his decrees that had lain hid from everlasting in his breast, and ordered the dispensation and administration of things to his Church; and then I shall have finished the 10th verse.

The text telleth us that he purposed in himself, in or *for* the dispensation of the fulness of time, to gather together all things in him.

Concerning this *time*, first, in general; the meaning is this, that God, that hath made every business under the sun, hath set a time for it. So you have it, Eccles. iii. 1, 'To everything,' saith he, 'there is a season, and a time to every purpose under the sun.' Here is now a dispensation of the fulness of seasons, (so the word signifieth,) and of the greatest purposes God had, not under the heavens, but before the heavens were, which he purposed in himself from everlasting. 'A time,' saith he, 'there is to be born.' If there be a time to be born, and a time to die, as the second verse saith, there was certainly a fulness of time when Messiah should be born, when all things should be gathered in the person of Christ in one, and when all should be scattered again, and he should die, as I opened before. 'There is a time,' saith he, ver. 3, 'to break down, and a time to build up.' So there is a time when he suffered all the world to lie scattered, and a time when he buildeth them up. The word *dispensation* is a family word, and is taken from rearing or building up a house. 'There is a time,' saith he, ver. 5, 'to cast stones away, and a time to gather stones together.' God let all the stones, both of Jews and Gentiles, lie scattered; but when the set time came he had pity upon those stones, as the expression is, Ps. cii. 14, and gathered them all in one. It was a 'dispensation of the fulness of times.'

I am to open here these three things :—

1. What is meant by *fulness of times.*
2. Why *dispensation of the fulness of times* is added.
3. *In,* or *for;* for indeed the word rather signifieth *for* the dispensation of times than *in.*

First, For the fulness of times, when this great project of God began to take its birth, as I may so speak. There were some shows of it before, but when the great delivery was, that was when Christ came first into the world, and after his ascension into heaven, then Jews and Gentiles were called, and angels fall down before him and acknowledge him their Head, and all things were gathered together in one. There was, first, a fulness of *times* when this was done; and, secondly, a fulness of *seasons,* for so the word in the original signifieth. It is not only a fulness of time, as you have it, Gal. iv. 4, but it is also a fulness of seasons; for so I say the word signifieth.

First, it was a fulness of *time* for this great work, when Christ came into the world. And why was it a fulness of time? What is meant by fulness of time here?

Then is time said to be full when all ages are run out, that God shall come to turn the glass, and set the lower end upwards, as I may so express it. Or, if you will have it in Gal. iv. 2, 'the time appointed by the Father,' so it is called there; it is called 'the fulness of time' in the fourth verse. There is a time, saith he, that God hath set; so many ages shall run out, and when they are run out, I will turn the glass, and begin a new dispensation and administration of things in the world; I will send my Son. When times appointed by God are run out, then is a fulness of times. I will give you a scripture for that phrase; it is Luke xxi. 24; he saith, 'Jerusalem shall be trodden down, till the times of the Gentiles be fulfilled;' that is, till the times be expired that God hath given to the Gentiles to enjoy the gospel alone; and when that time is expired, he will call the Jews, and till then Jerusalem shall be trodden down. So that this is the first signification of it, it is till all times be run out that God hath appointed. There is, as you know, the first age of the world, and the latter age of the world. You may justly compare it to your hour-glass, when the former age was expired, when all is run out, and the bottom glass is filled, then God cometh and turneth up a new administration, and beginneth another dispensation.

In the second place, it is not only a fulness of times, but it is a fulness of *seasons;* so the text hath it.

Christ came into the world in the centre of seasons, when the world was ripe, when all things called for him, the condition both of Jew and Gentile; the full time was come, the harvest was ripe, as our Saviour Christ doth express it to his apostles. When Christ came into the world to begin a new administration and dispensation of things, it is called a due time, Rom. v. 6, 'In due time,' or in due season, as the word is, 'Christ died for the ungodly.'

Now, why was it a fulness of time first; and, secondly, why was it a fulness of season?

It was a fulness of time—why? For the world had stayed long for it; they had stayed four thousand years before the Messiah of the world came. Great actions have long delays, so God doth order things in his dispensations; great mercies have long delays; the greatest mercy that ever was had four thousand years after it was promised, and then came the fulness of time.

But why a fulness of season? Why, my brethren, it was a fit season for the Jews, and it was a fit season for the Gentiles, that Christ should come into the world when he did, and that he should stay long before he came.

It was a fit season for the *Jews;* for the Church of God, which was only confined to the Jews, was, as a man, to grow up by degrees; to be a child first, and then to grow up to youth; and when a full age was come, then to receive their inheritance. This is the very reason the Apostle giveth, Gal. iv. 2, 3, which respecteth the Jews; he compareth the Jewish church there, God's first church, to a child, though an heir, but an heir under age. 'This heir,' saith he, 'so long as he is a child, differeth nothing from a servant, but he is under tutors and governors.' He is under the government, under the dispensation of what? Under the elements of the world, under his A B C; for so was Moses' law. The Church of God was an infant, and was to grow up by degrees, first to learn its letters, its A B C; for such, I say, was the ceremonial law, the types of it. And then came David and the prophets, and led them up further; but the Church was not grown to man's estate till Christ came. What followeth then? 'When the fulness of time was come,' ver. 4, 'God sent his Son, made of a woman,' &c. It was fit that the Jewish church, or whoever was a church, it was fit they should for a while be under nonage, and have a dispensation, an economy, a dispensation that was fit for a child; but when they were come up unto man's estate, then the great heir of the world, Christ himself, their elder brother, cometh into the world to bestow their inheritance upon them.

In the second place, it was a fit season in regard of the *Gentiles* too. For, you know, I said it was to gather together all things on earth, not Jews only, but Gentiles, as I have expounded. Now God ordered that Christ should not come into the world till about the time he meant to have the Gentiles called; and there was great reason that he should stay the experiment many thousand years before the Gentiles should be called; he would not have Christ come into the world till he should break up his decrees, till there should be the great birth of his everlasting purposes, that both Jew and Gentile should come in.

When Christ was to come into the world, he was not to stay long for his reward. What was his reward that he bargained for? Not for the Jew only, but also for the Gentile. Isa. xlix. 5, 6; it is driven there, by God the Father, bargainwise. When he saw that he was to die only for the Jew, saith he, ver. 4, 'I have laboured in vain, and spent my strength for nought.'

But what saith God in answer to him at the 6th verse, 'Is it a light thing that thou shouldest be my servant, to raise up the tribes of Jacob, and to restore the preserved of Israel? I will also give thee for a light to the Gentiles, that thou mayest be my salvation unto the ends of the earth.' Our Saviour Christ would have complained if he had not had the Gentiles brought in after his death; therefore God ordered his coming into the world then, when he meant to have both Jew and Gentile to be brought in; then should the 'desire of all nations come,' as you know he is called.

And there was a great deal of reason that God should suffer the Gentiles and all the world to lie in sin, long before Christ came, that there might be a fulness of season for his coming. Why? I will give you Scripture reason.

First, He would have mankind try all the ways they could for to be saved, and when they had tried all in vain, lo! your physician, saith he; there is he that shall help you. You have it, Acts xvii. 26–29. He speaks expressly to the point. To open the text; he telleth the Athenians there, ver. 26, that God had made of one blood all nations of men, and determined their times and the bounds of their habitation; and he was pleased to set such times wherein the Gentiles should walk in their own ways; he would afford them but the help of nature, 'that they should seek the Lord,' ver. 27, 'if haply they might feel after him,'—find him in his works by groping in the dark,—'though,' saith he, 'he be not far from every one of you.' Let them try all their works of nature, whatever might do them any good; when he saw all these would stand you in no stead, then, saith he, he sendeth his Son into the world. When they had tried all in vain, then there was a fulness of season. 'God now,' saith he, ver. 30, 'commandeth all men everywhere to repent.'

I will back this with another scripture; it is 1 Cor. i. 21. He had left the world, the Gentiles, to their philosophy, (the 'wisdom of the world,' he calleth it, ver. 20,) to find out the way to be saved. Where is the wisdom of this world? You philosophers, where are you? 'God,' saith he, 'hath made foolish the wisdom of this world.' All the light that nature hath, how made he it foolish? 'After that,' saith he, ver. 21, 'the world by wisdom knew not God,'—I will try you, whether by that wisdom I gave you by nature you will come to know me, I will turn nature every way. Mark now, 'After that,' saith he, when through their corrupt wisdom they did abuse that light God gave them, and instead of knowing God, worshipped idols, 'it pleased God by the foolishness of preaching to save them that believe' among the Gentiles; to send Christ, and by the preaching of the gospel to save these poor Gentiles, after they had tried all ways. So that it was the fulness of season every way.

I will but add one scripture more, and so I will leave it. It was fit that all men should corrupt their ways to the full before the Messiah came. As they should try all ways how they could grope after God, and pervert all the wisdom and light God gave them, so to be corrupted to the uttermost; for then the physician comes most seasonable to administer physic, when the disease is at the height. Read but the 14th and the 53d Psalms, and read the last verse of both. The Apostle quoteth both those two psalms in Rom. iii. 14, to shew that all mankind was corrupt. 'The fool hath said in his heart, There is no God. Corrupt they are, and have done abominable iniquity; they are altogether become filthy; there is none that doth good, no, not one; their throat is an open sepulchre,' &c. What followeth? 'Oh that the Redeemer would come out of Zion!' That is the last verse of those psalms. When David, by the spirit of prophecy, foresaw that all men should corrupt their ways, that they were all full of wickedness, and that the world could never be saved of themselves, and that they had tried all sort of ways to help themselves, and all in vain—then, 'Oh that the Redeemer would come out of Zion!' Now is the time for the desire of all nations, the Redeemer longed for, to come; he speaks it upon occasion of the universal corruption of all mankind. Here was a fulness of season, when God sent his Son into the world to gather in one both Jew and Gentile.

So now you see what is meant by fulness of time, and by fulness of season. Fulness of time is, when all the times appointed by God were run out, fulfilled. Fulness of season is, when there was the fulness of season for the Jews, that were to be a child grown to age; for the Gentiles, when they had all corrupted their ways, then it was a fit season for the Messiah to come. And that is the *first*.

But, *secondly*, What is meant by *dispensation;* εἰς οἰκονομίαν, *in*, or *for*, the dispensation of the fulness of times? The truth is, to read it *for* is more genuine and more natural; and what is the meaning of it? Some interpret it, 'in the dispensation of times,'—that is, say they, time wisely dispensed. God is the steward of time, and he did wisely dispense it; he gave every age a portion, and in the end brought forth this fulness of time wherein he dispenseth his Son. But I take it, it is not so much meant of the dispensation of times properly taken, of times ordered, although that is a true meaning of it; but it is taken metaphorically—the fulness of time is said to have a dispensation, a new dispensation; which new dispensation is to gather all things in one. The latter days, when Christ came into the world, it should have a new business, a new dispensation; there should be a new administration of those times, to begin from that time and continue to the end of the world.*

We know that *time* is said to do that which is done in time; as, for example, you find in Scripture a day is said *to bring forth*, so here it is said that *time doth dispense.* He compareth it to a steward; as in other places he compareth it to a womb, or a mother, so here to a steward that hath a dispensation. It is not meant of *dispensatio temporis*, so much as *dispensatio rerum*, of things in time. In the 6th verse of the Epistle of Jude, the great day of the Lord is expressed thus—'The judgment of the great day.' Why, the great day is not the judge. It is called the judgment of that day because it is done in that day. So here, 'the dispensation of the fulness of time' is not the dispensation of time properly taken, the ordering of time, though that is included; but it is meant the *business of time.* So that the scope is this—that God did appoint that the latter days, which is meant the fulness of time, from the time that Christ was born, and so on; he intended this to be the dispensation, the business, the administration of the world from that time, to gather all together in one.

It agreeth with what the Apostle saith, Heb. i. 1. 'God,' saith he, did 'at sundry times, and in divers manners, speak in times past unto our fathers by the prophets; he hath in these last days spoken unto us by his Son.' There is a new business, a new dispensation of things belonging to the fulness of time, to the latter days, from the time of Christ. He beginneth to alter the dispensation of himself to his Church; he turneth the Jewish church into Christian, out of one nation to another; he turneth all the types of the law into his Son, for his Son is nothing but the types of the law really expressed. This is now the dispensation of the fulness of time; he makes that the business of the last age, to send his Son into the world, to make

* *See* Jackson, Book vii. p. 42.

him the head of his Church visible; whom angels shall acknowledge, whom all things that are in heaven and in earth shall come into, that are his elect, both Jews and Gentiles. This was, saith he, reserved for the fulness of time, to be the business of the latter age. This is the meaning of it.

Obs. 1.—I will come to an observation or two, and so end. You see, my brethren, that there was a fulness of time when Christ came into the world; the world stayed long first, it stayed four thousand years. Learn this observation from it, *That if you wait for a great mercy, you must have many times and days run out before the fulness of time cometh to have it.* You cannot have a greater instance; for how long did the world stay for Christ? Four thousand years, as I said before. Thou art a poor soul that hast waited for Christ long to come into thy heart; how many years hast thou waited? The world waited four thousand years to have Christ come into it. It is the greatest mercy thou art capable of to have Christ come into thy heart; he is well worthy thy waiting for then. It is no argument that he will not come because he stays long; for should the world have argued, that because he stayed two parts of the three, therefore he would not come at all? No; great mercies are long a-coming, for the Messiah was so. The breaking up of God's heart, of the great design, of all the treasures there, you see it was hid in himself from the beginning of the world for so many thousand years. That is the first observation.

Obs. 2.—The second is this, *That God may let men go on in sin long, and give them Christ too, for all that.* You see, God let the world go on in sin, try all ways to help themselves, let all the world corrupt their own ways; he did it for a long time, and at last in the fulness of time sent his Son. Thou mayest try all ways; try duties, try what thou canst, how far corrupt nature may go, and God may give thee Christ at last. He did so by the world; after that by their wisdom they knew not God, he sent his Son, made of a woman. When God hath given thee light, and thou hast tried a thousand ways, thy duties, and this and that, to get Christ, and thou hast set up a ladder to heaven, to get Christ this way and that way,—after thou hast tried all things, he sends Christ into thy heart; when thy case is desperate, when thy heart is forlorn, then Christ cometh.

Obs. 3.—There is a third observation, that I will but mention; it is this, *That God is the Lord of all time.* He appointeth the fulness of times.

SERMON XIII.

In whom also we have obtained an inheritance, being predestinated according to the purpose of him who worketh all things after the counsel of his own will, &c.—VER. 11–14.

I WILL give you, first, the general scope of the words; and, secondly, I shall open them unto you particularly.

First, for the general scope of ver. 11–14, it is to apply all that he had doctrinally said in the first ten verses. He had spoken of predestination, of adoption to glory or an inheritance, of redemption, of vocation, and of gathering together all in one. Of these things he had discoursed in general, in a doctrinal way, from the 3d verse to the 11th. Now he beginneth particularly to apply all these; for in the opening of them you shall perceive there is nothing almost he had delivered doctrinally but he applieth and comforteth the people of God with it.

He had said that God had intended to gather all in heaven and all in earth to himself; that is the last thing spoken to in the 10th verse. To apply this to things in heaven there was no need, for he was not a preacher to angels, to speak directly unto them; therefore he applieth it only unto things on earth. All things on earth are divided into Jew and Gentile. First, therefore, he applieth it unto the Jews; 'in whom we,' saith he, 'have obtained an inheritance, that we should be to the praise of his glory, who first trusted in Christ.' Here are the Jews, whom God called first; we apostles, we Jews. Then he applieth it unto the Gentiles, and that under the Ephesians whom he wrote to: 'in whom ye also trusted,' ver. 13, 'after that you heard the word of truth,' &c.

He had spoken of a great gathering into one in Christ. Let us Jews, saith he, and apostles comfort ourselves, we have a part in it; and the Ephesians and the Gentiles, comfort yourselves, ye have a part in it too, (as you shall hear that the word signifieth by and by.) So much for the general scope.

Secondly, Now to open the words particularly; and first to begin with the application that he makes to the Jews in the 11th and 12th verses. The first word that we meet withal to be opened is this, 'in whom we have obtained an inheritance;' so it is translated, and rightly translated too; but I shall give you somewhat a larger meaning of it, which they that are scholars do well know agreeth with the meaning of the word; for I profess this rule and principle in opening of the Word, (though there be a more eminent scope of one thing than another,) yet to take in the most comprehensive meaning that can be given of things; for the Holy Ghost hath vast aims in writing of the Scripture.

'Εκληρώθημεν, that is the word here which is translated 'we have obtained an inheritance.' To open this word to you; there are two things to be opened concerning it.

The first is, what the word cometh from and importeth.

The second is, the kind of the verb, for it is a verb; I shall make it plain by and by to the easiest capacity.

That which is contained in the substance of the word, for the signification of it, is this. The word κλῆρος, which it cometh from, noteth out, first, having a *part* or a *portion* in a thing. I shall give you clear Scripture for every signification I give you of it. It noteth out, first, I say, having a part or a portion in a thing, being partaker with others of the same thing. That is the first signification of the word κλῆρος, and so it cometh in fitly here. He had spoken of gathering all things in heaven and in earth in one, in Christ: 'In whom we,' saith he, 'have a part;' in this Christ, in whom all are gathered; let us comfort ourselves, we have a part. That is the first. I shall give you a scripture where the word κλῆρος, whence this word cometh, is taken for a part, a portion in common. Read Acts viii. 21; speaking of Simon Magus, 'Thou hast no part or portion,' or lot or portion. It is the same word that this word cometh of.

Obs.—Now, my brethren, what is the observation from hence? Do but ask your own hearts; you have heard of this great gathering in the 10th verse; have you a part in it? have you a portion in it? You are to apply the word as you go; you see the Apostle doth so. When he had spoken of this general gathering of all things in Christ, now he cometh to apply it; 'in whom we have a part,' saith he; in whom ye also have a part, saith he. Hast thou a part in it? Let me ask thee the question; ask thine own heart the question. Oh, to be found not to have a share in this great gathering, what a misery will it be! That is the first thing it signifieth, a part or portion.

In the second place, it signifieth a part or portion of an *inheritance*. The word κλῆρος is often used for an inheritance, as Acts xxvi. 18, where he saith, 'an inheritance among them that are sanctified.' Therefore our translators well translate it, 'in whom also we have obtained an inheritance.'

In the third place, the word κλῆρος is taken for a *lot*. Inheritances, you know, use to go by lot. The Jews' inheritances were divided by lot; so Num. xxxiv. 13, 'This is the land which ye shall inherit by lot;' therefore it is called the 'lot of the inheritance,' Num. xxxvi. 3, and in many other scriptures.

Here, then, are three significations of this word. Here is, first, a part or portion; which part or portion is an inheritance; which inheritance cometh by lot. The word ἐκληρώθημεν doth imply all these: that is, in whom we have a part and portion; an inheritance annexed to that portion; and it cometh to us by lot. These three things are included in the signification of the word.

Now, my brethren, it is a word of a passive signification, and it implieth that we are passive in obtaining it; it is not a thing we seek for, but it is cast upon us. We have a word in the English, we say a man is disinherited; that is a passive word; there is no English word that shall answer it, to say a man is *inherited*, but he is endowed with an inheritance; he seeks not for it, it is cast upon him. Therefore in that place, Acts xxvi. 18, it is called receiving an inheritance; 'that they may receive,' saith he, 'an inheritance with those that are sanctified.' The word here used in this text (saith Beza) is used of magistrates that were chosen by lot to their places; even as Saul was chosen king by lot, so do we obtain this inheritance, a part or portion in Christ by a kind of lottery: it was not a thing we deserved, it was a thing came to us we never dreamed of. It was not so much as sought for by us; the word here is a mere passive word, it was cast upon us; we found a share in Christ before we were aware, as it were, not thinking of it. Not but God awakeneth men first, but they do no more towards it, they know no more of it, till God takes them and works upon their hearts, than a man asleep doth for the obtaining of an inheritance which is bestowed on him.

Obs.—What is the observation hence? This, *You have heaven cast upon you, you that are believers, as it were by lot.* Poor souls, you come hither to church, and here you put yourselves upon God's lottery; and you do well. What is the reason that a poor servant goeth away with Christ in her heart? She hath a draw for it, and she draweth eternal life; it is cast upon her. Ladies come here; here come men and women of great quality; perhaps they go away without it. It is cast upon men by lot. The greatest work that ever God did is to convert souls, and he carries it so as if he did it the most casually. You know the most casual thing in the world is a lot. A lot, you know, is a thing carried by a secret providence, for so he saith, Prov. xvi. 33, 'The lot is cast into the lap, but the whole disposing of it is of the Lord.' Here you come, and you are all cast into the bag of the Church, and God, by his secret providence, throws and casteth heaven upon thee, and letteth others go. Poor Zaccheus climbs up upon a tree (for he was a little man) to see Christ: 'Come down,' saith Christ, 'this day salvation is come to thine house.' Go, saith he, into the highways, and bring in the beggars; take whom you can find. God had predestinated them, yet it is carried so as if it came to them by lot; even as Saul, that went to seek his father's asses, and before he cometh home he was anointed king of Israel. 'What did ye go out to see?' saith Christ to John Baptist's hearers, 'a reed shaken with the wind?' They went out to see a novelty when they went to hear John; to see a reed shaken with the wind, or to see some great man clothed in gorgeous apparel, just as men go out to see shows; but yet John turned the hearts of the children to the fathers, turned many of their souls to God, that went thus out for other ends. Even thus God, I say, by a kind of lottery casteth heaven upon men; they obtained an inheritance by lot.

Now, my brethren, if you ask how and when it was that they came to have a part and portion in Christ; in whom we have obtained a lot, a portion, and an inheritance? Then, when they were converted and turned unto God; then it was that they came to have a right and portion in Christ and in this inheritance. It is not said expressly in the text, but the coherence carrieth it strongly. Why? For, first, he saith, they were 'predestinated' by God, that 'works all things by the counsel of his own will.' How came they to have it? Not simply by predestination, but by a work which was the fruit of predestination, and by a work of grace; therefore many interpreters translate the word here *vocati*, we were called to an inheritance. Then, secondly, he mentioneth faith: 'We,' saith he, 'did obtain this inheritance, who first trusted in Christ.' So now, when they began to trust in Christ, then they began to have a part and portion in this lot. Then, thirdly, when he applies this ἀπὸ τοῦ κοινοῦ to the Ephesians, ver. 13, 'In whom ye also had a part and portion in him,' (for that is the best reference of the words,) 'after ye heard the word of truth, the gospel of your salvation, and believed,' &c. So that then it is we come to have a part, and a portion, and right to this inheritance, when we are savingly converted and turned to God. That is the Apostle's scope, and is as if he had said, When we were converted, and ye were converted, then both ye and we came to have a part and portion in this gathering universal, and in this inheritance.

I will give you a scripture or two to back this. The first is Acts xxvi.

18. Christ from heaven speaks there, that he would send Paul to preach to the Gentiles, 'to open their eyes, and to turn them from darkness to light,'—here is conversion mentioned, you see; 'from the power of Satan unto God, that they might receive forgiveness of sins, and an inheritance'—that they might receive it, and obtain it by being thus turned—'among them that are sanctified by faith in him.' Mark, when they were turned, when men believe, when they begin to trust in Christ, as he saith here of the Jews, ver. 12; when after they have 'heard the gospel of salvation,' they believe, as he saith of the Gentiles, ver. 13; when they are called and sanctified, then it may be said that they began to receive or obtain this inheritance, though they were predestinated to it before. My brethren, you cannot without conversion either have a right to this inheritance, neither can you be made fit to be made partakers of it. In that place, Acts viii., where he speaks to Simon Magus, (Simon Magus lay still in sin, he was a carnal wretch;) 'Repent,' saith he; 'thou hast neither part nor lot in this matter.' He doth not say that he might not have for time to come. What reason doth he give why he had no part for the present? 'For thy heart is not right in the sight of God; repent therefore.' He doth not say but he might have: Thou that art yet still in thy unregenerate estate, thou that hast not obtained a lot, a part and portion, yet thou mayest have; 'repent therefore,' saith he, 'of this thy wickedness, and pray God, if perhaps the thought of thine heart may be forgiven thee;' and if once he repented, then he should come to have a part in this inheritance and in this Christ, and in being gathered together in one, with all things else, in heaven and in earth.

Obs.—From hence you see, to give you an observation upon it, what it is that giveth you a part and portion in the inheritance with the children of God; it is being called, it is having faith wrought in you, it is being sanctified; for by all these are you gathered to Christ as your head. 1 Pet. i. 3, 'Who hath begotten us again to an inheritance,' saith he, (those are his words.) You must be begotten again before you have right to this inheritance, before you can 'receive an inheritance among those that are sanctified;' so you heard out of the Acts. I will give you but one scripture more to convince you of it, and it is a parallel place to this; it is Col. i. 12, 'Giving thanks to the Father, who hath made us meet to partake,' to have a lot, to have a share, 'in the inheritance of the saints in light.' What is it that makes you meet? It is being holy. Why? Because it is an inheritance of the saints, and an inheritance in light; and while thy heart is carnal and walketh in darkness, thou canst never come to have a part and portion in this matter. In whom, therefore, saith the Apostle, (here is the sum of all,) we have a part or portion, an inheritance strangely cast upon us, we know not how; we never looked after it, it was cast upon us by lot. How? By giving us faith, by calling us, by turning us to God; and by means of that we are come to have a part and portion in this inheritance. So you have the first word explained, 'In whom we have obtained a lot,' a portion, an inheritance by lot, by being called, and sanctified, and renewed.

Now, the Apostle, when he had thus applied this for their and his own comfort, leadeth them to consider the fountain. For, my brethren, we are apt to think with ourselves, we have grace wrought in us, therefore we have interest in Christ, and in him a part and portion in this inheritance, and so look no further. But what doth the Apostle? He leadeth us up to the eternal love of God, (I pray, think of that;) for what followeth? 'In whom having obtained an inheritance—according to his purpose who worketh all things after the counsel of his own will.' Look to the fountain of all this, saith he; it is your being predestinated, and this from an everlasting purpose; and although it came to you, as it were, by a lot and by chance, and you were as far off from being called, when you were called, as any men in the world; but yet, saith he, it was a lot guided by God's eternal predestination. 'Being predestinated,' saith he, 'according to purpose.'

I shall open this a little. I handled predestination before, therefore I will not speak of it now; only this, remember that he speaks this of the Jews and apostles, for he applieth this to them: 'In whom,' saith he, 'we that first trusted in Christ have a portion, being predestinated.' You may read in the next verses, where he goes on to make the like application to the Gentiles, that he doth not mention predestination in that his application to them. He speaks of their calling indeed, but he doth not speak of their predestination; not but that they were predestinated, but why doth he choose to mention it in his speech to the Jews only? The truth is this, they had been the people of God, and had it by promise; they had God and heaven entailed to them; Abraham was their father. Yea, but saith the Apostle, for all this it was God's eternal love, it was his predestination, that was the cause of singling us out. And he mentioneth it not in his speech to the Gentiles, though he intendeth the same thing to them; for if the Jews and apostles had it by predestination, the Gentiles, that were without the promise and 'without God in the world,' had it from the same fountain much more. And he mentioneth it to the Jews, because election carried it away even amongst them, and election, the force of difference it puts amongst men was seen most amongst them, because, I say, they were the people of God by promise. Take two scriptures for it. First, Rom. xi. 7. You shall see there that he makes the calling of the Jews to depend especially upon election. 'What then? Israel,' saith he, 'hath not obtained that which he seeketh for,' (multitudes of the people of Israel did not;) 'but the election hath obtained it;' it is the elect amongst Israel that have obtained it. Do not think, saith he, it cometh to you by your father Abraham, as they thought; it is the election that obtained it. Secondly, Rom. ix. 11. He speaks there of Esau and Jacob; he saith the purpose of God according to election was it that stood. It was said to the mother of both, that 'the elder should serve the younger.' Election, you see, carries it among the Jews; therefore his mentioning of predestination here cometh in seasonably, for they would have thought the promise to their fathers would have carried it. No, saith he, 'being predestinated.'

But why 'predestinated according to his *purpose* who works all things after the counsel of his own will?' There is an opinion in the world that there is a twofold predestination; that God dealeth with some men according to purpose, as he did with the apostles—converteth them infallibly, and they persevere. They are, they say, chosen according to purpose. But others, God dealeth with them according to their works. It is a truth, God deals with none but according to their works; but yet he doth not predestinate men to be saved according to works, for if he did, he should predestinate them for their works. It is not therefore brought in here by way of distinction, to shew that there is one predestination according to works, and if you walk thus and thus then God chooseth you to life; and another predestination which is peremptory. But all the scope is this, to shew the stability of it, to shew that God's choosing of men is stable, and firm, and unalterable; therefore it is called predestination according to purpose.

For this look into Rom. ix. 11, the place I quoted even now; saith he 'that the purpose according to election might stand'—that is, that it might be unalterable; join *purpose* and *stand* together. What God doth purpose is immutable. 2 Cor. i. 17, saith Paul, (who was but a creature,) I promised, saith he, to come to you, to take you in my way as I came out of Macedonia. Paul did not come. 'When I therefore,' saith he, 'was thus minded, did I use lightness? or the things that I purpose, do I purpose according to the flesh, that with me there should be yea yea, and nay nay?' No, saith he, what I purpose, that I will perform. Why will Paul do it? Because he would have the gospel receive no prejudice; I preach the truth, and I would be true of my word; therefore, saith he, if I promise a thing, and purpose a thing, I will do it. Will Paul do thus? then God will do it much more; having predestinated us according to his purpose, it shall stand then;—'that the purpose of God according to election,' saith he, 'might stand;' so the word is in that Rom. ix. 11. It signifieth, therefore, the immutability of God's counsel; that is meant by being *predestinated according to his purpose.*

I come now to the last thing in the verse; 'who works all things according to the counsel of his own will.' This is a third thing here in the words. For the coherence of it, how it cometh in: it cometh in, first, as a reason why God had converted them; or, rather, why their conversion, and their faith, and their obtaining an inheritance, was by predestination. It is a reason that will convince any man, that they, having obtained a part and portion in so great a business as heaven was, having grace wrought in their hearts that did interest them in that inheritance, that it must needs be by a foreknowledge, by a decree of God. Why? Because, saith he, God works *all things else* according to the counsel of his own will; therefore certainly this. The reason is very strong; he would convince them that God did work grace in their hearts as the fruit of predestination, he would convince them that God had given them heaven, which came to them by lot, he had done it by a set decree, from everlasting. Why? For, saith he, 'he works all things after the counsel of his own will;' he plotted every thing beforehand, therefore certainly this; he hath done every thing advisedly, nothing falleth out but what he had laid the plot before. If he had a hand, saith he, in any thing, or in all things that ever he did, he must needs have a hand in working grace in men's hearts, for it is more than all. If he bestowed any thing upon any creature,—if he hath given the kingdoms of this world unto men, and that he doth according to his will among the inhabitants of the earth, as it is said, Dan. iv., then certainly they that have the kingdom of heaven promised, have it by his decree. Here lieth the reason, and thus he argueth: because God hath a hand in all things, therefore he hath a hand in the conversion of men, therefore he hath a hand in bestowing of heaven upon men. And that is the first way; it cometh in as a reason of what was said before.

It cometh in, secondly, to shew how great a power it was that wrought grace in their hearts, and how much God's heart was in it when he did it. He hath shewed as much power, saith he, in working grace in your hearts, as in working all things else; his heart is as much in this thing as in doing all things else. He doth put them altogether, you see.

How do you prove that to be the scope of such a phrase as this?

I will give you a scripture for it; it is Phil. iii. 21; he speaks there of changing of our vile bodies, which requireth a mighty power, to make them like Christ's glorious body. How doth he express the greatness of this power? By just such a phrase as this here: 'who shall change our vile body,' saith he, 'that it may be fashioned like unto his glorious body.' How? 'According to the working whereby he is able even to subdue all things unto himself.' This phrase cometh in to shew that God putteth forth the same power in changing our vile bodies and making them like the body of Christ—the same power I say, and no less than that power—that must subdue all things, that created the world, that ruineth the world in the end, and annihilateth or bringeth down kingdoms, and doth everything. Well, you have grace wrought in your hearts here; how had you it wrought? By him, saith he, that worketh all things; no less power than that which goeth to work all things, goeth to work this; the same proportion of power that goeth to work all things else, goeth to work grace.

So now you have the general scope how these words come in.—To open the words particularly to you a little, for I would fain make an end of this verse—

First, The word here that is translated 'worketh,' signifieth to work effectually; 'He worketh all things effectually,' that is the meaning of it; he doth it according to the counsel of his will, and that will shall stand, it shall not be resisted; whatsoever he will do he doth effectually; you have it Ps. cxxxv. 6, 'The Lord is great; whatsoever the Lord pleased, that did he in heaven, and in earth, in the seas, and in all deep places.' And Isa. xlvi. 10, he saith, the counsel of the Lord shall stand.

In the second place, he saith, 'He worketh all things;' what all things? I will not meddle with sin, what hand God hath in it, though the very same phrase is used of it, Acts iv. 28. The crucifying of Christ, the greatest sin in the world, it is said nothing was done in it but what his hand and counsel determined; there was both counsel and hand in it,—that is the expression there,—at least for the ordering of all the circumstances of it. I only mention that; and consider all things else, God worketh all things effectually, his hand casteth all things. Doth there a hair come off your heads? A hair is a small matter; it is by the Father, Matt. x. 30. Doth a man shoot an arrow, and there is one behind the bush, and he killeth him? It is God that delivereth that man into his hand, Exod. xxi. 13. He ordereth the thing that is done by chance, and doth it effectually. God foretold that Ahab should be slain when he went out to battle; yet the text saith plainly that the arrow that did kill him was shot by chance: 'A certain man drew a bow at a venture,' so you have it, 1 Kings xxii. 34, 'and smote the king of Israel between the joints of the harness,' whereof he died; it was a mere adventure, but God guided it effectually, for he had prophesied that Ahab should not go home from that battle.

Things that are of the merest chance, God works them all. When Nebuchodonozor went to destroy Jerusalem, it was the greatest design that could be, a thing foretold seventy years before, in Hezekiah's time. You shall find in Ezek. xxi. 20, 21, it was a mere matter of chance that Nebuchodonozor went thither. The prophet there describeth the king of Babylon's journey with his army; he describeth his coming to Jerusalem, and how doth he describe it? 'Son of man,' saith he, ver. 19, 'appoint thee two ways, that the sword of the king of Babylon may come: both twain shall come forth out of one land: and choose thou a place, choose it at the head of the way to the city.' There were two ways; Nebuchodonozor came out with his army,—he did not resolve whither he would go; God had foretold he should go to Jerusalem,—he cometh out, I say, with his army, and he cometh to the head of two ways, one to go to Egypt, (as some,) another to go to Jerusalem. He was undetermined; what doth he do? He goeth and useth divination. 'The king of Babylon,' saith he, ver. 21, 'stood at the parting of the way, the head of the two ways, to use divination: he made his arrows bright,' or, as some read it, he did, by mingling arrows together, cast a lot which way he should go; 'he consulted with images, he looked in the liver.' He opened beasts to see whether there was good fortune, as some call it, to go on the right hand or on the left. All this was foretold that he should do. Who knew what should be in the liver of that beast, and that his soothsayer should guide his way to Jerusalem, and assure him of good fortune in that way rather than in the other? The text saith, ver. 22, 'At his right hand was the divination for Jerusalem.' All his lots, shuffling of arrows, looking into the liver, all this did cast him to go to Jerusalem, and God had foretold this long before. You see he works all things, the most casual things that are, by his own appointment. 'The lot is cast into the lap, but the whole disposing thereof is of the Lord,' Prov. xvi. 33.

Come to the wills of men, they are more ticklish things than matters of chance are; for what say men? We have a liberty, we can do what we will. But what saith the Apostle? Say not, 'To-day or to-morrow we will go to such a city;' but, 'If the Lord will, we will do this or that,' James iv. 13, 15. But to give you an instance for it, that God ruleth the wills of men, for I cannot instance in many things; I will give you, to me, one of the greatest instances the Scripture affordeth. It is Exod. xxxiv. 24. God commandeth them that at three set times in the year all the men should appear before the Lord in Jerusalem. Now you know the Jews did live in the midst of their enemies; and might the enemies say, Now all the men are gone up out of the country to Jerusalem, we will go and destroy the women and children; this they might plot and order it many years before, what should hinder them? Why, saith God, go up three times in the year, and I will order it so that 'none shall desire thy land.' If God had not a strong hand upon the wills of men that he can turn them which way he pleaseth, how could he make that promise beforehand that they should not desire their land? If God did not effectually rule the wills of men, the inclinations of men's spirits, when they had all opportunity, all the reason in the world, all advantages, yet that they should not have a desire to the land,—how could God, I say, undertake this, unless he did rule the wills of men? My brethren, I profess I would not serve this God, if he did not rule the wills of men in this world. Why? Because I could have no temporal promise fulfilled; for most temporal promises depend upon men's will. If he did not rule the hearts of all the men in the world, of kings, of parliaments, what a confusion would this world run into? How could I sue out any promise that God makes, wherein I have to do with the wills of men, as in most we have? Therefore certainly he ruleth, and ruleth effectually, things wherein men are most free; he doth either take away desire, or put in desire; turns their hearts to hate his people, or, on the other side, gives his people 'favour in their eyes,' as the expression is; it is just such another instance, Exod. xi. 3. When the people of Israel had gone and brought ten plagues upon them, when all their first-born were slain; here was a fair way made for favour, was there not? That they should come after all this, and say, I pray, give us your jewels. What! after you have done us all this mischief? Yet, saith the text, God gave them favour in their eyes, and they gave them their jewels of silver, and their jewels of gold, and raiment, Exod. xii. 35.

What a mighty thing is this in God's ruling the wills of men! Doth not this God, think you, work effectually in all things, when he ruleth the most ticklish things of all, the wills of men, and so the hearts of kings? I need not instance. Now, my brethren, if God thus doth work all things, certainly then he works grace much more, when he turns the will to believe. If he put a desire in you, if he take away a desire, it doth not lie in the counsel of your own will, saith he. There are those that think grace is wrought by the counsel of man's will. God indeed giveth me power to believe, or not to believe, and then the counsel of my will casteth it. No! it is according to the counsel of his will, not according to the counsel of thy will; as you know the Apostle saith, he works both the will and the deed. If he brings forth the will into the deed of all things else, much more in the matter of grace, whereby you come to 'obtain an inheritance among those that are sanctified.'

I should shew you why counsel of will likewise is attributed to God. I shall be too long if I go on to open that,. I will therefore but make an observation or two, and so I will conclude.

Obs. 1.—Doth God work all things according to his will? Then give up thy ways to him. 'It is not in man,' saith Jeremiah, 'to direct his steps.' It is God that must direct them for thee, for he works all things according to his will. If any man in the world, if his understanding and will were a rule to mine, and I knew he were infallible, I would certainly go give up all my ways to what he saith. As you say you must be ruled by him that bears the purse, you must be ruled by him that bears the understanding. Certainly, if any man have an infallible understanding, I will be ruled by him. God hath; he works all things, and all effectually by the counsel of his own will; therefore in all thy ways give up thyself to him.

Obs. 2.—Again, in the second place, (I cannot prosecute many,) God works all things according to the counsel of his own will. It is an inference that Job makes of it, chap. xxiii. 13, 14. You shall find there, that Job professeth his sincerity, how fearful he was of offending God: 'My foot,' saith he, ver. 11, 'hath held his steps, his way have I kept, and not declined;' he obeyed him, he did not decline the least from his ways; 'neither have I gone back,' saith he, 'from the commandment of his lips: I have esteemed the words of his mouth more than my necessary food.' What is the reason of all this? It followeth, according to the coherence, as best interpreters give it, 'He is in one mind, and who can turn him? and what his soul desireth, even that he doeth; he performeth the thing that is appointed for me, and many such things are with him.' Saith he, I considered with myself this, that I were as good be subject to his will, for he will have his will upon me; I cannot resist his will, I were as good submit; 'he works all things according to the counsel of his will;' he performeth all things that are 'appointed for me;' he is of one mind, and I cannot turn him. I must therefore comply with him; hence it was that I have not gone from the commandment of his lips. I thought it was best to yield to him, and to give up my will to his. It is a strange argument, and you see the Scripture enforceth it.

SERMON XIV.

In whom also we have obtained an inheritance, being predestinated according to the purpose of him who worketh all things according to the counsel of his own will: that we should be to the praise of his glory, who first trusted in Christ. In whom ye also trusted, after that you heard the word of truth, the gospel of your salvation, &c.—VER. 11–14.

THE scope of these verses I shewed you in my last discourse to be this: An application of all that which he had doctrinally delivered about predestination, vocation, and the like benefits,—an application of them, with some interlacings of what was not said before,—unto both the Jews and the Gentiles. Unto the Jews, or rather the apostles put for all the Jews, themselves being Jews, in the 11th and 12th verses: 'In whom we have obtained an inheritance who first trusted in Christ.' And, secondly, unto the Gentiles in the 13th verse: 'In whom ye also,' Ephesians, speaking to them in the name of all the Gentiles, as speaking of himself and the other of the apostles in the name of all the Jews.

His application unto himself and the rest of the apostles, and so to the Jews, is in the 11th and 12th verses. I made entrance into them in my last discourse. The 11th verse containeth in it two particulars.

First, It sheweth what God had done for them, and that in *three things.*

Secondly, He illustrateth those three things which God had done for them, by a *general proposition,* whereof each particular in the one answereth to the other.

First, He sheweth what God had done for them in *three things;* he giveth them the comfort of three things.

1. By effectual calling of them, by sanctifying of them, and working faith in them, by their having trusted in him, they were interested in a glorious inheritance. 'In whom,' saith he, 'we have obtained'—namely, by this sanctification and faith, as I shewed you before—'an inheritance.'

2. He mentioneth the ground and the spring (he applieth that also, and brings it home to their hearts) of God's calling them, viz., predestination; we having 'obtained an inheritance, being predestinated.'

3. He mentioneth the immutability of God's predestinating them; it was 'according to his purpose.'

So much for what he sheweth God hath done for them before, of which he giveth them the comfort.

Secondly, He doth illustrate these things by a *general proposition,* which containeth three things in it, answerable to these three. 'In whom we have obtained an inheritance, being predestinated according to the purpose' (these are the three first particulars) 'of him who worketh all things according to the counsel of his own will.' I shewed the coherence of these latter words before. That which now I shall cast in is, that the apostle doth fit, and suit, and proportion this general proposition, *that God worketh all things according to the counsel of his own will,*—he fitteth it unto the particulars God had done for them. He had called them to obtain an inheritance, being predestinated according to his purpose.

The meaning is this: that by the same counsel of his will, and by the same power that he had wrought all things else, by the same power he had called them, and sanctified them, by which they had obtained an inheritance; and by the same counsel of his will he had predestinated them according to his purpose by the same wherewith he works all things else. He sheweth that the principle by which he works all things is the same principle by which he wrought grace in their hearts. First, in working all things, there is an omnipotent power, an efficacious hand; for he is said to work, ἐνεργεῖν, to work effectually; by the same power, saith he, did he work grace in your hearts. In the second place, all things that he doth work, he did contrive beforehand by his counsel; by the same counsel, saith he, he did predestinate. Then, thirdly, that which casteth all, according to his counsel, was his will; 'He works all things according to the counsel of his own will.' Why, according to that will, saith he, He hath predestinated you; 'He hath predestinated you according to his purpose,' namely of that will. So that now, *will* in the one answereth to the *purpose* in the other; and *counsel* in the one answereth to *predestination* in the other; for indeed predestination implieth an ordering, a disposing of things by counsel. And then, thirdly, his *working grace*, by which they were called, answereth to that *power* which he wrought all things by.

Here then, you see, there are three principles of God's working all things whatsoever he works, the salvation of men and all things else. Here is, first, an omnipotent power, which is *executionis*, as the thing that executeth and performeth all; he is said to work, and work effectually, so the word signifieth. Secondly, here is his will and the sovereignty of it, which is *imperationis*, that which giveth the command for a powerful execution. Thirdly, here is his wisdom, that is *directionis*, as that which giveth direction both to will and power. 'He works all things according to the counsel of his own will.'

And, first, for the *power of God* in working, which is the first thing briefly to be explained; secondly, his *counsel;* and thirdly, the *counsel of his will.* I shall speak briefly of all these three. He works all things by an omnipotent power; and by counsel; and by the counsel of his own will.

First, For the power wherewith he worketh all things. The first thing I shewed about it before was this, that God hath an effectual hand in all things. I went over things natural, things moral, things contingent, the wills of men, and the like; I shall repeat nothing now. That is the first thing that the text affordeth, that God works, and works effectually; he hath a hand in everything.

The second thing concerning his power that the text affordeth is, that God's power is limited in his workings by his will. He doth not work all things that he can work; 'Unto thee,' saith Christ, Mark xiv. 36, 'all things are possible.' It is possible, saith he, that this cup should pass from me, and that men should be saved another way; but his power did not work this, it was limited by his will; so you know that Christ saith, 'Thy will be done.' God can, saith John, Matt. iii. 9, raise out of these stones that you tread upon sons unto Abraham; he never did it, but do it he could. God doth not shew himself omnipotent by doing all he can do, but everything that he doth do, he sheweth an almighty power in it. Therefore divines use to say, that God, though he is omnipotent, yet he is not omnivolent; though he can do all things infinitely more than he hath done, yet he doth not will to do all things that he is able, for his power is limited by his will; so saith the text: 'He worketh all things according to the counsel of his will.' 'If thou wilt,' saith he, 'thou canst make me clean,' Matt. viii. 2. His power was able, but whether his will had determined his power to do it or not, that he knew not.

The third thing which this text holdeth forth concerning his power is this, that whatsoever God will do, that he doth effectually. 'He works all things according to the counsel of his will.' The meaning is, not only that all that he doth, he doth by counsel; but that all that his counsel and will decreeth, that he doth. 'My counsel shall stand,' saith he, Isa. xlvi. 10.

So much now for that first thing, his power; which are all bottomed full upon the text.

Secondly, The second is concerning *God's counsel* in working. You know counsel referreth to the understanding, to the judgment. It is a considering what one meaneth to do, how to do it, and to do it the best way and most wisely; that is properly counsel. There is something in counsel which is in man which we must not attribute unto God, and something in man which may be attributed to God; for we must cut off all imperfection in what we attribute to God. There are two things in counsel in a man. There is, first, a discourse and inquiry what is best; he setteth his reason a-work, and one thought cometh in after another. And then there is, secondly, a judgment, when he hath considered all, what is the best. Now the first part we must cut off from God; he doth not advise and deliberate as men do, to take this thing, or that thing, one after another, by way of inquiry into his mind. No, for 'known to God are all his works from eternity,' saith the Apostle, Acts xv. 18; as the word signifieth, 'he hath them all before him.'

How then is counsel attributed unto God?

Thus; that which is the result, that which ariseth in men's minds or judgments out of inquiry, a mature pitching upon what is best; this now, which is the perfection of counsel, which is the ripening and the maturity of it, this is attributed to God. This is *certum judicium*, a certain judgment of what is best to do. Thus God works all things according to his counsel. I will give you but one scripture for it; for we must still back everything with some parallel word, that in the mouth of two witnesses everything might be established. Isa. xxviii. 29; it is said there of God, that he is 'wonderful in counsel and excellent in working.' I cannot stand to open the coherence of the place, but it falleth in full to the business in hand. He is excellent in working, for whatsoever he willeth that he doth; and he is as wonderful in his counsel, for all that he doth is with the greatest ripeness of judgment, with the highest wisdom, that shall declare him as much to be God in the wise doing of it, as to declare he is God in the powerful doing of it. Thus you see in the second place what is meant by counsel.

Thirdly, Now then, in the third place, why is it said the *counsel of his will?* Here is a third principle, *his will;* and it is called the *counsel of his will*. I shall open it briefly. It implieth these particulars following:—

First, That God's will doth not pitch upon things blindly, but by an advised act; he knoweth what he doth, wittingly and willingly in all he doth; his will hath counsel joined with it.

It is said, secondly, to be the counsel of his own will, for so the text hath it, because he doth not go forth of himself for counsel; he neither doth regard the conveniency among the creatures one with another, but their conveniency depends upon his counsel. Men, when they counsel, look upon things; and as things are framed and fashioned, so they must frame their counsels; but with God it is otherwise, he frameth things according to the counsel of his own will, he adviseth with none: 'Who hath been his counsellor?' Rom. xi. 34.

In the third place, it is called the counsel of his own will, to shew that in casting whatsoever he meaneth to do, his will hath the supreme stroke. Still you shall find it in the Scripture, that all is attributed to his will; and observe the phrase here, it is not called the will of his counsel, but it is called rather the counsel of his will,—it is the observation of Catherinus and Musculus upon the place,—to shew the difference between man's will and God's. The law of man's will is still to be determined by the understanding, so that the will of a man is the will of his counsel. My brethren, when God considered whether he would make a world or no, the consultation was not whether it was best to make it or not to make it. Why? Because there was no best to God to do the one or the other; there is the greatest reason for it that can be, for it was all one to him whether he did it or no. What caused him then to do it? What did cast it? It was his will. His will setteth his counsel so to work, as it were, to do it the best way; but it is not his will being determined by his counsel as judging it best, for it was neither better one way nor other for God, for he standeth in need of no creature. So that in Scripture you have election attributed to his will, 'He hath mercy on whom he will;' you have creation attributed to his will, 'By thy will all things were created,' Rev. iv. 11.

But now, though his will had the casting of it clearly, and therein lieth the sovereignty and liberty of the will of God in his works *ad extra*, yet you will ask me, *How far did counsel attend his will?*

I answer in these particulars. First, God knew all that he could do, all that his power is able to do, and therefore did not pitch upon things that had a contradiction in them. As for example, that God should make a thing to be and not to be at the same time; his will did not pitch upon this, because his counsel dictated that they were not compatible; it was not fit for God to do. So likewise 'it is impossible for God to lie;' his understanding knew this, so his will did not pitch upon such a thing. Here is one act of counsel, he did not pitch upon things that have a contradiction in them.

In the second place, his counsel dictated to him, if I may so speak, that it was good to create, and to communicate himself to the creatures, to choose men to salvation, and that it is the property of goodness to communicate itself, and that it becometh goodness to do it. But yet still all this is not best, it is not best to God; we cannot say so; for he could be as happy without doing this as he is with doing of it; only I say his counsel said it was good.

Then, thirdly, if his will cometh to create and produce creatures, then wisdom dictates that it was best to do it the best way; if God will manifest himself, to do it to the uttermost; so will setteth counsel on work, or rather counsel presenteth to the will the utmost and best ways of glorifying of himself. Therefore, Heb. xi., you shall find there that all things that are made are said to be made of things not seen, namely, of God. 'By faith,' saith he, ver. 3, 'we understand that the worlds were framed by the word of God, so that things which are seen were not made of things that do appear.' The meaning is this, that his understanding did present to him models of worlds, as it doth to an artificer, if he will raise up a building, how to make it and contrive it. He made things out of things that did not appear, that were in his own mind,—the ideas, the mould, the pattern of things, such as men have in their heads when they make a house and the like; and he pitcheth upon what is best. And thus far now his counsel attends his will. If his will resolveth to create, to do a thing, then counsel is set a-work to do it the best way; although it may be said that God had other ways as good, for his wisdom is not limited to one world, or to the things that are or shall be.

To conclude with one scripture, and so pass off from this: Ps. civ. 24, 'Wonderful are thy manifold works; in wisdom hast thou made them all.' They are wonderful, and they are manifold, and he hath made them all in wisdom; and his wisdom sheweth itself to be as truly the wisdom of God, as his power shewed itself to be the power of God, in making them. And this is the subserviency or the concurrency that counsel hath with his will in working all things.

Obs. 1.—Now, my brethren, I should give you some observations from hence. I did anticipate some in my last, as namely this: If God works all things according to the counsel of his own will, you should not lean to your own will, nor to your own wisdom; give up yourselves fully unto God, as it is, Prov. xxiii. 4.

Obs. 2.—In the second place, more particularly, If God works grace by the same kind of counsel of his will, and by the same power that he works all things else, as the text plainly saith, then he works grace infallible; for we see he worketh other things infallible. 'Let there be light,' saith he, and there was light. Let there be light, saith he, in that man's soul, and there is light. He works in us the will and the deed; not only the power to will, but the will itself.

Obs. 3.—The third thing that I observed is this, That the same thing that cast it why he would work all things, it was his will, not as judging it best for him,—it was not following the dictates of his understanding, as always is in us,—but only he saw it was good so to do. So likewise, of his choosing men, this or that man, of predestinating you and you, (for so the coherence carrieth it,) it was merely his own will, his own goodness.

There is no reason why thou shouldst believe, and another not; no reason, I say, why God, having infinite things before him, should choose such and such; why he should take such and such of those he meant to make; why he should love such, and not others; there is no reason but his will. His counsel propounded that it was good to love these; but that it was better to love this man than that man, here his will determineth it. It is not the will of his counsel, but the *counsel of his will*. As when he came to create, (it is the comparison that Aquinas hath, and it is an exceeding good one,) Take, saith he, that first *chaos*, that lump of darkness, out of which God made all things; that out of this piece fire should be made, that that piece should go to make earth, that the other piece should go to make air; that such a piece of the element should make a tree, such a piece should make beasts, such fishes; that that dust should make a man, Adam, rather than other dust; there is no reason of it, it is his will. That of mankind, that nature of man should be assumed, that Jesus Christ hath now in heaven, it was his will. So, saith he, is it in election; for God works all things, not according to the will of his counsel, as judging this man better than that by an act of counsel; but it is the counsel of his will. But when he hath pitched his love upon these and these men, then counsel is set a-work indeed, to contrive all ways to shew love to them; and all the ways the wisdom of God takes, is but to vent that love that was in his heart. Therefore Christ is given to die, and you to fall into sin; there are a thousand contrivements that the counsel of his will had, to manifest the glory of his grace, and the riches of his love. —And so now I fall off from that, and come to the 12th verse.

That we should be to the praise of his glory, who first trusted in Christ.

Here are two things in this verse :—

1. Here are the *persons* whom he applieth this to, designed out with a special privilege. We, apostles and Jews, that had this privilege first to 'trust in Christ;' we, saith he, were thus predestinated and called, and have obtained an inheritance.

2. You have what ought to be the end, what is the duty that every man is obliged unto, that cometh unto these benefits, that is predestinated thus, and called thus. 'We should be,' saith he, 'to the praise of his glory.'

To begin with the latter, because it lieth first in the text. The coming in of these words, the coherence of them, is not so much to shew what was God's end in predestinating us, (that he had shewed before,) as what is the duty of every one that is predestinated; what this benefit should work upon their hearts; for here the apostle speaks by way of application; their duty is this, saith he, to 'be to the praise of his glory.'

I will not stand distinguishing *praise* and *glory;* I did it before, when I opened the 'praise of the glory of his grace.' Only first here; praise is all that God requireth. Ps. l., Wilt thou, saith he, offer to me the rams or the bullocks upon a thousand hills? They are all mine already; what do I care for them, I can make enough of them. Thou wilt offer God thy duties, what are they to him? What is it then that will please him? Saith he at the last verse, 'He that offereth praise, glorifieth me.' It is glory he would have, nothing takes God else. Do what you will, if you do not aim at the praise of his glory, it never pleaseth him. He turns away a chapman, that would have given him rivers of oil. What care I, saith he, for thy first-born, that is the fruit of thy body? Why, he would have glory. Nothing, I say, takes God else.

In the second place, observe, he doth not, as before, say, 'to the praise of the glory of his grace' only, he doth not limit it to that; but he saith, when he cometh to obedience, to the praise of his glory in the general. For though in our faith we do most magnify the glory of his free grace in the pardon of sin, which faith layeth hold upon; yet in obedience we should aim at all his glory, all the ways he can be glorified in. And he will have glory out of every thing you do. 'Whether you eat or drink, or whatsoever you do, do all to the glory of God,' 1 Cor. x. 31.

In the third place, observe this concerning it: he doth not say, 'to the praise of his glory,' by words and by thanksgiving only; but 'to *be* to the praise of his glory.' It is real things, things that have being, that God requireth. My meaning is this, that your being, all you are and have, should be to his glory, not only in word, so the force of the word will carry it: 'that we should *be*,' saith he, that all you are, that all you have, should be sacrificed and given up to God, 'to the praise of his glory.'

Now, though I might shew you how this is enforced from all the former, yet I should be too long. I will pass that by.—So much for the first thing.

Secondly, he cometh to *the persons to whom he applieth this*, designed out by a special privilege; namely, those 'who first trusted in Christ.' He hath predestinated us, called us, apostles and Jews, but to whom he vouchsafed this privilege, that we should first trust in Christ. He speaks, as I take it, especially of that *we*—that is, we apostles. Paul was an apostle; you know they were all Jews; but in their name and under them he meaneth all the Jews too that were believers. He applieth it to themselves first, and unto the Jews, as contained under them. As likewise, when he applieth it to the Ephesians, 'in whom ye also trusted,' he speaks but to the Ephesians only, but he meaneth all Gentiles. I speak this to reconcile two opinions of interpreters. Some say that the apostles are meant; others say that the Jews are meant. The apostles had the honour to be the first-fruits of the Christian church, of the church of the New Testament; and therefore, as Christ preached to them first, and called them first himself,—for so you know he did,—so when he prayeth for his church, how doth he pray? For the apostles first, and then for all them that 'shall believe on him through their word,' John xvii. 20. For the apostles were the first-fruits; therefore we are said to be 'built upon the foundation of the prophets and apostles,' Eph. ii. 20. They were laid as the first stones of this great building.

The word which we translate *trusted* is, in the original, and you may see it in your margins, *hoped;* 'who first hoped in Christ;' for, my brethren, hope is sometimes put for faith, as John v. 45, 'Moses, in whom ye trust;' in the original it is, 'in whom ye hope.' For the truth is this, I do not say the grace of hope is the foundation of faith, but it is most certain that a hopefulness *that it may be I,* founded upon the indefinite promise, is the foundation of faith. And, take the very apostles' faith, it was but at first a hoping in Christ; 'who first,' saith he, 'hoped in Christ.'

Now, the thing I would have you observe is this, that he mentioneth it as a privilege to be the first trusters or hopers in Christ, and he applieth it to the Jews and to the apostles. You shall see parallel scriptures fall in with this: Rom. i. 16, 'The gospel,' saith he, 'is the power of God to salvation to every one that believeth; to the Jew first,' mark! 'and also unto the Greek;' but to the Jew first. Take another place, Acts iii. 26. When Peter there first preacheth to the Jews, speaking of the resurrection of Christ, he saith, 'God, having raised up his Son Jesus, sent him unto you first, to bless you, in turning away every one of you from his iniquities.' The Jews, therefore, and the apostles, were the first that trusted in Christ; and then afterwards it was diffused from the Jews, by the apostles, unto all nations: 'Preach the gospel,' saith he, 'to every creature;' but 'to the Jew first;' they were to believe first—'who first trusted in him.'

I have wondered, when I considered this one thing, which will further open the text, that God should call so many Jews, and call them first,—for so he did, and there were multitudes of them, if you read the story of the Acts,—and after that cast off that nation. And why were they, when he meant to convert no more of them afterwards, to have this great privilege the apostle mentioneth here?

I will give you one reason of it. It is because they were the first-fruits of the Jews to be called afterwards in the fulness of time. Because God meant to call them afterward, as it is certain to me he meaneth to do, therefore he called so great a flush of them at first; and called them first, to shew that they shall be the elder brethren under the gospel, though they be cast off for so many hundreds of years. That which makes me think so is that which the Apostle saith, 1 Tim. i. 16; and I know them that interpret it as spoken of the Jews. Speaking of his own conversion, 'He shewed mercy,' saith he, 'to me first,' as one of the first-fruits of my nation, as in a type, (so the word is,) as in 'a pattern to them who should hereafter believe,' namely, to the Jews. They expound it particularly, as being a type of the conversion of his own nation; yea, and some have thought that in the same extraordinary way that he was called shall they be called too. So much now for the expounding of this—'who first trusted in Christ.'

Obs. 1.—I will give you an observation, and so pass off from it; and it is this, *That it is a great privilege, much to be valued by every Christian, to be before others in Christ.* You see the Apostle here mentioneth it as the only privilege, distinct, that the Jews had from the Gentiles, that they 'first trusted in Christ.' It is a privilege either to be before others in time; you shall find that, Rom. xvi. 7, where Paul giveth the upper hand of fellowship to Andronicus and Junia upon this ground: 'They were,' saith he, 'in Christ before me.' And so should younger Christians give unto elder, which may allay the pride and pertness of young ones, who are rather apt to censure old ones. Paul giveth it as an honour in that respect, 'who were in Christ before me;' as here it is made a privilege of the Jews, 'who first trusted in Christ.' Or, secondly, it is a privilege, not only when one is in Christ before another, but more especially when one is the first-fruits either of a family or of a nation that have believed. You shall read, 1 Cor. xvi. 15, of the household of Stephanas, that it was the 'first-fruits of Achaia.'

Hath God singled thee out of a family where never one was converted before? This is thy privilege, thou didst first trust in Christ, and thou art the first-fruits that hast sanctified that family unto God; it is likely he will have more out of it, for you know the first-fruits sanctified the lump. Certainly there is that covenant which God makes with nations, that where he beginneth to convert, there are the first-fruits of more to come; and God goeth on to continue that covenant to that nation for ever, though for a while he may cast them off; for they that are converted are the first-fruits. You may observe it, that scarce ever the gospel came to a nation, but it hath continued more or less to this day. The Christian name is as much over the world as ever it was; though Turks dwell with them, and domineer and tyrannise over them, yet the Christian name is in all nations where it once was, because the first converted were the first-fruits of those nations that sanctified the whole lump. Therefore was Abraham called the Father of the Faithful; he was one of the first great believers in a way of difficulty. Therefore was Eve the Mother of all Living, she was the first believer; we have a warrant that she believed, we have not a certain ground that Adam did; for the covenant is made with her, the promise is made to the woman; she is called, therefore, the Mother of all Living, because she first trusted in Christ.

Obs. 2.—Observe again, in the second place, *That if you have any privilege in grace* above another, it dependeth upon predestination, as well as your salvation doth; it dependeth upon an act of God's eternal love. The Apostle, as he ascribed their salvation to predestination, so this privilege, that they first trusted in Christ; it was ordered by the counsel of God's everlasting will, 'being predestinated,' saith he, 'who first trusted in Christ.' Therefore, not only have recourse to bless God and his eternal decrees for his love in saving thee, but for any particular privilege that thou hast before others in point of grace; have recourse to God's eternal counsel, for it was the fountain of it, as well of the degrees of grace as of glory; they have all their spring from God's eternal decree, as well as who shall be saved and who not.

Obs. 3.—*It may be made a motive to any one that hath been long in Christ, and in Christ before others, to be more holy than they.* Why? 'That we,' saith he, 'should be to the praise of his glory, who first trusted in Christ.' We that were the first-fruits of the world, we that were in Christ before you; we, saith he, should more especially be to his praise. As there is a more especial favour, which God in his predestination shewed us, so there is a more especial duty lieth upon us, to be to the praise of his glory. Therefore the Apostle findeth fault with them, Heb. v. 12, that whereas for the time they might have been teachers of others,—they might have had abundance of grace and knowledge,—they were dullards, they were dwarfs in respect of growth in grace.

Obs. 4.—And last of all: You that mean to repent, when you come to lie upon your death-beds, if you do so, what do you lose? You last trust in Christ, and so you shall be dishonoured. Is it not better to turn while you are young, and so to be of those that first trust in Christ? The apostle here, you see, makes it a privilege of the Jews, that they were those that first trusted in Christ.—And so much likewise for the application of what he had said unto the Jews.

To come now to his application of it to the Gentiles. 'In whom ye also,' saith he; he saith no more; you have it indeed put into your translation, 'trusted;' it is not in the original, but he speaks by way of ellipsis, shortly, and cutteth off his speech. 'In whom you also,' you Ephesians, you Gentiles—you also; which you may refer either unto *trusting*, which was in the verse before: 'In whom you also trusted,' as well as they, though they first, 'after you heard,' for so it followeth;—or else you may refer it, for the Holy Ghost hath a comprehensive meaning, and the Scripture is the shortest writing in the world, to what he had said to the Jews, cutting off this privilege, that they first trusted in Christ. 'In whom also you have obtained an inheritance, being predestinated according to the purpose of him who worketh all things according to the counsel of his own will, that you should be to the praise of his glory; having also trusted in him when you heard of the gospel of truth,' &c. You may refer it either to the one or to the other, and indeed to both. For, my brethren, the Apostle's scope is to make application of all he had said both to Jew and Gentile. Now, to go over the same thing twice to both had not been so comely; therefore he divideth them, and saith something of the Jew, which he applieth to them, and something of the Gentile, which he applieth to them, yet so as what is said of the Jew is applicable to the Gentile, 'In whom ye also had an inheritance, and were predestinated,' &c. And what is said of the Gentile, that 'after they heard the word of truth they believed, and were sealed,' is true also of the Jew; and because it would have been too long to mention them both, he divides it therefore, and cutteth it off with a short speech, 'In whom you also,' having reference to all that went before. So much for the coherence.

There are in this verse these three things:—

1. That the Gentiles did also trust in Christ and were called, and by calling had an inheritance as well as the Jews.

2. That this calling, and their faith, was by hearing the gospel; which he amplifieth by two encomiums of it:—

(1.) That it is the 'word of truth.'

(2.) That it is the 'gospel of their salvation.'

3. After that they had believed, they were 'sealed with the Spirit of promise.'

These are the parts of this 13th verse.

And first of all from this,—that he saith the same thing of the Gentiles that he saith of the Jews, cutting off that privilege that they were the first; the Jews trusted in Christ, and so did the Gentiles; the Ephesians trusted in Christ, as well as the apostles; they were by faith partakers of an inheritance, as well as the apostles,—what is the observation from hence? In a word this—

That we are all saved by the same faith that the apostles are. We have all the same common inheritance, the same common faith. I will give you a scripture for both.

First, that we have a like faith: 2 Pet. i. 1, 'Peter, an apostle of Jesus Christ, to them that have obtained like precious faith with us;' with us apostles, therefore he mentioneth himself as an apostle when he speaks it. We have likewise the same common salvation, the same common seal of the Spirit, 1 John i. 3, 'That which we have seen and heard declare we unto you, that ye also may have fellowship with us; and truly our fellowship is with the Father, and with his Son Jesus Christ.' We have assurance of the love of God, and walk in communion with him. You, saith he, are capable of having the same assurance, and we write to you these things, that you may have it; for the scope of that epistle is to beget assurance in the hearts of the godly. We are all saved by the same faith, and are capable of the same assurance, and shall have all the same salvation; it is called 'common salvation,' Jude 3. That is the observation from the coherence, 'In whom ye also trusted,' or 'obtained an inheritance,'—for you may put in both,—or obtained it by faith, or by trusting, 'after you heard,' &c.

After you heard.—He sheweth that their faith was wrought by hearing. I will not stand upon that, only this observation I shall give you out of it: That presently, as it were, after they heard, they believed; the gospel came no sooner to them but they were converted. It was the manner in the primitive times, God made quick work then. You shall find it backed by what is said to the Colossians, chap. i. 6. He saith there, that they had obeyed from the first day that they heard the gospel. Which, my brethren, may shame us; we live under the gospel many years; it is not after we have heard, but after we have heard and heard again, that we are turned unto God. How obedient were they! 'From the first day,' saith the apostle of the Colossians, there; 'after you heard,' saith he, here; as it were presently upon it.

I come, secondly, to the encomiums which here the apostle giveth the gospel by which they were converted. He calls it first a 'word of truth;' and, secondly, the 'gospel of your salvation.' I shall but briefly speak of these two, and shall shew you, first, singly, why the gospel is called *a word of truth*, and why the *gospel of their salvation*. Secondly, I shall shew you jointly *why both are here mentioned together*.

First, The gospel is called a 'word of truth,' not only because it is a true word, as being a Hebraism, but it is τὸν λόγον τῆς ἀληθείας, a word of an eminent truth. The greatest truth that ever God uttered, or shall utter, is the gospel of salvation by Jesus Christ; therefore it is called 'the gospel of that truth,' as we may so expound it. When our Saviour Christ told them that he was the Messiah, John viii. 40, what saith he? 'I tell you the truth,' saith he, 'which I heard of God;' the greatest secret, the highest truth that ever was, which I heard of God, and which came down from heaven; as he telleth Pilate, John xviii. 37, that for this cause he came into the world to speak the truth. What was that truth? That he was the Son of God and the Messiah of the world. 'In him,' saith the apostle, 2 Cor. i. 20, 'are all the promises of God yea, and in him Amen.' He doth not only say, 'in him they are yea;' if *yea* will not serve, saith he, you shall have *Amen* to it; it is a truth of truths, it hath yea to it and Amen to it too. To give you an instance more. My brethren, there is no truth that ever God swore to, but this. The law is all truth, but the law was made without an oath, for if it had been with an oath we had been in an ill case, for God could then never have recalled it; what is a mere threatening he recalleth, but what is done with an oath he never recalls. The gospel is sealed with an oath. God sweareth by himself, Heb. vi. 13. Never any truth was sealed with an oath but the gospel, the promise made to Abraham.

It may, secondly, be called a word of truth in opposition to the law; for the law represented but a shadow; but now, saith he, you have the truth, you have Christ, that is the substance of all the law, you have him revealed and tendered to you in the gospel. It is a word of truth, of Christ that is the truth. 'The law came by Moses,' saith he, 'but grace and truth by Jesus Christ,' John i. 17.

Let your hearts, my brethren, get hold by faith of this truth. There are many controversies in the world on foot, as about the worship of God and a thousand such things. Though there be a truth in them, and a truth thou must inquire into, yet if thou hast learned this truth to lay hold upon salvation revealed in the gospel, thou hast learned the greatest truth of all, more than all truths whatsoever.

And believe this gospel, that it is a word of truth. The greater truth it is the more it requireth faith, and the greater sin it is not to believe it; therefore the apostle aggravateth the sin of unbelief of the gospel, 1 John v. 10: He that believeth not this gospel, saith he, this record that God giveth of his Son, 'hath made God a liar;' for God hath uttered the greatest truth of all in the gospel, he hath bound it with an oath, which he never did any truth else. He hath really exhibited Christ in it. You had him in a promise before, but now you have him really; when he gave Christ into the world, there is the truth of all the promises; he therefore that believeth not the gospel makes God a liar. Unbelief is the greatest lie that ever was. Why? Because this is the word of truth in an eminent way.

Secondly, Why the 'gospel of your salvation?'

First, Why of salvation? Secondly, Why of *your* salvation? speaking to the Ephesians.

First, Why of salvation? Because the matter of it is salvation. Beza, therefore, whereas he useth to translate it as we do, the gospel or the evangel, translates it here—and he doth it nowhere else but here, and in one place more—the 'glad tidings of your salvation.' He giveth it in the signification. Why? Because salvation is the gladdest tidings in the world. My brethren, if a man were in danger of drowning, go and throw him a crown, and bid him take hold of that and come ashore, and he shall have all the kingdoms of the world with that crown, and throw him a rope; he will take hold of the rope, and let go the crown. No, saith he, I will take this rope. Why? It will save me, it will tow me ashore. I may be drowned for all the crown. What could God have said to have pleased you more, than that you poor sinners should be saved? than to fling out to you the gospel of your salvation, as a tow to lay hold upon to get safe over the sea of his wrath, and to obtain at last an everlasting salvation? The matter of the gospel is salvation; it is called *salvation*, the gospel is, Heb. ii. 3; as the writing wherein a man's pardon is contained, is called the pardon itself.

It is likewise called the gospel of salvation, because it doth bring men to salvation, and because it is the 'power of God unto salvation,' as the Apostle saith, Rom. i. 16.

Now, my brethren, what observation shall we draw from hence? It is the 'glad tidings of salvation,' so Beza translates it; because, saith he, this is the best tidings that ever was. Here I will give it in the signification of it, saith he. I will not use the word *gospel* or *evangel*, but take it thus—

it is the glad tidings of salvation. Oh, how should salvation, therefore, be valued by us! When the Apostle would set out the gospel to you, It is the gospel, saith he, of your salvation. What could he speak more to have moved the hearts of men than this? It is a word of truth, or it is a faithful saying; it hath truth and faithfulness in it, 'worthy of all acceptation,' that may draw you; but it is a gospel of salvation, saith he. When first this gospel was preached to these poor Gentiles, it is said, Acts xiii. 48, 'they were glad, and glorified the word of the Lord.' Oh, how glad should you be when you hear it preached! For you are not saved yet, you are not in heaven yet. It is the gospel which must save you and bring you there. It is the gospel of your salvation that works salvation in you, that bringeth you to salvation, that buildeth you up to eternal life, Acts xx. 32.

I should have likewise shewed you why it is called *your salvation*, but I will pass over that. I have shewed why it is called the 'word of truth,' why the 'gospel of salvation;' but why are both these here put together? You shall find it called the gospel of salvation somewhere else, as Heb. ii. 3, and the 'power of God unto salvation,' Rom. i. 16. And you shall find it often called 'the word of truth,' as Col. i. 5, and other places; but here both come in; for what reason? For two reasons—

First, Because if he had said only, 'the gospel of your salvation,' this is such mighty news to poor sinners that they would never have believed it, for men are not apt to believe too good news; therefore, saith he, it is the 'gospel of your salvation,' and the 'word of truth' too. As when the angel, Rev. xix., told John glorious things, because he thought they were too good to be true, the angel clappeth upon them this seal, ver. 9, 'These are the true sayings of God;' so the Apostle here, when he commendeth the gospel as the gospel of your salvation, that brings you news of being saved, to draw your hearts to believe it, saith he, It is the word of truth, the greatest truth that ever God uttered. The greatest truth, my brethren, and our salvation are met in one. It is the *word of truth*, and it is the *gospel of our salvation.*

The second reason why he mentioneth both is this: he speaks of faith, as you see, 'who first trusted in Christ; in whom ye also trusted; and after you believed you were sealed,' &c. Now, faith is seated in two faculties, in the understanding and in the will. Answerably, what hath the gospel? To satisfy the understanding, it hath the greatest truth in the world; it is the word of truth; the understanding closeth with that. To satisfy the will, it hath the greatest good in the world; it is the gospel of salvation. So that now first a man being persuaded of the truth of the gospel, and that truth being matter of salvation, his will hath reason to close with it, and so he makes up the bargain with God; that is, believeth. Heb. xi. 13, after they saw the promises, and were persuaded of them, they embraced them. There was seeing and being persuaded of them, as being the word of truth; there was embracing of them, as being the salvation of their souls.

Thus you see why the gospel is a word of truth and the gospel of salvation, and why the apostle here joins them both together.

There remains the third thing in the text to be handled: 'After that you believed you were sealed,' which sealing is an 'earnest,' for so it followeth ver. 14.

SERMON XV.

In whom also, after that ye believed, ye were sealed with that Holy Spirit of promise, which is the earnest of our inheritance until the redemption of the purchased possession, unto the praise of his glory.—Ver. 13, 14.

I have proceeded unto these words in opening of this chapter. The coherence of these words with the former is both natural and elegant. He had spoken of an inheritance which they were predestinated unto, so ver. 11; which inheritance was purchased for them by Jesus Christ; so, ver. 14, it is called 'the purchased possession.' Being appointed them and purchased for them, he telleth them, in the 13th verse, that the gospel brought the first news of it to them: 'After you heard,' saith he, 'the word of truth, the gospel of your salvation.' Upon their hearing of it, their faith closed with it, and by believing they obtained that inheritance; so saith the 11th verse. Now, because that this inheritance, though the right unto it was obtained by believing on Jesus Christ, though it was appointed for them from everlasting,—they were 'predestinated according to his purpose,' so saith the 11th verse,—although purchased by Jesus Christ, yet they stood still out of the possession of it. In the meantime, therefore, 'till the redemption of this purchased possession,' till the time should come that they should enjoy it, he giveth them the Holy Spirit, who had both sealed them up to it, and had given them the earnest of it in their hearts. 'After you believed,' saith he, 'you were sealed with that Holy Spirit of promise, who is the earnest of our inheritance.'

For the division of these words,—I mean the first part of them, viz., those in the 13th verse, 'In whom after ye believed, ye were sealed with that Holy Spirit of promise,'—they fall naturally into these parts:—

First, Here is A work of the Holy Ghost distinct from faith: 'After you believed, you were sealed.' There is a work of sealing, to open which will be the greatest difficulty that I shall have to do with at this time.

Here is, *Secondly,* The order of that work: it is 'after they had believed.'

Here is, *Thirdly,* The virtual cause, if I may so call it, in whom this sealing was wrought: it is *in Christ,* 'in whom after ye believed ye were sealed.' *In whom* referreth to sealing, as I shall shew you anon.

Fourthly, Here is The Person that is the sealer; it is the Spirit, the Holy Ghost, the third Person in the Trinity; and he is set forth unto us, as he is a sealer, two ways:—

First, He is the 'Spirit of promise.'

Secondly, He is a 'holy Spirit.'

Then, *Fifthly,* here are The persons sealed: 'After ye believed,' speaking to the Ephesians, 'ye were sealed,' &c.

I. To begin with the *first.* I shall profess merely to perform the part of an expositor, and but mention such observations concerning *sealing,* which in itself will afford a large field of discourse otherwise, as the text affordeth. And first, concerning this sealing, let us inquire what that is.

I shall *first* shew you *what it is not;* which some interpreters have given to be the meaning of it too.

Secondly, I shall endeavour to shew you *what it is.*

First, What it is not. I will not trouble you with what Popish interpreters make this sealing to be, because they are enemies to assurance of salvation. But, first, Piscator and some others do take it for the work of faith itself; and so they express the meaning of it to be, that in believing, in the work of faith, the Holy Ghost did seal up the truth of the promise unto their hearts. The like saith Calvin upon this place; and they have these two reasons for it. Because he is called the *Spirit of promise*, say they; because he sealeth up the truth of the promises, when men believe. And whereas he had called the gospel the 'word of truth' in the words before, he speaks, say they, to these Ephesians, and telleth them, Ye know it by this to be the truth, for the Holy Ghost did seal it up to you, when you believed.

Their meaning, that I may explain it to you, as I understand it, is this: there is a *twofold assurance.*

There is, first, an assurance of the truth of the promises,—and that is their meaning,—whereby a man's understanding is spiritually convinced that the promises are true and from God. And, secondly, there is an assurance of a man's interest in those promises.

Now, when they say that the Holy Ghost, in believing, seals believers, their meaning is, that he sealeth up the truth of the promises to them. Now to confute this interpretation in a word or two. I do grant them *three things* concerning it.

The first is, that it is a truth that in all faith there is an assurance of the *truth* of the promises wrought. I do not say there is an assurance of a man's *interest* in the promises. No, but whoever believeth hath unbelief thus far subdued, that he fully believeth this promise is true, and giveth up his soul unto it. There is a prevailing assurance of the truth of the promise, above all doubting, in every believer. I do not say it excludeth doubting; neither do I say it is an assurance of a man's own personal interest in the promise. I could shew you this by Scripture, but I must not insist upon it.

In the second place, I grant that this is a work of the Holy Ghost. It is not all the light of reason that can convince a man spiritually of the truth of a promise, or draw his heart into rest upon it. Speaking of the conversion of the Thessalonians, 1 Thess. i. 5, and of the Apostle's entrance among them when they first were turned to God, he saith, that 'the gospel came not unto them in word only, but in the Holy Ghost, and in much assurance.' The *Holy Ghost* and *assurance* are both there joined together.

Nay, in the third place, the Holy Ghost's convincing a man of the truth of any promise is called a sealing. I grant that likewise. Job, chap. xxxiii. 16, speaking of the manner of God's converting men in those times, which was done by visions and by dreams, 'then,' saith he, 'he openeth the ears of men, and sealeth their instruction.'

But yet, though all this be granted, this is not the meaning of the place, to speak of the work of faith. For, first, if you mark it, it is not a sealing up of the promise, the truth of it, a sealing of *instruction*, that the Apostle here speaks of; but it is a sealing of their *persons*, and so their personal interest in the promise: 'by whom,' saith he, '*ye* were sealed;' he doth not say the promise, or the truth of it, was sealed to them, but *their persons* were sealed.

Then, secondly, it cannot be meant of that sealing of instruction that is wrought in believing, for it cometh after believing; 'after ye believed,' saith he, 'ye were sealed with the Spirit of promise.' I know Piscator readeth the words otherwise, but I shall meet with his interpretation anon, (for the order of it,) when I speak to that point.

Again, it is evident he speaks of this sealing as a distinct thing from faith. For suppose this sealing were at the same time that men believe; suppose he had said, When you believe you were sealed; yet it is evident that it must needs be a distinct thing from faith. If a man saith that he did such a thing when such a thing was, it argueth he speaks of two things.

Lastly, if he had spoken of the sealing of the Spirit as the cause of faith, he would not have said, 'when you believed you were sealed with the Spirit,' but 'through sealing you did believe.' He would have spoken of faith as an act of theirs, and of sealing as an act of the Spirit, the cause of faith. And so much to confute that interpretation.

I find, again, in the other place, that Zanchy doth acknowledge—as a man must needs do—that sealing here is a distinct work from faith. But then he interpreteth it of the work of regeneration, and of sanctification, and renewing the image of God upon a man's heart; and his reason is this: for, saith he, a seal doth import the impression of an image; he giveth many reasons, but that is the main. Now, because that sanctification beareth the image of God, therefore, saith he, the sealing of the Spirit is the stamping of holiness and of all the frame of graces upon the heart; which, saith he, is upon believing, is wrought in a man by faith.

Now, my brethren, to confute this. I do grant that the seal here mentioned doth imply and import, in a secondary sense, the stamping of the image of God upon the heart, and therefore this attribute of *holy* is given to the Spirit as he is a sealer. But yet it is not the meaning of the Holy Ghost here, not the principal meaning of it, especially not the first work of sanctification; and the reasons are these:—

For, first, besides that many divines hold—and I think not without ground—that all the principles of sanctification are wrought in the heart before an act of faith, they are all wrought together; this is a truth, that the acts of sanctification depend upon the acts of faith foregoing them, (it will decide a controversy;) I say the acts of sanctification, our acting of love to God and obedience, do follow the acts of faith, laying hold upon Christ, and free grace; but yet the working of the image is presupposed before faith in order of nature. I might prove this unto you at large.

But, secondly, if the working of the image of God upon the heart were the thing here intended to be the seal, he would not say, 'after ye believed.' Why? Because that believing and faith is part of the image of God, part of the image of Christ, as well as any other holy disposition in us. It is said, we 'receive grace for grace' of Christ, John i. 16. That is, look what graces he had, we also have, and faith amongst the rest; and therefore, 1 John v. 1, he that believeth is said to be born of God.

And then there is this third reason for it also, why the first work of regeneration is not here intended in this metaphor; for the Apostle followeth an allusion of making sure an inheritance. Now, when the Scripture speaks of the work of sanctification and of regeneration, he nowhere calls it the seal of the Spirit, but he calleth it the writing of the law in the heart. For you know, when you will make a thing sure, you write the covenants, and when you have done, you seal to it. Now sanctification is the writing in the heart, as the scripture is written in the book. So you have it, 2 Cor. iii. 3, 'Forasmuch,' saith he, 'as ye are declared to be the epistle of Christ, written not with ink, but with the Spirit of the living God.' Here is sanctification; now the Holy Ghost is as ink, and that is as writing; but here the Holy Ghost is as the seal, and the work here which the Holy Ghost works is as the thing sealed.

That which occasioneth this mistake is this: because every seal hath an image in it, it was therefore supposed that the main intent of sealing was this stamping of an image; but that is not the main intent of a seal. It is true every seal hath an image upon it which it leaveth upon the wax; but yet the main intent of a seal is to assure or ascertain, to certify and make known, and to convey and make sure a thing; that is the intent of a seal, that is the primary intent of it; only, *ex consequente,* by way of consequence, and because you may know this seal is true, you have an image annexed to it. So I have confuted those interpretations that put most fair. It was necessary for me to do it, for they that read comments will find that these are the great interpretations.

Secondly, Now then, in examining *what it is,* I shall do that first in general.

It is, first, a work of the Holy Ghost. That is certain, he may be called an *earnest,* the Holy Ghost's person may be so called; but he is not called a *seal,* but in relation to an act of sealing. It importeth a work of the Holy Ghost upon the heart. This giving of the person of the Holy Ghost to a man is the highest earnest of heaven, more than all your graces. But if you speak of the Holy Ghost as a seal, it importeth a thing sealed, an act of his, a work upon a man's spirit. That is the first.

Secondly, It is a metaphorical expression, or a similitude; and if you will open this similitude, you must have recourse to the use of seals, what use seals serve for.

Divines give many uses of a seal that they apply to this particular in the text. They say, God sealeth his children, because he owneth them to be his by way of appropriation, setteth them apart to be his, as you merchants seal your goods, and so distinguish them from other men's goods; as, Cant. iv. 12, the spouse is called a sealed fountain unto Christ. The meaning of which metaphor is this: the Jews, you know, whose drink was water, there were some fountains and springs more delicate than others. Those that were great men, such as Solomon, the kings and others, if they had a delicate spring of waters, they rolled a stone upon it, (so you read they did of their wells, Gen. xxix. 3,) and then when they had done they would seal that stone, that their servants or others, walking in their enclosed gardens, might not taste of that spring. They would reserve it for themselves. As in Matt. xxvii., 'they sealed up the stone that was rolled upon the sepulchre to make it sure;' so they used to do to their fountains—rolling a stone upon them, they sealed them up. It is an allusion to what one's wife or spouse should be to him. She should be as a sealed fountain, appropriated unto him alone; and so, saith Christ, is the Church to me. Prov. v. 15, 18, 'Drink waters out of thine own cistern;' 'Let thy fountain be blessed,' saith he, speaking of a man's wife; 'rejoice with the wife of thy youth.' And so now, to appropriate the soul to Christ, to make the soul that sealed fountain, this is one interpretation they give of it.

So likewise for *estimation,* and for *security,* and the like. They give many such. But, my brethren, I cut off all such interpretations in a word or two.

And the first is this: that you have all these upon believing, as well as after believing. You are distinguished from other men, you are sealed in that sense, you are appropriated to God when you are first converted; but this sealing is after believing: therefore still this hitteth it not.

Secondly, let there be never so many uses of a seal, that which is proper to the scope here is sealing of an inheritance. You see the Apostle speaks of an inheritance, whereof the Holy Ghost is a sealer. 'We have obtained,' saith he, 'an inheritance by faith,' and having believed, we are 'sealed with the Holy Spirit of promise.'

So that now, if you would know the proper meaning of the word, you must have recourse to the use of a seal in sealing up of an inheritance.

What use is there of a seal in sealing up of inheritances?

There is a double use of it. There is, first, a making the inheritance sure to a man in itself; and there is, secondly, a making the man know that it is his, to confirm and settle his spirit that it is his. Now let us see which of these two is the seal here meant.

First, it is not the sealing of it to make a thing sure, to make salvation sure, that is not the scope principally here, *to make it sure in itself;* and the reason is this: for to make salvation sure there needeth no seal after believing. No, there was a seal set to make salvation sure long before his believing, therefore that is not the Apostle's scope here. Look into 2 Tim. ii. 19, 'The foundation of the Lord standeth sure, having this seal, The Lord knoweth who are his.' He speaks of God's eternal election; there is the seal now by which salvation is made sure in itself; therefore now for the Holy Ghost to seal it up, to make it sure in itself afterward, it needed not; there needed not a second seal to that end. No, upon thy believing, and by being sanctified, and receiving the Spirit at first, thy salvation is made as sure as by all the works of the Holy Ghost for ever after.

Well then, secondly, there is nothing, therefore, that is left that should be the meaning and the principal scope of the Holy Ghost here, but this, that they are sealed by the Spirit *to make them sure,* to make their persons sure of their salvation, to persuade their hearts, to put them out of question that this inheritance was theirs, that they might be able to claim it. In Jer. xxxii. 10, when Jeremiah did buy land, you read there that he had both the evidences written, and he had witnesses to them, and he had them sealed too; and all this in public, before public notaries, before the magistrate. It is the manner amongst men still; and the Holy Ghost alludeth to what was done then; he doth, I say, mention his sealing there unto that end, that there might be a public and a general notice, that he himself might be able to claim that land for ever.

Now, my brethren, this is that that I pitch upon to be the meaning of the Holy Ghost here. You must know that in ancient times, as likewise now, as the Scripture recordeth, when there should be a public certificate made that all men should take knowledge that such an act is authentical, it was done by a seal and without hands sometimes. Look into Esther viii. 8, 9, when a decree was made by the Persian monarch, it is said it was written in the king's name,—there was not the king's hand to it,—and it was sealed with the king's ring. Read on in that chapter; he wrote (at the 10th verse) in the king Ahasuerus' name, and sealed it with the king's ring. All acknowledged that to be the king's seal when they saw it. The end of the seal was to make a certificate, that it might be known by those whom it did concern. And therefore now, to this day, you see, where the king's broad seal is, the king's hand is not to it; but there is the seal set, and it is enough to assure all that see it that it is the king's act. The end of a seal here, therefore, is to make known, to assure, to persuade, and to certify that such a thing is an act of God's.

And, my brethren, not to make salvation *sure in itself*, but to make *us sure of it*, is plainly the meaning of the Holy Ghost here; for, first, you shall see that in other Scriptures sealing is so taken. Take but one or two places; I will name one eminent one, 2 Cor. i. 21, 'Now he which stablisheth us with you in Christ, and hath anointed us, is God; who hath also sealed us, and given the earnest of the Spirit in our hearts.' As Musculus well observeth upon the place: There are, saith he, three similitudes used to express what he had said plainly at first; he had said, 'he that stablisheth us with you;' this same establishing is expressed both by anointing (for the Holy Ghost is given to teach us all truths, 'the anointing teacheth us all things,') and by sealing, 'who hath also sealed us,' saith he; he assureth us of our interest in them, and he hath given us an earnest of them in our hearts; and thus, saith he, the Holy Ghost establisheth a man. It is not making salvation sure, but it is making the person sure; it is therefore expressed by 'establishing us with you.' And the scope of the Holy Ghost in this place is evident to be so, for mark by what degrees he setteth forth the revelation of salvation to believers. He telleth them, first, that the gospel brought them the first news of it; it was the happy news of 'your salvation,' as the 13th verse hath it, and so Beza expoundeth it; and as usually the first news of a thing is but confused, so is the first news of the gospel; it is but an indefinite hint; there is salvation, this salvation is offered to you, it may be yours. Well then, secondly, cometh faith, and that closeth with this salvation. 'You believed,' saith he, you gave your souls up unto it to be saved by it; then cometh the seal of the Spirit after believing, and confirmeth a man, settleth and establisheth the soul (as the Apostle's phrase is in that of the Corinthians) that this salvation is his.

And then again, in the second place, if you observe it, he doth not say that your *inheritance* is sealed, as if it were made sure in itself; but he saith the *persons* are sealed; 'he sealed *us*, he sealed *you*;' those are the phrases both here and in that of the Corinthians; therefore the end of this sealing is to seal up their peculiar interest.

And then, again, there is this third reason for it likewise, that it is not making salvation sure in itself, but to make us sure of it, because that the inward work here of sealing answereth to the outward work of baptism. It is Zanchy's observation, though he doth not apply it: I say, the Apostle, instead of saying you are baptized and so sealed, mentioneth the inward work of baptism rather. You are sealed, saith he, by the Spirit. Now the end of baptism is to be a seal; that is the outward seal, for it succeedeth circumcision, as appeareth, Col. ii. 11, 12, compared. Now, circumcision is called the 'seal of the righteousness of faith,' Rom. iv. 11. Now every ordinance hath his proper work; the proper work of baptism, the inward work that answereth to baptism, is the seal of the Spirit, for that is the seal of the righteousness of faith. Now baptism supposeth regeneration, supposeth salvation sure in itself first. Sacraments are never administered to begin or work grace; you suppose children to believe before you baptize them. Read all the Acts; still it is said, 'they believed and were baptized.' I could give you multitude of places for it. Now then salvation is made sure upon believing; but you are baptized, that is the seal to confirm. Answerably, salvation is made sure upon believing; but the seal of the Spirit cometh as the fruit of baptism, which is the proper work of it. The inward seal answereth to the outward. You shall therefore find in the Acts, that upon baptizing of men that were at years, the Holy Ghost fell upon them; as, when the eunuch was baptized, Acts viii. 38, 'he went away rejoicing,' so saith ver. 39. He had 'joy in the Holy Ghost.' You have the jailor baptized, Acts xvi. 33; you have him rejoicing, ver. 34. So that now the seal of the Spirit in those primitive times did accompany the outward seal of baptism; and so, to this day, the proper fruit you are to expect of your having been baptized, is to be sealed with the Spirit of promise; it is not to work regeneration, but supposeth it. So now you see that sealing is an assurance of salvation.

But now there is a twofold assurance of salvation, that we may yet go further in examining what is intended in it; for I must sift things to find out what is the proper scope, what is the *elixir* of the Holy Ghost's intention. There is, first, an assurance by sense, by conditional promises, whereby a man, seeing the image of God upon his heart, to which promises are made, cometh comfortably to believe that he is in the estate of grace. That there is a use of sense all acknowledge. But then, secondly, there is an immediate assurance of the Holy Ghost, by a heavenly and divine light, of a divine authority, which the Holy Ghost sheddeth in a man's heart, (not having relation to grace wrought, or anything in a man's self,) whereby he sealeth him up to the day of redemption. And this is the great seal of all the rest. The one way is *discoursive;* a man gathereth that God loveth him from the effects, as we gather there is fire because there is smoke. But the other is *intuitive*, as the angels are said to know things; it is such a knowledge as whereby we know the whole is greater than the part, we do not stand discoursing. There is light that cometh and overpowereth a man's soul, and assureth him that God is his, and he is God's, and that God loveth him from everlasting.

Now the question is, Which of these two is intended here? I shall give you an answer to it by consulting that in 1 John v. 8. He saith, 'There are three that bear witness' to a man's conscience, to a man's spirit. There is the *Spirit*, saith he, that is the Holy Ghost; and there is the *water;* and there is the *blood*. By water he meaneth sanctification, as all agree; and by blood he meaneth the blood of Jesus Christ, by faith laid hold upon, which hath a witness in it: 'He that believeth,' saith he, 'hath the witness in himself,' ver. 10. You shall find both these in Heb. x. 22: 'Let us draw near with a true heart in full assurance of faith, having our hearts sprinkled from an evil conscience,'—there is blood, for, Heb. ix. 14, the blood of Christ is said to purge the conscience from dead works,—'and our bodies washed with pure water,' that is, our whole man sanctified, alluding to the types of the ceremonial law. But you see here, beside the testimony of blood, when a man cometh to believe, he layeth hold upon the blood of Christ; when a man looks to Christ, though with a weak faith, Jesus Christ doth somewhat look upon him; as when a man looks upon a picture, if he eye the picture, the picture seemeth to look upon him too; this becometh some quiet to the soul. A man that is elected, and cometh to lay hold upon the blood of Christ, look as a man that is guilty of murder, when he cometh to the dead body the blood floweth: so when a man that is a believer looks upon Christ, there is a fresh flowing of the blood, and that strengtheneth faith; no man looks upon Christ but cometh off more cheerly; but this is a weak witness. Then cometh in water, that witnesseth too; but yet, I say, if you mark it, here is the Spirit, that differeth from both these, therefore there is a further testimony than either from a man's sanctification or from mere faith. The

Holy Ghost witnesseth with both the other: for your sanctification cannot comfort you, if it were not for the Holy Ghost; no, your faith could not comfort you, but that it is a work of the Holy Ghost. I will give you but one place for it, Rom. xv. 13. He prayeth that God would make them 'abound in hope through the power of the Holy Ghost.' If thou hast any hope wrought in thee, either by looking to Christ's blood, or by seeing grace in thy heart, it is by the power of the Holy Ghost. Well, why doth he say *Spirit,* differing from both *blood* and *water?* Because there is an immediate testimony beyond all these, which the Holy Ghost works in a man's soul.

Now, my brethren, to answer you which is meant here by the sealing of the Spirit. I answer in two things.

First, I say, that in a large and in a general sense all assurance wrought, whether by *water* or by *blood,*—for there are no other ways,—any assurance, what way soever it be, is a seal of the Holy Ghost. I shall give you something to confirm it. If you will take sealing for a *giving in witness* in a large and common sense, so whatsoever giveth a testimony through the power of the Holy Ghost is an irradiating of a believer, and is the work of the Holy Ghost, that may be said to be a seal. In John iii. 33, you shall see the use of the phrase of sealing. It is used there for the giving of a testimony: 'He that hath received his testimony,' namely, by believing, 'hath set to his seal that God is true.' So that now, in a large and common sense, any witness that is given to confirm a truth is expressed in the Scripture by *setting a seal unto.* Therefore now, when the Holy Ghost doth give in a witness that you have grace *by blood,* laid hold on by faith, that you have grace *by water;* if it be a witness, it may be called a seal. I will not exclude these two other ways of assurance. Witnesses did use to set to their seals as witnesses, as well as the conveyer of an inheritance, in ancient times. Therefore divines make degrees of sealing. They say there is a sealing by blood, and there is a sealing by water, by sanctification, and there is a sealing by the Spirit. They make them several degrees; as in passing a thing at court, it passeth the king, and then it passeth the privy seal, and then it passeth the broad seal. These are but three several degrees of confirming the same thing; but the broad seal doth the business, whereby a man authentically claimeth it for ever. So that I say, in a large sense, I will not deny but that sealing here may be put for all kinds of assurance.

But yet let me say this, that that which is here more eminently meant is the immediate testimony of the Holy Ghost, the special thing that is here aimed at; and my reasons are these—

First, If you follow the metaphor close, every witness is not a seal in a strict sense; when there are witnesses and a sealer too, the witnesses come in to confirm the seal, or to confirm the writing. Every seal indeed is a witness, and it is the highest witness that is; and therefore, though the Spirit and his immediate testimony is called a witness, yet he is called a seal too; but yet, on the other side, every witness is not a seal, not in a strict sense. There are many things that are signs that are not seals, as you have it, Rom. iv. 11. There are many witnesses that are not sealers, especially in matters of inheritances, where there is a conveying over by the person that sealeth.

Then again a second reason is this: if you observe the phrase, it is said you are 'sealed by the Spirit,' he only is mentioned. Now, if you have recourse to that 1 John v. 8, water is said to be a witness, and blood a witness, and the Spirit a third witness; the witness of water and blood are swallowed up as it were in the witness of the Spirit, in respect of the immediate testimony of the Holy Ghost. His testimony, though it is joined with theirs, yet it is hid under theirs; it is not said so much to be the testimony of the Spirit, as the testimony of water and blood: whereas here it is said to be the testimony of the Spirit, therefore that third is rather meant than the other.

And then again, in the third place, in sealing of an inheritance, the witnesses, you know, are *extranei;* they are persons which are not the conveyers of the inheritance; he that selleth or conveyeth the inheritance is said to seal properly, he whose the inheritance is. Therefore now, though your grace and faith may come in as witnesses, yet when he speaks of a seal, he must mean the seal of the conveyer; which is therefore the seal of the Holy Ghost himself, as distinguished from these two, as principally aimed at.

Great persons, who stand upon their authority, use to seal without witnesses. If you will speak of the seal of a king, as this is the seal of God: so, Esth. viii. 8, they did but write in the king's name, and seal it with the king's ring: there was the seal, there was no hand to it. To this day the king writeth *teste me ipso,* 'witness ourself,' when he putteth his seal to. In some colleges, when they put the college seal to a thing, they put no hands to, neither of the fellows, nor of the master, but only the seal of the college. Saith Christ, John v. 33, 34, 'I receive not testimony from man.' Though John, saith he, hath given me a witness, yet I receive no testimony from him, I am witness enough myself. When the Holy Ghost cometh to seal up salvation, he will have no witness but himself; they may come in as under-confirmers of it; but he doth it himself; 'witness ourself.' That is the seal of the Holy Ghost.

God hath made a promise, and he hath made an oath, to confirm our salvation; he hath made a promise, and he hath set to his seal, to confirm salvation; now do but parallel these two. When God sweareth, he sweareth by himself, he will not swear by anything else. Will the Holy Ghost seal? he sealeth by himself, he will take nothing else: so you have it, Heb. vi. 13, 'Because he could swear by no greater, he sware by himself.' Will he seal? he will seal by himself. There may be other witnesses, but they are *extranei;* they have not to do with the bargain; but, saith he, it is my witness. I will seal by myself, I will receive testimony from none. He doth it himself.

So now, my brethren, I have opened this thing unto you, and all that I have said tendeth plainly and clearly but to open the words.

Now I shall come to some observations from what hath been said.

Obs. 1.—In the first place, you see that *the work of faith is a distinct thing, a different thing, from the work of assurance;* that is the least that can be gathered from it. He speaks of faith as one thing, of the sealing of the Spirit as another thing. Those that have held *that faith is assurance,* and others that have held the contrary; there is a double mistake in the point. I shall shew it in a word.

First, it must be granted, that in all faith there is an assurance; but of what? Of the truth of the promise. If a man doubt, if he 'waver,' as St James saith, in the truth of the promise, he will never act his faith. But the question here is about the assurance of a man's interest; that is not always in faith.

Again, all faith is an application of Christ. But how? It is not an application that Christ is mine, but it is a laying hold upon Christ to be mine. It is not a logical application in way of proposition that I may say

Christ is mine; but it is a real one, I put him on, I take him to be mine; and that is the better of the two. Faith, my brethren, is distinct from assurance.

Obs. 2.—In the second place, the sealing of the Spirit here intended, especially that immediate assurance which is mainly aimed at, is *a light beyond the light of ordinary faith*, that ordinary faith which a man liveth by. Why? Because he makes it to be a further work than believing. 'After ye believed,' saith he, 'ye were sealed;' he makes it a further thing; and because it is the next thing to heaven, you have no more, you can have no more till you come thither; for you are sealed, and it is the 'earnest of your inheritance.' Faith indeed doth give the soul up to Christ, it dependeth upon him, quieteth itself in the blood of Christ. A man feeleth the load taken off his conscience while he believeth, and while he washeth himself in that blood, and eyeth that blood; but this of the seal of the Spirit is more. At the 17th verse, (it may perhaps prove the meaning of it, I shall consider it when I come to it,) he is called the 'Spirit of wisdom'—I told you by *wisdom* is meant *faith*, in the 8th verse—'and revelation.' I will give you Job for an instance; Job had an ordinary light he lived by, and an extraordinary light that came into his soul. Look Job xlii. 5, 'Mine ear,' saith he, 'hath heard of thee, but now mine eye hath seen thee.' He calleth this *vision*, in comparison of what he had all his lifetime. I think Job speaks it in respect of a sight of God himself, but you may apply it to the sight of a man's interest; it is a sight by which a man seeth it, though he did but hear of it before. I have heard it whispered to me by the Holy Ghost,—for the Holy Ghost whispereth secretly by blood and by water,—that I am in the state of grace, but now I see it, saith he.

I yield, my brethren, that the sealing of the Spirit is but faith, if you compare it to heaven. It is not the vision of heaven, and therefore, 1 Pet. i. 8, it is said, 'Believing, you rejoiced with joy unspeakable and glorious.' It is but faith in comparison of heaven, it is believing when you are filled with joy; so, Rom. xv. 13, he prayeth that they may be 'filled with all joy through believing.' But let me tell you that it is faith elevated and raised up above its ordinary rate; as Stephen's eye with which he saw Christ was his natural sight, but it was his natural sight elevated, raised up above the ordinary proportion of an eye; so is this, a light beyond the ordinary light of faith. I will give you but one instance to difference it unto you, and it is a clear one. You read in 2 Sam. xii. 13, that Nathan came to David as a prophet, and when he spake as a prophet, David believed it, he had faith to entertain this word; and he telleth David plainly, that his sins of adultery and murder were forgiven, and he said that God had told him that he should not die. Well, this being a word of God, David had an ordinary light of faith to apprehend it, to believe it, as we believe the Scripture when it is read. Suppose thy name were written in the Book of God; that thou foundest it in the gospel, as Cyrus's name was in the prophets, that thou shouldst be saved; thou wouldst believe it with such a faith as thou believest there is a God out of the Scripture, and a Christ out of the Scripture. Well, but David for all this was not satisfied; he had a faith to believe that his sins should be forgiven, and that faith was an assurance that they should be pardoned; but it was not a seal of the Spirit. Therefore, Ps. li. 12, after Nathan came unto him, he prayeth, 'Restore unto me the joy of thy salvation, and establish me with thy free Spirit.' He knew it before by an ordinary light, but the thing he seeks for here is the witness of the Holy Ghost.

Now, when we say that it is a Spirit of *revelation*, we do not mean as the

Papists do; they say, a man cannot be assured of his salvation but by vision, and by an angel appearing to him, and by immediate messages from heaven. Neither do I mean such revelation as Paul had, when he was carried up to the third heaven. No; but it is such a light to know a man's own interest in salvation by, as wherewith the apostles wrote Scripture; not that he that hath it can write Scripture. It is not a revelation of new truths, but to apply those truths to a man's own heart. In 2 Cor. i. 21, 22; in the verses before, the Apostle speaks of the truth of his doctrine; as he was an apostle, he pawneth his apostleship upon it; I am confident in it, saith he, the gospel I preached is not 'yea and nay.' I am an apostle, and I delivered it unto you as an apostle; but now coming to those ordinary believers of the Corinthians, saith he, 'He that stablisheth us in Christ with you is God, who hath also sealed us,' &c. He hath given you that light to see your interest in those promises, the same light wherewith we see the truth of the promises, and have preached them unto you.

And so now you have the second observation from hence. The first was, that it is a distinct thing from faith; the second is, that it is a higher light than the ordinary light of faith.

Obs. 3.—The third is this, for I shall keep to the text. It is called a seal; now in reason every seal hath an impress upon it. *What is the impress of the immediate seal of the Spirit that it stampeth upon a man's heart?*

To help you to understand this, I must have recourse to that 2 Tim. ii. 19, 'The foundation of God standeth sure, having this seal, The Lord knoweth who are his;' that is, God knoweth whom he hath loved from everlasting. Here is God's seal. Well, what is the seal of the Spirit? It is the impress of this seal from everlasting; he cometh and stampeth upon a man's heart, The Lord knoweth thee to be his. It beareth the image of God's everlasting love, (it is news with a witness,) of God's everlasting love to a man, to him in particular; that is the motto, the impress about this seal. It hath holiness with it too, as I shall shew, but I say the impress, the motto is this, God knoweth thee to be his. For this seal of the Spirit answereth to the other seal, it is the copy of it, it is engraven from it. God's seal is, The Lord knoweth who are his (that is in general spoken of election;) the particular seal of the Spirit is, God knoweth thee to be his. As we choose God because he chose us, we answer his election in love, we love God because he loved us first; so this seal of the Spirit, Know thou that thou art God's, answereth that, God knoweth thee to be his, which was God's seal from everlasting. It is the electing love of God brought home to the soul; therefore, as election looks not to works nor graces, when God chose you to be his: so when he sealeth you up, the impress of that love of his is without the consideration of works; a man doth not know that he is God's by marks and signs, but by an immediate impress and light of the Holy Ghost's.—And so now I have fully, as I could, explained to you what this seal of the Spirit is.

II. Let me now in a word but observe *the order*. You see here it is *after believing;* 'after ye believed you were sealed,' saith he. I will not here enter upon that controversy,—because the text giveth not occasion for it,—whether assurance by signs be first, or assurance by the Spirit immediately be first? for I must still keep to what the text saith. Only this I raise out of it, and observe further to open the text, that the Spirit is after believing.

Piscator readeth the words, *Per quod etiam quum credidistis,*—When ye believed, at the same time that ye believed. But, my brethren, it is not πιστεύοντες, *believing*, as you have it, 1 Pet. i. 8, 'Believing, you were filled with joy in the Holy Ghost;' but it is πιστεύσαντες, it is of the time past, when ye *had believed;* having believed ye were sealed. 'After ye believed,' saith our translation rightly.

Take the greatest instance in the world for it, the apostles themselves; they were believers, and they trusted God by faith, before they were assured and had the seal of the Spirit. You know, ver. 12, Paul, speaking of the apostles, saith, 'who first trusted in Christ,' and the word is 'hoped in Christ.' Now do but look into the 14th of John, read but that chapter, and you shall find that the apostles had faith and the Holy Ghost long before they had assurance and the seal of the Spirit. Saith Christ there, 'Ye believe in God;' here they had faith, but it was a very poor faith, for, ver. 5, they said they did not know the way to heaven, so far were they off from this assurance here mentioned. Christ telleth them there also, that they had the Spirit, ver. 17, 'He dwelleth with you,' saith he, he is in your hearts. Well, but see what he saith in the 20th verse. At that day, namely, when I am ascended, ye shall know (I will give you the Comforter, the Spirit of truth, so he calleth him, he dwelleth with you now;) but 'at that day you shall know that I am in my Father, and you in me, and I in you.' Then they should have a full manifestation of their union with Christ, and their union with the Father, and of the union of Christ with the Father. 'Then you shall know,' saith he, 'at that day;' this was after their believing.

I will give you but one scripture more (it openeth that place to me clearly) in the same chapter. Christ promised them that do believe the Comforter. 'I will pray the Father,' saith he, ver. 16, 'and he shall give you the Comforter; whom the world cannot receive, because it seeth him not, neither knoweth him: but ye know him; for he dwelleth with you, and shall be in you.' I take the meaning of the words thus: I promise you the Holy Ghost as a Comforter, you have him already as a sanctifier; he dwelleth with you, you have him already as one that hath wrought faith in you; but as a Comforter the world cannot receive him as you shall. Why? Because the world hath not known him *as a sanctifier*, but so you have known him already; for till such time as the Holy Ghost hath wrought faith, and put a man into the state of grace, he cannot assure him, he cannot comfort him. For, my brethren, consider well the reason he giveth why the world cannot receive the Spirit is, because they do not know him. I ask this, When thou wert converted, wert not thou one of the world? Thou didst not know the Spirit. If this were the reason why men did not receive the Holy Ghost, no man in the world should receive him; therefore the meaning must needs be this, till men have some experience of the work of the Spirit upon their hearts; till he hath been a sanctifier in them, and caused them to believe, they cannot receive him as Comforter. Why? Because there is not matter wherewithal to comfort them; they must first be in the state of grace before they can be comforted by being in the state of grace. They must therefore receive him as a sanctifier before they can receive him as a Comforter.

I shall name one scripture more, it is Acts xv. 8, 9. You shall see there that the Holy Ghost was poured out in the primitive times after believing. At the 7th verse he speaks of the Gentiles, that they 'heard the word of the gospel, and believed;' and saith he, ver. 8, 'God, which knoweth the hearts,'—knowing they believed,—'bare them witness, giving them the Holy Ghost, even as he did unto us.' So that now the giving of the Holy Ghost, as he did to the apostles, as a Comforter, as a sealer to them of salvation, is when they have believed, when God, who knoweth their hearts, knoweth them to be holy.

And, my brethren, the reason is clear and evident; for Jesus Christ must first be mine, before I can say he is mine, the thing must be first; now he is made mine by faith, I then receive him to be mine. They were without Christ in the world, he saith of these Ephesians, till they believed; when they believed, then Christ is theirs, therefore necessarily an act of faith must go before an act of assurance; for assurance doth tell you that Christ is yours, and that according to the rule of the Word. Now, according to the rule of the Word, though he may be yours in God's secret purpose, yet you are without Christ before you believe. Things must be, before I believe them to be.

Then it is equal that God should be honoured first by mere trusting, by mere *believing*, before he honoureth your faith with setting to his seal. John iii. 33, he that believeth 'hath set to his seal that God is true.' Well, when a man hath done that, now, saith God, I will set to my seal that he believeth, and that he is my child. But God will have you trust him first with a mere act of trust, as the woman did that trusted the prophet: she had no more meal nor no more oil than would save their lives, one meal more. Well, saith he, I will be trusted; 'Make me thereof a cake first, and bring it to me that I may eat of it, and after make for thee and for thy son.' God will be trusted first; and when you have set to your seal that God is true in his Word, God will set to his seal after your believing.

SERMON XVI.

In whom also, after that ye believed, ye were sealed with that Holy Spirit of promise, which is the earnest of our inheritance, &c.—VER. 13, 14.

THE coherence of these words with the former, as I have shewed you, is easy and natural. He had spoken of an inheritance; he had spoken of it in the 11th verse, and he speaks of it likewise in the 14th verse; an inheritance unto which they were predestinated by God's eternal purpose, so ver. 11; in which inheritance they had, by faith and by believing, as I shewed, obtained an interest: 'we obtained an inheritance who first trusted in Christ,' ver. 11, 12. Now then, having been thus appointed to it, having obtained an interest in it, and the thing itself being made thus sure, and this by faith; now, saith he, 'After ye believed, ye were sealed with that Holy Spirit of promise.' This inheritance, as it was made sure in itself, so you had the inheritance made good to you by a work of sealing: ye were sealed with that Holy Spirit of promise.

I shewed the last time, in opening of the work of sealing, first what it was not, which some interpreters would have to be meant in this place.

It is not, first, the gift of the Spirit only, abstractedly considered, for it importeth a work of the Spirit upon the heart, which sealing always must needs do, and impression likewise. Indeed, the gift of the Spirit may be the earnest of the inheritance, merely and alone considered, as I shall shew you anon; but the sealing of the Spirit importeth an impression, a work upon the heart.

It is not, secondly, a work of faith, as some would have it; for besides that he doth not say, 'Believing ye were sealed,' (as elsewhere he speaks; so the apostle Peter speaks, 1 Pet. i. 8, πιστεύοντες, 'Believing, ye rejoice,' in the present tense;) but it is πιστεύσαντες, having believed, or, as our translation well rendereth it, 'after ye believed;' which at least implieth it is a distinct thing from faith.

Then, thirdly, I shewed it was not sanctification or regeneration; which though it be an image, yet the use of the metaphor of sealing, though it implieth an image, is taken principally from the use of a seal, which primarily is not so much to stamp an image, though it doth that, as it is to assure.

I shewed by this what it was not. I shewed, secondly, what I conceived it to be.

You must fetch the notion of it from the use of a seal amongst men, and you must confine it likewise to the use of a seal in matters of inheritance, for that is properly the Apostle's scope, he followeth that metaphor; therefore, though there be many uses of a seal,—for service, and propriety, and the like,—yet, I take it, they are not the proper scope here.

The use of a seal in point of inheritance is, first, to make the thing sure, to convey an inheritance, that the inheritance should be thereby conveyed, and made sure in itself. Now, though that is not excluded,—for every work of the Spirit doth make the thing over and over sure, still engageth God more and more,—yet that is not the proper and primary scope of sealing here. Why? Because there is an ancienter seal than that, the original seal of all, whereby salvation is made sure in itself, even God's eternal purpose. And this sealing is a distinct thing from that 2 Tim. ii. 19, 'The foundation of the Lord remaineth sure, having this seal, The Lord knoweth who are his,' speaking of eternal election; that is, rather a setting of us upon God's heart as a seal, (as the expression is, Cant. viii. 6, 'Set me as a seal upon thine heart,') than God's sealing our hearts by his Spirit. This is not the meaning here, for he had spoken of that before; he had spoken how by predestination they were appointed to it, ver. 11, and how by faith they had obtained it, and the thing was conveyed; they had 'obtained an inheritance,' ver. 11.

There is therefore another use of a seal. It is to ascertain the parties, or others, to whom the thing is made over unto, that they might have that to shew for it for ever. So, indeed, sealing is taken in the Scripture, not only so much for making salvation sure in itself, as to assure our hearts, as the phrase is that the Apostle useth in his epistles. It is parallel to what is in 2 Cor. i. 21, 22. 'He which stablisheth us with you in Christ, and hath anointed us, is God, who hath also sealed us.' *Sealing* and *anointing* is there put for *stablishing* us, making us sure of it, not making the thing sure.

Now, because there are two ways of making us sure of salvation; the one mediate, by the witness of our graces and the witness of the blood of Christ sprinkled upon the conscience, and laid hold upon by faith; and the other immediate, which is an immediate testimony of the Holy Ghost, as I shewed out of 1 John v. 8, where there are said to be three that bear witness that we have eternal life, as it followeth afterward, ver. 11; there is the water, blood, and Spirit. Now by Spirit there is meant the Holy Ghost, by water is meant our graces and sanctification, and by blood is meant the blood of Jesus Christ, looked upon by faith; when faith hath a recourse unto it, it leaveth a witness behind itself. A man never cometh to Christ but he goeth away somewhat quieted, somewhat comforted; he never layeth hold upon that blood but it easeth or pacifieth the conscience more or less. Now when *Spirit* is made a distinct thing from the other two, it must needs be an immediate witness of the Spirit distinct from the other two. Why? Because the Holy Ghost witnesseth with the blood and water; therefore when he saith *Spirit* as a third witness, it is differing from both these; it must be the Holy Ghost witnessing without these.

The question is then, Which of these are meant here, when he saith, 'Ye are sealed with the Spirit of promise?'

I answer, If you take it in a large sense, every witness, and all assurance of salvation by any of those witnesses, may be called a sealing of the Spirit; if you take sealing in a large sense, for testifying or witnessing a thing that is true, as John iii. 33, where the word is used, he that believeth, saith he, 'hath set to his seal that God is true.' If you will take it for witnessing anything, every one of these witnesses, in such a metaphorical sense, may be called a seal. Yet I take it, that which is principally aimed at here is an immediate testimony of the Holy Ghost. The metaphor of sealing an inheritance implieth as much; for you know, in conveying inheritances, as I shewed out of Jeremiah, there are witnesses that are as standers-by; but the act of sealing is the immediate act of the party that conveyeth it. And the seal of great persons is set to without witnesses; the seal of the king is without hand, as the broad seal amongst us, you know, is. And so, Esth. viii. 8, the seal of the king Ahasuerus was without a hand; there was no other witness but the king's seal to it. So now, when the great God of heaven and earth, when his Spirit will witness over and above water and blood, he will do it himself. My brethren, every seal is a witness, but every witness is not a seal, in a strict sense.

Now then, concerning this seal of the Spirit, we having found what is principally meant; for all this is but to find out the meaning of it; I gave you these three things:—

The first was, that it was a distinct light from the ordinary light of faith, a light beyond that light. It is indeed faith elevated, though not to vision, where faith shall cease, as it is in heaven; yet as Stephen's bodily eye was raised to see Christ beyond what the power of the ordinary sight could have done, so here is a light beyond what the ordinary light can reach unto.

In the second place, this immediate seal must have an impress that it stampeth upon the heart. Now I told you, that the motto, or the impression that this beareth,—to follow still the metaphor of a seal,—is the impress, it is the copy of that great seal in heaven, which God did set to our salvation before all worlds. Now what was that great seal, that original seal of all God's heart? Saith the Apostle, 'The foundation of God standeth sure, having this seal, The Lord knoweth who are his;' that is, he chooseth them out of love. Now then this immediate seal of the Holy Ghost beareth the impress of this original seal, stampeth this upon the heart,—The Lord knoweth thee to be his, and he hath known thee so from everlasting. And as God chooseth us, not looking to works or anything in us, so this light cometh in without reference to graces, or anything else.

Then, in the third place, as in a seal, the wax, you know, is passive unto the stamp of the seal, so is the heart, the understanding, and the will and affections to this work of sealing. That is a third thing I add now, still keeping to the metaphor of sealing, as being proper to the text. It is a light that doth not leave you to think, 'This may be my own thoughts,' but an overpowering light; for when the Holy Ghost will speak as a sealer, he will do his office, and therefore a man's own spirit is not active in it. He is active in it in the effect indeed, but in the light itself, and in the receiving of it, he is passive, as at the first conversion.

Having opened what the work is, I shewed in the second place the order of it; it is after believing. I gave you that one instance in the apostles themselves, which I shall repeat, because I should have use of it afterward. You may read, John xiv. 1–4, that they believed in Christ; yea, at the 17th verse, they had the Holy Ghost in them: yet at the 16th verse, he promiseth them, when he was ascended he would give them the Comforter; and, ver. 20, 'At that day,' saith he, 'ye shall know that I am in you, and you in me.' The apostles had not this seal of the Spirit till Christ ascended; they had the Holy Ghost before, they had some assurance before; for you know Peter appealeth to Christ, 'Lord,' saith he, 'thou knowest that I love thee,' and Christ telleth Peter, that he did believe so as 'flesh and blood had not revealed to him,' Matt. xvi. 17. He had the witness both of blood and water, yet the Holy Ghost was to come down as a Comforter. And in that day, saith he, ye shall know your immediate union with me, 'that I am in you, and you in me.'

III. The third thing concerning this sealing in the text is, *the* PERSON *in whom we are sealed.* There is, first, the *work of sealing,* that hath been opened. Secondly, there is the *order of it,* it is after believing. Then, thirdly, the person in whom, or the *virtual cause* in whom we are sealed. It is in Christ: 'In whom, after ye believed, ye were sealed.'

The words translated here, 'in whom,' ἐν ᾧ, are exceeding ambiguous in their reference, as in the Greek they are. They may refer unto the gospel, spoken of just before, and so Piscator would have it; that is, *by which gospel* ye believed; that ἐν ᾧ is put for δι' οὗ. Or, secondly, they may refer to Christ, 'in whom,' as our translation readeth it; and so they have a double reference: either that the meaning is, 'in whom, after ye believed,' and so it referreth to faith, to believing in Christ; or, secondly, they may refer to sealing, 'in whom, after ye believed, ye were sealed,' sealed in him after believing.

My brethren, there is not a verse but there are such ambiguities as these are; so comprehensive and vast a writer in his scope and aim is the Holy Ghost, yet still aiming at something peculiar. There is no book written so ambiguously, in that comprehensive way, as the Scripture.

If you ask now, to which I refer 'in whom?' Plainly, I say, unto sealing; and my reason is this, for he mentioneth sealing here as a new benefit distinct from faith. And as he had said of all other benefits, that they were in Christ; we are elected in Christ, adopted through him, redeemed through him, in whom God abounded in grace to us; still mark it, to every benefit, 'in Christ,' is added. Now speaking of a new benefit of sealing, this phrase, 'in whom,' referreth to sealing; so that this is the meaning of it, that the *work of sealing* is performed *in Christ.*

Now, my brethren, 'in whom' will still have a double reference, and a double meaning, if we refer it to Christ and to sealing in him, and both is the meaning and scope of the place.

First, Ἐν is all one with εἰς. In Christ you were sealed, that is, you were sealed *into Christ*, into him: so it importeth that the matter made known in the work of sealing, is a man's union with Christ. When the Holy Ghost sealeth a man up, the thing he makes known, the thing he sealeth to him is this, that he is in Christ, that he hath been elected in Christ by God the Father from everlasting, that he is one in Christ; he was one with him from everlasting, he was one with him when he hung upon the cross, he is one with him now in heaven. 'Into whom,' so the words will bear, as well εἰς as ἐν, you may read either, one as well as another; I speak for the scope and meaning of it.

I will give you a scripture for this interpretation: 2 Cor. i. 21, where he speaks of establishing and sealing our hearts, he putteth in this phrase, saith he, 'He who stablisheth us with you εἰς Χριστὸν, in Christ, is God.' He hath stablished us in Christ, or sealed us in Christ, (for that followeth, ver. 22, ὁ δὲ σφραγισάμενος,) into Christ. And, John xiv. 20, 'At that day ye shall know that I am in my Father, and you in me, and I in you.' So that a man's union with Christ, his being in Christ, is the matter sealed up to him; 'in whom ye are sealed.' My brethren, in the work of sealing there is the love of all the Persons manifested; God the Father's love, and Christ's love, and our union with him, he leaveth not him out. Therefore you shall find, 1 John v. 8, there are three witnesses in heaven that witness love to us, as well as three on earth. I remember that I shewed that the work of baptism is the outward seal, to which this inward seal most principally referreth; for baptism is not to work regeneration, that is a mistake, as circumcision was not. Rom. iv 11, he calleth circumcision 'the seal of the righteousness of faith, which Abraham had, being uncircumcised;' so that it is not to work, but to seal regeneration and salvation unto us. Now, as we are said to be 'baptized into Christ,' Rom. vi. 3, that is the outward seal: so this is the inward work, whereby the Holy Ghost sealeth a man into Christ. 'In whom we are sealed;' it may be as well εἰς as ἐν, as it is in that place of the Corinthians which interpreteth it.

Or, in the second place, this phrase, 'in whom ye are sealed,' importeth, and the intent of it is to shew, by virtue of whom this benefit is bestowed, that it is bestowed by virtue of Christ. The work of sealing is wrought in us by virtue of Christ; it is in him virtually, though by the Holy Ghost efficiently. The Holy Ghost is the author of it, but Jesus Christ is the virtual cause. In that 2 Cor. i. 20, the place I quoted even now for sealing and stablishing us, you shall find there, that 'all the promises are yea and Amen in him.' Now as all the promises are *yea* and *Amen* virtually in Christ, they had been worth nothing else, if he had not died to make them good, so the sealing of all the promises unto the heart of a believer is in him too. So the words that follow, 'He that stablisheth us, and sealeth us in Christ,' will bear both senses, as well as here it doth.

Now, my brethren, to open this a little, for it is a point of useful consideration. The work of sealing of the Holy Ghost is done by virtue of Jesus Christ. He, and his virtue, is left out in no work that is done for us. I remember that I gave you this rule in handling of the 10th verse, and it is a thing I have largely elsewhere handled, that whatsoever work God doth upon us, he doth unto Christ first. Now then, are we sealed virtually in Christ? Why then, we must find the same work upon Christ himself first. We died to sin, because he died; we rose from sin, because he rose; we are sealed, because he once was sealed, and by virtue of that we come to be sealed. This is necessary to be opened, if you will understand the full scope of this, 'in whom ye are sealed.' Now we read that Jesus Christ was sealed, John vi. 27, 'For him hath God the Father sealed.' Mark it, *him* hath he sealed. Now do but look into your margin, and see to what the translators have referred this sealing of Christ; to Matt. iii. 17. Do but read there, and you shall find that Jesus Christ, when he was baptized, which, as I told you, is the outward seal, heard a voice from heaven, saying, 'This is my beloved Son, in whom I am well pleased.'

My brethren, as Christ did partake of the same ordinances we do, so there was some effect that these ordinances had upon him, which he was capable of, answerable and suitable to what they have upon us. Therefore, as baptism is the outward seal, to seal up adoption to a believer, and the witness of the Spirit is the inward work, the fruit of baptism, to be waited for, (yet a man hath it not by virtue of his baptism;) so when Christ was baptized, what was the fruit of it? What was the inward work answerable to the outward upon him? This, 'This is my beloved Son, in whom,' &c. And as the inward seal of the Spirit to us is an immediate witness, so was this from heaven to Christ. Not that ours is an immediate voice from heaven, but a light of the Holy Ghost's superadded to the light of faith; other revelations cease, and they are the revelations that the Papists speak of.

That you may see your ground for this, look 1 John v. 9, compared with the verses going before. He saith there are three witnesses in earth, and three in heaven, that bear witness to two things (read the place, you will find it the scope.) First, that we have eternal life in Christ; and, secondly, as appeareth by the 9th verse, that Jesus Christ is the Son of God; 'This is the witness of God,' saith he, 'which he hath testified of his Son.' There are three in heaven that bore witness that Jesus Christ is the Son of God when he was baptized; there was God the Father, and God the Son, and God the Holy Ghost, all these three did bear this witness. There was God the Father; he speaks, the voice that came from heaven was his voice properly, for he called him his Son, 'This is my beloved Son;' there was God the Father's testimony. And, John i. 32, 'the Holy Ghost descended down upon him like a dove;' there is the Spirit's witness, and all at his baptism. And then, as 'he that believeth hath the witness in himself,' so Christ had the witness of his being Son of God from the second Person also; he had it in himself. All these three witnesses concurred then at his baptizing; and thus was Jesus Christ our Lord and Saviour then sealed. Will you have me speak plainly? Though he had the assurance of faith that he was the Son of God, he knew it out of the Scriptures by reading all the prophets; yea, and as Adam had it written in his heart that he was the son of God, so Christ had the like instinct and law in his spirit that he was the Son of God; yet to have it sealed to him with joy unspeakable and glorious, by the witness of all the three Persons, this was deferred to the time of his baptism. He was then 'anointed with the Holy Ghost,' as I remember the expression is, Acts x. 38; 'anointed with the oil of gladness' —that was the first beginning of it—'above all his fellows,' in a more peculiar and transcendant manner. Now mark it, answerably (compare 2 Cor. i. 22) he hath sealed and anointed us, just as he sealed and anointed Christ in his baptism. We are conformed unto Christ; look what was wrought upon him, is wrought upon believers. He did believe in God, and himself to be the Son of God by faith from his mother's womb, so he telleth us, Ps. xxii. 9. But this eminent, transcendant, heavenly witness of it from all three Persons, was deferred till now. So now we see we are sealed in him, by virtue of him, and by his being sealed.

IV. The fourth thing in the text is this, *The efficient cause by whom we are sealed.* By the Spirit, the third Person in the Trinity, who is described to us by two things. 1. That he is the *Spirit of promise.* 2. A *holy Spirit,* and this as a sealer, for so you must understand it. All these must be spoken to; for there is a mystery lieth in all these. First, here is the Spirit by whom we are sealed, there is the person. Secondly, here is his description as he is a sealer: 1. he is the Spirit of promise; 2. he is a holy Spirit. You shall find every one of these have their weight in the matter of sealing.

First, *For the person.* Let us speak to that a little. The Apostle had mentioned the work of the other two persons before: he had mentioned the work of God the Father; 'Blessed be God the Father, who hath blessed us with all spiritual blessings;' so ver. 3 and 4. He had mentioned God the Son before; 'In whom we have redemption through his blood,' and we are 'chosen in him,' &c. But he had not mentioned the Spirit before; yet he had mentioned the work of the Spirit before too, the work of faith and the work of vocation, working prudence and wisdom, as I shewed before out of the 8th verse. What is the mystery of this?

Obs.—The thing I observe out of this is, That it is the special work of the Holy Ghost to comfort and assure the hearts of believers of their salvation. It is a most special work of the Holy Ghost. I will give you but two evidences out of Scripture for it. The first is out of John xiv. 26. Our Saviour Christ did forbear to comfort them, for he telleth them there is a Comforter to come; 'But the Comforter,' saith he, 'who is the Holy Ghost, whom the Father will send in my name, he shall teach you all things,' &c. Our Saviour Christ would not take the office out of his hands, he is to be your Comforter, saith he, and I will refer all to him. As he is called by the special name of the Comforter, to shew what is his special work and office, so answerably you shall find that joy is called 'joy in the Holy Ghost,' 1 Thess. i. 6. It is the Father's love which is sealed up to us, it is the Son in whom we are sealed, so it is the Holy Ghost by whom we are sealed. The Father prescribed all the cordials, the Son tempered them, but the Holy Ghost applieth them. 1 Cor. ii. 10, 11, As the spirit of a man only knoweth the things of a man, and he to whom this spirit in him will reveal it: so, saith he, it is the Spirit of God that revealeth the deep things of God, that everlasting love of his. Who else but he is to do it? It is his office.

Therefore, my brethren, you must give the honour of all the comfort you have to the Holy Ghost in a more special manner. Give it not to your graces, though the Holy Ghost witnesseth with them; there is no comfort you have but in the power of the Holy Ghost; there is an express place for it, Rom. xv. 13. Therefore look not to your graces; I mean, do not ascribe it to your graces, do not pore and dote upon them; it is the Holy Ghost always comforteth when they comfort. As it would derogate from Christ to ascribe justification to any other, so it derogates from the Holy Ghost to ascribe comfort to any other. And remember, that the special thing upon which mention of the Holy Ghost is made is, when comforting, when assuring, when sealing cometh to be mentioned.—So much for that observation.

Come we now to the description of the Holy Ghost here, as he is a sealer. First, he is called *the Spirit of promise.* Secondly, he is called *the Holy Spirit.* 'Ye are sealed,' saith he, 'with that holy Spirit of promise.'

He is called the Spirit of promise for two reasons and considerations. First, because, take him as he is a sealer and comforter of them that believe, he is promised; we have a promise that the Holy Ghost shall comfort us and seal us. Therefore, because the Holy Ghost is the thing promised, and that as a sealer, we are said to be sealed by the Spirit of promise. And, in the second place, he is called the Spirit of promise as a sealer; because he never sealeth but by a promise, as I shall shew by and by; it is *ab effectu.* To speak of both these—

The Holy Ghost is called the *promise*, and that as a sealer, (that is the first thing,) because he is promised. Our Saviour Jesus Christ was the great promise of the Old Testament, but the Holy Ghost is the great promise of the New. I need not quote you places to shew you that Christ was the great promise of the Old Testament. You have it Acts xiii. 32, and Heb. xi. 39. Many places might be brought. The Holy Ghost is the great promise of the New; he is called the 'promise of the Father,' Acts i. 4, ii. 33, and Gal. iii. 14. 'That we may receive,' saith he, 'the promise of the Spirit.' He is called the promise there, because he is the thing promised.

My brethren, God doth give forth all three Persons in promises, (it is a good observation by the way.) He hath a Son, he promiseth him; well, he hath given him, that promise is ceased,—I mean in the exhibition of Christ in the flesh,—is fulfilled. He hath a Spirit, you shall have him one day fully; but in the meantime you have him under a promise. He hath given us his Spirit also, saith he; that also cometh in 2 Cor. v. 5. He had given us his Son before, he giveth us his Spirit too; he hath promised it. There is God the Father, you have him promised too; for the time will come, as it is 1 Cor. xv. 28, that 'God will be all in all.' You have all three Persons in promises. God hath put forth all out of himself, he hath more blessings than one, he hath promised all in himself. But the Holy Ghost is called the Spirit of promise, as he is a sealer. That is the point I must stand upon.

The word here is, in the original, *τῆς ἐπαγγελίας*, of that promise; he hath put the article to every word, τῷ πνεύματι, that Spirit, τῆς ἐπαγγελίας, of that promise—namely, of sealing, to seal believers. There is a special promise, my brethren, unto believers, that they shall have the Spirit to seal them, if they sue it out. Many want it, but there is a promise for it, that same 14th of John which I quoted before. The apostles, they were believers, ver. 1; they had the Spirit dwelling in them, ver. 17; yet he promiseth them the Spirit both in ver. 16, 20, and 26. He doth not promise him as a sanctifier, but under the notion and in the name of a Comforter; not only as one that should give gifts to them and make them apostles, but should comfort them. They believed already; but that the Holy Ghost should come unto them as a Comforter, here was a special promise yet to be fulfilled. Look into Acts i. 4, 5, and you shall find this to be true; he biddeth them there wait at Jerusalem 'for the promise of the Father, which,' saith he, 'you have heard of me; for John baptized with water, but you shall be baptized with the Holy Ghost, not many days hence.' And still observe it, for it is spoken of him as a Comforter; for so Christ promised him, though indeed he came with enlargement of gifts upon them too as apostles.

You will say, the apostles had this promise, who were extraordinary men, have believers the same?

Read first Acts ii. 33. Saith he, Christ being ascended, 'and having received of the Father the promise of the Holy Ghost, he hath shed forth this which ye now see and hear.' They were filled with the Holy Ghost as with wine, as the Apostle's expression is in the Ephesians, so that they said they were drunk. But doth this belong to believers? See what he saith to the men that were pricked in their heart, ver. 38, 'Repent, and be baptized every one of you, in the name of Jesus Christ, for the remission of sins,'—that is, for assurance of remission; for otherwise a man must believe before he be baptized, for so they did, and so they were, as appeareth, ver. 41, 'They that gladly received the word were baptized,' or, they should be baptized, that they might receive the remission, or the assurance of the remission of their sins,—'and ye shall receive the gift of the Holy Ghost. For the promise' (mark it, that promise that was made to us, and you have seen fulfilled to us) 'is unto you and to your children; and to all that are afar off,'—to the Gentiles afar off to the end of the world,—'even to as many as the Lord our God shall call.' Mark that, to all believers. There is a promise of it, you may sue it out; and therefore you shall find, Gal. iii. 14, there is mention of the receiving of the promise of the Spirit after believing, 'That they might receive,' saith he, 'the promise of the Spirit through faith.' What promise of the Spirit is it that a man receiveth through faith? A man must have the Spirit to work sanctification, (mark that;) then to have the Spirit as a worker of faith, as a beginner of sanctification, cannot be the meaning of it; but there is an eminent promise yet to be fulfilled to believers, for they received the promise of the Spirit through faith. What promise of the Spirit is that? The Spirit as a sealer, the Spirit as a comforter; for so he was promised to the disciples after they believed.

Obs.—What is the observation from thence? Plainly this: You that are believers, wait for a further promise of the Holy Ghost as a sealer, and sue it out with God; for you see here the great promise, it is the promise of the Spirit as a sealer. So you shall find, Acts i. 4, that the apostles were to wait for the promise of the Spirit: so do you. My brethren, those that did receive the word gladly, as the text saith, Acts ii. 41, had a promise of the Holy Ghost to be expected as a comforter, as a sealer, as the place there evidently implieth. Though you have some joy wrought in you by faith, yet there is some further promise still to be expected; 'For the promise,' saith he, 'is to you, and to all that are afar off, even to as many as the Lord shall call.' You shall find in John vii. 38—that I may not stand reckoning up many places—that our Saviour Christ saith, 'He that believeth on me, as the Scripture saith, out of his belly shall flow rivers of living water,' of water to comfort and refresh him. 'But this spake he of the Spirit, which they that believe on him should receive; for the Holy Ghost was not yet given' (mark,) 'because that Jesus was not yet glorified.' My brethren, let me vent that notion to you, for I believe it will hold, that the giving of the Holy Ghost as a sealer with joy unspeakable and glorious, was reserved to the times after Christ was glorified. Men had the Spirit to work faith before, they had faith under the Old Testament; but for the Spirit to come and work joy unspeakable and glorious in ordinary believers, was not till Jesus Christ himself was glorified. It is true that David and some other saints in the Old Testament had it, who were eminent types of Christ, that was to be anointed with the oil of gladness; but the ordinary saints under the Old Testament had a spirit of bondage upon them; there was a spirit of adoption too, but not to seal up to a man his sonship. This is the great promise of the gospel, which cometh to believers when Jesus Christ is glorified, when he is ascended up to heaven, and there is 'anointed with the oil of gladness above his fellows;' then he poureth out the Spirit upon men, which will sue out this promise.

My brethren, it is the great fruit of your baptism; you have not that great fruit of your baptism till you have this. The circumcision of old was a seal of the righteousness of faith, and of the promised seed, of Christ to come, of a bloody Saviour, to redeem by blood; for so circumcision was by blood. Now as circumcision was then, so now that Christ is come and glorified, our baptism is the seal of the Spirit; it is the proper work that answereth to baptism. Therefore you shall find it is called 'baptizing with the Holy Ghost,' because it is that which is the fruit of baptism, it answereth that outward seal; and therefore you may read that Peter biddeth them be baptized, and they should receive this promise, Acts ii. 38.

You that believe are to wait for this promise; as the Jews waited for the coming of Christ, so are you to wait for the coming of the Holy Ghost into your hearts. It is said that the fathers served God night and day, waiting for the promise, namely, Christ to come, Acts xxvi. 6. Serve your God day and night faithfully, walk humbly; there is a promise of the Holy Ghost to come and fill your hearts with joy unspeakable and glorious, to seal you up to the day of redemption. Sue this promise out, wait for it, rest not in believing only, rest not in assurance by graces only; there is a further assurance to be had. It was the last legacy Christ left upon earth. Look John xiv. 16; he saith there that he would send the promise of the Father; this very promise of sending the Comforter; read Luke xxiv. 49. Therefore sue out the will of Christ, sue out that last legacy of his. It was the fruit of his ascension; when he was ascended up and received this promise, then he poured it out.

And let me add this too—I thought to make it a distinct observation—from *the persons here that were to be sealed.* 'Ye were sealed;' ye, who? Ye Ephesians; they were ordinary believers, they were not apostles, they had not all miraculous gifts, yet he saith of them, 'Ye were sealed with the Spirit of promise after ye believed.' Read over all the epistles, and you shall find almost all the saints in the primitive times sealed; thus the Corinthians they had it, 2 Cor. i. 22, 'God hath stablished us with you, and hath also sealed us.'

The Ephesians had it you see, they were sealed; for afterward, chap. iv. 30, he exhorts them not to grieve the Holy Spirit, by which they were sealed. The Thessalonians had it, 1 Thess. i. 10. They received the word with such joy, that he saith they waited for the coming of Jesus Christ from heaven; for that is the next step, heaven is next unto it, and to wait for Christ when you are thus sealed. Those that Peter wrote to had it, 1 Pet. i. 8, 'In whom believing, ye rejoice with joy unspeakable and full of glory.' Thus ordinary it was in the primitive times; where the defect lies God knows; but certainly it might be more common if men would sue it out; such a promise there is. He is therefore called the Spirit of promise, because he is promised as a sealer.

Only, my brethren, let me give you a direction or two. First, believe this promise, wait for it by faith, make it the aim of your faith; we are said to 'receive the promise of the Spirit through faith,' Gal. iii. 14. Believe there is such a thing, aim at it, wait for it, and serve God day and night in all humility to obtain it, rest in no other lower and under assurance; and in the end the Lord will give it. The reason why men attain it not is, because they rest in other assurance, and they do not aim at this; they content themselves with bare believing, and that their consciences are quieted. But, my brethren, there is such a work as sealing by the Spirit, if you have faith; there is a Spirit, and a Spirit of promise made to believers, which you may receive by faith. This is the first reason why he is called a Spirit of promise, because he is promised to believers as he is a sealer.

I mentioned *a second reason* why he is called the Spirit of promise as he is a sealer. What is that? Because he always sealeth by a promise. These truths, my brethren, are worthy your laying up, not only to clear the doctrine of this great work of the Spirit, (and I still speak what is proper to the text,) but also to direct you, and to try whether you have it, you that boast of it. It is always, I say, by a promise; when he sealeth he bringeth a promise home to the heart. He is therefore called the Spirit of promise, because he useth a promise in sealing; as we say of a soldier, he is a man of the sword, because a sword is the weapon he useth; so he is called the Spirit of promise because he useth a promise. As we are said to be heirs of the promise, because the promise belongeth to us, so he is called the Spirit of promise because he comforteth us by a promise. There is a Spirit lieth hid and dwelleth in the promise to comfort us, if faith could but draw him down to come into our hearts and set them on.

My brethren, we heard that Jesus Christ was sealed when he was baptized; but he was sealed by a promise, it was not by an immediate revelation only, but by bringing home a truth to his heart. What was it? 'This is my beloved Son, in whom I am well pleased.' This is a Scripture promise, you shall find it in Isa. xlii. 1, 'This is my servant, in whom I delight; my elect, in whom my soul is well pleased.' That which had been spoken before of the Messiah is brought home to his heart. He sealeth not up his Son when he speaks from heaven immediately, but he doth it by a promise; therefore much more, my brethren, doth he seal up you. The Word and the Spirit are joined; they are joined in the new Jerusalem, much more now. Isa. lix. 21, the promise there, that 'my Word and my Spirit shall not depart out of thy mouth,' is spoken of the calling of the Jews plainly, for the Apostle quoteth it in Rom. xi. 26, and it is the only place he quoteth for their call. 'The Redeemer shall come out of Zion,' are the words just before. When Jesus Christ gave the promise of the Holy Ghost as a sealer and Comforter to the apostles, he calleth him a Comforter indeed; but how?

Saith he, 'He shall bring all things to your remembrance, for he shall take of mine and shew it unto you;' for if the Holy Ghost do not come with a word, and take of Christ's and set that upon your heart, it is a delusion; he sealeth by a promise still, and therefore in all that discourse of Christ, where he promiseth him as a Comforter, in John xiv., he calleth him a 'Spirit of truth,' as well as a Comforter. Therefore when we say, it is an immediate testimony, the meaning is not that it is without the Word; no, it is by a promise; but the meaning is, it is immediate in respect of using your own graces as an evidence and witness: but he bringeth home a promise to the heart, some absolute promise or other; he 'rideth upon the wings of a promise,' as you may read in the Book of Martyrs, concerning Bilney. He is a Spirit of promise, my brethren, when he sealeth. Therefore let me tell you this, all your revelations that are without the Word, or would draw you from the Word, are naught and dangerous. We do not speak for enthusiasms; it is the Spirit applying the Word to the heart that we speak of. It is not to write new Scripture, to make words, to be guided by the Holy Ghost without the Word. No, we detest all such; but it is to draw you to the Word; he fasteneth the Word upon your hearts, sealeth you by a promise; therefore he is called a *Spirit of promise.*

There is one thing more that I must make an end of; it was necessary to open these truths unto you, for I could not open the words else. The last thing he is described by as he is a sealer is, *that he is a holy Spirit.* The Holy Ghost hath put a mighty emphasis upon this, as you shall see by and by; he hath put an article upon every word, as they that understand the Greek know, it is τῷ πνεύματι τῆς ἐπαγγελίας, τῷ ἁγίῳ, 'sealed with that Spirit of that promise, that holy.' There is not the like again in any place. There is a special promise of him as a sealer; and he sheweth himself to be a holy Spirit, if in any work, in sealing. And, which is more, he doth not say, 'that Holy Spirit,' τῷ πνεύματι ἁγίῳ; indeed we translate it so, we put holy to Spirit; but the truth is, the word *holy* cometh in divided from the other, and *promise* cometh in between, in the Greek, τῷ πνεύματι τῆς ἐπαγγελίας, τῷ ἁγίῳ, it is 'that Spirit of that promise, that holy.' This is the true reading of it according to the original, to shew that this title of holy is not given to the Spirit himself, but as an effect of his in sealing. It is true, indeed, he is holy in himself, and it argueth him to be so, if he make us so when he sealeth us; for look what impress is left upon the wax must needs be in the seal much more; if he make us holy when we are sealed, he himself must be holy much more originally. But that is not the aim of it, only to shew that he is holy; but to shew that when he sealeth then he works holiness; therefore the Holy Ghost here putteth an emphasis upon it, by putting to the article 'that.'

Observe from hence this, that all assurance that is true assurance, and the true seal of the Holy Ghost, it makes a man holy. If ever anything makes him holy, this doth it. Is he a holy Spirit in working faith? Doth he purify your hearts by believing? He will purify your hearts much more when he sealeth you, when he works joy in believing, unspeakable and glorious.

Yea, my brethren, God doth not give this promise of his Spirit as a sealer till a man be very holy. John xiv. 21, 'He that hath my commandments, and keepeth them, he it is that loveth me; and he that loveth me shall be loved of my Father, and I will love him, and manifest myself to him.' God doth not put these cordials into a foul stomach; and when a man hath these, they make him wonderful holy. Take the apostles for an instance. The apostles, as I told you, were believers, they had a promise of the Holy Ghost as a sealer and a Comforter; but they were to wait for it, as you read in Acts i. 4. Now all the while they waited for it, what did they? They continued all the while, till they had it, in prayer and supplication; the text saith so; they were exceeding holy, especially before. Well, when they had it, how holy did it make them! It is of purpose made the preface to the Book of the Acts. You see how full of boldness they were, how full of zeal, because full of the Holy Ghost, and full of the joy of the Holy Ghost. The apostles were poor low Christians as any are, almost. When Jesus Christ was to die, how sleepy were they! When Christ was administering the sacrament to them, and told them what he should suffer, they talked presently 'who should be the greatest amongst them.'

Thus carnal were they, they had not received the Spirit as a sealer; but when once they had received him as a sealer, read the story of the Acts, read their Epistles, and see what a spirit of boldness and zeal they had. 'When thou art converted, strengthen thy brethren.' It is a new conversion, it will make a man differ from himself in what he was before in that manner almost as conversion doth before he was converted. There is a new edition of all a man's graces, when the Holy Ghost cometh as a sealer. Self-love bustleth before, and keepeth a coil to secure itself; but when once self-love is secure, and the love of God is shed abroad in a man's heart, it makes a man work for God ten times more than before, or else at least more kindly. I know there are ways wherein the soul can glorify God more, in a way of recumbency, when he hath not assurance, by submitting himself to God whatsoever becometh of him, and by pure trusting of God, though he know not whether he will save him or not, which is the greatest trust in the world. But yet in matter of holiness and obedience, the assurance of the love of God, when it is shed abroad in the heart, will constrain a man, as the apostle's phrase is. 'He that hath this hope,' he speaks of assurance in that 1 John iii. 3, 'purifieth himself, even as he is pure.' My brethren, it is the next thing to heaven, therefore it must needs make a man heavenly. If there were nothing but self-love in a man, it is true he would abuse it when he hath assurance; but when this love shall stir up love to God, and bring a greater increase of love to God above a man's self, how will that work! I appeal to you, good souls, if Christ do but look toward you a little, how holy doth it make you! Much more, then, when the Holy Ghost is poured out upon you, and when you are baptized with the Holy Ghost as a Comforter. Look, as when the sun cometh near to the earth, then is the spring; it was winter before; so when the Holy Ghost cometh in this manner upon the heart, it was winter before, but it will be spring now.

My brethren, to end this, therefore all those comforts,—mark what I say, try yourselves, and try others by it,—all those revelations and comforts that make men loose and unholy, unclean and carnal, are not these comforts of the Holy Ghost. I confess, a holy man may, when they are gone, abuse the remembrance of them; but while they are upon the heart, they do carry a man's soul in all up to God. The apostle Jude doth not know how to speak words bitter enough against those men that turn the grace of God into wantonness. 'They are ordained of old,' saith he, 'to this condemnation.' Read how bitterly he speaks of such men from the third verse to the end of his epistle; especially when men shall be loose in their opinions, as he saith, 'corrupt themselves' in what they know naturally to be sin. My brethren, he is a holy Spirit, nothing is more opposite to this holy Spirit than looseness, than uncleanness, and such sins are. 'If we say,' saith he, 1 John i. 6, 'that we have fellowship with God, and walk in darkness, we lie.' What doth he mean by fellowship here? He meaneth assurance plainly. These things we write to you, that you may know ye believe in the Son of God; (it is the scope of that epistle,) he that saith he hath fellowship with God, and walketh in darkness, lieth; let him be what he will. The apostles are vehement, their spirits are up against no men more. He is a holy Spirit of promise that sealeth men to salvation.

Let this therefore be made a motive to seek it at God's hands; urge him with this, besides his promise; tell him it will make you holy. It is a great motive to seek it, it is a motive to you to seek it, and it is a motive to you to urge God to obtain it.

I conclude with this: a seal hath two ends and uses, the first is to assure and certify, and the other is to stamp an image; for so always a seal doth. Now they are both here. He is called the Spirit of promise, because he bringeth home the promise to a man's heart and assureth him of an interest. He is called the Holy Spirit of promise in sealing, because he stampeth the image of holiness upon you, and makes you more holy than before.

So you have the meaning of these words, 'In whom ye were sealed with that holy Spirit of promise,' with all those concurring scriptures that were necessarily to be brought for the opening of them.

SERMON XVII.

Who is the earnest of our inheritance until (or, *for*) *the redemption of the purchased possession, unto the praise of his glory.*—VER. 14.

IN the first place, For the reference of these words to the former; 'who is the earnest.' It referreth not unto Christ, 'in whom you are sealed,' as Faber Stapulensis would have it; but they refer to the Spirit of promise mentioned immediately before. And to put us out of doubt in it, in 2 Cor. v. 5, it is called the 'earnest of the Spirit.' Christ is called nowhere an earnest.

Then, secondly, For the scope of his words. The verse I have read to you is the conclusion of all about the benefits bestowed upon us, and of the Apostle's application of these benefits both to Jew and Gentile. He had enumerated all sorts of benefits,—election, predestination, our redemption by Christ, our vocation, and faith, and sealing. In enumerating of all these benefits, his scope is to mention the special glory that all the three Persons have, and are to have, from us in the work of our salvation. And so his scope is here to shew how great a gift of the Holy Ghost is added unto all that Christ hath done for us, and unto all the Father hath done for us, of which he had spoken in the former verses. As he had set out the Father's work in election in the 4th, 5th, and 6th verses, Jesus Christ's work in redemption in the 7th and the 10th verse, so here his scope is to set forth the great benefit we have by the Holy Ghost: the greatness of that gift, 'We are sealed by him, who is,' saith he, 'the earnest of our inheritance.' It is the conclusion of all, and so comprehendeth all that either the Spirit is to us, or works in us. It expresseth the greatness of the gift of the Holy Ghost to us, and the use that that gift is to us.

So you have the reference of the words; you have the coherence and scope of the words.

Now for the division of the words. You have three things contained in this verse eminently.

I. The first is, *That the Holy Ghost is an earnest.*

II. The second, *Of what he is an earnest?* of an inheritance. *Until when?* 'Until the redemption of the possession' of that inheritance.

III. And then, thirdly, *The end of all;* 'to the praise of his glory.'

I. I must first begin to explain *the Holy Ghost's being an earnest.* And, *first,* I shall explain the phrase unto you, what that importeth in itself. And, *secondly,* how it is to be understood that the Holy Ghost is an earnest.

And, first, for the phrase *earnest,* what is meant by that? 'Ἀῤῥαϐὼν; it is a word which the Greeks had from the Jews; and although it is not only used in the New Testament by the Holy Ghost, but by profane writers also, yet the Greeks had it from the Tyrian merchants, and so used it in their bargains as an earnest of the whole sum in bargaining. They used it likewise for any other kind of earnest whatsoever.

The Hebrew word is of a larger signification; it takes in a *pledge* or pawn, as you call it. You know in your English phrase a pawn is one thing, an earnest is another. Now the word that the Jews used, from whence this is fetched, signifieth a pledge, a pawn, as well as an earnest. As Gen. xxxviii. 17, there Tamar doth require of Judah a pledge that he would give her what he promised her. But the Grecians use it especially for an earnest. Ἐνέχυρον is put for a pledge, but ἀῤῥαβὼν for an earnest.

Now you will ask, how these two, a pawn and a pledge, do differ from an earnest?

I will shew you, first, *what is common to them both*, which will help to open the thing; secondly, *wherein they differ*.

In common, the nature and use of a pledge and an earnest is this, both are to give assurance, to give security. If a man borroweth money of one, oftentimes they leave a pawn; that pawn giveth assurance, giveth security for the payment of so much money. On the other side, if a man goes to bargain with one, the buyer giveth an earnest to the seller, and that also doth bind the bargain. They are both for security, they are both for assurance, that is the scope of both.

How do they differ then?

A pawn is properly for money borrowed, or promised to be paid, and must always be worth as much as the money that it is engaged for; who will take a pawn else? But an earnest is not so; an earnest is but a part in hand. You shall have a bargain that is worth a thousand pounds, and the earnest it may be is but sixpence, or a shilling, or a piece. It is but part of the payment.

In the second place, a pawn or a pledge may be something of another kind from money. One may pawn his jewels, his clothes, for money; but an earnest always is a piece of money, for money to be paid. It is a thing of the same kind.

Then, thirdly, a pawn is restored again when the money is paid; but an earnest is never restored, for it is part in hand; a man keepeth it for ever by him.

So that now, by this, you will come to understand what is meant by an earnest. It is, first, a part in hand, part of payment, it is not the whole. It is, secondly, something of the same kind; it is part of the same we shall one day receive. And, thirdly, it is never restored again as a pawn is. I shall have use of these, as you shall find, in opening how the Spirit is an earnest.

The second thing for opening the phrase is this: I have shewed you how a pawn and an earnest differ; now let us see what reference this phrase hath, in the place it cometh in, both to what is before and what is after.

An earnest is of use in two cases, and they are both here glanced at.

An earnest is of use in case of buying and selling, when the buyer hath not money ready, or the seller hath not his commodity ready, then you give money as an earnest of the bargain.

Secondly, an earnest doth not hold only in buying and selling; but it holdeth in conveying of inheritances. This is the latitude of the Greek phrase. You shall see it amongst ourselves, as I take it, at this day. When an inheritance is conveyed to another man, there is first a writing drawn, with hands unto it. Answerably, there is now for the inheritance of heaven sanctification and faith wrought in the heart, which are the finger of the Holy Ghost; they are his work. There is, secondly, the seal, which is after you have believed and have been sanctified. And, thirdly, in conveying inheritances, if I be not mistaken, they use to carry a man unto the ground. If you sell land or convey an inheritance, if you will give possession, what do you? You carry him unto the ground, and there you give him a turf of earth, something that grows upon the ground,—not money, but something of the same kind with the inheritance he is to possess,—and that bindeth the party, as lawyers know; and it is said to give possession, to give the buyer a further degree of right.

Now see how aptly the Holy Ghost followeth this similitude here in these words. He aimeth at both, he glanceth at both. First, at that way of bargaining; and that is evident by two expressions, the 'redemption which is by price,' ἀπολύτρωσις, and the 'purchased possession.' Yet he chiefly aimeth at conveying an inheritance, for so the words are expressed; it is the earnest, saith he, of our inheritance; and the word *possession*, that relateth to inheritances: 'The earnest of our inheritance, until the redemption of the purchased possession.' He glanceth, you see, at both, and takes in both.

And, first, to speak a little to that of bargaining. It is true, my brethren, that heaven is a free gift, and there is no buying and selling between us and God about it in a proper sense. Yet let me tell you of this first, that Jesus Christ bought it, it is his *purchased possession* for us. Now as we sinned, Jesus Christ paid the debt, and he purchased the possession, and we have the earnest of the bargain.

And it was exceeding proper it should be so. Why? Because we are Christ's, we are one with him. It is my purchased possession, saith Christ; give them the earnest of it for whom I purchased it, and it is all one as if you give it me. So now, though in a contrary way to bargaining,—for there the buyer useth to give the earnest of the money, not the seller of the commodity; but here God doth accept of Christ's money, and giveth us an earnest, part of the commodity in hand;—yet if you will take it in respect of bargaining, it is an earnest between us and God; the Scripture is not abhorrent from that metaphor. You shall find in Matt. xiii. 44, 45, the kingdom of heaven, saith Christ, is like to treasure hid in a field, which a merchant man espieth, selleth all that he hath, and buyeth the field. It is not a proper buying indeed; but it is a buying what in him lieth, it is a parting with all he hath; God can have no more. He giveth up all his lusts, all the interest he hath in this world, and all the comforts of it, he giveth up himself; it is a buying without money, as the phrase is, Isa. lv. 1. Now then, when we have given up ourselves thus to God; sold ourselves to him to work righteousness, as Ahab sold himself to work wickedness, then doth God come; there is an earnest for you, saith he; he giveth us an earnest of the commodity which we give up ourselves for. That is the first use of it, it is in respect of bargaining; how it is in respect of inheritances I shall shew afterward.

Observe now how properly and pertinently the Holy Ghost followeth these two similitudes or metaphors of *sealing* and *earnest;* he placeth his words most fitly. When he speaks of heaven as a thing promised, then he mentioneth the seal of the Spirit; 'Ye were sealed,' saith he, 'with the Spirit of promise.' When he speaks of heaven as a thing to be possessed and enjoyed, he useth the metaphor of an earnest, or part in hand, that doth give a kind of possession beforehand.—So much now for opening the phrase, and the correspondency that one phrase hath to another, which giveth much light to the whole.

The second thing, as I told you, to be done is this, to shew *how the Holy Ghost is an earnest.*

The great question I had with myself a long while was this, Whether the Holy Ghost is said there to be an earnest only in respect of working assurance of salvation in the hearts of men; so as the meaning should be, that whereas before the Apostle had expressed the work of assurance by *sealing,* now he doth do it by a new metaphor of being an *earnest*, importing only the same thing: so as this similitude should be limited to the same thing only that sealing is, namely, to work assurance. But when I had fully considered it, the upshot of my thoughts is this:—

It is true, indeed, he mentioneth this of the Spirit being an earnest in a special manner, in respect of assuring us of salvation; for the scope of an earnest is to assure as well as a seal; yet so as it is not to be limited only to the work of assurance, though he hath that especially in his eye; but it is spoken in a large and more general sense, as when I shewed the scope of the words I mentioned; he speaks of the Spirit in respect of all he is to us, and all the work in us. In a word, he is not only an earnest in respect of working an assurance in our hearts,—though so and more particularly,—but he is an earnest in his person given unto us, in his graces wrought in us. An earnest takes in all these. It is a general proposition, brought in indeed upon an occasion of the mention of the Holy Ghost as a sealer in the words before; and it doth second that phrase, and doth more peculiarly suit and comply with it, for an earnest is ordained to assure, yet it is taken in a larger sense. Therefore, now I am to do two things in opening how the Holy Ghost is an earnest.

I am first to shew in general, *how the Spirit and all his workings are all the earnest of our inheritance.*

Yet, secondly, that there is a work of *assurance*, in which he is *more particularly* an earnest.

The scope of an earnest is both to assure the thing, and it is to assure the party to whom the earnest is given. Now in the general sense, take the gift of the Spirit, the graces of the Spirit, they all *assure the thing;* but then the work of assurance which the Holy Ghost works, that *assureth the person.* He is an earnest in both.

The metaphor of a seal only respecteth the work of assurance, as I shewed when I handled it; but the similitude of an earnest doth import assuring the thing. It is an earnest of heaven, to make that sure in itself; and it is an earnest of heaven to us, to make us sure of it too. Now therefore I shall speak of these two things.

First, in general to shew you that the Holy Ghost and all his graces are an earnest of our inheritance, that makes sure the thing to us.

And, first, the Holy Ghost himself, abstractedly taken from all our graces, being given to us, is the greatest earnest of heaven to make it sure of all other. My brethren, the gift of the Holy Ghost is the greatest earnest of heaven that ever was or could be.

You must know that in the Greek ὅς there is a varying from grammatical rules in relation to what he had spoken of; for he had spoken of the Spirit, πνεῦμα, in the neuter gender; but yet he saith ὅς ἐστιν, 'who is,' it is not 'which is.' I know the observation, and I took it as an excellent one, which Beza makes out of it, that to shew, saith he, that the Holy Ghost is a person, though πνεῦμα be in the neuter gender, yet he speaks of him in the masculine, as of a person, as elsewhere in John xvi. 13, 'When he shall come,' speaking of the Spirit of truth; he speaks of him as of a Person, 'when he,' saith he. Which should teach us to speak reverently of the Holy Ghost;—it is a good observation, that we should not say of him, *it*, as is the usual manner amongst us to say, Lord, give us thy Spirit, that it may work this or that. No, that HE may work this or that; he is a person. The original word varieth, as they that know it know well; he doth not say, *that* or *which*, but *who* or *he;* we should speak still of the Holy Ghost, not as of a thing, but as of a person. I thought, I say, it was a good observation, that which is gathered from it; but, my brethren, it is not all the meaning of it, when he saith, he, or who, (speaking of his person,) is an earnest. His meaning is, that the gift of the person of the Holy Ghost, taken severed from all his works in us, his person given to us to dwell in us for ever, as he is, this is the greatest earnest that God could bestow upon us, of our inheritance to come. And that is the first thing wherein the Holy Ghost is an earnest; he is an earnest in the gift of his person.

You shall find, 2 Cor. v. 5, the Apostle speaks there of the person of the Holy Ghost, as an earnest given to us distinct from his graces and works in us. Mark the phrase, 'He that hath wrought us for this selfsame thing,' namely for heaven, which he speaks of ver. 4, 'is God.' Here is you see the work of God upon us; he hath wrought, he hath fashioned graces in our hearts. Are not they the great earnest? No, not comparatively, for it followeth, 'who also hath given unto us the earnest of his Spirit.' You shall find in another place, as I shall shew anon, when he speaks of working assurance, he calleth it the earnest of the Spirit in our hearts; but here is the person of the Spirit mentioned distinct from his works; 'who hath also given us the earnest of his Spirit.'

The giving of the Holy Ghost is the greatest earnest of heaven to come, and that considered as distinct from his graces wrought in us. I will make this plain to you in a word or two.

He is the greatest earnest of heaven. Why? Because he is more than heaven. And in this, if you will, he is a pledge rather than an earnest; that signification will come in, for it will bear both. It is a rule in the civil law, a pawn must always be worth more than the money it is pawned for. My brethren, the Holy Ghost is more than heaven, let me tell you so. The Apostle argueth in Rom. viii. 32, If he have given us his Son, how shall he not with him give us all things also? I will argue likewise, Hath he given the person of his Spirit to you to dwell—not personally, take heed of that—but to dwell in your persons for ever; why, will he not give heaven and all things else, which are less than his Spirit? The gift of the Holy Ghost is the foundation of all grace and glory.

And more, my brethren; we have two of the greatest pawns of our going to heaven that ever was. First, we have the Lord Jesus Christ in heaven with our nature, to shew that man's nature shall come there; there is a pawn in heaven for it. He sendeth down the Holy Ghost into our hearts, the third Person, to shew we shall come thither likewise; for this Spirit will fetch us up. If he be given to your persons once, as I shall shew you by and by, he will never rest till he hath brought you thither. So he is called an earnest, because he is the great gift, and will draw on the less.

And, secondly, if he be given you simply, his person to your persons, why then he is engaged to bring you to heaven. You think, if you get grace in your hearts, there is an earnest of heaven. Why, grace in itself might be lost, if it were not for the Holy Ghost that dwelleth in your hearts; that is the fountain of it; the stream may be cut off, but if the stream have a fountain that continually bubbleth up, the stream will never be dried up, the perpetuity of the stream dependeth upon the fountain. Now, who is the fountain of all grace? It is the Holy Ghost, the gift of the Holy Ghost. John vii. 38, 'He that believeth on me, as the Scripture hath said, out of his belly shall flow rivers of living water.' Here is a fountain, you see, whence shall flow rivers of living water. Who is this fountain? Read on, 'This he spake of the Spirit, which they that believe on him should receive.'

It is the same Spirit, my brethren, that works grace and works glory. In Rom. viii. 23, we are said to have received the 'first-fruits of the Spirit.' Why is grace there called the first-fruits of the Spirit, but because if you have the Spirit you shall have glory? The same Spirit that works grace works glory, as the same ground that beareth the first-fruits beareth the crop.

Learn, therefore, to value and prize this great gift of the Holy Ghost. If he dwell in you, and hath begun to work grace in your hearts, which is an argument his person is given to your persons for ever, he will never leave you. The Spirit doth not dwell in us as he did in Adam, so long as we shall be holy; but he dwelleth in us to work holiness, he cometh down to us therefore when we are unholy.

I will name but one place; it is Rom. viii. 11: 'If the Spirit of him that raised up Jesus from the dead dwell in you;' what then? 'He that raised up Christ from the dead shall also quicken your mortal bodies by his Spirit that dwelleth in you.' My brethren, doth the Spirit dwell in you now? When you are laid in the grave, that Spirit dwelleth in you as he did in the body of Christ; I do not say in the same high manner. The Spirit of God did dwell in the body of Christ in the grave, and raised it up, he never left him; though his body was a dead carcass without a soul, yet that body was hypostatically united to the Godhead, therefore it is called Holy One: 'My Holy One shall not see corruption.' Now, the comparison is, If we have the Spirit of Christ, and if he dwell in us, the same Spirit shall never leave our bodies till he hath raised us up also. Nay, while thy body is dead and rotten in the grave, the Holy Ghost dwelleth in it. So that now the gift of the Holy Ghost is the greatest earnest of heaven that could be. That is the first.

As the Spirit is an earnest of heaven, so the graces of the Spirit are to assure the thing still, for that is one use of an earnest. My brethren, grace is part of heaven, as I have oft expressed it; it is that to heaven which colours are to varnish, that is grace to glory. 'He that believeth hath eternal life.' Love, you know, is said to remain, 1 Cor. xiii.; and grace is called the first-fruits of the Spirit, Rom. viii. 23.—And so now in general you see how the Holy Ghost is said to be the earnest of our inheritance in a more large sense than the work of assurance; he is an earnest both in the gift of his person, and likewise in his graces.

What graces? you will say.

Why, in faith and love. You would look for some glorious thing now; faith and love are the graces that God works by the person of the Holy Ghost given unto thee. The Apostle instanceth in these two in the next verse to the text: 'For this cause,' saith he, 'I have given thanks for your faith in Christ, and love to all the saints.' Hath the Holy Ghost wrought these in thy heart? These are an earnest that the person of the Holy Ghost is given unto thee; and the person of the Holy Ghost being given unto thee, is an earnest that that inheritance that God hath appointed for his children shall be thine. That Spirit dwelling in thee that dwelt in Christ, shall raise up thy mortal body as it raised up Christ's.

Now, my brethren, I must come to the *second* place, and shew you how, though, in general in a more large sense, the Holy Ghost is said to be the earnest of our inheritance; yet in a more proper sense it is spoken *in respect of the work of assurance which the Holy Ghost works in us.* That is the peculiar, special thing that the Holy Ghost hath in his eye; and why? Because he coupleth it with sealing. Saith he, 'He hath sealed us by his

Spirit, who is the earnest,' namely as a sealer, as one that giveth assurance; we have assurance in us of our redemption, &c. Compare but Eph. iv. 30 with this verse; there you read, 'We are sealed to the day of redemption;' that is, God hath wrought assurance in us that we shall be redeemed, and he hath sealed us up to the day of redemption. Here it is, 'Who is the earnest of our inheritance, until the redemption,' &c. So that both import the work of assurance.

The end of an earnest is to work assurance in the party that it is given unto, as well as a seal. You shall find in 2 Cor. i. 21, 22, speaking of establishing us in Christ,—it is a place I have often quoted,—of his working assurance in our hearts of being in Christ, he calleth it in the next verse sealing us, and giving us the earnest of the Spirit in our hearts. He mentioneth them both, and putteth them both together, as being that whereby the Holy Ghost doth establish us. And in that he addeth, 'He hath given us the earnest of the Spirit in our hearts,' for that is the phrase there—the place in 2 Cor. v. 5 I quoted even now mentioneth only giving of the Spirit; but in that place of 2 Cor. i. 22 he is said to give the earnest of the Spirit in our hearts,—what is the meaning of that? It importeth a work upon the heart, to assure and establish the heart; that it is not only an earnest from God to the person to make the thing sure to him, but it is an earnest wrought in the heart of the man to whom the thing is given in a special manner. And that that is the meaning of it, read the next verse in that 2 Cor. v. 6, 'Therefore,' saith he, (because we have this earnest,) 'we are always confident.'

Now, my brethren, the great business is this, seeing the earnest of the Spirit is put for giving assurance, and the sealing of the Spirit is put for the giving assurance too, how to distinguish these two; or rather, what is it that the one similitude holdeth forth more eminently, and what doth the other mainly import? I had thought sometime that the earnest of the Spirit had been some further thing than the sealing of the Spirit; but certainly it importeth the same thing, only, as the manner of Scripture similitudes is, wherein one simile falleth short the other helpeth it out. So they both imply the work of assurance. He hath sealed us by the Spirit, who is an earnest—that is, as a sealer he is an earnest; yet sealing implieth one thing in assurance, the earnest of the Spirit implieth another.

You will ask me, how we shall distinguish these two?

I shall do it briefly, as God hath given me light. You know the soul of man hath two great faculties that are wrought upon; he hath an understanding, he hath a will and affections. Now, as we believe with the whole heart, so we are assured with the whole heart too. There is a work both upon the understanding and upon the will; by the one a man knoweth his estate in grace, his understanding is fully convinced of it; the will and affections do taste the sweetness of it beforehand. You shall find, Rom. v. 5, speaking of assurance, which he calleth hope, as he doth elsewhere, he saith, 'Because the love of God is shed abroad in our hearts;' not only into one faculty, but into all faculties, both into the understanding and will.

Now then, if you will know what sealing holdeth forth more especially, it is the work upon the understanding. The seal, though it assureth, yet it is not part of the inheritance; but the earnest so assureth as it giveth you part of the inheritance; it works that joy in the heart which the saints shall have in heaven. You have both these mentioned in assurance in some places of Scripture. The work of assurance upon the understanding, (that is properly sealing,) Col. ii. 2, it is called πληροφορία τῆς συνέσεως, 'the full assurance of understanding.' So, Heb. x. 22, it is called the 'full assurance of faith.' It is an overpowering light, whereby a man's understanding is fully convinced that he is God's, and that God is his; as God knoweth who are his, he knoweth himself to be God's. That is sealing properly or more eminently. Now what is earnest? It is a giving you part in hand, part of that joy and comfort, that taste of heaven. When he thus sealeth he accompanieth it with a taste, with 'joy unspeakable and glorious.' It is a part taken up beforehand, as heirs take up money upon their lands beforehand. It is not a bare conviction that a man shall go to heaven; but God telleth him in part what heaven is, and lets the soul feel it. There is nothing sweeter than the love of God, and the tasting of that sweetness is the earnest of the inheritance.

I shall give you scripture that holds forth both these. Look into Ps. iv.; there first you have the work upon the understanding of a man, ver. 6, 'Lord, lift thou up the light of thy countenance upon us;' then followeth the work upon the will, ver. 7, 'Thou hast put gladness in my heart,' saith he, 'more than in the time that their corn and their wine increased.' In Col. ii. 2, you have two things mentioned: you have first 'that their hearts may be comforted'—there is the earnest of the Spirit; then you have, 'unto all riches of the full assurance of understanding'—there is the seal of the Spirit. The Spirit, John xiv., as promised by Christ, is called both a Comforter and the Spirit of truth; the one for working upon the will, putting comfort there; the other for working upon the understanding, convincing that. 1 Thess. i. 5, 6, compared, there is receiving the word 'in much assurance'—that is the work upon the understanding; and there is with 'joy in the Holy Ghost'—that is the work upon the will and affections. Here is sealing, here is earnest.

You shall find in 1 Pet. i. 8, 9, he had said that 'believing, they rejoiced with joy unspeakable and full of glory;'—therefore this is no less than heaven, part of heaven. When Paul was in heaven, what did he hear? Things unspeakable; so is this joy, and it is called glorious because it is a part of heaven;—here now is the earnest of the Spirit. Yea, if you observe the phrase that followeth in the 9th verse, 'Receiving,' saith he, 'the end of your faith, the salvation of your souls.' I find that the best expositors interpret this receiving of salvation not to be meant of heaven, for then he would have said, you *shall receive* salvation; but to be meant of assurance, which is the end of faith, it is the reward of faith. When a man hath been long tried, (the trial of your faith, which he speaks of, ver. 7,) in the end he cometh to be assured, he receiveth the end of his faith, which is the assurance of the salvation of his soul. Why is it called salvation? It is heaven, my brethren; that is the reason of it. So now you see what is meant by the earnest of the Spirit, both in respect of assurance and also in respect of assuring the thing, and the work of assurance.

I shall now come to some observations. The first observation is this:—

Obs. 1.—There is no falling from grace. Why? Because the gift of the Holy Ghost, and his graces, and the work of assurance, are an earnest. Pledges indeed are restored again; if he were only a pledge or a pawn it were something, but he is said to be an earnest. Now, what saith Christ, John xiv. 16? 'I will give you the Comforter, that he may abide with you for ever;' never to be returned again, as you know an earnest is not.

The truth is this: if men to whom he giveth the Spirit should not be saved, God must lose his earnest, he must lose his Spirit. As he would not lose the death of his Son, that he should die in vain; so he will not lose his Spirit, whom he giveth as an earnest unto believers. Luke x. 42, saith Christ to Mary, 'Thou hast chosen the better part, which shall never be taken from thee.'

Obs. 2.—Secondly, As joy in the Holy Ghost and assurance is an earnest, it is part of payment. You know in an earnest, if you have part in hand, you have the less when you come to receive the full sum. I will not say that it is so here, that those that have most comfort here shall have less in heaven; but this I will say, if they do not improve this earnest, if they do not put this talent out to use, they shall have less, let me tell them so. I may say in this case, just as Christ said to Thomas, John xx. 29, 'Because thou hast seen me, thou hast believed; blessed are they that have not seen, and yet have believed.' Thou hast seen Christ, thou hast an earnest of heaven, thou hast some sight, some taste; it is well thou art obedient; but let me tell thee that they that are obedient as thou art, and yet have not this earnest, there is more behind. Therefore, poor soul, comfort thyself; hast thou not had this earnest penny, and yet thou hast been obedient to God? There is the more behind.

Obs. 3.—You that have the earnest of the Spirit, prize it. You use to lay up your earnest money, by which you may sue for the bargain, safely and carefully, you prize it more than all your other money, as you do your bonds more than all your other papers in your study besides, because you have that to sue for your debt. Value, therefore, the Holy Ghost's graces, especially the earnest of him whereby he works assurance.—So much now for this, that he is said to be the earnest of our inheritance.

II. Now, to come to the second thing mentioned, *of what he is said to be the earnest, and until when*. He is said to be 'the earnest of our inheritance until the redemption of the purchased possession.' I put both these together, of what the Spirit is an earnest, and until when, as under a second head.

First, Of what? Of an inheritance. What is the inheritance? Will you know what it is, my brethren? Look Rom. viii. 17, we are said there to be heirs of God. It is a mighty speech; I do not know how to speak more of your inheritance. 'Heirs of God,' saith he, 'and co-heirs with Christ;' that is, God himself is your inheritance. Why, how do you prove that this is the meaning of it? Because you are co-heirs with Christ. Now, who is Jesus Christ's inheritance? Who makes Christ happy? God. Ps. xvi. 5; it is a psalm of Christ plainly: 'The Lord is the portion of mine inheritance, and of my cup;' and so he concludeth, 'At thy right hand there are pleasures for evermore.' Now, my brethren, if God be the inheritance, you see a just reason why that the person of the Holy Ghost should be the earnest, that he that is God should be the earnest of the inheritance, which is God too.

I will give you one scripture more; it is Rev. xxi. 7, 'He that overcometh shall inherit all things, and I will be his God.' God and all things are a man's inheritance, whereof the Holy Ghost is the earnest.

He is the earnest 'until the redemption of the purchased possession.' The word εἰς, our translators do rightly interpret it; they read it *until*, for so, Eph. iv. 30, 'Ye are sealed,' saith he, 'unto the day;' εἰς ἡμέραν, until the day, until then; for that indeed is the proper scope of an earnest when the full payment and possession is deferred, to assure in the meantime, to assure until then; therefore, Rom. viii. 23, we are said to wait for the redemption of the body, having received the first-fruits of the Spirit.

The second thing to be explained is redemption. What is meant here by redemption?

That is easy. It is not the redemption by Christ's blood; there needeth no earnest until that, for that is past, that is done already. That you read of ver. 7, 'In whom we have redemption through his blood,' that is not actual redemption, it is the paying of the price once for all; but the redemption here is actual and complete full redemption; as Luke xxi. 28, 'When your redemption draweth nigh, lift up your heads.'

There is a twofold redemption. The one is a redemption by price, the paying of the price. In Heb. ix. 12, it is said that Jesus Christ, before he went to heaven, obtained redemption for us. And there is a redemption of application of that price unto us, which is the redemption meant here; as Eph. iv. 30, they were sealed unto the day of redemption; it is to come.

And let me say this to you, the reason why Musculus would have this word possession added to redemption is, saith he, to distinguish it from that redemption of Christ's by price, that was *redemptio solutionis*, the redemption of paying the price; but this is *redemptio possessionis*, whereby we are put into the possession of it. It is εἰς ἀπολύτρωσιν τῆς περιποιήσεως. And that is the account that he doth give of the phrase.

Or if you will, I will distinguish it thus to you, that I may magnify the Holy Ghost unto you. There is a redemption by Jesus Christ's paying the price, and there is a redeeming us by the Spirit, applying that price; therefore he is said to be the earnest of our inheritance for the redemption—that is, to work redemption; so some interpret εἰς ἀπολύτρωσιν, he is the cause of redemption, he is ἀῤῥαβὼν εἰς ἀπολύτρωσιν, on purpose to work it, not as an idle earnest that lieth by us, but as a hostage; being a person that works the redemption of the party, he is a hostage for us. Therefore if you read Rom. viii. 9, 10, 23, you shall find that the redemption of our bodies, and the raising up of our bodies, is ascribed unto the Spirit of God. So now you easily understand what is meant by redemption.

But then why should the Holy Ghost put in this word *possession*, and 'purchased possession,' as the word indeed signifieth? Certainly he is not redundant, it is not an overplus. Eph. iv. 30, where he speaks of the same thing, he saith merely this, they were 'sealed to the day of redemption;' but here it is 'until the redemption of the possession.' There is a mystery in it.

First, Beza makes it a mere *hypallage*, that is an inversion, a speaking backward; or, as I may express it in English, instead of saying *possession of redemption*, he saith *redemption of the possession;* and it is, as scholars know, a frequent thing in Scripture to use such inversions of speech; as 'the law of righteousness,' for 'the righteousness of the law,' or the righteous law; a man of blessedness, for a blessed man; Lev. v., there 'the silver of the shekel' is put for a 'shekel of silver,' &c.

And there is this to confirm Beza's interpretation, that in 1 Thess. v. 9, where he useth this phrase, we are, saith he, ordained εἰς περιποίησιν σωτηρίας, for the possession, or obtaining salvation. It is the same word used here. So that the possession of salvation in that of the Thessalonians is all one with the possession of redemption here, redemption being ordinarily called salvation. Therefore, as I said before, Musculus saith it is put by way of distinction, that whereas in the 11th verse he said we had obtained an inheritance, here in the 14th verse he saith the Spirit is an earnest of the possession of that redemption, or of that inheritance.—That is the first interpretation.

But, my brethren, because that this may seem to be a harsh phrase, we will see if there be anything that expositors give that will run more smoothly and currently. I find that there are two interpretations that are given of it yet more.

It is called, in the first place, 'the redemption of the purchased possession,' by *purchased possession* meaning the people of God; so that the meaning is this, that the Holy Ghost is the earnest of our inheritance till all God's people, his purchased possession and inheritance, be all redeemed, and then we shall receive the full inheritance together with them all. And this, the truth is, most interpreters run upon, and Calvin himself; and he giveth this good gloss upon it too: 'You should not,' saith he, 'think much to stay a while, and only to be content with an earnest, for you stay but till God hath gathered in all his people whom he hath purchased; when he hath once perfectly redeemed them all, you yourselves shall be estated in the inheritance.' The Spirit is an earnest of the inheritance, until the redemption of the purchased possession.

To give you some scripture to confirm this interpretation. First, in 1 Peter ii. 9, there he calleth the people of God—he useth the very same phrase that is used here—λαὸς εἰς περιποίησιν, 'a peculiar people,' or a purchased possession to God, so you may read it. He doth allude unto that in Exod. xix. 5, whence he takes the word, where they are said to be 'a holy people, a peculiar treasure,' or an inheritance unto God. And so now, as he calleth heaven our inheritance in the former words, so he calleth us that are redeemed God's inheritance in these words.

I shall name no more places, but that Deut. xxxii. 9, 'The Lord's portion is his people, Jacob is the lot of his inheritance.' And then, whereas it is said they are a purchased inheritance; my brethren, it is well added, for the people of God are so; they are not only God's inheritance by choice, but they are his by purchase. The word περιποιεῖν, as all Grecians acknowledge, is to get a thing by labour, by cost, and by conquest, and so it is more than κλῆρος. They are not only his inheritance, but they are his purchased possession, his purchased inheritance. Look into Acts xx. 28; saith he, 'The church whom he hath purchased with the blood of God.' The word used for *purchased* there, is the same word that is used here. This is the glory of the people of God, that they are God's purchased ones; not only his inheritance, but his *purchased* inheritance.

A second interpretation is this. By 'purchased possession' here is meant heaven itself. The same thing which he had spoken of before, calling it there an inheritance, here he calleth it a purchased possession. For this there is as express a scripture as for the former: Heb. x. 39, 'We are not of those that draw back to perdition, but of them that believe,' εἰς περιποίησιν, 'unto their salvation;' it is the same word that is here; we translate it 'unto the salvation of their souls,' which salvation is purchased by the blood of Christ. So that now his scope is, to note out the glory of heaven to consist in two things. First, in a perfect redemption, freeing us from all sin and misery; and, secondly, in a glorious possession, purchased by the blood of Christ. Now, saith he, 'He is the earnest of our inheritance, until the redemption of our purchased possession.'

But only the phrase, you will say, is harsh to interpret it of *heaven;* for how, you will say, is there a *redemption?* for heaven is not said to be redeemed; it is *bought* indeed, but how is it said to be redeemed?

I answer two things. In the first place, it is said to be the *redemption* of this possession in respect of the persons to be redeemed and possessed of it. That is sometimes attributed to heaven which is not meant of *it*, but of the *persons* that shall come thither. As, for example, it is called an inheritance immortal and undefiled. Why? Because we shall be undefiled when we come thither. 'I go,' saith Christ, 'to prepare a place for you.' It was prepared from the beginning of the world; he saith so, because *they* were to be prepared. So, because we are to be redeemed and to be possessed of it, therefore it is called 'the redemption of the possession;' that is, by which, when we are redeemed, we shall be possessed of it.

And, my brethren, it is not an improper phrase to say, 'the redemption of this possession,' of heaven. Why? Because there lieth a great many clogs in our way to it which must be removed: there lies sin and Satan, in whose hands we are, and death; and all these we must be redeemed from, all these must be removed before we have clear and quiet possession; therefore it is said, the Spirit is a seal until the redemption of the purchased possession. As a man that hath an estate, and right to it good enough, but he is troubled with suits in law that keep him from the possession of it; it may be called the redemption of his possession, when all is paid, and all suits are at an end.

If you ask me which of these two the Holy Ghost meaneth? Clearly and plainly, my brethren, he meaneth both, and it is the greatest elegancy in the writings of the Holy Ghost that he should intend both; as you shall see by and by.

For, first, if you take this purchased possession to be meant of heaven itself, that inheritance he speaks of, which the Spirit is the earnest of, it is the most elegant expression that could be. Why? For whereas you have not the actual possession of heaven until you are redeemed from sin and misery; and an earnest doth use to give interest in a possession beforehand, it giveth a right unto the land, you may claim the land by it. Hence he fitly saith he is the earnest of our inheritance aforehand, before we come to possess it, and being redeemed to possess it.

Then, again, if you take it for the church and people of God, for God's inheritance, it is as elegant every way and as proper. For, first, the Apostle's meaning is this, 'Ye have the earnest of the Spirit,' saith he, 'until the redemption.' Do you think much to stay for it? you do but stay till the redemption of all God's people; it is a common case, and God himself stayeth for them; they are his peculiar, they are his treasure, they are his purchased ones; he stayeth till they be redeemed: therefore, saith he, you may well stay. They were his redeemed people, his people purchased by the blood of Christ; but though purchased by the blood of Christ, yet they are 'sold under sin,' as the Apostle saith; they are *pawned*, the word is; and therefore they are detained from him by sin, and death, and Satan. Now therefore he in the meantime giveth them an earnest until the redemption of this possession, until he hath redeemed unto himself, and vindicated by his Spirit his people unto himself.

My brethren, whereas God is fain to stay for his own inheritance, what doth he do to make sure of the commodity? He giveth an earnest. It is an elegant expression, and infinitely comfortable to us. As the Holy Ghost is an earnest to us of *our* inheritance, he is an earnest to God of *his* inheritance too. The Apostle hath both in his eye, for our hearts are slippery commodities. God hath bought us by the blood of Christ, we would give him the slip; therefore, to make sure of us, he giveth us his Spirit, to be an earnest of our redemption too, to redeem us, and to bring us to heaven at last. And the word περιποίησις, 'purchased possession,' signifieth a guard, those that are guarded and defended; it signifieth *tueri*. He giveth us the Holy Ghost to guard us to heaven: an earnest, not to lie still, but as a hostage to accompany us thither. God is loath to lose you, as you are loath to lose him, therefore he giveth you his Spirit as an earnest; therefore nothing can be more to the comfort of God's saints. Thus vast and various is the Holy Ghost in his writing, and in his aims in both these expressions. We are God's inheritance; he is our inheritance: the Holy Ghost is an earnest to *us;* he is an earnest to *God,* 'until the redemption of the purchased possession.'

Now you have the meaning of the words, I will give you an observation or two from them.

Obs.—First, see the love of God.

1. That God should not only bestow an inheritance upon us, but bestow himself upon us, for himself is this inheritance; and not only make us heirs of him, but make us his own inheritance too, for so the word *possession* will bear it; that that God, who is blessed for ever and needeth no creature, should call his people his inheritance, which he liveth upon as it were,—for you know that a man's inheritance is that he liveth upon,—call them his purchased possession: here was love.

2. That he should purchase this inheritance by the blood of Christ, and pay so dear for it. They are not only his inheritance, but his purchased inheritance too; he did it to shew his love the more.

3. When he had bought us by Christ, he sheweth yet a further love; for though we were bought, and the price was paid, we still lie in sins, and therefore he sendeth his Spirit into our hearts to rescue us thence, to subdue us, to redeem us; until the redemption of the purchased possession he giveth the Spirit as an earnest.

4. He doth this to make sure work, that he might not lose us.

5. He giveth us this Spirit as an earnest to assure us in the meantime, to comfort us. He doth not only reserve heaven for us, (as it is 1 Pet. i. 4,) but he is careful to give us the Comforter while we are here, beforehand. You see the love of God.

Obs.—In the second place, do but observe, from what hath been opened, some arguments of the greatness of the glory of heaven.

1. Heaven is an inheritance given, and God's inheritance. Great men give inheritances answerable to their greatness; what inheritance then will God give? Himself, my brethren, as you heard before: 'heirs of God, and co-heirs with Christ.' You cannot be more happy than God can make you, or than Jesus Christ is, and you are co-heirs with him.

2. How great must that inheritance be, when 'joy in the Holy Ghost' is but the earnest! The earnest, you know, is but part in hand; it is but a sixpence, it may be, to a thousand pounds. Then, as a father well saith, how great is the possession, when the earnest is thus great! Take joy in the Holy Ghost, it filleth your hearts fuller of joy than all the good things in the world will do. So David telleth you, more than corn, and wine, and oil. Are you in distress? It carrieth you above all those distresses: 'We rejoice in tribulation,' saith the Apostle; they made nothing of tribulation. Nay, saith he, rejoice when you fall into divers of them. This the Holy Ghost doth. If the earnest do this, shall a little piece of it do this, what will the possession itself be? If you mark it, the great inheritance is to come.

3. It is called the purchased possession, if you interpret it of heaven. Purchased by what? By the blood of Christ. What think you will the purchase of Christ's blood come to? Do but think. A king's ransom is used to express a great sum; what will the ransom by the blood that was made a ransom,—so the text saith, 1 Tim. ii. 6,—what will the ransom by the blood of God come to? When Jesus Christ laid down his blood, saith he,

Let my heirs take out all that blood of mine in glory and grace. What will that glory come to, think you?

4. It is both a redemption and a possession. Two things in hell make men miserable, and divines know not which is the greater. The one is *pœna damni*, that they have lost heaven and happiness, and that wringeth them; the other is *pœna sensus*, the feeling of the wrath of God. The glory of heaven answerably, which makes us happy, consisteth of two things: a redemption from misery, and the possession of happiness.

III. There is yet one thing more in the text, which I must speak something unto ere I conclude; they are the last words in the 14th verse, *Unto the praise of his glory.*

It is a thing mentioned as *the end of all.* It is mentioned in the 6th verse as the end of election; 'to the praise of the glory of his grace.' It is mentioned in the 12th verse, in his application to the Jews; 'that we should be to the praise of his glory, who first trusted in Christ.' It is mentioned here again in the 14th verse, when he maketh application of all unto the Gentiles; 'in whom ye also trusted, &c. unto the praise of his glory.'

You shall find that, in all the enumerations of the benefits of God towards us, these two things come in again and again, 'in Christ,' and 'to the praise of his glory.' That 'in Christ' cometh in nine times; 'to the praise of his glory' cometh in thrice. There is a trinity of glory unto God, as there are Three Persons whom he had distinctly mentioned as the authors of our salvation; both God the Father, and God the Son, 'in whom we have redemption through his blood,' at the 7th verse; and God the Holy Ghost, 'by whom ye are sealed,' 'who is the earnest of our inheritance,' ver. 13.

To the praise of his glory. It referreth first to the persons; when he had spoken of the salvation of the Jews, ver. 11, 12, there he mentioneth their salvation to be 'to the praise of his glory.' When he speaks it again to the Gentiles, there he sounds it out again, 'to the praise of his glory.'

That the Gentiles should be added to the Church, therein was God exceedingly glorified. So it is said in the Acts, when they saw that God had given repentance to the Gentiles, then they glorified God. And though in making application both to the Jew and Gentile, he reckoneth apart something of the one and something of the other, that are in common to be applied to both; yet in his application he distinctly mentioneth, 'to the praise of his glory.' So in the conclusion of his application to the Jew, in the 12th verse, 'to the praise of his glory.' So in the conclusion of his application to the Gentile, in the 14th verse.

As it referreth thus to the persons, that God should have glory for converting the Gentiles, turning them; so likewise it referreth to the special benefits he had mentioned. He had mentioned their believing, he had mentioned their being sealed up, and having the Holy Ghost as an earnest of their inheritance: 'to the praise of his glory,' saith he.

Every new benefit should have 'to the praise of his glory' added to it in our hearts. Dost thou believe? Live to the praise of his glory. Hast thou assurance added to thy faith, and a being sealed by the Holy Spirit of promise? There is a further expectation that thou shouldest be to the praise of his glory; for God hath in that, if thou beest sealed, glorified thee, for to that it hath reference. He that is sealed up to the day of salvation, and hath 'joy unspeakable and glorious,' that hath his heart filled with it, hath not only the Spirit of grace, but, as the Apostle saith, 1 Peter iv. 14, he hath the Spirit of glory resting on him. He hath the beginnings of glory in his heart, therefore it is expected that he should live much more to God's glory. It is the expression of Peter, in that 1 Peter i. 9, as by the coherence appeareth, and as I have shewed already, that those which are filled with 'joy unspeakable and glorious,' which are the words just before, do receive the end of their faith; they do receive it at present, they have part of their wages; they are partly in heaven, especially at the time when they have it. Therefore if God glorify them, it is expected much more of such that they should live to his glory. And self-love in these is secured, it is provided for, which useth to bustle in those which want assurance; but God hath quieted and secured that principle in thee, that now thou must lay out all for God's glory.

Or else, in the last place, 'unto the praise of his glory' may have relation—and so Piscator carries it, and there is none of these references but it is to be taken in—to the 'redemption of the purchased possession.' There is a purchased possession to the praise of his glory; God hath appointed us and sealed us up unto it.

My brethren, why hath God appointed an inheritance, a heaven to his children? It is to the praise of his glory. God will be glorified in nothing more than in the greatness of that glory which he bestoweth upon his children at last. How great therefore shall their glory be, when the utmost glory of God, the utmost *praise of his glory*, of his manifestative glory,—for that is meant by the praise of his glory; glory is his essential glory, the praise of it is the manifestation of his glory,—when this must arise out of his glorified creatures? We shall by this see how glorious a God he is, by seeing how glorious and happy he can make creatures to be. In 2 Thess. ii. 14, he saith there, that we are 'ordained unto the obtaining,' εἰς περιποίησιν, 'of the glory of the Lord Jesus Christ.' The words may be read, as in the original they are, and interpreters read them, either to the obtaining glory in Christ, or else to the obtaining the same glory Jesus Christ hath; and either of both argue this glory to be infinitely glorious. 2 Thess. i. 10, 'When he shall come,' saith he, 'to be glorified in his saints, and to be admired in all them that believe.' This same purchased possession is to the praise of his glory. Then will Jesus Christ be manifested how glorious he is; but where and how? In them that believe; in shewing how glorious he can make them to be.

SERMON XVIII.

Wherefore I also, after I heard of your faith in the Lord Jesus, and love unto all the saints, cease not to give thanks for you, making mention of you in my prayers, &c.—VER. 15, 16.

General coherence and parts of the words:—

In the former verse he had set forth the causes of salvation and the original and fundamental benefits of election, predestination, redemption, calling, &c., from the 3d verse to the 11th. And then from the 11th to this 15th verse he had made application of it, both to the Jews, of which nation he was,—'in whom *we* have obtained an inheritance,'—and then to the Gentiles, under the persons of those Ephesians, 'in whom *ye* also trusted,' and so obtained an inheritance. After which, at the 15th verse, he beginneth to express his own particular affection to them, upon God's having endowed them with all those blessings before, thereby provoking these Ephesians, unto whom he had applied these great benefits, unto two great duties.

1. *Unto thanksgiving unto God*, who had bestowed such great things on them.

2. *To the further increasing in grace*, through the knowledge of them both; which he provokes them to by shewing what his own prayers and thanksgivings were to God for them.

Now he provokes them to these two duties most strongly, and yet but secretly and impliedly. He doth not say in express words, Wherefore, do ye give thanks, and do ye pray, &c.; but he doth more, he lays before them his own example, 'Wherefore,' saith he, 'I also do give thanks for you, and have not ceased to pray for you since I heard of your faith and love.' And this must needs strike all their hearts. Hath Paul, that is but as a stander-by, such a sense of the greatness of those things God hath bestowed upon us, that he giveth thanks for us, and out of his love to God and our souls prayeth that we may attain the knowledge of, and an increase in that knowledge of these things? How much more should we ourselves do it! If I, saith Paul; for he frameth his expression to such a meaning, καὶ ἐγὼ; even I, saith he,—or *I also*, as it is here translated,—do give thanks unto God for you, making mention of you in my prayers, then you yourselves much more should do it.

There are three things in these 15th and 16th verses.

First, *What Paul did for them;* which are two. 1. He gave thanks for them. 2. He had prayed for them; both amplified by this, 'without ceasing.'

There is, secondly, *The occasion of these;* Having heard, saith he—1. Of their faith in Christ; 2. Of their love to all saints.

Then, thirdly, there is *The subject-matter or cause of his thanks*, noted out in this particle 'wherefore,' διὰ τοῦτο, or 'for this,' I give thanks, which referreth to all those benefits he had before enumerated, made theirs hereby.

Exposition of the words :—

Wherefore.—This holds out the cause of his thanksgiving; and, first, it referreth to what he saith in the next words, 'hearing of your faith and love.' You shall find in that parallel epistle to the Colossians, chap. i. 3, 4, the same in the very same words: 'We give thanks to God, the Father of our Lord Jesus Christ, praying always for you, since we heard of your faith in Christ Jesus, and of the love you have to all the saints.' This was the cause of his giving thanks, their faith in Christ, and the love which they had to all the saints, as graces which did evidence their interest in all those benefits.

It referreth also, secondly, to all that went before. Paul had a comprehensive eye to all the benefits mentioned in the former verses, which God had bestowed upon them; this *wherefore* draweth all in. When I consider, saith he, how God hath elected you, predestinated you, redeemed you by the blood of his Son, given you faith, sealed you up by his Spirit, which Spirit is the earnest of your inheritance; διὰ τοῦτο, 'for this cause,' saith he, since I heard of your faith and love, and of your increase in these things, and so was confirmed thereby of the certainty of your interest in all these, I do give thanks for you, and I cease not to do it. Paul's giving of thanks for those he writes to, although usual in other epistles, yet is with this difference here from what elsewhere, namely, in respect of his ordering the bringing of it in. In other epistles it comes in in the preface or beginning, and stands alone and entire by itself; but here he ranks it in the midst of a discourse, after a large, exact, doctrinal enumeration of the great benefits we have in Christ, and withal after an application to the Ephesians, by shewing them their personal interest in those benefits; and so it comes in a way of coherence to all the rest foregoing, and upon occasion of those benefits. So as indeed Paul, looking back through this small particle, διὰ τοῦτο, *for this cause*, upon all the former beams of grace and benefits mentioned, and having taken a full and a summary prospect of them, gives thanks in the consideration of them for these Ephesians.

Yea, and, thirdly, this particle referreth to the very last words immediately before, 'to the praise of his glory.' God, saith he, had made this the end of all the benefits of our salvation, that himself should be glorified for them: *wherefore* I give thanks to God for you, and give him the praise of his glory on your behalf. God is not to lose his end, it is therefore my duty: wherefore I cease not to give thanks for you, &c. These three particulars, to which the words refer, are the cause of his thanks.

Obs.—Now the observation and meditation from hence is this: That the consideration of the greatness of the benefits of God towards us, when we take a full prospect of them, such as here the Apostle had given them, and withal our interest therein, with application to ourselves, which the Apostle here likewise made, together with this, that the end of all these is the praise of his glory,—when the soul considereth all this, it is provoked to give thanks to God. Learn, then, by this the way of stirring up your hearts to thankfulness to God. Take a view of all his benefits to you in Christ, labour to see your interest in them, and then consider that all this God hath ordained not for my salvation only, but for the praise of his glory. All this, if thoroughly apprehended by a fresh view of faith, will at any time move a good heart to give thanks to God.

Wherefore I.—Let us a little take notice of the grace of Paul, to quicken our own hearts by the example of it,—he was the highest example of grace, but Christ, that ever was upon earth,—and consider how enlarged his heart was in thankfulness to God for the salvation of the souls of others, as well as in desires to save them. 2 Thess. ii. 13, 'We are bound,' saith he, 'to give thanks,' to give glory, 'to God always for you, brethren beloved of the Lord, because God hath from the beginning chosen you to salvation through sanctification of the Spirit and belief of the truth.' It was not a matter of liberty, it was a matter of duty, as Paul here speaks of it; we are bound. And he speaks this, not as having been moved so much by his own interest in being the instrument of converting them; but he speaks of it as a brother, a member of that body, and accordingly, when he utters this thanksgiving, he calls them brethren: 'We are bound to give thanks always to God for you brethren, for you beloved of the Lord;' and the ground of it which he mentions is, that God hath loved them and chosen them. Here lieth much of the communion of saints, this is one great and high part of it. This is the angels' grace, to rejoice at the conversion of sinners; and this will be one great exercise of our grace in heaven, that we shall be thankful to God for his having chosen and saved every soul there. This will make up one great part of the happiness of heaven, that each saint shall rejoice in the salvation of all and every one as in his own; which will be like the reflection of a multitude of looking-glasses, so placed and disposed as every one reflects the image of itself upon the other in a moment. To return to Paul. In 1 Thess. iii. 9, he is so deeply affected this way, that he doth not know how to express his thankfulness to God: 'What thanks,' saith he, 'can we render to God again for you, for all the joy wherewith we joy for your sakes before our God?' It was when he heard of their faith, ver. 5, 6. My brethren, this is the happiness of a Christian, and of a holy heart, when made exceeding spiritual; he hath all that concerneth God's glory to rejoice in; the joy that we joy is 'for your sakes,' saith he; and yet not for their sakes simply, but 'in the sight of God,' having an eye to him too. This did fill his heart so full of joy, that he saith it kept him up in the midst of all his distresses; so, ver. 7, 'We are comforted over you in all our afflictions and distresses by your faith.' Oh, my brethren, where is the spirit of Paul?

Wherefore I also.—Καὶ ἐγώ, or, as the Syriac expresseth it, *Lo I.* He holds it up, *tanquam notandum*, that he should thus do it. I that am a looker-on, yet, saith he, through the grace of Christ, as it is my duty, I do give thanks to God for you; much more ought you yourselves. You see, saith he, how my heart is affected about you with the consideration of these great things which God hath bestowed upon you; therefore much more should your souls be thus affected unto God for yourselves.

Obs.—It should be a mighty argument to move the heart of any one to work out his own salvation, when he shall see another take care for it. Thou that art an ungodly son or servant, perhaps thy parents or thy governors, as thou mayest perceive, and thy conscience telleth thee, aim to bring thee to God, and to save thy soul. Do they do it, and wilt thou not do it much more? Should not this strike thee? Saith the Apostle, Phil. ii. 13, 'Work out your own salvation.' There is a motive with an emphasis, *your own.* We apostles labour about it; you are engaged much more to work out your own salvation.

After I heard.—This is the third thing, the occasion; the other was the cause. 'After I heard,' saith he, 'of your faith in the Lord Jesus Christ.' Acts xxi., we read that Paul had been the means of their conversion, and therefore must needs have been an eye-witness of their faith and love at that their first conversion. Why then, may some say, doth he here only mention, as matter of his thanksgiving, what he had by hearsay of them? It holds forth two things to us:—1. A further eminent grace and gracious practice of this apostle towards the saints, especially those to whom he was a means of conversion; namely, that when he had converted any, his calling of apostleship enforcing him to leave them, still his heart was longing, yearning after them, solicitous and inquisitive about them, to hear of their continuance in that faith, and growing up in grace. You shall see this too in 1 Thess. iii. 5, 'For this cause, when I could no longer forbear,'—mark his affection, he could not hold, he could have no rest in his spirit,—'I sent to know your faith;' and then, ver. 6, 'When Timotheus came from you unto us, and brought us good tidings of your faith,' &c., it was even as gospel unto me, 'and we are comforted in all our afflictions by your faith,' so ver. 7. 'And what thanks,' saith he, 'can we render to God again for you?' so at the 9th verse. You shall find the like, my brethren, in all his epistles. News of the saints thriving in grace kept Paul alive. 'Now do I live,' saith he, 'if ye stand fast in the Lord;' so it is ver. 8 of that chapter to the Thessalonians. It comforteth me in all my distresses; though I have I know not how many personal distresses, yet I draw that comfort out of the news of your faith, which upholds my heart, and doth counterbalance my afflictions.

2. It holds forth, that not only the work of conversion in others, but withal their growing up in faith and love, and walking suitably, is a great cause and matter of thanksgiving to God; for that this is both an evidence of the truth of conversion at first, without which it proves itself to be unsound, as also that whereby God is as much glorified.

Of your faith in the Lord Jesus Christ, and love unto all the saints.—1. In general. You shall find the same words to the same purpose used both in Col. i. 4, 5, 'We give thanks, since we heard of your faith in our Lord Jesus Christ, and love unto all saints;' and in his Epistle to Philemon, a particular person, 'Hearing of thy love and faith, which thou hast toward our Lord Jesus Christ, and to all saints.' He coupleth faith and love, you see, together, both as the two eminent graces, and as the two great evangelical commandments, summing up all in these two. Thus, in 1 John iii. 23, 'This is his commandment, That we should believe on the name of the Lord Jesus Christ, and love one another, as he gave us commandment.' Thus, likewise, the whole work of conversion: 'The grace of our Lord Jesus Christ was exceeding abundant in faith and love,' saith the Apostle of his own conversion, reducing all to these two, 1 Tim. i. 14.

2. Particularly—

Faith.—That goeth first, you see; for faith works by love, and it is love out of faith, 1 Tim. i. 5. Faith brings home the love of God to the heart, or else fixes the heart in a dependence upon it, and pursuit after it; and then these do cause love to all the saints. Be sure thou find faith in Christ coupled with love to the saints, yea, and to be the rise of it.

Faith in our Lord Jesus Christ.—It is Christ that is the object of faith. Faith, indeed, takes in, and looks at all things else in the world; but faith, as justifying, preyeth and seizeth upon Christ, as its proper object. This is, therefore, the usual style of the Scripture, speaking of or describing faith: 'Faith that is in me,' saith Christ, Acts xxvi. 18, for Christ is the more immediate object of faith; we believe in God through Christ, that through him our faith might be in God, 1 Pet. i. 20, 21. And it is not only upon the person of Christ simply considered, but it is upon Christ as *Jesus;* so here, 'faith in our Lord Jesus.' It is faith on Christ as a Saviour, for as such only he is fitted to a sinner's faith. Take Christ in his personal excellencies, he is rather the object of love than of faith; but take him as a Saviour, and as made justification to the ungodly, so justifying faith looks upon him. But of this elsewhere.

Yet further, by 'faith,' as he meaneth the work of faith, so he meaneth constancy in faith, persevering in faith; he doth not speak simply of their believing at first, for then he would have spoken of it, as out of his own experience himself had seen that. It was of the continuation of their faith, whereof he had heard. And thus the Apostle of the Thessalonians also; he calleth their continuing in faith, their faith, 1 Thess. iii. 6. Timothy, says he, 'brought tidings of your faith.' He had said in the first chapter, they had believed,—and himself was their converter, as of these here,—but yet afterwards he sent, and had heard by Timothy of their faith: that is, of their continuance and their constancy therein.

Your faith.—Here is one phrase more to be taken notice of. That which our translators have rendered *your faith*, in the original is καθ' ὑμᾶς, faith which is *amongst you*. And it denotes the eminency and renown of their faith. Faith in Christ being held out amongst them as the great and main business and matter of salvation, and not the doctrine of it only professed, but in the work of it; and this generally and ordinarily by them that were believers, so that it was notorious. *Passim apud vos*, as we in Latin speak, frequent or current amongst you; so eminently in the generality of believers, that their faith was renowned *tanquam fides Ephesina*, as the Ephesian faith. As in like phrase of speech, when we would speak of the learning in a university or society, as generally eminent, we say, The learning that is amongst you; as Paul of the Romans' faith, 'Your faith, which is spoken of in all the world,' Rom. i. 8.

Musculus carrieth it to this sense, that because Paul did not think them all godly, therefore he doth use a more wary expression; not saying, the 'faith that is in you,' but the 'faith that is among you.' Others, that the Apostle intended only an outward profession of faith, common to carnal Christians; because many wicked men may be—as it is certain *de facto* they are, though *de jure* they should not—in the Church, yet so as still it may be said, *apud ecclesiam est fides*, it is amongst them. But, besides the former interpretation given, and that if he should mean outward profession of faith by 'faith' here, such a profession is like to have been in all and every one, I answer—1. If you consult his style in other epistles, he speaks of all and every one of other churches as having true grace, as of the Philippians: 'Even as it is meet for me,' saith he, 'to think of every one of you,' chap. i. 7. And it is not merely an outward profession of faith he speaks of there, but a persuasion of a good work of faith, which God would fulfil to the day of Christ. So, at ver. 6, 'Being confident of this very thing, that he which hath begun a good work will perfect it;' and then follows, 'even as it is meet for me to think this of you all.' In 2 Thess. i. 3, there is yet a more distinct phrase to this purpose: 'We are bound,' saith he, 'to thank God always for you, brethren, as it is meet, because that your faith groweth exceedingly, and the charity ἑνὸς ἑκάστου πάντων ὑμῶν, of every one of you all aboundeth.' 2. If Musculus' criticism should have place here, yet there may be this account given of the variation of his style to the church of the Ephesians, that in a special manner Paul had it revealed to him by the Spirit of prophecy, of this church of Ephesus, that many, or some of them at least, should prove unsound in the faith, and so useth here a more wary and indefinite phrase. For look into Acts xx. 29, in a speech he made to the elders of Ephesus, he saith plainly, 'I know this, that after my departure there shall enter in among you grievous wolves, not sparing the flock: also of your own selves shall men arise, speaking perverse things, to draw away disciples after them.' And, 3. If any would make use of this his interpretation, that therefore the rule for receiving men into churches is not put upon a judgment of their holiness, but outward profession only; then let us see such a profession of faith in any such as is mentioned here, that hath 'love to all the saints' joined with it, and I affirm they ought to be received. But when men are enemies to the saints, and do make them the men of their hatred, then let them profess what they will, there is not that faith which the apostles gave signs of for to judge of others by. When men do discover a spirit contradictory to the power of religion, of such, or in the like cases, I may say as 1 John iii. 17, 'How dwells the love of God in him?' Truly, says John, I know not. It is to me, says he, a contradiction which I know not how to believe; nor would all the charity in John, the beloved disciple's heart, have relieved him. Neither was the testimony the Apostle gives here of these Ephesians, and, in the fore-cited places, of those he writ to, a judgment of mere charity, such as useth to be pleaded for, founded upon an outward profession, and a knowing nothing to the contrary. For as Calvin well observes upon this place, In that he gives thanks thus solemnly before God for their faith, it was not a bare testimony of charity, but of judgment.* Paul gives thanks here for what was positive—namely, their faith in Christ, and love to all the saints. Such was the judgment the apostles gave of men, and so grounded.

And love unto all the saints.

To saints.—You see he mentioneth not love to God, and why? for if there be a love to all saints, as saints,—as if it be to all, it is to them as saints,—they must needs be supposed to love God also, as the Apostle saith, 1 John v. 1, 'He that loveth him that begat, loveth him also that is begotten of him.' As, on the contrary, the same John had said in the chapter before, ver. 20, 'If a man say he loves God, and hateth his brother,' (that is, any saint,) 'he is a liar: for he that loveth not his brother whom he hath seen, how can he love God whom he hath not seen?' That is, if men do not love them in whom they see the image of God, certainly they love not God himself, whom they see not; as on the contrary also, if they do love that image, certainly they love God. If men's eyes cannot endure the light of a candle, I will never believe they would endure the light of the sun.

Again, the Apostle mentions not love to every man, though that be a duty, but love to *saints*. It is a duty to love a man's neighbour, as Matt. xxii., Luke x.; but that is not mentioned here as a sign of their interest in Christ; there is a humanity in man's nature to love his kind; but it is, you see, loving the saints, under that notion as saints. Our Saviour is very accurate in distinguishing it thus, as you find it, Matt. x. 41: 'He that giveth,' saith he, 'a cup of cold water to a prophet, in the name of a prophet, shall receive a prophet's reward: he that receiveth a righteous man in the name of a righteous man'—that is, as we in the Latin express it, *eo nomine*, under that notion and abstracted consideration that he is a righteous man, and therefore loves him—'shall receive a righteous man's reward.' In another Evangelist it is yet more emphatical to this purpose: Mark ix. 41, 'Whosoever shall give you a cup of water to drink in my name,' (because you are Christ's,) 'he shall not lose his reward.'

* Hæc gratiarum actio non modo testimonium *amoris* erat erga Ephesos, sed etiam *judicii*, quod de illis habebat Paulus. Nam ita coram Deo illis gratulabatur.

Obs.—My brethren, look upon saintship as the greatest excellency to love it. So Christ did, Ps. xvi. 1. His eye was 'upon the excellent ones in the earth;' that is, upon the saints, who were excellent to him; yea, also, even when not saints, because God loved them, as Isa. xliii. 4. It is strange to hear how men by their speeches will undervalue a saint as such, if without some other outward excellency. For whilst they acknowledge a man a saint, yet in other respects they will contemn him; he is a holy man, they will say, but is weak, &c. But is he a saint? And can there be any such other imperfection or weakness found as shall lay him low in thy thoughts in comparison of other carnal men more excellent? Hath not Christ loved him, bought him, redeemed him?

To all saints.—All those they judged to be saints. And this universal love unto all the saints, to be a certain evidence of true faith, follows from what was mentioned even now. For if a man love a righteous man, or saint, in the name or under the notion of a righteous man, as Matthew, or because he is Christ's, as Mark, then he will love all saints and righteous men, and all that are Christ's; for *à quatenus ad omne valet consequentia,* he will love the *totum genus,* the whole kind and tribe of them, in whom ever he sees the image of God, and upon whomsoever the love of God is pitched.

Here then lieth the trial of grace indeed, to love all kind of saints. There are saints that are froward, and peevish saints, and proud saints, &c.,—that is, they express a great many of these corruptions in their converses with men,—yet as we must love these, so it is a great sign of grace notwithstanding to love them, merely because they are saints, and that they are Christ's. A brother loveth his crooked brother, and a lame brother, and a little brother, as well as those brethren that have none of these defects; and they do it because they are brethren, and for the parents' sake who love them. Rich saints and poor saints, gifted saints and weak saints, these all together must be loved. Or, as the Holy Ghost's expression is, Rev. xix. 5, 'the servants of God, small and great.' Some are great saints, some are small saints; there is little holiness appears in them, and yet love them all, for God and Christ doth. It is an excellent argument which the Apostle hath, urging of Christ's example to this purpose, in Rom. xv. 1: 'We that are strong,' saith he, 'ought to bear the infirmities of the weak, and not to please ourselves; for,' ver. 3, 'even Christ pleased not himself, as it is written,' &c. There are saints that have infirmities, and great infirmities. He had instanced in the chapter before in differences of opinion and judgment, and discoursed thereof throughout that chapter, and upon that occasion thereof it was he makes this exhortation. 'One believes,' saith he, 'that he may eat all things,' that is, believeth it fully; others—speaking of the Jewish ceremonies that continued to some men's consciences—eat not flesh, but they eat herbs rather. These were opinions opposite, and which produced contrary practices; each of these must bear the infirmities of either—they are saints. Yea, further, some of them were censorious, and judging all others rashly that were not of their minds, as these words import, ver. 3, 'Let not him that eateth not, judge him that eateth.' And again, others were apt to despise their brethren, as the following exhortation implies, 'Let not him that eateth despise him that eateth not.' The word there used is so to despise as to set at nought, disdain, vilify, as Herod and his soldiers did Christ, Luke xxiii. 11; it is the same word, μὴ ἐξουθενείτω. These were high and great infirmities, not in respect of difference in opinion only, but distempers in affection also.

In chap. xv. 1, the Apostle lays this command upon each, to bear the infirmities of either. The word βαστάζειν is used of porters carrying burdens. We must be as 'porters' for our brethren; the worst and irksomest of services; and bear their greatest burdens, that may consist with their being brethren. And thus, Gal. vi. 2, you have the word used, and to this sense there again explained: 'Bear ye one another's burdens.' For what he calls 'infirmities,' Rom. xv. 1, he calls 'burdens' here; and in both commands our bearing them, because they are brethren, as ver. 1. And as for the measure and proportion of bearing, the word refers us even to what porters do, who of all mankind are inured to the greatest strainings and stretchings of their limbs. And for the obligation and motive thereunto, the metaphor insinuates that also. Kindness and common humanity in men, who are of a knot, and travel in company, doth afford to any of their companions mutual assistance. If there be any among them who through his having an infirmity, or a burden too heavy for him, which himself cannot carry alone, and so comes *lag*, as we say, or faints in the way, then the rest of his fellows that are stronger will do what they can to ease him in it, and bear it with him, or take it off from him. And then, in that Rom. xv.—for we walk to and fro, from one of these places to another—it follows, 'and not to please ourselves.' If a man consults with self-love, a man will find this irksome to self, that useth to seek pleasure in itself and in its own opinions, and boasts itself in its own understanding, and cannot bear contradiction from others, minds not others' good, much less is pleased with bearing others' infirmities, or supporting them in them; but seeks to depress another for them.

But to enforce this, and the rest of these exhortations, he propounds the disposition and example of Christ too, ver. 3, 'For even Christ pleased not himself.' Never was any one burdened, and so oppressed with the burdens of others he converseth withal, as Christ was with those he walked with. His human nature coming into the world, was to take and cleave to such company as God had chosen for him; and take them all, from first to last, and how unsuitable and unpleasing consorts they were, and must needs be unto him! First, his parents, of mean birth and breeding, of low understandings. He could have taught them, for at twelve years he posed the doctors, yet he was obedient to them. The next which we read of that he conversed with were his disciples; all of them men of contrary spirits to his. Of two of them he says, 'You know not what spirit you are of.' Fire must come down from heaven presently, to satisfy their zeal, upon those that were opposite to them, and their master Christ; which was as contrary to his spirit as any one thing can be to another. He was perfectly of another spirit; he was meek, they were fiery; yet he loveth them, still holds in with them. Yea, one of these fiery sons of thunder and lightning was peculiarly his beloved disciple, and lay in his bosom. Then also Peter, how bold and saucy was he with him, and so great a provocation to him, that he once with full mouth cried out against him, 'Get thee behind me, Satan;' yet he loves him, dies for him. In a word, he bitterly complains of all his disciples at once, Matt. xvii. 17, 'O faithless and perverse generation, how long shall I be with you? how long shall I suffer you?' He had borne so much, and so long, as he now at length speaks as one overpressed, as a cart with sheaves, groaning under it as weary.

Nor was there, or ever could there be supposed, any man so put to it this way as he; wisdom to converse with folly, perfect holiness with sin and impurity, truth with errors and mistakes. In converses of near relations, contrarieties and antipathies of dispositions, how burdensome are they! He could have much better and more suitable company in heaven; yet Christ with an unwearied patience bore all this, and loved them not a whit the less in the main; but died for them after all, and in dying bore their sins, and all ours also, 1 Pet. ii. 24, with an infinite far deeper and higher kind of suffering for them, when 'God laid on him the iniquities of us all,' than this of ours from our brethren he here speaks of; which was his righteous soul's being vexed with seeing and hearing what was contrary to the perfect transcendant holiness thereof. And now he is in heaven, those his saints that are on earth are of cross natures one to another, bad-natured creatures to God and man; yet he holdeth in with all sorts of saints, useth them kindly, and maintaineth such a fellowship with them all, as they all speak well of him.

Now follow, saith the Apostle, this example of your Lord and Master. And according to this his exhortation, in the 5th verse, he frameth his prayer for them: 'The God of patience and consolation grant you to be like-minded one towards another, according to Christ Jesus.' He mentions such attributes in God as were suitable to the thing prayed for: to be like-minded, when differing thus in judgment, and needed patience; therefore he prays to God, as the God of patience, to give and bestow on you the grace of patience towards your dissenting brethren, who himself is a God of patience towards you, in bearing with you that differ from him in infinitely more things than you from your brethren; and also to be a God of consolation to you, and that will help you to bear the infirmities of the saints, and to love and cherish them; for if once the heart be filled with the comforts of the Almighty, 'if there be any comfort in love,' as the Apostle speaks, Phil. ii. 1, they will be like-minded, and then they will bear with their brethren. He adds, 'according to Jesus Christ;' that is, the example of Jesus Christ, of which you heard out of Rom. xv., and also according to the law of Jesus Christ; for upon that ground,—if now you return again to Gal. vi. 2, and to what immediately follows there, 'Bear one another's burdens,' says he, 'and so fulfil the law of Christ;' and thus to love, and love *all* the saints, is commended to us by Christ, by that great and special law of his, which you find enacted by him, John xiii. 34, 'A new commandment I give unto you, That ye love one another; as I have loved you, that ye also love one another'—you will find he urgeth it under the old law: they were to love every one, because they had one and the same God their Creator. Moses commanded to love every one as their neighbour, whether they were Samaritans or Jews; but Christ hath brought up a new law, and new motives thereto, and a new way of loving, by his example. 'A new commandment I write to you,' says John, 1 Epist. ii. 8, 'which is true,' and so holds good, 'in him,' who began to set us the copy of it, 'and in you,' the followers of him. And when he was on earth, all his delight was in the saints, Ps. xvi. 3.

A new motive we have also for it—namely, our participation and communion together in Christ's blood. Men were before united in one God, their Creator, and in being 'made of one blood,' Acts xvii., and upon that ought to have loved one another as men, or if of the same nation. But the saints are all made of Christ's blood, and in that respect are a royal generation, a chosen nation, having of his blood all of them running in their veins. And accordingly he hath chalked out a new way of loving also. He gave his life for us, yea, himself, and all his glory; and so it follows in that John xv. 12, 13, 'Love one another, as I have loved you. Greater love hath no man than this, to lay down his life for his friend;' and so should we do, as 1 John iii. 16, for the spiritual good of our brethren. And as Christ singled out the saints thus to love them, and that with a special love, and all and every of the saints, so should we.

The last thing I observe, which gives light to the text, and instruction to us, is from the style the Apostle useth: 'Love to *all* saints.' That this was the primitive language, and this then made the great outward sign of a man's being in Christ in those times, as may appear both by this Apostle's so frequent mention of it in his Epistles, as Col. i. 4, Philem. 5, so also in that our Saviour Christ himself made it his badge, in that fore-named John xiii. 35, 'By this shall all men know that you are my disciples, if you love one another.' The disciples were known by some peculiar badge: as John Baptist's disciples, by austerity of life; and those that were the disciples of the Pharisees, by their habit and traditions; and thereupon saith Christ to his disciples, I will give you a badge whereby ye shall be known, and that by all men. It shall not be miracles. I will give you a greater sign. What is that? *Love one another*. Let that love be amongst you saints that is not amongst any generation in the world else; and so shall not I only know you that you are mine, and own you, nor you yourselves only know that you are mine, but all men shall know. The love of those first times to saints was such, according to this prophecy of Christ's, that the very heathen, taking notice of their mutual love, did distinguish and decipher them out by it. Tertullian, in his Apology for the Christians, writes: 'The love,' says he, 'amongst us is such, so great, that it is set as a mark and brand upon us. See,' say they, speaking of the heathens, their usual saying of us Christians, 'how they love one another.' Whereas they, the heathens, hate one another, saith he. 'And see,' say they, 'how they are ready to die one for another;' whereas you heathens, says Tertullian, 'are ready to kill one another.'

Application:—

My brethren, how far are these times off from this temper; wherein a little difference in judgment, what a great deal of judging one another and despising one another doth it breed in the hearts of men professing Christianity, in the hearts of saints! As the Apostle's words are there, in that Rom. xiv.,—and the discourse in that chapter, and his exhortation to forbearance, is not only in point of things merely indifferent, but in matters of exceeding great moment and consequence, namely, about the Jewish ceremonies and ceremonial worship: one would have them in the Church as once instituted of God, and another not; one esteemed one day above another; these were not matters of indifferency;—yet, saith he, receive one another for all this, own one another for all this; for God, saith he, hath received him into his own family. That is one motive he useth there in ver. 4. He is God's servant; the word is not δοῦλος, a servant any way, at large spoken, but οἰκέτης, he is a household servant. Jew and Gentile, both differing in opinion and practice, were both of the same family to God, whereof Christ is named; therefore do not you dare to cast him out from you.

Yea, at the third verse of chap. xiv. the Apostle, upon this ground, would not have them so much as judge them for such kind of opinions as might stand with their continuing the true servants of Christ, and the power of holiness in them. 'Judge not him that eateth,' speaking to the ceremonious Jew, 'for God hath received him;' that is, into his favour and grace, notwithstanding that opinion and practice of his: so as though he should die in that error, which thou thinkest such, through want of conviction, and never repent of it, yet God would save him. God accepts of him, and shall the subject take on him to reject and condemn him, when his king doth not? Yea, ver. 4, 'Who art thou that judgest another man's servant?' To judge thy fellow-servants in matters of this nature is an invasion of, and intrusion upon God's proper right, according to the law of nations; which therefore no power, civil or ecclesiastical, is to meddle in. He is, notwithstanding this, as faithful a servant to God as thou art. And who art thou? and, Who are ye? Be you the major part, and have the power in your hands; yet matters of difference from you of this alloy are not in your cognisance. And who are you, to assume this? Give to God the things that are God's, and to the magistrate, and to churches, what are theirs. But we would keep them, will men say, from falling into error. Let God look to and take care of that; saith he, 'He stands or falls to his own master,' who in a judicatory way is only to deal with him, without thy judging of him.

Yea, but he is in an error, which will prejudice and endanger him; but yet, not his salvation, says the Apostle. All sins for which a man shall be judged in the church are of that nature as, unless repented of, a man shall not be saved, as is strongly insinuated, 1 Cor. v. 5. For though you that are contrary-minded are apt, in the severity of self, to condemn what is opposite to you, as that which will endanger, or not stand with grace, yet he shall be holden up: and he speaks it with a peremptoriness, 'Yea, he shall be holden up, for God is able to make him stand;' so as an error of invincible ignorance shall not endanger him, he embracing all the principles and practices that are necessary to salvation. What! is there nothing but presently casting out for this? No, saith he, receive one another notwithstanding. 'Let not him,' saith he, 'that eateth,' or is strong, 'despise another that eateth not,' or set him at naught, and say he is weak and silly, and I know not what: and let not the other 'that eateth not, judge him that eateth.' In these two lieth the rule of peace between them. Now, it is not likely that these men should presently be brought to one and the same mind or judgment; but let this rule be pressed in the meantime, not to judge one another for such things. There will be one believing one thing, and another believing another thing; and it will be so to the end of the world. In that Rom. xv. there is this expression in ver. 7, 'Let us receive one another,' saith he, 'as Christ hath received us, to the glory of God.' When the difference is but in such things as these, in God's name, saith he, if one heaven must hold us all, let churches hold us all. At least, let none dare to hinder the children from that bread, the children's bread, which Christ left as his last legacy for all whom he hath received at present. Yea, says he, *unto glory:* let the same land hold us all. Christ, saith he, 'hath received us to glory;' even now whilst the saints are as yet on earth, with their infirmities and differences, both from himself and one another. If he think men meet for glory, and that they shall live together in heaven; then, if the difference will never exclude them from heaven, they may not be excluded from the food of heaven; how far off is this from what the Apostle saith here, 'Love to all the saints?'

Ver. 16, *Cease not to give thanks for you, making mention of you in my prayers.*

In this verse are—1. The two duties he performed for them; 2. The constancy of his performance of them.

First, The duties: he prays for them, and gives thanks for them.

Secondly, The constancy, expressed twice by these two words, 'always,' and 'I cease not.'

General scope:—

Since I heard.—Musculus observes that Paul had himself been the instrument of their conversion, as Acts xix. And he used to pray for those churches which he had converted,—as you may see in his epistles, as to the Philippians also, chap. i.,—and that so his meaning should be, says he, my prayers have ever been for you. But, secondly, since I heard of your perseverance in faith and love, and increase in both, I have been abundantly more enlarged, and have added new petitions to my prayers, which follow after, as those which befitted the estate of grown and sealed Christians. And, thirdly, I have given thanks accordingly, and have been enlarged in that duty also.

First duty, Prayer—In my prayers.—It is private personal prayer he means. 'My prayer;' so in Philemon, 'in every prayer of mine;' not those prayers which he made in public, as the mouth of those congregations. To distinguish it from which he says, *my prayers;* that is, which he made alone by himself, as also in Philem. 4.

Making mention of you.—The word here signifieth either *remembrance*, or it signifieth *mention*. When it is taken for remembrance, then it is joined with the word 'to have' remembrance; ἔχω μνείαν, as you have it, 2 Tim. i. 3, but here that which is joined with it is *making*, ποιούμενος, and not *having*. For to say, *to make remembrance* of one, is not proper; therefore they translate it rightly, 'making mention.' Only this you must know, this same word here used signifieth remembrance, and signifieth mention, and are both applied to prayer for others; the one in 2 Tim. i. 3, the other here.

Obs. 1.—Observe out of it, in general, The *remembrance* of another in prayer is as the inward part, which is a special work of the Holy Ghost, bringing to mind a man, or persons, for whom he would have one to pray; and *mention* is the outward part, a praying for them by name; as whom the Holy Ghost doth set upon a man's heart,—as Paul, telling the Philippians how he prayed for them, and gave thanks for them, as he doth here, adds, 'I have you in my heart,' says he, chap. i. 7,—those, I say, whom God hath specially set upon a man's heart, and whom the Holy Ghost in prayer bringeth to his remembrance, a man should in a special manner make mention of. This from the signification of the word, both *remembrance* and *mention*. And withal know, to encourage you in the practice hereof, that the particular, express mention, especially in private prayers, of persons that are in our heart, and of whom the Holy Ghost bringeth the remembrance to us in prayer, is that which is exceeding acceptable to God, as being conformable to the mind of the Holy Ghost, who guides us in praying. The Apostle doth not only pray thus for, and make mention of churches by name; but you shall find he makes mention of particular persons in his prayers by name, as of Philemon, ver. 3, 4, 'I thank my God,' saith he, 'making mention of thee always in my prayers, hearing of thy love and faith.' The like he did of Timothy, 2 Tim. i. 2.

Obs. 2.—Secondly, observe the largeness of Paul's heart in his private prayers, as he had the care of all the churches. Read all his epistles, and you shall see almost every church that he writeth unto, he telleth them he prayed for them. And he telleth some special, particular persons so too, whom he had in his heart. And not only he, but other ministers did the same. Thus he tells the Thessalonians, that Timotheus and Sylvanus likewise made mention of them in their prayers, 1 Thess. i. Paul, my brethren, was nearest to Christ of any saint that ever was, and near unto Christ in this; for Jesus Christ in heaven hath the names of all saints in his breast, as the high priest had, and makes intercession for them. Paul maketh intercession for all the churches, and for many particular persons; he was abundant this way; and what a large time did he then spend in private prayer! Oh, think of the largeness of Christ's heart for us in his intercessions; as he knows his sheep by name, so every one that comes to God by him, he ceaseth not always to intercede for them, even every one of them in particular; as it follows there, 'He ever lives to make intercession.'

Since I heard of your faith and love, I have not ceased, &c.—From this coherence observe, The remembrance of eminent faith and love in Christians, or in churches, should provoke us to give thanks to God for them, and to pray much for them. And withal, it is a great encouragement to every saint to be very holy. For then God will stir up the hearts of many, to pray for them that are so, and the Holy Ghost will bring them to remembrance. Paul makes an argument for himself, Heb. xiii. 18, 'Pray for us,'—why?—'for we trust we have a good conscience in all things, willing to live honestly.' Seeing in all things we have a good conscience for the time past, but willing for the time to come to preserve it, you shall not lose your prayers in your praying for me. And in his Epistle to Timothy, he telleth him, that this moveth him to pray for him without ceasing; remembering, saith he, thy tears and thy faith, 2 Tim. i. 3, 4. Those that have much, shall have much added to them, and that by the prayers of others for them. And to that end God will stir up many to pray for them. This, among others, is a great motive and encouragement to holiness. Thou desirest many prayers for thee, this is the way to procure them.

Second duty, Giving of thanks.—By prayer we shew our dependence upon God for what we want. In thanks, we return an acknowledgment to God of what we have already received. Thanks is for mercies bestowed and past; and prayer is a seeking of God for mercies to come.

Now, first, mark the coherence. The words he had immediately before uttered were, that God had done thus and thus for them, 'to the praise of his glory.' And so it is as if he had said, The end of all the benefits God bestoweth being to the praise of his glory, and I, having this praise of his glory in mine eye and heart, as dearest to me, and 'having heard of your faith and love, cease not to give thanks for you.' My brethren, the highest way that we in this life are able to give glory to God is by thankfulness, Ps. l. 14, 15, compared with ver. 23, 'Offer unto God thanksgiving; and pay thy vows to the Most High: and call upon me in the day of trouble, and I will deliver thee, and thou shalt glorify me.' And this glorifying is offering thanks: so, ver. 23, 'Whoso offereth praise doth glorify me.' So that now you are obliged unto this duty, upon the highest obligation, because of all duties else it doth tend so much to the glory of God.—I have despatched the two duties.

The second thing in the word is, *his constancy in praying;* 'I cease not.'

The meaning is this: In every prayer, as oft as I have prayed solemnly, which I have not ceased to do, 'I have not ceased to give thanks to God for you;' so Phil. i. 4, 'Always, in every prayer.' If we seek a great blessing at God's hand, we cease not praying for it till we have an answer. The parable so teacheth us, Luke xviii. 1. And then—

Obs.—The observation is, That (which we are wanting in the performance of) great mercies, either upon ourselves or others, which we are bound to thank God for, we should do it without ceasing a long while after. When you are to seek to God for a great mercy, then you cease not to make mention of it in your prayers; but the Apostle, you see, ceaseth not to give thanks: they are both alike to the glory of God. And according to your prayers, so are your mercies; great and long prayers bring down in the end great and lasting mercies. And on the other hand, if your mercies be great and lasting, your thanksgivings should be great also.

Besides the reason I formerly mentioned,—that thanksgiving glorifieth God so much, and is to the praise of his glory,—take the measure of the duties themselves. Prayer and thanksgiving are of an equal latitude; they are both duties of the first commandment. And as we say of God's attributes, they are all of a like extent; so are those duties that are duties of the first commandment. It is a shame for us, that if we have been long and much in prayer for great mercies before we obtained them, we should make short and small work of our thanksgivings for them; that when you have not ceased to be instant in prayer to obtain them, you should cease to give thanks for them when you have received them. The glory of God is concerned alike in both. If they be great mercies, and such as have influence into the whole course of a man's life, whereof he hath the daily benefit, he should not cease to remember them, and to give thanks for them daily. If they be occasional mercies, they should work as occasional afflictions do. It is not to be said that every affliction a man should be continually thinking of, or making use of. No, but they are specially to operate till another affliction cometh. A man should make use of the last. So it is in mercies and thanksgivings. God stroweth some benefits, some mercies in our life, as a rhetorician doth flowers in his orations, here and there, up and down. Now the last mercy, till God hath put down that mercy by some greater, we should still remember it. Only, on solemn days of fasting, upon God's calling thereto by some eminent affliction, we should then take notice and a survey of as many former afflictions as we can call to mind, to humble ourselves under God's displeasure in multiplying of them. And thus of mercies, in days of thanksgivings.

Secondly, There are two words to shew this constancy: 'I cease not,' applied to his giving thanks, and 'always,' spoken of his prayings; and either denotes a constant set solemnity of praying and thanksgiving, but especially both joined do import it; which was morning and evening, as the worship of old was, 'night and day,' 2 Tim. i. 3. And though Daniel prayed thrice, and others seven times, yet the general constant custom, principle, and manner of the private worship of all the Jews was twice a-day, being conformable to the public institution of the sacrifices and incense twice a-day, which was termed 'continual sacrifice;' by which 'pray continually' may be interpreted, which was the rule of Paul's practice, Acts xxvi. 7, 'Unto the which promise our twelve tribes, instantly serving God day and night, hope to come.' But of that I have spoken more upon Phil. i. 4.

SERMON XIX.

That the God of our Lord Jesus Christ, the Father of glory, may give unto you the Spirit of wisdom and revelation in the knowledge of him. —VER. 17.

I COME now to the 17th verse, and that is the prayer itself which Paul here did put up for them, 'since he heard,' &c.

I will give you the division of the words, and some short analysis of them.

First, here is the person whom he prayeth to, that is, God; whom he doth set forth under the apprehension and notion, for the strengthening of his faith, for the obtaining of what he asks,—as we are always to do in prayer,—of 'the God of our Lord Jesus Christ, and the Father of glory.'

Secondly, you have the things he prayeth for. Concerning which, in the general, all the things he prayeth for are *spiritual knowledge,* he mentioneth nothing else: 'That he would give you the Spirit of wisdom and revelation in the knowledge of him,' so saith the 17th verse; and that he would give you *enlightened eyes,* as I shall shew you the words may be read, and I think are rather to be read, 'that you may know what is the hope of his calling,' &c., so saith the 18th verse. In general you see it is for *knowledge.* More particularly, here are four things he doth especially pray for:—

1. For the *Spirit of wisdom and revelation in the knowledge of God;* which, as I shall open to you, I take it is in personal communion with God.

2. *That they might know what is the hope of his calling;* what grounds they had to hope for eternal life, that they might see more clearly into them every day than other.

3. That they might have great and enlarged apprehensions working in their hearts, and telling their spirits, of *the riches of glory which God had laid up for them.* 'That ye may know,' saith he, 'what is the riches of the glory of his inheritance,' &c.

4. That they might know *the power that was engaged,* and had begun to work in them, that would subdue all their lusts, that would never leave them till it had brought them to the same place where Christ was. Whereas they might look upon themselves as men, and sinful,—and how shall we come to this glory you speak of?—he prayeth that they might know the exceeding greatness of that power which works in those that believe, even the same that wrought in Christ in raising him from the dead. And, further to encourage them, he setteth forth Jesus Christ, not only in glory, raised up by the power of God, and that the same power is engaged to raise them up, but he setteth him forth as their Head, in whom therefore they have interest, who sat at the right hand of God in the heavenly places,—so saith the 20th verse,—and whose heart was engaged to them. For, saith he, ver. 23, you are the fulness of Christ, and Christ will not lose one of them. That they might know all these things, and live in the comfort of them; this is the sum and matter of the Apostle's prayer.—So much now for the short and brief analysis of the words to the end of the chapter.

But I come to the first thing which is in the 17th verse. He prayeth that they might have the 'Spirit of wisdom and revelation in the knowledge of him.' The person he prayeth to I shall handle afterward, because the understanding of it hath influence into what followeth, as well as this first petition; why God is called the 'God of Christ,' why the 'Father of glory;' why Paul setteth him up under both these considerations to strengthen his faith, that these particulars shall be granted, I will shew this afterward; but I will now handle what is meant here by giving them the 'Spirit of wisdom and revelation in the knowledge of him.' For the opening of this, and likewise of all the rest, I will give you these general premises :—

First, As I said, the thing he prayeth for is *knowledge.* He doth not mention grace and holiness, not in all this prayer; yet it is most strongly included in it, and it is the most necessary effect and concomitant of *that knowledge* he prayeth for here.

Secondly, That he doth not pray so much that they might increase more and more in the knowledge of their interest in God and in heaven, though some think that that is the meaning of the 'hope of their calling;' but the main thing he prayeth for is, that they might know the things themselves; that they might know God, that they might know what riches of glory is laid up for them in heaven, have enlarged apprehensions of the things themselves to be known, and so that they might know the 'power that works in them that believe,' &c.

Thirdly, That the things he prayeth for here were things that befitted the state of grown Christians. He doth not pray for them as for men to be converted. No; for it is a prayer he framed for them 'since he heard of their faith and love,' of whom he had said, they were 'sealed' too 'with the Spirit of promise;' as in the former verses. Now, my brethren, this the Apostle doth; he considereth with himself to what pitch Christians that are to grow in grace should be brought, and what is the greatest means to cause them to grow in grace; and for the working and effectual knowledge of these things he prayeth here. He doth not pray that they might know sin, as in the first conversion, that they might repent and believe, &c. But he prayeth that they might increase in the 'knowledge of him,' in an experimental communion with God and acknowledgment of him; for so, as I take it, it is to be meant, as I shall shew you afterwards. He takes the utmost things that his own light reacheth to, and he putteth them into his prayer for these Ephesians. And read all the prayers that he makes for others in several epistles, as Col. i. 10, Phil. i. 9, and they all fall short of the prayer here. The Apostle's mind is more filled with a higher and a further light; he expresseth more glorious things; his eye was upon the utmost pitch of Christianity which he would have these Ephesians aim at, and which he desired God to bestow upon them.

And yet, in the last place, let me tell you, that here is nothing that he doth pray for, but that common Christians, *vulgus Christianorum*, the Ephesian women and men, all the saints there, were capable of. This I put in, because of the word *revelation*, which might seem to carry things to somewhat extraordinary, proper unto apostles. What is the meaning of it I shall shew afterward.

Now, my brethren, take an observation or two before I come to the particulars.

Obs. 1.—The first is this, *That spiritual knowledge is the great, the main thing in the working of grace, or in the increasing of grace.* He mentioneth not a word of holiness, but you see all he prayeth for is knowledge; but it is such a knowledge as no carnal heart in the world hath. He certainly prays for the highest thing, and the best thing he could pray for, that his light suggested to him. He prayed for holiness elsewhere with knowledge; but here you see for knowledge alone, because knowledge in the Scripture sense includeth the affections, includeth the whole heart to be carried after it—true knowledge doth; to know things as a man ought to know them, as the Apostle distinguisheth it in 1 Cor. viii. 2, to know the truth as 'the truth in Jesus,' as the truth is in the things themselves. The more knowledge and light a man hath in his understanding, the more his whole life is carried after such a knowledge. He need pray for nothing else if he have such a knowledge, for all else will fall in with it.

Look in all the prayers he makes for the churches: for the Philippians, chap. i. 9, 10, he prayeth that their 'love may abound,' but how? In all knowledge and sense, an experimental knowledge, that sees and tastes the things that a man knows,—'that you may approve the things that are excellent,' so saith ver. 10. So for the Colossians, chap. i., he prayeth, that they might 'walk worthy to all well-pleasing,' so at the 10th verse; but at the 9th verse first he prayeth they may be 'filled with all spiritual wisdom and understanding.' So that still, I say, observe, that all his prayers in these epistles, it is for knowledge in the first place, that is the main spring of all the rest.

My brethren, there is indeed a notional knowledge, or, as I may call it, a phantasmatical knowledge of spiritual things—that is, whereby a man knows them; but it is by such a kind of light as is in any knowledge and science whatsoever, whereby he knoweth the rationality of things, but by images as the fancy delivereth up to the understanding to work upon, by hearsay. But then there is a real knowledge that bringeth down the things into a man's heart. Saith Paul, 2 Cor. iii. 18, 'With open face we behold the glory of the Lord as in a glass, and are changed into the same image.' Put but the difference in the similitude that the Apostle expresseth it, and you shall see how all knowledge falleth short of spiritual knowledge, which changeth the heart. Take a man now that is a rational divine, and no more; he knoweth the truth of the Scripture, and the reason and the harmony that is between one principle and another, as a man doth of things by hearsay, and the understanding works upon the reason that is in them, and the concordance and harmony that is in them. Take a temporary believer, and his knowledge hath more life in it; it is as the knowledge that one hath of a man in a dream; he hath heard much of a man, and he dreams of him, and fancieth him to be such a man, and thinks he sees him lively and really, and is affected by being in his presence. But spiritual knowledge the Apostle expresseth to 'beholding as in a glass.' Now mark, if you were looking in a glass, and a man you never saw before stood behind you, and you see his face, here now is such a real sight as putteth down all hearsays, all pictures, all dreams of a man; yet you do not see this man face to face. Now vision in heaven is seeing God face to face; but, saith he, in the meantime we behold him as in a glass. We have a real knowledge of him through the artifice of the Holy Ghost, and this knowledge now changeth the heart into the same image; therefore no wonder if the Apostle here prayeth for spiritual knowledge, and for that only, for these Ephesians.

There is a knowledge, my brethren, by way of gifts, that is in Christians, that is not this spiritual knowledge. Men may have large gifts, and yet be babes in respect of this knowledge, and they themselves be saints. That instance of the Corinthians is full to this purpose. The Apostle telleth them, 1 Cor. i. 5–7, that in every thing they were enriched 'in all utterance and in all knowledge.' Mark it, it was such a knowledge which they had as served for utterance; they could express their minds fully and punctually, stamp their minds upon another man about spiritual things, which was from a distinct knowledge of the things. 'And,' saith he, 'you come behind-hand in no gift.' Well, but these knowing men, how doth the Apostle talk to them afterward? He tells them first, that there is another manner of knowledge than this, which is a spiritual knowledge; which, saith he, chap. ii., the spirit of the world doth not teach us, but the Spirit of Christ in a more eminent manner, and that to a man as a spiritual man. This you have in the 12th, 13th, 14th, and 15th verses of that second chapter. We have not, saith he, 'received the spirit of the world;' we do not know spiritual things by that understanding only, in a notional way that a man understandeth worldly things; but, saith he, there is a peculiar revealing of them by the Holy Ghost to a man's heart made spiritual, suited to the things. Now, when he had told them there was a spiritual knowledge, what saith he to them? Why, saith he, chap. iii., you that have all this knowledge, yet 'I cannot speak unto you as unto spiritual, but as unto carnal.' For all they were enriched in all utterance, and in all knowledge, and came behind in no gift; yet, saith he, ver. 3, 'you are yet carnal;' they were but as babes in Christ, so ver. 1. They were not spiritual, they wanted this spiritual knowledge in a great measure. Now, take a good heart that hath many notions in his head. Oh, thinks he, had I but a drop of that elixir that would turn all these notions into pure gold, into spiritual knowledge! That were excellent. Unbelief, my brethren, makes the knowledge of spiritual things to be but as dreams, though a man have much; whereas faith turns them all into realities, and works upon the heart accordingly. The Apostle telleth the Corinthians in that second chapter, ver. 9, that the eye hath not seen, nor the ear heard, nor ever entered it into the heart of a natural man; men may have much knowledge by the eye and by the ear, which entereth into their fancies, and so is delivered up to their understandings about spiritual things; but this is a knowledge that never entered into the heart of a carnal man. And this is the knowledge the Apostle here prayeth for.

Obs. 2.—The second thing I would have you observe is this: That that knowledge which makes a man holy is especially of spiritual things themselves. Though the knowledge of a man's interest that they are his, carrieth abundance of holiness with it, yet it is the revelation of the things in a spiritual way that doth it in a more eminent manner. Paul, you see here, doth not so much pray that they might know heaven was theirs,—he took that for granted,—but that they might know it, have glorious apprehensions let into their souls of what heaven was, and that they might increase in the knowledge of it, that they might know what God was more in his glory, as the God of Christ and the Father of glory. It is, I say, the knowledge of the things themselves that doth it. You think now that the want in knowledge is the want of application, that you know not till you have made them your own by application, and that therein lieth the great defect of faith. I acknowledge it is a defect of faith; but, my brethren, the main thing in faith is to see spiritual things really, to behold the glory of the Lord. Saith the Apostle, Heb. x. 39,—it is a place I have often upon occasion quoted to this very purpose,—'We are not of them that draw back unto perdition, but of them that believe unto the saving of the soul.' Now what is this faith that is to the saving of a man's soul? Read the whole 11th chapter to the Hebrews; it is seeing the things, the evidence of the things themselves; it is—you will wonder at it—to believe that God is; so he telleth us at the 6th verse. 'He that cometh to God,' saith he, 'must believe that God is.' It is to believe that the world was made. It is to believe all spiritual things by a divine light, by a spiritual light. Now, my brethren, when once things are thus strongly and really represented to a man's mind, it will carry them all to the heart. The Apostle, in 1 John v. 5, saith, that by faith we overcome the world; what is the faith that overcometh the world? It is not so much believing Christ is yours, as it is believing that he is; for who is he that overcometh the world but he that believeth that Jesus is the Son of God?

You will say unto me, that this is to preach only for general faith.

No, my brethren, if you will come now to the faith that justifieth you, it must be with the whole heart; and although all that is required to justification in the understanding be to believe the thing really and spiritually, yet the will must concur; and how must that concur? It must cast itself upon God for it, for justification; there, indeed, cometh in application. Nay, let me tell you further, that it is the strength of seeing the things themselves that draweth in the heart to give itself up to Christ. As now, take a poor soul that hath little evidence that Christ is his; it may be he is altogether out of hope of it; yet he hath a light that representeth such excellencies to be in Christ as he can never leave him; this is it that makes him give up his soul to him. Take a man that hath assurance,—I will exemplify it there too,—he believeth that heaven is his, Christ is his. Well, this assurance oftentimes lieth by him dead. Why? Because he wanteth a spiritual knowledge of the things. Let God come in now with a light, and reveal what himself is, and what heaven is to him, then assurance works in him. So that it is the knowledge of the things themselves is the main thing in Christianity, and the main thing in faith.—And so much in general for the observations which I do premise.

I come now to the particular opening of the things he prayed for. *He prayeth for the Spirit of wisdom and revelation in the knowledge of him.* This is the first thing.

I must explain three things here:—

1. What is meant by *the knowledge of him.*

2. The ways by which he prayeth that they may know; by *wisdom* and by *revelation.*

3. The *Author of this knowledge,* and wisdom, and revelation, and all; the Spirit of Christ, whom he prayeth might be given to them as such. 'That he may give you,' saith he, 'the Spirit of wisdom and revelation in the knowledge of him.'

The first thing you see he prayeth for, as the conclusion of all, is *the knowledge of him.* Whether you take it of God or of Christ, it is first of him; which implieth that all human knowledge of human things, if you know all the secrets in nature, is nothing to this. Paul, you know, desired to know nothing but Christ, and him crucified, 1 Cor. ii. 2. This is the eminent knowledge, the knowledge of him, that the Apostle here prayeth for. He prayeth not, you see, that they might have the knowledge of their own graces so much, nor the knowledge of their own corruptions so much,—though all these will follow upon the knowledge of him,—but the thing he pitcheth upon for grown Christians to grow up in, is the knowledge of him. The eminent thing in a Christian is to desire more knowledge of God and of Christ especially. If they know their own corruptions, what use do they make of it? To drive them to Christ, to make them know him more: 'I thank God through Jesus Christ,' saith Paul, when he saw himself a miserable man. If they know their own graces, it is that by those beams they might look upon that sun. If they know the law, it is to direct them to Christ.

The end, my brethren, of all duties,—mark what I say,—the end of grace itself, is the knowledge of God and communion with him; therefore you hear, and therefore you pray. If you rest in the duties, without communion with God and the knowledge of him, your soul will be found empty, and will sit down in sorrow at the last. In Col. i. 9, you shall see what the Apostle saith there, where he makes the very same prayer parallel to what is here. He prayeth 'that they may be filled with the knowledge of God's will in all wisdom and spiritual understanding,' (this is grace now,) that they may know their duties more, 'for this is the will of God, even your sanctification;' that husbands may know their duties, what is the will of God to them, and wives theirs, what is the will of God concerning them; take the whole will of God in the whole compass of it, he prayeth for that. To what end? 'That you might walk worthy of the Lord to all pleasing,' so it is, ver. 10, 'being fruitful in every good work.' But, mark it, what is the end of all this knowledge and of all this walking? 'Increasing,' saith he, 'in the knowledge of God.' That cometh in last, as being the perfection, the reward of all obedience, to know God more. A Christian, a holy heart, improveth the knowledge of all truth to know God more perfectly, and to have more communion with him by it. Wicked men oftentimes see the great wisdom that is in the knowledge of God; they see the harmony and the agreement of one truth in divinity with another, how one kisseth another, and they are mightily taken with it,—as nothing will take a man's understanding so much as matters of divinity,—and the rationality of it. But still they pick not God out of all this; they do not know him spiritually and personally. Or, take a man that is an atheist,—as the one studieth the Scripture, the other studieth the works of God,—let a man be an arrant atheist, he will see a mighty wisdom that nature hath in all the works of nature; in all the causes and effects of things, and how in weight and measure they are all made, and one thing is subordinate to another; but still he picks not God out of all this, but so a Christian doth. So that it is the knowledge *of him*, you see, in distinction and opposition to all things else, which the Apostle here prayeth for these Ephesians.

But now 'of him.' *Of whom?* Is it God the Father, or Christ? for αὐτοῦ will bear either of them.

My brethren, he speaks of God the Father just before, 'the God of our Lord Jesus Christ, the Father of glory, that he may give you the Spirit of wisdom and revelation in the knowledge of him.' He spake both of God and he spake of Christ. Who is the *him* here then? I take it especially God the Father; for in the 19th verse he speaks of Christ, while he is praying this prayer, as of a distinct person. 'That you may know,' saith he, 'the power that he wrought in Christ.' That same *he* there, is the *him* here; yet so as because it may refer to either, take both. It is the knowledge of God and Christ, or rather of *God in Christ;* to know God as he is the God of Christ, and as he is the Father of glory, and so to have the heart taken with him, to have the heart drawn into communion with him. This is the knowledge the Apostle here meaneth; you have them both put together, 2 Cor. iv. 6, 'God, who commanded the light to shine out of darkness, hath shined in our hearts, to give the light of the knowledge of the glory of God, in the face of Jesus Christ.' How came you to know him here but in and through Christ? So that it is the knowledge of both, but especially of the Father. And so in Col. i. 10, where the same words are used, it is called ἐπίγνωσις, as here; 'increasing,' saith he, 'in the knowledge of God.' You have them both mentioned, 2 Pet. i. 2, 'Grace and peace be multiplied through the knowledge of God, and of our Lord Jesus Christ.' Therefore, I say, take both in. So much now for this *of him*, of God in Christ, of 'the glory of God in the face of Jesus Christ,' as the Apostle expresseth himself in that 2 Cor. iv. 6.

Now let us consider *what is meant by the knowledge here he speaks of.* It is certainly meant an excellency of knowledge, as γνῶσις is often taken, not merely for a knowledge, but for an *excellency of knowledge*, as Grotius well observeth. Rom. iii. 20, 'By the law is the knowledge of sin.' The word there is the same that is used here, ἐπίγνωσις. That is, though a man know what is sin by the light of nature, yet he cometh to an exact, to a perfect knowledge by the law. 'I had not known sin,' saith the Apostle, Rom. vii. 7, 'but by the law.' Well, then, the thing the Apostle prayeth for here is, an exacter knowledge, a more perfect knowledge of God.

Yea, but *what manner of knowledge?*

My brethren, if you will have me plainly speak what I think the Apostle chiefly aimeth at, it is this. It is not only a more enlarged knowledge about the things of God, as it is said of Christ, Luke xxiv. 27, that he expounded the Scriptures concerning himself; so it is not to know more things concerning God, to have their knowledge enlarged for the matter of it; but the thing he aimeth at here, being the perfection of knowledge, and the end and issue of all knowledge to grown Christians, to sealed Christians, it is communion with God, is such a knowledge as the Apostle here meaneth. Not such a knowledge as shall enable you to express God to others, but such a knowledge as makes you personally holy, and hath personal communion with God joined with it.

The reason why I interpret it so, is not only because the word will bear it, for γνῶσις is indeed an acknowledgment or owning. One knoweth a stranger, but he doth *agnoscere*, he doth acknowledge, as some interpreters well distinguish, one he knew before, his friend. So that the intimate knowledge of God as of a friend;—as he said of Moses, 'I know thee by name,' and Moses knew God again; as the phrase is, John x. 14, 'I know my sheep, and am known of mine;'—to have this mutual knowledge, God knowing me, and I knowing God, and so to converse with God, and to have communion with him as with a friend; this intimate knowledge, I say, is the thing the Apostle meaneth. And my reason, besides what the word will bear, is this, because in Col. i. 9, 10, where he prayeth for the same thing, he makes it the consequent of holy walking; he prayeth before that they might walk worthy of the Lord to all well-pleasing, and then followeth, 'increasing in the knowledge of God;' the word is the same, ἐπίγνωσις, there and here; that is, increasing, as the reward of holy walking and being filled with the knowledge of his will, in communion with him, or in growing up to know him as your God, and his glory and excellency, and converse familiarly with him as with your friend. They were sealed Christians he wrote this to, for whom he prayeth, that knew God to be their God. Now, take a man that hath assurance, what is the next thing he desireth? To have much communion with God, to have much intimate converse with him; to see that God of whom he is assured, by a spiritual light revealed to his soul, to see him, and to see the excellency and the glory of him; as Moses, you know, it was his great desire. 'Shew me thy glory,' saith he, when God had used him once familiarly as a friend. Now, because this is the next great thing that sealed Christians, as these Ephesians were, do desire, therefore the Apostle prayeth for this knowledge.

There is a parallel place to this likewise. 2 Pet. i. 2, 'Grace and peace,' saith he, 'be multiplied' (the word is, be fulfilled) 'through the knowledge of God, and of Jesus Christ our Lord.' The word *knowledge* there is the same word that is used here. Now, my brethren, what is the meaning of it? 'Grace and peace be fulfilled,' for so the word signifieth, πληθυνθείη. How are they fulfilled, perfected? The meaning of it is this: God doth fulfil the utmost intent of his grace and favour to a man, by causing him to know him, and to have intimate communion with him. God doth fill a man's soul with perfect peace and joy in believing, through an intimate knowledge of God and of Christ. You see there the knowledge of God and of Christ is put for the utmost perfection, for the utmost issue both of God's grace, and of peace of conscience, and of joy in the Holy Ghost; they are fulfilled, saith he, through the knowledge of God and of Christ.

So that, my brethren, in one word, that is meant by the knowledge of God here which he prayed for for these Ephesians that were already sealed; which the apostle John meant, 1 John i. 3, where he saith, 'Our fellowship is with the Father, and with his Son Jesus Christ.' That is, that you may have communion with God, know him as a friend, converse daily with him, have an intimacy of knowledge, that he owns you, and you own him, he knows you, and you know him; and upon this knowledge of him, that you do *agnoscere*, that you acknowledge him, cleave to him, give up yourselves to him, and delight to converse with him. This is the knowledge of God here meant.—And so much for what is meant by the *knowledge of him.*

The next thing is, *What is meant by the Spirit of wisdom and revelation?*

By 'Spirit,' I take, is meant the Holy Ghost. Why? Because he is called a Spirit of *revelation.* Indeed, if it were only a Spirit of *wisdom*, it might have been taken for a gift of the Holy Ghost, for a principle of faith infused into us, inherent in us; but that he is called the Spirit of revelation, that is not a gift inherent; for revealing is an act of one without us, of a person distinct from us; therefore, 1 Cor. ii. 12, 'He hath given us,' saith he, 'his Spirit to reveal the things that are given unto us of God.' So that by Spirit of revelation must necessarily be meant the Holy Ghost, who is the author of such revelation, and of such wisdom in a man's heart as causeth him to have intimate communion with God. This is the meaning.

Now you will say, What is meant by *wisdom?* And what is meant by *revelation?* And why is revelation added to wisdom? By wisdom, as I shewed in the 8th verse, is meant a principle of faith; and so some take it here. To open this of revelation—

It is not *extraordinary revelation* that he meaneth here, such as Paul had, Gal. i. 12, where it is said that he knew the gospel by revelation, he never heard any man preach it. 'I neither received it of man,' saith he, 'neither was I taught it, but by the revelation of Jesus Christ.' It is not such a revelation he meaneth, though indeed this revelation beareth some analogy with it; for 'they shall be all taught of God;' yet so as it is by the word, and it is revelation which the light of the world leadeth him to. And the reason why it is taken here for ordinary revelation is clear; because it is that which he would have all the Ephesians whom he wrote to, to grow in, and to have bestowed upon them, as ordinary Christians; therefore he doth not mean the extraordinary revelations of those times.

Now then, *What is meant by wisdom and by revelation?*

There are several interpretations of it, which will hold forth to us the Apostle's meaning.

First, You must know that all spiritual true knowledge is called revelation, and therefore many interpreters think that wisdom and revelation is all one; only he calleth it revelation, to shew that it is such a knowledge as is peculiar to Christians, and such a knowledge as is by a special revelation of the Holy Ghost proper unto them. Matt. xi. 25, 'I thank thee, O Father, that thou hast hid these things from the wise and prudent of the world, and hast revealed them to babes.' All spiritual knowledge, even of the meanest Christians, is called revelation.

Now it is called *revelation* in three respects.

First, For the peculiarity of it; for that you know is properly said to be by revelation which is hid to another, but is made known to me, and which I could else no way have come to know if it had not been revealed to me. This is plainly the meaning of revelation. Matt. xi. 25, 'Thou hast hid these things from the wise, and hast revealed them unto babes;' and ver. 27, 'None knoweth the Father but he to whom the Son revealeth him.' So that it importeth a peculiarness of knowledge proper unto saints, which the Holy Ghost giveth, and which the Apostle prayeth they might grow up in.

Secondly, It doth import still a further newness of knowledge; for if I know a thing but as I did afore, it is not revealed to me, it is not a knowledge by revelation; for revelation I say implieth still some further new thing. Now read Rom. i. 17. He telleth us there that in the gospel the righteousness of Christ is revealed from faith to faith. What is the meaning of that? Why, it is revealed from one degree of faith to another. Why is every new degree of faith called a revelation? Why? Because a further degree of faith makes the thing new. That is the property of spiritual knowledge; when a man increaseth in it, he sees something new in it; when that which is more perfect cometh, saith the Apostle, that which is imperfect is done away. My brethren, in notional knowledge, when a man doth know a thing, he cannot be said to know it again, for he knoweth it already, because the mind of man is all for news. Well, but in spiritual knowledge, if thou knowest God spiritually, though thou knowest no more of him materially, yet thou hast a new light come in, and God becometh again a new thing unto thee, as if thou hadst not known him before. Therefore it is called revelation, this knowledge that is joined with wisdom whereby we know God. As when a man seeth a beauty, though he sees all parts and all proportions, yet if he be in the dark, let light come in, he sees a further excellency; it is, as it were, a new face to him to what it was when he had but a glimmering light. So though you see no more of God, no more of his attributes, yet if you rise to have a new light from the Holy Ghost, all that knowledge will become new, you will see a further excellency in God, and have your hearts anew drawn to him, as if they never had been drawn yet; you will say, when a new light cometh in, you see that in sin which you never saw before. A man will say, I saw not this before, though he did. Every new degree of light addeth a further degree of knowledge. Therefore it is said to be by revelation. He would have them to have new sights of God, which might lead them into communion with God.

Thirdly, But there is one meaning which I shall give you, which I think the Apostle in a special manner aimeth at. For the Apostle here seems not to make wisdom and revelation one and the same thing, as this interpretation doth, but to make them different. Therefore the meaning that I do think may more especially be aimed at, I shall open to you as briefly and clearly as I can.

The knowledge of God here, as I said at first, is *communion with God*, intimate knowledge of him, which he would have the Ephesians grow up in. Now, there are two ways of a Christian's having communion with God, which the Scripture holdeth forth, and which the saints have experience of. The one is *a way of wisdom*, and the other is *a way of revelation.* I shall open these to you as plainly as I can, and then prove it.

The way of wisdom is this; for he takes wisdom in a distinction from revelation. It is a knowing God by faith, making use of sanctified reason, taking in several truths of God, laying them all together, working them upon a man's heart by meditation, arguing God's excellency out of this and out of that, and so raising up a man's soul to admiring of him and delighting in him; by a way of discourse, by a way of wisdom; taking wisdom as opposed to and distinct from revelation, for so I now do. A man's understanding that is filled with many notions of God, a holy heart takes them and putteth them all together, and he boileth them together, and the concoction, the result of all is, that the soul is raised up to a communion with God and delighting in him whom he admireth. This is the ordinary way of communion with God; for wisdom, you know, is a rational laying of things together, to see the harmony of all those truths one with another; out of all which I gather how great and glorious a God he is, and so my heart is affected with him. When a man knoweth God out of a distinct consideration of several attributes, meditating of several passages, of redemption, &c., this is a way of wisdom, my brethren. And the Scripture is written so as it doth deal with a man *humano more;* a sanctified reason and meditation which the light of faith accompanieth, and by them converseth with God, resolveth all a man knoweth into God, by piecemeal, taking first this thought and then that.—This is knowing God in a way of wisdom, as I may so express it.

Then there is *a way of revelation,* which the Scripture and experience holdeth forth more or less, and it is a shorter cut. The Holy Ghost cometh down into a man's heart sometimes in prayer with a beam from heaven; he sees more at once of God, of the glory of God, astounding thoughts of God, enlarged apprehensions of God, many beams meeting in one and falling into the centre of his heart. They use to call these of old, comings down of God, whereby he slideth into a man's spirit by beams of himself; a man doth not come to have communion with God by way of many broken thoughts put together, but there is a contraction of many beams from heaven which is shed into a man's soul, so that he knoweth more of God in one quarter of an hour than he knoweth the other way in a year, and hath more communion and converse with God.—This, I take it, is the way of revelation, as it is distinguished from wisdom.

The Apostle, because he would have them perfect Christians, prayeth for both; that they may grow up both in a way of wisdom, so to have communion with God, and in a way of revelation likewise, that God might often come and visit their spirits in a more immediate manner, and shew himself to them. The one, my brethren, the way of wisdom, is *more humano,* accommodated and suited unto the reason of man, knowing God by way of discoursing; yet reason sanctified, for that it doth still. The other is *more angelico,* as some of the schools, distinguishing of these two knowledges, use to speak. The one is discoursive, the mind runneth to and fro, compareth one thing with another; but the other is more intuitive, hath a prospect of

God at once. The one is acquisite, wherein God useth a man's industry, by many considerations working upon a man's heart, which the Holy Ghost accompanieth, leadeth a man's heart into communion with God; but the other is infused, more immediate. In the one, the Spirit works in us, by applying himself to our own thoughts, goeth our own pace. But in the other, a man is in the Spirit; as the phrase is of Paul, he went 'bound in the Spirit,' and as it is said of John, he was 'in the Spirit;' and being so, his heart having this communion with God, then his revelation was made to him. The one is your commons, as I may say; the other is your exceedings. The one is the common standing light of faith that goeth to sermons with you, that goeth with you to all your prayers, more or less, and causeth your heart to cleave to God. But the other is comparatively an extraordinary light. 'We walk by faith,' saith he, 'and not by sight;' yet Christians now and then get a sight; a sight comparatively; it is a revelation comparatively to that of wisdom, though it be not that sight that we have of God in heaven.

I shall express it to you by this similitude. The ordinary constant course of a Christian, that is, a holy believer; he walketh in light, as we walk in light in the day. Whether the day be dark and cloudy or not, we have light enough to do our work, to go about our business; though we do not see the sun, yet we know the sun shineth. So there is an ordinary standing light of faith, that causeth you to cleave to God and obey him, and it is enough for you to help you to do your work. But suppose now upon a sudden, in a cloudy day, a cloud should break, and a beam be let in that you see the sun; such kind of irradiations hath the Spirit of God into the hearts of his people sometimes. Sometimes you pray to God, my brethren, and there is, as it were, a curtain between God and you; you know he is behind the curtain, you know you pray to him, and you have so much knowledge and faith in him, that you believe he heareth your prayers, and accepts of you. But another time you go to prayer, and all the windows are set open, all the curtains are drawn, as I may so express it. Now this is a way of *revelation*, more than by a way of *wisdom*.

This Christians have experience of; and this the Scripture holdeth forth.

First, *Christians have experience of it.* My brethren, take a Christian of a weak understanding, but exceeding holy; he hath little knowledge of God by way of wisdom, by a way of discourse, and by a way of laying this thing to that thing, and so knowing God. He is hardly able oftentimes to speak wisely and rationally of things; yet notwithstanding, this poor soul, you shall have God breaking in upon his spirit sometimes, and he will know more of God in one prayer than a great scholar, though very holy, hath known of him all his life. And the truth is, that oftentimes God doth deal with weak understandings, that are very holy, in this way. For if they were shut up unto knowing God by a way of sanctified reason, those that have large understandings would have infinite advantage of them, and they would grow little in grace and little in holiness; therefore now God makes a supply by breaking in upon their spirits by such irradiations as these are.

You shall see it in temptations. A poor soul is tempted that there is no God, he doubteth whether there be a God. You may come, and bring forth arguments by way of wisdom, and sometimes they will convince him, he will get a little light from them; but sometimes God will come into his soul with an immediate beam and scatter all his doubts, more than a thousand arguments can do. The way of wisdom thus of knowing there is a God, that untieth the knot, but the other cutteth it in pieces, doth it presently. So it is in all temptations; as, whether a man be a Christian or no? A man goeth the way of wisdom, of sanctified reason, and he looks into his own heart and there sees the work of grace, argues from all God's dealings with him, and all these satisfy not a man. Well, God cometh with a light into his spirit, and all his bolts and shackles are knocked off in an instant. Here now you see is a way of wisdom, and here is a way of revelation.

Take those Christians that have great parts and understanding, and have grown up to much communion with God in a rational way, by way of meditation and sanctified digestion of their knowledge; yet do but ask them, if at some times they have not had such mighty impressions of God upon their hearts, have been lifted up to the mount, so that they have seen that in God which hath left that impression upon them, that all their lifetime they had not before. Now, even in them here is a way of wisdom and revelation in the knowledge of God.

Now to prove it to you by Scripture. I will give you one out of the Old Testament, and another out of the New; and then I will give a caution or two, not to be misunderstood, and so I will end.

First, out of the Old Testament. Job xlii. 5. I quoted it by way of illustration, indeed, in the point of sealing; but it properly belongeth to this head I am now on. There you shall find, that Job, who was a holy man, and lived holily all his days; when God had spoken to him out of the cloud, preached a sermon to him; what was the issue of it? 'I have heard of thee,' saith he, 'by the hearing of the ear, but now mine eyes see thee.' He doth not mean that he had any outward vision of God; that is plain, for you read of no such thing made to Job in the whole book; and if there had, that vision had not been comparable to the knowledge of faith. He speaks therefore of an inward light, that now upon this sermon fell upon his spirit. That, saith he, all the knowledge I have had of God in comparison of this, is but hearsay; not but that it was real, but so he compareth it: 'I have heard of thee by the hearing of the ear, but now mine eyes have seen thee.'

The other place that I shall mention to you is that in John xiv. 21, 'He that hath my commandments, and keepeth them, he it is that loveth me: and he that loveth me shall be loved of my Father, and I will love him, and will manifest myself unto him.' My brethren, here is a promise made not only to apostles, but to believers; for it is to them that keep the commandments, and have out of much love obeyed God's law. He that hath my commandments, saith he, and keepeth them, he loveth me: him do I love, and him will my Father love; that is, we will take him into a more special nearness, to express more love to him; and how will he express more love to him? 'I will manifest myself unto him.' Here is now some further manifestation than what they had before; yet they had faith before, that is plain, for they loved God. The promise is to him that hath the commandments and keepeth them, and it is to one that loveth God, and that God loveth before; yet there will be some further expression of love, and that by some special manifestation of God himself and of Christ to a man's soul; which is the reward of having the commandments written in his heart, and kept in his life. 'He that hath my commandments, and keepeth them: I will love him, and manifest myself unto him.' The word ἐμφανίσω, as Beza readeth it, I will set myself *in medio lucis*, in open light to him; and it is used of those apparitions, Matt. xxvii. 53, that were after

Christ's resurrection; not that there are such apparitions of God or of Christ, but because they hold a kind of similitude with this, for it is wholly by the Spirit. 'And,' saith he, ver. 23, 'we will come unto him, and make our abode with him.' Mark, *We will come,* as if he had never come before, so the expression implieth and carrieth it. As you know a martyr said, 'He is come, he is come!' He cometh in such a manner, with such a manifestation of himself unto a man as he never saw him before. So you have it likewise Rev. iii. 20, 'I will come in and sup with him, and he with me.' *I will come;* it is a manifestation of the presence of God rather in a notional way. And it is a supping with him; he cometh, and cometh suddenly, as when a great person sendeth his meat and will sup with a man, and converse familiarly with him, and letteth him taste of his cheer.

I will give you but a limitation or two to what I have delivered. For this I have delivered, all divines, Popish and Protestant, acknowledge, and the experience of Christians doth confirm it, and the Scripture itself holds it forth. Only, let me say this to you:—

By revelation you must not understand as if there were *visions* made. No, brethren; 'Henceforth, though we have known Christ after the flesh, we know him no more.' How had Paul known Christ after the flesh? He had seen him in heaven. But mark it, that knowledge which he had by faith he valued more than that sight he had of him when he was converted. All the wicked men in the world shall see Christ one day, but that will not save them; but to know him by faith is more. And there is no such revelation now.

And then, if you mark it, he doth not pray that they may have the Spirit of wisdom and revelation in the *knowledge of truths,* to open Scripture, to have an immediate light thus from heaven; to be able to say, This I know by divine revelation to be the meaning of such a place: or in matters of controversy to be able to say, This I know by divine revelation immediately that this is the truth. No, there is no such revelation now. It is the *knowledge of him,* it is only this in a way of personal communion between God and a man's soul. And for God to make such revelations as these to a man's spirit, to take him up to a nearness with himself; to come and sup with him, and manifest himself to him beyond the ordinary light of faith, going about by a long rational way of discourse and meditation; there is no harm in this, no absurdity in it. All truths that you know, you know them by a way of wisdom, and by such a way indeed a man's heart is settled in them; but when you come to converse with God, oftentimes God will in a more especial and immediate manner reveal himself to you.

It is not a revelation to draw men from the Word. No, but usually God cometh down upon the wings of some promise, or some word of his; and in that promise, putting an immediate beam of light from heaven into it, revealeth himself to a man's soul, that a man knoweth more of God in half an hour than he hath done in all his life.

And because the Apostle would have the Ephesians grow up in both, aim at both, he prays for both. He prays that they might know God both in a way of wisdom and revelation, and both joined together make perfect Christians indeed. Weak understandings oftentimes know God much in such a way of revelation, when they cannot in a way of wisdom; but to know him in a way of wisdom, and to have personal communion with him in that way of revelation, as I have opened it, it makes a strong Christian, fit for the profit of others. For this other knowledge, a man saith, Indeed I have seen God and his goodness, and I have tasted of it; but I can scarce give an account of him in a rational way, as a man may do by the knowledge he hath of God in a way of wisdom. Both together therefore make perfect Christians.

And so much for the opening of this, which I have been the longer about because I desired to finish this 17th verse; and it was necessary also to insist so long, for the explaining these things.

SERMON XX.

The eyes of your understanding being enlightened; that you may know what is the hope of his calling, and what are the riches of the glory of his inheritance in the saints.—VER. 18.

THIS is part of one of Paul's prayers; for the words just before are, 'Making mention of you in my prayers, that the God of our Lord Jesus Christ,' &c.

In the prayer that he makes, which reacheth to the end of this chapter, there is first the *person* he prayeth to, it is God the Father, under two considerations, as he is the 'God of our Lord Jesus Christ,' and as he is the 'Father of glory.' And, secondly, here are the *things that he prayeth for* unto this God; he prayeth for spiritual knowledge, that is the general; and that in these four particulars:—

1. In the *knowledge of himself*, in communion with God; and that by two ways, a way of wisdom, and a way of revelation; as I have already shewn in the 17th verse.

2. *That they may know what is the 'hope of his calling.'*

3. *What are the 'riches of the glory of his inheritance in the saints.'*

4. *What is the 'exceeding greatness of his power,' that works in the saints, and that will bring them to this glory.* The Apostle enlargeth his heart, according to the utmost experience himself had, what was requisite and necessary for sealed and grown Christians, and accordingly frameth his prayer for these Ephesians.

I have opened to you the meaning of the first petition, 'That he would give unto you the Spirit of wisdom and revelation in the knowledge of him.' By knowledge of him, I shewed, was meant an excellency of knowledge, as the Apostle calleth it, Phil. iii. 8, which consisteth in communion and fellowship with God. The way of which knowledge is, either in a way of wisdom, or in a way of revelation. I despatched this in the last discourse.

Now I come to the 18th verse, where there is a new petition. Our translators read it, 'The eyes of your understanding being enlightened, that you may know what is the hope of his calling,' &c. But I read it otherwise, and I shall give you an account of it afterward. I read it thus, 'And that he would give you eyes of your understandings enlightened, for you to know what is the hope of his calling,' &c.

To open these words, 'To give you eyes of your understandings enlightened,' I shall but mention to you how others would interpret the coherence of these words with the former.

They would make this and the former to be but one entire petition; and so indeed our translators carry it: 'That he would give unto you the Spirit of wisdom and revelation in the knowledge of him; the eyes of your understandings being enlightened, that you may know,' &c. They would make it, I say, but one entire petition or sentence, both this in the 18th verse and that in the 17th. And their meaning is this, 'That in the knowledge of God and Christ, their eyes being enlightened by a Spirit of wisdom and revelation,'—all these being means by which we come to knowledge,—'they might know what is the hope of his calling.' To such a purpose or sense as this do many interpreters usually read it.

But I rather cut it off from the former, and make it a new and distinct petition. He had finished one petition, when he prayed that God would give them a Spirit of wisdom and revelation in the knowledge of him, or communion with him. And now he prayeth for knowledge of the hope of his calling; for a taste and prelibation, or foreknowledge, of the greatness of that glory they were ordained unto. And as he prayed they should have a Spirit of wisdom and of revelation given them to know God, so now he prayeth God to give them eyes of their minds enlightened, to know the hope of his calling, and the riches of his inheritance.

Only I yield thus much to the other interpretation, which I desire you to observe: that of the two, the Apostle putting knowledge of God, and communion with God, the 'knowledge of him,' as the text hath it, before the knowledge of what is the riches of his inheritance,—I say, I yield thus much to it, that communion with God, and knowledge of God, is the highest way to come to know what heaven is, and what the riches of his inheritance are; and therefore it is a meaning agreeable to the analogy of faith to read it thus, That in the knowledge of him their eyes might be enlightened to know what heaven is. It is, I say, a meaning agreeable to the analogy of faith: the knowledge of God, and communion with God, is the high way to know what is the hope of his calling, and what the riches of his inheritance are.

But yet, my brethren, that interpretation of theirs is certainly to me not the meaning; and my reason is this, because they would make the knowledge of God but as a way and means only subordinate to the knowledge of what heaven's glory is: 'In the knowledge of him, the eyes of their understandings being enlightened,' say they, 'that they may know what is the hope of his calling, and what are the riches,' &c. But though it is true that by the knowledge of God, and communion with him, we come to know what heaven is; yet of the two, communion with God is the greater. I shall explain myself to you thus:—

There are two things to be considered in heaven. There is either the happiness that the saints themselves shall enjoy, which is 'in the saints,' saith the text, their happiness and their blessedness. And there is, secondly, communion with God, which is the cause of this happiness. Now of the two, communion with God is the greater. There is *beatitudo objectiva*, the thing possessed, which is God himself; and there is *beatitudo formalis*, which is the fruition of him; the happiness by enjoying God, and by knowing God. Now of the two, the knowing of God, communion with God, is more than our happiness; and therefore, if you mark it, the Apostle putteth that first, 'That you may have a Spirit of wisdom,' saith he, 'and of revelation in the communion and knowledge of him;' and then cometh, 'That you may know what happiness you shall have, what are the riches of the glory of his inheritance in you,' in the saints: there is *beatitudo formalis*, your fruition of it. Of the two, my brethren, it is the greater, therefore it is put first here, and therefore is not meant as a means only of knowing the other, but as a distinct thing from the other.

You shall find as much to this purpose in Rom. v., comparing the 2d and the 3d verses with the 11th. The Apostle speaks there of faith. By faith, saith he, 'we rejoice in the hope of the glory of God,'—that is, of that glory we shall have from God,—'and not only so, but we glory in tribulation also.' Though for the present we are miserable, yet through faith we see so much glory to come that the soul shall have, as it upholdeth us, we rejoice in the hope of glory, notwithstanding tribulation. Now mark the 11th verse, 'And not only so, but we also joy in God.' He riseth higher; to rejoice in hope of glory is a great matter; and not only so, but to do it in affliction too, that is more. But will you have the highest? saith he. 'Not only so, but we joy in God too.'

These words, 'Not only so, but we joy in God,' have an aspect, have a look to what is said in the 3d verse, where he bringeth in the same phrase, 'Not only so, but we rejoice in afflictions.' Not only so, saith he, but we rejoice in God. We do not only rejoice in our afflictions, in the hope of glory, but we rejoice in God too. Not only in the hope of our happiness, the inheritance in the saints, as the text saith, but in the knowledge of him. So that, 'in the knowledge of him,' is not the means only or simply whereby we come to know what heaven is, but it is a greater matter, for the top of heaven lieth in communion with God, and not only in your being made happy.

And so you see now why it is preferred here. So that here beginneth—this is all I have contended for—a new petition in these words, and I read them thus, and he that consulteth the original will find it will bear it: 'That he would give you eyes of your mind enlightened, to know what is the hope of his calling,' &c.

The words in the original are, πεφωτισμένους τοὺς ὀφθαλμοὺς τῆς διανοίας, 'eyes of your understanding enlightened,' in the accusative case, to give you the grammatical coherence of the words; it is not in the dative case, 'the eyes of your understanding being enlightened.' But take the words simply, and they lie thus, 'that God would give you eyes of your understanding enlightened.'

There are some that would make the words before, 'the Spirit of wisdom and revelation,' to intimate and import the causes of spiritual knowledge; and these words, 'the eyes of your understanding being enlightened,' the act of spiritual knowledge, which is the effect of those causes; and they would make that to be the coherence of these words with the other; and they open it handsomely thus. Say they, unto spiritual knowledge by way of causation, there are two things required. There is, first, a Spirit of wisdom, which is a Spirit of faith; and, secondly, of revelation, which is bringing light to that faith. They express it well by this similitude, which I shall afterward make use of. To bodily sight, say they, there are two things required. There is first an eye to see with, a faculty of seeing, that is meant by the 'Spirit of wisdom;' the Holy Ghost giving a power, an inherent principle, a habit, a disposition of spiritual wisdom. For you know he is a wise man, not that hath wise thoughts sometimes, but that hath wisdom habitually in him; as we use to say, he that is wise of himself, that hath a principle of wisdom in him, is properly wise. So now by a Spirit of wisdom, they mean that inherent principle of faith which makes a man wise, that infused habit which the Spirit works, that is as the new eye in the soul. And then, by the Spirit of revelation is meant, the light that the Holy Ghost acts this principle of faith by; and as the effect of both these, he mentioneth the 'eyes of their mind being enlightened to know him.' The one noteth out the causes, the other noteth out the effects.

But, my brethren, I will give you a reason or two against this interpretation, and so I will go on; for the coherence of these words is the greatest difficulty in this text; the rest will go on more easily.

If his meaning were to pray only for the principle of spiritual knowledge in the former words, and the act of knowledge in these latter words, 'the eyes of your mind being enlightened, to know,' &c., first, he would not have terminated the Spirit of wisdom and revelation in an act, in the 17th verse, as he doth; 'in the knowledge of him,' saith he. Then he cometh with a new business, 'the eyes of your mind being enlightened to know.' Here is a new cause of a second act; therefore certainly we must part them. Here is a Spirit of wisdom and revelation produceth one act, 'the knowledge of him.' Here are eyes enlightened, which produce a second act, 'that you may know,' saith he, &c. Certainly, therefore, the one doth not note out the causes and the other the acts; but here is an act answering the cause of knowledge in the one, and an act of knowledge, answering the cause of knowledge in the other.

So now, having shewed the coherence of the words, I come to the parts of the text.

The parts of this 18th verse are two.

I. Here is, first, *a new expression of spiritual knowledge;* 'that they might have enlightened eyes to know.'

II. Here is, secondly, *new objects to be known*, the knowledge of which would make them complete Christians. Which objects are three :—

1. *What is the hope of their calling.*

2. *What is the glory of their inheritance.*

3. *What the power is that is engaged to bring them to this inheritance.*

I. To begin with the first, *what is meant by spiritual knowledge*, as it is set forth to us here by giving them eyes of their mind enlightened, enlightened to know. As I take it, here are *four* things held forth to us :—

1. Here is the subject of spiritual knowledge, the mind, the understanding; 'the eyes of your understanding.'

2. Here is a double gift :—1. Of eyes unto the understanding. 2. Of light unto these eyes; for so I read the words, 'that he would give you the eyes of your understanding enlightened.'

3. Here is the act; to know.

4. Here are the persons; ye, saith he, εἰς τὸ εἰδέναι ὑμᾶς, 'that ye may know.'

I will open all these in order.

1. Here is, first, *the subject of spiritual knowledge;* it is the understanding, 'the eyes of your understanding.' Some copies read it τῆς καρδίας, 'the eyes of your *heart*.' There are *variæ lectiones* of the New Testament, as well as of the Old; that is, various readings. The king of Spain's Bible readeth it, 'the eyes of your heart.' Ordinarily we read it, 'the eyes of your understanding.' The truth is, the Hebrew word לֵב, which signifieth *heart*, the Septuagint usually translated it διανοία, *understanding*; as Gen. xxiv. 45. We use to call wise men *cordati ;* and fools in the Latin are called men without a heart, that is, without understanding; and it is called applying a man's heart to wisdom. Understanding, and a man's heart, in the Scripture phrase, are put both for one; they are both joined, διανοία καρδίας αὐτῶν, Luke i. 51, 'the understanding of the heart.' So indeed the words may be read there, which are translated 'the imaginations of the heart.'

Now, then, from hence the observation is but only this, That the heart followeth the understanding. They are put one for another, whether in a man's corrupt estate; when they err in their understandings, they are said to err in their hearts; for if their understandings err, their hearts will certainly do so. Saith our Saviour Christ, Matt. vi. 21, 'Where the treasure is, there will the heart be also.' Mark the reason, 'The light of the body is the eye.' How are these joined together? Plainly thus: look what the eye of the understanding of a man setteth up to be a man's good, his treasure, that the heart, the affections will follow. As we judge of things, so we are affected, and so the whole body, that is, the will and affections,—for he compareth the understanding to the eye, and he compareth the will and affections to the body, which is as the heart, and affections as the members,—look which way the eye goeth, saith he, the body will go as that directs. Look what the understanding pitcheth upon to be a man's treasure, there the heart will be. Therefore, now, it is all one to say, 'the eyes of your understanding,' as one copy readeth it; or, 'the eyes of your heart,' as another readeth it. If the understanding be once enlightened, the heart is enlightened, and so the whole soul is drawn; if that knoweth the excellency of heaven, where that treasure is, the heart will be also. I speak this to reconcile those diverse readings which the copies have.

And so much for the subject, the mind, or the heart, when that is once enlightened.

2. *Here is a double gift.* Here is an eye given, and here is an enlightened eye, light given to that eye too. There are some interpreters that do refer the words to the word 'give,' in the former verse, and do put some words in, and read it thus: 'That God would give the eyes of your mind, δῴη τοῦς ὀφθαλμοὺς φωτισμένους, to be enlightened.' Others, as Ambrose, read it, 'To have eyes of your mind lightened.' But I take the words nakedly and barely as they are in the Greek, and I read it thus, 'That he would give you eyes of your mind enlightened.' The gift, I say, consisteth of two things: first, of an eye of the mind; secondly, of light to that eye; and both these are requisite for us to know any spiritual thing, saith he, εἰς τὸ εἰδέναι, 'that you may know.' That a man may know heaven or any spiritual thing, he must have a new eye in his mind, and he must have a new light put to that eye; 'that he would give you eyes of your mind enlightened.' So that now cometh fitly in the interpretation that others would give it of the Spirit of wisdom and revelation; the one noteth out the principle, the other the light that the Holy Ghost bringeth in. To clear this to you—

In the first place, before a man can spiritually apprehend spiritual things, yea, or if he would grow in the apprehension of them, he must still have more of a new eye put into his mind. Read Deut. xxix. 4, 'God hath not given thee,' saith he, 'eyes to see, nor ears to hear, nor a heart to perceive to this very day.' If a man will understand spiritual things, he must have a new eye and a new heart. God must give him an eye of his mind, and to his mind; put into his understanding a new understanding.

In 1 John v. 20,—it is another place I bring for it,—saith the Holy Ghost there, 'He hath given us an understanding to know him that is true;' a peculiar understanding, not creating a new faculty. No, but enduing that faculty with a new disposition, with a quickness; for it is called by the prophet Isaiah, 'the understanding of the mind.' You shall find, therefore, in Scripture, that wicked men are said to be blind, they want an eye; and, so far as we are unregenerate, we want eyes as well as light to see heaven or any spiritual thing with. Saith he, John iii. 3, 'Unless a man be born again, he cannot see the kingdom of God;' for to see the kingdom of God a man must have a new light begotten in him, a man must have, as it were, a new understanding; and therefore you read, 1 Cor. ii. 14, that a carnal man 'cannot receive the things of God,' that is the phrase there; he cannot receive, he wants an eye, as a blind man he cannot receive in colours.

Well, that is the first gift, therefore, to have an eye, which in Ps. cxix. 18 is called opening the eye,—'Open mine eyes,' saith he, so we translate it; read the margin, it is 'reveal mine eyes:' Lord, take off the veil, and then I shall see the wonderful things of thy law; which answereth with what is in 2 Cor. iii. 16, the veil lies over all men's hearts; that, as there is film over all men's eyes that are blind that they cannot see, so there is over every man's heart by nature. Here, then, is the first thing to be done, to clear the eye, to give a new eye, to take the veil off.

But if a man have never so good an eye, if he be in the dark, he can see nothing; therefore the second thing that concurreth to spiritual knowledge here is, 'to give you eyes enlightened;' as to give you a new eye, so to give you a new light. For, Eph. v. 13, it is light that makes all things manifest. It is a philosophical speech the Apostle there useth, it agreeth with what Aristotle saith, *lumen* is *actus perspicui*, it is that which putteth life into colours and acts them. Let ever so good an eye be in the dark, it seeth not; therefore, now, here is a second work of the Holy Ghost, to enlighten this eye if ever a man cometh to see anything in a spiritual way; and as there cometh more light in, so a man seeth more or he seeth less. And therefore you shall find, in Acts xxvi. 18, the conversion of a sinner hath two expressions: the first is 'to open his eyes,' to take away the veil; and then 'to turn him from darkness to light.' You shall find the like in 2 Cor. iv. 6. God, saith he, that created light out of darkness, giveth 'the light of knowledge' (mark that phrase) 'of the glory of God in the face of Jesus Christ.' Will you have knowledge? There must be a light to accompany it. All men's experience that have grace agreeth with this. What is the reason that you shall see some things in a chapter at one time and not at another; some grace in your hearts at one time, not at another; have a sight of spiritual things at one time, not at another? The eye is the same, but it is the Holy Ghost that openeth and shutteth this dark-lantern, as I may so call it; as he openeth it wider, or contracts it or shutteth it narrower, and sometimes he shutteth it wholly, and then the soul is in darkness, though the soul have never so good an eye. Therefore, as the Apostle prayeth for an eye, so he prayeth for light; 'that he would give them eyes of their mind enlightened.' And so much for the gift: here is the subject of it, the mind or the heart, that was the first; secondly, here is the gift, to give them an eye, to give them light, eyes enlightened.

3. *Here is the act, both of this eye and of this light*—that is, 'to know,' εἰς τὸ εἰδέναι; to know, saith he. To every act of spiritual knowledge that you have in anything, my brethren, there is a giving you an eye to see it, and there is giving you a new light to see it with. It is a gift of the Holy Ghost, not only to give you a light and to give you an eye, but it is a gift for him to draw forth the act of knowledge, to give you for you to know, so the word is in the original, εἰς τὸ εἰδέναι. It referreth to 'give,' with the 17th verse, even this as well as the other.

Our dependence upon the Holy Ghost, consider what it is, in all spiritual things. It is, first, to have a new eye; it is, in the second place, to have a new light from the Holy Ghost to actuate, to inform that eye, to shine upon it, to irradiate it; and, thirdly, to draw forth the act of knowledge. In Phil. ii. 13, It is God, saith he, that giveth the will; that giveth τὸ θέλειν; the very act of the will is from him; and here τὸ εἰδέναι, an act of knowledge, is his too, it is a gift too. Saith our Saviour Christ, 'To you it is given to know,' δέδοται γνῶναι, it is given to know; the very act of knowledge is a gift. We see, I say, my brethren, the great dependence we have upon the

Holy Ghost; not only must he give us an eye and give us light, but he must give us to know too. It is a mighty expression that in 2 Cor. iii. 5: saith he, 'We are not able of ourselves to think a good thought;' he doth not say we are not able to *do*,—as Christ said before him, 'Without me ye can do nothing,'—but he saith, ye cannot *think*, if you come to spiritual things. No, *you cannot think;* of all things else it is easiest to think, yet this must be given too. Prov. xx. 12, 'The hearing ear and the seeing eye, the Lord hath made both of them.' Is it true in naturals that not only the eye is made but the seeing too? It is certainly much more true in spirituals. The scope of Solomon there is to let us see, as Cartwright well observeth, that in the smallest thing, in the very applying of sight to an act of seeing, 'the hearing ear and the seeing eye are of the Lord;' so it is much more in spirituals; he must give you an eye and he must give you a light, and he must draw forth that gift too, else we have no sufficiency to do it. 'We are not able to think a good thought, but all our sufficiency is of God;' and there cannot a greater instance be given that 'all our sufficiency is of God,' when we cannot so much as 'think one good thought' else.—So much now for the giving them both an eye and light and the act of knowledge.

4. Here is a fourth thing, and that is *the persons,* 'for you to know,' for so indeed it is in the original. He mentioneth *you* no less than three times: that he might give to *you,* ver. 17, the eyes of *your* mind; that *you* may know, ver. 18. All that I observe out of it is this, which some against the Papist have done out of the same text, against implicit faith. What do the Papists say? They would have you see with other men's eyes; they would have you believe the greatest thing in the world, and believe it because the Pope saith it. No, saith the Apostle, I would have you see with your own eyes, I would have him give you 'the eyes of your mind enlightened, that you may know.' There all these three *yous* in it. The just shall live by his faith, and nobody's faith else.—And so much for that.

II. I divided the words into these two parts: first, into spiritual knowledge, that he prayeth for; that you see I have despatched. The next, which is that I now come to, is *the objects he prayed they might know,* which I told you were three, and in this verse we have two of them laid down. The first is, *what is the hope of their calling;* the second is, *what is the riches of the glory of his inheritance in the saints.* There is nothing difficult in these words but only this, 'what is the hope of their calling.' I shall present the difficulty to you, and I will tell you what my apprehension and judgment of it is.

Hope is taken, say interpreters, for two things; either for the thing hoped for, as Col. i. 5, 'For the hope,' saith he, 'which is laid up in heaven;' that is, heaven itself, the thing hoped for: so Titus ii. 13, 'Looking for the blessed hope;' that is, the thing hoped for. Or else, in the second place, it is taken for the grace of hope; not for the object, but for the grace of hope, by which we do hope. And it is sometimes put for assurance of our interest in the thing hoped for; as 1 John iii. 2, 3, 'Now we are the sons of God,' saith he; 'and he that hath this hope in him,' that is, hath an assurance of this, is confident of this, 'he purifieth himself as God is pure.' And so likewise Rom. v. 4, 5, 'Experience worketh hope, and hope maketh not ashamed,' that is, it worketh an assurance that leaveth not the soul in confusion; 'because the love of God is shed abroad in our hearts,' so it followeth. So that by hope there, he meaneth assurance of salvation; as likewise Rom. xv. 13, 'That you may abound in hope through the power of the Holy Ghost.'

Now, my brethren, interpreters do generally carry it by hope to be meant here the thing hoped for. I find almost all interpreters go that way, restraining it to the thing hoped for; and, say they, the Apostle, what he calleth hope in these words, he more plainly explaineth in the next words, that he meaneth by hope the thing hoped for. He telleth you in the next words what it is, what is 'the riches of the glory of his inheritance,' saith he. So that what he meaneth by hope in the one, he plainly expresseth in the other. Only he calleth it hope here in the first sentence, to shew that it is but in hope, but it is to come in the world to come; and to shew that the highest joy that we have here is but in hope to what is to come. For as it is, Rom. viii. 24, 'What a man seeth, that he doth not hope for.' By hope there, he meaneth the object of hope.

And it is called the 'hope of your calling;' or, say they, the 'hope of his calling.' Why? Because it is that unto which we were called. Read 1 Thess. ii. 12, 'Who hath called you,' saith he, 'to his kingdom and glory.' So then the meaning of the Apostle, say they, is this: he prayeth that they may know what great things are laid up in heaven for them, which God calleth them to hope for, which are annexed to their calling.

I find Zanchy thinks the grace of hope should be here meant, not so much the thing hoped for, as the grace by which we hope for this thing hoped for. And so they interpret it thus, 'the hope of his calling;' that is, say they, the hope which God calleth us to have of that glory that is to come, which God commandeth us to have, and calleth us to. Therefore, say they, it is called the hope of his calling. And his meaning is this, he prayeth that they may know what great hopes and assurance God would have us Christians to have of the life to come.

Now to this interpretation of theirs, I add but this: that by hope is here meant the ground of hope; it is not merely the grace of hope by which we do hope, but the ground which God doth give us to hope upon; the grounds and the evidences that we have for eternal life, that that should be the Apostle's meaning. And I find that Zanchy falleth into this, and so hinted me indeed to it; for he explaineth it thus, 'That they might know their hope is founded upon the most infallible and certain grounds that can be.'

I must give you Scripture for this, to shew where hope is put for the ground of hope. I will give you but one, Rom. iv. 18; there it is said, that Abraham 'against hope, believed in hope.' What is the meaning of that? He did against all grounds of hope believe. He mentioneth the grounds that might discourage him in the next verse; saith he, his body was dead, being an hundred years old, and Sarah's womb was dead; yet against all hope, that is, against all grounds of hope, he believed in hope.

So then the interpretation I pitch upon is plainly this. The Apostle prayeth here, that they may know what great, what infallible, what multitudes of grounds of hope God had called them to; what grounds of assurance and evidence their souls might have that heaven is theirs. So that now, in this first part, he prayeth that they may have much assurance of their own interest in heaven, and see good grounds for it. And, in the second part, he prayeth that they may see the glory of his inheritance.

I will give you my reason why I interpret it thus, rather than for the thing hoped for; that this expression should mean one and the same thing, heaven in both. My reason is this: the Apostle seemeth to pray for three things distinctly, and he putteth a conjunctive, *καὶ*, between them all. First, he prayeth that they may see what is the 'hope of their calling,' and see what is the 'glory of his inheritance,' and see what is the 'exceeding greatness of his power.' Now, if 'exceeding greatness of his power' be a distinct thing from 'what is the glory of his inheritance,' then 'what is the glory of his inheritance' is a distinct thing from 'what is the hope of his calling;' therefore, the thing hoped for is not meant, but he intendeth three several sorts of things that he prayeth for. And he addeth τίς, and τί τὸ ὑπερβάλλον μέγεθος, *what*, and *how great*, to all three, to shew that they are distinct; what great grounds you have of your interest, and that you may see what a great and glorious inheritance it is that you have interest in, and that you may see thereby how great the exceeding greatness of his power is that he works in them that believe, and keepeth you for that glory.

Having thus opened to you what is meant by the hope of his calling, what grounds of hope you have, I will but shew you how it agreeth fully with the scope and with the phrase the Apostle here useth, that I may back this interpretation.

It agreeth fully with his scope; for, first, he prayed in the former verse for communion with God. Now, what is the next thing a good soul would desire, next to communion with God. To have the grounds of his assurance kept continually fresh in his heart, that he may 'know the hope of his calling;' that is the next thing any good soul would pitch upon, to keep himself in perfect peace and comfort; and then to know the greatness of that glory that he had an interest in. Link these three things together, this makes a complete Christian, full of comfort, full of joy and peace in believing.

It agreeth also with the phrase that followeth, 'the hope of his calling;' interpreting it for grounds of hope or grounds of assurance, what grounds of assurance you have.

By 'his calling' here is either meant that calling which God commandeth you to have; such grounds of hope as God calleth you, being Christians, to have, commandeth you to have; that is one meaning of the phrase. So the word 'calling' is used, 1 Thess. iv. 7; saith he, 'God hath not called us to uncleanness, but to holiness;' that is, he hath commanded us to be holy, for so you may interpret it by the third verse, 'This is the will of God, your holiness.' God's calling and his will is all one. If you did but know, saith the Apostle, the grounds that God calleth you to have the hope you have, the assurance God calleth you to have, and hath given you grounds to have; that is the meaning of his prayer.

Or, secondly, the hope of his calling may refer to the work of grace, which is called calling and conversion; and so the meaning is proper and very good, and it is thus: that you, being called by God, have all the grounds to have assurance that may be; and I pray, saith he, 'that you may know what is the hope of your calling.' A man effectually called hath multitude of grounds to be assured, if he be not negligent in it. So that that which I pray for, saith he, is that you may know the very calling itself, the very work itself; God's calling you affordeth you grounds enough of hope. I pray that you may know the grounds of your hope, keep that fresh in your eye, and so you will be comforted.

I come now to some observations out of this interpretation.

Obs. 1.—The first observation is this: *That every man in the state of grace is called to have assurance*, and there are grounds enough for it. Oh, saith the Apostle, would you did know what is the hope of his calling, what grounds you have of hope from that calling of God that hath put you into the state of grace! The state itself affordeth it, and the word of God upon you affordeth it, only you want eyes to see it; therefore I pray that the eyes of your understanding may be enlightened to know it, daily enlightened to see those grounds.

My brethren, every believer hath grounds enough of assurance if their eyes were but enlightened. There is a whole epistle written on purpose; God wrote one book to shew the vanity of the creature; he hath written another book on purpose to assure us and every believer of salvation. The first Epistle of John is written on purpose for that end; you shall see it is his scope both by the first chapter, ver. 4,—so he beginneth, 'These things write we unto you, that your joy may be full,'—and by chap. v. 13, 'These things have I written unto you that believe on the name of the Son of God, that ye may know that ye have eternal life.' And, saith he, I write to all sorts of Christians that are called; so he saith, chap. ii. 12, 13, 'I write to you, children,'—those that are babes are capable of assurance, to know the hope of their calling, if God enlighten them,—'because your sins are forgiven for his name's sake. I write unto you, fathers, because ye have known him that is from the beginning. I write unto you, young men,' &c. All sorts of Christians are capable of assurance if God enlighten their eyes, and if they be once called there is abundance of grounds to give them assurance, to give them hope of salvation. He telleth us in the 10th verse of the 5th chapter, 'He that believeth hath the witness in himself,' that is, he hath the matter of it. Yea, there is no act of faith but putteth forth a witness;—as when we come to a hollow place there is no voice but turneth back an echo, only if you speak low the echo answereth you low, but if you speak loud the echo is loud too; so if a man's faith speaks strongly, it will echo forth back again a strong witness;—there is the witness of blood and the witness of faith. 'He that believeth hath the witness in himself.' There is no grace a man hath but is a ground of assurance. There is no exercise of grace but is a ground of assurance. In your very not sinning you may fetch assurance from it; so John telleth us, 1 Epistle iii. 9, 'He cannot sin, he hath the seed of God in him;' you shall find that in your hearts that you cannot sin; there is an evidence of grace when you are tempted to sin. The grounds that every believer hath for assurance of salvation, if he did but know them, they are infinite ones and infallible.—So much for the first observation.

Obs. 2.—To give you a second observation. Though a man have never so much ground of hope from God's calling him, yet, notwithstanding, he must have the eyes of his mind enlightened to know what is his hope, what are the grounds of evidence and assurance of salvation; and further than he hath an eye and an act of knowledge drawn forth, he cannot see it; therefore the Apostle prayeth that 'the eyes of their minds may be enlightened, that they may know what is the hope of his calling.'

To make this plain to you. All graces, as they work with a borrowed strength,—not with a strength of their own, but with the strength of the Holy Ghost,—so they shine to comfort you with a borrowed light, as the stars do with the light of the sun. A man hath a natural power to know what is within him, so saith the Apostle, 1 Cor. ii. 11. Let any man ask me what I think, I can tell him, and so can you; it is from the natural spirit that is in every one. 'What man,' saith he, 'knoweth the things of a man, save the spirit of a man that is in him?' The spirit of a man that is in him doth know it, it can tell you a man's thoughts and affections; but if you would come to know whether faith be in you or not, or whether true love to Christ be in you or no, or zeal for his glory, now you must have the Spirit to enlighten your eyes; though it be in you, the mere spirit of a man will not do it; so it followeth, 'We have received the Spirit that is of God, that we may know the things that are freely given us of God.' If you will come to know whether you have grace or no, which God hath bestowed upon you, here you must have the eyes of your mind enlightened, 'that you may know,' saith the Apostle, or else you will not see it. Your graces shine with a borrowed light. You can tell, 'I think such thoughts as believers think;' but to tell that this is true faith and differeth from that of hypocrites, this you cannot tell without the Holy Ghost enlighten you. Therefore he prayeth 'that the eyes of their minds may be enlightened, that they may know.'

I will give you a scripture more for this, Rom. viii. 16,—mark that place, —It is the Spirit, saith he, that 'beareth witness with our spirits, that we are the children of God.' He doth not only say he beareth witness *to* our spirits, but he beareth witness *with* our spirits. Our spirits, our graces, (that which is born of the Spirit is spirit,) never witness unless the Holy Ghost witness with them; if he do not give in his testimony with them, your graces will give no witness at all; if he do not enlighten the eyes of your mind to know, you will not know the hope of your calling, you will have no assurance.

Likewise that other place, Rom. xv. 13; the Apostle prayeth there, that they may 'abound in hope, through the power of the Holy Ghost.' Doth a man abound in hope? Hath he any comfort? any assurance?—for I take 'hope' there for assurance, as I do here,—any confident persuasion? It is, saith he, through the power of the Holy Ghost.—So much for the second point.

I might interpret it thus. 'The scripture is not of private interpretation;' so saith the Apostle, 2 Pet. i. 20. Read another book, your natural understanding will help you to understand it; but, saith he, the scripture is not of private interpretation; that is, no man's private understanding will help to understand it, but that Spirit that writ it. Look into your own hearts, there is a word written in the heart, as here the word is written in our books; that word written in the heart, the law written there, is not of private interpretation; all the human wit that any man hath who hath grace, cannot help him to do it, to know the meaning of it, but that Spirit that wrote it there; for so you know we are called 'the epistle of Christ, written not with ink but with the Spirit of the living God,' 2 Cor. iii. 3. He only is able to read it; unless he enlighten your eyes, give you an eye, and give you light, and draw forth an act of knowledge, you will not know what is the hope of his calling, you will not know what ground you have for assurance of salvation.

Obs. 3.—To come to a third observation, and it is a good one. You know I interpreted the hope of his calling partly in this sense, to be that which God calleth you to have. Art thou a believer? He calleth thee to hope; as he calleth you to holiness, so he calleth you to assurance, to hope. What is the reason then that poor souls want comfort? It is God's mind you should have it, there is enough in the word to comfort you; there is enough in your own hearts to comfort you, there is a Holy Ghost that dwelleth within you. God, I say, calleth you to hope. Satan, my brethren, and Antichrist call you to doubt; so the Papists do; but God calleth you to hope, calleth you to assurance. The Papists exact of every man as necessary to salvation, to believe a harder point than the assurance of their own salvation; for they exact of them to believe that the Church of Rome is the only Church of Christ, to believe the mother, but they would have men to doubt of their Father; they would have men to be bastards, that is the truth of it. But, saith he, 'that you may know what is the hope of your calling;' he would have them know it. The Apostle writing to men that had assurance, to old men, saith he, you have known the Father from the beginning, not only the mother, but the Father. It is a harder point to believe that the Church of Rome is the only true Church of Christ, than to believe that thou art in Christ, and there is more evidence in thy own heart, if the Holy Ghost irradiate thy mind, than there is of the other, for that is an extrinsical thing, and yet they are strict in that point; upon pain of damnation a man must believe that that is the true Church : yet they would not have a man believe he is a true member of the Church, nor of Jesus Christ. No, it is 'what is the hope of his calling;' he calleth you to hope, that is his commandment.

Rom. xv. 13, 'The God of hope fill you with all peace and joy in believing.' God is a God of hope, and he would fill your hearts with peace and joy through believing. He is not only called the God of hope because he is the object of hope, but because he is the author of it; and all the Scripture is written to work hope in us, so saith ver. 4 of the same chapter. God's mind is, that the saints should have nothing else, 'that you may know what is the hope of his calling;' only your eyes are dark indeed, there lieth the defect, naturally you are dark and can know none of these grounds, therefore the Apostle prayeth that the eyes of their mind may be enlightened, that they may know what is the hope of his calling.

Obs. 4.—In the fourth place, if you observe it, it is what is the hope of *his* calling, it is not what is the hope of *your* calling, or what is the hope of your grace; he giveth it not that title. Take calling in that sense for God's work of conversion upon a man's soul, I do observe but this out of it, and it is to you a note of much consequence: If you come to have good assurance that the Holy Ghost giveth, he will draw your eye unto his work, rather than unto the work that is wrought in yourselves.

I will explain myself to you as well as I can. It is the property of the Holy Ghost when he doth give any man assurance and hope, and enlighteneth his eyes to see what the hope of God's calling is, not to make the heart pore upon the work in himself: but to draw his heart up to God as the worker of it, and to have a hint from thence to stand admiring of him that thus called him, and by his mighty power wrought these things in him through his free grace. When men look upon grace wrought in themselves, self-love rejoiceth in it, and they boast as if they had not received it. No, saith the Apostle, look not upon the hope of *your*, but upon the hope of *his* calling; as having received it from him, let it lead you to the fountain of his free grace. I do observe it there in 1 Cor. ii. 12, (I quoted the place before,) 'We have received,' saith he, 'the Spirit of God, that we may know the things that are freely given us of God.' Mark that expression; not only know the thing, that this grace is wrought, but with this addition, it is the free work of God's grace. This is the end always of the Holy Ghost when he giveth assurance, that is his manner, as he discovereth his graces to you, these things are in you, so that these things are freely given you of God, he leadeth you to the fountain of his grace, that you may admire it and fall down before it; that you may know, saith he, praying for assurance, what is the hope of his calling; he fixeth their eyes there.

Next to communion with God and knowledge of him, he prayeth they may know their own interest.

The next thing that is to be handled is this—and what is *the riches of that glory*, which is the glory which they had assurance of. Put but these three things together, my brethren, and do but think with yourselves, what mighty effects it would work, what comfortable Christians it would make you, if your hearts came up to what Paul prayeth for here: that you lived in the knowledge and communion with God day by day, to converse with him as he is the God of Christ and the Father of glory, as he calleth him in the next verse; and next to that add, the grounds and evidences of our assurance, and eyes enlightened to see them, admiring the love of God in you and toward you; and, thirdly, add the eyes of your understanding further enlightened, with mighty vast apprehensions of that heaven you have interest in, of the riches of the glory of his inheritance. If a man's soul would live but in these thoughts, what a mighty powerful Christian would that man be! Paul had all these things in his heart, and when he cometh to pray for men he prayeth after this rate, and this is the meaning of his prayer.

SERMON XXI.

And what the riches of the glory of his inheritance in the saints.—VER. 18.

As I told you, this is one of the Apostle's prayers, as he hath many other scattered up and down in his Epistles. In this prayer of his you have these two parts: First, the person that he prayeth to; the God of our Lord Jesus Christ, the Father of glory. He doth set him forth under such considerations as were suitable unto the matter of his prayer, as I shall shew you in the closure of this sermon. Then, secondly, you have the matter of his prayer, which is for knowledge. 1. Intimate knowledge of God, intimate communion with him, as I have opened to you; 'that he may give you the Spirit of wisdom and revelation, in the knowledge' (or acknowledgment) 'of him.' 2. He prayeth God to give them eyes enlightened, eyes of their understanding. That which is translated the 'eyes of your understanding being enlightened,' if you will read it according to the original, as many interpreters go, it referreth to the word *give*; 'that he would give you eyes of your understanding enlightened,' enlightened to know what is the hope of his calling; that is the second part of his prayer. And then, thirdly, what the riches of the glory of his inheritance in the saints are. And, fourthly, what is the exceeding greatness of his power to us-ward who believe.

I am yet in the 18th verse. It hath two parts. It hath first a description of spiritual knowledge. It is a 'giving of enlightened eyes of the understanding, that you may know;' which I handled the last time. There are, secondly, two several objects which these eyes of the understanding being enlightened do serve to know. The first is, What is the hope of his calling. The second is, What are the riches of the glory of his inheritance in the saints.

I opened to you the last time what was meant by the knowing of the hope of his calling. I told you, that by hope, as I understood it, was meant, not the thing hoped for, for that is expressed afterward, but the grace of hope, the grace of assurance, and the grounds of that assurance, the grounds of hope. Hope is taken for the grace of hope, and it is taken likewise for the grounds of hope, as well as for the thing hoped for. It is taken for the grounds of hope; I gave you one scripture for it. I will add but this: in your ordinary expression in our English dialect, when you come and ask a physician concerning a dying friend, or one that is sick, you will say, What hope is there? that is, what grounds of hope? 'There is hope in Israel concerning this thing;' that is, there are grounds of hope. Now then, the Apostle's meaning is plainly this: he prayeth they may know both what assurance and hope God calleth them to have; what is the hope of his calling, what his will, and mind, and command is, you should have; he commandeth that you should be assured, be men full of hope, and of great hope; for by 'calling' is sometimes in Scripture meant his command, as I have shewed you. Or else, in the second place, and together with it, for it is both meant, he prayeth that they may know all the grounds that may give them hope by virtue of

God's calling, for to God's calling there are a world of grounds of hope annexed. There is no man that is called of God but hath all sorts of grounds to be assured of his salvation, and that by virtue of his calling. Now, then, this is the first thing the Apostle prayeth for, that they may make their calling sure; that is the meaning, to know what is the hope of their calling,—what grounds their calling affordeth them, that are annexed to their calling, to being in the state of grace,—what hope is annexed to their calling, of their interest in salvation. So that this is the first petition, that they may know their own interest for themselves, a peculiar one, a particular interest in those great things to come.

Having prayed for this, he doth in the second place pray, that they may know what the riches of the glory of his inheritance in the saints are; that they may know what the greatness of that glory in heaven is, of which they have an interest, and for which they have grounds to hope.

Now, then, put but these two things together, I appeal: let a man's eyes be but enlightened to see all those grounds that God, by virtue of his calling, hath given him to hope for salvation by; to see his own interest clear, to have those grounds fresh in his eye. And then, let him have a light to see, a glorious light to see what the riches of that glory are; what mighty, strong, and glorious Christians would this make men! Now for both these doth the Apostle here pray.

Having then handled this first part, 'what is the hope of his calling,' I now come to the second, 'and what the riches of the glory of his inheritance in the saints' are. I come to these words, and so on. As the Apostle would have them know their own interest, and all the grounds of it, that they might be comforted, so he would have them know the thing. How happy would Christians be, if they knew their own happiness; if they knew both their own interest, and likewise if they knew what the riches of the glory of his inheritance in the saints are!

There are two things that are to be opened in the handling of these words. The FIRST is, to lay open to you, so far as the word openeth it, and doth give you a sight of it, *What the glory of heaven is by the description here that the Apostle makes of it;* he calleth it 'the riches of the glory of his inheritance in the saints.'

The word here, ὁ πλοῦτος, the article that is put to 'riches,' is not only to know what it is for the substance, but how great it is. 'That you may know,' saith he, καὶ τίς ὁ πλοῦτος, 'how great the riches are,' that is the Apostle's meaning. I was in heaven, saith the Apostle,—so he might have said to them,—and I saw things, saith he, that I am not able to utter. When he came down again, he could tell no news of it; so you may read 2 Cor. xii.; they were too big for his mouth to utter. Therefore here the Apostle is as it were in travail, he bringeth forth great words, *riches*, and *glory*, and *inheritance*, and knoweth not how to express it, heapeth up one word upon another.

And then the SECOND thing that is to be considered in the text is, *Of what use the knowledge of the glory of his inheritance is to saints;* for he would not pray for it unless it were of mighty use. There are these two things to be handled in the words. And—

FIRST, *For the description*, for that the Apostle doth; as he doth pray that they may know it, so he doth interlace in his prayer such descriptions of it whereby they may know it. Now, concerning the description he giveth of it, I divide that into two parts:—

Here is, *first*, *The state itself that the saints shall be in.*

Here are, *secondly, The persons to whom it belongeth.*

First, The state itself, set forth to us by these three things :—

1. An inheritance.
2. A rich inheritance.
3. A glorious inheritance : 'the riches of the glory of his inheritance.'

Secondly, here are *the persons whom it belongeth unto.* Here is, first, the Person whose it is more properly and most eminently, it is *his inheritance.* Secondly, here is the subject in whom this inheritance is. He is the great inheritor; but who come in as heirs too under him? It is 'his inheritance in the saints.' And so now you have the division of the words.

First, To begin with the first, *an inheritance.*

'Inheritance' doth note out the substance of this glory, which is the subject of which the other two are predicated or attributed to. There are two attributes of this inheritance, *rich* and *glorious;* but *an inheritance* is the substance of it; therefore he saith, 'the riches of the glory of his inheritance.' *Riches* is attributed to *glory;* but both are attributed to *inheritance.*

In the first place, because we have a title to it, being saints, as sons have to their natural inheritance; in respect of *our title* to it therefore, it is called an inheritance. My brethren, God, to make heaven sure, and that his children might have mighty hope of their calling, hath made heaven sure by all sorts of ways that are found amongst men to make a thing sure. He hath made it sure by a purchase of the blood of Christ; so saith ver. 14, he calleth it 'the purchased possession.' He hath made it sure by an inheritance too; not only by a way of sale, it was sold to Christ, and it is his inheritance too, but it is an inheritance to us though he purchased it; so saith the text too. It is likewise by way of gift, that is the third way of conveying of it; for 'the gift of God is eternal life,' Rom. vi. 23. Lastly, it is given by will of a man that dieth, Heb. ix. 15. You read there that Jesus Christ died, and made his will, that all those that believe in him should have eternal life. 'For this cause,' saith he, 'he is the Mediator of the new covenant,' or testament, 'that by means of death, for the redemption of the transgressions that were under the first testament, they which are called might receive the promise of eternal inheritance.' As it is an inheritance, and purchased by Christ, and given by God, so bequeathed by Christ at his death. Read the next verses : 'For where a testament is, of necessity there must be the death of the testator; for a testament is of force after men are dead; otherwise it is of no strength at all whilst the testator liveth.' So that Jesus Christ died, and left it to us by will. We have it by all ways; you cannot have God made over to you more surely than by way of gift, than by way of inheritance, (if a man make no will, yet the heir succeedeth him,) than by way of purchase, than by way of will. All these ways is heaven conveyed to us.

In the second place, an inheritance noteth out *a perpetuity.* You know your style of inheritance runs thus, 'to a man and his heirs for ever.' So doth heaven; and therefore in the same place I even now quoted, Heb. ix. 15, it is called an 'eternal inheritance.'

In the third place, an inheritance noteth out *a whole possession;* it doth not note out a part, it doth not note out a portion. Abraham, you know, gave portions to his youngest children; but an inheritance he gave to his eldest son Isaac, to his first-born. Now read Heb. xii. 23; he calleth the saints there the first-born of them whose names are written in heaven. They have all inheritances as first-born.

You will say, how is that possible? For if one saint inherit all, how do the rest do so too?

Yes, my brethren. Look Col. i. 12, it is called an 'inheritance in light.' Now those that are sons of Adam born into this world, one man doth not inherit part of the light of the sun and another man another; but all men are heirs alike of the light of the sun. If God be the inheritance, if he be the light of it, as you shall hear anon in Rev. xxi. 23, then all may be heirs; for 'God,' saith he, 'is all in all.' He can be whole happiness to one man and whole happiness to another, and no man shall complain; every man possesseth whole God to himself. An inheritance is of the whole, it is not a portion.

So much now for the word *inheritance.* I have touched upon such things as are most material for the opening of it.

I come now to the attributes of it. First, it is *a rich inheritance.* Secondly, it is a *glorious inheritance.* Thirdly, there are *riches of glory* in it: for the word 'riches' may either be attributed to 'inheritance' (and so 'glory') apart; or you may join both together, 'riches of glory of our inheritance.' In the general, my brethren, the Apostle speaks here pertinently, after the manner of men; for all inheritances here below consist either of riches or glory. We see that men inherit both: the children of rich men inherit their riches, if they be noble men they inherit their honour; both honour and riches go by descent, he joineth them both here, you see; and where both these meet there is fulness. When the glory of the greatest monarch upon earth is described, Esth. i. 4, it is done both by riches and by glory; he saith, 'Ahasuerus made a feast, when he shewed the riches of his glorious kingdom, and the honour of his excellent majesty.' There are but these two things which the world pursueth, riches and glory; riches will compass all sorts of pleasures; and if you have these two you want nothing. Read but Eccles. vi. 2; he makes a supposition of a man to whom God hath given riches, wealth, and honour, so that, saith he, he wanteth nothing—if he have these he wanteth nothing—that his soul can desire in this life. Hence, therefore, because these two are things inherited, and because these two put together do fully make up a satisfaction to a man's desires, he describeth heaven to us both by riches and by glory; 'what are the riches of the glory,' saith he, 'of his inheritance.' And therefore you shall find that the reward of heaven is set forth to us by these two, by our Saviour Christ, and these two alone, Matt. xiii. 43, 44. At ver. 43, he layeth forth there the glory of that kingdom, 'Then shall the righteous shine forth as the sun in the kingdom of their Father;' there he mentioneth their glory. 'Again,' saith he, 'the kingdom of heaven is like to a treasure hid in a field;' there are riches. Therefore, Prov. viii. 18, Wisdom is said to have in her left hand riches and honour; for these are the great things the world desireth. You have both here.

First, to begin with *riches,* and secondly with *glory,* apart; and then, why 'riches of glory.'

It is, first, a rich inheritance. The Holy Ghost in this doth descend; he speaks as to children, he expresseth heaven by riches and by glory, because they are the great things, the only things we are capable of to understand heaven's glory by, and the abundance of good things there. First, for *riches.* You shall read in Rev. xxi. a description of the new Jerusalem. Whether it be an estate of glory of the Church here on earth yet to come, which is but the forerunner, is but the harbinger to that great glory after the day of judgment,—which I rather incline to,—or whether it be the glory of the saints in happiness hereafter, I will not dispute that now, however it will serve my purpose. For if it be meant of the estate of the Church on earth in her perfect glory and beauty yet to come, it will argue much more what is in heaven; therefore it is all one for my purpose whether you understand it of the one or the other. Do but read out that chapter, and you shall find there that he rakes all the bowels of the earth, he fetcheth up all the precious stones out of it, and gold and crystal, all those things that the world hath turned up trump, as I may so express it, to commend all things else, wherein riches lie, he hath reckoned them up all as you shall find there; to what end? He mentioneth gold to pave the streets of that city, for men to tread upon, so you have it ver. 21. Nay, he is not only profuse in his expressions,—lavish, as I may so express it, to have a street paved with gold,—but he doth feign as if he were a poet, he saith it was such gold as did shine as crystal, such gold as the chymics say they can make; they can make gold, they say, to have the very transparency of crystal. But the Holy Ghost aimeth not at this art, for it was not in the world; but if gold had a resplendency in it, if it were as transparent as crystal,—for to that he compareth it,—it had a perfection in it. What a glorious creature gold were, if together with the weight it had a transparency as crystal, whereas gold hath a darkness in it. In Solomon's time, which was a time of riches, 1 Kings x. 27, he saith silver was in Jerusalem as stones in the street; here is the type now, but it is but of silver, it is not of gold; but here the streets of the new Jerusalem are paved with gold.

Well, the wall of that city, if you read ver. 18, he saith it was all of jasper-stone; there was never such jasper in the world to make one wall: still he feigneth; he is fain, as we say, to compound, to make golden mountains to express the riches of the new Jerusalem. And you shall find, ver. 21, that every gate of the city was a pearl. A pearl as big as a man's thumb, what a mighty value is it of! Here are city gates, broad gates, open gates, for he saith they were never shut at all by day, for there was no night there. They are every one of one pearl, each gate is but one pearl. Here are the strangest fictions that ever were; you see what visions the Holy Ghost makes to set out the riches of the new Jerusalem. And he saith that all the nations shall bring their glory and honour into it, so at ver. 26,—that is, they shall bring their riches into it, that is the meaning of glory there; for in Scripture we find often that glory is put for riches: Gen. xxxi. 1, we read there that Jacob 'heard the words of Laban's sons, saying, Jacob hath taken away all that was our father's; and of that which was our father's hath he gotten all this glory;' that is, all this riches. The allusion here is to Isa. lxi. 6; there you shall find it is called the glory of riches which the nations shall bring in; and so the Septuagint translateth it. The like you have in Isa. lx. 9. It is a manifest allusion, this in the Revelation, to those places. Now, my brethren, that which is the head city of a kingdom, as London; that which is the head city of the world, as Rome once was, all the nations of the world bring their riches thither. Heaven is the head city, it is the city of the living God, all riches are come thither; it is therefore a rich inheritance.

And let me but add one thing to you: all these same riches of which the Holy Ghost, condescending to our capacities, if we may speak so with reverence, is fain to make fictions,—for mountains of gold, and gates of one pearl, is a thing that never was, nor ever will be in this world, but he doth it to set things forth to us;—all these descriptions, what are they but false riches? Luke xvi. 11, he calleth only the riches of grace and glory the true riches, and he calleth the other the mammon τῷ ἀδίκῳ. It is translated 'of unrighteousness,' but the Hebrew word the Septuagint oftentimes translates it for 'falsehood;' as now in English we say a thing is right when it is true, and it is wrong when it is false, so the riches of unrighteousness or of wrong, in the Hebrew dialect, oftentimes is put for falsehood. All the riches here are but false riches, these only are the true riches, the other are but shadows of it.

To speak a little more home to it. It is a rich inheritance; rich, why? Because that God layeth forth all his riches in making the saints happy. In Phil. iv. 19,—it is a place I shall afterwards quote to a further purpose,—saith he, 'My God shall supply all your need according to his riches in glory by Jesus Christ.' You know God is said to be rich in mercy, and rich in grace, and rich in love, and rich in power; all his attributes are called riches in Scripture. Now mark, wouldst thou know what heaven is? Thou shalt have all God's riches; not in bullion, for that cannot be, they are incommunicable, thou canst not have them in species; but thou shalt have them in use, in comfort; thou shalt have all God's riches turned into comfort. The attributes themselves are incommunicable, thou canst not have it in money paid thee down, it is proper to God; but all the riches in God shall be to make thee happy. 'God shall supply all your need according to his riches,' saith the text; and if God's riches undertake to supply you, certainly you will be full.

In the second place, to describe these riches more full unto you, I will give you one place of Scripture; the other place that I mentioned is applied to God, that all his riches shall be turned into comforts; this place I now give is of Christ's riches, it is 2 Cor. viii. 9, 'Ye know the grace of our Lord Jesus Christ, that, though he was rich, yet for your sakes he became poor, that ye through his poverty might be rich.' He doth not mean riches in this world, for the saints are the poorest in this world; 'you see your calling,' saith the Apostle, 'how that not many rich, not many noble, are called;' therefore the riches he meaneth are the riches of glory hereafter. Now see, for I argue, as from God before, so now from this that Christ did, an infinite mass of riches are laid up for us in the world to come. To raise up your considerations, consider this, saith he; Jesus Christ that was rich became poor, to that end that you might be rich. Jesus Christ was rich, he was the heir of all things, he had all glory; he left himself not worth one groat, my brethren. 'The foxes have holes, and the birds of the air have nests, but the Son of man hath not where to hide his head.' He became poor, the word is *a beggar;* not that Christ was a beggar, or lived by begging, for there was to be no beggar in Israel, he had not fulfilled the law if he had; therefore the Papists have but an ill ground from this place to justify the calling of their mendicant friars; but he was in the estate of a beggar, he was ministered unto, he left himself worth nothing. If that this Christ who, saith he, was rich—it is πλούσιος ὤν, he did exist rich before he was poor—laid all aside, emptied himself to nothing; if he will put all the riches he was worth out to use, that you might be rich, saith he, and you shall have all the use of it; what will this come to? My brethren, the Apostle, in Eph. iii. 8, calleth them 'the unsearchable riches of Christ;' you cannot tell them over to all eternity, for if Christ will put forth all his riches, and become poor on purpose to make men rich, what riches will that be? So that you see it is a rich inheritance.

And let me add this too, which is a good meditation of Austin's upon this place, saith he, *quid facturi sunt*, &c.;—How rich will his riches make us when we shall meet with him in glory, when his poverty makes us thus rich! As the Apostle, I remember, expresseth, Rom. xi. 12, speaking of the Jews, 'If the fall of them be the riches of the world, and the diminishing of them the riches of the Gentiles, what will their fulness be?'—And so much now for this first attribute, that it is a rich inheritance. We come to glory; 'the riches,' saith he, 'of the glory of his inheritance.'

To open you the word *glory*. Glory importeth always an excellency of things; and it importeth a superexcellency too. It importeth an excellency, as it is said, Matt. iv. 8, that Satan shewed him the kingdoms of the world, and the glory of them,—that is, all the excellency of them. And it importeth a height of excellency, τῆν δόξαν, so is the expression, 2 Peter i. 17, 'the excellent glory.' Always glory hath an excellency, yea, and an excelling excellency too, or else it is not glory, saith he, 2 Cor. iii. 9, 10: This glory, speaking of the law, is no glory by reason of the glory that excelleth, 'and if the ministration of condemnation be glory, much more doth the ministration of righteousness exceed in glory.'

The word that is used for glory signifieth in the Hebrew and the Chaldee both, *a weight*, and the Apostle hath an allusion to the meaning of the word according to the Hebrew phrase in his expression, 2 Cor. iv. 17, where he calleth it a 'weight of glory.' Very well, now to make use of this to set forth to you the glory of heaven.

First, it noteth out all excellency in man. The glory of men, he calleth it, 1 Peter i. 17, 'the flower of the grass,' that is the excellency of men; all sorts of excellencies are meant by glory. And it is an exceeding weight of those excellencies too, or else it is not glory. To instance in some. As—

First, for *beauty;* it is an excellency of man; when his beauty doth arise to a brightness, to a splendour, it is called glory, when it riseth to such a glory as dazzleth the eyes. Therefore, 2 Cor. iii. 7, you may read that Moses' face did shine that they could not behold the glory of his countenance. It is not an ordinary beauty that is called glory, but when it ariseth to such a height as it dazzleth the eyes that they cannot behold it, it hath a weight in it; it oppresseth the eyes. So likewise Acts xxii. 11; it is said there that Paul could not see by reason of the glory of the light; it is not an ordinary light, but that light that dazzleth the eyes that a man cannot see it; that is superexcellency of light, that is called glory. So likewise if you come to *pomp;* if it riseth, if it be such a pomp as is transcendent, which all men fall down before as they do before a king, then it is glory; it is not only pomp, but it is a superexcellency, a transcendency, beyond what is ordinary. You read of the queen of Sheba, 1 Kings x. 5, when she saw all the riches of Solomon, his glory, as it is described there, 'that there was no more spirit in her;' yet she herself was a queen, she came into the city with a great train and with much riches, yet when she saw Solomon exceeded her, he did so exceed her that she had no spirit in her. Now what saith Christ of the state, of the pomp of Solomon, Matt. vi. 29? 'Solomon in all his glory,'—it is in the original 'in all his royalty;' it was a glory such as no king else had, it was not only pomp, but it was a pomp that made her even swoon again, when she saw it she had no spirit in her; this was glory. So if you take it for *power and strength;* ordinary strength is nothing, but if you come to a superexcellency of strength, it is called glory; therefore, in 2 Thess. i. 9, it is called the glory of Christ's power; when he hath such strength as is not in all creatures again, this is not power only, but the glory of power. The word glory noteth out the superexcellency of every good thing. So likewise, take *joy and pleasure;*

if it come to joy which hath a superexcellency in it, which the mind of man cannot imagine how great it is, nor cannot utter, then it is called glorious: 1 Peter i. 8, 'With joy unspeakable and glorious,' or 'full of glory.' So now, whatsoever doth exceed the expectation of the creature, that is admired, that is called glory. In 2 Thess. i. 10, speaking of Christ, saith he, 'When he shall come to be glorified in his saints, and to be made wonderful,' or admired, 'in all them that believe;' when it cometh to wonderment, then it is glory.

So that now you have a complete definition of glory. It signifieth first all excellences whatsoever; and all excellences in the height, and such a weight as they do oppress, that the ordinary understanding of man cannot bear. So strength, in the glory of it, is superexcellency of strength; and joy, when it excelleth, is called 'joy full of glory.'—So much for the opening of the phrase.

Now, if you would know the glory of heaven, you are to do two things. You are first to fancy all sorts of excellences, of beauty, of strength, of joy, of holiness; take what you will, and when you have done, it is a superexcelling excellency; there is that glory in it beyond all what you can imagine in all these.

To exemplify it a little. First, in the body; for indeed the Scripture doth not hold forth the glory of the soul, nor are the words of men able to express it; but the Scripture sets forth the glory of the body. The world hath but one thing, that is a creature, that truly deserveth the name of being glorious, and that is the sun. Now, saith he, Matt. xiii. 43, 'The righteous shall shine as the sun.' And our Saviour Christ giveth them an instance of it, Matt. xvii. 2; there he transfigured himself before them, and it is said, 'His face did shine as the sun, and his garments were as white as the light, so white as no fuller could white them.'

Now, my brethren, to what end doth the Scripture give us one instance of what glory there is in the body, but thereby to raise up our minds to think what the glory of the soul will be in all sorts of perfection? For consider with yourselves; the sun, you do not call it a beautiful creature, as you call a woman; but it is a superexcellency of beauty, it is glorious. Saith he of the Church, Ps. xlv. 13, she is 'all glorious within;' what is the meaning of that? It is not a painted beauty, it is not extrinsical; it is innate, it is within. I take that to be the meaning. He instanceth only in the glory of the body, because from that you may argue the glory of the soul. The body shall shine as the sun, which is the most glorious thing the world hath; what will the soul be then? The body, that is but the sheath of the soul. Look Dan. vii. 15, 'I was grieved in my spirit in the midst of my body,' so it is translated. Look in your margins, and it is 'in the midst of my sheath;' he calleth his body but the sheath of his soul, but the garment. Now in the transfiguration of Christ there is mention made that his garments were white, so white as no fuller could white them; and, Luke ix. 29, it is said they were white and shining. Now, if his body shining as the sun made his garments white; and the body is but as the garment of the soul; and if the body shineth as the sun, how will the soul be then? Here lieth the comparison: his body did shine as the sun, his garments were white, and they were glittering too; the body is but the garment of the soul; if that shine as the sun, what will the soul do? 'Riches of glory,' saith the Apostle here. My brethren, the soul is the glory of man. Gen. xlix. 6, 'My soul,' saith he, 'come not into their secret, nor my glory into their counsel.' Now, if the soul be the glory of man, and the body, which is but a vile thing, ('our vile bodies,' so he calleth them, Phil. iii. 21;) if they shall shine as the sun, how will the soul, that is the glory of man, in all sorts of perfection? Therefore the Apostle here saith 'riches of glory.'

I will name but one place, and so leave it; it is 2 Cor. iv. 17. That word there, which is translated *exceeding*, is καθ' ὑπερβολὴν εἰς ὑπερβολὴν, 'one hyperbole upon another;' that is, one hyperbole of speech will not express it; as when you say, a wall up to heaven, or a high wall. Saith the Apostle, express heaven by hyperboles, and when you have done, tumble one hyperbole upon another hyperbole, and it will not express it. This he saith of the glory there; it is exceeding, it is hyperbolical, it is hyperbole upon hyperbole. I remember he speaks of sin, and saith it is καθ' ὑπερβολὴν ἁμαρτωλὸς, 'above measure sinful,' Rom. vii. 13; the sinfulness of it hath an hyperbole in it, man's wit cannot reach it. When he cometh to speak of the glory of heaven, it hath one hyperbole upon another; it is an exceeding hyperbolical glory.

So much now for the opening of that.

I told you likewise, that as it is a rich inheritance, and a glorious inheritance, so it is 'riches of glory;' you may join both together if you will. For riches, you know, are external things; but the saints in heaven, *omnià sua secum portant*, their riches are within, inherent riches, therefore glorious riches; the which glory importeth excellency and a superexcellency of all good things. And then to add riches to this glory, which noteth abundance, this overwhelmeth the mind of man; how can he look further? 'What are the riches of the glory of his inheritance?'—So I have done with that.

Secondly, Now I come to *the persons whom this belongeth to.* Here are two persons mentioned.

First, it is said to be 'his inheritance;' namely, God's, Christ's.

But, secondly, 'in the saints.'

This little pronoun here, αὐτοῦ, is put in, one would think, against the hair; for look elsewhere and he calleth it 'our inheritance;' so ver. 4, 'the earnest of our inheritance;' but when he would set out heaven to the uttermost, it is, 'what are the riches of the glory of his inheritance,' not of the saints' inheritance so much, it is but in them; but *his inheritance in the saints.*

I have read over all the comments that I can meet with,—and I think I have almost all,—and I do not find them insist at all upon this particle; but I may truly say of it, that which they refuse is the head of this corner; it argueth the glory of heaven more than all the words besides: that it is *his* inheritance, take it either of God the Father,—of whom I think it is principally meant here, as I shall shew you by and by,—or take it of Christ.

To shew you in what senses it may be called *his inheritance*, and that all these senses argue to you what an infinite glory it is—

First, It is *his inheritance*, because he is the Father of it; therefore, if you mark it, he prayeth to God the 'Father of glory' in the words before. He calleth him the Father of glory, because he, as the Father, doth give and bestow this inheritance, and therefore it is called his, his that bestowed it; for it is his originally, you know, rather than the Son's, that inheriteth. And you shall see how that must needs argue an infinite glory that saints must have, because it is his inheritance, his gift, and his as the Father of glory (take that in too.) Men give inheritances according to their estates; you shall know whether a man be rich or no when he dieth, by his inheritance he giveth. He is God, the Father of glory, so saith the 17th verse. He is God, the God of glory, so saith Acts vii. 2. He is Christ, the Lord of glory, so saith 1 Cor. ii. 8. He is King of glory, so saith Ps. xxiv. 7. If he will give an inheritance, he will do it like himself; therefore it must needs be a glorious inheritance and a rich one, that which God meaneth to give as a Father.

I will give you a scripture for it. It is Phil. iv. 19. I quoted it before, but it cometh in now full for our purpose. 'My God,' saith he, 'shall supply all your need,' or, as the word is, all your desires, the word signifieth both, 'according to his riches in glory by Jesus Christ.' What is the meaning of this? God, saith he, is a rich and a glorious God, and he is a Father of glory; so the 17th verse calleth him here. Now, saith he, he will not have these riches of glory lie by him. You know Abraham, when he had no son, saith he, Lord, thou hast given me these riches, but behold to me thou hast given no seed; I have never a child to inherit it; therefore God giveth him Isaac, upon whom he might bestow his riches and inheritance. So God had all these riches of glory lying by, he chooseth him sons to inherit, and when he bestoweth an inheritance upon them, it is according to that glory of his, in proportion to his riches that lie by him. Here is, you see, riches and glory, and accordingly doth he bestow an inheritance rich and glorious. It is therefore called his inheritance, and this argueth it to be great. Every man, you know, if he mean to give, will give according to his estate. If the Apostle had said *our inheritance*, alas! we are poor creatures, what inheritance is ours? But he doth say, 'his inheritance,' he argueth the greatness of it from his gift. I remember, Alexander the Great, when he had given a city to a mean man that asked it of him, said, 'I do not give a city away according to the proportion of the man, but as it is fit for me to give.' If Alexander will give gifts, he giveth cities; if God will give gifts, it is according to the riches of his glory. It is 'his inheritance.'

Secondly, It is called *his inheritance*,—which mightily doth argue this to be a glorious inheritance which the saints shall have, for it is 'in the saints,' still take that, it all aggravateth the glory of it,—I say it is called his, because he is in a special manner the possessor of it, and the maker of it.

I will give you Scripture for it: it is Ps. cxv. 15, 16, 'Ye are blessed of the Lord which made heaven and earth'—he made both, you see. 'The heaven, even the heavens,' (or the heaven and the heavens, as most read it,) 'are the Lord's: but the earth hath he given to the children of men.' What do I observe out of this place? This: as for the earth, saith he, and all the good things in it, God doth give that away; let the sons of men take it; I will let out that, saith he; nay, I will give it freely; let them take it and do what they will with it. But, saith he, the heaven and heavens are the Lord's; he reserveth that to himself, as his possession, it is his inheritance; the earth he hath given away to men, that is their inheritance, and let them take it, saith he; I made them both. Now, if you observe the coherence of these words, this saying, 'the heaven and heavens are the Lord's,' that is the third heavens, it is brought in to shew how blessed the saints are; he argueth it from this, for, saith he, 'ye are blessed of the Lord which made heaven and earth.' Why? 'The heaven and the heavens are the Lord's, and the earth he giveth to the sons of men.' The meaning is plainly this: how happy must the saints be that must be taken up to heaven, whenas heaven is reserved for God himself; this world he careth not what becomes of it, he giveth that away. He argueth the blessedness of the saints from this, that heaven is the Lord's inheritance: 'The heaven and heavens are the Lord's,' the earth is not good enough for him, but the heavens are his. Now, my brethren, what a mighty glory then must that be which the Lord who made both heaven and earth reserveth to himself! and this glory he takes the saints up to. Therefore now in that it is *his inheritance,* he is the possessor of it, he hath reserved that to himself, blessed must they needs be that do fear the Lord.

I could enlarge this, that God is the maker of it too, out of Heb. xi. 10, where it is said that God is the maker and builder of this city; it is his in that respect too, he hath shewed all his art upon that; so the word signifieth. Heaven was the first thing made. 'In the beginning he created the heaven and the earth,' heaven first. It was that he had in his eye from all eternity, as the τέλος, the perfection of all, as it is called, Rom. vi. 22, and therefore, Matt. xxv., it is said to be prepared from the beginning of the world, from the foundation of the world. The first thing that God ever made was that glorious state that he reserveth for himself, which is called his dwelling-place, 1 Kings viii. 39, and his throne, Ps. xi. 4, (I will not stand upon that;) it is called likewise his inheritance in that sense too.

That which setteth forth the glory of heaven here is, that it is the inheritance, κληρονομίας, of him in the saints; and so the meaning is this, that God himself is the inheritance of the saints: 'what is the riches of the glory of the inheritance of him by the saints,' that is, which the saints have by inheriting him. My brethren, will you know what heaven is? It is the inheriting of him, it is the inheriting of God. 'He that overcometh shall inherit all things; I will be his God,' Rev. xxi. And therefore, in scripture phrase God is called heaven; saith the prodigal, 'I have sinned against heaven and before thee.' And Dan. iv. 26, 'till thou knowest the heavens rule,' that is, that God ruleth. The saints shall inherit God, they have the possession of him; κληρονομίας will signify so too.

Now, my brethren, what an infinite argument doth this afford of the glory of heaven, that it is the possession of God! Saith he, Matt. xxv. 23, 'Enter into thy Master's joy;' that is, into that joy God hath materially; it is the inheriting of him, the inheritance of him. And the word 'entering' is a phrase that alludeth to an inheritance; for then we enter into an inheritance when we take possession of it; it implieth the full possession of it; and it is not to partake of it, but to enter into it, and to take possession of it, it implieth a fulness, it is not a participation so much.

My brethren, do but think with yourselves now, what heaven must needs be when a man's soul shall possess God as his inheritance. An inheritance, you know, is a thing for a man to use freely, and to be one's to the uttermost for his comfort; you shall have God, and all his attributes, set before you. Lo, there is your inheritance. Ps. xvi. 5, 'Thou art the lot of mine inheritance; at thy right hand there are pleasures for evermore.' A man hath God set before him; improve him, be as happy as he can make you.

I have wondered at those expressions in the Scripture: Rom xv. 7, we are said to be received to the glory of God; 1 Thess. ii. 12, we are said to be called to his kingdom, and to his glory; Rev. xxi. 11, the city is said to have the glory of God. Materially, God's glory is the glory of the saints, it is not the glory of creatures, or created glory, it is the glory of God that makes them happy. And ver. 22, 23, it is said there that the city hath no need of the sun, neither of the moon to shine in it, for it is enlightened by God. 'The glory of God doth enlighten it, and the Lamb,' saith he, 'is the lamp thereof;' so the word signifieth. They shall need no other happiness but to have God to be all in all, he is their happiness, it is the inheritance of him.

And let me yet further express this out of the place last mentioned. The original here in the text, when the Apostle saith it is the riches of the glory of his inheritance, is τῆς δόξης κληρονομίας αὐτοῦ. He meaneth God the Father, or God the Son; I think God the Father. I will give you my reason why: because he prayeth to God as the Father of glory, that he would open their eyes to see what are the riches of his inheritance. Now mark the expression there in that Rev. xxi. 23; he saith, God is the light of it, but the Lamb, he saith, is the lamp of it, and in Rev. ii. 28, you shall find him called the morning star; Christ is but the lamp, he is but the morning star. Who is the chiefest happiness in heaven now? God; a happiness beyond what Jesus Christ as God-man affordeth; he is but the lamp, but the morning star; God is all in all, when he hath given up the kingdom to his Father. It is his inheritance, it is not the inheriting of Christ only, as possessing him.

I will convince you by this. Who is it that makes Christ as God-man happy? It is God; it is God immediately participated; God is all in all to the Lord Christ. Now he that is the happiness of Christ shall immediately be our happiness too; for 'Christ hath received us to the glory of God,'—that is the expression, Rom. xv. 7,—into the glory that himself hath. So that now there is abundance in this, that it is the inheritance of him, of the Father of glory; 'what are the riches of the glory of the inheritance in him,' so the word will likewise signify.

I will give you but one meaning more, my brethren, and, I take it, it is the most proper here, and it is as great as any of the former, and it is this; 'what are the riches of the glory of his inheritance in the saints.' The meaning is this: that the glory that the saints shall have, God reckoneth it to be his inheritance; his inheritance, saith he, in the saints. The meaning is plainly this, that that glory that shall arise to God, which he shall for ever live upon, as upon his inheritance, shall arise out of theirs; it is not said to be *their* inheritance, but *his inheritance in them.* My brethren, there is much in this; not only are the people of God called God's inheritance, but the glory of the people of God in heaven is called God's inheritance too. In 2 Thess. i. 10, it is said that he 'shall come to be glorified in his saints, and admired in all that believe.' Mark his expression, the saints shall be glorified, but how? So as Jesus shall be admired in them and glorified in them. And, Rom. ix. 23, What if God, willing, saith he, to make known the riches of his glory on the vessels of mercy, which he had before prepared unto glory? Bringing vessels of mercy unto glory is but to make known the riches of his glory; his glory shall arise out of theirs; therefore it is said to be 'his inheritance in the saints.'

Now think with yourselves this: it is not a small deal of glory that will content God as his inheritance; for if he mean to manifest himself, he will do it like God. Ahasuerus, when he made a feast, would do it like a king, to shew forth the riches of his glorious kingdom, and the honour of his excellent majesty, as Esther i. 4. Now therefore, when God shall set himself to glorify himself to the uttermost, and all that glory that he meaneth to glorify himself in shall be in the saints, and their glory shall be his inheritance, what will this rise to?

To explain this to you in a word; there is an essential happiness and glory in God, which none can see. 'Thou canst not see my glory,' saith he, Exod. xxxiii. 20. And there is a manifestative glory that ariseth out of his works. Now this manifestative glory he counteth his inheritance, as well as the other. 'My glory I will not give to another.' He hath formed all for his glory, that is, for the manifestation of his glory; he counteth it his, his incommunicable; it is his inheritance.

Now then, if God will shew how glorious a God he is, by shewing how glorious a creature he can make, how glorious must those creatures be! Especially when their glory must come up to be an inheritance to God, that he may say, Lo, I have a goodly heritage. He that is the great God, and hath such vast desires of glory, shall say, I am satisfied, here I will rest; this is mine inheritance that I will live upon for ever, even the glory that I have bestowed upon these souls in heaven. Think with yourselves what these things are—'what the riches of the glory of his inheritance are in the saints.'

My brethren, it is the last of his works. He takes this world here for none of his inheritance, he will burn it to ashes, consume it, turn it to its old chaos. He takes devils and wicked men, and flingeth them to hell; they are lost, they are cut off from his hand, they are none of his inheritance. He takes Christ and the saints up to heaven and glorifieth them. Here is mine inheritance, saith he, here is my rest. As when he had made this world, which was to be but a type of this which is to come, he looks over all that he made, and the text saith 'he was refreshed,' Exod. xxxi. 17.

Now God will fling this world away; he flings wicked angels and men away; they are lost, they are gone from him, he hath no more to do with them; he reckons not of them, he reckons them as refuse things, as lumber which he only layeth by for the fire. Then he takes the saints up to heaven, and there he resteth, keepeth an eternal Sabbath; therefore it is called 'entering into his rest,' that is the phrase, Ps. xcv. 11. Oh, my brethren, what is that, think you, what glory must that be that must come up to be an inheritance for God to rest in for ever! In all these senses this particle here, 'his inheritance,' or 'inheritance of him,' what doth it arise to? The Lord open the eyes of our understanding, that we may know what the riches of the glory of his inheritance are.

I have but one thing more to handle, and that is, 'in the saints.' He meaneth, as Camero hath well observed, saints perfect, for they are the subjects of this glory. It is plain he meaneth so by what followeth in the next verse; for when he speaks of saints below on earth, he changeth his phrase; 'that you may know,' that is, here below, 'the greatness of his power to us-ward that believe.' So that here may be this cast in likewise to make heaven a glorious condition, that men's spirits, to possess all this, shall be made perfectly holy. 'The spirits of just men,' saith he, 'made perfect.' It is an inheritance in the saints. 'I shall behold,' saith he, 'thy face in righteousness, when I awake,' at the resurrection, Ps. xvii. 15. There is nothing but perfect holiness there.

But that is not the thing I aim at. But let us consider heaven from hence too, what the riches of his glory must needs be that God hath provided for saints; take an argument from them. I will give you an instance of it. You heard before that the earth God hath given to the children of men, but the heaven of heavens he hath reserved for his saints. Well, raise up your thoughts now; this earth here hath many good things in it, there is abundance of glory and riches in it, so much as, the truth is, it draweth all the hearts of the sons of men after it. To whom hath he given this earth? To the wickedest of men, to the ungodliest of men. 'He giveth kingdoms,' saith he, 'to the basest of men;' so it is, Dan. iv. 17. Nay, and the devil himself is the king of this world, and he hath all the things here. He undertook to give the kingdoms of the world and the glory of them to Christ. He is the prince that ruleth in the air, the god of the world; carrieth all before him.

Now raise up your thoughts; hath God given such a world as this is, and all the glory of it, to his worst enemies, to the very devils themselves, that were worshipped for about four thousand years by all the world, and had all the glory and riches of it? What hath he reserved then for the saints? What must be the riches of the glory of his inheritance in the saints, whom God loveth, whom he loveth from everlasting, when they shall be made perfectly glorious without spot and wrinkle; glorious so as God can fully delight in them, and they delight in him? What will be the riches of the glory of his inheritance in the saints?

And so now I have done with opening this, to shew you from all the arguments the text affordeth, what the riches of the glory of heaven are. I have kept merely to what the text saith; and I have made this vow with myself, if I meet with heaven in a scripture, I will speak of it so far as that scripture shall give me scope to do; for no subject will quicken the heart more than to lay open the riches of God's mercy, and the riches themselves, glory, and the unsearchable riches of Christ.

SERMON XXII.

And what is the exceeding greatness of his power to us-ward who believe, according to the working of the might of his power, which he wrought in Christ, when he raised him from the dead, and set him at his own right hand in the heavenly places.—VER. 19, 20.

THIS is one of Paul's prayers, and, as I take it, at this 20th verse doth this prayer of his end; for the rest is but a doctrinal enlargement of what he said last concerning Christ's exaltation.

I have divided this prayer into two parts :—

First, *The Person that he prayeth to:* 'That the God of our Lord Jesus Christ, the Father of glory.' When he would pray for all these glorious things, he thus styleth God, representeth God under these considerations to his faith, the God of our Lord Jesus Christ, the Father of glory.

Secondly, Here are *the things he prayeth for*. He prayeth first, that in a way of intimate knowledge and communion with God, they might have the Spirit both of wisdom and revelation whereby to obtain it, to obtain intimate knowledge and communion with God : 'That he may give to you the Spirit of wisdom and revelation in the knowledge of him.' I have opened this at large.

In the second place he prayeth, that he would give them eyes of their understanding enlightened, for so I read the words, to know three things.

The first is, 'to know what is the hope of his calling,' (so at ver. 18;) that is, what grounds from the calling of God they had to hope for eternal life, and to see their interest by them. That this was the meaning of it, I have likewise handled, and shewed at large.

The second thing he prays for is, after he had prayed that they might know their interest, and the grounds of it, that they might know the glory, and the greatness of that glory which they had interest in; and what the riches of the glory of his inheritance are in the saints.

And then, thirdly, that they might know that almighty power, which both had begun the work in them, and would go on to bring them unto all this glory : 'And what is the exceeding greatness of his power to us-ward who believe, according to the working of the might of his power,'—instancing in the power that raised up Christ from death to life,—'which he wrought in Christ when he raised him from the dead, and set him at his own right hand in the heavenly places.'

The last thing I did was to open these words, 'what the riches of the glory of his inheritance in the saints,' which the Apostle prayeth they might know. In the handling of these words I propounded two things.

The FIRST is, How great and glorious the happiness of the saints in heaven is, so far as the Apostle here representeth it, while he calleth it 'the riches of the glory of his inheritance in the saints.' It is an inheritance, a rich inheritance, a glorious inheritance, and the riches of it consist in glory; and it is an inheritance of God's bestowing, and the inheritance of himself indeed, for so the words will bear; and, last of all, in the saints. How the glory of heaven is set forth to us by all these things I shewed the last time.

The SECOND is, That the knowledge of this is useful to believers, to have enlarged thoughts of the glory of heaven, experimental working thoughts in their minds about it. Therefore you see, as he setteth forth heaven to them, it is in a way of prayer, 'that they may know it;' and to help them to know it, he describeth it thus largely, and under so many words. So that now the second thing that I am to handle and speak to is this, *The knowledge of the riches of the glory of this inheritance, what this is to the saints;* for as he setteth out the thing itself, so he prayeth for their knowledge of it.

Concerning the knowledge of it, which here he prayeth for, I shall but speak these few things:—

The first is this, that it is proper to the saints to have genuine and true thoughts of what the glory of heaven is. There is a peculiar knowledge that the saints have of heaven's glory, which wicked men have not. The Apostle, you see here, prayeth for these converted Ephesians, that they may know what are the exceeding riches of his glory, &c.

I shall name but one scripture; it is Heb. x. 34, 'You took,' saith he, 'joyfully the spoiling of your goods, knowing in yourselves that you have in heaven a better and an enduring substance.' Other men may know it by way of notion, but the saints know it in themselves: they have a prelibation by faith of heaven's glory. When their goods were taken away, God sealeth them bills of exchange in their own hearts to receive a better substance in heaven. They know it in themselves, so as no carnal heart in the world doth. 'Eye hath not seen, nor ear heard, nor hath it entered into the heart of man,' saith the Apostle—that is, of a natural man, for so he expoundeth himself in the following verses—'to know the things which God hath prepared for them that love him; but,' saith he, 'God hath revealed them unto us by his Spirit,' 1 Cor. ii. 9, 10.

Therefore, brethren, it is a great mistake for men to say now, I seek God for heaven's sake, and therefore I am a hypocrite. No; if thou knowest what heaven is; if thou hast such a knowledge of it as Paul here prayeth for, that lieth in communion with God, and in fellowship with him; and that he is the happiness, and that thou findest a spirit suited to find happiness in him alone; the more thou desirest heaven, the more holy thy heart is. It is so far from being a sign that thou art a hypocrite, that there is no greater sign that thy heart is holy. 'Whom have I in heaven but thee?' saith David, 'and whom in earth in comparison of thee?'

You will only make this objection: Do the saints know what heaven is? Why, heaven, it passeth knowledge!

I answer. Herein lieth their uttermost knowledge of it, by that little they feel and believe, for they see it passeth their knowledge, and that is it which takes their heart so much. The very objection doth prompt matter to my answer. I answer that objection with that which the Apostle saith, Eph. iii. 18, 19. He prayeth that they may be able to comprehend with all saints what is the breadth, the length, and depth, and height, and to know the love of Christ; but he addeth, 'which passeth knowledge.' So that now, to say that heaven passeth knowledge, that it is the hidden manna, the manna in the pot,—for that is meant by the hidden manna, the manna that was hid in the ark, which no man ever saw after it was put there,—to say that it is within the vail, unto which no man entered, as the Apostle's allusion is in the Hebrews; their knowledge lieth in this, that it passeth knowledge, and yet they are said to know it; 'we know in part,' saith he, but they know so much of it that it swalloweth up all their thoughts in the taste and apprehension they have about it.—And so much for the first observation concerning this knowledge, 'what are the riches of his inheritance,' the Apostle prayeth for.

The second observation I make about it is this: That to have a tasting knowledge what heaven is, is one of those things that have the greatest efficacy to carry on the heart to holiness. Why doth the Apostle mention that when he would set himself to pray? His aim is to pray them holy, and to fit them for heaven; you see he inserteth this, he prayeth that they may know what the glory of heaven is, and have working thoughts filling their hearts continually about it.

I will only give you one, and that the highest instance for this. It is the instance of our Lord and Saviour Jesus Christ. What was it that had a mighty power upon his heart to bear out all his sufferings, to be obedient to the death, to the death of the cross? The Apostle telleth us in Heb. xii. 2, 'Looking to Jesus the author and finisher of our faith; who for the joy that was set before him endured the cross, despising the shame, and is set down at the right hand of the throne of God.' I know that the words may be read as well, that instead of the joy which he might have had, he did endure the cross; but this interpretation suiteth most with the coherence, with what went before, that *for* the joy,—apprehending what joy that was that was set before him,—he endured the cross, and despised the shame; it was that which bore him up. That this is the scope of the Apostle appeareth by the connexion of this chapter with the former. In the former chapter he had shewed how by faith all the saints had lived; he instanceth how they sought a country, professed themselves strangers, their eyes were upon heaven still: he instanceth in all the patriarchs; in Moses, who did choose rather to suffer affliction with the people of God, esteeming the reproach of Christ greater riches than the treasures of Egypt, for he had respect to the recompense of reward. Now, in the conclusion of all, when he had brought in all his cloud of witnesses that lived thus by faith and eyed the recompense of reward, he bringeth in, last of all, Christ himself; who likewise, saith he, for the joy that was set before him, endured the cross, &c.

My brethren, when our Saviour Christ came to die, when he stood before the high priest to answer for his life, the high priest asked him whether he were the Son of God or no? He knew the words would condemn him, yet he would speak them: 'Nevertheless,' saith he, 'you shall see the Son of man come in his glory.' It upheld him in his suffering; he speaks it as to dash them, so to comfort himself. For that joy which he had then in his eye, he endured the cross and he despised the shame. Our Saviour Christ had a representation made him of all the glory of the world, so as never yet man had of it, either before him or since. Satan, that is the god of the world, took him up into a high mountain, on purpose to make landscapes in the air of the glory of the world, and caused it all to pass before him; it moved him not this. But God setteth the glory of heaven before him, and this moveth him; and for that glory, and for that joy he endured the cross, he despised the shame, so great an encouragement is it. Nay, I will go further with you, brethren; under enduring the cross is not meant only bodily death, but it is enduring the wrath of his Father; he was content to endure hell itself, so far forth as the Son of God was capable to bear the wrath of his Father without desperation, and all such circumstances cut off; he endured all this, for hell is loss of the joy of heaven. And what joy was it that he endured all this for? He might have been glorious in heaven, as he was the Son of God, without it; for it was his right the first moment that he was made flesh—a right that could not be taken from him. It was but the glory of the mediatorship that made him endure all this; it was but an additional glory, yet so great it was as it upheld his soul to endure the cross and to despise the shame, and to bear with all the contradictions of sinners, and to be obedient all his life.

I will not stand urging other places upon you. Therefore we faint not, saith the Apostle, 2 Cor. iv. 18, because we look upon things that are eternal, and not upon things that are temporal. Therefore we are always confident, saith he in the 5th chapter following, because we have an house with God not made with hands, but eternal in the heavens. In 1 Cor. xv. 58, when he had spoken of the glory of the saints after the resurrection, he exhorteth them there to all holiness, 'Therefore, my beloved brethren, be ye always steadfast, abounding in the work of the Lord, forasmuch as you know that your labour is not in vain in the Lord.' If this be the reward of it, saith he, it will not be in vain; you have good wages, and he that giveth good wages will look to have his work done well; it is an inference that he makes from the glory he will bestow upon the saints after the resurrection; read the whole chapter.

There are but two men we read of, beside our Lord and Saviour Christ, that had any more eminent knowledge of heaven than other men. The one was Paul, the other was Moses. Paul knew what were the riches of that glory, for he was rapt up to the third heavens; you read of it 2 Cor. xii.; and God vouchsafed Moses that privilege, to see his glory; therefore their grace wrought more than any man's we ever read of. It so much quickened the heart of Paul, saith he, I that have been in heaven, I could be contented to be accursed from Christ for the glory of God, and for the conversion of my brethren. And Moses, who had seen his glory,—which one would have thought would have made him so much the more to desire it,—'Blot me out of the book of life,' saith he. It enlarged his heart so much the more to the glory of God. I can ascribe these large dispositions of spirit to nothing else, but that God took the one up to the mount, and shewed him his glory, and took the other up to the third heavens. So that there is no consideration almost that will have more working and powerful effects upon the souls of men, to make them holy, than the knowledge of heaven hath. As likewise, Phil. iii. 18, 'Many walk,' saith he, as those that are 'enemies to the cross of Christ, whose end is destruction, whose god is their belly, who mind earthly things;' but, on the contrary, saith he, 'our conversation is in heaven, from whence we look for the Saviour, the Lord Jesus Christ, who shall change our vile body, that it may be fashioned like to his glorious body.' That will make a man heavenly-minded, if he look for the Lord and Saviour Jesus Christ, and the glory that is to come. Therefore doth the Apostle pray here that they may know what are the riches of that glory of his inheritance. —And so much now for the use that the knowledge of heaven is unto believers, and so I have done with the second particular the Apostle prayeth for.

I am behind-hand in one debt to you. I slipped over that first part of Paul's prayer, the titles he giveth God in the beginning of his prayer. I must pay this debt. I will therefore do it briefly. I therefore choose to bring it in here, after that I had spoken of heaven and the glory thereof, because those titles do agree with the particular matter of his prayer more especially.

The titles he giveth to God when he prays to him for these Ephesians, for these great things, are, as he is the *Father of glory* and the *God of Christ*.

'Making mention of you in my prayers,' saith he, 'that the God of our Lord Jesus Christ, and the Father of glory' would do so and so for you. The manner of the apostles is this in all their prayers, to give such styles and titles to God as was suitable to the matter that they prayed for. Paul here prayeth for knowledge, spiritual knowledge of glorious things; he prayeth that they may know what are the riches of the glory of his inheritance, and all this to be bestowed upon them in and through Christ; therefore in the beginning of his prayer he calleth him the God of Christ and the Father of glory.

And, first, why he calleth him the God of Christ? It is spoken in relation to his human nature; for take Jesus Christ as he is the second Person and God, it is an improper speech to say he is the God of him as he is God; but as he is a man, so he is the God of Christ. I opened this when I handled the third verse, therefore I will not insist upon it now; 'blessed be the God,' saith he there, 'and the Father of our Lord Jesus Christ,' &c. I will pass over that now; only in a word, he is called the God of Christ in distinction from the style in the Old Testament. How did the old covenant run? I will be the God of Abraham, and of Isaac, and of their seed. How doth the New Testament run? I will be the God of Christ, and of his seed. Abraham was therein a type of Christ; and the covenant was made with him. Now, because he is the God of Christ as of a public person that hath seed, all the faithful, just as he was the God of Abraham that was to have seed; hence, therefore, when he prayeth to God for any mercy or blessing which is to be conveyed to them in and through Christ, he presenteth God to himself and to his faith as the God of Christ, to shew the foundation of obtaining all blessings.

What is the observation from this, in a word? This: join the third verse and the sixteenth verse together. In the third verse, when he would bless God, under what notion doth he do it? 'Blessed be the God and Father of our Lord Jesus Christ, who hath blessed us with all spiritual blessings in heavenly things.' Here, in the 16th verse, when he would pray to God, he useth the same style, that 'the God of our Lord Jesus Christ' may give unto you so and so. The observation, then, is plainly this: That all mercies from God do descend down to us in and through Christ, and all prayers and blessings we put up to him should be all as to the God, and in the name of the Lord Jesus Christ. Therefore saith he in his blessing, 'Blessed be the God of our Lord Jesus Christ,' who has blessed us with all spiritual blessings in Christ; therefore saith he in his prayer, that 'the God of our Lord Jesus Christ may give unto you' thus and thus.

But, secondly, 'Father of glory,' that is the second title which here he giveth God. We find in other scriptures that he is called the God of glory, Acts vii. 2; that Christ is called the Lord of glory, 1 Cor. ii. 8. There are many other scriptures where he is called King of glory, Lord of glory, God of glory; but there is not one other where he is called Father of glory but only here.

There are some would read the words thus—they would make a parenthesis in these words, the God of our Lord Jesus Christ, and the Father of glory; that is, 'The God (of our Lord Jesus Christ, the Father) of glory,' and so they make the sense thus: 'The God of glory, and the Father of our Lord Jesus Christ,' joining *God* and *glory* together, because it is an uncouth phrase, the like is not in all the Scripture again. But, my brethren, we may well adventure upon the phrase as it is; and, indeed, it lieth more fair in the original, and that is thus, that God is the Father of glory.

He is called, first, the Father of glory by way of eminency of fatherhood; there is no such father as he, he is a glorious Father; and so by way of Hebraism, he is a Father of glory; that is, a glorious Father, such as no father else is. He is called the King of glory; there are other kings, but he only is the glorious King. There are other fathers, he only is the Father of glory; he is therefore called the heavenly Father. It is an expression the Scripture in the New Testament often useth, and in the Lord's Prayer it is. It is such a kind of expression as you use to children; when you would commend the excellency of a thing to them you use to call it golden: you shall have a golden ball, or a golden girdle, or a golden coat, because that is a notion under which they apprehend the excellency of a thing. Heaven and glory are the highest things we are comprehensive of; when he would set out how great a God, how glorious a Father he is, he calleth him heavenly Father, a Father of glory in distinction to all fatherhoods.

My brethren, the use or observation, call it which you will, shall be in a word this: Never be ashamed of your Father, you that are the sons of God, you are the highest born in the world; no nobility riseth to glory; your Father is the Father of glory; and therefore walk worthy of him, and let your good works so shine before men that you may glorify your Father, the Father of glory, which is in heaven. That is the first.

He is, secondly, called the Father of glory, that is, the Father of the Deity, taking Father for the spring, the fountain; the head, as it is often taken in the Scripture. He is not the Father of the Godhead of Christ, as if he did beget the Godhead of Christ. No; the object of his fatherhood in that sense is only the person of Christ. But we may say he is *Fons Deitatis*, he is the fountain of the Deity; and so divines express it, and the word Father will import it. We find that glory in Scripture is put for the Deity, for the divine nature. Exod. xxxiii. 20, 'No man can see my glory,' that is, my Deity, 'and live.'

Now, my brethren, to consider that God is the Father of the Deity, that he is *Fons Deitatis*, when we come to pray to the Father,—and therefore, indeed, all prayers are put up to him in a more special manner,—it is a mighty strengthening of a man's faith. Why? He that is the fountain of glory, of the Deity itself, communicated that Deity to the Son, and unto the Holy Ghost, that is to strengthen a man's faith that he will communicate grace and glory to a poor creature; therefore, he prayeth here for grace and glory, glorious grace; he prayeth to him as the Father of glory, in that sense as I take it now. My brethren, it is a great strengthening to our faith, that those things which are only in God himself, between himself and himself, yet may be props to our faith, that he will be our God, and do that for us in our measure that he hath done to the Persons and to himself. For example: one of the greatest and strongest arguments we have to support our faith is, that God is the Father of Christ. But how is he the Father of Christ? By eternal generation; yet this is put in as an argument to strengthen faith, that he will be the Father of all those that are Christ's. When you come likewise to pray for grace at his hands, consider it; he is able to give me, a poor creature, grace, for he was the fountain of the Deity itself; he was the Father of glory, taking in that sense. He that is able to communicate the Godhead to the Son and Holy Ghost, he is able to communicate grace and glory to me. You know that God is just, it is an attribute in him; we may plead this attribute as it is in himself, he having declared himself to be our God; if he be just, he must forgive sins now; if he be God, he must forgive sins. So that all those intrinsical things in God himself, all his attributes, those ways which indeed were natural between him and his Son, to be the Father of glory, they are all made engagements, we being in Christ, and strengtheners to our faith to obtain and seek things at his hand.

A third reason why he calleth him Father of glory is, he had spoken here, you see, of riches of glory, and riches of glory as his inheritance; so he calleth it. Now, what so proper, if he speaks of a rich glorious inheritance, which is God's inheritance given by him, as to call him, when he putteth this into his prayer, the Father of glory? That is, the author of all that glory, the contriver of all that glory which the saints have in heaven. Likewise in his discourse following, he mentioneth all the glory that Jesus Christ hath; he saith he had raised him from the dead, he hath set him at his right hand, far above all principalities and powers, given him a name above every name, given him to be the head over all things to the Church. He was the Father of the glory of Christ. Because he was to speak of our glory, and of the glory of Christ, and was to insist upon it in the following words, therefore he premiseth and calleth God the Father of glory.

My brethren, this is the honour that God the Father hath, that, take Christ as he is man and mediator, all the glory he hath the Father has given him by an act of his will; and so, in that sense, he is more peculiarly the Father of glory; he is the Father of all the glory Christ hath, of all the glory the saints have. And because the Apostle speaks of both these, therefore he mentioneth this in his title, 'Father of glory.' Look in Matt. xvi. 27, he saith that the Son of man shall come in the glory of his Father with his angels; though Christ calleth the angels his, as being their Lord; yet the glory himself shall have, he calleth his Father's.—And so much now for the opening of the phrase, why it is put into this prayer, 'Father of glory.'

I now proceed unto the 19th verse: *And what is the exceeding greatness of his power to us-ward who believe, according to the working of the might of his power*, (so it is in your margins,) *which he wrought in Christ, when he raised him from the dead*, &c.

Here is a third thing that the Apostle prayeth for, 'That they might have enlightened eyes, to know the exceeding greatness of his power to us-ward who believe,' &c. I must first give you the coherence of the words, why this cometh in here; and next it shooteth through the whole chapter, it shooteth up small roots, it hath coherence higher than the words just before.

The reference of these words is manifold. He had spoken much of God's good-will to his children in the former verses. Read all his discourses from the 3d verse to the 15th: he telleth them there how God had chosen them before the world was, had redeemed them by the riches of his grace; he had forgiven their sins, had accepted them in his beloved; he had predestinated them to a glorious inheritance. Here is enough spoken of his good-will. Now, to strengthen their hearts and their faith so much the more, he addeth, *the greatness of his power*, which his will putteth forth in their salvation. As he had doctrinally taught them and instructed them in the good-will of God from everlasting, so now he likewise prayeth that they may know the power of God, 'the exceeding greatness of his power to us-ward who believe.'

My brethren, do but join *power* and *will* together, and it breedeth strong consolation. 'If God be for us,' saith he, having spoken of his predestinating us from everlasting, 'who shall be against us?' They are the two ingredients in those strong cordials, Rom. viii. Now he strengtheneth their faith in this power of God, to be as much engaged for their good as his will. He strengtheneth their faith in it by two things.

First, by what already he had wrought. He had wrought faith in them; 'to us-ward who believe.'

In the second place, he strengtheneth their faith by what he had wrought in Christ, and in Christ as a Common Person and head representing us. He raised up Christ your head, gave him to be to you as a public person in heaven. He that raised up Christ personally, will raise up Christ mystically; and the same power that wrought in one, shall work in the other. Here is *power* and *good-will* joined, you see. Here is one scope, why he mentioneth his power, and bringeth it in to this prayer so solemnly.

A second scope the Apostle had was *to provoke them to thankfulness.* You may be sure that that was one of his great scopes, for he telleth them that he gave thanks for them; 'I also,' saith he, 'give thanks for you,' and cease not to do it, for the great things God hath done for you; so he telleth them, ver. 15. Now, that they might know how much they were beholden to God, as he had laid open to them the love of God, the riches of his grace, in the former verses; so now he layeth open to them the greatness of his power which he had, and would put forth in their salvation. He had told them before, they had obtained an inheritance by faith. But, saith he, you little think how much power this faith cost the working; it cost the 'exceeding greatness of his power.' He mentioneth that to make them thankful for the work of faith; that when they shall consider the guilt of sin that once they lay in, they might know it is of the riches of his grace that they had forgiveness; so when they look but upon the power of God that wrought faith in them, whereby they obtained that forgiveness, and which was engaged to bring them to salvation, they might magnify the exceeding greatness of his power. Put but both these together, and how thankful will it make a man to God! How will it provoke a man to glorify God for the power he putteth forth in working faith, and in bringing a man to salvation!

I will give you a scripture that falleth in with this coherence. It is Col. i. 12, 13; he there giveth thanks to God, as here likewise; 'Giving thanks,' saith he, 'unto the Father, which hath made us meet to be made partakers of the inheritance of the saints in light.' How made us meet? 'He hath delivered us from the power of darkness, and hath translated us into the kingdom of his dear Son.' He magnifieth God here, as in ordaining them to an inheritance, so in translating them, and rescuing them, as it were by force and violence, from the power of sin and Satan they once lay under. And that is the second scope why he mentioneth the exceeding greatness of his power here.

In the third place, the last thing he had mentioned was, 'the riches of the glory of his inheritance;' and he had set out the riches of the glory of it by many arguments, as I shewed in the last discourse: here he mentioneth the 'exceeding greatness of his power' engaged to glorify them, even the same that he put forth in Christ, when he raised him up to life and glory, as one of the highest arguments to let them see what heaven was, and the glory of it. Why? For that must needs be an infinite mass of glory which hath the exceeding greatness of God's power engaged to work it, the same power which raised up Christ from death to glory; for the effect must be answerable to the cause. Now, saith he, if you did but consider what an exceeding greatness of power there is engaged to glorify you, you will fall down before the apprehension of what glory this power must work in you. The work must be answerable to the cause; if there be an exceeding greatness of power goes to glorify saints, then the glory must bear some proportion with it. That is a third coherence.

In the fourth place, a fourth scope, coherence, or reference, is this. When he had prayed that they might know what interest they had to heaven, what the hope of their calling was, and that they might know how great the glory was; might some soul begin to think, Alas! we are poor creatures; looking upon their vile bodies, Shall these vile bodies of ours ever come to be filled with so much glory? How is it possible? Carnal reason will be considering, as Abraham's carnal reason would have him consider the deadness of his own body, and the deadness of Sarah's womb: so carnal reason will consider the vileness of a man's body and of his soul, and the lowness and meanness of it, and argue, as Mary did, when she was told she should be the mother of the Messiah, Luke i. 34, 'How can this be?' Saith he, ver. 31, 'The power of the Highest shall overshadow thee;' and 'with God,' saith he, 'nothing is impossible.' He mindeth her of the power of God. So here, when he had laid open the glory of that inheritance, to take away all doubting that they might be raised up to it, he prayeth that they might know what the exceeding greatness of his power is that will work this.

I will give you a scripture answerable to this coherence too. It is Phil. iii. 21, 'Who shall change our vile body, that it may be fashioned like to his glorious body.' How? 'According to the working whereby he is able to subdue all things to himself.' He doth suggest to their doubting faith the exceeding riches and greatness of his power, whereby he is able to subdue all things to himself, as that which was able, if to do all things, then this; and also certainly would change their vile bodies, and raise them up to this glory.

There were worser doubts than this that might rise in their hearts; for they might not only consider the vileness of their own bodies, but the sinfulness of their own hearts, and that is the worser doubt of the two. They might not only say, How shall such vile creatures as we ever come to be made glorious? but, We are sinful creatures, and though we see for the present the hope of our calling, and that we have interest in heaven, and though we see what a glorious estate it is, yet we may miscarry before we come thither, and 'we shall one day perish by the hand of Saul,' as David said: some sin or other may undo us, and make us fall from God. Therefore, to take this doubt away, what doth he do? He prayeth next, that they might 'know what is the exceeding greatness of his power in them that believe,' to bring them unto his glory; a power, which as it had been put forth infallibly in raising up Jesus Christ from death to life, and bringing him to glory, should as infallibly be put forth in bringing them to glory also. And so now, this added to the former, it makes a man have strong consolation.

Do but see all these three things put together, and what strong confidence must it needs work in a Christian's heart! If he seeth the hope of his calling, what grounds he hath that he is one to whom this inheritance belongeth. If he seeth, secondly, what the glory of this inheritance is, and hath mighty, vast, and stunning thoughts of it working in his heart. And, thirdly, if he seeth the exceeding greatness of that power that is engaged to keep the soul, that for the present hath this interest to eternal life. Put all these together, what could be more prayed for? Therefore the Apostle bringeth in that next, 'that you may know the exceeding greatness of his power,' &c.

I will give you a scripture that agreeth with all these scopes too, and mentioneth the very same things in the same order, 1 Peter i. 3; only there he mentioneth it by way of blessing God, whereas he mentioneth it here by way of prayer to God; but he bringeth in all three things there in a way of blessing, that he doth here in a way of prayer, and in the same order. 1. 'Blessed be God,' saith he, 'who hath begotten us by the resurrection of Jesus Christ from the dead to a lively hope;' that is, to have an assurance and hope of salvation that putteth life into a man's soul. Here is the 'hope of their calling.' 2. 'To an inheritance incorruptible, and undefiled, and that fadeth not away, reserved in heaven for you.' Here are the 'riches of the glory of his inheritance,' described; that is the second thing, you know, in the text. 3. 'Who are kept,' saith he, 'by the power of God through faith unto salvation.' Here is the third, that ye may know, saith he here, what is the hope of your calling; that you may know what is the riches of the glory of his inheritance in the saints; and that you may know the exceeding greatness of that power that keepeth you thus to salvation. So now you have the full scope and coherence of these words in the general.

The parts of these words in the 19th verse are these four:—

I. Here is, first, a more general amplification or *description of the power of God* as here it is set forth.

II. Here is, in the second place, *the persons whom this power is engaged to*, to work their salvation and their good; it is to us that believe.

III. Here is, thirdly, *the things wherein this power is seen*, both in Christ's resurrection and in working faith; it is in them that believe, and in raising them up at last to that glory that Christ in heaven hath.

IV. Fourthly, here is *the use that the knowledge of this will be of to a Christian;* wherefore the Apostle prayeth they may know it.

I. To begin with the first, he prayeth they may know what is the exceeding greatness of his power to us-ward. He describeth the power while he prayeth they may know it. Even just as before while he prayed that they might know what heaven's glory is, he giveth the strongest description of it that could be, 'that ye may know what are the riches of the glory of his inheritance in the saints.' So here, when he would have them know what the power of God is that is put forth to believers, he setteth it forth in words, he wrappeth in such a description of it in his prayer, that might open their eyes to see what it was; 'what is the exceeding greatness of his power.'

First, the description of the power of God here set forth hath two parts in it. I reduce it to two heads.

1. *The excellency and sublime greatness of the power of God engaged to believers.* He calleth it not only great power, but 'greatness of power,' and not content with that, it is τί τὸ ὑπερβάλλον μέγεθος, the exceeding, superexcellent, sublime, overcoming, triumphing greatness of his power.

2. He describeth it by *the infallible efficacy of this power*, that it will certainly bring to pass the thing which you believe and hope for, and which God hath intended to you. 'According,' saith he, 'to the effectual power,' for so the word signifieth, κατὰ τὴν ἐνέργειαν, the effectual working of the might of his strength; so you may interpret it, and the original bears it; 'according to the effectual working of the might of his strength, of the force of his strength.' He setteth forth, I say, this power, first, by the *excellency* and sublime greatness of it; and, secondly, by the *efficacy* of it, it is efficacious, it bringeth things to pass.

1. Now to open these a little unto you, and to begin first with the description of *the excellency of this power*. I shall open the phrases to you, for that will make way for the rest.

He calleth it first the 'greatness of his power.' When he speaks of the power of creating, he never giveth such a phrase to it; he sheweth forth his power there indeed; he saith, 'his power and Godhead,' Rom. i. 20. When he speaks of the work of grace and salvation, then he calleth it the 'greatness of his power.' You shall find that usually, ὁ πλοῦτος, as we call it, that is *number*, is attributed to the *mercy* and to the *wisdom* of God; but μέγεθος, namely *greatness*, is attributed to the *power* of God. You nowhere read the riches of his power, you nowhere read of his powers; but you read of his mercies, and riches of mercy; but his power consisteth of greatness. Ps. cxlvii. 5, 'Great is our Lord, and of great power;' look how great God is in himself, so great is his power, if you would know the greatness of his power. But when he speaks of his understanding in the next words, 'his understanding,' saith he, 'is infinite.' Look in your margins, in the Hebrew it is, 'Of his understanding there is no number;' he attributeth an infinity of number to understanding, and so to his mercy; but when he cometh to speak of his power, it is a bulk, 'great is the Lord, and great is his power.' School-men have laboured to give reasons why God is omnipotent; but, as divines well observe, all their reasons fall short to prove it, and there is no reason to prove it but this which the psalmist giveth, 'The Lord is great,' and therefore, 'great is his power.'

If you will know therefore how great his power is, consider how great a God he is, and all the power that is in this God is engaged to save a poor believer. All being hath some power that doth accompany it to do something; there is no creature that hath a being but hath a power to do something; only, because the creatures have limited beings, one creature hath power to do one thing and another creature hath power to do another thing. Now give me one of an infinite being, and he must have an infinite power; as he is in being so must he be in working. The Lord is great, and great is his power; his power is as great as himself.—So much now for the first thing, the greatness of his power.

He doth not only say the greatness of his power, but he addeth, ὑπερβάλλον. That word hath these three forces in it:—

In the first place, it signifieth an excelling power that putteth all power else down. 2 Cor. iii. 10, the same word is used where he speaks of the glory of the gospel. The glory, saith he, that the law hath is no glory, in comparison of that which excelleth; it is the same word which is translated here 'exceeding.' Take all created powers, my brethren, and they are nothing to God.

I will give you a scripture for it; it is in 1 Cor. i. 25. 'The weakness of God,' saith he, 'is stronger than man's strength.' He hath a power that excelleth, that exceedeth, that all the power of the creature is no power to it. That is the first thing.

In the second place, the word τοῦ κράτους doth signify sometime *overcoming, prevailing*. He hath an exceeding greatness of power in him, engaged to believers, which is a prevailing power, nothing can resist it. Saith he, Phil. iii. 21, where he speaks of the power that shall glorify believers, 'According to the working whereby he is able even to subdue all things to himself;' he is able to subdue them, to conquer them. It is κράτος; it is a conquering, prevailing greatness of his power that is able to subdue all things. It makes nothing rise to something; it makes all things arrive to whatsoever he will have them come to; they have all an obediential faculty in them to obey him; he is able to subdue all things to himself, and by that power he will glorify believers.

Again, in the third place, it is called ὑπερβάλλον, a supereminent, surpassing greatness of power, because it passeth our knowledge. In Eph.

iii. 19, he useth the same word, τὴν ὑπερβάλλουσαν τῆς γνώσεως ἀγάπην; you translate it, 'the love of God that passeth knowledge.' It is the same word that is used here. It is a power that exceedeth all our thoughts, as it is Eph. iii. 20, 'To him that is able to do exceeding abundantly above all that we are able to ask or think;' it is so exceeding, what he will do for believers, that they are not able so much as to think. 'As far as the heavens are above the earth, so are his thoughts' (and so his power) 'above ours.' It doth not only exceed the power of the creature, and excel it,—all that which is in the creature is as nothing to it,—but it excelleth all their thoughts. I have quoted scriptures that imply all these significations of the words.—And so much for the first part, that description of the exceeding greatness of his power, the excellency of it.

2. In the second place, he setteth forth this power by *the efficacy of it* in the next words; 'According,' saith he, 'to the efficacious working of the might of his strength.' As I take it, the scope of these words is to shew that it is such a power that works in believers as will always do the things that God intendeth to do with it, as hath an efficacy, a thorough working in it; every word is emphatical to imply so much.

First, the word that is translated working, ἐνέργειαν, implieth an efficacy of working, such as bringeth the thing to pass. To give one instance, 2 Thess. ii. 11, 'God shall send upon them ἐνέργειαν πλάνης, efficaciousness of error,' an efficacy of error; they shall be given up to delusions efficaciously and strongly, so as their understandings shall not resist them. More plainly, Phil. iii. 21, 'According,' saith he, 'to the efficacy, the energy whereby he is able to subdue all things.' So that now that is the first thing, it doth note out an efficacy which is implied in the first word which we translate working, it is *energia*.

The words that follow do as plainly and manifestly express an efficacy and an ability to do what he will for believers; he calleth it an efficacy of the force of his strength, or of the might of his strength. Look in your margins, and you will find it so translated out of the Greek. Τοῦ κράτους τῆς ἰσχύος αὐτοῦ. It is 'the energy of the might of his strength.' One word was not enough to express the power that works thus strongly; he therefore doubleth it, as the manner of the Hebrews is. He doth not say, 'according to the working of his power,' or 'according to the working of his might;' but he putteth two words together, 'of the might of his strength;' that is, as the doubling in the Hebrew phrase implieth, the uttermost of a thing; as thus, 'the Holy of Holiest,' that is, of the Most Holy, so the 'might of his strength,' that is, his uttermost strength.

You shall find it is doubled of God to shew the greatness of his strength when he works a thing infallibly and bringeth it to pass. Isa. xl. 26, 'Lift up your eyes on high, and behold who hath created these things,' (the heavens he meaneth,) 'that bringeth out their host by number, and calleth them all by names by the greatness of his might, for that he is strong in power; not one faileth.' When he doubleth the attribute, makes him strong in power, as here he doth, then always followeth an efficacy, a thorough working the thing. 'Not one faileth,' he never faileth when he putteth forth the might of his strength, as the word here is. And you shall find the Septuagint use the very same words that are used here in their translation of those words. As likewise in Job xii. 16, 'With him is strength and power,' the Septuagint read it, κράτος καὶ ἰσχὺς, the same words that are used here. It is doubled to shew the mighty effectualness of his power; when God will do a thing so as to put forth the might of his strength, he will certainly bring the thing to pass. Now, saith he, the might of his strength works efficaciously in all them that believe; 'the exceeding greatness of his power, according to the working of the might of his strength.'

Now, that his scope is to shew the efficaciousness, the irresistibleness of his power in working what he meaneth to work in believers, it appeareth by what followeth. For what doth he instance in? He putteth forth, saith he, the same power toward you believers that he wrought in Christ when he raised him from the dead to glory. Now, I appeal to all your thoughts what power it was that was put forth when God raised Christ from the dead; a power that could not be resisted; a power that should as certainly raise him up as God is God, and it was impossible it should be otherwise. I will give you Scripture for it and reason.

The scripture is, Acts ii. 24, 'Whom God hath raised up, having loosed the pains of death, because it was not possible he should be holden by it.' Now, the power that works in a believer is such a power as works according to the efficacy of the might and strength that wrought in Christ in raising him from death to life.

Now, to gather up this. The Apostle here would have them apprehend two things concerning the power of God that is engaged to them. He would have them first to apprehend the excellency of it, that they might admire it as it is in God. That is the scope of the first word, 'to know the exceeding greatness of his power to us-ward who believe;' that, as it is Eph. iii. 20, 'To him that is able to do exceeding abundantly above all that we ask or think, unto him be glory in the churches for ever.' He layeth open the greatness of his power as it is in itself in the first words, that they might admire it in God, and thank him for it. But, secondly, he addeth the efficacy that this power will have in them to bring them to salvation in the next words, 'according to the working of the might of his power,' to the end to comfort them. He addeth the one that they might admire the power in God; he addeth the other to comfort them, when they shall see such a power works as shall efficaciously bring a thing to pass, and as effectually and irresistibly as it wrought in raising up Christ from the dead. That as it was impossible that God should lose his Son, and his eldest Son, as he had lost him when he was not raised up again; therefore when he raised him up, he saith, 'Thou art my Son, this day have I begotten thee;' he was lost before. This power, saith he, shall work in you, and bring you to salvation; that power that wrought in Christ when he raised him from death to glory.

II. I will but add one thing more, with which I will end; and that is, *the persons* whom this great power of God, this exceeding greatness of his power, a power as great as God himself, a power as efficacious as what wrought in Christ when he was raised from the dead; to whom is all this power engaged? It is engaged *to us-ward:* that is the second thing. I will but speak a word or two to it, and so conclude.

Obs. 1.—The first observation is this: That the simple consideration of what power is in God, of mercy or any other attribute, will never comfort a man's heart, *unless that he have a knowledge that it is to us-ward*, and for our good. The Apostle doth not, you see, pray simply that they may know what is the exceeding greatness of his power in itself; that would have done them no good; but he prayeth that they may know what is the exceeding greatness of his power *to us-ward.* The devils know what mercy is in God; yea, but, say they, it is not to us-ward; therefore all their knowledge of it doth them no good. So likewise you may read, 2 Peter iii. 9, speaking of the mercy of God to men, and, as is thought, peculiarly to the Jews to whom he there writeth, saith he, it is his 'long-suffering to us-ward, not willing that any should perish, but that all should come to repentance.' Here lieth that which works the comfort in a man's heart; that it is the power of God to us-ward. 'To us a child is born, to us a Son is given;' and 'peace on earth,' not in hell; because there is peace on earth to us-ward; this is it that draweth a man's heart; this is it which giveth the comfort.—That is the first observation.

Obs. 2.—But the second is the main observation, and it is this: *That toward the saints, and for their good and their salvation, God doth engage the uttermost of all his attributes;* engageth the uttermost of power, the exceeding greatness of his power to us-ward. It is not so in any work else, saith he, or toward any creature else; but it is *to us-ward.* He doth engage the greatest of his mercies, the uttermost of them, to us-ward. I shall give you Scripture for both by and by. He had mentioned in ver. 11 the power of God that works all things. He worketh all things by the counsel of his will, saith he. But there is a peculiarness of power, the power that works in us that believe; it is the exceeding greatness of his power to us-ward. The mercies of God are mercies to us-ward, such as to none else; they are called therefore by way of distinction 'the sure mercies of David;' that is, of David and his seed, the faithful; such mercies as to no creature else, singular mercies, special mercies: others are common mercies, as divines use to call them, but these are mercies to us-ward, sure mercies of David. So now, when he speaks of power in other scriptures, he putteth a singularity of power that works in believers, a power equal to that which works in all things else. Look Phil. iii. 21 and Eph. iii. 20, 'According to the power that works in us,' so it is in the Ephesians: 'According to the working whereby he is able to subdue all things to himself,' so it is in the Philippians. Take all the power whereby he is able to do all things else, and it is but equal to that which he works in the saints.

My brethren, the grace of God in Christ, and the salvation of mankind by Christ, was a new stage God set up to bring all his attributes upon, to act their parts to the uttermost. He had shewed them all before, he had shewed power in creating the world, and a great power; but when he cometh to make the new creation, then cometh in the exceeding greatness of his power; he speaks superlatively of it. He sheweth mercy, nay, he sheweth riches of mercy to wicked men; it is called 'the riches of his goodness and long-suffering,' Rom. ii. 4. But when he cometh to speak of mercy to the saints, what doth he do? Read Eph. ii. 7. He doth not only call it riches of mercy, but he calleth it by the same word that is used here, τὸν ὑπερβάλλοντα πλοῦτον, the exceeding great riches; what is said of power here, the same is said of mercy there when he speaks of mercy to believers: the 'exceeding riches of his grace to us-ward,' there; the 'exceeding greatness of his power to us-ward,' here. All the attributes of God that he bringeth upon the stage, he acts them to the uttermost now in and through Christ.

My brethren, the works of the new creation put down the old. 'I create,' saith he, 'a new heaven and a new earth, and the former shall not be remembered;' he will put forth such power in them. Nay, let me yet go further; go to hell, you shall read indeed that he sheweth his power there; so it is, Rom. ix. 22, 'What if God, willing to shew his wrath, and make his power known;' and believe it, a blow struck in wrath hath a great deal of power in it; for anger stirreth up power, draweth forth the mighty power of God. But what followeth comparatively to hell in his working toward the saints? It followeth, ver. 10, 'and the riches of his glory upon the vessels of mercy.' Though he sheweth a glorious power in his wrath in condemning men, yet he sheweth a greater riches of glory, of mercy and of all attributes else, in saving men and bringing men to heaven. The power that God will shew in glorifying his saints will infinitely exceed the power he sheweth in condemning wicked men. The power that love stirreth up is a greater power than what wrath stirreth up in God.

I will give you the reason of it: nothing commandeth power and strength more than love; it commandeth it more than wrath, 'Thou shalt love the Lord thy God with all thy strength,' Mark xii. 30. Doth God love thee? He loves thee with all his strength, as thou lovest him, and art to love him. Jer. xxxii. 41, 'I will rejoice over them to do them good, with my whole heart and with my whole soul;' his love makes him to love them with all his strength, with all his heart. Now, when he sheweth forth the power of his wrath when he cometh to condemn men, yet let me tell you this, it is not with all his heart, there is something that regrets within him; for he considereth that they are his creatures, and he doth not will the death of a sinner simply for itself, for there is something in him that makes a reluctancy; there is not his whole power in this, though it be the power of his wrath. But when he cometh to shew forth his power out of love, that draws his whole heart; therefore you shall find in Scripture that mercy is called God's strength, because when he will have mercy, all the strength and power of God accompanieth it. Num. xiv. 17, 'Let the power of my Lord be great.' What to do? To destroy them? To do some great work for them? No, but 'according as thou hast spoken,' saith he, 'saying, The Lord is long-suffering and of great mercy; pardon, I beseech thee, the iniquity of this people, according to the greatness of thy mercy.' His mercy is there called his strength, because that love doth draw forth all the strength of God.

Now, my brethren, to gather up to an end and to a conclusion: you therefore that believe, comfort yourselves with the exceeding greatness of this power that is engaged to you; know the exceeding greatness of his power to you-ward. It is a power will do for you above all your thoughts; it exceedeth that way, it is ὑπερβάλλον in that sense. It is a power that will do beyond all resistance. 'If God be for us, who shall be against us?' saith the Apostle. 'The Father,' saith Christ, 'is greater than all, and no man is able to pluck them out of my Father's hand,' John x. 29. It is a reigning, a domineering power, a power that carries all before it. The word τοῦ κράτους τῆς ἰσχύος may signify the sovereignty, the dominion, the absoluteness of his power, such as a monarch hath. Suppose a monarch had strength to do all by himself, and had authority joined with that strength, it were a power that would carry all before it, and command all. Such a power it is that God putteth forth to believers. It is a conquering power: 'He will have mercy upon whom he will have mercy, and who hath resisted his will?' When you come to beg pardon for your sins, what say you? 'Lord, forgive us our trespasses.' What arguments do you use? 'For thine is the kingdom, the power, and the glory.' Sovereignty and dominion and strength are both his, and out of both these he will pardon your sins and save you; and if all that power of God will bring you to salvation, and keep you to salvation, you shall be surely kept.

And, my brethren, let me raise up your thoughts to consider with yourselves, if the exceeding greatness of his power be engaged in you and to you to do for you, what then is the thing that is answerable to this power? If that power that wrought in Christ, to raise him from death to glory, shall work in us, Lord, whither will it bring us? What, will God bring you to salvation? It must, then, be a thing answerable to the power. What glory, therefore, must it be which God will shew forth in the saints at the latter day! The heavens declare the power and glory of God; yea, but the estate of the saints in heaven declares the exceeding greatness of his power; and what a glory, then, must that needs be!—And so much now for the second thing, *the persons;* 'the exceeding greatness of his power *to us-ward.*'

There are these two things yet behind—

First, to shew wherein, in what it is, that this power is put forth: it is put forth both in working faith and in keeping them to salvation, glorifying them at last. All that work and power that God putteth forth toward a believer, first and last, from his conversion to his salvation, is that which the Apostle here intendeth. This I shall shew the next day.

The second thing that remaineth is this: that it is a power that answereth to the power of raising Christ from death to life, and from death to glory. And therein I must shew these two things—

1. That the greatest work that ever God did, and the greatest power that ever was shewed, was in the resurrection of Jesus Christ, and raising him up to glory.

2. That the working in the hearts of believers grace and faith, and keeping them to salvation, and glorifying them at last, will hold a proportion with that great power that was shewed in Christ's resurrection. And when I have handled these, I shall have done with the 18th, 19th, and 20th verses.

SERMON XXIII.

And what is the exceeding greatness of his power to us-ward who believe, according to the working of the might of his power, which he wrought in Christ, when he raised him from the dead, and set him at his own right hand in the heavenly places.—VER. 19, 20.

I SHEWED the last day, the reference or coherence that these words have with and to the former. I did it in many particulars; the chief whereof is this: whereas he had spoken, in the former verses, of the riches of the glory of that inheritance that is provided for the saints, that their hearts might be strengthened against all doubts of attaining that glory, he prayeth that they might see, as the riches of that inheritance, so what is the exceeding greatness of his power to us-ward who believe, &c. And he propoundeth, for their comfort, two things to them: the greatness of the power, and the efficacy of it; whereof already they had some experience in their first conversion; which power was engaged to perfect and finish their salvation, and bring them to that glory. And to confirm their faith thus, he presenteth Christ to them as their Head, (as the 22d verse hath it,) whom, as their Head, God hath raised up from the dead, to that surpassing glory which he hath in heaven, far above all principalities and powers, as a pawn that they should one day come thither as well as he; for the same power that wrought in him in raising him from the dead, is engaged, saith he, by virtue of him, and of his being a Common Person for you, to work likewise in you. This, in brief, is the main scope of the Apostle in these and the following words, to the end of the chapter.

The parts of these 19th and 20th verses, or, if you will, of this 19th verse, in a more especial manner, are these four:—

Here is, first, a magnific and glorious description—one word heaped upon another—of the power that is in God. And take it, first, as it is a general description of it; he setteth out concerning it three things—

First, the superexcellent greatness of it. He calleth it not only a greatness of power, but he calleth it an exceeding greatness of power.

He setteth it out, *secondly*, by that infallible and irresistible efficacy of it in its working: 'according,' saith he, 'to the energy or effectual working,'—working that always hath success, faileth not,—the thorough 'working of the might of his power.'

Then the *third* thing concerning the description of this power is the proportion of its work: 'according to its working,' saith he. Those are the three things concerning this power in the general. I despatched two of them the last day.

I shewed, *first*, the excellency of this power; it is a greatness of power, it is ὑπερβάλλον μέγεθος τῆς δυνάμεως, it is a superexcelling power. I shewed that the force of those words contained three things in them: it was a power above all we are able to ask or think in that sense—above all our knowledge, as I shewed the word is used in this epistle to the Ephesians; it is a power above all resistance which any creature can oppose; and it is so great a power, so excelling, as in comparison of it the creature hath no power. This I shewed to be the force of the words from parallel places of the New Testament.

Then, *secondly*, here he setteth forth the efficacy of this power; he calleth it the effectual working of the might of his power; κατὰ τῆς ἐνέργειας τοῦ κράτους τῆς ἰσχύος αὐτοῦ. I shewed you that the phrase is put for efficacy of working, such as hath always success, takes effect, and brings the things to pass. And therefore now, to shew that God when he thus worketh, worketh effectually, he doth put two words together; 'the effectual working,' saith he, 'of the might of his strength,' the might of his power; so you may see the words varied in your margins.

The word that is translated power, ἰσχύος, signifieth natural strength; the word κράτους τῆς ἰσχύος, the might of that strength, is the utmost extension of it; as when a man is said to do a thing with the might of his strength, the meaning is, he putteth as it were the utmost strength but that he will effect it. The word κράτος is so taken in the Virgin Mary's song, Luke i. 51. That which is here translated might, is taken there for the extension, the stretching forth of the arm of God, ἐποίησε κράτος ἐν βραχίονι, 'He hath shewed strength,' saith she—it is the same word—'with his arm.' Now the arm, you know, is the strongest part of a man; he wrought strength with his arm, he put it forth to the full; and she speaketh it of the greatest work that ever God did, which was the incarnation of the Son of God.

Or the word ὑπερβάλλον is the authority, the command of his strength, the prerogative of his strength. He doth not work in this with an ordinary power; but as kings work with their extraordinary power, and they will stretch their prerogative, so doth God in this; it is the working of the prerogative of his might and of his power.

So now you see, first, the excellency of this power in those words, 'the exceeding greatness of his power.' You see the efficacy of it in those words, 'according to the working of his mighty power.'

Now, then, in the *third* place, observe concerning the power of God in general, *that God hath proportions of work, putteth forth his power more or less.* When he speaks here of the power toward believers, saith he, it holdeth proportion, it is according to the working of his mighty power which he wrought in Christ when he raised him from the dead. Always God proportioneth the putting forth of his power to his work, sheweth more power in one work than in another. Therefore you find in Scripture sometimes mention of the finger of God; as in those miracles in Egypt, Exod. viii. 19, the magicians acknowledge that it was the finger of God. And our Saviour Christ, when he wrought miracles here below, Moses being his type, and those magicians that opposed Moses being types of the Pharisees, therefore useth the same phrase; 'If I,' saith he, 'by the finger of God cast out devils.' Here is the finger of God you see. Well, sometimes God putteth forth his hand, which is more than his finger; as it is said he brought the people out of the land of Egypt with a strong hand. But then in other works he putteth forth his arm, which is more than his hand, and then he cometh to his might, 'He sheweth might with his arm,' saith she, Luke i. 51. And Ps. lxxxix. 13, 'Thou hast a mighty arm,' saith he, speaking of God. So that you see there are proportions of power God putteth forth, and in this work, whatever it be, there is the might of his arm, the might of his power, there is the prerogative of his power; there is the exceeding greatness of his power exercised toward believers, as I shewed the last day.—And so much now for the consideration of the power of God as here in general it is spoken of God.

The second head that I observed in these words is, *the subject of this power*, whom it works upon, the persons; 'what is the exceeding greatness of his power to us-ward'—to us whom he had spoken of in the former verses, elected in Christ before all worlds; and the observation I raised from thence was this: That of all the works of God, seeing he hath the same proportion of power, more in some works and less in others, in the works of salvation toward believers, therein he sheweth the exceeding greatness of his power. The power of God, as I shewed, is seen in hell; the power of his wrath. The power of God was seen in creating the world; but the greatness of his power, the exceeding greatness of his power, to us-ward. The love that is in God calleth forth all his strength, and engageth it for the good of believers. As he sheweth forth, not only mercy, but riches of mercy, yea, exceeding riches of mercy; as it is Eph. iii. 8, it is the same word, ἀνεξιχνιαστος πλοῦτος, that is here; so likewise it is said of his power to us-ward, he sheweth forth the greatness of his power, the exceeding greatness of his power.

Now, my brethren, raise up your thoughts, you that are believers. If exceeding greatness of mercy shall be the contriver of what good you shall have, and if the exceeding greatness of power shall be the worker, and undertake to work all that mercy doth contrive; what will God do with you then? What will God bring you to, upon whom he will shew forth, ere he hath done, the exceeding riches of his grace, the exceeding greatness of his power? —And so much now for the persons; 'to us-ward.'

III. The third head which I propounded to be handled out of these words, and which is indeed the most difficult, is *wherein this greatness of God's power is shewed.* One instance you have of it, wherein it was shewed, in raising up our Head, our Lord and Saviour Jesus Christ, from death to glory; that he instanceth in plainly; 'The same power,' saith he, 'that wrought in Christ when he raised him from the dead, and set him at his own right hand, in the heavenly places;' there is no question made of that by none that open these words. But then, in what work this greatness of power, proportionable to the raising Christ from death to life, can be spent as wrought in us; of that there is a great controversy about the words.

There are some of our divines and interpreters that restrain the Apostle's scope only to the working of faith at first, and they make the coherence of the words thus and thus only, 'that you may know what is the exceeding greatness of his power to us-ward.' There make a stop. 'Who believe according to the working of his mighty power;' joining, 'who believe,' and, 'according to the working of his mighty power,' together. Their meaning is this: who have had faith wrought in them, according to the working of his mighty power. So that now all this mighty power is in the working of faith at first, and so they restrain it; as if the Apostle had said, You know what power went to work faith in you; it was not the power of your own will, but it was the exceeding greatness of his power; you believed according to the working of the might of his power, such as was in Christ when he was raised from the dead. That is the first sense given of it.

The Remonstrants, or those whom you call the followers of Arminius, go a clean contrary way, and they quote Calvin himself against the former opinion; and indeed to restrain it only to faith and the working of faith, which Calvin is against. But then they contend the scope of the Apostle to be only to shew what the power of God shall be in us, in raising us up at the last day to glory, and that that is the Apostle's scope and his only scope here. They would cut off all the power of God working in us at first when we believe, yea, and cut off from the Apostle's aim here all the power that works in us before the latter day; but that power that shall raise us up from the dead, and set us in glory, that is the power which the Apostle meaneth here, which is answerable to the raising up of Christ from death to life. And there is a great deal of appearance for it, that this should be the Apostle's scope. He had spoken of heaven in the very words before, 'what are the riches of the inheritance of the saints;' now he speaks therefore of that power that raiseth the saints up to that glory; then in the words following you have the instance of Christ raised up from death to glory as your Head, as a pawn that God will raise you up likewise from the bodily death of the grave to life and glory; and it is a great comfort to believers to know that the same power that raised up Christ shall one day raise up them.

Now, for my own part, if you would know my thoughts of these words, and what the scope of the Apostle is, wherein the power to us-ward is shewed,—as usually all truth lies between two extremes, and yet takes something of both extremes,—I think this, that the Apostle's scope is to shew that all the saving workings of God, both of grace and glory, from first to last, from the first act of conversion to the setting of a man upon the highest pinnacle of glory in heaven, raising of him up at the latter day, and the like; they are all the plain scope and meaning of the Apostle here. He meaneth both that efficacious power put forth in working faith at first; 'who believe according to the working of his mighty power.' He meaneth that mighty power that keepeth us to salvation; 'who are kept by the power of God through faith to salvation,' 1 Peter i. 5. And last of all, he meaneth that almighty power that shall 'change our vile bodies, that they may be fashioned like to the glorious body of Christ,' Phil. iii. 21. The Apostle looks not forward only to the glorious resurrection to come, nor backward only to the work of conversion and first believing, but likewise to their present keeping in the state of grace, that those whom God had already by such a power converted, he would by the same power keep them to salvation, and raise them up at the latter day. And all these works are works of the exceeding greatness of his power, and they all hold proportion with raising up Jesus Christ from death to life.

So that now I do grant to both sides what they would have; and the truth is, that this sense doth Vostrius, one of the Remonstrants' side, in his comment upon this place, incline unto in his paraphrase; though afterward in his *scholia* upon his paraphrase he denieth it. 'The exceeding greatness of his power,'—that is, saith he, partly already put forth, and which shall be put forth in us.

Now, my brethren, the reason why I interpret it is, because you see the Apostle neither restrains it to the time past,—he doth not say, 'who have believed,'—nor doth he restrain it unto the time to come. He doth not say, 'the power that shall work in you;' but he speaks indefinitely, because he would take all in, 'what is the power,' saith he, 'to us-ward who believe.' And that which is translated 'to us-ward,' εἰς ἡμᾶς, is either *towards us*, or *in us*. The words will signify either, because the Apostle's scope is for either, either the power that is towards us for the future, to keep us for heaven and raise us up at the latter day, or the power that works in us for the present; the words bear both. And those other words, 'according to the effectual working,' we shall find are applied both to conversion, to growth in grace, and to raising us up at last; and so what is elsewhere said in parcels, is all meant here. You have it applied to conversion, Eph. iii. 7, where he saith, that he was made an apostle and converted according to the effectual working of his power; 'whereof,' saith he, 'I was made a minister, according to the gift of the grace of God, given to me by the effectual working of his power.' It is the same word that is used here. His meaning is, either by that effectual working that wrought upon my heart, or that effectual working he works upon the hearts of others to convert them. He speaks of conversion. So likewise for growth in grace; Eph. iv. 16, he saith, 'The whole body increaseth with the increase of God, by the effectual working in the measure of every part.' Here it is applied to growth in grace. And then, last of all, Phil. iii. 21, he saith, 'He will change our vile bodies,' (speaking of glory,) 'according to the effectual working of his mighty power,' (it is the same word still,) 'whereby he is able to subdue all things unto himself.' So that indeed the Apostle here takes in all the works of God upon believers first and last; and that I take to be most properly the scope of the Apostle here, that in them all he sheweth the exceeding greatness of his power, the same that wrought in Christ when he raised him from the dead.

Now, my brethren, because there is a controversy about the words, and that the Remonstrants, as I told you, would cut off all aims that the Apostle should have to the work of faith and conversion at first; they would not have it to be understood of that by no means, and of that only is the controversy; therefore I will take some pains to clear unto you that that is one part of the meaning the Apostle here takes in, and a great part too. You shall give me leave to do it, for it is the gaining of one of the strongest forts we have, and the fortifying of it, for the glory of the grace of God in conversion.

Whereas our divines, some of them, would read the words thus, 'who believed according to the working of his mighty power,' as if their faith and believing were wrought by such a mighty power; here, say they, the words 'who believed' do not come in to any such sense; it is not to shew what power goeth to work faith, but to describe who they are whom God will shew his power upon one day; they are those that believe. It supposeth them already believers; he doth not speak, say they, at all of faith, as the fruit of this power, in which this power is put forth, but as the qualification of the persons in whom it shall be put forth: so that those that are believers may comfort themselves that one day the same power that was put forth in Jesus Christ to raise him from the dead to glory, shall raise them up too. So that they make the words, 'who believed,' a mere *exegesis*, a mere explanation of what persons he meaneth, in whom this power shall be put forth.

There is a great reason that they should contend against this. Why? For if it should prove to be the meaning of it, that all this power of God, the same that wrought in Christ in raising him from death to life, that that power should be put forth in conversion at first, and that that power should be engaged to keep a man to salvation; all the doctrine of free-will, as they hold it, and of falling from grace, falleth to the ground instantly. For if there be a power that is efficacious, and such a power as wrought in Christ, which was such a power as it was impossible but he should be raised from the dead; if such a power converteth a man at first, and afterward is engaged to keep him to salvation, then both conversion and faith is wrought maugre all opposite power in the creature, whatsoever it be: and likewise they are kept by the same power to salvation, and shall never fall away. Here will therefore be a power beyond the power of moral persuasions or enlightenings; here will be a power that doth infallibly, efficaciously work faith in men.

Now, my brethren, in arguing which of these two is the scope of the Apostle, viz., whether that the power of God in converting a man at first, be not the aim of the Apostle in this place—in arguing this, I shall launch no further into the controversy than to clear the place; which as an interpreter I must do, and I shall do it with all fairness and simplicity, as in all controversies we ought to do.

To come, then, to the reasons of it. There are three sorts of arguments which I shall bring to prove that the Apostle's scope is *to take in the power of God working conversion at first.*

1. The first is taken from the very *letter* of the words.

2. The second shall be taken from the *coherence* of the words with what is before.

3. The third sort of arguments shall be taken from *what followeth after.*

1. First, that the Apostle here intendeth to speak of *the exceeding greatness of his power in the first working of faith;* take the letter of the words, and it will evidently bear this sense; 'who believe,' saith he, 'according to the working of his mighty power.' And whereas they say you should put the stop at 'who believe,' and read it thus, 'what is the exceeding greatness of his power to us-ward who believe;' and should not join them with what followeth, 'who believe according to the working of his mighty power,' it cometh all to one. We see that 'who believe' is hedged in with an almighty power on one side, 'the exceeding greatness of his power to us-ward who believe;' and with an almighty power on the other side, 'who believe according to the working of his mighty power.' So that certainly his mighty power in working faith should be intended.

Then again, in the second place; whereas when he spake of the riches of the glory that is in heaven, the persons there in whom he had said this glory is, he calleth saints; 'the riches of the glory of his inheritance in the saints;' that is, as I interpreted it when I handled it, in saints made perfect; for it is only in those saints that are now perfect in heaven. But mark it, when he cometh to speak of the power that is to us-ward, he doth not say the power in saints, or toward saints made perfect, but *to us-ward who believe;* he changeth the phrase. What is the meaning of that? We that believe at present, we have this power put forth in us; he distinguisheth believers on earth from saints in heaven. When he speaks of the power that wrought before, and works at present in them, he calleth them believers; when he speaks of the riches of glory hereafter, he calleth them saints. Why? You know that perfect holiness is in heaven, but faith is not there; faith ceaseth there, saith the Apostle. So that his meaning in a word is this: that as there are riches of glory in the saints in heaven, so there is an exceeding greatness of power towards us that believe on earth. As we believe at present, so the power is at present.

Again, thirdly, if you mark it, he doth not say the power that *shall work* in you, as if it were to be confined only to the raising men up at the latter day. He doth not speak it in the future, as if he restrained it to the glory of heaven to come; but, saith he, 'that ye may know what is the power,' τῆς δυνάμεως, the power at present. If he had meant the power only that shall work hereafter, he would have expressed it in the future tense; for so he doth express the resurrection of Christ in the time past; 'which hath wrought in Christ,' saith he.

Then, in the fourth place, there is something in this word 'to us-ward;' at least the Apostle's meaning must be to include himself who was an apostle, he shuffleth himself in with these Ephesians, and with all believers; 'to us-ward.' Now, how was Paul converted? When he was converted, he had experience of the exceeding greatness of his power, if any man in the world ever had, or shall have. Nay, his example is acknowledged by many of those that are contrary-minded to be an exception. God did work, say they, infallibly in his conversion. For a man to be taken in the height of his persecution; Christ met him in the field, he was going out against him armed; he strikes him off his horse at first blow, turned him clean contrary; 'I that was a persecutor and injurious,' I had nothing else in my heart; 'Lord,' saith he, 'what wilt thou have me to do?' 'The exceeding greatness of his power to us-ward,' Paul among the rest. And the Scripture seemeth to lean that way, that Paul had an effectual work, as our translators translate the word ἐνέργεια there, in the place I quoted even now, Eph. iii. 7, 'I was made a minister of the gospel,' saith he, 'according to the gift of the grace of God given unto me, by the effectual working of his power.'

To open these words a little. He speaks, as I take it, with Rollock and Calvin, of his conversion, together with which he received his apostleship and commission for it. You shall find that Paul's conversion is expressed by receiving his apostleship, and the one is put for the other. You have many places for that; whenever almost his conversion is mentioned, you have his apostleship likewise, and the commission for it put in. When our Saviour Christ would convert him from heaven, what doth he say to him? Read Acts xxvi. 16, 'Stand upon thy feet,' saith he; 'for I have appeared unto thee for this purpose, to make thee a minister and a witness both of these things which thou hast seen, and of those things in the which I will appear unto thee.' In his conversion here Christ telleth him that he would make him an apostle; he expresseth his conversion by it. You may find the like in Acts ix. 14, 15, where his conversion is likewise related; when Ananias was sent to him, Christ speaks of him as of a man new struck. 'Go thy way,' saith he, 'for he is a chosen vessel, to bear my name before the Gentiles,' &c. The like you may find, 1 Tim. i. 12. Read his conversion there; how doth he express it? Saith he, 'He counted me faithful, putting me into the ministry, I that was before a persecutor and blasphemer; and the grace of our Lord Jesus Christ was exceeding abundant.' He expresseth his conversion by being put into the ministry of apostleship, such as Paul had.

Now therefore, when he saith here in Eph. iii. 7, 'Whereof I was made a minister, according to the gift of the grace of God given to me, by the effectual working of his power;' this is the Apostle's meaning, that he was converted by the effectual working of his power. And as here in the text it is said, the exceeding greatness of his power to us-ward who believe, the same that wrought in raising Christ from the dead, so compare with this Gal. i. 1, 'I was made an apostle,' saith he, 'not of men, neither by men; but by Jesus Christ, and God the Father.' I was converted, saith he, and what followeth? 'Who raised him from the dead.' Why cometh that in? The same effectual working, saith he, that raised up Jesus Christ from the dead, made me an apostle, converted me to the faith. Now then, the Apostle, out of his own experience of 'the exceeding greatness of his power,' putteth himself in too; 'to us-ward,' saith he, the same power that converted me, converted you; although there was some extraordinariness in it in respect of the manner of doing it, yet the power is the same. As we receive like faith, as the apostle Peter saith, so the same power is no less to work in the poorest believer's faith, than what wrought in the heart of Paul. And so much now for the reading of the words, that they will bear that sense; not to relate only to the power put forth in believers at the resurrection, but in the first work of faith.

2. The second sort of arguments shall be taken from the scope of the Apostle here, in *the coherence of these words with the former*, and with those that follow after; for you shall see that the coherence of both will carry it, as well to refer it to the *working of faith* at the first, as to the *raising us up* at the last.

One scope of the Apostle, which I mentioned when I shewed the coherence, was this, to comfort believers in the weakness of their faith for the obtaining this glory, against all doubting. Now, my brethren, what is the great doubt that possesseth the hearts of Christians, that usually takes up their thoughts? It is not so much a questioning the power of God to raise them up hereafter, as it is the power of God to keep them for the present. Therefore, when the Apostle would comfort their hearts, that they should attain this glory, he doth not pray only that they may know the power that should raise up saints at the latter day; but the power that should keep them, that they might know the power that is engaged to us-ward that believe, to preserve us to this glory. I say, believers are not so much, or not so usually, taken up with doubtings or questionings about the power of God in raising them hereafter with Christ; all men's thoughts take that for granted; but the doubt is about keeping them until then.

I will give you a scripture for it, John xi. 23. Poor Martha there, when Christ came to raise up Lazarus, and told her, 'Thy brother shall rise again;' 'I know,' saith she, 'that he shall rise again at the resurrection of the last day.' She doubted not of this; this did not trouble her at all, but she only doubted of the power of Christ to raise him presently, her faith stuck at that. 'By this time,' saith she, 'he stinketh, for he hath lain four days in the grave.' It was the present resurrection she doubted of, and the power of Christ in that. 'Therefore,' saith he, ver. 40, 'said I not unto thee, that if thou believest, thou shouldst see the glory of God?' see it presently. I quote it for this purpose, to shew that if the scope of the Apostle be to take away the doubting of Christians concerning their attaining this glory, it is not so much he prayeth that they may see the power that shall raise men at last, for that few men doubt of,—ordinarily they do not,—but how they shall be kept by the power of God to this salvation; the present power that shall keep them and preserve them, that they doubt of. This is that, therefore, that the Apostle prayeth for that they may see. Therefore, 1 Peter i. 5, after he had mentioned the glory of that inheritance, he comforteth them with this, that they are 'kept by the power of God unto salvation;' he speaks to their hearts, for that is the great thing they doubt of. Now then, mark how I argue. If this be the scope of the Apostle to comfort believers, that there is an almighty, an omnipotent power that shall keep them in the state they are in, that they shall attain to glory, the argument is strong, that if such a power as this be to keep them and preserve them, that much more such a power was put forth in their first conversion, when they first came to believe. If to preserve them in faith after they have believed, and were sealed; then much more, to persuade them to believe at first, when they were heathens, to bring them to the faith, would require an exceeding greatness of power.

My brethren, there is as great a power, and a greater, if we may make comparisons, in converting at first, than in keeping afterward, Rom. v. 9, 10. The Apostle makes it there a greater work to reconcile us, being enemies, than to keep us friends, being reconciled. It is a greater work to put life into a dead man, of which the comparison is there, than to keep life in him; you know heat will do that. Conversion is a greater work in some regards than glorifying a man is. Why? Because the glorifying a man is but a gradual change, it is but from grace to glory; but to convert a man is a special change, it altereth the state of a man, a wolf becometh a lamb; it altereth the kind, the other addeth but a new degree. Now therefore, if the Apostle's scope be, as most evidently it is, they may know his power, to the end to comfort them, to take all doubts away;—they knew the hope of his calling before, he prayed for that in the former verse; that they might know the riches of the glory of his inheritance, that he prayed for in the last words before; now, that they might know the power that would keep them, according to their hope, unto that salvation;—so that now it agreeth well with this scope of the Apostle.

Again, in the second place; suppose the Apostle's scope be to comfort them, and to strengthen their faith in this point, that there shall be an almighty power put forth in them, to raise them up at the latter day; you shall find—take this in too—that they may know the power that first converted them, is the strongest argument that can be to persuade them of the other. My meaning is this: that the strongest argument that could be brought to persuade the Ephesians, to strengthen their faith, that an almighty power should one day work to raise them from death to glory,—I say, the strongest argument to work this in them, is to see the power that first converted them. Here is one argument indeed to strengthen their faith, namely, they saw by faith their Head, Jesus Christ, to have been raised from death to glory; but then add but this to it, We saw as great a power, and found as great a power in working faith in us, and conversion in us, in changing our hearts, as was put forth in raising of Christ from death to life; here is a double argument. And so, indeed, I find most of the Greek fathers run that way in their interpreting this place. The Apostle, say they, doth declare what God already hath done for them and in them; how he had wrought them to believe by an almighty power, to strengthen and confirm their faith for the future, that he would shew forth the same power in raising them up from death to life.

To this purpose Theophylact and Chrysostom,—I name him because he was as much for the freedom of will as any other, being an orator to persuade men to turn to God; a holy and a good man, as good as Austin, that was of another mind, living in the same age with him,—yet he interpreteth this place of working faith at first; for to this purpose is his speech. The Apostle's scope, saith he, is to demonstrate by what already was manifested in them, namely, the power of God in working faith; to raise up their hearts to believe what was not manifested, namely, the raising of them up from death to life: it being, saith he, a far more wonderful work to persuade a soul to believe in Christ than to raise up a dead man, a far more admirable work of the two. To raise up a dead man, saith he, God made but one word of it,—I speak it to shew that that is his scope,—'Lazarus, arise; and he that was dead arose, and came forth bound hand and foot,' &c. Saith Peter to Tabitha, 'Arise; and she opened her eyes and sat up.' But here it costs God many words when he cometh to convert a man, 'How often would I have gathered you under my wings?' I allege it to this purpose, to shew that they likewise interpret it to this sense, that by what they had already experience of in their own hearts, they might from thence see and believe that great power that would work in them hereafter. And whereas now,—take the other sense,—all the weight of the argument to persuade their faith of the truth of this, that they shall one day be raised up from the dead, lieth upon their mere faith to believe that God raised up Christ, which is a thing they did not see, nor had experience of; take this argument in too, that a believer hath found the same power in him in working faith that wrought in Christ; he hath not only a double argument, but an argument in his own experience of that power, and so more suitable to him for his heart to be more taken with it, and he hath this comfort besides, that that power which converted me is engaged, and will certainly keep me, and raise me up at the last day. So that the Apostle's scope will be every way more full.

And then another scope the Apostle hath—as appeareth by the 15th and 16th verses—is to provoke them to thankfulness. He saith that he thanked God for the work of grace in them, whereby they had obtained an inheritance, ver. 13. Now, to the end that they may be thankful, and thankful to purpose, he prayeth that they might know this great power that thus wrought faith in them, whereby they were interested in that inheritance, that thus they might be thankful also. Did you but know, saith he, what power it was that works in you that believe, you would be astonished with the love of God toward you; you would be overcome with it; how thankful would you be! It is Austin's observation upon this Eph. i. 16. He argueth from it because Paul gave thanks. If God's power, saith he, were not in it, in turning a man to God; and were it not the cast of his own will, and yet the will of man work freely too, how could a man heartily give thanks unto God? There is one absurdity put upon his opinion. Say they, If you do not hold that the will of man casteth it freely, to what end are all exhortations made by God to man? But on the other side, If the power of God do not cast it, and yet the will work freely too, why are thanks given to God, as the author of all, more than to man's own will? And the truth is, there would less absurdity fall upon the other than upon this.

So now you have two sorts of arguments despatched. First, from the letter of the words; secondly, that this agreeth with the scope of the Apostle here in the words before.

3. I will name one more, and that is a great one, and it is *the coherence of these words with those that follow after;* that the Apostle doth here evidently mean the exceeding greatness of his power in converting a man at first, that he takes this in eminently in his aim. To make this plain unto you. After that the Apostle had discoursed of the power of God in raising up Christ from the dead, from the 20th verse to the 23d; having said likewise that the same power works in us that wrought in Christ when he was thus raised; mark what he saith in the 2d chapter, ver. 1 and 6, 'And you who were dead in sins and trespasses, wherein in time past ye walked, hath he quickened. Even when we were dead in sins, hath he quickened us' (so ver. 5) 'together with Christ, and hath raised us up together, and made us sit together in heavenly places in Christ Jesus.' Here the Apostle plainly declares that his scope and meaning is, speaking of the exceeding greatness of power that works in those that believe, the same that wrought in Christ in raising him from the dead, and set him at his own right hand in the heavenly places; the same power, saith he, hath quickened you, when you were dead in sins and trespasses, the same power, saith he, hath raised you up, and set you with Christ, your Head, in heavenly places. When he saith, 'You hath he quickened,' as he doth at the 1st and 5th verses of the 2d chapter, his mean-

ing is, he hath put life into you, put a principle of godliness into you: 2 Peter i. 3, 'According as his divine power hath given unto us all things that pertain unto life and godliness.'

Now, to shut up this discourse, the Apostle, from the 19th verse of this chapter to the 6th verse of the 2d chapter, saith these two things, and all is summed up in them—to give you the coherence, and mark it. First, he layeth down a general proposition in the 19th verse, That they may know what is the exceeding greatness of his power in them that believe, according to the working of his mighty power, which he wrought in Christ, when he raised him from death to glory. Here is the general proposition, that God sheweth the same power in them that believe that he shewed in Christ in raising him. Well, there are two enlargements of this. First, he telleth and explaineth what a great power was shewed in Christ; and that he doth from the 21st verse to the end of the chapter; how he was raised up, and set far above all principalities and powers, and above every name that is named in heaven and in earth. Then, secondly, he explaineth how it was, and when, this same power wrought in them that believe. 'And you,' saith he, 'hath he quickened, when ye were dead in sins and trespasses, together with him, and hath raised you up,'—not only *will* but *hath* done it. Therefore evidently the Apostle speaks of the conversion of believers; the same power that wrought in Christ and raised him up, is that which works in them and raised them up also.

Now, my brethren, to back this with one parallel place, which I ever love to do, and so I shall go off from this. As here in the text he makes mention of the greatness of his power in working faith, and paralleled it with the power that raised up Christ from the dead; so read Col. ii. 12, 13, and you shall find the very same thing said there too. Saith he, 'Ye are buried with him in baptism, wherein also ye are risen with him through the faith of the operation of God, who hath raised him from the dead.' Parallel this with the words of the text. Saith the words of the text, 'the power that works in you to believe;' he speaks of faith. Saith the Apostle here, 'Ye are buried with him, but ye are risen through faith.' Again, secondly, he compareth believing in the text (being compared with those following verses in the 2d chapter) to a rising from the dead. So here in the Colossians, 'Ye are risen with him through faith,' saith he. Then again, in the third place, as in the text he makes a parallel of the work of faith with the resurrection of Christ; 'who believed,' saith he, 'according to the power that wrought in Christ when he was raised:' so he makes the same parallel here in the Colossians, 'through the faith of the operation of God, who hath raised him from the dead,' viz., Christ. And, fourthly, as we are said to believe according to the efficacious work, the word ἐνέργεια is likewise here in the Colossians called faith of the working, or efficacious working of God. And as here God is said to be the author, the same that raised up Christ did work faith in them, so likewise in this place it is faith of the operation of God, who raised up Christ from the dead. So that every way the one place is parallel with the other.

I will give you but one evasion of some against this place, and shew the weakness of it, and presently conclude.

Say they, the meaning of the phrase, 'through faith of the operation of God,' doth not note out that the operation of God is the efficient cause of faith; but that the operation of God that raised up Christ from the dead is the object of faith, therefore it is called faith of the operation of God; that is, say they, that hath the power and operation of God that raised up Christ from the dead for its object, to believe that we shall likewise be raised up.

But, my brethren, that the Apostle when he saith, 'faith of the operation of God,' meaneth that faith was wrought by God, and that he takes it in that sense, appeareth plainly by comparing it with the 11th verse that went before. Speaking there of sanctification, as he doth here of faith,—of sanctification under the notion of circumcision, for you know it is called circumcision of the heart,—saith he, 'In whom also ye are circumcised with the circumcision made without hands, in putting off the body of the sins of the flesh by the circumcision of Christ.' Now, to open these words unto you. Here is an allusion of the work of sanctification and faith to be the fruits and effects of two sacraments, the Old Testament circumcision, and the New Testament baptism. When he speaks of sanctification as the work and fruit, the inward work of the old circumcision, he distinguisheth of circumcision. There is one, saith he, that is outward, made with hands, of those that did circumcise the child with their hands, that is outward circumcision; but then, saith he, there is a circumcision that is by the power of God immediately, and that is called a circumcision without hands, an inward circumcision that is without hands. What is the meaning of that? Whereof God is the immediate author, that is the Apostle's meaning; wherein a man doth make no resistance, wherein a man is, as it were, passive, for so you know in circumcision he was. Now then, the very same thing which he had said of sanctification in allusion to the old circumcision,—that sanctification was a work without hands, that is, of God's power immediately,—the same he expresseth of faith in the next words under the notion of baptism, calling it faith of the operation of God. So that when he saith, 'faith of the operation of God,' his meaning is, that it is wrought, as the inward circumcision is, by the immediate power of God, and by that very power that raised Christ from death to glory.

To open this yet a little further. This phrase, 'made without hands,' noteth out in Scripture still God's immediate power, and above the course of nature; an immediate power above second causes. When he speaks of heaven, 2 Cor. v. 1, he calleth it a house made without hands, that is, the glory we shall have shall be the immediate work of the power of God. He useth just the same phrase of the grace we have; it is circumcision without hands, and it is faith of the operation of God, which is all one. In Heb. ix. 11, you shall find that Christ's body, the framing of it and uniting of it to the Godhead,—which was the greatest work that ever God did, 'The power of the Highest,' saith he, 'shall overshadow thee;' he shewed strength with his arm when he did that,—it is said to be a 'tabernacle made without hands;' that is, it was done by the immediate power of God. So now, circumcision without hands is a circumcision immediately by God, and is all one with what he saith afterward of faith; 'faith of the operation of God.'

Now then, my brethren, to make an observation out of all this, and so to end at this time. There are three things that now remain to be handled:—

1. That God in converting and keeping of believers unto life, hath an efficacious working of his power. It is a work of the might of his power, working efficaciously and infallibly.

2. That there is an exceeding greatness of power put forth therein.

3. That the proportion of power put forth therein is the same that raised up Christ from death to glory. These are the three things that remain to be handled. I will only speak a word to the first, and so conclude:—

You see here, if that be taken, as it is evident it is, for the working of faith and converting a man at first, that conversion is by an efficacious work, an infallible work. I shewed you that the meaning of this phrase, 'according to his working,' implieth so much, I cannot repeat that; and to instance in that, he backs it with the same power that wrought in Christ, strongly confirms it; for, saith the Apostle, Acts ii. 24, it was impossible that he should be holden of the grave; so that there is an efficacious work that works faith in a man at first that shall not be resisted.

But you will say, similitudes are not to be stretched too far. But if it be not stretched to shew the efficacy and infallibility of the success,—that God doth as infallibly convert a man as he raised up Christ,—you stretch it to nothing; for if that be not the scope, nothing is, supposing it to be meant of conversion.

We do acknowledge that there is a power of God working in men's hearts that is resisted, as he saith, Acts vii. 51, 'Ye always resist the Holy Ghost.' There is a work of the Holy Ghost upon corrupt nature, enlightening it so far to see spiritual things as to effect self-love, and it is a work of power too. And look how far God putteth forth this power, so far it works; it works so far as to move a man when he is moved; if God had intended that it should save a man effectually it should save him. Those enlightenings spoken of, Heb. vi., and tasting of the powers of the world to come, are all works tending to salvation; they are works of the power of God, they are called the powers of the world to come, which are powerfully set on upon a man's heart; but they are not according to the rate and proportion of this efficacy of power here mentioned, which raised up Christ from death to glory. To give you an instance:—

Deut. v. 28, 29: You shall find there that the people were exceedingly moved; We will do all, say they, that God by thee shall command us. What saith God? 'They have spoken well,' saith he; 'but oh that there were such a heart in them, that they would fear me, and keep all my commandments always.' Compare with this now Deut. xxix. 2–4, 'Thou hast seen,' saith he, 'all that the Lord did in Egypt; the great temptations, the signs, and those great miracles: yet the Lord hath not given thee a heart to perceive, and eyes to see, and ears to hear, unto this day.' Here now was a work of the power of God, and it wrought upon self-love, they quaked and trembled, and it was the power of God to make them do so, and so far as God intended it, so far it wrought, it moved them; but still they had not a heart. To give a man a heart to perceive, and a heart to turn, and turn effectually, this is from the exceeding greatness of his power. So that now indeed there is a work and a powerful work too, which is and may be resisted; 'Ye always resist the Holy Ghost; as your fathers have done, so do ye;' but then there is a power that is not resisted, it is according to the effectual working of the might of his power, the same that raised up Christ from death to glory.

All those of the Remonstrants do acknowledge that God doth infallibly enlighten the mind of a man to see spiritual things; that likewise he doth work upon the affections of a man, and works good motions there. But, say they, the will, though thus beset both by the understanding and affections, must still be free, and God must, according to the law and course of things, so work upon it as to leave it to its liberty; therefore that may refuse for all this, and the only way of working upon it is but by moral persuasions.

On the other side, all the Jesuits almost, they acknowledge an efficacy and infallibility in conversion in those that are elected, predestinated; but they ascribe it all unto a congruity; that is, that God doth take a man at an advantage, spieth out a time wherein a man being under such and such circumstances and considerations, he may certainly convert him. Now, say they, mere moral persuasions, mere arguments would not be enough, though they were never so abundant. On the other side, if God should put forth a power to turn the will, that were too much; that would spoil the liberty of it, say they. Therefore he spieth, say they, an opportunity, takes a man at such a time as he hath a good disposition, and putteth him into such circumstances as he shall be converted.

My brethren, that which dasheth both these is this: the efficacy of working upon a man's heart is ascribed to the might of his power; so the text saith, 'according to the efficacy of the might of his power.' It doth dash first the working by moral persuasions only, for that is but a metaphorical working, so far as the objects propounded worketh; the will being set free by a power of grace. But such a kind of working doth no way require an exceeding greatness of power. If there were no other working upon a man's heart when he is turned, where should this exceeding greatness of power, Paul speaks of here, be spent? Not in assisting and accompanying moral persuasions or oratory arguments. The Apostle you see attributeth it to the might of his power, an efficacious power; therein lieth the efficacy of his grace. On the other side, take the congruity of the Jesuits; they say that when God doth mean infallibly to convert a man, he doth take him at such an advantage when he is so disposed, and every way so circumstantiated that it shall work. Saith the Apostle, it is according to the power of his might; therein lieth the efficacy of it too. He dasheth that likewise; for do but consider a little, to put the efficacy of the working of grace upon such circumstances as a man is cast into at such a time and not at another, is to cast the work upon mere accidents that will fall out; whereas here it is ascribed to the might of his power, not to his power only. And it may be a man is in such a disposition but once in his lifetime; suppose he be then converted, and he be out of that disposition the next day, how shall his heart be carried on to persevere in grace? Therefore certainly the efficacy of working grace and carrying it on lieth not in congruity,—it were ill for us if it did,—but it lieth in the power of his might. 'According,' saith he, 'to the efficacious working of the power of his might;' so saith the text.

My brethren, to end this; you shall find that the Scripture still attributeth it to the power of God. What saith the Apostle, 2 Thess. i. 11? 'That your faith,' saith he, 'may be perfected with power;' if perfected with power, then certainly begun with power. The thing I quote it for is this, he ascribeth it to power. Now, if a man carry a thing by power, you know it is beyond the force of arguments; we use to say, he carried it by force, by strength; I will not say by violence, for God works sweetly, and according to the nature of the will; but he saith, he carried it with power. Faith is perfected with power, and it is begun with power; yet God doth clothe his power with arguments and persuasions. You shall find likewise in Scripture, that the keeping of a man so as temptations do not overcome him, is not attributed to moral persuasions, to the liberty of the will being assisted and strengthened; but the victory that casteth it, whereby we overcome the world, the devil, and all, is attributed to the strength of God that is in us. 1 John iv. 4, 'He that is born of God overcometh the world, because greater is he that is in you, than he that is in the world.' It is a victory, my brethren, (that which casteth the act still,) for that is properly victory to give a man power to overcome, but the victory itself is not attributed to the liberty of a man's will put into such a condition that he may turn or overcome, but it is attributed to the strength of him that is in us, because he is greater, because he is stronger. How is he stronger if he do not overcome? Wherein is strength else seen? And so now as Paul in 1 Cor xv. 57, giveth thanks, triumpheth over Death, and Hell, and the Grave; 'Thanks be to God,' saith he, 'which giveth us the victory through our Lord Jesus Christ:' so come to the work of faith and believing, and preserving a man to salvation; whence cometh the victory? Even from God, from strength, a greater strength that is in you than is against you, in your own hearts, or in the devil; therefore saith Paul, 'Who shall deliver me? I thank God through Jesus Christ our Lord.'

It is a mighty instance that Austin hath. Take Adam, saith he, whom God did leave to shew the liberty of his will, according to the course and law of nature, to shew that he was a creature. He had all helps, he had habitual grace inclined his will to good, he had no corruption to tempt him, he had all sorts of encouragements, he had tasted how good God was; yet his will was tempted with the knowledge of a seeming good, and overcome. Take now a poor believer; he, saith he, hath but a little grace in him, and a great deal of corruption in his own heart; he hath habitually as much against him as for him, he is ensnared with all the pleasures of the world, he hath all the evil of it set against him; nay, he is put to deny himself: yet this man's will holdeth, when Adam with all his grace and no temptation fell away. What is the reason of this? It is the mighty power of God that worketh in him, that keepeth him, saith he. I use to say, that the weakest Christian and Jesus Christ are too hard for all the world and all their lusts. 'I am able to do all things,' saith Paul, 'through Christ that strengtheneth me.'

But you will say, the will is *a will*.

What then? Do you think that God made any creature that he doth not know how to rule it? Take the instance of Christ. He had a will and free, and more free it must be than any man's in the world; because if he had not that same full liberty that we have naturally, he had not merited, if his obedience had not been in the same nature free that ours is. For that is the argument; they say a man must have a free will, because his actions else are not worthy of praise or dispraise. Our Saviour Christ's actions had no merit in them (that is more than praise) if he had not the same liberty in working that we have; the human nature I speak of. Well, this human nature is joined to the Godhead. If God did not know how to carry on the will of the creature infallibly, what had followed here? That God now dwelling in the human nature might have sinned; for if the human nature had sinned, it had been attributed to him, as it is called the blood of God. The will of Christ therefore was an instrument, as we say his humanity was, which assuredly the power of God, which had engaged itself long before Christ came into the world, could rule and keep in obedience; yet keep it free, and most free, and free in that sense that we in this life are free. For otherwise, how could God have made the promises to all the seed, if he had not the will of this creature in his power to rule, and rule effectually, and yet the will be a will too? All the saints in the Old Testament must come down again else, all the promises must have been void, not a man had been saved, God could not undertake this, if he could not work upon the will to turn it to holiness, and yet be a will still. Therefore, certainly God hath a way to work upon the will of man efficaciously by the power of his might, by an omnipotent sweetness to carry a man on, and yet the will remain a will still.

In a word, my brethren, herein lieth liberty, when a man doth not only do actions out of his own inclinations as beasts do, but when he doth actions out of choice, and seeth full reason to do them ; because they are done with knowledge, they are therefore free. That it is both an exceeding greatness of power and an efficacy of power that works faith in us, the same that wrought in Christ when he was raised from the dead ; and the efficacy of it is ascribed to power and to the power of his might, that so you may give all the glory to God in the great work of conversion : 'Who according to the exceeding greatness of his power, according to the working of his mighty power, which he wrought in Christ, when he raised him from the dead, and set him at his own right hand in heavenly places.'

SERMON XXIV.

And what is the exceeding greatness of his power to us-ward, who believe, according to the working of the might of his power, which he wrought in Christ, when he raised him from the dead, and set him at his own right hand in the heavenly places.—VER. 19, 20.

I SHALL repeat nothing I have delivered, but only lay open the method I have proceeded in handling of these words.

I propounded these four things to be considered in them:—

The *first* is, some general considerations about the power of God. I named three—

1. The excellency of that power, described in these words, 'the exceeding greatness of his power.'

2. The efficacious working of his power, in these words, 'according to the effectual working'—the energy of his power—'of the might of his power.' They are all words to note out an efficaciousness in the thing here mentioned.

3. The proportions of the power of God; 'according,' saith he. He putteth forth more or less power in some works than in other, as himself pleaseth.

The *second* was, the persons toward whom this exceeding greatness of his power is exercised; it is *to us-wards.*

Thirdly, here is the work wherein it is exercised. It is all the works that God hath upon Christians, both from first to last; this I shewed in the last discourse, especially the work of conversion; 'who believe, according to the working of the might of his power.'

And when he had discoursed at large, from the 20th verse to the end of the chapter, what a power wrought in Christ when he raised him from the dead,—he having said that he putteth forth the same power in them that believe,—he telleth them in the 2d chapter, from the 1st verse to the 7th, that he put forth the same power in raising them up, in quickening their hearts, in working grace in them. Read over the coherence, and you will find it to be especially meant of the work that he had wrought in them, when he converted them and brought them to believe.

I am yet upon the *third* thing, viz., *wherein this power is manifested.* I proved in the last discourse—and I thought to have added something, but that the time cut me off from what I have now to deliver—that the thing wherein this power is manifested, this exceeding greatness of power, is at the present in believers; it is not only meant, as some would have it, of his power in raising them up at the last day. For this I shewed reasons, which I will not repeat.

I proved it, *first,* to be the scope of the Apostle.

Now, the *second* thing will be, *What it is in the work of conversion that doth draw forth the exceeding greatness of the power of God.*

And the *third* thing is this, *That it holdeth proportion with that power that raised up Jesus Christ from death to life.*

Now then, to handle, in the first place, that *second* thing mentioned, viz., What it is in the work of conversion,—which I have proved to be the scope of the Apostle to take in, and especially to aim at,—I say, *What is that should draw forth so great a power from God*, to have all these high and mighty expressions of it: 'the exceeding greatness of the might of his power.'

There are great disputes in the world, what power God putteth forth in converting men to him. My brethren, believe not discourses of it, but believe the Holy Ghost himself. If you would know what power is put forth in any work, ask the agent himself. Who is he that lets fall these words but he that hath converted millions of souls, who is 'the power of the Highest,' as he is called, Luke i. 35? He it is that hath indited this scripture, and he saith no less goeth to it than the 'exceeding greatness of his power.' Oftentimes the standers-by discern it not. When the woman was healed by a touch of the hem of Christ's garment, those that stood by discerned no such thing. Hear Christ speak: saith he, 'Virtue is gone from me.' He could best tell; because the Holy Ghost doth work oftentimes in men's hearts in a trice; like unto a strong man that hath a sleight of hand, takes up a weight in show easily; hence therefore, men think that there is no great power goeth to the work, but the man himself that doth the thing thus slightly, he can tell you what strength he putteth to it. So the Holy Ghost, he that was the inditer of this epistle, telleth us that the exceeding greatness of his power went to the converting of you.

Now, my brethren, though this be enough to settle your hearts in it, yet consider the work itself: what it is that requireth this power. All wise agents do proportion their power unto the work they have in hand; he that spends more power than the thing requireth, it is folly. And God, you know, works all things in weight and measure. Let us consider, therefore, what there is in this great work should draw forth the exceeding greatness of the power of God.

'According,' saith he, 'to the exceeding greatness of his power to us-ward.' The word εἰς ἡμᾶς either is *toward us*, as noting an extrinsical agency, an agency without us, yet which concerns us; or it noteth out *in us*. We will consider, first, *what God doth when he bringeth a man home to him, which is an extrinsical work out of him;* and, secondly, *what he doth in him:* and so we shall by degrees shew you that there is an exceeding greatness of power required to this work.

In the first place, *what God doth extrinsically toward a man, and for a man*, besides what he doth in him.

First, when he converteth a man, he casteth the devil out of him; that is one thing that is done for a man, besides what is done in his own heart; and there is an exceeding greatness of power goeth to this. In Matt. xii. 28, our Saviour Christ there, from his having cast out a devil, and their saying he did it by the prince of devils, he clears the point, and he riseth up to the point of conversion,—for that is his scope likewise,—and he sheweth that it must be a divine power that must cast the devil out of a man, and when you are turned to God the devil is cast out of you. Saith he, 'If I cast out devils by the Spirit of God, then the kingdom of God is come unto you; else,' saith he, 'how can one enter into a strong man's house, and spoil his goods, except he first bind the strong man, and then he will spoil his house?'

To open this place unto you a little:—

Every man before his conversion, as he is a child of Satan, so, as chap. ii. 2 of this epistle hath it, the devil works effectually in him while he is a child of disobedience; he doth ride and act, and fill the hearts of men, as you have it, Acts v. 3. You shall find this in Scripture, that the wickedness of men is expressed to you by how many devils they have in them; as, Luke xi. 26, when he would describe a man's state to be in a worse condition than his former, he takes seven devils worse than himself, and they enter into the man. According to the proportion of a man's wickedness in the state of nature, accordingly hath he devils that possess his soul; that is certain. 'According,' saith he in that Eph. ii. 2, 'to the prince of the power of the air, the spirit that works now in the children of disobedience,' works not in you as he was wont to do, for he is cast out; he works now, but not in you; you walk thus and thus, not according to the power of the prince of the air. Therefore, in John xvi. 11, he saith that the Spirit shall convince the world of judgment, for, saith he, 'the prince of this world is judged.' When a man is converted, Satan is judged, is cast out. Before, a man was 'taken captive of him at his will,' 2 Tim. ii. 26.

My brethren, this is a mighty power, to throw the devil out of a man. In Matt. xii. 28, he saith, 'If I by the Spirit of God cast out devils.' Look Luke xi. 20, 'If I by the finger of God.' The finger of God, you know, was applied to a miracle that no creature could do, Exod. viii. 19. He is called 'the strong man;' and, saith he, if I throw the devil out of any man, I must overcome him by strength, for he is a strong man. He compareth him to a giant, and, saith he, he will never yield; he must be bound; there is no quarter, no moral persuasions will turn the devil out of a man's heart. And he saith—I remember it is an expression in Luke xi. 22—that he hath πανοπλίαν, armour; he hath all sorts of armour for to defend himself, and to keep the heart, which, in the 21st verse, is compared to his castle. He compareth him to a strong man that hath his castle, and he hath goods there; for so he calleth them there, a spoiling of his goods, for every sin is the devil's goods; it is more the devil's work than ours, he is gratified in it more than we; it is our loss, but it is his gain, for he is the father of all sin. Now, saith he, if I cast the devil out of a man's heart, he must be bound, it must be by main strength; therefore, saith he, a man must enter in that is stronger than he, and bind the strong man, and then he will spoil his house. Here is, you see, one part of the greatness of power put forth in the work of conversion; but here is but the finger of God, it is no more in comparison of what followeth; yet this is somewhat toward it. Here is the exceeding greatness of his power toward us, or to us-ward.

But, secondly, let us come to *the exceeding greatness of his power in us.* To open that to you, for indeed that is the main. You shall find there are exceeding great expressions of Scripture about the work of grace in us.

It is compared to creating at the first,—that expression is often used,—to a metamorphosis, a transformation. It is a word that is used Rom. xii. 2. It is such a transformation as when beasts are turned into men; for so you know the word *metamorphosis* is. It is the title of a book that describeth the metamorphosis, the change of men into beasts, and beasts into men. So it is described Isa. xi. 6; he telleth us there that the wolf and the lamb should dwell together, and the lion and the calf should lie down together; that is, God under the gospel would change these creatures, the wildness of them; he would metamorphose them. And Isa. xliii. 18, 19; it is a place that the Apostle doth allude to, and therefore I quote it. You shall find in 2 Cor. v. 17, saith the Apostle, 'If any man be in Christ, he is a new creature: old things are passed away; behold, all things are become new.' Now, that place in Isaiah is quoted for this; and if you read there, where he useth the same words much to that purpose, he telleth you that the beasts of the field shall honour him. He had mentioned before, 'Remember ye not the former things, neither consider the things of old;' here old things are passed away. 'Behold, I will do a new thing; the beasts of the field shall honour me, the dragons and the owls.' He would go and convert heathenish men, men that were beasts, that were as remote from honouring God even as beasts are in some regard. But how would he do this but by a creation? Saith he, ver. 21, 'This people have I formed for myself; they shall shew forth my praise.' Here is that the Apostle saith, old things are past, all things are become new; it is with a transformation.

Now, my brethren, where have you in Scripture—mark what I shall now say—any one that fell away from God, that it is said of him he was a new creature, or was born again, which is the infusion of a new life, or a new soul; or that he was quickened and raised from the dead? All these phrases are put to express the greatness of his power. It is nowhere said in all the word of God, of any such man, that he fell away. Why? Because to that work that shall never fall away goeth a power answerable to the work of creation; it is the infusion of a new nature, it is the raising of a dead man. There is a counterfeit of it indeed, which these phrases are never applied unto.

But, you will say, these are metaphors.

Suppose they be but metaphors many of them, yet still in this they agree, that the same power that created, the same power that shall change a beast into a man, makes that transformation; the same power that shall quicken a dead man, the same power doth go to convert. In this they agree.

My brethren, I ask you this question, To what end doth God set forth the work of grace to us by these metaphors? He setteth them forth that he might have real thanks; therefore certainly there is something in these expressions that answereth the work of creation that is real; for God would not have you give thanks above his proportion, above what his power in working is. Do but compare Eph. ii. 10 with Col. iii. 10. In Eph. ii. 10, saith he, 'We are his workmanship.' How? Produced by creation. If he had meant any other working,—will you mark my reason?—if he had meant any other working than creation, he would never have said, 'his workmanship created;' it had been enough to have said, 'his workmanship,' for that implieth the power of God. Why doth he add 'created?' Certainly, to shew that is as great a work as creation. Therefore, in Col. iii. 10, (compare with this likewise Eph. iv. 24,) he compareth the image of God before the fall to the image of God now renewed in the heart of a Christian. Saith he, 'We are renewed,' so it is in the Colossians, 'after the image of him that created him,' namely at first. All the world grants that it was an immediate power of creation wrought that image at first. Now then, look Eph. iv. 24, and there you shall find that this image is said to be created likewise, 'after the image of him that created them' at the first. So that this is his meaning; as it is the same image, so there is the same power goeth to work it; it is a creation works it now, as a creation wrought it before. He useth the same expression both of the one and of the other.

Will you come to particulars, this is but in general, you shall find it is a power exceedeth the creation. I will but take for my ground Ezek. xxxvi. 26; you shall see there what goeth to convert a man. The power of God is put forth there in three things:—

It is put forth, first, in the *removing of what hindereth;* there is *amotio impedimenti;* it is called the taking the stony heart out of your flesh, so ver. 26.

There is, secondly, *a giving of a new capacity to perform*, a new nature and new disposition, which is called giving a new spirit, and by 'new spirit' he meaneth another thing than the Holy Ghost. Why? For he mentioneth him afterward; 'I will put my Spirit within you, and cause you to walk in my statutes.' That is at the 27th verse, but this new spirit is at the 26th verse.

And then, thirdly, there is not only a power given, new and holy dispositions that shall make a man capable by the actings of the Holy Ghost to do well; it is a workmanship created to good works, it is fit for it; but he telleth us, 'I will put my Spirit within you, and cause you to walk in my statutes,' so saith ver. 27. And to shew that he it is that doth all this by an almighty power, what saith he at ver. 36? After he had set down enlargements of promises, saith he, 'I the Lord have spoken it, and I will do it;' as he is Jehovah he will do it.

Now, let us but consider these three things, and you shall see what a mighty power goeth to turn a man to God.

Consider, first, *what God takes away;* 'I will take,' saith he, 'the stony heart out of your flesh.' It is not a hardness, such as is of wax, that by an extrinsical power may be melted; the fire will melt it, the sun will melt it; but no fire, no sun, will melt a stone; you can deal with that no way but by taking it away; therefore that is the phrase, I will, saith he, take away the heart of stone, or 'the stone of the heart.' You see here is something to be destroyed, therefore it is called a new creature, 2 Cor. v. 17. Why new? Because all new respecteth all old to be taken away, as Heb. viii. 13, 'In that he saith a new covenant, he hath made the first old;' he abolisheth that: so the words following imply, and so indeed it followeth in 2 Cor. v. 17, 'He that is in Christ is a new creature: old things are passed away; behold, all things are become new.' There is a passing away, a taking away of old things, and there is not a whit of the old remaineth in the new; all is become new, saith he; not a stick, not a stud that was in a man's natural estate will serve afterward, more than the soul and the faculties of it. All old things pass away, and all are become new.

Now, my brethren, will you compare it with the creation, that you may see it is a thing far exceedeth it? God sheweth forth power in creating; he sheweth forth here greatness of power, and exceeding greatness of power; it will appear before we have done.

Herein lay the power of God in the creation, that he created something out of nothing, as it is Rom. iv. 17, 'He called things that be not as if they were;' yet that is made even and equal with the raising of the dead in that very place. But here is a calling things that are *to nothing* first, and when he hath done that, then there is a calling things that are *out of nothing*. There is a doubling of his power in this; there is not only a calling things out of nothing, but there is a bringing to nothing old things. Now, it is a rule in politics, and it holdeth true in philosophy likewise, *Ejusdem potestatis est destruere cujus est constituere*,—The same power that goeth to make laws is it which destroyeth laws, disannulleth laws; there is as much power goeth to bring old things to nothing, as there is to create new things out of nothing. Now then, here is a double power, you see; here is not only power, but greatness of power; it will come to exceeding greatness anon.

The conversion of a sinner is not expressed only by putting in a *new heart*, but the Scripture doth usually express it by destroying *old things;* and as much by that as the other, because the power of God is seen as much in that as in working grace, that is, as in working grace simply: it is not but that the working of grace is at the same time with this destroying old things; but it is to shew that there is a doubling of his power in it. It is more than to create grace in Adam or in the angels. He therefore calleth it the 'destroying of the body of sin,' Rom. vi. 6; 'the circumcision of the heart,' he cutteth off something, Col. ii. 11; 'the taking away of the vail.' I might give you many like instances.

In one word, I do parallel justification and sanctification together. There goeth more to justify a sinner than went to justify an angel that never fell, or Adam in innocency. There is not only an active obedience, 'Do this and live;' but there is a satisfaction to the punishment of the law, which was an appendix to the law; there is a passive obedience too; if you will justify a sinner you must put these in. Come to sanctification likewise; there is not only required a power to put grace into a man, but to destroy sin. Therefore now, as when he would magnify the mercy of God in justifying us, he mentioneth the state of sin we were in: so when he would magnify the power of God in conversion, he considereth the estate we were in before conversion. So you see here is now a power to create a new creature, here is a power to dissolve the old. Here is power, and greatness of power.

Well, but consider in the third place this, that the thing to be destroyed—viz., sin—is opposite, is *enmity* to the grace that God bringeth in, and to God and his law. It is not simply to destroy old things, to bring a creature to nothing; but it is to destroy enmity. In the first creation, when all things were made out of nothing, there was nothing to oppose, though there were nothing to help it. It had no matter to be wrought upon, yet there was not matter to oppose, for all was made out of nothing. But here, that which is destroyed is the highest, the greatest enemy that can be. You may see for this Rom. viii. 7, 'The carnal mind,' saith he—or indeed, the carnal disposition of the mind, for the word implieth so much—'is enmity against God; for it is not subject to the law of God, neither indeed can be.'

Here are two things, you see, said of the disposition of a man's mind by nature. The first is, it cannot be subject; and the second is, it is enmity.

In the first place, *it cannot be subject.* A wolf will sooner marry a lamb, or a lamb a wolf, than ever a carnal heart will be subject to the law of God, which was the ancient husband of it, as in Rom. vii. 6. It is the turning of one contrary into another. To turn water into wine, there is some kind of symbolising, yet that is a miracle. But to turn a wolf into a lamb, to turn fire into water, or rather flesh into spirit; what saith the Apostle, Gal. v. 17? 'These are contrary.' Between nothing and something there is an infinite distance; but between sin and grace there is a greater distance than can be between nothing and the greatest angel in heaven.

To exemplify this unto you: to destroy the power of sin, how great a power must it needs be! You all yield that to take away the guilt of sin requireth an infinite power, an infinite righteousness. Saith our Saviour Christ, Matt. ix. 6, 'Whether is it easier to say to the man,'—and make it good when you have done,—'Thy sins are forgiven,' or to say, 'Arise and walk?' It was a harder thing to forgive sins; only, saith he, 'that ye might know that the Son of man hath power to forgive sins,' for they would deny that he had power to forgive sins, he exemplifieth it by a miracle; but to forgive sins, saith he, that is his meaning, is infinitely harder.

Now, as we say of the attributes of God that they are alike, of equal extent, so are the two attributes of sin, as I may call them; the guilt of sin and the power of sin are of a like extent. To destroy the power of sin in a man's soul is as great a work as to take away the guilt of sin; all miracles are in it, saith he: 'the blind receive their sight, the lame walk, and the poor receive the gospel;' it is easier to say to a blind man, See, and to a lame man, Walk, than to say to a man that lies under the power of sin, Live, be holy, for there is that that will not be subject.

You will say to me, that the expelling of sin is but the putting in of grace, as of darkness by light.

But let me tell you this, that sin is too hard for grace, if grace had not a back. Adam had grace enough, but sin seized on his heart, threw it out. 'The strength of sin is the law,' saith he, and sin would keep possession; it hath the law to plead for it; but, saith he, on the contrary, 'the strength of grace is the gospel;' and that is it that keepeth grace now that it is not thrown out, otherwise sin would quickly throw your grace out, it is too hard for it.—That is the first thing, it is not subject to the law of God.

Not only so, but it is said to be *enmity*. It is not only said, it cannot be subject, and it must be destroyed, or else it will never yield, but *it is enmity in the abstract*, it is in the nature of it. In Col. i. 21, we are not only said to be 'enemies by evil works,' it is not a grudge, but we are said to be 'enemies in our mind' too.

Now, my brethren, if there be such an enmity, and if there be such a power in sin as there is, to detain a man, that will not yield, will hold a man to the utmost, there must be *an almighty power of God to subdue it*. You shall find in Col. i., the Apostle at the 11th verse having mentioned the glorious power of God that enabled the saints to do what they did; upon occasion of it what followeth? 'Giving thanks,' saith he, ver. 12, 'unto the Father, who hath made us meet to be partakers of the inheritance of the saints in light: who hath delivered us from the power of darkness, and translated us into the kingdom of his dear Son.' When he cometh to give thanks for the works of grace upon them, what doth he mention? Not only making them holy, making them meet for the inheritance of the saints in light, but likewise for delivering them from the power of darkness. The word ἐῤῥύσατο implieth not merely a delivering or freeing, but a freeing by violence, a snatching out of a power that else would never yield. I remember Zanchy saith upon it, They are freed, saith he, not only that have a desire to be free, but they are snatched out, *eripiuntur*, that have no desire to be free. And that is the condition of a man in the state of nature.

But you will say, all these are but metaphors; all that is spoken of the state of corruption and the power of God in delivering a man.

Shall I tell you in a word? When you come to hell, you will not then say they are metaphors; you will then find all these things true of your natural condition. And let me tell you this too. If ever you come to be humbled, you will not find them metaphors, but realities; for the soul of a man is humbled under the real sense of all these things when he turneth unto God; and yet when it cometh to a dispute upon the power of God in working upon a man's heart, creation, and the like, these are you say but metaphors. My brethren, they have the greatest reality in them in the world.

To give you but an instance, that now your own hearts may be judges: go take all the powers of man, when a man cometh to turn unto God, and do but see what a mighty opposition there is; go take the *understanding* of a man. God beginneth there; what doth he find there? He findeth not only ignorance of all spiritual principles, and such an ignorance as a man is not capable of knowing; he cannot know, so saith the Apostle, 1 Cor. ii. 14, 15, he is blind. 'Now it was never heard,' saith he, 'from the creation of the world, that any man opened the eyes of one that was born blind;' yet this is the power that must convert a man. But, I say, that is not all, there is not only an incapacity, a blindness, but there is an opposition, and the strongest that may be; and this must be taken away.

I will quote but one place for it; it is in 2 Cor. x. 4. He describeth there, as the text doth here, the mighty power of God in converting of a man. 'The weapons of our warfare,' saith he, 'are mighty through God.' Mighty? Wherein lieth their might? That he might shew the might that is drawn forth, he describeth the opposition that the understanding of a man makes against the ways of God; he telleth us that there are strongholds: 'Pulling down of strongholds,' saith he; 'casting down imaginations, and every high thing that exalteth itself against the knowledge of God, and bringing into captivity every thought into the obedience of Christ.' Here lieth the power, the might that God sheweth; he speaks of that opposition that is in the understanding of a man, as the word *νόημα*, reasonings, implieth; high thoughts, a devil to a strong man. He compareth the opposition to what is in a besieged town; there are strongholds, and there are such as plainly will take no quarter, they must die for it, or else they will never yield; therefore he calleth it pulling down the holds; there is no way else to get them, the Holy Ghost must batter them about their ears, yield they will not. They consist in reasonings and in imaginations; a bottom light doth it. When a man cometh to turn to God, let him have never so much knowledge, when he shall come to turn to God in earnest, he hath a thousand dislikes and not fancyings of the ways of God, he hath a world of arguments and objections, and an infinity of reasonings against them. My brethren, when a man's heart is put to it what is the right way of worshipping God and serving him, personally and otherwise, there is nothing but a world of reasonings that come in against it; and there are high thoughts that exalt themselves likewise. These must all be brought into subjection.

My brethren, when a man turns to God,—I will express it to you in a parliamentary language,—you must have this fundamental law, this bill pass, this must be the predominate rule, the *suprema lex*, the highest law that must guide a man's whole life; namely, that it is best to obey Christ in all things, at all times, and in all conditions, whatsoever the state be. This bill must pass with the consent of the whole heart. Now, to advance Christ, to bring all, every high thought into captivity, into subjection to the obedience of Christ; this will never be without an army, without the mighty power of God, that must throw all these strongholds down; 'our weapons are mighty through God,' saith he; they must be mighty through him, they will never do else. Now, do but think with yourselves what an uproar there must needs be in the state of the soul at the introducing such a law as this into a man's heart, if it be in earnest, if he sees he must live by it for ever. You shall have all the three states against it, both the understanding, will, and affections; you shall have big swelling reasonings and thoughts of absurdities. What? If this law take place, we must all come down then; all projects, all corruptions must go down.

My brethren, if all the apostles were now alive, and should set themselves to persuade one man; and, besides them, if God should send all the angels down from heaven to the earth to persuade one man, they could not make this law pass in a man's heart, they could not persuade him to it; it must be the might of God to throw down all opposite reasonings. And God doth this, he doth come with a little light, a bottom light into a man's heart,—for he createth there,—and letteth him see that excellency that is in himself and in his ways; and he doth not stand reasoning much with him neither, though all reasonings are for it; but God letteth in a light, answereth all objections, throweth down all strongholds, bringeth every thought into the obedience of Christ. Paul was in his height; how opposite was he unto God? What a world of reasonings had he against Christ in his heart? Jesus Christ did but tell him, 'I am Jesus whom thou persecutest,' and there was a light shone in his mind, as much as that which shone round about him, and in an instant saith he, 'Lord, what wilt thou have me to do?' All the disputations in the world would never have wrought thus. So the poor jailor cometh in trembling at midnight, 'Sirs, what shall I do to be saved?' He was converted before morning. All the reasonings in the world, and all the moral persuasions that men or angels could have brought, would never have done this; it was the mighty power of God casting down strongholds, putting in a light that goeth beyond all a man's objections.

Come to a man's *will*, and you will have as much to do there. A man's will must have a new end put upon it. And come to the will and affections, you shall find as much difficulty there to oppose. For example, there are two great principles in the heart of a man, that if ever God's Spirit cometh to deal with in good earnest, will hold tug with him as long as they can. What are they? You shall have them in 2 Tim. iii. 2, 4, 'Men shall be lovers of their own selves;' there is the first; and then followeth, 'covetous, proud, boasters,' &c. And the last is at the 4th verse, 'lovers of pleasures more than lovers of God.' Here are the two principles that are in a man's will and affections, and they will try it too. This same Self-love, that is the General, that goeth before, the captain; and Love of Pleasure, that is the lieutenant, that followeth after this army. One is the first, the other is last, backs all these lusts that are between.

Love of a man's self; first begin with that. It is the great devil; absolutely it is Beelzebub, it is the prince of devils, it is the bottom of original sin; and to throw this devil out of a man's heart, to depose him, to bring him down, it must be a mighty power indeed to do it. It was a great power to cast the devil out of a man; but to cast out this great devil out of a man's heart, to depose him, and bring another king in, this is a hard work. When God was thrown out of a man's heart when Adam did sin, then Self-love was next heir, and stepped up into the throne. All that God had, saith Self-love, I will have, I will serve myself as much as ever I did God. Now, as all the heart was for God before, in the same manner it is for itself now. All the strength that a man hath doth back Self-love, stands for the king. It is a king of an absolute sovereignty; and because it is a king, therefore when God cometh and tells a man, You must be subject to me, Self-love bustleth. What? I am absolute, saith he. It is enmity against the law and against all that shall proclaim war against Self-love in a man. I am for myself, saith he, and all that is within me is for me; there is but poor Conscience, that standeth contesting a little; but the whole heart is for it, that is certain. Now, when the Holy Ghost shall come to depose this great king, this absolute monarch, as it is in a man's heart, especially it shall be a foreigner that shall go about to do it, as God and the Spirit of God is. 'Love is strong as death,' it is a proverb, Cant. viii. 6. Self-love much more; all the strength that a man hath is for himself, he will give all for his life, for the life of this king; a man will never yield; all in nature will rise up against him that shall go about to depose it, all will be in arms. Yet notwithstanding, though the heathen imagine a vain thing, though the people and kings of the earth rage against Christ, and though all in a man thus be up in arms, yet God will set his Son upon this holy hill, upon a man's heart, before he hath done.

My brethren, this must be an almighty power that must do it; it is not all the persuasions in the world will do it. You may persuade Self-love to much; to serve God, and to do many things so far as will stand with its prerogative, so that he may remain king still; but to depose him, and that God shall be king, and he God's favourite, this must be an almighty power to do it.

So likewise for the love of pleasures, that is the second thing. When Self-love cometh to be deposed thus, as in conversion it is, from being king, saith every lust, every poor inferior lust, If this government be altered, I shall lose this pleasure and that pleasure, if you turn the world upside down thus. There is nothing in the heart, my brethren, but is for pleasure in some kind or other. A man liveth in pleasure, that is the expression, as a fish doth in its element. Take him out of carnal natural pleasures in some creature or other, his soul dieth; it will fight for pleasure as for his life. Saith the Apostle, 2 Peter ii. 14, 'They have eyes full of adultery, they cannot cease from sin;' they cannot, till a further power cometh. Luke xiv. 20, 'I have married a wife,' saith he, and in plain terms, 'I cannot come;' he makes that his excuse; for such lusts as these are have a mighty power upon a man's heart. How great? See what Christ's own expression is, that was the Saviour of souls, and knew what belonged to the converting of them, for he died for them. In Matt. xix. 24, there was a rich man came to him, and he was an ingenuous man. Christ preached the gospel to him, moved his heart a little, he used all moral persuasions to him that could be, told him that he should have eternal life; yet he goeth away. What doth Christ infer upon this? You shall find the story of that young man is the introduction to the words I quote this place for; 'A rich man, saith he, 'shall hardly enter into the kingdom of heaven.' Hardly? That is no great matter. What doth our Saviour Christ? He riseth higher in his expression: 'And again I say unto you, It is easier for a camel to go through the eye of a needle, than for a rich man to enter into the kingdom of God;' not for one that is rich simply, but Mark telleth us, chap. x., for one that 'trusteth in his riches,' that is his expression.

First, he saith it is *hard*.

Secondly, it is *so hard*, as it is easier for a camel to go through the eye of a needle. It was a proverb among the Jews, and it is in many of the rabbins extant to this day. You will say that it is an absurdity to use such an expression, a camel to go through the eye of a needle; the more absurdity there is in it, the more it expresseth the impossibility.

In the third place, saith Christ, 'with men this is impossible, but with God all things are possible;' it is impossible for all men in the world to do the work for another man; that is simply impossible; but with God all things are possible: why doth he say *all things?* If it were a slight work he would not say so; but, saith he, with God that works all things else, that hath an omnipotent power to subdue all things to himself, with him it is possible, he must do this.

I find this word, 'all things are possible,' used but in one or two cases. It is used upon the incarnation of Christ; when the angel had told Mary that Jesus Christ should be born of her, saith he, 'with God all things are possible,' and that was the highest work that ever he did, he 'shewed strength with his arm' there. So it is said of his working in us, Eph. iii. 20; and the like you have, Phil. iii. 21, 'According to the power whereby he subdueth all things unto himself,' that is the power that works in us; that is the power that must work a man off whose heart is set upon his riches, and is set upon any pleasure.

My brethren, it is not the offers of eternity, it is not all the persuasions of men and angels, nor of the Holy Ghost himself, if they be but mere moral persuasions, will make a man part with a bird in the hand for two in the bush. My meaning is, that will make a man part with his lusts, or his pleasures and sin, and take and accept the offers of eternity; but it must be the power of God, with whom all things are possible, and he must put forth as much power to work this as he putteth forth to work all things else.—And so now you have seen the power that is shewn in destroying this opposite, sin.

I will but speak a word of *the power that is in creating*. There is yet something to be done, there must be a new creation besides this destruction. There is a taking away the old heart; old things pass away, you see what a power that requireth. The second thing in Ezekiel that I mentioned, because that place holdeth this out, is a new heart and a new spirit, and to work that is a work of creation; it is an almighty power of God. Now, creation is a work that hath no matter to work upon, that is properly creation, and therefore requireth an infinite power. 'Create in me,' saith he, 'a clean heart,' Ps. li. Saith he in Job xiv. 4, 'Who can bring a clean thing out of an unclean?' If a man's heart be unclean, if he come to have a clean heart, certainly it must be created. We are therefore said to be the 'workmanship of God, created to good works,' in that second to the Ephesians. Mark it, it is not only a working upon the heart, but a workmanship it is called. And if you will know the manner of setting up and producing it, it is by way of creation.

I might be large in shewing you, that besides this destroying old things, there is a creating of new principles and gracious dispositions in the heart before a man turneth to God, which are the foundations of his turning to God. 'Turn me, and I shall be turned.' I will name but a scripture or two; and then I will shew you the mighty power that goeth to create this disposition.

First, I will shew to you—because those that make the power of God to be only external, assisting, do detract from the power of God—that it lieth in *creating new dispositions* in the heart, and then *assisting*, and then working upon them. I will name a scripture or two. I have shewed you what goeth to destroy the old; I will shew you then what power also goeth to the creating and rearing up of the new.

First, I will shew you that *there must be a new principle created*. Saith he, John iii. 6, 'That which is born of the flesh is flesh, that which born of the Spirit is spirit.' See how I argue out of these words. Here you see there is flesh and corruption, which is by one birth; here is spirit, a distinct thing from the Holy Ghost, that is a fruit of a second birth. Now, my brethren, take a man in his first birth; all the world yieldeth that there are habitual principles and dispositions unto evil, there is a habitual aversion from God, and conversion to the creature; there are dispositions and inclinations only to what is evil. Now then, in the second birth, answerably the spirit that is made and born by the Holy Ghost must be oppositely holy, and have dispositions to the contrary; for otherwise, nature is not healed if the Holy Ghost only works acts in a man, and did not work habits; the second Adam did not answer the first. And therefore you shall find, Gal. v. 17, the Apostle saith, 'The flesh lusteth against the spirit, and the spirit against the flesh; for these are contrary.' I appeal; dare any man say the Holy Ghost lusteth in us against the flesh? No, it is the spirit, a habitual frame of heart that lusteth in us against corruption. So now there is a new spirit wrought; that is, there are dispositions that are contrary unto sin, as sin is unto grace. As there are habitual dispositions to sin, both through nature and custom; so there are habitual dispositions to good that do lust against the flesh in a man. Therefore he compareth this spirit in that 5th to the Galatians to a root, 'The fruit of the spirit is love, joy, peace, long-suffering, gentleness, goodness, faith,' &c. He compareth the spirit or frame of grace, begotten by the Holy Ghost, unto a root.

Now mark you, to follow this, in Matt. xiii. 21, speaking of those that are temporisers, what doth he say of them? He saith they wanted a root in themselves; that is, they had not habitual dispositions of grace created in their hearts, that might be a root to the fruit of the spirit; for you know the root and fruits answer one another. Nay, if you ask me what that root is, the parable there explaineth it, a good and honest heart, a heart made holy; therefore our Saviour Christ saith, Matt. vii. 17, compared with Matt. xii. 33, 'make the tree good, and the fruit will be good,' but the tree must be good first. Therefore you may read in Matt. xxv., the foolish virgins had lamps, they had assistance from the Holy Ghost for present performances; but the wise virgins took oil in their vessels with their lamps. When themselves were asleep, and their lamps were out, yet they had a holy disposition, a spirit of grace; they had oil remaining in their hearts. I will not stand to open this; it is the law written in their hearts. I could shew you that the written law in the heart is not the Holy Ghost, for he is the writer, as it is 2 Cor. iii. 3. It is called the 'inner man' renewed daily. It is the Holy Ghost that strengtheneth the inner man; it is not the soul that is the inner man properly, but the inner man is that which is opposite to corruption; and he saith, Eph. iii. 16, 'they were strengthened with might by the Spirit in the inner man.'

Well, here therefore is an inner man to be wrought, to be created. Now if there be an inner man to be created, and holy and gracious dispositions, here is an almighty power to do it.

My brethren, you know that John Baptist was sanctified in the womb; he had not the Holy Ghost only working upon him in way of acts, for he did not actually believe and actually repent; children do not. If you take away habits of grace, you must take away all grace from infants, from that pure part of the Church as one calleth them, *purissima ecclesiæ*, for so they are.

Now for the creation of these habits of grace, all holy dispositions, there must be an almighty power go to do it. I will give you a scripture for it; it is 2 Peter i. 3, 'According as his divine power hath given unto us all things that pertain to life and godliness, through the knowledge of him that hath called us to glory and virtue: whereby are given unto us exceeding great and precious promises: that by these you might be partakers of the divine nature, having escaped the corruption that is in the world through lust.'

Here you see wherein the mighty power of God is seen in working upon a man's heart; it is in giving him all things belonging to life and godliness. The meaning is this, he furnisheth him with tools; it is called a workmanship. If you would set up a man's trade, you will furnish him with all instruments, with all utensils necessary to a trade; so here, it is a workmanship created, he hath all habits in him necessary, all things pertaining to life and godliness, and this a mighty power must do answerable to the creation. Yea, let me tell you this, that although the creation of the world and of a man's soul be a mighty work, yet to create grace, especially the second time, to fit a man for heaven, is a greater work, it is more than all the first creation; it is a transcendent thing. There is no work that God doth so great as this, especially this new creation of grace, for it fitteth a man for heaven. Therefore saith the Apostle, 2 Cor. v. 5, 'He that hath wrought us for the selfsame thing;' he hath wrought us for heaven. Adam's grace did not fit him for heaven. That which must carry a man into heaven is a grace, as the grace of faith is, higher than what Adam had in this world. He was not fitted for heaven by what he had; but we are 'made meet for the inheritance of the saints in light.' It must be a more transcendent grace than what Adam had; raised up to higher acts at least.

Though grace be but an accident in the soul of a man, yet it is more worth than all men's souls. It is not so in philosophy; that will tell you otherwise, that will tell you that a substance is better than an accident. But it is so in divinity. Saith he, James i. 18, 'Of his own will hath he begotten us, that we should be a kind of first-fruits of his creatures.' The meaning is, Hath he put grace into us? To what end hath he done it? He hath made us thereby, saith he, the choicest of all his creatures: as Christ is called the first-fruits of them that sleep, the choicest of them; so, saith he, we are made the choicest of all the creatures, having grace wrought in us, he having begotten us. Israel is called, Jer. ii. 3, the first-fruits of God, because he was the choicest of all the world; and though that word seemeth to be a diminishing, yet the truth is here it heighteneth it,—it is ἀπαρχή τινα, and it is of the creatures, κτισμάτων, in the plural number,—it makes a man most excellent of all creatures whatsoever. It is a good saying of Aquinas: 'The good of grace,' saith he, 'is a greater good than the good of the world; it excelleth all creatures.'

And therefore, my brethren, let me but add this: Of all creations, the creation of grace is the greatest next to that of glory; and, for my part, I must profess unto you, I think as great, for it is that which fitteth a man for glory; it is the beginning of glory. Of all creations it is the greatest, there are but two to be compared with it. I shall give you Scripture for it. I remember the last day I quoted the second to the Colossians, and the 10th, 11th, 12th verses, where it is said that faith is of the operation of God, and speaking of sanctification, he saith, it is a 'circumcision made without hands.' There are but two things in the Scripture that are said to be made without hands, and it is to shew the excellency of their creation above all creatures else, as you shall see by and by. It is a phrase used of the glory of heaven: 'We look for a house not made with hands,' saith he, 2 Cor. v. 1. It is used likewise of the framing the body of Christ, and uniting it to the Godhead: Heb. ix. 11, it is said to be 'a tabernacle made without hands.' And what is the meaning of 'made without hands' there? The Apostle himself explaineth it; 'that is,' we translate it, 'not of this building,' but in the Greek it is, 'not of this creation.' Adam's body was made and created; but, saith he, his was made with hands in comparison with the body of Christ, take it with all his graces. It is not of this creation, saith he, it is a higher creation, so the phrase 'made without hands' implieth; and it is used but of the body of Christ, and of the glory of heaven; and to create grace is as much.

To confirm this to you, that it is so taken; 'made without hands,' is not only in opposition to the work of man, but to the work of God too, and to the work of the first creation. I will give you a scripture for this,—compare but two scriptures together,—that the phrase is so taken, Acts vii. 49. There

Stephen doth quote Isa. lxvi. 1, to prove that God would not dwell in a temple made with hands; saith he, ver. 47, 'Solomon built him a house; howbeit the Most High dwelleth not in temples made with hands.' That is, you will say, in temples made with man's hands; but you shall see it is not made with God's hands by the first creation: 'As saith the prophet,' he quoteth the prophet for it, 'Heaven is my throne, and earth is my footstool: what house will ye build me, saith the Lord? Hath not my hands made all these things?' 'Not made with hands,' hath an opposition not only to the temple made with man's hands, but to the whole creation made with God's hands at first; for otherwise how cometh in this phrase, 'Hath not my hands made these things?' That is, these are but my own creatures; heaven and earth are an ordinary sort of creatures, and all the things in the world you see are but an ordinary sort of creatures; and these, saith he, my hands have made: but I will have something to dwell in made without hands; that is, it shall not be of this creation, it shall be of a higher creation. What is that? Look in Isaiah, 'With him will I dwell that is of a poor and a humble spirit, that trembleth at my word.' Doth God create anew? Doth he create grace in the heart? It is not of this creation heaven and earth were made of; it is of a higher creation: yet there was an almighty power in creating them; and yet, saith he, it is not of that creation; the making of heaven and earth is but an ordinary sort of work; but the making grace in a man's heart is a creating without hands in comparison of heaven and earth.

To use but a scripture more, and it is but a false testimony; when the false witnesses brought an accusation against Christ, they said, 'We heard this man say, I will destroy this temple made with hands, and within three days I will build another made without hands;' which though it were a false testimony, yet it may serve for this.

But I say the phrase is only used of us, and of the framing of the body of Christ, which are all transcendent and above the first creation. So that to work grace, to work the love of God in the soul, to put the least life of grace into the soul, is a new creation; it is a work made without hands.

My brethren, I will end all this in one word. You see here is a work of a new creation, that doth put into a man's heart that which is above all creations; you will ask me what that is?

I will answer you in a word: it is putting in all things belonging to life and godliness; so the apostle Peter expresseth it, 2 Peter i. 3. The vast ocean of the heart of man, let his heart be never so far wrought upon by self-love, never so much stirred, there is not the least drop of godliness in it, the least drop of the love of God in it, not the least aiming at God more than at a man's self, of having a man's affections stirred upon considerations drawn from God and not from a man's self. All such dispositions of heart cost more power to work them than the making of the frame of heaven and earth. 'All these things have my hands made;' this is made without hands; it is not of that creation, it will never go to hell with thee.

I should make this more manifest to you, it is a practical point this which I have handled, and I have stood the longer upon it to this end, not only to stand disputing with men of the greatness of the power of God in conversion, but to give you an account of it; and I have spoken the things we have known, and felt, and seen, and to go and dispute with reasons will never convince a man. I remember that ecclesiastical story. There was a man that was a philosopher, and he held out disputing against fourscore bishops that met together in a council, held them all work, answered all their reasons. There came but in a poor, mean man that gave him but an account of his faith, and of the work of God upon him. Saith he, While these bishops with all their words spake words, I had words to answer them, but this man's words came with power that I cannot resist. My brethren, to dispute what power goeth to the work of grace, men will put it off easily, but to give you an account of it, wherein it lies, and to do it out of the Word, and out of a man's heart, and the experience of the people of God; this oftentimes hath a power going along with it that no man can resist.

SERMON XXV.

And what is the exceeding greatness of his power to us-ward, who believe, according to the working of the might of his power, which he wrought in Christ, when he raised him from the dead, and set him at his own right hand in the heavenly places.—VER. 19, 20.

WE are handling of this, the 'exceeding greatness of the power' which God in this life putteth forth toward believers. I have proved at large that the power here extended toward believers is not to be restrained only to the resurrection at the latter day,—that he will raise up our mortal bodies, as he raised up Christ's body unto glory,—but that he speaks of the power of God in this life, as the same Apostle expresseth it, chap. iii. 20, 'according to the power which worketh in us,' that worketh at present; that is the power he here meaneth.

The power of God is either seen in the first work of turning us to God, and that is mainly and eminently in the Apostle's eye; for, saith he, in a coherence to these words in the second chapter, ver. 1, 'And you who were dead in sins and trespasses' (it must have a verb) 'hath he quickened,' speaking of their conversion; and so at the 5th and 6th verses you find it plainly expressed.

Or else this power is shewed toward us in continuing the work of faith; and it is hard to say in which more power is shewn and spent.

I have made entrance upon the first, as an instance and a demonstration enough of all the power that works afterward; for we are kept by the power of God unto salvation, so saith the Apostle.

The power that God sheweth, the 'exceeding greatness of his power,' I propounded for the method of handling it these two things—

The former, That there is an exceeding greatness of power shewn in it.

The second, That it holdeth proportion with that power which wrought in Jesus Christ when he was raised from the dead.

For the former, for the demonstration that an exceeding greatness of power is shewn in working faith, and in quickening us at our first conversion unto God; that power, I said, was shewn in two things—

Either, first, (I went by degrees in it,) in what he doth for a believer, though not upon a believer; the word εἰς ἡμᾶς will not only bear what is done *in him*, but what is done *for him*, and done *toward him*. As the throwing out of Satan out of a man, as I shewed out of Luke xii., is a work that is done *for* a Christian; but it is not a work so much *upon* him as upon Satan that is cast out. 'Now,' saith he, John xii. 31, 'is the judgment of this world, now shall the prince of this world be cast out;' he speaks, when the world should be converted to Christ, that conversion is called the judgment of the world; as in John xvi. 11, 'He shall convince the world of judgment,' that is, of that holiness and righteousness which they ought to take up and walk in; and he addeth, 'for the prince of this world is judged.' That this is done by a strong hand, I shewed in the last discourse: 'If I by the finger of God cast out devils.' The finger of God must go to it.

Then, secondly, if you come to the work that he doth in us, it ariseth not only to a greatness of power, but to an exceeding greatness of power. I paralleled it with the first creation, in which there was a greatness of power shewn; there was a making of something, yea, of all things out of nothing, and between nothing and the least thing there is an infinite disproportion. But when he comes to work upon the heart of a man that is dead by nature in sins and trespasses, he doth not only find nothing to work upon, but he findeth all things against him, so that his power is not simply drawn out in creating grace out of nothing, but in subduing and destroying of corruption; and so I shewed you the Scripture expresseth it. There is not only nothing to help or further, but there is all things to oppose. I shewed this at large in the last discourse, and how to subdue that which opposeth there is required a greatness of power.

But then, in the second place, there is an exceeding greatness of power, there is a doubling of power. There is not only a power to destroy what is opposite,—as I shewed both upon the understanding, the will, and affections,—but there is a putting in and a creating of a new principle, a contrary principle, maugre all the opposition that the heart of man makes against it. And so, because there is a doubling of power, there is an exceeding greatness of power cometh to be spent in this work.

In handling of this I shewed that the very creation itself of the new creature was of a higher kind, as the Scripture expresseth it, than the first creation was; because that grace is the most excellent of all God's creatures. James i. 18, speaking of the work of conversion, and of God's begetting us again, 'Of his own will,' saith he, 'he hath begotten us.' And what followeth? 'That we should be a kind of first-fruits;' but, as I shewed you in the last discourse, the eminent first-fruits of all his creatures, the choicest of all; for so doth the grace given by regeneration make a man.

And that it was a higher creation than the first, the putting in of new principles thus into the heart, I shewed you by the phrase that is used, Col. ii. 11, where he calleth the sanctification of a sinner the circumcising the heart, which, as in Deuteronomy, is that we may love God. He calleth this new work in us sinners a circumcision made without hands. I observed this upon it, that that phrase, 'made without hands,' is used only of three things, whereof grace or the new creature is one. It is used of that glory which God will put upon his saints and children hereafter in heaven; which all the world must acknowledge is a work transcending that first creation: 'We have a house not made with hands,' saith he, 2 Cor. v. 1. It is used, secondly, of that framing the body of Christ, the human nature of Christ, both body and soul, and uniting it to the Godhead; that human nature, so united, is called a tabernacle made without hands, Heb. ix. 11. And then, thirdly, here, in this Col. ii. 11, he calleth the sanctification of a sinner, and working holiness and grace in him, circumcising the heart to love God; he calleth it a circumcision made without hands.

You have the like, as you shall see by and by, in Isa. lxvi. 1, 2. Only observe first what followeth there in Heb. ix. 11, when he said that the body of Christ is a tabernacle made without hands. What doth he add by way of explication? He saith that it is 'not of this creation;' so the word in the original is; as if he should say, the tabernacle and the bodies of men, of ordinary men, though the one made by man and the other made by God, yet they are a more slight, a more ordinary kind of work. But, saith he, this body of Christ is made without hands; that is, it is not of this creation, it is not of the old creation, it is of a more transcendent creation. And so is grace.

I backed this interpretation with Acts vii. 48, compared with Isa. lxvi. 1, 2. In Acts vii. 48, Stephen proveth that God will not dwell in temples made with hands. Saith he, 'Howbeit the Most High dwelleth not in temples made with hands; as saith the prophet,'—now mark what the prophet saith,—'Heaven is my throne, and earth is my footstool; what house will ye build me, saith the Lord of hosts? or what is the place of my rest?' Therefore man's hands cannot make him a house good enough. Nay, heaven and earth, the old creation, is not good enough for him; for, saith he, 'Hath not my hands made all these things?' Well, what is it that he will have now to dwell in, that both exceedeth all the houses man can build, and exceedeth the house that himself hath made, if you take the material heavens, and the earth that is his footstool? Look in Isa. lxvi., you shall find that it is a gracious heart, that is a thing made without hands; that is not of this ordinary creation of God, for it is spoken in opposition to things made with hands. 'All these things,' saith he, 'hath my hand made;' he slighteth them so, these are but an ordinary sort of works, I will not dwell in them; 'but to him will I look that is poor and of a contrite spirit, and trembleth at my word,' so it is ver. 2.

So that now, to have the least spark of grace begun in a man's heart is a work made without hands, in comparison. It is of a higher kind of work than all the works of men and angels—yea, than the works of the first creation. These things hath mine hand made; but I will dwell in a circumcised heart made without hands; that is not of this creation, that is of a higher creation than all this.—And so much for the general, That the putting in of grace into the heart is a matter of more transcendent power than the first creation was.

Now, my brethren, as I shewed you in particulars the power of God in destroying what opposeth;—I went over the understanding, shewed what opposeth there, what a mighty power went to destroy the strongholds there; I went over the will and affections, shewed you what opposeth there likewise—self-love, and all inordinate affections and love of pleasures, and the like;—as I did this in the negative part, in the destructive part, so I will do the same also in this positive part. And I will shew you, this is the scope, that for God to work grace in your understandings, to know things aright, which you think is most easy, there is an exceeding greatness of power going to it, no less than went to the first creation; yea, much more; it is not of this creation: so likewise to put in holy principles into your will and affections. Therefore, all that goeth to frame a Christian from first to last must needs be an exceeding greatness of power. I am forced thus to repeat things, that I may clear my method as I go along.

And, first, *What God doth upon your understandings when he doth convert you.* Why, it requireth an exceeding greatness of power, though you little think it, to believe: 'Who believe,' saith the Apostle, 'according to the working of his mighty power.' I will not run over all things that may be said of believing, but I will speak of spiritual knowledge, to know things spiritually and aright as Christians do, that it requireth an exceeding greatness of power to work it. I shall demonstrate this unto you, in the first place, in a more general way; and, secondly, more particularly by two things.

In the first place, *in the general.* For to make a soul to take a thing upon God's bare authority, and therefore to believe it, is as great a work as any God doth; and it requireth as much power,—mark what I shall say to you,—it requireth as much power to work faith in the heart to believe God will do such a thing, as it is for God to do it.

For instance, to explain myself,—though I shall not follow my instance in the opening of it, but for illustration's sake,—this is my meaning: at the latter day, God will raise up all our bodies from the dust to glory. To believe this spiritually and aright, and to work your hearts to believe it, requireth as much power as for God to do it, when he cometh to do it. So you have my meaning.

I shall give you a place of Scripture for it, and it is in Mark ix. 21, 22. There is a poor man cometh to Christ to have a miracle done for him; what doth he say to Christ? If thou canst do anything, saith he, wilt thou heal my son, and throw the devil out of him? 'If thou canst do anything;' so he saith to Christ. Then mark what Christ saith to him: 'Jesus said unto him, If thou canst believe, all things are possible to him that believeth.' To open these words a little. You see when the man said, If thou canst do anything, help my child; saith Christ again, If thou canst believe, all things are possible. He makes it of equal possibility for him to do the thing, and for the man to believe. It was as hard a matter for the man to believe this, and required as much power to work faith in him, as it was for Christ to effect it. Therefore our Saviour addeth, 'To him that believeth, all things are possible,' for faith commandeth all the power in God; as if he should say, There is as great an infinity of power required to work faith in thee to believe it, it is all one, and to do the thing. So far as anything is possible, so far it is credible, it is believable.

Let me put you a supposition. If God should reveal by me infallibly, as he did speak by the prophets and apostles, that he would make a new world to-morrow, it were as hard a thing for God to work this faith in you, as for him to make this world; he might make this world upon the same rate as he would work this faith in your hearts. To believe a thing upon divine authority doth require an omnipotent power. To believe things upon slight grounds, that is easy; 'The fool believeth everything,' saith Solomon in the Proverbs; but to believe this in earnest is a work of an almighty power.

And so much in general, that the power of God in doing anything for us is but proportionable to the working of faith in us that he will do it, or that he is able to do it; yet you think this is easy, and yet you see what the Scripture saith.

To come now *particularly* to shew you what a mighty power goeth to work faith and spiritual knowledge; and it is but to believe the thing, not to believe that it is yours; but to believe the thing in a spiritual manner requireth an exceeding greatness of power. I shall shew you it by two things:—

The first is, to work *a principle of faith.* You know I told you in the last discourse that this new creation, much of the power of it was spent in working habits as we call them,—that is, inward abilities,—to work a formal principle, such as is to work sight in a blind eye. You know there is the act of seeing, or seeing itself, and there is a principle of seeing, a power to see; a framing of an eye and of a soul to see, as I may so express it, or of a faculty of seeing. Now in the understanding, to understand things spiritually and aright, there must be an almighty power go to it, to put a new principle in you, to make you capable to believe and know spiritual things.

I remember in the last discourse, when I shewed what expressions the Holy Ghost useth to express the work of conversion, I quoted Rom. xii. 2, where it is called a transformation, an altering the form of the mind, the shape of the mind; it is a metamorphosis, as I then expressed it, and indeed the word is so in the Greek. Now the transformation there, what is it applied unto? It is applied unto the understanding of a man, it is but the changing of the understanding that that word is used of. You think that to believe and to know spiritual things is no great matter, and that all the difficulty lies in doing of them, and in being affected with them. But the Apostle saith plainly, that you may know things aright, that you may approve of them in a spiritual way, of their goodness and excellencies; you must be metamorphosed, saith he, in your minds, you must have a new form come in to your understanding; so the word signifieth.

He useth two words there: 'Be not conformed to the world,' saith he; and the word he useth for that is *συσχηματίζεσθαι*; it signifieth an outward form, an artificial form; for the world is but an empty show, an empty shape, as the Apostle calleth it: 'The fashion of the world passeth' away; it is the same word. But when he speaks of the other, the transformation of the understanding, the word is *μεταμορφοῦσθαι*; it signifieth an inward cause, such as the soul is to the body, a natural form, not an artificial; an inward one, not an outward one.

So that now, for a man to approve of spiritual things in a spiritual manner, look as if he would make a beast understand as a man, you must bring a new soul, a new form: so if you will make an unregenerate man understand spiritual things aright, you must bring a new form, a new soul, as it were, into his understanding. The Apostle expresseth it, 1 John v. 20, 'He hath given us an understanding that we may know him:' not but the same for substance, the same natural power of understanding, is in a wicked man and in a godly man; but there is a new ability, a new principle, a new quality put in that fits him to understand spiritual things, which the other cannot do.

To illustrate this further unto you, and to shew you that to work this requireth no less power than in the creation. Look first into 1 Cor. ii. 14. I shall tell you to what purpose I quote that by and by. 'The natural man,' saith he, 'receiveth not the things of the Spirit of God, neither can he know them, because they are spiritually discerned; but he that is spiritual judgeth all things, yet he himself is judged of no man.' To open these words: by a natural man he meaneth a man that is not regenerate, that is not born again, for he doth oppose him to a spiritual man; a man that hath no other principles in him in respect of grace than what he brought into the world; he hath the same natural understanding he had without any spiritualness put upon it by the Holy Ghost. This is a natural man. Now, saith he, this man receiveth not the things of the Spirit of God; nay, saith he, he cannot know them. But he that is spiritual is both able to receive them, and he can know them; so the opposition runneth. And all cometh to this, that there must be a new principle put into the understanding of a man; not only a new light come in, but a new principle, if you would have this man understand spiritual things aright. And that is the scope I quote this place for—that the understanding must be altered, a new principle must be put into it, a new habit as we call it. All the expressions do carry it to that sense.

For, first, he saith, otherwise, if he be not made spiritual he cannot receive spiritual things; that is, he wants a capacity. It is such a phrase, as if you would speak to a deaf man, you will say he cannot receive what you say, for he wanteth a faculty of hearing. If you bring a blind man into the sun, he cannot receive the light of it, for he wants a natural faculty so to do. He expresseth it in a way of nature; he is not capable of it, which argueth, I say, a want of a principle whereby to do it.

And not only so, but he saith in the following words, 'he cannot know them,' he wants a δύναμις, a power; οὐ δύναται γνῶναι, a *potentia*, as the philosopher calleth it; for the Apostle speaks suitably here to philosophical principles; that, as we say in philosophy, nothing can work but it must have a principle of working, a man cannot see without the faculty of seeing: so this man wants a faculty of knowing spiritual things, therefore he cannot know them.

Thirdly, the reason he giveth evidenceth this; for what is the reason why a natural man cannot know them? Because, saith he, they are spiritually discerned. He speaks just like our school-men, for we use to express in a way of distinction, in a spiritual manner, that is, spiritually. The meaning is, to see it in its own spiritual nature, abstracted from all considerations besides, so he cannot see it; that is the meaning of this, 'he cannot discern it spiritually.' If he would know it aright, he must know it as it is in itself; now so he hath not a principle suited and fitted to this object as it is spiritual in itself, he may know it otherwise in other considerations, but take it as it is spiritual and he cannot know it.

As, for example, it is as if he should say, the mind of a man, or the eye of a man rather, cannot see an angel. Why? For an angel is spiritually discerned. One angel can see another; but take an angel merely as he is a spirit, let him not take a shape, take him in his spiritual nature, and the eye of man cannot see him. Why? For he is a spirit, and he must be discerned spiritually. Just so it is here. Take spiritual things in their own nature, and he wants a faculty, a spiritual principle, to see them with, to know them with.

Therefore, in the fourth place, which is a fourth reason why that the Apostle here would have a spiritual, a new principle to go to help a man to see spiritual things spiritually; this is a fourth reason, in that he calleth him that discerneth, a spiritual man. 'He that is spiritual,' saith he, 'discerneth all things.' What doth he mean by a spiritual man? You have it interpreted John iii. 6, 'That which is born of the Spirit is spirit.' What is it that is born of the Spirit? It is not an act of knowing, but it is a principle of knowledge; for always that which cometh by birth is nature, it is natural dispositions that are derived to us by our birth; therefore we use to say of what is a man's disposition, he hath it by nature. Therefore now his meaning is this: he is a spiritual man, he is regenerate, he hath a new understanding, a new principle put into him, a quickness, a disposition of understanding, which a carnal man wants, and therefore he is not fitted to know spiritual things as he is. You shall find in 1 Cor. xv. 44, that the Apostle saith, 'There is a natural body, and there is a spiritual body;' they are the same terms in the Greek that are used here, a natural man, and a spiritual man. Now by spiritual body there, what is meant? Spiritual endowments; as to shine like the sun, to have agility and nimbleness to move as an angel, to have all such spiritual endowments put upon it; herein lieth the spiritualness of the body, in opposition to this natural body of ours. So a spiritual understanding lieth in having new endowments, which enableth a man to know spiritual things in such a manner as no natural man in the world can know them.

Well then, this is the scope of this place, and so I will leave it: That if you desire to know spiritual things aright, you must have as great a change wrought in your minds to make them spiritual, as your bodies one day shall have to make them spiritual at the resurrection; new qualities and endowments put upon your understandings, new forms, so the Apostle expresseth it—to be 'transformed in the renewing of your minds to know him'—in that 12th of the Romans.

Now then, to gather up this first head, this must necessarily be done by a creation, no less power than went to create at first. Nay, it is not of this creation neither.

To make that plain to you, that a man cannot know spiritual things, cannot have this principle of knowledge unless he be made a new creature; it must be a creation that must do it. For this I do quote 2 Cor. v. 16, 17. Read what the Apostle saith there; he speaks of the different knowledge he had when he was an unregenerate man, and a regenerate man. See how he expresseth it. 'Wherefore,' saith he, 'henceforth,' ἀπὸ τοῦ νῦν, that is, hence from the time of my conversion, for indeed a Christian reckoneth his life from his conversion; 'Wherefore henceforth,'—that is, from the time of my conversion,—'know we no man after the flesh; yea, though we have known Christ after the flesh, from henceforth know we him no more.' He speaks of knowledge, you see, and of such a knowledge as he had wrought in him from the time and instant of his conversion, differing from that before.

Before, I knew men after the flesh. That phrase, 'after the flesh,' referreth both to the things known; that is, I valued all men and things as they were in the flesh: if I looked upon a man that was rich and honourable, I valued him by his riches and honours, and what he was in fleshly things, by this I did set my esteem upon men, and accordingly upon things also; and this was all the understanding I had both of things and persons. Or the phrase referreth unto his manner of knowing, or notes out the principle by which he knew them; knew them after the flesh, saith he,—that is, from carnal principles; my understanding was nothing but flesh; 'that which is born of the flesh is flesh.' And so was my understanding, like the things I valued, suited to them; as the things were fleshly, so I valued them as such, by reason of my fleshly understanding: and so the Apostle useth the phrase, Rom. viii. 5, 'They that are after the flesh mind the things of the flesh;' that is, the disposition of the mind, and the things, are suited each to other, as a natural object and the faculty, as the eye in the body and corporeal objects. A man that is nothing but of a fleshly understanding, all his delight, and knowledge, and approbation of things is according to the flesh. As on the contrary, in the same place, he that is 'after the Spirit,' he savoureth and knoweth the 'things that are after the Spirit;' valueth them according to what they are in God's Book, at a spiritual rate.

Now, saith he, when I was thus carnal, I knew all things thus after the flesh; I counted myself, saith he in Phil. iii. 5, 6, to have these and these privileges; I was a Benjamite, a Hebrew, touching the law a Pharisee, concerning the righteousness which is in the law, blameless. He was a scholar, and profited more than his equals; and these things he valued himself and others by. And the truth is, a carnal man, take him practically, and thus he knoweth and esteemeth of things. Yea, saith he, I knew Christ after the flesh. It is the highest instance that can be. One would think, that if he should know anything spiritually, he should know Christ spiritually, if he knew him at all; for there is no carnal comeliness in him to desire him; that object is so spiritual as is not capable of fleshly knowledge. Yes, saith he, I knew Christ after the flesh; for the truth is, when he was a Pharisee, he thought the Messiah would have been a great king, and should have come in pomp and state to deliver his nation, as you know the opinion of the Jews was, Luke xvii. 20, 'The kingdom of God cometh not with observation,' or with pomp, for so good interpreters render it, and the opposition in the 21st verse makes for it: 'The kingdom of God is within you,' it is spiritual. Now, as the rest of the Jews, so I valued the Messiah thus, and I thought thus carnally of him; but, saith he, when I came to be converted, from henceforth, from the time I was converted, I knew him so no more. I saw then the Messiah to be such a one as the 14th and 15th verses hath described him; not one that should come with pomp, but one that should be crucified, and die, and rise again, and thereby take away our sins, for so in the 14th verse he is described, which is the occasion of this speech. This was the Messiah I began to know when I was converted, and I valued him according to pardon of sin and working grace in me. He came to know this Messiah spiritually, and after another manner.

Well now, to draw up to that I aim at: how came the Apostle, or what was the reason the Apostle, after his conversion, should have this change in his knowledge, that before he should know all things after the flesh, and now he knoweth all things in another manner?

Read the next words, 'Therefore,' or, as the word ὥστε will bear, 'Therefore, because,' (so Piscator renders it, and says it is an illative particle put for a rational, or the reason of what went before, 'wherefore', or 'because,') 'he that is in Christ is a new creature: old things are passed away; behold, all things are become new.' As if he should have said, Will you have the reason why that I know nothing any more after the flesh; no, not even Christ himself? It is because I am a new creature, that is the reason of it. I have had a new principle wrought in my understanding, by which all my thoughts are turned; all my former thoughts perish, as a man's doth when he dieth. I do not set a value upon men for honour and riches, and for their comforts in this life. I set that value once upon Christ himself, and judged of him; but now I judge of men and things in a spiritual way, according to what they are in holiness and the world to come. I judge by God's books, and not what they are in men's books or in the world's books. You see that which caused this was a new creation. 'Old things are passed away; behold, all things are become new.'

So that for a man to have true spiritual knowledge, which yet men are apt in their thoughts to slight, and think to be the least of all things to be wrought, it must have no less power than what went to the creation, it must have the exceeding greatness of the power of God to go to it.—So much for the first particular, the work on the understanding.

Now then, secondly, when this new creature is wrought,—that is, when a man hath a new eye given him,—there must be another creation before a man will know anything actually, before he will see it. This new creation, this new understanding gives him a new eye, a capacity indeed which a natural man hath not; the other is blind, he hath an eye. But still his eye will not help him to see; this new understanding will not see, except God doth somewhat more, it will not see aright and spiritually. You will ask, what is it that is further required?

As great a thing as the former. It is this: it is for the Holy Ghost to create in your understandings a new image of things, a new *species* or representation of things, such as never any carnal man in this world had; and this must go to spiritual knowledge, or you will never know things aright; you all come easily by it, but this power goeth to work it. It is the point in hand. You shall find, too, that an act of faith is expressed by an act of sight: 'He that seeth the Son, and believeth on him,' that is the expression of Christ, John vi. 40. There is such a sight of God and of Christ, by the understanding of a man renewed, when he doth know them, when his mind works upon them spiritually,—there is such a sight wrought in his mind of them as all the men in the world have not, nor are any way capable of. If all the angels in heaven—mark what I say—should go and describe God and Christ upon their own knowledge, and all their excellences; they saw Christ upon earth, they see him now he is heaven; and if a man should go and quicken up his understanding and natural parts, yea, and have the utmost assistance of the Holy Ghost, so as not to renew his understanding; all these will but raise up a shadow of Christ, in comparison of what a godly man hath of him in his heart. It will be but a φαινόμενον, it will be but as we call a false sun. You know there are sometimes more suns than one appear in the clouds; look what that is in comparison of the true sun, such will all that knowledge be that a man hath that is merely a natural man. Take a man in nature, raised never so high, all his knowledge is but a false Sun of righteousness in comparison of what a godly man seeth; because the Holy Ghost createth in him, stampeth upon his mind another manner of image and representation of him, than he doth in the heart of the most enlightened men in the world.

To open this unto you a little.

I told you even now of raising up a false sun, and seeing the true sun; they are like you know, but they are mighty vast, wide, different things. Saith the Apostle, Eph. iv. 21, when he exhorteth them to put off the old man, and to put on the new: 'If so be,' saith he, ver. 20, 'that ye have heard him, and have been taught by him, as the truth is in Jesus: that ye put off concerning the former conversation the old man,' &c. These words, 'If so be ye have heard him, and have been taught by him, as the truth is in Jesus,' are a correction of himself in what he said before. All Christians, saith he, are taught not to walk as the Gentiles walk; 'Ye have not so learned Christ;' but yet, because many Christians do learn Christ, and know Christ, and yet do otherwise, he correcteth himself,—'If so be,' saith he, 'ye have heard, and have been taught by him, as the truth is in Jesus.' If you have seen him in truth, saith he, if you have seen the true Jesus as he is in himself, if you have seen spiritual Jesus spiritually; then, saith he, it will have this fruit upon you, that ye will put off the old man, and put on the new; it is impossible it should be otherwise.

The thing I gather from hence is this: the Apostle, you see, distinguisheth the knowledge of Christians; all have learned Christ in the outward learning of him; but there is, saith he, a learning of him in the mind, 'as the truth is in Jesus.' There is a false knowledge, a knowledge of a false Jesus, but of an appearance of him, a shadow of him, which all carnal men that live under the preaching of the gospel have; but if you have seen Jesus in truth, this followeth upon it, you will put off the old man, and put on the new. So that from hence it is evident that there is such a knowledge of Christ, which a man is taught, and hath wrought in his heart by the Holy Ghost, such an image and representation of him which is in truth, and in comparison of which other knowledge is a false knowledge.

My brethren, shall I shew you the difference wherein this lieth?

All the world yieldeth that the difference of men's knowledges ariseth from the different image or picture of things, if you will so call it, which the mind takes in. That you will easily grant. If you take two men, and the one sees the picture of a man, and the other sees the man himself, he that hath seen the man himself hath such a knowledge of him as he that hath seen but the picture hath not, nor cannot have, except he see the man himself. Why? Because there is a different image begotten in the mind and fancy of him that hath seen the man, and him that hath only seen the picture. Hence ariseth different knowledges.

Here then is the thing I infer: that the Holy Ghost, when he reneweth the understanding of a man, doth beget in him by his almighty power another representation of Christ and of God, and of all spiritual things in their spiritual nature; whereas other men have but the pictures of them, they do not know them as the truth is in Jesus, as I said even now.

All knowledge is either *per species acceptas à rebus*, when we take the images off from the things themselves; as when we see a man himself, or when I take the image of him at second-hand from something that representeth him. Now herein lieth the difference of the knowledge of a godly man and others, that the Holy Ghost createth *proprias species*, a proper likeness and representation of spiritual things, of God and Christ; whereas all men else know him at second-hand, they hear of him, and have been taught by him, but not as the truth is in Jesus.

Hence is that phrase of the Apostle in 1 Cor. ii. 9. I take it, that which I am now handling openeth that phrase, and is pertinent to the meaning of it. Saith he, 'Eye hath not seen, nor ear heard, neither hath it entered into the heart of man'—that is, a natural man—'to conceive the things which God hath prepared for them that love him; but God hath revealed them unto us by his Spirit.' I plainly take the meaning to be this. There are such revelations, so the Apostle here calleth them, such images, such representations of spiritual things begotten in a godly man's heart, as never entered into the heart of any carnal man in the world, and that is the reason why he cannot know them. Now Jesus Christ, you know, is absent; 'in whom, though we have not seen,' saith he, 'we believe;' he is in heaven. And God is absent; he is a thing not seen: you hear his word and see his works; but beyond all these, the Holy Ghost begetteth in your minds an image of God and Christ, makes him real to you, makes him subsist; makes God that is absent, present, Christ that is absent, present. Therefore it is called *a sight*, so the Scripture expresseth it. 'He that seeth the Son, and believeth on him;' therefore, Heb. xi. 1, where there is a description of faith, he calleth it 'the substance of things hoped for;' they have a substantial image of the things begotten in them. It is not a mere notion.

Now, my brethren, this is the highest art, the greatest power—consider what I say—to beget a real and substantial notion and image of God, and of Christ, and of any spiritual thing, in the mind and heart of a believer, and is more than to create a world. Why? The excellency of any creature lies in this, in its ability to represent God to a man; therein lay the excellency of the creation at first, that it declareth God and his glory, and sheweth forth his handiwork, as the Psalmist saith.

Now the image that the Holy Ghost begetteth in a man's heart of himself, of God and Christ, and of all spiritual things, doth more lively represent God to a man than all the Scripture, simply, or than all the works of God, yea, than it was done to Adam. For, saith he, 'the eye hath not seen, neither hath the ear heard, nor hath it entered into the heart of man from the beginning of the world,' (so it is in Isa. lxiv. 4,) no, not into the heart of Adam himself.

This all divines acknowledge, that faith is a knowledge of God *in se*, not of God by his works at second-hand, but a knowledge of God in himself, as when you know the sun by a beam of himself; and this is the knowledge that the Holy Ghost works, and therefore there is required as much to it and more, than to create a world.

To give you a scripture for this, and that pertinent and proper to the thing in hand. It is in 2 Cor. iv. 6. The Apostle there compareth the spiritual knowledge which was in his own heart, and which by his ministry the Holy Ghost had begotten in the heart of others, he compareth the very knowledge of it to no less than the creating light out of darkness at first. Read the scripture: 'For God,' saith he, 'who commanded the light to shine out of darkness, hath shined in our hearts, to give the light of the knowledge of the glory of God in the face of Jesus Christ.' He compareth, I say, the knowledge which God wrought in his own heart being converted, and which by his means, being an apostle, was begotten in the heart of others, to that great work of creating light out of darkness. Saith he, the God, the same God that commanded light to shine out of darkness, the same God hath caused us to have the knowledge of God; and, mark it, why doth he add, 'in the face of Jesus Christ?' The word in the original is, 'in the person of Jesus Christ,' ἐν τῷ προσώπῳ. It is a personal knowledge, it is a real knowledge of God; that knowledge I have described all this while, it is not a notional knowledge, it is the knowledge of his person brought down into our hearts by the Holy Ghost, which is an artifice that transcendeth the power of any creature; it is peculiar to the Holy Ghost to give a subsistence of Christ to a man's soul.

And that the Apostle speaks here of a mighty power that works this knowledge is evident in the next words; for going on in the next verse, he saith, 'We have this treasure in earthen vessels.' That we should have such a knowledge in us, and be able to convey it to others, it is a treasure indeed this gift, and it is in earthen vesssels. To what end? 'That the excellency of power'—hyperbole—'that the greatness of the power may be of God,' may be ascribed to him that thus createth by an almighty power the light of the knowledge of the person of Christ in the heart of a man.

So that now you see, that the working of knowledge,—I do not tell you of all the great difficulties, for to draw a man to believe in Christ, and to lay hold on Christ, and to love Christ, all which require the same power; but I speak simply of spiritual knowledge, to believe the things themselves in a true, real, substantial manner,—this is from an almighty power. 'That ye may know,' saith he, 'what is the exceeding greatness of his power to us-ward, who believe, according to the working of his mighty power.' To work faith in the very understanding of a man, all this is required.—So much now for the first part: that to believe, to have spiritual knowledge wrought in a man, requireth exceeding greatness of power. I could not have made this plain under less time than what I have now spent upon it, and faith, you see, is in the text; for it is *to us-ward who believe;* I have therefore a little larger insisted upon it.

I come now, in the second place, to *the will* of a man; I will be brief in it; and that which is put in there too it requireth an exceeding greatness of power to make that holy, to make a man conformable to the things he knoweth. I will instance but in one thing:—

That the will of man should be raised up to aim at God's glory in all that he doth, and to make God the chiefest good, it must be an almighty power that must put this principle into a man's heart, a higher power than simply was in the first creation, to do it as believers are enabled to do it. Go, take all creatures that were made by God's almighty power; take men, take beasts; they have nothing of this in them at all, not of holiness to aim at the glory of God; take nature simply considered in itself, as man hath it now, there is no such thing in him, nor in all the creatures besides man; but angels that had it created in them at first after the image of God that created them, indeed they had it, and Adam had it so too. To put therefore such a principle as this is into a man, that his spirit shall love God naturally as now he loveth himself, and subordinate himself unto God,—and herein lieth holiness,—my brethren, this is the greatest work in the world.

You may easily know the greatness of the work from the excellency of the thing. This putteth down all creatures; it makes a man differ from other men, as a man doth from a beast. A man hath three lives that he liveth: the life of a plant, the life of a beast, and the life of reason; here is a fourth life, to aim at the glory of God. It is called 'the light of life,' John viii. 12.

My brethren, this is bringing in a new form indeed, a new soul indeed, to put this principle into a man's heart; this is transformation indeed. Why? It bringeth a new end into a man's heart; and *idem est finis in moralibus, quod forma in naturalibus*, and so *quod anima nova;* that is, what the form is to natural things,—that is, what the soul is unto a man's body,—that is a man's end to his soul when he is converted. It is the best definition I ever heard of conversion, that it is the change of a man's utmost end, and upon that a man's soul is turned to God. A man was before for himself, and so long as himself is his end, let him have never so many changes, yet still he turneth upon himself. Now, do but put holiness into him, to aim at God in all things, it changeth the whole man presently; it changeth all his course, all his affections, everything in him. It is a new loadstone, it will make him sail after another compass. Now, to work this, to make a man's heart to be for God as he is naturally for himself, it requireth a mighty power of God to do it. Saith the Apostle in 2 Peter i. 3, 'According as his divine power hath given to us all things that pertain to life and godliness.' Hast thou any godliness in thy heart? a principle of godliness to aim at God? for that properly is godliness, to set him up. It must be a mighty power that must do it; according, saith he, to his divine power; it is a power that only belongeth to God to do this.

Aquinas saith well, *elevat hominem,* saith he; when a man hath grace to aim at God, it raiseth a man up above all the being and power of nature. Therefore it is more than all the creation of nature simply considered; it is called, therefore, a 'divine nature.'

My brethren, you may know the great power that goeth to work this from the excellency of it; for the more excellent a thing is in being, certainly the more power goeth to work it. This excelleth all beings, raiseth a man beyond all beings; for it raiseth a man up *to live the life of God.* A man liveth the life of a beast when he liveth in pleasures; of a man, when he liveth in honour and in things the reason is capable of; but all this while he is a stranger to the life of God. But to add to the life of a beast the life of reason, and to the life of reason the life of God, you will say that there must be an exceeding greatness of power to do this. To make a man to aim at God and his glory, is more than to make a man, or beast, or stocks, or stones, or worlds. Saith the apostle James, chap. i. 17, 18, 'Every good gift and every perfect gift is from above, and cometh down from the Father of lights.' Ἄνωθέν ἐστι, it is from above, wholly from above; those gifts that are good, κατ' ἐξοχὴν, by way of eminency, are wholly from above, they are wholly by a divine power. He speaks of grace, read the words after: 'he hath begotten us again according to his will, that we should be the first-fruits.' And he speaks of grace before, as well as in the words after; it is a thing wholly from above, no power can do it. I told you before that the phrase, 'made without hands,' noteth out a transcendency of working; it is applied to Christ's body, and to the glory of heaven. Well, this phrase, ἄνωθέν, from above, is applied to none but Christ, and it is to argue the excellency of Christ above all others. Read John iii. 31. When John would prove Christ to be greater not only than himself, but greater than all, what saith he? 'He that cometh from above,' saith he—he useth the same phrase that the Apostle doth here of grace—'is greater than all;' so here, 'Every good gift is from above,' it is wholly divine, and cometh from the Father of lights. For a man to aim thus at God, I say it cometh wholly from him.

I will shut up this point only with this. Do but now look into your hearts; have you any of this perfect gift that is thus wholly from above, and draweth you up to above, to aim at God more than yourselves, and that that steereth your course? My brethren, to be thus turned to God is to have a new end, it throweth the soul upon new hinges, it toucheth the soul as a loadstone that toucheth the knife, draweth it toward God in everything. There is nothing of it in nature, no disposition of it, there is nothing of it in all the creature. Go, take man as simply considered, as reasonable; and take beasts, and all this inferior world, there is no such thing. There is a world indeed, a being, where there are those that aim at God. But take this world, all the creatures, sun, and moon, and stars, take all the sons of men, they have not such a principle as this. It is a higher principle than reason itself, it is the life of God; the other is but the life of reason, or the life of beasts. Do but examine now whether you have any such thing in you, if you would know whether the exceeding greatness of his power hath wrought in your hearts or no.

I may compare a man that is turning to God to one that is going with full sail to such a country or port, and hath taken in lading fitting and suitable to that country, and he hath a compass to guide him thither; he hath the wind fair for him. By nature a man loadeth himself with a world of vanities; he is shipped for this world, and that is it which his eye aimeth at, to make himself happy in the world in some thing or other. Now, my brethren, God meets with him by the way, takes him off from all his ends that were for himself, putteth in a new pilot, setteth up a new loadstar, giveth him a new compass, sendeth his blessed Spirit into his heart, that as a wind bloweth him clean another way; all the lading he hath by nature he cannot vent any of those commodities, he throweth them all overboard. Thus God dealeth with a man when he turneth him.

Paul was a ship richly laden. I was a scholar, saith he, and profited in the Jewish language more than all my teachers; I had much to boast of. God comes, and he throweth them all overboard; 'I count all things but as dross and dung in comparison of the knowledge of Christ,' &c. What made Paul do this? God had touched his heart with this loadstone, to the direction of which all must be conformed. He turneth out all old commodities, putteth in a new rudder, a new pilot, a new compass; and now, saith he, I must needs aim at God's glory in all things. My brethren, herein lieth the work of conversion; wherein lieth it else? Then it lieth in this, or it lieth in nothing. Now to work such a work as this in a man, to touch a man's heart thus, is as much as to throw the earth off its centre. Take the earth, if it move as some suppose it doth, if it move still upon its centre, this is no great matter; but if you should see the earth go off his centre, and fix itself in the same sphere with the sun, and go along with the same pace and with the same motion, you would think an almighty power must go to do all this. This God doth. A man moveth himself; move him which way you will, if you will move him to God, as self-love will sometimes do, yet still he is upon his own centre, all is for himself. God cometh and turns him off his own hinges, takes him from his own bottom, placeth him in the same sphere with himself, makes him aim at him in all things. This is holiness; and to put this principle into a man's heart, nothing but the almighty power of God can do it. It is above all the creation.

SERMON XXVI.

And what is the exceeding greatness of his power to us-ward, who believe according to the working of his mighty power, &c.—VER. 19, 20.

CONCERNING the working of his power to us that believe, here mentioned, I have shewn already that, first, it is not to be restrained only to the raising up of believers at the latter day. Nor, secondly, only to the power of the Spirit of God keeping us unto that day, as it is in Peter; 'kept by the power of God to salvation.' But that, thirdly, and more eminently, the power he prayeth here they might know was that power which wrought in them when first they were turned and converted unto God; for so he explaineth himself in the 2d chapter, from the 1st verse to the 11th. Here he speaks of the power that raised up Jesus Christ from death to glory, from the 20th verse of this chapter to the end; he saith, the same power that wrought in Christ in raising him up, works in us. And then, in the 2d chapter, he makes up the comparison; 'And ye,' saith he, 'who were dead in sins and trespasses;' there he describeth their death, and, when he hath done, speaks of their quickening and being raised up together with Christ. And indeed, as in the 2d chapter, from the 1st verse to the 11th, he sheweth the greatness of the work of grace and describeth it; so here he sheweth the greatness of the power that goes to work it, which that they may be thankful for, as he provoked them thereunto by his own example, 'I cease not to give thanks for you,' saith he, ver. 16; so he prayeth that they may know it.

In opening of this I have already done two things. I have first shewn that this is the intention of the Apostle in this place,—that I did at large,—namely, to speak of the power of God in quickening and converting men.

In the second place, I came to shew you what work it is that doth draw forth so great a power as here is spoken.

I shewed this two ways:—

First, *by subduing the old frame of heart,* which is enmity to God. In the *understanding,* casting down strongholds, as in 2 Cor. x. 4. In the *will,* deposing of self-love from that predominancy and regency, killing the great king, indeed the great devil, that is in all men's hearts. Not to root it out, but to depose it from being the predominant principle; which, when God cometh to do, all in a man is up in arms against him.

Secondly, *by mortifying all lusts,* giving them a death's wound, by destroying in part the body of sin, the love of pleasures, or whatsoever else is nearest or dearest to a man, as something or other is. That there is an almighty power in all this I have shewn at large.

I shewed, in the second place, besides the negative works which God destroyeth, what it is he putteth into the heart instead of this—new principles and habitual dispositions, which must be at least created. Not only old things pass away, but all things become new, as the Apostle saith.

Concerning this, I shewed in the last discourse that in the understanding there must be a new spiritual disposition, to make that capable of spiritual things in their spiritual nature; else a man cannot know them spiritually, as the Apostle saith, 1 Cor. ii. 14, 15. And this will require no less than a creation, for which I quoted 2 Cor. v. 16, 17.

Secondly, in the will; to put in a new and great principle, to put a new spring into the watch, that shall turn all the wheels another way naturally; to put in love to God. And, my brethren, God will be loved more than yourselves, or he will not be loved at all. To touch the heart with this is more than to create heaven and earth. This I shewed, and gave you proof for it.

So, now, you see what it is in the work of conversion that doth draw out this exceeding greatness of his power. Two things, then, are despatched. First, to clear it, that it is the meaning of the place. And then, secondly, what it is that draweth forth the almighty power.

There is a *third* thing, and that is this, *What it is that occasioned this great controversy and mistake, that there is not so great a power as this spoken of that goes to the converting of men.* That is the third thing, I say, which yet remaineth to be spoken to, which some have denied—that there is so great a power as this needful to conversion. I do not say what occasioneth the mistake of their interpretation of this place, that is not my meaning; but of the thing that doth misguide men in interpreting this place. There would never have been so great a stir concerning the manner of conversion, and the work of it, and about the power of God put forth in it, had not there been such workings upon the hearts of men as have less power than this here spoken of.

I have, ever since I discerned into matters of this nature, judged the occasion of the mistake in this controversy, as likewise in that other of falling away from grace, that the ground of the mistake in both hath been this, to speak plainly, that there are *certain inferior and lower sorts of works of the Holy Ghost upon men's hearts,* movings of the Spirit of God upon men's hearts, which do not hold proportion with this exceeding greatness of power here spoken of, which yet are works above nature, are works of power indeed; but they do not come up to this exceeding greatness of power here spoken of. There are workings of the Spirit of God upon men that hold proportion with the doctrines of those men that hold there is not such a power put forth.

In handling of this point, which will conduce much to the clearing of all, my scope is not to shew you exact differences between these inferior and lower workings of the Spirit of God, which men take for grace, and true grace itself; but my main scope is to shew that there is a different proportion of power requisite to the producing of inferior works of the Spirit of God upon men's hearts, and that effectual saving work which puts men into the state of grace. To those embryos that never have a reasonable soul in them, as we express it, there is less power goes to those false births that do miscarry than to a perfect conception, which putteth a man into the rank of mankind. There goeth this exceeding greatness of power, here spoken of, to the one, but to the other a lesser power serveth.

You may remember I observed out of the words, 'according to the working of his mighty power,' that God had several proportions of working; he putteth forth more power in some works than in others. Why doth he say else, this work holdeth proportion with the exceeding greatness of power which he shewed when he raised Christ from the dead? In some actions God putteth forth more power, and in some less. There is less power needed to the producing of some things than of others. Now, that this exceeding greatness of power is not needful in working in these lower ways, inferior works of the Spirit, is the main thing I am now to handle.

That I may proceed the more clearly in it, you must know this, that there are workings of the Spirit of God, by the word, upon men's hearts under the gospel, which are above nature, which are works of a great power, make a great deal of bustle in the hearts of men, and cause men to make a great noise in their professions in the world, and yet there is not an 'exceeding greatness of power' put forth in working such works.

I shall need to instance but in that place, Heb. vi. 4–6, for that is the highest instance; which I shall open by and by. You may read here of men enlightened, that are made partakers of the Holy Ghost, and have tasted of the heavenly gift, have tasted the good word of God and the powers of the world to come, if they should fall away it is impossible to renew them again unto repentance. Here is you see a work of the Spirit; for they are partakers of the Holy Ghost, and how else do these men, when they fall away, sin against the Holy Ghost? It is a work above nature, for it is a tasting of the heavenly gift. It is a work of power, for they taste of the powers of the world to come, and the things of another world which they are enlightened to apprehend have a powerful impression upon their hearts.

But though they be works of the Holy Ghost, yet you must know that the Holy Ghost hath works of several sizes, as all artists have; they have slighter works, and they have more exact and curious works. The Holy Ghost is not as a natural agent that works *ad ultimum virium*, to the uttermost he can work, in all the works he putteth forth in a man's heart, or as fire that burneth as much as it can burn. But he is *agens liber*, he worketh freely, so saith the Apostle, 1 Cor. xii. 11. There are diversities of operations, and 'all these,' saith he, 'worketh that one and the self-same Spirit, dividing to every man severally as he will.' He worketh according as he will, and hence therefore he putteth forth more power or less power as himself pleaseth.

Now then, *the different proportion of power that the Holy Ghost putteth forth in these slighter works*,—as I shall prove that in the Hebrews to be, but a slighter work in comparison of true grace,—and that not so great a proportion of power is requisite to work them as is to work true grace, converting, saving grace; that is the thing which now I am to handle. And perhaps that may be one reason why it is called the 'power of godliness,' 2 Tim. iii. 5. He doth difference it from a form. Why? Because there is a greater power from God that goeth efficiently to work it. So that as the Apostle saith of ministers, 1 Cor. iv. 19, that seemed to be something, but were flat, and yet took upon themselves to be apostles; 'I will come,' saith he, 'and know, not the speech of them that are puffed up only, but the power.' So now let us consider the power that goeth to the working upon the hearts of these men, and you shall find that it doth not hold a proportion with that exceeding greatness of power here spoken of.

To explain this unto you yet a little more, that I may be understood before I come to the point. You must know this, that man's nature being now corrupted and fallen into sin and misery, the Holy Ghost makes a trial of all sorts of conclusions upon corrupt nature, besides that of conversion. God propoundeth this to himself; saith he, I will make trial how far corrupt nature, remaining such, unchanged, without a principle of the love of God put into it, how far it will go, how far it may be elevated and raised and yet not converted, how much supernatural good and working toward salvation it is capable of, without making it a new creature.

I will quote but a place for this; it is Gen. vi. 3, 'And the Lord said, My Spirit shall not always strive with man, for that he also is flesh; yet his days shall be a hundred and twenty years.'

To open these words unto you—'

He speaks these words not of all mankind in the generality. Mark but the words before; he saith that the sons of God saw the daughters of men that they were fair, and they took them wives of all that they chose; snatched them away by force and violence; mingled themselves in unlawful marriages. Who were they he speaks of? Those that were the sons of God. Whom meaneth he by those? Not they that were his own children by regeneration, for the text expressly saith in Peter, speaking of those that were drowned in the flood, that he swept away the 'world of the ungodly.' But you must know this, that there were Cain's seed and Seth's seed. There were Cain's seed; speaking of that generation, he calleth the daughters of them the daughters of men. Cain was banished from the ordinances, Gen. iv. 14, cast out from the presence of the Lord; and so was his posterity, and therefore they are called men; that is, men left wholly to the swing of their natural corruption, without ordinances, without the enjoyment thereof, to work upon them or restrain them, and to convey the Spirit to that end. Then there were the sons of Seth; those that lived in the church, enjoyed the means of grace, the preachings of Noah and other of the patriarchs; and those were the sons of God; for so, you know, they that do so are called the sons of God, 'I have brought up sons, and they have rebelled against me;' and 'ye are the children of the Lord your God,' Isa. i. 2, Deut. xiv. 1; for God had taken them into the bosom of the visible church. Now then, those sons of God, living under outward means and in a sort the gospel,—I may call it so, for they lived under the preaching of Noah, a preacher of sure righteousness, Christ namely, and under the preaching of other patriarchs, —it is said the Spirit of God did strive with them, the Spirit of God going home to their hearts with the word.

Compare therefore with this 1 Peter iii. 18. It is a difficult place, and it is opened by this. Speaking of Christ there, saith he, 'He was put to death in the flesh, and quickened by the Spirit;' that is, quickened by the Holy Ghost and by the Godhead; 'by which also he went and preached to the spirits in prison, who sometime were disobedient, when once the long-suffering of God waited in the days of Noah, while the ark was a preparing.' I say these words in Genesis open those in Peter. Our Saviour Christ after his death was raised by the Spirit, by the Holy Ghost; for that Spirit that raiseth up our bodies dwelt in him and raised up his, as it is Rom. viii. This Spirit of his, saith he, went with the ministry of Noah, who preached the same gospel we do, and preached in the days of the old world. Moses saith here, that his Spirit contended or strove with them; and Peter alludeth to it that this Spirit by which Christ was raised had formerly preached to these men, who were now but spirits; for that was their estate, they were now dead, they were in hell; 'the spirits that now are in prison,' that is his meaning. And as Moses here saith, that God gave them a hundred and twenty years' warning to repent, 'The days of man,' saith he, 'shall yet be a hundred and twenty years;' so Peter saith, he was long-suffering, and that he waited; 'when once the long-suffering of God,' saith he, 'waited in the days of Noah,' waited a hundred and twenty years, 'while the ark was a preparing.'

Now then, that which I quote this place for is this, to come to it: that this Spirit of God contended or strove with these sons of God that lived in the church. It did strive, that is all his phrase; he put forth so much strength as to try whether he should overcome corrupt nature, or corrupt nature overcome him; he put forth only a striving strength; as in wrestling, you know, if a man only strive, he doth, as it were, feel the strength of another. There is a striving strength that the Holy Ghost putteth forth upon the hearts of men, and there is an overcoming strength. There is a striving strength, as here; there is an overcoming strength, as in 1 John iv. 4, 'He that believeth overcometh the world; for greater is he that is in you, than he that is in the world.' But here he putteth forth so much power as shall be a striving, and yet they remain flesh still, (mark that;) that is, he doth not put forth so much strength or power as doth alter corrupt nature, they shall remain flesh still; for so you know it followeth, 'he also is flesh;' and so the Septuagint puts an emphasis upon it, 'he also is but flesh.' These sons of God that had all this means, saith he, I have tried how far it will go, and I see they are but flesh still, they are corrupt still; and while I deal with them thus in a lower way, it will not overcome their corrupt nature, they remain flesh for all that; therefore Peter saith, they were disobedient, and are now in hell. And upon this, what conclusion doth God make? I have tried, saith he, all conclusions with corrupt nature, all but one, fully to overcome it; I have given it all helps, I have striven, I have contended, I have wrought thus far, I have given them a hundred and twenty years yet longer, and the conclusion of all is in the 5th verse: 'God saw that the wickedness of man was great upon the earth, and that every imagination of the thoughts of his heart was only evil continually;' and that corrupt nature would be corrupt nature still, would be flesh still, unless he put forth an almighty power, beyond striving, to change it.

To clear this yet a little more unto you, because it is the foundation of what I shall afterwards proceed in: you may observe that God hath tried all sorts of conclusions with the hearts of men, according to several sizes. He afforded corrupt nature a little light of truth, which the Apostle speaks of, Rom. i.; a light that shined in a dark place, whereby they knew many things of the law, as that there was a God, and that that God must be worshipped; this the heathens and all men more or less have in their hearts. He tried what corrupt nature would do with this, and he finds that generally they did imprison it in unrighteousness, they put this prophet of God into prison; that is, they went against their knowledge, they slighted it. The light of conscience, then, will not do it. Yea, he went so far with one man, he gave instance of one man in the world that went so far as to die for this, that there was but one God, and yet knew nothing of the Scripture. So Socrates was the highest instance how far the light of nature would go. God tried this conclusion first with the heathens.

I will give you a scripture for that. It is 1 Cor. i. 21, 'After that in the wisdom of God, the world'—that is the world of the Gentiles, for he speaks of them there—'by wisdom knew not God;' then when he had tried this conclusion, that all the light of nature, which he calleth the 'wisdom of God,' yet because of that corrupt carnal wisdom in men's hearts, would not turn them; then he sendeth preaching to convert them. After this, saith he, 'it pleased God by the foolishness of preaching to save them that believe.' This was trying a conclusion, you see; for after that he saw that this light of nature would do no good, then he sendeth Christ into the world, and by the preaching of the gospel to convert them.

Well, having tried the light of nature, and seen that will do no good, he cometh to the light of the law, and tries that with the Jews. He gave the law to them; 'he dealt not so with any nation, neither have the heathen the knowledge of his law.' This was but trying a conclusion too, as the other was. He would see how far the light of nature, improved by the light of the law added to it, would go. Now what saith the Apostle in Rom. viii. 3? 'What the law could not do, in that it was weak through the flesh.' He would try what the law would do; he gave them a perfect rule, they had the same help for the external means that Adam himself had, (mark it,) for they had the same law. How cometh it to pass that the law could do no good, could not work upon men's hearts, though a Spirit went with it? For so the law had, Neh. ix. 20. Saith he, it was weakened through the flesh; corrupt nature weakened all the power of it, it was too hard for that light of the law. He tried that conclusion too; and for that, as he gave Socrates the highest instance under the light of nature, so he gave Paul the highest instance under the law; a man that never sinned against his conscience in his life, but was concerning the law blameless till his conversion. 'I have kept a good conscience,' saith he, 'to this day;' he speaks it to the Pharisees that knew him before.

Well, he hath given us the gospel; he will try how far corrupt nature will go there too, will be wrought upon by the gospel, which hath a power of the Spirit accompanying it, as all these had; for certainly they were all supernatural, that must be acknowledged; it was more than corrupt nature of itself would have done. He makes a trial, I say, with the gospel too; for that you have that eminent instance in the 6th of the Hebrews, of men that are 'enlightened, and partake of the heavenly gift,' &c., and yet the Apostle tells us plainly, at the 9th verse, that there are better things than these which God works in men's hearts when he saveth them. 'We are persuaded,' saith he, 'better things of you, and such as accompany salvation.' The Holy Ghost elevateth and raiseth and works upon corrupt nature, to see how far it will go under the gospel.

And here he hath several sizes of working too. That parable in Luke viii. and Matt. xiii. sheweth it. The stony ground receiveth the word with joy, but falleth off in persecution. The thorny ground holdeth out in persecution, but cares, and riches, and pleasures grew up with it and choked the word. God hath several works upon nature, and trieth these conclusions with it.

And what is the reason he doth it?

In one word the reason is this: because he would shew, by a comparison of the work of grace with other lower workings of his upon men's hearts, what an excellent thing grace is; that it is 'precious faith' indeed, which is the faith of God's elect, as the apostle Peter calleth it, 2 Peter i. 1. There is nothing in nature but hath a counterfeit. Go up to the heavens, there you see the beams of the sun, and you have streams in the air; you have stars, you shall have falling stars and comets. Go down to the earth, you have precious stones, and you have the counterfeit of them, Bristol stones like to diamonds; and the excellency of the one is set off by the other. And God endeareth his children so much the more to him by this. Saith he, I have wrought so far upon another man's heart, but it was not grace; I might have done so with you, but I overcame you, I stretched forth the exceeding greatness of my power to you.

And he doth do it too for this end, that all may see their own weakness, that as the Apostle saith the law was 'weak through the flesh,' so the gospel shall be weak through the flesh, and all sorts of assistances, but what doth the deed, shall all be weak through the flesh too. God may strive with men, but if he doth not put forth a power to overcome them, they will overcome him. He doth it, I say, to shew the corruption of man's nature, and to shew the weakness of it, the utmost pravity of it, how it weakeneth all means of grace. Therefore he complaineth, 'What could have been done more in my vineyard, that I have not done in it?' that is, by way of means.

And, which most of all I would have you observe for the understanding of this, whereas you will say, If God give not sufficient grace to convert, why doth he try these conclusions?—

I answer you thus: though it is not sufficient grace to convert a man in the state of corruption, yet take a man as he was in Adam, and God considereth every man as he was in him, the same helps he affordeth now to corrupt nature would be sufficient to have kept Adam, and God is not bound to do any more. It is sufficient, I say, not in regard of the state of corruption to convert; but in this sense it is sufficient, that the same abilities and assistance given to Adam in innocency—and it is the fault of all mankind, their sin, that they are fallen from it—would have enabled him to have stood; and God, as I said, is not bound to any more.

And to clear God in this too, let me add this: that all these workings upon men's hearts, as they are trials of corrupt nature, so they mightily tend to lessen men's punishments, for they keep them from many sins. Yea, that which is wrought in the heart is in some way acceptable to God; this is more, God accepteth of it, though not for grace itself, yet he likes it well that corrupt nature will be wrought upon so far, though it be not turned to him effectually. You know he loved the young man that said he had 'kept all those things from his youth;' and so to see a man affected at a sermon, God is pleased with it, he accepts it according to its kind. As bring me a brass shilling, I say it is not a shilling, it will not pass for coin; but if you ask me whether it be worth anything, I say it is worth something in its kind, it is worth something as brass, though it is not worth something as a shilling: so these workings are acceptable unto God in their kind, though he takes them not for grace, they are not current money.

Having thus explained to you and laid this foundation, that the Holy Ghost hath lower kinds of workings upon the hearts of men, which yet notwithstanding do not arise to true grace, I will come now to shew you, *That God doth not put forth the same power in these as he doth put forth in a saving work.* That is the point which I am next to handle.

To demonstrate this unto you. The explication of it I refer to two heads:—

First, *That all lower workings of the Holy Ghost upon the hearts of men are but a restraint of corruption in them, and an elevation of corrupt nature.* A restraint and an elevation—that is, it is not a destroying corruption, but a restraining corruption. Nature remaineth corrupt still as it was. And it is not a changing of corrupt nature into its contrary, into grace, but it is an assisting of it, an elevating of it, a strengthening of it to go so far as he is pleased to carry it, remaining corrupt, and the same it was before.

And then the second thing that will demonstrate that not the same power is needful, is this, *That there is not a putting in of new principles of grace into the heart,* such as love to God, that was not there before; a new spiritual disposition in the understanding to take in spiritual things, as I shewed in the last discourse; but it is only working upon the old principles, improving them. And to both these, there is not so great power required as is there mentioned to conversion.

For the *first head*, you see it consisteth of *two parts.* There is, first, but a *restraining of corruption, not a killing of it.* You know, when I shewed you what power lay in working of grace, I told you it was a putting off the old man, it was a passing away of all things that were old, it was a circumcision made without hands, it was a destroying of the body of sin, a deposing of that corrupt principle of self-love; and let me tell you this, till that be deposed, a man is an unregenerate man. Now you shall see, that in all these inferior workings of the Spirit, these strivings of the Spirit, there is not a taking away of corruption; there is but a restraining of it, the heart remaineth the same that it was.

To make this plain unto you, I will but give you one scripture which speaks of these kinds of workings. It is 2 Pet. ii. 20. He speaks of men that have been enlightened and wrought upon by the knowledge of Christ. Saith he, 'If after they have escaped the pollutions of the world through the knowledge of our Lord and Saviour Jesus Christ, they are again entangled therein, and overcome, the latter end is worse with them than the beginning.' This is a place that is mightily alleged for falling away from grace; whereas, say we, the work here mentioned, namely, the escaping of the pollutions of the world through the knowledge of Christ, did not rise up to true grace.

You will say to me, How do you prove out of this place that here is only a restraining of corruption, or a driving of it in? As I remember he said of Abimelech, Gen. xx. 6, 'I kept thee in, and suffered thee not to touch her,' speaking of Sarah, Abraham's wife; he restrained his lust.

I prove it thus: by the similitude that the Apostle useth in the following words, 'It is happened unto them according to the true proverb, The dog is turned to his own vomit again; and the sow that was washed to her wallowing in the mire.' Here is escaping of the pollutions of the world, here is a washing of the sow, a washing off her dirt; here is a keeping of her from going into the mire again for a while after she is washed; but here is not a changing of the swine's nature, here is a swinish disposition still; for, saith he, the swine is returned again to wallow in the mire.

To confirm it yet more unto you, you shall find in 2 Pet. i. 3, that I may speak pertinently to the point in hand, and compare that place with this in the second chapter, ver. 20, and so to the end; he speaks there of the work of grace indeed, and what saith he of it? 'According,' saith he, 'as his divine power hath given to us all things that pertain to life and godliness, whereby are given unto us exceeding great and precious promises: that by these you might be partakers of the divine nature, having escaped the corruption that is in the world through lust.' I confess I was much puzzled at this a long while,—for he useth in appearance the same phrase here that he doth in 2 Pet. ii. 20, 'If after they have escaped the pollutions of the world through the knowledge of Christ, they return again,' here is one work; 'having escaped the corruption that is in the world through lust,' here is another,—till this reconciled it; and I pray consider it. Here is a work upon men's hearts which makes them escape. But what? The pollutions of the world; the word in the Greek is μιάσματα, signifying the gross defilements, the outward defilements that in men's lives they run into; 'through the knowledge of Christ,' without changing of their nature; for you see they are swine still, though they do not wallow in the mire. But compare this other power, which giveth us all things pertaining to life and godliness; he telleth us, we are also made 'partakers of the divine nature.' And he doth not say only, they escape the *gross defilements* of the world, as I said the word there signifieth, but ἀποφυγόντες τῆς ἐν κόσμῳ ἐν ἐπιθυμίᾳ φθορᾶς, they have escaped *the corruption that is in the world through lust.* Therefore there is a change not only in respect of outward defilements, but a change in respect of inward dispositions; the corruptions that are in the world through lust; these, a man having a new nature put into him that lusteth contrary, is free from the bondage of in some measure. Here is now a world of difference between washing of a swine from the outward defilement of the mire she hath wallowed in, and altering her swinish nature; there is no such work of power comparable in the one that is in the other. To wash off the pollutions, the gross defilements of the world that men lived in formerly, though it be through the knowledge of Christ, is nothing to the stamping of a new nature upon them, to the making them partakers of the divine nature, that they shall escape the corruption that is in the world through lust; that is, to kill the inward dispositions of sin, to destroy them, to alter the root and frame of the heart; this, saith he, is a divine power.

In a word, the one is but like laying Samson asleep, and then bind him, all his strength remaining, and when he awakes he breaks asunder all his bonds. But if you come to the work of the Holy Ghost, which is effectual upon corrupt nature, it is killing of Samson, it is giving him a deadly blow, which all in corrupt nature doth oppose; it doth not oppose the other so much, therefore it is not a work of so great a power.

So much for that first particular. It is but a restraint of corrupt nature, whereas the other is a passing away of old things, a destroying in part of the body of sin. Now to destroy, and subdue, and bring to nothing, therein lies the exceeding greatness of power; not in restraining, though it be a work of the gospel 'through the knowledge of Christ.'

In the second place, *There is an elevation, or an assisting of the Spirit of God,* whereby the Holy Ghost doth join with a man's spirit, and enableth him to perform actions above nature, which of himself he would not do. And, my brethren, there are those in the world that say that grace is nothing else but an assisting, an acting of the powers of a man. They acknowledge an inward calling as well as an outward; but the inward calling is nothing else but an elevation; the Holy Ghost elevateth a man's spirit, and joineth with it, and strengtheneth it with a supernatural strength put into it, and so by his assistance and joining with it, it is enabled to do that which of itself it would not do.

To express the difference concerning this, because much dependeth upon it. You know, in the Old Testament, that angels did appear in the likeness of men, and perhaps had the bodies of men for that time created for them by God, as some divines think. Make that supposition. They did all things as a man, the angels acted that body, used the tongue to speak with, and the feet to move, and the hands to do this and that, to pull in Lot, as you know they did, when they struck the others with blindness. They were created angels that did it, that the text is clear in. Now there is a great deal of difference between their assisting and joining with these bodies, and that work of God when he did create a soul, and breathed it into man's body at first: there is an infinite difference between them in the power put forth, for an angel can do the one; but to breathe the breath of life, the soul, into a body thus formed and fashioned, God only could do it. The one is a work of exceeding greatness of power; but merely to assist *tanquam forma,* and not *informans,* as the philosopher speaks,—an *assisting form,* and not an *informing form,* as the soul is to the body,—this is not a work of such great power, for you see an angel can do it.

I shall not need to stand explaining of it largely. You shall find, Eph.

iii. 16, that there is not only a strength put to the inner man, but there is an inner man too which God createth in a man, and then to strengthen it indeed is something. But simply to join, and strike in, and mingle itself with corrupt nature, as fire doth with water, according to the opinion of some, when it makes it hot,—though water be cold in itself, yet fire can and doth mingle itself into the pores of the water and heat it; for there are pores in the water, as philosophers do acknowledge; yet the principle of heat is in the fire, not in the water, which of its own nature is still as cold as it was, for it returns to its coldness again. So here, for the Holy Ghost to insinuate himself into the spirits of men, and act them, and raise them up to do things above nature, but yet put not into them a formal principle of life; thus, I say, to join with men's spirits, is no such great work of power, in comparison of that which I have described formerly unto you—viz., to put in a new light, the light of life; to give you all things belonging to life and godliness, to put in that great principle of the love of God into the heart, which is more than all the creatures themselves without it. This is a new life, a new principle, my brethren.

Those, who as you think in their opinions do deprave the grace of God, and you speak of them as such, the Arminians; they do not hold that a man can do anything of himself; they acknowledge that which Christ saith, 'Without me you can do nothing.' But, say they, it is but an assisting, it is but the joining with men a supernatural strength; it is not putting in of a new principle, say they. Why, say I, this is not such a work of such mighty power. Why? Take cordials, they will join with a man's spirit, to strengthen you. Take an angel, he will join with a man's spirit, and strengthen you; as we see in wicked men, the devil joineth with their corruption; a man shall have his affections blown up with Satan, like the waves of the sea by the wind, stronger than by nature they would be. You shall read of an angel, Dan. xi. 1, a good angel it was, and whether it was Christ or a created angel I need not dispute; certainly a created angel can do as much; he strengthened or confirmed the spirit of the king of the Medes; it was in a good business for the Church, and he joined with the spirit of the king in it. And, Luke viii., you shall find a man so strengthened by Satan, that no man could hold him, no, though he were bound with chains. And as one said of him that killed Henry the Fourth of France, that he had the strength of ten men in him; 'Satan filled his heart,' as the expression is, Acts v. So, on the other side, for the Holy Ghost to strengthen a man's spirit by an external assistance, enabling him to do these and these actions, by mingling himself with a man's spirit; this is not so great a power, for an angel can do it. But to make a 'workmanship created unto good works;' to put a new soul into a man, as the Scripture compareth it, and therefore I may so express it,—that is, to put a new principle of life and grace into a man, and then to enable him to act that grace,—here lieth that work that beareth proportion with the exceeding greatness of his power; that other doth not.

Now, my brethren, I will instance in particulars. I will shew you a work upon *the understanding* of a man, that a man shall be enlightened (as it is Heb. vi.) with a new light about spiritual things, and yet not have a work of grace that answereth to the exceeding greatness of God's power to work it.

To make this plain unto you. You may read in Num. xxiv. 2, that the Holy Ghost is said to fall upon Balaam. 'Balaam,' saith he, 'the son of Beor hath said, and the man whose eyes are open hath said,'—the Hebrew is, as it is in your margins, 'the man who had his eyes shut, but now are opened,'—'he hath said, which heard the words of God, which saw the vision of the Almighty, falling into a trance, but having his eyes open.' And the thing he saw was the happy condition of the people of God, as you may read afterward. Here was a man that had his eyes opened by a new light, a new work of the Spirit upon him, yet remained flesh for all this; there was no new creature wrought upon him at all, for you know he is brought in as an instance of one that went after the ways of unrighteousness; yet you see what glorious things he saith of himself.

My brethren, mark it, here is new light indeed cometh in, and the mind is raised up to new objects it never knew before; but here is no new eye made, no understanding given, as the Apostle expresseth it; here is not a being *born again* to see the kingdom of God, here is not the image of God created, here is not that new creature, as I described it in the last discourse; a new spiritual understanding, and disposition in the mind to receive spiritual things as they are in themselves. And, my brethren, thus merely to put a new light in the mind, to suggest things that never were before; this is not a thing that requires an almighty power. Whereas he knew worldly things before, now to propound spiritual things to him, and to open his eyes to see them; the old eye is capable of this, for you see Balaam's was.

I said before, an angel can do as much. An angel can fall upon the understanding, irradiate an object and present it to the mind. There were no fantastics, enthusiasts, if the devil could not do this; he turneth himself into an angel of light, and he can do it. I will give you Scripture for it: 1 Sam. xviii. 10, it is said, 'an evil spirit came upon Saul, and he prophesied.' Here was Saul's eye opened, as Balaam's was; here was prophesying, as he did. Herein lieth not then the greatness of God's power to enlighten them, and to reveal to them the things of the world to come; though they knew nothing before but of the things of the present world. Here is a new light brought in, like the bringing of a candle into a room; but here is not a new eye, as there is in a godly man, and such a representation made as answereth to the creation.

My brethren, to work faith in men to believe the things of the world; to work a faith that a man shall be fully convinced and believe this is the word of God; simply to do this, is not a work of an almighty power. Why? Because the devil can make a man believe a lie; he can work upon the understanding so, who hath not an almighty power in working. Look in 2 Thess. ii. 9, 10, where, speaking of Antichrist, 'whose coming,' saith he, 'is after the working of Satan, with all power and signs and lying wonders, and with all deceivableness of unrighteousness in them that perish; because they received not the love of the truth, that they may be saved; and for this cause God shall send them strong delusion, that they shall believe a lie.' He speaks indeed of the Papists, the learned sort of them, who are knowing men. But here you see Satan cometh with 'deceivableness of unrighteousness,' and maketh them 'believe a lie,' through God's permission. 'Who shall persuade Ahab, that he may go up and fall at Ramoth-Gilead? And there came forth a spirit, and stood before the Lord, and he said, I will go forth, and be a lying spirit in the mouth of all his prophets. Go,' saith God, 'and do so, and thou shalt prevail.' He went, and did so work upon the understandings of the false prophets as he made them believe it; he imitated God so. So, on the other side, for God to come and fall upon a man's spirit, and enlighten it so as he shall be fully convinced of the truth, that he is persuaded that these things that are delivered in the word are true, which he did not before; this is no more a work of an almighty power than that other by Satan is; he can do as much in another way, as the Holy Ghost in this way. So that to work upon the understanding is not a work of an almighty power.

My brethren, let me tell you this, if a man have never so much knowledge wrought in him by the Holy Ghost in a way of enlightening, when he cometh to turn to God, he findeth all that knowledge new, and it differeth as much from the other as the reason of a man from the fancy of an ape; let me so express it, there is a reality in the proportion that this expression holds forth. It is called the light of life. Take but the poorest soul that hath but the understanding of Jesus Christ given unto him by the Spirit of God, he hath that knowledge which all the learned men in the world have not. The one is a work of an almighty power by creation, the other is but an enlightening. So then, God may work upon the understanding, and not by an almighty power.

Come to *the will and affections.* In a man, you know, there is love, there is joy, there is fear, there is desire. The Holy Ghost by way of an assistance may stir all these affections in a man, and yet not in a way of an almighty power. You shall find in 1 Sam. xi. 6, it is said there, that 'the Spirit of the Lord came upon Saul, and he was exceeding angry.' It was upon a just occasion, upon an indignity offered his people by Nahash the Ammonite; he would make a covenant with the people, but the terms were that he might thrust out all their right eyes. Hereupon now the Spirit of the Lord fell upon Saul, and raised up his anger. The Holy Ghost sometimes raiseth the affections of wicked men,—Saul was so,—without creating anything, but merely insinuating himself and joining of himself with their spirits; as the wind joining with the waves of the sea, you see it makes them rise: so doth the Holy Ghost blow upon men's affections sometimes at a sermon, upon their fear, he terrifieth them, upon their love, upon their desires, as he did upon Balaam's: 'Oh that I might die the death of the righteous!' This is not a work of an almighty power. Why? Still, because an angel can do as much to the spirit of a man, an angel can stir a man's affections. There are many instances in histories how the devil hath raised men's affections to love women, and women's to love men, so long as the enchantment hath lasted. 'Who hath bewitched you?' It was a bewitching, that of the Galatians, chap. iii. 1. In 1 Sam. xvi. 15, you shall read there that an evil spirit from God troubled Saul; it did terrify his spirit.

By this you see, my brethren, that the Holy Ghost can, and doth work upon the affections of men; yet all this while there is not an almighty power put forth. Here is an elevation of a man's spirits, a stirring of his affections; but yet all this is without an almighty power. Why? Because there is no change wrought in him, there is nothing of a new creation to make him suitable to spiritual things as spiritual wrought in him.

And that is the first head. He works either by way of restraint or outward assistance. Assistance I may call it, but I call it outward assistance, because it is not a vital disposition put into the soul, but only a bringing in of a new light, and a stirring up of the affections. That is the first way whereby I demonstrate that these inferior works of the Holy Ghost have not an almighty power accompanying them.

The *second head* I propounded is this, and I would have you mark it most of all, if I shall be able to explain myself in it: *The Holy Ghost, when he works these inferior works, these strivings with the spirits of men, doth not put in new principles, only works upon the old, and improves them in a supernatural way.* It is an *eduction,* as I may call it, it is not a *creation.*

I will give you an instance to express it. The sun works upon the principles that are in the mud by its heat, and there are living things begotten in it. The sun, as some think, doth not create a new life. The truth is, a sensitive life is but the spirits of the element, which the sun concocts and boileth up to such a height. But when God made creatures, then indeed there was creation. The sun doth but merely work upon the principles in nature, and boileth them up and concocts them, and there is a creature produced that hath some life. But when God created at first, he made living creatures immediately. This is the difference between eduction, as philosophers call it, out of principles in nature, and putting in of new principles. The work of grace is a work of *creation*; and why a creation? Because it is *ex nihilo*. It doth not depend upon any pre-existent matter, but it is a putting in of all new. When Adam's body was made, God did not draw the soul out of the body, as the sun doth these creatures out of the mud, *ex putridâ materiâ*, there being some seeds of them in it before. But it is creation, and so the schools say; it is a thing that doth not depend upon matter; God putteth it in of nothing.

This helpeth to express clearly and fully the difference between the work of the Holy Ghost upon corrupt nature in a lower way, and in this higher way; and it differenceth the power, that there goeth not so much power only to work upon the old principles, as doth to put in new. There is almighty power goeth to the one; there doth not go an almighty power to the other.

In James i. 17, he saith, that 'every good and perfect gift cometh from above.' He speaks of the work of grace, of regeneration; that is plain, for it followeth, 'of his own will begat he us.' I quoted this place in the last discourse, and it is now full for my purpose. I told you then, that the phrase 'from above' is applied to none but Christ, whose birth was altogether heavenly, and unto grace, in the whole Scripture. It is applied to Christ, John iii. 31, 'He that cometh from above is above all.' And here he saith, every perfect gift, speaking of grace, is from above. 'Every perfect gift;' why doth he put in the word perfect? My brethren, you must know there are gifts that do come partly from above that are not perfect. Look into Heb. vi. 4. He speaks of men that are enlightened, that have 'tasted of the heavenly gift.' Here is a gift you see from heaven, and yet he plainly saith, that a little love of God is worth all these things he speaks of; for so he saith, ver. 9, 'We are persuaded better things of you, and things that accompany salvation.' Better than what? Better than all these enlightenings; that is his meaning plainly. There are graces, saith he, that the Holy Ghost works, that have salvation in them, so the word signifieth. And what are they? Read ver. 10, 'God is not unrighteous to forget your work and labour of love, which you have shewed toward his name.' Men despise signs altogether; you see the Holy Ghost mentioneth love to God, and obedience springing from that love, to be better than all those enlightenings and tastings of the powers of the world to come, which corrupt nature is capable of.

Now then, the one is a heavenly gift as well as the other. Why? Because that corrupt nature could not have any such thing in it, if the Holy Ghost from heaven did not work it; but yet it is not wholly from above, it is partly from heaven and partly from earth. I may say of it, as John saith of himself, comparatively to Christ, John iii. 31, 'He that cometh from above,' saith he, speaking of Christ, 'is above all.' His coming is wholly from above; he is the Lord from heaven, he came not from the earth, as other men; the Spirit of God made his body in the womb of the virgin, and put in his soul; but 'he that is of the earth is earthy, and speaks of the earth.'

All other men, and he includeth himself too, are partly from heaven; their souls are from thence, but their bodies are made after the ordinary sort of men's bodies. These inferior gifts are partly from above and partly from below; that is, they partly arise from the principles of corrupt nature, improved by the Holy Ghost; hence now they are not perfect, but every perfect gift cometh from above, wholly from above.

But compare with this Luke viii., where he speaks of these inferior workings in the parable of the sower; and he saith of the stony ground, that they did not 'bring forth fruit to perfection.' These are perfect gifts, and wholly from above; those other works are imperfect, because not wholly from above; only the Holy Ghost takes the same old corrupt heart, and works upon principles already in it.

I could give you many similitudes, which I omit, as that of the chemist. The chemist will fetch salt out of any body, out of a man's arm; give him but leave to use his art, to put fire to it, he will extract and draw spirits out of it. You would think here were a mighty alteration. Here is no great alteration, no alteration like the creation. Why? Because he works but upon what is in it already, only he draws it out.

So it is here. The Holy Ghost falleth upon a carnal heart; he would extract joy in the word, make an affection taste of the powers of the world to come; it is but an elevating, it is but a raising and boiling up principles that are there already.

Now to make this plain unto you. I shall do it by these three things. The work of grace, as I told you, is wholly new, all becometh new; it is not a working upon the old. Indeed, there is the old nature, I mean there is the same substance of nature, the understanding, and will, and affections, that were before. A man could not love God if they were not in him; but, I say, here is but a working upon the principles that were in nature, without putting in new.

To make this plain, I will shew you—

First, What principles are in corrupt nature capable to be wrought upon by the Holy Ghost.

Secondly, I will shew you that there are things in the word suitable to work upon these principles of nature, if the Holy Ghost setteth them home.

Thirdly, That the Holy Ghost doth but improve these principles, by setting home those things in the word suitable to them.

You will say, What are those principles in a man's nature that are capable thus to be wrought upon and improved by the Holy Ghost, without putting in of new, that a man shall seem to have abundance of religion, and be exceedingly affected with spiritual things?

I will go over some. Take a man's *understanding;* there is a light of conscience in it, whereby a man knoweth there is a God; as you may read, Rom. i. There is the letter of 'the law written in their hearts,' Rom. ii. 15. Now the Holy Ghost, without putting in of a new eye, can reveal more and further things of the law to their conscience, than nature of itself ever knew, and yet is capable to take in. Here is now but a work upon the old principle, a raising of it up higher, a revealing new objects to it.

There is naturally in a man's heart *the knowledge that there is a God.* There is naturally in all men's hearts devotion to a deity. The Holy Ghost cometh and works upon this principle, and convinceth a man's heart that the God that made heaven and earth is the true God, and that Jesus Christ is the Saviour of the world. Now, take a man that is brought up in Turkey; the same principle of natural devotion to a deity carrieth him to worship

Mahomet, that carries another that is brought up in the Church to worship Christ. The principle is one and the same, only here is the difference—the one hath the happiness to live in the Church, and to have the knowledge of the true Messiah. But, I say, the principle is the same in him that is in the heart of a Mahometan. Then the Holy Ghost cometh and works further upon this principle, and convinceth it with more supernatural knowledge concerning this Christ, that through it he escapes the pollutions of the world. This is for knowledge.

There is likewise in a man *a natural desire of happiness.* All men have a desire of the chiefest good. What is the reason else you go and heap up so many things together, riches and honours, &c. Now, the Holy Ghost cometh and works upon this principle in nature, and convinceth a man that heaven, and to be with God, is the only happiness. And a man out of love to himself listeth after this happiness; and, 'Oh that I might die the death of the righteous!' as Balaam said.

So likewise for the matter of believing that a man is the child of God; there is such a self-flattery in the heart of a man, that if he hear any good news out of the word that men shall be saved, I am the man, thinks he, that God will honour, as Haman thought himself the only man whom the king would honour; and so every man thinketh; this self-flattery makes out the conclusion presently. The Holy Ghost comes and terrifieth a man's conscience, letteth it see sin as it is; for conscience is to be subject to God, for it is his vicegerent. When the conscience is terrified, he heareth of the gospel and of pardon of sin, the Holy Ghost makes him believe it, and thereupon he is filled with joy. And that very natural principle, which in a man condemned to die, if he hear of a general pardon, makes him believe himself to be in the number of those that shall be pardoned, and so is joyful in believing it; the same will make a man joyful at the hearing of the gospel, as you have it in Matt. i. 31.

And, besides, a man's spirit is capable of a joy by the presence of the Holy Ghost; they are said to 'taste of the powers of the world to come.' You know naturally a man's conscience, if he do well, hath peace in it; so in the law. So in the work of the gospel too, if a man hears of a pardon, and doth any way reform through the knowledge of Christ, to encourage him he hath a joy in his spirit, which the Holy Ghost works, and yet still the principle is the same, for God doth it to encourage men; men shall not go a step toward him, but he will come a step toward them.

I should shew you, that all this is far from the exceeding greatness of power that goeth to the putting of new principles in the heart, to give a new understanding to see spiritual things as spiritual, to put in that great principle of the love of God; not only stir up old self-love.

Believe it, my brethren, that the same affection that makes men to love worldly things, when conscience is convinced, diverteth a man to spiritual things, though not as spiritual. As for instance, Felix trembled when Paul preached to him of judgment to come; the same affection that made him tremble when Paul arrested his conscience, would have made him tremble if Paul had arrested him with sentence of death from Cæsar. It is but the same affection diverted to a new object.

SERMON XXVII.

And what is the exceeding greatness of his power to us-ward, who believe, &c.—VER. 19, 20.

FOR the opening of these words, I have despatched two things already. Whereof the *first* is, that they are meant and intended principally by the Apostle of the power that God putteth forth in the work of conversion, or quickening us when we were dead in sins and trespasses, as himself interpreteth it in the chapter following, from the 1st verse to the 11th.

The *second* thing that I have already despatched in opening of these words is this, what it is in the work of conversion that draweth forth and requireth the manifestation of so great a power; 'the exceeding greatness of his power.' I shall repeat nothing of these.

In the *third* place, I entered upon this, to shew you what was *the occasion of the mistake,* as I apprehend it, why that it is denied by some that so great a power as there is mentioned is not needful to convert men unto God.

The ground of this mistake I resolved much into this: that there are indeed inferior workings of the Holy Ghost, wherein so great a power is not manifested; not such a power as raised up Christ from death to life. There are workings of the Holy Ghost upon corrupt nature, wherein he works but upon the common principles that are in corrupt nature already, and he doth proportion and apply those workings to the liberty of man's will exceeding much, he doth but strive with them, that oftentimes they do resist them, and yet they close with them; yet because he works but upon flesh, it remaineth flesh still. Their turning to God, if I may call it so, is but a fruit of the flesh, and therefore withereth and decayeth as all fruits of the flesh do. There is indeed an under work of the Holy Ghost which men fall from, wherein God doth not put forth, in the manifestation of his power, so great a power as this here mentioned. And, my brethren, although the preservation of man's natural liberty of his will be the great armoury whence all the arguments are fetched to shew that the power of God in conversion is not infallible, yet the groundwork which occasioneth and strengtheneth men in this dispute—a real experience, which the most men's hearts that live under the gospel, more or less, can seal to—is this, that there are workings upon their hearts which they oftentimes do resist, which have higher effects in some than in others. Some are so far overcome as to close with them, and yet because flesh is only wrought upon, it remaineth flesh still; hence they fall away; and these workings men take for all the work of conversion, therefore they deny any further power in a further work.

Now, the scope of my undertaking is this. It is not to discourse so much of the work itself, and of the particular differences between a true work and a false, or rather an under inferior work of the Spirit and that which putteth a man into the state of grace; as it is to shew the different make or workmanship, the different woof, or the different power rather, that goeth to these two works. And to handle this I judged not impertinent to the text, for when he saith, 'the exceeding greatness of his power to us-ward, who believe, according to the might of his power, which he wrought in Christ when he raised him from the dead,' he seemeth to make a kind of difference from all other workings that are upon the hearts of other men.

These inferior workings of the Holy Ghost upon the hearts of men, the highest of them that are mentioned in the Scripture are in Heb. vi., from the 4th verse and so on. He speaks of men enlightened, that taste of the powers of the world to come, and are partakers of the heavenly gift, and taste of the good word of God, if they shall fall away; he makes a supposition of it. And you shall find it likewise in the parable of the sower, Matt. xiii., Mark iv., Luke viii. There is the stony ground that received the word with joy, and there is the thorny ground that held it out in persecution.

For the understanding fully my scope, what I aimed at, to clear my meaning concerning these inferior works of the Holy Ghost upon men's hearts, I did the last time give you two premises.

The first was this: That the Holy Ghost in his working,—being a free agent, for he worketh according to his will; so saith the Apostle, 1 Cor. xii. 11, 'There are diversities of operations, but all these worketh that one and the selfsame Spirit, according as he will;'—though there be the same omnipotent power, that is, for the root of it, in all the works the Holy Ghost doth, for all are works of omnipotency in that sense; yet compare work with work, there is a greater manifestation of power in one than in another, according as he willeth; as, though his mercy be the same he sheweth to all mankind, to all his children,—it is the same mercy in God, and there is no difference, take mercy in the root of it, as it is an attribute of God,—yet in the manifestation of it, he sheweth more mercy to one man than another, to godly men than to wicked men, upon whom yet he sheweth a great deal of mercy.

The second premise I gave was this: That seeing he works according to his own will, and proportioneth his work accordingly, he meaneth to try conclusions with corrupt nature in all things where he doth not mean to convert. He will try how far corrupt nature will be raised and elevated to good, and yet not changed, and will therefore proportion his working accordingly. He tried, as I shewed before, how far the corrupt nature of man would go under the mere light of nature; so he did in Socrates. He tried how far corrupt nature would go under the mere light of the law; so he did in Paul. And he trieth how far corrupt nature will go, being assisted,—yet remaining corrupt, take in that too,—under the gospel; as in these, Heb. vi., and the parable of the sower. Which he doth to convince all mankind of that weakness and impotency that is in corrupt nature to attain to true good of itself; that when he shall carry it on to all the good it is capable of, yet it falleth short of that true good that is saving, all might see their own weakness and fly unto Christ. This is intimated as the reason in Rom. viii. 3, 'What the law,' saith he, 'could not do, through the weakness of the flesh.' Men are apt, corrupt nature is, to boast they can do something. God trieth the weakness of it, and how is it tried? By nothing more than this: saith the Holy Ghost, I will assist you, I will help you thus and thus far, and yet all that help, if I will not put forth more, shall be but weak through the corruption of your flesh, it shall not be able to save you. That was the second premise.

These two things being premised, I come to particulars of this great point in hand, which is this: *That there is an under work of the Spirit of God,* in which, compare work with work, there is not that exceeding greatness of power shewn as there is in true grace. What power is shewn in working true grace I have shewn formerly; I must not now repeat it. Compare, I say, work with work, for that is the state of the question, and there is not that proportionable measure of power put forth—manifested, I mean, take that too—in the one as there is in the other.

There are two parts of corrupt nature, and so there are answerably two parts of the image of God, or rather of the work of grace upon us. There is subduing corruption, and there is a quickening us to good, a raising of man's nature to what is good, to what is holy. Now there is an under work, an inferior work of the Holy Ghost, of a lower alloy, wherein—

First, He subdueth corruption by restraint, keepeth it in, which yet ariseth not to a killing of corruption; there is a driving in of the disease, but he doth not take it away. I expressed this in my last; I shall not need to repeat it. Then, secondly, in raising up of corrupt nature to good, there is a working upon it by way of assistancy; he joineth with corrupt nature, elevateth it, when yet he doth not work in it new vital principles of life. And merely to elevate and assist it requireth not so much power, or at least so much power is not manifested, compare work with work, as there is in putting in of a new principle of life. For example, suppose a dead body lay here before us, you might chafe it and bring heat into it. Let an angel come and take up that body, it shall speak, it shall walk, it shall, by an assistance which he putteth into it, perform all the actions of life; yet the body is dead still. So doth the Holy Ghost join with corrupt nature; he raiseth it up to good, to much good, yet the heart remaineth dead, because he doth not put in a new principle of life, which is the thing in the text; for he saith it is the same power that raised Christ from death to life, putteth a new vital principle in him. That was the first thing I shewed, and I was large upon it.

The second particular of the demonstration concerning the Holy Ghost's working good in the hearts of wicked men, in men remaining still in the state of nature, to shew that it is not the same power manifested that is manifested in converting truly and savingly, was this: That all the workings of the Holy Ghost in inferior works are but by *improving the principles that are in nature already;* by adding to them, but raising and winding up to a higher key what is in the heart already without putting in a new creature; and so it is but by way of eduction—that I may speak as philosophers do—out of principles there already; *ex potentia materiæ,* as they say, out of the power of the matter that is wrought upon; the seeds, the principles are there already; or, if you will, winding up of those principles, it is all one. But in a saving work *there is a putting in a new principle, and so it ariseth to a way of creation;* and therefore it is that there is that exceeding greatness of power manifested in the one that is not in the other.—And that is the thing that I shall clear to you at this time.

Consult with philosophy and divinity, and what else you will, all will acknowledge, experience will do it too, that the extracting of anything out of principles already, winding them up, stretching them, and not adding new, is not a work of that difficulty answerable to a new creation. As, for example, to beget a beast, and to beget a man. To beget a beast, there is, as some say, but the raising up of those principles that are in the seed of such a creature to a sensitive soul, through natural heat, a boiling them up to life; for what is the soul of a beast? It is but the spirits of the elements, it is but a bodily thing, and therefore of beasts it is said their soul is in their blood, because the spirits run in the blood, and that is their life. But if a man come to be begotten, there must be a new soul from heaven put in. There is not only an extraction, a winding-up of the spirits of the elements to a soul of sense, which is common to us with beasts, but there is a putting in by God a new soul, a reasonable soul, transcendent above all the workings of sense. Therefore, Heb. xii. 9, he calleth God the Father of spirits, in opposition to other fathers, that are but fathers of our bodies. The soul of man is immediately created and infused by God.

Now then, all creation, we say, is *independenter a subjecto;* it is a work that doth not depend at all upon a subject; it is not to work upon principles already, to wind up them; but creation is out of nothing. Therefore creation is incommunicable to any creature; God never used any creature to create, but he hath used the power of a creature to work upon the power of the matter, to stir up principles already in nature, and to beget something beyond what was in it at first. As, for example, to clear it yet further, the sun in the summer falleth down with the beams of it upon mud; there is a natural power accompanieth the beams of the sun so to heat with such a kindly warmth those principles that are in the mud that a living creature is begot: for you may see in mud a great many such things crawling that have life in them. This is but merely winding up the spirits of the elements that are in the mud already, and these philosophers call *animalia ex putridâ materiâ,* things begotten out of putrefied matter, and so come to a life. But when God came to make man, and the first beast that was, he used then no creature to do it; he did it himself immediately, he did not work upon the principles in nature in a natural way; but he wrought upon nothing, and so created.

Now, my brethren, this difference I have always thought to hold true in this very thing, that in those inferior works of the Holy Ghost which you read of in Scripture, there is indeed an educing forth of the principles that are in the heart already, a winding them up beyond what they would be, but there is not a new creation.

I gave you before that scripture, in James i. 17, 'Every good and perfect gift,' saith he—he speaks of regeneration plainly, read the next verse, 'Of his own will begat he us'—'is from above.' It is ἄνωθέν, wholly from above, and therefore it is a perfect work. But there are other works which are temporary works, in opposition to which James seemeth to speak, for he speaks of a temporary believer in the 8th verse, of a double-minded man, that is unstable in all his ways, a man that hath a heart, and a heart that is sometimes moved to good, but yet falleth back again. And it appeareth likewise, by the 22d and 27th verses, that he speaks this in opposition to temporaries, to inferior works of the Spirit; for, ver. 22, he speaks of men that are hearers of the word and not doers, that have not pure religion; so is his expression, ver. 27. Now here lieth the difference: the one is wholly from above; as Christ is said to be from above, so is grace. But these lower works are indeed partly from above, for if the Holy Ghost would not stir corrupt nature thus, it would not have any good in it; but they are partly from below; therefore they are not perfect gifts, for every good and perfect gift is wholly from above.

Now, my brethren, I shall explain myself, to open this thing unto you more fully, by these particulars:—

The first thing I shall say unto you by way of premise is this: That if the Holy Ghost will be pleased to work upon the heart of a corrupt man, and not change it, create nothing anew, then necessarily he must work upon some principle that is in corrupt nature already. This all will yield. If corrupt nature remain corrupt, and the Holy Ghost mean not to change it, and yet will work upon it, he must work upon some principles that are in it already. That is the first thing.

The second thing I premise to understand it is this: There are in all men natural faculties of will, and understanding, and affections, which are both the subjects of grace, and of these inferior works too; therefore they are not the principles I mean, simply considered. A man could not love God but he must have in him the affection of love; a stone could not love God. A man could not understand spiritual things unless he had an understanding. Therefore, when I say he works upon the principles of corrupt nature already, there my meaning is not only to express this, that he works upon the faculties of the soul, and the substance is the soul in which these faculties are seated; that is not all, for that is common both to an inferior work and to this other saving work.

Therefore, thirdly, that I may speak clearly, there is in the will and understanding, besides the natural power of it, principles,—whether left in corrupt nature as relics of the image of God, as men call them, or whether put in, I will not now dispute,—but there are principles in them which the Holy Ghost works upon and windeth up as far as they will go, yet there is no true grace, no thorough change; the heart remaineth flesh notwithstanding.

Now, that which I am to do is this: I am to shew you these two things:—

First, *I am to shew you what these principles are that are left in corrupt nature that may be wrought thus upon.* And—

Secondly, *How far they are wrought upon and the heart not changed.* And when I have shewed these two things, this will plainly appear unto you, that, in a lower work of the Holy Ghost, he only works upon principles there already; whereas, in a true work, he changeth the heart, putteth in new principles instead of them. The one is but improving what is there already, the other is a putting in of new.

First, Let us consider *what principles there are* in the heart—I mean besides mere nature, that is, understanding, will, and affections—by which a man is capable to be wrought upon by the Holy Ghost, and raised up to some good. First, I will shew you what the principles are. Secondly, I will shew you plainly that the Holy Ghost may work upon these principles, and raise them up to much good without changing the heart or putting in a new.

First of all; *there are in every man's understanding seeds of truth;* not only of truth to understand things of this world, but there are seeds of truth to understand the Godhead, to understand many pieces of the law of God.

This you have plain by two scriptures, which I will not stand long upon, for you all know them. The one is Rom. ii. 14, 15. 'The Gentiles,' saith he, 'which have not the law, do by nature the things contained in the law; these, having not the law, are a law unto themselves: which shew the work of the law written in their hearts, their conscience also bearing witness, and their thoughts in the meanwhile accusing or else excusing one another.' This is by nature, you see; that he plainly expresseth; that is, it is from a man's birth. I will not say it is from nature, for it is said to be a thing written, I believe it is by the finger of God put in, for man hath lost all light. But this is in every man's nature more or less, here is one principle whereby he knoweth many things of the law. Then here is another principle in Rom. i. 17–19, and so on. He saith, there is a truth which was withheld by all the Gentiles in unrighteousness; so he saith at the 18th verse. What truth was that? It was a glimmering light that there was a God; 'Because,' saith he, 'that which may be known of God is manifest in them;' this was not from nature, though it was by nature, for he saith, 'God hath shewed it unto them.' It was God put it in, over and above what was the due of corrupt nature; yet there it is, and it is, you see, in all men's hearts.

Now, as there are in every man's heart seeds and principles of reason, which by education and living in the world may be improved; a man may be exceeding wise, and yet wise only so far as those principles will go and be stretched, he shall be wise in his generation: so bring this light of conscience which a man hath by nature, bring it to the word of God to be improved, it will be mightily enlarged; and yet still all the light that is added to it by the word will be but of the same kind; it will not rise to grace, to a new principle, it is but enlarging the old. As for example, take the Jews; the Apostle in Rom. ii., after he had shewed in ver. 14 what the light of nature is, in the 17th verse he saith, 'Behold, thou art called a Jew, and restest in the law, and makest thy boast of God, and knowest his will, and approvest the things that are more excellent, being instructed out of the law; and art confident that thou thyself art a guide of the blind, an instructor of the foolish, which hast the form of knowledge and of the truth in the law.' Here you see that if the light of nature be brought to the law of God, it is mightily improved. A man by nature hath some light that there is a God, let that light be brought to the law and he will be confident; he hath some light by nature about duties belonging to God, bring that light to the law and he will have a form of knowledge and of the truth in the law. So that those seeds of knowledge that are in the mind of a man by nature, of God and of the law, being brought to the law and lighted at that torch, his light is greater, but yet still it is of the same kind, there is but an improvement of the principles of nature.—There is one.

In the second place, *there is in man a natural devotion to a deity;* that is more. The heathens had it; they all would worship some god or other; though this was their fault, that when they knew God they glorified him not as God; so the Apostle saith, Rom. i. 21. You shall find in Acts xiii. 50, that there were devout women which the Jews stirred up against Paul and Barnabas. They had a devotion in them. There is a natural devotion in men; now bring that to the law, to the word of God, and it will come both to know the true God, and to have a reverence of the true God too. All this is by nature, nature improved.

Well, in the third place, *here is a seed of light in the heart of every sinner, that he deserveth eternal death for his sin,* and that this God will punish him. There is this light too, naturally, in every man's heart. Rom. i. 32, he speaks of the Gentiles there plainly; 'Who knowing,' saith he, 'the judgment of God, δικαίωμα, that they which commit such things are worthy of death,' worthy of eternal death, for it is the judgment of God; where by 'judgment,' δικαίωμα, is evident he meaneth that part of the law whereby God is revealed as a judge inflicting punishment; the next words interpret it, 'they which do such things are worthy of death.' And so, chap. ii. 1, 2, it is evident that he goeth on to speak of the κρίμα, the sentence of God in punishing sinners. And so Aristotle useth the word in the 5th book of his Ethics; and in Rev. xv. 4 it is so used, speaking of the vials that were to be poured out; 'Thy judgments,' saith he—it is the same word—'are made manifest.'

Now, a man having that natural light in him, that there is such a God as is angry when he sinneth, and will punish him; bring this man to the law, to the word of God, then what followeth? Rom. ii. 1, 'We are sure that the judgment of God is according to truth against them which commit such things;' speaking of the Jews. A man that cometh to be enlightened by the word hath this natural principle mightily strengthened, confirmed, and enlarged.

Then again, in the fourth place, if a man come once to see his sin, *it is natural for him to think of a mediator;* to use somebody to intercede for him to God. There is that principle in nature. For that I will give you but a scripture or two. I instance in all that the heathens did; the heathens, the wisest of them, they acknowledged that there was but one God, but they said there were many that were lower gods, mediators; they were their κύριοι, it is a notion that Mr Mead did much enlarge. The scripture I will give you is 1 Cor. viii. 5, 'Though there be that are called gods, as there be gods many and lords many, yet to us there is but one God, and one Lord Jesus Christ.' They had many gods, or indeed rather one great God, and they called all other gods but as mediators to this great God. This was by nature; they could not tell how to go to God without lesser gods, which were their mediators, for so they called their lords. Therefore Simon Magus, you shall find, desired Peter to pray for him; and Pharaoh entreated Moses to intercede for him. And it was usual amongst the heathens to offer sacrifices to these lower gods, to mediate for them with the great God.

Well, in the fifth place, there is in every man's will and affections *a natural desire of happiness,* of a greater good than what this world hath; for it resteth not in anything in this world, it is like a bee that goeth from one flower to another, which sheweth that it cannot be satisfied with anything that is here.

There are all these principles in nature that is corrupt, and so you see the principles; which was the first thing I undertook to shew you.

Now, in the *second* place, let me shew *how the Holy Ghost may work upon these principles, mightily raise them, and yet not change a man's heart;* raise them to a great deal of good, and yet all that he addeth to these is but of the same kind; it is not of this creation, it is not grace. To make this manifest unto you—

There are two sorts of men that live in the Church under the gospel, who pretend to any good, that have not grace.

First, you have those that are a civil kind of men; that is, all that they have to shew for their salvation is abstinence from gross sins, and they have an ingenuity and honesty of nature, and they believe in Christ, and they profess the religion of the State. To bring men to this, to improve the principles in nature, so far, is a work of the Holy Ghost. But yet, my brethren, this falleth mightily short of true grace. I will lay my foundation in these; you shall see how far they are carried on to God.

I told you before that there is a natural light in every man whereby he knoweth that there is a God, and being educated in the Church, he is directed to know the true God. But this man's principle of knowledge is the same that is in the heart of a Turk, who acknowledgeth the true God, and doth ordinarily profess him, and his service to God is no more but what an honest Turk doth; only here is his happiness, he is directed by his education to the true God.

Well, a man living in the Church is enlightened by the law how to worship this God, more than what heathens are; he knoweth the Sabbath, and the duties of public worship and private prayer. Education, likewise, and living under the preaching of the word, teacheth him this. Now, the heathens had ways of worshipping their gods; they had prayers, and sacrifices, and fast-days: he, by his education, is directed to the right worship, and there is all the difference.

Then, thirdly, take heathens, take a Turk; there is a natural devotion, you heard before, in every man's heart: that natural devotion that is in every man's heart to a deity he bestoweth upon the true God, being directed to him by education, and worshippeth him with no more devotion than what a Turk doth his Mahomet. There is a devotion in every man's heart, which, being improved, may be raised up to the true God.

And then, fourthly, look what is the religion of the nation, he is zealous for, as all nations in the world are. Saith the Apostle, Rom. x. 2, speaking of the Jews, 'they have a zeal of God;' they have for their religion, for it is natural for every man to have so, to be zealous for that God he professeth, and for that religion he is educated in. The Gentiles had so.

Thus you see how far, in a civil man, these natural principles are improved.

Now, my brethren, the Holy Ghost falleth upon the hearts of many men living in the Church with a further work than this; the same common principles he windeth up still higher, and yet still that work falleth short of grace. There are the same false strings still, only he windeth them up to a higher key; but the strings are the same still, but as false in the one as in the other, only mightily improved and wound up.

To manifest this unto you—

I told you, first, that there is *a light of conscience* naturally in every man, whereby he hath a natural knowledge of the judgment of God, which being improved by education, a man cometh to know for certain that those that do such things deserve death. Now, the Holy Ghost goeth with the law of God that is preached, falleth upon a man's heart, and setteth this law home upon the conscience, and becometh a Spirit of bondage to a man. But yet he works but upon a principle of nature, improves it. So you have it, Rom. viii. 15, 'We have not received the Spirit of bondage again to fear.' The Holy Ghost becometh a Spirit of bondage to a man, bindeth his sins upon his conscience. And whereas now he hath naturally a glimmering light that there is a judgment of God against such sinners as he is, and having heard it out of the word, and learned it by education, he is confirmed in it so much that he knoweth for certain that the judgment of God is according to truth; yet he shifteth off this light. The Holy Ghost cometh upon him, and conscience is a tender thing; it is God's throne, and it is as tinder to sparks; the Holy Ghost, I say, cometh and setteth this conscience on fire, all on a light flame. He works but upon the same matter that is in it already in all this, as he will do in hell at the latter day: he will then set all the consciences of wicked men on fire; all their sins shall be as so many barrels of gunpowder in their consciences, all on a light flame presently. And therefore, whereas he had before but a glimmering light of the punishment of sin, now he feeleth it; God letteth into his conscience, which is a tender thing, scalding drops of his wrath. Here now a man beginneth to be mightily wrought upon, but yet it is but the same principle still thus wrought upon; for before natural light did but whisper, but now it crieth aloud.

Now, to do this, the Holy Ghost shall not need to infuse a new principle into you, or give you a spiritual understanding; the old understanding and the old conscience will serve to apprehend all this. 'The word of God,' saith he, 'is quick and powerful,' Heb. iv. 12. It will try and search every vein in a man's heart. He speaks it of temporary believers plainly; it is a threatening against them, the types of whom were those that fell away in the wilderness, of whom he speaks in the verses just before. The comparison the Scripture useth will help us in this. It is in 2 Pet. ii. 22. I opened it in part in the last discourse; but that I shall quote it now for I did not open. He speaks of men that leave their sins through a great deal of light. He compareth them, first, to swine; I shewed that before; they were outwardly washed, it was but restraining of corruption. He compareth them, secondly, to a dog; 'The dog,' saith he, 'is returned to his own vomit again.' He compareth the natural conscience of a man to the stomach; do but make this stomach sick, give it but a pill or two to quicken nature, and it will vomit up all. So will a man's conscience, if the Holy Ghost fall upon it; if he give it but two or three of those pills of mercury. The word of God is quick and powerful, no quicksilver is like it; it will make a man sick, and sick to death. Here is no new principle put in; it is a working upon the old stomach and humours thus, for though he vomit as the dog doth, yet he loveth it still. Sin and his soul are as nearly united as before; the dog returneth to his vomit again.

I might enlarge it to you by that example of Felix, that trembled when Paul discoursed of judgment to come, which I leave, because I will hasten.

Now, when conscience is thus wrought upon, and a man feeleth by a light of the Holy Ghost put into his conscience, which his conscience is capable of, what the wrath of God is, what saith the soul next? Oh for a physician! and nature itself, if it be thus wrought upon, will do this, will drive a man to the physician. 'The whole need not a physician, but they that are sick.' You heard before, there is a natural principle in us to use a mediator unto God. Now, a man living under the gospel hath heard that Christ is the mediator; education hath taught him that, even as it teacheth a Turk that Mahomet is the mediator to God. And by the same principle that Agrippa believed Moses and the prophets, he believeth the gospel and Paul's epistles, and there he readeth of a mediator, and that this mediator is Christ.

Now, my brethren, in this case, a man's soul having a further light, that natural principle being further enlightened, that light of faith which he had by education being now further improved by the Holy Ghost, a man cometh to remember his Redeemer; he forgat him all his days before.

There is an excellent expression for this in Ps. lxxviii. 34, 35: 'When he slew them, then they sought him: and they returned and inquired early after God. And they remembered that God was their rock, and the high God their redeemer.' That Christ which a man, before he was sick, had neglected, he would use him complimentally; but now he hath need of him, he remembereth him as never he remembered him before; he remembereth that he is his Redeemer, if ever he be saved. When men do come thus to stand in need of Christ, they consider him after a new manner, they remember him anew.

Well then, in the fourth place, the gospel that he knows doth not only reveal Christ to be a Redeemer to him to pardon his sin, but that there is a happiness which he bringeth with him. This standeth fully with a principle of nature too; for I told you there was this principle in nature to desire happiness beyond what is in this world, for no man is satisfied with what is here. All this suiteth with what is in nature, and nature improved by the light of the Holy Ghost will rise hitherto; therefore they are said to be 'partakers of the heavenly gift;' the heavenly gift is Christ. 'If thou knewest the gift of God,' saith he, John iv. And they are said to 'taste of the powers of the world to come,' Heb. vi. As they taste of hell, and know certainly there is a hell; likewise there being a natural principle in them to desire a happiness beyond what is in this world, it is confirmed when they hear out of the word that there is a happiness; and there are some tastes of it too, of which this principle is capable.

Now, lay this for a conclusion, that all these principles in nature are but improved, and see how easily a man will be wrought upon. For there is in every man, besides all this, self-love, which is the predominant principle in man by nature; he loveth himself more than he loveth God; herein lieth the bottom of man's corruption,—mark what I say unto you,—that makes him flesh for all this. Now, if a man's conscience be thus awakened, he seeth a need of a physician; he seeth a happiness which cometh with him, to which a man hath a natural principle suited; the news of it is: If this conviction be wrought upon a man's understanding, self-love will strike in presently, and all the affections in a man; the whole heart will be exceedingly set on work, and carried on to spiritual things revealed in the word, though not as spiritual, as I shall shew you anon. Do but once awaken self-love, make it but apprehensive of the danger he is in of the wrath of God; make self-love apprehensive of a Saviour and a Redeemer, which now he remembereth, and seeth he stands in need of, and a happiness that cometh with him, besides the avoiding of danger; this natural principle of self-love will bustle, and set all other principles afloat, and yet remaineth unregenerate.

For the reason is this: unregeneracy lieth in the predominancy of self-love. Now, what will this man say out of self-love? Is there a physician to heal me, will he say; send for him; oh, who will help me to him! It may be he loves not the physician. It is one thing to send for him to marry him, another thing to send for him to heal one; in this extremity, self-love will make a man do the one, but it must be grace to make you do the other. It is nature doth this; 'Skin for skin, and all that a man hath will he give for his life;' all that he hath, in hot blood, when he is put upon it. This is nature, and this nature stirred to spiritual things, to things out of this world, so I should rather express it.

To give you a plain scripture for it. It is Ps. lxxviii. 35, 36, compared. 'When he slew them, then they remembered that God was their redeemer;' he remembereth that Christ is his Redeemer; what followeth? 'Nevertheless they did flatter him with their mouth.' What is the meaning of *flattering?* It is this, when one seeks one merely out of self-love. You know there is *amor amicitiæ*, a seeking of one out of friendship; and when one hath an enemy, if he have need of him he will seek him, but it is but flattery, it is out of self-love. Thus they sought after God, and remembered that he was their Redeemer. This, my brethren, nature calleth for; if a man be in any extremity, if nature be stirred, if conscience be made thus sick, nature calleth for it.

I will give you a scripture for it. Jonah i. 5, when they were all in a storm, —and men are often sea-sick at a sermon, and remain so a long while after, —what do they do? The text saith, 'They cried every man unto his god;' and, ver. 6, they awakened Jonah, and bade him arise and call upon his God, if so be that God would think upon them, that they perished not. A man's conscience being convinced that Christ is the Mediator and Redeemer, remembering him, self-love being thus stirred, will put a man upon it to seek after Jesus Christ; and, Oh, what shall I give for this physician!

Especially, in the second place, when he heareth too that Jesus Christ bringeth happiness with him. Balaam, you know, was enlightened to see the happy estate of the people of God hereafter, Num. xxiv.; then nature works this, 'Oh that I might die the death of the righteous!' There is a principle in nature, if once stirred, that will desire this happiness for self's sake. And if but for self's sake, mark it, still a man is an unregenerate man; for the predominancy of self-love is the very bottom of original sin, whether it be turned to worldly things, or to things out of this world, it is all one. Therefore you read in John vi. 33, when our Saviour Christ had told them that he was the bread of life, and that he was able to make them happy; oh, say they, 'Lord, evermore give us this bread.' Yet he tells them, ver. 36, that they did not believe; and, ver. 41, they 'murmured at him;' and, ver. 66, 'many of them went back, and walked no more with him.'

Well, when Jesus Christ is sent for, the physician cometh to treat with the soul; he prescribeth to him, for so the word of God doth; first, saith he, you must leave these and these sins. He is sick, he hath taken a vomit, as I told you before. Well, it shall all come up. Peter telleth of some that 'escaped the pollutions of the world through the knowledge of Christ;' it is an expression of men that fall away, whom he calleth afterward swine and dogs, unchanged for all this, nature remaineth corrupt; yet through the knowledge of Christ, through the dictates of the holy commands of Christ, they leave these sins, refrain from what they have a mind to.

Yea, when they are thus sick they have no mind to their sins, that is more; yet it is but nature improved still. For if you should be sick in body or in old age, you will say of all your pleasures, 'We have no pleasure in them,' Eccles. xii. 1. So when a man is sick in his conscience, he is dead to all the pleasures in the world; and yet this is not mortification, the lusts are not killed; for when he grows well again, his lusts grow well with him, and gather up their crumbs.

Jesus Christ likewise tells him, the word tells him, and the ministers tell him, and good books that he reads tell him, when he is in this case, that he must fall to these and these duties, that he never practised in his life. If self-love be thus stirred by these principles of nature thus enlightened, thus wrought upon, he will do any thing; take up all sorts of purposes. I will give you scripture for it. Deut. v. 27, when God there had appeared to the people, and had appeared dreadfully, and their consciences were struck with the greatness of his majesty; 'If we hear the voice of God any more,' say they, 'then we shall die. Go thou near, and hear all that the Lord our God shall say: and speak thou unto us all that the Lord our God shall speak unto thee; and we will hear it, and do it.' They take up all good purposes of doing; and yet mark what God saith of them, ver. 29, 'O that there were such a heart in them, that they would fear me, and keep all my commandments always!' They wanted still a principle of regeneration; it was but self-love stirred that made them do all this.

And then, thirdly, that I may end this thing, in doing a man shall have a great deal of joy. For as the heathens in doing according to the light of their natural conscience, had peace, they had an excusing; so it is said, Rom. ii. 14; so if a man in this case shall fall to good duties, and reform his life, the Holy Ghost will give him joy. No man shall do any thing for God but he shall have a reward, joy to encourage him; you know the stony ground, they received the word with joy.

Now then, all nature being thus wrought upon, a man falling thus a-doing and reforming, and finding himself thus kindly used to encourage him, self-flattery in a man makes up a conclusion, that he is in a state of grace. And the principles of nature being thus wrought upon by the Holy Ghost, thus doth a man come to be a professor of religion, launcheth forth, walketh on strongly; and yet all is but the principles of nature improved, and but an under work of the Spirit.

I have made up the demonstrations of it unto you. I will but give you some corollaries from it, and so conclude.

Corollary 1.—The first is, That, which indeed is the point in hand, if there be such principles in nature, which the Holy Ghost works with, raiseth and elevateth, so as he need not put in new principles, but only stir nature; the Holy Ghost beginneth indeed, but flesh endeth;—then, my brethren, such a work as this doth not hold proportion with what the text here speaks of, wherein a man is raised up from death to life, as Jesus Christ was; or whereby he is made a 'workmanship created to good works,' as the 10th verse of the 2d chapter hath it. For in all this working, if you mark it, there is but an artificial kind of working in comparison. As for example, to express the difference to you between one and the other: go take an old piece of cloth; by dressing of it you may raise a new tuft upon it out of the old piece, and it will seem new; but yet it is but the same principle newly raised up. But come to the work of regeneration, what is it? It is not a dressing of the old garment, but it is a putting off the old man, and putting on the new, that is the expression the Apostle hath, Eph. iv. 22–24, 'That ye put off, concerning the former conversation, the old man, which is corrupt according to the deceitful lusts; and be renewed in the spirit of your mind; and that ye put on the new man, which after God is created in righteousness and true holiness.' To dress the old garment, to dress old nature and make it seem new; here is not a work now proportionable to the creation, here is but a raising up the principles there already. But to put it off, and to put on the new man in all holy and gracious dispositions suited to the spiritual part of the word; this is by creation: 'Put on the new man, which after God is created,' &c.

Here is indeed a new gilding over of the old heart, which a goldsmith, you know, can do; he hath an artifice in that, but to turn this heart into gold, as I may so express it, this is the difficulty; the base metal remaineth under all that gilt still; it is but flesh still, self-love still, and while that remaineth, the predominant principle in a man's heart is not changed. But to put in that which is more precious than gold and silver, the love of God, into a man's heart, this is that which turneth base metal into gold; it is not gilding of it over. The old principles do contribute to such a work as I have described. Take the old frame of the heart, hang some new weight upon it, as I may express it by a clock, and you may move it the clean contrary to what it went formerly: so here is but an artifice in this, hang but the consideration of hell and heaven upon corrupt nature, and self-love will move contrary to what it did. But, my brethren, it is a different thing for a man to be a 'workmanship created unto good works;' to take this old frame in pieces, and put in a new workmanship 'created to good works,' to move naturally another way, as the word *created* implieth. The other is a work of *skill* rather than a work of *power*, though it is a work of great power too; for it doth but apply such considerations as shall work upon the heart, but putteth in no new principles.

In a word, such a work as this is not wholly 'from above,' as was the expression, James i. 17. It is partly from beneath, and partly from above; the fleshly will of a man, take self-love as the predominant principle in him, contributeth to this work, and the Holy Ghost only hangs a weight upon self-love, and so stirreth it; but where there is a perfect work, it is wholly from above, the Holy Ghost cometh and putteth in a new principle. Compare for this but the 18th verse of that 1st of James with the 13th verse of the 1st of John, that I may express to you from the phrases used in both those scriptures the difference in these two works. Every perfect gift, saith James, is wholly from above. What is that gift that is thus wholly from above? It is regeneration; 'Of his own will begat he us,' and that by creation, 'that we should be a kind of first-fruits of his creatures;' the choicest of the creatures; so it is in the original, ἀπαρχήν. Now compare with it John i. 13, where he speaks of true regeneration, 'To become the sons of God that believe in his name; which were born, not of blood, nor of the will of the flesh, nor of the will of man, but of God.' What is that 'but of God' opposed unto? It is opposed unto three things—

First, it is not by 'blood,' those that are noble or the sons of holy men; it goeth not by blood. 'Say not, We have Abraham to our father;' that is, it is not therefore that you are godly, though God may draw election through the loins of his children.

Nor is it, secondly, of the 'will of man.' Thou art a holy man, and thou hast many children. Abraham would have Ishmael saved, 'O that Ishmael might live in thy sight!' God would have Isaac; he is not born of the will of man; Abraham could not have his will.

But here is a third thing; it is not a work of the 'will of the flesh. What is flesh? Professedly it is this: it is self-love in the height of it, when a man hath nothing in him but love of himself; it is the bottom of original sin, if you study it a thousand years. Well, there cometh the Holy Ghost upon a man's heart, and there is indeed a work partly from above, yet it stirreth but the flesh; it is partly from the Holy Ghost's stirring it, and partly from the will of the flesh stirred too. In opposition to which, saith James, 'Every perfect gift is from above;' that is, *wholly from above;* but these imperfect works, they work upon the 'will of the flesh,' they work upon self-love, and so far as that will carry a man to good, so far a man is carried. Whereas true grace is not a work of the will of the flesh, but of the will of God; it is wholly from above, for it deposeth the will of the flesh, deposeth self-love, and setteth a man on work from a new principle.

So I have done with the first corollary.

Corollary 2.—The second corollary is this: Go, take any man that hath had never so high a work, where only the principles of nature have been wrought upon and improved, wound up to the highest; if God turn this man truly to him, there needeth as much power yet to do it, after all this that I have mentioned, as to create a world, as to raise up Christ from the dead.

To make this plain unto you.

All other kinds of workings upon the principles of corrupt nature, some say, are dispositions preparing for grace. And I will yield it thus far they are, that whenever God works upon any man, he beginneth to stir self-love first; for there is no other principle to begin withal. But let the Holy Ghost wind up all these principles in man never so far, never so high, yet if he will savingly convert that man, he must put a new principle into him; that requireth as much power as to make heaven and earth, and all the other will not contribute *this* to it. I will yield that such workings as these make a man nearer to the kingdom of heaven; but you shall see what Christ saith in Mark xii. 34. He speaks of an ingenious scribe; he went beyond the Pharisees, they put their religion in duties. No, saith the scribe; it lies in loving God above a man's self. 'Thou art near,' saith Christ, 'unto the kingdom of God.' But how near? Suppose there be two kingdoms, and one man liveth in the borders of his kingdom, next the other; he is indeed nigh to the other kingdom, nigher than one that liveth in the head city, or in the heart of it. So here, this man is at the borders, at the utmost confines of the kingdom of death; but if he come to be translated into the kingdom of life, this an almighty power must do. Col. i. 12, 'Giving thanks unto the Father, which hath delivered us out of the power of darkness, and translated us into the kingdom of his well-beloved Son.' He is nearer indeed, but he is in the borders still.

I will make a supposition or two unto you to explain my meaning.

Suppose that opinion were true, I do not say it is, which some philosophers say concerning the forming of a man in the womb. They hold there are three souls in a man: the soul of a plant, whereby he groweth; the soul of a beast, whereby he hath sense; and the reasonable soul, which is put in over and above all these. Now, saith Aristotle, the child in the womb liveth first the life of a plant, and it groweth; then afterward it liveth the life of sense, the life of a beast; there is a sensitive soul added to that, as they interpret him. Yet when it is grown up this far, to bring the reasonable soul in requireth the almighty work of creation; it is created, and with creation infused, and with the infusion created. Just so it is here. If the Holy Ghost have wrought upon corrupt nature never so far, to bring in a true principle of spiritual faith, and to bring in a true principle of love to God above a man's self, wherein holiness lies; all this is no way conducing to it, it must be a creating anew, it can never be educed out of man's nature; no principle in man will be wound up to this; it must be, as the reasonable soul is, infused from heaven.

I will give you another instance. And the instance I shall now give is more proper to the similitude in the text, which is an allusion to the raising of Christ from death to life. Go, take two dead bodies. I will give you instances of two dead bodies in the Scripture that were raised to life. Take one, just as the prophet Elisha did, 2 Kings iv., newly dead, within an hour after, when the soul is newly out of the body; and take Lazarus' body, that had been dead four days, and did stink. Take this child's body; the soul was newly out of it; there were a great many preparatory dispositions to a resurrection, to bring life again, one would think. What was there? There was natural warmth left still; there was the blood remaining fresh in the veins uncorrupt; there was a body fitly limned in all the parts of it: yet for all this, if you will make this child live you must put the soul anew into it; that 'power that raised up Christ from the dead' must raise up this child newly dead. Come to Lazarus; he stinketh, the text saith; he had been buried four days. Then here is indeed a greater work in this respect, that the putrefaction is to be taken away more, but yet still there must be a putting in of a new life to both. And to put a new life into this dead child, there was as much power required,—that is, as almighty a power,—as into Lazarus' body that had been longer dead, though there were some dispositions in the one that made a fitness, more than in the other.

So that still,—let corrupt nature be wrought upon, raised never so high,—if God will save a man, there must be a new principle put in by an almighty power, and all this will not help toward it, not to abate of the power.

Corollary 3.—I come to a third corollary, and that is this: That look over all the scriptures where you find inferior workings which men fall from, and seem to be converted and fall away, you shall find in all those scriptures that those men are still unregenerate, they are but flesh. Look over them all.

I shewed how that corrupt nature may be thus wrought upon, remaining such; I shewed the reasons of it; you shall see the Scripture reckoneth those to be flesh and unregenerate. My meaning is not that there is flesh in them, for so it is in godly men; but that they remain still corrupt, unregenerate, unrenewed. Take that for a rule: while self-love is the predominant principle, though a man go never so far in supernatural actions, he is but flesh still.

It is a question that learned Camero starteth upon Heb. vi., 'Whether that a man enlightened, that falleth away, be a regenerate or an unregenerate man, or a third thing between them?' He dare not say he is a third thing. Why? Because then there must be a third place, there must be some third thing between the state of nature and the state of grace; but he would make him to be one that is in order to conversion, and so he is in the way of it, and so he is neither; as the embryo in the womb, before the reasonable soul cometh into it, is neither a man, nor a beast, nor a third thing, but a thing in order to be a man. But I do not suppose always that God useth such works to prepare men for grace; many a man that hath never been a temporary is wrought upon at first. So Paul was, and so the thief upon the cross, and the jailor, and many others.

Now this third thing, which I have mentioned by way of consequence from the former doctrine, tendeth to two things—

First, *To answer all those places that are alleged for falling away from grace.* The Scripture speaks of glorious works they fall from; but if it be manifested to you that they are all this while but flesh, then here is no falling from grace. Here is falling from the work they had indeed; but they are where they were, they are in a state of nature still.

The second thing for which I alleged the point is this,—it is the greatest comfort in the world,—you are troubled at these doctrines, many of them; comfort yourselves with this, *Let them go whither they will go, let them be wound up never so far, they are but flesh, they are but unregenerate men still.* I shall make application of it by and by. But—

First, I say, I mention it *to answer all those places that are urged for falling away.*—There are three places in Scripture which are more eminently alleged for falling from grace; that men have true grace wrought in them, and yet fall away.

The first is in 2 Pet. ii. 20. I opened that before. I shewed they were unrenewed, they were swine and dogs, and escaped but the gross defilements of the world, not the corruptions that are 'through lust.' I shall not need to stand upon that now.

The second place is the parable of the sower, where there are four sorts of grounds; three were wrought upon by the Holy Ghost in hearing of the word. There is the stony ground that received it with joy; and there is the thorny ground, that goes further, and yet bringeth not forth fruits to perfection.

Then, thirdly, there is that place in Heb. vi. that hath troubled all men almost that have had any work upon them, where he speaks of men that were 'once enlightened, and have tasted of the heavenly gift,' &c. Now this is it I will prove, that all those that had these workings upon them were unregenerate men still; and that will be home to the point.

To manifest this unto you, I will begin first with the parable of the sower. It is in Matt. xiii., Mark iv., Luke viii. There are three sorts of grounds wrought upon, whereof the last is said to 'receive the word with a good and an honest heart;' and the other, one of them received it into a 'stony ground,' and received it 'with joy.' They allege this to prove falling away, for in the end they fell away, yet 'believed for a time.' Then there is the thorny ground; 'and the thorns grew up and choked it.'

The difference between these two grounds, in a word, is this: As I take it, the stony ground was one that was not much humbled, but when he had first news of heaven, and happiness, and promises of the gospel, having a new light opened to him, the news being agreeable to his natural principles, he runneth away with joy. The thorny ground being more deeply humbled, and having a sense of the wrath of God upon their consciences, they hold out in persecution; for all persecutions are less than that wrath they feel upon their consciences.

Now to prove that both these grounds remain still unregenerate men—

First, for the *stony ground;* it is evident they were unregenerate men, because that corrupt nature is compared to the stony heart. The same comparison is used elsewhere: Ezek. xi. 19, 'I will take the stony heart out of their flesh, and give them a heart of flesh;' that is, I will convert them. There is still a stony heart remaining, for they fall away, saith Christ, because it was sown upon stony ground. It is said, 'they had not much earth;' that is the expression, Mark iv. 5. But a stone lieth at the bottom of the earth. What is the meaning of that, 'There is a heart and a heart?' That is, there are some principles in them that are affected with the things that are good, that lie in the uppermost part of their affections, the slabby part, and they receive the word there with joy. But then they cannot deny themselves, there is a heart of stone lieth at the bottom, the stone is not taken away. Still, therefore, they are unregenerate, say I. I may compare them just to the earth in frosty weather. When the sun in the day-time thaweth a little, you shall find the uppermost part of the earth slabby, melting a little; but thrust but your finger in, it is hard underneath. Men are so far wrought upon as to have good desires and affections; for carnal principles in nature will afford thus much, when yet the heart is unchanged, it is stony still.

Then for the *thorny ground;* it is more evident that they are unregenerate; and if it be evident of them, it is much more of the other, for the thorny ground went beyond the other. He saith plainly of the thorny ground, that the thorns grew up together with the word; therefore their roots of lust were not grubbed up, there was a cutting off of the tops indeed, but the roots were not digged up. Read but Jer. iv. 4, and compare it with that place in the parable. Saith he, 'Break up your fallow ground, and sow not among thorns.' Here is the same expression the Holy Ghost useth, and what followeth? 'Circumcise yourselves to the Lord, and take away the foreskins of your hearts.' If you mark it here, it is all one to sow among thorns, and to have the foreskin of the heart remain still. What is it to have the foreskin of the heart remaining? To be unregenerate. That man is not sanctified, is not circumcised. Corrupt nature, the power of it is not abated in him, for it is called a 'circumcision made without hands.' Now then, if an uncircumcised heart, and a heart that is full of thorns, though there be a sowing upon it,—if that be all one, then the thorny ground must needs be an unregenerate heart, an uncircumcised heart. Compare but the phrase of the prophet with that in the parable.

Come we next to the 6th of the Hebrews, and that will interpret the parable, and interpret all this. There you have mighty, glorious things spoken of; they are 'enlightened,' they 'taste of the powers of the world to come,' &c. Here is the highest kind of unregenerate men mentioned that are in the whole Book of God, yet they are no other than flesh; there is still a thorny heart remaineth, there is but a sowing among thorns. They are still corrupt, and have not that true grace which the power of God works in men's hearts.

How do you prove this?

Read the place. When the Apostle had spoken such great things of men that fall away, what doth he say? That they might not be offended, he addeth two things. First, he doth give them a similitude to distinguish them from godly men that are truly sanctified, truly regenerate. And he giveth the very same similitude that is in the parable of the thorny ground. Paul interpreteth Christ. 'For the earth,' saith he, 'that drinketh up the rain that cometh oft upon it, and bringeth forth herbs meet for them by whom it is dressed, receiveth blessing from God; but that which beareth thorns and briers is rejected, and is nigh unto cursing; whose end is to be burned.' Here is the parable interpreted. Your good earth, what is that? The earth that doth bring forth fruit meet for the dresser, which God may relish, may delight in. Here is the honest and good heart in the parable. What is the earth that bringeth forth thorns and briers, that is nigh unto cursing if they do not repent, but those that have such dews from heaven, enlightenings, tastings of the powers of the world to come, and yet bring forth thorns? Their hearts remaining still unregenerate; they sow among thorns. Here you see the Apostle explaineth what Christ saith in the parable; and both express them to be unregenerate men.

In the second place, that he may bring it more home to them, saith he at the 9th verse, 'We are persuaded better things of you, and things that accompany salvation, though we thus speak.' He had spoken great things, about enlightenings of men that might fall away, discouraging things. Notwithstanding all this, saith he, we are persuaded better things of you. What better things? He speaks of graces, better than all these enlightenings in them, that accompany salvation, or, as the words in the original are, *ἐχόμενα σωτηρίας*, that have salvation in them. He that truly believeth hath eternal life. He that truly repenteth hath eternal life. But all these enlightenings had not salvation annexed to them, that is his scope; they were not saving works, they did not put a man into a state of grace, into the state of salvation. So that they remain still unregenerate; for why doth he say, We expect better things of you? Not better in the event only, for that is the only evasion that is for this; better, say they, in the event, because they fell away and the others held out. No, better things in themselves, things that have salvation in them. And he instanceth in two graces. The love of God, and of his saints. You will say these were poor things to be put in comparison with those glorious things spoken of before? Yet he doth. Read the 10th verse, 'For God is not unrighteous to forget your work and labour of love,'—this is a better thing than all those enlightenings,—'which you have shewed toward his name, in that you have ministered unto the saints.' To give a cup of cold water to a disciple in my name, saith Christ; so to do the least good to a saint in Christ's name as he is his, is more than all these enlightenings; these are things that accompany salvation, these are better things.

I could much more enlarge upon this point, to shew you that they are unregenerate men out of these places. Only observe this, which is a corollary drawn from this Heb. vi.: That saving workings, and all these inferior workings wherein a man remaineth still flesh,—for they are nothing else but a principle of nature wrought upon, he remaineth corrupt still,—are different *kinds* of things. Here he expresseth them to be better things, the things themselves are better than all those enlightenings, &c.

In Luke viii. 18, you shall find that when Christ had ended the parable of the sower, how he concludeth, 'Take heed therefore how you hear.' It is in the closure of that parable; take in that first, and so I will open it. 'Take heed therefore,' saith he, 'how ye hear: for whosoever hath, to him shall be given; and whosoever hath not, from him shall be taken even that which he seemeth to have.' Mark it, he speaks it directly to interpret the parable. Take heed how you hear; for there are three sorts of hearers that are not good. There is the highway side, but we will not mention that. There is the stony ground, they receive the word with joy. There is the thorny ground, and they endure persecution; they have a greater work upon them, that is spoken in Heb. vi. Yet our Saviour Christ saith plainly in the closure of the parable, *when they fall away* that is taken from them that they seem to have. He seemeth to have true grace, but he hath it not; yea, he himself thinketh he hath it; he is not a perfect hypocrite in that sense; yet take him in comparison of what is true, it is but seeming to have, it is but a gilding over of corrupt nature, as I may speak. It doth differ from the other in kind.

I come now to the last thing, with which I conclude. They are *unregenerate men.* I speak this for the comfort of you that are saints, and have but the least labour of love in your hearts, the least love to the name of God. You read Heb. vi., and you are terrified at it. Read the 9th verse, 'We are persuaded better things of you.' What better things? You will expect some great thing? 'Your work and labour of love, which you have shewed towards his name,' saith he. Hast thou any love of God in thy heart, which is the root of thy actions? Hast thou love to the name of God in his saints and children? However men slight such signs as these are, the Apostle, you see, opposeth them to all enlightenings. I charge you therefore, and I charge you again, you that are poor good souls, never read the one but read the other too, and there is not a place in all the whole Book of God may comfort you more. That which always hath discomforted Christians so much, there is no place will comfort them more, if they have love of God in their hearts.

If you hear ministers preach of this, if they still make these to be unregenerate men, let them speak their worst, let them speak the highest; they cannot discourage thee, if thou have the love of God in thy heart. And if they wind it up further, believe them not, for you see the Holy Ghost saith there are better things than these. My brethren, they remain unregenerate men still; it is but working upon the principles that are in corrupt nature; it is but raising them up.

You will expect I shall give you some differences. I shall not do it. I will give you some *rules.*

They are unregenerate men; they were *never emptied of themselves, nor of their own righteousness.* If not in righteousness past, yet they trust in what is to come, or what is in them at present. Phil. ii. 3, 'We are of the circumcision,' saith he, we have true grace and are truly circumcised; 'for we have no confidence in the flesh.' All the duties these men perform they do them after the flesh, in this, that they do them upon legal motives and they rest in them. It is made a difference between the state of nature and the state of grace: he that is under the law, turneth the gospel into law; he is moved to all duties by the law. The one is under the guidance of grace, the other is under the guidance and stirrings and workings of the law upon the conscience. So he remaineth still an unregenerate man; he is married to the law still, he is not dead to the law, and emptied there, and married to Christ.

Then again, he is an unregenerate man, for *self-ends are the most predominant things in him.* It is said likewise here in Phil. iii. 3, 'We worship God in the Spirit, and have no confidence in the flesh.' What is it to worship God in the Spirit? The Apostle expoundeth it, Rom. vii. 6, 'When we were in the flesh we did fulfil,' &c.; that is, when we were unregenerate, all was lust, all was self-love, nothing else was the ground of all our obedience to God; but now, saith he, 'we are delivered from the law, that being dead wherein we were held; that we should serve in newness of spirit, and not in the oldness of the letter.' What is it to serve in newness of spirit, that is opposed you see to the oldness of the letter? It is this in a word, to be made a spiritual man, and then to serve God spiritually. What is it to be made a spiritual man that is opposed to flesh, which all these men are, though they are wrought never so much upon? In a word, a spiritual man is he that hath a heart suited with spiritual things as spiritual;—I can give you no other differences,—so the Apostle defineth it, 1 Cor. ii. 14; he that hath a spiritual understanding to take in the spiritual excellencies of the things revealed in the word; it is to see the excellencies of the things themselves.

You must know this, my brethren, there is a twofold goodness in the things revealed in the word; there is a proper goodness, and there is an accidental, a by-goodness. There is a proper goodness: as now take the instance in Christ; there are his proper excellencies, as he is holy, as he is righteous, as he is the Son of God, for which God loveth him; and all these glories that are proper and respective to his person. Now, to have an eye to see all these, and to have the heart taken with them, this is to be a spiritual man; here is a new principle. Then there is an accidental goodness cometh by Christ; you shall escape hell, you shall be happy; these things the word revealeth too; there is the bread of life, and there is the sauce. Now, the heart that is carnal, that loveth himself only, may be taken with that by-goodness that is in Christ, but never with the goodness that is in Christ himself. If thou hast a heart suited to the spiritual things revealed in the word, and thou findest thy heart taken with them, it is certain thou art not flesh, but spirit.

Would you try your hearts then? Observe what considerations they are that set your affections toward spiritual things, that set them afloat, that set your will a-work. If they be spiritual considerations of the excellencies of the things themselves revealed in the word, which you see and find a suitableness in your souls to them, it is certain thou art a spiritual man, thou art more than flesh; this is not working upon the principles in nature, for the natural man cannot receive the things of the Spirit, for they are spiritually discerned. If thou seest them spiritually, and art affected with them as such, certainly thou art spiritual.

I will end with a word or two. If any of you be yet troubled, you will say, I find nothing in me, but merely these natural principles, for ought I can perceive, stirring in me.

If thou dost not, let me but gain this of thee first. Though thou findest no more, yet thou mayest have more. For when God beginneth to work first upon any man, there is nothing but self-love in him, and all the motives used in Scripture to seize upon a man's self are suited unto him. But when he stirreth self-love thus in thee, he putteth love in thee to himself secretly, which will stir thee though thou perceive it not. For you must know that a great deal in a man's heart at first is but a temporary work; and as at the first raising the bells there is such a jangling that the great bell cannot be heard, so the love of God that is the foundation of all, at the first it may not be discerned. But however let me obtain thus much, that because thou findest no more, do not conclude there is no more.

Secondly, let me give this counsel to thee more. Thou seest the defects of thine own heart fall short of any true work. Make this use of it; stand not examining thy heart, and poring upon it endlessly, but let all these drive thee to Christ, and thou shalt find that faith in him will cut the knot. Go to Christ for supply of all the things thou wantest, and trade with him still, and while thou dost thus live by faith, thou wilt find in the end the comfort of all thy graces come in before thou art aware of it.

Thirdly, in that God hath begun thus to work upon thee, it may help thy faith thus to go to Christ,—not as a thing to rest upon, but thus far,—that it is more probable he will own thee and receive thee to mercy than another. Why? Because he hath begun to work upon thee, whether it be a true work or no; I dare not say it is, neither oughtest thou, till the Holy Ghost reveal the contrary. Go therefore to Christ, and labour to make up the match with him, and to get all things agreed on; for this is the misery of it, when men hear of these things they are tossed up and down like a wild bull in a net, and know not how to disentangle themselves. Go to Jesus Christ to help thee to do it. Consider this, that it is more probable God may be more merciful to thee than to others, not for any good in thee,—that is not my meaning,—but because he hath begun to work in thee, which he hath not done in another; and work it out by faith, for you must live by that and die by that, and your comfort must come in too by that; and when you have renewed acts of faith, the Holy Ghost will come and renew the evidences of your graces to you before you are aware.

SERMON XXVIII.

And what is the exceeding greatness of his power to us-ward, who believe, according to the working of the might of his power; the same which he wrought in Christ, (or, *put forth in Christ,*) *when he raised him from the dead, and set him at his own right hand in the heavenly places,* &c.—VER. 19, 20.

I SHALL repeat nothing unto you of what I delivered in the last discourse. I will only give you the general heads.

These words, 'And what is the exceeding greatness of his power,' &c., refer, as you have formerly heard, to the words in the 18th verse, where Paul prayeth, 'that the eyes of their understandings might be enlightened, that ye may know what is the hope of his calling, and what is the exceeding greatness of his power to us-ward,' &c. So that, indeed, these words are the last part of Paul's prayer, which consisteth of three things which he prayeth for.

1. That they may know what was the hope of their calling, the ground of their hope.

2. What were the riches of that inheritance they were called unto, and had ground to hope for; 'what are the riches of the glory of his inheritance in the saints.'

3. What power it was had both begun to work in them and was engaged to bring them to this inheritance; and that in the words I have read.

There are five general heads—I propounded but four at first—unto which I reduce all the opening of these words; whereof I have despatched three already.

The *first* general head is the reference of these words, their various aspect; they look several ways, both to what is before and what is after. That I have handled formerly.

Secondly, There are the parts of the words.

First, Here is a more general description or amplification of the power of God manifested to believers, and that in two things.

1. There is the exceeding greatness of it; 'the exceeding greatness of his power.' That I have handled.

2. There is the efficacy of it, in those words, 'according to the effectual working of the might of his power.'

So much in general, concerning the power of God here set forth.

Secondly, Here are the persons to whom it is drawn forth; 'to us-ward,' believers. I have opened that likewise, and given those observations that arise from thence.

Here is, *thirdly,* The work wherein this great power is manifested in believers. It is not to be restrained only to the resurrection at the last day, but enlarged also to their conversion, and all God's gracious dealings with them from first to last. And because there was a controversy upon that, whether conversion should be taken in, yea or no, I have therefore done three things to clear that.

The first was to prove that conversion is meant and intended here by the Apostle, as that wherein God sheweth forth the exceeding greatness of his power.

Secondly, for the opening of this, I shewed you wherein the exceeding greatness of power is drawn forth; or what it is in conversion draweth forth so exceeding a great power.

Thirdly, which was the thing I handled in the last discourse, I shewed how that by way of difference there are inferior works of the Holy Ghost upon men's hearts, which have not in proportion (compare the works) so exceeding greatness of power manifested in them. I shewed this to clear the text, for he saith it is 'the exceeding greatness of his power to us-ward;' to none else, in all works that are wrought upon them, let them go never so far. And likewise I did it to shew the occasion of that controversy. And all these things I have despatched.

There are yet these things remaining to be handled:—

I. The *first* is, I must speak something concerning *their knowledge of this power;* for if you mark it, he prayeth in the 18th verse that God would give them enlightened eyes, to know what is the exceeding greatness of his power in them that believe. I spake something concerning the knowledge of every particular else he prayeth for, and therefore I must do something about the knowledge of the power of God in them.

II. The *second* thing which remaineth is this: *The parallel* or *the pattern* that the Apostle prayeth they might have in their eye, when they consider how great a power works in them; even the same power, saith he, that wrought in Christ, in raising him from death to glory.

III. Then the *third* thing to be handled, which belongeth to the 20th verse, is this: *The resurrection and exaltation of Jesus Christ from death to glory;* which he continueth to the end of the chapter.

I. I must begin then with that, which is *the knowledge that believers have*, or which he prayeth they should have, *of the power of God working in them.* And concerning that I shall give you, for the explication of it, these three particulars; whereof some will be considerations about it, some will be observations.

I will give you, *first,* this distinction, that you may understand it the better, because the Apostle's scope here in his prayer is, that they may know the power that works in them that believe. You shall find in Phil. iii. 10, that the Apostle himself expresseth his own desires; 'that I may know,' saith he, 'the power of his resurrection, and the fellowship of his sufferings, if by any means I might attain unto the resurrection from the dead.' The Apostle here prayeth, 'they might know the exceeding greatness of his power to us-ward that believe, the same that wrought in Christ when he raised him from the dead.' You would think now, that the knowledge the Apostle speaks there and speaks here are all one, but they are not. Therefore, in the first place, I will give you a distinction of the knowledge, both from what is there meant and what is here meant.

There is a twofold knowledge of the power of Christ's resurrection. The one is a *knowledge of faith*, the other is a *knowledge of experience.*

In that place, Phil. iii. 10; the knowledge he prays for there is a knowledge of *experience;* that he might know the power and virtue of Christ's resurrection in the effects of it; that he might find those effects upon his heart which Christ's resurrection is ordained to work in him; and therefore, saith he, ver. 11, 'If by any means I might attain unto the resurrection from the dead;' that is, to be as perfectly holy as those that are risen from the dead. I would find, saith he, this effect of the resurrection of Christ. That is meant by the power of his resurrection there.

There is likewise a knowledge of *faith;* and that is this, for a man by faith to take in and understand that he may glorify God, and believe what a great power it was that raised up Christ from death to life, and that no less power works in believers when it works faith; and that is the knowledge the Apostle meaneth here. His meaning is not, that you may know more and more—if you will, you may take it in, it is not the chief scope—the effects of the resurrection of Jesus Christ; but from the effects that were in their hearts by faith, they might see the power that wrought it. This is the Apostle's scope here. As there is a double knowledge of a physician, who hath already oftentimes cured you of a disease. You know what skill is in him, that you may thank him; but then you send for him anew, and you desire to know the power of his medicines, and to know his skill rather by giving you new physic, and restoring you to health anew. That is the knowledge the Apostle meaneth in the Philippians; the other is the knowledge he meaneth here. And therefore, if you observe it, the words, 'what is the exceeding greatness of his power,' are referred to what went before, 'that you may have your eyes enlightened to see,' or to know, 'what is the power,' &c. Not only to have hearty experience of the effects of that power in them, but eyes to know the power that hath wrought in you already the faith you have, and will further work in you. It is a knowledge of faith, to believe it is so great a power, the same that wrought in Christ that works in you.

And so much now for that first particular, which is the first thing to clear this concerning the *knowledge of the power that works in us.*

The *second* thing I propound to clear is this: *How useful this knowledge is to Christians,* to know the power that works in them to be the same that wrought in Jesus Christ, when he was raised from the dead.

For that I must refer you to what I delivered concerning the Apostle's scope and reference of these words, as it here cometh in. I shall repeat it to you with enlargement.

It is useful, first, to the end you may be *thankful.* So at the 15th verse, Paul giveth thanks because God had converted them, that they might give thanks too, and see the more cause to do it; he prayeth here, they may know the power that wrought in them, the same power that wrought in Christ. You use to value a kindness by the love that is shewn in it; and you are to value a work of God upon you by the power that is put forth in it, and accordingly to be thankful. And, therefore, you shall find that the Scripture doth speak of the power of God in converting a man at first. The Apostle here in this second chapter, when he applieth all this to the Ephesians, goeth over the greatness of the work, that they might see the power. You were dead in sins and trespasses, and you hath he quickened; and faith is the gift of God, it is not in yourselves; you are his workmanship, created to good works. It is all to this end, that they might see the greatness of this power. And therefore, 1 Cor. i., from the 18th to the 26th verse, the Apostle saith, that God hath chosen out the most foolish means in the world, and the weakest means; to what end? To shew his wisdom and power in saving men. The preaching of Christ, saith he, is of all means the most foolish, for it preacheth and teacheth you to believe in a crucified God; it is so for the matter of it, most foolish. And of all means else it is the most weak, for it is saving men by the breath of a weak man. And why hath God chosen out these two? To shew, saith he, that 'the foolishness of God is wiser than men, and the weakness of God stronger than men.' It was to magnify his power so much the more in the work of conversion. 'The Jews,' saith he, 'require a sign,' that is his expression there, ver. 22. A sign, what is that? It is some extraordinary miracle to make them believe. What doth he oppose to a sign? 'It hath pleased God,' saith he, 'through the foolishness of preaching to save them that believe.'

Now then, his meaning in a word is this: let there be never so many signs and miracles wrought before you, they will never work faith; they may work an historical faith indeed. Look how far education prepareth you to believe, that you are brought up in the knowledge of the true God and the true Christ by education; so far miracles did bring the heathens and the Jews. They did serve instead of education to work in men an historical faith; but yet, saith he, when it cometh to the point, it is not a sign that will do it, but it must be the power of God to work faith.

Then again, another end which this knowledge of God serveth for, as to magnify the power of God, so it serveth *to strengthen your faith for the future;* that from the experience of that power you have found already in your hearts, you might gather and collect what a mighty power was engaged, and would continue still to work in you. And therefore, you shall find in Scripture, that the Apostle doth often come in with this; 'To him that is able to keep you,' so you have it in Jude 24. My brethren, you are not to look what your own weaknesses are, but what the power of God is in bringing you to salvation. As in the point of mercy you are not to look what your sins are, but what the grace of God in Christ is, you are to eye that; so now the Apostle, when he would draw up these believers' hearts, and wind them up to the height, consider, saith he, as Abraham did, not his own weakness of body, but the power of God. So do you, saith he, consider not your own sins, not your own distresses; these will all argue to you that you will fall short at last; but consider the power that works in you, to strengthen your hearts for the future.

I mentioned other things in the coherence, all which come under this head, how useful this knowledge is to a believer. I will only add one thing more, and that is this: you should to that end endeavour and pray to know what is the power that works in you, *that you might have dependence continually on that power.* That is the scope of the Apostle, why he would have them know it; it is useful to this end, that they might see what continual dependence they had upon the power of God, not only to see that without him you could do nothing, but that it is he that works all you do. Your will beareth not one part, and his power another, but it is he that works in you both the will and the deed, as it is Phil. ii. 13. God doth not only work *with* the will, but he works rather *by* the will. And therefore, you should labour to know the power that works in you to this end, that you might see your dependence upon God for every good thing he works in you.

There is a notable place to this purpose, which I confess I should have more enlarged upon. Here you see the same power works that wrought in Christ when he was raised from the dead. Now, you shall find in Heb. xiii. 21, that it is the same power goeth to work every good thing in you; not only the principle of grace, but every act of grace. Therefore the Apostle prayeth they might know the power that wrought in them, to this end that they might have a dependence upon that power for the working of all good in them, not only at the first, but to the end of their days. Read the words there in the Hebrews, 'The God of peace, that brought again from the dead our Lord Jesus Christ, the great shepherd of the sheep.' Why is this preface used of Christ's resurrection? Mark what followeth, 'make you perfect in every good work to do his will, working in you that which is well-pleasing in his sight.' Why doth he mention the title of Christ's resurrection, when he speaks of working in them, not only grace at first, but every good thing that is pleasing in his sight? Because the same power that goeth to convert your souls at first, goeth to increase every degree of grace in you, and to work every good work. As suppose I am to pray, I am to have that power put forth in my soul—if I make a prayer pleasing in his sight—that was put forth in raising Christ from death to life. Therefore, saith the Apostle, 'the God of peace, that brought again from the dead the great shepherd of the sheep, make you perfect in every good work.' So now, to the end you might see your dependence upon God for everything you do,—not only for the beginning of your faith, to praise him, but for the finishing of your faith, to depend upon him,—he prayeth that they might see and know what this power was.

In 2 Thess. i. 11, the Apostle prayeth that God would 'fulfil all the good pleasure of his goodness, and the work of faith with power.' So that the fulfilling of the work of faith is with power, as well as the beginning of it. They had found the power of God in working faith in them at first; read 1 Thess. i. 5, 'Our gospel came unto you not in word only, but also in power.' Here he speaks of their first conversion. Now, in 2 Thess. i. 11, he prayeth that God would perfect this faith with the same power he had begun it. Therefore he prayeth here that they might know what this power is that wrought grace at first, to the end they might depend upon the same power to perfect it, for no less would do it.

I might be large upon this point, for indeed I had intended to be so. I could shew you that every act of grace must have an almighty power go with it to draw it forth. I will only give you in another scripture, that as here you see the work of faith is with power, so you shall see the work of patience and long-suffering, to bear afflictions, to do it so as to please God, is a work of an almighty power too. The place is Col. i. 11. It is one of Paul's prayers too. He prayeth that they may be 'strengthened with all might, according to his glorious power, to all patience and long-suffering with joyfulness.' To make a man patient and long-suffering, patient under afflictions, long-suffering to bear with the faults of others, and to expect the promise, though much time be spent before we obtain it, he saith it is a work of power, and a work of glorious power, wherein God sheweth the glory of his power, the exceeding greatness of his power, for then it cometh to glory when an exceeding greatness of power is manifested, an overcoming power; for that is properly glory when victory attendeth power, when power overcometh. 'I am able to do all things,' saith Paul; it is a proud word, a very proud word, but what followeth? 'Through Christ that strengtheneth me.' So in 2 Tim. ii. 1, 'Be strong,'—he speaks to Timothy, and he speaks to him as if he spake to a giant that had all strength in himself; be strong, be valiant; but what followeth?—'Be strong in the grace that is in Christ Jesus.'

Now then, that you might know your dependence you have upon the Lord Jesus Christ, he prayeth that ye may know the power that wrought in Christ in raising him from the dead works in you.

My brethren, you must know this, that you are not only dead in sins and trespasses in respect of justification, but you are so in respect of sanctification also. If a man have never so much grace and holiness, he is to look upon himself as ungodly in respect of being justified; so saith the Apostle, Rom. iv. 5, 'To him that worketh not, but believeth on him that justifieth the ungodly.' He speaks of Abraham's faith. Abraham looked upon himself as ungodly when he went out of himself to be justified; and this after he had grace, for in himself he was so. You are to do the like in respect of your dependence upon God for sanctification; you are to look upon yourselves as dead creatures, dead in sins and trespasses you were once, and of yourselves you are so still; and all grace that is wrought in you, though it be a principle of life, is dead when it cometh to work, if the almighty power of God assist it not.

Not but that a regenerate man hath a capacity in him which a wicked man hath not; for he is a charcoal that hath been in the fire already, therefore he is capable to take fire sooner,—he hath habitual grace more fitted to be stirred up, but yet the coal is a dead coal of itself; so that a new life to every action must be put into you, if you have any life and stirring in you.—And so much now concerning the second head, the use that this knowledge is unto men, to know the power that works in them.

Thirdly, I shall give you two observations about that knowledge which will further clear it.

Obs. 1.—The first observation is this, That believers that have true grace wrought in them, may yet be much ignorant of the power that works it. You see the Apostle here prayeth for them that were believers already, that they might have enlightened eyes to know what was 'the exceeding greatness of his power to us-ward who believe.' What Job saith of the works of nature, chap. xxvi. 14, is much more true of the work of grace. He speaks in the former part of the chapter of the works of nature, and how doth he conclude it? 'Lo, these,' saith he, 'are parts of his ways: but how little a portion' (or how little a drop, as some read it) 'is heard of him? but the thunder of his power who can understand?' In working all these works of nature, saith he, God makes as still a noise as when a drop falleth which we can scarce hear; but the thunder of his power, that is, the force of his power,—it is not the noise of his power; thunder is put for force, so it is in that book of Job often, as chap. xxxix. 19, and elsewhere,—who can understand? So I may say to you, when you hear great things spoken of conversion, yet how little a drop of his power is that; how little a noise doth it make in men's spirits! There is a thunder of power goes to work it, a mighty force goeth to work it, but yet it makes but the noise of a drop, it is but a little drop which we hear; there is a still voice in which God is, and in which his mighty power is, and he passeth by, and we know it not.

My brethren, when we tell you there is such a mighty power in conversion, your thoughts run to nothing but thundering works; you think presently this power must lie in thundering men down to hell with terrors. No, it lies in changing men's hearts by an omnipotent power, but that power is but a still work, it is but a drop, and it falleth as a drop; for so conversion is compared. 'My doctrine shall distil as the dew;' it soaks into men's hearts, and there is a thunder of power goeth with it, though it is not heard.

The conversion of a sinner, the power of it, and his not feeling it, I may compare to that change which shall be at the latter day. 'We shall not all die,' saith he, 'but we shall all be changed.' Suppose you lived at the latter day, and were saints and believers when Christ came to judgment, you should see some men's bodies raised out of the grave, but your own bodies and spirits will be changed, changed in an instant; you will not find a mighty power upon you sensibly, but you will find a mighty work whereby you shall find yourselves not to be the men you were; your bodies will shine as the sun in an instant. So is it here, my brethren; there is a change wrought in a man's heart in a still way; this is a mighty thing. If a man will judge it by what he feeleth, if he will judge it by any violent power put forth in it, there is exceeding little, a man feeleth nothing. He feeleth stirrings and workings in his spirit indeed, as there will be when a man is thus changed; there will be an elevation of the spirit and of the body at the latter day; but for any violent work there will be none. So oftentimes is it here; yet it is the same power that changeth men that doth raise them out of the grave, from the dust, and as much is the one as the other.

And as I may very well compare it thus: men that have dispositions never so near grace, yet, as I said before, and I will give you this comparison now, to put grace into their hearts and to change them truly is like the change that will be wrought at the latter day in men's bodies and minds that are believers. They have life already, but to change them there must go an almighty power, and the same power that goes to raise others out of their graves.

Now, my brethren, what is the scope of all this? It is not only to comfort poor believers, though they have not found a work of so much noise in their hearts, of so much violence and disturbance; that is not it, wherein God cometh forth in the exceeding greatness of his power; he came in the still small voice when he was not in the earthquake and in the rending of the rocks. Thou mayest have a mighty work upon thee, and yet not know the exceeding greatness of power that goes to work it. This, I say, is not the scope so much; but it is that you should not censure such whose judgments are that there is not so great a power put forth in conversion; they may have grace for all that: for the Apostle prayeth here that they may know, they that had grace, that they may know what is the exceeding greatness of his power to us-ward that believe. You are not to censure them therefore, not simply for that. That is the first observation that belongeth to the third head.

Obs. 2.—The second is this, That in the matter of salvation men do as much stick in an ignorance and unbelief of the power of God towards them, as his will and mercy. Here you see the Apostle prayeth as heartily they might know the power that works in them, both that they may be thankful, and likewise that they may depend upon it for the future, as you would do to know the riches of the mercy that is in God, and his good-will towards you.

There are two things mainly which are the object of men's faith; both put together draw men in to believe. The one is to believe that the *power* of God is able to do it; and the other to believe his *good-will*. Now, men do stick as much at the belief of the power of God in working, that he is able to work, as at his good-will, that he will work. Therefore the Apostle prayeth here, you see, that they may have eyes enlightened to know the exceeding greatness of his power. Abraham's faith is described to us, Rom. iv. 21, by his trusting in the power of God. 'He was strong in faith,' saith he, 'being fully persuaded that, what he had promised, he was able also to perform.' This was the great faith of our father Abraham; it was placed upon the power of God, as well as upon his good-will. Now, take a poor sinner that hath lived long in doubt whether God would own him or no; he sticks only at this, I know God is able to save me, saith he, but I do not know whether he will or no. But I tell you, my brethren, you stick as much at the power of God to save you, as you do at the mercy of God, and it is an equal difficulty to believe the one as the other; and therefore, when such a soul findeth himself pardoned, what doth he use to say? Is it possible that such a one as I should have mercy? 'Let the power of my Lord be great,' saith Moses, Num. xiv. 17, 'to forgive the iniquity and transgression of this people.'

I might illustrate this point unto you, but I shall be prevented in what followeth. Only this, therefore you have it in Scripture so often, the Apostle mentioning it; as 2 Tim. i. 12, 'I know whom I have believed, and I am persuaded that he is able to keep that which I have committed unto him.' His faith, you see, is founded upon the power of God. 'To him that is able to do exceeding abundantly above all that we ask or think,' Eph. iii. 20. 'To him that is able to keep you from falling, and to present you faultless before the presence of his glory,' Jude 24. And, speaking of the conversion of the Jews, Rom. xi. 23, 'God is able,' saith he, 'to graff them in again;' he doth not only say God is willing to do it, but he is able; that is his expression there. This alludeth to what was said to Ezekiel, when the dry bones were presented to him, Ezek. xxxvii. 3, those dry bones are the Jews; 'Son of man; can these bones live?' Yet, saith Paul, he is able to engraff them, able to raise them.

I speak this to this purpose, to shew that the Scripture holdeth forth as much the power of God for the object of our faith as the mercy and good-will of God. Dost thou believe that I am able to help thee? It was the question that Christ asked the poor man that brought his possessed child to be cured, Mark ix. 23. And the thing he propounded to Christ was his ability to help him, his power. 'If thou canst do anything,' saith he, 'have compassion on us.' Therefore the Apostle prayeth here that they may know what is the exceeding greatness of his power to us-ward that believe. So much now concerning that fourth general head, which is the knowledge of this power which the Apostle here prayeth for.

II. I come now in the next place to *the parallel between these two.* He compareth, you see here, the resurrection of Jesus Christ and his exaltation to glory, the power of it, to that that works conversion in us, and all other good works.

The parallel, then, between what power wrought in Christ and works in us,—or rather, that Christ is the pattern of; what God wrought in him he will work in us; which he would have Christians have in their eye,—that is the next thing to be spoken to: 'that you may know,' saith he, 'what is the exceeding greatness of his power to us-ward, who believe according to the working of the might of his power that he wrought in Christ.' That Jesus Christ is the pattern, the common instance or evidence, that look what he had wrought in him, the same power should work in us, that is the Apostle's meaning. Now, this parallel is but hinted to us only in a touch here in the 19th verse; 'according,' saith he, 'to the working,' &c.

For the opening of this I shall give you likewise these few considerations, whereof the first shall be more general, and yet raised out of the text.

The general consideration is this, which hath two things in it: That Christ is set forth to us as a pattern, as a standard set up by God, both of what he will be to us, and what he will work in us. I say, he set up Jesus Christ as a common standard, a common pattern to himself, that look what he putteth forth toward Christ out of himself, the same he will put forth to us; look what works he wrought in Jesus Christ, the same he will work in us. He is a pattern both of the affections of God,—the same affections, the same disposition he beareth to Christ he beareth to us,—and likewise the same works he wrought upon Christ he will work upon us.

This is an infinite comfort to believers, that God hath not only set up Jesus Christ as a pattern that we should love him as Christ hath loved us, that we should follow Christ's example and imitate him in all things, our works should be like Christ's : I say, this is not all, but for our comfort—the other is for matter of duty—but for our comfort, God hath set up Jesus Christ as a pattern to himself, that look what he hath been to Christ, that he will be to us ; look what he wrought in Christ, he will work in us.

He is a pattern, first, *of the attributes that God manifested in Christ;* the same shall be manifested in us ; that the text is clear for. Hath he shewn exceeding greatness of power in Christ ? 'I pray that you may know,' saith he, 'what is the exceeding greatness of his power to us-ward ;' the same he wrought in Christ. Here is the same attribute put forth, the same power that wrought in Christ works in us.

Then, secondly, he is set up by God as a pattern *of the same works;* that is implied in these words, 'which he wrought in Christ when he raised him from the dead.'

First of all, *Jesus Christ is the pattern set up by God to himself, that of the same attributes he sheweth forth and manifesteth in Christ, the same he will shew forth in us.* Here is an instance of power ; I will give you but one instance more of love, and so I will pass from that. Here he saith the exceeding greatness of that power which wrought in Christ works in us. Look John xvii. 23, and there you shall find the same love wherewith he loveth Christ he loveth us. 'I in them,' saith he, 'and thou in me, that the world may know that thou hast sent me, and hast loved them as thou hast loved me.' So that Christ is set up by God as a pattern to himself, to shew forth the same attributes in us that he did in him ; here is, you see, the same power put forth to Christ and to us in the words of the text ; here is the same love put forth towards us as was towards him ; 'that thou hast loved them,' saith he, 'as thou hast loved me.' He sheweth how they are one ; as he is one with the Father, they are one with him in their proportion ; now always love followeth union, and therefore accordingly as he hath loved him he loveth them. We use to love the members and the head with the same love, because we love the members in relation to the head. A father-in-law loveth the husband and the wife, the daughter-in-law, with the same love, because he loveth her in relation to his son, her husband. So doth God love his children, members of Christ, with the same love he loveth Christ the Head ; and he loveth the Church, the spouse of Christ, his daughter as he calleth her, Ps. xlv., with the same love as he loveth Christ her husband, that is, his Son. As in Eph. v. 25, &c., speaking of the peculiar love men should have to their wives, 'Husbands, love your wives, even as Christ also loved the church, and gave himself for it ; that he might sanctify and cleanse it with the washing of water by the word, that he might present it to himself a glorious church, not having spot, or wrinkle, or any such thing ; but that it should be holy and without blemish. So ought men to love their wives as their own bodies ; he that loveth his wife loveth himself.' So doth God love us, as he loveth Christ ; 'that thou hast loved them as thou lovedst me.'

So that, my brethren, you see in general, that God hath set up our Lord Jesus Christ as a pattern to himself of the same affections and attributes as he manifested in him, to manifest in us.

He is a pattern likewise of the same works ; the same power that wrought in Christ works also in us. Here you see he raised up Christ from death to life, he set him at his own right hand in heavenly places. Read chap. ii. 5; saith he, 'You, that were dead in sins and trespasses, hath he quickened together with Christ, and hath raised us up together, and made us sit together in heavenly places in Christ Jesus.' The same power that wrought in Christ, the very same work he wrought in Christ, he works in us also. This is the Apostle's scope.

But now here lies the great thing, more particularly: it is not so much to compare the work wrought in Christ and in us together, to shew that God works the same works in us which he wrought in Christ; but that which the text holdeth forth is, that the same proportion of power that was put forth in raising up Christ from death to life, is put forth in converting us and bringing us to heaven. Therein lieth the parallel especially. So that now this is the thing I am to speak to: it is not to shew the likeness of Christ's resurrection and exaltation to the work of conversion; that is not the scope in hand; but to shew that the *same power* that God putteth forth in the one, he putteth forth in the other. That is it which makes the parallel, as it is intended here.

To shew you this I must do two things.

First, I must shew you *the greatness of power that was required to raise up Jesus Christ from death to glory.*

Secondly, That there is *a like proportion of power put forth in working upon our hearts* to the power that was put forth in Christ's resurrection. I have spoken much of the power of God in conversion, in general; 'the exceeding greatness of his power.' That which now remaineth is to shew, that it holdeth proportion with that power which raised up Christ from death to glory. 'According to the working of his mighty power, which he wrought in Christ,' saith he.

For the first of these two, That there was an exceeding greatness of power put forth by God in raising up Christ from death to glory; there is a great difficulty in opening this point unto you clearly, to shew you wherein this power lay. I will give you a parallel place of Scripture, wherein you shall see that of all works that God did do for Christ, the raising of him up from death to glory was a work of the most power,—set aside that of the incarnation,—did manifest and declare the greatest power of all other. The scripture is Rom. i. 3, 4, 'Jesus Christ our Lord, who was made of the seed of David according to the flesh, and declared to be the Son of God with power, according to the Spirit of holiness, by the resurrection from the dead.' I quote this place for this, as you shall see in the opening of it, that of all works else, Jesus Christ was declared with the greatest power, to be the Son of God, by the resurrection from the dead.

I will open these words unto you a little, for the scope of the place here is the same with what is in my text.

He speaks of two natures that are in Christ, his human nature and his divine nature; that is the first thing tendeth to open these words. His human nature is expressed in these words, 'he was made of the seed of David according to the flesh;' that is, take him according to his human nature, he was the son of David: and, saith he, declared to be the Son of God by the Spirit of holiness; by Spirit of holiness he meaneth his divine nature; that is, as concerning his divine nature he was declared to be the Son of God. Every parcel, if I may so speak, in the Trinity is called *Spirit;* you see his divine nature is called here the Spirit of holiness, for God is a Spirit; and so is the second Person as well as the third, he is a Spirit too;

he is God, and therefore called the Spirit of holiness. 'God is a Spirit,' saith he, John iv. 24.

Now observe the difference, 'He was made of the seed of David according to the flesh.' Take his human nature, *he was made;* but take his divine nature, the Spirit of holiness in him, he was only 'declared to be the Son of God;' he was not made the Son of God, he was begotten, not made. Now he was declared with power to be so.

I will not stand to open those words, 'declared,' &c., and the various acceptation of them. Only observe, that he was declared with power to be the Son of God, with an omnipotent power; as, in Luke iv. 36, it is said, 'with power he commanded the unclean spirits, and they came out;' such a power as is only proper to God. But the main thing I quote the place for is this, what it was that declared Christ with so much power to be the Son of God? It followeth, 'by the resurrection from the dead,' saith he. Why doth he instance in this? He had wrought miracles, you know; he had raised Lazarus, and he had raised another from the dead; doth not that argue him to be the Son of God with as much power as his own resurrection? No; if you will have, saith he, an instance of an almighty power, and that he was the Son of God, take his resurrection from the dead; he was declared mightily to be the Son of God by his resurrection. Therefore the apostles, if you observe it, when they would prove him to be the Son of God, the Messiah, still you shall find they open his resurrection. Look Acts ii., from the 22d verse, and so on; when they would convince the Jews that he was the Messiah, they do it by his resurrection. And look Acts iv. 2, you have the like, where it is said, 'They taught the people, and preached through Jesus the resurrection from the dead.' You shall find the like Acts xiii. 33, where Paul proveth him to be the Messiah by the resurrection from the dead. And therefore, in 1 Tim. iii. 16, Christ is said to be 'justified in the Spirit;' that is, having been put to death in the flesh, and quickened by the Spirit, his Godhead, he was justified, he was declared that righteous one that had died for sin, and to be the Son of God, to all the world.

Now then, how doth the resurrection of Christ argue him to be the Son of God with power, that the exceeding greatness of his power should be put forth in his being raised from the dead? That is the thing I must speak to.

Interpreters upon that place, Rom. i. 4, put it upon this: say they, he raised up himself by his own power; that is the gloss they put upon it; therefore he was declared to be the Son of God, because he raised up himself. And indeed it is a strong argument, that he was the Son of God with power, if he raised up himself.

But you will say, How doth that prove it?

It proveth it thus: suppose there had been no more in his own resurrection than in any man's else, yet because he raised up himself, it was declared with power that he was the Son of God.

But how might that appear to the Jews that he was the Son of God? Why might not the Jews think that Christ had been raised up by the power of God, as Lazarus had been raised up, or those in the Old Testament had been raised up? How doth it prove that he is the Son of God in his resurrection, more than in anything else? And how doth it appear that he raised up himself as the Son of God?

I will shew you how it appeareth. He had said before, he had given it out, it was that he died for, he had told them that he was the Son of God; and the witnesses brought in this witness, that they heard him say, 'Destroy this temple, and in three days I will build it again.' Now if he had lied, if he had not been the Son of God, God would never have raised him up; therefore it was a manifest argument that he was the Son of God, by his being raised up again; and being the Son of God, raised up himself by that power that is in God himself. Therefore, in John ii. 19, saith he, 'Destroy this temple, and in three days I will raise it up;' and John x. 18, 'I have power to lay down my life, and I have power to take it again.' Had he lied, had he not been the Son of God, certainly God would never have raised him up; therefore seeing he was raised up by God, certainly he was the Son of God.

But yet still the objection remaineth; for you will say, though he was declared to be the Son of God by being raised up again, he having given it out, which is all that interpreters put upon that place; but yet what special power was there put forth in his resurrection, more than in any man's else, that he should be said to be declared to be the Son of God with power by his resurrection, and that God should shew forth the exceeding greatness of his power in raising of him up? That is the thing I am to speak to.

To that I will but suggest two things unto you, wherein the power lay of raising up Christ from death unto life; and a special power, more than in raising up all men else besides, that were before him, or shall come after him.

My brethren, our Lord and Saviour Jesus Christ undertook never to rise or enter into his glory till such time as he had satisfied for the sins of all his elect; they lay all upon him; therefore to raise him up from death to glory must needs be a work of a greater power than ever yet was to raise up any man, whatsoever he were; for he had all the sins of all the elect, that he was to satisfy for, meeting in him.

My brethren, let me speak unto you. We are dead in sins and trespasses; but let me tell you this, he was to die for sins and trespasses, that is the phrase the Apostle useth, Rom. vi. 10. We read it, 'He died unto sin,' or, 'He died for sin,' the word will bear it. He was by his death to satisfy for sin, or he must never rise again.

Now then, take Jesus Christ not only as an ordinary man, but take him as he is made sin, as he is made a curse, there must a mighty power go to bring him to glory; for he must suffer for that first, he must have a power to endure that first before he be capable of being raised up again; which all angels and men could never have borne; therefore there is so great a power declared in his rising again.

In Rom. iv. 24, 25, 'We believe on him that raised up Jesus our Lord from the dead, who was delivered for our offences, and was raised again for our justification.' Mark that; the resurrection of Christ was not an ordinary resurrection, for it was not an ordinary death: for, saith he, when he died he was delivered for our offences, and he must satisfy for them by his death; and when he was raised again, he was not raised as a particular person, it is not like the raising up of an ordinary man; but, saith he, he was raised for our justification, for the justification of all that he died for, and therefore he must satisfy for sin, and pay the uttermost farthing before he rise again. Hence now cometh there to be so great a difficulty in raising up our Lord and Saviour Jesus Christ to that glory he was raised up unto.

I will omit some confirmations of this truth, and give you but one scripture, which will present it unto you. It is Acts ii. 24, 'Whom God hath raised up, having loosed the pains of death; because it was not possible he should be holden of it.' It is Peter's speech concerning Christ and his resurrection. And, ver. 27, 'Because thou wilt not leave my soul in hell, neither wilt thou suffer thy Holy One to see corruption.'

To open these words, and to prove the thing out of them which I intend

—viz., That in raising up Jesus Christ from the dead there was an infinite power put forth, more than in raising up any one that ever yet was raised up. The Apostle's scope here is to prove that Jesus Christ is the Son of God, and he proveth it by his resurrection, and by the difficulty that was in it, which is implied in these words, 'Because it was not possible he should be holden of death,' or of 'the sorrows of death.' If it had been possible, they would have held him, but it was not possible; there was so mighty a power came to have his *mittimus*, that though they put forth all the power they could, yet it was not possible they should hold him.

Now, to open the words a little unto you, I will give you what I think to be the sense of the place. The difficulty of raising up of Christ lieth in these words, that first the pains of death were to be loosed. They are ὠδίναι, as Beza and others, and I find that Zanchy ran the same way. The meaning of them is this: God raised him up, say they, being loosed; it is not the pains of death being loosed, but *him* being loosed; *solutus doloribus mortis*, for *solutis doloribus mortis*. He ascribeth that to the pains of death which properly belongeth to Christ; he was freed from the pains of death, and then God raised him up. As in the gospel it is said, 'his leprosy was cleansed;' that is not a proper speech, but 'he was cleansed of his leprosy:' so here, having 'loosed the pains of death'—that is, he was loosed from the pains of death, he had scattered, he had dissipated all the pains of death, and then he was loosed, and he was raised.

Now, what is meant by the *pains of death* here? Let us examine that a little, for, if you mark it, the difficulty of his resurrection lies in the pains of death. After Christ was in the grave,—consider what I say,—there were no pains of death that held him, he had no pains in the grave after he was dead. What pains are they, then, that are here called the pains of death, which he was freed from, and then God raised him up, upon which he putteth the difficulty of his resurrection?

The word in the Greek, ὠδίναι, is the birth-throes of death. Isa. liii. 11 interpreteth it well; 'He shall see,' saith he, 'of the travail of his soul.' They were the birth-throes which his soul had, which he must be loosed from and overcome, before he is capable to be raised up by God. It is not an ordinary death he is to undergo, or ordinary sorrows of death that hinder his resurrection, but there are the birth-throes of death to be overcome. What are those birth-throes of death? The travail of his soul. All our sins met in him, and the chastisement of our peace was upon him, as you have it in the 5th and 6th verses of the same Isa. liii. All those pangs that were in his soul—they tended to death, they would have carried his soul to hell, kept him from ever rising again, he had never come to glory; therefore they are called the pains of death—held him: yea, they would have held his soul had he not been God; had not God upheld him, they would have carried his soul instantly away, and held him from ever being capable of rising up again. Therefore, before he be capable of being raised, he must be freed from these pains of death; therein lieth the difficulty of his resurrection.

They are called the 'sorrows of death' too; not only of the first death, but of the second. I do not say he died the second death, the Scripture doth not say so. But that the sorrows of the second death took hold upon him, and upon his soul, to me is a certain truth. 'My soul,' saith he, he points to what was it, 'is heavy unto death;' he doth not say, My soul dieth, but it is heavy unto the death; it was at the point of death, when our sins and the wrath of God came in upon him.

In Isa. liii. you have his *deaths* mentioned,—look into your margins,—not death only, but deaths; and in Heb. ii. 4, it is said, 'he tasted of death.' What death? It appeareth by the following verses, *that death* which the devil hath power of; he tasted of it, but he was not overcome by it, that is the second death. It is that death which men are afraid of all their life long, which the Jews were afraid of: read the 9th, 14th, and 15th verses of that second to the Hebrews; and that was the second death.

Now, my brethren, in this death, and the pains of it, lieth the danger that Christ should never be raised up again, should never come to heaven; for those pains of death would have fetched his soul away, and made all angels and men to have died the second death, never to have been raised, never to satisfy the wrath of God. They were sorrows of death; deadly sorrows, as some interpret it, as he himself is called a man of sorrows, which is attributed to none but to him, because none endured the sorrows he did, deadly sorrows: as it is called the 'abomination of desolation,' that is, abominable desolation; so the sorrows of death, that is, deadly sorrows, hellish sorrows, infernal sorrows, if you will so express it; for there was the cause of it, the wrath of God; there was the substance of it.

Now, in a word, to gather up this. Saith he, God hath raised him up, he being free, or having freed himself by the power of the Godhead from these pains of death, which, if it had been possible, he should have been held by them, but hold him they could not; therefore the words in the 27th verse interpret it without all straining. There is a great deal of do what should be meant by 'leaving his soul in hell,' and his 'Holy One not to see corruption,' that is, his body. Say I, the 24th verse interpreteth it, 'him hath God raised up,' being freed from the sorrows of death, of the second death, the birth-throes of it; God delivered his soul of it, left not his soul in hell; then he raised up his body that it should not see corruption. Herein now lieth the difficulty of raising up our Lord and Saviour Jesus Christ, more than all the men in the world; for if all the angels in heaven, and all the men in the world, had encountered with those sorrows of death he encountered with, they had never been raised up, for they could never have overcome them. Therefore saith the text here, the 'exceeding greatness of his power' was shewn in raising up Christ from death to glory.

And this is one sense in respect of which there is an exceeding greatness of power attributed to the resurrection of Jesus Christ.

But, secondly, if you will know wherein the exceeding greatness of power lieth,—if you observe the coherence,—it is not only in raising him up simply from death, there is but a little said of that here, but it is attributed to *the glory he was raised up to.* Therein lay the power; it lies not simply in the *terminus à quo*, the term, the state from which he was raised; but if you take in withal this, that God hath 'set him at his own right hand in the heavenly places, far above all principalities and powers;' take but the compass of the distance between the state he was raised from, and the state he is raised unto, and then you will all acknowledge what the text saith here, there is an exceeding greatness of power indeed.

So that if you ask me now, What this power was that was shewn upon Christ?

I answer, first, merely in his raising him up; for he was to overcome that which no creature could overcome, before he was capable of being raised; he was to pay the last farthing, whereof the sorrows of death were part, and the greatest sum.

And then, secondly, if to raise him up merely had been no more than to raise another man, yet to raise him up to glory, there lieth the exceeding greatness of his power. Take the *terminus ad quem*, the state wherein he is now. Eph. iv. 9, 'He that ascended, he descended first into the lower parts of the earth.'

Now then, go and make a pair of compasses, make a proportion between these two; put one foot of the compass in heaven, whither he is ascended, far above all principalities and powers, and put the other foot of the compass in the lower parts of the earth, in the grave in which he lay; and to raise him up from the one to the other is the exceeding greatness of power the Apostle here speaks of. Measure from the lowest part of the earth, to far above all principalities and powers, and therein lieth the power put forth in raising Christ here spoken of.

Now I have shewn you wherein the power of raising up Christ lieth; that is the first thing. The second thing I should shew you is this: That to bring a sinner from the death of sin to live again,—Christ lay under the guilt of sin imputed to him, we lie under the *power* and *guilt* too,—to raise up a sinner from this, 'we who were dead in sins and trespasses,' and place us in heaven with Christ, holdeth a proportion with the resurrection, and with the power put forth in raising up Christ from death to glory.

This is the second thing I should shew to make up the parallel.

SERMON XXIX.

And what is the exceeding greatness of his power to us-ward, who believe, according to the working of the might of his power; the same which he wrought in Christ, (or, *put forth in Christ,*) *when he raised him from the dead, and set him at his own right hand in the heavenly places,* &c. —VER. 19, 20.

THAT which is said here of the resurrection and exaltation of our Lord and Saviour Jesus Christ is to be understood two ways. Either—

First, comparatively; as he compareth the work in our hearts, or upon us, with the power that wrought in Christ when he raised him from the dead. Or—

Secondly, the words in the 20th verse, and so on, are to be considered simply as setting before us the resurrection and exaltation of Jesus Christ.

I must first handle these words in their comparison. The meaning whereof is this: that the same power that wrought in Jesus Christ in raising him from the dead, and setting him at God's right hand, works in our faith, in our believing. 'Who believe,' saith he, 'according to the working of his mighty power, the same which wrought in Christ,' &c.

You shall find that the Apostle handles both parts of this comparison. He speaks of the resurrection and exaltation of Christ, what a great work that was, from the 20th verse to the end of this chapter. And then he speaks what a great work it is to raise up our hearts and to work upon them, that *us*, who were dead in sins and trespasses, God should quicken and raise up together with Christ, and make us sit in heavenly places; this he speaks of in the second chapter, from the 1st verse to the 11th.

That which is proper to the opening of this 19th verse is, to speak only of the power, both which raised up Christ from death to life and which works in us that believe. And to that I am to keep at this time.

There are therefore two things to be spoken to—

First, That there was *an exceeding greatness of power* shewn forth in Christ's resurrection and setting him at God's right hand.

Secondly, That in a proportion, there is as exceeding greatness of power shewn to us-ward when God bringeth us to believe.

I must begin with the first, to shew you the exceeding greatness of power in raising up Christ. I quoted for that, Rom. i. 4, where it is said he was declared to be the Son of God with power by the resurrection from the dead. And a parallel place to this, which I then omitted, is that in 2 Cor. xiii. 4, where it is said that 'though Christ was crucified through weakness,'—he was left to all the weakness of man's nature, so as to take in sufferings, though the power of God was seen in upholding him under it,—'yet he liveth by the power of God.' Though he was crucified in weakness, yet his life, his raising up again, was by the power of God. So you see express scripture that in the resurrection of Jesus Christ there was shewn forth a great power; and such a power as he was declared by nothing more to be the Son of God.

Now, you will ask me wherein was the power shewn, both in raising up of Christ from the dead and in exalting him? For you must take both in; it is not only the power that was shewn in raising him from the dead, but also the power that exalted him. Take both in, I say; and so there was an infinite power in it: to raise him up, him that was laid so low in the grave, and to exalt him to sit at God's right hand, to wield all the affairs of heaven and earth, and who shall be the judge of the world, that is far above all principalities and powers. Take the distance between these two terms, the grave, and what he is in heaven, and there is an exceeding greatness of power indeed, the highest instance of power that can be imagined.

First, then; to shew you the power that was put forth in his resurrection, in his raising up from death to life. Of all works still the raising one up from death to life hath been counted an evidence of an omnipotent power. Our Saviour Christ had done many miracles, yet, saith he, John v. 20, 'My Father will shew me greater works than these, that you may marvel.' And what are those greater works? Look ver. 21, 'As the Father raiseth up the dead, and quickeneth them, even so the Son quickeneth whom he will.' To raise one from the dead therefore is a greater work than all those miracles Christ wrought; and therefore though he was declared to be the Son of God by all his miracles, yet that which struck the stroke, and put it out of question that he must needs be the Son of God, was that he was raised from death to life.

But you will say, wherein lieth so extraordinary a power in raising of Christ as was never shewn in raising of any man? For that is the thing the text holdeth forth; for otherwise the raising up of Lazarus, the raising up by the prophets, shew an omnipotent power. But here is a peculiar exceeding greatness of power attributed to the raising of Christ from death. Wherein, you will ask, was that shewn?

It was shewn in this, that Jesus Christ rose not as a single person, but he rose as a Common Person for all his elect; and therefore in 1 Cor. xv. 20–22, he is called 'the first-fruits of them that sleep;' and it is said that in Christ all shall rise, and all did rise when he rose. Now, if when Jesus Christ rose he broke open all graves, set them all open,—Dead men, saith he, your bonds are loosened, you shall come forth one day by virtue of my resurrection,—then the raising up of Christ was as much as the raising up of all mankind at the latter day; for he took the gates of hell and death, and carried them up to the hill, as Samson did; therefore saith the Apostle, 1 Cor. xv. 55, 'O death, where is thy sting? O grave, where is thy victory? Thanks be to God, which giveth us the victory through our Lord Jesus Christ.' He spoke of Christ's resurrection. When he rose all rose, and his resurrection had all the power of all resurrections contracted in it.—That is the first.

But then, secondly, you must know that when Jesus Christ rose, he rose not like an ordinary man; he rose for our justification, he rose in the stead of sinners, to justify sinners, as having borne their sins and satisfied for them. He was not to rise—mark what I say—unless he had fully satisfied God for all the sins of his elect; and to satisfy for those sins, which must be done before he riseth, required an infinite power. I take it that Peter holdeth forth this in Acts ii. 24. I opened the words in the last discourse. I shall but in a word or two repeat the sum of what was then said. Speaking of the resurrection of Christ, saith he, 'Whom God hath raised up, having loosed the pains of death, because it was not possible he should be holden of it.' He telleth us first, that there were certain sorrows of death,—that is, deadly sorrows, or, as the word in the Greek signifieth, there were birth-throes of death, that were deadly. They were not pains he endured after he was dead, for then you know the body endures nothing, and his soul was in Paradise; therefore, these pains of death, these deadly pains, must be endured before; yet there were those that hindered his resurrection, that had he not overcome those pains first, God had never raised him up. Now, our Saviour Christ did scatter, did dissipate all these pains of death; he paid them to God, he bore all our sins, and God's wrath; and when he had done this, Now, saith God, I can raise him up when I will; now let him die. When that was finished, he gave up the ghost; for when he hung upon the cross, you know he said, 'It is finished.' I take it, he had relation to that great brunt which the Apostle to the Hebrews saith he feared, which was these pains, these deadly pains of enduring the wrath of God for man's sins. Now, saith he, the great brunt is over, it is finished; and when these were scattered, then did God come and raise him up; and herein lay the greatness of the power shewn in the resurrection of Christ, that God raised him up, he having loosened the pains of death first, or Christ being loosened, or having overcome,—the words will bear all this,—then God raised him up. Therein, I say, lay the power, and therein lay more in his resurrection than in all men's else besides.

Or else, secondly, the power that wrought toward Christ mentioned here referreth to his exaltation; for you see he doth not only say the power that wrought in Christ in raising him from death, but in setting him at his own right hand; you must take both in. Now, what is wanting in the one is supplied in the other. Suppose there was but a small power in raising him up from death to life; yet to take a poor carpenter's son, whom all would have despised, and to carry him up to heaven, where he flingeth off flesh, the frailty of the human nature, and appeareth more glorious, infinitely more glorious, than all the angels, and is filled with more knowledge, and that all that God meaneth to do shall run through the hand of that human nature; here was a power, to raise him up thus high, beyond what the thoughts of man can reach.—And so much now for the power that was shewn in raising up Christ from death to glory. That part of the parallel is despatched.

Now, to come to the *second* part, and that is this, *That in God's working upon us there is a proportion of power to us-ward who believe, answerable to the power that raised up Christ from death to glory.*

For my clear proceeding in this, I will set limits to myself, which shall help you to understand my scope.

First, I will not speak of the likeness that is between Christ's resurrection and the working of grace in our hearts, although the Scripture telleth us, in Rom. vi. 4, that like as he was raised up from the dead, so we are raised up to walk in newness of life; he makes a likeness between the one and the other. The words, 'according to his working in Christ,' note not so much a likeness, as a proportion, and therefore it is κατὰ τὴν ἐνέργειαν τοῦ κράτους τῆς ἰσχύος αὐτοῦ, 'according to his effectual working,'—the proportion of working that efficacy of power put forth,—'which he wrought,' saith he, 'in Jesus Christ.' So that now it is not my design to handle a likeness between Christ's resurrection and our conversion,—that is not the scope, though that other scriptures hold forth, for I must speak pertinently to what this place holds forth,—but that it is the same power, in a proportion, that works in the one and in the other.

And then, in the second place,—let me add that too,—it is not a proportion of equality; that is, that an equal proportion of power is put forth in us and in Christ. No, let Christ have the pre-eminence above all his brethren; he is the wisdom of God, and the power of God, as he is called, 1 Cor. i. 24. But yet there is so great a nearness as that when God would speak of the power that goeth to quicken our hearts, to work faith in us, of all the works that ever he did he chooseth rather to instance in his power in raising up Christ from death to life, than in any work else whatsoever.

Then, thirdly, I shall not mention the power of God in general, in converting,—I have handled that already, and handled it largely,—but only so far as the similitude will hold forth a like power in the point of believing, in the point of faith. That is the thing I am now to speak to.

If you ask me now wherein there is the like proportion of power put forth toward us that was toward Christ? I answer you, first, that you must take in all the works of God upon us first and last; you must take in the first resurrection and the second resurrection, both which the Scripture seems to hold forth. You must take in all the works of God upon a believing soul from his first conversion till God hath set him in heaven; take them altogether, and the power that raised up Christ from death to life and glory, holdeth some proportion with that power that shall work in us first and last, before God hath done with us.

Now, to shew you that all the works of God upon us are a resurrection. You all take for granted, therefore I shall not need to speak much of that, that the raising up of our bodies at the latter day will hold proportion with the raising up of Christ. But, my brethren, the work of conversion holdeth proportion with it, and our growth in grace and carrying us on in holiness holdeth proportion with it.

I shall give you Scripture that both these are called resurrections. John v. 20, 21; you shall read there of the Father's raising up of the dead at the 21st verse, and the Son's likewise quickening whom he will. Now read on the chapter to the 29th verse, and you shall find a double resurrection there mentioned. You have first the resurrection of conversion, whereby he works faith in men's hearts; that you have at the 24th and 25th verses, 'He that heareth my word, and believeth on him that sent me, hath everlasting life, and shall not come into condemnation; but is passed from death to life.' So saith the 24th verse; then he addeth at the 25th verse, 'Verily, verily, I say unto you, The hour is coming, and now is, when the dead shall hear the voice of the Son of God; and they that hear it shall live.' Here is the first resurrection. He telleth us at the 20th verse, that the Father would shew him greater works than any he had yet done. Now, in the 11th chapter, you shall find he raiseth up Lazarus, when Lazarus stank, and had lain four days in the grave. Then read chap. xiv. 12; you shall find he tells his apostles, You have seen, saith he, Lazarus' raising,—for he was raised at the 11th chapter,—when I am gone, you shall do greater works than that. What were those greater works they should do? They should convert souls; men that were dead in sins and trespasses, they should be turned unto God. Our Saviour Christ converted few, but the apostles had three thousand converted at one time, as you know there were at the first sermon that ever Peter preached. It is hard to instance what was a greater work than what Christ did, but only that which here our Saviour calleth, that 'the dead shall hear the voice of the Son of God, and they that hear it shall live.' He speaks, my brethren, of conversion; for if you mark it, he had said in the verse just before, that 'he that heareth my words, and believeth on him that sent me, is passed from death unto life.' He useth the same phrase, 'I say unto you, The hour is coming, and now is, when the dead shall hear the voice of the

Son of God; and they that hear it shall live.' And then, comparing it with the 28th verse, it appeareth more manifestly he speaks there of a second resurrection, of a general resurrection. 'Marvel not,' saith he, 'for the hour is coming in the which all that are in their graves shall hear his voice, and shall come forth; they that have done good, to the resurrection of life; and they that have done evil, to the resurrection of damnation.' There is this difference between these two resurrections mentioned, the one in the 25th, the other in the 28th verse, that that in the 25th verse is spoken but of some, for all men are not converted, they do not rise in that sense; 'they that hear his voice they shall live;' but the truth is, all do not hear his voice. But when he comes to speak of the resurrection at the latter day, saith he, 'The hour is coming in which all that are in their graves shall hear his voice, and shall come forth,' &c. And then he putteth a difference between their deaths; the one, he saith, is a bodily death; therefore, by way of difference, he expresseth it thus, 'All that are in the graves shall hear his voice,' so it is ver. 28. But when he speaks of the other in the 25th verse, he saith they are simply dead; 'The dead,' saith he, 'shall hear his voice, and they that hear it shall live.' Yea, in this 25th verse, he corrects himself, 'The hour is coming,' yea, 'and now is,' saith he,—it is coming, and coming presently,—wherein those that are dead shall hear his voice and live; therefore, he doth not speak of the general resurrection.

Here, you see, is a double resurrection. Now, take both these together,—the first resurrection, wherein men are quickened that were dead in sins and trespasses; and the last resurrection, when all that are in the graves shall rise,—take, I say, both these works together, and you have a mighty power put forth; for you have the work double.

Our Saviour Christ had a double resurrection: he had one of his soul, as I may so call it, when he overcame the pains of death,—that I spake of in Acts ii. 24,—'Thou wilt not leave my soul in hell;' and there was a resurrection of his body, 'Thou wilt not suffer thy Holy One,' namely, his body, 'to see corruption.'

Now, my brethren, we likewise have a double resurrection too. We have a resurrection of our soul, which is done in this life, whereby grace is wrought in our hearts, being dead in sins and trespasses; and at the latter day we have a resurrection of our bodies. Now, as the greatness of his power in Christ's raising lay not in taking him out of the grave so much as in rescuing his soul from what he feared,—from those pains, those birth-throes of death, the wrath of God which he was to undergo,—that resurrection of his soul was the great resurrection; so Peter quoteth it. So it is here; the great resurrection is the first resurrection.

That you may yet see this clearer, you shall find in Scripture that our new birth and the resurrection are parallel expressions, they are put one for another; and Jesus Christ's resurrection is called a begetting, and our being begotten again is called a resurrection, because that the same power that is put forth in the one is put forth in the other.

It is evident that Christ's resurrection is called a begetting of him in Acts xiii. 33: 'God,' saith he, 'hath raised up Jesus again; as it is written in the second psalm, Thou art my Son, this day have I begotten thee.' Here you see Jesus Christ's resurrection is called a begetting; and you shall find, in Col. i. 18, he is called 'the first-begotten from the dead.' Mark it, his resurrection is called a begetting.

Now, as his resurrection is called a begetting of him again, or a begetting him rather, so our being born again, our conversion, is called a resurrection, as you have it Col. ii. 12. I shall come to it by and by. Yea, Matt. xix. 28, he calleth the resurrection of the just, when they shall rise again at the latter day, their regeneration, their being begotten again; saith he, 'Ye which have followed me, in the regeneration, when the Son of man shall sit in the throne of his glory, ye also shall sit upon twelve thrones,' &c. Those words, 'in the regeneration,' refer to the time when Jesus Christ will come to judgment. There the general resurrection is called the regeneration, the new begetting of the sons of God; and therefore one of the Evangelists calleth them sons of the resurrection, because it is a begetting them again.

You see, my brethren, how the Scripture speaks of conversion; it calleth it a regeneration, it calleth it a resurrection, and it calleth the resurrection at the latter day a regeneration; it calleth Christ's resurrection, likewise, a begetting of him again.

You see, therefore, now, that conversion is called a resurrection, as well as that at the latter day. Now, I am to prove this likewise, that all our growth in holiness is called a resurrection too. And for that I shall quote you Phil. iii. 11, 12; 'If by any means,' saith he, 'I might attain to the resurrection of the dead.' Interpreters do most of them carry it to this sense, namely, that Paul had in his eye the reward at the latter day, and that is his meaning when he saith, that he 'might attain to the resurrection of the dead.' But it is evident, by his scope, that he meaneth perfect holiness, growing in grace; his aim was to grow as holy as men shall be when they are risen from the dead. It appeareth so plainly; for, saith he, 'not as though I had already attained, either were already perfect: but I follow after, if that I may apprehend that for which also I am apprehended of Christ Jesus; forgetting those things which are behind, I reach forth to those things which are before.' His meaning is this: saith he, Our Lord and Saviour Jesus Christ hath taken me to work so much grace in me, such a portion and measure of grace is to be wrought in me by Jesus Christ; and, saith he, I desire to know the power of his resurrection to that end, as the 10th verse hath it; I would fain, saith he, have that holiness presently, and stay no longer for it, 'for which I am apprehended of Christ.' I would be as holy as I shall be when I shall rise again at the latter day. So that every degree of holiness he doth account a part of the resurrection from the dead; and that this is his meaning appears by those words, 'not as though I had already attained.' All the world knew that he had not attained the resurrection from the dead,—that is, the glory of the world to come; what need he have corrected himself if that this were the meaning? Therefore he speaks of holiness in this life, which is a continual resurrection till he cometh to be perfectly holy: 'Not as though I had already attained, either were already perfect,' in holiness, namely; there was a perfect holiness in his eye,—which he calleth the resurrection from the dead,—to be as holy as they shall be that shall rise again, which he followed after, forgetting what is behind, and pressing at what is before, at what is to come.

And in this sense, as you read in Ezek. xxxvii., the dried bones were not raised at once, but by degrees; the bones first came together, and then the sinews and the flesh came upon them, and then the skin covered them above. So, the truth is, this power raiseth us up by degrees; every new degree of grace is as after the bones came together in conversion, then flesh cometh, and then sinews, and so by degrees we attain the resurrection from the dead.

You see now that all the works of God upon us, both of conversion at first, degrees of grace and growth in grace afterward, are called a resurrection; and, lastly, the great work at the latter day, when he will raise up our bodies, and bring our souls to them, and raise both up to glory. Now then, take all the work of God upon a Christian, first and last, and before God hath done with him, there will be so great a power found working in him as no pattern can hold forth the like, but the raising of Christ from death to glory.

And, my brethren, if you doubt of the proportion of power between the working on us and on Christ, do but consider the state that God raiseth us from. He saith we are dead in sins and trespasses before; the Apostle insisteth much upon that; he runneth out at large upon it in the second chapter, where he makes out the comparison; and you shall observe that he makes the difference between God's raising up of Christ and of us to lie in this. When he speaks of the power that was shewn in raising Christ, he runneth out here, in this first chapter, much upon his glorification, as if the greatness of his power was chiefly spent there. When he speaks of his power in raising us up in the second chapter, he spendeth a great part of his discourse in shewing that we were dead in trespasses and sins; the *terminus a quo,* the term from which we were raised, that is it which setteth forth the exceeding greatness of his power to us-ward. Consider, I say, what we were, —dead in sins and trespasses,—that these men should be converted to God, should be carried on in holiness till they be perfectly holy, till they attain to that estate which men risen from the dead shall have in holiness, and withal have their bodies raised out of the grave, bodies that have seen corruption: Jesus Christ's body never saw corruption, he was never dead in sins and trespasses; he died for sins and trespasses indeed, but we were dead in sins and trespasses. Now then, compare the state out of which we are raised, and all the works of God upon us, and all the degrees of it, which are all little resurrections, and put them all together, first and last, they will hold a great proportion with the power that raised up Christ from death to life and glory, so as there is no work that ever God did, holdeth the like proportion in power with this as the resurrection of Christ doth.

Now, I should indeed lay open to you the greatness of the death in which we were in sins and trespasses; it would set forth this power, how low we were in this respect; but because that belongeth to the second chapter, I will therefore pass it over.

I come now more particularly to shew you—for the point is worth the insisting upon, for these are but generals—that in a more especial manner in the work of faith (for, if you observe it, the text here instanceth only in believing) there is a like power put forth as was in the raising of Christ from death to life. 'Who believe,' saith he, 'according to the working of his mighty power, which God put forth in Christ when he raised him from the dead.' *Who believe;* so that to handle the power of God in working of faith is that which is proper to the text, and is certainly the scope of the Apostle; for read the second chapter, where he makes up the comparison, at the 5th, 6th, and 8th verses, 'You who were dead in sins hath he quickened: by grace ye are saved through faith; and that not of yourselves, it is the gift of God.' That was the life which had quickened you, in working which lay the greatness of his power to us-ward. And, my brethren, I shall shew you that the work of faith, if any other work of God upon us should be a resurrection, then there is a resurrection in that. The work of sanctification is a resurrection, and a great deal of power is put forth in it; but the work of faith is in a special manner a resurrection from the dead, and the like power put forth in the working of it that was put forth in raising Christ from the dead. This you see is proper to the text.

I shall first prove it from Col. ii. 12. It is a place I quoted before. Saith he, 'Buried with him in baptism, wherein also ye are risen with him.' *Risen*, how? 'Through the faith of the operation of God, who hath raised him from the dead.' Here, you see, he makes believing to be a resurrection; risen, saith he, through faith; and this faith, he saith, is of the operation of God. He saith they were dead in sins and trespasses; they were dead in the guilt of sin, and they rose by faith from under that guilt. That is his scope, as I shall shew you by and by.

To open these words unto you a little, and to shew you the parallel between the work of faith and the resurrection of Christ, and that in point of power. It is called 'faith of the operation of God,' because it is especially wrought by God. As when you commend a receipt, you will say it is a receipt of such a man's making, it is a precious thing, there is none makes it but such a one that is an eminent physician. So he saith here of faith. 'Faith,' saith he—which is a precious grace, for it is called precious faith, 2 Pet. i. 1—'of the operation of God,' and of such a power as raised up Christ from death to life; 'Faith of the operation of God, who hath raised him from the dead.' You see he speaks only to the point of believing.

Now, my brethren, to shew you how faith is a resurrection, and from such a power put forth in the working of it as was in the resurrection, you must know this, that a man is said to be dead, as well in respect of the guilt of sin, as of the power of sin. As thus: take a man condemned to die, the man is alive still, there is not the power of death upon him, but there is the guilt of death upon him, and you will say he is a dead man; his pardon now would be a resurrection from death to life. You find it in John v. 24, that 'he that believeth is passed from death to life;' and, in John iii. 18, you find that 'he that believeth not is condemned already;' that is, really he is condemned, he is under a state of death whether he believeth it or no. Now, on the other side, look in Rom. v. 18, and you shall find our being justified is called 'justification of life.' Here, you see, he that believeth not, take him in his former estate, is a dead man; he is condemned already. He that is justified is a living man; it is justification of life, it is thus really. Now then, what is it whereby a man is raised up from this state of condemnation, and brought into this state of life? It is faith. 'He that believeth,' saith he, 'is passed from death to life;' and 'He that believeth hath eternal life.'

Now, my brethren, as really and indeed a man in the state of nature is a dead man, and a man in the state of grace is a living man, is in the state of life; so now, that God may make the soul to apprehend his love, what he doth for him, he doth not only change a man from a state of death to life by a real pardon,—as a king useth to do, he only pardoneth a man outwardly; he was a dead man before, he is a living man now, he is passed from death to life,—but God doth so deal with his soul in working faith in him, that what he doth really the soul may apprehend it, and in making him apprehend it, which is the work of faith, there is truly a resurrection from death to life. And therefore, in that Col. ii. 12, 13, faith is called a quickening of a man. 'You, being dead,' saith he, 'in your sins and uncircumcision of your flesh, hath he quickened together with him,'—he speaks of faith, which he mentioned in the verse before, where he saith, 'Ye are risen with him through faith,'—'having forgiven you all trespasses.' Mark those words. So that now, that faith whereby a man looks out for forgiveness of all his trespasses, apprehendeth pardon of sin, that faith is said to be a resurrection; for it makes a man to apprehend the justification of life; it makes a man that apprehends himself to be a dead man, to be a living man, and putteth a new life into his soul.

You shall find often in the Scripture that it is said the just shall live by faith.

Now, when he saith in this place of the Colossians, we are 'risen by faith,' and that we are 'quickened by faith,' ver. 13, it is plain he meaneth faith as it hath justification for its object, as we believe to be justified; because, 'having forgiven you all your trespasses' cometh in in the 13th verse.

Now then, having given you this general proof that faith is a resurrection from the dead, I will particularise you the work of faith, and shew you that it is truly a work of resurrection. I must open it by these two things:—

I must shew you, first, that when God bringeth a man to believe, he strikes him stark dead to get life in him again, and he putteth such a new life into him, as all creatures, men and angels, can never put into his soul: so that you do rise through faith,—faith of the mere operation of God, which none else could work,—when you do lay hold upon Christ for forgiveness of sins. First, I say, he strikes the man dead. I will explain that unto you by these particulars.

You must know, first, that every man, though he be dead in sins and trespasses, as you all are, yet he is alive in himself. Through that great self-flattery that is in all men's hearts, you think well of yourselves, and that you are living men. I will give you an instance for it. You would think that a man that is used to nothing but the preaching of the law, and knoweth nothing but the law, that that man must needs be a dead man in his own thoughts, and that he must apprehend nothing but the sentence of death, and that he is a child of wrath, for the law is a killing letter. Yet take the instance of Paul: he was a man that had as exact a knowledge of the law as any unregenerate man in the world hath. Now, saith he, Rom. vii. 9, 'I was alive without the law.' He saith two things of himself: first, that he was without the law,—that is, I was without the spiritual knowledge of the law, without the knowledge of the law in the spiritual strictness of it. And then, saith he, I was a living man; I thought I should have gone to heaven as certainly as any man in the world. It is strange that a man should be able to bear the law, and should yet think himself a living man; yet, you see, Paul did. He could not deny but that his sins had deserved death; but yet he framed to himself such an interpretation of the law as to think himself to be a living man.

Well, you live under both law and gospel; I assure you this, that all of you by nature, though you have never so much outward light by the preaching of the word,—though you think yourselves living men, and you frame to yourselves what is faith, and what is repentance, and what will save you; that you will live, and think yourselves to be living men,—yet if you have not an inward spiritual light struck upon your hearts, you are but dead still.

Now, my brethren, in the second place, whensoever God cometh to work faith in any man's heart, what doth he? He killeth him, strikes him dead; whereas naturally, through self-flattery, a man apprehendeth, whatsoever the word saith, that he is a living man. 'I was alive,' saith he, 'without the law,' that is, without the true spiritual knowledge of the law. God cometh and killeth him, slayeth him. In Gal. ii. 19, 20, saith he, 'I through the law am dead to the law.' This was when Paul came to understand it aright; he was struck stark dead with it; he that thought that if any man living should have gone to heaven, he should, he received the sentence of death in himself, and now you may know where to have him; 'Behold, he prayeth,' saith he. He was struck off his horse, and there he lay stark dead; that is, all the sinews and principles of life, the heart-root of it was struck; he saw that interpretation of the law of God that made him to see that he was a dead man, and that if any man in the world went to hell, he should. This was Paul's case, my brethren; you may find this in Rom. vii.,—it followeth there in the same place,—how he was struck dead. 'I was alive,' saith he, 'without the law once, but when the commandment came,' and arrested me, 'sin revived, and I died: and the commandment, that was ordained to life, I found to be unto death.' I went upon a mistake, saith he; I thought I should have been saved by my works, by doing: Do this, and live. I was mistaken; I saw the law did nothing but condemn me, and that all my works were dead works; the commandment came, came in the spiritual knowledge of it: he saw the spiritual holiness the law required, when this commandment came into his heart, as you see the sun cometh and shines into a house; then it struck him stark dead.

Now, my brethren, to work this, to kill a natural man thus, that is alive through self-flattery, and to lay him for dead, it is a mighty work. Why? Because every man having self-love in him, self-flattery will never give up the ghost of itself; all the reason a man hath will fight for arguments to prove himself a living man. This same self-flattery, which you are all born with, will struggle for life; it must be killed, it will never yield of itself; and to kill it is a mighty power. What, to kill the Benjamin of original sin; what is a man's Benjamin? To think well of himself, that he shall be happy. Now, to make him think that the state he is in is a state of damnation, if he go on in it, and to strike all self-flattery at the root, to lay the axe at the root of the tree and kill it; my brethren, what saith the soul? Nay then, saith he, if this Benjamin be once killed, I shall go with sorrow to my grave; I shall never recover that, I shall never have a good day more, if I entertain such a conceit, that I am in a state of death. To keep up this opinion in a man's heart, that he is a living man, all in a man will fight for it.—So that, first, to kill the man is a mighty work.

And the truth is, my brethren, it is never thoroughly done till there cometh in a spiritual light created in a man's heart. For my part, I think that which strikes a man dead, and dead to purpose, and prepareth ultimately for grace, it is a spiritual light, the same light wherewith I see Christ afterward; there is nothing else will kill a man. God indeed may come with terror upon a man's conscience, knock him into a swoon; but self-flattery will revive again when the terrors are off, and he will have a good opinion of himself again. But to kill a man wholly from ever rising again, that a man shall say, as Paul, I am dead to the law for ever, I can never recover this wound, I can never have a good opinion of my former estate more, or of myself more; nothing can do this but a spiritual light: the commandment must come, there must be a spiritual light to discover a man's sin, and his state of death, or he will never die.

Well, when a man is thus laid dead, what followeth? Saith the Apostle, 'sin revived.' Why, I was guilty of sin before, it never troubled me; I had thoughts of God's being merciful, I could set my good works amongst them, and one should answer the other; but when God had laid me for dead thus, all my sins revived. I looked upon my sins before as dead serpents that had no stings; but now they are all living serpents, and they begin to revive, and to kill me, and sting me worse. For when a man seeth himself in a state of death, all his sins come in upon him; I died, saith he, and sin revived. And as when self-flattery is once killed, a man is dead for ever from having any opinion of himself: so when a man is once dead thus, he is apt to be swallowed up with despair, as the Apostle's expression is of the incestuous person, 'swallowed up with sorrow;' not only dead, but buried. If God be not merciful to the poor soul, he is not only killed, you see, but he is likely to be buried.

Now then, when the soul lieth thus,—to come to the second head,—when a man is thus dead, thus killed, to work faith in this soul is a resurrection; 'Ye are risen,' saith he, 'through the faith of the operation of God, that raised up Christ from the dead.' It must be a resurrection, my brethren. For, first, you can never fetch life into this soul again, if he be rightly wounded. A man terrified may, for he is but in a swoon; but he that hath a spiritual insight into his condition, all the world will never fetch life in him again—that is, he will never have a good opinion of his former estate, nothing but the resurrection of faith will do it, a new light put in; a new light through the righteousness of Christ for the forgiveness of sins, that will revive his heart.

Nay, he will not only never have a good opinion of his former estate; but set him a-work to do new things, that which he never did before, from all his doing of them he will never come to have life again; nothing but faith will do it. Tell him thus, You were a dead man before, because you did not these and these things, you had not these and these workings which now you have; but all these new workings, of themselves considered, merely as workings in him, will never fetch life in him; it must be faith, and faith on him that raised up Christ from the dead, that must do it. In this case nature is apt to fall a-doing, and to fall upon new duties, evangelical duties, never practised before, to wash the heart, to reform the life, and twenty such things; when it hath tried all these, all is in vain; when the soul is rightly wounded, it will never live by all these. If he could weep his eyes out for sin, if a man could be all holy, as I may so express it; if his heart could set itself to all sorts of duties, all these would never fetch life in him again; nay, holiness itself would never fetch life into this heart. It must be faith only that must recover this man out of the deadness that God hath struck him with. So that there is a rising again by faith. Saith the Apostle, Gal. ii. 19, 'I am dead to the law through the law,' I am dead to it for ever, I can never live to it again. What doth he mean by *law* there? He doth not only mean merely the law of Moses, but he disputeth there against the opinion of the Galatians, who did not only take in the law of Moses to be justified by, but they took in works after conversion to be justified by them. That is clear out of Gal. i. 9. He telleth us, in the preface of the epistle, what his scope was; it was not to confute another law, but another gospel. 'If any man,' saith he, 'preach any other gospel unto you; yet not another,' saith he. They would have made another gospel, they would have joined works with Christ. Saith he, I can never live by this other gospel; I must have pure gospel, saith he; it must be Christ alone that must revive me; mere faith in the Son of God, as he saith chap. ii. 20. I am dead to all new laws whatsoever. Take the gospel itself, the law written in the heart; sanctification will never revive me again, I am dead to all those courses, it must be nothing but sheer faith. If ever you will fetch life into that soul again, you must have a cordial of Christ purely, and no mixture of law, or works, or qualifications, or anything else in it.

Now, my brethren, a man goeth and trieth all sorts of duties—sometimes men do so—to get life in themselves; but they do but set up new wares in old shops, while they turn these duties into a legal way. A man is not only dead to the condemning power of the law, but he is dead to the law as it is a covenant. A man is not dead to it in respect of the precepts of it, the matter of it, but in respect of the form; to the covenant of it he is dead. And if you will turn all the duties of the gospel, repentance, and all sorts of qualifications, into works of the law, a man is dead to them for ever; all these will never fetch life into that man again. Now mark what the Apostle saith in that same second to the Galatians, ver. 19. To what end was he dead to the law thus? 'That I might live unto God,' saith he. This death was to this end, that there might come a new life to him from God, and to God; which life he describeth afterward in ver. 20. It is the life of faith in the Son of God. 'The life that I now live,' saith he, 'I live by the faith of the Son of God.' Here, you see, now cometh in a resurrection, which all the world could not work in him. Dead, you see, he was. I am dead to the law for ever, nothing will recover me, all the legal ways in the world will never do it. 'The life I now live is by the faith of the Son of God.' Here is death and life, and here is faith, a resurrection from death to life. He saith, a man cannot live to God till he is thus dead to the law; and by death to the law I do not understand terrors, my brethren. No, they do but stound a man; but it is a spiritual insight into a man's natural condition, taking him off from whatsoever he is, or can be supposed in himself to be at present, or hereafter, that he can never have life in any of these,—this is a being dead to the law. And being so, he is now fit for a resurrection, to live by the faith of the Son of God alone.

Now, my brethren, there was a mighty power to kill a man thus; but now there is as great a power to raise up this man's soul, to believe only, and purely, and nakedly on Jesus Christ, and to come alone to him, and to set him only in his eye; there is as great a power as answereth his resurrection. I will but give you a scripture or two for it in general, and then make it good by particulars.

This man being thus dead, twice dead, as I may say;—for he is dead in his own righteousness, past, present, and to come; he is dead in the guilt of sin, all sin cometh in upon him, as the deadly sorrows came in upon Christ, to hinder him from rising again by faith: for when a man attempteth to believe, all his sins, like those deadly sorrows you heard spoken of in Christ's soul to hinder his resurrection, revive and come about him. Now, I say, to raise this man up requires a mighty power. Take one instance; it is in Ps. lxxxviii. It is a place to the purpose, for I shall quote those scriptures that speak in the language of the resurrection, of raising from death to life, and that in the business of faith, in the point of justification; for that is the point in hand. In that psalm you shall find a poor man lying in desertion, a man that was dead in his own apprehension, killed as Paul was. It is Heman; he was a godly man, but he lay under desertion; he had faith already, he had some revivings, but yet so as he was given up to desertion. Now, see what he saith of himself, ver. 4, 5: 'I am counted with them that go down into the pit; free among the dead, like the slain that lie in the grave, whom thou rememberest no more.' His meaning is this: I am a man that do apprehend myself to be one of those that are free of hell, 'free among the dead;' a man that am slain, stabbed with the guilt of sins reviving, like to the slain that lie in the grave, that lie in hell. And what saith he at the 10th verse: 'Wilt thou shew wonders to the dead? Shall the dead arise and praise thee? Shall thy loving-kindness be declared in the grave?' Can my soul ever come to think, I shall live in thy favour, in thy free grace and loving-kindness, to be justified by it, to apprehend myself a living man, and all my sins forgiven? To do this, saith he, is as great a wonder as to raise a man up from death to life; therefore he useth that expression, 'Wilt thou shew wonders to the dead?' He calleth it a wonder; for of all works else, still in Scripture you shall find the resurrection from the dead hath been counted the greatest wonder.

Now, my brethren, if this poor soul under desertion was left thus dead, then much more at first. I do not mean that there is the same sensibleness of it; but a man is much more unable to lay hold on Christ when he beginneth to believe at first, than this man was in temptation. The phrase in the 10th verse, as the Septuagint translates it, is exceeding emphatical. Saith he, 'Wilt thou shew wonders to the dead? Shall the physicians arise and praise thee?' So they read it, and so some good Hebrecians read it also; that is, Go send for all the college of physicians, all the angels out of heaven, all the skilful ministers and prophets that were then upon the earth, Gad and David, for he lived in David's time; send for them all. All these physicians may come with their cordials and balms; they will never cure me, never heal my soul, never raise me up to life again, except thou raise me; for I am 'free amongst the dead,' saith he. Now then, my brethren, to work faith in such a one; for this poor soul, being thus dead, to go out of himself, and by naked and sheer faith to go to Jesus Christ alone, whom God raised from the dead, and to believe on him alone; this is now as great a power as indeed to raise a man up from death to life.

I should have enlarged myself much here, by giving you some general scriptures that prove it a work parallel with raising up Christ from the dead; and shewed it likewise by the faith of Abraham, Rom. iv. 24, and Rom. x. 9. But at present I shall only demonstrate it unto you in particulars.

To raise up this soul now, what will do it? My brethren, nothing in a man's self will do it, therefore God's power alone must do it. Saith he in Gal. ii. 20, 'The life which I now live, I live by the faith of the Son of God.' It is not I that live, saith he. Mark those words, 'It is not I.' All in myself, saith he, could never have wrought this faith, could never have begotten this life; but it is faith in the Son of God only, and faith alone that must put this life into me.

My brethren, all in a man's self is against believing, therefore it must be put in immediately by God. All in a man is against it. To demonstrate this unto you—

First, The way of living by faith, merely upon Christ, which only shall raise this man, is clean contrary to the way of nature, to what *self* was brought up in. What, to go out of myself, to live in another; that all the comfort I have, all the power I have, must arise out of myself, in another, and not in myself. Nature was never thus brought up at its best; take pure nature; saith Nature, I was never brought up to that, for Adam did not live so, he lived in himself; he might say, 'It is I that lived.' But to make this *I* a cipher to all eternity, all in a man's self a cipher, and a man to be nothing in himself till this figure *Christ* be joined to him! He that knows this, knoweth it is the hardest thing in the world; for to live in himself is the way that pure nature itself took, therefore corrupt nature much more.

You shall find this, my brethren, try it when you will; when you go to believe nakedly upon Jesus Christ, you had rather do anything else; you will go I know not how far about, you will take all the pains in the world that you might find comfort from doing. Why? Because by believing you must go out of yourselves, and look for all your comfort in another. And a man will never go out of himself, to cast himself wholly and merely upon Jesus Christ, that all the comfort he hath shall come from thence. Saith Christ, John v. 40, 'You will not come unto me that you might have life.' They would take all pains, pray and fast twice a-week, for so you know the Pharisees did; they would fetch all the circuits they could, by way of doing; but to come to Christ nakedly and sheerly, to trust their souls with him, and not to look to themselves, this they would not do. Let another man come in his own name, saith he, him you will receive; but 'ye will not come unto me that ye might have life.'

My brethren, the Galatians, to see the vanity of corrupt nature in this way, are an instance. They had believed in Jesus Christ, yet they found a more easy way by way of doing, and looking into themselves; and they had rather subject themselves to the whole ceremonial law again, and join that to Christ, than take Christ alone. What a miserable thing is this! This is the way of nature. Therefore now there is nothing in a man's self to help him to believe, all is against it.

Nay, my brethren, secondly, If a man come to believe and live, he must have no ground in himself upon which he buildeth, laying hold upon Jesus Christ. When you come to believe, you will find that self will be interposing a great many grounds. This same *I* will trouble you. Look, as when you come to a sick friend, you will be bringing this and that with you, and say, Take this, and take that, it will do you good. So this self, this same *I*, will be interposing, it will be putting you upon this duty and that duty, and upon doing such and such things, that so you may come to live. Now for a man to come to say, 'Not I, but Christ,' I will live no life else; here lieth the work of faith. In Rom. iv. 5, 'To him that works not,' saith he, 'but believeth on him that justifieth the ungodly, to him faith is imputed for righteousness.' *That works not;* what is the meaning of that? The meaning is not, that a man that hath no grace in him, or no good works,—for then Abraham should not have been saved; he instanceth in him, faith wrought with his works, you know James telleth us so. What is meant then by it, Not to him that works? That is, when a man cometh to believe, he looks not to any works in himself. My brethren, I will tell you this: when you come to believe, you will find this, that if self have nothing else to help you to believe, it will tell you it hath nothing, it is humbled, &c. If you now take that as a ground why you believe,—indeed it is that which driveth you to believe,—then your faith is founded upon that which works. Now, saith the Apostle, 'To him that works not'—that is, when he cometh to believe, he looks to no works, he looks upon himself as if he had nothing at all, no works, no qualifications whatsoever, to ease his heart in point of believing. No, he looks upon himself as ungodly; 'that works not,' saith he, 'but believeth on him that justifieth the ungodly.' Those are the terms he believeth upon at first; nay, and the terms upon which he must exercise faith all his days; if he come to exercise naked faith, he must look upon him that justifieth the ungodly. Now, my brethren, this is a miserable case, when a man must have life put into the soul again out of another, from nothing in himself; there is no ground at all in himself that must help him to believe.

Nay, I will go further with you, to shew you that this faith is a pure resurrection, merely put in by God. When a man cometh to the point of believing, he hath not only no grounds in himself to help him, to ease him in it, but he hath no power at all to put forth a hand to lay hold upon Christ. A man is as a dead branch cut off, there he lieth; if God will take that dead branch and 'graff it in,' he is able to do it, as the Apostle's expression is, Rom. xi. 23. But, my brethren, when he cometh to believe, as he is a dead man in his own apprehension, condemned, so he hath no strength to lay hold upon life in Christ. What saith Heman in that Ps. lxxxviii. 4? 'I am,' saith he, 'as a man that hath no strength.' I remember once a man in great distress of conscience; a friend of mine said unto him, 'Believe you in Christ.' Saith he, 'Yonder is a star; bid me lay hold upon it;' for, indeed, to lay hold upon the Lord Jesus Christ, to close with him nakedly and sheerly by a hand of faith, a man hath no power of himself to do it; but as God findeth you Christ, so he must find you a hand too. The Apostle telleth us, Rom. v. 6, 'When we were without strength,' saith he. My brethren, there is not only a deadness in respect of the sentence of death, but in respect of the power of another life; 'when we were without strength,' saith he.

I have often compared the state of such a man to one that is falling off from a pinnacle; there is a rope, if he can catch hold on it, but he wants hands, his hands are cut off, and so he falleth down and crusheth himself to pieces. Now, for God to create hands, to create faith in a man's soul, whereby he may lay hold upon Christ, my brethren, here is an almighty power; there is nothing in a man's self to be a ground for it, there is nothing in a man's self to give him ability.

And, that I may conclude, it is the conclusion of the Apostle in the second chapter of this epistle, where he makes up the comparison of the power of God in working faith, the same that wrought in Christ when he was raised from the dead. What doth he say? Compare the 1st, 5th, 6th, and 8th verses together. When we were dead, saith he, in sins and trespasses, he hath quickened us together with Christ, and raised us up together; by grace ye are saved, through faith. And what saith he of that faith? 'And that not of yourselves, it is the gift of God.' Here is all I have been speaking of all this while. No man, saith he, is able to raise himself; he is dead in sin, in the guilt of it. Is he raised up with Christ? It is by faith; so he saith in Col. ii. 12, 13. How cometh he by this faith? Not of yourselves, it is the gift of God. 'It is not I,' saith he, 'but Christ liveth in me: and the life which I now live, I live by the faith of the Son of God.' Here is now a resurrection, you see, clearly and plainly; for a poor soul that is thus killed and dead, to be raised up, to come nakedly to the Lord Jesus Christ.

Now, my brethren, let me speak a little; for it may be in describing the work thus in a high way, though the truth is you may have and may spy something in you that is agreeing to it, yet to take off all doubts in your hearts, let me but add a caution or two, and so conclude.

My brethren, it is not as if God did always at once work this resurrection in the soul of a man; that is, so and so. No; in many God goeth by degrees to kill him, to empty him, to slay him. It may be he had a great death's-wound at first, when he was humbled; he had a good knock, and was terrified, and his soul began to think of Christ, and he reformed his life. Now God leadeth him on by degrees, and never leaves him till he causeth him to see nothing in himself to help him to believe, and enableth him to lay hold upon Jesus Christ nakedly. Here is a work of resurrection. It may be wrought in thee by degrees; thou art emptied, struck dead day after day, week after week, year after year; but so as God goeth on to perfect the work of faith with power: and if thou belongest to him, he will never leave thee till he hath fully emptied thee of thy self, and till thou canst say, It is not I, nor any power in me, but the faith of the gift of God; and the life I now live is the life of the Son of God, which is by faith.

My brethren, Abraham, when he was grown a strong Christian, lived by this faith; for that place, 'To him that works not, but believeth on him that justifieth the ungodly,' is spoken upon occasion of Abraham. God is teaching us this lesson all our lifetime. It is the great lesson of the gospel. And, my brethren, leave not till you have gotten this resurrection; it is the great resurrection of all the rest, wherein the power of God is most seen.

If I were asked how I would define faith, truly I would tell you, that it is the *power of God drawing a man's heart to rest upon the Lord Jesus Christ nakedly and alone for life and salvation.* I say, it is the power of God drawing a man's heart. A man can tell no reason; he hangeth upon Christ, and knoweth not why. 'As many as are taught of God,' saith he, 'come unto me, and they come whom the Father draweth.' There is a drawing of the heart. A man cannot rest in himself till he cometh unto Christ, and there he lieth, and the power of God holdeth him fast to Christ, he cannot get off.

Look upon temptations, (a little to help you,) when you come to be tempted. It is said, 1 Pet. i. 5, that we are 'kept by the power of God through faith.' Here you see it is the power of God that holdeth a man to Christ; and wherever faith is, either first or last, God tempteth, as it is ver. 7. Now in temptation you shall find—if you were not thus laid dead at first, at first humbling, yet one time or other in temptation you shall be—that all the grace in you will stand you in no stead. There are times wherein, as Jesus Christ was in the garden alone with his Father, and the disciples and all comforters were asleep; so your graces will lie asleep, you can have no comfort from them, you are to deal with God alone. Now, in such times as these are, to find your hearts drawn to Jesus Christ nakedly and alone, to have quickenings from the consideration of what is in Christ, and in him only, looking upon nothing in yourselves; here are some sparks of the resurrection, here is a dew from heaven upon your souls, to make faith spring, which nothing else could do.

Of all works else, *to believe is the easiest and the hardest.* If a man find it out, it is the easiest; that is, it is the shortest cut. Go which way you will else, go by your graces, you will have a great deal of pudder in yourselves without comfort. Go to duties, I do not say but you should use them as means; but to find a life in them you cannot, you will find a restlessness indeed. But now to go to Jesus Christ for life is the easiest way, it is the shortest cut; there is a resurrection from the dead. And yet of all else it is the hardest, for you must come off from this *I;* this *I* would live, this self would live, it would give you grounds of life; but to throw away a man's self, and that nothing shall live in a man but the Son of God, and I live in him by faith, this is the hardest thing in the world, yet the easiest when a man hath found the way, and none findeth it but those whom God teacheth. 'They shall all be taught of God.'

Thus I have opened unto you, as plainly as I could, that in the very work of believing—and that is proper to the text—there is a proportion with that power that raised up Christ from the dead; there is a resurrection. 'Ye are risen,' saith he, 'by faith of the operation of God.'

SERMON XXX.

Which he wrought in Christ, when he raised him from the dead, and set him at his own right hand in the heavenly places, &c.—VER. 20.

THESE words in the 20th verse are in their coherence to be considered by us two ways—according to their coherence with the words before, and the words that follow after.

In respect of their coherence with the words before, they come in by way of comparison, or analogy, or similitude, to shew that the same power that wrought in Christ, in raising him up and setting him at God's right hand, works in us believers, and is engaged to do so.

Or else, secondly, they are to be taken in and considered simply, and as spoken absolutely of Christ, as setting out his death, or resurrection and exaltation, and sitting at God's right hand.

Now, that this latter, the simple or absolute consideration of Christ, as laying forth to us these great articles of our faith concerning his resurrection and glorification, is the main scope that the Apostle here intendeth, and to represent these things to the Ephesians' eyes, and to pray they may know them, is evident by this, that when he had spoken in a few words of the parallel power in both, he hinteth that but in a word or two; but he runneth out upon the other, and spendeth, you see, four whole verses of the chapter in the enlarging himself upon the resurrection and exaltation of our Lord and Saviour Jesus Christ.

The comparative consideration of the same power, that that which wrought in Christ works in believers, I have despatched; but that which I am now entering upon is the simple consideration of the main grounds of faith which are to be known about Christ. These now come to be considered.

Now I have given you the coherence and scope of the words, I will give you the parts of them in general, as much as now needeth, to the end of the chapter.

First, He doth run over, I say, the great articles of your faith concerning Jesus Christ. He sheweth how he was dead,—he intimateth that,—and remained in a state of death, for he was 'raised from the dead,' saith the text.

Secondly, He setteth before us his resurrection; 'whom God raised up,' saith he.

Thirdly, His exaltation, the exalting of Christ, the glorifying of Christ; set forth in these words, 'and set him at his own right hand in the heavenly places.' So he expresseth it, first under a metaphor; he calleth it 'setting at God's right hand.' But then he explaineth himself in the 21st and 22d verses, and he sheweth how high that exaltation is; he saith it is 'far above all principalities and powers.' He sheweth both the extension of it, it is over 'all things,' all things in this world, and in the world to come; and he instanceth in the greatest things, both principalities and powers, might and dominion. He sheweth, secondly, the height of it, as the other was the breadth of it; he saith he is so far advanced that all these things are under his feet, so saith the 22d verse.

In the fourth place, As he shewed his death, and resurrection, and exaltation, so he sheweth the relation that Jesus Christ beareth to his Church: in the midst of all this exaltation, saith he, he hath all things under his feet indeed, but he is a head to his Church, that is for their comfort; and this doth Jesus Christ account as great a part of his exaltation as any other, that he is a head to his Church, for so it followeth in the last verse, 'which is his fulness;' though he be full of all this glory, he is pleased to account his relation to his Church to be his fulness, without which he is not perfect.

Lastly, He telleth us the influence that Jesus Christ hath now he is in heaven; he sitteth not there as possessing glory and happiness in himself, but he hath an influence into all things; 'he filleth,' saith he, 'all in all.'

So now you have the parts of the words to the end of the chapter. Before I come to handle these particulars, as I have often done, so I shall now give you one observation in general, and the observation riseth from this: both that the Apostle here runneth out so much when he had mentioned the power that wrought in Christ, he runneth out upon his resurrection, and exaltation, and sitting at God's right hand, &c., and prayeth that they might know these things, for that is part of his scope also. Hence observe this, my brethren—

That the knowledge of these common articles of our faith,—of Christ's being raised again, his sitting at God's right hand, and having all things under his feet, and the like,—that the true knowledge, the constant apprehension of these, take them in the relation that Christ hath to us as a head—take that in—is of all knowledges the most necessary, the most useful, the most comfortable; and therefore the knowledge of this is the last of the Apostle's prayer, for all this cometh in his prayer to God for them; necessary for sealed Christians as these Ephesians were, Christians grown up, for them to spend the deepest and the dearest of their thoughts upon.

My brethren, they are common points, and you have them in your creed, and every child knoweth them, and you take them for granted; whereas if they were but digested by faith constantly and daily, if you would make constant meals of them, there are no points in religion more strong, more powerful to quicken men's hearts than these. It would never else have been, that by universal consent of the Church in all ages, these should be put as the common articles of our faith, as you know they are.

Whatever account you make of them, let me tell you this, they were the great points which took up the thoughts of the faith of the primitive Christians,—that their Christ was risen, newly ascended up to heaven, and sitting there at God's right hand. They were fresh news then, and did mightily quicken their hearts; and it was that which took up their sermons; read their sermons in the Acts, chap. v., and you shall find they insist upon these things.

When Paul came to Corinth, you shall see in 1 Cor. xv. what an emphasis he putteth upon these common points, Christ's being dead and risen again. Saith he there, 'I declare unto you the gospel which I preached,'—so it is at the first verse,—'which also ye have received, and wherein ye stand; by which also ye are saved;' and he addeth, 'if ye keep in memory,' that is, if you exercise your thoughts daily upon what I have delivered,—for it is a great point, it is not only necessary to salvation for their first believing, but for their keeping in memory, and whetting their souls upon them,—'if ye keep in memory,' saith he, 'what I preached unto you, unless ye have believed in vain.' 'For,' saith he,—if ye would know what this gospel is which he putteth this weight upon,—'I delivered unto you first of all that which I have received, how that Christ died for our sins according to the scriptures; and that he was buried, and that he rose again according to the scriptures;' and, saith he, ver. 11, 'So we preach, and so ye believed.' It was the great thing in their preaching, and it was the great thing in the eye of their faith.

Read all Paul's Epistles, you shall likewise find he runneth out upon these points. Here is but a small occasion given; you see how he enlargeth himself upon it. When he cometh to speak of these points his heart swelleth and mightily riseth up, for indeed his heart was full of them.

These were the cream of notions in the primitive times, both in the sermons of the apostles, and in the daily talk and thoughts of the Christians. They were the great notions in that golden age. These made them comfortable, heavenly, spiritual Christians, to have their conversation in heaven, ready to sacrifice their lives at an hour's warning, because so the apostles preached, and so they believed, as he telleth them in that place of the Corinthians.

Other doctrines, my brethren, that are the great doctrines of this age, that you may see what children we are, the Apostle professeth that they are but the beginnings, the principles of the knowledge of Christ. Do but look into Heb. vi. 1–4: 'Leaving,' saith he, 'the principles of the doctrine of Christ, let us go on unto perfection.' What are the principles of the doctrine of Christ? Saith he, 'Not laying again the foundation of repentance from dead works, and of faith toward God, and of the doctrine of baptisms, and of laying on of hands, and of resurrection of the dead, and of eternal judgment.' These,—the laying open of faith, the works thereof, and of repentance and sanctification, the laying open of the doctrine of church government, which imposition of hands, as some think, is put for,—although they are all necessary and useful, and so likewise to terrify men's consciences, and preach hell to them, and judgment, and wrath, and the like; these, saith he, are but the principles of the doctrine of Christ, and he chideth them that they should stick at these. In chap. v. 10, 11, he speaks of Christ, that he was called of God a high priest after the order of Melchisedec; 'of whom,' saith he, 'we have many things to say, and hard to be uttered, seeing ye are dull of hearing,' (he chideth them presently,) while ye are preaching and talking of faith, and repentance from dead works, and imposition of hands, and the like. But to lay open the great things of Christ, his resurrection from the dead, and sitting at God's right hand,—which the Apostle makes the sum of this Epistle to the Hebrews, read chap. viii. 1; the sum of those things that he had spoken, and to be spoken, the word in the original beareth both, is, that Christ is set down at the right hand of the Majesty in the heavens;—to lay open, I say, the death and resurrection of Christ, and his sitting at God's right hand, and all the mysteries thereof, these are the great points that the Apostle would have them go on to the knowledge of; this is a going on to perfection.

Now, how contrary is the strain of Christians in this age! They, on the other side, account these doctrines, because you have them in your creed, the principles of Christ, and of the doctrine of Christ, and therefore they leave them, and go to insist altogether in their thoughts, and every way, upon the other. My brethren, though those other are not to be neglected, yet these are the great things of the gospel, as our Saviour speaks in another case. And know these will be the current truths of that age that is to come, and men will rejoice in them, and the true knowledge and constant apprehension of these points will make men to live in heaven.

So much now for the general observation. Only I will add this: The reason why men's thoughts are no more taken up with these common points about Christ, is because they do not mingle them with faith. For you must all acknowledge this for a most certain truth, that they are all the greatest things the gospel revealeth; now if they be the greatest things of the gospel, if you had faith answerable they would make your minds great, they would have a proportionable influence upon your souls, both to comfort them and to quicken them. But the error lieth in this, not that these are not the great points of religion, but because you have not faith to rise up to them, to make use of them, that is the truth of it.

My brethren, are you troubled with the guilt of sin? If you could but see by faith Jesus Christ rising from the dead, and sitting at God's right hand, and crowned with glory and honour, the guilt of sin would vanish with the real and serious thoughts of these, more than by all the assurance of your own graces. Doth the power of sin trouble you? That Jesus Christ died for sin, for this very sin that I am committing; you are now a-sinning; why, did not Jesus Christ rise again from the dead, in whom I believe to be saved? Have but faith in it, and it would presently quash the rising of a lust, and instantly fire your souls. Is Jesus Christ sitting in heaven, in glory, and am I a member of his, and hope to be with him, (or else why do I believe in him?) what do I then sinning upon earth?

You know how the Apostle urgeth it, Col. iii. 2, 'If ye be risen with Christ, seek those things which are above, where Christ sitteth at the right hand of God. Set your affection on things above, and not on things on the earth.' This our hearts will do if we believe these great things. My brethren, you make conscience of sin, and you do well; but had you but faith in those great things about Christ, that faith would make more quick riddance of your sins than your consciences can do; the one would direct you what is sin and what not, but the other would strengthen you against it. If these common principles were held forth and professed, if they were lived upon by believers, you would find that the holiness of your lives would have, as in your own hearts, so in the hearts of others, more power to convince you. The believers in the primitive times, as they were holy in their lives, so they professed this still to be the foundation of their holiness: Christ is dead, Christ is risen, Christ is in heaven, therefore we must live so and so; and this was their great profession; read but the writings of those first times, and you shall find it. It dasheth all the carnal gospellers in the world; it would shame men out of their sins, or out of their professing of Christ. If Paul were alive, he would spit in any man's face that will say that he believeth in Christ that died and rose again, and yet lived in sin. I cannot demonstrate this unto you as I would. I must leave the point: so much in general.

Now, I come to the particular articles concerning Christ laid open in the text. I shall not be able to insist on the several uses the knowledge of them will be unto you, but I will open them and handle them by way of exposition; and that is all I shall do, because I must keep to the point in hand.

You have these articles of your faith concerning Christ explained from the 20th verse to the end of the chapter:—

First, you have him here *dead, truly dead, perfectly dead,* not a spark of life left before he was to be raised; or else what need there be so great a power to work in him? 'The greatness of the power,' saith he, 'which wrought in Christ, when he raised him from the dead.' Here is his death.

Secondly, here is *his remaining in a state of death* after his dying; he doth not say simply, who raised him from death, but 'raised him from *the dead*,' from amongst the dead amongst whom he lay. That is the second.

Thirdly, you have *his resurrection*, and you have two things concerning it. First, the resurrection itself; secondly, the raiser of him, God the Father: 'who raised him from the dead,' saith he.

Lastly, you have *his exaltation;* his setting him at God's right hand, &c.

This is the more general division of the 20th verse.

First, to begin with his death which is hinted here. *He was dead, and truly dead.* I will not speak of the kind of his death, crucifying,—it is not in the text,—but of that act of dying, that he died. To confirm which article, that the eye of our faith might be upon it, and in a special manner take notice that he was not only crucified, but dead, I will give you but a scripture or two about it, that shall shew you the necessity and the reason of it, why he died. I do not now speak of all his sufferings, why he was crucified, or why he was a man of sorrows, the manner of his death, or the kind of his death, but simply the act of dying, his giving up the ghost.

It was a prophecy in the Old Testament that the Messiah should be slain, cut off out of the land of the living, as the expression is, Isa. liii. 8, which is an apparent prophecy of his death. 'He died,' saith he, in that 1 Cor. xv. 3, 'according to the scriptures.' The Old Testament prophesied of it. It was necessary he should die. What saith Christ himself, John xii. 24? 'Verily, verily, I say unto you, Except a corn of wheat fall into the ground and die, it abideth alone: but if it die, it bringeth forth much fruit.' Our Saviour Christ speaketh it of himself. He compareth himself to a grain of corn that falleth from heaven; it dropped from thence, for he is called 'the Lord from heaven,' 1 Cor. xv. 47. And as the corn that falleth into the ground, if it doth not die, it remaineth alone,—that is, it remaineth fruitless, it bringeth forth nothing,—so if I would have been alone in heaven, I needed never to have died, yea, I needed never to have come from thence; but, saith he, if I will have others come up thither, look as the corn must die before such time as grain grow up out of it, so must I. And though corn indeed in dying seeth corruption, for you cannot suppose a death of a grain of corn but by corrupting; which in a way of analogy to what he meant to express about himself he calleth a dying of the grain; so as though he saw no corruption in the grave, yet die he did, and in those terms expresseth the similitude. He expresseth it, therefore, by way of such a similitude as of his death, not that he suffered corruption, but that he, as a man, had a death answerable to it; he died by breathing out his soul; and if he had not done that, he must have been in heaven alone, but having died, not a hundred-fold or a thousand-fold only cometh up, but an innumerable company of believers in all ages, throughout all the world, both Jews and Gentiles.

To give you a reason or two to shew you the necessity of it—

The first was to confirm the covenant of grace, and to make it of a covenant a testament, which was much for our advantage. There are two reasons; I will only mention them. In Heb. ix. 15-17, 'And for this cause,' saith he, 'he is the mediator of the new testament, that by means of death, they that are called might receive the promise of eternal inheritance,' &c. He compareth here, you see, the covenant of grace not to a covenant simply, but to a testament, to a man's will. That word *Berith*, which the Hebrew useth for *covenant*, the Greek expositors and the Septuagint still translate it *testament*, and the Apostle, therefore, keepeth to their translation, and he keepeth indeed to the intent and scope of the Holy Ghost, for it was not simply a covenant God made but a testament. And therefore, if you mark it, at the 18th verse he putteth Exod. xxiv., where Moses took the blood and sprinkled it on the people, and said, 'Behold the blood of the covenant which the Lord hath made with you;' now, saith the Apostle, there in the 18th verse, 'Neither was the first testament dedicated without blood;' by blood he meaneth death, for they did not only take the blood of the beasts from them by letting of them blood, but they killed them, and then took the blood and sprinkled the covenant. Now, all this was done in a type, that although it was a covenant, yet it was such a covenant as must have the death of him with whom and for whose sake the covenant was made; and so it was both a covenant and a testament. Now, it being a testament, mark what the Apostle saith in the following verses to shew you the necessity of Christ's death. 'Where a testament is,' saith he, 'there must also of necessity be the death of the testator.' Of necessity; why? Because if it be a testament, it is never made immutable till the testator dieth, as the civil lawyers say; it is but a changeable thing till the testator is dead, but after he is dead it standeth immutable. If it had been barely a covenant, it would not have comforted us so much; but it is proved a testament now because Christ died.

You see then one reason why it was necessary Christ should die, that he might make the covenant of God a testament. And why was the covenant of God to be made a testament?

I will tell you. In God's covenant with us and for our salvation, and with Christ likewise for us, there was both free grace,—in respect of free grace it is called a covenant,—and there was justice to be satisfied, and that requireth death, and in that respect it is called a testament. I make my covenant with you, saith God to Christ, but the condition is your death; but it shall not only be a covenant, but a testament; you shall die, and you shall make your will when you die, and the covenant I make with you shall be a testament to them that belong to you. Now, this testament, this will of his, would not have been in force if he had not died. The typical covenant was not ratified but by death; it was blood, not simply drawn from the beasts by blood-letting, but killing of the beasts, and then taking their blood and confirming the covenant. So the blood of Christ still noteth out his death in the Scripture, as the blood in the old testament noted out the beasts slain. He was to die to make the covenant a testament.

I should have mentioned another reason, which is in the latter end of that 9th chapter of Hebrews, ver. 27, 28; for he goeth on to speak of the death of Christ. 'As it is appointed unto all men once to die, but after this the judgment; so Christ was once offered'—that is, he died once, he was offered up by dying, so is the opposition, and so much the similitude implieth—'to bear the sins of many;' and therefore, in Rom. vi. 10, we shall find that phrase is used, 'He died unto sin once.' You know the curse was, that man should die the death; 'In the day thou eatest thereof thou shalt die the death.' Our Saviour Christ was made the whole curse because he would redeem us from the whole curse. There was a curse went out against his soul, he paid deadly pains, as I told you out of Acts ii.; and then he cried out it was finished, when he bore the wrath of God in his soul after that. Here now was that whereby our souls were redeemed; but our bodies must be redeemed too from death; therefore after all this he must die, as it is appointed for all men once to die. Is that a law, saith he, and will Christ be a mediator? He must die too. This is the Apostle's reasoning in Heb. ix. 27, 28.

Hence it was, and it is an observation worth your marking, that God, because his death, the expiring of soul from body, was the completing of that sacrifice, ordered it to be at the hour of the evening sacrifice, which was his type. The evening sacrifice was offered up at the third hour, that is at three of the clock, then did Christ breathe his soul out and offered up himself to be a sacrifice, for dying was essential to a sacrifice.

So much for the first, that he is said to be dead. I shall give you but small touches and hints.

The second thing concerning Christ, which is a great article of our faith too, is, *that Jesus Christ remained in a state of death.* If you mark it, he doth not say simply that he raised him up from death, but *from the dead;* that is, he was a companion with the dead; that is, look what estate their bodies were in, his body was in: he was free among the dead, though in another sense than Heman speaks of himself; he was in the company of the dead, he was raised from the dead.

This, my brethren, was likewise to fulfil the curse. The curse was not only that Adam should die, but he was to return to his dust, so Gen. iii. 19. And therefore, you shall find that they are made two things by the Psalmist, Ps. cxlvi. 4: speaking of man, saith he, 'his breath goeth forth,' there is the act of dying, 'and he turneth to his earth.' Every man is not buried, but the common sepulchre of all mankind is the earth, though a man lieth on the top of it; that is *commune sepulchrum,* the common sepulchre of all mankind. Now, our Saviour Christ was in a state of death, not only dying, but he remained in a state of death. It is a strange speech in Acts xiii. 34, where, speaking of our Saviour Christ, saith he, 'He raised him from the dead, now no more to see corruption.' Here he expresseth what it is to be raised from the dead, no more to return to corruption. Why, did our Saviour Christ ever see corruption? No, the text expresseth the contrary, in the 35th verse, 'Thou wilt not suffer thy Holy One to see corruption.' Why doth the Apostle then say, 'He raised him from the dead, no more to see corruption?'

His meaning is plainly this: though indeed his body was not corrupted,— for as his body was free from sickness while he lived, so it was free from corruption when he died, it became not his honour, it was exempted from sickness and infirmities,—yet, saith he, take that state of the dead which tendeth to corruption, and he was under it. He was raised from the dead, no more to return to corruption; not that he corrupted before, but that he remained in a state in which men's bodies use to be corrupted. Our Saviour Christ was not only to get a victory over death, but over the grave, over a state of death; now corruption is the state of death, and that the Apostle meaneth by corruption, when he saith to return no more to corruption; yet actual putrefaction, that he meaneth afterward, when he saith, 'He will not suffer his Holy One to see corruption.'

To exemplify this unto you thus: If Jesus Christ presently after he had died, if his soul had come into his body again, he had died indeed, but he had not risen from the dead; he had been quickened indeed, as the Scripture sometimes speaks, but he had not been raised from the dead; therefore that he might be raised from the dead, he must continue in a state of death. As if he had come off the cross before he had died, it might be said he had been crucified, but it could not be said that he died; so if his soul had come to him again when it went first out of his body, it might have been said he had been quickened indeed, but it could not have been said he was raised from the dead, for that implieth a lying under a state of death.

You shall find therefore that death is said to have dominion over him, as over his prisoner. It is the phrase, Rom. vi. 9, 'Christ being raised from the dead dieth no more; death hath no more dominion over him;' which implieth that death not only killed him, but it had dominion over him, had him in his power, he was in the state of death, he was death's prisoner. You must know that death had him in his power, dominion it had a while over him; but, saith he, it was impossible that he could be holden by it. Therefore, in 1 Cor. xv. 20, he is said to be 'the first-fruits of them that sleep.' Why of them that sleep? Because he did not only die, but he slept, he took a nap, he was a while under the state of death; therefore it is said he was raised from the dead.

And herein, my brethren, lay the last of the humiliation of Christ. It lay not simply in his being buried; there was an honourableness in that, for he had an honourable funeral, he was embalmed with sweet odours and spices, which the Jews used to call a burial; not only so, but he was and continued in the state of death. Therein lieth the bottom and the last of his humiliation. It is said, in Eph. iv. 9, that he descended into the lower parts of the earth before he ascended. The lower parts of the earth is not meant his grave; for the truth is, his grave was not in the lower parts or in the bottom of the earth, for it was above the earth, it being their manner then to make their tombs in rocks; but it implieth a state of death that our Saviour Christ was in. He did return to dust, to a state of death, to his earth, which was the curse; he was a while dead, death's prisoner, death had dominion over him; therefore he is here said to be raised from the dead.

My brethren, Christ did run through all estates with us; he was not only born into the world, but he lived in it as we do; he might have been born into it and gone out again, but he lived in it three-and-thirty years. When he came to die, he might have died and taken his soul up again presently. No, but he would remain in death; look what befalleth us did befall him, setting aside what was dishonourable to his person, as corruption would have been. The same state our soul shall be after death, his soul was in; it went to Paradise, so likewise do our souls; therefore you read of Paradise as well as the third heavens, 2 Cor. xii. Look what state our bodies were in, that state was his body in too; and God did it, that, as we might see he should be conformed to us and we to him, so that we might be satisfied he was dead indeed.

So much for the second thing: he was raised from the dead; therefore as he died, so he was reserved in a state of death.

I come, in the third place, *to his resurrection*, for I shall run over these things more briefly. There are two things concerning it that I shall speak unto you of, for the opening of these words.

The first is the *necessity of his resurrection.*

The second is the *author of his resurrection.* The author of his resurrection is said to be God; 'which he wrought in Christ,' saith he, 'when he raised him from the dead.' He speaks of God the Father.

First, For the *necessity of Christ's resurrection.* I shewed you why it was necessary for him to die; I shall shew you, in a word or two, why it was necessary for him to rise.

First, it was needful for him to rise again *in respect of God.* It was the title that God had in the Old Testament, that he was the God of Abraham, of Isaac, and of Jacob. Now from thence doth our Saviour Christ, Matt. xxii. 32, prove the resurrection, and that Abraham, and Isaac, and Jacob, must rise again; not Abraham's soul only, but Abraham, body and soul, must live; for that makes Abraham, the body and soul together make the man. 'For God,' saith he, 'is not the God of the dead, but of the living;' therefore certainly Abraham must rise again.

Now look into the New Testament, and you have the style altered. Now it is, 'The God and Father of our Lord Jesus Christ.' So then, as from that style in the Old Testament Christ proveth that Abraham must rise; so from this style in the New Testament it was necessary that Christ should rise, for God is not a God of a dead Christ, but of a living Christ. Therefore rise he must in respect of God. Saith he, 'Thou art my Son, this day have I begotten thee:' as if he should say, I was loath to lose my Son; therefore God raised him up again, he begat him again; 'This day have I begotten thee.' It is spoken of his resurrection expressly in that Acts xiii. God had as much work for him to do after as before; he had the world to be governed by him, the Church to be saved, and the kingdom to be ruled, and then to be delivered up to God the Father. Therefore there was a necessity that Christ should rise in respect of God.

Then, secondly, *in respect of Christ himself* it was necessary he should rise, it was meet he should; there was a great deal of reason, that he that suffered so much for God, in obeying of him, should rise again to enjoy the fruit of it. It is the reason given Isa. liii. 11, 12, 'Because he made his soul an offering for sin,' and died so willingly, 'he shall see of the travail of his soul, and be satisfied;' he shall live to see it. Therefore he was to rise again, that he might enjoy and possess what by his death he had purchased.

There are some of the school-men that have argued it, though it is a falsehood, that a mere creature might have satisfied the wrath of God. Take an angel filled with grace; if that angel would have lost himself, given up himself to ruin and destruction, this might have been taken as sufficient to procure the salvation of another, of a sinner. But there is this great reason why God, if it could have been done, would never have accepted it, because that pure creature could never have risen again. Why? Because though it might have satisfied, yet it must have taken an eternity of time to have done it, it must always have been a satisfying, it could never have risen to see of the travail of his soul: but Jesus Christ could despatch the work of satisfaction in a few hours, and die, and rise again, and live to see of the travail of his soul.

And, my brethren, there was no reason,—I will not say no reason in respect of him, for he may do what he pleaseth,—but there was no reason he should be beholden to any creature so much as to put him to the highest, the greatest self-denial, of dying and being accursed, and not rewarded; therefore, that he might be rewarded, he rose again. And therefore you read in Acts ii. 24, which indeed is another reason, 'It was impossible for him to be holden of death.' Impossible, not only in respect of his power, that he was able to raise himself, but impossible according to justice. For when he had paid the sorrows of death, as there he speaks of it, death could not hold him; the law of God, the justice of God said, Deliver the prisoner, for he had satisfied; there was an impossibility but that he must rise again in that respect.

Next, he did rise *that he might be Lord of all*, and it was fit it should be so. You shall find in Rom. xiv. 9, 'To this end,' saith he, 'Christ both died, and rose again, and revived,'—that is, had a new life, for his life in heaven is another kind of life than what he had here below,—'that he might be Lord both of the dead and living.' He died to purchase a lordship, he rose again to possess it, and it was fit that he that purchased it should possess it.

Last of all, *it was exceeding necessary for us poor souls and creatures.* I will give you but one scripture for it, for I must not stand upon these things. In Acts xiii., where the Apostle preacheth the resurrection to the Jews, do but mark how he terms it; 'We declare unto you,' so it is in ver. 32, 'glad tidings.' That which we are preaching, saith he, is good news for you, it is glad tidings. What is that? 'How that the promise which was made unto the fathers, God hath fulfilled the same unto us their children, in that he hath raised up Jesus again.' Here is the glad tidings; it was good for us that Christ rose again. And then he quoteth a proof for it out of the second Psalm, 'Thou art my Son, this day have I begotten thee.' And in ver. 34, mark that likewise, 'As concerning that he raised him from the dead, now no more to return to corruption, he said on this wise, I will give you the sure mercies of David.' He proveth the resurrection out of these words, 'I will give you the sure mercies of David.' One would wonder how that this should prove the resurrection; but he doth not only go about to prove the resurrection, but to shew them that it was glad tidings to them; he saith, that if Christ had not risen again you had never had the sure mercies of David. So that now, by the resurrection of Christ, all the sure mercies of David are confirmed unto us. In Ps. lxxxix. 1–3, to open this place a little, and so pass from the point, saith he, 'I will sing of the mercies of the Lord for ever;' so beginneth the first verse. 'For I have said, Mercy shall be built up for ever: thy faithfulness shalt thou establish in the very heavens.' How is this proved? Wherein lieth this mercy? 'I have made a covenant with my chosen, I have sworn unto David my servant, Thy seed will I establish for ever, and build up thy throne to all generations.' Here now is the sure mercies of David, that God meant to raise up Jesus Christ, and to set him at his own right hand in the heavenly places, and so convey all mercies to us his seed and children. Read now but Acts ii. 30; saith he, 'David being a prophet, and knowing God had sworn with an oath that of the fruit of his loins, according to the flesh, he would raise up Christ to sit on his throne; he seeing this before spake of the resurrection of Christ.' Compare these three places one with another, and you see how they prove the resurrection. That which I observe out of them is this: that he rose to convey to us the sure mercies of David, to execute and apply all mercies to us, which had been nothing worth if Christ had not risen. I will give you but one place more for that, that you may see it was good news for us that Christ rose; it is a parallel place to the other three. It is Acts iii. 25; saith he, 'Ye,' meaning the Jews, 'are the children of the prophets, and of the covenant which God made with our fathers; unto you first God, having raised up his Son Jesus, sent him to bless you.' Mark, his resurrection was to bless you. Hence now we tell you good tidings, saith he; Jesus Christ is risen from the dead; for, saith he, 'I will give you the sure mercies of David.' You could never have had your sins pardoned, if Christ had not risen. 'If Christ be not risen, you are yet in your sins;' it is his expression, 1 Cor. xv. 17.

My brethren, if Christ had not risen, we had not risen. In the same 1 Cor. xv., 'in Christ all rise.' Now Jesus Christ is risen, how doth the Apostle teach you to argue? I will only quote that place in Rom. vi. 9, 11, and will end with it; 'Knowing,' saith he, 'that Christ being raised from the dead dieth no more. Likewise reckon ye also yourselves to be dead indeed unto sin, but alive unto God through Jesus Christ our Lord.' Is Christ, saith he, risen; then consider with yourselves, have you faith in you? hath that power begun to work in you? Then, saith he, look as death had no more dominion over Christ, you may as soon have Christ pulled out of heaven and nailed again to the cross, as that death shall ever have dominion over you. And is not this good news, my brethren? We bring you glad tidings, saith he, that God hath fulfilled the promise made unto the fathers; he hath raised up Christ from the dead; and, saith he, by this he bestoweth upon us the sure mercies of David; for he riseth for our sanctification, he riseth for our justification, he riseth for our resurrection, and as he rose we shall rise again. Reckon not yourselves dead, but alive unto God; as death had no more dominion over him, so shall it not have dominion over you. So that, my brethren, there is no point of greater use than this, that Jesus Christ is risen from the dead. You shall find in Scripture that it is made the great object of our faith; as, Rom. x. 9, 'If thou shalt confess with thy mouth, and believe in thine heart, that God hath raised up Christ from the dead, thou shalt be saved.' I shall have occasion to shew you the reason of it by and by.

And so much now for the resurrection itself, the necessity of it, and the end of it; which I have done most briefly.

Secondly, consider *the raiser of him*, that is the next thing; the raiser of him is said to be *God the Father*. You shall find that this work of raising up Christ from the dead is accounted so great a work that you have it still attributed to God. It is his name that he is the Father of Christ, as you heard before, and it is a name that by way of periphrasis is used for God; when he speaks of God, he putteth this in still, that 'he raised up Christ from the dead.' You have it in four places of Scripture: Rom. iv. 24, viii. 11, Col. ii. 12, 13.

There is only this one difficulty to be explained here: how the Father is said to be the raiser up of Christ, when yet the Scripture telleth us that Christ raised up himself; that is, the second Person, united to that soul and body, brought them both together again and quickened it. That Christ raised up himself, you have express Scripture for it: John ii. 19, 'Destroy this temple, and in three days I will raise it up.' He spake of the temple of his body. John x. 17, 18, 'I have power to lay down my life, and I have power to take it again.'

And the truth is, my brethren, it was necessary that he that was your Mediator should be able to raise up himself. Why? Because in the works of mediation, whereof this was one, he was to borrow nothing, it must all be his own. If he had borrowed anything, mark what I say, it had not been a Mediator's work, for he had been beholden to God. If there had not been some sense wherein what he did, and what he was, had been his own so as not his Father's, all his works had not been works of mediation; his satisfaction had not. If in dying he had not offered up himself, if by his own power he had not overcome those sorrows of death, he had not satisfied. Why? For if it had been a borrowed power, then all the satisfaction he offered had been God's already; he could not have paid, for no man could pay one with what is not his own: so when he came to rise again, if he had not raised himself by his own power, it had not been a Mediator's action.

Now, brethren, how then is it that here it is said God raised him up from the dead, whenas he raised up himself; and it was necessary that he should do so, if he be Mediator?

That wicked heretic, Socinus, denieth that Christ did raise himself from the dead, because he knew that this would pinch him, that therefore he must be God; for to raise one from the dead is made a work of omnipotency, as Rom. iv. 17, 'He believed on him, even on God, who quickeneth the dead, and calleth those things which be not as though they were.' It is the property of God to quicken the dead, even as much as to create; therefore, to avoid this (he denieth that he is God) he goeth against express Scripture, and denieth that Christ raised himself, and he hath cunning evasions for it; but I will not stand upon it.

But to answer this, and to reconcile it, how both the Father is said to raise Christ, and Christ is said to raise himself, I will give you these three several answers to reconcile it :—

First, you must know that all the works of the Three Persons, what one doth the other two are said to do. It is a certain rule, that *opera Trinitatis ad extra sunt indivisa*, all their works to us-ward, of creation and redemption, and whatsoever else, are all works of each Person concurring to them. As they have but one being, one essence, so they have but one work; yet as they have three several subsistences, so they have three several manners of working. Hence now the Father is said to raise Christ, so it is here; so likewise Christ is said to raise himself, as you have it in the place I quoted even now; and, thirdly, you have as express a place of Scripture that the Holy Ghost raised him too: Rom. viii. 11, 'If the Spirit of him that raised up Jesus from the dead dwell in you.' He speaks of the Holy Ghost, and he saith this Spirit raised up Christ from the dead.

Now therefore these two may very well stand together, that both God the Father raised him up, and he raised up himself; for all Three Persons concur in every work. The Father is said to create, the Son is said to create, and the Holy Ghost is said to create. And so likewise, the Father is said to raise him, the Son is said to raise himself, and the Holy Ghost to raise him too. To give you a scripture punctual to the point in hand, the matter of the resurrection, that both Father and Son do jointly concur in it: John v. 19, 20, 'The Son can do nothing of himself, but what he seeth the Father do; for what things soever he doth, these also doth the Son likewise.' The Son doth the same things the Father doth; if the Father raiseth him, the Son raiseth himself. And mark what followeth at the 21st verse, 'For as the Father raiseth up the dead,'—there is an instance,—'and quickeneth them, even so the Son quickeneth whom he will.' If the Father and the Son both concur to the quickening of them, then certainly Father and Son concur to the quickening and raising up of the human nature; therefore, 1 Cor. xv. 45, he is called a quickening spirit. 'The first Adam,' saith he, 'was made a living soul, the second a quickening spirit.' The Godhead that is meant by *spirit* did quicken him, quicken him when he was dead, and raised him up.

And, my brethren, let me only give you this consideration about it: it is not in this raising of Christ as it is in our conversion, therein there is a difference. You see in raising up of Christ, that Christ himself, namely the Son of God, and the Father did in a joint manner concur to it; indeed the body concurred nothing to it, for that was dead, but the Son of God, the second Person, concurred and raised up that body and soul. But so it is not in our conversion; our wills and God's power are not joint workers together; though he paralleleth them in respect of power, yet in this point they are not alike.

In the second place, although God the Father did raise up Jesus Christ, yet Jesus Christ as God-man did that by virtue of which he was raised up, and therefore may be said to raise up himself; though the power was the Father's, yet he did that which merited, as I may so say, which purchased that power to raise him up again. Look Heb. xiii. 20, 'Now the God of peace, that brought again from the dead our Lord Jesus Christ.' Here you see that God is said to do it; and he useth a fit phrase, he calleth it 'bringing him again from the dead,' for he calleth him 'that great shepherd of the sheep.' The phrase whereby his death is expressed in Isa. liii. is, that he was 'led as a sheep to the slaughter;' he was led to death, therefore how fitly doth he use a phrase when he speaks of him as the shepherd of the sheep when he was brought again from the dead. 'Brought again' is an allusion to the phrase used in the prophet, 'led away.' Here is God the Father's work. What followeth? 'Through the blood of the everlasting covenant.' Here is Jesus Christ's work for his own resurrection; he had his hand in it, that it was by blood, his own blood, by virtue of which it was done. God had made a covenant with him: if he would shed his blood he would raise him; therefore now as he is raised by God, so he is said to be raised by his own blood, he was raised by the 'blood of the covenant.' So that Jesus Christ himself had a hand in it in this respect also, as well as the Father. And though I know divines say he merited nothing for himself, because all was his due as he was the Son of God, and it is a truth; but I cannot see but he might have a double title to glory, and resurrection, and all, and might purchase it and merit it; it was by the blood of the everlasting covenant. So in Zech. ix. 11, it is said, he will 'deliver the prisoners out of the pit by the blood of the covenant.' Look by what power he doth deliver poor souls out of distress, deliver captives out of the pit; by the same blood of the covenant doth he deliver Christ himself, brought again from the grave, from the pit, from the dust, 'that great shepherd of the sheep.'

Then again, for a third answer; go, take several considerations about Christ, and in one consideration God the Father is said to raise him, but in others he raiseth himself. Consider him—I remember it is Camero's answer—as a Common Person, as the first-fruits of a company of members that are raised with him as a common Head; and so God the Father is said to raise him, saith he, and we are raised in him by God the Father. But then consider him as a Mediator, in respect of satisfaction to be performed, and to do the work of a Mediator himself, whereof resurrection is one; so, saith he, he overcometh death by his own power, he broke open the gates of death and hell, he hath the keys at his girdle, and he shewed that he had the power of death. Here are now two considerations wherein Jesus Christ is said to be raised up by God the Father, and by himself. And then, thirdly, here is another: take Jesus Christ as he is to be a satisfier for sin, to perform the work of mediation, so he raiseth himself; but take him as he is to be rewarded for all the services he had done, as it is fit he should be, and the rewarder is God, for to him he did the service; now, saith God, you have done your work I will raise you up; so he concurreth in his resurrection as a rewarder of him. 'And him,' saith he, 'hath God raised up.'

I will add but these considerations about it to quicken your faith, and so make an end instantly.

It is a matter of great comfort to us, first, that Christ raised himself, for it is a sign that he hath satisfied God; for otherwise death would have held him: if he had not loosed the pains of death, those deadly pains, if he had not fully paid a price, it had been possible for death to have held him; but having paid them it was not possible that he should be held by them. 'He rose again,' saith he, 'for our justification;' it is good for us that Christ raised himself. Herein doth our Prophet excel that cursed prophet of the Turks, Mahomet, whom they would have to be their great prophet. He promised them to rise again a thousand years after his death, and in our age, in these times wherein we have lived, have those thousand years been expired, and now they have no way to solve the matter, but that when he was dying, his voice being weak and faint, they mistook him, and that he said two thousand years, when they thought he had said one thousand. But we have no such prophet as this. Our Saviour Christ, because he would shew himself to be the Son of God, appointed to rise again three days after, and he kept his word. 'This Jesus,' saith he, Acts ii. 32, 'hath God raised up, whereof we all are witnesses.' He rose again for our justification. Here is the great Prophet that was to come into the world.

In the second place, it is great comfort to us that God raised him up from the dead. You shall find it to be one of the names of God, that he is said to be God that raised up Christ from the dead. And you shall find it to be the great object of our faith, 1 Peter i. 21, 'Who,' saith he, speaking of believers, 'do believe in God, that raised him up from the dead, and gave him glory; that your faith and hope might be in God.' Observe these words. The object of your faith is, that God hath raised up Christ from the dead and given him glory, and he addeth that this was done for that end, that you might have faith and hope in God. You could never have looked up to God with comfort, if you had not looked upon him as God that raised up Christ from the dead, for thereby we know now that God is well pleased with Christ, is satisfied, for he hath raised him up again; therefore your faith may be in God that he accepteth Christ's satisfaction for sinners, so to believe on him to be justified by it; and in that he raised him from the dead and gave him glory, your hope may be in God for the time to come that he will give you glory too. Hath he raised up Jesus Christ? He will raise up you also. He makes Jesus Christ a pattern, as here indeed in this very verse the Apostle doth, of what God will do to us; 'which he wrought in Christ when he raised him from the dead.' Did he raise up Christ? He will justify thee, which is a resurrection, as you heard. Did he raise up Christ? He will sanctify thee, which is an attaining unto the resurrection from the dead. Did he raise up Christ? He will raise up thy dead body out of the grave, he will glorify it. We believe on that God with a great deal of comfort that raised up Jesus Christ and gave him glory, now we come to have hope that we shall have the like.

I have often wondered what should be the meaning of that place, Rom. iv. 19,—let me open it unto you a little,—where he speaks of justifying faith, faith that layeth hold on Christ for justification; and he instanceth in Abraham's faith. 'Abraham believed,' saith he, 'and it was counted unto him for righteousness;' and he was your father. Now what was it that Abraham believed? Saith he, 'Not being weak in faith, he considered not his own body now dead, when he was about a hundred years old, nor the deadness of Sarah's womb: he staggered not at the promise of God through unbelief; but was strong in faith, giving glory to God; and being fully persuaded that what he had promised he was able also to perform.' The Apostle here speaks only of faith in the power of God to give him a son, to give him Isaac. What was this to justifying faith? For I count that to be faith justifying that hath justification for its object, and the faith whereby Abraham was justified we are justified; and certainly it must be so, or else the Apostle proveth nothing in bringing the instance of Abraham's faith that we must have the like. But if you observe the coherence of one thing with another, you shall see this doubt is taken off, and that the faith here spoken of is plainly faith laying hold upon justification, and doth, according to the pattern of Abraham's faith, require the like of us.

Read, first, the 17th verse. The text saith that Abraham was 'the father of us all, (as it is written,' saith he, speaking of the promise of Isaac, 'I have made thee a father of many nations,) before him whom he believed, even God, who quickeneth the dead, and calleth those things which be not as though they were.' Abraham saw the resurrection of Christ in two things. He saw it first in the birth of Isaac; for though Sarah's womb was dead, and his own body was dead, yet he believed that God would raise up Isaac, a type of Christ, out of this dead body, out of Sarah's womb. Here was one quickening of the dead. Abraham had a promise that of this very Isaac the Messiah should come. What saith God to him? 'Go take thy son,' saith he, 'and offer him for a burnt-offering.' Abraham made full account to do it; he had no refuge in the world but this, that God was able to raise up Isaac again; for it was as much as if God had said to him, Go kill the Messiah: for if Isaac had been killed, if Isaac should not live and get a child, and so child after child, the Messiah should not come out of the loins of Abraham, and so his faith had been void, all the promises must be let go. Now, look in Heb. xi. 17–19: 'By faith,' saith he, 'Abraham, when he was tried, offered up Isaac,'—he is said to offer him up, because it was as good as done, Abraham thought it was so,—'and he that had received the promises offered up his only-begotten son.' Here was his faith now. If Isaac die, he must lose all the promises; yet he that received the promises, saith he, offered him up: therefore he is said to believe against hope; against hope, because the Messiah was to come out of Isaac's loins, and if Isaac did not live he was to lose his Messiah, his interest in heaven, his justification and salvation and all. Here is his trial now.

Read on, ver. 18, 'For in Isaac shall thy seed be called.' It is not only Abraham's seed, but it is the seed of Isaac; therefore Isaac must live, I am gone else, I must never look for salvation else. In this strait what doth Abraham do? Ver. 19, 'Accounting that God was able to raise him up from the dead.' Here was all his refuge. And when God did bid him spare Isaac, he looked upon this as a type of the resurrection of the Messiah, so saith the next words; 'from whence also he received him in a figure,' in a type. A type of what? Of the Messiah to come out of his loins.

So then, when Abraham first believed the promise, the begetting of Isaac was a resurrection from the dead; when he offered him up it was the death of the Messiah to him, for Isaac was the figure of the Messiah; he was a figure of him in his resurrection, therefore in his death. Now then, when God did give him Isaac again, saith he, even thus shall that seed promised be put to death and rise again; and this faith was counted to Abraham for righteousness. This was faith, believing in a figure upon God that raised up Christ from the dead, for Isaac was in this a type of Christ, and Abraham saw Christ's day in this.

That this is the scope of the Apostle in that Rom. iv., being thus compared with Heb. xi., appeareth by this: saith he, ver. 22, therefore this faith was 'imputed to him for righteousness.' Here is justifying faith. 'Now,' saith he, 'it was not written for his sake alone, that it was imputed unto him, but for us also, to whom it shall be imputed,'—like as it was to Abraham,—'if we believe on him that raised up Jesus our Lord from the dead.' Here is your object of faith that justifieth; this was Abraham's faith in a figure, and this is a believer's faith, to believe on him that raised up Christ from the dead. Why? To be justified by him, 'who was delivered,' saith he, 'for our offences, and was raised again for our justification.'

You see, then, my brethren, that the faith of your father Abraham was a believing in God that raised up the Messiah from the dead for his justification. Herein now lieth your faith, to eye Jesus Christ in his resurrection for your justification.

And then, lastly, if the Holy Ghost raiseth up Christ, then,—in a word, if this Holy Ghost dwell in you,—he will raise up your hearts also, he will raise up your bodies. That you have, Rom. viii. 11, with which I will end: 'If, saith he, 'the Spirit of him that raised up Jesus from the dead dwell in you, he that raised up Christ from the dead shall also quicken your mortal bodies by his Spirit that dwelleth in you.' The same Spirit that dwelt in Christ and raised up him, the same Spirit shall raise up your mortal bodies.

So now I have opened these three things:—

1. The death of Christ.
2. His remaining in a state of death.
3. His resurrection; and the necessity of all these, and how God the Father raised him up, and how he raised up himself; and some observations and uses from all.

SERMON XXXI.

The same which he wrought in Christ, when he raised him from the dead, and set him at his own right hand in the heavenly places, far above all principality and power, &c.—VER. 20, 21.

THE power that wrought in Christ in his resurrection, I have spoke to that. As also of the several articles which are laid down here in these words: as, namely, that Jesus Christ was dead; that he was not only dead, but remained in the state of death, for he was 'raised from the dead;' and, lastly, that he was raised up, and that by God. I have despatched and explained these things out of these words. I come now to that state of exaltation which is here set forth to us; 'and set him at his own right hand in the heavenly places, far above all principality and power,' &c.

There are five things in these first words, 'and set him at his own right hand in the heavenly places.'

The first is, *What is meant by setting him at his own right hand;* wherein we must consider both something about the phrase, and something about the thing itself imported thereby.

The second thing to be considered is, *The author of it*, GOD; it is he that set him.

The third is, *The subject of it, him;* 'when he raised him from the dead, and set him at his own right hand.'

Fourthly, *When it was he was set by God at his right hand.* It is plain, after his resurrection; 'which he wrought in Christ, when he raised him from the dead, and set him,' &c.

Lastly, *The place where;* 'in the heavenly places.'

These are the parts which remain of the 20th verse, concerning the exaltation, which I hope to despatch, and so likewise to proceed to the 21st verse, which is an explanation of the great dignity that our Lord and Saviour Jesus Christ enjoyeth in heaven. What he saith but metaphorically in the 20th verse, 'he set him at his own right hand in the heavenly places,' he expresseth more really in the 21st verse, 'far above all principality and power,' &c.

First, To begin with the phrase, 'and set,' καὶ ἐκάθισεν. The word is sometimes used, as we say in grammar, either intransitively, for the sitting of him that sits; or else transitively, to *make to sit*, to *cause to sit.* So it is here taken; for it is spoken of God the Father's setting of Christ, or making Christ to sit at his own right hand. It is used on the other side of Christ's own sitting; the same word καθίσαι, Acts ii. 30, as the Septuagint well readeth it, 'he raised him up to sit,' so they read the words. Yet so as that here are two things implied: one, that Jesus Christ doth sit at God's right hand; and the other, that God the Father hath set him there. Ps. cx. 1, 'He said unto him, Sit thou.' Now always God's word hath a causation with it; 'he said to him, Sit,'—that is, 'he made him sit,' or as it is here expressed, 'he made him sit with a mighty power,'—for where the word of a king is there is power, and where the word of God is there is power; it had the greatness of power going with it, the exceeding greatness of power, even the same that raised him up from the dead.

Further, for the phrase too, as it noteth out Christ's sitting at God's right hand, it is not a proper phrase of speech, it is but a metaphor, but a similitude to express that height of glory to us that Jesus Christ hath in heaven with God, by what is done by kings here on earth to those whom they will honour. It is but a metaphorical speech; that is clear by this, because you know God properly hath no hand, nor right hand; and if God have no right hand, then Christ's sitting at God's right hand must needs be a similitude likewise; for they are relatives, if the one be not real, the other cannot be. That Christ hath 'all things under his feet,' which is another phrase used in the 22d verse, is but a metaphorical speech; those who are below one, infinitely below one, are said to be under his feet; so is it said here, that both Christ sitteth at God's right hand, and that he hath all things under his feet.

So that now, to gather what posture of his body Jesus Christ hath in heaven, or what posture he shall have when he cometh to judgment, though it is expressed by *sitting*, and *sitting at God's right hand*, and at the *right hand of power*, yet this phrase will not infallibly determine what shall be the posture of his body. Rather, if I would deliver what out of other scriptures seems to be more clearly held forth about it, it would seem to be *standing* rather than *sitting;* if you take it in its proper sense, as he is a man, standing is the properest posture of a man.

I know not well what to say to that in Acts vii. 55, where it is said that Stephen 'looked up into heaven and saw the glory of God, and Jesus standing at the right hand of God.' It seemeth to be a vision of his eye elevated supernaturally, such as Paul had when he was converted, when Christ from heaven spake to him. 'Last of all,' saith he, 'he was seen of me.' Therefore his bodily face did shine, because he saw him with his bodily eyes. And they saw a representative glory of God; for you shall find that likewise in the Old Testament and in the New there was a place to represent the presence of God, as 1 Kings viii. 10, and Luke ii. 9, it is said the glory of God shone round about the shepherds.

Now, the like representation Stephen had when he saw heaven opened. 'I see the heavens opened,' saith he, 'and the Son of man standing on the right hand of God;' he seemeth to speak clearly of what he saw, and the manner of it. I do not know what to say to this place. Sure it was not a seeing of him by faith only, such as is spoken of, Heb. ii. 9, 'We see Jesus crowned with glory and honour;' this is more. There is only this that may be said of it, that it was such a kind of vision as was presented to John in the Revelation. He saw a throne, and he saw a Lamb slain; so Rev. v. 6, and chap. i. 15, 16. He saw a man that had a sword come out of his mouth, his feet like unto fine brass, and his countenance was as the sun that shineth in his strength, &c. He speaks of Christ; for, saith he, ver. 17, 'He said unto me, I am the first and the last, I am he that liveth and was dead.' This was but a vision; now the like it may be was this of Stephen's only. And as those visions in the Revelation were but suited to the present occasion, so this vision was but suited to the present condition Stephen was in; he was to suffer for Christ, and he seeth Christ *stand*, as being ready to help him.

But, however, we may learn this from it, which is to the point in hand, that these words *sitting* and *standing* being used thus promiscuously, the

Holy Ghost varying the phrase, that therefore the word *sitting* is not to be understood of the natural posture of his body. He would not vary the phrase so of standing and sitting, and being at the right hand of God, if it were taken properly and strictly.

If therefore, to come to the thing itself, for I have done with the phrase, it be meant by way of similitude, I shall open this similitude, what it is, thus :—

You must consider that it is spoken to us after the manner of men, and when he is said to sit at God's right hand, God is represented to us as a king, as the Lord Sovereign of heaven and earth; as, 1 Tim. i. 17, he is called, 'the King eternal, immortal, invisible, and only wise God.' A king that is full of glory, which glory is always represented to us under the same words and expressions that are familiar among men to represent glory by; and therefore when we speak of a king, we say 'His Majesty :' so when the Scripture speaks of God, this King, it calleth him 'the Majesty on high ;' so Heb. i. 3. And as kings have their thrones, as Solomon had, to set forth his glory, and 'throne' in the Scripture is still put for kingly power, so likewise is God said to have a throne. The Scripture representeth the sovereignty of God, by having a throne that he sitteth on; therefore you shall still read, both in the Old Testament and in the New, that he appeareth upon a throne. Now this glory of God, and this throne of his, is said to be in the heavens, because it is certain that the glory of God and his sovereignty is there represented more, infinitely more than in this world it is. This is but his footstool, heaven is his throne; so you have it in that 7th of the Acts,—it is but some five verses before this vision of Stephen's,—'Heaven is my throne, and earth is my footstool ;' and then he looks up and seeth the glory of God, and Christ standing at his right hand.

You see, now, how the glory of God is set forth in the way of kingly power, having a court where he manifests it; in which court standeth his throne, for heaven is so.

Now then, after the same manner of men is the glory of the man Christ Jesus set forth unto us by sitting at God's right hand. So, Heb. i. 3, it is said that he is 'sat down on the right hand of the Majesty on high ;' as I said, majesty is put for the kingly power of God, and Christ is sat down on the right hand of that Majesty, that is, of God himself, as you call the king 'His Majesty.' And as in Heb. i. 3, he is said to sit down on the right hand of Majesty, so in Heb. viii. 1, he is said to sit on the right hand of the throne of the Majesty in the heavens, that is, of God, who displayeth his glory in the heavens. Therefore Stephen saw the glory of God first, and Jesus standing on the right hand of God; and in Matt. xxvi. 64, it is called 'sitting on the right hand of power ;' and in Luke xxii. 69, it is explained 'the right hand of the power of God ;' that is, of the powerful God.

It was the custom of the eastern nations for kings to express their respect to those whom they favoured by setting them at their right hand, as you know Solomon set his mother, 1 Kings ii. 19; and therefore it was the request of the mother of the sons of Zebedee for her children, that Christ would let them sit, the one at his right hand, the other at his left. And that in 1 Esdras iv. 29, though it be Apocrypha, it representeth what the manner of those nations was: it is said that Apame, the king's concubine, 'did sit on the right hand of the king.' So among the Romans, we read in Suetonius, in the Life of Nero, when the king of Parthia came, he set him at his right hand. But Christ's sitting at God's right hand is not only a token of familiarity, but it is more; for these, though they were set at the right hand, yet they were not invested with power by it, only a respect was shewn to them;

therefore we further read that the manner of those eastern nations was for the king's son always to sit upon the throne of his father, and that upon his right hand, for that was his hand of respect.

So we read in Exod. xi. 5, when he would express the eldest son of Pharaoh, he saith thus: 'From the first-born of Pharaoh that sitteth upon his throne, unto the first-born of the maid-servant that is behind the mill.' And the like we have Exod. xii. 29, 'It came to pass, that the Lord smote all the first-born in the land of Egypt, from the first-born of Pharaoh that sat on his throne, unto the first-born of the captive that was in the dungeon.' Here you see how the eldest son is expressed; it is all one to say, the eldest son of a king, and to say, one that sat upon his throne. And accordingly you have it of Christ, being the eldest Son of God, Rev. iii. 21, 'To him that overcometh, I will grant to sit with me in my throne, as I also overcame, and am set down with my Father on his throne.' And therefore, as Solomon, 1 Kings i. 34, was crowned king, and was set upon his father's throne while his father was alive, and remained king, so is Jesus Christ, and in that Solomon was a type of Christ, and David of God the Father; and though God be king still, yet he, as it were, hath given over the government, as David did, to his Son. Read Acts ii. 30, 31, &c. David 'being a prophet, and knowing that God had sworn with an oath to him, that of the fruit of his loins, according to the flesh, he would raise up Christ to sit on his throne; he seeing this before spake of the resurrection of Christ.' And, saith he, 'This Jesus hath God raised up; therefore being by the right hand of God exalted,' &c. Here, you see, he doth apply this type of Solomon unto our Lord and Saviour Jesus Christ.

Therefore you shall find in Dan. vii. 9, 13, where the kingdom of Jesus Christ, and his inauguration into it, is set forth; there 'the Ancient of days did sit,' and the Son of man was brought to him. And what saith he, ver. 19? 'I beheld till the thrones were cast down.' There are those that find fault much with this translation, and say it is clean contrary; it is, 'till the thrones were set;' and so the Septuagint reads it, 'till the thrones were set;' as the Rabbins say, one throne for God the Father, and one for God the Son. The Ancient of days did sit, and then the Son was brought to him, and another throne was set for him, and he did give him dominion, and glory, and a kingdom, &c., so ver. 13. So that to sit at God's right hand is not only a matter of favour, such as kings sometimes shew to those whom they would honour, but it is a matter of prerogative belonging to the eldest son; the same that was performed to Solomon, that was crowned king and sat upon his father's throne in his father's lifetime; his father withdrew, as it were, and so doth God the Father, and lets Christ execute the government. It was a prerogative that was never given to any creature. See for this, Heb. i. 13, 'To which of the angels said he at any time, Sit on my right hand?' Not an angel had this privilege; it is, therefore, a privilege peculiar to the eldest Son of the King of heaven, to sit at the right hand of God; as you heard before, out of the place in Exodus, that to be the eldest son of a king, and to sit upon his throne, is all one. So that whereas God hath translated some into heaven, as Enoch and Elijah, and those that rose with Christ; they are indeed translated to heaven, but none sat at God's right hand, that is peculiar unto Christ himself, that is God's own Son. And, indeed and in truth, when the thrones were set in that 7th of Daniel, you shall find that the angels stood; so the expression is there, ver. 10, 'There were thousand thousands ministered unto him, and ten thousand times ten thousand stood before him.' And now, in comparison of this, for they are all metaphorical expressions, the saints are said to stand; but it is the prerogative of Christ alone to sit: 'Sit thou at my right hand, till I make thine enemies thy footstool.'

In general, therefore, you see there are two things imported by Jesus Christ's sitting down at God's right hand. The first is the exaltation of Christ, as God's eldest Son. Not only to be next him, to be second in heaven to him; not only so, but as God's eldest Son to be invested with all God-like power and authority, to sit upon his throne alone, and to do there as Solomon did upon David's throne, even in David's lifetime; to be taken up to the participation of all that happiness, blessedness, glory, majesty, and power, which the great God himself enjoyeth, and that in such a manner as no creature is capable of. To none of all the angels did he say, Sit, as he saith to Christ. That is, I say, the sum of the meaning of these words, 'he set him at his own right hand.'

Now to come to the particulars of this advancement of Christ, that this, 'his being set at God's right hand,' holdeth forth.

First, It noteth out *the enjoyment of all blessedness* in an infinite manner; that God is immediately his happiness. And this the words, 'being at his right hand,' implieth. And then he is said to *sit*, because he doth quietly possess and enjoy all this happiness. That this is part of the meaning of the phrase is evident by that in Ps. xvi. 11, a psalm made of Christ, and quoted by Peter in that second of the Acts to which I have often had recourse. Now, what saith Christ there? 'Thou wilt shew me the path of life; in thy presence is fulness of joy.' But this doth not speak home to that I would have, but that which followeth doth. 'At thy right hand there are pleasures for evermore.' It is spoken assuredly of such pleasures as Jesus Christ by way of prerogative enjoyeth beyond all the saints and angels, he being at God's right hand so as none of them are. It was that peculiar encouragement that Jesus Christ had, not to be in heaven only as a common saint, but to be in heaven at God's right hand, and to have pleasures answerable, far above all the pleasures of men and angels, as I shall shew you when I come to handle that point.

There are said to be 'pleasures at God's right hand.' The right hand, you know, is that wherewith a man is bountiful; if he will lay out himself and distribute of his riches, he doth it with his right hand: 'Let not thy left hand know what thy right hand doth.' When Jesus Christ speaks of God's distributing and communicating to him fulness of pleasures, he saith, 'At thy right hand are pleasures,' &c. Jesus Christ is at God's right hand, and therefore God doth communicate and impart to him, to the utmost, all his happiness, so far forth as that human nature is capable of. 'Length of days are at her right hand,' that is, eternal life; 'and at her left, riches and honour.' So Wisdom speaks in the Proverbs; for we are said to be at God's right hand. The happiness of the saints at the latter day, how is it expressed in Scripture? 'He will set them on his right hand.' I speak it for this, that happiness, and being in heaven, is expressed by being at God's right hand; and Christ is said to be at God's right hand: what happiness and pleasures then hath he? On the other side, the highest misery of wicked men is said to be in their being at God's left hand.

As it implieth the fulness of pleasure, so it importeth *honour* and *glory*, and a fulness of the participation of that. For that you may take those expressions I gave you before, of Queen Bathsheba being set at Solomon's right hand; it was in a way of glory and respect unto her. 1 Kings ii. 19, when Bathsheba came to the king, 'the king rose up to meet her, and sat down upon his throne, and caused a seat to be set for the king's mother; and she sat on his right hand.' Therefore our Saviour Christ, when they, Matt. xx. 21, desired one to be on his right hand and the other on his left, interpreteth it in ver. 27 to be a desire of being chief; that is the interpretation he himself putteth upon it. He is therefore in that first of the Hebrews, ver. 11, said to be 'set down on the right hand of Majesty,' having imparted to him a God-like and a royal majesty, such as appeareth in no creature. So now, to be set down at God's right hand, which is a second meaning of it, is this, for Jesus to be crowned with glory and honour; 'We see Jesus,' saith he, Heb. ii. 9, 'to be crowned with glory and honour'—that is, he is set down at the right hand of Majesty.

In the third place, to be set down at God's right hand is not only to have a fulness of happiness, to enjoy the Godhead; to have rivers of pleasures from his right hand, and to have glory and majesty to be set above all; but it is to have a real *rule*, and *power*, and *dominion* put into his hands too. Kings oftentimes make no other use of their kingdoms but to enjoy pleasures, and glory, and state; but for their rule they leave it unto others, as Pharaoh did to Joseph. 'In the throne,' saith he, 'I will be above thee.' But now it is otherwise; when Jesus Christ is set down at God's right hand, he hath the rule, the dominion over all things imparted to him, he is invested with it. And this is a different thing from majesty; therefore they are both mentioned in Matt. xxiv. 30, 'Ye shall see,' saith he, 'the Son of man coming in the clouds with power and great glory.' Power is one thing, and glory is another, although it is power that doth make glorious. And hence, therefore, one evangelist calleth it, 'sitting on the right hand of power,' Mark xiv. 62, because that Christ is invested with the power of God, and the right hand is in a more especial manner put for power in Scripture. As, to give you but one place for it, though there be multitudes of them, Exod. xv. 6, 'Thy right hand, O Lord, is become glorious in power.' The right hand is still put for power. So that for Christ to sit at God's right hand, is for him to have all power and dominion put into his hands. Therefore both in Ps. cx., where God's placing Christ at his right hand is mentioned, there he is called Lord: 'The Lord said unto my Lord, Sit thou on my right hand.' David was a king, he was one of those principalities and powers that the 21st verse mentioneth, but he acknowledgeth Christ to be over him; nay, David was his father, that is more. Parents that are kings do not call their children lords; but Christ had such a prerogative by sitting at God's right hand that he was the Lord of David. And the apostle Peter interpreteth it, Acts ii., speaking of the exaltation of Christ; 'Being,' saith he, ver. 33, 'by the right hand of God exalted;' and he quoteth David for it too, 'The Lord said unto my Lord,' saith he, 'Sit thou on my right hand.' Now what saith he, ver. 36? 'Therefore let all the house of Israel know assuredly, that God hath made that same Jesus, whom ye have crucified, both Lord and Christ.' So that sitting at God's right hand is interpreted to be making of him Lord, and that is evidently held forth in the text; for he saith that he is over principalities, and powers, and might, and dominion, and whatsoever else is named in heaven or in earth, and he hath them all under his feet. And to shew forth the excellency of Christ, he saith he is over all these; that is, as a ruler, as a lord over all these.

My brethren, what is the reason the Pope is called Antichrist? You cannot call episcopal government antichristian in that sense the Pope is called Antichrist. But the Pope is plainly called that great Antichrist; and what is the reason? Because he doth usurp the very same authority, the very imitation of it, which our Lord and Saviour Jesus Christ hath in heaven. For what is that which Christ is invested with? It is to be over all powers, and principalities, and dominions in this world and the world to come; and to sit in heaven, advanced to God's right hand, and to have all these under his feet. Now if you read 2 Thess. ii. 3, 4, you shall find the description of that man of sin to be this: 'That man of sin,' saith he, 'the son of perdition, shall be revealed, who opposeth and exalteth himself above all that is called God,'—that is, above principalities and powers, above angels themselves, for they have undertaken to command angels,—'so that he as God sitteth in the temple of God, shewing himself that he is God;' taking upon him the same power which our Lord and Saviour Jesus Christ challengeth to himself. Others do take that which God hath given his Church to themselves, and place church power in a subject it ought not to be in; and it may be said they are *antichurchian*, but not *antichristian*. But this is that which makes the Pope Antichrist, that he assumeth to himself, as far as possibly he can, directly, that power that Jesus Christ himself is invested withal.

Then again, in the fourth place, God's calling Christ to sit at his right hand importeth *all those abilities, all those royal, glorious endowments*, which God filled the human nature with when he came first to heaven, to make him fit to be the governor of all the world. That infinite wisdom and power that is in the human nature, and all other prerogatives whereby he is able to manage the government of this world and the world that is to come, and to have all those things run through his hands which all creatures could not do if the wit and power of them all were put together,—that he is able to wield this sceptre, this is a fourth thing which 'sitting at God's right hand' importeth.

This the text holdeth forth unto us; for, if you mark it, he doth not only say, that God did set him at his right hand as a king doth advance his favourite, or as he doth set his son in his throne with him, give him the same authority himself hath, whereas he doth not give ability; but the text speaks of a power that wrought in Christ when he set him at his own right hand, a physical power, as I may so call it, which can be exercised and put forth in nothing but in this. As when God set up Saul to be king, he gave him not only power, but a heart to be a king; so God, as he gave Jesus Christ power over all might and dominion, so he hath given him a heart also. And, my brethren, to take that man Christ Jesus, that carpenter's son, as I may so express him, speaking of him in his meanness and lowness, that sorry man, as the prophet speaks of him, and to fill him with such wisdom and power as that he is fit to govern all the world, to have the power of all the doings in the world in his own hands,—this is that 'which God wrought in Christ, when he raised him from the dead, and set him at his own right hand.'

Now this is a mighty alteration, to fling off all the flesh, and to endow him with all these abilities. As it is said, 1 Cor. xv. 43, our bodies are sown in weakness, but they shall be raised again in power; they are sown a natural, but they shall rise a spiritual body; that is, furnished with all new abilities to make them to be spiritual bodies: so is Jesus Christ furnished with all abilities fit for the managing of all the affairs of the world; that look whatever God meaneth to do, that the man Jesus Christ, joined to the Godhead, is able to do; and look whatever God knoweth concerning the government of the world, that the man Jesus Christ knoweth. Brethren, nor saint nor angel had this.

You shall find this set forth to you in Rev. v.; do but duly weigh that chapter, the scope of it is clearly this. You must know that the Revelation, the general story of which beginneth at the 4th chapter, and so to the end, is the acting over of the story of the world that was to come, and things are set forth to us comedy wise. There is first a stage set up, a throne, and there are the elders about God, that is chap. iv. Then there is a prologue to it, and that beginneth in this 5th chapter; and what is the prologue? It is clearly nothing else but the instalment and coronation of Jesus Christ, as he that should govern the world, and so should be able to give the revelation to John. And although his coronation was a thing past, for it was done when he ascended, yet it is here represented to John, because it was the foundation of all the story that followeth. How is it represented? There is a book held forth with seals upon it; that book containeth God's decrees to be executed, and he that takes the book must undertake to fulfil what is written in the book, and to make it good. There is a proclamation made to all in heaven and in earth, whether any were worthy to open the book, and to loose the seals thereof. It seemeth to be an allusion to the admission of a judge to his place—they give him a roll, or a book; or to the ceremony that is used in the University, when they admit the proctors to their places—they give him a statute. So here, speaking of the instalment of Christ into the government of the world, he alludeth to some such kind of ceremony. Here is a book held forth, and proclamation made that whosoever takes this book must fulfil and make good whatsoever is contained in it. Now, saith he, there was none found either in heaven or in earth that was able to know God's decrees, much less to execute them. None was found worthy to do it but the Lamb. And how cometh the Lamb to be able to do it? He hath 'seven horns and seven eyes.'

There are two things goeth to kingly power: first, knowledge; secondly, power. He hath knowledge answerable to his power, for he hath 'seven eyes;' that is, as it is there interpreted, 'they are the seven spirits of God, sent forth into all the earth.' His eyes run to and fro in the earth, he knoweth all that is done, so no angel in heaven can do, he seeth every man's heart. And he hath 'seven horns;' he is as able to perform (for the horn in Scripture phrase still signifieth power) whatsoever he knoweth, whatsoever he meaneth to do. And he takes the book out of the right hand of him that sat upon the throne, for he standeth at God's right hand. And upon his taking it, what a song was sung! you may read it at ver. 12. They all fell down before the Lamb, being glad there was found one that was able to administer the affairs of the world; 'and they said with a loud voice, Worthy is the Lamb that was slain, to receive power, and riches, and wisdom, and strength, and honour, and glory, and blessing.'

To open these a little; they are all ensigns of kingly power.

First, He is only worthy to receive *authority* to do it; that is meant by power. 'All power,' saith he, when he ascended, when he was taking his flight to heaven, 'is given unto me in heaven and in earth.'

Secondly, He is only worthy of *riches*, which kings have; he only was worthy to possess all creatures. 'He hath obtained an inheritance,' a better name than the angels, for he is the 'heir of all things.' And as he hath authority, so he is able now, he hath a natural right unto it, to dispose of all creatures as his own proper goods and riches.

Thirdly, He is worthy to receive *strength;* he hath not only authority and power to dispose of all, but he hath strength too. Kings have not strength answerable to their power,—that is, to their authority,—but what they do, they must do by others. But Jesus Christ hath strength, personal strength, he is able to do it alone.

Fourthly, *Wisdom;* that is as large as all these.

Fifthly, *Honour.* Honour is due to him from all the creatures, they fall all down before him.

Sixthly, *Glory,* from his Father that hath thus joined him in commission, and set him up to be sharer with him in the kingdom. And—

Lastly, *Blessing,* from all his saints, for they only bless him. And this he hath given him by 'sitting on God's right hand.'

I will give you but one instance. He was able, when he was set down on God's right hand, to send the Holy Ghost into men's hearts. What a mighty ability was this—could any creature do it?—that the Holy Ghost should be his ambassador, to despatch his business here! Yet this is made the fruit of being set at God's right hand. Acts ii. 33, 'Being by the right hand of God exalted, and having received of the Father the promise of the Holy Ghost, he hath shed forth this, which ye now both see and hear.' Could any creature have done this? No mere creature could have done it, nor he as mere man could have done it; but he being man joined to God, so he hath right to do it.

You see now what is imported by 'sitting at God's right hand.' This is the substance of it. It importeth—

First, *Fulness of all pleasure.*

Secondly, *A communication of God-like majesty.*

Thirdly, *Power and dominion over all things.*

Fourthly, *Ability to execute that power.*

So much for the substance of it. There are two circumstances that sitting on God's right hand doth yet imply, to make up this fully:—

First, *That he doth quietly possess all this.* The word *sitting* still implieth quiet possessing. As 1 Kings ii. 38, when Shimei was in Jerusalem quiet and undisturbed, we translate it, 'he dwelt at Jerusalem;' the Hebrew word is, 'he sat at Jerusalem,' he quietly enjoyed his house; as David is said to 'sit in his house.' That same phrase there in Acts iii. 21, which we translate 'whom the heavens must receive,' or contain, 'until the times of restitution of all things;' it is strange to see how ambiguous the Holy Ghost speaks; the words may be as well read thus, and as clearly, and no man can deny it, 'who must possess the heavens till the times of the restitution of all things.' It is as true and as full a sense, and the Lutherans answer us home in that place, for we would bring it against their *ubiquity,* and they say, and say truly, 'who must possess the heavens till,' &c. It is a phrase used in Greek and Latin, to *receive the city,* or *receive the kingdom,* speaking of kings or conquerors, when they come to possess a kingdom or a city. David useth the phrase, Ps. lxxv. 2, 'When I shall receive the congregation, I will judge uprightly;' that is, when I shall come to possess the kingdom. So Jesus Christ possesseth heaven, he sitteth and quietly enjoyeth his kingdom. This is implied by sitting on the right hand of God.

Secondly, He doth not sit only quietly, but *he sitteth surely.* When his kingdom is mentioned, still you shall find this added, Thy throne is for everlasting; it endureth for ever; it is from generation to generation, &c. And this the word *sitting* implieth. As, Isa. xvi. 5, speaking of the kingdom of Christ, 'In mercy,' saith he, 'shall the throne be established; and he shall sit upon it in truth.' To have him sit upon it, and to have the throne established, is all one. It implieth the firmness of his kingdom; it is such a kingdom as shall break all kingdoms.

So you have what it is to have Christ sit at God's right hand, as briefly as I could, explained. The uses that this affords are infinite, which the Scripture giveth; but I must not run out into this thing, for I must merely expound.

The *second* thing in the text is, *who it is that set him at his right hand.* I have done with the first; opened the phrase of sitting at God's right hand. I come now to the second, his exalter and advancer. It is God, namely the Father, that set him at his own right hand, and that by his exceeding greatness of power.

You know our Saviour Christ acknowledgeth that all his power is from the Father. 'All power,' saith he, 'is given unto me;' that is his expression, Matt. xxviii. As he is the natural Son of God simply considered, so he doth not sit at God's right hand, and so indeed power is not given to him, for so he hath it by nature. But take him as he is Mediator, and that as he is God and man too,—for he is Mediator in both natures, and so all the power that he hath is given unto him,—and so he is only said to begin to sit at God's right hand after his resurrection; whereas, as he is the natural Son of God, he had power equally with the Father from before the world was. Therefore you know God boasteth of it; 'I have set my king upon mine holy hill.' Other kings are by human institution and creation; but this same Jesus Christ, he is my king, saith he.

Now, my brethren, though the Father did but give it him, let me say this for Christ on the other side, he hath a right to it. So indeed it is carried between the Father and the Son; it is the Father's gift, and so the Father is honoured, but yet it is the Son's due. All power is given unto him; yet he saith plainly in Luke xxii. 29, that he hath power to give a kingdom, he useth the same expression of himself that he doth of his Father. 'I appoint unto you a kingdom,' saith he, 'as my Father hath appointed unto me.' And as the Father quickeneth whom he will, so the Son quickeneth whom he will too, John v. 21. Only there is a reconciliation of free-will; God's will and Christ's never differ, for Jesus Christ exerciseth the highest liberty of will, and not only so, but he exerciseth a sovereignty of will, and it is his right and due so to do; yet he doth nothing but what the Father willeth.

It is his Father that set him at his own right hand. I desire you to observe the difference of these two phrases the Scripture holdeth forth. The exaltation of Christ is not only said to be *at* God's right hand, but it is said to be *with* God's right hand. As in Acts ii. 33 he saith, he was 'by the right hand of God exalted;' and Acts v. 31, 'Him hath God exalted with his right hand to be a Prince and a Saviour,' &c. So that being at his right hand implieth that he hath all power committed to him; and being exalted *with* the right hand, or *by* the right hand of God, implieth it was an answerable almighty power that raised him up to this.

My brethren, our Lord and Saviour Jesus Christ did not only live by the power of God while he was here. 'Man liveth not by bread only, but by every word that proceedeth out of the mouth of God.' I do so, saith he; that is his meaning. But you shall read, that since he is gone to heaven, he liveth by the power of God. It is in 2 Cor. xiii. 4, 'He was crucified through weakness, yet he liveth by the power of God.' And because that God the Father is he that exalted him, therefore Paul calleth him 'the Father of glory' in the beginning of this prayer in this chapter.

I might enlarge this. You see how the Persons honour one another: the Father's honour, that he doth give him this power; the Son's honour, that he is worthy; and it was fit, and comely, and necessary for his Father to do it. Consider of it thus: that the Son of God should be chosen (take it so) to be the Mediator of the world, that the Son, that that person should be singled out, it was but an act of choice; though it was comely it should be the Son rather than the Holy Ghost. That the man Christ Jesus, that he was chosen to it, that was merely of God, as much as the choice of us was to eternal life; yet now, when this man Christ Jesus was united to the Son of God, he had right to all this, it was his due. Heb. i. 2, 6, compared together; as he is called in the second verse, the appointed heir of all things, so he is called in the sixth verse the natural heir of all things.

Now, it being his due the first day, what doth Christ? He layeth aside all his glory, takes the form of a servant, voluntarily doth it to honour his Father. What honour doth his Father do to him for it when he cometh to heaven? Have you obscured your glory, saith he, withdrawn it for my sake? I will do as much for you, I will commit all judgment to you; I will not be seen, the eyes and thoughts of all creatures shall be next upon you: 'The Father judgeth no man, but hath committed all judgment unto the Son,' John v. 22, that is, visibly to execute it. So that God did as it were give up the kingdom, as David did to Solomon while he was alive. Because that he glorified God in suffering himself to be made obedient to the death, therefore it was justice for God to glorify him likewise, by withdrawing himself from the affairs of the world; that is, in respect of visible execution of it.

And Jesus Christ had this in his eye when he was to die upon the cross; he suffered for it, as I said in the last discourse. 'You shall see,' saith he, 'the Son of man sitting on the right hand of power.' And 'for the joy that was set before him, he endured the cross, despising the shame, and is set down at the right hand of the throne of God,' Heb. xii. 2. He had this honour of his in his eye, and therefore as his reward the Father gave it him, and it was comely the Father should give it him; and because that he, while he was here below, was made lower than the angels, much lower, a little lower for the time, but much lower otherwise, therefore God hath set him above the angels. And because while he was here he suffered himself to be insulted on by Satan, to have power on his body to hurry it up and down; and when he came to die, saith he, 'The prince of this world cometh, but he shall find nothing in me,' yet come he did; therefore now he is exalted far above all principalities and powers, &c. And it was his due to have it, it was his reward, it is but his condign reward; and it is yet a reward therefore given by the Father.

Thirdly, The next thing in the text that is mentioned is, *who it is that is here exalted.* It is *him.* Whom? Christ. Some would restrain this exaltation of Christ's sitting at God's right hand only to the human nature. For, say they, as he was the Son of God simply considered, he did always sit at God's right hand. But the mistake lieth in this. It is true, take him as he is Son of God, he hath an equal power with the Father from everlasting, but that power is never expressed by sitting at God's right hand, for then the Holy Ghost should be said to sit at God's right hand as well as God the Son, which is never said. But the sitting at God's right hand doth imply that power that is committed to him as Mediator, both God and man, —that is, as he is the Son of God, clothed with man's nature, exalted now in heaven,—so that what is attributed to the one is attributed to the other by communication of properties; as we say that God and man died, though the manhood only did die, yet it is attributed to the whole, it is called the blood of God; and we say God-man rose, though his body only rose, yet it is attributed to the whole; *totus Christus*, though not *totum Christi*. Whole Christ rose and whole Christ sitteth at God's right hand; he exalted him, though not the whole of Christ.

I will not insist longer on this. There is only a scripture or two I will give why not only the manhood is said thus to be exalted, but the Godhead too as considered joined with the manhood. The first, that his Godhead is thus exalted, I mean that the Son of God is exalted, is that Ps. cx. 1, 'The Lord said unto my Lord, Sit thou,' &c. Now, he was David's Lord only as he was Son of God. I mean that the foundation of his being Lord is laid in that; therefore, Heb. i. 13, the Apostle proveth him to be God from this, because he was bidden to sit down on God's right hand; 'To which of all the angels said he at any time, Sit on my right hand, until I make,' &c. 'But unto the Son he saith, Thy throne, O God, is for ever and ever,' &c. And then it belongeth to him likewise as man; that you have a clear place for, John v. And our Saviour putteth it in on purpose. Saith he, at ver. 22, 'All judgment is committed unto the Son;' and lest that we that know him to be both God and man should take this to be spoken of him in regard of his Godhead, as he was second Person only, he telleth us plainly, ver. 27, 'He hath given him authority to execute judgment also, because he is the Son of man.' So that take him as he is Son of man, so he hath authority given him to execute judgment; and he putteth in this to open the prophecy, Dan. vii., for, saith he there, at ver. 14, to the Son of man was given dominion, and glory, and a kingdom which shall not be destroyed, and to this Son of man, saith he, is all judgment given.

Now, you will ask how it is said, take him as he is the Son of God, that he should be exalted, for he is but as he was?

Yes, my brethren, he is exalted in this sense, because his Godhead was obscured and hidden while he was here below. It was his due to have shined in his manhood instantly as he doth now in heaven, that all men should behold his glory as the glory of the only-begotten Son of God, as the apostles Peter, and James, and John did when he was transfigured. Now he veileth all his glory; when he cometh to sit at the right hand of God, there he sheweth it; so that in respect of manifestation he is said to be exalted, for then he was manifested to be the Son of God.

So much for the Person that is exalted, how it is true of him both as God and man.

The *fourth* thing to be explained is, *when it was that he began to be exalted*. The text plainly saith, after his resurrection; the same power, saith he, 'which he wrought in Christ when he raised him from the dead, and set him at his own right hand.'

There are some divines that are mightily mistaken in this, for they would make the sitting at God's right hand to be the prerogative of the hypostatical union, and so would make him to sit on God's right hand when he was in the womb. But, brethren, the Scripture runneth clean otherwise. It was his due indeed then, and his right; but in respect of its execution, he was but as a king under age, till he rose again and ascended up to heaven. Therefore you shall find, Heb. i. 3, it is expressly said, 'After he had purged our sins, he sat down on the right hand of the Majesty on high.' *After*; mark that phrase; it was not till then: so Heb. x. 12, 'After he offered one sacrifice for sin, he sat down on the right hand of God;' it was after that. He was like one that is born a king, that cometh to act the part of a servant upon a stage; but when he cometh to such a period he throweth off the form of a servant, and sheweth himself to be a king: and so doth Jesus

Christ; therefore you have it, Phil. ii. 9, 'He took on him the form of a servant, and was obedient unto the death;' and then it was that God exalted him, he did not enter upon this glory till he had suffered death; so Heb. ii. 9, and in Rev. v. 12, it is said there expressly, he was worthy to receive honour, and glory, and riches, &c., because he was slain. He was first to be slain. It became him first to suffer, and so to enter into his glory. Therefore his sitting at God's right hand was not before God had raised him.—That is the fourth thing.

The *fifth* is, *the place where he sitteth.* It is expressly said, in heaven. The word in the original is not heavenly *places;* the word *places* is put in; but, he 'set him at his own right hand in the heavenlies.'

The Lutherans therefore interpret it, 'he sitteth in heavenly things;' that is, they say, all his power is exercised in things heavenly. But, my brethren, that which followeth confuteth it in part, for he saith he is over 'every name that is named, not only in this world, but also in that which is to come;' not only heavenly things, but earthly things; so that not only heavenly things are meant, though they are not to be excluded, but answerable to the phrase of *sitting* is properly intended *heavenly places,* and so notes out the very place where he thus sits, even in heaven. Heaven is the court of the great God, where his throne is, as you saw out of Acts vii. 49; and it is the place where God hath appointed Jesus Christ to be honoured. Only let me say this: when he cometh to judge wicked men, because he will not bring them up to heaven, for none of them shall ever enter into the third heavens, then he cometh down, and bringeth heaven down with him, for all the angels come with him, and he shall come in the clouds with all the glory of his Father, in the greatest glory and majesty that can be. But the proper seat and place of Christ is at God's right hand. 'I see the heavens opened,' saith he, 'and the Son of man standing on the right hand of God.'

Therefore still the Scripture calleth us to look up to Christ as sitting at God's right hand in the heavens. The Lutherans would have him everywhere even as man, which is to maintain that opinion of his bodily presence in the bread you eat in the sacrament, which is a mighty gross absurdity, for so he should be as much in the bread you eat every day as in that of the sacrament; and, accordingly, they further make his ascension into heaven a mere metaphor; they say he did not remove his place locally, whereas the text saith expressly they saw him ascend up into heaven.

That the sitting of Christ at God's right hand is in heaven, and that that is the place appointed for him, I will give you but one scripture for it. I therefore quote it because I will open it a little unto you; it is Acts ii. 34. When he would prove that those words in Ps. xvi., 'At thy right hand are pleasures for evermore,' &c., were not meant of David, what expression doth he use? 'For David,' saith he, 'is not ascended into the heavens: but he saith himself, The Lord said unto my Lord, Sit thou,' &c. My brethren, David was ascended into heaven, for his soul was there. How, then, doth this argument hold? The truth is, he putteth ascension into heaven to be all one with sitting at God's right hand, because that heaven is the place where God hath appointed to manifest his glory and the glory of Christ; and therefore, Mark xvi. 19, it is expressly said he was received up into heaven and sat on the right hand of God. So, in 1 Pet. iii. 22, 'He is gone into heaven, and is on the right hand of God.' I could give you multitudes of places for it.

It is a wild opinion of the Lutherans, that would have heaven also everywhere, as Christ is everywhere. But the Apostle telleth us plainly, 1 Thess. i. 10, that we expect and wait for Christ from heaven. If Christ were everywhere, and heaven were everywhere, how could we expect to 'meet him in the air,' when he shall descend from heaven, as the Apostle saith, 1 Thess. iv. 17, speaking of the air as a distinct place from heaven?

So you have all these five things opened that belong to this part of the 20th verse. First, What is meant by sitting on God's right hand. Secondly, Who it was that raised him; God the Father. Thirdly, The subject that was thus exalted, both considered as God and man. Fourthly, The time when it was begun; it was when he ascended into heaven after his resurrection. Fifthly, The place where; it is in heaven, in heavenly places.

I will now make a little entrance into the 21st verse, so much indeed as shall give a light into it:—

Far above all principality, and power, and might, and dominion, and every name, &c.

Here he expresseth more really what he had said in the other speech more figuratively; there he expresseth the dignity of Christ by sitting on God's right hand, here he speaks more plainly, 'far above all principality,' &c.

There are two general heads of this verse.

Here is, first, *The eminence of Christ's exaltation;* and, secondly, *The universality of it.*

The *eminency* of it is set forth two ways:—

First, For the intention, *the height of it as it is personal in him;* it is not only above, but 'far above all principality, and power, and might, and dominion,' &c.

Secondly, It is expressed by *the lowness of the subjection of all things to him;* he is far above, for 'all things are under his feet.'

Then there is the *universality* of it; he instanceth in the chiefest things that are in this world and in the world to come, in might and dominion, in principalities and powers, and in every name that is named, not only in this world, but also in that which is to come.

First, To open unto you *the eminency of this exaltation of Christ.* He is said to be far above, not only above, but far above, not ἄνω only, but ὑπεράνω, far above; so far that the Apostle knew not how to express it, but, as we use to say, infinitely above. So now that which in Acts ii. 33 is called simply the exaltation of Christ, in Phil. ii. 9 is called superexaltation, so the word is in the original; not only an exalting, but an exalting to the highest, an infinite exalting; and therefore, Heb. vii. 26, we are said to have such a high priest as is 'made higher than the heavens.'

I told you before, that sitting at God's right hand noted out, first, *fulness of pleasure;* secondly, *glory;* thirdly, *power and dominion.* Now, you shall see that in all these Jesus Christ is advanced far above all creatures, and enjoyeth them all in that transcendent manner as no creature doth, either angels or men.

First, *Jesus Christ hath such pleasure as no creature hath.* For that, take Ps. xlv., where he speaks of Christ as exalted at God's right hand, and speaking of his throne, saith he, ver. 6, 'Thy throne, O God, is for ever and ever; the sceptre of thy kingdom is a right sceptre.' He speaks of him as installed into his kingdom. What followeth? 'Because thou lovest righteousness and hatest wickedness, therefore God hath anointed thee with the oil of gladness above thy fellows.' Here is, you see, an anointing with joy and gladness above his fellows; in this regard, therefore, he is above all principality and power, and all things else. Why? Because he is nearer the fountain than all creatures are, for he is one Person with the Son of God; and the communication of God, and all the fulness of the Godhead, to him must needs be so much the greater by how much the union is nearer. As he had the nearest union that any creature could have to be one Person with the Godhead, so he hath the joys of God, which none else can have. While he was upon the earth he was a man of sorrows, such as no man had; so now when he cometh to heaven, as his sorrows abounded, so his joys also abound. As he was the first of many brethren in respect of affliction, so he is anointed with the oil of gladness above his fellows: for he hath not only the joys of God to be his, but the joys of all his children; they are also his, therefore he bids them be holy, that my joy may be full, saith he; I rejoice in it, saith he—I rejoice in it, saith he, more than you; for, as the Apostle saith, 'you are my crown and my joy;' so Christ hath joy in all.

Secondly, Take rule and dominion, that is most proper to the text indeed; *he hath a rule and dominion far above all things.* Rev. iii. 21, 'Ye shall sit with me in my throne, even as I also am set down with my Father in his throne.' What is the meaning of that scripture? This in a word: As I am glorified, so shall ye be glorified, and I have communicated to you a kind of rule, a kind of suffrage at the day of judgment; but this is peculiar to the Son, to the Lord Jesus Christ, to sit in the Father's throne.

So likewise for *glory;* which is the third thing meant by sitting at God's right hand. He hath such glory in heaven, that could a man see him sitting in heaven, and all the angels about him, he would say, That is the Son of God, presently. Set a king among his nobles, and you could not know one from another, if he would conceal his outward state; but set the Person of Christ amongst angels, you would presently say, That is the Son of God. 'We saw his glory,' say they, 'as the glory of the only-begotten Son of God,' when they had but a glimpse of it in his transfiguration. There is such a glory shineth in the person of Jesus Christ as he is far above all angels and men, he is the Sun of righteousness; therefore he is said to be the 'image of the invisible God,' so as no men or angels are; and 'the brightness of his Father's glory,' which they are not; it is spoken of him as he is man; for otherwise as he is God, he is as invisible as God himself. Therefore as the actions of the Son of God are higher than the actions of men,—for you see they are of infinite worth, which men's good works and angels' are not,—so the glory of God-man, the Son of God, is more than all the glory of angels or the glory of all the sons of men whatsoever; it is of another kind.

Hence it cometh to pass that our Saviour Christ is to be worshipped, for you see he hath that glory that no creature hath; take him as he is man sitting at God's right hand, he is to be worshipped, which no creature is. Saith he, Heb. i. 6, 'When he bringeth his Son into the world he saith, Let all the angels of God worship him.' It is spoken of his second coming, as I could open at large. And Ps. xlv. 11, there the Church is said to stand at Christ's right hand, and one would think she were mightily exalted; what followeth? Ver. 12, 'Daughter,' saith God, 'he is thy Lord, and worship thou him.' You shall find that this is part of Christ's exaltation in Phil. ii. 10, that all worship that is to be performed unto God should be done in his name. 'Wherefore,' saith he, 'hath God highly exalted him, and given him a name above every name, that in'—it is not *at* the name, but *in*—'the name of Jesus every knee should bow;' that is, that all worship should be put up to him in the name of Christ. This is that prerogative which no creature hath or was fit to have; this glory God would give to none but to the man Christ exalted in heaven; yea, let me add this, that this began to be done when he did ascend up into heaven.

I have wondered sometimes at that speech, John xvi. 24: 'Hitherto ye have asked nothing in my name.' When he taught them the Lord's Prayer, one would have thought they should have been taught to make their prayers in the name of Jesus Christ, as we are taught to do by the Apostle; but he was not then ascended; this 'at his name every knee shall bow,' he must suffer for it first, and then enter into this glory. Therefore, Rom. viii. 34, you have his sitting at God's right hand and his interceding for us joined together.

This is the reason why Jesus Christ is so jealous that he will not use the mediation of saints in heaven as the Papists do, which is flat idolatry. Why? Because he is in heaven the only Mediator. Here on earth you must indeed speak to men to pray for you, but if you speak to any in heaven to pray for you, Christ is jealous of it; for it is part of his glory to sit on God's right hand and to be the only Mediator, and that not only in his name should prayers be put up, but that none else should be employed to put up prayers besides. Therefore the worshipping of saints is flat idolatry, because Jesus Christ is in heaven, and it is his only prerogative to intercede for us, it is a part of his right and glory.

These prerogatives are far above what ever any creature hath: and so now I have done with the intention of his exaltation; 'he is exalted far above all principality,' &c.

SERMON XXXII.

Far above all principality, and power, and might, and dominion, and every name that is named, not only in this world, but also in that which is to come: and hath put all things under his feet.—VER. 21, 22.

THE scope of the Apostle in these words is, by way of amplification, to set forth unto us the glorious exaltation of our Lord and Head Jesus Christ. He had described his exaltation in the words before under this metaphor, 'he set him at his own right hand in the heavenly places.' Here he goeth on to amplify and set him forth, as before, under a similitude of sitting at God's right hand, comparing God to a great king, and Christ to his eldest son that sitteth in his throne, invested with that power which God himself should execute. But here now in these words he setteth him forth to us by these three things:—

In the *first* place, by instancing in the greatest powers, in the most excellent things that are; he instanceth in the best, to shew that he is set over all: 'He is exalted,' saith he, 'far above all principality and power, might and dominion.'

In the *second* place, lest he should not have mentioned all, he addeth, 'and every name that is named.'

Thirdly, to shew that it is, as over all, so everywhere, he mentioneth both worlds: 'not only in this world,' saith he, 'but also in that which is to come.'

Fourthly, he addeth the lowness of the subjection that all principality and power, &c., hath to him, in the 22d verse; 'and hath put,' saith he, 'all things under his feet.'

Now then, to begin *first* with this, to shew you the exaltation of Christ in respect of all persons, degrees of persons whatsoever; 'he is exalted far above.' I opened that 'far above' in my last discourse, and I will not now repeat anything. The persons here are 'principalities and powers, might and dominion.'

He goeth on here indeed to follow the similitude he had begun. He had compared God to a great king, heaven to his court where he hath his throne, Jesus Christ to his eldest son that did use to sit in the throne, and no subject else; and yet these kings had nobles, they had rulers of great place and authority under them in all their dominions. He presenteth here Christ sitting upon the throne of God the Father as his eldest Son, so he mentioneth all sorts of under-rulers, of nobles that belong to any of his dominions 'principalities and powers, might and dominion.' He instanceth in these as being the most excellent; and if he be over these, and far above these, and hath these under his feet, then how high must this exaltation of Christ be?

The glory of a king, you know, lieth not only in having subjects, but in having subjects of subordinate ranks. There are the common people; and there are the *noblesse*, as they call them, the gentry; and then there are the nobles over them; and so by this subordination of powers doth the glory of a king appear. As you see it is in this kingdom, and so especially in those eastern monarchies, the language of which the Scripture speaks in, which remain to this day more absolute than our European princes are; as in Persia, you read in Esther i. 14, of seven that were counsellors of Media and Persia, and then you read of nobles and rulers over all the one hundred and twenty-seven provinces, that were under them. And to this day, the Great Turk hath his bashaws, whereof every one is as great as European kings are, and under them they have their governors likewise, and it is a tyranny, a superiority downward; and by all these—when they appear before the Great Turk, they fall down upon their faces and lie at his feet—doth appear the greatness of that monarch. So it is here; here is God's eldest Son having all principalities and powers in any world you can imagine lie at his feet.

Now then, to open unto you, first, what is meant by these expressions, *principalities, powers, might, and dominion.* It is as if you should speak according to the language of England, there are deputies, as you know there is the Deputy of Ireland, and dukes, and marquises, and earls, &c. Or in Turkey there are viziers, bashaws, and beglerbegs, these are the titles of their nobles. So is it here, here is principality, and power, and might, and dominion.

A parallel place with this is that in Col. i. 16; the order indeed is inverted, for that the Apostle stands not upon. 'By him,' saith he, 'all things were created, that are in heaven, and that are in earth, visible and invisible, whether they be thrones, or dominions, or principalities, or powers.' Here in the text, he leaveth out *thrones*, but instead of it putteth in *might*, there is all the difference; and he meaneth authorities of governments, both visible and invisible, in this world and the world to come.

It is hard to distinguish the subordination of these; only we are certain of this, that by ἀρχῆς, which we translate here *principality*, supreme magistrates are meant; that by ἐξουσίας, powers, ordinary powers, inferior magistrates are meant. By 'might,' may be meant any power that hath force in it, as your tyrannical power hath. And by 'dominion,' those lower kinds of lordship that masters have over families, parents have over children. So as he doth instance both in the highest and in the lowest. His scope is to take all governments in, that is certain. Therefore in 1 Cor. xv. 24, he speaks there how that Jesus Christ will put all governments down, and he mentioneth three of those that are here in the text. 'He shall deliver up the kingdom to his Father, when he shall have put down all rule'—the word is ἀρχῆς, that which we translate *principality*—'and all authority'—the word is the same which we translate *power* here in the text—'and power,' the word is the same that is translated *might* in the text.

Now, it is enough to us that the Apostle doth here intend these two things:—

First, A subordination of powers, of higher powers and lower powers.

Secondly, That he doth intend all sorts of power, all rule, power, and authority whatsoever, and that in either world.

Now, to open what should be meant by these powers here that are thus subordinate one to another which the Apostle here intendeth—

We find these names, principalities and powers, might and dominion, given to three sorts of rulers—

To good angels.

To bad angels.

To men that are magistrates in this world.

Then the question will be, Which of all these should be meant here?

I will shew you, first, that these titles and terms here used are given to all these three sorts.

They are first applied to men, to magistrates: Tit. iii. 1, he biddeth them 'be subject to principalities and powers, to obey magistrates.' And in the 8th verse of the Epistle of Jude you have κυριότητα, which is another word here used; you have that mentioned there too, dominion. So that these are applied to magistrates upon earth.—That is the first.

Then we have them applied to good angels; they are called principalities and powers too. Besides that place in Col. i. 16, which I mentioned even now, 'all things visible and invisible, whether they be thrones, or dominions, or principalities, or powers,'—there are invisible thrones, and dominions, and principalities, and powers,—besides that place, take that in Eph. iii. 10, 'To the intent that now unto the principalities and powers in heavenly places might be made known by the church the manifold wisdom of God.' He sheweth the scope of the preaching of the gospel; it was that the angels who are employed about the affairs of this world,—which he calleth therefore principalities and powers,—they coming to the sermons preached in the church, as they do, having occasion to come down into the world, that to them 'might be made known by the church the manifold wisdom of God.'

Then, thirdly, you find these are put for bad angels, for devils; for that take Eph. vi. 12, 'We wrestle not against flesh and blood,'—that is, with mankind only, we do not only wrestle with kings and emperors, and the great men of the world,—'but against principalities and powers, against the rulers of the darkness of this world.' And if you will have a clear place for it, it is Col. ii. 15, where it is said, that Christ 'spoiled principalities and powers, and made a show of them openly, triumphing over them in it.'

Here now is the question, Which of all these three should be here meant, whether the rulers of this world, or whether bad angels, or good angels, or all of them?

In a word, my brethren, that which I shall tell you is this, that the Apostle meaneth here all these. I will give you my reasons why: for he speaks of the advancement of Christ, not only above one sort of principality and power, but 'above all principality and power, might and dominion;' not only in one world, but he 'hath set him,' saith he, 'in heavenly places, far above all principalities and powers,' therefore above good angels that are principalities and powers in heavenly places. And because he would be sure to include all, saith he, 'every name that is named;' because he would take in all worlds, saith he, 'in this world and in that which is to come;' and as in his Epistle to the Colossians he expresseth it, 'visible and invisible, in heaven and in earth.'

I will give you but one parallel place for it, where you shall find that Christ is said to sit at God's right hand, above angels and all principalities and powers whatsoever. It is 1 Peter iii. 22: 'He is gone into heaven,' saith he, 'and is on the right hand of God,'—it is the same that the text saith,—'angels and authorities and powers being made subject unto him.' Here, you see, all sorts are taken in, angels and men on earth. That which the text saith, 'all principalities, and powers, and every name that is named in this world, and in the world to come;' Peter saith, 'angels and authorities and powers,' be they what they will be. So that now all is meant.

Only, my brethren, for explication sake I will say but these two things, whereof the first is this: That the Apostle's scope is not to reckon up all the orders and ranks of powers on earth, or powers in heaven, or amongst the devils, for what they are we know not; he doth not instance in all the particulars, therefore he bringeth in this general, 'every name that is named.' It doth not follow that there are no more, and but so many; neither indeed is it much how we distinguish them; it is enough that there are subordination of powers in all these worlds, and that all these subordinations are subject unto him.

The second thing that I would add is this: That the governments of this world, which are called, you know, principalities and powers, they are used as expressions to signify out unto us the governments in the other worlds, or, if you will, invisible governments; that is the better expression of the two: that though there be a subordination of angels amongst themselves, yet he doth express it by the same names that the governments here below are expressed, of principalities and powers, and might and dominion; for this world is a scheme of the other world, and the government of this visible world is a shadow of the government of the invisible world.

I will add a third thing, and that is this: That if the Apostle speaks here of angels,—as certainly he doth, both good and bad,—his scope is not to shew by these several titles several actions of angels, but several ranks of angels distinct, though expressed to us under what is here in this world. That is clear from Col. i. 16; 'Things visible or invisible, whether,' saith he, 'they be thrones, or dominions, or principalities, or powers.' That same word εἴτε, *whether*, implieth that they are distinct. It is not the same angel is sometimes a 'throne,' and sometimes a 'dominion,' used in several works; but as amongst men there are several offices, so likewise amongst them.

So much now, in the general, for the explication of this, 'principality and power, might and dominion.'

Now then, of the governors of this world there is no question; but all the question is of the invisible governments,—the angels, good and bad, which here Jesus Christ is said to have under his feet,—that are called principalities and powers. I will handle them both together, and manifest unto you that there is a subordination—what, we know not—of angels, of invisible governments, both good and bad, in respect of which they are, as the Scripture calleth them, principalities and powers, both the one and the other. I shall shew you the subordination or the superiority that there is both amongst themselves, and also over this world in ordering the affairs thereof. There is a subordination both of good and bad angels amongst themselves, and there is likewise a subordination in respect of ordering the affairs of this world; and over all these is Jesus Christ so far above, as that they are all under his feet.

First, for the angels among themselves. It is a clear case of the bad angels; for of the devils it is said, Matt. xii. 24, that there is Beelzebub, the prince of the devils: and in the same place,—for it was an objection made against Christ, that he cast out devils by the power of the prince of the devils, —our Saviour Christ answereth at the 25th verse, 'Every kingdom divided against itself cannot stand: if Satan cast out Satan, he is divided against himself; how shall then his kingdom stand?' He compareth them to a kingdom; and he compareth them to a kingdom for this, that as in a kingdom there is a power superior and subordinate, so there is amongst them.

In Eph. ii. 2, the Apostle speaks of the 'prince of the power of the air.' By *power* there he certainly meaneth the devils, who are called principality and power, the same name, ἐξουσίας; and by ἄρχοντα, their prince, he certainly meaneth the great devil, that great serpent that tempted Adam: he calleth all the rest in the singular number, because they all agree together in one for mischief, they are as one army, and as one kingdom, whereof he is the general, he is ἄρχων. Therefore our Saviour Christ calleth him, 'the prince of this world.' And, if you mark it, our Saviour Christ doth not deny, in that place I quoted before, but that the great devil could have commanded the lesser devils out; only he saith this, he confuteth them another way: saith he, It is impossible he should be so foolish to do so; for then he must divide his kingdom against himself. There lieth our Saviour's reason: he denieth not but that the great devil could have commanded the lesser; for he is the prince of devils, he is the prince of the power of the air; that is, of all the whole army of devils that are in the air, who are but one power, one force, as you call it.

I might urge this likewise from that in Eph. vi. 12, where they are called, as principalities and powers, so they are called the rulers of this world. As rulers of the world,—they are rulers in that respect,—so principalities and powers amongst themselves; ἀρχὰς and ἐξουσίας, they are both principalities and powers—some are chief, and some are inferior; for by ἐξουσία, or *potestas*, is meant inferior magistrates, unless the word 'higher' be added for distinction's sake; as Rom. xiii. 1, 'Let every soul be subject to the higher powers.'

So much now for the devils, that there is a subordination amongst them, there are principalities and powers among them, and there is one chief, ἄρχων, that is, the 'prince of devils'—the 'prince of this world,' as our Saviour calleth him, and the 'prince of the power of the air.'

Then come to the good angels, and you shall find the like. In Dan. x. 13, there cometh an angel to Daniel, and, as I shall shew you anon, he was a created angel; but, however, that is not to the purpose whether he was or no. He cometh to Daniel, and speaks of another angel besides himself. He saith, there was an angel that touched him, and bade him not fear, and excuseth why he had not come to him sooner, though his prayers were heard many days before; so you read, ver. 12. Saith he, ver. 13, 'The prince of the kingdom of Persia withstood me one-and-twenty days; but, lo,' saith he, 'Michael, one of the chief princes, came to help me; and I remained there with the kings of Persia.'

To open these words unto you:—

Here are two angels spoken of, whereof one mentioneth the other. There is one appeareth to Daniel, and telleth him a story of Michael, another angel; and, if you mark it, he saith this Michael is the *first* of the chief princes. Certainly he is compared with those of his own rank; he is not compared with the chief princes of this world, with men; it is certainly in respect of angels; if so, then there are chief princes amongst them. And in Dan. xii. 1, 'Then shall Michael stand up, the great prince, &c., who is the first of the chief princes;' and they are called chief princes, too, in respect of others of their own rank—namely, angels—who are not of the chief magistracy, as those princes are said to be; for you must make all comparisons in respect of the same kind. This word here, *the first*, or *one*, doth not always imply one that is above the rest in authority, but it is used of the first in number; as in all bodies where there is an aristocracy, where you have many that are chief magistrates, there is one that is first in rank, first in number, as Peter was amongst the apostles; and as it is in Gen. i. 5, that which we translate the *first day* is *one day*,—so the word signifieth, that is, the first number, for we say *one* in reckoning, two, three, &c. So this great angel here was the first of the rank of the chief magistracy of heaven.

I will not determine, as some have undertaken to do,—not Papists only, but Protestants, and that of late,—that there are seven of these chief princes, angels. There is an old tradition amongst the Rabbins,—it is older than Christ, and it is in the Book of Tobit,—where the angel is brought in speaking to Tobias: 'I am Raphael,' saith he, 'one of the seven angels that stand ministering before the Holy One.' I will not, I say, insist upon that, for I know indeed no full ground for it in the Book of God, though there are many pretty allusions to make it good; as the 'seven spirits that stand before the throne of God,' mentioned both in Zechariah and in the Revelation, which, say they, are these seven chief angels.

I will not stand confuting of this, only there is one argument against it which I never yet saw answered. That in the Revelation cannot be meant of the seven angels; for in the first chapter, he wisheth 'grace and peace from God, and from the seven spirits that are before his throne, and from Jesus Christ,' &c. He would never have wished grace and peace from archangels, and left the Holy Ghost out, and so rank them with the Father and the Son. We find, evidently, that this Michael, that is here in Daniel called the 'first of the princes,' in the 9th verse of the Epistle of Jude is called an 'archangel;' as Christ, you know, is called the great shepherd and bishop of our souls; or as you say here an 'archbishop,' so he is called here an archangel.

And it is certain the angel there mentioned in Jude was not Christ. Why? Because it is said, that when he disputed with the devil about the body of Moses, he durst not bring a railing accusation; mark that word, *he durst not.* Our Saviour Christ was not incarnate when Moses died; how can it be said of the Son of God that *he durst not?* It must be spoken of the second Person if that interpretation hold, for he was not then incarnate; therefore it is certain he was a created angel that is called there an archangel. And in 1 Thess. iv. 16, you shall find mention made of the voice of the archangel, not the voice of an archangel; but 'the Lord shall descend with the voice of the archangel;' so that he is distinguished from Christ, so as it is not Christ.

Now the notion I drive it to is this: Here is a subordination, you see; here are your chief princes, which for my part I think are archangels, whereof this Michael is one, the first in order, as Peter was the first of the apostles, though they were equal. For I find this in Col. i. 16, where he reckoneth your invisible magistracy, he doth not reckon any one in heaven as supreme and alone above all the rest; but he reckoneth thrones and dominions. What is meant by *thrones?* Those that have kingly power, superior power; for by thrones is always meant the power of kings. Now he doth not say, there is one throne, one angel in heaven above all the rest in authority, as a king is over his subjects; but he makes an aristocracy of it, he saith they are thrones, like so many kings; for the seven counsellors of the kings of Persia are called kings in Dan. x. 13. 'I remained there,' saith he, 'with the kings of Persia;' which were the seven counsellors mentioned in Esther i. 14. Therefore the king of Persia is called a king of kings.

So now, there are thrones indeed in heaven amongst the angels; there are those that are the chief princes, that are as kings in comparison of the rest, whereof this Michael is the first; but there is not in heaven one angel above all the rest, I know no ground for that.

And I have this further reason to second it, the difference between heaven and hell. For in hell there is a kingdom set up against Christ, and that is resolved into a monarchy; but in heaven, though some, I know not how many, are thrones, yet they are all under one king, who is the King of kings, the Lord Jesus Christ; he is the King of angels, the Head of all principalities and powers; and there is not one created angel over all the rest. They are called *thrones*, I say, not *a throne*, when he speaks of invisible governments, Col. i. 17.

Only there is that objected in Rev. xii. 7, where it is said that Michael and his angels fought against the dragon and his angels. And it is certain, though angels are not intended there, yet it is an allusion unto them. It is plain angels are not intended there, for it is said, ver. 11, that those angels 'overcame by the blood of the Lamb,' and that they loved not their lives unto the death. Yet, however, the allusion is to this great angel, that is, the first of the chief princes; and because he is the first, the first in order, the first in number,—that pre-eminence indeed Daniel giveth him,—therefore the rest are called his angels; but yet he is not their prince by way of authority, as the great Beelzebub is amongst the devils.

You shall find this, to confirm this notion, that the angels are in their several charges, a multitude of them, subordinate to some one; and that those have the government of the rest, it should seem by that in Daniel, where there is mention made of many that are chief princes.

I will give you a scripture or two. You shall find in Luke ii. that to the shepherds in the field an angel is said to appear, one angel is still mentioned for a long while. 'And, lo, the angel of the Lord came upon them,' so ver. 9. 'And the angel said, Fear not,' so ver. 10. But at ver. 13, 'And suddenly there was with the angel a multitude of the heavenly host.' He doth not say all the heavenly host; this was not the chief angel of all the rest of the angels that brought them all down; it was but a multitude of them. The truth is, here is the host, and their general, their colonel, as you may call him; those angels that were of his company, it goes under his name, he saith it: 'And suddenly there was with him,' that is, there appeared together with him; he appeared first and spake, but they all came down from heaven together. And in Ps. xxxiv. 7—to speak still in the language of soldiers, for they are called the heavenly host, amongst which there is the greatest order—it is said, 'The angel of the Lord encampeth about them that fear him.' Yet you shall find in Ps. xci. 11, 'He shall give his angels charge over thee.' Nay, one man hath more than one angel; these little ones, saith Christ, they have their angels. And, Luke xvi. 22, the angels, not angel only, but the angels did fetch the soul out of Lazarus' body, and carry it to heaven. But why is it said in that Psalm xxxiv. one angel encampeth? His meaning is, the angel and his host; as you say, such a colonel besieged such a city, or quartered in such a town, meaning him and his host: so one angel and his company; for one angel, you know, cannot properly be said to encamp; there must be, to encamp or besiege a place, a multitude; yet it goeth under his name because he is the chief.

So that now, both among good and bad angels you see there are some that are chief: there is the angel and his host, his company; that are centurions, as it were, or, if you will, that are governors of more. So much now for their subordination one to another, for that was the first thing. They are principalities and powers; by principalities is meant your chief magistrates, and by powers is meant your lower magistrates. You see there are chief of the princes amongst angels, that have others under them; therefore, in Zech. ii. 3, 4, you find that one angel appeared and another met him, and the first angel speaks to the other as one speaks to one that is under him: Go, saith he, run and tell the prophet that Jerusalem shall be inhabited. He speaks as the centurion did to his servants; he saith unto one, Go, and he goeth. So much, I say, for this first thing, that both good and bad angels have subordination amongst themselves.—There is 'principalities and powers.'

But, in the second place, they are said to be principalities and powers, as amongst themselves, so in respect of their government of the affairs of this world. My brethren, you do not know all the governors you have; you have not only kings, and parliaments, and men to rule over you, or that do despatch and manage the affairs of this world; but you have good angels and bad angels, you have principalities and powers of both sorts, that do manage the affairs of the world invisibly; 'visible and invisible,' saith he, Col. i. 16.

First, for the bad angels; there is a most express place for it; it is that in Eph. vi. 12, he calleth them, as 'principalities and powers,' so 'rulers of the darkness of this world;' we translate it so, but those that know the original know it is this, κοσμοκράτορας; they make but one word of it, 'rulers of this world,' and the darkness of it. And if the bad angels be thus, the good angels are much more, my brethren.

I will give you but a scripture for it, and it may be it will include both; it is Heb. ii. 5, 'Unto the angels hath he not put in subjection the world to come, whereof we speak.' Mark his expression, he distinguisheth; there is a world indeed, saith he, that is not subject to the angels, 'the world to come;' implying that this world is subject to the angels, to bad angels, as to plunderers, and robbers, and murderers from the beginning, and sowers of all dissension in kingdoms and nations, as you shall see by and by, that set king and people, and all together by the ears.

And there are likewise good angels that this world is subject to; the world to come is not, as I shall shew you anon likewise, and it is subject unto them as the preservers of it, and as the opposers and fighters against these evil angels that would bring all to confusion.

You therefore find that the angels, both good and bad, are called *gods;* it is a title you know given to magistrates: 'I have said ye are gods.' And it is only due to the civil magistrate; it is not due to spiritual rulers, they are nowhere called gods. Why? Because their power is not in a way of command, but their power is in a way of revealing the truth, and so working upon men's consciences; they are therefore nowhere called gods; no, not the apostles themselves, for they have not dominion over the faith. But ye have good angels and bad angels called gods as well as magistrates here below, and they are therefore called so because they are rulers. Of the devil there is an express place, 2 Cor. iv. 4, where the Apostle calleth him 'the god of this world;' it is all one with that in John xii. 31, where he is called 'the prince of this world.' He is by the Apostle in one place called the god of this world, and by Christ in another the prince of this world; and you have as clear a place that the good angels are called gods too, and that in this respect; it is in Ps. xcvii. 7, 'Worship him, all ye gods;' now look in Heb. i. 6, where the Apostle quoteth it, and interpreteth it to be meant of the good angels, 'Let all the angels of God worship him;' they are gods, and gods because they are chief princes, as you heard before.

The Scripture is exceeding express for this. It is true that God ruleth the hearts of his children by his Spirit only in matters spiritual, for he will have none have the credit of being the author so much as of a good thought, take it spiritually, but only his own Spirit. But yet he ruleth the world and the spirits of men so far forth as concerneth civil things; yea, and their actions so far forth as they are *in ordine ad spiritualia,* in order to spiritual things; the hearts of kings, and princes, and people, for the good of his Church, he ruleth them much by angels.

I will open to you but that place of Daniel I quoted even now, Dan. x. both the 13th and the 20th and the 21st verses, and chap. xi. 1, compared all together. In chap. x. 13, there is, as I said before, an angel—and to me it is plain he was a created angel—that cometh and telleth Daniel that the prince of the kingdom of Persia had withstood him twenty-one days; and, ver. 20, 'I will return,' saith he, 'to fight with the prince of Persia;' and, chap. xi. 1, I am that angel, saith he, that in the first year of Darius the Mede did stir him up, and I did confirm and strengthen him when he gave out the edict to let the people of God out of captivity; for it was Darius did it, you read indeed of Cyrus, but Darius was the king, and Cyrus was his general. Now this angel here was certainly a created angel. I will give you these reasons for it:—

First, he doth excuse himself to Daniel why he did not come sooner to bring him the message from God which he brought. I was disturbed, saith he, I had other business,—the prince of the kingdom of Persia withstood me twenty-one days,—so that I could not come sooner, though thou prayedst, and thy words were heard sooner. He was therefore a created angel, for had he been the Son of God he could both have revealed it to Daniel and withstood the prince of Persia too.

And then he was a created angel, because he saith, ver. 13, that Michael came to help him. If he had been the Son of God he might have done it alone.

And then, which is as much as any of the rest, when he left me, saith he, I remained with the kings of Persia. If he had been the Son of God he had been everywhere, he could not have been said to remain there alone, still to transact that business he was employed in. So that to me it is clear he was a created angel.

Now the question is, What is meant by the prince of Persia? for, if you mark it, there are both the prince of the kingdom of Persia and the kings of Persia mentioned distinctly in ver. 13.

There are some—and if it be true, it is all one to my purpose—that say, that this prince of the kingdom of Persia that withstood this angel was Cyrus himself, or Cambyses his son, whom he left in his room to govern the kingdom while he was in Scythia; for though that Cyrus, in the first year after he had taken Babylon, being general of the army, had given liberty to the people of the Jews to come out of captivity, yet you shall find elsewhere that this Cyrus recalled his grant; for we read in Nehemiah that they were forced to cease the work from the days of Cyrus. Now, saith the angel, when the enemies came and suggested to Cyrus to recall his grant, and there was a great consultation about it, a consultation of twenty-one days, I remained, saith he, at the court of Persia, and did all I could to persuade and strengthen the heart of Cyrus; but I was withstood in what I would have accomplished by the hard and obstinate spirit of the prince of the kingdom of Persia, but there came one to help me, and then I prevailed; and, saith he, because the spirit of the prince is slippery, and apt to return to itself again, I am left with him and his counsellors.

Here you see now that this was a created angel that dealt with the hearts of princes; he dealt with the heart of Cyrus in the great affairs of the kingdom of Persia, to move him to deliver the people out of captivity.

You have likewise this same Michael whom I have mentioned so often, that archangel that came to help him; and to shew you that this Michael was a created angel,—I shewed you it before out of the Epistle of Jude,—you shall find in ver. 21 that he is called their prince, and chap. xii. 1, 'At that time shall Michael stand up, the great prince which standeth for the children of thy people;' he was the great angel that did transact the affairs for the Jews. For my part, I know not otherwise how it should be: it is plain he was a created angel; and it is as plain that he is called their prince in a special manner, the prince of this people of the Jews; therefore this other angel that was left with the kings of Persia to transact the affairs there, when he could not prevail with Cyrus, he called in this Michael, one of the chief of the princes, to help and assist him. And read chap. xi. 1, there you shall see this angel saith that he did deal with Darius the Mede, and caused him to grant out that decree for the building of the temple; 'I stood,' saith he, 'to confirm and strengthen him.'

So you see that these good angels, for these were all good businesses, have a great stroke in kingdoms for the good of the Church; yea, they are called their princes,—'Michael your prince,'—as having a special care over that people of the Jews, and by God, for that time at least, designed unto it.

Now, my brethren, for my part I must confess that I rather think this prince of the kingdom of Persia to be an evil angel than to be the king of Persia himself, and my reason is this: because the kings of Persia, both Cyrus and Cambyses, for there were two of them, are afterward mentioned by a distinct word from what is used of the prince of the kingdom of Persia. 'I was left,' saith he, 'with the kings of Persia;' there he speaks of men. Now when he saith 'the prince of the kingdom of Persia,' as distinct from them, I think he meaneth plainly the devil.

And I have this further reason for it, because he saith, 'I will return to fight with the prince of Persia;' not that angels in matters of the Church do oppose by way of fighting, for he saith, chap. x. 13, that the prince of the kingdom of Persia withstood him; he could not suggest that which he would to Cyrus but the devil did oppose him; as now in Rev. xii. it is said that Michael and his angels fought with the dragon and his angels. Though it be an allusion, yet it argueth thus much, that there is opposition between angel and angel. And so when it is said, ver. 20, 'When I am gone forth, the prince of Grecia shall come,' there will another wicked angel come, for they call one another; as Michael helped the other good angel, so the prince of Grecia would help the bad one, for the devil knew well enough that the empire would come to Greece, and that the Jews, if they were kept in captivity, would fall into the hands of the Grecian monarch, and so their captivity should have been continued I know not how long; and so the prince of Grecia, that wicked angel that was deputed at that time for the affairs of Greece, cometh and joineth with the prince of the kingdom of Persia both against this angel, for the prince of Persia withstood the delivery of the people out of captivity.

Now, my brethren, if this interpretation will not hold,—the other place in Eph. vi. shewed that the bad angels do deal and are rulers in this world,—I have at least made this good out of this place, that the good angels deal in the government of the things of this world, and they have a peculiar allotment. Michael is called their prince. The like you have in Rev. xii., where Michael and his angels fought against the dragon and his angels.

Now, I yield you that this is but an allusion, and that the scope is to set out the opposition that is made by wicked men on earth against the godly here; but yet the allusion is to the fight that is between good and bad angels. And I will tell you what the occasion was in Daniel. The occasion was, whether the people of Israel should be delivered out of captivity or no, whether the temple should go on to be built; the devil opposed it, and that angel that appeared to Daniel, and Michael, furthered this, and dealt with the kings of Persia to this purpose.

So in that Rev. xii. there is the like fight,—there beginneth the book prophecy, and it beginneth, as almost all interpreters agree, with the primitive times,—there is the dragon and his angels; it is plainly meant of the devil, for he calleth him 'the old serpent, the accuser of the brethren.' If you read the 3d verse of that chapter, you shall see that this dragon had seven heads and ten horns, by which is always meant the Roman empire. So that it is evident that it was the devil in the Roman empire stirring up that state against the Church. The devil and his angels is said to have ten horns and seven heads, and seven crowns upon his heads; it is the hierarchy of the Roman empire; for while it was heathenish the devil always wrought in it, therefore that empire is called the dragon and his angels.

On the other side, you have the apostles and the faithful men that did endeavour to set up Christ, and you have Michael and his angels assist these men against the devil in the Roman empire; even just as you saw before in that place of Daniel there was angel against angel, so there is here in this of the Revelation.

Read the whole book of the Revelation, this which I now say will be one key to it. You shall find that all that is said to be done is done by angels. Such an angel sounded his trumpet, such an angel poured out his vial, &c. He speaks of things done here below, judgments upon wicked men, and good things for the Church. Why are they said to be done by angels? Because these angels do guide men, act kings and princes to do that they do against Antichrist. And the government of this world of the New Testament is represented to us rather under the notion of angels than of men, because that angels do stir up men to do what they do.

I will give you one instance more. You see now how angels, both good and bad, deal in the Persian and the Roman monarchy. I will give you one instance how they did deal in the Babylonian monarchy, and it is about cutting down Nebuchadnezzar. Angels were to execute that. Read Dan. iv. 17; he saith it was by 'the decree of the watchers.' Who were the watchers? It was not the Persons in the Trinity; they were angels, for it is said, ver. 13, 'the watchman came down from heaven.' Though one angel was the executioner more especially, yet he saith it was by the decree of the watchers; they decreed in heaven, the council of angels did, as being of counsel to the great king, and one watcher came down to execute it. Thus, you see, angels have their hands in the great things of the world, in ruling of kingdoms and the affairs here below.

Let me add but one instance about evil angels: it is in Judges ix. 23, 24. You read in the former chapter how Gideon had delivered Israel, and he had seventy sons; but the men of Shechem set up Abimelech, a bastard son of Gideon's, begotten of a strumpet out of their own town, and put to death seventy of the sons of Gideon, who were lawfully begotten. Now, to avenge this what doth God do? There was a mighty division followed, a great war; who was the cause of it? There were other visible pretences, but the truth is, the stirrer up of all this was an evil spirit: for so it is said, 'God sent an evil spirit between Abimelech and the men of Shechem; and the men of Shechem dealt treacherously with Abimelech: that the cruelty done to the seventy sons of Gideon might come, and their blood be laid upon Abimelech their brother, which slew them, and upon the men of Shechem, which aided him in the killing of his brethren.' Here you see that good angels and bad angels do stir up kings and states, one one way, and the other another way. And they have thus dealt in the great monarchies of the world, and they deal so in Popery too.

I will give you a clear instance for it. It is said, Rev. xiii. 1–3, that the dragon did give his seat to the beast, the same dragon and his angels that is called the old serpent, chap. xii.; he saith plainly that he did give the Pope his power and his seat and great authority, and he ruleth and acts that state to this day; and therefore, in 2 Thess. ii. 10, it is said that that man of sin works with all deceivableness of Satan, and that God giveth him up to the deceivableness of error by the devil.

Thus you see the devil hath wrought in all the monarchies, and doth to this day, and that kingdom or state, or any part of it, that opposeth the Lord Christ, it is the devil that works in it; and good angels and bad angels, where there are wars, have as much to do as men have, and do oppose by suggestions to the spirits of men, and have as great a hand in the affairs of the world as men have. They are the rulers, the invisible rulers of this world; they are the principalities and powers here in the text, which our Lord and Saviour Christ is set over.

So, then, I have made this plain unto you, that there are not only principalities in this world, visible ones, but invisible ones over this world. Now, in a word, to manifest this too, that our Lord and Saviour Jesus Christ is above all these, he is above kings and angels and devils, they all but serve his turn; he is exalted, saith he, far above all principalities and powers, and every name, be it what it will, be it visible or invisible; they were all made by him, and all made for him, and they all serve him. You think kings rule the world; it is certain that good and bad angels rule the world more, and it is certain that Jesus Christ ruleth the world more than all these.

First, That he is above, far above *good angels*, I shall not need to insist much upon it; you have a clear place for it, Heb. i. 6, 'Let all the angels of God worship him.' Now, to give you a scripture out of the Old Testament, that all the angels of God worshipped Christ; in Isa. vi. 1, he saith, I saw God sitting upon his throne, and about it stood the cherubim, and they covered their faces with their wings; covered their faces in token of subjection; as women cover their faces in the church in token of subjection, so did the angels. Now, who was this that appeared then upon the throne that the prophet here speaks of? Read John xii. 41. Christ plainly saith it was himself; 'These things,' saith he, 'said Esaias when he saw his glory,' having reference to that Isa. vi. So then, my brethren, they worship him, which argueth an infinite distance; for though worship be but a created thing, yet my desire is infinite, because I cannot reach to glorify God as I would, and therefore it is proper only to God.

Secondly, You shall find that he useth them as agents at his pleasure. Look in Heb. i. 7. It is said there, he made 'his angels spirits, and his ministers a flame of fire.' This place is quoted out of Ps. civ. 4. He makes his angels, he made them on purpose to be his spirits, or, as the word is in the Hebrew, his winds; that, look as the winds execute the will of God, so do these angels at any time; they are his winds to fly up and down the world. You see Christ here upon earth commanded the winds, and they obeyed him; so he commandeth angels, and they obey him. They are 'his winds, and his ministers a flame of fire.' Look as thunder and lightning obey God, they all do his will; so do these obey Christ, and they have power like to winds and to thunder and lightning. Lightning, you know, is a subtle thing;

it killeth, and a man knoweth not how; so do angels, they have the same force and much more; therefore he compareth them to it. And in the last verse of that Heb. i. they are said to be sent out. By whom? By Christ, of whom he had spoken in all that first chapter.

Then come to *bad angels;* and he is far exalted above these. When he first ascended, he left them in the air, they are under his feet indeed. I will give you but a place or two. Col. ii. 14, it is said he spoiled principalities and powers; he made a show of them openly, and triumphed over them. He spoiled them, ἀπεκδυσάμενος, he took away their weapons; the word alludeth to that, for that was the manner of those that conquered, they took away the weapons of those that they conquered.

He did this when he ascended; for I take it these words have reference to his ascension, and my ground is, because then he led captivity captive, as he saith, Eph. iv. 8. He spoiled devils then, and he made an open show of them. As we are made spectacles unto angels and men and unto God, as the Apostle saith; so before angels and men and before God, Jesus Christ made an open show of them. As they used to do that triumphed over the conquered, they tied them at their chariot-wheels, and so led them openly after them in way of triumph; so did Jesus Christ triumph over devils when he ascended. Yea, my brethren, before-hand. Saith Christ, 'I saw Satan fall down from heaven like lightning,' when the gospel was preached. And this great Bishop of our souls silenced Satan presently: for before, the devil spake in the oracles, in trees, and he spake in temples; as God did in the Holy of Holiest, so he had done all the world over. But when Christ came, all the oracles were mute, the heathens wondered at it. Plutarch writeth a book of it.

And let me tell you this, that all the great design of God, since Christ hath been in heaven, hath been to ruin Satan, to throw him down out of *his* heaven. You heard before that he was in the Roman empire, and he was worshipped there as God. Jesus Christ in three hundred years flung him out thence. The accuser of our brethren is come down to earth. All his idols were flung from thence, he was thrown down from heaven; that is, from being worshipped as God.

Well then, the devil turned Christian, and gives the Pope his power in the West; setteth up the Turk in the East. My brethren, our Lord and Saviour Christ will never leave till he hath thrown him out of these seats too. Therefore you read, Rev. xix. 19, 20, at the end of the great war against both, I saw, saith he, the beast, and the false prophet that wrought miracles before him, with which he deceived men that dwelt upon the earth; and the kings of the earth were taken that stood for them, these were cast into the lake that burned with fire and brimstone. And then what followeth? Chap. xx. 2, there was an angel came from Christ, with authority from him, for Christ needeth not do it himself, it is but giving an angel commission to do it: 'And he laid hold on the dragon, that old serpent, which is the devil, and Satan, and bound him,' saith he, and flung him into hell. This power hath our Lord and Saviour Jesus Christ.

And, my brethren, to shew you in a word that Jesus is above all power, you shall find in 1 Cor. xv. 24, that he will reign till he hath put down all rule, and all principalities and powers, and especially the devil, for he speaks of a power that is an enemy unto him; for it followeth in the next words, 'he must reign till he hath put all enemies under his feet.' All the power and principality the devil hath in the world, and not only he, but what angels have, will be put down, but especially he. Why? Because he is an enemy; for he must reign, saith he, till he hath put all enemies under his feet. And at the day of judgment the devils tremble, and that great devil shall be brought forth that set himself up against the Lord Jesus Christ, and shall be judged, and every poor saint shall tread him under his feet, as it is Rom. xvi. 20: and everything in earth and under the earth, men, and angels, and devils, shall bow their knees before the Lord Jesus Christ; that is, they shall acknowledge him to be the great Saviour, the great King of the World, as it is Phil. ii. 10, and repeated Rom. xiv. 9, and interpreted of the day of judgment, when the angels shall be judged. Therefore fear not, my brethren, our Lord Jesus Christ is above devils, and men, and angels, and all.

So much for opening of these words, 'far above all principality, and power, and might, and dominion.'

In a word to this, *and every name that is named.*

What is the reason the Apostle addeth this?

He addeth it for two reasons—

The first is this: If I have not reckoned all sorts of power, saith he, think of anything else that I have not mentioned; if there be any that I have not named, as assuredly there are, I will comprehend it under one general: 'every name that is named, not only in this world, but also in that which is to come,' whatsoever it be. And by name is meant often in Scripture, *authority;* as in the name of Christ, that is, in the authority of Christ; and as we say, in the king's name, that is, in the king's authority. I will not stand upon it. In earth there were some he had not reckoned, in heaven amongst angels there were some he could not reckon; therefore if there be any name, saith he, it is all subject to Christ. That is the meaning of these words.

And then, again, there is another reason why he addeth this, 'every name that is named,' to 'principalities and powers,' because *name* is a larger word than *powers.* There may be names in this world, persons there may be and excellencies that have not power; and so there may be excellencies in the other world that have not power and authority. Therefore, saith he, be it what it will, be it what excellency it will, be it whatsoever it will, Jesus Christ is exalted far above it, so far that all is under his feet.

Now, by *names,* as I take it, is meant both persons and excellencies or dignities.

First, All persons are meant by this 'every name.' I will give you a scripture or two for it: Acts i. 15, 'The number of the persons'—we translate it so; in the Greek the word is, the number of the names—'were one hundred and twenty.' So that when he saith 'every name,' he meaneth every person. That is the first.

Secondly, It is put for *excellency, dignity, glory,* be it what it will. Gen. vi. 4, the men of the old world are called 'men of name;' so the word is in the Hebrew, and therefore the Grecians call men famous and of renown, 'men of name;' and, chap. xxx. 8, Job calleth base men, 'men without name.'

Now then, the meaning is this, that not only Jesus Christ is advanced above all power and authority, but above all persons, and all excellencies and dignities, or whatsoever thing doth excel; suppose not power only, but wisdom, learning, or whatsoever it be. Let one be famous, have a name for what he will have; any angel in heaven, or any man in this world, or the world to come; all creatures whatsoever, and all excellencies of creatures, Jesus Christ hath a better name than they. So saith the Apostle, Heb. i. 4, 'He hath obtained a more excellent name than the angels,' and he hath this by inheritance, which now he is exalted unto; and therefore, in the same chapter, he speaks of his sitting at the right hand of God. The scope of the chapter is to shew both the excellency of his person, that he hath a better name than all things, and the superiority of his place; he sitteth at the right hand of God. 'And to which,' saith he, 'of all the angels said he at any time, Sit on my right hand, until I make thine enemies thy footstool?'

So now, my brethren, I have opened that. I should come to have shewn likewise what is the meaning of these words, *in this world, and the world that is to come*, but I will omit that now, and make some observations upon what hath been delivered, and so conclude.

The *first* observation that I should have made is this: That there are *two worlds*. But I must reserve that.

But the *second* is this: That there are differing names and excellencies in this world and that which is to come. Men that have great names in this world will be, many of them, without names in the world to come; they will be vile persons, without names, as you heard out of Job. Men that shall be saved, and have great names for saints here, yet they may be the least in the kingdom of God, in the world to come; the first are oftentimes last, and the last are first. What names you shall have in the world to come, let that be the main care of your souls.

Now what have men names for? For famous acts done. Do famous acts which shall have renown, if you will have a name in the world to come. After the day of judgment, though there be no power and principality, yet there are names for ever; therefore, I say, the word 'name' is larger than that of principality and power. Christ will put down all principality and power, both of angels, and men, and of devils, but there will be names remaining still. Paul will have a greater name in heaven for ever than other saints have.

My brethren, seek not after names here, to be great and famous in the Church of God; but desire that, and it is sincerity only doth it, which shall get you a better name in the world to come. What do I care to be judged by man's day, saith the Apostle,—he speaks so slightly of it,—there is God's day. It is not, saith he, how things appear now, and what name I have now; but what it will be in God's day and in Christ's day in the world to come. Who shall sit at Christ's right hand, and who at his left, as it was not Christ's to give, so it is not ours to know. Poor saints that stand in the alley may sit at Christ's right hand, when another, one that yet goeth to heaven, and hath a great repute in this world, not only civil, but in repute otherwise too, may stand at his left in comparison. There will be names, my brethren, different from what is in this world.—That is the second observation.

Thirdly, You see that all principalities and powers are subjected to Jesus Christ. Then fear not devils, fear nothing. It is the use the Apostle makes, Rom. viii. 38: 'I am persuaded,' saith he, 'that neither angels, nor principalities, nor powers, nor things present, nor things to come, shall be able to separate us from the love of God, which is in Christ Jesus our Lord.' It is not as if the good angels would hinder you; but the Apostle, though he knew they would not, yet he makes that supposition, as he doth Gal. i. 8, 'If an angel from heaven,' saith he, 'preach any other gospel.' He might well think a good angel from heaven would never preach any other gospel; but he makes a supposition of it, merely to shew the truth of this gospel. So here, to shew the certainty of the estate of the elect, he makes a supposition. Suppose, saith he, they should, yet fear not. Why? Because Jesus

Christ sitteth at the right hand of God, and hath angels, and principalities, and powers under him; so you have it, 1 Peter iii. 22.

And as good angels shall not, so it is certain likewise that evil angels shall not; good angels will not, and bad angels shall not. Matt. xvi. 18, saith he, 'I will build my church upon this rock,'—that is, this faith and confession that Christ is the Son of God, and a heart and life answerable,—'and the gates of hell shall not prevail against it.' They may assault it, but they shall not prevail. My brethren, this devil whom you fear, and who tempteth you, as Jesus Christ hath him under his feet, so he will have him under your feet too one day; do but stay a while, he shall tread down Satan under your feet shortly, Rom. xvi. 20. You need fear nothing therefore, either in heaven or in earth.

The *fourth* observation is this. I have told you there are two sorts of rulers in this world. There are visible ones, whom you all reverence and adore, as indeed you ought to do, principalities and powers here in this world, the higher powers, superior dignities; but there are greater than these, there are higher than they, as Solomon saith in Ecclesiastes; there are angels, both good and bad, that are greater princes than these. Do but think with yourselves now, how little you know of the story of this world; you know much, it may be, of the plots and policies of the princes of this world; but do you know those conflicts of Satan, those underminings the good angels have against him? Do you know the transactions whereby this world is governed? You do not know them; but the day of judgment will be a gallant day for that, for then you will have the story of all the world broke open; you will not only have the story of all the actions of princes, what they have done in their bed-chambers,—not only the reason of this petty thing, and that petty thing,—but all the agitations between angels good and bad shall be all made known to you.

The bad angels, these wicked spirits that do us all the mischief, have plots beyond the plots of princes; they have methods, as the Apostle calleth them; art beyond the art of princes; and there are transactions between good angels beyond all what the men of the world have. The story of this world, how pleasant would it be to a man; but the story of the world to come, my brethren, will be far more pleasant; you shall not only be ear-witnesses of all, but judges of it. The Apostle saith expressly, 1 Cor. vi. 3, that the meanest saint shall judge the angels; that is, the bad angels shall all be brought before the judgment-seat of Christ,—nay, for ought I know, the good angels shall be brought too, to give an account of what they have done,—for it is spoken of all in general at the day of judgment, that to him 'every knee shall bow, both things in heaven, and things in earth, and things under the earth.' Now then, what a story will the world produce at the latter day, that hath had two such governments run all along in it!

Lastly, you see here, when the Apostle reckoneth up the best things that are, what are they he reckoneth up? Powers and names, when he would reckon up the greatest excellencies; for indeed these are the greatest excellencies, therefore the men of the world contend so much after them, after name, and glory, and honour, and principality, to subdue men; these are the great pursuits of the wisest of the sons of men. It is not so much pleasure of the body; that fools pursue after most; but men of wisdom and parts pursue after power, and name, and principality: these are the best things. According to the account the Holy Ghost himself maketh when he instanceth in things that are great, 'A good name is better than great riches.'

The devils do not live upon pleasures of the body, and riches, and such things as these are; but what they live upon, what they please themselves with, is in having power, in subduing nations, ruling kings, as you saw in Daniel, and to have his name set up; as the devil was worshipped four thousand years in the world before our Saviour Christ came. What a name had he! Power and name, you see, are the greatest things that are; which therefore the best of creatures, good angels and bad angels, pursue after; therefore here they are instanced in. He doth not mention riches, but 'principality, and power, and every name that is named,' &c.

SERMON XXXIII.

Far above all principality, and power, and might, and dominion, and every name that is named, not only in this world, but also in that which is to come: and hath put all things under his feet, &c.—VER. 21, 22.

THESE words do set forth unto us and proclaim the supremacy of our Lord Jesus Christ, the King of kings, over all persons, by what names or titles soever distinguished and dignified, in all God's dominions, belonging either to this world or the world to come.

His kingly dignity is set forth unto us first, for the substance of it, by that usual metaphor of sitting at God's right hand. This in the 20th verse.

In this 21st verse, as likewise in the beginning of the 22d, you have the amplification, or an enlarged explication of it—

First, by the sublimity of the condition he is exalted unto; he saith it is not only *above,* but *far above.* And that—

Secondly, amplified by the quality and dignity of the persons above whom he is thus far advanced; 'principalities and powers,' &c. And because all particulars of power in this world and the world to come could not be mentioned nor rehearsed; therefore, to be sure to take in all, he addeth this general, 'every name that is named.'

Thirdly, it is set forth unto us by the extent of this his advancement, of his dominion and sovereignty both of place and time; this world, and the world that is to come, in all ages and in all God's dominions.

Fourthly, by the lowness of the subjection of all these principalities, and whatsoever else, unto him; 'they are under his feet.'

Lastly, by the universality of all this: it is 'far above all;' 'and hath put all things under his feet.'

So you have the division of these words in the 21st, and in the first part of the 22d verse.

I have despatched, *first,* what is meant by 'sitting at God's right hand.' And—

Secondly, I have gone over two heads of the amplification of this exaltation of Christ:—

First, The sublimity of his condition personally; 'far above.'

Secondly, I have opened to you the quality of these persons whom he is set over; angels, good and bad, and magistrates in this world, whatsoever they be. I shewed you, that by principalities and power, might and dominion, he would include all sorts whatsoever. That all these three were called by these names, I opened; likewise, what was meant by 'every name in this world, and the world to come.'

So now the third thing, and that which remaineth, cometh to be opened, *the extent of his dominion;* 'in this world, and the world to come.'

Upon the first consideration of these words, 'in this world, and the world to come,' I thought to have found no difficulty, but to have slipped them over lightly and generally.

Concerning their coherence there is only this to be said. Some refer it only to the words immediately foregoing, 'every name that is named in this world, and the world to come.' But certainly that is too narrow. I rather therefore, with Beza and others, refer it to the whole that he had said of Christ's exaltation; 'he sitteth at God's right hand, over all principalities and powers, and over every name that is named in this world, and the world to come.'

Now then, the great thing to be opened is this: *What is meant by the world to come; and the difference of these two, this world, and the world to come.*

There are these *three* senses and interpretations of it, and I love to take, especially where there is a comprehensiveness, as here there is of all, all in.

This world, and the world to come, may be taken, first, for *heaven and earth;* this state of the world on earth, and that state of the world in heaven, which are two worlds. So that, as the Apostle, in Col. i. 16, when he would divide all things that are created in heaven and in earth, visible and invisible, mentioneth thrones and dominions, principalities and powers; so answerably here, when he speaks of Christ's exaltation, he saith he is exalted far above all these in this world, and in the world to come; that is, in heaven and in earth. And so it cometh all to one with what Christ himself saith, Matt. xxviii. 18, 'All power is given me in heaven and in earth;' that is, in this world, and the world to come, in all God's dominions.

Only then here is the question, why heaven should be called the *world to come*, whereas it is extant now as well as earth is, which is called, in this interpretation, the *present world?* And Christ has now actual power in heaven as well as in earth. Why is it therefore called the world to come?

To this the answer is: though it be a world now extant, yet to us poor creatures here below it is a world to come. It was a world created at the same time that this lower world was: 'Gen. i. 1, 'In the beginning God created the heavens and the earth.' By 'heavens' he meaneth the angels and the higher world; as by 'earth' all that chaos out of which all this world was made that is under it, sun, moon, stars, and the lower elements.

This is the comfort of the saints,—to scatter some observations by the way,—that this great world is *to come.* The Psalmist, Ps. xvii. 14, calleth wicked men, 'men of this world, whose portion is in this life.' This world is theirs, and let them take it; this is 'your hour,' saith Christ, 'and the power of darkness.' 'If we had hope only in this life,' saith the Apostle, 1 Cor. xv. 19, 'we were of all men the most miserable;' but we have a world to come.

It is a world to come in respect of us; as likewise you have it, Luke xviii. 30; speaking of him that shall deny himself, saith he, 'he shall receive manifold more in this present time, and in the world to come life everlasting.' And so, 1 Tim. iv. 8, he hath the 'promise of this life, and that which is to come;' that is, heaven. Now this is one part of the meaning.

Yet let me say this of it. The Apostle's scope being to speak of Christ's actual reign, and having mentioned that it is in heaven,—for so he saith ver. 20, 'He is set at God's right hand in heavenly places,'—as the special place of it, and that at present; to call heaven the world to come, because *to us* it is to come, Beza himself saith it is somewhat too harsh; therefore he seeks out another interpretation.

Then the *second interpretation* is this: that this phrase should note out the duration of Christ's kingdom, that it is for ever, in all ages to come whatsoever. It is a phrase the Scripture often useth to express eternity; as, Matt.

xii. 32, their sin 'shall not be forgiven, neither in this world, nor in the world to come;' that is, never. As in Rev. xx. 10, there are two *evers* put, one *ever* for this world, and the other *ever* for the world to come. They shall be 'tormented for ever and ever;' for ever in this world, and for ever in the world to come. And that it noteth out eternity, there is that likewise I quoted even now, Luke xviii. 30, 'in the world to come eternal life.' Therefore that place, Isa. ix. 6, which we translate, and rightly, 'Eternal Father,' or 'Father of eternity,' the Septuagint reads, the 'Father of the world to come.'

Christ's kingdom, to back this interpretation also, is said to be 'for ever.' Luke i. 33, saith the angel to Mary, speaking of Christ's kingdom, 'The Lord shall give him the throne of his father David, and he shall reign for ever;' not for one *ever*, but for all *evers*. And that he meaneth eternity, he addeth, 'and of his kingdom there shall be no end;' having indeed relation to that in Isa. ix. 7, where he saith, 'of his government and peace there shall be no end.'

And so I find some that bring that place, Heb. x. 12, 'After he had offered one sacrifice for sins, for ever he sat down on the right hand of the Majesty on high.' They allege that place for his sitting at God's right hand for ever, not only in this world, but in the world to come. Although I think there is never a place of Scripture where I find that he sitteth for ever at God's right hand, in the sense the article of the creed hath it. And 'for ever' there seemeth to refer to 'after he had offered up one offering for sin for ever;' for he saith in the verse before, that their sacrifices could not take away sins, never made an end of them, but they returned again. 'But he,' saith he, 'by one sacrifice took away sins for ever.' So that 'for ever' referreth rather to that than to sitting on God's right hand; and ver. 14 confirmeth it likewise, where he saith, 'He hath perfected for ever them that are sanctified.'

Now, against this interpretation I will give you the objections and the resolutions, for I cannot pass over them.

The objections are these:—

If his meaning were this, that he sitteth on God's right hand, above all principalities and powers for ever, then there is this objection, that there are no principalities and powers for ever that Christ should sit over; for the truth is, when this world endeth, there will be an end of all principalities and powers. You have an express place for it, 1 Cor. xv. 24, 'Then cometh the end, when he shall have delivered up the kingdom to God the Father; when he shall have put down all rule and all authority and power.' How then can it be said, he sitteth on God's right hand over all principalities and powers in this world, and the world to come, taking it in this sense, 'for ever?'

There are but two things to help this objection.

The first is this: that though there be no principalities and powers for ever, but rule ceaseth, as it is certain they do, both of good angels and bad, and magistrates and men; yet there are several names, several dignities and excellencies, as I shewed you the word 'names' implieth, that are in this world, and the world to come. And so in that sense it is true, that he is for ever on God's right hand, above all names that are named in this world, and the world to come.

Then the second thing that answereth this objection is this: the Apostle speaks by way of supposition, as it were; as in that other speech of our Saviour's, 'Their sins shall not be forgiven in this world, nor in the world to come.' It is not as if there were forgiveness of sins in the world to come; but his meaning is, suppose there would be forgiveness then, they should never be forgiven. So, suppose never so many names, or principalities, or powers in this world, or the world to come, he is over them all.

But then there is a second objection, and that is this: that in the same 1 Cor. xv. 24, it is said thus, 'Then cometh the end, when he shall have delivered up the kingdom to God the Father;' and, ver. 25, 'He must reign, till he hath put all his enemies under his feet: and when all things are subdued unto him, then shall the Son also be subject unto him that put all things under him, that God may be all in all;' so saith ver. 28.

Here is now a worse objection against this interpretation of the phrase, 'in this world, and the world to come.' And indeed and in truth I find great interpreters, both upon this place and the other, to confine and determine the phrase of sitting on God's right hand, to end after the day of judgment, when he giveth up his kingdom to his Father. And the reason is this, because it is evident that the Apostle quoteth that which he saith, 1 Cor. xv. 25, 'He must reign, till he hath put all his enemies under his feet,' out of Ps. cx. 1, 'Sit thou on my right hand, till I make thine enemies thy footstool.' They interpret that *reigning*, which he must then give up to his Father, by that *sitting* mentioned there.

There is this will help that likewise :—

That the word 'until' doth not note out that then he shall not reign; for the word is not always interpreted exclusively to exclude the time after, but inclusively to include all the time before, whereof there might be a doubt, whether he reigned or no till then, because he had so many enemies. After the day of judgment he shall have none; but there might be this doubt, whether he reigned yea or no till then, because his enemies were so many and so strong. So we find the word used, 2 Sam. vi. 23, where it is said, 'Michal had no child until the day of her death;' it is not as if she had any afterward. It is taken therefore for an undetermined time.

But yet there is this still will take away that: that it is plainly said, he doth *give up the kingdom to God*, and likewise that then *Christ shall be subject unto him.*

Thus perplexed, you see, is the opening of these words, and there must be some pains to resolve this doubt.

The best reconciliation which I shall give you, shall be in these few distinctions, which, I suppose, will clear to you in what sense Christ hath a kingdom, and indeed sitteth on God's right hand for ever, and in what sense he giveth up the kingdom to the Father.

The *first distinction* I give you is this: there is a *natural kingdom* due to Jesus Christ as he is God, yea, and by natural inheritance is due to him being man, as joined to the Godhead; for he inheriteth the privileges of the second Person.

Of this natural kingdom, founded upon his being the Son of God,—which the Apostle, to the Hebrews, chap. i. 4, saith 'he hath obtained by inheritance,'—he saith, ver. 8, 'But unto the Son he saith, Thy throne, O God, is for ever and ever.' And though the right of it is devolved merely because he is God, yet it is by inheritance; being the natural Son of God it is his natural inheritance, therefore he is, as it were, in joint commission for ever with God, as he is God and man. This natural dominion therefore over all things,—for all things were made by him and for him, be they what they will, whether principalities or powers, or whatever else,—this right remaineth for ever, that is certain. And accordingly many of those privileges, which I interpreted to be understood by his sitting on God's right hand, must likewise remain. As, first, fulness of joy; 'At thy right hand is fulness of joy for ever:' so he is at God's right hand for ever; for he doth enjoy—the manhood doth—a fulness of joy immediately in God himself, and this for ever. And, secondly, all that personal honour and glory, and glorious authority which he was filled with, which he was crowned with indeed when he came first to heaven; all these remain to eternity likewise, and they are a natural due to him, though bestowed actually then when he came up to heaven. And he is thus in commission with his Father likewise, so far as natural rule goeth, as a natural inheritance to him; though less than his Father as he is God-man.

But now, secondly, there is a *dispensatory kingdom*, as divines use to call it, as he is considered as Mediator between God and his Church; which kingdom is not his natural due, but it was given him, and given him by choice; yea, as he was second Person and Son of God, that that person was chosen out to execute the office of Mediator. And this kingdom is more properly and strictly noted out by sitting at God's right hand in the Scripture: and God gave it him as a reward of his obedience; he hath it by commission. John v. 22, 23, 'The Father himself judgeth no man, but he hath committed all judgment unto the Son;' he is God's *Dominus facere totum*, as I may so express it; he is that Lord whom God hath set up to do all his business for him visibly and apparently to the day of judgment. And this kingdom is in a more especial manner appropriated to Jesus Christ. It is so his as it is not the Father's in a more eminent manner.

In this will that common axiom of divines help us, that what works all three Persons do towards us *ad extra*, though they have all a joint hand in them, yet they are attributed more especially to one Person than to another: as sanctification, you know, is attributed more specially to the Holy Ghost, redemption to the Son, creation to God the Father, though all three Persons have a hand in it. So likewise is it here; though the Father ruleth till the day of judgment, and the Holy Ghost with him, yet it is in a more especial manner appropriated unto the Son.

Yea, let me add this, that seeing to appropriate thus a work more especially to one person than to another is an act of God's will, hence it is that one person may have it for a time appropriated unto him, and afterward given up unto another person more properly. So now until the day of judgment Christ hath the kingdom committed to him; after the day of judgment it is appropriated more eminently unto God the Father, yet so as that God the Father ruleth now; so on the other side, though the Father is all in all after the day of judgment, yet the Son is said still to judge.

Now, the reason, to touch it in a word, why God the Father did thus appropriate a time for the reign of Jesus Christ more especially, and that all men's thoughts should be drawn unto him, and the Father should, as it were, withdraw himself, was this, that all men should honour the Son as they honour the Father; so you have it, John v. 22; that as for every work there is a season, so there should be for every person a season wherein they shall be in a more especial manner more glorious.

And there is this second reason for it likewise,—it was a reward indeed that was exceeding due unto Jesus Christ,—that he should have the kingdom appropriated unto him for a season, that he should draw all men's eyes to him, and have all the glory and honour as it were in a more immediate manner, because he veiled his Godhead in obedience to his Father; therefore his Father now, when he cometh to heaven, doth answerably, to recompence him, withdraw himself, and appeareth not so much in government, but hath committed all judgment unto the Son. Let my Son have it, saith he. And then, that you may see the equity of this, founded upon that place of Scripture, 1 Cor. xv. 28, because the Father hath committed all judgment unto the Son for so long a season, until he hath made all his enemies his footstool, therefore again doth Jesus Christ, to honour his Father, give up the kingdom to him, and he himself becometh subject to him that hath put all things under him.

My brethren, though Jesus Christ hath this kingdom committed to him for this reason,—he went into a far country to receive a kingdom,—yet when he is in the height of his kingdom, and hath all his enemies down under him, he will not carry it like a conqueror home, as if he had gotten it by his own sword and by his own bow only; but even then, when he is in the height of all, he giveth it up unto his Father before men and angels. It will be the last thing he will do at the latter day before he goeth to heaven, when he hath cleared all the world's accounts; for they shall all be judged by the man Christ, and it is a greater service than all his sermons he made on earth; then, when he hath done and is in his full triumph,—which should teach us when we are highest and most raised then to fall down,—when he hath all his enemies under him, to death, to the meanest and lowest subjection, every one subdued, when he hath judged all the world, and pronounced the sentence both upon just and unjust, and every knee hath bowed to him; then he subjecteth himself unto his Father, and delivereth up the kingdom to him, and God becometh all in all; and this is the last and great solemnity of all.

This is the first distinction. His natural kingdom remaineth for ever, which is a due to him even as he is man joined to the Godhead; but you see there is something of a mediator-like kingdom which he doth give over.

The *second distinction* is this, to clear it yet further: this Mediator's kingdom, as I may so call it, *regnum œconomicum,* receiveth a double consideration. First, consider him as he is Mediator of his Church *considered under imperfection,* either of sin or misery, or any other want, till his Church shall be complete. Or, secondly, consider him as he is a Head of his Church made complete and *fully perfected* in all parts and in all degrees.

Or, that I may explain my meaning to you, I remember when I opened the 3d and 4th verses compared with the 7th of this chapter, I told you that I thought in election there were two great designs involved. The one, that which was more principal and primitive, which was the choosing of us in Christ as a Head to that absolute glory which with and in Christ we shall have in the highest heavens for ever after the day of judgment. But then, secondly, to illustrate and set off this glory the more, God letteth us fall into sin, into misery; body and soul are parted, the one liveth in heaven in a blessed condition, the other lies in the grave; Jesus Christ hath not all his saints, he hath them but by degrees. Now, then, answerably hath Jesus Christ a double relation to his Church; the one as a Head *simply considered*; for we are chosen in him as a Head and Common Person to that condition which for ever we shall have in heaven; and he hath the relation of a Redeemer and Mediator for us *as we are sinners,* and under misery, and under distress, and under imperfection.

Now, my brethren, while the Church remaineth thus imperfect;—Christ hath not all his members up to him, nor are they out of all danger, as I may so express it; for though at the day of judgment to the saints there is no real danger, yet they are to give account of their actions, and there remaineth a final sentence to be pronounced upon them by the great Judge, and in that sense there is a forgiveness of sins then; therefore Paul prayeth that he may find mercy at that day;—now, I say, while there is any such thing as guilt, or the appearance of it, or any imperfection, as till that final sentence there is, so long is Jesus Christ a Mediator for us to God, as under some misery, some want, some danger. He standeth between God and us, and God hath given him all power in heaven and in earth, that he may give eternal life to them that believe,—we could not be trusted more safely than with him that is our Saviour,—that he shall be able to free us. And so long Jesus Christ ruleth in a way of conquest, destroying sin and death and all enemies, and redeeming the body, and bringing body and soul together, and lastly pronouncing a final sentence; and in this sense it is that the Scripture usually speaks of his sitting at God's right hand to intercede for us,—as it is, Rom. viii. 34, and by sitting there he meaneth reigning,—to destroy enemies, to put us out of danger of death and condemnation. But when once this final sentence is passed, then this work of a Mediator, his reigning thus as a Redeemer of us considered under sin and misery, ceaseth,—for when once that final sentence is passed then all sins are for ever and ever forgiven, never to be remembered more; God then looks upon us as in his first project, without spot or wrinkle for ever,—then Christ presenteth us to his Father. 'Lo, here I am, and the children thou hast given me; here they are just as thou didst look upon them in thy primitive choice.' And so now considered, I say his kingdom ceaseth, for there will be no need of it; and this indeed is an answer which learned Cameron delivereth upon that place, 1 Cor. xv.

But yet then, take Jesus Christ as our Head, as he is spoken of in the next words, and indeed as a distinct thing from his sitting at God's right hand, so he is for ever a Head. We were chosen in him at first,—I shewed in what sense when I opened those words, 'chosen in Christ, and elected in Christ,' in the 3d and 4th verses,—and as we were chosen in him at first, so we are considered in him for ever, and exalted in him, our persons in his Person; and God then, having forgiven all sin and misery, and the Mediator's office for intercession, &c., being laid aside, he is all in all both to Christ and us, and so now he delivereth up the kingdom unto God the Father.

I will add but this one third thing to it, to make this point—how he is a King, and sitteth at God's right hand for ever, and how not—clear. When he hath delivered up this kingdom of his redeemership unto God the Father, yet he sitteth down with this honour for ever, that it was he that did execute this office of a Mediator, so as not a soul is lost, not a sin left unsatisfied for, not an enemy unsubdued; he sitteth down like a mighty and glorious conqueror. He is not a General in war longer, that kind of kingdom and rule ceaseth, yet he hath this honour for ever, that he it is that did these and these exploits, brought in all those rebels, subdued all enemies, and remaineth a glorious dictator. So that indeed and in truth Jesus Christ shall then reign more gloriously with his Father, though it is more especially appropriated to him till the day of judgment, than ever he did before; for then he reigneth triumphantly, whereas before he reigned as one that was conquering and to conquer. And as David said, when all his enemies were subdued, Am I a king this day? so will Jesus Christ say, He was never kinged so much as now. Therefore some interpret those words, 1 Cor. xv. 24, 'Then shall the end be;' that is, say they, the perfection and accomplishment of his kingdom then cometh. Yea, in some sense, my brethren, he then setteth the crown upon his Father's head again, for his Father was put out of rule, as it were, by the devil, who got all this world, and by wicked men, that did what they list; but his poor saints, whom he chose to eternal life, lay under sin and misery. Jesus Christ now subdueth all these enemies, rescueth these poor souls whom he loved from all evil, and presenteth to him a peaceable kingdom and government, and so he with his Father enjoyeth it to all eternity.

So much now for the opening of these words, 'this world, and the world to come,' in that second sense given, and the explaining how Jesus Christ is a king in both.

I will only add this: whereas it is said, 'of his kingdom there shall be no end,' his meaning is, as it is interpreted Dan. vii. 14, it shall not be destroyed for ever. It is a kingdom to give way to no kingdom else; it is continued, he reigneth for ever, though he himself giveth up the kingdom to his Father, and becometh visibly and apparently more subject than he was unto him. In this sense, that I may explain that too, it is not meant in respect of his Godhead, for so he was never subject; it is not meant in respect of his manhood, for so he is always subject: but whereas he so reigneth now as if God the Father reigned not visibly and apparently,—that is, he doth all visibly, although it is the Father's glory he cometh with,—yet he hath the glory of it, he runneth away with it, as it were; but when he shall have given it up, with this acknowledgment, that his Father is the author of this kingdom, and that he gave it him, and so setteth his crown upon his Father's head, then it shall appear to men and angels to be his Father's kingdom in a more eminent manner.—And so much for that second interpretation.

I will add a *third*, and so leave it: namely, what should be meant by the 'world to come' here; speaking of Christ's sitting at God's right hand, over all principalities and powers, in this world, and the world to come.

My brethren, there is a special world, called the world to come, appointed for Jesus Christ eminently to reign in; and therefore though all these senses are true and good, and must be taken in, yet let me add this to it, that God did not content himself to bestow this world upon Christ, for him to rule and reign in, and to order and dispose the affairs of it as he doth, and after the day of judgment to reign in that sense you heard spoken of before for ever, more gloriously than he did before. But he hath appointed a special world on purpose for him, between this world and the end of the day of judgment,—and the day of judgment itself is part of it, if not the whole of it, —wherein our Lord and Saviour Jesus Christ shall reign; which the Scripture eminently calleth the 'world to come;' Christ's world, as I may so call it: that as this present world was ordained for the first Adam, and God hath given it unto the sons of men, so there is a world to come appointed for the second Adam, as the time after the day of judgment is God the Father's in a more eminent manner, who then shall be all in all.

I mention this third interpretation both because the height of Christ's kingdom is in the world to come when that cometh once, and because that is more properly his, and also is to me, by comparing other scriptures, evidently intended in this place. It is the height of his kingdom; for in this world he hath principalities and powers of angels under him, by whom he ruleth; after the day of judgment, God is all in all; but there is a world to come which the angels have nothing to do with at all, which is not subjected as this world is unto the angels, but is made on purpose for Jesus Christ.

I will give you for this two parallel places of Scripture, Heb. ii. 5, compared likewise with 2 Peter iii. 7.

In Heb. ii. 5, 'To the angels,' saith he, 'hath he not put in subjection the world to come.' Whom hath he subjected it to then? 'But,' saith he, 'one in a certain place testified, saying, What is man, that thou art mindful of him? or the son of man, that thou visitest him? Thou madest him a little while lower' (so it is in the margins) 'than the angels, and hast crowned him with glory and honour, and didst set him over the works of thy hands: thou hast put all things in subjection under his feet. Now we see not yet all things put under him; but we see Jesus, who was made a little lower than the angels by the suffering of death, crowned with glory and honour.'

Compare now this place in the Hebrews with this in the text. First, you see, he speaks of Jesus Christ as made Lord of all; what here in the text he calleth 'sitting at God's right hand,' there he expresseth by being 'crowned with glory.' Here he saith 'he was raised from the dead,' there he saith he was 'made a little while lower'—indeed, for the measure, far lower—'than the angels by the suffering of death,' a worm and no man.

In the second place, he quoteth out of Ps. viii. that passage which likewise is here in the text, 'He hath put all things under his feet;' so saith ver. 22, and that sentence is nowhere else found in the Old Testament, and it is quoted thrice by the Apostle; here in the text, in Heb. ii., and in 1 Cor. xv.

Thirdly, he saith that there is this world to come ordained for this man: 'What is man, that thou art mindful of him? or the son of man, that thou visitest him?'—that thou hast subjected this world to come unto him, and put all things under his feet? He saith the like here in the text: he sitteth at God's right hand, over all principalities and powers, in this world, and the world to come, and he hath put all things under his feet. So that, you see, that place in the Hebrews and the words in the text agree, quoting both the same place.

These words, 'having all things under his feet,' are, as I said, nowhere in the Old Testament but in Ps. viii. You shall observe therefore that in 1 Cor. xv. 25, where the Apostle beginneth to quote Ps. cx., to prove that Christ must reign 'till all his enemies be put under his feet,' that the word 'all' is not in Ps. cx., nor is it said there 'under his feet,' but it is 'make thine enemies thy footstool.' The Apostle therefore being to prove that all enemies are to be destroyed, which Ps. cx. doth not fully serve for, what doth he do? He helps it out with Ps. viii., where the phrase is used, 'he hath put all things under his feet.' So that now Ps. viii., and Heb. ii., and 1 Cor. xv., and these words of my text, are all parallel places, and therefore I could not pass over this interpretation.

I will give you another place for it: 2 Peter iii. 7, compared with ver. 13, 'The heavens and the earth, which are now,'—here that which in the text the Apostle calleth this world, is expressed by 'the heavens and the earth which are now,'—'by the same word are kept in store, reserved unto fire,' &c. And ver. 13, namely, in opposition to the heavens and the earth which now are, mentioned ver. 7, he saith, 'Nevertheless we, according to his promise, look for new heavens and a new earth, wherein dwelleth righteousness.' The Jews still express *world* by saying *heaven and earth;* therefore, when the Apostle would express this world, he calleth it heaven and earth, meaning the world that now is; but, saith he, 'we look for a new heaven and a new earth,' that is, a world to come. Now the words which in Heb. ii. 5 the Apostle useth of 'world to come' are οἰκουμένην τὴν μέλλουσαν, wherein dwelleth righteousness.

And that this place in Peter and that of Heb. ii. fall all to one, appeareth by this: that when the apostle Peter had gone and alleged this, that there is to be 'a new heavens and a new earth,' that is, a world to come, 'wherein dwelleth righteousness,' so it is ver. 13.; at the 14th verse he makes use of it; at the 15th verse he quoteth Paul for it in his Epistle to the Hebrews,—for Peter writeth to the Jews,—'Even also,' saith he, 'as our beloved brother Paul, according to the wisdom given unto him, hath written unto you;' that is, of this new heaven and new earth, of this world to come.

Now, read that Epistle to the Hebrews;—for our divines usually quote this place to prove, and it is the best that can be, that Paul was the author of that epistle; for Peter writ to the Jews, that is plain, for he writ to the strangers dispersed, which were the ten tribes, throughout the lower Asia and those countries, as you may read, 1 Peter i. 1–3. He hath written to you, saith he, of this new heaven and new earth, wherein dwelleth righteousness;—now in the second of the Hebrews he writeth of it, proving it out of the 8th Psalm.

Thus you see, going from one place to another, that scripture and that in Heb. ii. are parallel, and that in Heb. ii. and this in 2 Peter iii. are parallel likewise.

My brethren, I will not stand discoursing to you about this new world; I shall only speak what is pertinent to the thing in hand. Unto this did all the prophets give witness, and therefore I am not ashamed to give witness to it too.

In Rev. v. 10,—I opened that chapter to you when I explained Christ's sitting at God's right hand,—as soon as ever they saw Christ take the book, and was installed king, what do their thoughts presently run to? The world to come; 'he hath made us kings,' say they, 'and priests, and we shall reign on the earth.' To be sure, at the day of judgment they shall; which will be a long day certainly, when all the accounts of the world shall be ripped up, and the world new hung against the approach of the King to it. There will be new heavens and new earth indeed, and the glory of the creatures then will put down the glory of this old world of Adam's; it was not good enough for this great Lord, our Lord and Saviour Christ. But I say I will not much insist upon it; I will only open so much as is pertinent to the thing in hand.

You see this place and that in Heb. ii. how parallel they are, and that the second of the Hebrews quoteth Ps. viii.

Now, consider but the scope of the psalm, as the Apostle quoteth it to prove the world to come. Any one that reads that psalm would think that the Psalmist doth but set forth old Adam in his kingdom, in his Paradise, made a little lower than the angels,—for we have spirits wrapped up in flesh and blood, whereas they are spirits simply,—a degree lower, as if they were dukes and we marquises; one would think, I say, that this were all his meaning, and that it is applied to Christ but by way of allusion. But the truth is, the Apostle bringeth it in to prove and to convince these Hebrews, to whom he wrote, that that psalm was meant of Christ, of that man whom they expected to be the Messiah, the man Christ Jesus.

And that he doth it I prove by the 6th verse,—it is the observation that Beza hath,—'one in a certain place,' quoting David, *διεμαρτύρατο*, 'hath testified;' so we may translate it, hath testified *etiam atque etiam*, testified most expressly: he bringeth an express proof for it that it was meant of the man Christ Jesus; therefore it is not an allusion. And indeed it was Beza that did first begin that interpretation that I read of, and himself therefore doth excuse it and make an apology for it, that he diverteth out of the common road, though since many others have followed him.

Now the scope of the psalm is plainly this: in Rom. v. 14 you read that Adam was a type of him that was to come. Now in Psalm viii. you find there Adam's world, the type of a world to come; he was the first Adam, and had a world, so the second Adam hath a world also appointed for him; there is his oxen and his sheep, and the fowls of the air, whereby are meant other things, devils perhaps, and wicked men, the prince of the air; as by the heavens there, the angels, or the apostles rather; 'the heavens declare the glory of God,' that is applied to the apostles, that were preachers of the gospel.

To make this plain to you, that that psalm, where the phrase is used, 'all things under his feet,' and quoted by the Apostle here in the text,—therefore it is proper,—was not meant of man in innocency, but of the Messiah, the Lord Jesus Christ; and therefore answerably, that the world there is not this world, but a world on purpose made for this Messiah, as the other was for Adam—

First, it was not meant of man in innocency properly and principally. Why? Because in the first verse he saith, 'out of the mouths of babes and sucklings hast thou ordained strength.' There were no babes in the time of Adam's innocency, he fell before there was any.

Secondly, he addeth, 'that thou mightest still the enemy and avenger;' the devil that is, for he shewed himself the enemy there to be a manslayer from the beginning. God would use man to still him; alas! he overcame Adam presently. It must be meant of another therefore, one that is able to still this enemy and avenger.

Then he saith, 'How excellent is thy name in all the earth, who hast set thy glory above the heavens!' Adam had but Paradise, he never propagated God's name over all the earth; he did not continue so long before he fell as to beget sons; much less did he found it in the heavens.

Again, ver. 4, 'What is man, and the son of man?' Adam, though he was man, yet he was not the son of man; he is called indeed the 'son of God,' Luke iii. 38, but he was not *filius hominis*. I remember Ribera urgeth that.

But take an argument the Apostle himself useth to prove it. This man, saith he, must have all subject to him; all but God, saith he; he must have the angels subject to him, for he hath put all principalities and powers under his feet, saith he. This could not be Adam, it could not be the man that had this world in the state of innocency; much less had Adam all under his feet. No, my brethren, it was too great a vassalage for Adam to have the creatures thus low to him. But they are thus to Jesus Christ, angels and all; they are all under his feet, he is far above them.

Secondly, it is not meant of man fallen, that is as plain; the Apostle himself saith so. 'We see not,' saith he, 'all things subject unto him.' Some think that it is meant as an objection that the Apostle answereth; but it is indeed to prove that man fallen cannot be meant in that Psalm viii. Why? Because, saith he, we do not see anything, all things at least, subject unto him; you have not any one man, or the whole race of man, to whom all things have been subject; the creatures are sometimes injurious to him. We do not see him, saith he; that is, the nature of man in general considered. Take all the monarchs in the world, they never conquered the whole world; there was never any one man that was a sinner, that had all subject to him. 'But we see,' saith he,—mark the opposition,—'but we see Jesus,' that man, 'crowned with glory and honour;' therefore it is this man, and no man else; the opposition implieth it.

The philosophers themselves complain that nature was a stepmother to man; they did not see that subjection of the creatures unto him, but many miseries and incursions of miseries upon him. But, saith the Apostle, 'we see this man, Jesus, crowned with glory and honour.'

And then it is not an angel to whom all this is subject; it is a man, plainly; a man made a little while lower than the angels, and then crowned with glory and honour far above all, for so the opposition runneth.

And it is not this world only that shall be subject to this man, but it is a world to come; so the Apostle saith plainly, ver. 8, 'We see not yet all things put under him,' therefore it is not this world, saith he, but Jesus Christ is in heaven, crowned with glory and honour already; and there will be a world, and a world there is beginning, that shall be subject to him, as well as this present world.

So now it remaineth, then, that it is only Christ, God-man, that is meant in that Psalm viii. And indeed and in truth Christ himself interpreteth that psalm of himself; you have two witnesses to confirm it, Christ himself and the Apostle. Matt. xxi. 16, when they cried Hosanna to Christ, or 'Save now,' and made him the Saviour of the world, the Pharisees were angry; our Saviour confuteth them by this very psalm, 'Have ye not read,' saith he, 'Out of the mouths of babes and sucklings thou hast perfected praise?' He quoteth this very psalm which speaks of himself, and Paul, by his warrant, and perhaps from that hint, doth thus argue out of it, and convince the Jews by it.

What the meaning of that is, 'out of the mouths of babes and sucklings,' I refer to what Mr Mead in his *Diatribæ* hath written upon that Psalm viii. He interpreteth it of men, of the man Christ Jesus principally, who was but a babe, by whom God would still the enemy and avenger, under whose feet he hath put all things; therefore he is the man who is prophesied of.

You know how the prophecy of the Messiah runneth, Gen. iii. 15: He shall bruise thy head, and thou shalt nibble at his heel; which implieth plainly that he that was to be the Messiah should have Satan under his feet, he was to tread upon Satan's head; the nibbling at the heel sheweth that he should wind up his head and bite him by the heel, being thus under his feet.

Now, my brethren, he is the sole man that, as the Psalmist and Apostle saith, hath a world to come ordained for him. To speak a little of that now that I have shewed it to be the meaning of both—

As Adam had a world made for him, so shall Jesus Christ, this second Adam,—Adam being a type of him that was to come,—have a world made for him. This world was not good enough for him; he hath a better appointed than that which old Adam had, a new heaven and a new earth, according to the promise, Isa. lxvi. 22, where the saints shall reign. 'Thou hast made us kings and priests, and we shall reign on earth.' And this world he hath not subjected unto angels; no, there are none of those principalities and powers in it, or shall be in it, when it cometh to its perfection.

Do but mark the harmony of one thing with another. There are two Adams: an earthly Adam, he hath an earthly world; a heavenly Adam, and he hath a heavenly world. There are two covenants, the Law and the Gospel. The angels delivered the first covenant; 'The law was given by the ministration of angels.' But the second covenant, the gospel, declareth and speaks of this second world made for the man Christ Jesus. God hath not used the angels to preach the gospel, they do not meddle with it; but he hath appointed men to do it. He is so far from subjecting this world that is to come to angels, that they are not the declarers of it. 'Unto the angels,' saith he, Heb. ii. 5, 6, 'hath he not put in subjection the world to come, whereof we speak,' though they gave the law. Men that were babes and sucklings, out of their mouths he hath ordained strength to begin to create this new world.

Why is it called the *world to come*, and yet we speak of it, saith he, and the gospel beginneth it?

Because as the other world was six days a-making,—there was a chaos first, and so it went on by degrees,—so it will be in this world likewise; we are now but in the first day's work as it were, the perfection of it is to come. 'The kingdom of heaven is like unto a grain of mustard seed, which is the least of all seeds,' and yet the greatest in the end. The Apostle, speaking of conversion, Gal. i. 4, calleth it a delivering us from this present evil world. 'Old things are passed away,' saith he, 'and all things are become new.' Here is a creation, a beginning, here is the first day's work, and God will never leave till he hath perfected this world; and because the perfection of it is not yet, therefore it is said to be a world to come.

And because it is a new world begun thus, and thus begun when Christ began to preach; which first began, saith the Apostle to the Hebrews, to be preached by the Lord himself here upon earth; therefore it is, that as the first world had a seventh day for the celebrating of the creation of it, so hath this new world now a Lord's day; and of that Lord's day doth the Apostle speak, Heb. iv. 4, as here he doth of this new world in Heb. ii. And the Holy Ghost, when Christ was set in heaven, fell down then upon the feast of Pentecost, which was upon the first day of the week, our Lord's day, as Lev. xxiii. 15, 16.

Now, my brethren, this world, when it is finished, shall not be subject to the angels, but to Christ and his babes and sucklings, to that man Christ Jesus, Lord Paramount of it, for whom it was made, and those citizens of this world, as Pareus expresseth it. Therefore Christ is called τὸν ἄρχηγον, the Captain of our salvation, for he in this is a Common Person; and as he by suffering was made a little while lower than the angels, so are we to suffer with him, and having suffered with him, to reign with him.

My brethren, you do not read of the angels judging the world, and sitting upon the throne; do but take that part of this world, however, we are sure of that, that the saints then shall reign, and reign on earth. They are said to sit, and to sit on twelve thrones, Matt. xix. 28. And in Rev. xx. it is said the thrones were set, and those that were beheaded for the testimony of Jesus sat upon them; therefore Christ promiseth to give the government of ten cities to him that had made his five talents ten. The devils will be shut out; he hath taken and locked out that great devil: those principalities are gone during that time; and being they are gone, there needeth no principalities of good angels to oppose them.

Will you have me speak what I think? I think this, that that office which the angels do in this world here below, men risen from the dead shall do to men that are saints. For the first part of this reign, of this kingdom of Christ, of this world to come; that world shall be subject, not to angels, but to men, after that first resurrection which the 20th chapter of the Revelation speaks of.

And it is no absurdity at all; for if the angels that behold God's face are busied about things here below, I see not but that the saints may be so too; it is an honour rather than otherwise. The angels begin it indeed, they gather the elect from all the four corners of the earth; and they end it, they are the executioners to fling wicked men and devils into hell. But they to whom this world is subject, that are the judges, that are the principalities and powers in this world to come, are men. They shall judge the angels, so saith the Apostle.

And, my brethren, in this world will be the height of the kingdom of Jesus Christ; and when that is ended, he delivereth up the kingdom unto God the Father.

Now I will make but a short use or two, an observation, and so I will end.

Here, *first*, you see two worlds for you. You that look for happiness, methinks you should be satisfied with the expectation of this. Alexander wept because he had half conquered one world,—this world,—that there were no more for him to conquer, out of a supposition when he had conquered all what he should do, one world would not satisfy him. If thou hadst the same desire, thou needest not care for this world, there is another world, there are more worlds than one; 'by whom he made the worlds,' saith he, Heb. i. There are things present, and the comfort is there are things to come; there is a present world, and there is a world to come. Care not for this world, it is old Adam's world, it is loss to the saints; it is well if thou canst get handsomely rid of it with little sinning, if thou canst be but delivered out of this present evil world, as the Apostle speaks, Gal. i. 4.

It was all that Christ desired, all that he prayed for; saith he, John xvii. 15, 'I pray not that thou shouldest take them out of the world, but that thou shouldest keep them from the evil.' But, my brethren, there is a world to come. Abraham and all his seed, not only the Jew, but the Gentile, are not only heirs of Canaan, but of the world; it is expressly said so, Rom. iv. 13.—That is the first observation.

In the *second* place, admire we this man Christ Jesus whom God hath thus advanced,—yea, and, to set him up, hath made a world on purpose for him, peculiar for him and for his to enjoy, and for him to use them as under him to rule and govern.

It is the observation of Chrysostom upon the place, admiring that that man that was the scorn of death, so he was here below, and when he hung upon the cross, that was the derision of men; we shall see no beauty in him, that we should desire him, as it is, Isa. liii;—yet that God should take up this man, raise him up from the dead, and set him at his own right hand, and subject all principalities and powers under him, give him this world, a world to come in a special manner, and to reign likewise for ever and ever after the day of judgment, to use him in all his great businesses, to judge the world by this man. If this, saith he, had been spoken of God, there had been no wonder, for all the nations of the world are but as a drop of a bucket to him; but to hear it spoken of a man, of a drop of that drop, one man out of all nations, who himself was but a drop, a tear when he was in the womb first; to raise up this babe, this suckling, thus to still the enemy and avenger, to conquer death, to subdue angels, to have all principalities and powers under him, and not to still them with arms but with his mouth,—'out of the mouths of babes and sucklings,'—and to make a world thus on purpose for him; oh, how excellent is thy name in all the earth, and thy glory above the heavens!

This was it that made the Psalmist himself admire at the Lord Jesus Christ, that God should thus visit him, carry him to those depths, make him a little while—as the word βραχύ τι signifieth; as the orator saith, 'hear me a little while'—lower than the angels, though a great deal for measure lower than they, to let him down to the lowest parts of the earth, to the nethermost hell, and lay all our sins upon him and all his wrath. 'Lord,' saith he, 'what is man, that thou visitest him?' Visiting is sometimes put for visiting in anger, as Ps. lix. 5. So God visited Christ first, made him thus lower than the angels in this sense for a little while; and when he had done, he visited him in favour as much, takes that broken man, shattered man,—for his soul was broken, 'my heart is broken;' it is the expression that Christ himself useth in one of the psalms,—takes him and raiseth him up to heaven, crowneth him with glory and honour, setteth him in all that glory you have heard. Oh, what is man and the son of man,—he speaks of the nature of man as it is united to the Godhead in Christ, foreseeing it by a spirit of prophecy,—that thou shouldst visit him thus, first in anger, then in favour? What is this babe, this suckling, that thou shouldst raise him up to this glory and honour?

My brethren, all this concerneth us, for what saith the Psalmist here in the first verse? He calleth him the *Lord our God*, this man Christ Jesus. How excellent is the name of God for doing this, how excellent will it be in all the earth one day, and founded in the heavens now, and will be for evermore after the day of judgment. It will be that which will take up, swallow up the thoughts of men and angels to all eternity.

That I may set it out a little. I thought to have done it when I handled those words, 'under his feet,' but I will touch it now a little, and be the briefer then. Take all this that hath been said of Christ as the text setteth it forth here, take it all together, and here is the most glorious prospect of a kingdom that ever was; it putteth down all the kingdoms of the world that were shewn to Christ by Satan. Do but take the prospect of it.

First, here is a Father of glory, to whom he prayeth, ver. 17; a God that is the fountain of all glory, and himself the Father of our Lord Jesus Christ, whom he makes a man, visiteth him, you heard how low; layeth him in the earth, raiseth him up, setteth him in his throne at his own right hand. There is your King, the eldest Son of God. Here is God the Father, the Father of glory, and here is his Son at his right hand. Here are worlds for his dominions, this world and the world to come. To set forth the glory of this kingdom, here are nobles, who you know set out the glory of a kingdom by their being under the king and under his son; here are principalities and powers, might and dominion; and here is the highest exaltation that ever was, all these nobles under his feet, under his Son's feet. All things, saith he, are under his feet. Those that are his friends are under his feet too, under him as subjects; they fall down and kiss the dust of his feet,—'to him be glory and honour,'—and they throw down their crowns, as you read, Rev. v. Those that are his enemies, he hath the most glorious conquest over them that ever was; he treadeth upon them, he sitteth and makes them his footstool, that he may sit the easier; and Satan, that great devil, he triumpheth over him, so that he makes his children to set their feet upon his neck.

What is there now, my brethren, that you will say, or that you will think, can be added to make this man Christ Jesus more glorious? One would think now that he hath enough: he is advanced, you see, to the highest throne of majesty, he is established a king for ever; he hath worlds for his dominions, this world and the world to come; he hath the highest power, he hath all things under his feet. What is it, I say, that should make this man yet more glorious?

Take Adam, that was his type. Adam had a world about him, he had a paradise, a court which was his peculiar. If he had had sons, Paradise had been his court properly, for he was the father of the world. What wanted this man? Plainly he wanted a wife, he wanted a helper; God himself saith so. My brethren, all this was in a type. This man Christ Jesus, thus advanced far above all principality and power; here is the Father of glory, here is his Son set in glory, here are nobles all under him, here are dominions enough; where is the queen? What saith the words following: 'He hath given him to be the head over all things to the church, which is his body, the fulness of him that filleth all in all.' *Over all to be the Head of his Church;* so some translate it, and I think it to be a part of the meaning, that above all privileges else he accounteth this, as it were, the highest flower in his crown, that he is a Head to his Church, his body. It is as if our Lord and Saviour Christ should have said, I have all this honour, I am thus full, I am at my Father's right hand; if I have not my Church I want a body, I am not yet full. Therefore now, above all this glory and exaltation, hath God given him to be Head of his Church. I sit at God's right hand; come up, saith he, to his Church, that by nature and by desert is under his feet; come up, saith he, and sit on my right hand, as I sit on my Father's right hand.

Read Psalm xlv. There, when he is anointed with the oil of gladness above his fellows, the queen standeth at his right hand: and, saith he, as I sit in my Father's throne, so my Church sits upon my throne; and though I have all things under my feet, I will have my Church, my queen, which is flesh of my flesh,—therefore she is called his body,—she shall have her seat at my right hand, for she is my fulness, I am not full without her. My brethren, Jesus Christ delighteth more in love than he doth in power, though he be King of kings. Let me yet once more break forth into what the Psalmist doth: Oh, what is man, that thou art mindful of him? and the son of man,—the Lord Christ, and his Church, made up of men,—that thou art thus mindful of him?

SERMON XXXIV.

Far above all principality, and power, and might, and dominion, and every name that is named, not only in this world, but also in that which is to come: and hath put all things under his feet, and given him to be the head (or, *a head*) *over all things to the church, which is his body, the fulness of him that filleth all in all.*—Ver. 21–23.

Our Lord and Saviour's exaltation is set forth unto us in these three last verses, and the verse before, in a double relation.

The first is, *His exaltation above all creatures*, and the distance he standeth in to them; he is 'far above all principality, and power, and might, and dominion, and hath all things under his feet.'

Secondly, His exaltation is set forth to us *by his relation and pre-eminence which he hath to his Church;* 'he hath given him to be a head over all to his church, which is his body, the fulness of him that filleth all in all.'

If you will have it, Jesus Christ, the great King, his supremacy in all matters, and over all persons, civil and ecclesiastical; 'far above all principality,' &c. There is his supremacy over all creatures, and all civil government, and a Head to his Church also. These are the two general parts of these words.

Concerning his exaltation, as it is laid down in the 21st verse, I have already shewn these two things:—

First, *How he is advanced far above all things*; for his own personal dignity is far above all principality and power. And this is amplified by the *persons* over whom he is exalted: it is over all principality and power, both good angels and bad, and the most excellent of creatures here on earth—kings and magistrates, whatsoever they be, by what names or titles soever distinguished; 'every name that is named.'

Then the third thing, which I considered in the last discourse, was *the extent of it;* 'not only in this world, but in the world to come.'

Of those words, 'in this world, and the world to come,' I told you interpreters gave two interpretations; whereof the

First was, that by *this world*, and the *world to come*, should be meant heaven and earth; as he himself saith at last, 'All power is given unto me in heaven and in earth.' And what might be objected against this interpretation, I answered in my last discourse, and how it would not wholly and fully suit the scope of the Apostle here.

Then, in the second place, 'in this world, and the world to come,' I told you was a phrase that imported *for ever*, and so should imply all time after the day of judgment, not only in this world, but in all the worlds to come, be they what they will be. Now, because there was that great objection against it in 1 Cor. xv., that he is to reign, to sit, until his enemies be made his footstool, and then to give up the kingdom unto God the Father,—so it is expressly said, ver. 24, 25,—I therefore explained how far his kingdom was eternal, and how far not, and how to be given up at the latter day.

To these two interpretations I added a third, which is not to exclude the others, but is indeed a kind of middle between both, taking in both the one and the other. Or, if you will, thus: that between the state of this world, as now it is, and the state of things after the day of judgment, when God shall be 'all in all,' there is a world to come, which is on purpose, and in a more especial manner appointed for Jesus Christ to be King in. And seeing there is such a world to come, certainly this is to be taken in here, if there were no other reason.

But I told you that there was a more especial reason why that this interpretation must be here taken in with the rest. For I find all interpreters, almost with one consent, to refer me for the words that follow, 'hath put all things under his feet,' to Ps. viii., as the only place in the Old Testament where those words are spoken concerning Christ; ver. 6, 'Thou madest him to have dominion over the works of thy hands; thou hast put all things under his feet.' So as, say they, these words, 'he hath put all things under his feet,' are a testimony borrowed from Ps. viii., which the same apostle Paul quoteth and citeth in two other epistles to the very same purpose. He quoteth them Heb. ii. 8, where he speaks of his kingdom, and in 1 Cor. xv. 27.

Now therefore, I was led to look into Heb. ii., where indeed I find the same words quoted out of Ps. viii.; and I found this likewise, that the Apostle's scope was to prove that the Psalmist prophesied of a world to come, ordained for Christ; and proveth it by this, that he was to have a world wherein all things were to be subject to him; the very same thing that followeth here in the 22d verse. And, saith he, though we now see Christ crowned with glory and honour,—so it is at Heb. ii. 8, which is all one and to 'sit at God's right hand,'—yet, saith he, all is not subject unto him. Though God hath put all under his feet, yet all is not yet subject; therefore there is a world to come, saith he, wherein all things shall be subject to Jesus Christ.

Now then, I finding here a 'world to come,' wherein Christ is King over all, and 'all things put under his feet,' which are the next words, and that in the judgment of all interpreters it is taken out of Ps. viii., which Heb. ii. quoteth, there is no rational man could imagine but that, in the same sense that 'world to come' is taken in Heb. ii., in the same sense it must be taken here.

I did in my last discourse, indeed, with more modesty pass over what I thought was meant by that 'world to come' than perhaps is here meet. Perhaps, likewise, I might not be so well understood. I will therefore explain myself unto you, professing not to be long upon it; for I will not discourse of it, but merely take what is pertinent and apposite to the expression in hand, 'the world to come,' as it is held forth unto us in Heb. ii.

I also proved that that *man* prophesied of in Ps. viii., that was to have all things under his feet, was only Jesus Christ. I shall speak now more to this, that he hath a world to come ordained for him, in which 'all things' are to be understood. And I shall express myself, all that I mean to say about it, in these two heads:—

The first is, That that 'world to come,' mentioned Heb. ii. 5, wherein Christ is to have 'all things under his feet,' is *not this world that now is, or merely the government that Christ now hath; neither is it the world after the day of judgment*, and yet is said to be a 'world to come.'

And then, secondly, *I shall shew you what I think is meant by that world to come*, and the several steps and degrees of its perfection, its growing up, in respect of which it is said to be a world to come.

And, first of all, that the world to come, mentioned in Heb. ii. and prophesied of, Ps. viii., which this text referreth us to, *is not the world that now is*, that is plain; for the Apostle distinguisheth this world that now is from that world that is to come by this: saith he, now we do not see all things subject unto him,—and it is his argument by which he proveth that there must needs be such a world to come subject unto Christ,—'We see not,' saith he, 'all things put under him yet,' Heb. ii. 8; therefore it is a world to come. Here lies the Apostle's reason. That same word 'not now,' or 'not yet,' implieth evidently that there is a world to come in which this is to be fulfilled, wherein all things shall be subject unto Christ. It is true, this world to come is begun, as I shall shew you by and by, but it is not grown up to its perfection. We see Jesus crowned indeed, but we do not see all things subject unto him yet. This is the Apostle's scope in Heb. ii.

So that, first, it is not this world that now is.

Then the second thing is this, to prove *that it is not the estate of the world after the day of judgment*. I shall only prove it out of Heb. ii. and this place; I will go no further, for I will still speak pertinently to the text.

First, then; the world to come, that is ordained for Christ to have all things subject to him, is not the world after the day of judgment, I mean the state after the day of judgment. My reason is this, because that of this world that is to come for Christ, Adam's world was the type. Now mark it, my brethren. Look into Rom. viii. 19–22, the Apostle sheweth you plainly there that Adam's world, this very world wherein now we are,—which is the type of Christ's world to come,—this earth and this heaven, these creatures do groan 'for the manifestation of the sons of God; for the creature,' saith he, 'was made subject unto vanity, not willingly, but by reason of him,' namely, Adam, 'who hath subjected the same in hope, because the creature itself also shall be delivered from the bondage of corruption into the glorious liberty of the children of God. For we know that the whole creation groaneth and travaileth in pain together until now.' So that you see there is a world to come which is not that after the day of judgment,—for what will become of these creatures then, no man can tell me,—but it is this very individual creation, where we live and are, that doth groan for a restitution; and the restitution of it is the world to come, as the present corruption and bondage of it is this world.

And then, if you look into Ps. viii., you shall find there, that in the type of Christ's world to come, it is said that heavens, and stars and moon, and sheep and oxen, and fowls of the air, and fishes, these are all subject unto him. This cannot be meant after the day of judgment; no, not in the type. There is nothing after the day of judgment which heavens, and stars and moon, and sheep and oxen, and fowls of the air, and fishes should signify or typify out to us.

So that it is a world to come, between the state of this world, which is yet in its ruff and in its height to this present, and the day of judgment.

I will give you a second reason for it, and it is this: For when this world to come shall come, and Christ shall have all subject unto him in it,—for he only, saith he, shall have all subject,—then he shall 'deliver up the kingdom unto his Father,' namely, at the end of the day of judgment. This is plain, 1 Cor. xv. 24, 25, &c. He saith plainly there that when he hath put all things under his feet,—when he hath done it, when he hath brought him fully into possession of this world to come, wherein all things are to be subject unto him,—then, ver. 28, 'when all things shall be subdued unto him, then shall the Son also himself be subject unto him that hath put all things under him.' So that now, this world of his doth cease when the day of judgment ceaseth, for 'then cometh the end,' saith he, ver. 24.

And then, thirdly, answerably out of the very words of the text you have this world, and the world to come, wherein there are principalities, and powers, and might, and dominion; 'not only in this world,' saith he, but 'in the world to come.' Why now, after the day of judgment there will be no principalities and powers, or might and dominion; therefore not this world to come, if you take it in a proper and strict sense.

That there will be no principalities and powers after the day of judgment is ended, is plain thus: for in 1 Cor. xv. 24, 'He shall deliver up the kingdom to the Father, when he shall have put down all rule, and authority, and power.' Here are three words, according to the Greek, of those four which are in the text.

So that now, I say, that world to come, which the Apostle speaks of, Heb. ii., and quoteth Psalm viii. for it, wherein Christ is actually to have 'all things under his feet,' is not that time after the day of judgment. It is not this world neither, nor the state of things now; for we do not see yet all things put under him; therefore there is a world to come between these two.

And so much now for that first general head, namely, that by 'world to come,' both here and in Heb. ii., is not meant the state of things after the day of judgment simply or only, but another world besides.

Now, in the second place, I come to explain *what it is that is meant by this world to come.* I shall do it as briefly as possibly the thing will bear, and indeed but to explain the text.

I will shew you, first, in *general* why it is called *a world;* and, secondly, why *a world to come.*

Then more *particularly* I shall shew you *the several degrees of the coming on of this world;* and when it is at its perfection, that Christ shall have all in subjection to him, and then that world to come shall cease; of that the second of the Hebrews speaks.

First, Why it is called *a world.*

My brethren, you must know this, that as God made this world for Adam, and put all things under him, though not under his feet; so God appointed a world for the second Adam, his Son Christ Jesus, and Adam's world was but the type of this world to come. Rom. v. 14, it is said that Adam was the type of him that was to come. Answerably this old Adam's world,—which now good angels and bad angels, and sinful men, these principalities and powers, rule,—it is but the shadow of that world which is to come, prophesied of in that 8th Psalm, and mentioned in that second of the Hebrews.

Yea, my brethren, let me add this to it also, that God doth take the same world that was Adam's, and makes it new and glorious; the same creation groaneth for this new world, this new clothing; as we groan to be clothed upon, so doth this whole creation. And as God takes the same substance of man's nature, and engrafteth the new creature upon it, the same man still; so he takes the same world, and maketh a new world, a world to come, for the second Adam. For the substance of the same world shall be restored to a glory which Adam could never have raised it unto, the same world that was lost in Adam. And this God will do before he hath done with it; and *this restitution is the world to come.*

Now then, Why is it called a *world to come?*

It is called a world to come because, though the foundation of it is now laid,—it was laid then, when our Lord and Saviour was upon the earth,—the foundation of it is laid in the new creature. Why is it called the *new creature*, but because as the first creation began the old world, so this new creature beginneth the new world? And as the old world was not perfected in a day, but in six days, so this new world to come is not perfected at once, the new creature is but the beginning of it; the new creature there below is in your hearts.

Saith the Apostle there in that second of the Hebrews,—do but mark the coherence, and you shall see that this new world is begun, and it is but begun, and you shall see when it began,—ver. 2, 'If the word spoken by angels was steadfast,' meaning the law, 'how shall we escape,' saith he, ver. 3, 'if we neglect so great salvation; which at the first began to be spoken by the Lord, and was confirmed unto us by them that heard it?' &c. 'For,' saith he, 'to the angels hath he not put in subjection the world to come, whereof we speak.' He had spoken of the preaching of the gospel in the words just before; he saith it was begun to be preached by Christ, and accompanied with the miracles and signs of the Holy Ghost; and this gospel, saith he, the angels did not deliver. They delivered the law indeed. 'The word spoken by angels,' saith he, 'was steadfast,' that is, the law; but, saith he, this gospel, which is the kingdom of heaven, is the beginning of 'the world to come, whereof we now speak.' This world, saith he, was not subjected to angels; they preached it not, neither shall they have anything to do in that world which the gospel beginneth. This world that now is, is subjected to them indeed, as I shewed you formerly; but the world to come is not.

It began therefore, you see, then, when Jesus Christ began to preach; and therefore you may observe the language of the gospel. 'Repent,' saith John Baptist, Matt. iii. 2, 'for the kingdom of heaven is at hand.' The world to come is coming upon you, when Christ shall come to preach the gospel, to make men new creatures. Here was the foundation of it. And saith Christ himself, Mark i. 15, 'Repent; the kingdom of heaven is at hand;' and, Matt. xvi. 28, 'There are some that stand here,' saith he, 'that shall not taste of death'—and all are dead that stood there long ago—'till they see the Son of man coming in his kingdom.'

The foundation of this world to come was thus laid by our Saviour Christ in bringing in the gospel, and it was prophesied of in Dan. ii. 44. He saith expressly there, that 'in the days of these kings'—while the principalities and powers stand of those monarchies; for he came stealing into the world when the Roman monarchy first began, in Augustus Cæsar's time; Christ, that meant to ruin it, came stealing in upon it—'shall the God of heaven set up a kingdom which shall never be destroyed; but it shall break in pieces and consume all these kingdoms, and it shall stand for ever.' This same new world, you see, began in the flourishing and height of the Roman monarchy. Now, what did Jesus Christ do when he came into the world and went up into heaven, when he began his new world? Consider what the world was before.

The devil was worshipped in all parts of the world, as the god of the world. Our Lord and Saviour Christ flingeth him down; 'I saw Satan,' saith he, 'fall down like lightning.' Where heathenism did not prevail, there did Judaism, all the ceremonial law; how zealous were the Jews of all their ceremonies, and of the temple! He throweth all them down; the apostle Paul calleth it, Heb. xii. 26, 'shaking of the earth.' Here is a great deal of this world gone presently, and falling down like Dagon before the new world.

He converteth by his apostles millions of souls over all the world; and how is conversion expressed in 2 Cor. v. 17? 'Old things are passed away; all things are become new.'

And this is but the first day's work of this world to come; the world is yet to come, for the Apostle, for all this, saith, we do not yet see all things subject unto him. This is but a delivering us out of 'the present evil world;' it is not a subjecting the present world unto Christ, it is a delivering them out of it that are converted, as it is Gal. i. 4.

And, my brethren, what is the reason that we Christians begin to reckon our time from Christ? We do not reckon from the creation; we do not say five thousand and five hundred and so many years, as it is since the creation; but we say one thousand six hundred, &c. as reckoning from Christ, for then our new world began.

This new world, that is but in the first day's work, when it had thrown down heathenism, the devil, flung out all those Jewish ceremonies, shook that earth, it is like a new nail that shaveth off by degrees the old one. Christ will not cease till he hath made all new. It is said there in that Dan. ii. 44, that it shall break in pieces and consume all those kingdoms, eat out the world and all the monarchies and glory of it, before it hath done.

Well, you shall see, when he had thrown down heathenism and Judaism,—which was his first day's work, as I may so say,—then cometh a night of Popery, and that steppeth up in the room of it. What will Christ do before he hath done? He will have a second day's work, and he will not cease till he hath thrown out every rag, the least dross and defilement, that Antichrist or Popery brought in or continued in the world. And we are under the second day's work, if I may so express it; we are but working up still to a purer world; it is this new world, this world to come, working up to its perfection. And, my brethren, Jesus Christ will never rest till he hath not only thrown out all the dross of this world, both in doctrine and worship,—which conforming to the world bringeth in, and hath brought into the world,—but for a second degree of this world, he will never rest till he hath brought all the world, that is, the generality of men, to be subject to him; which is another degree of this world to come.

The world, you know, consisteth of Jews and Gentiles. In the Apostle's time he had not conquered all the corruptions of the world, much less had he conquered the generality of mankind in the world. How bitterly doth the Apostle complain of the cutting off of the Jews; but a few of them at best came in, the generality of that nation was cast off. And for the Gentiles, 'Who hath believed our report?' say the apostles. But a very few in comparison. Therefore there will come a time when this new world shall have yet a further perfection; it shall grow up to a world, that the generality of mankind, both Jew and Gentile, shall come in to Jesus Christ. He hath had but little takings of the world yet, but he will have before he hath done; the world was made for him, and he will have it before he hath done.

In Rom. xi. 26, saith the Apostle, 'all Israel shall be saved,'—speaking of their second call,—for the generality of it. There is the new world of the Jews, a new world in that sense. And for the Gentiles, he telleth you that is but cast in. 'If the casting off of the Jews,' saith he, 'was the reconciling of the world,' that is, of the Gentiles, 'what shall their fulness be,' their taking in, 'but life from the dead?' The veil shall be taken off from all nations, so is the expression, Isa. xxv. 7. And that which is so much alleged for unity shall one day be fulfilled; but it will be when Christ is Lord of all the earth, never before. Christians will never agree till then, and then indeed there shall be 'one Lord, and his name one,' as it is, Zech. xiv. 9.

Here will be a brave world indeed, my brethren, and this is another degree of this world to come; one shepherd and one sheepfold of Jew and Gentile, and that sheepfold as large as all the world; so John x. 16. I speak of the generality, and the most. This was never yet fulfilled, for the Apostle expressly saith, that the casting off of the Jew was the receiving in of the Gentiles; therefore they were never yet one sheepfold together, but they shall be one.

My brethren, read the prophets, you shall find promises of strange and wonderful things: of glorious times, and that here upon earth; of all nations coming in to Jesus Christ; of all prosperity; of the mountain of the Lord set above all mountains, &c.

Disputing once with a Papist, he urged this upon me: saith he, If the Church of Rome be not the true church, and the church to which all churches shall submit, which hath had constant peace and prosperity, all riches, and glory, and honour, for this many hundred years; how hath this ever been fulfilled to your church, that all nations shall flow into it, that it is a mountain set above all mountains, that abundance of peace and prosperity is in it, which shall run down like a river; whereas you, saith he, have been in persecution? The truth is, my brethren, there is no answer for it but one, that the time is yet to come. And this one of their own, even Horrerius a Jesuit, though himself was for the Church of Rome, and made the prosperity of it one note of the truth of that church, yet he acknowledgeth, seeing such glorious things spoken of the Church of Christ in this world, that it is yet to be fulfilled, and was never yet fulfilled, no not in the Roman Church.

So now, you see, there is so much toward this world to come; yea, and the truth is, thus far we find many divines fall in, yea, and find those that do acknowledge that this state of glory, of a glorious church on earth, shall continue for a thousand years, during which time the Jews shall have it, and the Gentiles together with them.

There is a third thing, which is more controverted; and there is a fourth to be added to that, which I think that few will deny.

The *third degree* of this new world is this, that when this glorious time cometh, that Jesus Christ will thus call home both Jew and Gentile, and have a new world in respect of multitudes of men of all nations coming in unto him, to make this new world the more complete, he will bring part of heaven down to it. This, I say, is more controverted. I shall but express to you briefly some grounds for it, which I confess for these twenty years I have not known well how to answer, and that is all that I can say.

It is not that Christ himself shall come down—that is the old error of some—to reign at Jerusalem; which error indeed the fathers spake against, and which hath brought a blemish and absurdity upon that opinion. But that under Christ, reigning in heaven,—for certainly his court is there, and that is his temple, and he sitteth there both over this world and that to come,—yet that under him part of heaven shall come down and rule this world, to make the glory of it so much the more complete, to put down Adam's world, I shall give you rather those reasons.

I know not how to understand that place first, which shall be the foundation of all the rest; it is a known place alleged to this purpose; Rev. xx., indeed the whole chapter, but especially the 1st, 2d, 3d, 4th, and 5th verses. You shall find, my brethren,—and those that know that book acknowledge this,—that in chap. xix. both Pope and Turk are destroyed; so ver. 20 of that chapter. 'The beast was taken, and with him the false prophet that wrought miracles, and had deceived them that had the mark of the beast,' &c. And they were 'cast alive into a lake of fire burning with brimstone.' Here now the beast is gone, but the devil is left; therefore, chap. xx. 1, 2, 'I saw an angel come down from heaven, having the key of the bottomless pit and a great chain in his hand; and he laid hold on the dragon,'—that is, the devil, it is no other, and his angels, he is put for all the rest,—'that old serpent,'—that now doth traverse the world, going up and down, and is the ruler and the god of this world,—'which is the devil, and Satan, and bound him a thousand years, and cast him into the bottomless pit, and shut him up, and set a seal upon him, that he should deceive the nations no more, till the thousand years should be fulfilled: and after that he must be loosed for a little season.'

Here you see the devil cooped up, and why? Not to deceive the nations any more. It was never fulfilled yet. When was it fulfilled? Not during the times of Antichrist, he never more deceived than he did then; and the order you see is after the beast is taken, the beast is not yet destroyed: so that this thing is to come. It is not after the day of judgment, for he is to be loosed for a little season; so saith the text. And the truth is, you shall find that which we call properly and strictly the day of judgment, when all shall arise and be judged, followeth, as ver. 12, 13, and that after the devil hath been loosed a little season again.

Now, when the devil is gone, and is thus shut up for a thousand years, what is done for this thousand years?

Read the 4th, 5th, 6th, and 7th verses. 'I saw thrones,' saith he, 'and they sat upon them, and judgment was given unto them.' What is judgment, but reigning? And what were they to whom judgment was given? 'I saw,' saith he, 'the souls of them that were beheaded for the witness of Jesus, and for the word of God,'—namely, in the primitive times, under the Roman empire,—'and which had not received the mark of the beast upon their foreheads, or in their hands,'—those which stood out unto the days of Antichrist, which argueth that this is to fall out after the times of Antichrist too,—'and they lived and reigned with Christ a thousand years. But the rest of the dead lived not again until the thousand years were finished. This is the first resurrection.' Now, it is said that the first resurrection is a spiritual resurrection of men's souls from the death of sin; such interpretations are put upon it. But consider with yourselves a little. First, it is the souls of men dead; that is plain, for he saith they were 'slain with the sword,' they were 'beheaded' for the witness of Jesus: and as their death is, so must their resurrection be; their death was certainly a bodily death, for they were beheaded, therefore their resurrection must be answerable to it. And, to mention no other arguments, they 'reigned with Christ a thousand years;' this is not the glory of heaven, for that is for ever, and so they had reigned from the first time they were slain, if that glory were meant; but they reign upon their rising; for he saith, 'the rest of the dead lived not again till the thousand years were finished.' Therefore the opposition implieth, that it is a living again, and a proper resurrection.

Now, where do these reign? It should seem on earth by this argument; because, why else is the devil bound up? He need not be bound up for their reigning in heaven; but as a preparation to this, the devil is bound up, so the text saith. This is one place out of which I could urge multitude of things, but I forbear.

Well, I know not how to answer another, and that is that I quoted in my last discourse, Rev. v. 10, where the saints expressly say in John's time, 'Thou hast made us unto our God kings and priests, and we shall reign'—not, *we do*, but *we shall reign*—'on earth.' And then go join with this 2 Pet. iii. 13: 'We, according to his promise, look for new heavens and a new earth, wherein dwelleth righteousness.' We,—we apostles, we saints that live now,—we look for it. How do I prove that? Because the use he makes of it is this: 'Wherefore, beloved, seeing you look for such things, be diligent to be found of him in peace, without spot, and blameless.' It could not be an argument then, in those times, to be holy and blameless, if they themselves personally were not to look for it; and he saith expressly, 'seeing you look for it.'

And what is that which, according to his promise, they look for? A new heaven, and a new earth. Not heaven itself properly taken; there is not a new heaven to be made; it is the old heaven, that was made from the foundation of the world, in which we shall for ever be with Christ after the day of judgment. However, how is there a new earth there? 'We look for a new heaven and a new earth, wherein dwelleth righteousness,' wherein righteousness reigneth and ruleth; because, as I said before, it will be a new world subjected unto Jesus Christ, when the new Jerusalem cometh down from heaven.

You will ask me now, What shall they do here in this new world?

I shall give you such considerations as shall take off the absurdity. First, I will tell you what they shall not do. They shall not eat and drink, nor marry, nor give in marriage. Our Saviour saith expressly, that the children of the resurrection do none of these things. Therefore to imagine a Turkish heaven here below, a Turkish paradise, is that which hath been the absurdity put upon that opinion; and which indeed made many of the fathers, after the first three hundred years, to fly out against it. There was an opinion then that Christ himself should again reign personally at Jerusalem a thousand years, that they should abound in all sensual pleasures, in marrying wives, eating and drinking, &c., and that the Jewish ceremonies should be then restored. And it was this opinion that the fathers confuted, and did so much fly out against; for otherwise the truth is that Austin himself saith, that if you will grant only spiritual delights to come from heaven for them, it is an opinion, saith he, that may be tolerated. And Tertullian saith the like in his third book against Marcian, which he wrote in his best time, before he turned Montanist; and he calleth it, 'a heavenly kingdom upon earth, in abundance of spiritual good things.'

I have told you what they do not; I will tell you what they do, and take off the absurdity of that likewise. He saith they shall be kings and priests, so Rev. v. 10. And chap. xx. 6, 'Blessed and holy is he that hath part in the first resurrection: on such the second death hath no power,'—they are out of the danger of it, both body and soul being raised and in a celestial estate,—'but they shall be priests of God and of Christ, and shall reign with him a thousand years.' To open this a little to you—

First, to be *kings*. You heard this in Heb. ii. 5, that he hath not put this world to come in subjection to the angels. The angels, now, are the thrones and principalities, and the kings and the great ones that rule this world that is now. But the truth is, he saith, they shall be kings then; he hath not put this new world in subjection unto the angels, but unto them. And for them to take the angels' office, to be as angels after this resurrection, is no absurdity.

They shall be *priests*. I shall take off that absurdity by this. Our Saviour Christ, when he took up his body here out of the grave, continued forty days upon earth; what did Christ Jesus all that while? He did perform the part of a priest and of a prophet, he did instruct them in the worship of God; so you read expressly, Acts i. The apostles, my brethren, had a brave teacher, Christ risen from the dead; he began this new world, and he remained forty days on earth before he ascended, on purpose. Now, think with yourselves, for the saints to be conformed unto Jesus Christ their Lord and King, to run through but the same state he doth. He ran through this world, he was poor and miserable; so are you. When he died, 'Into thy hands, Father, I commend my spirit;' whither his soul went, ours go. When he rose again, and took up his body, and remained forty days upon the earth, he instructed his disciples in the great things of the kingdom of God. If the saints do so, when they first take their bodies, here is but a conformity unto Christ. He then ascended; so shall they, and for ever be with the Lord.

My brethren, consider this further, for I shall mention all that doth alleviate it; the great objection lies in this, that the souls of men, that now are in heaven and see the face of God, should come down and do such a service as this, to reign on earth here below, in such a glorious church as I have told you; here lieth the absurdity. To take this off, consider this: that even this estate will be a better estate than what their souls now have. I will give you reason for it; for otherwise our Lord and Saviour Christ, when his body and soul was here also below after his resurrection, was not in a better estate than his soul was before his resurrection, which certainly it was. You will say, They are now in heaven. Yes, as the angels are; but as the angels come down here below, and yet always see the face of their Father,—so saith the gospel, Matt. xviii. 10, 'Their angels do always behold the face of my Father which is in heaven,'—so may these still be in heaven and behold the face of God. Stephen, you know, beheld the face of God, and the glory of God, and Christ standing on his right hand, though he was a mortal man, and here below.

In one word, let me say this: God hath eternity of time to reveal himself in, he doth advance his favourites by degrees; first glorifieth their souls apart, takes soul and body, when they are united they have a better condition than the glorifying of their souls simply. How many of these ways God hath to manifest himself by degrees; how many worlds to come he hath to do all, the more the better; for you will say, you are so happy in every one, that you know not how to be happier. He leadeth us by a kind of wonderment from one glory to another: as in masques you draw away one board, and a glorious sight appeareth; you draw away another, and another is presented to you: so doth God with his children, because he hath an eternity of time to make all these shows and representations to them, and in doing this he doth not lessen, but increase their happiness.

This is the greatest service that can be done, for it is the angels' work, they do it now. And let me add this: then will come to be fulfilled that which you pray for in the Lord's Prayer, 'Thy will be done on earth as it is in heaven.' At the day of judgment, during that time we are not so much doing God's will, as giving account of our ways, and of having performed it. If, therefore, this prayer be fully and exactly fulfilled, that the will of God shall be done on earth as completely as in heaven, it must be the time of the first resurrection; which Paul therefore, when he would express his desire of being perfect, saith he would 'attain to the resurrection of the dead;' that is, to be as holy as men shall be then.

My brethren, I have spoken these things unto you rather as that which hath a great show of truth in it, than as if I could answer all objections that might be made against it. But, as I said in the last discourse, if this hold not, as it is exceeding probable it will, yet there is *a fourth degree* of this world to come, which I am sure will hold, and that is this: during the day of judgment, strictly taken, after the general resurrection both of just and unjust, then, my brethren, to honour this new world, God will not only come down, but Jesus Christ himself will come down, and he will abide a long day here too; therefore it is no absurdity for saints to live on earth, even when Christ himself shall do so; neither will it diminish from his happiness at all, for he will come and bring all his glory with him.

The day of judgment will be a long day, my brethren; and let yourselves judge whether it will not or no. For do you think that the accounts of the world can be cast up in the twinkling of an eye? Doth not Solomon say expressly, that every work, whether it be good or evil, shall be brought to judgment? Eccles. xii. 14. And doth not the Apostle as expressly say, 1 Cor. iv. 5, that things shall be so brought to judgment, as every one shall be able to judge the secrets of all men's hearts? And do you think this will not take up time? Shall we ourselves take in the accounts of all men's hearts in an instant? No, my brethren, this will be a long day; wherein Jesus Christ will do that great service, a greater service than all his preaching, the examining of the accounts of all the world, and convincing of all mankind, and sending them speechless to hell, so as they shall have nothing to say, and so as we too shall be able to 'judge the world;' so the Apostle saith, 1 Cor. vi. 2.

Now here is this new world in its height and perfection. Here is Christ, and all his angels round about him; yet this world is not subject unto them. They begin it, they gather together those that have died during the 'thousand years,' from all quarters, and they execute the sentence that Christ hath pronounced, and the saints have assented unto, and they fling them all into hell. But the truth is, they do not sit as judges, they *stand*, —so the expression is used, Dan. vii. 10,—whereas the saints are said to 'sit upon twelve thrones;' and in 1 Cor. vi. 3, they are said to 'judge the angels.'

And here now is Adam's world in the perfection; that creature that hath groaned under all men's lusts shall be then fully restored to the 'glorious liberty of the sons of God.' During that time the world shall be new hung, when Christ her Lord shall come into it. And if the other will not hold; and thus far I am persuaded it will hold, that there is the world to come in to Christ, wherein all heathenism, superstition, error, and whatsoever else, shall be rooted out of the world, and the generality both of Jew and Gentile shall come in to Jesus Christ; and that is a glorious world, my brethren, without that of the day of judgment.

Here then is Christ's *world to come*,—I have given you an account of it as briefly as I can,—wherein he shall have all things subject unto him, for the Apostle expressly saith, that then, at the day of judgment, all things shall be under his feet, and never fully till then, for the last enemy that is to be destroyed is death, and then he shall give up the kingdom to God the Father. And what the world to come shall be after then, no man knoweth; only the Scripture saith, God shall be all in all, and Christ himself shall be subject unto him. So I have done with these words, 'this world, and the world to come.'

I come now to the 22d verse, which is the latter part of Christ's exaltation over all creatures; for that which followeth afterward is his exaltation in relation to his Church. The last part of it is this, *He hath put all things under his feet.*

Here are two things contained in this—

1. The lowness of the subjection of all things; they are 'under his feet.'

2. The universality; 'all.'

I shall not handle these two distinctly, for they will fall in promiscuously and miscellaneously one with another; therefore I shall handle them one with another.

First, For the *coherence* of these words with the former.

The Apostle, as he had set forth the exaltation of Jesus Christ, in respect of *personal excellency,* more eminently in the former verses, 'far above all principality and power,' &c.; so here he setteth forth his *dominion* more eminently, that all is 'under his feet.' If you ask what the personal excellencies of Christ are, they are such as are far above all principality, power, might, and dominion; he excelleth in glory, in majesty, in wisdom, in power, in holiness, all principalities and powers; I confess *dominion* is included too under it, but more eminently personal excellencies. If you ask what dominion he hath over all these, he telleth us plainly, all is under his feet.

There are these two parts of his exaltation, mentioned in that second of the Hebrews, which chapter is parallel with this. He saith there, ver. 9, he was 'crowned with glory and honour;' that which the Apostle here expresseth by setting him at God's right hand, that is there expressed by being 'crowned.' For there are these two ceremonies in the installation of kings; there is a crowning of them, and a setting them upon the throne. Now Jesus Christ had a crown, first, of glory, set upon his head; he had all personal excellencies poured out upon him. And then, secondly, he had a crown of honour set upon his head. He was crowned with glory and honour, saith the text; that is, he had dominion given him; for, as it followeth there, 'thou hast put all things under his feet.'

I do but observe this from it, and I will do it briefly: That the personal worth that is in Jesus Christ is the ground and foundation of his dominion over all. Why are all things so low as under his feet, but because his personal worth excelleth all principalities and powers and every name whatsoever? You shall find in Heb. i., where he speaks of sitting down at God's right hand, he first premiseth his personal worth. 'He is the image of the invisible God,' saith he, 'the express character of his person,' 'he by whom he made the worlds,' &c.

Is Christ's personal worth the foundation of his dominion over all things; because he is far above all things in his person, therefore are all things under his feet? My brethren, observe this from it, that though Jesus Christ was worthy of the kingdom of all the world, yet, as the Apostle telleth us, Heb. v., he took not this honour upon himself, but he was called to it. Which should teach us the greatest modesty in assuming any honour or dignity upon ourselves above others. No such example as Christ's to teach it. He did not assume a jot of power beyond his commission. He would not have had power over all, if *all* had not been in his commission. Kings should not go a jot beyond their commission; Christ himself did not, though his own worth is the foundation of his being king over the world.

And let me add this too, that God himself was not partial. He had a Son, whom he preferreth; yet if he had not had personal worth in him, as the foundation of it, he had never raised him up unto this. My brethren,

Christ is a better king than you could have chosen for yourselves. He is my king, saith God, Ps. ii., a king of my appointing. Aristotle saith, that nature makes kings, as nature makes servants; meaning those that are the most wise and the most excellent; they are kings by nature, so is Christ. In hell, the greatest devil, the strongest devil, the wisest devil, he is the prince of devils. So in heaven, Christ, that is far in his person above all principalities and powers, and deserveth it, his worth carrieth it, hath all under his feet.

It should therefore grieve none to be subject unto Jesus Christ. You are to be subject unto men that have power, to kings and those that are in authority. Wives are to be subject to their husbands, though they be froward, servants to their masters, &c. But our Lord and Saviour Jesus Christ, he is the holiest, the wisest, he is far above all principalities and powers; in all these, therefore, he deserveth to have all things under his feet. None will grudge to be subject to such a king as he is, if they knew what a king he were. Therefore, those that will not be subject unto him, how do they deserve to be destroyed! 'Those that will not have me to reign over them,' saith he, 'bring them hither, and slay them before my face.'—So much for the coherence.

I shall now open the phrase to you, *all things are under his feet*.

You may understand it either *locally*, in respect of place, under his feet; or *imperially*, in respect of power, they lie at his feet to dispose of as he pleaseth.

Now it is not true that all things shall be under the feet of Christ locally; for when Christ shall come to judgment into this world, the highest heavens will be above him, they will not be under his feet locally; therefore that cannot be so properly the meaning of it.

Yet let me add this to that, that even in respect of place he is advanced far above all angels and men. I know not how otherwise to understand that place, Eph. iv. 10. It is said there that he 'ascended far above all heavens;' it is spoken in respect of place. Therefore we argue against the Lutherans, who would have Christ to be in every place; we say he did ascend, unless we make his ascension imaginary; he must be in the heavens, as his proper place, where he is circumscribed. Now, he saith here, he ascended far above all heavens, not heaven only, but all heavens. He ascended up on high to the top of the heavens, to his throne, so eminent that all may see him, all angels and saints, they are all under his feet even in that respect; for in John xvii. he prayeth that they may see his glory, which, if he were not thus eminently set up above them all, how could they see him? Yet so as it should seem he is in the midst of them; for he is said to be the 'tree' in the midst of the 'paradise of God,' and the expression still runs thus, 'I will be in the midst of you;' yet so too as he is in heaven. It is not so above all heavens, as he is out of heaven, as some fondly and foolishly dream, for it is in the heavenly places; so the text saith. The mercy-seat, that typified out Christ's seat, was the highest thing in the Holy of Holiest; so certain is the throne of Christ; therefore there may be something in it, that even in that respect locally all is under his feet.

But, my brethren, the main thing is, that it is metaphorically taken to express his power. Christ's sitting at God's right hand is a metaphor, for God hath no right hand: so answerably, his having all things under his feet is a metaphor too, and both taken from the manner of the eastern monarchs. To be under his feet signifieth in general subjection to him; so Ps. viii., where the phrase is first used of Christ, ver. 6, 'Thou madest him to have dominion over the works of thy hands; thou hast put all things under his feet.' To have all things under his feet, is to have dominion over the works of his hands. And if that will not carry it, yet the Apostle's own interpretation in Heb. ii. will. He, to explain it, putteth in the word 'subjection:' 'Thou hast put all in subjection under his feet.' So that to be under his feet importeth in the general a subjection.

As it noteth out a subjection in the general, so to be under one's feet noteth out utmost subjection. You know that in nature it is so: to bow the head is a token of reverence, but to fall down upon the earth at one's feet is the lowest you can go, and it is to express the utmost subjection. And, indeed, this was the custom of those great monarchs of the East, and it was peculiar to imperial and monarchial power, to absolute monarchies, which they then had; which the western kings not professing to have, therefore they have not men fall down at their feet, though they have men kneel to them. But the manner of those eastern kings was to have their subjects fall down at their feet; and it is the manner of the Turks at this day.

It is an expression that setteth forth two things; to come to shew it more particularly; it expresseth—

1. The subjection of subjects.
2. A triumph over enemies.

First, it expresseth the subjection of subjects to their princes, according to the custom of the East. Take the kings of Egypt: Exod. xi. 8, saith Moses there to Pharaoh, 'All the people that are at thy feet;' read your margins and you have it so; it is all one as to say, all the people that are thy subjects. So it is said of Benhadad the king of Syria; look in your margins there too, 1 Kings xx. 10.

The manner was, and we have it upon good record, both out of Xenophon of Cyrus, lib. xviii., and of Herodotus, when they came to their kings, to throw themselves down, and to kiss the pavement where their feet stood. The phrase you have likewise in Isa. xlix. 23. And therefore now that worship that is due to God alone is expressed by falling at his feet, Rev. xix. 10. So that it noteth out, first, a subjection of subjects.

Secondly, it noteth out a triumph over enemies. For this I shall give you two instances in Scripture: the one is Joshua x. 22–24. There you shall read that when Joshua had overcome those five kings, saith he, 'Open the mouth of the cave, and bring out those five kings unto me out of the cave. And they did so, and brought forth those five kings unto him out of the cave. And it came to pass, when they brought out those kings unto Joshua, that Joshua called for all the men of Israel, and said unto the captains of the men of war, which went with him, Come near, put your feet upon the necks of these kings; and they came near, and put their feet upon the necks of them. And Joshua said unto them, Fear not, nor be dismayed, be strong and of a good courage: for thus shall the Lord do to all your enemies against whom you fight.' He did not use it as a right of barbarism and cruelty, but as that which was to hearten out those people and encourage them, to assure them that God would do so with the rest. And Joshua, you know, was Jesus' type, who was to tread upon all his enemies, and to make them his footstool.

And in the eastern empire of Greece, which lasted till within these two hundred years and upward, this custom was continued. Therefore we read of Michael Balbus, that he called for a rebel that had usurped the crown, and having him in his power he bade him lie down upon the pavement; and, as the historian saith, according to the custom of those kings, he set his feet upon his neck. It is true, it is used in Europe only by the Pope; it is,

feet. Here lies one of the reasons. But, my brethren, although the Church may be under his feet in way of subjection to her sovereign Lord, yet she may be his body likewise. For, as a queen hath a double relation to her husband; one as he is a king, and so she is subject; if she ask anything at his hands she kneeleth down as well as the meanest subject, she is at his feet presently: yet for all that, she is flesh of his flesh, she is his queen, she is his wife notwithstanding, and her being his wife hindereth not her being a subject. You have it in Ps. xlv. applied to the Church, 'At his right hand,' saith he, 'is the queen;' yet saith God to her, 'He is thy God; worship thou him. She is at his right hand, she is advanced as a queen; yet she is to know her distance, she is to be subject, for all that she sitteth together with him in the heavenly places; yet she must worship him, she must be at his feet.

If it be urged, that to shew the Church's dignity, she is said to be Christ's body, and therefore not at his feet, I say it followeth not; for as the one is put to shew forth her dignity, so the other is put to shew forth Christ's dignity. Her dignity is set forth by what she is advanced to, that she is his body; but her dignity must not impair his, she must know her distance, for all this she is under his feet. Even as Christ's satisfaction swalloweth not up free grace, so the dignity of the Church, sitting together with Christ, swalloweth not up that exaltation of Christ over her; she is under his feet notwithstanding.

Yea, my brethren, I may say, even as Abigail said unto David, 1 Sam. xxv. 41, when he sent to take her to him to wife: Tell him, saith she, I am his servant to wash his feet. So may the Church say. She is a queen indeed, and she is his body, but she is a servant, she is his subject, she is under his feet for all that.

Yea, it was necessary to express her subjection as well as her dignity; for whence is her dignity but from his free grace? Therefore, to exalt that free grace was her subjection to be intimated. She is laid thus low, she is under his feet; but then Christ takes her off the dust, setteth her at his own right hand, makes her his queen; this sets off the other, makes the grace of Christ the more glorious; therefore the Apostle, Eph. ii., when he saith, We are set together with Christ, addeth, 'by grace ye are saved;' for your place is under his feet, saith he, however you are called up to sit at his right hand.

So much for the answering that question. I had another, which I cannot now handle.

I will but make an observation or two, and so I will end.

Obs. 1.—The first is this: Are you all under his feet, my brethren? Then learn to worship him: 'He is the Lord thy God; worship thou him.' How is worship expressed? Fall down at his feet. In Rev. v., the elders are said to 'cast down their crowns,' and to 'fall at his feet;' and, Ps. xcix. 5, which is a psalm of the kingdom of Christ, 'Exalt him,' saith he, 'worship at his footstool.'

Not only the excellency of his person calleth for this, 'Let all the angels of God worship him;' but consider with thyself, it is necessary for thee. Thou must either be under his feet as an enemy, to be trodden upon, to be destroyed; or under his feet in way of subjection, to worship him, and to worship him purely too, according to his law; therefore look to it that you do what you do according to law. Choose now, either to be subject to him as a friend, to worship him according to his law, or to be destroyed, to be trodden under his feet as enemies.

Obs. 2.—A second observation is this: All things are under his feet. He is your sovereign; you are in the lowest subjection that may be. Is there ever a poor soul a suitor to him for grace? Wilt thou know how to obtain it? Acknowledge his sovereignty, lay thyself at his feet, acknowledge as a creature thou art subject to him, he may do with thee what he will. And as thou art a sinner, say, Thou mayest tread upon my neck, thou mayest crush me to pieces as an enemy; acknowledge that he hath not power only to crush thee, but provocation to do it. If you will but lay yourselves thus at his feet, give up your souls to him, he will pardon you. You must do it; he hath all your lives in his hand, he hath the keys of hell and of death; there is no way but to submit. It is the expression used, Lam. iii. 29, 'Put thy mouth in the dust;' what is the meaning of that? It is plainly this,—as the Scripture useth to express it,—lick the dust of his feet; for it is a metaphor, taken from what they used to do when they came before their great kings; they licked the dust of their feet, and spake submissly, as out of the earth: so they do to the Great Turk at this day. Do so to God: put thy mouth in the dust; thou art at his feet.

Obs. 3.—Thirdly, consider here, and admire the grace of Jesus Christ to his Church, sinners and enemies unto him: they are not only at his feet as creatures, but they are at his feet as enemies too; he could crush them and tread upon them if he would. Christ himself said he was a worm, and no man; God might have trod upon him and quashed him presently. To be sure we are so: Jesus Christ, with his brazen feet, might tread thee in the wine-press of the wrath of God; and thou art a poor worm, and canst make no resistance. Hath the Lord Jesus Christ taken thee up to be a member of him, to be part of his body? Consider what a grace this is, that that Church in the next words should be called *his body* which in the former is reckoned up among those that are under his feet; herein is the grace of Jesus Christ.

In that Heb. ii., where it is said all things are under his feet, and he himself is crowned with glory and honour, it followeth presently, 'He is not ashamed to call them brethren.' Oh, let us remember our original! Are we married to Jesus Christ? Remember whence thou art taken. As Hannah saith, 1 Sam. ii. 8, 'He raiseth up the poor out of the dust, he lifteth up the beggar from the dunghill, to set them among princes, and to make them inherit the throne of glory.' This Christ hath done for thee: thou wert in the dunghill, in hell; he hath raised thee up to be his body, to sit with him in the heavenly places.

I will give you the reason why Jesus Christ makes his wife and his spouse of those that are under his feet. It is the greatest reason in the world. What is the reason that kings will not marry so low,—they affect to marry kings' daughters,—but yet great, absolute monarchs will not do so. Go among the Turks and Persians, read the Book of Esther; they never affected to marry kings' daughters. Why? Because they would acknowledge none greater than themselves, therefore they would marry slaves, such as were under their feet: so Turks do at this day; it is to shew their greatness. It is all one to them to choose a king's daughter or a slave; for they acknowledge themselves so high that no king else could come up to them.

So it is with Jesus Christ: he is so high in dignity that no worth can commend any creature to him; therefore he takes those that are under his feet, poor sinners,—upon whom he can tread as upon those in hell, it is all one to do it,—and he can love them as heartily and as familiarly, make them his queen, set them at his own right hand. Therefore, be not discouraged, though you be laid never so low at his feet in the sense of your own vileness, for it is all one to Jesus Christ. The truth is, he hath none else to marry but those that are under his feet; he must have no wife, if he have not those that are perfect slaves: yea, if he will have the sons of men, he must have enemies upon whom he might tread, and trample under his feet.

So much for that third observation.

SERMON XXXV.

***And gave him** to be the head* (or, *a head*) *over all things to the **church**, which is his body, the fulness of him that filleth all in all.*—VER. 22, 23.

FOR the coherence, sum, and scope of these words, which is the only part that remaineth now to be handled, it is this: it containeth the most excellent part of Christ's supremacy, who is the King of kings; it treateth of the supremacy which he hath over the Church, and over all churches whatsoever that are his body. And yet—do but observe the condescending of Christ speaking by his Spirit, when he speaks of the height of his own dignity—he expresseth his own dignity with those terms of respect to his Church, as it is apparent he would shew forth withal her dignity also. As he would set out his own greatness, that he is a Head, so he would set forth her nearness to him, and her advancement with him. It is worth your observing, that he calleth him a 'head over all,' here is his dignity; but withal he addeth, to her, 'which is his body.' He is not a mere external Head to rule her, as a king is a head of his kingdom; but he is a Head to her as to a body, a natural body, a conjugal body, as a husband is to his wife, or as the head is to the natural body.

He had before expressed his dignity in other words: he saith, he hath all things under his feet; he had laid the Church itself as low as at his feet, as low as could be. Now, whereas he might have said he is a head over all the Church, he doth not say so; but he saith he is a 'head over all to the church;' *over all*, but to her. Still to express her dignity; if he be over all, it is for her, for her good, for her comfort.

He expresseth again his excellency in another phrase; he saith, 'he filleth all in all;' but withal still he expresseth it with terms of respect to her, he giveth her her due, and her utmost due; for all this, saith he, she is *his fulness.* He involveth the Church's dignity together with his own. All which, my brethren, put together and opened, there is nothing can afford greater comfort unto us.

I divide the words into these three general parts:—

Here is, first, *The dignity of Christ and his relation to his Church;* he is a 'head over all to his church,' and he 'filleth all in all.'

Here is, in the second place, likewise, *The Church's relation to Christ, and her dignity:* her relation, 'which is his body;' her dignity, she is his spouse.

And then, thirdly, here is *The founder of both*, both of the Church and of Christ too, as a Head; it is the gift of the Father. 'And hath given him,' saith he, or 'gave him to be a head to the church, which is his fulness, even of him that filleth all in all.' Even both these are founded upon the Father's gift. And do but observe that too, when he saith, he 'gave him to be a head to the church,' he doth express it so ambiguously, as the question is whether he meaneth more favour to Christ in giving him to be her Head, or more favour to the Church in giving him to be a Head to her.

The words will bear both in the Greek, καὶ αὐτὸν ἔδωκε κεφαλὴν ὑπὲρ πάντα τῇ ἐκκλησίᾳ. It may be translated as well, 'given him to the church to be her head,' making the greatness of the gift lie there, that it should be to her. Or it may lie, 'given him to be a head to the church,' making the greatness of the gift to be in giving him this privilege, this dignity. So that still he involveth Jesus Christ's dignity with his Church's; and let them for ever go together.

So you have the scope, and coherence, and sum of these words. I told you there were three parts of the text; and lest I should forget the founder, which is the last of the three, I will begin first with that, for indeed it will not come in so properly afterward, and it is the first thing in the text; 'and gave,' speaking of the Father.

Herein there are two things to be considered:—

The first is, that it was a gift to either. For God to give the Head, to give Christ to be the Head to the Church, was a gift to her; for God to give to Jesus Christ to be the Head of the Church, was a gift to him. The words do ambiguously refer to both. The greatness of the gift I shall shew, when I come to open those words, 'over all,' above all gifts; that is one part of the meaning.

But take it first thus. It was *a gift to the Church*, that God gave Jesus Christ to be her Head, and her to be his body. You will easily see that, for you heard in my last discourse she was 'under his feet;' therefore to advance her so far as to be his body, to be his queen, you must needs acknowledge this to be a great advancement, and a mere gift on her part. Do but think of Esther's advancement, read her story, from a slave to be a queen, and think what the advancement of the Church is, to be a body unto Christ, her Head.

Then, secondly, it is *a gift to Christ* to be a Head, and to have a Church to be his body. I will instance in both severally.

It was a gift, first, that God would give Jesus Christ a body, whereof he might be the Head. You read in Adam's story, who was Christ's type, that God brought the woman to him; you know Adam was the type of 'him that was to come,' Rom. v. 14, and that in marriage, as Eph. v. 32. As soon as he saw her, he knew her, knew God's meaning; saith he, 'This is bone of my bone, and flesh of my flesh.' He took her thankfully, as a gift from God; though afterwards, when he was fallen, he most impiously upbraided God with this gift. 'The woman,' saith he, 'whom thou gavest me,' Gen. iii. 12. I quote it only for this, that she was a *gift;* for even in these words Adam, when he was fallen, acknowledgeth her to be so. Now this is as true of the second Adam too, Eph. v. 23, 30, 32, compared. The Apostle speaks there of Adam and Eve, and he compareth Christ and his Church, and saith that was the mystery enfolded in Adam's marriage. Now you shall find this second Adam acknowledging this gift more thankfully than the first doth. What saith he, John xvii. 6? Speaking of his Church, saith he, 'Thine they were, and thou gavest them me;' and, Heb. ii. 13, 'Lo, here am I and the children that God hath given me.' He doth it more thankfully; but still it argueth that the Church was a gift to him.

As a gift to him, so for him to be a Head to the Church was a gift too. Ἔδωκε κεφαλὴν, he gave him to be the Head,—so Beza reads it, and so you see our translation renders it,—that is, appointed him to be the Head, set him in the place of a Head, *constituit*, as Gen. iv. 1; the word *give*, for so it is in the original, נָתַן. It is said that Pharaoh set Joseph over all the land of Egypt; and the Septuagint saith, he appointed him, made him a head over all the land of Egypt. Now this translation our translators have followed: 'he made him to be the Head;' it might be read as well, 'made him to be a Head;' but they put the gift upon Christ, it was a gift to him to be made a Head, which certainly is the more direct scope of the place.

Now let me only add this concerning it. It was as a great gift to Jesus Christ to give him a body, so to advance him to that great dignity to be their Head. Although for his own excellency none else was fit for it, it was his due; yet still, as I have often said, so it is carried, because he is less than the Father, as he is God-man. That which is his due is a gift; therefore the school-men do exceeding well in this. They say there was a threefold grace bestowed upon Christ.

First, There was the grace of union, that the manhood should be united to the Godhead; it was a great grace that, and the foundation of all the rest.

Secondly, That this manhood should be filled with all personal graces, which they call *habitual grace*, as they call the other *gratia unionis;* that that should be full of grace and truth, as it is in John i. 14. It is a great grace too.

But then, say they, thirdly, There is *gratia capitis;* there is this grace bestowed over and above all these, that he should be a Head, that he should have a Church, to whom he might communicate all his grace; that as the Apostle speaks of himself, Rom. i. 5, 'By whom we have received grace and apostleship,' that is, the grace of apostleship: so Jesus Christ, he received the grace of headship. It is therefore a gift.

I will not stand to open this further; I will come to some observations.

Obs. 1.—The first observation is this: That Christ, you see, reckoneth it a new gift and grace, besides his having personal communion with God, to be united to him, to have a body, whom he might fill, whom he might communicate unto. It is a new grace to be a Head, and to have a body. 'He gave him to be the head to his church, which is his body.'

My brethren, do but think this good thought from hence. Is it a gift, is it a grace, that God should make Christ a Head, as you see it is? Then never doubt of his willingness to communicate anything to you; for it is a grace to be put into the office, to be a Head to fill you. It is given him, you see, given him as a matter of grace, that he should be a Head to his Church, and fill all in all. As it is the office of the liver to communicate blood to the whole body, it were unnatural for it to keep it within itself: so for the head also not to diffuse spirits into the whole. There is no consideration can more comfort you than this. How willing then must our Lord and Saviour Jesus Christ needs be to communicate to his Church; it is a grace that he should do it, it is an honour that he should do it; it is the greatest advancement, the highest of all the rest that his Father hath bestowed upon him. 'My goodness,' saith he, 'extendeth not to thee,' but my comfort is, it extendeth to my saints; it is Christ's speech, Ps. xvi. 2.

Do but consider, to make a little use of it to yourselves further, wherein lieth the excellency of grace? It lieth in communicating to others; so Christ reckoneth it, and so should we. Hast thou grace in thy own heart, as Christ hath habitual grace in his? There is one mercy. Doth God make thee an instrument to do good to others? There is another mercy. It is the gift given to Christ, to be a head to communicate to members. See what the Apostle saith, 1 Cor. xii. 7, 'The manifestation of the Spirit is given to every man to profit withal.' All the manifestations of the Spirit, whereby a man profiteth another, it is a gift, it is given to him; the text plainly holdeth forth that.—That is the first observation.

Obs. 2.—In the second place, Is it a gift that Jesus Christ himself should be the Head of the Church? It is given to him; although none else is fit for it but he, and though it be his due, yet it must be given. Then do but make this consequence from it: it is certain an office or dignity, in the Church, or over the Church of God, must hold of the Head Christ; it must be given too, it must be appointed too—that is all one: *constituit*, he did make him, constitute him, or give him. If the great office of all the rest is by way of gift appointed, then certainly all the rest, they must all hold *in capite*, hold of the Head Christ. The Pharisees knew this well enough; you shall see how they put Jesus Christ to it, for when any come to usurp authority over you, as you are a Church, ask the same question that the Pharisees did Christ. They put him to it that was the Head of the Church. Matt. xxi. 23, 'When he was come into the temple, the chief priests and the elders of the people came unto him as he was teaching, and said, By what authority doest thou these things? and who gave thee that authority?' The principle they knew well enough. No man was to exercise any authority over the Church, but it was to be given him. Who hath given thee this authority? say they to the Head.

What answer doth Christ give them? He knew it was a folly to tell them, for it would not satisfy them. But I will ask you another question, saith he; and that also makes for what I say. 'The baptism of John, whence was it? from heaven'—that is, by divine institution—'or of men?' Here was a shrewd question. 'And they said, We cannot tell;' for they were in a doubt; you may read what their reasonings were. I only quote it for this, that Jesus Christ himself, that was made the Head of the Church, was asked by what authority he did it. Therefore you may very well ask any other men, if they take any authority over the Church, Will you shew your office, that it is warranted in the word? John could not baptize, you see, but he must have it from heaven. This is our Saviour Christ's scope and meaning.

Now, my brethren, that you may see the ground of the equity of this, you must know, that all officers of a Church are in a further distance from the Church, to have any authority over it, than Jesus Christ is over the whole Church. Now, if that Jesus Christ doth not take upon him to be a Head, who deserveth it, but it is given him, certainly no man is to take any office over the Church of God, but he must have a warrant for it; the thing will necessarily follow. All the kings and princes in Christendom, and all the parliaments in the world, cannot set up an office over the Church which Christ hath not set up. It is God, saith he, that hath set in the Church some apostles, and some prophets, and some teachers, 1 Cor. xii. 28. Or, if you will speak in the language of the text, 'given them,'—that is, appointed them, so the phrase in Eph. iv.

You that cannot add a hair to your head, can you think you can add a member to the Church of Christ, which shall have an office, that he never appointed? Take the natural body; can any man invent, all men, take all their wits together, a member that is not natural to the body, that God hath not already made? For in his book all our members are written. Can you make a different member from the hand or the eye, that the body hath not, that you can say will be useful to the body? Go to the Church; all the men in the world cannot find out by their wisdom and appointment an officer that shall rule in the Church, that doth not depend merely upon God's command; you must have all these members written in his book. The head is written, you see; it is given to him; certainly then all the members must.

This kingdom is pulling down, it is setting up a power over churches; what else makes all the commotions and stirs that are among us? All that I will say is this. Have a warrant for what you do, that it may be said, 'By what authority do ye these things?'. My meaning is this: by what authority do these appointments exercise jurisdiction over the Church of God? If Christ himself have it by gift, certainly they must. All our tenor holdeth *in capite*, that I may speak in law; holdeth of him that is Head of the Church. I do not say that if there be officers in the Church which God hath not appointed, that presently they deny Christ to be the Head, and that they do not hold the Head itself. Far be it from us to say so; that is the expression in Col. ii. 19. Speaking of idolaters, he saith they do not hold the Head Christ; but we may say that those officers do not hold of the Head, as it is expressed, Eph. iv. 15, 16. In which two places you may see the different phrases.

So much now for that first thing, he had it given to him to be the Head. He had his body given to him, and he had his headship given to him too.

Now I come to the dignity itself; it is *headship*. 'He gave him to be a head over all to the church.' There are three things to be explained in this.

First, *What is intended by Church.*

Secondly, *What being a Head to the Church importeth.*

Thirdly, *To what purpose 'over all' cometh in.* It is put, you see, between his being a 'head,' and 'to the church.' 'He is a head,' saith he, 'over all to the church.'

I will begin with the first, *What is intended by the Church.* Therein I shall only open this distinction to you of the differing acceptation of the word *church*. In general you must know this, that the word church hath a relation to an assembly of men uniting in one; that is properly a church, apply it to what you will, whether to a church of saints, or a church of men, a civil assembly of men; it is applied to both in Scripture.

Now, it being taken here of *saints*, that are members of Christ, it hath this double acceptation in Scripture; I shall mention no other: if any man can find any other, I would see it.

It is taken, first, for the general company and assembly of all saints, united together by several bonds to Christ their Head, or united by one band. If you speak of the church of men, united they are by a common band unto Jesus Christ their Head. This we call the Catholic Church, which you have in the Creed. It is called in this epistle, chap. iii. 15, the whole family of all that are named in heaven and earth, which are united by one common bond. In chap. iv. he saith, there is one body, and one Spirit, and one Lord; it is all one with what is here in the text: he is a Head to his church, which is his body.

And, my brethren, that this general assembly of all saints is the church universal; to give you a place for that, it is Heb. xii. 23, 'Ye are come to the general assembly and church of the first-born, which are written in heaven.' The general assembly of saints, this is here in heaven; take it in earth, take it wherever saints are,—they are either in heaven or in earth,—this 'general assembly' is the church universal. That is the first acceptation of the word.

But, secondly, we find in the New Testament particular assemblies and companies of saints, and that on earth, to be dignified with the name of churches, and to be dignified with the name of *bodies to Christ;* not one body, but if they be several churches they are distinct bodies to Christ. We read, therefore, of the churches of Galatia, chap. i. 2; of the churches of

Judea elsewhere; of the churches of Asia, Rev. i.–iii.; of all the churches of the Gentiles, Rom. i. 5. Now these I call, as divines do, particular churches in a distinction from the general church of all saints. I will give you my warrant for it, for that very phrase of a particular church. It is 1 Cor. xii. 27, 'Ye are,' saith he, speaking to the church of Corinth, 'the body of Christ, and every one of you members of Christ in particular.' That same phrase, καὶ μέλη ἐκ μέρους, it is, you are a part, you are in particular; our translation rendereth it well, it is the most genuine reading of the words. The meaning is this: as every one of you are members of Christ in particular, so go, take you altogether, as you are the church of Corinth, you are a body of Christ in particular too. Here you see is a particular church mentioned in distinction from the general assembly whereof you heard out of Heb. xii.

You must know this,—for the scope of this place in 1 Cor. xii.,—the Apostle had shewn that the church of Christ is a body unto Christ, he had discoursed under that similitude throughout the whole chapter in all the verses before. Read the whole chapter from the very 1st verse to the 27th, and you shall find that he compareth the church of Christ to a body, and Christ to the head; but he had so discoursed as he had meant the universal church all the way in all the former or the chief part of the chapter. Now, because they might say, How doth all this discourse of Christ and his body, when you mean the church universal, concern us? And how doth your similitude hold of us? It holdeth indeed of the church in general, but doth it hold of us? Yes, saith he, 'You are the body of Christ, and members in particular;' and, therefore, all that I have said of the church universal under the similitude of a body holdeth good of you, of your church in particular, every particular church being the model, and bearing in its proportion the resemblance of the universal.

And he doth it to prevent all disorder, and schism, and rent, which was among that church, and he useth and enforceth that similitude of a body. There is the same reason of a particular body, that Christ is their head, and of the whole body, as there is the same reason of a drop of water and the whole ocean; they are *totum homogeneum.* A church, a particular church, the church of Corinth is the body of Christ in particular, as well as the whole church is a body to him in the general. This is the scope of that place. Therefore, saith he, you may apply all that I have said of the body of Christ in general to your own; you are the body of Christ and members in particular, though you are not the whole body of Christ—that is, the church universal.

Now, you see that in respect of the universal church, a particular church of Corinth is said to be a body to Christ. I will give you a place that saith it is his whole body; as it is a part in respect of the church universal, so it is within itself an entire whole body. The place is 1 Cor. xiv. 23, 'If therefore the whole church be come together into some place;' mark it, the place is express. As this church of Corinth was but a part of the universal church, yet within itself—as he saith 1 Cor. v. 12, 'Do not ye judge them that are within?'—it was a whole church. 'If the whole church be come together in one place;' the church of Corinth was not the whole church of Jesus Christ in heaven and in earth, neither can the whole church of God (take it so) meet together in one place; yet he calleth it, you see, a whole church: 'if the whole church come together into some place,' to that end to edify one another, as the scope of the place is. This church of Corinth, therefore, was as truly a body to Jesus Christ, and a whole body to him, as the church universal was the whole body, and had all the privileges of the body.

As for example, to exemplify it unto you. In your city you have many several companies, as mercers, &c. All these companies are several bodies, yet they are all parts of the city; they are companies in particular if you compare them to the whole, yet they are entire and distinct companies amongst themselves; so is it here of particular churches.

And, my brethren, that you may see what the limits of this whole church of Corinth were, what the bounds, the *terriers* of this whole church were; it is of no more than could meet together in some place. 'If the whole church,' saith he, 'be come together into some place.' Some say that the meaning of this ἐπὶ τὸ αὐτὸ is only this, that they came together to one purpose in unity. But it is clear, by comparing other scriptures, that it is a distinct thing from meeting in unity; it is meeting in one place, as Acts ii. 1, 'They were all with one accord'—there is their unity—'in one place.' Here are the *terriers* of this church.

There is a place in 1 Cor. xi. 20, 'When you come together in one place,' ἐπὶ τὸ αὐτὸ, saith he. I will tell you how they answer this. Say they, there might be many churches in Corinth, and yet it may be truly said, 'When you come together into one place;' as if you should speak to all the churches in London, 'When you come together into one place,' taking it in a distributive sense. But come to this place, 1 Cor. xiv. 23, 'If the whole church be come together into some place;' that cannot be in parts, it is a contradiction to say that the whole church should meet together in one place and yet meet in several congregations, for if the whole meet, and meet together, they do not meet in parts certainly.

Now, my brethren, this is a particular church; and let me add this, you see here is but one church at Corinth, and there was another church not far off from Corinth, not two miles, that was a distinct church too, a whole body to Christ, as Corinth here was. Rom. xvi. 1, 'I commend unto you Phebe our sister, which is a servant of the church which is at Cenchrea.' Where, do you think, stood this same Cenchrea? It was situated by the water; as near as Ratcliff is to London, so near it was to Corinth, as Strabo in his 18th book sheweth. These were two distinct particular churches. That church of Corinth was a whole church, as many as met in one place. That church of Cenchrea was a whole church too, though it was so near it; for Cenchrea was to Corinth as Leith is to Edinburgh in Scotland, a haven town.

I will give you another instance of a particular church that met only in one place for their public ordinances, and it is the greatest instance of the biggest church that ever was in the world, for it was the first church. I do it to explain to you the difference of a universal church and a particular church, and to shew you what the bounds of it is. My brethren, the church of Jerusalem—of which you shall read from the second chapter of the Acts to the eighth—may for the bigness of it and number seem a monster, yet in one place still; and it certainly being the first church that ever was under the New Testament,—it consisting of some of all the tribes, as appeareth, Acts ii. 5, 9–11, &c., they were men of Israel out of all nations,—it was to be the mother church, and so the epitome of the Catholic Church. It had all the apostles as ministers of it in it; therefore it was *maximum quod sic*, as we say in philosophy; we say of the natural body, there is a stature, a bigness, which the body may be stretched to, beyond which it cannot go; so, certainly, that was a church that was stretched to the utmost wideness that the sides of a church could be stretched to. There was the greatest reason in the world for it: it was the first church, to be the mother church, from thence to go out into the whole world; they had all the apostles to be their ministers, and it was the epitome of the Catholic Church: therefore it was stretched, I say, to the utmost wideness that a particular church could be stretched to; yet the Holy Ghost doth carefully put in this, and distinctly and often, that however their number seem to be great, yet they met in one place; he expresseth it so from the first to the last. Do but walk the Scripture around with me and you shall see it.

In the beginning of that church their number was but one hundred and twenty; so Acts i. 15. They were in one place, ver. 13. 'They went up into an upper room, and they abode there,' or continued there, 'with one accord;' so he saith, ver. 14. They were in one place and with one accord, for these are still things distinct.

Go on to Acts ii. 1: 'They were all with one accord in one place.' What their houses and their places were we know not, the Holy Ghost doth not record it, but certain it was so big as he saith, ver. 6, 'It was noised abroad, and the multitude came together;' namely, where the apostles were. And the place was so big that, ver. 14, Peter standing up lifted up his voice to speak to them all, that they might all hear, and there was no less than about three thousand converted at that sermon and added to that church, ver. 41; and many thousands else did surely come, and when they were increased to this number of three thousand, yet still in one place; for, ver. 44, 'all that believed were together;' it is the same word in the Greek that is translated elsewhere 'in one place.'

Well, chap. iv., there is this number of three thousand increased to five thousand, so ver. 4; yet still in one place, the Holy Ghost diligently noteth out this. He telleth the story there how that Peter and John were apprehended by the priests and by the rulers and elders, and then at ver. 23, he saith, that 'being let go, they went to their own company,' where they 'prayed together with one accord;' and, ver. 31, he saith, 'when they had prayed, the place was shaken where they assembled together, and they were all filled with the Holy Ghost.' Here still this church is in one place.

Here is a mighty church you see now; as full, one would think, as the seats could hold. Read chap. v. 11, 12, and you shall see how diligent the Holy Ghost is to note this plainly that they were in one place. Saith he, 'Fear came upon all the church,' &c., 'and they were all together in Solomon's porch;' here is still this great church in one place.

Well, let them be multiplied to what they will, for we know not what they were multiplied unto, but this is the upshot of the story: Acts vi. 1, 'When the number of the disciples was multiplied;' make them as many as you will, yet it is said, 'the twelve called the multitude of the disciples unto them;' they called them not in parts, but the whole together. How prove you that? Plainly, ver. 5, 'The saying pleased the whole multitude.' Here was the whole multitude gathered in one place; you see how diligent the Holy Ghost is in this great church to put in still that they were in one place. And, my brethren, let what exceptions be made that can be, I will believe the Holy Ghost. Let men say, How could possibly so many be in one place, what one place could contain such a multitude? I could send you to Charenton in France, where you may see many thousands come together at once. I could send you to the Books of Esther and Nehemiah, where all Israel met together; but certain it is that here they all met together in one place, ἐπὶ τὸ αὐτὸ.

And let me add this too, that the members of this church were fleeting, they did not dwell constantly at Jerusalem. For the great objection is, they say that it was not a church consisting of fluid members, but of men that constantly dwelt there, and this objection they have from Acts ii. 5, 'There were dwelling at Jerusalem devout men out of every nation,' whereof three thousand were converted. My brethren, this hinders not. Mr Mead, in his *Diatribe*,—which I refer all readers to, he is far enough off from this notion that I draw it to,—in his last discourse but one upon this very place, saith that by dwellers at Jerusalem is not meant men that had a fixed habitation there; but he saith the word κατοικοῦντες will signify men that sojourned, that were there for a while, and he bringeth two instances out of the Septuagint for it in Genesis. And he giveth this reason, which to me seems to be unanswerable, that they did not dwell at Jerusalem fixedly, for, ver. 9, it is said that they 'heard in their own tongue wherein they were born, Parthians, and Medes, and Elamites,' &c. Now, how could they be both dwellers at Jerusalem and dwellers in all these countries too, if they had not been sojourners there for a time? The truth is, it was a land-flood, it was a fluid church, occasioned by their coming up to Jerusalem at the feast. I give this instance for this purpose, that the greatest church in the world, the first that ever was, was but one church, a church that could meet in one place; the Holy Ghost, you see, is diligent to express it, and I have shewed you how it might be.

You see, therefore, there are two sorts of churches. There is, first, the church universal, which is the whole body of Christ upon earth; and there is a church in particular, as you heard of the church of Corinth, and you have heard it exemplified by the church at Jerusalem.

I will in a word give you the reason why that, beside the church universal, God hath instituted a particular church as a body too. It is in a word this, because the whole church universal cannot meet together for ordinances. You cannot call all the saints upon earth to hear and to pray together; yet that God may have a constant worship upheld in the world, and in a constant way, and known where to be had, and by whom, he hath appointed his people to meet in several bodies; and, saith he, I will account all these several bodies to be several churches to me, and I will be a Head to them. As for instance, the king is king of the whole kingdom, but withal hath granted charters to this corporation, and to that corporation, and to the other corporation; he is king of all, and they are so many several bodies unto him.

Now, I having explained to you the difference between a particular church and a universal church,—for that they that meet in one place together are a particular church no man denies,—you will ask me, which of these two are meant here? for I have brought this distinction but to explain the text.

I answer, that here the church universal is meant in a primary manner, the whole church both in heaven and in earth, whereof Jesus Christ is the Head. It is plain that the church universal is here primarily meant; it needeth no proof, for he speaks of that church that is his fulness; now it is only the universal church, when they shall be all put together, that makes up the fulness of Christ. Take all churches in all ages, when they meet together, as they shall do one day; take the general assembly of saints and angels, they only are *his fulness*. And that he speaks here of the universal church, the phrase implieth it, 'he filleth all in all;' that is, the universal church.

But yet, secondly, so that all particular churches, that are bodies to Christ and churches too, are not excluded, but so far as they bear relation unto Christ as a body, so far he is their Head and filleth them all. For if they have this honour to be churches and a body to Christ in particular, then assuredly Jesus Christ is their Head and filleth them as well as he doth the whole church, even as a king is as well a head of several corporations as he is of the whole kingdom. And for this I will give you Scripture : Eph. iv. 10, he telleth us there that Jesus Christ is ascended up on high, that he may fill all things ; here is the same phrase that is used in the text, and he calleth him a Head afterward, ver. 15. To fill all. Who? Not only the universal church, but all the officers and members of the particular church. How prove you that? Saith he, ver. 11, he gave some prophets, some evangelists, and some pastors and teachers; which you all know are the officers of particular churches. So that by 'filling all in all,' he doth not only mean filling the universal church, but a particular church with all the officers of it, till it come to that proportion of stature that he hath appointed it to.—So much for the explication of this, what is meant by *church*, and whether both be meant or no.

Now, my brethren, how far the word *church*, set aside the universal church, may reach,—whether or no it may not reach beyond a particular congregation that do meet together in one place,—is the great question of these times. And I know that some have expected that I should speak to this, because, and merely because, the word *church* is here in the text. As, that I may state the question to you, for I shall do no more, whether, yea or no, besides a particular congregation that meet together in one place,—which you see is reckoned a church and the whole church,—many congregations, many churches united in one, may not be called one particular church. When I say many churches, the meaning is this : many churches, though they do not meet together in one place for ordinances of worship, of prayer and sacraments, and hearing the word, yet are but one in respect of discipline and goverment; whether or no these are not to be reckoned one church merely for discipline sake, excommunication, and the censures of the church. Here is the question. As, for example, whether many churches under one diocesan bishop, in order to being governed by him, though all the churches in that shire cannot meet together to pray and receive the sacraments, &c., yet whether in respect of discipline and government they might not be united in one under him as their governor.

Or, secondly, whether, yea or no, many churches that do not, nor cannot meet together to pray or to hear in common, or to receive the sacrament in common, yet being to be subject to all the elders and ministers within such a circuit, whether they may not be said to be one in that respect, as being under those elders and ministers; which is a Presbyterian church. Whether doth the Scripture allow this, yea or no?

Or, whether that only a particular congregation—taking in both the elders and ministers and the congregation itself together, that enjoy both worship and discipline together—is said to be a particular church, and none else. This is the great controversy of the times, and this you expect, it may be, that I should answer.

If you will take the answer of my judgment, you know that already. If you will take an answer out of other scriptures, I have no ground to run out into it from this text. For all that this text saith is but this, that he is the Head of his church, which is his body. He doth not determine whether a diocesan church be his body, or whether a Presbyterian church be his body, or only a particular congregation. Only, my brethren, to determine this I will but give you this one rule out of the text, and that is this : that nothing is or can be reckoned the Church of Christ but what may be called a distinct body to Christ. Now then, take many congregations united together in one under a diocesan bishop, you must make that one man the church and a body to Christ. Take likewise many congregations united in one under many ministers, you must make these ministers met together the body of Christ. Now then, the rule I shall give you will be fair and easy. In Matt. xviii. 17, there our Saviour Christ doth first let fall the institution of a particular church; that is clear of all sides. And I speak to the church in hand, for it is a church not only for prayer and the sacraments, but for discipline, for he speaks of one that is to be cast out. 'If any man offend,' saith he, 'go tell the church.' Now by church here he cannot mean the universal church, that is plain. Why? Because you cannot call all the men in the world together that are saints to tell them; you cannot call men and angels together, that is without question. What then is meant by church, for he speaks of a new institution under the New Testament? My brethren, what is meant by church in that Matt. xviii. you must find in the apostles' writings, for Christ left it to them to interpret; you must go and find in the Epistles of Paul, and in the Acts of the Apostles, for they interpreted Christ and his meaning.

Now then, read all over the Acts of the Apostles, read over all the Epistles; if you can find one man called a church and a body to Christ, if you can find the elders of several churches met together called a church, and may be called a body of Christ,—for that is still necessary to a church, to be a body to Christ, 'the church, which is his body,'—if you can find this, then embrace and submit to that as a church; for it is that which Jesus Christ intended, it is an ordinance which you may warrantably be subject to, and apply all those places to: obey your elders, &c. Apply it thus; they are the church, they are our elders.

This rule, my brethren, to begin with the first institution of a church under the New Testament, and to take the interpretation of it afterward, is the fairest rule that can be given, and it is fair upon two grounds. For when Jesus Christ mentioneth a church where he would have men go for discipline, for excommunication, certainly he doth not speak in obscurity,—that is, that it should not be interpreted by the examples of the New Testament, namely of the apostles that followed him,—for there was no church extant under the New Testament in Christ's time while he lived, therefore it was left to be interpreted by what was called church afterward.

Now, look what was familiarly called a church by the apostles, look into the Acts, and from thence to the end of the Revelation,—that which, I say, is usually called a church, and is a particular church, a body to Christ, certainly that is the church Christ meaneth; otherwise we were still to seek what church Christ sendeth us unto. If we cannot find that those which should exercise discipline over us are called a church somewhere or other in the Acts of the Apostles, or in some of the Epistles, how can our consciences be satisfied? Here we have a church mentioned; Go, tell the church, saith he; the consciences of men, therefore, must have it expressly determined by the apostles what church we must rest in. Now go all over, I say, and see to what thing they give most familiarly that name.

And the fairness of this rule appeareth likewise in this, that certainly that must have the name of a church which carrieth the authority of a church; will you call any one a king that hath not the authority of a king? They that have the authority of a church must have the name of a church, especially when Jesus Christ will first institute and give a name to it. Now, look and see to what the name of a particular church is given, and let that be the decider of this great controversy. That is all I will say of that point. I have avoided discoursing upon it, because it is not natural to the text; only it was necessary to give you this distinction of this word church for the comfort of all churches particular, that Jesus Christ is their Head as well as he is of the church universal, that they may look at Christ to fill them,—and he is their head to fill them, and all the members and officers of them,—as well as he filleth the universal church.

I will add but two cautions, to inform you concerning two divisions; the one from the universal church, and the other from particular churches. It is proper to the thing in hand, 'church,' 'the church, which is his body;' and there is no schism to be in the body, no schism from the universal church, no schism from particular churches that are truly churches of Christ. I will tell you of two great divisions from either. You have heard of two sorts spoken of, the one of old, the other of latter years; the one the Donatists of old, the other the Brownists of late. You call the Brownists the new Donatists, and the Donatists the old Brownists. I will explain that which is the worst in either opinion, and you shall see it is proper to the thing in hand.

First, for the Donatists that were in Austin's time. I have examined diligently the writings of Austin; among them I find the highest venom of their opinions to lie in this, and it is high enough,—if we may know men by the writings of their adversaries against them, for there is none of their own writings extant,—the truth is, they denied the church universal, they denied that the church was anywhere but in that part of Africa where they were, and this inflamed that holy man Austin against them. They might have put out of their creed, 'I believe the Church Catholic,' and put in 'I believe a little part of the world to be the Church.' Here you see a schism hath been from the church universal.

Now, go take the Brownists; they never deny the church universal, as the Donatists do; they have always affirmed that there is a church universal in all places, yea, and in England the most glorious church of saints of any in the world. But yet herein hath lain their error; they have sinned against particular churches, as they of old did against the universal church. And against these I, for my part, and many of my brethren, profess that they are in an error; and it is evident by Rev. xv., that, from the first time of the separation from Popery, there hath been a temple built to God, churches to God, in all the Reformed Churches.

I come to the next thing, and that is, *The Head of the Church.* How great a dignity this is to Christ, and benefit to the Church, I shall shew when I handle those words, 'over all.' I must speak to this, *he is a Head to the Church.*

It is a similitude, as all that are made of Christ have the greatest reality in them. A head in Scripture is to be taken in three several senses. There is, first, a *political head,* a ruling head, as a king is said to be the head of his loyal subjects; as I remember there is a place in one of the Books of the Kings which makes the kings of Israel heads of the people. And in this sense is God said to be a head to Christ, 1 Cor. xi. 3.

Secondly, there is a *conjugal head,* as the husband is the head of the wife, in the same 1 Cor. xi. 3.

Thirdly, there is a *natural head,* which I need not quote Scripture for; that is, the head of the natural body, as a man's head is of the members of his body.

In all these senses is our Lord and Saviour Jesus Christ head of the church in a peculiar manner. He is, first, a head of the church as a king is head of his loyal subjects; for he is not so much a head to rebels, he treads them under his feet, but he is a head to his loyal subjects. Now he is in a peculiar manner a king to the church. Ps. xliv. 4, 'Thou art my king,' saith the church, my king in a more especial manner. He is so a king to the church as he is not to all the world besides. A head in that sense. And in this large sense, take a head for a king, and Jesus Christ is a head to the angels too, as Col. ii. 10. It is said there he is the head of all principalities and powers; that is, he is their king. Of this headship that Christ hath over the angels, I shewed when I opened the 10th verse, where all in heaven and in earth are said to be gathered together in one, as in a head, to Jesus Christ.

Secondly, there is a conjugal head; so the husband is said to be the head of the wife, and that is nearer than of kings to their subjects, nay, though they be loyal subjects; you find this in Eph. v. 23. The headship of Christ to his church is nearer than that of a king to his loyal subjects; it is the headship of a husband to a wife; even as the relation of a king to his queen is nearer than to all his subjects: he is a head to them, but he is in a nearer manner a head to his queen. So is it here.

Thirdly, there is a natural head; that as in nature the head is the head of the body, so is Jesus Christ a head to his members and to his churches; they are all as members of that one body, and therefore he saith plainly in 1 Cor. xii. 12, that as the body is one and hath many members, so also is Christ. And this is meant here, for it follows, 'which is his body.'

Now, my brethren, if you will take it in this latter sense of a similitude taken from a natural head, so our Lord and Saviour Jesus Christ is a head only to the church of men who are of the same nature with him, so he is not to angels; neither is it anywhere said that angels are the spouse of Christ, neither is it anywhere said that they are the members of Christ. He is neither a conjugal head to them, neither is he a natural head to them, but he is a head to them as a king is to his loyal subjects; he is the head of all principalities and powers.

Yet so, let me add this, to open this similitude, when we say that Jesus Christ is a head to his church, which is a similitude drawn from the natural head, the meaning is not but that in reality Jesus Christ hath a greater nearness to his church than the head hath to the natural body. Though it be but a similitude, yet it importeth a greater reality, a greater nearness. Why? Because that all the similitudes that are drawn from things here below and applied to Christ do hold more really of Christ than of the things whence the similitude is drawn. Is he called a vine? He is the true vine, the other is but a false vine in comparison. Is he called a head, and the church his body? There is more reality and nearness betwixt the church and him than between the natural head and the body; that other is but a shadow of this. Only he is not a natural head, though the similitude be drawn thence; but he is a mystical, a spiritual head.

I cannot now enter into all the particulars for which Jesus Christ is called a head. I will mention only one. It is proper to a head of a body to be but one, natural reason will tell you so much; for the similitude is drawn here from the natural body; 'the church,' saith he, 'which is his body.' If there were many heads to a body, it would be a monster.

Do but look upon Popery a little; what doth it? It clappeth another head upon the universal church, the Pope; makes him a head of the church. It is the greatest derogation from our Lord and Saviour Jesus Christ that can be, to make or name any other head of the church but himself. Magistrates are heads in the church; but to make any man a head of the church is the greatest derogation to Christ that may be. That he that hath 'all under his feet,' so it is before; God hath given him over all to be a head; above all privileges else this is the greatest, that he is a head to his church, it is the chiefest flower of his crown. How can this, therefore, be given to a vile man, as the Pope is? In Col. i. 18, it is reckoned there among the great prerogatives of Jesus Christ, among the flowers of his crown, that he is the 'head of the body, the church, who is,' saith he, 'the beginning, the first-born from the dead.' He is, saith he, αὐτος, *ipse*, *he*, and *he alone*, as the Greek emphasis is. And if the Pope can say that he is the beginning, and the first-born from the dead, let him challenge it and wear it, that he is the head of the body, the church. But *he*, he *Christ*, is the beginning, the first-born from the dead; he is the Head of the body, the church.

I will give you another place, Eph. iv. 11, 12, where you have all the greatest officers that ever were upon earth, the rulers of a church mentioned, 'He hath given some apostles;' certainly here is Peter mentioned, from whom the Pope claimeth his supremacy. To what end was this? Read ver. 12, 'For the edifying of the body of Christ;' and ver. 15, 'That we may grow up to him that is the head.'

My brethren, they themselves, though they say the Pope is the head of the church, dare not say, 'which is his body.' They say he is a head for external government; they dare not say that the church is his body. They dare not say, he is Lord of the church, that is Christ's title only; for, 1 Cor. xii. 15, there is but one Lord, namely to the church. They dare not say, he is the husband of the church, for then they would make the church that cleaveth to him a whore; for there can be but one husband of the church. But to be the head of the church is more than this; it is a nearer relation, and will they go and give him this then? It is *crimen capitale*, a capital crime, and all the distinctions they can make will never acquit them of high treason against our Lord Jesus Christ. It is a wonder that ever men of learning should give this title to the Pope; there can be no reason given of it but one, and that is this: it was to make up a complete character that he is Antichrist, that the Scripture might be fulfilled. Ignorant times did give him this title, and it hath been long the unhappiness of the world, that what the ignorance of former ages hath said and established, that the learning of succeeding ages must maintain; therefore the learnedest wits of the world, the Jesuits, have gone about to maintain this title of the Pope.

You know, when I opened those words, that Christ is advanced 'far above all principalities and powers,' I told you, that that was it that made the Pope Antichrist, because he was an imitation of Christ in this, and took on him the power which was personal in Christ alone. As Jesus Christ is said to 'sit at God's right hand,' so he 'sitteth in the temple of God;' as Christ is over all principalities and powers, so likewise doth the Pope sit above 'all that is called God,' 2 Thess. ii. Afterwards I gave you a prospect of all the glory of Christ; I put all together out of this chapter. I will give you a prospect of all the glory of Antichrist, as it is parallel with that of Christ's, set forth in this chapter. You shall see how he doth usurp and arrogate to himself all that is attributed to Christ here in this chapter, that you may see that he hath the full and complete character of that great Antichrist upon him.

When I set out Christ unto you, I told you his exaltation lay in this: he was advanced at God's right hand above all principality and power; that all things are under his feet; that he is a Head to the Church, &c. Now do but compare Christ and Antichrist together.

First, Doth Jesus Christ sit in heaven, which is the holy of holiest, the temple of God, and the inward part of it? Look in 2 Thess. ii. 4, and you shall find that he is the Antichrist that sits in the temple of God, the whole temple of God on earth, for so the Pope challengeth to do, and if he could he would sit in heaven itself; he would, as his predecessor, the king of Babel did, make his throne above the stars, if he could; but he cannot come to heaven. However, he sitteth in heaven here below, he arrogateth to himself all power in the Church of God.

Secondly, Doth Jesus Christ sit at God's right hand in his temple, above all principalities and powers? So doth this Antichrist; he exalteth himself above all that is called God; above all kings and emperors, be they what they will.

Thirdly, Hath Jesus Christ this world and the world to come to rule in? Lo,—we will follow the Pope still,—he arrogateth to rule all in this world; for he saith, all the kingdoms of the world are given to him, and he is to dispose of the crown of them in order to the church. And, which never any monarch ever did before him, he arrogateth power in the world to come, just as Jesus Christ; and he and his divines have fancied to themselves a world to come for him to have the keys of,—that is, purgatory, which men's souls go to when they are dead. He putteth down all the monarchs in the world; they rule men, but men here below, they never followed men's souls into the world to come; the Pope professeth a power there. Nay, they have said they can command angels, and sometimes they have let men out of hell.

Fourthly, Hath Jesus Christ all under his feet? Go to Rome; there is no prince in Europe, none of the Roman emperors required that men should fall down and kiss their feet; but yet this subjection doth the Pope require above all princes else. It is a strange thing, that he of all others should arrogate this, which was proper to the kings of the East. None of the emperors or kings of Europe require this of their subjects; they kneel to them, but never fall down to kiss their feet; this is the lowest subjection, and this the Pope requireth.

Nay, Doth Jesus Christ set his feet upon his enemies? Doth he make them his footstool? You know the story of a Pope that did it to Frederick the emperor, whom he caused to lie down on the ground, and set his feet upon his neck, and blasphemously used that passage in the psalm, which is meant of Christ, *Calcabis super aspidem et draconem*, &c.,—'Thou shalt tread upon the dragon and the serpent, and everything that hurts thee.'

And lastly, that nothing may be wanting, there is but one prerogative of Christ's left. He is over all a Head to the Church. This title doth the Pope arrogate to himself too. My brethren, I will say, but one thing to you, as they said to Christ that were sent to know whether he was the Messiah, 'Art thou he that should come, or do we look for another?' So, is this he, or do we look for another Antichrist? For my particular, I look for no other.

SERMON XXXVI.

And gave him to be a head (or, *the head*) *over all things to the church, which is his body, the fulness of him that filleth all in all.*—VER. 22, 23.

I DIVIDED these words into these two parts :—

First, *What concerneth our Lord and Saviour Jesus Christ as a Head;* he is a head to his Church over all, and he filleth all in all.

Secondly, *What concerneth the Church;* it is his body, and it is his fulness.

First, Concerning the headship of Christ: I shewed you, that by head here was meant a similitude drawn from the natural head of a man's body. There is a conjugal head, as the husband is the head of the wife. There is a political head, as the supreme magistrate is the head of the commonwealth. But this similitude hath relation to the natural head of the body of man, which is the nearest relation of all others. I opened so much in general in the last discourse. Now I shall shew you more particularly *the relation of headship that Jesus Christ hath to his Church.*

I have often had many discussions with myself, whether that this relation of headship should not import some distinct office from that of king, priest, and prophet, to which three all divines do reduce the offices of Christ. But I have at last resolved my thoughts thus: that this relation of headship doth import all his offices, but with that peculiarness, and with that eminency, as no other relation in Scripture doth. For—

First, to begin with his *kingly office;* there is this difference between a king and a natural head of a body, that a king ruleth only externally by commands, and by laws, and by proclamations declared; but the rule of a head is natural. Therefore now, if you reduce it to the kingly office of Christ, it is with an eminency, with a peculiarity. It is our advantage that we are not ruled by Christ as a king simply considered, so far as that similitude will carry it, by external laws revealed, or by way of promises or rewards; but we are ruled by Christ naturally and inwardly, as the members are ruled by the head, which of all rules is the best and most eminent. So that it noteth out the peculiarity of his kingly office.

Secondly, come to his *prophetical office.* His headship noteth that too, and that with a peculiarity. The head doth not teach the members by outward dictates, or by way of doctrine; but it doth teach the members by way of impression, a secret impression, carrying them on to do the thing it teacheth. So Jesus Christ, as a head, doth not only teach by way of doctrine, but by efficacy. I need not write unto you, saith he, for you are all taught of God to love one another. And this is the most glorious teaching in the world.

Thirdly, go to his *priestly office,* and his headship importeth that too. There are two parts of his priestly office. There is, first, offering of sacrifice; secondly, there is intercession, a pleading of that sacrifice before God for us. And of the two, intercession is the most eminent part of the priesthood of

Christ; for that part of his priestly office was resembled by Melchisedec, who, we never read, offered sacrifice, but he blessed Abraham, as Christ doth us from heaven, and now intercedeth for us.

Now, intercession is noted out by headship, for it is natural to the head to speak for the members; the tongue speaks, if speaking will prevent any danger; the head takes care of the members by intercession and by pleading. It noteth out, therefore, his priestly office, and that with an eminency and by a peculiarity.

I might shew likewise how it noteth out his being God and man; but I would finish the chapter at this time, therefore I must cut off many things. Only there is this question, which I know not well how to pass over,—I find it not started by interpreters upon the place, but I find it started by some divines in other discourses of theirs,—and it is this, When it was that Christ began to be Head of his Church? Say they, it was when he did ascend; and the text, say they, is clear for it: for having raised him from the dead, he gave him to be a head over all things to his church, when he had first set him at his own right hand in the heavenly places.

To solve this doubt in a word or two:—

In the first place, headship is taken either largely for one that *representeth* another, who is a common person for others. The head, you know, standeth for the whole body; therefore you give the name of the whole man to the head: it is so in all languages. In Latin, *caput* is put for the whole person; so likewise in Greek, the word κεφαλὴ is put for the whole person: so Jesus Christ, being the head, is put for the whole body, as 1 Cor. xii. 12; and as you see oftentimes in princes' coin. Now then, take Christ as he is a common person, a person representative, so he was a head before his incarnation. In election we were all chosen in him as in a common person, standing for us, and undertaking for us, as I shewed when I opened those words, 'chosen in him.' And so, likewise, he was a common person when he was upon earth, and every action of his was capital, as the school-men say; every grace of his was *gratia capitis.* Now, as headship is taken thus for a common person representing another, so I say Christ was a head before his incarnation; and so he was a head while he was upon earth.

But then, secondly, headship importeth *an influence into members;* and that influence is either virtual or actual, as I may so distinguish. It is virtual, as before Christ was incarnate; yet the virtue of his being God-man and a head to his church was it that filled all the saints then as well as now. Therefore he was a 'Lamb slain from the beginning of the world,'—that is, he was considered as such; so he was a head from the beginning of the world, from Adam's fall.

But then there is an actual influence, whereby the Godhead, dwelling in the manhood, doth actually fill all things through his manhood, as the instrument of it: and so he began to fill all things when he ascended; for then the human nature was enlarged to take into his care every member of his church, and to send commission that this soul should be filled with this good thought, and that soul with this; which was not before.—And so I have cleared that thing.

Now, this similitude of a head importeth many things; but I will keep to what the text saith. There are two things imported in the text whereby the headship of Christ is represented to us—

First, He is said to be a Head *in respect of eminency;* and that is plain in the text; he gave him to be 'a head over all.'

Secondly, He is said to be a Head *in respect of influence into his members;*

that is plain in the text too, 'he filleth all in all.' I shall open those words afterward; but only, because the text giveth us hints of these two, I will first speak a little of them.

First, He is a Head *in respect of eminency*. The head, *caput*, is oftentimes put for the *beginning*. Christ is a head in that sense; he is the beginning of his church, he hath that eminency: so Col. i. 18, 'He is the head of the body, the church: who is the beginning, the first-born from the dead; that in all things he might have the pre-eminence.' Here is one eminency. Now, he is the beginning of the church. As Adam was the beginning of the creation, so is Christ of the new creation; he was first in order intended, he was not ordained for us, but we for him; the text is plain for it, for we are 'his fulness.' The head is not ordained so much for the body, as the body for the head. He hath the first in that sense.

He is likewise head in respect of eminency, for he is worth all the body. Oh, my brethren, think what Jesus Christ is! The head of a man is infinitely more worth than his body. Divide them you cannot; but if you could divide them, the head is of more worth than all the body, for all reason, and wisdom, and whatsoever is glorious, all the senses dwell in the head; there is but one sense dwelling in the body,—namely, the sense of touching,—but the perfection of all the senses is in the head, it is the seat of the understanding. All the beauty is in the head; therefore the civil lawyers, in their language, call whatsoever is excellent, *caput*, the head.

All beauty, you know, lieth in the face, and the face and head is all one. You may read, 1 Cor. xi., of uncovering the head, that is, uncovering the face; covering the head is covering the face with a vail, as the custom of those times was. Such a one, my brethren, is Jesus Christ. You see saints, and you see but few of them, and you do not see them in their ruff, in their glory, as they shall be in their robes at the latter day; when you have thoughts of them all, put them all together, what are they? They are but the toes, the fingers, the hands of this head. Christ is worth all this body, and a thousand bodies more, if you could suppose them. In him is all the beauty: for it is said, the glory of God shineth in the face of Jesus Christ,—the face is put for the head,—so 2 Cor. iv. 6.

The image of God appeareth in the head more than in all the body; so it doth in Christ. God is very well pleased when he looks upon the Head, though the members be scabbed, and diseased, and full of humours; but in him I am well pleased, saith he. He is *primum amabile*, that makes the body beautiful in the eyes of God; and he will never leave it till he hath cleansed it, and made it like himself. He is 'fairer than the children of men,' than all the children of men put together, Ps. xlv.

And whereas you will say, All the grace we have Christ hath; but, my brethren, how hath he it? Not as you have it; for the fulness of the Godhead dwelleth in him, and dwelleth in him bodily. The body hath all the use of the reason of the head, so that when you see a man do actions, he doth them rationally; as when a man playeth on a lute, it is a rational act, which made one say that the soul is in the fingers' ends: but now he doth these actions by way of participation; it is the soul that guideth all. So we have grace, but it is by participation; the spring of all is in Christ the Head. All the counsel, all the wisdom is in the Head; and he is 'made unto us wisdom,' we have none of ourselves; he is the mighty Counsellor, as you know he is called.—So that he is a Head in respect of eminency, a Head over all, body and all.

Secondly, He is a Head *in respect of influence;* which is imported in these words, 'he filleth all in all.' He is a Head in respect of influence these three ways: in respect of communicating—

1. Of life.
2. Of motion.
3. Of strength.

First, *All our life is from him; that is, spiritual.* The body indeed liveth a natural life without the head, but it doth not live an animal life, a sensitive life, all that is from the head. You have a natural life from Adam, but all your spiritual life is from the Head, Christ. My brethren, the very bands by which we are united to this head all come from him, as all the nerves and sinews, by which the members are united to the head, spring from the head. You have a plain place for it, Col. ii. 19, speaking of men that did not hold the Head, Christ, by which, saith he, 'all the body by joints and bands having nourishment ministered, and knit together, increaseth with the increase of God.' He doth not only communicate all life to us, but he knitteth us to himself; first he apprehendeth us, and then we apprehend him, as in the Epistle to the Philippians.

Secondly, The head you know is *the principle of motion,* as well as the principle of life and union of the members. There is no motion in any little member but it is formed in the head first, and the head, the fancy first formeth it, and then sends the spirits to the toe, and biddeth it move this way or that way; or to the hand, and bids it act this thing or that; and it is more the action of the head than it is of the toe or of the hand. So it is here; all the spiritual actions which you do are from Christ, that 'worketh all in all,' 1 Cor. ii. 6, as he is here said to 'fill all in all.' What a mighty vast comprehensive Head have we, that should think all the good thoughts of every member; that is, give directions that any should think them. He sendeth his Spirit down, who is said to be that same ἐνέργεια, that same inward working, Eph. iv. 16; he sendeth his Spirit down, and that works every thing that Christ would have wrought.

I find in some of the school-men, handling Christ's headship, that they would make the Holy Ghost to be the heart, and Christ to be the head; they would follow the similitude so far. But it is an absurd one, for to make the Holy Ghost the heart in this body is indeed to make him a member whereof Christ is the head; he beareth no such part. But what part doth he bear in this body then? He beareth the part of the spirits, that run up and down in the nerves and sinews and blood, which is called the life of a man, that carry all the commissions for actions to be done, and that part indeed the Holy Ghost hath between the head and us.

Now, my brethren, do but think with yourselves what a head Christ is, in respect of motion. Suppose—it is a supposition may be made to illustrate the thing—there were a man as high as that his head were in heaven, and his feet were here upon earth, and his hands stretched all over the world. No sooner did the head that was in heaven think of moving the toe, but it would move in an instant. Even such a one is Christ, he is a head, he hath a part of his body in heaven, he moveth them as he pleaseth; he hath another part on earth here, and he moveth them as he pleaseth too, and he doth it in an instant. He is the principle of all motion. He is the head in that respect.

Thirdly, *He is the fountain of all strength likewise.* All the strength of the body lieth in the spirits. Take away the animal spirits that come from the head, the body is a weak thing; 'it is sown in weakness;' when the spirits are gone, the body dieth. Further than Christ strengtheneth us, we are all dead; therefore the Apostle prayeth, Eph. iii. 16, 'that they may be strengthened with might by his Spirit in the inner man.' And I am able, saith he, 'to do all things through Christ that strengtheneth me.'

And so much for the headship of our Lord and Saviour Jesus Christ. He is, first, the fountain of all spiritual life, the uniter of us to himself, the principle of all union is from the head; he is, secondly, the fountain of all motion; and, thirdly, of all strength.

The second thing to be considered in Jesus Christ's headship is this, *He is said to be a Head over all;* 'gave him to be a head over all.'

There are many senses of them, and they are all full of comfort to us. The words note out first, as I said before, an eminency, an excellency, a superexcellency. As Eph. vi. 16, 'Above all things take the shield of faith,' that is the most eminent thing of all the rest; so Jesus Christ is a head above all. And so it referreth to the gift; that above all gifts that God hath given him, this is the greatest gift, to be the head of the church. That is one meaning. It was the greatest gift that could be given to Christ to be a head of the church, which is his body; more than sovereignty over all things else, which he had mentioned before. And it was the greatest gift that could be given to the church, the words will bear either; *καὶ αὐτὸν ἔδωκε κεφαλὴν ὑπὲρ πάντα τῇ ἐκκλησίᾳ.*

Or else, in the second place, 'he gave him to be a head over all to the church,' hath this sense in it. It noteth out his sovereignty and superiority over all in relation to his church, that God gave him to be a head to the church, who is above all; and so indeed the Syriac translation readeth it, 'he that is above all, God gave him to be a head to his church.' And this seemeth to be the meaning more properly, for he had set him out before, how he was over all principalities and powers, far above all; yet he repeateth it again in this, he gave him to be a head over all to his church; that is, he that was Lord of all, God added this to him, to be a head to the church; noting out, that none was fit to be a head to the church but he that was over all; he is over all that belongeth to his church for her good; over all that are against her to hurt her. And it was needful for the church to have such a head, for we have enough against us; but who shall be against us if Christ our head be for us?

There is a third meaning yet, and it is for our comfort. It is this: it hath relation to headship; that is, above all relations else he gave him to be a head and to act that part. He doth not say, he gave him to be a lord simply, nor a king, nor a brother, but above all these, though he is all these, he is a head. God gave him to be above all things else a loving, and kind, and natural head to his church, which is his body.

Every one of these senses, my brethren, how full of comfort are they! If you refer 'above all' to gift, 'he gave above all him to be a head;' how full of comfort is it! That this should be the greatest gift that ever God gave, Christ to be a head to his church; and Christ reckoneth it so. Look into John xvii., read over that chapter; you shall see there, as it is a prayer, so it is a thanksgiving too; it is an acknowledgment of mercies and benefits given him by his Father. He telleth his Father indeed he had given him glory; saith he, ver. 1, 'Glorify thy Son, that thy Son also may glorify thee,' 'with the glory which I had with thee before the world was,' ver. 5; which, ver. 22, he calleth 'the glory which thou gavest me.' And this indeed Jesus Christ valueth most, therefore he mentioneth it first in ver. 1; for his own person being worth more than ours, he hath reason to value his own glory more than all ours; he should not love himself regularly else. But next to that, what valueth he? Ver. 2, 'Thou hast given him power over all flesh;' here is his being over all; but to what end? Mark what followeth: 'That he should give eternal life to as many as thou hast given him.' And, ver. 22, 'The glory which thou hast given me I have given them.' So that he useth this power that he hath in order to our salvation. And if you read that chapter, observe it, what is it that Christ mentioneth oftenest in that chapter as the greatest gift? It is the giving of his church to him. He mentioneth it, ver. 6, 'I have manifested thy name to them which thou gavest me; thine they were, and thou gavest them me.' So again, ver. 8, 'I have given thy words to them which thou gavest me, and they have received them;' ver. 9, 'I pray for them which thou hast given me;' ver. 10, 'All mine are thine, and thine are mine;' still he pleadeth his interest in them as by way of gift. So ver 11, 'That those which thou hast given me may be one;' still he mentioneth this as the greatest gift of all the rest which God hath bestowed upon him.

My brethren, Jesus Christ reckoneth his being a head to the church more than all his temporal dominions, more than his being over all things else. What use shall we make of it? In a word thus, let us prize our relation to Christ, seeing Christ prizeth so much his relation to us; he prizeth it more than his being over all things, than his being far above all principalities and powers; let us prize it more than all worldly greatness and riches, or what else soever. Our being members of Christ is more than our being all things, as Christ's being a head to us is more than being Lord of all the world.

And then again, let the Church value this gift of Christ being a head to her, for it beareth that meaning too; there is an emphasis in that word *him*. 'He gave *him* to be a head,' so saith the text. He had set him forth as Solomon in all his royalty, sitting at his Father's right hand over all principalities and powers; 'and he hath given him,' saith he, 'to be a head over all to the church.' What should the church do now? It should go over all the excellencies of Jesus Christ to make her prize the gift of Christ to her as a head. And let me tell you, he hath given him to be a Saviour, the Saviour of his body, but to be a head is the greater, to be a head is an everlasting thing. When sin will be remembered no more, when his priesthood is at end, he will be a head for ever when he hath given up the kingdom to God the Father. It is a peculiar blessing. To which of all the angels hath he said he is a husband to them, or a head to them, as a body? To none of them. It is only to this body, the church, the sons of men.

Oh, my brethren, when you are in heaven and when sin shall be forgotten,—you love him now because he saveth you, justifieth you, and cleanseth you, and you will love him at the latter day because he pronounceth you blessed, forgiveth you all sins, and suffereth you not to enter into condemnation;—but when all these shall be over, what will be the sweetness for ever? That he is your head. 'Above all he gave him to be a head to his church.'

And do you but consider what a head you have. There is I know not how many *alls* in him. In his person there dwelleth all the fulness of the Godhead bodily; so he saith, Col. ii. 9. In his relation to you he is *all*, and he is *in all*, Col. iii. 11. In his power for you he is *above all;* so saith the text. In his communicating his goodness, 'he filleth all in all;' so saith the text too. He is one that hath all the Godhead; that is all in all, that is above all, that filleth all in all. What would you have more? Here are *alls* enough for you; value this gift, that Jesus Christ is your head.

Last of all; take that other sense, that of all relations else he is above all a head, performeth that part the best, and nothing is more comfortable to his church. He is not only above all other heads, above husband, above the natural head of the body, puts them all down, they are but shadows to him; but above all offices belonging to himself he is above all a head to his church. It is as if a wife should say of her husband, He is the best warrior in the world, he is a king, he hath the power and command of all the world, he is wise, he is rich, he is above all in everything, and he hath all sorts of excellencies in him; but above all he is the best husband in the world, he putteth himself down in that, he acts that part the best. So it is with Jesus Christ; he is the king of all the world, he is wise, &c.; but above all he is a head, he excelleth in that above all things else.

I should have made this use of it and pressed it upon you: If he be a head above all, it is fit you should be subject to him in all. 'Wives,' saith he, 'be subject to your husbands, as the church is to Christ.' One would wonder at that, that the church's obedience to Christ should be made the pattern of wives' obedience to their husbands. Certainly it argueth that the church is more naturally, more willingly subject to Christ than wives are to their husbands. Yet let any wife consider, How do I obey Christ? how do I obey my husband? But I pass from that.

I have done with the relation of Christ to his church; he is a head, a head over all to his church. I come now to the office of Jesus Christ to his church imported in these words, 'he filleth all in all.'

First, I must explain to what kind of thing this word *all in all* is restrained or limited.

Secondly, I must explain the phrase of *filling*.

Thirdly, the phrase itself, *all in all*.

First, This word 'all' is not to be extended to all things in the world, though that be true that Christ doth put all the fulness into the creature; Adam brought an emptiness. But that is not the meaning here. It is to be restrained to his body, to believers, they are the *all* here mentioned. As in Col. iii. 11, Christ is said to be 'all in all,' but what meaneth he? To his church; 'There is neither Greek nor Jew,' saith he, speaking of the new creature in the words before, 'Barbarian, Scythian, bond nor free; but Christ is all in all;' namely, in his saints, be they what they will. So, Eph. iv. 10, 11, it is said he filleth all things, but by 'all things' there is meant his saints, his church, as it followeth, 'He gave some to be apostles, &c., for the edifying of the body of Christ.'

Secondly, For the phrase *filling;* to open that, 'he filleth all in all.' It is Christ's work in heaven, my brethren. 'He ascended far above all heavens, that he might fill all things,' saith the Apostle in Eph. iv. 10. He gave him to sit at his own right hand, that he might fill all things, saith the text.

It implieth, first of all, *an emptiness in us* that are filled by him. Not only a real emptiness, that we have nothing in ourselves; 'without me,' saith he, 'ye can do nothing;' we are but valleys, 'every valley must be filled,' Luke iii. 5. But he filleth only those that have a sensible emptiness, that have a feeling of their own wants: 'He filleth the hungry with good things,' Luke i. 53. Hunger is not only a real emptiness, but hunger is a sensible emptiness.

My brethren, the church, take all the saints in heaven and in earth, they are all empty things without Jesus Christ. We are not able to think a good thought, we are all but mere empty vessels brought to a conduit pipe to be filled; we have not a drop of good, not so much as one good thought, further than Jesus Christ filleth us. This is the glory of our Head.

Secondly, consider *what he filleth us with.* He filleth us with his Spirit. Read from Luke i. 15, to the end of the Revelation, you shall find that phrase used many a time. They were filled with the Holy Ghost, filled with him as with wine, Eph. v. 18; 'filled with the fruits of righteousness,' Phil. i. 11; 'filled with the knowledge of his will, in all wisdom and spiritual understanding,' Col. i. 9; 'filled with joy,' Acts xiii. 52. And if this be not enough, you shall be 'filled with all the fulness of God' one day, and a little of God will fill you, Eph. iii. 19.

But thirdly, *How is it that Christ filleth his Church?*

He doth it two ways.

He filleth them first *meritoriously*, by what he did here upon earth; he purchased power and grace to fill them with these. For, my brethren, you must know this, that Christ doth nothing for us but he himself had something in him proportionable that might merit why it should be done. Doth he make us rich? He was first poor. Doth he fill us? Himself was first empty, so saith Phil. ii. 7. It is said there, 'he emptied himself;' so the words ἑαυτὸν ἐκένωσε signify.

Then again he filleth *efficiently*, and that while he is in heaven. He sendeth down the Holy Ghost, and he works all; the manhood doth it instrumentally, the Godhead doth it virtually. The fulness of the Godhead dwelleth in him, and runneth, overfloweth through the human nature as the instrument of it, and filleth all in all.—And so much now for his filling.

Thirdly, I come now to the phrase, *filleth all in all.* There are two things in that to be considered distinctly.

First, Here is *an all which is filled.*

Secondly, Here is *all with which it is filled.*

First, He filleth all, that is, as I said before, *all saints*, all the members of his body. And that importeth these particulars:—

First, It importeth that he filleth *every saint;* there is not one but he filleth. There is not a saint, my brethren, but hath a measure of the stature of the fulness of Christ, which God hath appointed him to have, and Christ filleth him top full before he hath done, he leaveth not one saint out. We are all vessels, 'vessels of mercy,' that are to be filled; and you may read Eph. iii. of a sea of love, a sea that knoweth neither shore nor bottom. 'That ye may be able to comprehend,' saith he, 'what is the breadth, and length, and height, and depth,' of what? 'Of the love of Christ, which passeth knowledge, that ye may be filled,' saith he, 'with all the fulness of God.' Every saint shall be thus filled one day, thrown into that sea of the love of God, and Jesus Christ, and of the knowledge of him, and take in all that he can hold; he shall be filled top full according to his measure.

Secondly, This word 'all' importeth *all sorts of saints*, that both Jew and Gentile, rich and poor, men and women, shall all be filled. Thus you find the word 'all in all' used, Col. iii. 11, 'There is nether Greek nor Jew, circumcision nor uncircumcision, Barbarian, Scythian, bond nor free: but Christ is all, and in all these.'

Then, thirdly, he filleth all, that is, *all the powers and faculties*, both of body and soul, that are in every one of these members. Thou hast an understanding, a memory, a will, a fancy, thou hast outward senses, thou hast a body; Jesus Christ will fill every one of these top full. He will empty thee of every one of thine own thoughts before he hath done. He will fill thine understanding with none but his own thoughts, top full; thou shalt think no thoughts but what Christ himself thinketh. He will fill thy will, thou shalt have no desires, no affections, but what Jesus Christ hath; he will fill thee with all his own joy, with all his own delights, with all the pleasures himself hath at God's right hand. I tell you, my brethren, he will turn a man's self out of doors, and fill a man's self with himself, that as the iron that is red hot, all the pores of it are filled with heat, there is nothing but iron and fire, so at last there will be nothing but Jesus Christ and the man. As the cloud filled the temple, so will he fill your bodies and make them temples of the Holy Ghost; he will glorify you with the same glory that he himself hath; he will fill all parts in a man at last.

Secondly, He will fill all in all. I have shewed you what *all* is to be filled, Now then, what is the *all* with which he will fill *all?* He will fill you with all sorts of graces, he will fill the whole with all sorts of gifts, so the word is taken, 1 Cor. xii. 6: 'God worketh,' saith he, 'all in all.' It is not that every one hath all gifts, but take the whole body, and amongst them they have all. He worketh in the eye, and filleth that, and he filleth the hand as a hand, according to the use of every part. So that put all together, and he is all in all, and so in this life, and in the world to come it is said, God will be all in all, 1 Cor. xv. 28.

So much now for that head likewise; 'he filleth all in all.' And so now I have done with Christ's part, wherein he is said to be a Head over all, filling all in all.

Now then, will you come to *the Church's relation?* The church, saith he, which is 'his body, the fulness of him that filleth all in all.' You see that in Jesus Christ's relation there were two things. There was, first, his *headship*; there was, secondly, his *office*, filling all in all. Now if you come to the church's relation, she hath something to answer both. Answerable to his headship, she is called his body; 'which is his body.' Answerable to his filling all in all, she is called his fulness.

In my last discourse I handled what was meant by the word *church.* There was a necessity that lay upon me to open that distinction of church, universal and particular. I gave you two cautions about two errors concerning each of these, both toward the church universal and toward particular churches. Concerning which I must necessarily say something to take away some mistakes and misapprehensions of meaning; for I walk by this rule, to give no offence to Jew or Gentile, or to the churches of God, as the Apostle speaks.

The first error, I told you, was of the Donatists of old, who denied the Church Catholic, and restrained it to one part of the world; and yet the imputation of this error lieth upon those whom you call Brownists to this day. This I cleared them from, and it is as great a clearing as can be.

The second error was of those who hold particular churches—those you call parish churches—to be no true churches of Christ, and their ministers to be no true ministers, and upon that ground forbear all church-communion with them, in hearing or in any other ordinance. And as I acquitted these from that other error, so I acquitted myself from this, and my brethren in the ministry. I would not now have touched upon it again, but, as I said, to clear, not myself so much, as some mistakes about it.

The first is this: it was understood as if I said that all parish churches and ministers generally were churches and ministers of Christ, such as with whom communion might be held. I said not so. I was wary in my expressions. I will only say this unto you about it. There is no man that desireth reformation in this kingdom,—as the generality of all godly people do,—but will acknowledge and say, that multitude of parishes, where ignorance and profaneness overwhelm the generality, scandalousness and simony the ministers themselves; that these are not churches and ministers fit to be held communion with. Only this, the ordinances that have been administered by them, so far we must acknowledge them, that they are not to be recalled or repeated again.

But here lieth the question, my brethren, and my meaning. Whereas now in some of the parishes in this kingdom, there are many godly men that do constantly give themselves up to the worship of God in public, and meet together in one place to that end, in a constant way, under a godly minister, whom they themselves have chosen to cleave to,—though they did not choose him at first,—these, notwithstanding their mixture and want of discipline, I never thought, for my part, but that they were true churches of Christ, and sister churches, and so ought to be acknowledged. And the contrary was the error that I spake against.

Secondly, for holding communion with them. I say, as sister churches, occasionally as strangers, men might hold communion with them. And it is acknowledged by all divines, that there is not that obligation lying upon a stranger, that is not a member of a sister church, to find fault in that church, or in a member of it, as doth on the church itself to which one belongeth.

I will give you my reasons that moved me to speak so much. It was not simply to vent my own judgment, or simply to clear myself from that error; but the reasons, or rather the motives and considerations, that stirred me in it were these:—

First, if we should not acknowledge these churches, thus stated, to be true churches of Christ, and their ministers true ministers, and their order such, and hold communion with them too in the sense spoken of, we must acknowledge no church in all the Reformed Churches; none of all the Churches in Scotland, nor in Holland, nor in Germany; for they are all as full of mixture as ours. And to deny that to our own churches, which we do not to the churches abroad, nothing can be more absurd. And it will be very hard to think that there hath been no church since the Reformation.

Secondly, I know nothing tendeth more to the peaceable reformation amongst us, than to break down this partition wall; for there is nothing provokes more than this doth, to deny such churches to be true churches of Christ. For do but think with yourselves, and I will give you a familiar example. You come to a man whom you think to be a godly man; you tell him he hath these and these sins in him, and they are great ones; it is as much as he can bear, though you tell him he is a saint, and acknowledge him so. But if you come to him, and say, besides this, You are a limb of the devil, and you have no grace in you; this provokes all in a man, when there is any ground in himself to think so, or in another to judge him so. So it is here; come to churches and say, You have these defects amongst you, and these things to be reformed; but if you will come, and say, Your churches and your ministers are antichristian, and come from Babylon, there is nothing provokes more. Therefore, if there be a truth in it, as I believe there is, men should be zealous to express it; for this is the great partition wall that hindereth of twain making one.

Then again, this is that which I consider, and it is a great consideration also. I know that Jesus Christ hath given his people light in matters of this nature by degrees. Thousands of good souls that have been bred up and born in our assemblies, and enjoy the ordinances of God, and have done it comfortably, cannot suddenly take in other principles; you must wait upon Christ to do it.

In this case men are not to be wrought off by falsehoods, God hath no need of them. No, rather, till men do take in light, you should give them all that is comfortable in the condition they are in; we should acknowledge every good thing in every man, in every church, in every thing, and that is a way to work upon men, and to prevail with them; as it is Philem. 6, 'That the communication of thy faith may become effectual by the acknowledgment of every good thing which is in you in Christ Jesus.' It is that which buildeth men up, by acknowledgment of every good thing that is in them.

Lastly, the last inconvenience is this: it doth deprive men of all those gifts that are found amongst our ministers, and in this kingdom, that they cannot hold any communion or fellowship with them. So that I profess myself as zealous in this point as in any other I know. And, for my part, this I say, and I say it with much integrity, I never yet took up religion by parties in the lump; I have found by trial of things that there is some truth on all sides. I have found holiness where you would little think it, and so likewise truth; and I have learned this principle, which I hope I shall never lay down till I am swallowed up of immortality, and that is that which I said before, to acknowledge every good thing, and hold communion with it, in men, in churches, or whatsoever else. I learn this from Paul, I learn this from Jesus Christ himself, he 'filleth all in all;' he is in the hearts of his people, and filleth them in his ordinances to this day; and where Jesus Christ filleth, why should we deny an acknowledgment, and a right hand of fellowship and communion?

My brethren, this rule that I have now mentioned, which I profess I have lived by, and shall do while I live, I know I shall never please men in it. Why? It is plain, for this is the nature and condition of all mankind; if a man dissents from others in one thing, he loseth them in all the rest; and therefore if a man do take what is good of all sides, he is apt to lose them all, but he pleaseth Christ by it, and so I will for this particular.

I come now to 'his body' and his 'fulness.'

First, It is said to be *his body.*

Secondly, It is said to be *his fulness.* I shall speak to both.

Our Saviour Christ's body is either taken for his *natural body*, which he weareth in heaven now and was laid in the grave, or it is taken for his *mystical body*, namely his saints. Concerning this distinction I will add but this: That what Christ did to his natural body, that he doth to his mystical body, to conform them to him.

Again, for a second distinction, our Lord and Saviour Christ hath a *sacramental body.* Saith the Apostle, 1 Cor. xi. 24, speaking of the bread, 'This is my body, which was broken for you.' And he hath a *ministerial body*, which is an assembly of his children incorporated to enjoy ordinances. 1 Cor. x. 17, speaking of the church of Corinth, 'You,' saith he, 'are one bread, and one body; for we are all partakers of that one bread.' This is a ministerial body to Christ. As he hath a universal church, a mystical body, whereof only his saints are members, so he hath a ministerial body, which is his ordinance, which are saints incorporated and made one, either really or verbally; really, by eating that one bread, as the Apostle saith.

Now to leave these distinctions; only I will give you one observation upon the last distinction, as I did upon the former. There is a sacramental body, that is, the bread which is broken. There is a ministerial body, which is the ordinance of church-fellowship. Here you see the same thing said of saints that is said of the sacrament. It is said of the saints, 'which are his body;' there is no more said of the bread in the sacrament, which is his body. Yet the Pope and the Papists give more reverence to the sacramental bread,—and that bread, they say, because it hath the appellation of *body*, must needs be transubstantiated,—to the sacramental body of Christ, than they do to the mystical body. As of old,—it was an argument used long before the Reformation in England,—they do give more reverence to images of Christ than they do to the image of Christ in men's hearts, than they do to saints; so now they give more reverence to the sacramental body of Christ—and both these errors are correspondent and proportionable—than they do to the mystical body.—And so much for those two distinctions.

Now, why doth this come in, 'which is his body?'

It cometh in upon a twofold consideration—

First, To shew the nearness of the relation that Jesus Christ hath to his Church, and his Church hath to him. He is not a head only as a ruler, but he is a head as a natural head to a body; he is so a head to his church, which is his body.

Secondly, To shew that he is affected to them, to the saints, as the head is to the body.

I might handle many things here concerning the church's being a body to Christ wherein the similitude holdeth, but I shall not be able to do that and despatch what I am yet to do. I shall only make this use of it: That a body and the members of it are united one to another by the nearest union, by a union of sense; so saith the Apostle, 1 Cor. xii. 12, 'As the body is one, and hath many members, and all the members of that one body, being many, are one body; so also is Christ.' Here is a union. And the inference of the Apostle from thence is this, ver. 25, 'That there should be no schism in the body, but that the members should have the same care one of another; and whether one member suffer, all the members suffer with it.' This is the inference the Apostle makes of the church's being a body.

Now let me make but an observation upon the former distinction mentioned. I told you there is a sacramental body of Christ; 'This is my body.' And there is a ministerial body of Christ; you are 'one body, for you are partakers of that one bread.' My brethren, it is strange to see and to consider how that these two have made the greatest divisions in the world. Those things that are for communion—for Christ hath appointed church-fellowship for communion; he hath appointed the sacrament for the communion of his body; you shall be one body, saith the Apostle, by it; 'Ye are one bread and one body; for ye are all partakers of one bread,' 1 Cor. x. 17—are that which hath caused the schism of the body, as I may so express it in the Apostle's words. For what hath bred the greatest difference between the Papists and us of all other points? It is, 'This is my body.' It was that chiefly about which all the martyrs suffered. Amongst the Protestants, what hath made the greatest dissension between the Lutherans and the Calvinists? It is, 'This is my body.' There is, though not a transubstantiation, yet a consubstantiation—he is in and with the bread; so the Lutherans hold. Amongst ourselves, what hath been the great division? Still though not about the sacramental body, yet about the ministerial body of Christ, church-fellowship. The body of Christ hath been the occasion of the rending of the body of Christ. As the dispute was about the body of Moses, so are the disputes about the body of Christ. My brethren, if you cannot agree in judgment, yet agree in heart. Let me but mind you of the relation you bear to Christ; remember you are his body, and there should be no schism in the body; and there would be no schism if you did not judge one another for these things. Though you are of different minds, here is no schism, for this will be while the saints are upon the earth; but the schism is in judging one another, in not being at peace because you differ in judgment.

Let me say to godly men, agree; you are the body of Christ, remember that; let your mystical relation to Christ, that mystically you are his body, prevail over all considerations whatsoever. It is the strongest tie in the world. Shall I prophesy unto you? Either agree, or God will make you agree; either with the sword, or with fire and fagot. And let me edge it with this a little, 'which is his body.' Oh, my brethren, this word, *his body*, is a sweet word. You are not only a body among yourselves, but consider whose body you are, you are the body of Christ, *his body;* the body which he owneth, which he filleth, which is more his body than yours; and if you will do nothing out of love one to another as becometh saints, yet do it out of love unto him.

I will add this: this word *his* is added also to shew that it is the relation this body beareth to Christ that giveth the excellency to it. This body would have no beauty, no excellency in it if this head stood not on it. 'The church, which is his body.'—So I pass from that.

I have nothing now remaining, but only this last point, *which is his fulness.* He beareth the relation of head, she of body: he performeth the office of filling her; she performeth this to him, she is his fulness.

These words, 'his fulness,' are either taken actively or passively. If you take them actively, they refer to Christ, and then the meaning is this, that *he filleth her.* If you take them passively, *she is his fulness.* I cannot stand to shew you how the word is taken in both senses, either for that which filleth, or that which is filled. I pitch rather upon that which this translation holdeth forth, viz., that this body is said to be Christ's fulness.

Why doth the Holy Ghost add this? He doth not content himself to say, that Christ is the Head of the Church, which is his body, but he must needs bring in this, that she is *his fulness.*

He mentioneth it, my brethren, as an honour to his church, that she is such a body to him, as that though he be a head that filleth her, yet he is not complete without her. He would shew that Christ needs her not, therefore he saith he filleth her; he 'filleth all in all:' and yet because he is in some sense imperfect without her, she is as an ornament to him, therefore he addeth she is his fulness; 'the fulness of him that filleth all in all.'

Now she is called the fulness of Christ in the same sense that it is said, 2 Cor. xii. 9, 'My strength is made perfect in weakness.' What, is not God's power perfect without our weakness? Yes, it is perfect in itself; but it is said to be made perfect, because it is declared to be perfect in weakness. So when the church is said to be Christ's fulness, what, is not he full without her? Yes, for he 'filleth all in all;' yet his fulness she is, and she setteth off his fulness, because she serveth as an empty vessel for him to fill, and to shew his fulness in; that he is not full only in himself personally, but that he hath enough overflowing to fill all his body, to fill all in all.

Now then to open this, Jesus Christ hath a *threefold fulness*—

He hath, first, a *personal fulness;* the fulness of the Godhead dwelleth personally in him, so Col. ii. 9.

He hath, secondly, a *dispensatory fulness*, mentioned here in the text; he filleth all in all. 'Of his fulness we all receive grace for grace.'

Then, thirdly, he hath a *relative fulness*, which ariseth from a relation to his church. He is the head, and the church is his body. And, as if you would make a man, you must not only have a head, but you must have a body too, or it is not a perfect man: so if you would make up Christ,—take Christ mystically,—you must not only have the person of Christ, but there must be a body too; and so there ariseth a perfect full stature of Christ, as the Apostle calleth it, 1 Cor. xii. 12.

Now, my brethren, when, and how, doth the church become the fulness of Christ?

It becometh his fulness by these three things—

First, when Jesus Christ hath every saint brought to him, and gathered about him, united to him, and all joined in one with him, every saint that God hath given him. If there were one saint wanting, Jesus Christ should not be full. Mark what I say to you, if there were this joint of the little finger cut off, this body of mine would be imperfect: so if Jesus Christ should want but one of his members,—the joint of the little toe, as I may so express it,—the least saint, (comfort thyself,) Jesus Christ should not be full; thou makest up Christ's fulness.

Secondly, the church is then said to be his fulness, when she shall have all variety of all gifts and graces dispersed amongst them. As now, take the members of a man's body, there is not a member but hath its use, there are variety of uses for the several members; put them all together, and there is a completeness for all sorts of uses the body needeth. So it is here. Take all the saints together at the latter day, and there will be nothing wanting of grace, or of any measure of gifts, that is needful for glory, and excellency, and ornament.

Thirdly, to make up this fulness of his body yet more complete; as there must be all the members, not one wanting; as there must be all variety of uses that members serve for, none lame or imperfect: so likewise there must be a fulness of growth to a stature, to a proportion, or else the body is not full. For example; if this hand of mine, or this little finger were writhen shorter in its proportion, if it did not grow to the full measure of the proportion of a little finger, there would be an uncomeliness and a disproportion, the body would not be full. So it is in the body of Christ; therefore to make up this fulness so much the more, you read, Eph. iv., that the Apostle, in the 10th verse, having said that he filleth all in all, saith, ver. 15, that the saints are to 'grow up into him in all things, which is the head, even Christ;' and, ver. 13, 'till they all come to a perfect man, unto the measure of the stature of the fulness of Christ.' To open these words a little:—

The fulness of Christ lieth not only in having every member, but every member growing up to a full stature that God hath appointed him. You see some little saints, and you see some great saints; there are saints great and small, as they are called in the Revelation. You wonder at this disproportion. Now mark; when you come at the latter day, and all the saints are round about Jesus Christ, you will find a perfect body; you will say, if this saint had grown anything more, he had not stood well among his fellows; if this saint had been anything less, there had not been a fulness. They are all to grow up to the fulness of the stature of Christ.

Why is it called the fulness of the stature *of Christ*, and not of *the body?* Because the fulness of the body is in the fulness of the head, therefore he rather calls it the fulness of Christ than of the body.

The corollaries from thence are in a word these:—

Is the body the fulness of Christ, and so his fulness, that he will have every part, every member? *Here is then a certainty of salvation.* A man may lose his clothes, and suffer them to be taken from him; but if he can help it, he will never lose his members. My brethren, Christ will never lose his members; 'My Father,' saith he, 'is greater than I, and none shall pluck them out of my Father's hand.' But if his sheep were his very hands themselves, to be sure he would not suffer them to be pulled off; they are not only his sheep, but his members; they are not only in his hands, but his hands and his feet; they are the members of his body, yea, they are his fulness.

Secondly, Learn from hence this: *Thou shalt certainly have thy measure in the growth of grace.* Thou art humbled in thyself because thou growest not according to the means; that which God hath appointed thee to, thou shalt, either by afflictions, or by the word, attain to that stature; for the members of Jesus Christ are all written in God's book, and the stature that they are all ordained unto, that when they are all met the body may be full. That doctrine is not true that telleth us that Christ might have died and been in heaven to want a body; for you see it is his fulness, he cannot want so much as one member but he had been imperfect.

I will give you but some observations, and so end.

First, See the love of our Lord and Saviour Jesus Christ. He might have taken all the glory and honour to himself here; the Holy Ghost might only have said, He is the head of the church, which is his body, that filleth all in all; but he would needs put in that is his fulness, 'the fulness of him that filleth all in all.' He would not take all the honour to himself, he would give her her due; his body, saith he, which is his fulness. Certain it is, my brethren, that our Lord and Saviour Jesus Christ accounteth you his fulness. Doth he see a soul converted to God? It is a part of my fulness, saith he; his joy is full by it. Doth he see you get a little grace at a sermon? Here is one step more to my fulness, saith he. He needed not anybody, he was perfectly glorious in himself; but he hath taken upon him such a relation as he were imperfect without a body, he standeth in need of a body. What saith the Apostle, 1 Cor. xii. 21? 'The head cannot say to the feet, I have no need of thee.' Jesus Christ, though a head, cannot say to the least saint, I have no need of thee. It was his love to enter into this relation. And learn from hence to give everything his due praise; you see here, though the Apostle saith that Christ filleth all in all, yet he giveth the church her due praise; he mingleth that with his. Christ filleth all, yet the church serveth for him to empty himself into.

Secondly, Is every degree of grace in a saint a part of Christ's fulness? Doth it add to his fulness? Is the addition of every member a part of his fulness? Then conversion of souls, adding grace into the hearts of men, is the best work in the world, for it is an adding to Christ's fulness; and what can be a greater work? It is not only doing good to a poor soul, though that would move one; it is the motive that James useth: 'He that converteth a sinner from the error of his way, shall save a soul from death,' he pulleth him out of the fire; but besides this, he addeth to Christ's fulness, which is the highest motive that can be. That as the apostle Paul saith, that it moved him to take all that pains he did, to suffer persecutions for preaching of the gospel, and to be glad of it too; I bear, saith he, the afflictions of Christ in my flesh, for his body's sake; this was Paul's motive: but here is a higher motive; here is not to do it for his body's sake only, but for Christ's, to make up his fulness. If there were a piece of work, a statue that were to last to eternity, would not all the cunning artists in the world be glad to have a hand in carving but a finger in that statue? My brethren, to build up the saints, to joint in the saints to Christ, is to add to the fulness of Christ. The work of the ministry is the best work in the world; God had but one Son in the world, and he made him a minister.

Thirdly, What a glorious sight, my brethren, what a glorious meeting will there be at the latter day, when Jesus Christ shall have all his fulness, all his body fully and perfectly united to him in all their glory, perfectly cleansed, not a member wanting, and all grown to their full stature! To see the man Christ, as I may so call him, that perfect man the Apostle telleth us of, Eph. iv. 13, and in 1 Cor. xii. 12,—that is, Christ and all his members making one perfect man, he the head and they the body,—there was never such a sight as this; not only to see this head crowned with all glory and honour, sitting at God's right hand, and having all things under his feet; and how beautiful will that head be to behold! Our Lord and Saviour Christ is more worth than all this body, when it hath all her graces, and all her perfections; and the least member of this body is more worth than all the world, let me tell you that too; but when you have viewed the head, to view every member limb by limb, to see all the beauty and perfection of every part, when there shall not be a saint wanting, nor a degree of grace wanting, but a body proportionable to this head; the head being so excellent, if he had not a body suitable he were deformed. Christ's beauty, my brethren, will add to the beauty of this body; and the beauty of this body, put all together, will set off the beauty of the head. How doth our Lord and Saviour Jesus Christ himself long for this day, when he shall be full, when he shall come to be glorified in his saints, as the Apostle saith, 2 Thess. i. 10.

My brethren, if you had heard of a piece of work that all the cunning carvers in the world had been about these six thousand years, and it had been wrought limb by limb, and all the Bezaleels in the world, filled with the Holy Ghost, had been carving of it, and this piece had not been complete and put together, as you know in working arras there are many pieces put together to make the picture of a man; if you heard of such a piece of work, what mighty, what infinite expectation would you have! Let me tell you this, that this body of our Lord and Saviour Jesus Christ hath been carving and working by all the prophets, and apostles, and ministers, by all the Bezaleels of the world, filled with the Holy Ghost, to this day, limb by limb; and, as the Psalmist saith, 'I am wonderfully and fearfully made in the lower parts of the earth,' God hath wrought it in the lower parts of the earth, as he did his body in the womb. When all these shall be brought together, and Christ the Head set upon them, then view them all together, what a sight will it be! Oh, but let me say one thing more. What will it be to be a member of this body, though but the little toe, though but the least part of it, to be one that shall go to make up the fulness of our Lord and Saviour Jesus Christ!

So I have done with this text, and thus likewise I have, together with this chapter, finished that course of this exercise which I undertook at first; and I have so done it, as I am not conscious to myself of having offended any.

END OF VOL. I.

BALLANTYNE AND COMPANY, PRINTERS, EDINBURGH.

www.ingramcontent.com/pod-product-compliance
Lightning Source LLC
LaVergne TN
LVHW011338110826
845153LV00011B/452

* 9 7 8 1 5 8 9 6 0 1 3 9 0 *